THE GOVERNMENT CONTRACT COMPLIANCE HANDBOOK

FIFTH EDITION

By

Seyfarth Shaw LLP,

Harlan Gottlieb,

and

Kevin L. Phelps

THOMSON REUTERS™

For Customer Assistance Call 1-800-328-4880

Mat #41358173

© 2014 Thomson/West

For authorization to photocopy, please contact the **Copyright Clearance Center** at 222 Rosewood Drive, Danvers, MA 01923, USA (978) 750-8400; fax (978) 646-8600 or **Copyright Services** at 610 Opperman Drive, Eagan, MN 55123, fax (651) 687-7551. Please outline the specific material involved, the number of copies you wish to distribute and the purpose or format of the use.

This publication was created to provide you with accurate and authoritative information concerning the subject matter covered; however, this publication was not necessarily prepared by persons licensed to practice law in a particular jurisdiction. The publisher is not engaged in rendering legal or other professional advice and this publication is not a substitute for the advice of an attorney. If you require legal or other expert advice, you should seek the services of a competent attorney or other professional.

ISBN: 978-0-314-64056-7

About the Authors

Seyfarth Shaw was founded in 1945 in Chicago by three lawyers and has grown to over more than 800 attorneys in 13 offices in the United States, Australia, England and the Peoples Republic of China. Seyfarth Shaw is a full-service firm with attorneys who specialize in Government contracts, commercial litigation, construction, corporate and finance law, employment and labor law, employee benefits, environmental law, real estate, securities litigation, trade secrets, trusts and estates, and workouts and bankruptcy.

Seyfarth Shaw's Government Contracts Practice Group has been part of the firm since 1979. We represent domestic and international clients in the high technology, defense, construction, commercial item, and service industries in a wide range of counseling and litigation matters. We lecture extensively on the compliance topics discussed in this Handbook, and have presented in-house compliance training to clients and to the general public.

Harlan Gottlieb has spent 28 years practicing Government contract law with extensive experience in government procurement, source selections, foreign military sales, intellectual property and fiscal law. He has appeared numerous times before the Government Accountability Office on contractor protests and before the Armed Services Board of Contract Appeals on contractual disputes.

Mr. Gottlieb currently serves as the Senior Attorney Advisor for the Aviation and Missile Command (AMCOM) in Huntsville, AL. He was formerly the Chief Counsel for the Program Executive Office for Simulation, Training and Instrumentation (PEO STRI) where he supervised an office of 6 attorneys, a paralegal and administrative assistant. He is responsible for providing legal advice to AMCOM Aviation program offices and Contracting Officers on billion dollar helicopter programs, from requirements inception to "retirement," as well as issues in ethics and fiscal law. From 1987 to March 1995, he served as an Attorney Advisor with the U.S. Army Aviation and Troop Command, now the Aviation and Missile Command. He provided contract and programmatic legal advice to the Program Mangers for the CH-47 and Apache programs.

Mr. Gottlieb has earned many government recognitions and awards for his work. He graduated on the Dean's List at Washburn University School of Law in 1985. He earned a Bachelor of Arts at Tulane University in 1978. He is a member in good standing of the Missouri Bar Association.

Kevin Phelps earned his Juris Doctor in 2006 from The George Washington University Law School. Mr. Phelps has worked for two top-five defense contractors, with extensive experience negotiating and managing, from cradle-to-grave, large-dollar complex U.S. Government, international, and commercial contracts as well as purchase orders and agreements with both large and small business vendors. Mr. Phelps is a member in good standing with the Court of Appeals of Maryland, where he resides with his wife and two sons.

Acknowledgments

This Fifth Edition of The Government Contract Compliance Handbook builds on the efforts of the many attorneys in the Government Contracts Practice Group of Seyfarth Shaw LLP who contributed to the First Edition and to the intervening editions and annual updates. We would like to acknowledge their efforts.

Mr. Gottlieb would like to acknowledge his many mentors who taught him over the last 28 years. He would also like to acknowledge his wife, Nan, whose enthusiasm for his editing here knew no bounds.

Mr. Phelps would like to thank his parents, Susan and Larry--for instilling the constant drive to learn, the GW Law Government Contracts faculty--for providing their invaluable knowledge and experience, and above all his wife Kerry--for her unwavering support in his Government Contracts profession and the several tangents along the way.

Finally, we would like to acknowledge the continuing support of the Thomas West editors who edited the manuscript and guided this project to completion.

Joseph J. Dyer on behalf of the
Government Contracts Practice Group
Group of Seyfarth Shaw LLP
Harlan Gottlieb
Kevin Phelps

Preface

On publication of the Fourth Edition of The Government Contract Compliance Handbook, the authors reflected on various of the then recent procurement scandals and mused on the renewed focus on compliance that such scandals would bring. Their musings were on point. Perhaps most significant is the requirement, implemented in 2007, that contractors establish formal compliance procedures and undertake regular training. At the same time, case law developments have made it increasingly easier and attractive for private persons to sue on behalf of the Government for violations of various of the procurement related laws - so-called qui tam actions. As the Fifth Edition goes to print, the nation is facing significant budget deficits with calls from Congress that agencies do more with less. As part of the "more," agencies have stepped up their efforts to ferret out suspected fraud and abuse. They will certainly do so with increasing vigor in the coming years. Thus, a thorough understanding of the rules and regulations that control the award and performance of Government contracts, especially as they pertain to issues of integrity and transparency of the process, continues to be critical for all Government contractors.

This Fifth Edition of The Government Contract Compliance Handbook endeavors to provide in-depth substantive information as well as practical advice to you, the contractor, to help you avoid liability to the Federal Government. The focus of the book therefore remains on company compliance programs, practices and procedures.

A substantive compliance program can reduce the chances that someone in your company will engage in improper practices. And although a compliance program cannot absolutely insure against incurring criminal, civil, or administrative liability to the Government, it can provide contractors an effective shield against the worst consequences of a Federal fraud investigation.

The Handbook consists of four Parts containing 20 chapters and a separate Appendix section.
  Part I: Compliance Basics
  Part II: Obtaining Government Contracts
  Part III: Contract Performance
  Part IV: Special Problems
Part I provides information on developing and managing a compliance program. It includes a discussion of the principal procurement fraud civil and criminal offenses and penalties. It also covers the basics of setting up a company compliance

program and conducting a compliance audit. In addition, Part I discusses how to respond if the Government institutes a criminal investigation of your company, and the importance of recognizing, understanding, and resolving the parallel criminal, civil and administrative proceedings you potentially could face.

Part II discusses preaward compliance issues that may result in liability even before you obtain a Government contract. This part will help you to understand the requirements of procurement integrity statutes and regulations, how to avoid bribery, illegal gratuities, and conflicts of interest, and how to avoid submitting fraudulent or misleading cost or pricing data to the Government in the course of obtaining a contract award.

Part III includes material on compliance in all aspects of contract performance, from the submission of invoices for work performed to the requirement in some contracts to conform your cost accounting practices to special Government standards.

Part IV covers some special problems in compliance, such as issues that may arise when you submit contract claims to the Government or when one company merges with or acquires another company that is a Government contractor. This Part also discusses the special rules related to the export of U.S. products and technology to foreign entities and domestic and foreign source preferences.

A separate Appendix section follows the main text. It is a comprehensive source for forms, certificates, charts and other illustrative material to be used as a reference with the text of the Handbook or as a separate independent ready reference.

As in the past four editions of the Compliance Handbook, our aim here is to present comprehensive compliance information in a straightforward form accessible to the layperson and as free of "lawyer speak" as possible. Each chapter includes case examples or scenarios to help illustrate the major procurement fraud and compliance issues raised in that chapter. In addition, at the end of most chapters you will find a brief list of key compliance "recommendations" for use as a checklist to review the principles discussed in the text.

Although the Handbook provides general guidance on compliance issues, it does not take the place of advice from your own legal counsel on specific issues affecting you or your company. In addressing specific compliance questions, you should consult with counsel to verify the current status of applicable laws and regulations and to obtain an assessment of the relevant facts.

PREFACE

We hope this new edition of The Government Contract Compliance Handbook provides assistance to you and your company in ensuring your compliance with Federal laws and regulations. The cliché "an ounce of prevention is worth a pound of cure" is more true today than ever before.

The Authors
November 2014

Summary of Contents

PART I. COMPLIANCE BASICS
Chapter 1. The Offenses & Penalties
Chapter 2. Your Response to a Criminal Investigation
Chapter 3. Parallel Proceedings & Global Settlements
Chapter 4. Your Compliance Program
Chapter 5. Conducting a Compliance Audit

PART II. OBTAINING GOVERNMENT CONTRACTS
Chapter 6.   Handling Procurement Information
Chapter 7.   Influencing Government Actions
Chapter 8.   Conflicts of Interest
Chapter 9.   Defective Pricing
Chapter 10. Selling Commercial Items

PART III. CONTRACT PERFORMANCE
Chapter 11. Cost Allowability
Chapter 12. Cost Accounting
Chapter 13. Time Charging
Chapter 14. Progress Payments
Chapter 15. Product Substitution

PART IV. SPECIAL PROBLEMS
Chapter 16. Contract Claims
Chapter 17. Domestic & Foreign Product Acquisition Preferences
Chapter 18. Acquisitions & Mergers
Chapter 19. International Sales
Chapter 20. Foreign Military Sales

Appendices

Appendix A.   Summary of Criminal and Civil Statutes Applicable to Procurement Matters

Appendix B.	Representations and Certifications Chart
Appendix C.	Sentencing Guidelines for Organizations
Appendix D.	List of the Federal Inspectors General
Appendix E.	Sample Code of Business Ethics and Conduct
Appendix F.	DoD Hotline Poster
Appendix G.	Sample Company Policy Statement on Bribery and Gratuities
Appendix H.	FAR 52.203-2: "Certificate of Independent Price Determination" Clause
Appendix I.	Department of the Army Memorandum, Procurement Fraud Indicators, SELCE-LG-JA (27-10i) (Feb. 20, 1990)
Appendix J.	FAR Table 15-2: Instructions for Submitting Cost/Price Proposals When Cost or Pricing Data are Required
Appendix K.	DCAA Form 1: "Notice of Contract Costs Suspended and/or Disapproved"
Appendix L.	FAR 52.242-4: "Certification of Final Indirect Costs"
Appendix M.	FAR 52.242-3: "Penalties for Unallowable Costs Clause"
Appendix N.	Form CASB-DS-1: "Cost Accounting Standards Board Disclosure Statement"
Appendix O.	Time Card Analysis Attribute Test
Appendix P.	Sample Time Card
Appendix Q.	Sample Time Cards Which Exhibit Violations
Appendix R.	Standard Form 1443: "Contractor's Request for Progress Payment"
Appendix S.	GAO, "DOD Fraud Invesgitations: Characteristics, Sanctions and Prevention" (Jan. 1988)
Appendix T.	DOD Office of Inspector General, "Indicators of Fraud in DOD Procurement" (June 1987)
Appendix U.	DFARS 225.872-1: List of Current DOD Qualifying Countries
Appendix V.	FAR 25.003: List of Designated Countries
Appendix W.	DOD Security Assistance Management Manual Form Letter

SUMMARY OF CONTENTS

Appendix X.   Defense Security Cooperation Agency, "Guidelines for Foreign Military Financing of Direct Commercial Contracts"

Appendix Y.   Contractor's Certificiation and Agreement with Defense Security Cooperation Agency

Table of Laws and Rules

Table of Cases

Index

Table of Contents

PART I. COMPLIANCE BASICS

CHAPTER 1. THE OFFENSES & PENALTIES

I. OVERVIEW
§ 1:1   Scope note

II. CRIMINAL FRAUD
§ 1:2   Generally
§ 1:3   False statements
§ 1:4   —Examples
§ 1:5   —Frequently asked questions
§ 1:6   Mail & wire fraud
§ 1:7   —Examples
§ 1:8   Major fraud against the United States
§ 1:9   —Frequently asked questions
§ 1:10   Criminal false claims
§ 1:11   —Examples

III. CONSPIRACY
§ 1:12   Generally
§ 1:13   Examples

IV. CIVIL FRAUD
§ 1:14   Generally
§ 1:15   Civil False Claims Act
§ 1:16   —Examples
§ 1:17   Qui tam lawsuits
§ 1:18   —"Relators"
§ 1:19   —Procedures
§ 1:20   —Whistleblower protections
§ 1:21   —Frequently asked questions
§ 1:22   The Foreign Assistance Act
§ 1:23   Program Fraud Civil Remedies Act
§ 1:24   —Examples

V. CORRUPTION
§ 1:25   Bribery & illegal gratuities

§ 1:26 Conflicts of interest
§ 1:27 Kickbacks
§ 1:28 Foreign Corrupt Practices Act
§ 1:29 Lobbying restrictions & collusive bidding

VI. IMPROPER ACCESS TO GOVERNMENT PROPERTY & INFORMATION

§ 1:30 Procurement Integrity Act
§ 1:31 Theft of Government property statute
§ 1:32 Espionage statutes

VII. OBSTRUCTION OF JUSTICE

§ 1:33 Generally
§ 1:34 Obstruction of federal audit
§ 1:35 —Example
§ 1:36 Obstruction of judicial proceeding
§ 1:37 —Example
§ 1:38 Witness tampering
§ 1:39 Obstruction of pending administrative proceeding
§ 1:40 Perjury & false declarations under oath
§ 1:41 —Examples

VIII. CRIMINAL PENALTIES

§ 1:42 Generally
§ 1:43 Sentence of Fine statute
§ 1:44 RICO
§ 1:45 —Example
§ 1:46 Federal sentencing guidelines
§ 1:47 —Sentencing of individuals
§ 1:48 —Sentencing of organizations

IX. CIVIL PENALTIES

§ 1:49 Generally
§ 1:50 Forfeiture of claims
§ 1:51 Foreign Assistance Act
§ 1:52 Voiding contracts

X. ADMINISTRATIVE PENALTIES

§ 1:53 Debarment
§ 1:54 —Grounds & mitigating factors
§ 1:55 —Procedures
§ 1:56 Suspension

TABLE OF CONTENTS

§ 1:57 —Grounds & mitigating factors
§ 1:58 —Procedures
§ 1:59 Contractual remedies

CHAPTER 2. YOUR RESPONSE TO A CRIMINAL INVESTIGATION

I. OVERVIEW

§ 2:1 Scope note

II. INVESTIGATORS AND DEVICES

A. INVESTIGATORS

§ 2:2 Generally
§ 2:3 Defense & civilian agency investigators

B. INVESTIGATIVE DEVICES

§ 2:4 Generally
§ 2:5 Grand jury investigations
§ 2:6 Subpoenas
§ 2:7 Search warrants
§ 2:8 Wiretaps
§ 2:9 Field interviews

III. PREPARING FOR AND RESPONDING TO AN INVESTIGATION

A. BE PREPARED

§ 2:10 Retain documents
§ 2:11 Appoint a records custodian
§ 2:12 Educate employees
§ 2:13 Maintain contact with former employees

B. DETECTING AN INVESTIGATION

§ 2:14 Generally
§ 2:15 Inquiries by federal auditors
§ 2:16 Allegations by contracting officers
§ 2:17 Requests for employee interviews
§ 2:18 Receipt of grand jury subpoena
§ 2:19 Receipt of company hotline calls
§ 2:20 Lawsuits by current or former employees

C. INITIAL STEPS AFTER AN INVESTIGATION IS UNDERWAY

§ 2:21 When the investigators arrive
§ 2:22 Selection of counsel
§ 2:23 Avoid obstructing justice
§ 2:24 Preliminary internal inquiry
§ 2:25 Insurance & indemnification requirements
§ 2:26 Advise government investigators that they are bound by local ethics rules
§ 2:27 Notify your employees of the investigation
§ 2:28 Advise your employees how to respond
§ 2:29 Counsel for your employees

D. COMPANY & EMPLOYEE RIGHTS DURING AN INVESTIGATION

§ 2:30 Generally
§ 2:31 Unreasonable search & seizure
§ 2:32 Self-incrimination
§ 2:33 Employees' right to counsel

IV. CONDUCTING AN INTERNAL INVESTIGATION

§ 2:34 Generally
§ 2:35 Authorization by company management
§ 2:36 Choosing the internal investigators
§ 2:37 Interviewing current & former employees
§ 2:38 Report of the investigation
§ 2:39 Communications with the prosecutor
§ 2:40 Voluntary disclosure of wrongdoing

V. RESPONDING TO A GRAND JURY PROCEEDING

§ 2:41 Witness & document subpoenas
§ 2:42 Motions to quash or modify subpoenas
§ 2:43 Preparation of witnesses
§ 2:44 Averting an indictment

CHAPTER 3. PARALLEL PROCEEDINGS & GLOBAL SETTLEMENTS

I. OVERVIEW

§ 3:1 Scope note

TABLE OF CONTENTS

II. RISKS OF PARALLEL PROCEEDINGS

§ 3:2 Generally
§ 3:3 Transfer of information
§ 3:4 Protecting privileged information
§ 3:5 Burdensome litigation
§ 3:6 Inconsistent defenses
§ 3:7 Frequently asked questions

III. GLOBAL SETTLEMENT

§ 3:8 Generally
§ 3:9 Benefits
§ 3:10 Negotiating the agreement
§ 3:11 Elements
§ 3:12 Criminal liability & penalties
§ 3:13 Civil liability & penalties
§ 3:14 Suspension & debarment
§ 3:15 —Appointment of ombudsman
§ 3:16 —Reporting requirements
§ 3:17 Frequently asked questions

IV. MITIGATING FACTORS

§ 3:18 Generally
§ 3:19 Recommendations

CHAPTER 4. YOUR COMPLIANCE PROGRAM

I. OVERVIEW

§ 4:1 Scope note

II. DEVELOPING A COMPLIANCE PROGRAM

§ 4:2 The FAR compliance requirements
§ 4:3 Your "compliance book"
§ 4:4 Defense contractors
§ 4:5 Requirements imposed by settlement agreements
§ 4:6 Mechanism for future modifications
§ 4:7 Employee screening

III. RECOVERING COMPLIANCE COSTS

§ 4:8 Cost allowability

IV. STEPS TO ACHIEVE COMPLIANCE

§ 4:9 Corporate code of ethics

§ 4:10 Corporate procedures & policies
§ 4:11 Compliance officer
§ 4:12 Company hotline
§ 4:13 Audits & investigations
§ 4:14 Disciplinary action
§ 4:15 Reporting violations to the government
§ 4:16 Cooperating during government investigations
§ 4:17 Education & training
§ 4:18 Updating

CHAPTER 5. CONDUCTING A COMPLIANCE AUDIT

I. OVERVIEW

§ 5:1 Scope note

II. PLANNING THE AUDIT

§ 5:2 Forming the audit team
§ 5:3 Establishing the audit's scope
§ 5:4 Developing audit work programs
§ 5:5 Developing audit deliverables

III. PERFORMING THE AUDIT

§ 5:6 Major tasks
§ 5:7 Reviewing existing policies & procedures
§ 5:8 Interviewing personnel
§ 5:9 Testing controls
§ 5:10 Sampling transactions
§ 5:11 Documenting the audit

IV. IMPLEMENTING & REPORTING THE AUDIT RESULTS

§ 5:12 Key steps
§ 5:13 Recommendations for improvement
§ 5:14 Corrective action
§ 5:15 Follow-up
§ 5:16 Reporting audit results to the government

Table of Contents

PART II. OBTAINING GOVERNMENT CONTRACTS

CHAPTER 6. HANDLING PROCUREMENT INFORMATION

I. OVERVIEW

§ 6:1 Scope note

II. PROCUREMENT INTEGRITY ACT & RULES

A. BASIC PROHIBITIONS

§ 6:2 Generally
§ 6:3 Restrictions on disclosing procurement information
§ 6:4 Restrictions on obtaining procurement information
§ 6:5 Restrictions on employment contacts
§ 6:6 Prohibition on official's acceptance of compensation

B. EFFECTS OF VIOLATIONS

§ 6:7 Criminal penalties
§ 6:8 Civil Penalties
§ 6:9 Administrative penalties
§ 6:10 Restrictions on procurement protests

C. FREQUENTLY ASKED QUESTIONS

§ 6:11 Questions & answers

III. IMPROPER ACCESS TO GOVERNMENT PROPERTY & INFORMATION

§ 6:12 Theft of government property statute
§ 6:13 Espionage statutes

IV. HOW TO RECOGNIZE THE PROBLEM

§ 6:14 Generally
§ 6:15 Examples

V. COMPLIANCE INITIATIVES

§ 6:16 Generally
§ 6:17 Establish policies & procedures
§ 6:18 Educate your employees

§ 6:19   Establish a training program
§ 6:20   Recommendations

CHAPTER 7. INFLUENCING GOVERNMENT ACTIONS

I. OVERVIEW
§ 7:1   Scope note

II. BRIBERY & ILLEGAL GRATUITIES
A. STATUTORY FRAMEWORK
§ 7:2   Generally
§ 7:3   Bribery
§ 7:4   Illegal gratuities

B. FREQUENTLY ASKED QUESTIONS
§ 7:5   Questions & answers

C. HOW TO RECOGNIZE THE PROBLEM
§ 7:6   Generally
§ 7:7   Examples

D. COMPLIANCE INITIATIVES
§ 7:8   Generally
§ 7:9   Establish policies & procedures
§ 7:10 Monitor employees' activities
§ 7:11 Require government employees to pay
§ 7:12 Recommendations

III. LOBBYING RESTRICTIONS
A. STATUTORY FRAMEWORK
§ 7:13 Generally
§ 7:14 Byrd Amendment
§ 7:15 Lobbying Disclosure Act

B. FREQUENTLY ASKED QUESTIONS
§ 7:16 Questions & answers

C. HOW TO RECOGNIZE THE PROBLEM
§ 7:17 Generally

TABLE OF CONTENTS

§ 7:18 Examples

D. COMPLIANCE INITIATIVES

§ 7:19 Generally
§ 7:20 Byrd Amendment
§ 7:21 Lobbying Disclosure Act
§ 7:22 Recommendations

IV. COLLUSIVE BIDDING

A. STATUTORY FRAMEWORK

§ 7:23 Generally
§ 7:24 Sherman Antitrust Act
§ 7:25 Clayton Act
§ 7:26 Federal Trade Commission Act
§ 7:27 Other statutes & regulations
§ 7:28 Exceptions
§ 7:29 —Affiliated companies
§ 7:30 —Teaming agreements & joint ventures
§ 7:31 —Defense production pools

B. FREQUENTLY ASKED QUESTIONS

§ 7:32 Questions & answers

C. HOW TO RECOGNIZE THE PROBLEM

§ 7:33 Generally
§ 7:34 Examples

D. COMPLIANCE INITIATIVES

§ 7:35 Generally
§ 7:36 Recommendations

V. KICKBACKS

A. STATUTORY FRAMEWORK

§ 7:37 Generally
§ 7:38 Anti-Kickback Act
§ 7:39 —Elements
§ 7:40 —Contractor responsibilities
§ 7:41 —Penalties

B. FREQUENTLY ASKED QUESTIONS

§ 7:42   Questions & answers

C. HOW TO RECOGNIZE THE PROBLEM

§ 7:43   Generally
§ 7:44   Examples

D. COMPLIANCE INITIATIVES

§ 7:45   Generally
§ 7:46   Establish policies & procedures
§ 7:47   Develop policies for auditors & accountants
§ 7:48   Recommendations

CHAPTER 8. CONFLICTS OF INTEREST

I. OVERVIEW

§ 8:1   Scope note

II. PERSONAL CONFLICTS

A. PROCUREMENT INTEGRITY ACT

§ 8:2   Generally
§ 8:3   One-year ban on hiring former agency officials
§ 8:4   Restrictions on employment discussions
§ 8:5   Penalties
§ 8:6   Frequently asked questions

B. ETHICS REFORM ACT

§ 8:7   Generally
§ 8:8   Communications and appearances with intent to influence, generally
§ 8:9   Lifetime ban on communications and appearances
§ 8:10   Two-year ban on communications and appearances
§ 8:11   One-year ban on communications and appearances
§ 8:12   Penalties

C. CRIMINAL "REVOLVING-DOOR" STATUTES

§ 8:13   Generally

III. ORGANIZATIONAL CONFLICTS

§ 8:14   Generally

TABLE OF CONTENTS

§ 8:15 Government responsibilities
§ 8:16 Contractor responsibilities
§ 8:17 Frequently asked questions

IV. HOW TO RECOGNIZE THE PROBLEM
A. PERSONAL CONFLICTS

§ 8:18 Generally
§ 8:19 Examples

B. ORGANIZATIONAL CONFLICTS

§ 8:20 Generally
§ 8:21 Examples

V. COMPLIANCE INITIATIVES
A. PERSONAL CONFLICTS

§ 8:22 Generally
§ 8:23 Recommendations

B. ORGANIZATIONAL CONFLICTS

§ 8:24 Generally
§ 8:25 Recommendations

CHAPTER 9. DEFECTIVE PRICING

I. OVERVIEW

§ 9:1 Background

II. CURRENT REQUIREMENTS
A. TRUTH IN NEGOTIATIONS ACT

§ 9:2 Generally
§ 9:3 Applicability
§ 9:4 Defining "cost or pricing data"
§ 9:5 Submission of data
§ 9:6 Certification of data
§ 9:7 Exceptions & waiver
§ 9:8 —Adequate price competition
§ 9:9 —Prices set by law or regulation
§ 9:10 —Commercial item acquisitions
§ 9:11 —"Exceptional case" waiver

§ 9:12 —Modifications
§ 9:13 Information other than cost or pricing data
§ 9:14 Subcontractor data
§ 9:15 Price adjustment for defective pricing
§ 9:16 —Burden of proof
§ 9:17 —Measure of government's recovery
§ 9:18 —Your defenses
§ 9:19 —Offset
§ 9:20 Other penalties
§ 9:21 —Civil fraud
§ 9:22 —Criminal fraud
§ 9:23 —Suspension & debarment

B. FREQUENTLY ASKED QUESTIONS

§ 9:24 Questions & answers

C. ADDITIONAL DOD REQUIREMENTS: ESTIMATING SYSTEMS

§ 9:25 Generally
§ 9:26 Applicability
§ 9:27 Disclosure & government review
§ 9:28 Correction of deficiencies

III. HOW TO RECOGNIZE THE PROBLEM

§ 9:29 Generally
§ 9:30 Examples

IV. COMPLIANCE INITIATIVES

§ 9:31 Generally
§ 9:32 Recommendations

CHAPTER 10. SELLING COMMERCIAL ITEMS

I. OVERVIEW

§ 10:1 Scope note

II. COMMERCIAL ITEM ACQUISITIONS

§ 10:2 Generally
§ 10:3 Defining commercial items
§ 10:4 Defining commercial services

TABLE OF CONTENTS

A. EXEMPTION FROM STATUTORY COMPLIANCE

§ 10:5 Generally
§ 10:6 Exemptions for prime contracts
§ 10:7 Exemption for subcontracts
§ 10:8 Other exemptions
§ 10:9 Application of the Truth in Negotiations Act

B. COMMERCIAL ITEM CONTRACT CLAUSES AND DATA RIGHTS

§ 10:10 Contract terms and conditions
§ 10:11 Implementation of statutes and executive orders
§ 10:12 Representations and certifications
§ 10:13 Subcontract clauses
§ 10:14 Rights in technical data & computer software

C. FREQUENTLY ASKED QUESTIONS

§ 10:15 Questions & answers

III. SPECIAL CONTRACTING METHODS

A. GSA'S MAS PROGRAM

§ 10:16 Generally
§ 10:17 MAS pricing
§ 10:18 Contract price reductions
§ 10:19 Industrial funding fee
§ 10:20 Competition requirements

B. SMALL PURCHASES

§ 10:21 Generally
§ 10:22 Laws inapplicable to simplified acquisitions

IV. HOW TO RECOGNIZE THE PROBLEM

§ 10:23 Generally
§ 10:24 Examples

V. COMPLIANCE INITIATIVES

§ 10:25 Generally
§ 10:26 Gratuities
§ 10:27 Access to information
§ 10:28 Recommendations

PART III. CONTRACT PERFORMANCE

CHAPTER 11. COST ALLOWABILITY

I. OVERVIEW

§ 11:1   Scope note

II. CURRENT REQUIREMENTS

A. FAR COST PRINCIPLES

§ 11:2   Generally
§ 11:3   Coverage
§ 11:4   "Allowable" costs
§ 11:5   Specific unallowable & restricted costs
§ 11:6   Apportioning costs
§ 11:7   Accounting rules

B. LIABILITY FOR UNALLOWABLE COSTS

§ 11:8   Disallowance of unallowable costs
§ 11:9   Certificate of final indirect costs
§ 11:10   "Penalties for unallowable costs" clause
§ 11:11   Referral of fraud cases

C. FREQUENTLY ASKED QUESTIONS

§ 11:12   Questions & answers

III. HOW TO RECOGNIZE THE PROBLEM

§ 11:13   Generally
§ 11:14   Examples

IV. COMPLIANCE INITIATIVES

§ 11:15   Generally
§ 11:16   Upper management
§ 11:17   Supervisors & middle management
§ 11:18   Nonsupervisory employees
§ 11:19   Accounting department
§ 11:20   Recommendations

TABLE OF CONTENTS

CHAPTER 12. COST ACCOUNTING

I. OVERVIEW

§ 12:1 Scope note

II. CURRENT REQUIREMENTS

A. COST ACCOUNTING STANDARDS

§ 12:2   Background
§ 12:3   Do the CAS apply to your company?
§ 12:4   —Exempt contracts
§ 12:5   —Waiver
§ 12:6   —Full CAS coverage
§ 12:7   —Modified CAS coverage
§ 12:8   CAS contract clauses
§ 12:9   Disclosure statement
§ 12:10 Educational institutions
§ 12:11 Accounting changes & contract adjustments

B. CFAO COMPLIANCE DETERMINATIONS

§ 12:12 Generally
§ 12:13 Types of noncompliance
§ 12:14 Initial finding of noncompliance
§ 12:15 Agreement with CFAO's initial finding
§ 12:16 Disagreement with CFAO's initial finding
§ 12:17 Unilateral accounting changes

C. COST ACCOUNTING STANDARDS VS. COST PRINCIPLES

§ 12:18 Generally

D. CONTRACTOR LIABILITY

1. Liability For False Statements

§ 12:19 Generally
§ 12:20 Solicitation representations & certifications
§ 12:21 Proposals where cost or pricing data are required
§ 12:22 Disclosure statements
§ 12:23 Overhead or final indirect cost certifications
§ 12:24 Cost impact proposals

2. Liability For False Claims

§ 12:25 Generally

§ 12:26 Errors in progress payment billings
§ 12:27 Overbilling on cost contracts & invoices

E. FREQUENTLY ASKED QUESTIONS

§ 12:28 Questions & answers

III. HOW TO RECOGNIZE THE PROBLEM

§ 12:29 Generally
§ 12:30 Examples

IV. COMPLIANCE INITIATIVES

§ 12:31 Generally
§ 12:32 Develop a system of internal controls
§ 12:33 Employ CAS-qualified personnel
§ 12:34 Educate your employees
§ 12:35 Recommendations

CHAPTER 13. TIME CHARGING

I. OVERVIEW

§ 13:1 Scope note

II. CURRENT REQUIREMENTS

§ 13:2 Generally
§ 13:3 Administrative requirements
§ 13:4 Certifications
§ 13:5 Penalties for mischarging for companies
§ 13:6 Penalties for mischarging for individuals
§ 13:7 Frequently asked questions

III. HOW TO RECOGNIZE THE PROBLEM

§ 13:8 Generally
§ 13:9 Dramatic changes in time charging
§ 13:10 Lack of change over extended period
§ 13:11 Adjustments in recorded time entries
§ 13:12 Clear undercharging to a visible account
§ 13:13 Reclassification of employees by labor category
§ 13:14 Charging patterns that affect your CAS disclosure statement
§ 13:15 Unexplained adjustments in labor standards
§ 13:16 Overly rigid budgetary controls

TABLE OF CONTENTS

§ 13:17 Contract provisions that limit costs
§ 13:18 Contract definition contracts
§ 13:19 Examples

IV. COMPLIANCE INITIATIVES
A. SYSTEM OF ACCUMULATING & REPORTING LABOR COSTS

§ 13:20 Generally

B. UPPER MANAGEMENT

§ 13:21 Establish policies & procedures
§ 13:22 Cost allocation policy
§ 13:23 Education of employees
§ 13:24 Enforcement through internal audits

C. MIDDLE MANAGEMENT

§ 13:25 Review all charges carefully
§ 13:26 Assignment of work
§ 13:27 Review & approval of time cards
§ 13:28 Review of transfers of labor charges

D. NONSUPERVISORY EMPLOYEES

§ 13:29 Submit accurate time cards

E. ACCOUNTING DEPARTMENT

§ 13:30 Screen for invalid charges
§ 13:31 Effective designation of project numbers
§ 13:32 Maximum automation of systems
§ 13:33 Control of invalid labor charges

F. AVOIDING PROBLEMS

§ 13:34 Recommendations

CHAPTER 14. PROGRESS PAYMENTS

I. OVERVIEW

§ 14:1 Scope note

II. CURRENT REQUIREMENTS

A. OVERVIEW

§ 14:2 Generally

B. PROGRESS PAYMENT REQUESTS

§ 14:3 Generally
§ 14:4 Submission of accounting data
§ 14:5 Certification

C. PROGRESS PAYMENT RATE

§ 14:6 Generally

D. CALCULATING PROGRESS PAYMENTS

§ 14:7 Generally
§ 14:8 Cumulative total costs
§ 14:9 Progress payments to subcontractors
§ 14:10 Allowable, reasonable, and allocable costs

E. LIQUIDATION OF PROGRESS PAYMENTS

§ 14:11 Generally
§ 14:12 Subcontractor progress payments

F. TREATMENT OF "LOSS CONTRACTS"

§ 14:13 Generally

G. TITLE TO PROPERTY

§ 14:14 Generally

H. SUSPENSION & REDUCTION OF PROGRESS PAYMENTS

§ 14:15 Generally
§ 14:16 Failure to comply with material contract requirement
§ 14:17 Failure to make progress or unsatisfactory financial condition
§ 14:18 Excessive inventory
§ 14:19 Delinquency in paying costs of performance
§ 14:20 Unliquidated payments exceed fair value of work
§ 14:21 Actual profit less than estimated
§ 14:22 Substantial evidence of fraud
§ 14:23 Setoff

TABLE OF CONTENTS

I. FREQUENTLY ASKED QUESTIONS

§ 14:24 Questions & answers

III. HOW TO RECOGNIZE THE PROBLEM

§ 14:25 Generally
§ 14:26 Examples

IV. COMPLIANCE INITIATIVES

A. OVERVIEW

§ 14:27 Generally

B. UPPER MANAGEMENT

§ 14:28 Generally
§ 14:29 Segregate subcontractor progress payments
§ 14:30 Establish cut-off dates for accumulation of costs
§ 14:31 Segregate allowable from unallowable costs
§ 14:32 Monitor contract performance
§ 14:33 Retain accounting records

C. ACCOUNTING DEPARTMENT

§ 14:34 Compliance with company's procedures

D. INTERNAL AUDITORS

§ 14:35 System oversight

E. AVOIDING PROBLEMS

§ 14:36 Recommendations

CHAPTER 15. PRODUCT SUBSTITUTION

I. OVERVIEW

§ 15:1 Scope note

II. CURRENT REQUIREMENTS

A. CONTRACT QUALITY REQUIREMENTS

§ 15:2 Contractor's responsibilities for quality control
§ 15:3 Types of contract quality requirements
§ 15:4 Contractor inspection requirements for commercial item contracts

- § 15:5 Contractor inspection requirements for small contracts
- § 15:6 Standard inspection requirements
- § 15:7 Higher-level quality requirements

B. PENALTIES

- § 15:8 Generally
- § 15:9 Penalties for individuals
- § 15:10 Penalties for companies

C. FREQUENTLY ASKED QUESTIONS

- § 15:11 Questions & answers

III. HOW TO RECOGNIZE THE PROBLEM

- § 15:12 Examples

IV. COMPLIANCE INITIATIVES

- § 15:13 Upper management
- § 15:14 Middle management
- § 15:15 Quality assurance personnel
- § 15:16 Recommendations

PART IV. SPECIAL PROBLEMS

CHAPTER 16. CONTRACT CLAIMS

I. OVERVIEW

- § 16:1 Scope note

II. CERTIFYING & PRICING CONTRACT "CLAIMS"

- § 16:2 Definition of "claim"
- § 16:3 Certification
- § 16:4 —Effect of defective certification
- § 16:5 —Certification language
- § 16:6 —Who must certify?
- § 16:7 —Defense contracts
- § 16:8 Pricing methods
- § 16:9 Pricing CDA claims or requests for equitable adjustment
- § 16:10 Fraud liability
- § 16:11 Frequently asked questions

TABLE OF CONTENTS

III. HOW TO RECOGNIZE THE PROBLEM

§ 16:12   Generally
§ 16:13   Examples

IV. COMPLIANCE INITIATIVES

§ 16:14   Establish a claims team
§ 16:15   Maintain records
§ 16:16   Corroborate & document the facts
§ 16:17   Claim negotiation
§ 16:18   Claim litigation
§ 16:19   Recommendations

CHAPTER 17. DOMESTIC & FOREIGN PRODUCT ACQUISITION PREFERENCES

I. OVERVIEW

§ 17:1   Scope note

II. PRINCIPAL LAWS & RULES

A. TREATIES, STATUTES & RULES

§ 17:2   Generally
§ 17:3   BAA requirements
§ 17:4   The Berry Amendment
§ 17:5   TAA (WTO GPA) requirements
§ 17:6   Free trade agreements

B. OTHER EXCEPTIONS

§ 17:7   Generally
§ 17:8   BAA exceptions
§ 17:9   TAA exceptions

C. IDENTIFYING END PRODUCTS

§ 17:10   Generally

D. DETERMINING COUNTRY OF ORIGIN

§ 17:11   Generally
§ 17:12   BAA—"Domestic" end products
§ 17:13   —"Qualifying country" (DOD) end products
§ 17:14   TAA—Designated country end products
§ 17:15   U.S.-made end products

§ 17:16   NAFTA marking rules—FAR vs. Customs

E. PENALTIES
§ 17:17   BAA penalties
§ 17:18   TAA penalties

F. FREQUENTLY ASKED QUESTIONS
§ 17:19   Questions & answers

III. "MADE IN USA" LABELS
§ 17:20   Generally
§ 17:21   FTC requirements
§ 17:22   Penalties
§ 17:23   Frequently asked questions

IV. HOW TO RECOGNIZE THE PROBLEM
§ 17:24   Generally
§ 17:25   Offers to supply products
§ 17:26   Postaward activities & contract performance
§ 17:27   Examples

V. COMPLIANCE INITIATIVES
§ 17:28   Generally
§ 17:29   Create a "history" of end products & their components
§ 17:30   Keep inventories separate
§ 17:31   Establish a compliance monitor & oversight procedures
§ 17:32   Plan ahead
§ 17:33   On-site review
§ 17:34   Recommendations

CHAPTER 18. ACQUISITIONS & MERGERS

I. OVERVIEW
§ 18:1   Scope note

II. PLANNING & EXECUTING THE ACQUISITION OR MERGER

A. COST ISSUES
§ 18:2   Generally

TABLE OF CONTENTS

§ 18:3   Planning & execution costs
§ 18:4   Financing costs
§ 18:5   Depreciation of the combined assets
§ 18:6   Cost of money
§ 18:7   Restructuring costs: defense contracts
§ 18:8   Adjustment of prices of contracts subject to CAS

B. NOVATION AGREEMENTS

§ 18:9   Generally
§ 18:10   Requirements
§ 18:11   Failure to execute a novation agreement

III. SPECIAL CONCERNS FOR THE RESULTING COMPANY

§ 18:12   Organizational conflicts of interest
§ 18:13   Small-business size status
§ 18:14   Responsibility to perform contracts
§ 18:15   Facilities that violate environmental requirements
§ 18:16   Liability for acquired company's prior actions

IV. FOREIGN ACQUISITIONS OF U.S. COMPANIES

§ 18:17   Generally
§ 18:18   Restrictions on ownership
§ 18:19   Restrictions on access to classified information
§ 18:20   Methods to protect classified information

V. DUE DILIGENCE REVIEW

§ 18:21   Generally
§ 18:22   Due diligence checklist

CHAPTER 19. INTERNATIONAL SALES

I. OVERVIEW

§ 19:1   Scope note

II. EXPORT REGULATIONS

A. INTERNATIONAL TRAFFIC IN ARMS REGULATIONS

§ 19:2   Exports
§ 19:3   Deemed Exports

§ 19:4   Re-exports
§ 19:5   Significant Military Equipment
§ 19:6   Brokering
§ 19:7   Registration
§ 19:8   Temporary imports
§ 19:9   Penalties

B.   EXPORT ADMINISTRATION REGULATIONS

§ 19:10   Exports
§ 19:11   Deemed Exports
§ 19:12   Re-exports
§ 19:13   Non-Country Specific Restrictions
§ 19:14   Other
§ 19:15   Penalties
§ 19:16   Office of Foreign Assets Control Regulations
§ 19:17   How To Recognize The Problem

C.   COMPLIANCE INITIATIVES

§ 19:18   Both the DDTC and the BIS provide guidance regarding the initiatives that companies might undertake to ensure their compliance with U.S. export control laws. Briefly, companies should:

III.   FOREIGN CORRUPT PRACTICES ACT

A.   ANTI-BRIBERY PROVISIONS

§ 19:19   Prohibited Payments
§ 19:20   Permitted Payments
§ 19:21   Your Affirmative Defenses
§ 19:22   Penalties
§ 19:23   International Initiatives

B.   ACCOUNTING PROVISIONS

§ 19:24   Required Records And Controls
§ 19:25   Penalties

C.   HOW TO RECOGNIZE THE PROBLEM

§ 19:26   Generally
§ 19:27   Examples

D.   COMPLIANCE INITIATIVES

§ 19:28   Educate your employees

TABLE OF CONTENTS

§ 19:29 Beware of misconduct
§ 19:30 Seek an advisory opinion from the government
§ 19:31 Implement adequate recordkeeping

IV. ANTIBOYCOTT PROVISIONS.

A. EXPORT ADMINISTRATION REGULATIONS

§ 19:32 Prohibitions
§ 19:33 Penalties

B. INTERNAL REVENUE ADMINISTRATION

§ 19:34 Generally

C. HOW TO RECOGNIZE THE PROBLEM

§ 19:35 Generally
§ 19:36 Examples

D. COMPLIANCE INITIATIVES

§ 19:37 Educate your marketing staff
§ 19:38 Review contract documents carefully
§ 19:39 Refuse to supply boycott-related information
§ 19:40 Monitor your agents' and partners' actions
§ 19:41 Report boycott requests

V. RESTRICTIONS ON AGENTS & REPRESENTATIVES.

§ 19:42 Generally
§ 19:43 How to recognize the problem
§ 19:44 Examples
§ 19:45 Compliance initiatives
§ 19:46 Recommendations

CHAPTER 20. FOREIGN MILITARY SALES

I. OVERVIEW

§ 20:1 Scope note

II. CURRENT REQUIREMENTS

A. FMS SALES

§ 20:2 Statutory Basis
§ 20:3 Mechanics of the sale

§ 20:4   Types of government-to-government FMS case sales
§ 20:5   Pricing the FMS Sale
§ 20:6   FMS commissions and "bona fide" agent contingent fees

B. DIRECT COMMERCIAL SALES

§ 20:7   Generally
§ 20:8   FMS credit-financed (FMF) sales
§ 20:9   —Credit guidelines
§ 20:10 —Certification
§ 20:11 —FMF commissions and contingent fees
§ 20:12 "Pseudo" FMS Cases

C. NONRECURRING COSTS RECOUPMENT

§ 20:13 History of recoupment policy
§ 20:14 Current policy
§ 20:15 Waiver of recoupment charges

D. OFFSET ARRANGEMENTS

§ 20:16 Generally
§ 20:17 Reporting requirements
§ 20:18 FMS offsets
§ 20:19 FMF offsets

III. HOW TO RECOGNIZE THE PROBLEM

§ 20:20 Generally
§ 20:21 Examples

IV. COMPLIANCE INITIATIVES

§ 20:22 Generally
§ 20:23 FMS and direct commercial sales
§ 20:24 FMS credit-financed (FMF) sales
§ 20:25 Recommendations

APPENDICES

Appendix A.   Summary of Criminal and Civil Statutes Applicable to Procurement Matters
Appendix B.   Representations and Certifications Chart
Appendix C.   Sentencing Guidelines for Organizations
Appendix D.   List of the Federal Inspectors General

Table of Contents

Appendix E.   Sample Code of Business Ethics and Conduct
Appendix F.   DoD Hotline Poster
Appendix G.   Sample Company Policy Statement on Bribery and Gratuities
Appendix H.   FAR 52.203-2: "Certificate of Independent Price Determination" Clause
Appendix I.   Department of the Army Memorandum, Procurement Fraud Indicators, SELCE-LG-JA (27-10i) (Feb. 20, 1990)
Appendix J.   FAR Table 15-2: Instructions for Submitting Cost/Price Proposals When Cost or Pricing Data are Required
Appendix K.   DCAA Form 1: "Notice of Contract Costs Suspended and/or Disapproved"
Appendix L.   FAR 52.242-4: "Certification of Final Indirect Costs"
Appendix M.   FAR 52.242-3: "Penalties for Unallowable Costs Clause"
Appendix N.   Form CASB-DS-1: "Cost Accounting Standards Board Disclosure Statement"
Appendix O.   Time Card Analysis Attribute Test
Appendix P.   Sample Time Card
Appendix Q.   Sample Time Cards Which Exhibit Violations
Appendix R.   Standard Form 1443: "Contractor's Request for Progress Payment"
Appendix S.   GAO, "DOD Fraud Invesgitations: Characteristics, Sanctions and Prevention" (Jan. 1988)
Appendix T.   DOD Office of Inspector General, "Indicators of Fraud in DOD Procurement" (June 1987)
Appendix U.   DFARS 225.872-1: List of Current DOD Qualifying Countries
Appendix V.   FAR 25.003: List of Designated Countries
Appendix W.   DOD Security Assistance Management Manual Form Letter
Appendix X.   Defense Security Cooperation Agency, "Guidelines for Foreign Military Financing of Direct Commercial Contracts"
Appendix Y.   Contractor's Certificiation and Agreement with Defense Security Cooperation Agency

Table of Laws and Rules

Table of Cases
Index

Part I

COMPLIANCE BASICS

Chapter 1

The Offenses & Penalties

I. OVERVIEW
§ 1:1 Scope note

II. CRIMINAL FRAUD
§ 1:2 Generally
§ 1:3 False statements
§ 1:4 —Examples
§ 1:5 —Frequently asked questions
§ 1:6 Mail & wire fraud
§ 1:7 —Examples
§ 1:8 Major fraud against the United States
§ 1:9 —Frequently asked questions
§ 1:10 Criminal false claims
§ 1:11 —Examples

III. CONSPIRACY
§ 1:12 Generally
§ 1:13 Examples

IV. CIVIL FRAUD
§ 1:14 Generally
§ 1:15 Civil False Claims Act
§ 1:16 —Examples
§ 1:17 Qui tam lawsuits
§ 1:18 —"Relators"
§ 1:19 —Procedures
§ 1:20 —Whistleblower protections
§ 1:21 —Frequently asked questions
§ 1:22 The Foreign Assistance Act
§ 1:23 Program Fraud Civil Remedies Act
§ 1:24 —Examples

V. CORRUPTION

§ 1:25 Bribery & illegal gratuities
§ 1:26 Conflicts of interest
§ 1:27 Kickbacks
§ 1:28 Foreign Corrupt Practices Act
§ 1:29 Lobbying restrictions & collusive bidding

VI. IMPROPER ACCESS TO GOVERNMENT PROPERTY & INFORMATION

§ 1:30 Procurement Integrity Act
§ 1:31 Theft of Government property statute
§ 1:32 Espionage statutes

VII. OBSTRUCTION OF JUSTICE

§ 1:33 Generally
§ 1:34 Obstruction of federal audit
§ 1:35 —Example
§ 1:36 Obstruction of judicial proceeding
§ 1:37 —Example
§ 1:38 Witness tampering
§ 1:39 Obstruction of pending administrative proceeding
§ 1:40 Perjury & false declarations under oath
§ 1:41 —Examples

VIII. CRIMINAL PENALTIES

§ 1:42 Generally
§ 1:43 Sentence of Fine statute
§ 1:44 RICO
§ 1:45 —Example
§ 1:46 Federal sentencing guidelines
§ 1:47 —Sentencing of individuals
§ 1:48 —Sentencing of organizations

IX. CIVIL PENALTIES

§ 1:49 Generally
§ 1:50 Forfeiture of claims
§ 1:51 Foreign Assistance Act
§ 1:52 Voiding contracts

X. ADMINISTRATIVE PENALTIES

§ 1:53 Debarment
§ 1:54 —Grounds & mitigating factors
§ 1:55 —Procedures

THE OFFENSES & PENALTIES § 1:1

§ 1:56 Suspension
§ 1:57 —Grounds & mitigating factors
§ 1:58 —Procedures
§ 1:59 Contractual remedies

> **KeyCite®:** Cases and other legal materials listed in KeyCite Scope can be researched through the KeyCite service on Westlaw®. Use KeyCite to check citations for form, parallel references, prior and later history, and comprehensive citator information, including citations to other decisions and secondary materials.

I. OVERVIEW

§ 1:1 Scope note

The Federal Government remains committed to using the criminal, civil, and administrative processes to eliminate procurement fraud. Historically, the Government used only civil and administrative remedies to attack the problems of fraud, waste, and abuse. Criminal sanctions were reserved for only the most aggravated cases. Beginning in the 1980s, however, the law enforcement climate changed, and the Government began using criminal enforcement tools much more aggressively. That policy shift dissipated somewhat in the 1990s but returned in the early 2000s and should continue to be an area of focus for firms doing business with the Federal Government.

The Civil False Claims Act has emerged as one of the major enforcement tools for combating perceived procurement fraud. In part, this is because of its lower burden of proof than in the criminal false claims statute. Moreover, its qui tam provisions allow a private party to initiate an action on behalf of the Government.

In general terms, "procurement fraud" can be defined as any deceptive or corrupt conduct related to the procurement of goods or services by a Government agency. Such conduct can occur in any type of Government procurement, ranging from the purchase of sophisticated defense systems to basic maintenance services.

The Government typically focuses on five categories of procurement fraud by contractors: (1) mischarging (either labor or materials); (2) product substitution (sometimes referred to as defective products); (3) corruption in contractor-Government dealings; (4) eligibility for, and compliance with special Government contracting program requirements; and (5) defective pricing. In addition, the Government has also alleged contractors have obstructed justice through destruction of records or providing false information after an audit or investigation has commenced. It is important to keep in mind that both the individual employees and the entity can be held liable for fraudulent conduct.

In making a decision to charge a corporation, the Government has wide discretion in determining when, whom, how and whether to prosecute for violations of Federal criminal law.[1] Disclosure is mandatory, and often viewed favorably, while real or perceived efforts to impede an investigation will expose you and your company to further liability.[2] Sanctions for procurement fraud and related offenses include damages, probation, restitution, exclusion from contracting with the Government, penalties for individuals and organizations, and in some cases incarceration for individuals.

This chapter provides an overview of the major criminal and civil procurement fraud offenses and outlines the various criminal, civil, and administrative sanctions the Government may employ to combat procurement fraud.

II. CRIMINAL FRAUD

§ 1:2 Generally

There are several key criminal statutes under which the Government typically prosecutes "procurement fraud." The following section describes and discusses these criminal provisions in a general fashion, focusing on the way these offenses are most commonly charged. This information is summarized in a chart in Appendix A to this Compliance Handbook.

Note that this chapter discusses criminal statutes that apply specifically to Government contractors in their relationships to the Government, not criminal statutes that apply to *businesses generally*. In other words, this chapter does not address the criminal provisions of civil rights, environmental, labor, immigration, occupational health and safety, pension, social security, and tax laws.

§ 1:3 False statements

The statute the Government uses most frequently to address all categories of procurement fraud is the False Statements Statute.[1] This statute prohibits lying to the Government, i.e., knowingly and willfully making a false statement concerning a matter within the jurisdiction of the executive, legislative, or

---

[Section 1:1]

[1]Memorandum of Deputy Attorney General Larry D. Thompson, January 20, 2003.

[2]Memorandum of Deputy Attorney General Larry D. Thompson, January 20, 2003.

[Section 1:3]

[1]18 U.S.C.A. § 1001.

The Offenses & Penalties § 1:3

judicial branch of the United States. To establish a violation, the Government must show the following:
   (1) You willfully made a false, fictitious, or fraudulent statement or used a document knowing that it contained any false, fictitious, or fraudulent statement or entry;
   (2) Concerning a matter within the jurisdiction of an agency or department of the United States;
   (3) The statement was false, fictitious or fraudulent; and
   (4) You knew the statement was false, fictitious, or fraudulent when made.

A "statement" under the False Statements Statute may be oral or written, and either sworn or unsworn. For example, a signed form is a "statement." In any Government procurement there are numerous forms, certifications, invoices, letters, time cards, receipts, price quotes, etc. that, if false, the Government can use as a basis for a prosecution under the False Statements Statute. Beware. It does not matter, for False Statements purposes, whether a contractor uses words such as "certifies," "represents," or "affirms." If the statement to the Government is untrue, the Government can seek criminal and civil penalties under the False Statements Statute as well as assert its rights to other remedies. Therefore, you should always verify the accuracy of any oral or written representation you make to the Government as of the date the representation is made. A chart listing some of the representations and certifications required of Government contractors is set forth as Appendix B to this Handbook. While it is not necessary for you to "certify" before the False Statements Statute is invoked, you should pay special attention to certifications because the Government has deemed them important and you will therefore be less able to characterize inaccurate statements therein as immaterial or inadvertent.

For the statement to relate to "a matter within the jurisdiction of an agency or department," you need not make the statement directly to the Government. It need only be a statement that could *affect* some aspect of an agency's function. Thus, a subcontractor that submits false invoices to a prime contractor may be liable to the Government under the False Statements Statute even if the prime does not furnish the invoices to the procuring agency because the subcontractor's false statement of costs could affect the agency's auditing of contract costs—a matter clearly within its jurisdiction.

For a false statement to be actionable, it must be "material." A statement is material if it has a natural tendency to influence or is capable of influencing a decision or function of the Government. The materiality requirement thus excludes trivial falsehoods from the reach of the False Statements Statute. However, the

§ 1:3   GOVERNMENT CONTRACT COMPLIANCE HANDBOOK

materiality requirement does not require that the Government know about, rely on, believe, act on, or be deceived by the statement. Nor does it require that the Government suffer any loss or damage because of the statement; it only requires that the false statement be made.

The False Statements Statute also prohibits falsifying, concealing, or covering up, by means of some trick, scheme, or device, a material fact that you had a duty to disclose. The traditional rule has been that a statement or action in accordance with a reasonable interpretation of a regulation is not "false." However, the Ninth Circuit has taken the position that the meaning of a regulation is for the court to determine.[2] A statement inconsistent with the court's interpretation is false. While the Eleventh Circuit has rejected that view, you do not want to be in a position of making such an argument if you can possibly avoid it.[3]

The statutory *penalty* for violation of the False Statements Statute is up to five years' imprisonment, unless the offense involves terrorism, for which a maximum penalty of eight years applies. A violation of the False Statements Statute can also trigger fines of $250,000 for individuals and $500,000 for companies (see the discussion of the Sentence of Fine statute in § 1:43).

Note that one of the largest criminal fines ever imposed on a defense contractor resulted from a False Statements Statute prosecution. A contractor paid $400 million for making false statements regarding its processes and procedures on Foreign Corrupt Practices Act (FCPA) compliance, while knowingly circumventing FCPA requirements.[4]

Cases & Commentary: As noted in Appendix B, the provision set forth at FAR 52.209-5, which must be included in all solicitations where the resulting contract is expected to exceed the simplified acquisition threshold, requires that the contractor and/or its principals certify that they have (or have not) been suspended or debarred, indicted, convicted, or found liable for certain enumerated civil and criminal violations in the last three years or had a contract terminated for default in the last three years. Reacting to Congressional concerns, the FAR Councils enlarged the scope of the certification to include unsatisfied federal tax liabilities. Specifically, the regulations require that the contractor and/or its principals certify whether they have (or have not) within the preceding three-year period been notified of

---

[2]*U.S. ex rel. Oliver v. Parsons Co.*, 195 F.3d 457 (9th Cir. 1999).

[3]*U.S. v. Whiteside*, 285 F.3d 1345 (11th Cir. 2002).

[4]*See* DOJ, "BAE Systems PLC Pleads Guilty and Ordered to Pay $400 Million Criminal Fine" (March 1, 2010), *available at* http://www.justice.gov/opa/pr/2010/March/10-crm-209.html.

§ 1:3

any delinquent federal taxes in an amount that exceeds $3,000 for which the liability remains unsatisfied. The regulations state that federal taxes are considered "delinquent" if the liability has been finally determined and assessed and if the contractor and/or its principals have failed to pay the assessment when it was due. FAR 9.406-2 and 9.407-2 were likewise amended to add an unsatisfied federal tax liability as a basis for debarment and suspension.[5] From a compliance perspective, while it is not uncommon for companies, particularly large concerns, to have ongoing federal tax disputes, it is necessary to monitor the status of those matter very carefully to assure the required certification is accurate. Further, the definition of "principals" is broad, including officers, directors, owners, partners and persons having primary management responsibilities. Thus, it is important for the contractor to obtain assurances from those individuals regarding their personal tax liabilities before executing the certificate.

The impact of the failure of one of the members of a contractor's team—whether an individual employee or a corporate partner—to make an accurate and complete certification under FAR 52.209-5 was illustrated where one member of a joint venture, TOA, failed to disclose that a Japanese agency had recently fined it approximately $1 million for bid rigging. The contracting officer was apparently unaware of this and made an affirmative finding of responsibility by awarding the contract to the joint venture. Even after learning the facts, the contracting officer failed to reconsider the responsibility determination, testifying (to an amazed court) that "[B]ecause bid rigging is common in Japan it does not rise to a level serious enough to render the corporation not responsible." The court concluded that making a decision on such a crucial issue without seeking guidance from the highest levels within the agency was arbitrary and capricious. The court enjoined performance of the contract until the contracting officer obtained further guidance and made a new responsibility determination. The Government implemented the court's decision by designating a new contracting officer. The contracting officer was directed to treat the two instances of bid rigging as being a "commission of an offense lacking business integrity or business honesty" in evaluating TOA's "present responsibility" and to determine whether its record of integrity and business ethics was satisfactory in light of the criteria for debarment contained in FAR 9.406-1. The contracting officer interviewed the head of TOA and its parent company and concluded that the bid rigging were conducted by a sister company of TOA and that none of the TOA executives were involved in, or even aware of, the illegal activities of the other company. The contracting officer also examined

---

[5]*See* 73 Fed. Reg. 21791.

evidence of measures to ensure compliance with legal and ethical standards by the company and ultimately concluded that TOA was presently responsible. The court accepted these findings and lifted the injunction prohibiting the award of the contract to the joint venture.[6]

§ 1:4 False statements—Examples

False certifications: You sign a Buy American Act (BAA) certificate that states that each end product to be submitted under the contract is a domestic end product although you know that some of the end products are not domestic.

You may be liable for a violation of the False Statements Statute. (A chart setting forth many of the required representations and certifications for fixed-price supply contracts is included in Appendix B to this Handbook.)

False written statements: You write a letter to a Government official that states you plan to provide exclusively domestic end products when you know that part of the end products are not domestic. Again, you may be liable for a violation of the False Statements Statute even though you did not make the statement in a formal certification.

False oral statements: At a meeting with the Contracting Officer and other Government officials regarding BAA issues, the Contracting Officer asks you where your product is manufactured. You tell her it is a domestic end product, even though you know it is not considered as such for BAA purposes. You may be liable for a violation of the False Statements Statute if by the time of contract performance you do not provide the Government with a BAA-compliant product. (For a more detailed discussion of the Buy American Act, see §§ 17:1 et seq.)

§ 1:5 False statements—Frequently asked questions

Question 1: Can I be convicted under the False Statements Statute even if I do not personally sign a certification stating that a product complies with all contract requirements?

Answer 1: Yes. In one case, for example, a contract specified the number of plastic bags per box that would be delivered by the contractor to the Government. The contractor's president ordered production workers to deliver boxes to the Government that contained fewer bags than the contract required or than were set forth on the box labels. The company president refused to sign a certificate with each shipment stating that the shipment complied

---

[6]*See Watts-Healy Tibbitts A JV v. U.S.*, 84 Fed. Cl. 253 (2008), dismissed, 329 Fed. Appx. 269 (Fed. Cir. 2009).

with all contract requirements. The shipping manager signed the certificates instead. The president was convicted under the False Statements Statute and appealed, arguing that there was no evidence he made a false statement or ordered anyone else to do so. The U.S. Court of Appeals for the Ninth Circuit held that ordering the production and shipment of boxes, with knowledge that they would need to be accompanied by signed certificates and that the certificates would be false, was sufficient to violate the statute.[1]

Question 2: Am I violating the False Statements Statute if I make a promise to perform a future act without any intent to perform that act?

Answer 2: Yes. The Fifth Circuit, for example, has held that a promise made without the intent to perform may violate the False Statements Statute.[2] In this particular case, the defendant contractor certified in a bid that it would not disclose its bid prices to other offerors. However, the evidence showed that at the time of making the certification, the defendant was in the process of trying to convince another offeror to exchange price information with the defendant so that they could rig the bids for the contract. The defendant argued that its promise could not be a false statement because it was merely a prediction of future performance. The court rejected that argument, explaining that it is not the breaking of a promise that exposes a defendant to criminal liability but making a promise with the intent to break it.

Question 3: Can a hypothetical representation qualify as a false statement?

Answer 3: The Ninth Circuit has said that an expressly pro forma financial statement, based on assumptions and projected future events, can nevertheless support a conviction under 18 U.S.C.A. § 1014, which, like the False Statements Statute, proscribes false statements on loan and credit applications.[3] There, the Court held that a hypothetical financial representation could be a false statement if the underlying assumptions were known to be false. It also concluded, however, that such assertions are not held to the same standards of "rectitude" as other statements.

Question 4: Is the question of whether an allegedly false statement is "material" submitted to the jury to decide?

[Section 1:5]
[1] *See U.S. v. Fairchild*, 990 F.2d 1139 (9th Cir. 1993).
[2] *See U.S. v. Shah*, 44 F.3d 285 (5th Cir. 1995).
[3] *See U.S. v. Sarno*, 73 F.3d 1470 (9th Cir. 1995).

Answer 4: The Supreme Court has held that the materiality of a defendant's false statement is an issue of fact that must be submitted to the jury.[4]

§ 1:6 Mail & wire fraud

Typically an "add-on" to other charges, the mail and wire fraud statutes prohibit the use of the mails or wires (telephone, internet, etc.) to further a scheme to defraud.[1] To establish a case of *mail* fraud, the Government must demonstrate that you:

(1) Knowingly and willfully devised or participated in a scheme or artifice to defraud another or to obtain money or property by means of false or fraudulent pretenses, representations, or promises; and

(2) Used or caused to be used the United States mails or any private commercial interstate carrier in furtherance of the execution of that scheme.

For *wire* fraud, the first element is identical to the first element of mail fraud—devising or participating in a scheme to defraud. The difference in the two statutes is the use of different means of interstate communications. Under wire fraud, the Government must prove that you used interstate or foreign wire communications to further the scheme to defraud, whereas under mail fraud, the Government must only prove that you used the mails or any interstate carrier.

Any scheme or artifice to defraud will be sufficient to satisfy the first element of these fraud statutes. Courts have consistently refused to narrow the definition of these terms, preferring broad interpretations to ensure that every conceivable scheme to defraud can be addressed.

The "mailing" or "wiring" elements of the statutes are satisfied when you mail or wire anything in furtherance of the scheme. As long as you "cause" the mailing or wiring, you have satisfied this element of the statutes. You are deemed to "cause" use of the mails or wires whenever you know or should reasonably foresee that mailing or wiring will follow in the ordinary course of business. Note that the victim does not need to be the recipient of the communication, although in procurement fraud cases, a Government representative is usually the recipient.

A representation or promise is "false" or "fraudulent" within the meaning of the mail and wire fraud statutes if it relates to a

---

[4]*See U.S. v. Gaudin*, 515 U.S. 506, 115 S. Ct. 2310, 132 L. Ed. 2d 444 (1995).

[Section 1:6]

[1]18 U.S.C.A. § 1341 (mail fraud); 18 U.S.C.A. § 1343 (wire fraud).

THE OFFENSES & PENALTIES   § 1:7

material fact and is known to be untrue or is made with reckless indifference as to its truth or falsity. "Half truths" and statements that effectively conceal material facts are also "false" or "fraudulent" for purposes of these statutes. A material fact is a fact that would be important to a reasonable person in deciding whether to engage in a particular transaction.

In 1987, the U.S. Supreme Court held that the mail and wire fraud statutes were limited in scope to the protection of "property rights" and did not reach "schemes to defraud citizens of their intangible rights to honest and impartial government."[2] In 1988, Congress passed legislation that effectively overruled this decision, enacting a new definition applicable to the mail and wire fraud statutes. This statute—18 U.S.C.A. § 1346—provides that "the term 'scheme or artifice to defraud' includes a scheme or artifice to deprive another of the intangible right of honest services." For example, if you mailed tickets to a sports event to a Department of Agriculture official in the hopes of winning a contract, and the official attends the event but awards the contract to a competitor, you could be charged under the mail fraud statute with defrauding the Government of its intangible right of the official's honest services, even though the Government suffered no economic loss as a result of your conduct. (You may also have violated the bribery or gratuities provisions of the U.S. criminal code, see § 1:25.) Broadly speaking, the Government relied on this provision to prosecute individuals for alleged violation of fiduciary duties owed to a party even though the actions of those individuals did not necessarily involve a violation of the criminal law. The Supreme Court determined that applying the statute to such a broad range of actions rendered it unconstitutionally vague and that it could only be used where the underlying activity involved bribes and kickbacks.[3]

The statutory *penalties* set forth for mail or wire fraud are up to twenty years' imprisonment and fines under the Sentence of Fine statute (see § 1:43). If the violation affects a financial institution, statutory penalties provide for fines up to $1 million and imprisonment up to 30 years. Each use of the mails or wires constitutes a separate offense, even if the communications are part of a single fraudulent scheme.[4]

§ 1:7 Mail & wire fraud—Examples

Defective pricing: When submitting cost or pricing data to the

---

[2]*McNally v. U.S.*, 483 U.S. 350, 107 S. Ct. 2875, 97 L. Ed. 2d 292 (1987) (mail fraud statute extends only to schemes to defraud someone of property).

[3]*See Skilling v. U.S.*, 561 U.S. 358, 130 S. Ct. 2896, 177 L. Ed. 2d 619 (2010).

[4]*E.g., U.S. v. Tadros*, 310 F.3d 999 (7th Cir. 2002).

Government pursuant to the Truth in Negotiations Act (see §§ 9:1 et seq.), you inform the Government that you will pay more for the material involved in the contract than you know you will. You do so by mailing false cost or pricing data to the Government and placing a phone call to the Contracting Officer in which you make false representations concerning your costs. Such a mailing or phone call by you to the Contracting Officer could be charged as part of a scheme to commit mail or wire fraud.

Mischarging: You instruct employees who are working on a fixed-price contract to charge their time to a cost-plus contract. You then mail invoices relating to the cost-plus contract to the Government. Your mailing of false claims for labor costs under your cost-reimbursement contract could leave you liable for mail fraud.

Kickbacks: You hold a prime contract with the Government and conspire to award subcontracts in exchange for 13 percent of all subcontract payments, then file false tax returns hiding the matter.[1]

§ 1:8 Major fraud against the United States

The Major Fraud Act of 1988[1] created a new criminal offense, "Major Fraud Against the United States."[2] To establish a case of Major Fraud, the Government must show the following:

(1) You knowingly executed or attempted to execute a scheme or artifice;

(2) With the intent to defraud the United States, or to obtain money or property by means of false or fraudulent pretenses, representations, or promises;

(3) In a procurement of property or services where you were a prime contractor, subcontractor, or supplier on a contract with the United States; and the value of the contract, subcontract, or any constituent part thereof for property or services was $1 million or more.

In contrast to the mail and wire fraud statutes discussed in the

---

[Section 1:7]

[1]*See* DOJ "Two U.S. Contractor Employees Sentenced for Kickback Conspiracy and Tax Crimes Related to Iraq Reconstruction Efforts" (October 10, 2012), *available at* http://www.justice.gov/opa/pr/2012/October/12-crm-1220.html (Two former Parsons Corp. employees were ordered to pay over $2 million and sentenced to 15 months and 27 months for conspiring to commit mail and wire fraud, and filing false tax returns as part of a subcontract kickback scheme in Iraq.).

[Section 1:8]

[1]Pub. L. 100-700, § 2(a), 102 Stat. 4631.

[2]18 U.S.C.A. § 1031.

THE OFFENSES & PENALTIES § 1:8

preceding section, under the Major Fraud Act there is no need to show use of the interstate mails or wires in the "scheme or artifice" to defraud the U.S. The legislative history of the Major Fraud Act suggests that the "knowing" standard is intended to include not only actual knowledge, but also "willful blindness or deliberate ignorance."[3] The penalty provisions of the Major Fraud Act have a *statute of limitations* of seven years[4] because of the complexity of investigations involving Major Fraud against the United States.[5]

The Major Fraud Act Amendments of 1989[6] permit the Attorney General in his sole discretion to pay up to $250,000 to *whistleblowers* who furnish information relating to a possible prosecution for a major fraud. The payments are made from Department of Justice appropriations, but a court may order reimbursement to the Department from criminal fines imposed. Persons ineligible for such payments include (a) Government employees who furnish information in the performance of official duties, (b) individuals who, without justifiable reasons, fail to furnish the information first to their employer, (c) persons who furnish information based on allegations already publicly disclosed (unless they were an "original source" of the information), and (d) individuals who participated in the violation. These "reward" provisions have not been utilized extensively. The probable reason is that available financial bounties to individuals are much more easily available under the Civil False Claims Act. (See Part IV below.)

The statutory *penalties* set forth for violations of the Major Fraud Act are greater than those for violations of many other criminal statutes. The Major Fraud Act provides generally for fines of $1 million and 10 years' imprisonment. However, the fine may increase to $5 million if (1) the gross loss to the Government or the gross gain to a defendant is $500,000 or greater, or (2) the offense involves a conscious or reckless risk of serious personal injury. The maximum fine imposed a defendant under the Major Fraud Act (including multiple counts) is $10 million.

In addition, the Major Fraud Act contains a whistleblower protection provision.[7] This section allows individuals discharged, demoted, suspended, threatened, harassed, or in any other manner discriminated against in the terms and conditions of employ-

---

[3] H.R. Rep. No. 610, 100th Cong., 2d Sess. 6 (1988).

[4] 18 U.S.C.A. § 1031.

[5] S. Rep. No. 100-503, 100th Cong., 2d Sess. 3, reprinted in 1988 U.S. Code & Admin. News 5969, 5971.

[6] P.L. 101-123, § 2(a), 103 Stat. 759 (codified at 18 U.S.C.A. § 1031(g)).

[7] 18 U.S.C.A. § 1031(h).

§ 1:8 GOVERNMENT CONTRACT COMPLIANCE HANDBOOK

ment because of their cooperation in or furtherance of a Government Major Fraud investigation to sue their former employer for civil damages.[8]

§ 1:9 Major fraud against the United States—Frequently asked questions

Question 1: Is there a private right of action under the Major Fraud Act?

Answer 1: No. Even though the Major Fraud Act allows the Justice Department to pay specified amounts to "whistle-blowers" for information leading to possible fraud prosecutions, there is no statutory basis for concluding that Congress intended to imply a private right of action. In an unpublished opinion, the U.S. District Court for the Southern District of New York dismissed a Major Fraud Act claim where the criminal allegation was brought by a private citizen, holding that the citizen did not have standing to bring such a claim.[1]

§ 1:10 Criminal false claims

To establish a violation of the criminal False Claims Act,[1] the Government must prove the following:

(1) You made or presented a claim to certain Government officials or to a Government department or agency;
(2) The claim was asserted against the United States or its agencies or departments;
(3) The claim was false, fictitious, or fraudulent; and
(4) You knew the claim was false, fictitious, or fraudulent when presented.

The definition of the term "claim" is a broad one. As a practical matter, any attempt to get money from the Government is a claim.

You do not have to present the claim *directly* to the Government to trigger a violation of the statute. Submission of a claim to a private entity with the knowledge that the entity will pass the cost on to the Government is enough for you to be charged with a criminal false claim. For example, submission of falsified

---

[8]*See, e.g., Moore v. California Institute of Technology Jet Propulsion Laboratory*, 275 F.3d 838, 160 Ed. Law Rep. 304 (9th Cir. 2002).

[Section 1:9]

[1]*Pentagen Technologies Intern., Ltd. v. CACI Intern. Inc.*, 1996 WL 435157 (S.D. N.Y. 1996), adhered to on reconsideration, 1996 WL 434551 (S.D. N.Y. 1996).

[Section 1:10]

[1]18 U.S.C.A. § 287.

invoices by a subcontractor to a prime contractor with the knowledge that the prime will pass the cost on to the Government may expose the subcontractor to criminal liability for submission of a false claim.

The statutory *penalty* for violation of the criminal False Claims Act is imprisonment of up to five years. The criminal False Claims Act can also trigger fines of $250,000 for individuals and $500,000 for companies (see Part VIII below).

§ 1:11 Criminal false claims—Examples

Product substitution: You deliver to the Government parts that you know are refurbished under a contract that you know calls for delivery of new parts. You deliver invoices to the Government claiming payment. Any invoice requesting payment under these circumstances may be charged as a criminal false claim.

False testing: You send the metal bolts that you are making for the Government to an outside laboratory for testing, as required by the contract specifications. When the bolts fail the tests, you falsify the results to indicate that the bolts in fact passed the tests. You ship the bolts to the Government and send an invoice to the Government for payment. Each invoice sent to the Government under these circumstances may be charged as a criminal false claim.

III. CONSPIRACY

§ 1:12 Generally

There are two federal statutes governing illegal conspiracies to defraud the Government. The more popular of the two, the general federal conspiracy statute[1] makes it a crime for two or more persons to "conspire either to commit any offense against the United States, or to defraud the United States, or any agency thereof in any manner or for any purpose." To establish an offense under § 371, the Government must show the following:

(1) An *agreement* between two or more persons to commit any offense against the United States or to defraud the United States; and
(2) The commission by one conspirator of an *overt act* in furtherance of the conspiracy.

There is no need for a formal conspiratorial agreement. All that is required is a *mutual understanding*—stated or tacit—to try to accomplish a common and unlawful plan. This understand-

---

[Section 1:12]
[1] 18 U.S.C.A. § 371.

ing may be inferred from the facts and circumstances of a given situation.

An *overt act* in furtherance of a conspiracy is any act that aims to advance the conspiratorial scheme. Only one conspirator need commit an overt act. The overt act need not itself be an illegal act. Neither the overt act nor the conspiracy as a whole need be successful; the defendant need not complete the substantive offense to be guilty of a conspiracy to do so. The overt act requirement simply ensures that the law does not punish mere thoughts or agreements unaccompanied by any action on those thoughts or agreements.

Regardless of when a conspirator joins a conspiracy, the conspirator is considered a full-fledged member of the conspiracy from the time the conspiracy began until the time he or she actively *withdraws* from the conspiracy. Withdrawal is accomplished by taking an affirmative action inconsistent with the object of the conspiracy, such as the communication of withdrawal to the other co-conspirators.

Unless you withdraw from a conspiracy, you may be liable as a conspirator, even if you did not know every detail of the conspiratorial agreement or the other conspirators' precise actions in furtherance of the conspiracy. Indeed, you need not even know the identities of all the other conspirators. Simply stated, a person who actively participates at the inception of the conspiracy and then merely ceases his or her activity, a person who performs one small role in the conspiracy, or a person who joined the conspiracy in its last stages all may be liable for the entire conspiracy.

A *conspiracy to defraud* the United States under § 371 is interpreted to include any conspiracy to defraud the Government of money or to obstruct or impair a legitimate Government function. Thus, conspiracies to bribe a federal official are often characterized as conspiracies to defraud the United States of the honest and faithful services of its employees. Conspiracies that involve the submission of false documents to the Government are often characterized as conspiracies to obstruct the legitimate function of the affected Government agency. Additionally, conspiracies involving bid-rigging among contractors are often charged as conspiracies to defraud the United States under § 371.[2]

The other conspiracy statute is the false claims conspiracy

---

[2]*See U.S. v. Gosselin World Wide Moving, N.V.*, 411 F.3d 502 (4th Cir. 2005), cert. denied, 126 S. Ct. 1464, 164 L. Ed. 2d 246 (U.S. 2006).

statute.[3] This special conspiracy statute is applied less frequently than the general conspiracy statute (§ 371); it applies only when the conspirators agree to defraud the Government in a specific manner—by obtaining payment of a false claim. However, when the Government charges conspiracy under § 286 it does not need to establish an overt act in furtherance of the conspiracy as an element of the offense.

The penalties for conspiracy are fines under the Sentence of Fine statute (see § 1:48) and imprisonment for up to five years (under § 371) or up to 10 years (under § 286).

§ 1:13 Examples

Conspiracy to commit an offense against the U.S.: Because more than one person is often involved in many of the examples of crimes discussed in earlier sections of this chapter, a charge of conspiracy can in many instances be added to another offense. For example, if you instruct employees to mischarge on a contract, and the employees know they are mischarging on a contract, the Government could charge you and your employees with a conspiracy to violate the criminal false claims statute as well as charge you with submitting false claims. Moreover, since most conspiracies involving Government contractors are directed against the Government, these conspiracies could also be charged as conspiracies to defraud the United States under § 371 (or, if the conspiracy involves the payment or allowance of a false claim, under § 286).

If an employee sells confidential bid data and other related information to representatives of competing contractors, and the competing contractors use that data to underbid you, the individuals and the contractors involved can be charged under § 371 for subverting the Government's procedures for competitively awarded contracts.[1]

Unsuccessful conspiracy to defraud the U.S.: As a member of your company's marketing organization, you discuss with one of your colleagues your idea for bribing a Government procurement official by directing your company's travel business to a travel agency owned by the procurement official's wife. The following week, your colleague tells you that she met with the person in your company responsible for selecting a travel agent and that "the switch is in the works." Your colleague also tells you that the procurement official told her he is "pleased as punch that you're giving my wife so much business," and that the company

---

[3]18 U.S.C.A. § 286.

[Section 1:13]

[1]U.S. v. Cartwright, D. Md., indictment unsealed January 7, 2008.

should expect no problems on an upcoming procurement. The next month, the Government procurement official gets a new assignment and is no longer responsible for making awards to your company. Your company has kept as its travel agent the travel agent who had served it all along. Even though your company never switched travel agents, you could be liable for conspiracy to bribe or conspiracy to defraud the Government of the honest services of the procurement official because you and your colleague agreed to bribe the official, and because your colleague took an overt act (meeting with the person responsible for selecting a travel agent) in furtherance of the illegal agreement.

The "little guy" and "late participant" as full-fledged conspirators: Smith and Cooper work on different shifts. Their foremen, on instructions from management, direct Smith and Cooper not to perform contractually required tests on the product they are manufacturing but to write up the test reports anyway. Smith and Cooper do as they are told for several months. Then Smith, who has read an article about Government procurement fraud investigations, decides to leave his job. He tells his foreman that he is doing so because of the false test reports; he also writes a letter to the company president to inform him of the scheme. Jones comes to replace Smith and, per instructions from supervisors, fails to perform the tests and writes up false test reports. The scheme is discovered a week later. Cooper and Jones may be liable for conspiracy to make false statements, conspiracy to submit false claims, or conspiracy to defraud the Government, even though (a) they were "just following orders," (b) they do not know each other, (c) they never entered into a formal agreement, and (d) Jones entered the conspiracy at a late date and participated in it for only a short period of time. Smith may be liable for his participation in the conspiracy up to the time he quit and notified the company president.

IV. CIVIL FRAUD

§ 1:14 Generally

In addition to the criminal fraud statutes discussed above, there are several civil statutes that provide for multiple damages awards, heavy civil fines, and administrative penalties for procurement abuses. These statutes are examined below and the information is summarized in the chart in Appendix A to this Handbook.

§ 1:15 Civil False Claims Act

The past several years have seen very active courts nationwide issuing decisions on a plethora of issues arising under the False

§ 1:15 THE OFFENSES & PENALTIES

Claims Act. Those decisions and analysis of them would fill a treatise, which is not the purpose of this chapter. Instead, this chapter is intended to give the reader an understanding of what compliance pitfalls lurk.

Under the civil False Claims Act,[1] the United States may recover treble damages and penalties for the submission of false claims to any federal agency or entity using federal funds to pay such claims. Specifically, a person (or company) may be liable under the Act if he or she:

(1) Knowingly presents, or causes to be prese nted, to a Government official a false or fraudulent claim[2] for payment or approval;

(2) Knowingly makes, uses, or causes to be made or used, a false record or statement to get a false or fraudulent claim paid or approved;

(3) Conspires to defraud the Government by getting a false or fraudulent claim allowed or paid; or

(4) Knowingly makes, uses, or causes to be made or used, a false record or statement to conceal, avoid, or decrease an obligation to pay or transmit money or property to the Government.

The civil False Claims Act defines "knowingly" to include reckless conduct or conduct in deliberate ignorance of the truth. In addition, *no specific intent* to defraud is required.

The main differences between the civil and criminal false claims statutes are the *level of intent* required, the *burden of proof*, and the *penalties*. The criminal False Claims Act (see

---

[Section 1:15]

[1]31 U.S.C.A. § 3729; *see generally* Sylvia, The False Claims Act: Fraud Against the Government 2d (2010).

[2]The U.S. Court of Appeals for the Fourth Circuit in *Harrison v. Westinghouse Savannah River Co.*, 176 F.3d 776 (4th Cir. 1999), held that the phrase "false and fraudulent claim" in the False Claims Act should be construed broadly because the FCA is intended to reach all types of fraud that might result in financial loss to the Government. Therefore, it is not necessary that a false demand for payment be submitted to the Government. Instead, it was sufficient in this case that the qui tam plaintiff alleged that a knowing misrepresentation by the contractor to the Government about the need to hire and the cost of hiring a subcontractor had a material effect on the Government's decision to approve the subcontract, and these false statements caused the Government to pay a higher price for the work than it would have paid had the contractor performed the work itself. Because the false statements caused the Government to incur higher costs than it would have paid absent the alleged fraud, the allegations were sufficient to state an FCA claim. *But see U.S. ex rel. Karvelas v. Melrose-Wakefield Hosp.*, 360 F.3d 220, 57 Fed. R. Serv. 3d 1262 (1st Cir. 2004), cert. denied, 543 U.S. 820, 125 S. Ct. 59, 160 L. Ed. 2d 28 (2004) (finding an actual demand for payment necessary for an action under the FCA).

§ 1:15 GOVERNMENT CONTRACT COMPLIANCE HANDBOOK

§ 1:10) requires the Government to prove that the defendant *knew* the claim was false, fictitious, or fraudulent. Courts have held that criminal knowledge of the claim's falsity can be inferred from a reckless disregard for the truth of the claim combined with a conscious effort to avoid learning the truth.[3] This standard is very similar to the civil False Claims Act's definition of "knowingly," which (as stated above) includes "reckless conduct" or conduct "in deliberate ignorance of the truth."

Under the civil False Claims Act, the Government need only show a violation by "a preponderance of the evidence." Under the criminal False Claims Act, as in all criminal cases, the Government must prove its case "beyond a reasonable doubt."

The statutory text of the civil False Claims Act does not explicitly address the necessary nexus between an allegedly false statement and a "false" claim. However, several circuits deciding the issue have found that a civil action brought under the False Claims Act, and predicated on a false statement, does include a materiality requirement.[4] "Materiality" has been defined as "having natural tendency to influence, or being capable of influencing, the decision of the decision making body to which it was addressed."[5]

The *penalties* for violation of the civil False Claims Act include (a) a fine of between $5,500 and $11,000 for each false claim, (b) an amount equal to three times the amount of damages the false claim caused the Government, and (c) the costs of prosecution. Because penalties may be imposed for *each* false claim (e.g., every invoice), they can quickly accrue to a large sum.[6]

The civil False Claims Act further provides that the court may assess a *reduced penalty* of not more than two times the amount

---

[3]*See, e.g., U.S. v. Nazon*, 940 F.2d 255 (7th Cir. 1991); *U.S. v. Gold*, 743 F.2d 800, 17 Fed. R. Evid. Serv. 669 (11th Cir. 1984); *U.S. v. Raymond & Whitcomb Co.*, 53 F. Supp. 2d 436 (S.D. N.Y. 1999).

[4]*See U.S. ex rel. A+ Homecare, Inc. v. Medshares Management Group, Inc.*, 400 F.3d 428, 2005 FED App. 0120P (6th Cir. 2005), cert. denied, 126 S. Ct. 797, 163 L. Ed. 2d 630 (U.S. 2005); *U.S. v. Southland Management Corp.*, 326 F.3d 669 (5th Cir. 2003); *U.S. ex rel. Costner v. U.S.*, 317 F.3d 883 (8th Cir. 2003); *Luckey v. Baxter Healthcare Corp.*, 183 F.3d 730 (7th Cir. 1999); *U.S. ex rel. Berge v. Board of Trustees of the University of Alabama*, 104 F.3d 1453, 1459, 115 Ed. Law Rep. 344 (4th Cir. 1997); *U.S. v. TDC Management Corp., Inc.*, 24 F.3d 292 (D.C. Cir. 1994).

[5]*U.S. v. Southland Management Corp.*, 288 F.3d 665 (5th Cir. 2002), on reh'g en banc, 326 F.3d 669 (5th Cir. 2003).

[6]In *U.S. v. Mackby*, 339 F.3d 1013 (9th Cir. 2003), cert. denied, 541 U.S. 936, 124 S. Ct. 1657, 158 L. Ed. 2d 356 (2004) (finding $730,000 penalty for $55,000 in damages does not violate the Excessive Fines Clause of the Eighth Amendment because it was not grossly disproportionate to the defendant's level of culpability).

THE OFFENSES & PENALTIES § 1:15

of actual damages sustained by the Government if the defendant *cooperates* with the Government. Specifically, the penalty may be reduced if (1) the person committing the violation furnishes investigating officials with all information known to that person about the violation within 30 days of obtaining the information, (2) the person committing the violation fully cooperates with any Government investigation of the violation, (3) at the time the information is furnished, no criminal prosecution or civil or administrative action has commenced with respect to the violation, and (4) the person did not have actual knowledge of the existence of an investigation into the alleged violation.[7]

Cases & Commentary: On May 20, 2009, Congress significantly expanded the coverage of the civil False Claims Act as part of the Fraud Enforcement and Recovery Act of 2009, P.L. 111-21, 123 Stat. 1621. In large part this was done to legislatively reverse certain court decisions that Congress viewed inconsistent with the overall purposes of the act. As revised, 31 U.S.C.A. § 3729 now states:

(a) LIABILITY FOR CERTAIN ACTS

(1) IN GENERAL.—Subject to paragraph (2), any person who—

(A) knowingly presents, or causes to be presented, a false or fraudulent claim for payment or approval;

(B) knowingly makes, uses, or causes to be made or used, a false record or statement material to a false or fraudulent claim;

(C) conspires to commit a violation of subparagraph (A), (B), (D), (E), (F), or (G);

(D) has possession, custody, or control of property or money used, or to be used, by the Government and knowingly delivers, or causes to be delivered, less than all of that money or property;

(E) is authorized to make or deliver a document certifying receipt of property used, or to be used, by the Government and, intending to defraud the Government, makes or delivers the receipt without completely knowing that the information on the receipt is true;

(F) knowingly buys, or receives as a pledge of an obligation or debt, public property from an officer or employee of the Government, or a member of the Armed Forces, who lawfully may not sell or pledge property; or

(G) knowingly makes, uses, or causes to be made or used, a false record or statement material to an obligation to pay or transmit money or property to the Government,

---

[7]31 U.S.C.A. § 3729(a).

or knowingly conceals or knowingly and improperly avoids or decreases an obligation to pay or transmit money or property to the Government, is liable to the United States Government for a civil penalty of not less than $5,000 and not more than $10,000, as adjusted by the Federal Civil Penalties Inflation Adjustment Act of 1990 (28 U.S.C. 2461 note; Public Law 104-410), plus 3 times the amount of damages which the Government sustains because of the act of that person.

(b) DEFINITIONS—For purposes of this section

(1) the terms "knowing" and "knowingly"—

   (A) mean that a person, with respect to information—

      (i) has actual knowledge of the information;

      (ii) acts in deliberate ignorance of the truth or falsity of the information; or

      (iii) acts in reckless disregard of the truth or falsity of the information; and

   (B) require no proof of specific intent to defraud;

(2) the term "claim"—

   (A) means any request or demand, whether under a contract or otherwise, for money or property and whether or not the United States has title to the money or property, that—

      (i) is presented to an officer, employee, or agent of the United States; or

      (ii) is made to a contractor, grantee, or other recipient, if the money or property is to be spent or used on the Government's behalf or to advance a Government program or interest, and if the United States Government—

         (I) provides or has provided any portion of the money or property requested or demanded; or

         (II) will reimburse such contractor, grantee, or other recipient for any portion of the money or property which is requested or demanded; and

   (B) does not include requests or demands for money or property that the Government has paid to an individual as compensation for Federal employment or as an income subsidy with no restrictions on that individual's use of the money or property;

(3) the term "obligation" means an established duty, whether or not fixed, arising from an express or implied contractual, grantor-grantee, or licensor-licensee relationship, from a fee-based or similar relationship, from statute or regulation, or from the retention of any overpayment; and

(4) the term "material" means having a natural tendency

§ 1:15

to influence, or be capable of influencing, the payment or receipt of money or property.

Structurally, the provisions § 3729(a)(1)(A)–(H) of the amended act correspond to the previous provisions in § 3729(a)(1)–(7).

One issue leading to the substantive changes in the amended FCA was the "presentment" requirement in the former 31 U.S.C.A. § 3729(a)(1). That section provided for liability for any person who:

> knowingly presents, or causes to be presented, to an officer or employee of the United States Government or a member of the Armed Forces of the United States a false or fraudulent claim for payment or approval.

U.S. ex rel. Totten v Bombardier Corp., 380 F.3d 488 (D.C. Cir. 2004) involved a contractor who manufactured products for Amtrak trains. The court held in that case that a the contractor could not be held liable under § 3729(a)(1) for submitting an allegedly false claim to Amtrak because Amtrak was not a Government entity and thus the claim had not been "presented" to the U.S. Government. The effect of this decision, and others similar to it, was to force the Government to rely on § 3729(a)(2) in FCA cases where the defendant was a subcontractor or other third with no direct contractual relationship to the Government. (As noted below, other court decisions made it increasingly difficult to utilize this provision in such cases.) To remedy this situation Congress revised the definition of "claim" in § 3729(b)(2) to include demands "presented" not only to "an officer, employee, or agent of the United States" but also demands made to "a contractor, grantee, or other recipient" of Government funds. Thus, proof of presentment to the Government is no longer necessary in order to establish liability under the new § 3729(a)(1)(B).

In *Allison Engine Co., Inc. v. U.S. ex rel. Sanders*, 553 U.S. 662 (2008), the Supreme Court confirmed that § 3729(a)(2) did not requires proof that a defendant's false statement had been physically "presented" to the Government. However, the Court then said that the presence of the phrase "to get a false or fraudulent claim paid" required a showing that the third party "intended" the Government to rely on the statement as a condition of payment. Because of the similarity of language this conclusion also applied to liability for conspiracy under the former § 3729 (a)(3). As a practical matter, this would be a difficult standard to meet because in many cases the third party, say a third tier subcontractor who manufactures a commercial product, might not be aware that the Government is the ultimate customer.

In enacting the amendment to the FCA, Congress expressly stated that it wanted to overturn this portion of the *Allison* decision. Thus, the revised § 3729(a)(1)(B) deleted the "to get"

§ 1:15   GOVERNMENT CONTRACT COMPLIANCE HANDBOOK

language. Instead to constitute an FCA violation, the false record or statement now need only be "material" to a false or fraudulent claim. Likewise, § 3729(a)(1)(C) was also reworded to eliminate the need to prove an intent to defraud in conspiracy cases. Previously, courts had read a "materiality" requirement into the FCA. Section § 3729(b)(4) of the amended FCA specifically defines "material" as having a natural tendency to influence, or be capable of influencing, the payment or receipt of money or property. Thus, now, a subcontractor or other third party can be liable under the FCA if its false claim would influence the Government's decision to make payment, even though the claim had not been directly submitted to the Government and there was no evidence that the contractor intended the Government to rely on it.

To emphasize its intent to legislatively overrule *Allison*, Congress made this specific change retroactive to "claims" that were *pending* on June 7, 2008, two days before the Supreme Court issued its decision remanding the case to the district court.

The other provisions of the amended FCA do *not* apply to events that took place before May 20, 2009. However, after the 2009 amendments to the FCA and the enactment of the Patient Protection and Affordable Care Act of 2010, Pub. L. No. 111-148, 124 Stat. 119 (PPACA), the knowing retention of such funds would arguable constitute a violation of 31 U.S.C.A. § 3729(a)(1)(G).

Another issue that had arisen out of various court decisions over the years concerned the *source* of the funds that would used to pay an allegedly false claim. The question was "At what point do monies lose their identity as "Government funds?" This was a recent issue in cases involving contracts with the Coalition Provisional Authority (CPA) in Iraq. The Fourth Circuit in *U.S. ex rel. DRC, Inc. v. Custer Battles LLC*, 562 F.3d 295 (4th Cir. 2009) held that the crucial issue was whether the Government had initially provided the funds, not whether it still retained "control" over them at the time defendants submitted the false claims. The new definition of "claim" in § 3729(b)(2) statutorily confirms the Fourth Circuit decision. Thus, a person can now be liable for a false claim if the money is to "be spent or used on the Government's behalf or to advance a Government program or interest" and if the Government provides or reimburses any portion of that money.

The amendments to the FCA also enlarged the scope of the original "reverse false claims" provision in § 3729(a)(7) by making the retention of funds that were known to be paid in error a violation of the act. Previously, in order to establish liability the Government had to demonstrate that a contractor used a false record to "conceal, avoid, or decrease an obligation" to pay or transmit money or property to the Government. As amended,

The Offenses & Penalties § 1:15

under § 3729(a)(1)(G) a person is liable if he or she "knowingly conceals or knowingly and improperly avoids or decreases an obligation to pay" the Government. In other words, liability is not predicated on the creation or use of a record, but simply the act of concealing or avoiding an obligation to pay.

In addition, the amendments to the FCA significantly expanded the "whistleblower" provisions of the act. Previously, under § 3730(h), whistleblower protection extended only to an "employee" who was engaged in lawful acts "in furtherance of an action under this section." Under this provision, a good faith subjective belief that there was a basis for a FCA action was not sufficient and if it were ultimately determined that there was no viable action against the employer, discharging the employee would not constitute an unlawful retaliation. See § 1:20, Qui tam lawsuits—Whistleblower protections, *infra*. The amended act now extends coverage not only to employees, but also to contractors and agents. In addition, it no longer focuses on actions aimed at initiating a qui tam action, but rather protects all legal acts "in furtherance of other efforts to stop 1 or more violations of this subchapter." The amendment thus shifts the emphasis from exposing the consequences of improper activity to preventing it from occurring in the first place.

The amendments to the FCA also modified the operation of the statute of limitation provisions set forth in § 3731(b). Reportedly there is currently a backlog of hundreds of pending qui tam actions. Because of the sheer number of cases and their complexity, it has become difficult for the DoJ to make an informed judgment as to whether to intervene within the six year statute of limitations. DoJ has argued, for the most part unsuccessfully, that date on which it filed its own action "relates back" to the date of the filing of the original qui tam action, i.e., for purposes of the statute of limitations, that the DoJ action would be deemed to have been filed at the same time as the original suit. See, *e.g.*, *U.S., ex rel. Ramadoss v. Caremark Inc.*, 586 F. Supp. 2d 668 (W.D. Tex. 2008). Congress has now added a new § 3731(c) to the FCA which expressly states that the Government pleading "shall relate back to the filing date of the complaint of the person who originally brought the action" so long as the Government claim "arises out of the conduct, transactions, or occurrences set forth, or attempted to be set forth, in the prior complaint of that person."

Finally the FCA amendments modified the provisions of § 3733 of the act by making it easier for investigators to obtain a Civil Investigative Demand. A CID is an investigative tool available to the DoJ in FCA cases that can be issued for the production of documents, interrogatories, oral depositions or any combination of these. Under the previous act, only the Attorney General had the authority to issue a CID; he or she was expressly prohibited from delegating that authority. Now § 3733(a)(1)(D) expressly authorize the AG to do just that.

Whether taken individually or collectively, the amendments to the FCA constitute a breathtaking expansion in the coverage of the act. Consider this: Demonstrating that a claim was "presented" to the Government to establish liability under the § 3729(a)(1)(A) is no longer necessary, thereby making that section applicable to subcontractors and other third parties as long as the Government pays or reimburses that party for some portion of the amount claim. Demonstrating that a subcontractor or other third party "intended" to defraud the Government is no longer required for § 3729(a)(1)(B) as long as that party "makes or uses" a false document that would be capable of influencing the Government's decision to make payment. Likewise, it is no longer necessary to show an intent to defraud in order to establish a conspiracy violation under § 3729(a)(1)(C). Further, it is not necessary to demonstrate the Government "controls" the funds that are the subject of the false claim or even to show that the Government has title to those funds; all that is necessary is a showing that some portion of the money was "provided" by the Government in order "to advance a Government program or interest."

To establish liability under the "reverse false claims" provision of § 3729(a)(1)(G), it is only necessary to show that a person avoids repaying any funds known to have been paid in error. Thus, the pool of persons to whom the act now applies has increased tremendously beyond the relatively small number of traditional Government prime contractors. Clearly, persons involved in the healthcare industry, grantees, and in general anyone who is a direct or indirect recipient of Government funds falls within the scope of the act. The outer limits of this group is difficult to define: Does it include defrauding a charitable organization that is partially funded by the Government? Quite possibly. What about corruption in foreign countries involving humanitarian programs that are partially funded by the Government? Again, quite possibly. And, with the expanded definition of "protected activity" under the whistleblower provisions of the act, the expanded availability of CIDs, and the increased amount of time now available for investigation before the Government must make a decision on whether to intervene, the number of FCA actions is almost certain to increase. For a more detailed discussion of these amendments, see Laura Laemmle-Weidenfeld and Michael J. Schaengold, "The Impact of The Fraud Enforcement and Recovery Act of 2009 on The Civil False Claims Act," 51 The Government Contractor ¶ 224 (July 8, 2009).

The FCA creates liability for a "person" who defrauds the Government. Courts have interpreted that term based on the

§ 1:15

FCA's history and purpose. In *Cook County, Ill. v. U.S. ex rel. Chandler*, 538 U.S. 119 (2003) for example, the Supreme Court found that counties and municipalities were "persons" subject to suit under the Act. Three years earlier, the Supreme Court found that states were *not* "persons" under § 3729. *Vermont Agency of Natural Resources v. U.S. ex rel. Stevens*, 529 U.S. 765 (2000). In *U.S. v. Menominee Tribal Enterprises*, 601 F. Supp. 2d 1061 (E.D. Wis. 2009), judgment entered, 2009 WL 2877083 (E.D. Wis. 2009), the court held that there was no affirmative evidence that Congress intended to allow Indian tribes to be sued under the FCA and thus concluded that tribes are not "persons" under 31 U.S.C.A. § 3729. However, while an entity such as a state or Indian tribe may not be a person within the meaning of the FCA, nothing prohibits a suit against an individual who committed the fraud simply because he or she was employed by such organizations. *Stoner v. Santa Clara County Office of Educ.*, 502 F.3d 1116 (9th Cir. 2007), cert. denied, 128 S. Ct. 1728, 170 L. Ed. 2d 515 (2008) and cert. denied, 129 S. Ct. 46, 172 L. Ed. 2d 22 (2008).

The most fundamental requirement of the FCA is that the "false or fraudulent claim" must be *objectively false*. *In U.S. ex rel. Wilson v. Kellogg Brown & Root, Inc.*, 525 F.3d 370 (4th Cir. 2008), the relators claimed the contractor was liable under the FCA because it had failed to maintain a fleet of vehicles as required by its contract. The court found that the maintenance provisions of the contract were very general and that the allegations of poor maintenance did not qualify as an objective falsehood.

Similarly, a claim cannot be "false" when the law is unclear or when there is a legitimate "good faith" disagreement about the applicable law. In *U.S., ex rel. Ramadoss v. Caremark Inc.*, 586 F. Supp. 2d 668 (W.D. Tex. 2008) the Government contended a "pharmacy benefit manager" had allegedly violated the reverse false claims provisions of the FCA by failing to reimburse Medicaid for certain costs that should have been paid by a private insurance company. The court rejected this argument, noting that the law in the area was complex and had been the subject of prolonged litigation.

Likewise, courts have generally required that the false claim be "material," *i.e.*, that the fraudulent statement or action by the contractor is required to be made in order to receive payment or some other benefit. "Materiality" has been a particular issue in cases in which the contractor has allegedly failed to comply with a contract requirement even thought the product or service furnished to the Government fully complied with all of the contract specifications. The question basically becomes: Are all contract requirements "equal?" Courts have generally answered this by saying "The failure to perform a contract requirement will only be considered material, and thus give rise to potential FCA liability, if payment was conditioned on compliance with that requirement." See, *e.g.*, *Science Applications Intern. Corp.*, 653 F. Supp. 2d 87 (D.D.C. 2009) rev'd on other grounds 626 F.3d 1257 (D.C. Cir. 2010) (Government presented sufficient evidence to support the jury's finding that contractor's OCI representations were critical to the Government's decision to pay). At least one court has held that the issue of materiality is a legal issue to be decided by the court, not a factual question for a jury. See *U.S. ex rel. Berge v. Board of Trustees of the University of Alabama*, 104 F.3d 1453 (4th Cir. 1997). Note the recent amendments to the FCA discussed in § 1:15, *supra*, explicitly defines "materiality" as an element of a violation of the new § 3729(a)(1)(B).

The American Recovery and Reinvestment Act, Pub. L. No. 111-5, 123 Stat. 115, which was signed on February 17, 2009, provided billions of dollars for a wide variety of projects to stimulate the U.S. economy. The law directed the President and heads of Federal agencies to "commenc-[e] expenditures and activities as quickly as possible consistent with prudent management." Section 1512 of the Act imposes extensive reporting requirements on recipients of Recovery Act funds. In particular, contractors must report on a quarterly basis (1) the amount of funds received from each agency, (2) the amount of funds that were expended or obligated to projects, (3) a detailed list of all projects for which funds were expended, including the name and description of the project, an evaluation of the completion status of the project, and an estimate of the number of jobs created and retained by the project, and (4) detailed information on any subcontracts or subgrants awarded by the recipient. Significantly, § 1512(f) specifies that this information must be provided "as a condition of receipt of funds under this Act." It appears, then, that contractors will be unable to contend in a FCA suit that false statements contained in these reports were not "material" to the Government's decision to make payment. On April 23, 2009, OMB provided guidance on the application of these requirements. See 74 Fed. Reg. 18449. These provisions have been implemented in a new clause at FAR 52.204-11 entitled "American Recovery and Reinvestment Act—Reporting Requirements."

The Government can initiate a FCA action as a separate suit or assert it as a counterclaim in a court action brought by the contractor. See, e.g., *Daewoo Engineering & Const. Co., Ltd. v. U.S.*, 73 Fed. Cl. 547 (2006), judgment aff'd, 557 F.3d 1332 (Fed. Cir. 2009), cert. den., 130 S. Ct. 490 (2009). The DoJ can raise the counterclaim in a contract dispute that is subject to the Contract Disputes Act, 41 U.S.C.A. §§ 7101 to 7109, without first obtaining a contracting officer's final decision on that matter. See

The Offenses & Penalties § 1:15

Martin J. Simko Const., Inc. v. U.S., 852 F.2d 540 (Fed. Cir. 1988). The three-year statute of limitation period under 31 U.S.C.A. § 3731(b)(2) is triggered by the Government's discovery of the fraud. However, the "discovery" is not the knowledge of the fraud by any government official, but knowledge by an official having the authority to initiate litigation under the Act. This is generally considered to be an official at the Civil Division of the DoJ since it has exclusive litigating authority under the FCA. See *Jana, Inc. v. U.S.*, 34 Fed. Cl. 447 (1995); *Veridyne Corp. v. United States*, 86 Fed. Cl. 668 (2009).

Liability under the civil False Claims Act does not hinge on whether the Government actually paid the claim. In *Bridges v. Omega World Travel, Inc.*, 2009 WL 5174283 (E.D. Ark. 2009), the relator, a government employee, contended that a travel agency failed to offer him the lowest available airfare in violation of the terms of its contract with the Government. The travel agency contended that the allegations did not constitute a claim under 31 U.S.C.A. § 3729(a)(1) because the Government was never charged the higher fare price. The court rejected this, holding that the FCA does not require fraudulent charging; it was meant to reach all types of fraud that might result in financial loss to the government, even if there is no actual loss.

The FCA provides that the a defendant who submits a false claim is liable for both civil penalties and three times the amount of the damages the Government sustained as a result of the false claim. Regarding the penalty, 31 U.S.C.A. § 3729(a)(1)(A) states that any person who submits a "false or fraudulent claim for payment" is liable for a civil penalty of not less than $5,000 and not more than $10,000 as adjusted for inflation.

The civil FCA provides in 31 U.S.C.A. § 3729(a)(2) that the penalty can be reduced from three times the actual damages to twice the amount of damages if the defendant furnishes "officials of the United States responsible for investigating false claims violations with all information known to such person about the violation within 30 days after the date on which the defendant first obtained the information" and meets certain other requirements. In *U.S. ex rel. Maxwell v. Kerr-McGee*, 2010 WL 3730894 (D. Colo. 2010) the court held that the defendant had the burden of proof to establish by a preponderance of the evidence that it furnished the "officials" with such information. Further, the court stated that the disclosure must be made to the Attorney General since DoJ had the responsibility for investigating such matters. Since the defendant had only made disclosure to its customer, the Mineral Management Service, it did not qualify for the reduced penalties.

§ 1:16 Civil False Claims Act—Examples

Product substitution: Your employees submit parts that are refurbished on a contract that calls for new parts, not because you or they set out to breach the contract, but because your company does not have a good system for identifying which contracts call for new rather than refurbished parts. Government officials have previously told you that your system is inadequate. If you continue to send the Government invoices for new parts when you actually supplied refurbished parts, are you liable to the Government for submitting false claims? While your intent to defraud the Government is probably insufficient to establish a criminal false claims case against you, you may be liable for violation of the civil False Claims Act arising out of your reckless disregard for the truth inherent in your conduct and submission of invoices on the contract.

Product substitution where the Government does not reject the substituted materials: Your employees submit invoices to the Government for tools known to be other than the brand-named tools the Government ordered. The Government accepted the tools on delivery without complaint. The U.S. Court of Appeals for the Eighth Circuit addressed a case with these facts and ruled in an unpublished opinion that the submission of such invoices violated the False Claims Act, and that the Government's acceptance of the tools was not a defense to civil liability under the Act.[1]

Defective pricing: When selling a product to the Government that falls within the "commercial item" exemption for application of the Truth in Negotiations Act (see §§ 9:1 et seq.), you certify to the lowest price at which you sold the product to the public during the period in question. Unbeknownst to you, your salesmen have informally been extending discounts to valued customers which you would have known about if you had been more careful about reading their sales reports. You could be liable for violation of the civil False Claims Act in connection with the submission of any invoices to the Government for your product.

Cases & Commentary: "Fraud-in-the-inducement": Another example of a factual setting that can give rise to a false claim allegation occurs when a contractor makes factual representations in its proposal concerning the resources it will apply to the contract and then after award significantly departs from its stated plan, presumably to its financial advantage. In *U.S. ex rel. DRC, Inc. v. Custer Battles, LLC*, 472 F. Supp. 2d 787 (E.D. Va. 2007),

---

[Section 1:16]

[1] *See U.S. v. Advance Tool Co.*, 86 F.3d 1159 (8th Cir. 1996).

aff'd, 562 F.3d 295 (4th Cir. 2009) the *qui tam* plaintiffs alleged that the contractor had fraudulently represented that it would use 138 persons in performing a fixed-price contract for "screening" operations at Baghdad International Airport but that it used fewer persons than it had represented. The court found that the only indication of the number of planned personnel set forth in the proposal was derived from the contractor's estimate of its costs which were based on the salaries of 138.5 security personnel. The court concluded that this was insufficient to constitute a representation of the number of personnel that would be utilized, noting that courts have held that a legitimate estimate by a contractor of work that is to be performed is not a false claim. Further the court found that liability requires that a person "knowingly" make a false statement and that in the context of a "fraudulent inducement" claim, "the requisite intent must be coupled with prompt, substantial nonperformance." The court found that in fact the contractor had staffed the project with around 138 people for much of the time and thus there was no evidence of "prompt, substantial nonperformance." Finally, the court found that even had the contractor falsely represented the number of personnel, such misrepresentation was not "material" as required for a false claim. The court noted that the official in charge of evaluating proposals stated that the contractor was chosen because of its price and its commitment to meet the overall objectives of the contract, and that "the number of security personnel the contractor would provide was never a prerequisite for awarding the contract."

See *U.S. ex rel. Hooper v. Lockheed Martin Corp.*, 688 F.3d 1037 (9th Cir. 2012), where the U.S. Court of Appeals for the Ninth Circuit determined that in a proposal, "false estimates, defined to include fraudulent underbidding in which the bid is not what the defendant actually intends to charge, can be a source of liability under the FCA."

Exaggerating or overstating one's experience and resources in a proposal can also constitute an FCA violation under a "fraud in the inducement theory." *U.S. ex rel. Longhi v. Lithium Power Technologies, Inc.*, 530 F. Supp. 2d 888 (S.D. Tex. 2008), aff'd, 575 F.3d 458 (5th Cir. 2009), cert. denied, 130 S. Ct. 2092, 176 L. Ed. 2d 722 (2010), involved four proposals under the Government's SBIR program. The court found that the offeror continuously misrepresented the arrangements between itself and another contractor and between itself and a university. It also misrepresented the amount of related work it had performed prior to submitting these proposals. The contractor argued that the Government was trying to make "a mountain out of a group of small molehills." The court explained that that was the nature of the fraud, and not an excuse for it:

§ 1:16   GOVERNMENT CONTRACT COMPLIANCE HANDBOOK

But that encapsulates exactly the overall misrepresentation that [the contractor] made in its proposals. It embellished a whole series of molehills so it could present a mountain of experience, facilities, and novelty to attract the reviewers.

The court also concluded that the Government had received no benefit from the work the contractor performed and thus determined that the Government's damages were equal to the three times the amounts paid out under the four contract as specified under the FCA, for total damages of almost $5 million. Finally, in calculating the statutory penalty, the court concluded that the contracts, rather than the individual payments under those contracts, triggered the forfeiture and assessed the single penalty for each of the four contracts. See also *U.S. v. United Technologies Corp.*, 2008 WL 3007997 (S.D. Ohio 2008) rev'd on other grounds, 2010 WL 4643244 (6th Cir. Nov. 18, 2010) (contractor's statements in its BAFO regarding how it calculated certain costs were false and gave rise to liability under the FCA).

Falsely certifying entitlement to an exemption to TINA can potentially lead to liability under the False Claims Act. In *U.S. ex rel. Ubl v. IIF Data Solutions*, 2007 WL 2220586 (E.D. Va. 2007) a whistleblower alleged that his employer had falsely claimed that it qualified for the commercial item exemption in FAR 15.403-1(b)(3) and that the prices the Government paid were substantially higher than they would have been had the contractor submitted cost and pricing data as required by TINA. The court found that these allegations, if true, would support liability under the FCA.

In another "fraud-in-the-inducement" case, the contractor submitted a price proposal for a cost-plus-award fee contract based on a hypothetical skill mix set forth in the solicitation. The *qui tam* relator contended that the contractor recognized that the specified skill mix was probably not adequate to accomplish the engineering tasks that were to be performed and that the costs billed to the government would far exceed the amounts specified in its proposal. The court held that "[w]ithout more, a contract underbid is not a false claim" and that in order to succeed on a "fraud-in-the-inducement" theory, the relator had to prove that the contractor "had no intention to perform the research contract according to the terms of [its proposal]." Since there was no evidence of this, the court concluded that the contractor was entitled to summary judgment. *U.S., ex rel. Laird v. Lockheed Martin Eng'g & Sci. Servs. Co.*, 491 F.3d 254 (5th Cir. 2007).

In *U.S. v. Eghbal*, 548 F.3d 1281 (9th Cir. 2008), defendants bought and resold foreclosed properties for profit. In order to obtain financing, the purchasers applied for HUD mortgage insurance. As part of obtaining this insurance, the defendants falsely certified to HUD that they had not advanced funds to the purchasers for use in making down payments. In defense to a FCA suit, defendants argued that the false statements were not, by themselves, "claims" since the mere agreement to insure a loan did not require the disbursement of funds. The court rejected this, holding that a lending institution's demand for reimbursement on a defaulted loan originally procured by a fraudulent application would be a "claim" covered by the FCA.

The DoJ reported that a District Court ordered a construction company to pay $1.661 million as treble damages for breaching its agreement to abide by the Davis-Bacon Act requirements to pay electricians agreed-upon wages in constructing buildings at a military base in violation of the FCA. The contractor had agreed to pay the workers a base hourly rate of $19.19 plus fringe benefits of $3.94 per hour. However, the company only paid them between $12 and $16 per hour.*U.S. v. Circle C Construction*, No. 3:07-CV-00091, (M.D. Tenn. March 16, 2010).

Individuals and companies who participate in Medicare, Medicaid and other Government health insurance programs also face liability under the False Claims Act for improper behavior. For example, an Ohio corporation and two Cleveland hospitals agreed to pay $13.8 million to settle a False Claim Act suit that accused the hospitals of paying illegal kickbacks to doctors for patient referrals. The Government alleged that subsequent claims for reimbursement for the cost of caring for these patients violated the Act because the hospitals had no entitlement to payment for referrals from the illegal kickbacks. United States ex rel. Kirby v. University Hospitals Health Sys, Inc., No. 03-CV-05179, settlement announced (N.D. Ohio, Aug. 18, 2006).

More recently, a pharmaceutical firm agreed to settle two *qui tam* suits for more than $650 million, one of the largest settlements ever obtained under the FCA. One suit alleged that the company had failed to pass on to the federal Government and various state governments the benefits of lower prices that had been given to other purchasers of certain drugs. The other claimed that the company offered incentives to hospitals to use one of its drugs in an effort to encourage patients to continue using that drug after leaving the hospital. See: *Nevada ex rel. Steinke v. Merck & Co., Inc.*, 432 F. Supp. 2d 1082 (D. Nev. 2006), and *U.S. ex rel. St. John LaCorte v. Merck & Co., Inc.*, 2008 WL 818982 (E.D. La. 2008).

Expressing Congressional concern over fraud in federally financed healthcare programs, the Deficit Reduction Act 2005, Pub. L. No. 109-171, §§ 6031 to 6033, contains provisions that encourage states to enact false claims laws with *qui tam* provisions patterned on the federal statute that would allow states to share in any recovery. These provisions, which became effective

§ 1:16 Government Contract Compliance Handbook

January 1, 2007, also require certain entities that participate in Medicaid programs to provide instruction to employees about the state and federal false claims statutes and how to commence actions under them. For a more complete discussion, see Boese and McClain, New False Claims Law Incentives Pose Risk For Contractors And States, 20 No. 10 Andrews Government Contract Litigation Reporter (September 11, 2006).

The violation of one anti-fraud statute does not necessarily give rise to a violation of the civil FCA. In *Kellogg Brown & Root Servs., Inc. v. U.S.*, 2011 WL 2739776 (July 6, 2011) the Government alleged that the general legal presumption that a bribe paid in violation of the Anti-Kickback Act was included in the contract price necessarily meant that subsequent invoices were "false claims." The court rejected the Government's efforts to bootstrap a legal presumption applicable to the AKA in order to demonstrate a violation of the FCA. The court noted, "No presumption applies to the FCA that would relieve defendant of its burden to plead facts supporting the elements of an FCA claim. Defendant must claim the threshold requirements under the FCA, i.e., that a false or fraudulent claim was submitted and that plaintiff had knowledge of its falsity."

§ 1:17 Qui tam lawsuits

The civil False Claims Act contains a "qui tam" provision authorizing private citizens with evidence of fraud against the Government to file lawsuits in their own names (on behalf of themselves and the Government) and then keep a share of the Government's recovery.[1] Since the 1986 amendments to the False Claims Act, which were revised to encourage the filing of qui tam suits, there has been an explosion in the number of these actions. From 1987 to 2005, 5,129 qui tam cases were filed, leading to the Government's recovery of over $9.6 billion. The number of qui tam actions initiated in 2005 was almost six times the number filed in 1987. The rise in qui tam litigation, however, is not surprising, given the financial incentives for doing so, and because the Justice Department may decide to take the case forward, and because personal participation in the wrongful conduct does not disqualify an individual from benefiting financially from the action.

Cases & Commentary: Contractors must appreciate that facing a *qui tam* lawsuit is more than just a remote possibility. On November 22, 2010 the Department of Justice reported that it obtained $3.0 billion in settlements and judgments in fiscal year

---

[Section 1:17]
[1] 31 U.S.C.A. § 3730(b).

THE OFFENSES & PENALTIES § 1:17

2010, and another $3.0 billion in fiscal year 2011. About $2.3 billion of the total involved *qui tam* actions in 2010, and $2.8 billion in 2011. *Qui tam* relators received $385 million of the total recovery. As an example, a court awarded a *qui tam* relator 30%—the maximum permissible in cases in which the Government does not intervene—of the total damages and penalties awarded in the case or approximately $2.76 million. *U.S. ex rel. DRC, Inc. v. Custer Battles, LLC*, 2009 WL 3756343 (E.D. Va. 2009). In another recent case the DoJ announced it had reached a $2 million settlement with Lockheed Martin, Inc. in a *qui tam* action. The suit alleged that prior to the issuance of a solicitation for computer support services, and then after it had been issued, two Government employees conspired with Lockheed Martin and Science Applications International. Corp. to assure the contract was awarded to those companies by sharing non-public information with them and by including language in the solicitation that biased the selection in their favor. The *qui tam* relator, a former Government employee, received $560,000 as his share of the recovery. DoJ noted that, as in recent years, health care accounted for the lion's share of fraud settlements and judgments, amounting to 80%, or $2.5 billion of the $3.0 billion that was recovered. The total recovery since the 1986 amendments to the FCA has been $27 billion.

Section 3731(b) of the FCA contains a statute of limitations:

> A civil action under section 3730 man not be brought
> (1) more than 6 years after the date on which the violation of section 3729 is committed, or
> (2) more than 3 years after the date when facts material to the right of action are known or reasonably should have been known by the official of the United States charged with responsibility to act in the circumstances, but in no event more than 10 years after the date on which the violation is committed.

A large majority of courts have held that § 3731(b)(1) applies to qui tam cases whereas the longer time period allowed under § 3731(b)(2) applies only to actions brought or joined by the United States because of the reference to when the facts became "known" as opposed to when they "occurred." *U.S. ex rel. Sanders v. North American Bus Industries*, 546 F.3d 288 (4th Cir. 2008). The statute of limitations and the backlog of *qui tam* cases (and those brought directly by the Government) have created their own problems for DoJ. In *U.S., ex rel. Ramadoss v. Caremark Inc.*, 586 F. Supp. 2d 668 (W.D. Tex. 2008), the relator filed its *qui tam* action on August 25, 1999, but the Government did not intervene until August 19, 2005. Following an earlier decision in *U.S. v. The Baylor University Medical Center*, 469 F.3d 263 (2d Cir. 2006), the court ruled the Government was prohibited from pursuing alleged violations occurring more than six years before

§ 1:17   GOVERNMENT CONTRACT COMPLIANCE HANDBOOK

it intervened in the case, *i.e.*, prior to August 19, 1999. The court rejected the argument that the relator's initial action "tolled" the statute or that the Government's complaint "related back" to the date of the relator's complaint. This ruling did not affect the right of the relator to pursue the claims prior to that date. But, as practical matter, relators can seldom afford the cost of litigating these complex claims. Thus, to some degree, the Government's failure to promptly file would deprive the Government of a remedy and the relator from a monetary recovery for its efforts. Congress recognized these problems in the 2009 amendments to the FCA. As noted in § 1:15, *supra*, § 3731(c) of the FCA now explicitly provides that the Government's complaint relates back to the date of filing of the original action "to the extent that the claim of the Government arises out of the conduct, transactions, or occurrences set forth, or attempted to be set forth, in the prior complaint of that person."

§ 1:18   Qui tam lawsuits—"Relators"

The qui tam provisions permit any "person, partnership, corporation, association or other legal entity, including any State or political subdivision of a State" to bring a qui tam action. However, the Act also sets forth several jurisdictional bars to qui tam suits. It precludes (1) suits brought by a former or current member of the armed forces against a member of the armed forces arising out of that person's military service, (2) suits against Government officials based on information already known to the Government, (3) suits based on allegations or transactions that are the subject of a civil suit to which the Government is already a party, and (4) suits based on the "public disclosure" of information in hearings, reports, audits, investigations, or the news media unless the relator is the "original source" of the information.[1] An "original source" is defined as "an individual who has direct and independent knowledge of the information on which the allegations are based and has voluntarily provided the information to the Government before filing" the qui tam suit that is based on the information.[2] It should be no surprise that most qui tam suits are filed against employers by employees or

---

[Section 1:18]

[1] 31 U.S.C.A. § 3730(e); *See U.S. ex rel. Laird v. Lockheed Martin Engineering & Science Servs. Co.*, 336 F.3d 346 (5th Cir. 2003) (Suit dismissed where relator did not have "direct and independent knowledge of the information upon which the allegations" were based and thus could not qualify as an original source), and; *Seal 1 v. Seal A*, 255 F.3d 1154 (9th Cir. 2001) (addressed issue where relator's original disclosure involved one entity but investigation led to suit against another entity).

[2] 31 U.S.C.A. § 3730(e)(4)(b).

former employees.

Cases & Commentary: In *Rockwell Int'l Corp. v. U.S.*, 549 U.S. 457 (2007), the Supreme Court for the first time addressed what constitutes an "original source" for purposes of the False Claims Act. This is important because the courts only have jurisdiction to hear cases where the allegations have been publicly disclosed if they are brought by the "original source of those allegations." The relator in this case, while still employed by Rockwell, prepared a report predicting that the company's planned method of disposing of toxic materials by mixing them with concrete would not be successful because defects in the piping system would not allow the proper mixing of the sludge and concrete. The relator subsequently reported environmental violations to the FBI and provided the agency with a copy of his report. The Government confirmed that the concrete blocks were leaking, but not because of a problem with the piping system. Rather, the Government attributed the problem to an employee's alteration of the prescribed concrete/sludge ratio. The relator's initial complaint had focused on the assumed piping problem, but during the course of the litigation, he amended the complaint to take into account the employee's actions. The Supreme Court held that whether the relator was an "original source" had to be judged against the amended complaint and since the relator had apparently had no "direct and independent knowledge of the information" regarding the employee's actions, the Court had no jurisdiction over the matter. The Court noted that if the question of "original source" hinged on the contents of the *initial* allegations in the complaint, it would allow person to plead a "trivial theory of fraud for which he had some direct and independent knowledge and later amend the complaint to include theories copied from the public domain." Also, the Court rejected the argument that it had jurisdiction over *all* claims raised by the relator simply because he was the original source regarding *one* of those claims. See *U.S. ex rel. DeKort v. Integrated Coast Guard Systems, LLC*, 2010 WL 4363379 (N.D. Tex. 2010) ("[T]he first set of shaft alignment issues, does not translate to direct and independent knowledge of an unrelated defect that manifested itself more than a year later."). See also *U.S. ex rel. Boothe v. Sun Healthcare Group, Inc.*, 496 F.3d 1169 (10th Cir. 2007) (The fact the relator was *not* an original source for three claims does not deprive court of jurisdiction over remaining claims in which relator was an original source); *U.S. Department of Transportation ex rel. Arnold v. CMC Engineering*, 2010 WL 3942488 (W.D. Pa 2010) (court rejects theory of "common scheme" that would make relator the "original source" of allegations against all defendants even though he had no direct knowledge regarding certain defendants). In *U.S. ex rel. Davis v. Prince*, 2011 WL 63899 (E.D. Va. 2011) the court emphasized that the analysis of whether there had been a "public disclosure" and, if so, whether the plaintiff was the "original source" of the allegations had to be done on a "claim-by-claim" basis and that a plaintiff could not "package" its claims to avoid such an analysis:

> The first step in determining whether the public disclosure bar eliminates federal court jurisdiction over a putative FCA action is to identify the claims in the relator's complaint. This is an important step, as the public disclosure bar must be applied on a claim-by-claim basis. *See Rockwell Int'l Corp. v. United States*, 549 U.S. 457, 477, 127 S.Ct. 1397, 167 L.Ed.2d 190 (2007). To achieve this goal, a district court must identify each claim "based on a review of the substance of the complaint, not just how it may be formally structured." *United States ex rel. Boothe v. Sun Healthcare Group, Inc.*, 496 F.3d 1169, 1177 (7th Cir.2007). In other words, even if a relator groups multiple claims into a single count, a district court must apply the jurisdictional analysis to each "reasonably discrete claim of fraud." *Id.* (holding that jurisdictional analysis must be applied to ten discrete claims of fraud, even though the relator lumped all of her claims into a single count).

Under the FCA, and prior to the amendments under the Patient Protection And Affordable Care Act (PPACA), Pub. L. 111-148, 124 Stat. 119, § 10104(j)(2) discussed below, an "original source" is defined as "an individual who has direct and independent knowledge of the information on which the allegations are based . . . ." 31 U.S.C.A § 3730(e)(4)(b) "Direct" knowledge is generally considered to be knowledge that was obtained "first hand," by the relator's own efforts rather than by the labor of others, and not derivative of the information of others. "Independent" knowledge cannot rely on any public disclosures. A court applied these concepts in *U.S. ex rel. Lam v. Tenet Healthcare Corp.*, 287 Fed. Appx. 396 (5th Cir. 2008), holding that the relators were not original sources because most of their information was based on informal conversations with hospital personnel and the hospital records they examined would not have been sufficient to form the basis for an FCA claim. More recently, in *U.S. ex rel. Branch Consultants, L.L.C. v. Allstate Ins. Co.*, 668 F. Supp. 2d 780 (E.D. La. 2009), leave to appeal denied, (Dec. 22, 2009), a court concluded that a property inspector was an "original source" of alleged insurance fraud based on information he obtained during the inspection of 57 properties that were damaged during Hurricane Katrina. In *U.S. ex rel. Jamison v. McKesson Corp., Medicare & Medicaid P 303329*, 2010 WL 1276712 (N.D. Miss. 2010), the relator contended defendants violated the civil False Claims Act by setting up a sham durable medical equipment supplier solely to provide supplies and services to its captive patient base in violation of federal regulations. After finding that various agency and GAO reports were "public disclosures"

THE OFFENSES & PENALTIES § 1:18

and that the relator's suit was based directly on these reports, the court concluded that the relator was not the "original source" of these allegations:

> The burden is on Jamison to show that the information and allegations he discovered are "qualitatively different information than what had already been discovered" and not merely the "product and outgrowth" of publicly disclosed information. *** Jamison has not met this burden. The knowledge that Jamison brings to this case is almost entirely indirect—that is, based on research and review of public records, as well as second-hand interviews with Beverly employees and former employees. ***Jamison's extensive investigation did not put the Government "on the trail" of any new malfeasance; instead, Jamison took disclosures that had already been made by the OIG, and based on his own experience and research, claimed Beverly's relationship with CSMS and McKesson is fraudulent.

In addition to having "direct and independent knowledge of the information on which the allegations are based, an "original source" must also have "voluntarily provided the information to the Government before filing an action . . . which is based on the information." In *U.S. ex rel. Branch Consultants v. Allstate Insurance Co.*, 2011 WL 322367 (E.D. La. Jan. 24, 2011) the court found the relator's initial disclosure was "plainly inadequate" as to certain defendants and that these deficiencies could not be remedied by "supplemental disclosures" given to the Government after the initial complaint had been filed. Finally, the court noted that relator's statements in the disclosure that it had additional examples of fraud in its files and that the Government was welcome to review those files did not cure the deficiencies. The court stated "The original source provisions imposes disclosure requirements on the relator, and the government was under no obligation to comb through [the relator's] files to obtain the information upon which [the] allegations are based."

Section 3730(e)(4)(A) bars actions "based upon the public disclosure" of allegations or transactions in a criminal, civil, or administrative hearing, in a congressional, administrative or Government Accountability Office report, hearing, audit, or investigation, or from news media unless the action is brought by the Attorney General or the person bringing the action is the source of the information. For purposes of § 3730(e)(4), a public disclosure occurs when the critical elements exposing the transaction as fraudulent are placed in the public domain, through particular channels. *Glaser v. Wound Care Consultants, Inc.*, 570 F.3d 907, 913 (7th Cir.2009). Courts have generally held that the source of the disclosure must be one of the specified sources in order to constitute a "public disclosure." See *U.S. ex rel. Bondy v. Consumer Health Foundation*, 28 Fed. Appx. 178 (4th Cir. 2001) (response to FOIA request not identified as source of "public

§ 1:18   GOVERNMENT CONTRACT COMPLIANCE HANDBOOK

disclosure); *U.S. ex rel. Putnam v. Eastern Idaho Regional Medical Center*, 2009 WL 2901233 (D. Idaho 2009) (letters, faxes, and phone conversations between relator and state Department of Health and Welfare did not come within any of the fora set out in 31 U.S.C.A. 3730(e)(4)(A) and thus did not constitute a "public disclosure"); *Bridges v. Omega World Travel, Inc.*, 2009 WL 5174283 (E.D. Ark. 2009) (wide availability of the Government contract, price list, records of government travel transactions and federal regulations under which a travel company operated were not public disclosures because none fell in the categories specified in the statute), *U.S. ex rel. DeKort v. Integrated Coast Guard Systems*, 705 F. Supp. 2d 519 (N.D. Tex. 2010) (quoting *USA ex rel. Barrett v. Johnson Controls, Inc.*, 2003-2 Trade Cas. (CCH) ¶ 74176, 2003 WL 21500400 (N.D. Tex. 2003): "The plain language of the statute suggests that there are three sub-parts to the public disclosure prong: (1) the public disclosure; (2) in a particular form specified in the statute, such as an administrative report or hearing; (3) of allegations or transactions."). However, several courts have stated the "public disclosure" as used in the FCA "includes documents that have been filed with a court, such as discovery documents and a plaintiff's complaint" even though the statute mentions judicial "hearings" rather than "filings." *U.S. ex rel. McKenzie v. BellSouth Telecommun., Inc.*, 123 F.3d 935 (6th Cir. 1997); *Federal Recovery Servs., Inc. v. U.S.*, 72 F.3d 447 (5th Cir. 1995) and *U.S. ex rel. Springfield Terminal Ry. Co. v Quinn*, 14 F.3d 645 (D.C. Cir. 1994).

The Supreme Court resolved the conflict by reversing the decision in *Schindler. Schindler Elevator Corp. v. U.S. ex rel. Kirk*, 131 S.Ct 1885 (2011). The Court held that the agency's written response to a FOIA request was, itself, a report and that the documents that were attached to that response were part of the "report." Thus, a relator would have to show that it had independent knowledge of any incriminating information that it received in response to a FOIA request in order to avoid the public disclosure bar.

The Patient Protection And Affordable Care Act (PPACA), Pub. L. 111-148, 124 Stat. 119, § 10104(j)(2) enacted on March 23, 2010 significantly altered the definitions of "public disclosure" and "original source" in 31 USCA § 3730(e)(4). The revision also *may* give the DoJ new authority to block dismissal even where there has been a public disclosure or the relator could not demonstrate that it was an original source of the information. That section now states:

> (A) The court shall dismiss an action or claim under this section, unless opposed by the Government, if substantially the same allegations or transactions as alleged in the action or claim were publicly disclosed—

(i) in a Federal criminal, civil, or administrative hearing in which the Government or its agent is a party;
(ii) in a congressional, Government Accountability Office, or other Federal report, hearing, audit or investigation; or
(iii) from the news media, unless the action is brought by the Attorney General or the person bringing the action is an original source of the information.

(B) For purposes of this paragraph, "original source" means an individual who either (i) prior to a public disclosure under subsection (e)(4)(A), has voluntarily disclosed to the Government the information on which allegations or transaction in a claim are based, or (2) who has knowledge that is independent of and materially adds to the publicly disclosed allegations or transactions, and who has voluntarily provided the information to the Government before filing an action under this section.

§ 1:19 Qui tam lawsuits—Procedures

A qui tam lawsuit is brought in the name of the United States[1] and is filed under seal. On filing a qui tam complaint, the relator must provide the Department of Justice with the evidence underlying the suit.[2] Within 60 days (or any extension of this period granted by the court), the Government must choose either to take over the prosecution or to decline to prosecute the action.[3] However, extensions are common to permit the Government to investigate the allegations and determine whether to intervene. The Government will look at all aspects of the case when deciding whether to take over the prosecution.

Cases & Commentary: Section 3730(b)(5) sets out what is referred to as the "first-to-file" rule:

(5) When a person brings an action under this subsection, no person other than the Government may intervene or bring a related action based on the facts underlying the pending action.

The 10th Circuit held that the provision barred the second-in-time action only with regard to the defendants that had been named in the earlier action. See *In re Natural Gas Royalties Qui Tam Litigation (CO2 Appeals)*, 566 F.3d 956 (10th Cir. 2009). To the same effect is *U.S. ex rel. Branch Consultants v. Allstate Ins. Co.*, 560 F.3d 371 (5th Cir. 2009). In *Hampton v. Columbia/HCA Healthcare Corp.*, 318 F.3d 214 (D.C. Cir. 2003), the court held that § 3730(b)(5) barred the second suit if it was based on the "same material elements of fraud" as the earlier case. In *U.S. ex rel. Folliard v. CDW Technology Servs., Inc.*, 2010 WL 2593521

[Section 1:19]
[1] 31 U.S.C.A. § 3730(b)(1).
[2] 31 U.S.C.A. § 3730(b)(2).
[3] 31 U.S.C.A. § 3730(b)(2).

§ 1:19   GOVERNMENT CONTRACT COMPLIANCE HANDBOOK

(D.D.C. 2010), the court applied the *Hampton* test and concluded that the subject suit alleging fraudulent sales of computer equipment from non-designated countries was barred because an earlier action was based on the same general allegations, even though the earlier action involved different agencies and different contracts. Similarly, in *US. ex rel. Folliard v. Synnex Corp.*, 2011 WL 2836372 (D.D.C July 19, 2011) the court dismissed as to certain defendants because the complaint was based on the "same material elements" as an earlier filed case even though the earlier case involved different products an was still under seal at the time relator files its complaint in this case. In *U.S. ex rel. Batiste v. SLM Corp.*, 659 F.3d 1204 (D.C. Cir. 2011), the court affirmed dismissal of a complaint alleging the same material elements of fraud as a previous case, finding that an earlier-filed complaint need not meet heightened pleading requirements for fraud allegations as required in Fed. R. Civ. P. 9(b). Instead, the first complaint must only provide enough notice for the Government to begin an investigation into the alleged fraud. In *U.S. ex rel. Chovanec v. Apria Healthcare Group Inc.*, 606 F.3d 361 (7th Cir. 2010), two pending actions alleged defendant's main office implemented a nation-wide plan to overbill Medicare and Medicaid. The court held that the relator's current claim was a "related" because it involved the same "material" or "essential" facts of those earlier cases, even though the current action covered a different period of time and concerned just one of defendant's offices. In *U.S. ex rel. Piacentile v. Sanofi Synthehelabo, Inc.*, 2010 WL 5466043 (D.N.J. 2010), the court dismissed an FCA action against one of the two defendants under the first-to-file rule even though the earlier had eventually been dismissed. The court stated that the later case need not rest on precisely the same facts as a previous claim to run afoul of the statutory bar as long as the later allegation states all of the essential facts of the previously-filed claim. In *U.S. ex rel. Branch Consultants v. Allstate Insurance Co.*, 2011 WL 322367 (E.D. La. Jan. 24, 2011) the court held that whether an action was barred by the first-to-file rule had to be determined based on the facts existing at the time the action was filed. Thus, filing an amended complaint with additional allegations after the suit in another court had been dismissed did not avoid the jurisdictional bar. In an unusual case, a court held that the first-to-file rule barred the relator's case because the appeal of an earlier decision—*which had been filed by the same relator*—was still pending at the time he filed the subject action. *U.S. ex rel. Carter v. Halliburton Co.*, 2011 WL 2118227 (E.D. Va. May 24, 2011).

Section 3730(b)2) of the FCA imposes mandatory filing and service requirements on qui tam relators. Specifically, the statute provides that "[a] copy of the complaint and written disclosure of substantially all material evidence and information the person possesses shall be served on the Government and shall be filed in camera, shall remain under seal for at least 60 days, and shall not be served on the defendant until the court so orders." The courts are divided over whether the failure to comply with these provisions requires dismissal of the action. See *U.S. ex rel. Summers v. LHC Group, Inc.*, 2009 WL 1651503 (M.D. Tenn. 2009) (employee's failure to file qui tam action in camera or under seal was fatal deficiency resulting in dismissal with prejudice), aff'd 623 F.3d 287 (6th. Cir. 2010); *U.S. ex rel. Ubl v. IIF Data Solutions*, 2009 WL 1254704 (E.D. Va. 2009) (despite the use of "shall" in this provision, these requirements are not jurisdictional and the failure to comply with them will not cause the case to be dismissed). See also *U.S. ex re. Lujan v. Hughes Aircraft*, 67 F.3d 242 (9th Cir. 1995) where the relator filed the complaint under seal but approximately five weeks later apparently disclosed the substance of the complaint to a newspaper. The court stated that a violation of the sealing rule did not automatically require dismissal of the suit. Rather, the court fashioned a three part test to determine whether this sanction was appropriate: (1) the extent to which the Government had been harmed by the disclosure; (2) the nature of the violation in terms of its "relative severity"; and (3) the presence or absence of bad faith or willfulness on the relator's part. It returned the case to the lower court for consideration in light of this test. In *U.S. ex rel. Davis v. Prince*, 2011 WL 446869 (E.D. Va. 2011) the court held that the "under seal" requirement also applied to an *amended* complaint but refused to dismiss the case, stating that "Because the amended complaint was substantially similar to the original complaint, the policy arguments supporting dismissal for failure to comply with the sealing requirement do not apply.").

Although the FCA explicitly contemplates that the complaint will be unsealed once the Government has decided whether or not to intervene, it does not address whether the Government's motions for extensions of time and accompanying memoranda should remain under seal indefinitely. Courts that have directly addressed this issue have held that "by permitting *in camera* submissions, the statute 'necessarily invests the court with authority either to maintain the filings under seal or to make them available to the parties.'" *United States ex rel. Yannacopolous v. Gen. Dynamics*, 457 F.Supp.2d 854, 858 (N.D. Ill. 2006) (quoting *United States ex rel. Health Outcomes Techs. v. Hallmark Health Sys., Inc.*, 349 F.Supp.2d 170 (D. Mass. 2004)). Courts have analogized disputes over whether to unseal documents under the FCA to discovery disputes under FRCP 26(c), which authorizes protective orders for confidential trade secrets and similar information. In *U.S. ex rel. Rostholder v. Omnicare, Inc.*,

2011 WL 3236016 (D. Md. July 28, 2011) the court, after inspecting all of the documents *in camera*, concluded that they should be unsealed, rejecting the Government's argument that they contained confidential investigative techniques or substantive details regarding the Government's methods of investigation that could jeopardize the prosecution of the case.

Section 3730(b)(4) of the FCA states that the Government "shall" intervene in an action within 60 days after receiving both the complaint and material evidence. However, this is not a jurisdictional requirement and the Government's failure to meet this deadline will not bar the Government from proceeding with the case. See *U.S. ex rel. Siller v. Becton Dickinson & Co. By and Through Microbiology Systems Div.*, 21 F.3d 1339 (4th Cir. 1994) (rejected on other grounds by, U.S. ex rel. Findley v. FPC-Boron Employees' Club, 105 F.3d 675 (D.C. Cir. 1997)).

The settlement of a whistleblower action, which did not include an FCA claim, did not bar a subsequent FCA action by the relator or the Government on the basis of "issue preclusion." *U.S. ex rel. Lusby v. Rolls-Royce Corp.*, 570 F.3d 849 (7th Cir. 2009) (claim preclusion requires that the same litigants be involved in both suits; regardless of whether it intervenes in follow-on FCA suit, the Government is a real party in interest to that suit because its financial interests are at stake; hence resolution of whistleblower litigation, which did not involve the Government, does not prevent the follow on FCA action).

Section 3730(c)(2)(A) provides that "[t]he Government may dismiss the action notwithstanding the objections of the person initiating the action if the person has been notified by the Government of the filing of the motion and the court has provided the person with an opportunity for a hearing on the motion." The Government may seek dismissal both before and after the relator has served its complaint on the defendant. The right of the Government to seek dismissal is nearly unreviewable, except, for example, where fraud on the court is alleged. *Ridenour v. Kaiser-Hill Co., L.L.C.*, 397 F.3d 925 (10th Cir. 2005). See *U.S. ex rel. Wickliffe v. EMC Corp.*, 2009 WL 911037 (D. Utah) (court granted Government's motion to dismiss based on Government's assertion that current case was duplicative of another pending case and thus barred by the "first-to-file" rule) and *U.S. ex rel. Schweizer v. Oce, N.V.*, 681 F. Supp. 2d 64 (D.D.C. 2010) (court followed *Hoyle v. American Nat'l Red Cross*, 518 F.3d 61 (D.C. Cir. 2008), holding that Government's decision to dismiss after reaching settlement with defendant was "beyond judicial review").

A relator can appeal the dismissal of its case to the appropriate court of appeals. The Federal Rules of Appellate Procedure provide that the appeal must normally be filed within 30 days after the case is dismissed, but when the Government is a party to

THE OFFENSES & PENALTIES § 1:20

the action, the period is extended to 60 days. In *U.S. ex rel. Eisenstein v. City of New York*, 129 S. Ct. 2230, 173 L. Ed. 2d 1255, 73 Fed. R. Serv. 3d 1132 (2009), the Court held that since the U.S. was no longer a "party" after declining to intervene, the relator had to file an appeal from the dismissal of its own action within 30 days. The effect of that decision on pending appeals that were filed between 31 and 60 days of dismissal has been harsh. In *U.S. ex re. Haight v. Catholic Healthcare West*, 602 F.3d 949 (9th Cir. 2010), *cert. den.* 131 S.Ct. 366, 178 L.Ed.2d 150 (2010), the court held that the decision of the Supreme Court applied retroactively and thus required dismissal of appeals that had not been filed with the 30 day period:

> Under *Eisenstein*, Plaintiffs' notice of appeal was untimely when filed. The Supreme Court knew that *Eisenstein* could affect pending appeals. Indeed, Plaintiffs in this case filed an amicus brief with the Supreme Court asking that it prohibit retroactive application of its decision in *Eisenstein*. *** Despite acknowledging that its decision would have "harsh consequences" for some plaintiffs and "unfairly punish those who relied on the holdings of courts adopting the 60-day limit in cases in which the United States was not a party," the Court expressly refused to limit its decision to prospective application. *Eisenstein,* 129 S. Ct. at 2236 n. 4. Those harsh consequences are now concretely before us: Plaintiffs' appeal is untimely and must be dismissed.

§ 1:20 Qui tam lawsuits—Whistleblower protections

The False Claims Act also protects employee relators from retaliation by their employers. The Act provides:[1]

> Any employee who is discharged, demoted, suspended, threatened, harassed, or in any other manner discriminated against in the terms and conditions of employment by his or her employer because of lawful acts done by the employee on behalf of the employee or others in furtherance of an action under this section, including investigation for, initiation of, testimony for, or assistance in an action filed or to be filed under this section, shall be entitled to all relief necessary to make the employee whole.

A claim of retaliatory discharge under the FCA requires that the employee show that the employer knew the employee was investigating fraud by the company and discharged her *because of* the protected activity. An employee cannot prevail on a claim for retaliatory discharge simply by showing that she was terminated after investigating possible wrongdoing by the employer.[2] If a whistleblower would have been fired regardless of engaging in protected activity, the whistleblower cannot recover

---

[Section 1:20]

[1]31 U.S.C.A. § 3730(h).

[2]*See Yuhasz v. Brush Wellman, Inc.*, 341 F.3d 559, 57 Fed. R. Serv. 3d

§ 1:20

under the Act.[3]

Noting an agreement among many of the U.S. courts of appeals, the Supreme Court acknowledged that the actual filing of a false claim action is not a prerequisite to relief under the False Claims Act prohibition against retaliation.[4]

Cases & Commentary: Prior to the 2009 amendments to the FCA discussed in § 1:15, *supra*, in order to receive "whistleblower protection" against retaliatory discharge, the employee need not have filed a *qui tam* suit or even have contemplated initiating such a suit. However, at a minimum, the employee must been investigating matters that reasonably, and objectively, could lead to a viable FCA case. In *Fanslow v. Chicago Mfg. Center, Inc.*, 384 F.3d 469, 21 I.E.R. Cas. (BNA) 1326 (7th Cir. 2004), the Seventh Circuit explained the test:

> An employee need not have actual knowledge of the FCA for her actions to be considered "protected activity" under § 3730(h). If so, only those with sophisticated legal knowledge would be protected by the statute. *United States ex rel. Yesudian v. Howard Univ.*, 153 F.3d 731, 741 (D.C.Cir.1998) ("... only [lawyers] would know from the outset that what they were investigating could lead to a False Claims Act prosecution."). In the past, we have said that an employee must show that an FCA action is a "distinct possibility" at the time of the investigation for her actions to be considered "protected activity." *Neal*, 33 F.3d at 864. This was not meant to contradict the rule that does not require actual knowledge of the FCA, however. It implied instead that there is an objective component to the test for a claim under § 3730(h), as well as a subjective one. We agree with several of our sister circuits, which have held that the relevant inquiry to determine whether an employee's actions are protected under § 3730(h) is whether: "(1) the employee in good faith believes, and (2) a reasonable employee in the same or similar circumstances might believe, that the employer is

---

342, 2003 FED App. 0297P (6th Cir. 2003).

[3]*See Wilkins v. St. Louis Housing Authority*, 314 F.3d 927 (8th Cir. 2002).

[4]*See Graham County Soil & Water Conservation Dist. v. U.S. ex rel. Wilson*, 545 U.S. 409, 125 S. Ct. 2444, 162 L. Ed. 2d 390 (2005) (citing *U.S. ex rel. Karvelas v. Melrose-Wakefield Hosp.*, 360 F.3d 220, 57 Fed. R. Serv. 3d 1262 (1st Cir. 2004), cert. denied, 543 U.S. 820, 125 S. Ct. 59, 160 L. Ed. 2d 28 (2004) (holding that protected conduct is "conduct that reasonably could lead to a viable FCA action"); *U.S. ex rel. Yesudian v. Howard University*, 153 F.3d 731, 128 Ed. Law Rep. 1030 (D.C. Cir. 1998); *Childree v. UAP/GA CHEM, Inc.*, 92 F.3d 1140 (11th Cir. 1996) (holding that disclosure to employer of possible FCA violation protected conduct where litigation is a "distinct possibility" at the time of the disclosure); *Fanslow v. Chicago Mfg. Center, Inc.*, 384 F.3d 469 (7th Cir. 2004) (protected conduct is where employee had reasonable, good-faith belief that the employer is committing fraud against the United States); *Wilkins v. St. Louis Housing Authority*, 314 F.3d 927 (8th Cir. 2002); *Moore v. California Institute of Technology Jet Propulsion Laboratory*, 275 F.3d 838, 160 Ed. Law Rep. 304 (9th Cir. 2002)).

THE OFFENSES & PENALTIES   § 1:20

committing fraud against the government." *Moore v. Cal. Inst. of Tech. Jet Propulsion Lab.*, 275 F.3d 838, 845 (9th Cir. 2002). See also *Wilkins v. St. Louis,* 314 F.3d 927, 933 (8th Cir. 2002) (adopting the *Moore* standard)

Despite the statement in *Fanslow* that a person should not have to have "sophisticated legal knowledge" of the FCA for her actions to be considered "protected activity," some cases would seem to require exactly that. For example, in *Hoyte v. American Nat. Red Cross,* 518 F.3d 61, 27 I.E.R. Cas. (BNA) 385 (D.C. Cir. 2008), the relator contended that the defendant had failed to report mishandling of blood in violation of FDA regulations and the terms of a Consent Decree. The plaintiff claimed this gave rise to a "reverse false claims" action under 31 U.S.C.A. § 3729(a)(7) which imposes liability on person who "knowingly makes, uses, or causes to be made or used a false record or statement to conceal, avoid, or decrease an obligation to pay . . . money or property to the Government." The court held that defendant's alleged violation of FDA regulations would have, at most, only given rise to a potential penalty which would not constitute an "obligation" that would give rise to a viable FCA claim under (a)(7). Similarly, the Consent Degree did not impose an obligation on defendant to tender money or property to the Government, but only to follow the prescribed blood handling and reporting regulations. Since there was "no viable action against [defendant] under [(a)(7) of the FCA], Hoyte's investigation and reporting of [defendant's] conduct did not constitute 'protected activity' . . . and her subsequent discharge was therefore not unlawful retaliation under section 3730(h)."[5]

The whistleblower protections not only prohibit affirmative retaliatory action, but the failure of the employer to take steps to stop it. See *U.S., ex rel. Howard v. Urban Investment Trust, Inc.*, 30 I.E.R. Cas. (BNA) 918, 2010 WL 832294 (N.D. Ill. 2010) where the court stated:

> Synergy argues that, in order for liability to attach, the employer must engage in some sort of affirmative retaliatory action, and Howard's claims of "intentional inaction" on Synergy's part are insufficient. However, the statute is not limited solely to affirmative action, but also covers situations in which an employee is *"in any other manner discriminated against* in the terms and conditions of employment.

However, where the employer has complete discretion with

---

[5]*See also U.S. ex. rel Owens v. First Kuwaiti General Trading & Contracting Co.*, 2010 WL 2794369 (4th Cir. 2010) ("Whatever other conclusions the record could support, it gives no indication Owens was concerned about fraud while he was working for First Kuwaiti or that the treatment he complains of was driven by fear that he was laying the groundwork for a suit like this one.").

§ 1:20   GOVERNMENT CONTRACT COMPLIANCE HANDBOOK

regard to action, the exercise of that discretion generally will not be considered "retaliatory." Thus, in *Turner v. DynMcDermott Petroleum Operations Co.*, 2010 WL 4633403 (E.D. La. 2010) the court held that the denial of a monetary perk—in this case a $5,000 bonus—was not a retaliatory action because giving a bonus was wholly within the employer's discretion. Also, an audit of an employee's performance—which could be considered "retaliatory"—did not occur here because it was initiated in response to complaints from finance department employees regarding the performance of the human relations department in which the relator worked.

Section 3730(h)(3) did not originally impose a statute of limitations on retaliation claims. Instead, courts usually applied the closest analogous state law statute in deciding whether a suit was "timely." *U.S. ex rel. Dyer v Raytheon Co.*, 2011 WL 3244489 (D. Mass. July 29, 2011). However, the Dodd-Frank Wall Street Reform and Consumer Protection Act, Pub. L. No. 111-203, 124 Stat. 1376 (2010), amended § 3730(h) by adding a statute of limitations for FCA retaliation claims. 124 Stat. 2079. As a result, § 3730(h)(3) currently provides that "[a] civil action under this subsection may not be brought more than 3 years after the date when the retaliation occurred." There appears to be a split in authority as to whether this provision is to be applied retroactively. Compare *Saunders v. District of Columbia (D.D.C. June 6, 2011)* (suggesting, without deciding, that it should be applied retroactively, noting "there is some reason to believe that Congress' specification of [that statute] obviates the need to resort to the 'borrowing' doctrine") with *Riddle v. DynCorp Int'l Inc.*, 733 F.Supp.2d 743 (N.D. Tex. 2010) (holding that the statute of limitations contained in the Dodd-Frank Act is *"not* retroactive").

Prior to the 2009 amendments to the FCA discussed in § 1:15, *supra*, the employer must have known that the person was investigating fraud by the company and must have discharged that person for that reason. In *U.S. ex rel. Marlar v. BWXT Y-12, L.L.C.*, 525 F.3d 439, 27 I.E.R. Cas. (BNA) 1172 (6th Cir. 2008), the court held that relator's complaints to superiors of inaccuracies in health records at a nuclear facility likely would not have been sufficient to put her employer on notice the employee was investigating matters that could lead to an FCA case. However, a subsequent letter to the president of the company complaining that the under-reporting of injuries and illnesses had resulted in large incentive payments to the contractor was sufficient to put the company on notice that the employee was engaged in "protected activity."

The amendments to the FCA discussed, in § 1:15, *supra*, now extends coverage not only to employees, but also to contractors and agents. In addition, it no longer focuses on actions aimed at initiating a qui tam action, but rather protects all legal acts "in furtherance of other efforts to stop 1 or more violations of this subchapter." The amendment thus shifts the emphasis from exposing the consequences of improper activity to prevent it from occurring in the first place.

In addition to whistleblower protections under the Civil False Claims Act, the Federal Acquisition Streamlining Act of 1994, Pub. L. No. 103-355 amended and revised 10 U.S.C.A. § 2409 and 41 U.S.C.A § 265 to prohibit reprisals against employees of a contractor for disclosing to a Member of Congress and other Government agencies or officials information relating to a substantial violation of law related to a Government contract. A person who believes he or she has been subjected to a prohibited reprisal can submit a complaint to the agency's Inspector General who will then conduct an investigation. If it is determined that a violation has occurred, the head of the agency may order the contractor to take appropriate remedial action including reinstating the employee. If the contractor fails to comply, the agency can seek enforcement of the order in a district court. These provisions have been implemented in FAR 3.901 to 3.906. Note that these protections extend to retaliation for complaints made to the Government. However, employees who make a complaint to the employer on a company hotline about activities that are unconnected to a potential FCA violation, would not appear to be protected under either of these provisions.

The American Recovery and Reinvestment Act, Pub. L. No. 111-5, 123 Stat 115, which was signed on February 17, 2009, provided billions of dollars for a wide variety of projects to stimulate the U.S. economy. The law directs the President and heads of Federal agencies to "commenc[e] expenditures and activities as quickly as possible consistent with prudent management." One goal of the act was to encourage employees of contractors to report not only illegal actions by the contractor, but also instances of gross waste and mismanagement. To protect workers against retaliation for reporting such events, § 1553 of that act contained its own "whistleblower protection" provisions:

> An employee of any non-Federal employer receiving covered funds may not be discharged, demoted, or otherwise discriminated against as a reprisal for disclosing, including a disclosure made in the ordinary course of an employee's duties, to the Board, an inspector general, the Comptroller General, a member of Congress, a State or Federal regulatory or law enforcement agency, a person with supervisory authority over the employee (or such other person working for the employer who has the authority to investigate, discover, or terminate misconduct), a court or grand jury, the head of a Federal agency, or their representatives, information that the employee reasonably believes is evidence of—
> (1) gross mismanagement of an agency contract or grant relat-

§ 1:20 GOVERNMENT CONTRACT COMPLIANCE HANDBOOK

    ing to covered funds;
    (2) a gross waste of covered funds;
    (3) a substantial and specific danger to public health or safety related to the implementation or use of covered funds;
    (4) an abuse of authority related to the implementation or use of covered funds; or
    (5) a violation of law, rule, or regulation related to an agency contract (including the competition for or negotiation of a contract) or grant, awarded or issued relating to covered funds.

These provisions have been implemented in FAR Subpart 3.907. See 74 Fed. Reg. 14634.

More recently, § 846 of the National Defense Authorization Act for Fiscal Year 2008, Pub. L. No. 110-181 and § 842 of the National Defense Authorization Act for Fiscal Year 2009, Pub. L. No. 110-417 amended 10 U.S.C.A. § 2409 to establish protections for DoD contractor employees that differ from those specified for civilian agency contractor employees in 41 U.S.C.A. § 265. The differences include an expansion of the types of information to which the protections apply, expansion of the categories of Government officials to whom information may be disclosed without reprisal, establishment of time periods with which the Inspector General and the agency head must take action with regard to a complaint filed by an contractor employee, and, most significantly, establishment of a *de novo* right of action in federal district court for contractor employees who have exhausted their administrative remedies under 10 U.S.C.A. § 2409. DoD issued an interim rule adding a new DFAR Subpart 203-9 to implement these provisions. 74 Fed. Reg. 2410. This rule was made final on November 9, 2009. 74 Fed. Reg. 59914.

The Sarbanes-Oxley Act contains its own whistleblower protection provisions at 18 USCA § 1514A(a)(1):

> (a) No [publicly-traded company] . . . may discharge, demote, suspend, threaten, harass, or in any other manner discriminate against an employee in the terms and conditions of employment because of any lawful act done by the employee—
>
> (1) to provide information, cause information to be provided, or otherwise assist in an investigation regarding any conduct which the employee reasonably believes constitutes a violation of section 1341 [mail fraud], 1343 [wire fraud], 1344 [bank fraud], or 1348 [securities fraud], any rule or regulation of the Securities and Exchange Commission, or any provision of Federal law relating to fraud against shareholders, when the in formation or assistance is provided to or the investigation is conducted by—
>
> (A) a Federal regulatory or law enforcement agency;
>
> (B) any Member of Congress or any committee of Congress; or
>
> (C) a person with supervisory authority over the employee (or such other person working for the employer who has the authority to

THE OFFENSES & PENALTIES § 1:21

investigate, discover, or terminate misconduct).

In *Tides v. Boeing*, 2011 WL 1651245 (9th Cir. May 3, 2011) the court held that the statute only gave protection if disclosure were made to the three specified categories of recipients and did not protect whistleblowers who made disclosures to the press.

On November 27, 2012, the President signed into law the Whistleblower Protection Enhancement Act of 2012, Pub. L. No. 112-199, 126 Stat. 1465, which broadened existing protections for federal employee whistleblowers such as: enhanced anti-retaliation rights, increased protection for individuals who come forward after the first disclosure is made, and increased penalties for retaliatory supervisors.

§ 1:21 Qui tam lawsuits—Frequently asked questions

Question 1: What do courts consider "publicly disclosed" information?

Answer 1: Courts have held that information obtained through Freedom of Information Act requests is publicly disclosed for purposes of the "original source" provision of the False Claims Act.[1] The Seventh Circuit has held that public reports that point to industry-wide abuse, but do not name specific defendants, still satisfy the "public disclosure" bar to qui tam actions.[2] The Second Circuit has held that if the information on which a qui tam suit is based is in the public domain, but the qui tam relator was not a source of that information, the suit is barred.[3] In that case, the district court had found that the qui tam complaint was based on a copy of a complaint filed against the defendants under the Racketeer Influenced and Corrupt Organizations Act (RICO). The RICO complaint did not rely on information provided by the qui tam relators. The Second Circuit held that to be considered an "original source," a relator also must have directly or indirectly been a source to the entity that publicly disclosed the allegations on which a suit is based. Accordingly, the Second Circuit upheld the district court's dismissal of the qui tam complaint.

The Fifth Circuit has summarized the split among courts of ap-

---

[Section 1:21]

[1]*See, e.g., U.S. ex rel. Burns v. A.D. Roe Co., Inc.*, 919 F. Supp. 255 (W.D. Ky. 1996), vacated, 186 F.3d 717, 1999 FED App. 0232P (6th Cir. 1999).

[2]*See U.S. v. Emergency Medical Associates of Illinois, Inc.*, 436 F.3d 726 (7th Cir. 2006).

[3]*See U.S. ex rel. Dick v. Long Island Lighting Co.*, 912 F.2d 13 (2d Cir. 1990) (rejected by *U.S. ex rel. Siller v. Becton Dickinson & Co. By and Through Microbiology Systems Div.*, 21 F.3d 1339 (4th Cir. 1994)) and (rejected by *U.S. v. Bank of Farmington*, 166 F.3d 853 (7th Cir. 1999)).

§ 1:21   GOVERNMENT CONTRACT COMPLIANCE HANDBOOK

peal in interpreting the statutory definition of "original source."[4] The majority of the Circuits hold that to qualify as an "original source," the relator must have indpendent and direct knowledge of the information on which the prior public disclosure is based.[5] By contrast, a miniority of the Circuits hold that the relator can only be an original source if he or she has direct and independent knowledge of the allegations in the qui tam complaint itself.[6] The United States Supreme Court has recently granted certiorari to consider the proper statutotry interpreation of "original source."[7]

Question 2: Can there be "public disclosure" when the information is not accessible in Government documents or news media accounts?

Answer 2: There is no clear answer to this question, and it depends on which court has the case. The U.S. Supreme Court has not addressed the issue and the U.S. courts of appeals do not agree. For example, suppose that Government agents interview your employees while executing a search warrant and tell the "innocent" employees about the fraud that the Government is investigating. Has there been public disclosure?

The Second Circuit held that, in this situation, once these "innocent" employees learned about the fraud from the agents, there was "public disclosure."[8]

The Fourth Circuit has taken a more expansive view of the jurisdictional limitation on qui tam lawsuits and held that a qui tam suit is "based upon" a public disclosure of allegations only when the qui tam relator has *actually derived* from the public disclosure the allegations on which the qui tam action is based.[9] The court further held, in disagreement with the Second and

---

[4]*See U.S. ex rel. Laird v. Lockheed Martin Engineering & Science Servs. Co.*, 336 F.3d 346 (5th Cir. 2003).

[5]*See Minnesota Ass'n of Nurse Anesthetists v. Allina Health System Corp.*, 276 F.3d 1032 (8th Cir. 2002); *Grayson v. Advanced Management Technology, Inc.*, 221 F.3d 580 (4th Cir. 2000); *U.S. ex rel. Findley v. FPC-Boron Employees' Club*, 105 F.3d 675 (D.C. Cir. 1997); *U.S. ex rel. McKenzie v. BellSouth Telecommunications, Inc.*, 123 F.3d 935, 1997 FED App. 0257P (6th Cir. 1997).

[6]*See U.S. ex rel. Hafter D.O.v. Spectrum Emergency Care, Inc.*, 190 F.3d 1156 (10th Cir. 1999); *U.S. ex rel Mistick PBT v. Housing Authority of City of Pittsburgh*, 186 F.3d 376 (3d Cir. 1999); *U.S. v. Northrop Corp.*, 5 F.3d 407 (9th Cir. 1993).

[7]U.S. ex rel. Stone v. Rockwell Int'l Corp., et al, Nos. 99-1351, 99-1352, 99-1353 (10th Cir., 2006), cert. granted Sept. 26, 2006.

[8]*See U.S. ex rel. Doe v. John Doe Corp.*, 960 F.2d 318 (2d Cir. 1992) (rejected by *U.S. ex rel. Siller v. Becton Dickinson & Co. By and Through Microbiology Systems Div.*, 21 F.3d 1339 (4th Cir. 1994)).

[9]*See U.S. ex rel. Siller v. Becton Dickinson & Co. By and Through Microbiology Systems Div.*, 21 F.3d 1339 (4th Cir. 1994) (rejected by *U.S. ex rel. Findley v. FPC-Boron Employees' Club*, 105 F.3d 675 (D.C. Cir. 1997)).

THE OFFENSES & PENALTIES   § 1:21

Ninth Circuits, that to be an "original source," a qui tam relator need only have direct and independent knowledge of the information on which the allegations in the public disclosure are based.[10]

The District of Columbia Circuit said that if the alleged fraud has been publicly disclosed, a qui tam action is barred, even if the qui tam plaintiff was not aware of the disclosure.[11] The court maintained that Congress intended to limit qui tam actions to those in which the relator contributes significant independent information not already in the public domain.

The Sixth Circuit has adopted the D.C. Circuit view, holding that to be an original source, a relator must inform the Government of the alleged fraud before the information has been publicly disclosed.[12] The Sixth Circuit found that the relator was not an "original source" because her complaint was filed three years after a case was filed with similar claims, and well after the allegations were made public. In another case, the Sixth Circuit held that a relator can lose "original source" status if the plaintiff alleged the misconduct in a prior civil complaint before notifying the Government.[13]

The Ninth Circuit held in one case that an original qui tam source, unimpeded by the public disclosure bar, is a person who "voluntarily provided the information to the Government."[14] The Ninth Circuit dismissed the case, holding that the relator there could not have disclosed the information "voluntarily" within the meaning of the False Claims Act because he was required to disclose it as part of his duties as an agency Inspector General employee[15]

In a subsequent case, the Tenth Circuit agreed with the en banc Ninth Circuit opinion.[16] The court found that the jurisdic-

---

[10]*See also U.S. ex rel. Springfield Terminal Ry. Co. v. Quinn*, 14 F.3d 645 (D.C. Cir. 1994) (sufficient if qui tam relator had direct and independent knowledge of *any* essential element of underlying fraud transaction).

[11]*See U.S. ex rel. Findley v. FPC-Boron Employees' Club*, 105 F.3d 675 (D.C. Cir. 1997) (relator's allegations that Government employees' clubs that earn revenue from vending services on federal property violate the False Claims Act by retaining monies owed to the Government merely echoed publicly disclosed transactions that already enabled the Government to investigate the case and decide whether to prosecute).

[12]*See U.S. ex rel. McKenzie v. BellSouth Telecommunications, Inc.*, 123 F.3d 935, 1997 FED App. 0257P (6th Cir. 1997).

[13]*See Walburn v. Lockheed Martin Corp.*, 431 F.3d 966, 2005 FED App. 0479P (6th Cir. 2005).

[14]*See* 31 U.S.C.A. § 3730(e)(4)(B).

[15]*See U.S. ex rel. Fine v. Chevron, U.S.A., Inc.*, 72 F.3d 740, 105 Ed. Law Rep. 885 (9th Cir. 1995).

[16]*See U.S. ex rel. Fine v. Advanced Sciences, Inc.*, 99 F.3d 1000 (10th Cir.

§ 1:21　　　Government Contract Compliance Handbook

tional bar on qui tam litigation was triggered when a relator disclosed allegations and transactions set out in a Department of Energy audit to the American Association of Retired Persons (AARP). The court explained that public disclosure occurs when the allegations of fraud or fraudulent transactions on which a qui tam claim is based are affirmatively disclosed to members of the public who are otherwise strangers to the fraud. Suffice it to say that the "public source" bar is a key issue and hotly debated in many qui tam cases.

Question 3: Does a qui tam claim survive a relator's death?

Answer 3: According to the U.S. District Court for the District of New Jersey, a qui tam relator's claims are remedial rather than penal, and, therefore, the claims survive the relator's death.[17]

Question 4: Does a qui tam relator have the authority to agree to a settlement releasing claims under the civil False Claims Act?

Answer 4: The Ninth Circuit has held that a qui tam relator's release of claims under the civil False Claims Act was not enforceable because it was *entered into without the Government's knowledge*.[18] The relator released False Claims Act claims as part of a "general release" of all claims against the defendant. The Ninth Circuit reasoned that enforcement of a release entered into without the Government's knowledge would frustrate an important purpose of the qui tam provisions: to encourage the Government to take action against a False Claims Act violator when its wrongdoing is brought to light by a relator's allegations.

However, if the Government had investigated allegations before the settlement, a qui tam plaintiff's settlement and release in a state court wrongful termination case precluded a subsequent qui tam suit based on the same allegations. In one case, the Government was fully aware of the relator's allegations that tubeshells manufactured by a defense contractor did not meet corrosion resistance requirements but declined to intervene after finding that the allegations were unsubstantiated.[19]

Additionally, the Eight Circuit has held that when a release is granted as part of a settlement arising in a bankruptcy context, the public interest concerns addressed by the Ninth Circuit are not implicated, and so the release will be enforced.[20]

Question 5: Can the Government veto settlement of a qui tam

1996) (rejected by *U.S. v. Bank of Farmington*, 166 F.3d 853 (7th Cir. 1999)).

[17]*See U.S. ex rel. Estate of Botnick v. Cathedral Healthcare System, Inc.*, 352 F. Supp. 2d 530 (D.N.J. 2005).

[18]*See U.S. v. Northrop Corp.*, 59 F.3d 953 (9th Cir. 1995).

[19]*See U.S. ex rel. Hall v. Teledyne Wah Chang Albany*, 104 F.3d 230 (9th Cir. 1997), as amended on denial of reh'g and reh'g en banc, (Mar. 19, 1997).

[20]*See U.S. ex rel. Gebert v. Transport Administrative Services*, 260 F.3d 909

THE OFFENSES & PENALTIES § 1:21

lawsuit despite its failure to intervene in the suit?

Answer 5: The Fifth Circuit has held that the Government has the power to "veto" a voluntary settlement in a qui tam suit even if it declined to intervene in the suit. The Fifth Circuit found that the Government had standing to appeal the settlement even though it had not intervened and so was not a party to the suit.[21] The court based its decision on the language in the False Claims Act stating that a qui tam suit "may be dismissed only if the court and the Attorney General give written consent to the dismissal and state their reasons for consenting."[22] The court held that this language is unambiguous, and that nothing else in the statute negates the import of this language. Furthermore, it determined that the Government has enough interest in the outcome to permit it to appeal even if it was not a party to the settlement. The Sixth Circuit agreed with this analysis, stating that "if Congress wanted to limit the consent requirement . . . we presume it knew the words to do so."[23]

The Ninth Circuit has held that the legislative history of the 1986 False Claims Act amendments militates against giving the Government the power to void a settlement because the Act encouraged private litigants to take more responsibility for enforcement.[24]

Question 6: Can an in-house counsel bring a qui tam suit against a former employer?

Answer 6: According to the U.S. District Court for the Eastern District of Virginia, the answer is yes.[25] The court held that nothing in the False Claims Act prevents in-house counsel from being a relator in a qui tam action, although state law attorney-client obligations and fiduciary duties independent of the False Claims Act may have the practical effect of precluding such actions.

Question 7: Can a Government employee be a relator?

Answer 7: Federal courts have considered the question of whether an employee of a federal agency Inspector General's (IG's) Office may act as a relator in a qui tam action under the False Claims Act. Take, for example the case of one federal em-

---

(8th Cir. 2001).

[21]*See Searcy v. Philips Elec. N. Am. Corp.*, 117 F.3d 154 (5th Cir. 1997).

[22]*See Searcy v. Philips Elec. N. Am. Corp.*, 117 F.3d 154, 159 (5th Cir. 1997) (citing 31 U.S.C.A. § 3730(b)(1)).

[23]*U.S. v. Health Possibilities, P.S.C.*, 207 F.3d 335, 2000 FED App. 0100P (6th Cir. 2000).

[24]*See U.S. ex rel. Killingsworth v. Northrop Corp.*, 25 F.3d 715, 28 Fed. R. Serv. 3d 1522 (9th Cir. 1994) (rejected by *U.S. v. Health Possibilities, P.S.C.*, 207 F.3d 335, 2000 FED App. 0100P (6th Cir. 2000)).

[25]*See U.S. ex rel. Doe v. X Corp.*, 862 F. Supp. 1502 (E.D. Va. 1994).

§ 1:21   GOVERNMENT CONTRACT COMPLIANCE HANDBOOK

ployee who, after retiring from the IG's Office at the Department of Energy, filed several qui tam actions against organizations that were audited by the IG while the relator was employed there. The defendants in at least three of those actions argued that IG employees should not be permitted to act as qui tam relators. In two different actions brought by the same former federal employee, two judges for the U.S. District Court in New Mexico disagreed on that issue. In one case,[26] the district court held that IG employees are responsible for detecting and reporting fraud under the terms of their employment, and to permit them to collect a bounty under the qui tam provisions of the False Claims Act for doing their jobs would create a conflict of interest that could undermine the effectiveness of the IG offices. However, in another case,[27] the district court held that the concern about conflicts of interest was best addressed to Congress. Because Congress had not made IG employees ineligible to serve as relators, the court concluded it should not read that restriction into the False Claims Act. Furthermore, according to this judge, permitting IG employees to bring qui tam suits would probably enhance, rather than undermine, enforcement of the Act.

Several courts have held that a Government employee whose job responsibilities include an obligation to report fraud cannot satisfy the False Claim Act's "original source" requirement for actions based on publicly disclosed information. The Ninth Circuit held that the former IG employee-relator discussed above could not bring a qui tam action because his job required him to supervise and edit audits that other employees had conducted and therefore his disclosure of fraud was not voluntary.[28] The Ninth Circuit also has found that a Contracting Officer cannot be an original source when reporting alleged fraud by a contractor over which the Contracting Officer has a duty under the Federal Acquisition Regulation and Navy rules to review and refer fraudulent claims to appropriate investigatory officials.[29] Similarly, the First Circuit held that a Government worker formerly employed as a Quality Assurance Specialist could not be an "original

---

[26]*See U.S. ex rel. Fine v. Advanced Sci., Inc.*, 879 F. Supp. 1092 (D.N.M. 1995), aff'd, 99 F.3d 1000 (10th Cir. 1996) (rejected by *U.S. v. Bank of Farmington*, 166 F.3d 853 (7th Cir. 1999)).

[27]*See U.S. ex rel. Fine v. MK-Ferguson Co.*, 861 F. Supp. 1544 (D.N.M. 1994), aff'd, 99 F.3d 1538 (10th Cir. 1996).

[28]*See U.S. ex rel. Fine v. Chevron, U.S.A., Inc.*, 72 F.3d 740, 105 Ed. Law Rep. 885 (9th Cir. 1995).

[29]*See U.S. ex rel. Biddle v. Board of Trustees of Leland Stanford, Jr. University*, 147 F.3d 821, 127 Ed. Law Rep. 596 (9th Cir. 1998), opinion amended and superseded, 161 F.3d 533, 130 Ed. Law Rep. 1093 (9th Cir. 1998) (adding dissenting view that Contracting Officer can be "original source" for qui tam purposes).

The Offenses & Penalties
§ 1:21

source" because the fruits of his effort at uncovering fraud belonged to his employer, the Government.[30] An unpublished decision from the Southern District of New York agreed with these decisions, holding that if a Government employee was obligated to report defects in the contractor's software, his reports cannot be called "voluntary" for purposes of the "original source" exception.[31]

Question 8: Are the qui tam provisions of the False Claims Act constitutional?

Answer 8: For a number of years after the 1986 Amendments, defendants in qui tam lawsuits regularly challenged the qui tam provisions of the False Claims Act as unconstitutional on essentially three grounds: the provisions violate (1) the standing requirement of Article II, § 2, (2) the separation of powers doctrine of Article II, § 3, and (3) the Appointments Clause of Article II, § 2. The Supreme Court held in 2000, however, that the qui tam provisions provide for constitutional standing because the relator serves as the assignee of the Government—the party who has suffered an injury.[32]

Question 9: What reward does a relator receive?

Answer 9: The amount a relator receives will vary depending on how the case proceeds and the total amount of the recovery. If the Government decides to pursue the lawsuit, it will have primary responsibility for prosecuting the action.[33] If the Government prosecutes the action and is successful, the qui tam plaintiff receives between 15% and 25% of the proceeds from any judgment or settlement, plus expenses, attorney fees, and costs.[34] The 15% minimum award has been called a "finder's fee" that the qui tam plaintiff receives as a matter of right for simply filing the suit. If the qui tam plaintiff confers a benefit beyond merely filing a complaint, then his or her portion of the total recovery may go as high as 25%. If the Government does not proceed with the action and the plaintiff proceeds alone to trial or settlement, then the plaintiff receives 25% to 30% of the proceeds, plus expenses, attorney fees, and costs.[35] If the Government does not intervene in the relator's lawsuit, but subsequently settles with the

---

[30] *See U.S. ex rel. LeBlanc v. Raytheon Co., Inc.*, 913 F.2d 17, 20 (1st Cir. 1990) (rejected by *U.S. ex rel. Williams v. NEC Corp.*, 931 F.2d 1493 (11th Cir. 1991)).

[31] *See U.S. v. Caci Intern. Inc.*, 1997 WL 473549 (S.D. N.Y. 1997), judgment aff'd, 172 F.3d 39 (2d Cir. 1999).

[32] *See Vermont Agency of Natural Resources v. U.S. ex rel. Stevens*, 529 U.S. 765, 120 S. Ct. 1858, 146 L. Ed. 2d 836 (2000).

[33] 31 U.S.C.A. § 3730(c)(1).

[34] 31 U.S.C.A. § 3730(d)(1).

[35] 31 U.S.C.A. § 3730(d)(2).

§ 1:21   GOVERNMENT CONTRACT COMPLIANCE HANDBOOK

defendant anyway, the Sixth Circuit has held that this constitutes an "alternate remedy" and does not bar the relator from receiving a reward.[36]

Whether or not the Government proceeds with the action, if the court finds that the action was brought by a person who planned and initiated the violation on which the action was predicated, the court may *reduce* (but not eliminate) the relator's share of recovery. If the person bringing the action is convicted of criminal conduct arising from his or her role in the violation of the False Claims Act, that person must be dismissed from the civil action and may not receive any proceeds.[37]

Question 10: Does the six-year limitations period contained in the civil False Claims Act also apply to retaliation claims?

Answer 10: No. The U.S. Supreme Court held in 2005 that the statute of limitations for a retaliation claim is the most closely analogous state limitations period.[38] There, the Court found that "at a minimum," the False Claims Act was ambiguous as to whether the six-year limitations period applies to retaliation claims and instead followed the most analogous state statute of limitations, as is customary when the federal statute is silent on the issue. Thus, the retaliation allegations may be subject to a substantially shorter limitations period.

Question 11: How specific does a relator have to be in alleging that the defendant committed fraud?

Answer 11: Rule 9(b) of the Federal Rules of Civil Procedures states "In alleging fraud or mistake, a party must state with particularity the circumstances constituting fraud or mistake." The "circumstances" required to be pled with particularity are "the time, place, and contents of the false representations, as well as the identity of the person making the misrepresentation and what he obtained thereby." *Harrison v. Westinghouse Savannah River Co.*, 176 F.3d 776 (4th Cir. 1999). In general, the purpose of Rule 9(b) is to ensure (1) that an opportunistic relator is unable to tarnish the reputation of a company by instituting a spurious lawsuit and (2) and to give the defendant sufficient facts to understand and respond to the allegations that are being made. Courts seem more likely to find that these goals have been met where the relator was directly involved in the allegedly fraudulent conduct.

Simply alleging that a contractor continually breached the

---

[36]*See U.S. ex rel. Bledsoe v. Community Health Systems, Inc.*, 342 F.3d 634, 56 Fed. R. Serv. 3d 1089, 2003 FED App. 0322P (6th Cir. 2003).

[37]31 U.S.C.A. § 3730(e)(3).

[38]*Graham County Soil & Water Conservation Dist. v. U.S. ex rel. Wilson*, 545 U.S. 409, 125 S. Ct. 2444, 162 L. Ed. 2d 390 (2005).

THE OFFENSES & PENALTIES § 1:21

contract and related regulations and that because of this every payment request constituted a false claim will not replace the "particularity" requirements of FRCP 9(b). *See U.S. ex rel. Wildhirt v. AARS Forever, Inc.*, 2011 WL 1303390 (N.D.Ill. Apr. 6, 2011).

Question 12: Can the conduct of the relator or its attorney during the course of the litigation affect the outcome?

Answer 12: Most certainly. In *Rhonda Salmeron v. Enterprise Recovery Systems, Inc.*, 579 F.3d 787 (7th Cir. 2009), the court affirmed a lower court decision which dismissed a false claim action after finding that the plaintiff's attorney had a "virtually unbroken pattern of dilatory and irresponsible conduct," consistently missing filing deadlines and failing to appear at status conferences, and that he had violated an "attorneys' eyes only" agreement by leaking a document to third parties.

Question 13: Can a defendant ever recover losses incurred as a result of the events underlying a civil False Claims Act against either the *relator* or its co-defendant.

Answer 13: Yes, under certain circumstances. *Cell Therapeutics Inc. v. Lash Group*, 586 F.3d 1204 (9th Cir. 2009) involved a situation in which Lash, a consulting firm, mistakenly advised Cell that it could market its cancer drug for "off-label" treatment of other diseases and that such off-label uses were reimbursable by Medicare. This led to a *qui tam* action against both Cell and Lash. Cell eventually settled the *qui tam* action with the Government and the *relator*. It then filed suit against its co-defendant seeking $12.3 million damages in business losses (beyond the $10.5 million it paid to settle the fraud claims) based on theories of breach of contract and negligence. Citing language from an earlier decision, the court held that there was no right to recover damages and penalties imposed under the FCA based on theories of indemnification or contribution.

Question 14: Can a member of the armed forces file a *qui tam* action against other another member for events relating to their services while in the military?

Answer 14: No. Section 3730(e) bars a *qui tam* action against current or former members of the military:

> No court shall have jurisdiction over an action brought by a former or present member of the armed forces under subsection (b) of this section against a member of the armed forces arising out of such person's service in the armed forces.

However, in *U.S. ex rel. Little v. Shell Exploration & Prod. Co.*, 690 F.3d 282 (5th Cir. 2012), the Fifth Circuit found that a federal auditor, "even one whose job it is to investigate fraud," may bring a qui tam suit based on evidence found during the course of employment.

§ 1:22 The Foreign Assistance Act

The Foreign Assistance Act was passed by Congress in 1961.[1] The Act established various assistance programs designed to promote stability abroad. Contractors who submit false claims under the banner of foreign aid can also face penalties under the Foreign Assistance Act (22 U.S.C.A. § 2399b). Any individual, corporation, partnership, association, or other legal entity who does so shall forfeit or refund the payment plus 25%, and the greater of $2,200 and double the damages or 50% of the payment for each fraudulent act together with the costs of suit.[2]

§ 1:23 Program Fraud Civil Remedies Act

The Program Fraud Civil Remedies Act establishes an administrative remedy for false claims and false statements cases under $150,000 that the Department of Justice (DOJ) declines to prosecute.[1] The Act aims to resolve small-dollar fraud cases in which the cost of litigation would exceed the damages the Government might recover.

The Act imposes civil *penalties* of up to $5,500 for each certified written false statement and false claim. In addition, the Act imposes a *damages* assessment of twice the amount of the false claim in cases where the Government has paid the claim. The Government does not need to show a specific intent to defraud; actual or constructive knowledge of falsity is sufficient.[2] However, a false statement cannot be prosecuted under this Act unless the statement contains or is accompanied by an express certification of affirmance of its truthfulness and accuracy.

Agencies designate an investigating official—usually the Inspector General—to conduct investigations into possible violations of the Act. This official has the power to subpoena documents. The investigating official transmits findings to a reviewing official within the agency who independently evaluates the allegations to determine whether there is adequate evidence that a false claim or statement has been made. If so, the reviewing official refers the matter to DOJ which reviews the charges and determines whether to litigate the case. The agency may commence administrative proceedings only with DOJ approval.

The Program Fraud Civil Remedies Act requires agencies to is-

---

[Section 1:22]

[1] 22 U.S.C.A. §§ 2151 et seq.
[2] 22 U.S.C.A. § 2399b(a).

[Section 1:23]

[1] P.L. 99-509, §§ 6101 to 6104, 100 Stat. 1874.
[2] 31 U.S.C.A. § 3802(a)(1), (2); 31 U.S.C.A. § 3801(a)(5).

sue implementing regulations specifying the identity of the investigating and reviewing officials, the procedures for conducting administrative hearings under the Act, and the like. Twenty-one agencies have issued implementing regulations.[3]

The Government has thus far made limited and infrequent use of the Program Fraud Civil Remedies Act to combat fraud by Government contractors. For example, the then-General Accounting Office—now Government Accountability Office—(GAO) reported that from October 1986, when the Act became effective, through September 1990, seven of the eight agencies that GAO reviewed had referred only 41 cases to DOJ for permission to prosecute. Of these 41 cases, 26 came from the U.S. Postal Service. The GAO reported that the Defense Department had resolved only one case involving contractor fraud under the Act, resulting in a total recovery of $15,139.[4]

§ 1:24 Program Fraud Civil Remedies Act—Examples

False statement: Assume you submit a false Certificate of Current Cost or Pricing Data to a Government official concerning a $550,000 contract. DOJ declines to pursue this matter. You can still be pursued by the Government, however, because you could be charged with making a false statement under the Program Fraud Civil Remedies Act (provided the Government does not seek more than $150,000) since the statement you submitted to the Government was certified.

False claim: In connection with the same contract, you submit a false invoice to the Government for $100,000 in materials when you know, or should know, that the actual value of the materials provided was $50,000. Again, you could be charged with making a false claim under the Program Fraud Civil Remedies Act.

V. CORRUPTION

§ 1:25 Bribery & illegal gratuities

The bribery statute prohibits giving and receiving bribes to

---

[3]*See* Office of Personnel Management, 5 C.F.R. pt. 185; Dept. of Homeland Security, 6 C.F.R. pt. 13; Dept. of Agriculture, 7 C.F.R. pt. 1; Nuclear Reg. Commn., 10 C.F.R. pt. 13; Dept. of Energy, 10 C.F.R. pt. 1013; Dept. of Commerce, 15 C.F.R. pt. 25; Dept. of State, 22 C.F.R. pt. 35; Agency for International Development, 22 C.F.R. pt. 224; Broadcasting Board of Governors, 22 C.F.R. pt. 521; Dept. of Housing and Urban Development, 24 C.F.R. pt. 28; Dept. of Justice, 28 C.F.R. pt. 71; Dept. of Labor, 29 C.F.R. pt. 22; Dept. of Treasury, 31 C.F.R. pt. 136; Dept. of Education, 34 C.F.R. pt. 33; Dept. of Veterans' Affairs, 38 C.F.R. pt. 42; U.S. Postal Service, 39 C.F.R. pt. 273; Environmental Protection Agency, 40 C.F.R. pt. 27; Dept. of Interior, 43 C.F.R. pt. 35; Dept. of Health and Human Services, 45 C.F.R. pt. 79; Dept. of Transportation, 49 C.F.R. pt. 31.

[4]GAO Rep. No. AFMD-91-73 (Sept. 13, 1991).

§ 1:25   GOVERNMENT CONTRACT COMPLIANCE HANDBOOK

public officials.[1] The illegal gratuities statute, like the bribery statute, is a criminal law that applies to offers and solicitations of gifts to Government officials.[2] Both statutes are discussed in greater detail in §§ 7:1 et seq.

§ 1:26   Conflicts of interest

The Ethics Reform Act of 1989[1] imposes criminal penalties on former Government officers and employees who engage in specified conflicts of interest. The Procurement Integrity Act places restrictions on private sector employment of former Government employees and requires agency officials to promptly disclose contacts with contractors regarding employment. Criminal, civil, and administrative penalties are prescribed for violations of these provisions.[2] These and other "revolving door" statutes, as well as organizational conflicts of interest, are discussed at greater length in §§ 8:1 et seq.

§ 1:27   Kickbacks

The Anti-Kickback Act imposes criminal and civil penalties for kickbacks in connection with contracts and subcontracts.[1] The Act essentially extends the anticorruption concepts that apply to dealings with "public officials" under the bribery and illegal gratuities statutes (mentioned above) to private persons in subcontract relationships. The Anti-Kickback Act is examined in greater detail in §§ 7:1 et seq.

§ 1:28   Foreign Corrupt Practices Act

The Foreign Corrupt Practices Act (FCPA) prohibits, among other things, bribery of foreign officials.[1] The statute essentially extends the anticorruption concepts that apply to dealings with U.S. "public officials" to "foreign officials." Of note, there is a recent rise in collective enforcement among countries, with the U.S. DoJ and SEC cooperating with the British Serious Fraud

---

[Section 1:25]
   [1] 18 U.S.C.A. § 201(b).
   [2] 18 U.S.C.A. § 201(c).

[Section 1:26]
   [1] 18 U.S.C.A. § 207.
   [2] 41 U.S.C.A. § 423.

[Section 1:27]
   [1] 41 U.S.C.A. §§ 51 to 58.

[Section 1:28]
   [1] 15 U.S.C.A. §§ 78dd-1, 78dd-2.

Office to enforce the FCPA here in the U.S. and the Bribery Act of 2010 in the U.K. The FCPA is discussed further in §§ 19:1 et seq.

§ 1:29 Lobbying restrictions & collusive bidding

In addition to the obstruction of justice statutes discussed below, you should also be aware of the following corruption-related statutes.

The so-called "Byrd Amendment,"[1] which imposes constraints on your use of Government funds to support "lobbying" activities, and the Lobbying Disclosure Act of 1995,[2] which sets forth comprehensive registration and reporting requirements regarding lobbying activities, provide for civil penalties for violations of their requirements. See §§ 7:1 et seq. for a detailed discussion of these laws.

The Sherman Antitrust Act imposes criminal penalties for collusive bidding activity and other anticompetitive conduct.[3] The Clayton Act and the Federal Trade Commission Act also authorize civil lawsuits against companies suspected of restraining trade and prohibit unfair methods of competition and unfair or deceptive acts or practices in or affecting commerce.[4] These laws regarding anticompetitive practices are discussed in greater detail in §§ 7:1 et seq.

VI. IMPROPER ACCESS TO GOVERNMENT PROPERTY & INFORMATION

§ 1:30 Procurement Integrity Act

The Procurement Integrity Act prohibits a company competing for the award of a Government contract or subcontract from knowingly obtaining, and current or former Government employees from knowingly disclosing, contractor bid or proposal information or source selection information before the award of a federal agency procurement contract to which the information relates. Criminal, civil, and administrative penalties are prescribed for violations of these provisions.[1] The Procurement Integrity Act is discussed in greater detail in §§ 6:1 et seq.

[Section 1:29]

[1] 31 U.S.C.A. § 1352.

[2] 2 U.S.C.A. §§ 1601 to 1612.

[3] 15 U.S.C.A. §§ 1 to 7.

[4] 15 U.S.C.A. §§ 12 to 27; 15 U.S.C.A. §§ 41 to 58.

[Section 1:30]

[1] 41 U.S.C.A. § 423.

§ 1:31 Theft of Government property statute

The theft of Government property statute penalizes the theft, conversion, and conveyance of Government property.[1] The Government has used this statute to prosecute conversion or conveyance of both tangible and intangible Government property. See §§ 6:1 et seq. for a more detailed discussion of this law.

§ 1:32 Espionage statutes

The criminal espionage statutes restrict the taking and dissemination of information relating to the national defense.[1] These laws are examined in §§ 6:1 et seq.

VII. OBSTRUCTION OF JUSTICE

§ 1:33 Generally

There are a number of statutes that address and penalize interference with federal judicial proceedings, investigations, and audits.

§ 1:34 Obstruction of federal audit

To establish a violation of the obstruction of federal audit statute,[1] the Government must prove the following:

(1) You tried to influence, obstruct, or impede a federal auditor's performance of his or her official duties;
(2) You did so with the intent to deceive or defraud the United States; and
(3) The official's duties related to a person receiving more than $100,000 in any one year under a Government contract or subcontract.

The purpose of the obstruction of a federal audit statute is to deter any destruction or fabrication of documents or intimidation of witnesses or employees undertaken to prevent a Government auditor from discovering irregularities. Penalties include fines under the Sentence of Fine statute (see § 1:43) and up to five years' imprisonment.

The statute defines "Federal auditor" as "any person employed

---

[Section 1:31]
  [1]18 U.S.C.A. § 641.
[Section 1:32]
  [1]18 U.S.C.A. §§ 792 to 799.
[Section 1:34]
  [1]18 U.S.C.A. § 1516.

THE OFFENSES & PENALTIES § 1:36

on a full- or part-time or contractual basis to perform an audit or a quality assurance inspection for or on behalf of the United States." Accordingly, the statute reaches efforts to obstruct the performance of quality assurance inspectors as well as efforts to obstruct the performance of financial auditors.

§ 1:35 Obstruction of federal audit—Example

Destruction of documents: You received more than $100,000 in contracts from the Government this year. In connection with one of your contracts, a Defense Contract Audit Agency auditor asks whether you have retained certain documents concerning the contract. You tell him that you have not. You then retrieve the documents from your file and instruct your secretary to destroy them. You could be liable for obstructing a federal audit as well as for making false statements.

Cases & Commentary: Section 871 of the Duncan Hunter National Defense Authorization Act for Fiscal Year 2009 (Pub. L. No. 110-417) added language allowing the Comptroller General to interview current employees regarding transactions being examined during an audit of contracting records. On October 14, 2009 the FAR Councils made final an earlier interim rule which revised FAR clauses 52.215-2, Audit and Records—Negotiation, and 52.214-26, Audit and Records—Sealed Bidding to add the required statutory language. 74 Fed. Reg. 52851. Thus, the previous scope of a GAO audit permitted by those clauses has been expanded to include "the right to interview any current employee regarding such transactions." A refusal to make employees available to GAO or intentionally discouraging them from cooperating could be viewed as obstructing a federal audit.

§ 1:36 Obstruction of judicial proceeding

It is a criminal offense to endeavor to influence, intimidate, or impede any grand or trial juror or court official; or to influence, obstruct, or impede or endeavor to influence, obstruct, or impede the due administration of justice corruptly or by threats of force, or by any threatening letter or communication.[1] To obtain a conviction for obstruction of justice, the Government must show that there was a pending judicial proceeding. Generally, the obstruction of a Government investigation not connected with an on-going judicial or quasi-judicial proceeding does not fall within

---

[Section 1:36]
[1]18 U.S.C.A. § 1503.

§ 1:36 GOVERNMENT CONTRACT COMPLIANCE HANDBOOK

the purview of the obstruction of justice statute.[2] For example, interference with execution of a search warrant does not constitute obstruction of justice. Likewise, a pregrand jury agency investigation by an inspector general, the Federal Bureau of Investigation, or the Internal Revenue Service does not qualify as a judicial proceeding but may be covered under other protection of justice provisions.

In one case, the U.S. Court of Appeals for the Fourth Circuit summarized the requirements of the obstruction of justice statute by explaining that a defendant must have knowledge or notice of a pending judicial proceeding, and must have acted with the intent to influence, obstruct, or impede that proceeding in its due administration of justice.[3]

The Supreme Court also has addressed the scope of the statute.[4] The Court held that simply lying to a federal agent, who might or might not eventually testify before a grand jury, did not constitute endeavoring to obstruct the due administration of justice. The Court held that if the defendant lacks knowledge that his actions are likely to affect the judicial proceeding, he lacks the requisite intent to obstruct. Furthermore, although the defendant knew that a grand jury proceeding was in progress, the Government did not show that the federal agent was acting on behalf of the grand jury or that the defendant knew his false statements to the agent would be provided to the grand jury. Therefore, simply lying to the federal agent did not have the "natural and probable effect" of interfering with the administration of justice.

In light of this case, the Second Circuit held that "to prove the accused was corruptly endeavoring to influence, obstruct or impede a grand jury investigation under 18 U.S.C.A. § 1503, the Government had to prove a connection between the defendant's intentional acts and the likelihood of potentially affecting the administration of justice: the action taken by the accused must be with an intent to influence judicial or grand jury proceedings; it is not enough that there be an intent to influence some ancillary proceeding."[5] In that case, the defendant, a manager for a securities underwriter, had allegedly ordered employees to destroy documents in an effort to obstruct grand jury and SEC investigations.

In one case, the Fourth Circuit affirmed a conviction for

---

[2]See U.S. v. Davis, 183 F.3d 231, 52 Fed. R. Evid. Serv. 732 (3d Cir. 1999), opinion amended, 197 F.3d 662 (3d Cir. 1999).

[3]See U.S. v. Littleton, 76 F.3d 614, 619 (4th Cir. 1996).

[4]See U.S. v. Aguilar, 515 U.S. 593, 115 S. Ct. 2357, 132 L. Ed. 2d 520 (1995).

[5]See U.S. v. Quattrone, 441 F.3d 153 (2d Cir. 2006).

THE OFFENSES & PENALTIES   § 1:38

obstruction of justice that involved the alteration of subpoenaed documents.[6] The defendant received a grand jury subpoena demanding the corporate minute books relating to two U.S. Navy contracts to refit several ships. The defendant produced them, but the Government discovered that the minutes had been altered. More than a year later, the defendant produced only parts of the original minutes, explaining that he had found them under a rug in his home. The court held that submission of evidence of such alterations to the original minutes was sufficient to sustain a conviction for obstruction of justice.

Conduct that violates the statute includes the fabrication of records in response to a grand jury subpoena and attempts to influence witnesses not to recall information, or even to invoke their privilege against self-incrimination under the Fifth Amendment of the U.S. Constitution, if the motive of the inducer is to shield his own criminal behavior.[7] This is a particularly complex issue on which you should seek specific legal guidance. While business entities do not have Fifth Amendment rights against self-incrimination, individual employees do, which creates obvious tensions.

§ 1:37 Obstruction of judicial proceeding—Example

Destruction of documents: A subcontractor calls to tell you that his company has received a grand jury subpoena that covers cost estimates for the contract on which you serve as the prime contractor. You received an identical subpoena, but destroyed your copies of the estimates many months ago before you knew there was any investigation. You say, "I can't believe you kept those estimates—they'll get me in a lot of trouble. If you know what's good for you, you'll put those estimates the same place I did—the shredder." If the subcontractor destroys the documents, the subcontractor could be liable for obstruction of justice. You could also be liable for causing him to destroy the estimates. You are probably not liable under the obstruction of justice statute for the destruction of the estimates in *your* file because you destroyed them when you were unaware of an investigation.

§ 1:38 Witness tampering

Federal criminal law proscribes as a felony the knowing use or attempted use of intimidation, physical force, threats, corrupt persuasion, or the engaging in "misleading conduct" toward an-

---
[6]*See U.S. v. Brooks*, 111 F.3d 365 (4th Cir. 1997).
[7]*See U.S. v. McComb*, 744 F.2d 555 (7th Cir. 1984).

other with the intent to:[1]

(1) Influence, delay, or prevent any person's testimony in an official proceeding;
(2) Cause or induce any person to withhold testimony or withhold documentary or physical evidence from an official proceeding; alter, destroy or conceal an object with intent to impair its availability for use in an official proceeding; or be absent from an official proceeding to which the person has been summoned by legal process; or
(3) Hinder, delay, or prevent the communication of information relating to the commission or possible commission of a federal offense to a law enforcement officer or judge.

Under this provision, one who intentionally harasses another person and thereby hinders, delays, prevents, or dissuades the person from attending or testifying in an official proceeding or reporting a commission of a federal offense is liable for committing a misdemeanor. As the U.S. Supreme Court discussed in *Arthur Andersen, LLP v. U.S.*, a finding that shredding documents impeded the investigation was insufficient by itself to establish guilt.[2]

"Misleading conduct" is very broadly defined to include, among other things: (a) knowingly making a false statement, (b) intentionally omitting information from a statement and thereby causing a portion of the statement to be misleading, (c) intentionally concealing a material fact and thereby creating a false impression by the statement, (d) knowingly submitting or inviting reliance on a writing that is false or altered with intent to mislead, and (e) knowingly using a trick, scheme, or device with intent to mislead.[3] However, a " 'knowingly corrupt persuader' for purposes of 18 U.S.C.A. § 1512(b) cannot be someone who persuades others to shred documents under a document retention policy when he does not have in contemplation any particular official proceeding in which those documents might be material."[4]

The witness tampering statute is similar to the obstruction of justice statute (see § 1:36) with two significant exceptions. First, the witness tampering statute may be invoked only if the defendant used *intimidation*, physical force, threats, harassment, or misleading conduct. The obstruction of justice statute, on the

---

[Section 1:38]

[1] 18 U.S.C.A. § 1512.

[2] *Arthur Andersen LLP v. U.S.*, 544 U.S. 696, 125 S. Ct. 2129, 161 L. Ed. 2d 1008 (2005).

[3] 18 U.S.C.A. § 1515(a)(3).

[4] *Arthur Andersen LLP v. U.S.*, 544 U.S. 696, 125 S. Ct. 2129, 161 L. Ed. 2d 1008 (2005).

THE OFFENSES & PENALTIES § 1:40

other hand, according to some courts, reaches noncoercive witness tampering.[5] Second, unlike the obstruction of justice statute, the witness tampering statute is not limited to "pending" official proceedings and, thus, covers *potential* witnesses.

§ 1:39 Obstruction of pending administrative proceeding

The statute that governs obstruction of pending proceedings before any department or agency of the United States (18 U.S.C.A. § 1505) parallels the obstruction of justice statute (18 U.S.C.A. § 1503, discussed in § 1:36), differing primarily in the types of proceedings they cover. The agency or departmental "pending proceedings" covered by § 1505 include preliminary and informal inquiries as well as formal proceedings.[1] These include both investigative and adjudicative actions by the Government. No formal stage of investigation or adjudication need have been reached for agency action to constitute a "proceeding" under this statute. Investigations by the Federal Bureau of Investigation[2] or the U.S. Attorney's Office[3] are not "proceedings" for purposes of this statute.

In one case, this statute was used to prosecute a contractor employee for false testimony provided in a deposition taken in connection with an Armed Services Board of Contract Appeals proceeding.[4] The defendant, a production supervisor, was convicted on perjury and obstruction charges and was sentenced to 16 months in prison.

§ 1:40 Perjury & false declarations under oath

The perjury statute[1] and the false declarations statute[2] define the crimes of perjury and false declarations under oath. The es-

---

[5]*See, e.g., U.S. v. Risken*, 788 F.2d 1361 (8th Cir. 1986) (and cases cited therein).

[Section 1:39]

[1]*See, e.g., U.S. v. Laurins*, 857 F.2d 529, 26 Fed. R. Evid. Serv. 1346 (9th Cir. 1988) (Internal Revenue Service); *U.S. v. Browning, Inc.*, 572 F.2d 720 (10th Cir. 1978) (Bureau of Customs Investigation); *U.S. v. Fruchtman*, 421 F.2d 1019, 8 A.L.R. Fed. 885 (6th Cir. 1970) (Federal Trade Commn.); *U.S. v. Abrams*, 427 F.2d 86 (2d Cir. 1970) (Immigration and Naturalization Service); *U.S. v. Tallant*, 407 F. Supp. 878 (N.D. Ga. 1975) (Securities and Exchange Commn.).

[2]*See U.S. v. Higgins*, 511 F. Supp. 453 (W.D. Ky. 1981).

[3]*See U.S. v. Wright*, 704 F. Supp. 613 (D. Md. 1989).

[4]*See U.S. v. Hobbs*, 922 F.2d 848 (11th Cir. 1990) (table).

[Section 1:40]

[1]18 U.S.C.A. § 1621.

[2]18 U.S.C.A. § 1623.

§ 1:40   GOVERNMENT CONTRACT COMPLIANCE HANDBOOK

sential elements of perjury are (1) an oath authorized by a law of the United States, (2) taken before a competent tribunal, officer, or person, and (3) a false statement, written testimony, declaration, or deposition willfully made as to facts material to the hearing. The essential elements of false declarations are (a) an oath, (b) a knowing false material declaration or the use of any other information, such as a document, knowing that it contains a false material declaration, (c) in a proceeding before or ancillary to a court or a grand jury.

There are several differences between the two statutes. The perjury statute applies to *all* proceedings under oath, while the false declarations statute applies only to declarations made in proceedings before or ancillary to court or grand jury proceedings. On the other hand, the false declarations statute covers not only written testimony but the submission of false documents. Finally, the false declarations statute relaxes the Government's evidentiary burden making it somewhat simpler to prove the crime in the vital arenas of court and grand jury proceedings. Perjury prosecutions are subject to the common law "two witness" rule. This rule requires that perjury be proven by either the independently corroborated sworn testimony of a single witness or the sworn testimony of two witnesses. The false declarations statute explicitly ignores that rule.[3]

§ 1:41   Perjury & false declarations under oath— Examples

Perjury: A firm with which you do business is faced with suspension and debarment proceedings before a Government agency. One of the issues in that proceeding is whether you ever transmitted your company's confidential bid information to that firm. The head of that firm asks you to submit an affidavit denying that you ever did so. You submit a sworn affidavit which so states, even though you know that you did transmit the confidential bid information. You could be liable for perjury, even though you did not testify in court.

False declarations: You receive a grand jury subpoena calling for certain invoices from your company. You submit invoices which, at the time you drew them up, did not accurately reflect the transactions the invoices purported to reflect. You could be liable under the false declarations statute.

VIII.   CRIMINAL PENALTIES

§ 1:42   Generally

In addition to liability for fines and imprisonment that are

---

[3] 18 U.S.C.A. § 1623(e).

expressly stated in the individual criminal statutes discussed earlier in this chapter, other laws and rules may affect the scope and severity of the penalties that may be imposed on criminal violators.

§ 1:43 Sentence of Fine statute

In addition to the penalties established for violations of specific criminal statutes (as noted in the individual sections above discussing the criminal offenses), the "Sentence of Fine" statute provides for a set of alternative fines that may be imposed.[1] Under the Sentence of Fine statute, the applicable fine for a criminal offense is not more than the greatest of:

(1) The amount established in the statute setting forth the offense;
(2) Twice the amount of gross gain derived from the offense (or gross loss caused by the offense to the victim); or
(3) In the case of a felony, $250,000 for an individual and $500,000 for a corporation.

See the chart in Appendix A to this Handbook.

§ 1:44 RICO

The Racketeer Influenced and Corrupt Organizations Act (RICO)[1] does not penalize any specific crime. Instead, RICO imposes *additional* criminal penalties on persons who engage in a "pattern of racketeering activity." A "pattern of racketeering activity" is defined as the violation, during the preceding 10-year period, of two or more of over 30 specified substantive federal and state criminal statutes. The crimes that can serve as the bases or "predicates" for a RICO violation include bribery, illegal gratuities, and mail and wire fraud, but not false claims or false statements.

To establish a criminal violation of RICO, the Government must prove the following basic elements:

(1) The existence of an enterprise engaged in interstate or foreign commerce;
(2) That you were employed by or associated with the enterprise; and
(3) That you participated, directly or indirectly, in the affairs of the enterprise through a pattern of racketeering activity.

[Section 1:43]
[1] 18 U.S.C.A. § 3571.

[Section 1:44]
[1] 18 U.S.C.A. §§ 1961 to 1968.

§ 1:44   GOVERNMENT CONTRACT COMPLIANCE HANDBOOK

Although RICO was enacted to combat the infiltration of organized crime into legitimate business, RICO is in no way limited to persons engaged in organized crime. An "enterprise" under RICO may be either a legitimate enterprise, such as a corporation engaged in Government contracting, or an illegitimate enterprise.

The statutory *criminal penalties* for a RICO violation (which are in addition to the fines or imprisonment for the underlying offenses that make up the pattern of racketeering activity) are a fine pursuant to the Sentence of Fine statute (see § 1:43) and up to 20 years' imprisonment (or for life if one of the racketeering activities is punishable by life imprisonment). RICO also provides for the *mandatory forfeiture* of the violator's interest in the enterprise. Thus, a corporation found guilty under RICO as a result of its Government contracting activities is subject to forfeiture of the division engaged in Government contracting; and individuals convicted are subject to forfeiture of their corporate offices, directorships, stock holdings, and the like.

In addition to criminal actions, the RICO defendant may be subject to a *civil* action for treble damages and costs by any "person injured in his business or property" (18 U.S.C.A. § 1964). However, according to the Second Circuit, the Government is not a "person" authorized to bring a civil RICO damages action.[2] Civil remedies available under RICO include treble damages, costs, and attorney fees. Equitable remedies may include orders of divestiture, restrictions on activities, and dissolution or reorganization of institutions.[3]

§ 1:45   RICO—Example

Product substitution and bribery: Assume you substitute inferior raw materials on one of your company's Government contracts and bribe a Government inspector to accept the product. You discuss the intended bribe with the inspector in a telephone call and you later use the mail to send payment to the inspector. The product substitution, if characterized as mail or wire fraud, could serve as one predicate of a RICO charge; the bribery could serve as a second. The enterprise whose affairs were conducted through a pattern of racketeering could be your corporation or one of its divisions.

§ 1:46   Federal sentencing guidelines

To remedy perceived disparity in sentencing of federal criminal

---

[2]*U.S. v. Bonanno Organized Crime Family of La Cosa Nostra*, 879 F.2d 20 (2d Cir. 1989).

[3]18 U.S.C.A. § 1964(a).

THE OFFENSES & PENALTIES   § 1:47

defendants, the Sentencing Reform Act of 1984 created the United States Sentencing Commission—an independent agency composed of nine members, seven voting and two nonvoting—to define sentencing policies and practices. The Commission's primary purposes are to achieve uniformity and proportionality in sentencing. The Commission created the Sentencing Guidelines to achieve these goals by establishing a system that creates categories of offenses and defendants and imposes different sentences for criminal conduct of differing severity. However in 2005, the U.S. Supreme Court held[1] that the guidelines cannot be mandatory on sentencing judges, to be consistent with constitutional principles. Changes in this area are possible as Congress reacts to the Supreme Court's decision.

The Guidelines rely on the seriousness of the offense, the role of the defendant in that offense, the criminal history of the defendant, and any mitigating circumstances present in formulating an appropriate sentence. The Guidelines rank all federal crimes numerically by severity level. These rankings constitute the offense level at which the crime is evaluated. Other numeric values are assigned to the criminal history of the defendant, the defendant's role in the offense, and any aggravating or mitigating factors occurring in the commission of the offense or background of the defendant.

§ 1:47 Federal sentencing guidelines—Sentencing of individuals

For the sentencing of individuals, the Guidelines set forth a calculation (which is prepared by the U.S. Probation Office) which includes base-level points for each offense and enhancement points for the value of the harm or gain and for aggravating factors and related offense characteristics.[1] The Guidelines also provide point reductions for an individual's acceptance of responsibility and cooperation.[2] The formula results in a calculation of a total offense level, which is used to determine the sentence. This offense level total is referenced on the Sentencing Table,[3] which charts the applicable range of incarceration for the

---

[Section 1:46]
   [1]*U.S. v. Booker*, 543 U.S. 220, 125 S. Ct. 738, 160 L. Ed. 2d 621 (2005).
[Section 1:47]
   [1]U.S. Sentencing Guidelines ch. 2.
   [2]U.S. Sentencing Guidelines ch. 3.
   [3]U.S. Sentencing Guidelines d., ch. 5, pt. A.

category of offender, and the Fine Table,[4] which establishes the range of applicable fines. (See Appendix C for sample worksheets, incarceration tables, fine tables, etc.)

Even though the Guidelines do not specifically discuss sentencing white-collar offenders, the Guidelines do reflect the Sentencing Commission's belief that imprisonment is the most effective deterrent for white-collar offenders and that severe economic crimes deserve harsher punishments. Particularly in the wake of scandals in the financial markets in 2000 and 2001, individuals convicted of "white-collar" offenses are receiving significant sentences including imprisonment.

§ 1:48 Federal sentencing guidelines—Sentencing of organizations

For the sentencing of organizations, the Guidelines concentrate on four general principles: (a) an organization must remedy any harm it causes to whatever extent possible, (b) if the organization operated for a primarily criminal purpose, the fine imposed should be high enough to divest the organization of its ability to continue to operate, (c) the fine should be based on the seriousness of the offense and the culpability of the organization, and (d) probation is appropriate in some circumstances to ensure that other sanctions will be fully implemented and that steps will be taken to reduce the likelihood of future criminal conduct.[1]

When preparing a presentence report on an organization, the U.S. Probation Office performs a calculation of an offense point total similar to the approach taken with individuals discussed above. The calculation for sentencing organizations is based on a three-step point system:

(1) *Establish a base fine*: A base fine is the *greatest* of: (a) the gain to the company from the offense, (b) the loss from the offense caused by the company, or (c) the amount specified in a base fine table (which currently provides for fines ranging up to $72.5 million but may be increased under pending revisions).[2] A calculation of an offense total similar to the calculation for individuals is used to obtain a base fine from the Fine Table for organizations.[3]

(2) *Calculate a culpability score*: The culpability score leads to adjustments of the base fine to be applied to the corporation. Minimum and maximum "multipliers" determine an organiz-

---

[4]U.S. Sentencing Guidelines § 5E.1.2.

[Section 1:48]

[1]U.S. Sentencing Guidelines ch. 8.
[2]U.S. Sentencing Guidelines § 8C2.4(a).
[3]U.S. Sentencing Guidelines § 8C2.4.

ation's culpability score. A number of factors may result in upward adjustments, such as the level of involvement in or tolerance of the offense by high-level personnel, the prior criminal history of the company, whether the offense violated a judicial order, injunction, or probation, and whether the company engaged in obstruction of justice during the investigation. The culpability score may also result in a downward adjustment if the organization has an effective compliance program, voluntarily disclosed the offense, and cooperated during the investigation.[4] The highest culpability score causes the court to apply multipliers of two-to-four to the base fine; the lowest culpability score causes application of multipliers of .05 to .20 to the base fine. A multiplier chart sets forth a range of multipliers for the range of culpability scores.[5]

Through the interaction of the culpability scores and multiplier table the Sentencing Guidelines for organizations create strong incentives for your company to establish a compliance program and to report any violations of law to the Government. For example, the Guidelines provide for downward adjustments to the culpability score, resulting in a substantial reduction in fines from a reduced multiplier, if the company had an effective program to prevent and detect violations, or if the company reported the offense prior to imminent threat of disclosure or Government investigation.

(3) *Restitution to the victim*: Restitution to the victim is another aspect of the Sentencing Guidelines' punishment provisions for organizations. Restitution should be addressed as part of every sentence, based on the defendant's ability to pay. Although the Guidelines for organizations call for courts to reduce fines as necessary to avoid interfering with the defendant's ability to pay restitution to the victims, the U.S. Court of Appeals for the Ninth Circuit has held that the Guidelines do not preclude courts from imposing fines that may threaten the defendant's continued viability.[6]

Although you need not be fully conversant with the intricacies of the Sentencing Guidelines, you should understand that judges will continue to look to them for guidance and that Congress may seek to legislate further in this area.

IX. CIVIL PENALTIES

§ 1:49 Generally

As discussed earlier in this chapter, there are a number of

---

[4]U.S. Sentencing Guidelines § 8C2.5.
[5]U.S. Sentencing Guidelines § 8C2.6.
[6]*See U.S. v. Eureka Laboratories, Inc.*, 103 F.3d 908 (9th Cir. 1996).

§ 1:49 GOVERNMENT CONTRACT COMPLIANCE HANDBOOK

statutes—the civil False Claims Act, for example—that provide civil remedies, such as fines and recovery of actual and enhanced damages, to the Government for certain offenses. In addition, civil penalties are provided under some procurement-specific laws and rules, such as the Contract Disputes Act's fraud provision (see § 16:10) and the Truth in Negotiations Act's defective pricing provisions (see §§ 9:1 et seq.). Some additional civil penalties that may be imposed, and issues that may arise in the imposition of civil penalties, are discussed below.

§ 1:50 Forfeiture of claims

The Forfeiture of Claims statute provides that a "claim against the United States shall be forfeited to the United States by any person who corruptly practices or attempts to practice any fraud against the United States in the proof, statement, establishment, or allowance thereof."[1] This provision applies to claims brought before the Court of Federal Claims. The question of whether the Government has suffered measurable damages as a result of the fraud is irrelevant to application of the forfeiture penalty; all that is required is the knowing submission of a false claim to the Government.[2] In addition, *any* fraud in connection with a claim results in the forfeiture of the all claims that arise from the contract, not just the fraudulent portion.[3] In one case, for example, the Court of Federal Claims held that a contractor who incurred statutory penalties under the False Claims Act forfeited, under the Forfeiture of Claims statute, any claim for equitable adjustment.[4]

Cases & Commentary: Improper conduct by a contractor under a contract can have devastating consequences on routine claims for price adjustments under that same contract. In *Morse Diesel Intern., Inc. v. U.S.*, 74 Fed. Cl. 601 (2007), the contractor had previously admitted to violations of the criminal False Claims Act and the Major Fraud Act in connection with claims for reimbursement of bond costs under several contracts for the construction of federal buildings. Furthermore, the court had

---

[Section 1:50]

[1] 28 U.S.C.A. § 2514.

[2] *E.g., Young-Montenay, Inc. v. U.S.*, 15 F.3d 1040 (Fed. Cir. 1994).

[3] *Supermex, Inc. v. U.S.*, 35 Fed. Cl. 29 (1996) (contractor's bribery of Government official placed a "stigma" on the contract sufficient to deem the contractor's equitable adjustment claims unenforceable due to public policy considerations). *But see N.R. Acquisition Corp. v. U.S.*, 52 Fed. Cl. 490 (2002) (distinguishing *Supermex*).

[4] *See Ab-Tech Const., Inc. v. U.S.*, 31 Fed. Cl. 429 (1994), aff'd, 57 F.3d 1084 (Fed. Cir. 1995) (table).

THE OFFENSES & PENALTIES   § 1:50

determined that rebates of portions of the claimed bond costs by the surety brokers to the contractor violated the Anti-Kickback Act. The current case involved 15 separate claims for added costs totaling over $53,000,000 that the contractor had submitted under the various construction contracts. The court found that the Government had established "by clear and convincing evidence" that the improper billing for bond costs violated the Forfeiture of Claims Act. As a consequence, the court found that the contractor forfeited all of these claims. Interestingly, 10 of the 15 claims had been filed with the GSA Board of Contract Appeals. The Forfeiture of Claims Act applies only to claims before the Court of Federal Claims. To remedy this jurisdictional issue, the court arranged for the transfer of those cases from GSBCA to the Court of Federal Claims pursuant to the Contract Disputes Act, 41 U.S.C. § 609(d) and proceeded to find that they were forfeited. Subsequently, the court imposed fines of approximately $260,000 for violation of the Anti-Kickback Act and $7 million in penalties and damages under the False Claims Act. The court rejected Morse Diesel's contention that awarding penalties under both statues would be "improperly duplicative." *Morse Diesel Intern., Inc. v. U.S.*, 79 Fed. Cl. 116 (2007). But see *Kellogg Brown & Root Services, Inc. v. U.S.*, 2011 WL 2739776 (Fed. Cl. July 6, 2011) ("The mere 'taint' of the kickback is insufficient to state a claim under the forfeiture statute when it is not alleged that the kickback is related to the "proof, statement, establishment, or allowance" of a claim.").

As discussed in § 16:10 of the main text, in *Daewoo Engineering and Const. Co., Ltd. v. U.S.*, 557 F.3d 1332 (Fed. Cir. 2009), petition for cert. den 130 S. Ct. 490 (2009), the contractor had submitted a claim totaling almost $64 million for added costs in constructing a road on a remote island in the Republic of Palau. The contractor claimed that over $13 million of added cost had already been incurred and that the remaining $50.6 million would be incurred in completing the project. During the course of the trial at the Court of Federal Claims, the DoJ filed a counterclaims pursuant to the False Claims Act, the Forfeiture of Claims statute, and the penalty provisions of the Contract Disputes Act alleging that the portion of the claim relating to future costs was fraudulent. The court agreed, finding that the calculation assumed that the Government was responsible for each day of additional performance beyond the original 1080-day contract period, without even considering whether there was any contractor-caused delay or delay for which the Government was not responsible. The calculation then simply assumed that Daewoo's current daily expenditures represented costs for which the Government was responsible. Daewoo apparently used no outside experts to make its certified claim calculation, and at trial made

§ 1:50   GOVERNMENT CONTRACT COMPLIANCE HANDBOOK

no real effort to justify the accuracy of the claim for future costs or even to explain how it was prepared. Further, Daewoo's damages experts at trial treated the certified claim computation as essentially worthless, did not utilize it, and did not even bother to understand it. The Court of Federal Claims pointed out that Daewoo's claim preparation witnesses inconsistently referred to and interchanged actual, future, estimated, calculated and planned costs. The court found that Daewoo's main witness, who certified the claim, gave false testimony. The court also found that the testimony of another witness regarding the calculation of Daewoo's certified claim "left no doubt that [Daewoo's] case was unsupportable and was pursued by Daewoo with fraudulent intent." Based on this, the court found that $50.6 million of the total claim was fraudulent and in accordance with the CDA assessed a penalty "in an amount equal to such unsupported part of the claim," *i.e.*, $50.6 million. In addition the court found Daewoo liable under the Forfeiture of Claims statute, thereby forfeiting the remaining $13 million of its claim. The court also assessed a $10,000 penalty for violation of the civil False Claims Act. The Federal Circuit affirmed the lower court decision in its entirety. See *Daewoo Engineering and Const. Co., Ltd. v. U.S.*, 557 F.3d 1332 (Fed. Cir. 2009), cert. den. 130 S. Ct. 490 (2009). With regard to the Forfeiture of Claims statute, the court noted that unlike the penalty provisions of the CDA, under which the penalty equals only the unsupported part of a claim, 28 U.S.C.A. § 2514 provides that the entire claim will be forfeited even though only part of the claim is found to be fraudulent. See also *Young-Montenay, Inc. v. U.S.*, 15 F.3d 1040 (Fed. Cir. 1994) (because a contractor had submitted a claim to the Government for $153,000 when it knew the Government was liable only for $104,000, forfeiture of a later damages claim was justified).

In *Veridyne Corp. v. U.S.*, 83 Fed. Cl. 575 (2008), the Court of Federal Claims noted that the statutory language of the Forfeiture of Claims statute had been construed as proscribing fraud in the prosecution of claims against the United States, not fraud in the performance of the contract. See *Baird v. U.S.*, 76 Ct. Cl. 599, 1933 WL 1901 (1933). Accordingly, the court concluded that the statute would not apply where the Government alleged the contractor had knowingly underestimated the likely cost of services in its proposal for and IDIQ contract in order to take advantage of an agency's ability to award contracts with a value of $3 million or less a sole source basis. In *Alcatec, LLC v. U.S.*, 100 Fed. Cl. 502 (2011), aff'd, 2012 WL 2826946 (Fed. Cir. 2012), The Court of Federal Claims penalized the contractor $347,050 based on the Forfeiture of Fraudulent Claims Act and the False Claims Act. Alcatec had filed a $3.8 million claim for costs incurred on a Federal Emergency Management Agency (FEMA) contract to deactivate temporary housing in Mississippi for Hurricane Katrina victims. COFC found that Alcatec acted with "specific intent to deceive FEMA with regard to the dates on which inspections were performed and a reckless indifference to the hundreds of duplicate inspections that were billed to FEMA." The Court found these actions amounted to fraud. Alcatec's $3.8 million claim was forfeit and the company was penalized for the fraudulent invoices.

§ 1:51 Foreign Assistance Act

If your company knowingly submits a false claim to a financial institution or Government agency for payment from funds made available under the Foreign Assistance Act, or a claim for payment for a commodity deemed ineligible under the act, your company could face penalties of (1) 25% of the amount sought (and not received); (2) forfeiture of goods or money received; and, (3) $2,200 for each improper act and double the damage sustained by the U.S. Government, or 50% of payments or advances received (whichever is greater) *in addition* to the costs of the lawsuit.[1]

§ 1:52 Voiding contracts

Where the Government believes that a contract was induced by fraud or is otherwise tainted, it may bring a civil action to declare the contract void and to recover all payments made to the contractor.[1] Although the contractor's conviction for crimes establishes the Government's right to cancel the affected contract, conviction is not required.[2]

Cases & Commentary: Long Island Savings Bank, FSB v. U.S., 503 F.3d 1234 (Fed. Cir. 2007), cert. denied, 129 S. Ct. 38, 172 L. Ed. 2d 19 (2008), was a so-called "Winstar" case in which the Government earlier had been found liable for breach of contract damages to thrift institutions which had suffered financial losses due changes in the law regarding the treatment of supervisory goodwill and capital credit. Long Island had previously obtained a $435,755,000 judgment on its "Winstar" claim from the U.S.

[Section 1:51]

[1]22 U.S.C.A. § 2399b(a).

[Section 1:52]

[1]*E.g., K & R Engineering Co., Inc. v. U. S.*, 222 Ct. Cl. 340, 616 F.2d 469 (1980) (cancellation of contract based on conflicts of interest); *Appeal of Schuepferling GmbH & Co.*, ASBCA No. KG, 98-1 BCA ¶ 29659 (bribery made contract void "ab initio" and cannot be ratified; Government not required to pay for work performed).

[2]*E.g., U.S. v. Acme Process Equipment Co.*, 385 U.S. 138, 87 S. Ct. 350, 17 L. Ed. 2d 249 (1966).

§ 1:52   GOVERNMENT CONTRACT COMPLIANCE HANDBOOK

Court of Federal Claims. On appeal, the Government contended that the CEO of the thrift institution had falsely certified he did not receive any income from a law firm in which he was a partner for work the law firm had done for the thrift. In fact, the CEO and family members had received at least $10.9 million from the law firm during the period in question. Thus, there was a clear conflict of interest between the CEO and the company. Further, the Government argued that the CEO's actions should be imputed to the thrift institution itself, thereby rendering the contract with the Government void *ab initio*. The court agreed, finding that had the CEO disclosed he was still receiving income from his firm the U.S. would have never entered into the contract with the institution. The court also imputed knowledge of the false statements to the thrift itself, noting that a principal can only escape responsibility for the actions of its agent if that agent, in this case the CEO, was acting entirely for his own purposes. Here, the Court found, the CEO's certification, albeit false, benefited the thrift as it was necessary in order to get Government approval for the take-over of the failed thrift and the work performed by his law firm also benefited the thrift since there was no question about the need for, or quality of the services. Since the contract was void *ab initio*, the thrift institution forfeited the entire $435,755,000 in damages. The Supreme Court declined to review this decision. *Long Island Sav. Bank, FSB v. U.S.*, 129 S. Ct. 38, 172 L. Ed. 2d 19 (2008).

Even though a contract is deemed to be void *ab initio*, the contractor may be able to retain past payments for work and obtain payment of pending invoices. In *Veridyne Corp. v. U.S.*, 83 Fed. Cl. 575 (2008), the Government contended that a contractor had knowingly underestimated the likely cost of services in its proposal for an IDIQ contract in order to take advantage of an agency's ability to award contracts with a value of $3 million or less a sole source basis. The Government's position was that it was that it was not only not obligated to pay approximately $2.7 million in pending invoices but was also entitled to recover over $31 million it had already paid the contractor. The court held that in situations in which a contract was deemed to be void *ab initio* because of fraud, the Government could only recover past payments or deny pending invoices if the underlying fraud involved allegations of bribery or contract conflict of interest. Citing *U.S. v. Amdahl Corp.*, 786 F.2d 387 (Fed. Cir. 1986), the court stated:

> The court in *Amdahl* recited the well-established proposition that, "though a contract be unenforceable against the Government, because not properly advertised, not authorized, or for some other reason, it is only fair and just that the Government pay for goods delivered or services rendered and accepted under it." *Id*. This is so

The Offenses & Penalties § 1:53

even where "an award is plainly or palpably illegal" and "made contrary to statutory or regulatory requirements because of some action or statement by the contractor." *Id.* at 395. Such a contractor is still "entitled to payment, either on a *quantum valebant* or *quantum meruit* basis." *Id.* The Federal Circuit did recognize the rule that fraud in procurement could obviate recovery: "[T]he remedy may be different in a case involving fraud or the like," citing to *K & R Engineering* and referring to situations involving conflicts of interest. *Id.* at 395 n. 8.

Defendant has not alleged a conflict of interest in the case at bar. Forfeiture is an inappropriate remedy for common-law fraud except when a conflict of interest is perpetuated by a contractor involved in facilitating and maintaining a Government agent's conflict of interest or where an agent of the contractor obtains a contract through a conflict of interest. The case law, properly read, does not support defendant's argument that the appropriate remedy for any contract that is void *ab initio* is forfeiture of monies already paid or the denial of recovery in *quantum meruit* or *quantum valebant*. Tellingly, defendant did not cite to *Amdahl*, even though it is the only case discussing the remedy for contracts that are void *ab initio*, and it involved a similar factual situation where a contract was awarded contrary to a statutory restriction on contract award.

Defendant has not pointed to any binding case law establishing that, absent a showing of bribe or a conflict of interest, voiding Mod 0023 *ab initio* would entitle the Government to forfeiture of all monies paid under the post-1998 modifications for services already performed by plaintiff. Thus, absent the required nexus to bribery or conflict of interest, plaintiff would not be liable for the amount of $31,134,931.12, representing forfeiture of all monies paid under Mod 0023, or forfeit its claim for unpaid invoices.

X. ADMINISTRATIVE PENALTIES

§ 1:53 Debarment

If you fail to abide by the Government's contract compliance laws and regulations or otherwise engage in improper business conduct, you can be prohibited from bidding on, entering into, or continuing to perform Government contracts. Debarment is the *total exclusion* of a contractor and its affiliates from Government contracting or subcontracting for a specific period of time—generally no more than three years.

Debarment (and suspension, see §§ 1:56 to 1:58) are Government-wide; agencies must honor the suspension or debarment of a contractor by another agency. The General Services Administration (GSA) is required to maintain a List of Parties Excluded from Federal Procurement and Nonprocurement Programs, which is a compilation of individuals and firms debarred, suspended, proposed for debarment, or declared ineligible by agencies or the Government Accountability Office. GSA's list is posted on the Internet. All Government Contracting Of-

§ 1:53   GOVERNMENT CONTRACT COMPLIANCE HANDBOOK

ficers are expected to check the list, which is updated daily, before awarding contracts.

Cases & Commentary: As noted in the principal text, contractors debarred, suspended, or proposed for debarment are excluded from receiving contracts, and agencies shall not solicit offers from, award contracts to, or consent to subcontracts with these contractors, unless the agency head determines that there is a compelling reason for such action. FAR 9.450(a). The FAR Councils issued a final rule revising FAR 9.405-2 to implement section 815 of the National Defense Authorization Act for Fiscal Year 2010, Pub. L. 111-84. 76 Fed. Reg. 39236. The implementing contract clause, FAR 52.209-6, Protecting the Government's Interest When Subcontracting With Contractors Debarred, Suspended, or Proposed for Debarment, generally prohibits the awarding a subcontract to any party that has or is currently suspended or debarred. The provisions further states a prime contractor shall require each proposed subcontractor to disclose its status in this regard as of the date of the award of the subcontract. The final rule revising these existing requirement makes clear they apply, and must be flowed down, to all subcontracts exceeding $30,000 with the exception of subcontracts for COTS items and second-tier or lower subcontracts for commercial items.

§ 1:54   Debarment—Grounds & mitigating factors

The Federal Acquisition Regulation (FAR) provides for debarment of contractors for a wide variety of causes, including a criminal conviction or civil judgment for a procurement-related offense, for violating federal or state antitrust laws, or for serious violations of the terms of a Government contract or subcontract.[1] The key technical factor for determining whether and for how long you will be debarred is your "present responsibility." The FAR includes a list of 10 examples of mitigating factors that Government debarring officials consider in determining whether to debar a contractor.[2] Specifically, the Government looks at whether the contractor targeted for debarment:

(1)   Had effective standards of conduct and internal control systems in place at the time of the activity that constituted cause for debarment or had adopted such procedures before any Government investigation of the activities cited as a cause for debarment.

[Section 1:54]

[1]FAR 9.406-2; *see generally* West, Hatch, Brennan & VanDyke, Suspension & Debarment, Briefing Papers No. 06-9 (Aug. 2006).

[2]FAR 9.406-1(a).

The Offenses & Penalties   § 1:55

(2) Brought the activity cited as a cause for debarment to the attention of the appropriate Government agency in a timely manner.
(3) Fully investigated the circumstances surrounding the cause for debarment and, if so, made the results of the investigation available to the debarring official.
(4) Cooperated fully with Government agencies during the investigation and during any court or administrative action.
(5) Has paid or agreed to pay all criminal, civil, and administrative penalties for the improper activity, including any investigative or administrative costs incurred by the Government, and has made or agreed to make full restitution.
(6) Has taken appropriate disciplinary action against the individual(s) responsible for the activity that constituted cause for debarment.
(7) Has implemented or agreed to implement remedial measures, including any identified by the Government.
(8) Has instituted or agreed to institute new or revised review and control procedures and ethics training programs.
(9) Has had adequate time to eliminate the circumstances within the contractor's organization that led to the cause for debarment.
(10) Recognizes and understands the seriousness of the misconduct giving rise to the cause for debarment and has implemented programs to prevent recurrence.

The regulations provide that if the decision to debar is based on a felony conviction, the period of debarment should be commensurate with the seriousness of the crime. However, the debarring official may reduce periods of debarment if the contractor has demonstrated that it has complied with certain requirements including full disclosure, cooperation with investigators, restitution, disciplinary action against involved employees, and the establishment of review and control procedures.[3] Conversely, although the maximum period of debarment is otherwise stated to be three years, that period may be extended if the debarring official "determines that any extension is necessary to protect the Government's interest."[4]

§ 1:55 Debarment—Procedures

If the Government intends to debar you, you are entitled to *notice* of the Government's charges. This right has been firmly

---
[3]*See, e.g.,* DFARS 209.406-1.
[4]FAR 9.406-4(b).

§ 1:55   GOVERNMENT CONTRACT COMPLIANCE HANDBOOK

established by the courts.[1] Consequently, the FAR has a notice provision that requires that before beginning debarment proceedings, the agency must give formal notice of the proposed debarment to you, stating the reasons for the proposed debarment in terms sufficient to put you on notice of the conduct on which the proposed debarment is based.[2] The agency is *not* required, however, to divulge its evidence. This lack of information as to the precise basis for the potential debarment may severely hamper your ability to defend yourself, particularly because there are no discovery rights in debarment proceedings.

To remedy this, you should request an informal face-to-face meeting with debarment officials to ascertain the agency's concerns. Note, however, that when attempting to deal with the Government informally, you must be careful to preserve your rights. One court found that by conducting numerous discussions and negotiations with the Government, the contractor waived its right to a hearing.[3] You should consult experienced counsel before you enter into any discussions with the Government concerning any aspect of a proposed debarment (or suspension, see the following section).

Under the FAR procedures, you are afforded 30 days after receipt of notice in which to submit information in opposition to the proposed debarment. The opportunity to rebut does not mean that you will be entitled to a hearing. Only when the proposed debarment is not based on a conviction or civil judgment and the information you submit in opposition raises a genuine dispute over material facts will you be granted the right to a fact-finding hearing.[4] Because most debarments are based on convictions, and it is difficult to dispute material facts when they are not disclosed in the Government's notice of debarment, you will rarely be afforded a predebarment hearing.

§ 1:56 Suspension

Suspension is the temporary exclusion of a contractor from Government contracting designed to be imposed "pending the completion of investigation and any ensuing legal proceedings"

[Section 1:55]

[1]*See Gonzalez v. Freeman*, 334 F.2d 570 (D.C. Cir. 1964).

[2]FAR 9.406-3(c). *See also* DFARS, app. H, setting forth guidelines to ensure uniformity in Department of Defense debarment proceedings.

[3]*See Adamo Wrecking Co. v. Department of Housing and Urban Development*, 414 F. Supp. 877 (D.D.C. 1976).

[4]FAR 9.406-3(b)(2), 9.406-3(d)(2).

against the contractor.¹ Suspension is often a preliminary step to debarment. Unlike debarment, however, which is for a specific period, the length of a suspension is open-ended, although the regulations require that if legal proceedings are not initiated within 12 months after the date of suspension notice, the suspension shall be terminated unless an Assistant Attorney General requests an extension.²

§ 1:57 Suspension—Grounds & mitigating factors

A contractor may be suspended if the Government has "adequate evidence" of certain improper conduct, including, among others, (1) commission of a fraud or a criminal offense, (2) violation of federal or state antitrust laws, and (3) commission of an offense indicating lack of business integrity that directly affects the present responsibility of the contractor.¹ The *indictment* of the contractor for any of the causes noted above constitutes "adequate evidence" for suspension.² Unlike the grounds for debarment, however, a contractor may not be suspended for a willful failure to perform a contract or for a history of poor contract performance. However, a suspension may be based on lesser evidence than a debarment, requiring merely an indictment rather than a conviction.

The FAR states that the existence of a cause for suspension does not necessarily require that the contractor be suspended.³ The suspending official should consider the seriousness of the contractor's acts or omissions and may, but is not required to, consider remedial measures or mitigating factors, such as those set forth in the FAR regarding debarment (listed above in § 1:54).

To illustrate, if a contractor or one of its employees is indicted, the suspending authority does not have to suspend the contractor from doing business with the Government. Further, a contractor has the burden of promptly presenting to the suspending official evidence of remedial measures or mitigating factors when it has reason to know that a cause for suspension exists.

§ 1:58 Suspension—Procedures

As in a debarment action, you must be very careful to protect

---

[Section 1:56]
¹FAR 9.407-4(a).
²FAR 9.407-4(b).

[Section 1:57]
¹FAR 9.407-2(a).
²FAR 9.407-2(b).
³FAR 9.407-1(b)(2).

§ 1:58   GOVERNMENT CONTRACT COMPLIANCE HANDBOOK

your rights in any suspension proceeding that is initiated against you on the basis of an indictment. Immunity from criminal charges will not protect you from suspension, and evidence gathered through a suspension proceeding may be used against you in a criminal proceeding. Because a suspension proceeding may prejudice your criminal defense, however, you may request that the suspension proceeding be halted pending the outcome of the criminal proceeding. A stay of proceedings is wholly within the suspending agency's discretion; it is not mandatory.[1]

Unlike the procedures for debarment, the FAR suspension procedures require *notice* to the contractor *on* suspension and *not before* suspension.[2] The agency must notify you that you have been suspended, specify the basis for the suspension, state that the suspension is for a temporary period of time, and explain the effect of the suspension. As in the case of debarment, you have 30 days in which to submit information in opposition to the suspension. Again, you face a very difficult task in defending yourself where the notice is unclear regarding the basis for the suspension.

There is no due process right to a *presuspension* hearing. Should you meet certain requirements, however, you may be granted a fact-finding proceeding once the suspension is in effect, with the opportunity to appear with counsel, submit documentary evidence, present witnesses, and confront any person presented by the agency.[3] However, the conditions for obtaining a suspension hearing are more stringent than those for obtaining a predebarment hearing. You are afforded this additional procedural right only if the suspension is not based on an indictment, the information you submit raises a genuine dispute over a material fact, and the Department of Justice has not advised the suspending agency that Government interests in other proceedings will be prejudiced if a fact-finding hearing proceeds.[4]

§ 1:59 Contractual remedies

There are a number of contractual remedies the Government has available when confronted by evidence of unlawful conduct on the part of a contractor. For example, among the most important of these is the "Price Reduction for Defective Cost or Pricing Data" clause, which implements the Truth in Negotia-

---

[Section 1:58]

[1] FAR 9.407-3. *See U.S. v. Kordel*, 397 U.S. 1, 90 S. Ct. 763, 25 L. Ed. 2d 1, 13 Fed. R. Serv. 2d 868 (1970).

[2] FAR 9.407-3(c).

[3] FAR 9.407-3(b)(2).

[4] FAR 9.407-3(b)(2)(d).

tions Act and gives the Government the right to price reductions in negotiated contracts for defects in cost or pricing data submitted by the contractor (see §§ 9:1 et seq.).[1] Similarly, General Services Administration Multiple Award Schedule contracts contain a "Price Reductions" clause which permits the Government to recover overcharges that result from inaccurate, not current, or incomplete preaward information submitted by a contractor (see §§ 10:1 et seq.).[2] The "Penalties for Unallowable Costs" clause, included in many large contracts, provides that if the Contracting Officer determines that a cost submitted by the contractor in its proposal is expressly unallowable under a FAR cost principle, the contractor shall be assessed a penalty of one to two times the amount of the disallowed cost (see §§ 11:8 to 11:11).[3]

[Section 1:59]
[1] FAR 52.215-10.
[2] GSAR 552.238-76.
[3] FAR 52.242-3.

Chapter 2

Your Response to a Criminal Investigation

I. OVERVIEW
§ 2:1   Scope note

II. INVESTIGATORS AND DEVICES
A. INVESTIGATORS
§ 2:2   Generally
§ 2:3   Defense & civilian agency investigators

B. INVESTIGATIVE DEVICES
§ 2:4   Generally
§ 2:5   Grand jury investigations
§ 2:6   Subpoenas
§ 2:7   Search warrants
§ 2:8   Wiretaps
§ 2:9   Field interviews

III. PREPARING FOR AND RESPONDING TO AN INVESTIGATION
A. BE PREPARED
§ 2:10   Retain documents
§ 2:11   Appoint a records custodian
§ 2:12   Educate employees
§ 2:13   Maintain contact with former employees

B. DETECTING AN INVESTIGATION
§ 2:14   Generally
§ 2:15   Inquiries by federal auditors
§ 2:16   Allegations by contracting officers
§ 2:17   Requests for employee interviews
§ 2:18   Receipt of grand jury subpoena
§ 2:19   Receipt of company hotline calls
§ 2:20   Lawsuits by current or former employees

C. INITIAL STEPS AFTER AN INVESTIGATION IS UNDERWAY

§ 2:21 When the investigators arrive
§ 2:22 Selection of counsel
§ 2:23 Avoid obstructing justice
§ 2:24 Preliminary internal inquiry
§ 2:25 Insurance & indemnification requirements
§ 2:26 Advise government investigators that they are bound by local ethics rules
§ 2:27 Notify your employees of the investigation
§ 2:28 Advise your employees how to respond
§ 2:29 Counsel for your employees

D. COMPANY & EMPLOYEE RIGHTS DURING AN INVESTIGATION

§ 2:30 Generally
§ 2:31 Unreasonable search & seizure
§ 2:32 Self-incrimination
§ 2:33 Employees' right to counsel

IV. CONDUCTING AN INTERNAL INVESTIGATION

§ 2:34 Generally
§ 2:35 Authorization by company management
§ 2:36 Choosing the internal investigators
§ 2:37 Interviewing current & former employees
§ 2:38 Report of the investigation
§ 2:39 Communications with the prosecutor
§ 2:40 Voluntary disclosure of wrongdoing

V. RESPONDING TO A GRAND JURY PROCEEDING

§ 2:41 Witness & document subpoenas
§ 2:42 Motions to quash or modify subpoenas
§ 2:43 Preparation of witnesses
§ 2:44 Averting an indictment

YOUR RESPONSE TO A CRIMINAL INVESTIGATION § 2:1

> **KeyCite®:** Cases and other legal materials listed in KeyCite Scope can be researched through the KeyCite service on Westlaw®. Use KeyCite to check citations for form, parallel references, prior and later history, and comprehensive citator information, including citations to other decisions and secondary materials.

I. OVERVIEW

§ 2:1 Scope note

Assume you are Vice President-Controller of a small corporation that does about a third of its business with the federal Government. You are sitting in your office late on a Friday afternoon when the receptionist transfers an "urgent" call to your line. The call is from the General Manager of one of your out-of-state facilities which manufactures aerospace parts for the Department of the Air Force. She tells you that six "agents" have appeared in the reception area of her facility and that they have a search warrant. They are seeking records related to the company's contracts with the Air Force. The agents have asked whether the General Manager would answer some questions, and they would also like to interview other employees.

What do you advise your employees? Should they answer questions asked by the agents? Will it appear that the company has something to hide if they do not? Does the company have something to hide? If so, what are the implications for the company? For the employees? How should you respond to the criminal investigation of your company that is obviously already well underway?

Companies involved in contracting with the federal Government to provide goods and services may find themselves in the position of having to make these decisions and others, often on short notice, when faced with the prospect of a Government investigation. Coordinating your response to such an investigation is often time consuming, frustrating, and fraught with traps for the unwary.

This chapter is not intended to be an exhaustive guide to handling a criminal investigation. Handling such investigations and coordinating a corporate response to them usually requires consultation with legal practitioners possessing special expertise in both criminal and Government contract law. Instead, this chapter provides you with basic information regarding the *types of investigators* and the typical *investigative tools* used by the Government. This chapter also offers suggestions on *detecting* the existence of and *preparing for* such investigations, and discusses important issues that arise during investigations. Although a company always hopes to avoid becoming the subject of a crimi-

§ 2:1   GOVERNMENT CONTRACT COMPLIANCE HANDBOOK

nal investigation, being prepared for one can directly affect the outcome if such an investigation does arise.

II. INVESTIGATORS AND DEVICES

A. INVESTIGATORS

§ 2:2 Generally

A Government investigation into contracting activities may arise from an array of sources, particularly in the area of defense contracts. An understanding of the entity conducting the investigation may provide insight into the scope of the investigation and possible outcomes.

§ 2:3 Defense & civilian agency investigators

1. *DCIS.* The Defense Criminal Investigative Service (DCIS) is a component of the Department of Defense (DOD) Inspector General's Office (IG). The DCIS and the criminal investigative agencies of each branch of the military have gained increased respect from federal prosecutors; a fact that has resulted in an increased number of investigations initiated independent of the Federal Bureau of Investigation (FBI).[1]

2. *NCIS.* The Naval Criminal Investigative Service (NCIS) is the Navy's criminal investigative agency that, like its Army and Air Force counterparts, generally reports incidents of alleged contractor fraud to either the FBI or the local U.S. Attorney's Office.

3. *AFOSI.* The Air Force Office of Special Investigations (AFOSI) is the investigative arm of the Air Force. AFOSI conducts criminal investigations for the U.S. Attorney's Office, the U.S. Congress (to supplement testimony) and for certain civil lawsuits.

4. *CID.* The Army's Criminal Investigation Command is the Army's investigative agency responsible for procurement fraud investigations.

5. *FBI.* The FBI is probably the most well-known procurement fraud investigator. The FBI provides investigative support to Justice Department attorneys and the U.S. Attorneys.

6. *GAO-OSI.* The Office of Special Investigations of the Government Accountability Office (GAO-OSI) is part of GAO's Office of the General Counsel.

[Section 2:3]

[1]A Memorandum of Understanding between the FBI and military investigative agencies was instituted in 1984. http://www.justice.gov/usao/eousa/foia_reading_room/usam/title9/crm00669.htm.

7. *DCAA*. The Defense Contract Audit Agency (DCAA) is the principal contract audit entity in the Federal Government. It performs contract audit functions for DOD and is used by most civilian agencies to perform contract audits as well. DCAA auditors are not "investigators" per se. Nevertheless, the DCAA is a powerful investigative agency because of its ready access to contractor books, records, and personnel. The auditors are not trained to perform investigations, nor are their audit procedures specially geared to the detection of fraud or other criminal conduct. The auditors are, however, instructed to maintain a proper degree of professional skepticism and to be alert to the possibility of fraudulent activity in the course of the audits they perform.[2] Thus, as a result of DCAA's access to and familiarity with defense contractors' books and records, the auditors often serve as the eyes and ears of investigative agencies.

8. *GSA OIG*. The General Services Administration Office of Inspector General (GSA OIG) is one of many agency IG offices that conduct and supervise audits and investigations relating to its own programs. The GSA's operations include significant procurement programs such as the Federal Supply Schedule. (See Appendix D for a listing of Federal Inspectors General.)

9. The American Recovery and Reinvestment Act, Pub. L. No. 111-5, 123 Stat. 115, which was signed on February 17, 2009, provided billions of dollars for a wide variety of projects to stimulate the U.S. economy. The law directs the President and heads of Federal agencies to "commenc[e] expenditures and activities as quickly as possible consistent with prudent management." Because of concern over the possibility of fraud and waste, the act granted the Government Accountability Office and agency Inspectors General wide ranging audit authority, including specifically, the right to interview officers and employees of contractors and subcontractors. Section 902 of the act states in part:

> ACCESS OF GOVERNMENT ACCOUNTABILITY OFFICE.
> (a) ACCESS.—Each contract awarded using funds made available in this Act shall provide that the Comptroller General and his representatives are authorized—
>> (1) to examine any records of the contractor or any of its subcontractors, or any State or local agency administering such contract, that directly pertain to, and involve transactions relating to, the contract or subcontract; and
>> (2) to interview any officer or employee of the contractor or any of its subcontractors, or of any State or local government agency administering the contract, regarding such transactions.

---

[2] *See* DCAA, Defense Contract Audit Manual 4-702.2 (June 30, 2006).

Similarly, § 1515 provides:

ACCESS OF OFFICES OF INSPECTOR GENERAL TO CERTAIN RECORDS AND EMPLOYEES.
(a) ACCESS.—With respect to each contract or grant awarded using covered funds, any representative of an appropriate inspector general appointed under section 3 or 8G of the Inspector General Act of 1978 (5 U.S.C. App.), is authorized—
> (1) to examine any records of the contractor or grantee, any of its subcontractors or subgrantees, or any State or local agency administering such contract, that pertain to, and involve transactions relating to, the contract, subcontract, grant, or subgrant; and
> (2) to interview any officer or employee of the contractor, grantee, subgrantee, or agency regarding such transactions.

Moreover, § 871 of the Duncan Hunter National Defense Authorization Act for Fiscal 2009, Pub. L. No. 110-417 amended the Federal Property and Administrative Services Act of 1949 and the Armed Services Procurement Act to authorize the Comptroller General to interview employees while conducting audits of contracts that were awarded after using procedures other than sealed bids. Note, that while the audit provisions of the Recovery Act apply only to contracts that are funded pursuant to that act, the § 871 provisions apply to all contracts that did not result from sealed bids.

From a compliance perspective, it becomes even more critical that you advise your employees of their rights and that you avoid even the appearance that you are trying to dissuade them from cooperating with GAO and IG auditors.[3]

The Recovery Act provisions have been implemented in the FAR in new alternate clauses to 52.212-5, "Contract Terms and Conditions Required to Implement Statutes or Executive Orders—Commercial Items," 52.214-26, "Audit and Records—Sealed Bidding," and 52.215-2, "Audit and Records—Negotiation. For the Comptroller General these alternate clauses provide specific authority to audit contracts and subcontracts and to interview contractor and subcontractor employees under contracts using Recovery Act funds. Agency Inspector Generals received the same authorization, with the exception of interviewing subcontractor employees.

The § 871 provisions have also been incorporated in FAR. Specifically, FAR 52.215-2, Audit and Records—Negotiation and FAR 52.215-2, "Audit and Records—Sealed Bidding have been modified to allow GAO to interview current contractor employees

---

[3]*See* § 2:28 for a further discussion on giving advice to your employees in this situation.

when conducting audits. This rule, however, will not be applied to contracts for commercial items and FAR 12.503, which lists statues that are inapplicable to such contracts, has been modified accordingly."

B. INVESTIGATIVE DEVICES

§ 2:4 Generally

The investigators have at their disposal a variety of investigative tools. The main goal of the investigator is to obtain information by a grand jury investigation, subpoenas, search warrants, wiretaps, and field interviews.

§ 2:5 Grand jury investigations

The federal grand jury is a very powerful investigative device for prosecutors and perhaps the Government's most effective investigative tool. The grand jury's power to subpoena documents and witnesses throughout the federal system is extremely potent.

A grand jury has broad investigative powers to determine whether a crime has been committed and, if so, who committed it. A grand jury consists of between 16 and 23 layman jurors, of which a concurrence of 12 is required for an indictment. The jury, which deliberates in *secret* without the presence of a judge, prosecutor, or defense counsel, may compel witness testimony and the production of documents. In evaluating evidence and deciding whether to indict, grand juries are not bound by the Federal Rules of Evidence.

Practically speaking, the grand jury's agenda is controlled by the prosecutor, and the grand jury is likely to follow a prosecutor's recommendations regarding indictment, especially in complex cases. Thus, the grand jury is very much an arm of the prosecutor and not truly an independent body.[1]

§ 2:6 Subpoenas

1. *Grand Jury Subpoenas.* Grand jury subpoenas are issued by a U.S. District Court at the request of the prosecutor. The subpoena will have a "return date" or deadline for compliance, usually 30 days, unless it is a "forthwith" subpoena that requires immediate compliance. Grand jury subpoenas are of two types. The first, a *witness* subpoena (*subpoena ad testificandum* in legal terminology) compels the appearance of a witness before the grand jury to provide testimony. The second, a *document*

[Section 2:5]

[1]*See,* IF IT'S NOT A RUNAWAY, IT'S NOT A REAL GRAND JURY, CREIGHTON LAW REVIEW, Vol. 33, No. 4 1999-2000, 821.

subpoena (*subpoena duces tecum*) requires the appearance of a witness for testimony and also compels the witness to bring certain documents or things to the appearance. Protected attorney-client or attorney work-product materials are not subject to disclosure under the grand jury's subpoena power.

You should contact counsel *immediately* if you receive a grand jury subpoena. When an investigator serves a document subpoena, no documents should be produced before review by counsel.

2. *Administrative Subpoenas.* Pursuant to the Inspector General Act of 1978 as amended,[1] each agency IG is authorized to subpoena documents to assist in the performance of the IG's regulatory functions. The Act establishes an Office of Inspector General in numerous federal agencies including HHS, the VA, the National Aeronautics and Space Administration, GSA, and other agencies to combat fraud, waste, and abuse in agency and federally-funded programs. The Act was amended in 1982 to include DOD and to centralize audit and investigative functions within each applicable federal department by granting IGs broad authority to ferret out fraud in agency operations.[2]

Unlike grand jury subpoenas, administrative subpoenas compel only the production of *documents*[3] and may *not* compel oral testimony.

Administrative subpoenas are not self-executing. When a party does not comply with a properly-issued administrative subpoena, the agency involved must institute an enforcement proceeding in U.S. District Court to pursue the demand in the subpoena.

The Inspector General Reform Act of 2008, Pub. L. No. 110-409 expanded the scope of the IG's subpoena authority to include "electronically stored information, as well as any tangible thing."[4]

§ 2:7 Search warrants

Search warrants are issued by a federal judge or magistrate.

[Section 2:6]

[1]5 U.S.C.A. app. 3, §§ 1 to 12.

[2]5 U.S.C.A. app. 3, §§ 2, 4.

[3]5 U.S.C.A. app. 3, § 6(A)(4).

[4]". . . to require by subpoena the production of all information, documents, reports, answers, records, accounts, papers, and other data in any medium (including electronically stored information, as well as any tangible thing) and documentary evidence necessary in the performance of the functions assigned by this Act, which subpoena, in the case of contumacy or refusal to obey, shall be enforceable by order of any appropriate United States district court: *Provided*, That procedures other than subpoenas . . . shall be used by the Inspector General to obtain documents and information from Federal agencies"; 5 U.S.C.A. App. 3, § 6(a)(4).

YOUR RESPONSE TO A CRIMINAL INVESTIGATION § 2:9

They are being used more frequently in procurement investigations, especially where there is fear that documents or other evidence will be destroyed or altered. Some prosecutors favor search warrants because warrants enable them to select and immediately obtain documents thought to be important for their case.[1]

Some prosecutors will use this device because of the dramatic and intimidating impact on a company of the surprise arrival of armed federal agents executing a search warrant. Corporate employees, unaccustomed to such scenes, often panic and make statements to the agents out of fear or nervousness. Although a search warrant can be executed immediately, the company and its employees have the right to contact an attorney before responding and should do so immediately.

§ 2:8 Wiretaps

The Government may also opt to obtain information via electronic means. Although telephone wiretaps are not common in the corporate setting, "consensual" telephone wiretaps appear to be increasing in popularity. In a consensual recording scenario, the calling party, working with law enforcement agents, permits the Government to record his conversation with another party, although the party called does not know of the intercept and does not give his consent.

Another electronic device that may be used by an investigator is the "body wiretap." This surreptitious recording device involves wiring a friendly witness and recording the conversations he has with the suspected individual.

§ 2:9 Field interviews

Government investigators find field interviews a most effective investigative device. An agent may arrive at your company unannounced, secure an immediate interview with an employee without defense counsel present, and obtain damaging admissions as a result. Experienced investigators will also approach employees at their homes, at night, or on weekends when company officers who might provide guidelines are inaccessible.

[Section 2:7]

[1]"The peculiar nature of electronic data is a further consideration. Electronic evidence poses an even greater danger of destruction or concealment than does traditional physical evidence. As the courts are discovering, electronic evidence can be overwritten, transferred, or expunged with little to no human effort, and if performed by a competent expert, may leave little trace that it ever existed." In re APPLICATION OF THE United States of America FOR AN ORDER PURSUANT TO 18 U.S.C. § 2703, (E.D. Virginia 2011).

§ 2:9   GOVERNMENT CONTRACT COMPLIANCE HANDBOOK

Note, however, that Ethical Standards for attorneys for the Government require prosecutors and other Government attorneys to follow state and federal court rules for ethical attorney conduct.[1] This law ultimately may prevent the Government from conducting field interviews of your current employees during an investigation of your company without your knowledge and consent.

Most states and federal district courts have ethical rules prohibiting a lawyer from communicating directly with a person the lawyer knows is represented by counsel. Government attorneys are cautioned to avoid communicating or conducting field interviews with your current employees without the presence of counsel or the counsel's consent.

III. PREPARING FOR AND RESPONDING TO AN INVESTIGATION

A. BE PREPARED

§ 2:10 Retain documents

Government investigations almost always include a review of pertinent records. Your company should have a specific document retention policy in place. Moreover, federal statutes and regulations require that you maintain and make your records available to the Government if you negotiate a contract with the Government that exceeds $100,000 in value.[1]

The length of time that documents must be retained varies depending on the specific class of records involved. Generally, however, the Comptroller General has access to and the right to examine any of your directly pertinent books and other records regarding transactions related to a federal contract for *three years* after the final payment on the contract.[2] You should be aware that specific retention periods for specific documents may be more or less than three years, however.[3]

§ 2:11 Appoint a records custodian

It is often helpful if your company appoints a permanent "records custodian" to handle Government document requests. The custodian should identify, locate, and retrieve the records called

---

[Section 2:9]

[1] 28 U.S.C.A. § 530B.

[Section 2:10]

[1] FAR subpt. 4.7, 15.209(b), 52.215-2.
[2] FAR 4.703(a)(1).
[3] *See* FAR 4.705 to 4.705-3.

for in the subpoena. The custodian should be familiar with the company's overall business operations as well as the way that the business records are kept. Ideally, the custodian should be someone who is *uninvolved* in the subject matter of the Government's inquiry.

§ 2:12 Educate employees

In addition to educating employees on overall compliance with Government regulations and contract requirements, you should encourage your employees to be alert to signs of active investigations. You should also instruct them on what to do if they are approached by Government investigators. (See below.)

§ 2:13 Maintain contact with former employees

To the extent possible, you should maintain contact with former employees who may have been involved in contracts and company pricing and billing actions. Former employees may be able to provide key information to you that is related to your company's defense. In addition, they may provide insight as to the Government's possible theories of prosecution because the Government may attempt to contact former employees before approaching current employees. A report by a former employee of contact by federal investigators may be the first sign that an investigation is underway.

B. DETECTING AN INVESTIGATION

§ 2:14 Generally

You should be alert to the signals that a Government investigation may be underway. Awareness of these signals may allow you to correct potential problems in-house before the investigation is concluded and the Government seeks an indictment. Moreover, monitoring the investigation will assist the company in conducting its own investigation and marshaling an effective response. Generally, the presence of any one of the factors discussed below may indicate that a federal investigation is underway.

§ 2:15 Inquiries by federal auditors

Although Government auditors are not trained investigators, unusual inquiries into specific business practices or procedures by auditors may indicate that a criminal investigation has been or is about to be initiated. DCAA auditors, for example, are instructed to look for indicators of fraud. In fact, the DCAA *Contract Audit Manual* specifically outlines an auditor's responsibilities for preventing, detecting, and reporting fraud, improper practices, or other unlawful activity.[1] An auditor is *required* to initiate an "investigative referral" when he or she becomes aware of circumstances that raise a reasonable suspicion of fraud or other unlawful activity.[2] DCAA also performs audits of CHAMPUS contracts.

§ 2:16 Allegations by contracting officers

All companies that contract with the Government have frequent contact with Government Contracting Officers (COs). Most defense contractors have frequent contact with the Procuring CO and the Administrative CO responsible for particular contracts or facilities. You may also have a CO Representative or a team of Government inspectors physically located in your facility.

Because your personnel have developed a close working relationship with these Government personnel, your employees will often receive clues that an investigation is underway. This may occur when the CO Representative happens to ask a seemingly routine question about a contract that was awarded and completed months or even years ago, or abruptly questions a previously-routine accounting practice.

The CO, a CO Representative, a local DCAA auditor or fiscal intermediary may even make an overt allegation of irregularities to one of your employees. You and your employees must be sensitive to such clues so that you can detect the existence of an investigation and assess your company's exposure to liability in a timely fashion.

§ 2:17 Requests for employee interviews

Federal investigators may contact you for the purpose of securing interviews with various employees to obtain information on a particular topic. If this occurs, it is advisable to ask the investigator to explain the purpose of the interview. The investigators may be interested in eliciting information about your company or perhaps about another company with which you do business.

§ 2:18 Receipt of grand jury subpoena

Obviously, the receipt of a grand jury subpoena is an unmistakable signal that an investigation is underway. You should *contact criminal counsel immediately* on receipt of a grand jury subpoena.

[Section 2:15]

[1]*See* DCAA, Defense Contract Audit Manual 4-700 (June 30, 2006).

[2]*See* DCAA, Defense Contract Audit Manual 4-702.2b.

§ 2:19 Receipt of company hotline calls

If you receive a report of an alleged wrongdoing on the company hotline (see §§ 4:1 et seq.), it is possible that a Government investigation is already underway. The same employee who made the hotline call may have already contacted the Government.

§ 2:20 Lawsuits by current or former employees

Current or former employees sometimes file complaints with the Equal Employment Opportunity Commission, the local Human Rights Commission, the Unemployment Compensation Commission, or other state or local agencies. A current or former employee may also file a "qui tam" suit under the civil False Claims Act.[1] In qui tam suits, the "whistleblower" employee sues the employer for fraud on behalf of the Government and is entitled to a percentage of the Government's recovery. (See §§ 1:1 et seq.)

Company counsel should be alert to the criminal implications of allegations by these individuals and should coordinate the company's response with criminal counsel. These complaints may indicate a broader pending or potential Government investigation. It is reasonable to assume that a current or former employee who is suing you may also have contacted federal authorities. If you believe that an employee has done so, you must be very careful about how you contact that employee. The whistleblower protection provision of the False Claims Act has been construed very broadly to prohibit any adverse reaction ("retaliation") by an employer against an employee.[2]

C. INITIAL STEPS AFTER AN INVESTIGATION IS UNDERWAY

§ 2:21 When the investigators arrive

The very first step you take when investigators call on your company-either to serve a search warrant or subpoena or to request interviews-should be to *contact counsel.* Although your employees should be polite and responsive to the investigators, they should be wary about volunteering information and unconditionally cooperating with the investigators. Your employees should focus on *obtaining* information from the investigator; it is better to do more listening than talking at this stage.

1. *Identify All Investigators.* At the outset, the investigators should present proper credentials and should provide their names, institutional affiliations, and contact information to the

---

[Section 2:20]

[1]*See* 31 U.S.C.A. §§ 3729 to 3733.
[2]*See* 31 U.S.C.A. § 3730(h).

company officials. Even in an apparently noncriminal investigation, all investigators present should be identified.[1] You and your employees should be alert to the presence of unknown persons accompanying auditors. For example, if an auditor with whom you have worked for years in a nonadversarial way has been tasked to assist in a criminal investigation, he or she may have an agent with him or her who is unknown to you. You may unwittingly, therefore, deal with this agent in the same general manner you would with the auditor, when in fact the agent is intent on gathering evidence against you.

2. *Determine The Purpose Of The Investigation.* The purpose of the visit should be established at the outset. Investigators often tend to start by asking general questions that may initially conceal the topic they really want to discuss. It is very important to determine the thrust of the Government's investigation by finding out which employees the investigators want to interview and to have counsel *monitor* the interviews.

3. *Determine Whether A Subpoena Or Search Warrant Has Been Issued.* It is also advisable to determine whether there is a subpoena or search warrant that the investigator is going to serve on you. An investigator may wait until *after* the interview to serve a subpoena, assuming that the subject will be far more willing to cooperate before he or she is aware of the existence of a subpoena. When the subpoena is served, you should *not* turn over any *documents* during the interview, even if the investigator suggests that the documents be turned over as a "courtesy."

If the investigator serves you with a search warrant, it is advisable to ask for; (1) a *copy* of the warrant, (2) the *identification* of the person serving the warrant, (3) *time to review* the warrant, and (4) *time to consult* with the company's attorneys. It is also important not to answer any substantive questions during the time a search warrant is being served or executed. Search warrants can be extremely disruptive and traumatizing to employees and the company. Be prepared to contact counsel immediately on receipt of a search warrant and do not take steps to comply with the warrant until counsel is available.

4. *What NOT To Do.* Do not attempt to *conceal* anything from the investigators and do not *lie* to them. Although you are perfectly free to refuse to answer questions put by investigators and refer them to corporate counsel, attempts to deceive investigators may subject you to collateral criminal charges for false statements and obstruction of justice. (See §§ 1:1 et seq.)

[Section 2:21]

[1]*See, e.g., U.S. v. Okwumabua,* 828 F.2d 950, 23 Fed. R. Evid. Serv. 1048 (2d Cir. 1987).

YOUR RESPONSE TO A CRIMINAL INVESTIGATION § 2:23

If you decide to answer the investigator's questions, do not give any answers unless you are certain that the response is accurate and complete in *every* respect. Before you answer, it is usually necessary to review the contract file and other documents because the event that is under investigation probably took place months or, more likely, years ago.

When served with a subpoena, never agree to provide anything not required by the subpoena. In the case of a search warrant, you should not speak with the investigator regarding the seized documents nor should you answer any substantive questions of any kind.

§ 2:22 Selection of counsel

Probably the most important decision to be made at the start of an investigation is the selection of counsel to represent the company. Most contractors' in-house legal departments do not have sufficient Government contract and criminal law expertise or resources to respond adequately to a criminal investigation.

Therefore, you must normally retain outside counsel. Such counsel should be brought into the process at an early stage. Critical decisions are often made at the beginning of the Government's investigation, and you should have the benefit of outside counsel at this important stage.

§ 2:23 Avoid obstructing justice

It is important to be aware of the potential for obstruction of justice during the course of an investigation. It is a federal offense to obstruct justice.[1] (See §§ 1:1 et seq.) The statutes governing obstruction of justice describe numerous offenses, some broad and some very specific. In a very general sense, the statutes make it an offense to endeavor corruptly or succeed in influencing, obstructing, or impeding the administration of justice in a pending judicial or quasi-judicial proceedings.

To establish that an obstruction of justice has occurred, the Government must show that the person charged had the *specific intent* to do so. Conduct that raises obstruction of justice issues includes the following:

(a) Altering or destroying documents sought in an investigation.
(b) Falsely denying knowledge of information.
(c) Corruptly influencing another person to exercise his or her Fifth Amendment privilege against self-incrimination.

[Section 2:23]
[1]*See* 18 U.S.C.A. §§ 1501 to 1518.

§ 2:23   Government Contract Compliance Handbook

(d) Intimidating a witness with the intent of influencing testimony, or retaliating against a witness for giving testimony in an official proceeding.

Tampering with a federal witness by seeking to "influence" a witness' testimony through "misleading conduct" is also a form of obstruction of justice and is specifically prohibited by the Victim and Witness Protection Act of 1982.[2] You should be sensitive to the serious implications of this statute when advising your employees of their rights in connection with a federal investigation, when interviewing employees and other individuals in the course of an internal investigation, and when preparing witnesses for Government interviews or grand jury testimony. The following conduct is also unlawful: (1) corrupting or endeavoring to influence jurors, officers of the court, or the administration of justice;[3] (2) obstructing or influencing proceedings before federal departments, agencies, and committees;[4] and (3) influencing, obstructing, or impeding a federal auditor in the performance of his or her official duties.[5] Familiarity with and sensitivity to these prohibitions can prevent you from turning what may have been a manageable investigation into serious criminal problems for the company and its employees.

§ 2:24   Preliminary internal inquiry

Often, corporate managers feel it is necessary to conduct their own initial inquiry of possible wrongdoing before contacting outside counsel. This can be counterproductive, however, because it creates evidence against the company and its employees that the Government may use later. Thus, any initial in-house inquiry should be limited. Usually, documents created and conversations held at this early stage will *not* be privileged and therefore may be available to the Government later. Keep in mind that any initial inquiry should generate just enough information so that a determination can be made whether to retain counsel and to conduct a full internal investigation in light of a company's responsibility to inquire into questionable conduct.[1]

§ 2:25   Insurance & indemnification requirements

A full awareness of any insurance and indemnification require-

---

[2]18 U.S.C.A. §§ 1512 to 1515.
[3]18 U.S.C.A. § 1503.
[4]18 U.S.C.A. § 1505.
[5]18 U.S.C.A. § 1516.

[Section 2:24]

[1]*Graham v. Allis-Chalmers Mfg. Co.*, 41 Del. Ch. 78, 188 A.2d 125 (1963).

ments is essential at the outset of an investigation. Make sure you understand company insurance policy provisions or buy-sell agreement indemnification provisions early-on in the investigation. For example, the company's insurer may require *immediate notification* of any pending investigation to trigger coverage. Failure to make the appropriate notification may waive the company's right to indemnification.

A company's obligation to indemnify employees for litigation-related expenses is governed by internal corporate charters, bylaws, employment contracts, and board resolutions, as well as by state law. Although under most circumstances such indemnification is discretionary, it is important to know at the outset the extent to which your company allows the advancement of legal fees to employees. It may be necessary for employees to retain counsel on very short notice, and the first question they will ask is "who will pay?"

§ 2:26 Advise government investigators that they are bound by local ethics rules

If the state in which the investigation is occurring prohibits "ex parte" communications with your current (and perhaps other) employees, corporate counsel should consider advising the investigative agency that it is bound by the Ethical Standards for Federal Prosecutors law and should not attempt to interview or communicate with any current employees without your counsel's presence or consent. Because violation of attorney ethics rules can cause an attorney to lose his or her license to practice, a reminder of the requisite ethical standards may deter the investigative agency from conducting field interviews of your current employees without your knowledge and consent. Although you need to avoid any appearance that you are obstructing justice, a fair request that the Government abide by such ethics rules will help to prevent any potential Government overreaching and mitigate the possibility that your employees will disclose damaging information regarding your company.

§ 2:27 Notify your employees of the investigation

News of a federal investigation spreads quickly in a company, forcing you to decide whether and how to notify your employees. Although it is tempting to delay or forgo completely the announcement of a criminal investigation to avoid disrupting the workplace, it is usually better to notify your employees of the investigation promptly and to advise them of their rights and obligations.

Failure to notify employees can result in untruthful or inaccurate responses by employees who may be approached by an

§ 2:27   GOVERNMENT CONTRACT COMPLIANCE HANDBOOK

investigator without warning. For example, an unprepared employee may be "ambushed" by federal agents for an interview at home or at work without any opportunity to refer to records or to respond to questions carefully. An unprepared employee may be intimidated if approached for an interview and may be reluctant to tell the employer of the encounter, especially if the investigators specifically ask the employee not to tell anyone about the interview. Thus, you would lose the opportunity to gain additional information about the investigation. Notifying your employees about a criminal investigation and giving clear guidance on how to respond to inquiries can only enhance your position in an investigation and preserve employee morale.

Employees should be advised by *written* notice of the existence of an investigation and of their rights and obligations. You should advise employees that they are *not* under any obligation to consent to an interview with a federal investigator, that if they consent to an interview the employee can *terminate* the interview at any time and for any reason, and that the employee can insist that *counsel* be present for any interviews. (See below).

§ 2:28 Advise your employees how to respond

When advising employees how to respond to Government inquiries, it is critical to remember that your advice must not exceed the bounds of lawful conduct. You cannot flatly advise employees to refuse to speak with Government investigators. Instead, you must advise employees that it is *their decision* whether to speak with Government investigators. They are free to speak with Government investigators if they desire to do so. They are also perfectly free to tell the Government investigator to contact your company's attorneys for information.

Your employees should be advised that their refusal to talk with Government investigators *cannot* be viewed as an admission of guilt or an implication that they have something to hide. They should also be informed that their refusal to submit to an interview cannot be used against them in any way by the Government.

Inform your employees that their agreement to talk with Government investigators in a voluntary interview does *not* mean that they will not also be *subpoenaed* by the grand jury to testify. Often, investigators will try to imply to your employees that if they agree to provide information voluntarily, it will not be necessary for them to testify before a grand jury. Some investigators will even suggest that the employees will have to travel to a distant location to testify, at their own expense, unless they agree to a voluntary interview. You should advise your employees that their compliance with requests for interviews will *not* relieve them of the requirement to testify before a grand jury, and that, if they are subpoenaed, the Government will bear their travel expenses, if any.

You should also advise your employees that they have an absolute right to *consult with an attorney* before they decide to submit to an interview. At this time, you may want to advise your employees of your policies regarding indemnification and advancement of attorney fees.

Above all, you must *avoid even the appearance* that you are attempting to dissuade your employees from cooperating with the Government or that they will be penalized in any way for cooperating with the Government. Aside from possible liability for obstruction of justice that could arise from such conduct, efforts to thwart the Government's investigation will surely be viewed by the investigators as a sign that the company has something important to hide.

§ 2:29 Counsel for your employees

After the initiation of a Government inquiry, it may become apparent that your employees, directors, and officers may be parties or witnesses and will require legal representation. Whether corporate counsel can or should undertake to represent such individuals depends largely on the extent to which your company and your employees have conflicting interests.

While there may be advantages in having corporate counsel also represent your employees, in the event that an actual conflict of interest arises, the *joint representation* should *not* continue. You may, however, advise your employees in making their selections of counsel to represent them by suggesting a list of experienced possible attorneys. It is important to note that having *separate* counsel represent the company and its employees does *not* preclude cooperation between the two defense teams; nor does a joint defense arrangement *waive* any privileges.[1]

The feasibility of joint defense arrangements arises when it appears that the interests of an employee in a criminal investigation are potentially different from those of the company, and the

---

[Section 2:29]

[1]*But see, U.S. v. Balsiger, Slip Copy*, 2011 WL 10879630 (E.D.Wis. 2011), citing *United States v. Agnello*, 135 F.Supp.2d 380, 383 (E.D.N.Y.2001) ("A client who is part of a joint defense arrangement is entitled to waive the privilege for his own statements, and his co-defendants cannot preclude him from doing so . . . . All that [his co-defendants] would be entitled to do, to the extent that a joint defense privilege did attach to the conversations, is stop [the waiving member] from directly or indirectly revealing the privileged communications of other participants.").

§ 2:29 GOVERNMENT CONTRACT COMPLIANCE HANDBOOK

employee has obtained counsel either with or without the assistance of management. To the extent that the employee's interests are consistent with the company's interests, a joint defense agreement should be considered.

The main advantage of entering into a joint defense agreement between company counsel and the attorneys for individual employees is the increased ease of *information sharing* without prejudice to any attorney-client privilege. While the joint defense agreement does not need to be complex, or even in writing, for the joint defense attorney-client privilege to be valid, its purpose must be to protect the interests and communications of the parties to the agreement.

D. COMPANY & EMPLOYEE RIGHTS DURING AN INVESTIGATION

§ 2:30 Generally

You and your employees have certain rights that may be exercised during Government investigations. It is important and appropriate for you to inform your employees of their rights and obligations during Government inquiries.

§ 2:31 Unreasonable search & seizure

You and your employees have a right to be protected from illegal searches and seizures. If material is seized without a search warrant or the warrant is unreasonably broad, your company and affected employees may be entitled to the exclusion of the seized evidence in a prosecution. You should be sensitive to the fact that your employees generally have a reasonable expectation of privacy in their offices, desks, and file cabinets, although the degree of privacy diminishes when a supervisor in your company rather than a Government official intrudes on the employees' privacy.[1]

§ 2:32 Self-incrimination

Although the Fifth Amendment to the U.S. Constitution does not protect companies against self-incrimination,[1] a company employee may assert the privilege against self-incrimination in cir-

---

[Section 2:31]

[1]*O'Connor v. Ortega*, 480 U.S. 709, 107 S. Ct. 1492, 94 L. Ed. 2d 714 (1987).

[Section 2:32]

[1]*See Curcio v. United States*, 354 U.S. 118, 77 S. Ct. 1145, 1 L. Ed. 2d 1225 (1957); *U.S. v. White*, 322 U.S. 694, 64 S. Ct. 1248, 88 L. Ed. 1542, 152 A.L.R. 1202 (1944); *Hale v. Henkel*, 201 U.S. 43, 26 S. Ct. 370, 50 L. Ed. 652

cumstances where he or she personally may be criminally liable for acts committed in his or her corporate capacity.[2] If such an employee or former employee asserts the Fifth Amendment privilege in a *civil* case involving the company, an adverse influence may be drawn against the company.[3]

§ 2:33 Employees' right to counsel

As discussed above, right-to-counsel issues may get complicated when an employee's and the company's interests do not coincide. For example, when conducting an internal investigation, employees must be advised at the outset that the interviewer is representing the *company* rather than the employee. Although the company may decide at a later date that it will represent the employee, the employee's right to counsel also entitles the employee to *separate* counsel.

IV. CONDUCTING AN INTERNAL INVESTIGATION

§ 2:34 Generally

Often, when a company is faced with a criminal investigation, counsel will advise that the company undertake an internal investigation to determine the facts. Assuming that the company has undertaken the initial steps outlined above, and that management has determined that a potentially serious situation exists, the internal investigation should be promptly initiated to determine what happened and why.

Initiating an internal investigation will not only assist you in assessing the company's exposure to liability and in responding to the Government's inquiries, it will also place you in an active rather than a reactive mode. In addition, an internal investigation will assist you in determining whether a voluntary disclosure to the Government regarding any wrongdoing or mistakes is warranted. It may also serve as an indication of your good corporate citizenship—which is often a pivotal factor in Government decisions to suspend, debar, or prosecute a contractor.

§ 2:35 Authorization by company management

The first step in conducting an internal investigation is to have

---

(1906) (overruled in part by, Murphy v. Waterfront Com'n of New York Harbor, 378 U.S. 52, 84 S. Ct. 1594, 12 L. Ed. 2d 678 (1964)).

[2]*See Curcio v. United States*, 354 U.S. 118, 77 S. Ct. 1145, 1 L. Ed. 2d 1225 (1957); *Wilson v. U.S.*, 221 U.S. 361, 31 S. Ct. 538, 55 L. Ed. 771 (1911).

[3]*See Rad Services, Inc. v. Aetna Cas. and Sur. Co.*, 808 F.2d 271, 22 Fed. R. Evid. Serv. 392 (3d Cir. 1986). *See also Baxter v. Palmigiano*, 425 U.S. 308, 96 S. Ct. 1551, 47 L. Ed. 2d 810 (1976); *Brink's, Inc. v. City of New York*, 539 F. Supp. 1139, 10 Fed. R. Evid. Serv. 1358 (S.D. N.Y. 1982).

corporate management authorize it formally. Before the investigation begins, corporate counsel should submit a written authorization request to management detailing the purpose of the investigation, establishing that communications generated in the course of the investigation will be *privileged,* and describing all potential forms of litigation related to the investigation, such as civil and criminal proceedings and subpoena compliance. Corporate management should then formally authorize the internal investigation and the request that all communications be kept confidential. Once authorized, all *costs* of the internal investigation should be *segregated* so that their allowability and allocability under the company's Government contracts may be addressed later.[1]

§ 2:36 Choosing the internal investigators

As a general rule, counsel should conduct the internal investigation because issues regarding whether particular conduct is a violation of law and the protection of confidential information are best handled by attorneys. You must weigh various considerations in deciding whether your corporate or outside counsel should conduct the investigation.

Corporate counsel may have a better understanding of the company's procedures, operations, and contracts. Your company's attorneys are also generally known to your employees and may be better received during interviews. *Outside counsel,* however, may be more impartial in their assessment of the questioned practices. Another major advantage of having outside counsel conduct your investigation is that Government prosecutors and investigators tend to perceive company counsel as part of the corporate management structure and thus, lacking in independence and objectivity.

Perhaps the most important factor to consider when selecting either corporate or outside counsel to perform as the "internal investigator" is the issue of *attorney-client privilege.* Corporate counsel is required to provide business as well as legal advice to the company. Accordingly, difficulties arise in establishing and maintaining the attorney-client privilege when a corporate lawyer may be viewed as a business advisor rather than legal counsel, or when the corporate lawyer collects information during the investigation that is shared with others such as accountants who are not involved in defending the case. Thus, investigation by in-house counsel may result in inadvertent waiver of the attorney-client privilege.

[Section 2:35]
[1] FAR 31.205-47 — Costs Related to Legal and Other Proceedings.

Often, the best choice for an "internal investigator" is outside counsel working closely with corporate counsel. This "team" best serves the company's interests because it takes advantage of the employees' familiarity with corporate counsel, of the wider experience of the outside counsel in criminal matters, and of the more secure protection of privileged information provided to outside rather than in-house counsel.

§ 2:37 Interviewing current & former employees

Reviewing the relevant documents and conducting employee interviews are the heart of a thorough internal investigation. The interviewers, who should be experienced, should be very wary of guiding witnesses' testimony by characterizing your corporate position regarding the criminal investigation one way or the other. Interviewers should be thorough, objective, forthright, and considerate—and should take careful notes.

Employees should be advised to be truthful and accurate. You should advise the employee of the purpose of the interview and request that the employee not discuss the interview with anyone. The employee should be informed that management intends the interview to be privileged, but that management might voluntarily disclose the contents of the interview if it serves the company's interests to do so.

Finally, the employee should understand that neither corporate counsel nor outside counsel represents the employee, and that the employee may wish to consider hiring separate counsel.

§ 2:38 Report of the investigation

After counsel have reviewed the relevant documents and interviewed knowledgeable current and former employees, the results of the internal investigation should be reported to management. It is ordinarily preferable to report the results in *writing* rather than orally.

The report should include a summary of the facts, an analysis of applicable legal principles, and an explanation of weaknesses, if any, in company procedures, an outline of legal arguments against criminal prosecution or civil sanctions, and recommendations for corrective and preventive actions. A report in the above format can be extremely beneficial to management by serving as a basis for decisions regarding the company's investigation strategy and whether to disclose voluntarily the findings of the investigation to the Government.

It is important, however, to structure the report so as to ensure the protection of the report's contents under the *attorney-client privilege* and the *attorney work-product doctrine*. In addition, you

§ 2:38   GOVERNMENT CONTRACT COMPLIANCE HANDBOOK

should be wary of disclosing the report outside your company; such disclosure may risk waiving privileges.

Maintaining the confidentially afforded by attorney-client privilege and the attorney work-product doctrine continues to be a difficult issue.

In the wake of the Enron debacle, the Department of Justice (DOJ) issued what became known as the Thompson Memo that listed nine factors prosecutors "should" take into account in deciding what charges to bring against a corporation. The memo indicated a company could receive "cooperation credit" if it had waived attorney-client and work product privileges and provided the results of any internal company investigation to prosecutors and cut-off payment of attorneys' fees for an employee under investigation.

Both Congress and the private sector strongly criticized this policy. As a result, on December 6, 2006, DOJ issued the "McNulty Memo" which revised this policy somewhat. The revised guidance did not prohibit seeking a waiver of the attorney-client privilege. Rather, it simply indicated that prosecutors should not routinely request corporations to take this step and required them to obtain higher-level approval before proceeding. Also, while it recognized that many state indemnification statutes authorize companies to advance legal fees prior to a formal determination of guilt and that compliance with these statutes "cannot be considered a failure to cooperate," it went on to add "[i]n extremely rare cases, the advancement of attorneys' fees may be taken into account when the totality of the circumstances show that it was intended to impede a criminal investigation."

These changes to the original policy satisfied almost none of its critics, and instead, led to the introduction of legislation in both the House and Senate that would have overturned the DOJ policy. On September 18, 2007, a DOJ representative testified before the Senate Judiciary Committee that the procedures set out in the McNulty Memo were working well and that legislation was not needed. However, at about that same time, a former chief justice of Delaware's Supreme Court reported to that same committee that anecdotal evidence suggested that some prosecutors were unfamiliar with the restrictions imposed by the McNulty Memo or, if they were aware, simply choose to disregard them.

Apparently bowing to widespread House and Senate opposition, DOJ, in a July 9, 2008 letter to the Senate Judiciary Committee, outlined several proposed changes in the McNulty Memo.[1] Among these, prosecutors would no longer consider whether a corporation waived the attorney-client privilege or agreed to disclose privileged information such as attorney notes and legal conclusions reached as a result of an internal investigation in determining what charges to bring against a company. Also, under the proposed change prosecutors would not consider whether a company reimbursed an employee for his/her legal expenses, continued to retain that employee during the pendency of the investigation, or entered into a joint defense agreement with employees in evaluating "cooperation credit." On August 28, 2008, DOJ formally issued its revised policy. That document continues to list nine facts that a prosecutor "should" (as opposed to "must" in the McNulty Memo) take into account in deciding what charges to bring. The new policy specifically states that "[T]he decision not to cooperate by a corporation (or individual) is not itself evidence of misconduct, at least where the lack of cooperation does not involve criminal misconduct or demonstrate consciousness of guilt . . . ." The policy further states that "Eligibility for cooperation credit is not predicted upon the waiver of attorney-client privilege or work product protection." Instead, the key element for consideration is "disclosure of the relevant *facts* concerning such misconduct" regardless of whether a waiver of privilege is involved. However, it continued, prosecutors may still take into consideration a company's willingness to disclose privileged documents in two situations: (1) where the company or employee asserts an "advices of counsel" defense; and (2) where the communications were made in furtherance of a crime or fraud. In addition, in evaluating cooperation "[p]rosecutors should not take into account whether a corporation is advancing or reimbursing attorneys' fees or providing counsel to employees who are under investigation." Finally, the revised policy stressed "A corporation's offer of cooperation itself does not automatically entitle it to immunity from prosecution or a favorable resolution of its case." Whether these revisions will satisfy critics is problematic as there is a feeling among business organizations that prosecutors will ignore DOJ guidance and that only legislation can resolve the issue.[2]

§ 2:39 Communications with the prosecutor

Communications with Government representatives are a good

[Section 2:38]

[1]For a full description of the McNulty Memo, see http://www.justice.gov/dag/speeches/2006/mcnulty_memo.pdf.

[2]To date, no such legislation has been enacted.

§ 2:39   GOVERNMENT CONTRACT COMPLIANCE HANDBOOK

way for management to learn the focus of the Government's investigation. The company representative conducting discussions should be a criminal lawyer who is capable of developing a comfortable, professional rapport with the prosecutor.

It is sometimes useful to talk with the prosecutor to determine whether your company is a *target* or merely a witness in the Government's probe. It is best not to permit corporate counsel to handle such discussions due to the reluctance of prosecutors to provide corporate counsel with information because of the Government's natural suspicion that corporate counsel may have been involved in the alleged wrongdoing.

It is also important to consider the advantages of *not* discussing the investigation with the prosecutor at all. You may decide that it is best to maintain a low profile with the Government rather than to arrange a meeting with the prosecutor to find out exactly where you stand in the investigation. Each case must be decided on its own facts.

§ 2:40   Voluntary disclosure of wrongdoing

If, in the course of the internal investigation—or at any time—you discover illegal conduct has occurred or is occurring, you should consider making a voluntary disclosure of the improper practice to the Government. First, however, you and your counsel should carefully discuss the advantages and the disadvantages of voluntarily disclosing violations to the Government, and, if you decide to make a disclosure, what the scope of that disclosure should be.

1. *Disadvantages.* The risks of participating in a voluntary disclosure program are significant. Voluntary disclosure programs are not amnesty or immunity programs. Voluntary disclosure of fraud and wrongdoing does not necessarily prevent your company from being prosecuted or from being excluded from contracting with the Government or participating in Government programs. In addition, voluntary disclosure may have an adverse effect on your employees' willingness to cooperate in your internal investigation. Employees may measure their responses very carefully if they know that the information they provide will be routinely disclosed to Government investigators. Finally, it is important to understand that voluntary disclosure to the Government may result in the waiver of the attorney-client privilege and attorney work-product protection.[1]

By way of example, TW Metals, Inc., a Pennsylvania company,

[Section 2:40]

[1]*See In re Martin Marietta Corp.*, 856 F.2d 619 (4th Cir. 1988).

reportedly voluntarily disclosed that it had supplied items with specialty metals from 2001 to 2005 in violation of the Berry Amendment. Even though the contractor had made a voluntary disclosure, the Government brought suit under the False Claims Act. The contractor reportedly settled the case by agreeing to pay $215,000 to the Government.

2. *Advantages.* Although voluntary disclosure does not provide amnesty for the contractor regarding the violations disclosed, the Government may be more lenient to companies that voluntarily disclose their wrongdoing. For example, out of the more than 360 defense contractors that participated in the DOD's voluntary disclosure program between 1986 and 1996, only three contractors were prosecuted based on information they provided to the Government.[2]

Another advantage of participating in a voluntary disclosure program is that your company's disclosure demonstrates present responsibility and integrity. Such disclosure minimizes the adversarial relationship between you and the Government and fosters a more cooperative spirit. This is especially important where the Government is your primary or only customer.

Under the Federal Sentencing Guidelines for organizations, voluntary disclosure of wrongdoing can reduce a company's exposure to penalties in the event of an indictment and conviction. (See §§ 1:1 et seq.) If there is a corporate plea of guilty or a conviction, the sentencing guidelines require the court to identify a base fine that follows a fixed schedule and then multiply that base fine by a "culpability multiplier" that is also based on a fixed schedule.[3] A voluntary disclosure that is made: (1) "prior to any imminent threat of disclosure or government investigation"; and (2) "within a reasonably prompt time after becoming aware of the offense" can result in a 50% to 95% reduction in the multiplier.[4] With scheduled fines that range up to $72.5 million, the savings can be substantial.[5]

3. *Contents of Disclosure.* If you decide to make a voluntary disclosure, you should provide a detailed description of how the illegal or improper practice arose as well as an outline of the relevant fraud issues. You should also identify all the divisions, contracts, and personnel involved. Most importantly, you must include a summary of the *company's response* to the alleged wrongdoing. Explain how the practice was identified, provide a

---

[2] DOD Inspector General, Semiannual Report to Congress 31 (Apr. 1, 1996 to Sept. 30, 1996).

[3] U.S. Sentencing Guidelines §§ 8C2.4, 8C2.5.

[4] U.S. Sentencing Guidelines § 8C2.5(g).

[5] U.S. Sentencing Guidelines § 8C2.4(d).

§ 2:40   GOVERNMENT CONTRACT COMPLIANCE HANDBOOK

description of the investigative process, and describe how the practice was terminated. This explanation should also set forth any disciplinary actions that the company took in addition to any corrective and preventive measures that were instituted. Also, be sure to submit a list of investigative, audit, and legal information to be provided to the Government.

Finally, you should assure the Government that you are willing to *reimburse* the Government for any damages suffered and that you are willing to *cooperate* with further Government investigative efforts.

As noted in the update to § 1:21, there is a split in authority as to whether the "voluntary disclosure" of wrongdoing amounts to a "public disclosure" within the meaning of § 3730(e) which would bar a *qui tam* action unless the realtor was the "original source" of the information.[6]

V. RESPONDING TO A GRAND JURY PROCEEDING

§ 2:41   Witness & document subpoenas

Grand juries have the power to subpoena documents as well as testimony. It is important for you, your employees, and your counsel to understand that *full and complete compliance* is essential; omissions in responding to a subpoena may result in charges of obstruction of justice.

§ 2:42   Motions to quash or modify subpoenas

If a document subpoena is objectionable because it is unreasonable or oppressive in some manner, you may move to quash or modify the subpoena under the Federal Rules of Criminal Procedure.[1] As the subpoenaed party, however, *you* have the burden of establishing the unreasonableness of the subpoena.[2] In assessing reasonableness, courts generally consider, among other

---

[6]*See U.S. ex rel. Lockhart v. General Dynamics Corp.*, 529 F. Supp. 2d 1335 (N.D. Fla. 2007), *U.S. ex rel. Rost v. Pfizer, Inc.*, 507 F.3d 720 (1st Cir. 2007) (voluntary disclosures to the Government of possible wrongdoing were not a public disclosure); and *U.S. ex rel. Cox v. Smith & Nephew, Inc.*, 2010 WL 4365467 (W.D.Tenn. 2010) (voluntary disclosure that contractor had supplied products from a non-designated country in violation of Trade Agreements Act was not a public disclosure). *But see U.S. ex rel. Fowler v. Caremark RX, L.L.C.*, 46 F.3d 730 (7th Cir. 2007) (disclosure of information to U.S. Attorney's office during an investigation of company's business practices constitutes a public disclosure).

[Section 2:42]

[1]*See* Fed. R. Crim. P. 17(c).

[2]*See generally U.S. v. R. Enterprises, Inc.*, 498 U.S. 292, 111 S. Ct. 722, 112 L. Ed. 2d 795 (1991).

factors, the relevance of the requested documents to the investigation, the particularity with which the documents are specified, whether production of the documents would be burdensome, and the period of time covered by the subpoena.[3]

§ 2:43 Preparation of witnesses

Your counsel should instruct all witnesses to answer questions truthfully during appearances before the grand jury. Your witnesses should understand the range of inferences that may be drawn from their responses. Counsel must be extremely careful when preparing their clients for grand jury testimony to abide by the attorneys' ethical obligation both to provide effective representation and not to engage in conduct that obstructs justice.

§ 2:44 Averting an indictment

Normally, you will have an opportunity to make a presentation to the prosecutor, either written or oral, in an attempt to convince the Government not to seek an indictment. This should be done through counsel. You have an obvious interest in convincing the Government that criminal prosecution is not warranted. You should prepare your presentation to the Government only after a thorough internal investigation and after the facts have been ascertained.

An effective presentation sets forth the facts and directly addresses specific questions raised by the prosecutor. You should consider furnishing helpful documents and proffers of favorable testimony only after carefully weighing the advantages and disadvantages of revealing such evidence to the Government. The hope, of course, is that your submission will persuade the Government *not to indict* your company or perhaps even to opt for a *global settlement* to resolve any criminal, civil, and administrative actions against you at the same time (see §§ 3:1 et seq.).

You may also plead your case to the prosecutor's *supervisor* if you believe the prosecutor is being unreasonable or acting improperly.

---

[3]*U.S. v. R. Enterprises, Inc.*, 498 U.S. 292, 111 S. Ct. 722, 112 L. Ed. 2d 795 (1991).

Chapter 3

Parallel Proceedings & Global Settlements

I. OVERVIEW
§ 3:1 Scope note

II. RISKS OF PARALLEL PROCEEDINGS
§ 3:2 Generally
§ 3:3 Transfer of information
§ 3:4 Protecting privileged information
§ 3:5 Burdensome litigation
§ 3:6 Inconsistent defenses
§ 3:7 Frequently asked questions

III. GLOBAL SETTLEMENT
§ 3:8 Generally
§ 3:9 Benefits
§ 3:10 Negotiating the agreement
§ 3:11 Elements
§ 3:12 Criminal liability & penalties
§ 3:13 Civil liability & penalties
§ 3:14 Suspension & debarment
§ 3:15 —Appointment of ombudsman
§ 3:16 —Reporting requirements
§ 3:17 Frequently asked questions

IV. MITIGATING FACTORS
§ 3:18 Generally
§ 3:19 Recommendations

> **KeyCite®:** Cases and other legal materials listed in KeyCite Scope can be researched through the KeyCite service on Westlaw®. Use KeyCite to check citations for form, parallel references, prior and later history, and comprehensive citator information, including citations to other decisions and secondary materials.

I. OVERVIEW

§ 3:1 Scope note

Parallel investigations are simultaneous and often overlapping private, criminal, civil, or administrative agency investigations arising out of the same or similar conduct. For example, you may find yourself the subject or target of a grand jury investigation for knowingly supplying defective parts to the Department of Defense (DOD). At the same time, you may face suspension or debarment proceedings at DOD and a separate lawsuit by the Civil Division of the Department of Justice (DOJ) seeking to recoup damages for the alleged false claims you submitted to the Government for payment for the defective parts.

Such parallel proceedings are difficult to defend because they often present defendants with conflicting goals. What may be appropriate and helpful to a defendant in response to a criminal investigation may be devastating in its impact on the civil side of the equation. For example, a voluntary disclosure of wrongdoing may avert the possibility of an indictment or even suspension or debarment from contracting with the Government, but it may provide useful information discoverable by your opponents in a civil suit arising out of the same transaction. Similarly, efforts to challenge an administrative suspension or debarment may provide free discovery to the prosecutor conducting a grand jury investigation regarding the same conduct underlying the suspension or debarment proceeding. This chapter discusses the problems and strategy considerations that may arise from defending and settling simultaneous proceedings.

II. RISKS OF PARALLEL PROCEEDINGS

§ 3:2 Generally

If you are a Government contractor confronted with parallel investigations, you face many problems. For example, the burden of having to defend multiple proceedings at the same time may impair your ability to prepare an adequate defense in any of the proceedings. Simultaneous proceedings may also adversely affect your right to a fair trial or compromise your right against self-incrimination. Moreover, when a company faces two or more proceedings, productivity and employee morale often suffer, and the risk of exhausting the company's resources looms large.

§ 3:3 Transfer of information

You should be aware that one of the serious risks of parallel proceedings is that agencies tend to *share information* with each other. Information may even be shared between agencies and a grand jury. Therefore, you should carefully weigh any voluntary disclosure decision, keeping in mind that disclosure may permit parties who otherwise would not have access to your information nevertheless to legitimately obtain it.

Parallel proceedings also make it difficult to shield *confidential* company information from disclosure during litigation. The disclosure of such information in one investigation may open the door to its use in a parallel proceeding. Because Government entities often share information, your attorneys should try to reach an agreement with the appropriate Government entity stating that the Government will avoid unnecessary disclosure of the information you provide to it or it will not disseminate the information at all.

The DOJ, for example, has established a policy of encouraging coordination between the DOJ and the Inspectors General of the various agencies.[1] Similarly, the DOD has undertaken efforts to coordinate procedures and to centralize information within its different branches with respect to civil, criminal, and administrative proceedings related to fraud cases.[2] The Inspectors General of administrative agencies are also authorized to share information among themselves and with the DOJ.[3]

§ 3:4 Protecting privileged information

One of the most serious pitfalls of parallel Government investigations is that the disclosure of privileged materials to one Government agency increases the danger of waiving applicable privileges in other proceedings. You should be particularly cautious when considering disclosing documents that are protected by the attorney-client privilege or the attorney work-product doctrine under an agency voluntary disclosure program. Courts usually find that the voluntary disclosure of privileged information

---

[Section 3:3]

[1]DOJ Manual § 9-42.500 (2000). *See* U.S. Attorney General, Memorandum to DOJ Attorneys, "Coordination of Parallel Criminal, Civil, and Administrative Proceedings" (July 28, 1997) (available on the Internet at http://www.usdoj.gov/ag/readingroom/970728.htm

[2]*See* DOD Directive 7050.5 (June 7, 1989).

[3]*Securities & Exchange Commission. v. Dresser Industries*, 628 F.2d 1368 (D.C. Cir. 1980).

§ 3:4　　　　　Government Contract Compliance Handbook

in one proceeding waives the privilege for all purposes.[1]

§ 3:5　Burdensome litigation

Parallel proceedings may be oppressive for contractors because of the need to coordinate the defense of a number of actions in different forums. For example, although the various investigating agencies may share information, there is no guarantee that they will coordinate discovery, so you may be faced with duplicate requests for your records. Your company also may have claims pending against the Government in connection with the contracts that are the subject of the pending investigation. In many cases, the Government will seek to stay discovery in your civil suit and effectively delay your potential recovery until the criminal matters are resolved.[1]

[Section 3:4]

[1]*See In re Columbia/HCA Healthcare Corp. Billing Practices Litigation*, 293 F.3d 289, 58 Fed. R. Evid. Serv. 1451, 53 Fed. R. Serv. 3d 789, 2002 FED App. 0201P (6th Cir. 2002) (rejecting selective waiver); *Westinghouse Elec. Corp. v. Republic of Philippines*, 951 F.2d 1414, 35 Fed. R. Evid. Serv. 1070, 22 Fed. R. Serv. 3d 377 (3d Cir. 1991) (disclosure of documents to Securities and Exchange Commission during internal, adversarial investigation waived attorney-client and work-product privileges); *In re Martin Marietta Corp.*, 856 F.2d 619 (4th Cir. 1988) (disclosure of investigation materials to the Government impliedly waived privilege as to all non-opinion work product related to the subject matter of disclosure); *U.S. v. Massachusetts Institute of Technology*, 957 F. Supp. 301, 37 Fed. R. Serv. 3d 711 (D. Mass. 1997), judgment aff'd in part, vacated in part, 129 F.3d 681, 48 Fed. R. Evid. Serv. 66, 39 Fed. R. Serv. 3d 4 (1st Cir. 1997) (disclosure of information to Defense Contract Audit Agency waived attorney-client privilege); *McMorgan & Co. v. First California Mortg. Co.*, 931 F. Supp. 703, 35 Fed. R. Serv. 3d 1170 (N.D. Cal. 1996) (disclosure of documents to Department of Labor waived privilege during litigation brought by private party); *U.S. ex rel. Mayman v. Martin Marietta Corp.*, 886 F. Supp. 1243 (D. Md. 1995) (attorney-client privilege covering evaluation drafted by in-house counsel waived during settlement negotiations by disclosure of document referring to in-house counsel's evaluation).

But cf. *Diversified Indus. Inc. v. Meredith*, 572 F.2d 596 (8th Cir. 1977) (en banc) (disclosure of information to Securities and Exchange Commission during formal investigation did not waive any privilege in subsequent litigation against private party); *McDonnell Douglas Corp. v. U.S. E.E.O.C.*, 922 F. Supp. 235 (E.D. Mo. 1996) (information given to Equal Employment Opportunity Commission during an investigation did not waive privilege for subsequent suit); *Boston Auction Co., Ltd. v. Western Farm Credit Bank*, 925 F. Supp. 1478 (D. Haw. 1996) (disclosure of information by bank to Farm Credit Administration did not constitute waiver under Hawaii law).

[Section 3:5]

[1]*See Aerospatiale Helicopter Corp.*, DOTBCA No. 1905, 89-2 BCA 21770. In some cases, the Government may assert counterclaims alleging wrongdoing in response to your contract claims; *see, e.g., Commercial Contractors, Inc. v. U.S.*, 154 F.3d 1357 (Fed. Cir. 1998); *BMY Combat Systems Div. of Harsco Corp.*

§ 3:6 Inconsistent defenses

The possibility that different attorneys acting on your behalf may act in an inconsistent manner increases when you hire different counsel to represent you in different proceedings. *Daily contact* and *coordination* with and among outside counsel helps ensure that no actions are taken in one area that are inconsistent with your company's position in another.

§ 3:7 Frequently asked questions

Question 1: What can I do to ensure that privileged documents disclosed during one proceeding remain privileged for another proceeding?

Answer 1: There is no easy answer to this question because protecting your privileges is tricky in the context of the complex web of parallel proceedings. It is important, at a minimum, that counsel experienced in the criminal, civil, and administrative ramifications of Government contract fraud proceedings provide advice on your overall approach. This will minimize the risk that you inadvertently waive your company's privileges or rights by disclosing information, by allowing employees to be aware of information, or by permitting employees to testify regarding confidential company matters. Under some circumstances, waiver is unavoidable, but it should be the result of an informed decision rather than an accident.

Question 2: Can the Government bring debarment or civil proceedings against me for conduct that already was the basis for previous criminal charges?

Answer 2: Yes, you can be debarred for the same acts that led to a criminal conviction. Debarment is generally considered by courts to be a civil penalty, and subsequent criminal charges for the same conduct that led to an earlier debarment are not considered to violate your rights against double jeopardy[1] (see §§ 1:1 et seq.). Similarly, except under fairly extreme circumstances, the Government may institute a civil action for recovery

---

v. U.S., 38 Fed. Cl. 109 (1997) (Government counterclaimed for violations of False Claims Act in response to contractor suit for equitable adjustment).

[Section 3:7]

[1]*See Hudson v. U.S.*, 522 U.S. 93, 118 S. Ct. 488, 139 L. Ed. 2d 450, 162 A.L.R. Fed. 737 (1997) ("Applying traditional double jeopardy principles to the facts of this case, it is clear that the criminal prosecution of these petitioners would not violate the Double Jeopardy Clause." It is evident that Congress intended the OCC money penalties and debarment sanctions imposed for violations of 12 U.S.C. §§ 84 and 375b to be civil in nature.); *U.S. v. Perry*, 152 F.3d 900 C.A.8 (Neb.), 1998 (SEC disgorgement "of all profits gained from sales or offers to sell interests in the trust" was a civil penalty and Perry's criminal conviction did not implicate the Double Jeopardy Clause.).

§ 3:7   GOVERNMENT CONTRACT COMPLIANCE HANDBOOK

of damages and penalties even after a criminal prosecution arising from the same facts. Claims of double jeopardy under such circumstances have generally not proven successful (see §§ 1:1 et seq.).

III. GLOBAL SETTLEMENT

§ 3:8   Generally

A "global settlement" of all the Government's claims against you is the most effective way to minimize your liability exposure if you are confronted with parallel proceedings in different forums. However, Government agencies have become increasingly reluctant to participate in global settlements. Consequently, in practice today, global settlements are more likely to be "parallel settlements" or "coordinated settlements." If the Government commences an investigation of your company, you should actively pursue a settlement to resolve all criminal, civil, and administrative disputes with each interested party, including the Civil and Criminal Divisions of the DOJ, the relevant administrative agencies, prime and subcontractors, and any "qui tam" private plaintiffs. You must understand, however, that reaching a settlement is difficult because no particular federal entity will spearhead and coordinate the effort for you. Rather, it is entirely up to you to bring together the various federal agencies involved, as well as any prime or subcontractors and qui tam plaintiffs, and convince them to enter into a settlement with you that will resolve all of your issues.

The sections below are intended to familiarize you with the nature, usefulness, and contours of such a settlement. Because of the complex and sensitive nature of settling parallel proceedings, however, it is critical that you obtain *effective representation* by counsel when negotiating a global settlement.

§ 3:9   Benefits

When the Government has multiple claims pending against you, settling as many of these claims as possible at the same time has several advantages. Such a coordinated settlement avoids the prohibitive *costs of litigating* multiple proceedings at the same time. It may also prevent the *suspension or debarment* of your company from Government contracting. Likewise, an early settlement of parallel cases offers you the opportunity to *control the negative publicity* regarding your company that a Government criminal charge or conviction would likely cause. Although you may try to keep the facts and circumstances of any investigation and settlement out of the public eye, the Government may and often does issue press releases regarding prosecutions or settlements.

In addition, a coordinated settlement may be your only means of *avoiding pleading guilty* to criminal charges. A guilty plea may provide conclusive evidence of your liability in later civil or administrative proceedings. A well-thought-out and comprehensive settlement agreement also may serve to protect your company's rights in a subsequent claim involving the same contract that was the subject of a criminal or civil investigation.[1]

§ 3:10 Negotiating the agreement

When your company faces multiple proceedings in different forums, you will need to deal with investigators from several Government departments and agencies, with each agency having its own attitude toward an appropriate settlement. Because you must deal with the varying interests, priorities, procedures, and demands of these independent governmental units when negotiating an appropriate settlement, you should approach any Government fraud investigation with the understanding that the settlement process will be complex and difficult.

Although the DOJ will *not* coordinate settlement efforts with other agencies, it will likely grant you sufficient latitude to resolve ancillary liabilities with other agencies. *You* must take the initiative, therefore, to negotiate a global settlement of multiple proceedings.

Your success in negotiating a satisfactory global settlement will often depend on your *speed* in commencing an internal investigation of your company at the first indication that improper conduct has occurred and in instituting negotiations with the Government. You cannot afford to wait for the inevitable Government investigation. Your company must implement procedures that will enable you to commence negotiations with the DOJ and other cognizant agencies quickly, to help you stay ahead of the Government investigators.

Your strongest asset in settlement negotiations will be your *past record* of contract *compliance* and *cooperation* with the

---

[Section 3:9]

[1]*See Rockwell Intl. Corp.*, EBCA No. C-9509187 et al., 97-1 BCA ¶ 28814 (finding that contractor's plea agreement did not prevent contractor from pursuing reimbursement for certain fees from the Government); *United Technologies Corp., Pratt & Whitney Group*, ASBCA No. 46880-84 et al., 95-1 BCA ¶ 27538 (holding that the plea arrangement did not bar UTC's subsequent breach of contract claim).

§ 3:10   GOVERNMENT CONTRACT COMPLIANCE HANDBOOK

Government.[1] It is important, therefore, that you have an adequate compliance program in place *before* you receive a grand jury subpoena from the Government. In many cases, you will be able to cast your company as the victim of the misconduct that is the focus of the investigation.

Government agencies know that a contractor's main concern is to avoid suspension or debarment from contracting with the Government, and agencies will use this leverage effectively during negotiations. That does not mean, however, that you will be unable to negotiate terms that will diminish the likelihood of suspension or debarment. Moreover, your status as a valued supplier of a commodity the Government needs may make you an attractive candidate for settlement.[2]

§ 3:11 Elements

Your success in obtaining a satisfactory settlement with the Government will, naturally, depend on the facts of each case. The primary subjects of a coordinated settlement, which are discussed in greater detail below, relate to (a) criminal liability and penalties, (b) civil liability and penalties, and (c) agreement with the suspension and debarment authority. You should recognize that, in many cases, you may not be able to settle one or more aspects of the case, such as the amount of civil penalties. You may, however, be able to obtain other valuable concessions from the Government, such as an agreement by the DOJ that it will recommend against suspension or debarment of your company or the revocation of your export licenses. The specific elements of the typical coordinated settlement are outlined in more detail below.

§ 3:12 Criminal liability & penalties

The focus of most Government procurement fraud investigations will be on the criminal case against your company. The scope of the civil and administrative agreements will, therefore, hinge on the criminal settlement, which is often cast in terms of a plea agreement. While not every criminal investigation will result in a criminal indictment or plea, it is not unlikely in the current contracting environment. Moreover, the Government is not likely to decline prosecution unless you can demonstrate that you are a victim of the alleged misconduct yourself. Plea agree-

---

[Section 3:10]

[1]*See Dantran, Inc. v. U.S. Dept. of Labor*, 246 F.3d 36 (1st Cir. 2001) (describing how respondent's cooperation with DOL during investigation and settlement prompted the ALJ to treat the company with leniency).

[2]*See U.S. ex rel. Barajas v. U.S.*, 258 F.3d 1004 (9th Cir. 2001).

ment negotiations typically focus on the number of criminal *counts* against you and the size of the criminal *fine*.

Plea agreements do not usually address suspension and debarment directly. Nevertheless, the language of the agreement is often of critical importance in influencing the subsequent action of the suspension and debarment authority.[1] You will often have latitude in choosing the count and the specific act to which you will plead guilty, and the choice you make will influence your subsequent liabilities. For example, prosecutors may (1) permit you to plead guilty to an act outside the statute of limitations, (2) agree to recommend against suspension and debarment, or (3) stipulate that the alleged misconduct did not involve one of your Government contracts.

Another important focus of the plea agreement is setting the amount of criminal fines and restitutional penalties to which you are liable. Criminal plea agreements may also require contractors to reimburse the Government for the costs of the Government's investigation and to remove from their indirect costs on Government contracts the salary and expenses attributable to any accountants, lawyers, or managers who were involved in conducting the company's own internal investigation.

You should take an aggressive negotiating stance to ensure that the agreement includes the standard provision that the Government agrees not to prosecute any of your *affiliates*, such as parent companies, subsidiaries, successors, or assignees. This provision may be crucial if your management decides to sell the operating unit at which the misconduct occurred.

It is important to note that a criminal plea agreement with Federal Government authorities does not bind *state or local* prosecuting authorities. The Government will often agree, however, to advise other prosecuting authorities of your cooperation.

§ 3:13   Civil liability & penalties

As part of the global settlement, you should attempt to execute a civil settlement simultaneously with the criminal plea agreement. In some cases, the criminal plea agreement may actually set forth the amount of the civil settlement. In other cases, however, you will need to execute a separate agreement that sets forth the amount and specific terms of the civil settlement.

The primary focus of a civil settlement is on the *amount* of civil

---

[Section 3:12]

[1]*See Facchiano Const. Co., Inc. v. U.S. Dept. of Labor*, 987 F.2d 206 (3d Cir. 1993) (stating that a plea arrangement in which Department of Housing and Urban Development debarred a contractor would not prohibit DOL from instituting its own debarment procedures).

§ 3:13

damages, penalties, and the *terms of payment*. It is often difficult for the Government to quantify damages in a complex procurement fraud case. For example, in a case involving falsified quality records, the Government may advance a number of theories to quantify actual damages so that the final damages figure will often include elements of several theories, including (a) the cost to the Government of the fraud, (b) the scrap value of the product, if any, and (c) any amount found due through audit. The Civil Division of the DOJ may also insist on treble damages and significant penalties under the False Claims Act.[1]

In addition to taking an aggressive stance on the amount of the fine, you should attempt to negotiate advantageous terms of payment. In many cases, the Government will accept an extended payment schedule that will ease the burden on your company of a substantial civil award.

Similarly, you should try to settle all outstanding claims with prime and subcontractors. Third parties are not bound by settlement agreements with the Government.[2] Qui tam relators who ostensibly bring their claim on behalf of the Government have the ability to object and be heard when presented with a proposed agreement negotiated by DOJ and the defendant.

The Government has taken steps to make it easier for your company to reach a civil settlement with the Government without resorting to litigation. The DOJ has emphasized its continuous obligation to evaluate settlement possibilities and has directed agencies to assess the possibility of settlement as soon as adequate information is available concerning the Government's litigation position.[3] Federal agencies are urged to promote increased use of alternative dispute resolution techniques.[4] Furthermore, the Administrative Dispute Resolution Act of 1996 encourages the Government to use alternative dispute resolution techniques to settle claims short of litigation,[5] while the Alternative Dispute Resolution Act of 1998 authorizes U.S. District Courts to develop

---

[Section 3:13]

[1] 31 U.S.C.A. §§ 3729 to 3733.

[2] *See generally* Sylvia, The False Claims Act: Fraud against the Government ch. 10; Huffman, Madsen and Hamrick, The Civil False Claims Act, Briefing Papers No. 01-10 (Sept. 2001).

[3] *See* 62 Fed. Reg. 39250 (providing guidance on and implementing certain provisions of Exec. Order 12988 (61 Fed. Reg. 4729), which directed agencies to establish methods and procedures for resolving fairly and efficiently civil litigation with the United States).

[4] Exec. Memorandum (May 1, 1998) (available on the Internet at http://www.npr.gov/library/direct/memos/dispute.html).

[5] *See* P.L. 104-320, 110 Stat. 3870 (Oct. 19, 1996) (codified as amended in various sections of U.S. Code, titles. 5, 10, 28, and 41).

§ 3:14

and offer alternative dispute resolution programs in civil cases.[6]

The importance of trying to resolve all actual and potential liabilities at the same time cannot be overstated. In *Morse Diesel Intern., Inc. v. U.S.*, 74 Fed. Cl. 601 (2007), the contractor had previously admitted to violation of the False Claims Act and the Major Fraud Act in connection with billing for surety bond costs under several contracts for the construction of federal buildings. However, neither of the two settlement agreements precluded further actions arising out of those facts. Accordingly, in subsequent litigation before the Court of Federal Claims for price adjustments under those contracts, the court held that those same actions constituted violations of the Forfeiture of Claims Act and directed that the contractor forfeit its pending claims totaling more than $53,000,000. Subsequently, the court imposed fines of approximately $260,000 for violation of the Anti-Kickback Act and $7 million in penalties and damages under the False Claims Act. The court rejected Morse Diesel's contention that awarding penalties under both statues would be "improperly duplicative." *Morse Diesel Intern., Inc. v. U.S.*, 79 Fed. Cl. 116 (2007). More recently, in *U.S. ex rel. Bunk v. Birkart Globistics GMBH & Co.*, 2010 WL 4688977 (E.D.Va. 2010), the defendant entered into a plea agreement in which it admitted violating the criminal conspiracy statute, 18 U.S.C.A. § 371 and the Sherman Antitrust Act, 15 U.S.C.A. § 1 and that the Government had experienced damages of $865,000 as a result of these actions. The court held that under both the doctrines of collateral estoppel and judicial estoppel the defendants could not challenge the amount of damages in a subsequent civil FCA action. But see *U.S. ex rel. Bunk v. Birkart Globistics GMBH & Co.*, 2012 WL 488256 (E.D.Va. 2010) (where the court dismissed the $50,248,000 mandatory FCA civil penalty as an "unconstitutionally excessive fine" in violation of the Eighth Amendment).

§ 3:14 Suspension & debarment

For a Government contractor, often the most crucial aspect of a global settlement is the agreement with the suspension and debarment authority assigned to the case. The primary focus of the settlement negotiations will be whether your company is "presently responsible" to perform Government contracts, and the primary indication of present responsibility is the effectiveness of your compliance program. As discussed in more detail in §§ 4:1 et seq., your compliance program should include (1) a corporate code of ethics, policies, and procedures to ensure compliance with federal procurement law, (2) appointment of a compliance officer,

---

[6]P.L. 105-315, 112 Stat. 2993 (Oct. 30, 1998).

§ 3:14　　　　　　　Government Contract Compliance Handbook

(3) establishment of a "hotline" for employees and others to use to report instances of suspected misconduct, and (4) internal audit and investigation mechanisms.

The suspension and debarment authority typically requires the inclusion of certain nonnegotiable provisions in any settlement agreement. *First*, the Government usually *reserves* the right to suspend or debar you (a) for any violation of the settlement agreement, (b) if you knowingly allow a debarred or convicted individual to hold a managerial or supervisory position in your company, or (c) if you deal with a company presently debarred from contracting with the Government. *Second*, an agreement usually makes clear that all of your *costs* related to the Government's criminal or civil investigation or administrative proceedings against you are unallowable under your Government contracts.[1] In addition, the suspension and debarment authority may impose additional (and often burdensome) requirements as "indicia" of your corporate integrity, such as requiring that you appoint an ombudsman to monitor or to help institute a "corporate integrity" compliance program and that you create a system for mandatory reporting of violations to the Government.[2]

Even if you are successful in persuading the Government that you should not be debarred for improper conduct, an individual contracting officer can still find that you are "not responsible" based on the same facts. In *OSG Product Tankers LLC v. U.S.*, 82 Fed. Cl. 570 (2008), the contractor's parent company pled guilty to 33 felony counts related to environmental violations. The Government designated the Maritime Administration as the lead agency for debarment proceedings against the parent. Because of various mitigating factors the Government agreed to a settlement in lieu of debarment. Subsequently, while evaluating a subsidiary's proposal for the lease of two ships, the contracting officer had concerns about the parent's record of integrity and business ethics, particularly in light of the recent criminal conviction. The contracting officer ultimately concluded that the subsidiary was "not presently responsible" and thus ineligible for award even though it had not been part of the debarment proceeding. The subsidiary brought suit, contending that the Maritime Administration had been designated as the appropriate agency to review the actions of the parent, that the agency had already found that these events did not warrant debarment, and that that decision preempted the contracting officer's finding of non-responsibility. The court first noted that FAR § 9.104-3(c) al-

---

[Section 3:14]

[1] *See* FAR 31.205-47.

[2] *See generally* Feldman, 4 Government Contract Guidebook ch. 12.

lowed the contracting officer to take into account the parent's past performance in making a responsibility determination for the subsidiary. It then pointed out that "debarment" and "non-responsibility" are two separate concepts:

> Debarment is distinguished from a finding of non-responsibility in that the latter excludes the contractor from a specific contract with a single Executive agency, and the former excludes the contractor from all Executive agency contracts . . . . [T]he contracting officer's "determinations of responsibility are based upon different factors [from that of the debarment official's] and have different underlying purposes."

Thus, the court ruled that simply because the Government exercised its discretion in settling with the parent did not preclude the contracting officer in fulfilling his/her responsibilities under FAR § 9.1 in finding that the contractor was "not presently responsible." Finally, the court concluded that the contracting officer had made a thorough investigation of the facts, including sending written questions to the subsidiary and allowing the subsidiary to make an oral presentation before a board of experts whom the contracting officer had convened for that purpose and thus refused to overturn the finding of non-responsibility.

§ 3:15 Suspension & debarment—Appointment of ombudsman

One of the most striking features of some settlement agreements is the requirement that contractors select and retain an independent ombudsman with no prior or future financial or other interest in your company who is charged with monitoring your compliance program as an impartial outsider. The procedures for appointing an ombudsman and the functions he or she is to perform may occupy several pages of the settlement agreement. The ombudsman's primary responsibilities are to (1) receive hotline calls from employees who have information on possible compliance violations, (2) conduct investigations of employee complaints, and (3) report the results of investigations and recommendations to your management and the cognizant Government agency. The suspension and debarment authority may also require that the ombudsman have access to any investigative file compiled by your management or counsel, and that the ombudsman submits periodic reports to the Government agency which summarize the number of investigations conducted, the results of those investigations, and the adequacy of your corrective action.

The ombudsman is an external watchdog who may have a negative impact on your day-to-day operations. The most effective means for avoiding this external oversight is to implement a

§ 3:15   GOVERNMENT CONTRACT COMPLIANCE HANDBOOK

proven and effective compliance program along the lines outlined in §§ 4:1 et seq. *before* any fraud investigation takes place. You cannot afford to wait until the Government commences an investigation to begin your compliance program. You should act now to develop internal mechanisms to receive and investigate employee allegations of impropriety in order to avoid any requirement of external oversight of your operations in future settlement agreements.

§ 3:16 Suspension & debarment—Reporting requirements

Whether or not the Government requires as part of the settlement agreement that you appoint a company ombudsman, it may require you to investigate any reported material violation of applicable law or regulation relating to Government procurement. The Government usually demands at least some form of access to your internal investigation materials, including interview notes, employee statements, and final investigation reports. Your negotiating skill will determine how extensive this access will be.

Disclosure of *privileged* investigatory files to the ombudsman or the Government may constitute a *waiver* of the attorney-client and attorney work-product privileges regarding that information (see above). You should attempt to protect your privileges by negotiating a settlement that minimizes the required disclosures to the suspension and debarment authority. For example, the Government may agree to review rather than obtain copies of your investigation files. Moreover, the suspension and debarment authority may state in the agreement that disclosure will not waive applicable privileges as to any other person or entity. The courts are unclear, however, whether such a reservation of rights will avoid a waiver of applicable privileges regarding the subject matter of the information.[1]

[Section 3:16]

[1]*Compare Fox v. California Sierra Financial Services*, 120 F.R.D. 520 (N.D. Cal. 1988) (rejected by, *In re Columbia/HCA Healthcare Corp. Billing Practices Litigation*, 293 F.3d 289, 58 Fed. R. Evid. Serv. 1451, 53 Fed. R. Serv. 3d 789, 2002 FED App. 0201P (6th Cir. 2002)) (disclosure of information to Securities and Exchange Commission without a reservation of rights waived any confidential privilege attached to the information), and *Jonathan Corp. v. Prime Computer, Inc.*, 114 F.R.D. 693 (E.D. Va. 1987) (disclosure of documents without a reservation of rights waived any attorney-client privilege), with *U.S. v. Miller*, 600 F.2d 498, 4 Fed. R. Evid. Serv. 867 (5th Cir. 1979) (privilege was waived even though documents were delivered to the Government subject to a reservation of privilege rights), and *Hartford Fire Ins. Co. v. Garvey*, 109 F.R.D. 323 (N.D. Cal. 1985) (declining to recognize as valid a reservation of rights regarding privilege).

§ 3:17 Frequently asked questions

Question: If the Government declines to intervene in a qui tam action, am I free to settle the action with the qui tam plaintiff?

Answer: Most likely, no. A specific provision of the False Claims Act[1] seems to indicate (and at least one U.S. Court of Appeals has explicitly found)[2] that the Government can veto any voluntary settlement entered into between you and a qui tam plaintiff, even if the Government declined to assume control of the case. You should be careful to ensure when crafting any settlement agreement with a qui tam plaintiff that the terms of the agreement do not "bargain away" claims on behalf of the Government. In other words, you should be mindful that the Government still has an interest in your settlement terms and you should seek Government consent to the settlement.

IV. MITIGATING FACTORS

§ 3:18 Generally

The best way to ensure that the Government will treat you fairly when negotiating a global settlement is to have in place *corporate policies and procedures* regarding compliance and reporting obligations. As stated earlier, one main factor that can contribute to your success in attaining a favorable global settlement is your *past record* of contract compliance. You should establish, therefore, a compliance program that stresses eliminating employee conduct that could lead to criminal, civil, or administrative inquiries by the Government. Remember, having an adequate compliance program in place *before* receiving a subpoena from the Government will help your company demonstrate its good faith attempts to prevent illegal conduct.

In addition, your ultimate success in negotiating a satisfactory global settlement against you will depend on how you handle the Government investigation of your company. Both the Federal Acquisition Regulation and the DOJ Manual outline certain mitigating factors that the Government should take into account when determining what remedial or punitive measures should be

---

[Section 3:17]

[1] 31 U.S.C.A. § 3730(b)(1).

[2] *Searcy v. Philips Electronics North America Corp.*, 117 F.3d 154 (5th Cir. 1997) (False Claims Act provides the Government with a unilateral right to veto a qui tam settlement regardless of the Government's declination to intervene). *But see U.S. ex rel. Killingsworth v. Northrop Corp.*, 25 F.3d 715, 28 Fed. R. Serv. 3d 1522 (9th Cir. 1994) (rejected by, *U.S. v. Health Possibilities, P.S.C.*, 207 F.3d 335, 2000 FED App. 0100P (6th Cir. 2000)) (where Government has declined to intervene, it must possess "good cause" to veto a settlement and have a court hearing on the settlement's reasonableness).

§ 3:18   GOVERNMENT CONTRACT COMPLIANCE HANDBOOK

imposed on a contractor.[1] These mitigating factors are reflected in the following recommendations for contractors that are the subject of a Government investigation.

§ 3:19 Recommendations

(a) Immediately commence your own *internal investigation*. Acting quickly to redress or explain any allegation of wrongdoing will be looked upon favorably by the Government.

(b) *Cooperate fully and willingly* with any Government agency investigation. You should make it apparent that you, like the Government, want to uncover any instance of impropriety.

(c) Recognize the *seriousness* of any uncovered misconduct. The Government does not take its investigations lightly, and neither should you.

(d) Take *disciplinary action* against any individual responsible for the illegal conduct.

(e) Make sure that you are adequately prepared to negotiate a *comprehensive resolution* with all interested parties whenever you are confronted by parallel proceedings involving several departments of agencies.

[Section 3:18]

[1] FAR 9.406-1(a); DOJ Manual § 9-27.420 (2000).

Chapter 4
Your Compliance Program

I. OVERVIEW
§ 4:1   Scope note

II. DEVELOPING A COMPLIANCE PROGRAM
§ 4:2   The FAR compliance requirements
§ 4:3   Your "compliance book"
§ 4:4   Defense contractors
§ 4:5   Requirements imposed by settlement agreements
§ 4:6   Mechanism for future modifications
§ 4:7   Employee screening

III. RECOVERING COMPLIANCE COSTS
§ 4:8   Cost allowability

IV. STEPS TO ACHIEVE COMPLIANCE
§ 4:9   Corporate code of ethics
§ 4:10   Corporate procedures & policies
§ 4:11   Compliance officer
§ 4:12   Company hotline
§ 4:13   Audits & investigations
§ 4:14   Disciplinary action
§ 4:15   Reporting violations to the government
§ 4:16   Cooperating during government investigations
§ 4:17   Education & training
§ 4:18   Updating

KeyCite®: Cases and other legal materials listed in KeyCite Scope can be researched through the KeyCite service on Westlaw®. Use KeyCite to check citations for form, parallel references, prior and later history, and comprehensive citator information, including citations to other decisions and secondary materials.

I. OVERVIEW

§ 4:1   Scope note

Beginning December 24, 2007, a new contract clause at FAR

§ 4:1

52.203-13 entitled "Contractor Code of Business Ethics and Conduct (DEC 2007)" made the establishment of a compliance program *mandatory* for contracts and subcontracts with an expected value of more than $5 million and a performance period of 120 days or more. These new requirements represent a significant shift from the Government's prior policy of expecting contractors to "voluntarily" establish ethics and compliance programs that demonstrated their present responsibility to be eligible for a contract award and their commitment to corporate integrity.

Even if you are exempt from the requirements of FAR 52.203-13, The array of penalties the Government may impose on contractors for violations of federal laws and regulations are a strong incentive for you to establish an effective program to ensure that your employees comply with all procurement requirements. A well-designed compliance program, properly communicated to your employees, monitored, and enforced, will reduce the likelihood of serious criminal, civil, and administrative disputes with your Government customer. Furthermore, if you have an established compliance program in place, you are more likely to receive favorable treatment from the Government and the courts in the event you are charged with a violation.

A compliance program is nothing more than a set of policies and procedures you put in place to ensure adherence to federal procurement law. At a minimum, a compliance program should include a corporate code of ethics, mechanisms by which questionable activities are brought to the attention of management, an education and training program for employees, and systematic reviews of existing practices and procedures.

As noted in Chapter 1 of this Handbook, the United States Sentencing Guidelines provide for a reduction in criminal penalties if you have an effective corporate compliance program in place.[1] Specifically, the sentencing court will reduce the fine if the company has an effective program to prevent and detect any violations of law. It is important, therefore, that you develop and implement an effective compliance program in advance of the Government audits and investigations that you are likely to face as a Government contractor. This chapter presents the FAR compliance requirements and then discusses a number of recommended approaches for designing your compliance program, with brief descriptions of the elements your program should include.

[Section 4:1]
[1] U.S. Sentencing Guidelines § 8C2.5(f).

II. DEVELOPING A COMPLIANCE PROGRAM

§ 4:2 The FAR compliance requirements

The FAR emphasizes Government contractors "must conduct themselves with the highest degree of integrity and honesty."[1] It goes on to state that contractors "should have" a written code of business ethics, a business ethics compliance training program, and an internal control system that is suitable to the size of the business and extent of its involvement in Government contracting.

According to the rule, an internal control system should "[f]acilitate timely discovery of improper conduct in connection with Government contracts" and "[e]nsure corrective measures are promptly instituted and carried out."[2]

FAR 52.203-13 must be included in solicitations and contracts where the value of the contract is expected to exceed $5,000,000 and the performance period is 120 days or more. This clause must be flowed down to subcontracts that also meet these threshold requirements. If a contract action establishes a maximum quantity of supplies or services to be acquired, the final anticipated dollar value must be the highest final priced alternative to the Government, including the value of all options. Thus, IDIQ contracts would be "covered" by the clauses if the estimated value exceeded $5,000,000, even though the "guaranteed minimum" was much less. Generally, small businesses and contracts for commercial items are exempt from the specific requirements of FAR 52.203-13.

Timing. Where applicable, FAR 52.203-13 requires contractors to have a written code of business ethics and conduct in place within 30 days of contract award, unless the contracting officer establishes a longer time period, and make a copy *available* to each employee engaged in the performance of the contract. Within 90 days of award, contractors must establish an ongoing business ethics and business conduct awareness program and an internal control system that are suitable to the size of the company and extent of its involvement in Government contracting.

Business ethics and disclosure requirements. In addition, under FAR 52.203-13(b), contractors must exercise due diligence to prevent and detect criminal conduct and otherwise promote an organizational culture that encourages ethical conduct and a commitment to compliance with the law Moreover, contractors are required to make a timely disclosure, in writing, to the agency

---

[Section 4:2]
[1] FAR 3.1002(a).
[2] FAR 3.1002(b)(2) to (3).

Office of the Inspector General, with a copy to the contracting officer, whenever in connection with the award, performance, or closeout of the contract or any subcontract thereunder, the contractor has *credible evidence* that a principal, employee, agent, or subcontractor has committed (1) a violation of the civil False Claims Act, or (2) a violation Federal criminal law involving fraud, conflict of interest, bribery, or gratuity violations found in Title 18 of the United States Code. in connection with the award, performance, or closeout of the Government contract or any subcontract thereunder.

If the contract is intended for use by multiple agencies, *i.e.*, as would be the case with an FSS multiple award schedule contract, the contractor need only make a disclosure to the OIG of the ordering agency and the IG for the agency responsible for the basic contract.

Finally, FAR 52.203-13(b) provides that the Government, to the extent permitted by law and regulation, will safeguard and treat disclosed information as confidential, if marked as "confidential" or "proprietary" and will not release such information to the public pursuant to a FOIA request without prior notification to the contractor.

Ethics and Business Conduct Awareness Program. FAR 52.203-13(c) first requires contractors to establish a program which includes reasonable steps to communicate periodically in a practical manner the contractor's standards and procedures and other aspects of the contractor's business ethics awareness and compliance program and internal control system, by conducting effective training programs and otherwise disseminating information appropriate to an individual's respective roles and responsibilities. The training under this program shall be provided to the Contractor's principals and employees, and as appropriate, the contractor's agents and subcontractors.

Next FAR 52.203-13(c) requires contractors to maintain an internal control system, which shall (1) establish standards and procedures to facilitate timely discovery of improper conduct in connection with Government contracts; and (2) ensures corrective measures are promptly instituted and carried out. At a minimum, the contractor's internal control systems must provide for the following:

- Assignment of responsibility at a sufficiently high level and adequate resources to ensure effectiveness of the business ethics awareness and compliance program and internal control system;
- Reasonable efforts not to include an individual as a principal whom due diligence would have exposed as having engaged in conduct that is in conflict with the contractor's code of business ethics and conduct;

- Periodic reviews of company business practices, procedures, policies, and internal controls for compliance with the contractor's code of business ethics and conduct and the special requirements of Government contracting, including:
  (1) Monitoring and auditing to detect criminal conduct;
  (2) Periodic evaluation of the effectiveness of the business ethics awareness and compliance program and internal control system, especially if criminal conduct has been detected; and
  (3) Periodic assessment of the risk of criminal conduct, with appropriate steps to design, implement, or modify the business ethics awareness and compliance program and the internal control system as necessary to reduce the risk of criminal conduct identified through this process.
- An internal reporting mechanism, such as a hotline, which allows for anonymity or confidentiality, by which employees may report suspected instances of improper conduct, and instructions that encourage employees to make such reports;
- Disciplinary action for improper conduct *or for failing to take reasonable steps to prevent or detect improper conduct*;
- Timely disclosure, in writing, to the agency OIG, with a copy to the contracting officer, whenever in connection with the award, performance, or closeout of *any* Government contract performed by the Contractor or a subcontractor thereunder, the contractor has *credible evidence* that a principal, employee, agent, or subcontractor of the Contractor has committed a violation of Federal criminal law involving fraud, conflict of interest, bribery, or gratuity violations found in Title 18 of the U.S.C.A. or a violation of the civil False Claims Act[3];
- The disclosure obligation continues until at least three years after final payment on the contact; and
- Full cooperation with any Government agencies responsible for audits, investigations, or corrective actions.

Similar to the disclosure provisions in subparagraph (b), subparagraph (c) specifies if the contract is intended for use by multiple agencies disclosure should notify the ordering agency's Office of Inspector General and the IG of the agency responsible for the basic contract of the violation. Subparagraph (c) also provides that the Government, to the extent permitted by law and regulation, will treat disclosed information as confidential and will not release it to the public under FOIA without notifying the contractor.

Suspension and Debarment. Applicable to all Government

---

[3] 31 U.S.C.A. §§ 3729 to 3733.

contractors, FAR 9.406-2 and 9.407-2 contain their own independent disclosure provisions. FAR 9.406-2 and 9.407-2 provide that knowing failure to disclose may be cause for suspension and debarment where there is a:

- Knowing failure by a principal, until three years after final payment on *any* Government contract awarded to the contractor, to timely disclose to the Government, in connection with award, performance, or closeout of the contract or subcontract thereunder, credible evidence of (1) a violation for the civil False Claims Act, (2) violation of Federal criminal law involving fraud, conflict of interest, bribery, or gratuity violations found in Title 18 of the U.S.C.A., or (3) significant overpayment on the contract, other than overpayments resulting from contract financing payments as defined in FAR 32.001.

Verifying Compliance. DCAA appears to be emerging as the agency most involved in verifying compliance with FAR 52.203-13. This is not surprising since DCAA has typically reviewed the adequacy of contractors' accounting and other business systems, including their systems of internal controls as part of its audit responsibilities. On July 23, 2009 DCAA issued "Audit Guidance on Federal Acquisition Regulation (FAR) Revisions Related to Contractor Code of Business Ethics and Conduct" (09-PAS-014(R)). This guidance revised the procedures for conducting overall accounting system control audits to reflect *each* of the new requirements of FAR 52.203-13. In addition to issues already addressed as part of a system control audit, DCAA will now:

- Verify the existence of a written code of conduct and review its contents to ensure it addresses ethical business practices, conflicts of interest and expected standards of ethical and moral behavior,
- Obtain evidence that the code of conduct was made available to each employee,
- Verify that written codes of conduct (a) are periodically communicated to all employees, (b) are formally acknowledged, and (c) cite consequences for violations,
- Verify that contractor's policies and procedures provide for a business ethics awareness and compliance program for all principals and employees and, as appropriate, the contractor's agents and subcontractors,
- Verify that the manager responsible for the ethics program reports to a high level official (*e.g.*, vice president/CFO),
- Verify that contractor's hiring policies prohibit appointing as a principal an individual who previously engaged in conduct that conflicts with the contractor's code of conduct and test the contractor's procedures to verify they include steps for exercising due diligence in identifying such conduct, *e.g.*, background

checks,
- Verify that the contractor performs periodic reviews, *i.e.*, at least annually, of company business practices, procedures, and internal controls for compliance with the contractor's code of business ethics,
- Verify that the contractor has an internal reporting mechanism, such as a hotline, which allows for anonymity or confidentiality,
- Verify that the contractor's policies and procedures provide for appropriate disciplinary action for improper conduct or failing to take reasonable steps to prevent or detect improper conduct,
- Verify that the contractor's policies and procedure provide for timely disclosure to the agency OIG and the contracting officer when there is credible evidence of a violation of Federal criminal law involving fraud, conflict of interest, bribery, or gratuity, or a violation of the civil False Claims Act,
- Request a copy of any disclosures made and verify that the contractor complied with its policies and procedures,
- Verify that the contractor's policies and procedures provide for cooperation with any Government agencies responsible for audits or investigations, and
- Verify that the contractor has flowed down FAR 52.203-13 to subcontractors where required.

Regardless of whether it is "voluntary" or "mandatory," it would be difficult to overemphasize the importance of having a good compliance program and utilizing the expertise of third parties in evaluating and updating that program, especially when faced with allegations of misconduct.

The first step in implementing an effective compliance program is to assess what compliance measures you may already have in place and decide what new measures are needed. A successful program must include all the requisite elements without becoming so overly detailed that it is unmanageable. You should evaluate existing procedures, policies, and operating environments at each of your contracting facilities and tailor your compliance program to the existing corporate environment at each facility.

The largest problem you face in designing a compliance program is balancing the need for a large number of policies and procedures to address all the procurement requirements with which you must comply against the need to implement a manageable program that your employees and the Government can understand. If the format of a program is accessible but the substance is lacking, violations will occur. On the other hand, if the substance is exhaustive but the form is excessively detailed or obtuse, violations are equally likely.

Specific procedures and internal controls will vary depending

§ 4:2   GOVERNMENT CONTRACT COMPLIANCE HANDBOOK

on the nature and size of your company, as well as the extent of your business with the Government. The Government will expect you to institute procedures and controls appropriate to your particular company that are sufficient to establish your commitment to corporate integrity.

§ 4:3   Your "compliance book"

The two primary objectives of a compliance program are (1) *reducing the likelihood of violations* of federal procurement law and (2) effectively projecting your *commitment to business ethics* to employees, the public, and the Government. The most effective way to achieve these ends is for you to design and implement a single-volume corporate "compliance book" that sets forth the standards of behavior you expect of the company and its employees. This compliance book should be brief but comprehensive and set forth your core procedures for adequate training and discipline of employees and your system of internal audits to ensure continued compliance.

Your corporate compliance book should include a *detailed overview* of your compliance program and a *statement of your commitment* to corporate integrity. Rather than including every policy and procedure, the compliance book should outline the basics of your program and emphasize the policies that signal your commitment to corporate integrity. You should include your core corporate policies and procedures related specifically to the compliance program itself, including the compliance officer's responsibilities, the corporate hotline procedures for reporting suspected violations, and the procedures for conducting both routine internal audits and more serious investigations.

The "compliance book" approach has been particularly successful for contractors with many operating divisions and subsidiaries. You can easily adapt the single-volume corporate compliance book to cover the particular policies and procedures at diverse operating units by including supplementary sections that pertain to a particular unit. You must determine initially, however, the core elements of a compliance program, as outlined below.

§ 4:4   Defense contractors

If you are a defense contractor, you should implement your compliance program and procedures in conformance with Department of Defense (DOD) Federal Acquisition Regulation Supplement (DFARS) Subpart 203.70, "Contractor Standards of Conduct." Although these regulations outline ostensibly "voluntary" compliance measures, they set forth explicit undertakings that the Government expects contractors, at a minimum, to implement. These regulations state that a contractor's system of

YOUR COMPLIANCE PROGRAM   § 4:6

self-governance should include the following:[1]

(1) A written code of business ethics and conduct and an ethics training program for all employees;

(2) Periodic reviews of company business practices, procedures, policies, and internal controls for compliance with standards of conduct and the special requirements of Government contracting;

(3) A mechanism, such as a hotline, by which employees may report suspected instances of improper conduct, and instructions that encourage employees to make such reports;

(4) Internal and/or external audits, as appropriate;

(5) Disciplinary action for improper conduct;

(6) Timely reporting to appropriate Government officials of any suspected or possible violation of law in connection with Government contracts or any other irregularities in connection with such contracts; and

(7) Full cooperation with any Government agencies responsible for either investigation or corrective actions.

The three key elements of the DFARS program described above are (a) a *written code of conduct*, (b) a mechanism for *comparing* actual *practices* with established *policies*, and (c) a mechanism for *reporting and investigating* suspected violations. A compliance program that includes these elements will go a long way toward demonstrating your present responsibility.

§ 4:5 Requirements imposed by settlement agreements

It has become increasingly common for the Government to use suspension and debarment proceedings[1] as vehicles for assessing contractors' compliance programs and imposing compliance requirements. For example, in addition to the general elements of a satisfactory self-governance program outlined in the DFARS (see § 4:4 above), DOD suspension and debarment authorities have delineated *additional* requirements for contractors involved in alleged violations of federal law that are *more burdensome* than the elements included in the DFARS.

§ 4:6 Mechanism for future modifications

It is important that your compliance program establish policies and procedures that can be modified to address new concerns as

---

[Section 4:4]

[1]DFARS 203.7001(a). *See generally* Goddard, Jr., Business Ethics in Government Contracting—Part II, Briefing Papers No. 03-7 (June 2003); Irwin, Ethics in Government Procurement/Edition III, Briefing Papers No. 99-8 (July 1999).

[Section 4:5]

[1]*See* FAR subpt. 9.4.

they arise because areas of emphasis in federal contract compliance are subject to change. In addition, your contract compliance program should include an effective mechanism to ensure that the program can be modified to conform with future administrative and congressional requirements in the federal procurement area.

§ 4:7 Employee screening

A successful compliance program should provide for the screening of employees assigned to sensitive or dangerous positions for drug and alcohol abuse. The program should also establish procedures for the careful evaluation of new employees for evidence of prior misconduct, particularly in such sensitive areas as subcontracting/vendor procurement.

III. RECOVERING COMPLIANCE COSTS

§ 4:8 Cost allowability

Often, one of your first concerns when establishing a compliance program is how much the program will cost and whether these costs are recoverable from the Government under your cost contracts. When designing and implementing your compliance program, you should remember that the resources you devote to developing and maintaining an effective compliance program are not only a good business investment, they are also a "cost of doing business" and thus are generally allocable and allowable indirect contract costs.[1] (Cost allowability is discussed in detail in §§ 11:1 et seq.)

The costs you incur in time spent by managers, employees, the compliance officer, in-house counsel, outside counsel, and accounting staff to plan and participate in compliance education and training programs, to develop and implement a code of ethics, and to administer the company's "hotline" are not designated as *specifically* unallowable, and thus are generally allowable as business expenses.

Under applicable FAR cost principles, *professional and consultant* service expenses you incur associated with your compliance program, such as for legal and accounting advice, are recoverable to the extent they are reasonable in relation to the services rendered and are not contingent on recovery of the costs from the Government.[2] When implementing your compliance program, you should be aware of the factors the Government considers in

---

[Section 4:8]
[1] FAR 31.203.
[2] FAR 31.205-33(b).

determining whether professional service costs will be allowable. These include (1) the nature and scope of the service rendered in relation to the service required, (2) the need to contract for the service, (3) your past pattern of acquiring such services and their costs, (4) the impact of Government contracts on your business, (5) the proportion of Government work to your total business, (6) whether the service can be performed more economically by your employees, (7) the qualifications of the individual or concern rendering the service, and (8) the adequacy of the contractual agreement for the service.[3]

Although compliance costs are generally allowable, you must be careful to distinguish professional services costs you incur associated with your compliance program from any professional services costs you may incur in the *defense* of fraud proceedings instituted against you. Costs incurred in the defense of civil or criminal fraud proceedings are almost never allowable.[4] To ensure that such specifically unallowable costs are not improperly charged to your contracts, you must establish procedures for separately charging such defense costs.

IV. STEPS TO ACHIEVE COMPLIANCE

§ 4:9 Corporate code of ethics

The corporate code of ethics is the heart of your compliance program and should be accorded the careful attention commensurate with its importance. The corporate code of ethics must first and foremost emphasize your *commitment to compliance* and corporate integrity. The specific provisions necessary to achieve that end vary widely from contractor to contractor, but an effective code must state explicitly that you are committed to complying with all procurement laws and regulations and to requiring strict compliance by your employees with the policies and procedures included in your compliance program.

Even more fundamentally, the code must provide clear notice that you will immediately *discipline* any employee or officer whose conduct violates applicable laws, regulations, or basic tenets of business integrity. This, coupled with procedures that require prompt reporting of perceived violations and that emphasize your commitment to investigate those violations, will reduce both the likelihood of violations and your potential liability for any improper conduct that does occur.

The code of ethics should be in *writing* and presented in a

---

[3]FAR 31.205-33(d). *See generally* Manos, Government Contract Costs & Pricing 2 § 40.

[4]FAR 31.205-47. *See generally* Manos, Allowability of Legal Costs, Briefing Papers No. 05-5 (Apr. 2005).

§ 4:9 GOVERNMENT CONTRACT COMPLIANCE HANDBOOK

format that both emphasizes its significance and communicates effectively its salient features to every employee. A Sample Code of Business Ethics and Conduct appears as Appendix E to this Handbook.

§ 4:10 Corporate procedures & policies

You must supplement the general ethics code with detailed written policies and procedures that ensure conformance with specific Government requirements and that define acceptable conduct in the workplace. These should include written procedures regarding, for example, time and expense charging, quality assurance reviews, bid and proposal preparation, and dealing with conflicts of interest.

You should draft procedures to cover *all* aspects of your operations and all of your operating units and subsidiaries. While you must tailor specific procedures and guidelines to your individual operating units, you must also ensure that all key areas are addressed in a consistent and effective manner. In most cases, the procedures should be tailored specifically to the activities at each operating unit. The best results are produced when personnel at each unit draft the policies and procedures applicable to that unit based on general, corporate-wide direction. Many contractors require that operating units submit each implementing procedure to a compliance board or officer for review and approval, but in larger corporations with a wide range of specialized activities and products, this may be an overly cumbersome approach.

§ 4:11 Compliance officer

Comprehensive policies and procedures without effective enforcement cannot achieve the desired effect of increased compliance. At the core of any effective compliance program, therefore, is the corporate compliance officer or compliance committee. The compliance officer or committee is responsible for ensuring that the compliance program is aggressively implemented and remains current. The compliance officer should work with management and human resources personnel to institute a comprehensive compliance program that creates an atmosphere enhancing compliance and instilling in your employees the understanding that management takes ethics and compliance seriously.

§ 4:12 Company hotline

One of the primary responsibilities of the compliance officer is designing and maintaining the internal "hotline" program for reporting suspected misconduct. You should implement a hotline program and make clear that it applies to every employee. The Government views the hotline as a vital component of a successful compliance program. Your commitment to establishing and maintaining a hotline, therefore, must be both clear and effective.

The company hotline program should include an institutionalized mechanism for *memorializing all calls or e-mails* to the hotline. You should delegate responsibility to the compliance officer to receive, document, and act on any allegations or reports of misconduct by employees. Many contractors designate a member of the law department to function as the compliance officer so that information will be protected from disclosure under the attorney-client privilege. You should note, however, that the involvement of an attorney will not necessarily protect all materials from disclosure under the privilege. In most cases, an employee using the "hotline" neither seeks legal counsel nor views the compliance officer as his lawyer. Thus, hotline information may not be privileged.

You should *publicize* the hotline widely as an effective alternative to normal reporting channels. Would-be "whistle-blowers" who fear retaliation are often reluctant to use normal channels to report suspected misconduct. An effective internal hotline can, therefore, act as an "early warning system" that violations are occurring and give you the opportunity to take steps to minimize the damage. To encourage employees to use your corporate hotline, calls or e-mails to the hotline must be completely anonymous. You should make certain, however, that you do not discourage, or appear to discourage, employees from reporting to a Government hotline as an alternative to the corporate hotline.

Further, you should integrate specific reporting requirements in your internal hotline procedures. For example, if you hold classified defense contracts, the *National Industrial Security Program Operating Manual* and the FAR and DFARS require that you prominently display posters that provide information on the DOD Inspector General Hotline. (See Appendix F.)[1]

§ 4:13 Audits & investigations

For an internal reporting mechanism to be effective, you must have in place procedures that ensure you will *thoroughly investi-*

[Section 4:12]

[1]DOD 5220.22-M; FAR 52.204-2; DFARS 203.7002, 252.203-7002. *See generally* Dover, Mergers & Acquisitions—Special Considerations When Purchasing Government Contractor Entities, Briefing Papers No. 04-8 (July 2004); Burgett & Sturm, Foreign Nationals in U.S. Technology Programs: Complying With Immigration, Export Control, Industrial Security & Other Requirements, Briefing Papers No. 00-3 (Feb. 2000).

§ 4:13   GOVERNMENT CONTRACT COMPLIANCE HANDBOOK

gate every report of misconduct. Your compliance program should, therefore, include detailed internal audit and investigation policies and procedures that forcefully articulate your intention to investigate every allegation of misconduct and provide resources adequate for completing that task.

The *compliance audit* is the vehicle by which you can best ensure that your corporate practices and procedures conform to federal procurement laws and rules and that your employees adhere to those practices and procedures. (§§ 5:1 et seq. addresses compliance audits in more detail.) Many contractors have established *audit teams*, comprised of outside counsel working in tandem with both corporate and outside accounting personnel, that review internal procedures and systems. Whether conducted by company personnel or outside counsel, your procedures should provide for three distinct audit phases: (1) a *business practice review*, (2) a thorough *document review*, and (3) a fraud, waste, and abuse *report to your management*.

You should conduct a comprehensive audit of the overall control environment in place at all of your operating facilities and subsidiaries that perform Government contracts. The review should focus on detecting and eliminating the occurrence of (a) mischarging of labor hours (see §§ 13:1 et seq.) and defective pricing (see §§ 9:1 et seq.), (b) product substitution (see §§ 15:1 et seq.), (c) improper testing, (d) improper communications with the Government (see §§ 6:1 et seq., 7:1 et seq., 8:1 et seq.), (e) improper contacts with Government personnel (see §§ 6:1 et seq., 7:1 et seq., 8:1 et seq.), (f) false claims (see §§ 1:1 et seq.), and (g) noncompliance with any new legislation.

If misconduct is uncovered during an audit or through a hotline report, your policies and procedures should require a thorough investigation of every allegation commensurate with the severity of the violation. You should have in place detailed procedures regarding employee interviews, investigative reports, and the use of outside counsel for more serious matters.

§ 4:14   Disciplinary action

Compliance procedures are only effective if properly enforced. Disciplinary procedures are necessary both to ensure fair enforcement and to reduce the likelihood of legal action against your company. You should establish a structured framework for disciplining employees who engage in misconduct and effectively communicate to employees that specific disciplinary action will flow from any misconduct.

It is important that you achieve *consistency* between the discipline policies included in the ethics code and the specific procedures implementing those policies. While it is important to erect an effective system of deterrence, it is equally important that the procedures and their application appear *fair* to employees in order to minimize labor conflicts. The disciplinary procedures you implement should be flexible enough to distinguish violations that are merely technical, inadvertent, or the result of negligence from more serious violations. Discipline should be progressive and should take into account the severity and frequency of violations as well as any mitigating circumstances.

§ 4:15 Reporting violations to the government

Once you establish mechanisms for discovering and reporting misconduct, you must develop and implement policies and procedures that focus on reporting that information to the Government. There has been a continuing debate in the Government contractor community as to whether reporting misconduct should be voluntary or mandatory. For contracts where FAR 52.203-13 does not apply (under FAR 52.203-13 contractors must timely report violations or suspected violations to the agency OIG with a copy to the contracting officer). Because many defense contractors are signatories to the Defense Industry Initiative on Business Ethics and Conduct, a program that promotes voluntary disclosure of all procurement-related misconduct, most contractors already have policies in place to disclose violations. The advantages and disadvantages of voluntarily disclosing wrongdoing to the Government are examined in greater detail in §§ 2:1 et seq.

§ 4:16 Cooperating during government investigations

If your disclosure to the Government results in an investigation of your company, or if the Government commences an investigation independently, the Government will view your cooperation during the investigation as an essential indicator of corporate integrity. Many administrative settlement agreements have included onerous provisions requiring contractors to cooperate with, and make disclosures to, the Government. (Settlement agreements are discussed in more detail in §§ 3:1 et seq.) You should, therefore, be prepared, on a case-by-case basis, to cooperate fully with Government investigators. You should adopt polices and procedures that explicitly implement your commitment to cooperate with the Government and satisfy all reasonable investigative requests.

§ 4:17 Education & training

The Government views the communication of compliance information to employees as the most important and effective means for raising compliance awareness. Therefore, you should implement a comprehensive training program for your personnel, particularly in areas where compliance has been neglected in the past. Thereafter, periodic retraining may be necessary to maintain and improve compliance awareness. Your training program should include *practical advice* for specific situations likely to be encountered by your employees.

Your training program must encompass several distinct parts. First, you must establish a training program that relates exclusively to *ethics and integrity*. You must train all your employees about the meaning and specific elements of the ethics code. Second, you must require training for each employee with respect to *particular policies and procedures* in substantive areas relevant to that employee.

Next, you must adequately *disseminate* each element of the compliance program. To ensure effective communication of that message, your chief executive officer should issue a corporate statement of ethical business conduct, followed by a series of corporate bulletins in key areas of compliance. Bulletins are an effective mechanism for ensuring adequate dissemination of specific policies and procedures developed by each operating unit.

To be sure that both the substance of the program and the seriousness of the message are communicated to employees, many contractors have required that employees *certify* that they have reviewed and understand the ethics code and all relevant policies and procedures, and that they have completed the designated training sessions. Documentation of employee training and awareness, whether by certification or other form, should be a routine part of any compliance program.

In some cases, the Government has required that a company make adherence to the company's compliance policies an element of each manager's and supervisor's performance standards.

§ 4:18 Updating

Finally, you should implement a mechanism to ensure continued compliance as requirements change. Even the best conceived compliance program can become ineffective if there is no mechanism for keeping track of *new requirements*.

Many contractors assign the responsibility for following new procurement requirements to the compliance officer. Another approach is to hold periodic compliance workshops that focus on integrating new legislative and regulatory requirements into an evolving compliance program. Supervisory and field personnel should attend formal seminars that explain prohibited conduct and include group discussions of new laws and rules. Well-structured workshops, coupled with creative educational aids, will help ensure continued compliance at your company.

Chapter 5

Conducting a Compliance Audit

I. OVERVIEW
§ 5:1   Scope note

II. PLANNING THE AUDIT
§ 5:2   Forming the audit team
§ 5:3   Establishing the audit's scope
§ 5:4   Developing audit work programs
§ 5:5   Developing audit deliverables

III. PERFORMING THE AUDIT
§ 5:6   Major tasks
§ 5:7   Reviewing existing policies & procedures
§ 5:8   Interviewing personnel
§ 5:9   Testing controls
§ 5:10   Sampling transactions
§ 5:11   Documenting the audit

IV. IMPLEMENTING & REPORTING THE AUDIT RESULTS
§ 5:12   Key steps
§ 5:13   Recommendations for improvement
§ 5:14   Corrective action
§ 5:15   Follow-up
§ 5:16   Reporting audit results to the government

> **KeyCite®:** Cases and other legal materials listed in KeyCite Scope can be researched through the KeyCite service on Westlaw®. Use KeyCite to check citations for form, parallel references, prior and later history, and comprehensive citator information, including citations to other decisions and secondary materials.

I. OVERVIEW

§ 5:1 Scope note

A key factor in the success of any ongoing Government contrac-

§ 5:1 GOVERNMENT CONTRACT COMPLIANCE HANDBOOK

tor compliance program is the periodic compliance audit. The purposes of a compliance audit are to (a) monitor and minimize the level of risk associated with company practices and procedures, (b) ensure that formal and informal company practices and procedures conform with Government procurement laws and regulations, and (c) determine whether employees are properly performing these practices and procedures. The benefits of conducting compliance audits as part of an ongoing compliance program include one or more of the following: (1) strengthened internal control systems, (2) enhanced company image, (3) reduced incidence of civil and criminal prosecution, and (4) reduced Government oversight due to the Government's reliance on compliance audit work performed by the company.

A compliance audit of a company is different from an internal investigation of a company. Investigations are designed to target specific issues and problems. Compliance audits are designed to identify systematically deficiencies in company processes, systems, and procedures and the underlying causes of such problems. Compliance audits takes a proactive approach by reviewing existing compliance systems and processes—the end goal being to prevent problems from occurring in the future by recommending improvements to existing systems and processes. The result of a compliance audit may take two forms: *recommended prospective changes* to processes or procedures if problems are identified or *quantification of past wrongdoing* identified as a result of the audit procedures applied. This chapter briefly examines both the planning and performance of an effective compliance audit and discusses how efficiently to communicate the results of the audit to company management and the Government and how to implement corrective action.

II. PLANNING THE AUDIT

§ 5:2 Forming the audit team

Forming the compliance audit team is the first step in the audit process. There are three issues to consider when forming the audit team: (1) whether to form a *steering committee* to oversee the audit, (2) whether to use *corporate personnel* to perform the audit, and (3) whether to use any *outside consultants* such as accountants or attorneys to assist in the audit process. Each of these issues needs to be carefully considered in light of the size, complexity, and frequency of the audits to be performed. To be successful, an audit must be properly planned and executed by competent personnel with the right skill mix so that existing problems, if any, will be detected and corrective actions put in place.

Steering Committee: The decision whether to appoint a steering committee depends principally on the scope, duration, and complexity of the compliance audit. Normally, a steering committee includes the director of the internal organization responsible for conducting compliance audit activity, the chief in-house counsel responsible for compliance matters, the chief financial officer for the organization, and, if outside consultants are retained, the ranking members of those organizations. Regular meetings of the steering committee should be scheduled to occur throughout the compliance audit to ensure that proper guidance, support, and overall direction are provided to the audit team. Developing a mechanism for interim reporting to the steering committee helps to ensure proper visibility of the audit to the company and real-time monitoring and disclosure of significant audit findings. The steering committee can help the compliance team set expectations regarding the final work product, as well as facilitate the process of implementing the necessary procedural changes resulting from the audit findings.

Company Personnel: Whether to use company personnel to perform the compliance audit involves careful consideration of several issues. First, the audit team must include the proper mix of skills and level of experience to fulfill the audit's objectives. Second, existing workloads and priorities need to be addressed for each member of the audit team. In the short term, an employee's participation in a compliance audit can be very demanding. Third, ensuring the independence of the audit team is essential, especially in smaller organizations. By utilizing personnel from the company's internal audit department or compliance office, the concern for independence can be addressed. Finally, an important consideration in determining the personnel for the audit team is protecting the company's claim of legal privilege regarding audit communications and findings in the event a Government investigation or legal proceeding is commenced related to compliance audit activity or procedures reviewed during the audit.

Outside Consultants: Many companies engage outside consultants (such as legal or accounting professionals) to perform or assist in performing a compliance audit. The advantages of retaining outside consultants include the benefits of specialized expertise, the availability of personnel solely dedicated to a specific project for a limited duration of time, and the participation of independent, objective professionals who may bring a fresh viewpoint to the audit. The disadvantages might include the cost of those services and the lack of familiarity outside consultants may have with the organization. Cost and lack of familiarity are two reasons why it is of the utmost importance when selecting outside consultants to ensure that the consultants have the requisite compliance audit experience and knowledge of the industry.

§ 5:3 Establishing the audit's scope

What areas should be audited and how often they should be audited? The factors to consider in determining the areas to cover in a company compliance audit include the size of the organization, the extent of the organization's Government business, the past history of problems, recent internal audit activity, and recent external audit activity (by the Defense Contract Audit Agency (DCAA) or an agency Office of Inspector General (OIG), for example). Audit activity in the industry may help guide the decision of what areas to audit and how frequently to perform the audits. Time and expense reporting, cost allocation, incurred-cost reporting, and cost estimating are examples of areas known to present high compliance risk. Other areas frequently reviewed as part of the compliance audit process include, but are not limited to, compliance with contractual terms and provisions, Cost Accounting Standards compliance, billing practices and procedures, and contract/proposal pricing practices. Input from the company's internal or external counsel, external accountants, audit committee, and board of directors may also prove helpful in determining where to focus audit efforts.

§ 5:4 Developing audit work programs

Work programs set forth the objectives to be achieved and outline the procedures to be performed in the areas within the scope of the audit. Developing work programs, therefore, is a critical element in planning an effective compliance audit. Work programs should include a sufficient level of detail so that all potential compliance risks are properly addressed for a given audit area and should provide guidance to any individuals who are unfamiliar with the areas under audit.

Several potential sources are available to assist in the preparation of work programs. These include Government sources such as DCAA work programs (defective pricing reviews, labor charging, incurred-cost audits), OIG work plans, and compliance reviews set forth in the Government procurement regulations (like the Department of Defense Contractor Purchasing System Review). Prior audit activity and results should be reviewed, as well as recent internal audit activity and findings, external audit activity and findings, special investigation audit activity, and formal audit reports.

§ 5:5 Developing audit deliverables

In addition to developing detailed work programs for a compliance audit, it is important to outline the expected deliverables resulting from the audit. For example, a common audit deliverable is a matrix of the issues or problem areas identified and their relative risk rating (high, medium, low). The matrix will then drive the prioritization of any corrective actions undertaken as a result of the audit. By establishing the format of deliverables at the outset of the audit, the Steering Committee can properly focus and direct the efforts of the compliance audit team so that unnecessary work is not performed.

III. PERFORMING THE AUDIT

§ 5:6 Major tasks

Performing a compliance audit generally involves five major tasks: (1) reviewing formal written policies and procedures, (2) interviewing personnel to confirm that existing written policies and procedures are adhered to, (3) testing controls, (4) sampling transactions, and (5) documenting the audit work performed. These steps are discussed below.

§ 5:7 Reviewing existing policies & procedures

The first step in performing a compliance audit is to review existing written policies and procedures to determine whether they adequately address compliance issues and to develop an understanding of how the compliance system in a particular area should be functioning. The audit team should pay particular attention to control features built into the system, the independence of interrelated functions, and system checks and balances. This initial step in the audit process should also provide the necessary background information to proceed to the next phase of the audit process, conducting effective interviews of key personnel in the area under review.

§ 5:8 Interviewing personnel

On completion of the review of the formal written policies and procedures, the next step is to interview company personnel to confirm that the compliance policies and procedures in place are functioning as they have been designed. Interviews also provide more detailed background information on transactions that may not be described in the particular policies or procedures themselves. Interview questions should be structured to determine what informal policies and procedures exist and are followed in addition to the written procedures. It is often found that, although formal written compliance policies and procedures are in place, over time the actual day-to-day operations have strayed from the established procedures. A detailed understanding of compliance system controls will permit the auditor to document and evaluate system flows and controls.

§ 5:9 Testing controls

The objective of the testing controls phase is to ensure that existing compliance safeguards are functioning as intended. Testing controls and procedures, often referred to as compliance testing, involves auditing specific transactions within the system to determine whether each of the specific controls and procedures functions properly to mitigate the risk of noncompliance. Compliance testing provides evidence of specific system strengths and weaknesses. Often, sampling techniques are employed to facilitate the controls testing.

§ 5:10 Sampling transactions

Sampling transactions is a means to accomplish the compliance testing element discussed above. Attribute sampling is the normal sampling method employed and involves defining what an acceptable error rate should be (for example, lack of an independent review and approval of a labor transfer) and then testing a sample of transactions for the specified attributes to determine whether the acceptable error rate has been achieved. Monetary Unit Sampling (MUS) is a sampling technique often used when the objective of the testing is to quantify the magnitude of an effort identified as a result of the compliance testing. MUS allows you to project the error rate on the total population by sampling a statistically valid, but typically limited, number of transactions.

§ 5:11 Documenting the audit

Documentation of the compliance audit normally involves process flows, system write-ups, tests of transactions, and evaluation of compliance procedures. Process flows depict procedures and controls in a simple, easy-to-understand presentation. System write-ups supplement process flows by providing a narrative description of procedures and controls. Tests of transactions provide evidence as to the actual operation of existing controls and are an effective ingredient in documenting the key aspects of a compliance system.

Clear and complete documentation is essential for proper evaluation of compliance and for reporting identified strengths and weaknesses effectively. Documentation provides a trail to audit findings and conclusions once the audit is completed. In the event of later Government review, documented evidence of compliance system effectiveness presents a more compelling argument for reduced Government oversight than unsupported compliance audit reports.

IV. IMPLEMENTING & REPORTING THE AUDIT RESULTS

§ 5:12 Key steps

Once you have completed the compliance audit work, problems identified during the course of the audit need to be communicated to management in an effective manner and resolved, if necessary. Typically, this involves four steps: (1) developing recommendations for improvement, (2) developing a corrective action plan to implement the audit recommendations, (3) developing follow-up mechanisms to verify that audit recommendations have been implemented to correct previously identified problems, and (4) reporting the results to the Government, if necessary.

§ 5:13 Recommendations for improvement

The principal byproduct of a compliance audit is recommendations to enhance existing compliance systems. Recommendations are normally developed from the results of the personnel interviews conducted and testing performed. Recommendations should address noncompliance with Government contract laws and regulations or other compliance control weaknesses and should include business process improvements as well.

Each recommendation should contain a description of the problem and why it presents a compliance or business risk and an evaluation of the current or potential impact of failing to implement corrective action. Each recommendation should also receive a priority ranking for management attention (low, medium, high) and identify the individual who will be responsible for implementing the corrective action and the timetable in which to do so.

§ 5:14 Corrective action

A corrective action plan sets forth specific measures that management or company personnel must take or analysis they must perform to implement audit recommendations successfully. These plans should also suggest a schedule or timetable of dates when the recommendations should be implemented. Certain audit recommendations may involve significant changes to existing business practices or involve alternative courses of action to be considered by management. Successful implementation of audit recommendations involves the review and integration of suggested changes into existing practices. Normally, one individual is responsible for the implementation plan, ensuring each corrective action is put into place in the timeframe established.

§ 5:15 Follow-up

A compliance audit is not truly complete until each audit rec-

§ 5:15   GOVERNMENT CONTRACT COMPLIANCE HANDBOOK

ommendation has been properly addressed. The steering committee should establish a date when follow-up work on the recommendations is to be completed. The follow-up work on the audit recommendations should confirm that recommended actions (or alternative courses of action) were implemented and, if not, why not. In all cases, the results of the follow-up work should be documented. The suggested timeframe for the follow-up review is three to six months after the recommendations were scheduled to be implemented.

§ 5:16   Reporting audit results to the government

Whether to report the results of a compliance audit to the Government is a sensitive issue. Relationships between contractors and Government personnel vary widely, and each situation should be treated based on its own merits. However, it is advantageous to have established policies in place regarding the disclosure of identified improper practices to the Government *before* commencing any compliance audit to ensure that the decision to disclose is not dependent on the audit's results. At a minimum, internal or external counsel should be consulted before disclosing any results to the Government.

Some contractors may be required—as the result of a prior administrative settlement with the Government, for example—to report the results of compliance audits to the Government. A contractor may also wish to demonstrate to the Government the effectiveness of the company's self-governance program and existing or newly established controls. Whether the contractor decides to disclose the audit results to the Government or not, well-documented audit workpapers will assist the company in presenting and defending audit findings to the Government.

DCAA may require access to defense contractor internal audit reports.[1] Such access is limited to evaluating contractor internal controls and business system reliability. DCAA auditors are not permitted to include the internal audit reports in their workpapers; auditors with a need to know are given read-only access to the internal audits.

Cases & Commentary: Contractors must keep in mind that voluntary disclosure programs are not amnesty or immunity programs. There is a split in authority as to whether the "voluntary disclosure" of wrongdoing amounts to a "public disclosure"

[Section 5:16]

[1]*See* DCAA Memorandum for Regional Directors, "Updated Audit Guidance on Access to Contractor Internal Audit Reports" (13-PPS-007(R)) (Apr. 23, 2013), providing guidance on implementation of § 832 of the National Defense Authorization Act for FY 2013, Pub. L. 112-239 (Jan. 2, 2013).

§ 5:16 CONDUCTING A COMPLIANCE AUDIT

within the meaning of 31 U.S.C.A. § 3730(e) which would bar a *qui tam* action unless the relator was the "original source" of the information.[2]

---

[2]*See U.S. ex rel. Lockhart v. General Dynamics Corp.*, 529 F. Supp. 2d 1335 (N.D. Fla. 2007), *U.S. ex rel. Rost v. Pfizer, Inc.*, 507 F.3d 720 (1st Cir. 2007) (qui tam actions brought after contractors had made voluntary disclosures to the Government of possible wrongdoing); and *U.S. ex rel. Cox v. Smith & Nephew, Inc.*, 749 F.Supp.2d 773 (W.D.Tenn. 2010) (qui tam action after contractor voluntarily disclosed supplying products from a non-designated country in violation of Trade Agreements Act). *But see U.S. ex rel. Fowler v. Caremark RX, L.L.C.*, 46 F.3d 730 (7th Cir. 2007) (disclosure of information to U.S. Attorney's office during an investigation of company's business practices constitutes a public disclosure).

Part II
OBTAINING GOVERNMENT CONTRACTS
Chapter 6
Handling Procurement Information

I. OVERVIEW
§ 6:1   Scope note

II. PROCUREMENT INTEGRITY ACT & RULES
A. BASIC PROHIBITIONS
§ 6:2   Generally
§ 6:3   Restrictions on disclosing procurement information
§ 6:4   Restrictions on obtaining procurement information
§ 6:5   Restrictions on employment contacts
§ 6:6   Prohibition on official's acceptance of compensation

B. EFFECTS OF VIOLATIONS
§ 6:7   Criminal penalties
§ 6:8   Civil Penalties
§ 6:9   Administrative penalties
§ 6:10 Restrictions on procurement protests

C. FREQUENTLY ASKED QUESTIONS
§ 6:11 Questions & answers

III. IMPROPER ACCESS TO GOVERNMENT PROPERTY & INFORMATION
§ 6:12 Theft of government property statute
§ 6:13 Espionage statutes

IV. HOW TO RECOGNIZE THE PROBLEM
§ 6:14 Generally
§ 6:15 Examples

V. COMPLIANCE INITIATIVES
§ 6:16 Generally

§ 6:17   Establish policies & procedures
§ 6:18   Educate your employees
§ 6:19   Establish a training program
§ 6:20   Recommendations

> **KeyCite®:** Cases and other legal materials listed in KeyCite Scope can be researched through the KeyCite service on Westlaw®. Use KeyCite to check citations for form, parallel references, prior and later history, and comprehensive citator information, including citations to other decisions and secondary materials.

I. OVERVIEW

§ 6:1 Scope note

The Government has available to it statutes and regulations that are intended to restrict the use and dissemination of procurement-related information by public officials and their contractor counterparts. The most important of these laws—the Procurement Integrity Act—represents Congress' effort to restore and maintain the public's confidence in the integrity of the federal procurement system. This chapter examines the Procurement Integrity Act's restrictions on obtaining or disclosing procurement information, as well as statutes that target the abuse of confidential information. The Federal Acquisition Regulatory Council recently added guidance to alert agency officials that the Procurement Integrity Act does not preempt other government ethics statutes and regulations in this area and to seek advice from agency ethics officials before engaging in certain activities that could have serious consequences including criminal prosecution.[1]

II. PROCUREMENT INTEGRITY ACT & RULES

A. BASIC PROHIBITIONS

§ 6:2 Generally

The Procurement Integrity Act, first enacted in 1988 and substantially revised in 1996, regulates the following activities:[1]

[Section 6:1]

[1]FAR 3.104 (FAR Case 1998-024). FAC 2001-06 (introduced March 20, 2002).

[Section 6:2]

[1]Pub. L. No. 100-679, § 6, 102 Stat. 4055 (1988), codified at 41 U.S.C.A. § 423 and amended by P.L. 104-106, § 4304, 110 Stat. 186 (Feb. 10, 1996). On January 4, 2011, the provisions of the Procurement Integrity Act were recodi-

(1) The *disclosure or receipt* of procurement information before the award of a contract to which the information relates.

(2) *Employment contacts* between Government contractors and current federal agency officials.

(3) The *acceptance of employment* by former federal agency officials from Government contractors.

This chapter addresses only the first issue—the restrictions on the disclosure or receipt of procurement information before the award of a contract. The other two issues, which involve the problems that may occur when contractors and agency officials discuss future employment opportunities, or when former agency officials accept employment from contractors following their Government service, are discussed in Chapter 8, "Conflicts of Interest."

The prohibitions on disclosure or receipt of procurement information are intended to maintain a level playing field in competitive procurements by preventing one potential competitor in a procurement from obtaining an advantage over others by having access to sensitive procurement information. The prohibitions are significant to contractors and to federal officials because they define the extent and content of the parties' exchange of information during the procurement process.

In revising the 1988 Procurement Integrity Act, the 1996 Act and its implementing regulations[2] repealed certain statutes relating to the employment of former agency officials, and streamlined the procurement integrity rules. The Act also eliminated the procurement integrity rules on gratuities (although the criminal penalties for illegal gratuities remain in effect; see §§ 7:1 et seq.) In addition, the Act eliminated the complex *certification* requirements, which required contractors in competitive procurements to certify that they are familiar with the Act's requirements and are not aware of any violations of those provisions. To comply with this requirement, contractors had to maintain and update procurement integrity certificates for each employee who was personally and substantially involved in the procurement process. Under the Act, contractors are no longer required to maintain and update individual certificates. Instead, contractors will only be required, under penalty of perjury, to "document" their compliance with the Procurement Integrity Act.

§ 6:3 Restrictions on disclosing procurement information

The Procurement Integrity Act prohibits a "person" from "knowingly" disclosing "contractor bid or proposal information" or

---

fied at 41 U.S.C.A. §§ 2101 to 2107 by Pub. Law 11-350, 124 Stat. 3726.

[2]62 Fed. Reg. 224 (Jan. 2, 1997) (amending FAR section. 3.104).

§ 6:3   GOVERNMENT CONTRACT COMPLIANCE HANDBOOK

"source selection information" before the award of a federal agency procurement contract to which the information relates.[1] The "person" to whom the disclosure restriction applies is defined as one who is a present or former U.S. official, or one acting on his or her behalf, or one who is advising the Government with respect to a federal agency procurement and who, by virtue of that office, has or had access to contractor bid or proposal information or source selection information.[2] A "Federal agency procurement" is defined as an acquisition using *competitive* procedures.[3] The information protected from disclosure is also defined. "Contractor bid or proposal information" is information submitted to a federal agency in connection with a bid or proposal, including cost or pricing data, indirect costs and direct labor rates, proprietary information, and other information marked by the contractor as "contractor bid or proposal information." "Source selection information" is information not previously made available to the public that is prepared for use by a federal agency in evaluating a bid or proposal, such as bid or proposal prices, source selection plans, technical evaluation plans and the results of technical evaluations or proposals, cost or price evaluations of proposals,

---

[Section 6:3]

[1]41 U.S.C.A. § 2102(a). *In East West, Inc.*, B-400432.7, B- 400325.7, B-400325.8, 2010 CPD 187 (Comp. Gen. 2010), the contract specialist advised an offeror that it had been selected for award, although no public announcement had been made and contract award was being withheld pending receipt of the required EEO clearance from the Department of Labor. GAO found that the notification did not constitute "source selection information" and that in any case "the protester has not shown that it suffered any prejudice—prejudice being an essential element of every viable protest—as a result of Integrity's having received notification of its selection several weeks prior to other offerors being notified." *See also, Assessment and Training Solutions Consulting Corp. v. U.S.*, 92 Fed.Cl. 722 (2010) (the protester contended that the Government had released data concerning the identity of its employees to competitors for a follow-on contract for medical training services at Ft. Bragg in violation of the Procurement Integrity Act. The court denied the claim finding that the resumes did not contain the names and contact information of the employees. Thus, there was no proof that the names and email addresses used by competitors to contact those employees had ever been "submitted to a Federal agency as part of or in connection with a bid or proposal to enter into a Federal agency procurement contract.").

[2]41 U.S.C.A. § 2102(a). GAO denied the protest of an incumbent contractor, finding the agency properly concluded that agency employee had not violated the Procurement Integrity Act by escorting representatives of a potential competitor on a site visit, which included a brief stop at the office of the protester's on-site manager, and a limited disclosure to the visitors about the firm's incumbent contract staffing. GAO noted that the information disclosed, as described by the protester, did not constitute contractor proposal information, source selection information, or a competition-sensitive trade secret. *Accent Service Company, Inc.*, B-299888, 2007 CPD 169 (Comp. Gen. 2007).

[3]41 U.S.C.A. § 2101(a).

§ 6:3 HANDLING PROCUREMENT INFORMATION

competitive range determinations, rankings of bids or proposals, and reports and evaluations of source selection panels, boards, or advisory councils.[4]

The regulations implementing the Procurement Integrity Act detail the procedures to be followed for protecting procurement information from unauthorized disclosure. The regulations include procedures for marking material as source selection or proprietary information and challenging inappropriate markings.[5]

The accidental disclosure of contractor bid or proposal information or source selection information by an agency to a competitor does not automatically invalidate the award of a contract. *Kemron Environmental Services, Inc., B-299880,* 2007 CPD 176 (Comp. Gen. 2007), involved a solicitation for the award of three contracts for emergency and rapid response services for the removal of hazardous substances. The solicitation called for proposals for fixed hourly rates for each of 15 different labor categories and fixed daily rates for 73 items of equipment. After evaluating Kemron's initial proposal the agency prepared an e-mail which posed questions about the pricing of one of 15 labor categories and seven of 73 pieces of equipment. The agency accidentally sent this e-mail to WRS, one of Kemron's competitors. WRS's treasurer read the e-mail and realized it referred to Kemron. After discussing the matter with WRS's president, the treasurer sent the e-mail back to the agency and destroyed all copies. He advised the agency that he did not remember any specific information in the e-mail. Subsequently, all offerors submitted revised final proposals. WRS's proposal was ranked third and received an award; Kemron was ranked fourth, leading to the subject protest. GAO noted that it would sustain a protest over an agency's refusal to cancel a procurement after the accidental disclosure of sensitive data "only where the protester demonstrates that the recipient of the information received an unfair advantage, or that it was otherwise competitively prejudiced by the disclosure." Here, GAO noted that the agency had only disclosed data for a small fraction

---

[4] 41 U.S.C.A. § 2101(2) and (7). See FAR 3.104-1 and FAR 2.101. In *McKing Consulting Corp. v. U.S.,* 78 Fed. Cl. 715 (2007), the contractor claimed the Department of Health and Human Services had violated the Procurement Integrity Act by publishing a list of dentists it used as consultants on a local university web site and by improperly discussing details of the procurement with a potential offeror after a pre-solicitation notice, but before the issuance of the actual solicitation. The court found that the list of consultants was not "proprietary" because the consultants had volunteered the information to the university two years earlier and thus was not subject to protection under the Procurement Integrity Act. Furthermore, there was no evidence that the agency had improperly provided the other potential offeror with proprietary consultant lists, price lists or any other potentially useful bid information that would amount to a PIA violation. Thus, the court denied the protest.

[5] FAR 3.104-4.

§ 6:3	GOVERNMENT CONTRACT COMPLIANCE HANDBOOK

of the labor and equipment categories covered by the solicitation. It found that in its revised final proposal, WRS had not changed the basic hourly rate for the one labor category and had made only small adjustments in the daily rates for some of the equipment categories that had been identified in the e-mail. GAO concluded that it would have been impossible for WRS to determine Kemron's initial total proposal price based on the limited data that had been disclosed and that it was even more unlikely that WRS would be able to determine how Kemron would revise its price after conducting discussions with the agency. Thus, Kemron had failed to demonstrate WRS had a competitive advantage resulting from the inadvertent disclosure. From a compliance perspective, it is important to note that GAO found that "WRS proceeded appropriately once the disclosure was discovered."[6]

In December 2010 the Air Force announced that due to a clerical error it had inadvertently sent Boeing and EADS the main competitors for the KC-X Tanker refueling program computer discs containing source selection information concerning the other party's Integrated Fleet Aerial Refueling Assessment data. The Air Force stated the information did not contain any pricing information. After conducting an investigation, the Air Force reportedly concluded that after discovering the error, both parties promptly isolated the discs to avoid further dissemination. Apparently neither party formally protested this disclosure and the Air Force subsequently awarded the contract to Boeing.

An agency must have a reasonable basis for the cancellation of a solicitation due to concerns over the possible violation of the Procurement Integrity Act. *Superlative Technologies, Inc.,*

---

[6]*Ocean Ships Inc., B-401526.4,* 2010 CPD 156 (Comp. Gen. 2010) involved the procurement of operation and maintenance services for Lot 1 of a number of supply ships used by the Military Sealift Command for "surge" operations. Prior to conducting discussions, the contracting officer sent an email to each competitor with a list of discussion items. The email sent to one of Ocean's competitors included a file containing Ocean's proposed prices for Lots 2 and 3. Within minutes of receiving the email, the competitor's vice-president, the sole recipient of the email, notified the contracting officer and explained that immediately upon recognizing its content he closed email. At the direction of the contracting officer he then deleted the email and emptied the "trash" folder on his computer. GAO denied the protest, concluding that, [Ocean] asserts that cancellation of the RFP and elimination of [the competitor] are required because of the *"appearance* that the integrity of the procurement process was compromised and unreliable." *** However, as indicated, we will sustain a protest based on an inadvertent disclosure of information only where it is shown to have harmed the protester. It is undisputed that the disclosure of [Ocean's] information was inadvertent, and that the agency and [the competitor] proceeded appropriately once the disclosure was discovered. Since, as discussed above, we find that [Ocean] was not competitively prejudiced by the disclosure, there is no basis for us to sustain the protest and recommend the suggested corrective action.

B-310489, B-310489.2, 2008 CPD 12 (Comp. Gen. 2008) involved a solicitation for technical services for the Department of Justice. SuperTec was the incumbent contractor; ManTech International was its principal competitor. During the course of negotiations, the agency's COTR, who had been involved in the development of the statement of work, advised that prior to the submission of proposals she had had discussions with ManTech regarding the contract requirements, pricing and labor categories and that these discussions may have provided ManTech an unfair advantage. Thereafter, the contracting officer cancelled the solicitation, citing both potential procurement integrity and organizational conflict of interest issues and a concern over a potential protest. Subsequently, the agency reissued the solicitation and eventually awarded a sole-source contract to TMR, an 8(a) concern, whose principal subcontractor was ManTech. GAO concluded that the decision to cancel lacked a reasonable basis because having used the procurement integrity and OCI concerns as a justification for cancellation, the agency did nothing to investigate or resolve those issues before awarding the contract to TMR/ManTech. "In fact," GAO commented, "the events, viewed as a whole, support the protester's allegation that the solicitation was cancelled to, in effect, avoid further review of the issues raised." GAO concluded by recommending the agency rescind the cancellation notice regarding the RFQ, document what consideration it gave to the OCI and Procurement Integrity issues, including determining what information was disclosed to one of the offerors prior to the issuance of the solicitation and whether that offeror should be excluded from the competition, and conduct a new competition under the original RFP if otherwise appropriate. In a subsequent protest, GAO chastised the agency for failing to implement GAO's recommendations and recommended that the agency refrain from awarding any subsequent contract for these services until the agency completed the recommended investigation. *Superlative Technologies, Inc., B-310489.4*, 2008 CPD 123 (Comp. Gen. 2008).

§ 6:4 Restrictions on obtaining procurement information

The Procurement Integrity Act also prohibits a "person" from knowingly obtaining "contractor bid or proposal information or source selection information before the award of a Federal agency procurement contract to which the information relates."[1] The definition of "person" in this part of the Act differs from the definition of "person" used in the nondisclosure provisions (discussed

---

[Section 6:4]
[1]41 U.S.C.A. § 2102(b).

§ 6:4 GOVERNMENT CONTRACT COMPLIANCE HANDBOOK

above) in that it includes persons who are not otherwise connected with the federal agency procurement in question. Specifically, the prohibition applies to any contractor, other business entity, or individual that obtains information even if that person is not participating in the procurement.[2] Neither the Act nor the implementing regulations define a "knowing" violation. In *GEO Group, Inc. v. U.S.*, 100 Fed.Cl. 223 (August 2011), the Court stated that the Procurement Integrity Act's prohibition on obtaining bid and proposal information only includes "present or former federal employees," H. Conf. Rep. No. 104-450, at 969 (1996), 1996 U.S.C.C.A.N. 238, 454.

§ 6:5 Restrictions on employment contacts

The Procurement Integrity Act also contains provisions to minimize and restrict conflicts of interest in the procurement process. First, the Act provides specific procedures that a Government official who is personally and substantially participating in a procurement must follow when he or she receives an *employment offer* from a bidder or offeror. The Government official must report the contact to the agency immediately and must either reject the offer or disqualify him or herself from further participation in the procurement.[1]

§ 6:6 Prohibition on official's acceptance of compensation

Second, the Act prohibits certain officials for one year following their performance of certain duties involving contracts in excess of $10 million from accepting "compensation" from those contractors.[1] These conflict-of-interest restrictions are discussed in greater detail in §§ 8:1 et seq.

B. EFFECTS OF VIOLATIONS

§ 6:7 Criminal penalties

If you, as a competing contractor, knowingly and willfully solicit or obtain, directly or indirectly, bid or proposal information or source selection information from a federal agency official, the Procurement Integrity Act provides criminal penalties of

---

[2]41 U.S.C.A. § 2102(b).

[Section 6:5]
[1]41 U.S.C.A. § 2103(a).

[Section 6:6]
[1]41 U.S.C.A. § 2104(a).

imprisonment for up to five years, fines, or both.[1] However, criminal penalties will be imposed only if the exchange of information (1) was for anything of value or (2) gave anyone a competitive advantage in the award of a contract. You may also be liable under the theft of Government property statute (see § 6:12) and the illegal gratuities statute (see §§ 7:1 et seq.) In addition, any related false statements or false claims carry the risk of additional criminal and civil penalties (see §§ 1:1 et seq.).

For a Government official to be liable for violation of the Procurement Integrity Act, the official must "knowingly" violate the law.[2] This is significant because, for there to be a "knowing" violation, an individual must intend to violate the procurement rules; the individual cannot have a "good faith" belief that he or she is acting in accordance with the statute. Agencies are required to establish procedures for employees to ask questions about the application of the Procurement Integrity Act.

§ 6:8 Civil Penalties

Civil penalties may be imposed for violating the Procurement Integrity Act if the exchange of information (1) was for anything of value or (2) gave anyone a competitive advantage.[1] A person who is shown to have engaged in such actions will be subject to no more than a $50,000 fine for each violation plus twice the amount of compensation he or she received or offered, while an organization will be subject to no more than a $500,000 fine for each violation plus twice the amount of compensation the organization received or offered.

§ 6:9 Administrative penalties

On learning that a contractor or other person has violated the Procurement Integrity Act, an agency may take any one of four actions. First, if no contract has been awarded at that time, the agency may *cancel* the procurement. Second, if a contract has been awarded, the agency may choose to *rescind the contract* if the contractor or one of his or her agents has been convicted of a criminal offense under the Act, or if the head of the agency has determined that the contractor or his or her agent has engaged in such conduct. Third, the agency may initiate *suspension or debarment* proceedings against the contractor. Finally, the agency

---

[Section 6:7]

[1] 41 U.S.C.A. § 2105(a); FAR 3.104-8.

[2] 41 U.S.C.A. § 2104(d); FAR 3.104-8(a).

[Section 6:8]

[1] 41 U.S.C.A. § 2105(b); FAR 3.104-8.

§ 6:9   GOVERNMENT CONTRACT COMPLIANCE HANDBOOK

may initiate an *adverse personnel action* against the agency employee.[1]

The Environmental Protection Agency temporarily suspended IBM Corp. from eligibility for Government contracts in March 2008. The suspension arose from allegations that IBM employees had obtained information from EPA employees concerning its competitor's proposal for a large contract to modernize EPA's financial systems in violation of the PIA. IBM reported that suspension had been lifted after it agreed with EPA to cooperate fully with ongoing investigations by EPA and the U.S. Attorney's office and to conduct an examination of its compliance program and take whatever corrective action was needed.

§ 6:10 Restrictions on procurement protests

The Act prohibits a contractor from raising alleged procurement integrity violations in a protest challenging the conduct of a procurement unless the alleged violation is reported to the agency no later than 14 days after the person first discovered the possible violation.[1] This requirement is intended to reduce the number of protests alleging violations of the Act.

The Procurement Integrity Act and GAO's bid protest regulations require as a condition precedent to a protest that a protester have reported the alleged violation of the PIA to the contracting agency within 14 days after becoming aware of the information or facts giving rise to the alleged violation. Failure to comply with this requirement will lead to dismissal of the protest at GAO. *Orbital Sciences Corporation*, B-400589, B-400589.2, (Comp. Gen. 2008); *Honeywell Technology Solutions, Inc., B-400771, B-400771.2*, 2009 CPD 49 (Comp. Gen. 2009). However, GAO has emphasized an allegation that the hiring of a former Government official constitutes a violation of the PIA is different from an allegation that hiring that individual constitutes a prohibited organizational conflict of interest. The 14-day notice requirement does not apply in the latter case. *Health Net Federal Services, LLC, B-401652.3*, 2009 CPD 220, (Comp. Gen. 2009) ("The focus on prohibited actions [under the PIA] is the very crux of the difference, since allegations dealing with apparent unfair competitive advantages do not necessarily turn on prohibited behavior, and, as noted above, arise without regard to the good faith behavior of all parties"). The COFC likewise emphasized

---

[Section 6:9]

[1]41 U.S.C.A. § 2105(c)(1).

[Section 6:10]

[1]41 U.S.C.A. § 2106; FAR 33.102(f).

HANDLING PROCUREMENT INFORMATION § 6:11

the difference between a PIA and OCI violation in *Jacobs Technology v. U.S.*, 100 Fed.Cl. 198 (August 9, 2011):

> An allegation of a possible PIA violation is a serious accusation and carries a different connotation than a potential OCI. For an OCI, a government contractor, by virtue of its contracts with an agency, may be accused of having access to or knowledge of information that gives it a competitive advantage on a new procurement. In comparison, a possible PIA violation requires the offeror to have *knowingly obtained* information that the agency intended to use in evaluating proposals on the new procurement. Thus, a PIA violation essentially requires an affirmative act by the offeror to obtain source selection information; simply having knowledge is not enough to support a possible PIA violation. A PIA violation also appears to be founded on improper or unlawful conduct. Indeed, an offeror who knowingly obtains information for purposes of achieving a competitive advantage in violation of the PIA may be subject to criminal penalties (i.e., imprisonment or fines) in addition to civil penalties and administrative actions. [footnote omitted.]

The requirement that a contractor first pursue a PIA issue with the agency before filing a GAO protest does not apply to protests that are filed at the U.S. Court of Federal Claims. *McKing Consulting Corp. vs. U.S.*, 78 Fed. Cl. 715 (2007).

C. FREQUENTLY ASKED QUESTIONS

§ 6:11 Questions & answers

Question 1: At what point during the conduct of a procurement do the restrictions on disclosing or obtaining procurement information apply?

Answer 1: The Procurement Integrity Act contains a simple bright-line rule prohibiting unauthorized disclosure or receipt of contractor bid or proposal information or source selection information *before the award of a contract* to which the information relates.[1]

Question 2: What exactly is a "federal agency procurement" and how do I know when there is a separate procurement for purposes of the Procurement Integrity Act?

Answer 2: A federal agency procurement is the acquisition (by using competitive procedures and awarding a contract) by a federal agency of goods or services (including construction) from nonfederal sources using appropriated funds.[2] For broad agency announcements and small business innovation research programs, each proposal received by an agency constitutes a sepa-

---

[Section 6:11]

[1] FAR 3.104-3(a)(1).

[2] FAR 3.104-1.

§ 6:11 GOVERNMENT CONTRACT COMPLIANCE HANDBOOK

rate procurement for purposes of the Act. Sole-source procurements and contract modifications are *not* federal agency procurements for the purposes of the Act.

Question 3: What constitutes "contractor bid or proposal information" under the Act?

Answer 3: Any of the following types of information submitted to a federal agency as part of a bid or proposal to enter into a federal agency contract, if that information has not been previously disclosed to the public, will be considered "contractor bid or proposal information" under the Act: (a) cost or pricing data, (b) indirect costs and direct labor rates, (c) proprietary information about manufacturing processes, operations, or techniques marked by the contractor in accordance with applicable law or regulation, or (d) information marked by the contractor as "contractor bid or proposal information" in accordance with applicable law or regulation.[3]

Question 4: What is "source selection information" under the Act?

Answer 4: "Source selection information" is any information prepared for use by a federal agency for the purpose of evaluating a bid or proposal to enter into a federal contract, if that information has not been previously made available to the public or disclosed publicly. Some examples are listed below:[4]

(a) Bid prices submitted in response to a federal agency invitation for bids, or lists of those bid prices before the bid opening.

(b) Proposed costs or prices submitted in response to a federal agency solicitation, or lists of those proposed costs or prices.

(c) Source selection plans.

(d) Technical evaluation plans and evaluations of proposals.

(e) Cost or price evaluations of proposals.

(f) Competitive range determinations that identify proposals that have a reasonable chance of being selected for award of a contract.

(g) Rankings of bids, proposals, or competitors.

(h) Reports and evaluations of source selection panels, boards, or advisory councils.

(i) Other information marked as "SOURCE SELECTION INFORMATION."

Question 5: Some large companies' internal structures include business units or operating divisions without separate legal identities. In practice, however, these divisions often operate in-

---

[3] FAR 3.104-1.
[4] 41 U.S.C.A. § 2102; FAR 2.101.

HANDLING PROCUREMENT INFORMATION § 6:11

dependently of each other. If one division is competing for a procurement, does one division of the company violate the Procurement Integrity Act by obtaining contractor bid or proposal information from another division?

Answer 5: The answer to this question will probably depend on whether the divisions operate independently of each other and in fact compete with each other for similar contracts. Practically speaking, this should not be a problem because the Procurement Integrity Act now states that the prohibitions do not restrict a "contractor from disclosing its own bid or proposal information or the recipient from receiving that information."[5] Therefore, a company could waive the prohibition even if one division receives bid and proposal information from the other division. Nevertheless, contractors should be aware that such conduct could violate antitrust and other anti-competition statutes or the independent pricing requirement and collusive bidding restrictions of federal solicitations.

Question 6: Do contractors still need to maintain and update individual procurement integrity certifications for all employees that are personally and substantially involved in the preparation of proposals?

Answer 6: No. The 1996 Act eliminated the need for procurement integrity certification in procurements after January 1, 1997.

Question 7: Does the Procurement Integrity Act prohibit contractors that are not participating in a particular procurement from obtaining source selection or contractor bid and proposal information about competitors that are participating in the procurement?

Answer 7: Yes. The Procurement Integrity Act prohibits a "person" from knowingly obtaining source selection or contractor bid and proposal information even if that person is not participating in the procurement.[6]

Question 8: Is it a violation of the Procurement Integrity Act for a contractor to solicit source selection or bid and proposal information if the contractor is unsuccessful in obtaining such information?

Answer 8: No. Under the Procurement Integrity Act, it is not a violation to solicit source selection or bid and proposal information if the information is not obtained.

---

[5]41 U.S.C.A. § 2107(2).
[6]41 U.S.C.A. § 2102(b).

III. IMPROPER ACCESS TO GOVERNMENT PROPERTY & INFORMATION

§ 6:12 Theft of government property statute

The theft of Government property statute penalizes the theft, conversion, and conveyance of Government property.[1] To prove this criminal offense, the Government must show that:

(1) You embezzled, stole, purloined, or knowingly converted to your use or the use of another, *or* you, without authority, sold, conveyed or disposed of;

(2) Any record, voucher, money, or thing of value of the United States, or any property made or being made under contract for the United States.

The statute also penalizes receipt, concealment, or retention with the intent to convert property that you knew was embezzled, stolen, purloined, or converted, with a fine, imprisonment of 10 years, or both, if the aggregate value of the stolen property is $1,000 or greater, but not more than one year if the value is below that threshold.[2] For a felony conviction, the Government must show that the thing converted, conveyed, or received had a value (face, par, or market value) in excess of $100.

If you stole a laptop computer from a Government employee's desk, for example, you might be liable under the statute. If you stole material at your plant that was purchased for use in performing a Government contract, you might also be liable.

What is less obvious, but probably more important for you to know, is that this statute extends to theft and conveyance of Government documents and information. The Government has prosecuted several cases under the theft of Government property statute where the "thing of value" that was stolen or received was procurement information or documents containing information.

For example, in the "Operation Ill Wind" Pentagon probe in the 1980s, Government contractors' consultants bribed Government officials to release procurement information, which the consultants then provided to the contractors. In "Operation Uncover" in the late 1980s, contractors' marketing executives exchanged Defense Department classified budgeting and planning documents, which had apparently been leaked by a Government official. These cases raised questions of whether "information," such as bid and budgeting information, can be a "thing of value" under the statute, and under what circumstances disclosure and

---

[Section 6:12]

[1]18 U.S.C.A. § 641.
[2]18 U.S.C.A. § 641.

§ 6:12

use of Government documents or information is "without authority."

Several appellate decisions have answered these questions. In one case,[3] the U.S. Court of Appeals for the Fourth Circuit held that conversion and conveyance of Government information can indeed violate the theft of Government property statute. Subsequently, the same court made clear that even if the Government does not have sole interest in a document or sole knowledge of the information, as is the case with bid information, the amount of a confidential, competitive bid is still a "thing of value" under the statute.[4] In another case, the Fourth Circuit held that for a conveyance of Government information to be "without authority," the disclosure need not be prohibited by specific published regulations; other categories of evidence (such as unpublished regulations and legends on the documents) are sufficient to show that the disclosure was without authority and that the defendant knew as much.[5] The District of Columbia Circuit has held that computer memory and usage time are Government property covered by the statute, but only if the defendant interferes with their legitimate use.[6] Subsequently, courts have found misprinted stamps that were useless to be a "thing of value."[7]

Thefts from organizations or governments receiving federal financial assistance can be prosecuted only under the theft of Government property statute if the stolen property still belonged to the United States when it was stolen. Another statute, 18 U.S.C.A. § 666, extends the Federal Government's reach in prosecuting theft, fraud, and bribery involving federal funds disbursed to private organizations or state and local governments pursuant to a federal program. Through this statute, Congress intended to protect "the integrity of the vast sums of money distributed through Federal programs from theft, fraud, and undue influence by bribery."[8]

---

[3]*See U.S. v. Fowler*, 932 F.2d 306 (4th Cir. 1991).

[4]*See U.S. v. Matzkin*, 14 F.3d 1014 (4th Cir. 1994).

[5]*See U.S. v. McAusland*, 979 F.2d 970 (4th Cir. 1992).

[6]*See U.S. v. Collins*, 56 F.3d 1416 (D.C. Cir. 1995).

[7]*U.S. v. Robie*, 166 F.3d 444 (2d Cir. 1999).

[8]S. Rep. No. 98-225, reprinted in 1984 U.S. Code Cong. & Admin. News 3182, 3510 to 3511.

§ 6:13 Espionage statutes

The criminal espionage statutes[1] restrict the taking and dissemination of information relating to the national defense. Most of the provisions relate to classic espionage situations; other sections of the statutes deal with situations in which persons with authorized access to national security information in effect betray their trust.[2] For example, one section prohibits those lawfully in possession of, or with access to, information relating to the national defense from communicating the information to any person not entitled to receive it when the possessor has reason to believe that the information could be used to injure the United States or to the advantage of any foreign nation.[3] Another section, which governs disclosure of classified information, includes a forfeiture provision under which a defendant forfeits to the United States any property derived from or used to commit a violation under this section.[4]

Although cases under these statutes are rare and difficult for the Government to prove, any contractor with a *security clearance* should be aware of these provisions. The Government takes the position that even a person with an appropriate security clearance is in unauthorized possession of a document if access to that document was *not necessary* to the performance of the person's official duties. The statute effectively prohibits those with security clearances from disseminating classified documents to other people with security clearances when the dissemination is not pursuant to the performance of official duties.

The espionage statutes also impose penalties on those who, through gross negligence, allow information relating to the national defense to be lost, stolen, abstracted, or destroyed, and who, knowing that such information has been lost, stolen, abstracted, or destroyed, fail to report its loss.[5]

IV. HOW TO RECOGNIZE THE PROBLEM

§ 6:14 Generally

Every company's ability to compete successfully depends on well-informed business decisions. In a competitive business environment, contractors obviously seek to obtain as much infor-

---

[Section 6:13]

[1] 18 U.S.C.A. §§ 792 et. seq.
[2] 18 U.S.C.A. § 793(d), (f).
[3] 18 U.S.C.A. § 793(d).
[4] 18 U.S.C.A. § 798(d)(1).
[5] 18 U.S.C.A. § 793(f).

mation as possible about their competitors to maintain a competitive "edge." Unfortunately, it is not always easy to determine where permissible research and marketing efforts end and improper intelligence activities begin. Moreover, information collection activities that are perfectly routine in a commercial setting may well violate the law in a federal procurement.

§ 6:15 Examples

Set forth below are some examples of where trouble may start for your company if you obtain or handle procurement-related information improperly.

Unsolicited source selection information: Assume you are the incumbent contractor competing for a follow-on contract involving facility maintenance services at an Army base. While performing the current contract, you receive an e-mail message with a Government cost estimate attached. You use the Government cost estimate as a guide in preparing your cost proposal. You submit your proposal to the Government without notifying the Contracting Officer that you have seen the Government cost estimate. Have you violated the Procurement Integrity Act?

Under the Procurement Integrity Act, the Government cost estimate is considered source selection information, which is protected under the statute. In addition, the statute broadens the prohibition to include obtaining source selection information regardless of the source of that information. However, whether your conduct violates the Act will depend on whether you actively solicited the information or inadvertently obtained it. In this situation, the best course is to notify the Contracting Officer on receiving the cost estimate information so that the Contracting Officer can level the playing field by releasing the cost estimate information to other competitors.[1]

Attempts to obtain proprietary information from a competitor's employee: You are the company project manager on a procurement involving administrative support services at a military installation. You are acquainted with an employee of the incumbent contractor (also competing for the follow-on award) whom you know to be dissatisfied with her current job. You approach the employee and suggest that there could be a position available for her with your organization. You also suggest that you would like to see her employer's proposal, as well as a list of employees and the salary structure. The competitor's employee begins compilation of the information, but another employee

---

[Section 6:15]

[1]*See*, IGT, Inc., Comp. Gen. Dec. B-271823, 96-2 CPD 51.

§ 6:15   Government Contract Compliance Handbook

learns of the activities and reports them to the incumbent's manager. The manager investigates and the employee admits to her supervisors that you requested the information.

Your competitor complains to Government officials who, in turn, conduct their own investigation. They are unable to determine whether you actually received any confidential information belonging to your competitor, but they satisfy themselves that you were at least attempting to obtain such information through a disgruntled employee.

Have you jeopardized your company's opportunity to continue to compete for the procurement at issue even though you did not actually receive any information and did not ask any Government official for it?

You certainly have. Under substantially similar facts, the U.S. Court of Federal Claims upheld a Contracting Officer's decision to disqualify a contractor that sought to obtain confidential business information from the disgruntled employee of a competitor. In that case, the Contracting Officer based his decision to disqualify the contractor on an appearance of impropriety in the integrity of the procurement process. The court rejected the disqualified company's arguments that the alleged conduct did not expressly violate any procurement rule or regulation.[2] However, in another case, the receipt of employee and compensation information was found not to violate the Procurement Integrity Act because it was not "procurement sensitive" information.[3]

Not only will such conduct jeopardize your company's opportunity to continue to compete for the procurement, but such conduct may subject your company and the individual involved to civil, administrative, and criminal penalties. The Procurement Integrity Act applies to all competitor or proposal information received before the award of a contract, not just to information received from a Government source.

Offers of gratuities for Government procurement information: Your company is demonstrating its newest personal computer at a trade show. You invite two Air Force computer specialists to see a demonstration and give them copies of a new commercial software program the computer is running. On the specialists' arrival, with no encouragement from you, they provide you with the Air Force's previously undisclosed planning paper regarding its personal computer needs over the next several years. You turn over the documents to a marketing person in your office. Do you face potential liability under the Procurement Integrity Act?

---

[2]*Compliance Corp. v. U.S.*, 22 Cl. Ct. 193 (1990), aff'd, 960 F.2d 157 (Fed. Cir. 1992).

[3]*Synetics, Inc. v. U.S.*, 45 Fed. Cl. 1, 14 (1999).

No. The Air Force planning information does not appear to fall within the definition of "source selection information" contained in the Act, and there are no gratuities provisions in the Act. However, the Government could still proceed against you on other grounds. Although the Procurement Integrity Act does not refer to gratuities, the free software may still constitute an illegal gratuity under federal criminal laws (see §§ 7:1 et seq.). In addition, your acceptance of the Air Force planning paper and its use by others in your company may expose both you and your company to liability under the theft of Government property statute.

Receipt of Government property with intent to convert: You were mistakenly copied on an e-mail message from a Government Contracting Officer with an attached internal memorandum concerning source selection issues. You use the memorandum in formulating a contract bid. You may be liable for receipt of stolen Government property with the intent to convert it to your own use in violation of the theft of Government property statute.

Transmission of classified information to unauthorized person: You are working on a "top secret" missile system. You have a friend who is a university engineering professor with a "top secret" clearance. You give your friend "top secret" documents that you obtained at work because he is interested in the missile system from an academic point of view. You could be liable for violations of the espionage statutes because your friend, while cleared, did not have a "need to know" the information and therefore was not entitled to receive it. You might also be liable under the theft of Government property statute.

Grossly negligent handling of national defense information: You are an engineer for a defense contractor with a "top secret" security clearance. In violation of classified document regulations, you take a secret document concerning weapons systems home over the weekend to review. The next week, you get a call from your cousin, who spent the weekend at your house. Your cousin tells you that he and others to whom he gave notes about the document found the document exceedingly interesting. You fail to report that your cousin appears to have abstracted the document. You may be liable for breach of the espionage statute that penalizes those who, in lawful possession of a document relating to the national defense, allow the document to be abstracted, or knowing that it has been abstracted, fail to make the proper report.

V. COMPLIANCE INITIATIVES

§ 6:16 Generally

It is not easy to know when you and your employees are

§ 6:16   GOVERNMENT CONTRACT COMPLIANCE HANDBOOK

entitled to take possession of or share specific procurement or other Government information. A Government official has said that companies and individuals should have no trouble complying with the laws in this area because they will know intuitively what kind of information to avoid. Although this may be an overly optimistic evaluation, this comment suggests that the Government expects your employees to become highly sensitized to the issue of handling procurement information properly. We have compiled suggestions for actions that your company can take to help ensure that your employees will not inadvertently violate relevant statutes and rules.

§ 6:17   Establish policies & procedures

Your company should have a written policy expressing the company's commitment to the requirements of the Procurement Integrity Act and other statutes protecting procurement information. This policy should be compatible with your other policies on offering illegal gratuities, hiring former Government employees, and obtaining and using competitors' proprietary information. The policy should make clear that prohibited activities apply to *all* federal procurements.

§ 6:18   Educate your employees

First, you must emphasize to your employees that they must act with caution when they encounter opportunities to obtain procurement-related information *through any unofficial channels*. In such situations, before the employees take possession of the information, they must determine whether they are supposed to be receiving the type of information at issue and whether they will be receiving it through the appropriate process. When in doubt, your employees should seek advice from your legal or compliance offices.

Second, you should thoroughly educate your employees concerning the *categories of information* that the Government has expressly labeled as "*off limits*" to contractors and their employees and agents. The Procurement Integrity Act is complex and requires careful reading and thought. To avoid compliance problems in this area, you must make an effort to inform your employees of the various types of information that they are prohibited from obtaining.

Third, your employees must understand the basic prohibition against offering or giving *gratuities* to Government officials. Although the Procurement Integrity Act no longer specifically governs the offering of gratuities, you and your employees are still prohibited from offering illegal gratuities under the federal

HANDLING PROCUREMENT INFORMATION § 6:19

criminal code and the Joint Ethics Regulation.[1]

Finally, your employees must understand that it is dangerous for them to engage in *discussions* with Government personnel regarding *future employment opportunities* with your company. The safest way to handle this issue is for your employees to decline all discussions with Government personnel regarding employment and to refer all such inquiries from Government personnel to an individual or department in your company designated to handle such matters.

§ 6:19 Establish a training program

The first step in assuring that your employees understand the rules regarding your receipt, use, or further dissemination of procurement-related information is to identify the employees who are involved, or will likely become involved, in your company's Government contract activities. You should provide training to such persons to cover all the statutory and regulatory requirements. Err on the side of inclusion rather than exclusion in choosing those whom you designate for training.

You should establish a training program format, together with written materials provided to each employee, which will allow you to document the specific efforts your company has made to instruct your employees in this area and the subjects covered. At a minimum, *written materials* provided to your employees should include the following items:

    (a) The text of the Procurement Integrity Act and the procurement integrity regulations, and definitions of key phrases and concepts associated with the statute and regulations.

    (b) The text of the theft of Government property statute and explanatory materials.

    (c) The text of the illegal gratuities statute and explanatory materials.

Your training materials should also identify the individuals within your company who can answer questions relating to the receipt or dissemination of procurement-related documents.

You should develop a system to ensure that all new employees who may be involved in the preparation of bids or proposals receive procurement integrity training so that they understand the Procurement Integrity Act and will comply with its requirements and prohibitions.

Develop a written record identifying each employee, agent, or

---

[Section 6:18]

[1] 5 C.F.R. §§ 2635.202 et. seq.

§ 6:19   Government Contract Compliance Handbook

consultant who you regard as involved in the federal agency procurements for which you are competing. You must be able to *cross-match* these individuals with those known to have received training.

Finally, you should *update* your training program as new developments in the law occur.

§ 6:20 Recommendations

(a) *Identify employees* who are or will become involved in your company's efforts to secure business from the Federal Government. Establish a *training program* for the identified employees that include information on the Procurement Integrity Act and other requirements that pertain to procurement-related and other official Government documents.

(b) *Keep records* of the employees that you have trained and the course materials you have used.

(c) Make clear, through a *written policy*, that your company strictly prohibits the unauthorized receipt of source selection information and competitors' bid or proposal information.

(d) Make known the identity of persons within the company who can *answer questions* regarding specific issues in this difficult area of Government contract compliance.

Chapter 7

Influencing Government Actions

I. OVERVIEW
§ 7:1   Scope note

II. BRIBERY & ILLEGAL GRATUITIES
A. STATUTORY FRAMEWORK
§ 7:2   Generally
§ 7:3   Bribery
§ 7:4   Illegal gratuities

B. FREQUENTLY ASKED QUESTIONS
§ 7:5   Questions & answers

C. HOW TO RECOGNIZE THE PROBLEM
§ 7:6   Generally
§ 7:7   Examples

D. COMPLIANCE INITIATIVES
§ 7:8   Generally
§ 7:9   Establish policies & procedures
§ 7:10   Monitor employees' activities
§ 7:11   Require government employees to pay
§ 7:12   Recommendations

III. LOBBYING RESTRICTIONS
A. STATUTORY FRAMEWORK
§ 7:13   Generally
§ 7:14   Byrd Amendment
§ 7:15   Lobbying Disclosure Act

B. FREQUENTLY ASKED QUESTIONS
§ 7:16   Questions & answers

C. HOW TO RECOGNIZE THE PROBLEM
§ 7:17   Generally

§ 7:18   Examples

D. COMPLIANCE INITIATIVES

§ 7:19   Generally
§ 7:20   Byrd Amendment
§ 7:21   Lobbying Disclosure Act
§ 7:22   Recommendations

IV. COLLUSIVE BIDDING

A. STATUTORY FRAMEWORK

§ 7:23   Generally
§ 7:24   Sherman Antitrust Act
§ 7:25   Clayton Act
§ 7:26   Federal Trade Commission Act
§ 7:27   Other statutes & regulations
§ 7:28   Exceptions
§ 7:29   —Affiliated companies
§ 7:30   —Teaming agreements & joint ventures
§ 7:31   —Defense production pools

B. FREQUENTLY ASKED QUESTIONS

§ 7:32   Questions & answers

C. HOW TO RECOGNIZE THE PROBLEM

§ 7:33   Generally
§ 7:34   Examples

D. COMPLIANCE INITIATIVES

§ 7:35   Generally
§ 7:36   Recommendations

V. KICKBACKS

A. STATUTORY FRAMEWORK

§ 7:37   Generally
§ 7:38   Anti-Kickback Act
§ 7:39   —Elements
§ 7:40   —Contractor responsibilities
§ 7:41   —Penalties

B. FREQUENTLY ASKED QUESTIONS

§ 7:42   Questions & answers

C. HOW TO RECOGNIZE THE PROBLEM

§ 7:43   Generally

§ 7:44   Examples

D. COMPLIANCE INITIATIVES

§ 7:45   Generally
§ 7:46   Establish policies & procedures
§ 7:47   Develop policies for auditors & accountants
§ 7:48   Recommendations

> **KeyCite®:** Cases and other legal materials listed in KeyCite Scope can be researched through the KeyCite service on Westlaw®. Use KeyCite to check citations for form, parallel references, prior and later history, and comprehensive citator information, including citations to other decisions and secondary materials.

I. OVERVIEW

§ 7:1 Scope note

Certain types of conduct may constitute the unlawful influence of a Federal Government procurement action. These include paying bribes or offering of gratuities to federal officials, offering or acceptance of kickbacks, engaging in collusive bidding, or using funds from Government contracts to support certain types of marketing activities. Some of the conduct—such as bribing a public official—is patently illegal. Other actions—such as taking a Contracting Officer out to play golf—are less obviously illegal. This chapter examines the laws and regulations that make certain activities unlawful and offers guidance on how to recognize them, particularly those that are not obviously illegal and may be perfectly acceptable in the commercial world.

Note that this chapter deals with statutes and rules that limit Government-contractor and contractor-contractor relationships. There are also a number of laws and rules that specifically govern the conduct of Government officials, including, for example, limits on gifts that Government employees can accept.[1] A discussion of these internal Government standards is beyond the scope

---

[Section 7:1]

[1]*See, e.g.,* Ethics in Government Act, 5 U.S.C.A. § 7351, implemented by Office of Government Ethics, "Standards of Ethical Conduct for Employees of the Executive Branch," 5 C.F.R. § 2635. For a discussion of the Ethics in Government Act, 5 U.S.C.A. § 7351 and the implementing Office of Government Ethics regulations, see Schulz, What Every Government Contractor Should Know About Gift Restrictions Applicable To Executive-Branch Employees, 20 No. 14 Andrews Government Contract Litigation Reporter (November 6, 2006).

of this Handbook.[2]

II. BRIBERY & ILLEGAL GRATUITIES

A. STATUTORY FRAMEWORK

§ 7:2 Generally

There are a number of statutes and regulations that pertain to the offer and acceptance of bribes, gratuities, and gifts between a contractor and a public official. There are two primary criminal statutes that prohibit a contractor from offering bribes or illegal gratuities and the Government employee's acceptance of them.

In the 1980s, the Government initiated increased enforcement of the laws and regulations that prohibit bribes and gratuities. Recent scandals involving improprieties in the award of major defense contracts have again prompted federal agencies to renew their bribery and illegal gratuities oversight and enforcement. As a result, Government contractors must be increasingly sensitive to the differences between doing business with commercial and Government customers.

The line between lawful activity and unlawful activity in the areas of bribery and illegal gratuities is not always clear. For example, if you make a contribution to an elected official with the hope of influencing his or her decision on a specific matter relating to your business, or if you offer a Government official a bottle of wine at Christmas—two types of conduct that are not patently illegal—you may nonetheless be violating the illegal gratuities and bribery laws. Therefore, you need to be particularly aware of and sensitive to conduct that might violate these laws.

§ 7:3 Bribery

The bribery statute prohibits the giving and receipt of bribes.[1] Thus, it punishes parties on both sides of the transaction (not just the person offering the bribe). To establish a violation by the person *offering* a bribe, the Government must show that the person: (1) corruptly gave or offered anything of value (2) to a public official, (3) with the specific intent to influence an official act or induce the public official to commit some fraud or violate an official duty. The statute is written in broad language and applies when the prohibited acts are performed "directly or indirectly" and when a person "gives, offers, or promises"

---

[2]18 U.S.C.A. § 201; 10 U.S.C.A. § 2207 (implemented by FAR section 3.2, "Contractor Gratuities to Government Personnel," and FAR 52.203-3).

[Section 7:3]

[1]18 U.S.C.A. § 201(b).

§ 7:3

something.

It is also a crime for a public official to ask for or accept a bribe. To establish a violation of the bribery statute by the person *seeking* a bribe, the Government must show essentially that the thing of value was demanded, solicited, agreed to, or accepted by the public official in return for being influenced in the performance of any official act.

Although the bribery statute does not require that the bribe actually be *paid*—only that it be offered, promised, asked for, or requested—there must be a clear "quid pro quo," i.e., a clear *connection* between the thing of value offered or received and the official act. The official act may be an act of commission or of omission. It is not necessary that the public official have the authority to act, only that the briber thinks he does.[2]

The bribery statute provides criminal *penalties* of a fine of the greater of either (a) $500,000 (for organizations) or $250,000 (for individuals), or (b) three times the monetary equivalent of the bribe and up to 15 years' imprisonment. An offender under the bribery statute may also be disqualified from holding a federal office.[3]

The Department of Justice (DOJ) continues to aggressively pursue Government employees and members of the military, as well as individuals and employees of contractors, for corruption arising out the conflicts in the Middle East. A Government contracting officer and a private contractor were sentenced to approximately six years in prison on bribery and wire fraud charges arising out of the payment of $40,000 in bribes by the contractor in return for the award of more than $4.7 million in contracts. The contractor attempted to conceal the payments by making checks payable to the contracting officer's wife and by paying some of his personal bills directly. *United States v. Harvey et al.*, 532 F.3d 326 (4th Cir, VA 2008) (Defendant's conviction for bribery affirmed; amount of restitution vacated and sent back to district court for findings consistent with the opinion).

More recently, DOJ announced that it had obtained indictments of a Major in the U.S. Army and two members of his family for allegedly accepting bribes amounting to over $900,000 in connection with the award of contracts for goods and services in Iraq and Kuwait. *U.S. v. Cockerham*, (W.D. Tex. 2007).

Also, on August 13, 2008, the DOJ announced that an Army Major pled guilty to bribery and conspiracy charges arising out of

---

[2]*See, U.S. v. Mirikitani*, 380 F.3d 1223 (9th Cir. 2004) (the existence of a nexus between the bribe and some federal money is not an element of the offense of bribery that must be proven to the jury beyond a reasonable doubt).

[3]18 U.S.C.A. §§ 201(b), 3559(a)(5), 3571.

§ 7:3

his activities as a contracting officer in Kuwait. The defendant admitted to having accepted about $5.8 million in bribes from five contractors who supplied bottled water and other goods and services. *U.S. v. Momon*, CR-08-187 (D.D.C. 2008).

A grand jury indicted two former employees of Kellogg, Brown, & Root for conspiracy to defraud the Government in connection with the delivery of fuel valued at $2.1 million in Iraq.[4]

Harold F. Babb, former Director of Contracts for Alaskan Native Corporation, Eyak Technology, was sentenced October 18, 2012 to 87 months in prison and ordered to forfeit over $600,000 for bribery and unlawful kickbacks for his part in a $30 million U.S. Army Corps of Engineers bribery and bid-rigging scheme, which DOJ called "the largest . . . in the history of federal contracting."[5]

§ 7:4 Illegal gratuities

The illegal gratuities statute,[1] like the bribery statute, is a criminal law that applies to offers and solicitations of gifts. Essentially, the illegal gratuities statute prohibits "tipping" Government officials. The main difference between the bribery and illegal gratuities statutes is the intent requirement. The bribery statute requires a showing of corrupt intent on the part of the offeror and a showing that the gift is a "quid pro quo" made directly in return for an act by a Government official. The illegal gratuities statute, on the other hand, requires only the offer or acceptance of anything of value "for or because of an official act."

As a practical matter, the illegal gratuities statute prohibits *all* gifts to public officials made as *rewards* for acts that they would perform anyway. Although prosecutors generally target gifts of substantial value under the illegal gratuities statute, the statute in theory proscribes *any* gift—even one as small as a meal—given for or because of an official act.

Criminal sanctions under the illegal gratuities statute include up to two years imprisonment and/or $500,000 in fines (for organizations) or $250,000 (for individuals).[2] In addition, under the Federal Acquisition Regulation's (FAR's) "Gratuities" contract clause (which is required to be inserted into every Government

---

[4]http://abcnews.go.com/TheLaw/FedCrimes/story?id=3997727.
[5]http://www.justice.gov/usao/dc/news/2012/oct/12-366.html.

[Section 7:4]
[1]18 U.S.C.A. § 201(c).
[2]18 U.S.C.A. §§ 201(c), 3559(a)(5), 3571.

contract over $100,000),[3] the Government has certain remedies against the contractor if it is found to have offered or given an illegal gratuity to an officer, official, or Government employee in order to obtain a contract award or receive favorable treatment under a contract. Violation of your contract's "Gratuities" clause allows the Contracting Officer to terminate your contract for default, recommend your suspension or debarment from contracting with the Government, and/or assess exemplary damages of up to 10 times the value of the gratuity given if the contract uses funds appropriated to the Defense Department.[4] The "Gratuities" clause penalties apply also to contracts tainted by bribery (see § 7:3 above).[5]

Generally it is the Government that alleges a contractor has violated the illegal gratuities statute. The standard of proof in such criminal prosecutions is proof "beyond a reasonable doubt." Occasionally, however allegations of illegal gratuities play a role in bid protests. As noted in the principal text, the general prohibition in the bribery and illegal gratuities statutes are implemented in FAR 3.101-2 "Solicitation and Acceptance of Gratuities by Government Personnel" and in the FAR 52.203-3 contract clause "Gratuities." In *Chenega Management, LLC v. U.S.*, 96 Fed. Cl. 556 (2010), Chenega alleged that the president of one of its competitors had given an illegal gratuity—two tickets to the Superbowl—to a Government official involved in the selection process and that as a result the contractor's proposal had been excluded from the competitive range. If true, this would have violated these FAR provisions. The court noted that the standard of proof in the context of a protest required showing a violation by "clear and convincing" evidence. The court held that Chenega had not presented any evidence to counter the findings of an Air Force investigation that the Government official had immediately reimbursed the competitor for the face value—$800—for each of the two tickets. The court also found that the Government official's role in the procurement was limited and that Chenega had not established how his limited involvement favored one offeror over another. Interestingly, though, the court did not address Chenega's allegation that the "street value" of the two tickets was over $6,000.

B. FREQUENTLY ASKED QUESTIONS

§ 7:5 Questions & answers

Question 1: What exactly is a bribe?

---

[3]FAR 3.202, 52.203-3 (implementing 10 U.S.C.A. § 2207).

[4]FAR 3.204(c), 52.203-3.

[5]*U.S. v. Muldoon*, 931 F.2d 282 287 (4th Cir. 1991) ("[p]ayment of an illegal gratuity is a lesser included offense of bribery").

§ 7:5   GOVERNMENT CONTRACT COMPLIANCE HANDBOOK

Answer 1: A bribe is a thing of value given with the specific intent to influence an official act (or failure to act) or to obtain favorable treatment under a contract. To be liable under the bribery statute, the Government must be able to prove a "quid pro quo" expectation by the offeror. In other words, the Government must demonstrate that money or something of value was offered by you in return for an exercise of the Government employee's official power.[1]

Question 2: What exactly is a gratuity?

Answer 2: In general, a gratuity is: (1) anything of value; (2) given, offered, or promised to a public official; and (3) because of any official act performed or to be performed.[2]

Question 3: What is the difference between a bribe and a gratuity?

Answer 3: The giver's state of mind distinguishes a bribe from a gratuity, but as one court has written, the distinction is slight. According to this court, proof of bribery requires a corrupt *intent* that is not required to prove the existence of an illegal gratuity. The intent element of a bribery claim need not be proven by direct evidence, but may be inferred from the surrounding circumstances. The evidence for proving bribery must establish that the giver or offeror *intended to receive* some benefit in return for the payment of something of value. On the other hand, to find an illegal gratuity, the evidence does not have to show that the offeror intended to exact action by the recipient.[3]

Question 4: Does a bribe have to be completed in order for you to be found guilty under the bribery statute?

Answer 4: No. Courts have stated that the Government only has to prove that you intended to bribe the public official. Failure to complete a bribe does not shield you from liability.[4]

Question 5: What does "anything of value" mean?

Answer 5: Generally, "anything of value" is an item that has monetary worth. However, one U.S. District Court has expanded this definition to include "intangible" benefits.[5] In that case, the

---

[Section 7:5]

[1]*McCormick v. U.S.*, 500 U.S. 257, 269–273, 111 S. Ct. 1807, 114 L. Ed. 2d 307 (1991); *U.S. v. Tomblin*, 46 F.3d 1369, 1379, 41 Fed. R. Evid. Serv. 964 (5th Cir. 1995).

[2]18 U.S.C.A. § 201(c)(1)(a).

[3]*U.S. v. Muldoon*, 931 F.2d 282 287 (4th Cir. 1991).

[4]*U.S. v. Tejada-Beltran*, 50 F.3d 105 (1st Cir. 1995); *U.S. v. Tomblin*, 46 F.3d 1369, 1379, 41 Fed. R. Evid. Serv. 964 (5th Cir. 1995).

[5]*U.S. v. Sun-Diamond Growers of California*, 941 F. Supp. 1262 (D.D.C. 1996), rev'd, 138 F.3d 961 (D.C. Cir. 1998), judgment aff'd, 526 U.S. 398, 119 S.

defendant, a large agriculture cooperative, allegedly expended money on various direct and indirect "gifts" for the then-Secretary of Agriculture, Mike Espy. The purported illegal gratuities involved, among other things, airline tickets for the Secretary's girlfriend that enabled her to accompany him to a trade association conference in Greece. The court found that the airline tickets constituted a "thing of value" to the Secretary even though the tickets were not given directly to him. Construing the illegal gratuities statute broadly, the court held that "monetary worth is not the sole measure of value."[6] Noting that a "thing of value" can be an intangible benefit, such as companionship, the court found that the airline tickets could have conferred a benefit on the Secretary and been considered an illegal gratuity.[7]

Question 6: Everything has some value. Does this mean that anything I give to a Government official could be an illegal gratuity?

Answer 6: Neither the illegal gratuities statutes nor the regulations define the term "anything of value." Nonetheless, the Office of Government Ethics (OGE) has adopted a number of exceptions for gifts that a Government employee *can* accept without violating the Office's ethical standards or the federal regulations against receiving gratuities.[8] These exceptions should serve as a helpful guide on the items that the Government considers permissible for a public official to receive, or, conversely, for you to give. Some of the gift exceptions include (a) modest items of food and refreshments, such as soft drinks, coffee and donuts, offered other than as part of a meal, (b) greeting cards and items with little intrinsic value, such as plaques, certificates, and trophies that are intended solely for presentation, (c) gifts of $20 or less, provided that the gifts do not exceed $50 per calendar year, and (d) awards or honorary degrees of less than $200 that are offered to the public on a regular basis.[9]

Some Government agencies have supplemented the OGE gift regulations with their own agency gift exceptions. The Department of Defense, for example, has two additional exceptions for attendance at state-sponsored events and for receipt of certain

---

Ct. 1402, 143 L. Ed. 2d 576 (1999).

[6]*U.S. v. Sun-Diamond Growers of California*, 941 F. Supp. 1262, 1270, (D.D.C. 1996), rev'd, 138 F.3d 961 (D.C. Cir. 1998), judgment aff'd, 526 U.S. 398, 119 S. Ct. 1402, 143 L. Ed. 2d 576 (1999).

[7]*See generally,* Klein, What Exactly is an Unlawful Gratuity After United States v. Sun Diamond Growers, 68 Geo. Wash. L. Rev. 116 (1999).

[8]5 C.F.R. § 2635.202(b) (discussing OGE standards in relation to 18 U.S.C.A. § 201(c)).

[9]5 C.F.R. §§ 2635.203(b), 2635.204.

scholarships or grants.[10]

Question 7: Is it a violation of the illegal gratuities statute if I want to give something of value to a Government official not because of or for performance of an official act but just because of the official's position?

Answer 7: For years, opinions from various U.S. Courts of Appeals concerning this issue were split.[11] However, in 1999, the U.S. Supreme Court issued a decision on this exact issue.[12] The Court held that to establish a violation of the illegal gratuities statute, the Government "must prove a link between a thing of value conferred upon a public official and a specific 'official act' for or because of which it was given." According to the Court, an "alternative reading . . . would criminalize, for example, token gifts to the President based on his official position and not linked to any identifiable act—such as the replica jerseys given by championship sports teams each year during ceremonial White House visits."[13]

Despite this Supreme Court decision narrowing the scope of the illegal gratuities statute, you should nevertheless be wary of offering any gratuities to a public official. The complex line-drawing between an acceptable gift and an illegal gratuity is not worth the risk of criminal liability for violating the gratuity statute.

Question 8: Is it illegal for me to give a gift to a friend who happens to be a Government employee with whom I work?

Answer 8: Maybe. The OGE considered this problem when the agency adopted its regulations concerning Government employees' acceptance of gifts. The OGE regulations state that a Government employee should not accept gifts based on personal relationships unless the circumstances of the gift-giving "make it clear that the gift is motivated by a family relationship or personal

---

[10] 5 C.F.R. § 3601.103.

[11] *See, U.S. v. Bustamante*, 45 F.3d 933 (5th Cir. 1995); *U.S. v. Standefer*, 610 F.2d 1076 (3d Cir. 1979), judgment aff'd, 447 U.S. 10, 100 S. Ct. 1999, 64 L. Ed. 2d 689 (1980) (en banc); *U.S. v. Secord*, 726 F. Supp. 845 (D.D.C. 1989); *U.S. v. Sun-Diamond Growers of California*, 138 F.3d 961 (D.C. Cir. 1998), judgment aff'd, 526 U.S. 398, 119 S. Ct. 1402, 143 L. Ed. 2d 576 (1999); *U.S. v. Williams*, 29 F. Supp. 2d 1 (D.D.C. 1998), judgment aff'd in part, rev'd in part, 183 F.3d 833, 52 Fed. R. Evid. Serv. 79 (D.C. Cir. 1999), vacated as moot, 240 F.3d 35 (D.C. Cir. 2001) and vacated in part, 240 F.3d 35 (D.C. Cir. 2001).

[12] *U.S. v. Sun-Diamond Growers of California*, 526 U.S. 398, 119 S. Ct. 1402, 143 L. Ed. 2d 576 (1999).

[13] *U.S. v. Sun-Diamond Growers of California*, 526 U.S. 398, 119 S. Ct. 1402, 1407, 143 L. Ed. 2d 576 (1999).

§ 7:5

friendship rather than the position of the employee."[14]

One court that has specifically addressed the issue of personal gift-giving between a contractor and Government employee noted that an illegal gratuity would not be found where a contractor could demonstrate that the gift was provided to the Government employee solely for the sake of friendship or some other innocent reason.[15]

Question 9: Does the illegal gratuity statute prohibit a gift that is permitted under another statute?

Answer 9: No, but you should ensure that in giving the gifts you abide by the letter of the particular statute that makes such actions permissible.[16] The Comptroller General decided a case essentially on this issue. In a bid protest over a contract award for travel management services for Government employees on official business, the protester alleged that the successful contract awardee offered illegal gratuities in the form of business class upgrades to Government employees who would be traveling long distances. The successful bidder had won the contract in part because of the upgrade offer. The Comptroller General held that providing upgrades to Government employees as part of contract performance was not an illegal gratuity because the Federal Travel Regulations allow Government employees to upgrade to business class service on long-haul flights.[17]

Question 10: Is a public official necessarily a Government employee or elected officer?

Answer 10: No. A "public official" need not be a Government employee or elected official. Rather, it is sufficient that the person be in a position to influence the outcome of a Government decision. For example, in a recent case in which the Government outsourced certain procurement functions to a private contractor, the contractor was convicted of soliciting a bribe from a Government vendor in exchange for allowing modifications to the vendor's contract which would provide cost savings to the vendor. The contractor was deemed to be a public official because its responsibilities included Government program management and procurement functions that the contractor was performing on

---

[14]5 C.F.R. § 2635.204(b).

[15]*U.S. v. Sun-Diamond Growers of California*, 941 F. Supp. 1262, 1271, (D.D.C. 1996), rev'd, 138 F.3d 961 (D.C. Cir. 1998), judgment aff'd, 526 U.S. 398, 119 S. Ct. 1402, 143 L. Ed. 2d 576 (1999).

[16]5 C.F.R. §§ 2635.203(b)(8), 2635.204(l).

[17]Omega World Travel, Inc., Comp. Gen. Dec. B-271262.2, 96-2 CPD 44, at 2-3.

§ 7:5   GOVERNMENT CONTRACT COMPLIANCE HANDBOOK

behalf of the Government.[18]

C. HOW TO RECOGNIZE THE PROBLEM

§ 7:6 Generally

Remember, what looks to you like a completely innocent offering to a Government employee may in fact be construed as an illegal gratuity or bribe. Thus, it is extremely important for you to be aware of your employees' and company's activities and to establish clear policies to prevent unlawful bribery and gratuities.

Each of your employees should be very wary about giving *anything* of value to a Government employee. For example, offering to train a Government employee for free on the use of your equipment may be a violation of the illegal gratuities laws or regulations. Although offering free training does not seem inherently unlawful, the law includes training within the definition of a "gift" that federal employees may not accept, depending on the circumstances.

Bribery is easier both to spot and to avoid. If you offer something to a Government employee with the expectation of receiving a specific favor, then you have violated the bribery statute. For example, if your employee takes the resident Government auditor to lunch with the expectation that he or she will give more favorable treatment to your books, your employee may have violated the bribery statute.

§ 7:7 Examples

Hiring a consultant: A senior Government official indicates that if you want an upcoming contract, you should hire his good friend Jones as a consultant. You do so. Jones does some consulting work for you, but not nearly the amount you are paying him for; in fact, you understand that Jones uses some of the money you pay him for the Government official's benefit. Even though the senior Government official approached you to hire his friend, you could be liable for bribery of the Government official under the bribery statute.

Offer of employment: Assume you have been in regular telephone contact with a Government representative with questions on a recently-issued solicitation. After going over a number of ambiguities in the solicitation, the Government representative

---

[18]*U.S. v. Kenney*, 185 F.3d 1217, 161 A.L.R. Fed. 765 (11th Cir. 1999). *See also, U.S. v. Thomas*, 240 F.3d 445 (5th Cir. 2001) (guard employed by private company that operated detention facility under INS contract was 'public official' within meaning of bribery statute; guard performed same duties as federal corrections officer and acted under INS authority, thus occupied position of public trust).

§ 7:7 INFLUENCING GOVERNMENT ACTIONS

mentions that he is fed up with Government bureaucracy and asks you about details of life in private industry. You mention that your company has a high turnover rate and is always looking for good contract managers. Is there anything wrong with that comment? You may have just violated the bribery statute. Because the intent to influence official actions need not be proven by direct evidence but may be inferred from the circumstances surrounding the action, you're hinting at the possibility of an offer of employment to the Government employee may be viewed as the offer of something of value in exchange for a favorable contract decision. (Furthermore, you may have violated the conflict-of-interest provisions of the Procurement Integrity Act concerning employment contacts with Government procurement officials (see §§ 8:1 et seq.).

Request for help: You are working under a fixed-price construction contract and have had some minor problems with your equipment and supplies. You also have been experiencing intermittent and frustrating delays due to changed and unforeseen site conditions. To make matters worse, an agency Contract Quality Control Representative (CQCR), who has been on your construction site since the initial stages of your contract, is constantly questioning and scrutinizing your work efforts. You know that without the presence of the CQCR you will get the work done faster, better, and, perhaps, at less cost to you. You decide to call the agency officer in charge of overseeing your contract and inquire if she can get the CQCR off your job site. You tell her that without the CQCR you will save a lot of time and money, and you offer her $100 to try at least once to get the CQCR off your construction site.[1] Do you face any potential liability under this scenario? Would the answer change if she called you back and told you she was unsuccessful? Regardless of whether the agency officer is successful in responding to your request, you have committed an act of bribery. Remember that failure to complete a bribe does not shield you from liability.

Request for help: Assume now that you did not offer any money to the supervising officer but you politely asked her to try to have the CQCR removed from your site. Would you have any potential liability if, after her unsuccessful attempts, you sent her a box of chocolates in thanks for her efforts? The answer to this question is unclear. You may be liable for giving both a bribe and an illegal gratuity. Your sending of the chocolates can be viewed as a

---

[Section 7:7]

[1]*See, Supermex, Inc. v. U.S.*, 35 Fed. Cl. 29, 34–35, (1996) (contractor pleaded guilty to bribery charges for paying $1,000 to a Navy officer in return for officer's elimination of Navy CQCR's "required" presence at contractor's construction site).

subtle request (or bribe) for the supervising officer to continue trying to have the CQCR removed. Perhaps more likely, the box of candy might also be considered an attempt to gain favor with the officer (an illegal gratuity) in anticipation of needing her "help" with other potential contract problems.

Wining and dining: You are a marketing representative on an electronics system. To cultivate your relationship with Government procurement officials, you take them out, on a regular basis, to expensive dinners, entertain them at your country club golf course, give them tickets to sporting and theater events, and send them cases of liquor to mark special events in their lives. Regardless of whether the Government could show that you got special treatment from these officials, you could nevertheless be liable for violating the illegal gratuities statute.

Business dealings with Government officials: A Government official with whom your firm routinely does business complains to you that he is having trouble selling a vacation home. You know that the home is worth far less than the asking price. Nevertheless, you direct a colleague to buy the home at the asking price, and you arrange for her to be compensated for the extra expense. You may be liable for conferring an illegal gratuity to the Government official.

Baby shower: Your company has been dealing with the same Government auditor for a number of years, and many of your employees have become good friends with her both on and off the job. When she announces that she will be taking maternity leave, your employees decide to have a baby shower for her and chip in to purchase a cake and gift for the baby. Is there anything wrong with throwing the baby shower? Yes. A violation of the illegal gratuities statute may have occurred. The baby shower may be interpreted as an illegal gift given to a Government official because of her Government position. Although the baby shower might have been given completely out of personal friendship, you would be responsible for overcoming the inference that the shower was an attempt to create an atmosphere for favorable auditing treatment by your friend.

Free tickets: Your company is one sponsor of a tennis tournament held to benefit the American Cancer Society. In exchange for your charitable contribution, you are given an allotment of free tickets, which otherwise cost $20 each. Not many of your employees are tennis fans, and you have extra tickets available. A team of Government inspectors has been reviewing your plant facilities for the past week, and because you know that several of them *are* tennis fans, you offer the tickets that would otherwise not be used. Have you done anything wrong? You may have committed a gratuities violation. Although the Office of Government

Ethics permits Government agency employees to accept unsolicited gifts having a market value of $20 or less,[2] your giving of these tickets to the inspection team during the week of your plant review hints at an attempt to create an atmosphere in which the inspection team might treat you more favorably than usual. (Note, however, that the OGE does except *certain* offers of free attendance to "widely attended gatherings" from the general prohibition against employee acceptance of unsolicited gifts.[3] Acceptance of the tennis tickets, nevertheless, probably would not be allowed under the OGE's ethics rules.)

D. COMPLIANCE INITIATIVES

§ 7:8 Generally

You and your employees must be fully apprised of the bribery and illegal gratuities laws, and your company should have written policies to implement these laws. It should be made clear that the purpose of the policy is not to inhibit or discourage normal, legitimate contact between your employees and Government personnel that is a necessary and desirable aspect of doing business. The purpose is only to prevent acts that are prohibited by law and regulation.

§ 7:9 Establish policies & procedures

You should establish a *written* company-wide policy concerning personnel interaction with Government employees and distribute copies of the policy to all employees. You should also have periodic general meetings or *training sessions* with your employees to explain the policy and answer questions. Have each employee *certify* that he has read the company's policy, understands it, and agrees to comply with it. A sample company policy statement on bribery and illegal gratuities is included in Appendix G to this Handbook. Include the policy in your consultant and agent contracts as well.

Assign a specific individual or office to be the *"Ethics Officer"* responsible for assuring compliance with the illegal gratuities and bribery rules. Notify each employee that when he is confronted with an ambiguous situation, any questions regarding the interpretation of federal statutes, regulations, and contract provisions on illegal gratuities and bribery should be directed to the legal department or the Ethics Officer. Encourage your employees to *consult* with the Ethics Officer freely, and make clear that all such inquiries will be kept confidential to the extent possible.

---

[2] 5 C.F.R. § 2635.204(a).
[3] 5 C.F.R. § 2635.204(g)(2).

§ 7:10 Monitor employees' activities

You must take affirmative steps to educate employees about the do's and don'ts of illegal gratuities and bribery, and you must set up procedures to help ensure that no violations occur. Clearly, the safest path is to establish a rule never to offer *anything* of value to a Government employee. Particularly with respect to illegal gratuities, it is too easy for you or one of your employees inadvertently to violate the prohibitions.

Monitor employees' *expense reports* to determine whether questionable gratuities are being given. Conduct *periodic spot checks* to verify, to the extent you can, that your company's policy is being followed.

Remember, illegal gratuities and bribery are frequently difficult to identify. The expenses can be disguised as something else and slipped through the company accounts. Nevertheless, a strong company policy against such activity and a good faith compliance program will protect you against accusations of "willful disregard" of the rules and will help limit such problems.

§ 7:11 Require government employees to pay

You should also take steps to encourage Government personnel to "pay their own way." If your interaction with a Government employee will include something more than coffee and doughnuts, be sure to make clear at the outset that you expect the Government employee to pay his or her own way.

§ 7:12 Recommendations

(a) Issue a *written policy* regarding the offering of anything of value to public officials.

(b) Distribute your policy to all employees and have them *certify* that they have read and agree to comply with its terms.

(c) *Appoint an individual* in charge of Government relations to whom your employees may *direct any questions* in this area.

(d) *Provide an opportunity* for federal officials to *pay* for in-house meals.

(e) Prohibit employees *absolutely* from offering *anything of value* to federal officials.

(f) *Monitor* employees' expense reports and conduct periodic spot checks to confirm that your policy is known by employees and is being followed.

III. LOBBYING RESTRICTIONS

A. STATUTORY FRAMEWORK

§ 7:13 Generally

Many companies routinely make marketing calls on Government agencies to keep abreast of potential Government needs and to keep the Government informed about their products or services. Unfortunately, this seemingly innocent activity potentially can lead to fairly severe liability. For example, suppose that you make a marketing call after the Government issues a presolicitation notice to discuss a specific product or service relating to a requirement in the notice. Your objective is to interest the Government in your product and ultimately receive the award. Depending on the funds that you used to "lobby" the Government about your product, you may have broken the law. In addition, if you failed to disclose your marketing call properly to the agency, you may face liability for failing to adhere to reporting requirements regarding your "lobbying" activities.

Two statutes (and their implementing regulations) govern the basic lobbying activities with which you may be involved as a contractor. The Byrd Amendment[1] deals with "improper influence peddling" by lobbyists on behalf of Federal Government contractors and grantees. The statute prohibits certain uses of Government funds if you lobby for Government contracts. The Byrd Amendment also requires you to disclose to the contracting agency the names of any registrants under the Lobbying Disclosure Act who lobbied for your particular contract. The Lobbying Disclosure Act of 1995,[2] which was enacted to create a more comprehensive scheme for reporting and registering lobbyists, may demand further disclosures to the Government about your lobbying activities.

§ 7:14 Byrd Amendment

The Byrd Amendment essentially can be divided into two parts. First, the statute prohibits an awardee of a federal contract, grant, loan, or cooperative agreement from using "appropriated funds" to attempt to "influence" any officer or employee of any federal agency or Congress in connection with a contract award or modification.[1] Second, the Byrd Amendment and implementing regulations require offerors in procurements of $100,000 or more to file a disclosure and certification that: (a) identifies any registrant under the Lobbying Disclosure Act (see § 7:15 below) who the offeror has paid from its own funds to make lobbying

---

[Section 7:13]

[1]1990 Department of the Interior and Related Agencies Appropriations Act, Pub. L. No. 101-121, § 319, 103 Stat. 701 (codified at 31 U.S.C.A. § 1352).

[2]Pub. L. No. 104-65, 109 Stat. 691 (Dec. 19, 1995, effective Jan. 1, 1996) (codified at 2 U.S.C.A. §§ 1601 to 1612).

[Section 7:14]

[1]31 U.S.C.A. § 1352(a)(1).

§ 7:14　　　　　　Government Contract Compliance Handbook

contacts on behalf of the offeror with respect to that procurement; and (b) certifies that the offeror has not used and will not use appropriated funds to influence, or attempt to influence, a member or employee of Congress, or an officer or employee of an agency in connection with the awarding of any federal contract.[2]

The Byrd Amendment covers federal awards to individuals, corporations, state and local governments, and a host of other groups and associations—whether operating for profit or not for profit. The law also extends to all subcontractors who participate in a federal procurement.

Under the Byrd Amendment, if you make prohibited lobbying expenditures from appropriated funds, you are subject to a civil penalty of "not less than $10,000 and not more than $100,000 for each such expenditure."[3] If you fail to file or amend a required disclosure or certification under the Byrd Amendment, you are subject to the same civil penalty for each reporting failure.[4] These penalties are enforced through the Program Fraud Civil Remedies Act (see §§ 1:1 et seq.); however, the Government reserves its other rights and remedies, which include criminal prosecution, suspension, and debarment.

§ 7:15 Lobbying Disclosure Act

Although not specifically targeted at federal contractors, the Lobbying Disclosure Act of 1995 (LDA) is broad enough to cover many contractor marketing and business development contacts, as well as routine communications relating to contract administration. It basically requires (with a few exceptions) individuals spending at least 20% of their time on lobbying activities and any organization employing at least one "lobbyist" to register with the Clerk of the House and the Secretary of the Senate within 45 days after making a lobbying contact or being employed to initiate a lobbying contact with a covered legislative or executive branch official.

A "lobbying contact" is defined as any oral or written communication to a covered legislative or executive branch official (including staff) on behalf of a client with regard to the administration or execution of a federal program or policy, including the negotiation, award, or administration of a federal contract, grant, loan, permit, or license. Covered executive branch officials are generally high-level officials and those who serve in a policymaking capacity, and include individuals serving in Levels I through V of the Executive Schedule and members of the uniformed ser-

---

[2]31 U.S.C.A. § 1352(b).
[3]31 U.S.C.A. § 1352(c)(1).
[4]31 U.S.C.A. § 1352(c)(2).

§ 7:15

vices whose pay grade is at or above 0–7 (a Brigadier General or higher). The definition of a covered legislative branch official includes all Members of Congress, any elected officer or any employee of Congress or its leadership staff, and any employee of a Member, committee, or working group.[1]

Each registrant under the Act must file semiannual reports with the House Clerk and Senate Secretary that disclose the specific issues being lobbied, his or her clients, estimates of lobbying income and expenses, and interests of foreign entities.[2] The LDA specifically enumerates "the negotiation, award, or administration of a Federal contract" as among the lobbying contacts that require a lobbyist's registration.[3]

Penalties for violations of the LDA include a civil fine of up to $50,000 for knowing failure to: (a) remedy a defective filing within 60 days of notification of the defect; or (b) comply with any other provision of the Act. The amount of the civil fine depends on "the extent and gravity of the violation."[4]

The Honest Leadership and Open Government Act of 2007[5] significantly amended the Lobbying Disclosure Act. From a Government contracts compliance perspective, the major changes include:

- The Act lowers the thresholds for registration from $6,000 to $2,500 with regard to the amount received from a client for lobbying work and from $24,500 to $10,000 with respect to expenses incurred by a company whose employees lobby on its own behalf;
- Lobbying reports, which previously had to be filed semiannually, must now be filed quarterly within 20 days of the end of the quarter;
- A new requirement obligates lobbyists to disclose any contribution over $200 to a Federal candidate, PAC or party organization and to certify that he/she has not violated any Rules of the House and Senate;
- The Act states that "the Comptroller General shall audit the extent of compliance or non-compliance with the requirements of this Act by lobbyists, lobbying firms and registrants through a random sampling of publicly available lobbying registrations and reports . . . ."; and
- The Act increases the fine for violations from $50,000 to

[Section 7:15]
 [1] 2 U.S.C.A. § 1603.
 [2] 2 U.S.C.A. § 1604.
 [3] 2 U.S.C.A. § 1602(8)(a)(iii).
 [4] 2 U.S.C.A. § 1606.
 [5] Pub. L. No. 110-81, codified as amendments to 2 U.S.C. § 1601, et seq.

§ 7:15   GOVERNMENT CONTRACT COMPLIANCE HANDBOOK

$200,000 and adds a maximum five-year criminal penalty.

These amendments raise significant compliance challenges for contractors. It is now more important than ever that a contractor use care in selecting an outside firm for lobbying assistance. For example, the Rules of the House can be complicated and no contractor wants to learn from a newspaper headline that its lobbying firm is under investigation for falsely certifying that it had not violated those rules. The same issues are of even more concern with employees who perform lobbying activities because they may be less familiar with these requirements than an independent lobbying firm.

B. FREQUENTLY ASKED QUESTIONS

§ 7:16   Questions & answers

Question 1: What are "appropriated funds" as used in the Byrd Amendment?

Answer 1: "Appropriated funds" are defined as Government contract-derived funds *other than* profit.

Question 2: Are there any exceptions to the Byrd Amendment's prohibition on the use of appropriated funds to influence or "lobby" for contract award?

Answer 2: Yes. The prohibition against the use of "appropriated funds" for lobbying does not apply to: (1) "reasonable compensation" paid to your officers or employees for agency or legislative "liaison" activities *not* directly related to a specific contract award, and (2) payment of either "reasonable compensation" to officers or employees or "reasonable payment" to nonemployee consultants for "professional or technical services rendered directly in the preparation, submission, or negotiation of any bid, proposal or application" for "meeting requirements imposed by or pursuant to law" as a condition for receiving an award.[1] The FAR describes more fully the liaison activities and professional services that can be paid from appropriated funds.[2]

For example, the FAR limits the definition of "professional or technical services" to "advice and analysis directly applying any professional or technical discipline" such as "drafting of a legal document accompanying a bid or proposal by a lawyer" and "technical advice provided by an engineer on the performance or operational capability of a piece of equipment." This exception is *not* limited to licensed professionals but includes advice and analysis directly applying any professional or technical expertise.

[Section 7:16]

[1] 31 U.S.C.A. § 1352(d)(1)(A).
[2] FAR 3.803.

INFLUENCING GOVERNMENT ACTIONS § 7:16

Excluded from the definition are "communications with the intent to influence" and communications that "advocate one proposal over another."[3]

Question 3: When do I have to file my Byrd Amendment disclosure and certification with the contracting agency or officer?

Answer 3: The statute states that your certification and disclosure must be filed: (a) with each "submission" that initiates agency consideration of your company, (b) on award of a contract that does not exceed $100,000[4] if there has been no prior filing, and (c) quarterly if there has been a "material change" in the accuracy of information you previously disclosed.[5] The Government Accountability Office (GAO) has specifically held that failure to submit a signed Byrd Amendment certification before award does not render a bid nonresponsive.[6] Rather, the GAO noted that the Byrd Amendment certification merely states that the bidder agrees to comply with the terms of the Act. In other words, regardless of whether a bidder signs the certification, it is bound by law to perform in accordance with the terms of the certification and is subject to the stated penalties for failing to do so. According to the GAO, by the terms of the certification itself, the relevant time for certification is contract award, not bid opening.

Question 4: Why should I, as a contractor, care about the LDA if the lobbyists, and not me, are required to register with the House Clerk and the Senate Secretary?

Answer 4: You should care about the LDA primarily for two reasons. *First,* the LDA potentially requires many federal contractors to register for the first time as lobbying organizations and to file semiannual reports on their lobbying activity. The LDA states that "an entity whose employees act as lobbyists on its own behalf is both a client and an employer of such employees." Your own employees, therefore, may qualify as lobbyists depending on the efforts that they put forth in attempting to secure a contract for your company. In other words, your own employees may have to register as lobbyists for you (as their "client"), and your company may have to register on behalf of your "lobbying" employees.

Second, under the Byrd Amendment, you generally must file with the Contracting Officer the name of the registered lobbyist under the LDA who has made lobbying contacts on your behalf. If you hire a lobbyist that should be registered and is not, and you fail subsequently to disclose the name of the lobbyist in your

---

[3]FAR 3.803(a)(2)(iii).

[4]31 U.S.C.A. § 1352(d)(2)(B).

[5]31 U.S.C.A. § 1352(b)(4).

[6]*Tennier Indus., Inc.*, Comp. Gen. Dec. B-239025, 90-2 CPD 25 (July 11, 1990).

§ 7:16   Government Contract Compliance Handbook

Byrd Amendment disclosure, you may be liable for penalties under the Byrd Amendment. Understanding the LDA's registration requirements, therefore, may help ensure proper disclosure under the Byrd Amendment.

Question 5: Who are considered "lobbyists" under the LDA?

Answer 5: "Lobbyists" are defined as individuals who: (1) are employed to provide services to their employers that include more than one "lobbying contact" in a semiannual reporting period, and (2) spend at least 20% of their time on "lobbying activities."[7] Individuals whose lobbying activities constitute less than 20% of their time during a six-month period are not required to register or report their activities. Registration and reporting requirements also do not currently apply to any lobbyist whose income on behalf of a particular client does not exceed $6,000 or, in the case of an organization whose employees lobby on its own behalf (this could be you), the total expenses in connection with lobbying do not exceed $24,500 during the semiannual period.[8]

Question 6: What are "lobbying contacts" under the LDA?

Answer 6: A "lobbying contact" is defined as any oral or written communication to a covered legislative or executive branch official (including staff) on behalf of a client with regard to the administration or execution of a federal program or policy, including (as stated above) the negotiation, award, or administration of a federal contract.[9]

Question 7: Are there any exceptions to the LDA's definition of "lobbying contacts" that are pertinent to Government contractors?

Answer 7: Yes. Some of the LDA's exceptions include: (a) a request for a meeting or for the status of an action, or any other similar administrative request if the request does not include an attempt to influence a covered official, (b) information provided in writing in response to an oral or written request by a covered official for specific information, (c) information required by subpoena, civil investigative demand, or otherwise compelled to be disclosed by statute, regulation, or other action of the Congress or an agency, (d) communications made in responses to a notice in FedBizOpps,[10] or other similar publication soliciting communications from the public and directed to the agency official specifically designated in the notice to receive such communications, and (e) a petition for agency action made in writing and required to be a matter of public record pursuant to established

---

[7]2 U.S.C.A. § 1602(10).
[8]2 U.S.C.A. § 1603(a)(3)(A).
[9]2 U.S.C.A. § 1602(8).
[10]Online at http://www.FedBizOpps.gov.

INFLUENCING GOVERNMENT ACTIONS § 7:17

agency procedures.[11]

Question 8: Is it possible that I would not have to disclose lobbying activities under the Byrd Amendment but my company or one of my employees would have to register under the LDA?

Answer 8: Yes. Remember that under the Byrd Amendment and implementing FAR provisions you are not required to disclose the lobbying efforts of an individual if the individual is receiving only reasonable compensation out of your own funds as a regularly employed officer or employee of your company. However, under the LDA, if your employees lobby on your behalf and the total expenses in connection with their lobbying exceed $24,500 during a semiannual period, you must register on their behalf. Your employees may be responsible, furthermore, for registering themselves. In addition, while the Byrd Amendment contains broad exemptions for routine business development, sales, and marketing activities (agency liaison activities), the LDA does not. Accordingly, communications with covered officials that are made in connection with a contractor's typical business functions may require LDA registration because the communications would constitute "lobbying contacts," and all the work done in preparation of such activities could constitute "lobbying activities."

C. HOW TO RECOGNIZE THE PROBLEM

§ 7:17 Generally

The interaction of the Byrd Amendment and the Lobbying Disclosure Act may appear to be rather confusing. If you remember the purposes of each statute, however, you should be able to understand generally what each law requires. Essentially, the LDA deals with the registering of lobbyists before Congress, while the Byrd Amendment involves making the federal agency aware of the funds and people that you are using to influence contract award.

Some of the requirements under the Byrd Amendment and LDA are fairly straightforward. For example, if you hire a registered lobbyist for the express purpose of persuading an agency to award you a contract, you must clearly disclose the activity and certify that the lobbyist was not paid with "appropriated funds." Or, if one of your paid employees is responsible solely for lobbying for contract awards, registration under the LDA most likely will be required. However, given the nuances of and exceptions to both the LDA and Byrd Amendment, there are many apparently innocent activities that may also require Byrd Amendment disclosure and certification and/or LDA registration.

---

[11]2 U.S.C.A. § 1602(8)(B).

You should be aware of these pitfalls so you can avoid inadvertent violations.

There have been only a few cases interpreting the Byrd Amendment and the LDA to date. Accordingly, if you think you may have a Byrd Amendment or LDA problem, you should consult your company's legal advisor. Get sound advice before you inadvertently stumble into a violation.

§ 7:18 Examples

The sales pitch: Your firm employs sales personnel to market and promote your products. Their traditional responsibilities include contacting various federal agencies both to learn about upcoming procurements and to inform the various agencies about your products. On learning that the Government has just issued a solicitation for a product, one of your employees contacts the Contracting Officer for more information, and in the course of the conversation explains how your product is different from (and better than) others in the marketplace. Has any violation of the Byrd Amendment or Lobbying Disclosure Act occurred?

Perhaps. This activity could fall under the Byrd Amendment because your agent has attempted to "influence the award" of a federal contract. If your agent is paid out of "contract funds" (overhead or general and administrative expenses charged to Government contracts) you would be in violation of the Byrd Amendment. However, in this situation, your sales personnel would not likely qualify as "lobbyists" under the LDA. A Contracting Officer is not generally a federal official of a sufficiently high level to qualify as a "covered executive branch official" under the LDA.

Contract options: Your company has been awarded a contract by the Government to produce radios. The contract contains an "Option" clause for additional units, and the Government may either exercise the option or resolicit. Your employees contact the Contracting Officer to explain why it would be more cost effective for the Government to exercise its option under the contract. Has your company done anything wrong?

It depends. If the employees who called the Contracting Officer are paid with appropriated funds, you may have violated the Byrd Amendment. Although the statute contains exceptions for agency liaison activities, the communication about the option contract probably would not be accepted. It is doubtful that you would have to register this activity under the LDA because this one-time contact most likely would be exempted from the LDA's registration requirements, and a Contracting Officer is not generally a "covered executive branch official."

D. COMPLIANCE INITIATIVES

§ 7:19 Generally

The Byrd Amendment and Lobbying Disclosure Act place onerous and, at times, confusing reporting, certification, and registration requirements on you. However, because of the substantial monetary penalties, you should ensure that your company complies with both statutes.

§ 7:20 Byrd Amendment

You must develop *procedures* to ensure that no prohibited payments are made to lobbyists, outside counsel, accountants, or any other consultants from contract direct, overhead, or general and administrative accounts. Payments to these personnel from contract funds may be made only after you have verified that the services were rendered for "professional or technical services" performed: (1) directly in the preparation, submission, or negotiation of a bid, proposal, or application, or (2) for "meeting requirements imposed by or pursuant to law as a condition for receiving that Federal contract." Similar but not identical controls must be placed on payments to in-house personnel for similar activities. Nothing in the Byrd Amendment, however, applies to selling activities by independent sales representatives before an agency, provided that the selling activities occur prior to formal solicitation by the agency.[1]

Furthermore, you must *monitor* your contracts on an ongoing basis to make sure that there has been no material change in the accuracy of any information previously disclosed to the Government. For this, you must ensure that there is good communication within your company with respect to all contract-influencing activities. You may want to establish a single point of control for this purpose.

You must also ensure that all declarations made under the Byrd Amendment include the required *certification* that appropriated funds were not used to influence or attempt to influence award, and that the required disclosures are filed. Remember that disclosures must be filed: (a) whenever action is initiated to obtain "agency consideration" for award, (b) on receipt of the contract if you did not previously file, and (c) quarterly if the information previously disclosed has materially changed since your previous submission.

If you are a prime contractor, you should identify your first-tier

---

[Section 7:20]

[1] FAR 3.803.

§ 7:20   GOVERNMENT CONTRACT COMPLIANCE HANDBOOK

subcontractors and let them know of their obligations both to: (1) submit their disclosure and certification forms to you, and (2) inform lower-tier subcontractors of their responsibilities. If you are a subcontractor, you must ensure that your certifications and disclosures are passed along to the prime or the next highest tier contractor.

§ 7:21 Lobbying Disclosure Act

Because the LDA requires lobbyists (or their organizations) to register themselves, you probably will not be too concerned about the LDA if you hire "outside" lobbyists to work for you—except for Byrd Amendment disclosure purposes.

On the other hand, you will be concerned with the LDA if you or your employees routinely do lobbying work for your own products. If one or more of your employees spends more than 20% of his or her time on "lobbying activities," and you spend more than $24,500 per six-month period for these activities, you or your employees probably would have to register under the LDA (even though you effectively are lobbying for yourself). Faced with this possibility, there are some procedures that you can initiate to ensure your compliance with the LDA.

Establish a *policy* that allows for lobbying *only* by outside lobbyists or lobbying firms. Such a policy would protect you from the need to comply with the requirements of the LDA, although you would have to keep aware of your Byrd Amendment disclosure obligations. Alternatively, you can ensure that all of your lobbying is initiated by your own employees. By doing this, you could either register under the LDA immediately or monitor your lobbying expenditures to ensure exemption from the LDA. In-house lobbying may be advantageous to you because the Byrd Amendment does not require disclosure of lobbying activities conducted by your own reasonably paid employees. Nevertheless, if you elect to use in-house lobbyists, be careful to avoid payments to them from appropriated funds.

§ 7:22 Recommendations

Each executive agency compiles contractor-submitted Byrd Amendment disclosure forms and passes them along to Congress annually. The disclosure form provides that lobbying information disclosed on the form "will be available for public inspection." To protect information that you consider *confidential*, clearly mark all disclosure forms with a *protective legend* stating that the information provided is "confidential, proprietary, commercial information exempt from public disclosure." You should also take exception to the public disclosure language of the form.

Set up an *internal monitoring system* "with teeth" to ensure that no aspect of Byrd Amendment or LDA compliance is neglected or forgotten. *Train* your managers to recognize potential Byrd Amendment and LDA situations and to follow through in resolving them with your general counsel.

When in doubt, get *legal advice*.

IV. COLLUSIVE BIDDING

A. STATUTORY FRAMEWORK

§ 7:23 Generally

The terms bid-rigging, price-fixing, and collusive bidding are often used interchangeably to describe a particular type of illegal, anticompetitive behavior that may constitute fraud or violate antitrust statutes. Engaging in these activities subjects you and your employees to criminal penalties, civil damages, and suspension and debarment of your company from contracting with the Government.

There are a number of mechanisms through which you can be penalized for any collusive bidding activity. The primary vehicle for *criminal* enforcement is the Sherman Antitrust Act.[1] The Clayton Act and Federal Trade Commission Act allow for *civil* actions against antitrust violators.[2] In addition, you may be liable under a number of other criminal, civil, and state laws if you or your company engages in collusive bidding. Thus, the Government has a large arsenal of weapons to use against collusive bidding which can cripple you or put you out of business. It is therefore critical that you take steps to protect yourself and your company from accusations of collusive bidding.

§ 7:24 Sherman Antitrust Act

Section 1 of the Sherman Antitrust Act provides that "[e]very contract, combination in the form of trust or otherwise, or conspiracy, in restraint of trade or commerce among the several States, or with foreign nations, is declared to be illegal."[1] To prove a violation of the Sherman Act, the Government must show that: (1) two or more real competitors had a common plan, agreement, or conspiracy, (2) to fix or stabilize prices, rig bids, allocate customers, or allocate territories or markets, and (3) the conspiracy or agreement of concerned goods or services in interstate or

---

[Section 7:23]

[1]15 U.S.C.A. §§ 1 to 7.

[2]15 U.S.C.A. §§ 12 to 27, 41 to 58.

[Section 7:24]

[1]15 U.S.C.A. § 1.

foreign commerce. There are four basic collusive bidding schemes that are most common to Government contract antitrust conspiracies.[2]

(1) *Bid suppression*: Bid suppression occurs when two or more competing contractors agree either not to bid on a particular contract or to withdraw their bids (for example, alleging a mistake in bid) so that a particular contractor wins the award.

(2) *Complementary bidding*: Complementary bidding involves an agreement among two or more competitors that a particular contractor will win an award. This takes two forms. Either the designated winner-to-be tells the other bidders what he plans to bid, thus allowing the others to submit higher bids, or the designated winner simply tells the other bidders what they should bid. This form of bid-rigging creates the impression that there is competition while ensuring that the designated contractor is successful.

(3) *Bid rotation*: In bid rotation, the contractors involved in bidding on the same contracts agree to take turns as low bidder. Sometimes the contractors create a cycle under which each successively becomes the low bidder in turn. More complex schemes involve changing the order of the cycle at regular intervals. Some bid-rotation plans allow the losing bidders to become subcontractors to the awardee of the contract.

(4) *Market division*: In this form of collusive activity, contractors agree to divide the market among themselves on the basis of criteria other than rotation. For example, the conspirators may agree that all contracts in a particular geographic region, or of a certain monetary value, will go to a particular contractor.

A Sherman Act violation carries substantial criminal penalties. Each person convicted under the Act is guilty of a felony. Corporations may be fined up to $100 million and individuals up to $1,000,000 for each violation, and individuals may be imprisoned for up to ten years as well.[3]

A defense contractor who supplied military tie down equipment reportedly entered into a plea agreement with the Department of Justice to pay a $275,000 fine to settle charges that it had conspired to fix prices on contracts in violation of Section 1 of the Sherman Antitrust Act. The company reportedly colluded with others to split the market between them by agreeing to refrain from bidding on certain work or by submitting intentionally high

---

[2]DOD Inspector General, Criminal Investigation—Policy Oversight, "Antitrust Enforcement in Department of Defense Procurement," 3-5 (IG/CIPO 5505.1-H, Jan. 1987).

[3]15 U.S.C.A. § 1. *See* Pub. L. No. 108-237, § 215(a) which increased the penalties from $10 million for corporations, $350,000 for individuals, and three years imprisonment to $100 million, $1 million, and 10 years respectively.

INFLUENCING GOVERNMENT ACTIONS § 7:26

bids on other work. U.S. v. Peck & Hale LLE, (E.D.N.Y., No. 08 CR 123-1 (JFB) March 26, 2008). In another case, a manufacturer of plastic marine pilings reportedly pled guilty to a bid rigging scheme. The defendant allegedly agreed with other contractors to allocate work among themselves and to not compete for one another's customers either by not submitting prices or bids to certain customers, or by submitting intentionally high prices or bids to certain customers. *U.S. v. Barmakian*, E.D.Va., No 2:08cr 197 (November 17, 2008).

§ 7:25 Clayton Act

Anticompetitive practices prohibited by the Clayton Act include "tying agreements" (conditioning the sale of a product on the buyer's agreement to purchase other products from the seller), exclusive dealing agreements (conditioning the sale of a product on the buyer's agreement to refuse to deal with the seller's competitors), and the joining together of competitors, through a merger or otherwise, who have a combined market share sufficient to substantially affect price competition in a particular market.[1] The Act allows individuals and the Federal Government and state governments to maintain *civil* actions against violators.

A private individual need not even be a competitor to be able to sue under the Clayton Act if he can show injury to business or property as the result of a violation.[2] Shareholders and officers of a corporation, however, have generally been denied standing to sue.[3] Federal and state governments must show that an antitrust violation has occurred and that the government was injured by the violation.[4]

The Act provides for the payment of treble the actual amount of damages, costs (including reasonable attorney fees), and prejudgment interest on the total damages.[5] Furthermore, a plaintiff may obtain injunctive relief if he can show "threatened" loss or damage to business or property.[6]

§ 7:26 Federal Trade Commission Act

The Federal Trade Commission (FTC) Act prohibits any "unfair

[Section 7:25]

[1] 15 U.S.C.A. §§ 12 to 27.

[2] *Reiter v. Sonotone Corp.*, 442 U.S. 330, 99 S. Ct. 2326, 60 L. Ed. 2d 931, 27 Fed. R. Serv. 2d 653 (1979).

[3] *Program Engineering, Inc. v. Triangle Publications, Inc.*, 634 F.2d 1188 (9th Cir. 1980).

[4] 15 U.S.C.A. § 15(a).

[5] 15 U.S.C.A. §§ 15a, 15c.

[6] 15 U.S.C.A. § 26.

§ 7:26   GOVERNMENT CONTRACT COMPLIANCE HANDBOOK

trade practice" and gives the FTC broad authority to regulate unfair competitive practices.[1] The FTC Act's standards mirror those of the Sherman Act.

§ 7:27   Other statutes & regulations

In addition to sanctions under the Sherman, Clayton, and FTC Acts, a contractor participating in a bid-rigging scheme may be subject to penalties under the False Claims Act[1] or False Statements Statute[2] (see §§ 1:1 et seq.), the wire fraud[3] or mail fraud[4] statutes if the telephone, telegraph, or mail, including e-mail, were used in furtherance of a bid-rigging scheme (see §§ 1:1 et seq.), the conspiracy statute[5] (see §§ 1:1 et seq.), and the civil remedy provisions of the Racketeer Influenced and Corrupt Organizations Act.[6] Collusive activity also can trigger federal and state debarment and suspension procedures. As discussed in §§ 1:1 et seq., a contractor may be debarred or suspended from doing business with the Government for a wide range of reasons, including conviction or civil judgment for the commission of fraud or a criminal offense with regard to Government procurement, or for violating federal or state antitrust laws.[7]

The FAR requires that each solicitation for firm-fixed-price contracts includes a "Certificate of Independent Price Determination" which calls for each bidder to certify that (a) the prices in its offer were reached independently and without agreement or consultation with other bidders, and (b) its offer will not be disclosed to other bidders or potential bidders before bid opening (the text of the FAR "Certificate" is set forth in Appendix H to this Handbook).[8] If a bidder alters the "Certificate," the bid must be rejected. In addition, if prices have been disclosed in violation of Paragraph (a)(2) of the "Certificate," a bidder must provide an explanation. If an offer is rejected because the "Certificate" was altered or modified, or if the Contracting Officer is concerned that the "Certificate" is false, the Contracting Officer must report the

---

[Section 7:26]
[1] 15 U.S.C.A. §§ 41 to 58.

[Section 7:27]
[1] 18 U.S.C.A. § 287.
[2] 18 U.S.C.A. § 1001.
[3] 18 U.S.C.A. § 1343.
[4] 18 U.S.C.A. § 1341.
[5] 18 U.S.C.A. § 371.
[6] 18 U.S.C.A. §§ 1961 to 1968.
[7] FAR 9.406-2.
[8] FAR 3.103-1, 52.203-2.

situation to the Attorney General.

§ 7:28 Exceptions

There are competitor relationships that may seem collusive in nature but are permitted nevertheless. For example, there are several types of contractor agreements that are allowable under the antitrust laws. These include company affiliations, contractor teaming arrangements or other joint venture agreements, and defense production and research and development pools.

§ 7:29 Exceptions—Affiliated companies

Affiliated companies are not prohibited either from bidding together or bidding against each other for a particular contract. For example, a parent company and its subsidiary, or subsidiaries of a common parent, may join together to submit a bid. The U.S. Supreme Court has held that it is not improper for affiliated businesses to submit a single bid where they function as essentially a single economic unit.[1] Similarly, it is not improper for affiliated companies to compete against each other,[2] as long as they submit independent offers in compliance with the FAR's "Certificate of Independent Price Determination," and each submits a bid that is competitive with all other bidders.[3]

§ 7:30 Exceptions—Teaming agreements & joint ventures

A teaming agreement is the joining of two or more contractors as a partnership or joint venture for purposes of acting as a potential prime contractor, or an agreement between a potential prime contractor and one or more companies to act as subcontractors. The FAR specifically permits these types of agreements, if the arrangement is disclosed in the offer or, where the arrangement is made after the offer, the arrangement is disclosed to the Government before it becomes effective.[1] Contractors enter into these types of agreements to reduce costs and improve performance, particularly in complex procurements where each participant has unique skills or capabilities.

[Section 7:29]

[1]*Arizona v. Maricopa County Medical Soc.*, 457 U.S. 332, 102 S. Ct. 2466, 73 L. Ed. 2d 48 (1982).

[2]Robbins-Gioia, Inc., B-274318, 96-2 CPD 222, pp. 20—21 (December 4, 1996).

[3]*David I. Abse, B-174449*, 1972 CPD 2, 51 Comp. Gen. 403 (January 12, 1972).

[Section 7:30]

[1]FAR 9.603.

§ 7:30 GOVERNMENT CONTRACT COMPLIANCE HANDBOOK

These arrangements are not automatically exempt, however, from the antitrust laws.[2] Where the purpose of the agreement is to further the Government's interest in reducing costs or improving performance, it will generally be acceptable.[3] However, where the arrangement serves to suppress competition, labeling it a joint venture will not avoid antitrust liability. If a joint venture or teaming agreement is challenged under the antitrust laws, the courts will examine the purpose and effect of the agreement to determine if the arrangement is legitimate.

The FTC has issued guidelines on the antitrust implications of joint ventures between competitors under its Joint Venture Project.[4] For the Government contracting community, the results of the FTC Joint Venture Project have a significant impact on teaming agreements between contractors. The Defense Department and Department of Health & Human Services have also alerted Contracting Officers to be cognizant of the amount of competition at the subcontractor level as well as the prime contractor level.[5]

§ 7:31 Exceptions—Defense production pools

Defense production pools are specific types of team arrangements or joint ventures that are specifically exempted from application of the antitrust laws.[1] The FAR defines a "pool" as an association of contractors joined together to perform a defense production or research and development contract, where the association is governed by a specific agreement and has obtained approval of the agreement by either the Small Business Administration or another designated official.[2] Pool members may submit

---

[2]*Northrop Corp. v. McDonnell Douglas Corp.*, 705 F.2d 1030, 36 Fed. R. Serv. 2d 102 (9th Cir. 1983); *Tower Air, Inc. v. Federal Exp. Corp.*, 956 F. Supp. 270 (E.D. N.Y. 1996).

[3]*Compact v. Metropolitan Government of Nashville & Davidson County, TN.*, 594 F. Supp. 1567 (M.D. Tenn. 1984).

[4]62 Fed. Reg. 22945 (1997); see FTC's Joint Venture Project web page at http://www.ftc.gov/sites/default/files/documents/public_events/joint-venture-hearings-antitrust-guidelines-collaboration-among-competitors/ftcdojguidelines-2.pdf.

[5]*See* "DOD's Gansler Directs Elimination of Anti-Competitive Teaming Arrangements" Government Contractor, 41 GC 16 (Jan. 13, 1999); HHS OIG Special Advisory Bulletin on Contractual Joint Ventures, Wednesday April 30, 2003.

[Section 7:31]

[1]FAR Subpart 9.7.

[2]FAR 9.701.

bids as part of the pool or individually.[3]

B. FREQUENTLY ASKED QUESTIONS

§ 7:32 Questions & answers

Question 1: Why is collusive bidding subject to the Sherman Act?

Answer 1: Collusive bidding is illegal under the Sherman Act because it is a form of "contract" that restrains trade by undermining the competitive process. In determining whether an activity is illegal under the Sherman Act, the Supreme Court has held that only those contracts, combinations, and conspiracies that operate to prejudice the public interest by unduly restraining competition are illegal.[1]

Question 2: What are some forms of illegal restraint-of-trade agreements?

Answer 2: While every restraint-of-trade agreement is potentially illegal, certain types of business arrangements, which by their very nature tend to restrict competition, are considered illegal per se. These include price-fixing, division of markets, group boycotts, and tying arrangements.[2] A tying arrangement is an agreement by a party to sell one product, but only on the condition that the buyer also purchases a different (or tied) product, or at least agrees that he will not purchase that product from any other supplier. As noted above in § 7:24, the Government has identified four prohibited collusive bidding schemes that are most common to Government contracts—bid suppression, complementary bidding, bid rotation, and market division.

Question 3: To be liable civilly for anticompetitive conduct, does a specific, anticompetitive intent have to be shown?

Answer 3: In a civil action under the Clayton Act, no proof of specific motive is required, and the general intent to restrain trade may be inferred from proof of either an unlawful purpose or an anticompetitive effect.[3]

Question 4: What if one of my employees is responsible for collusive bid-rigging and I do not know about it?

---

[3]FAR 9.703.

[Section 7:32]

[1]*Standard Oil Company Of New Jersey et al., Appts., v. United States*, 221 U.S. 1, 31 S.Ct. 502, 55 L.Ed. 619, 34 L.R.A.N.S. 834, Am.Ann.Cas. 1912D, 734 (1911).

[2]*Northern Pac. Ry. Co. v. U.S.*, 356 U.S. 1, 78 S. Ct. 514, 2 L. Ed. 2d 545 (1958). See *U.S. v. Microsoft Corp.*, 253 F.3d 34 (D.C. Cir. 2001).

[3]*U.S. v. U.S. Gypsum Co.*, 438 U.S. 422, 98 S. Ct. 2864, 57 L. Ed. 2d 854 (1978) (intent is an element of a criminal case). See *U.S. v. Container Corp. of America*, 393 U.S. 333, 337, 89 S. Ct. 510, 21 L. Ed. 2d 526 (1969).

§ 7:32   Government Contract Compliance Handbook

Answer 4: Be aware that the actions of employees involved in illegal activity can be imputed to the company.[4]

Question 5: If I have several outstanding contract claims against the Government but I am charged with collusive bidding, can I settle the contract claims with the Government's collusive bidding charges are pending?

Answer 5: Unfortunately, it is not that easy. When the Government alleges collusive bidding against a contractor, resolution of contract claims must be delayed until the Department of Justice (DOJ) concludes its investigation of the charges. Both the Contract Disputes Act of 1978[5] and the FAR[6] forbid Contracting Officers from settling, compromising, or otherwise adjusting any claim on a contract in which fraud is alleged. Fraud investigations are conducted by DOJ or another investigative agency, not by the Contracting Officer or the Comptroller General.

Question 6: Should I be concerned as a Government contractor, especially as a defense contractor, if I decide to merge with or acquire another Government contractor?

Answer 6: Yes. Although DOJ and the FTC are the vested agencies for antitrust enforcement, the Department of Defense (DOD) has become more actively involved in the review of mergers involving defense contractors. DOD now plays an influential advisory role in DOJ and FTC review of defense industry mergers. In fact, one source indicates that when DOD has supported a merger of competing defense contractors, the antitrust agencies have not taken contrary positions.[7]

If you are a defense contractor and are involved in a merger and/or acquisition, DOD support can be beneficial. You should try to gain a DOD review as early as possible in the negotiation of the merger or acquisition, particularly so that any recommendations from agency officials can be considered.

C. HOW TO RECOGNIZE THE PROBLEM

§ 7:33   Generally

The Government continues to investigate and prosecute violations of the antitrust laws affecting Government procurement. Therefore, it is important that both you and your employees who have bidding authority are in a position to influence your company's bidding policy to recognize potentially dangerous col-

---

[4]FAR 9.406-5.

[5]41 U.S.C.A. §§ 601 to 613.

[6]FAR 33.210.

[7]King, DOD Review of Mergers and Joint Ventures: Not Just for Antitrust Lawyers, Procurement Law (summer 1997).

INFLUENCING GOVERNMENT ACTIONS § 7:33

lusive bidding situations. While no industry is immune from collusive bidding, this activity historically has been found most often in the construction industry and certain other areas of Government contracting.

The procurement regulations provide some guidance for recognizing potentially collusive bids.[1] However, the Department of the Army has issued a memorandum on "Procurement Fraud Indicators" providing detailed guidance to procurement personnel which might be helpful to your employees in recognizing possible collusive activity (see Appendix I to this Handbook).[2] Indicators of collusive bidding and price-fixing set out in the memorandum include the following:[3]

(1) Bidders who are qualified and capable of performing but who fail to bid with no apparent reason.

(2) Certain contractors who always or never bid against each other.

(3) The successful bidder repeatedly subcontracts work to companies that submitted higher bids.

(4) Different groups of contractors appear to specialize in federal, state, or local jobs exclusively.

(5) There is an apparent pattern of low bids regularly occurring, such as corporation "X" always being the low bidder in a certain geographical area or in a fixed rotation with other bidders.

(6) A certain company appears to be bidding substantially higher on some bids than on other bids with no logical cost difference to account for the increase.

(7) Bidders frequently change prices at about the same time and to the same extent.

(8) A joint venture bids where either contractor could have bid individually as a prime.

(9) Competitors regularly socialize or appear to hold meetings or otherwise get together in the vicinity of procurement offices shortly before the bid-filing deadline.

(10) Bid prices appear to drop whenever a new or infrequent bidder submits a bid.

(11) Competitors exchange any form of price information among themselves, or bidders refer to "association or industry price schedules," "industry wide prices," or "market wide prices."

[Section 7:33]

[1]FAR 3.303.

[2]*See also* 32 C.F.R. Pt. 516 and 57 Fed. Reg. 31852 (July 17, 1992) Appendix F—Procurement Fraud Indicators.

[3]Dept. of the Army Memorandum, "Procurement Fraud Indicators," 5–7 (SELCE-LG-JA (27-10i), Feb. 20, 1990).

(12) Statements by a bidder that it is not its turn to receive a job or, conversely, that it is another bidder's turn.

This list is by no means complete. The Army memorandum states that antitrust violation indicators include agreements to adhere to published price lists, agreements to raise prices by a specified increment, agreements to establish, adhere to, or eliminate discounts, agreements not to advertise, and agreements to maintain specified price differentials based on quantity, type, or size of products.[4]

§ 7:34 Examples

Dividing the market: Your company and your competitors, Crown Custodians and Jones Janitorial Service, are all in the business of providing janitorial services to military bases. You learn that military Bases One, Two, and Three have recently requested bids on contracts for janitorial services. You agree with representatives of Crown and Jones that you will submit the low bid at Base One, Crown will submit the low bid at Base Two, and Jones will submit the low bid at Base Three. Is there a problem with this scenario?

Yes. You may be liable for collusive bidding in violation of the Sherman Act.

Unauthorized swap of information: One of your management employees used to work for a competitor and still maintains friendships with several former coworkers. Over lunch, they discuss how competitive the industry has become and how insecure their jobs are as a result of increased competition. To protect themselves and their companies from the financial hardship that could arise if several pending contracts are lost, they decide, without your knowledge, to exchange bid information to ensure that both companies will get a portion of the available work. Did your employee do something wrong?

Yes. This activity is clearly illegal because it constitutes a form of both bid rotation and complementary bidding. Furthermore, even though your employee was acting without your knowledge or acquiescence, his actions may be *imputed* to your company, and your company may be convicted of collusive bidding activity. This problem might have been avoided if your company had instituted a compliance program that explained the illegalities and the consequences of such activity to the employee. Also, your management oversight committee might have been able to prevent the problem if a pattern of bidding irregularity was timely detected.

---

[4]Dept. of the Army Memorandum, "Procurement Fraud Indicators," 5–7 (SELCE-LG-JA (27-10i), Feb. 20, 1990).

Dividing the territory: You have just purchased a trash removal company and intend to expand your market to Government agencies. The owner of a competing firm comes to your office and explains that "in this town" he does "all the trash removal on the west side." You agree not to infringe on his territory and to limit your participation to solicitations for contracts on the east side, where most of your market is anyway. Is there a problem with your acquiescence to the competing firm?

Yes. This behavior is illegal, even though you probably would have focused your efforts on the east side of town in any event. The fact that you might have sensed a threat from the competitor, or that you might have limited your efforts geographically in any case, does not excuse this geographic market division bidding scheme.

Submission of false bid: You receive a procurement solicitation that requires two bids to be submitted in order for any consideration of contract award. Unfortunately, you happen to be the only contractor interested in the procurement opportunity. You decide to ask your friend who operates a noncompeting business that could not perform on the contract to submit a bid just so that the solicitation can become effective. Is there a problem with this scenario?

Yes. Most likely you have committed an antitrust violation under the Sherman Act. In fact, one court has held on facts similar to these that conspiring with a non-competitor to submit a "false" bid was collusive bidding activity, even if the non-competitor could not perform.[1]

D. COMPLIANCE INITIATIVES

§ 7:35 Generally

The first step in avoiding collusive bidding is to recognize collusive bidding practices. Fortunately, this is not difficult in most cases. The two main groups within your company most likely to be involved in collusive bidding situations are employees with bidding responsibility and management employees with bidding oversight authority. Bid-rigging conspiracies often occur at the very highest levels within a company and, as a result, every employee with bidding authority or the power to influence bidding or bidding policy is a potential source of both bid-rigging conduct and its prevention. Establishing a company *ethics program* will help to solve the problem.

Your company must develop and adhere to a *code of conduct*

[Section 7:34]

[1]*U.S. v. Reicher*, 983 F.2d 168 (10th Cir. 1992).

§ 7:35   GOVERNMENT CONTRACT COMPLIANCE HANDBOOK

and antitrust compliance program that will prevent potential antitrust and collusive bidding activity within your company. You must be vigilant in avoiding *discussions* with competitors of bid information, pricing information, or your plans to bid or not to bid on a particular contract. Your anti-collusive bidding program must focus on supervision and *monitoring* of individuals within the company who either have *bidding authority* or are in a position to influence your company's bidding policy, including high-level management personnel. The management oversight committee must be familiar with all aspects of your bidding process, the markets in which you are competing, and the true costs of performance on the contracts for which you are competing. Only then will you be able to recognize and guard against improper activities of employees who are in a position to compromise your company by participating in a bid-rigging scheme.

A useful example of a contractor's compliance program formulated to cure past collusive bidding activities is the plan used by a contractor after two of its subsidiaries pleaded "no contest" to charges of bid-rigging.[1] Although these two subsidiaries represented only a small portion of the contractor's overall operations, the entire company could have been debarred from Government contracting. The risk of debarment, coupled with the fact that the contractor did not want its employees to engage in criminal conduct, caused the contractor to adopt a strict antitrust compliance policy. One of the key features was *central review* of all bidding practices and procedures. The plan can be summarized as follows:

(a) The company established a stringent antitrust compliance policy which makes clear that anticompetitive practice will not be tolerated and that violators of the law will be terminated.

(b) The company's chief counsel met with each employee who had bidding responsibility to explain the antitrust compliance policy and require each employee to sign a statement subscribing to the policy. The company plans to review these statements annually with each employee.

(c) The company's internal audit department will spend more of its efforts checking the business practices of each district office.

(d) The antitrust policy was reviewed with every manager, during which the company made clear that it will terminate the employment of anyone who violates the antitrust laws and will not pay for his criminal defense. Furthermore, the

---

[Section 7:35]

[1]*Peter Kiewit Sons' Co. v. U. S. Army Corps of Engineers*, 534 F. Supp. 1139 (D.D.C. 1982), judgment rev'd, 714 F.2d 163 (D.C. Cir. 1983).

company's policy is to cooperate fully with law enforcement agencies in their investigation of alleged antitrust violations.

§ 7:36 Recommendations

(a) *Make sure* employees and management personnel involved in the preparation or submission of bids *understand* the relevant laws, the situations in which potential collusive bidding may occur, and your company's policies with respect to such activity.

(b) Establish a compliance program and a *written company policy* that focuses on collusive bidding and make sure that *all* employees who are in a position to compromise your company are informed of the gravity of collusive bidding violations and the liability that they as *individuals* may incur if they engage in improper bidding activities. Distribute your policy statement to all employees concerned and have them sign *certifications* that they understand and agree to comply with the policy.

(c) Appoint an *oversight committee* (or individual) to control bidding policy and procedures and charge it with responsibility for all aspects of your company's bidding.

V. KICKBACKS

A. STATUTORY FRAMEWORK

§ 7:37 Generally

Assume that you are responsible for obtaining subcontracts for your company and are constantly trying to find new sources for business. You ask ABC Corporation to put you on its bidder's list, although you do not meet all of its technical requirements, and offer in exchange to provide a loan at a very favorable interest rate to enable ABC Corporation to expand its operations. You find nothing improper about this activity because you have not asked ABC Corporation to award you any specific contract. ABC Corporation declines your offer. Nevertheless, you may have violated the Anti-Kickback Act of 1986 because you have offered a thing of value (low-interest loan financing) in exchange for favorable treatment (placement on a bidder's list) in connection with federal contracts.

The Anti-Kickback Act of 1986 imposes criminal and civil penalties for kickbacks in connection with contracts and subcontracts. The Act essentially extends the anticorruption concepts applicable to dealings with "public officials" under the bribery and illegal gratuities statutes (discussed above in §§ 7:2 to 7:12) to private persons in subcontract relationships.

§ 7:38 Anti-Kickback Act

Congress enacted the Anti-Kickback Act of 1986[1] in response to concerns that the existing anti-kickback laws were ineffective. The Act strengthened, broadened, and clarified the provisions of previous legislation and attempts "to deter subcontractors from making payments and contractors from accepting payments for the purpose of improperly obtaining or rewarding favorable treatment in connection with a prime contractor or a subcontract relating to a prime contract."[2]

§ 7:39 Anti-Kickback Act—Elements

To prove a violation of the Anti-Kickback Act of 1986, the Government must establish the following:[1]

(1) You provided, attempted to provide, or offered to provide a kickback; or

(2) You solicited, accepted, or attempted to accept a kickback; or

(3) You included, directly or indirectly, the amount of a kickback in the contract price charged by a subcontractor to a prime contractor (or higher-tier subcontractor) or in the contract price charged by a prime to the United States.

The Act covers any individual or business entity.[2]

A "kickback" is defined as "any money, fee, commission, credit, gift, gratuity, thing of value, or compensation of any kind which is provided, directly or indirectly," to any prime or subcontractor or their employees "for the purpose of improperly obtaining or rewarding favorable treatment in connection with a prime contract or in connection with a subcontract relating to a prime contract."[3] The requirement that the kickback be provided for the purpose of "improperly" obtaining or acknowledging favorable treatment suggests that the statute does not apply to business transactions that are for legitimate purposes.

In some cases, business relationships that companies may think are customary commercial relationships, the Department of Justice considers kickbacks under the applicable statute.

On April 19, 2007, the DOJ announced it had intervened in

[Section 7:38]
[1] 41 U.S.C.A. §§ 51 to 58.
[2] FAR 3.502-2.

[Section 7:39]
[1] 41 U.S.C.A. § 53.
[2] 41 U.S.C.A. § 52(3).
[3] 41 U.S.C.A. § 52(2).

INFLUENCING GOVERNMENT ACTIONS § 7:39

three *qui tam* actions against Hewlett-Packard[4], Accenture LLP[5] and Sun Microsystems[6] which arose out of various information technology contracts these companies had with the Government. In general, the suits alleged that the contractors violated the Anti-Kickback Act and the False Claims Act when they recommended to the Government that the Government procure products and services from vendors with whom the contractors had "alliance relationships" and when these vendors then rebated a portion of the sales price to the contractors in return for those recommendations. The suits also generally alleged that vendors either made rebates or offered steep discounts to the contractors when those contractors furnished supplies and services directly to the Government under their prime contracts. Reportedly certain other large IT contractors have agreed to pay substantial amounts to settle other suits based on similar allegations.

More recently, the Armed Services Board of Contract Appeals agreed to stay a contractor's request for interpretation of its contract regarding whether it was entitled to retain "early payment" discounts that had been rebated by its vendors.[7] The Board took this action after learning that DOJ, in a separate investigation, had alleged that the vendors had increased their prices beyond what they would have otherwise charged and that the allegedly excessive prompt payments rebates were a disguise for illegal kickbacks.[8]

The typical "kickback" involves a payment by a subcontractor to a prime contractor in order to obtain a subcontract. Some cases are more complex: it is the prime contractor who is giving something of value to subcontractor. Defendants in Anti-Kickback Act cases have argued—without much success—that the act applies only to "upstream," but not downstream payments. For example, in *U.S ex rel. Garrison v. Crown Roofing Services, Inc.*, 2011 WL 1005062 (S.D.Tex. Mar. 16, 2011) a prime contractor allegedly awarded subcontracts to a company secretly owned by one of two COTRs in return for a favorable recommendation for

---

[4]Hewlett-Packard eventually settled this case for $55M. http://www.justice.gov/usao/are/news/2010/August/HPsettlement_083010.pdf

[5]Accenture settled this case for $21M. https://www.uspsoig.gov/sites/default/files/document-library-files/2013/sm-ma-13-005.pdf.

[6]http://www.washingtonpost.com/wp-dyn/content/article/2007/09/14/AR2007091402036.html.

[7]*Appeal of Public Warehousing Co.*, A.S.B.C.A. No. 56116, 2008 WL 355060 (A.S. B.C.A. 2008).

[8]*See also, Palm Springs General Trading and Contracting Establishment*, A.S.B.C.A. No. 56290, 2010 WL 1186022 (A.S. B.C.A. 2010) (stay of claim for unpaid contract amounts) and *Appeal of Kaman Precision Products, Inc.*, A.S.B.C.A. No. 56305, 2010 WL 2802406 (A.S.B.C.A. 2010).

the award of a prime contract. The court rejected the "upstream only" argument, stating:

> The Crown Defendants assert that the Government's claims under the AKA fail as a matter of law because "under the AKA, where payments are made between prime contractor and subcontractor in connection with the same contract, kickbacks can only go in one in one direction: to the prime contractor from its subcontractor or to a subcontractor from an equal or lower tier subcontractor." In other words, the Crown Defendants assert that Crown and Palmer could not have provided a "kickback" to USSE in return for preferential treatment because USSE was merely a subcontractor, and therefore was in no position "to provide Crown with preferential treatment under the Master Contract."
>
> * * *
>
> The Crown Defendants' argument that the AKA only forbids payments going up the contractual chain finds no support in the broad language of the Act. "Congress substantially rewrote the [AKA] in 1986 with the express purpose of extending the scope of the statute to any commercial bribery occurring anywhere within the federal procurement system." *United States v. Purdy,* 144 F.3d 241, 244 (2d Cir.1998). "The language of the amended statute lays bare this purpose." *Id.* It prohibits "any person" from paying "any kickback" to "any . . . subcontractor or subcontractor employee," "for the purpose of improperly obtaining or rewarding favorable treatment in connection with a prime contract." 41 U.S.C. §§ 52(2), 53. The 1986 Amendment defined "kickback" to include "any . . . thing of value" to "broaden the coverage of the Act." H.R.Rep. No. 99-964, at 11 (1986). The phrase "for the purpose of improperly obtaining . . . favorable treatment" was likewise "intended to expand the coverage of the [pre-1986] Act to kickbacks made in the Federal procurement process for *any* improper purpose." *Id.* (emphasis added). Nothing in the plain language of the statute prohibits kickbacks made from prime contractors to subcontractors. *See Purdy, 144 F.3d at 244* (finding that the AKA "impose [s] liability on any person who makes a payment to any other person involved in the federal procurement process for the purpose of obtaining favorable treatment").

See also U.S. ex rel. Compton v. Circle B. Enterprises, 2011 WL 382758 (M.D.Ga. Feb. 3, 2011) (defendant awarded subcontracts for mobile homes to competitors in return for agreement that they would not compete for prime contracts) and *U.S. v. Dynamics Research Corp.*, 2008 WL 886035 (D. Mass. 2008), (two employees of contractor that provided technical support services to the Government engaged in a scheme in which they recommended that contracts be awarded to a particular company, which, in turn, procured the equipment from a company that was owned by the wife of one of the employees).

§ 7:40 Anti-Kickback Act—Contractor responsibilities

The Anti-Kickback Act also places obligations on prime contractors and subcontractors to *report*, in writing, suspected violations of kickback laws either to the agency Inspector General, the head of the contracting agency, or the Justice Department.[1] Furthermore, the Act, as implemented in the FAR, provides that every prime contract exceeding $100,000 for other than commercial items must require that the prime contractor establish and follow *reasonable procedures* "designed to prevent and detect violations of the Act in its own operations and direct business relationships" such as company ethics rules prohibiting kickbacks, education programs for new employees and subcontractors, and audit procedures designed to detect kickbacks.[2]

The FAR also requires prime contractors to incorporate the substance of the anti-kickback provisions in its *subcontracts* that exceed $100,000.[3] Similar provisions exist in agency FAR supplements, and agencies on occasion implement further preventive measures against kickbacks.[4] Prime contracts covered by the Act also are required to have a provision stating that the prime contractor will cooperate fully with any Federal Government agency investigation of a suspected kickback.[5]

Under 1997 amendments to the Anti-Kickback Act, contractors with prime contracts under the simplified acquisition threshold ($100,000) and contractors with prime contracts for commercial items no longer are required to *certify* that they have not paid kickbacks, as was required under the Act before 1997.[6]

The Government also has broad powers to inspect your facilities and records to look for suspected kickbacks, and you are required to cooperate fully with the Government in any investigation of suspected kickbacks.

§ 7:41 Anti-Kickback Act—Penalties

Penalties for violations of the Act—criminal, civil, and administrative—are harsh. "Knowing and willful" violations of the Anti-Kickback Act are *criminal* offenses. Substantial criminal penalties may be imposed, including up to 10 years' imprison-

---

[Section 7:40]

[1] 41 U.S.C.A. § 57(c)(1).

[2] FAR 3.502-2(i).

[3] FAR 52.203-7, para. (c)(5).

[4] PHH Homequity Corp., Comp. Gen. Dec. B-240145.3, 91-1 CPD 100.

[5] 41 U.S.C.A. § 57(e).

[6] *See* 41 U.S.C.A. § 57, as amended by P.L. 104-106 (Feb. 10, 1996). *See* Federal Acquisition Circular 90-45 (Jan. 2, 1997).

§ 7:41   GOVERNMENT CONTRACT COMPLIANCE HANDBOOK

ment for individuals.[1] "Knowing" violations of the Anti-Kickback Act are *civil* violations. For a civil violation, the Government may recover as damages twice the amount of each kickback and up to $10,000 as a civil penalty for each occurrence of prohibited conduct.[2]

Furthermore, knowledge of illegal conduct may be *imputed* to your company; the Government can recover a civil penalty in the amount of the kickback from any person whose employee, subcontractor, or subcontractor employee violates the anti-kickback laws, equal to the amount of the kickback, without reference to the culpability of the person against whom the penalty is asserted.[3] The Anti-Kickback Act, therefore, imposes vicarious civil liability on a company whose employees are involved in making kickbacks, even when the company has *no knowledge* of its employees' conduct. This vicarious liability provision should act as an inducement for you to monitor vigorously the conduct of your employees.

When a kickback has been provided, accepted, or charged against a prime contract, the Act enables the Contracting Officer to *offset* the amount of the kickback paid against any amounts owed by the Government under the contract to which the kickback relates.[4] The Contracting Officer may also direct the prime contractor to withhold the amount of a kickback from the fees owed to a subcontractor.[5] These provisions are designed to provide the Government a full recoupment of any kickback amounts. The Government may also *terminate* a prime contract on the ground of kickback activity.[6]

Imposing civil penalties under both the Anti-Kickback Act and the civil False Claims Act is not "improperly duplicative." In *Morse Diesel International. Inc. v. U.S.*, 79 Fed. Cl. 116 (2007) the court found that the contractor's actions had violated both statutes and imposed fines of approximately $260,000 for violation of the Anti-Kickback Act and $7 million in penalties and damages under the False Claims Act.

[Section 7:41]

[1] 41 U.S.C.A. § 54.

[2] 41 U.S.C.A. § 55(a)(1).

[3] 41 U.S.C.A. § 55(a)(2).

[4] 41 U.S.C.A. §§ 55, 56.

[5] 41 U.S.C.A. § 56(b).

[6] *U.S. v. Acme Process Equipment Co.*, 385 U.S. 138, 87 S. Ct. 350, 17 L. Ed. 2d 249 (1966).

B. FREQUENTLY ASKED QUESTIONS

§ 7:42 Questions & answers

Question 1: What exactly is a kickback or kickback scheme?

Answer 1: In general, a kickback scheme usually involves an arrangement between a subcontractor and prime contractor or higher-tier subcontractor in which something of value (the kickback) is given by the sub to the prime or higher-tier sub as a payoff for ultimately receiving: (1) a subcontract award, (2) another kind of favorable treatment that can help lead to contract award, (3) continued contractual relations, and/or (4) the recovery of additional money from the Government through inflated bid prices. A kickback scheme also can involve arranged payments from a prime contractor to an agency official for prime contract award (or favorable treatment under the prime contract). Usually, with kickbacks, a subcontractor agrees to give back to the prime contractor (or let the prime keep) a percentage of the price charged to the prime for the subcontracts. Remember, however, that besides money, a "kickback" can include any "fee, commission, credit, gift, gratuity, thing of value, or compensation of any kind."[1]

Question 2: Why are kickbacks considered illegal?

Answer 2: Most kickbacks are considered illegal because payoffs for favorable contract treatment undermine the integrity and competitive nature of the procurement process. Furthermore, because kickbacks often are built into contract prices, the Government presumably will pay inflated costs.

Question 3: What are some examples of "favorable treatment" that contractors have paid for, other than outright contract award, that are illegal under the Anti-Kickback Act?

Answer 3: Some examples of illegal kickback schemes include payoffs for:

(a) Actions that assist in or help lead to contract award, such as receiving from a higher-tier subcontractor confidential information on competitors' bids (such as prices, delivery schedules, etc.),[2] obtaining placement on a bidders' list without meeting the requisite qualifications, or obtaining the removal of competitors who do meet the requisite requirements from a

---

[Section 7:42]

[1] 41 U.S.C.A. § 52(2).

[2] DOD Inspector General, Semiannual Report to Congress 35 (April–September 1995) (documenting one kickback scheme in which three contractor employees were paid by a subcontractor to open competitors' sealed bids and disclose inside information on pending contracts to ensure awards of contracts to favored subcontractors).

§ 7:42 GOVERNMENT CONTRACT COMPLIANCE HANDBOOK

bidder's list.

(b) Actions that allow for continued contractual relations, such as obtaining unwarranted waivers of deadlines or obtaining acceptance of substandard goods.

(c) Actions that, if undiscovered, may allow for recovery of additional money from the Government through inflated bid prices, such as obtaining unwarranted price increases or recovering improper expenses.[3]

Question 4: Does a kickback have to be completed to be prohibited?

Answer 4: No. The Anti-Kickback Act does not require a kickback to be completed. Mere *attempts* to provide or accept kickbacks may violate the law.

Question 5: What kinds of reasonable procedures can I implement to prevent and detect violations of the Anti-Kickback Act in my operations and business relationships as required by the Act?

Answer 5: The FAR and legislative history of the Act include examples of procedures to assist you in discovering kickback violations. They include: (1) developing and implementing internal company rules prohibiting kickbacks by employees, agents, or subcontractors, (2) creating education programs for employees and subcontractors that explain the company's policies against kickbacks and the consequences of engaging in such prohibited activity, (3) instituting periodic surveys of subcontractors to elicit information about kickbacks, (4) establishing purchasing procedures that minimize the opportunity for kickbacks, (5) developing audit procedures designed to detect kickbacks, (6) initiating screening procedures to detect employment applicants who have previously violated kickback laws, (7) limiting buyers' authority to approve bids, (8) starting information "hotlines" to allow employees to inform management of potential violations anonymously, and (9) mandating annual certifications by employees that they have not violated company anti-kickback policies and are unaware of any other person's violations.[4]

C. HOW TO RECOGNIZE THE PROBLEM

§ 7:43 Generally

Kickback violations may come from a variety of sources. Employees in a position to make or receive kickbacks include those who receive confidential information on competitors' bids, those who are charged with maintaining your bidders' lists, those in

---

[3] H.R. Rep. No. 99-634, 2d Sess., reprinted in 1986 U.S. Code Cong. & Admin. News 5960, 5968, 5969.

[4] *See* S. Rep. No. 99-435, 2d Sess. 20 (1986); FAR 3.502-2(i)(1).

INFLUENCING GOVERNMENT ACTIONS § 7:44

charge of bidding, or those who contract with or award contracts to subcontractors.

In 1987, the DOD Council on Integrity and Management Improvement issued a "Fraud Awareness Letter" that identified 20 indicators of potential subcontractor kickbacks.[1] The indicators, which can serve as a checklist for the types of activities Government investigators will be looking for, include the following:

(1) Restricted number of vendors allowed to bid.

(2) Certain bidders always bid against each other.

(3) "Broker" buying rather than direct purchase from suppliers/vendors.

(4) Buyers socializing with vendors/salespersons.

(5) All bidders represented by one or two brokers.

(6) Inadequate or missing cost or price analyses.

(7) Patterns where the last bidder to respond always receives the award.

(8) No "separation of power"—for example, the person who originates a requirement also places the order, or the person who places the order is responsible for receiving or authorizing payment for the order.

(9) Only one bid is at or below any fair cost estimation.

(10) Potential bidders complain that they are not notified of pending solicitations or subcontracts.

§ 7:44 Examples

Request for a commission: Assume you prepared a bid on your company's behalf to supply a Government agency with computer hardware and software. Soon after award, you called the subcontractor who provided the software, commented that you were instrumental in including her firm in your company's proposal, and suggested that she give you a commission in the amount of 5% of the contract's value. Have you done anything wrong?

Yes. You may be criminally and civilly liable for having solicited a kickback. If you accept the commission, your employer and the subcontractor might also be civilly liable.

Obtaining a subcontract: You are involved in obtaining subcontracts on behalf of your company. You are currently in the midst of discussions with representatives from RST Corporation concerning a possible subcontract on a large Government contract. Negotiations are difficult, and you try to tip the balance

---

[Section 7:43]

[1]DOD Council on Integrity & Mgmt. Improvement, "Fraud Awareness Letter" (September 1987).

§ 7:44   GOVERNMENT CONTRACT COMPLIANCE HANDBOOK

in your favor by making known to the RST representatives that if you are awarded this subcontract you will look favorably on that company's bid for a subcontract on a prime contract that you have with the Government. You are awarded the subcontract. Have you done anything wrong?

This transaction violates the kickback laws. You have given a thing of value (favorable treatment on the subcontract under your prime contract) for favorable treatment (award of the subcontract) under another Government contract. This activity will subject both you (the offeror) and RST Corporation (the acceptor) to criminal and civil prosecution under the Anti-Kickback Act. Remember that even if a kickback is accepted due to coercion or threat, you are not relieved of liability.

Attempting a kickback: You are actively seeking a major Navy subcontract. You know who your competitor is, but you don't know if the bid that you are going to submit is low enough to win the award. You have one of your employees call a friend of his at your competitor's plant to tell him that you will "take care of him" if he gives you an idea of what his company is planning to bid on the subcontract. The friend refuses to divulge the bid. Have you violated the law?

Yes. You and your employee are liable under the Anti-Kickback Act for attempting improperly to obtain favorable treatment in connection with the Government contract.

Nonconforming goods: You are an inspector for a major aircraft producer. A subcontractor delivers a component that does not meet specifications required by the contract. The component will function, despite the defect, and the subcontractor offers you $700 to accept the item as is. You take the $700, figuring that the component is noncritical and will function despite the noncompliance. Are you liable for this conduct?

Yes, both you and the subcontractor have violated the Anti-Kickback Act because he offered and you accepted a kickback for the purpose of improperly obtaining favorable treatment (acceptance of nonconforming goods).

Competitors: You are in fierce competition with another company for a subcontract. Because you know that the Anti-Kickback Act generally relates to kickbacks between contractors at different tiers, you decide to offer your competitor money if he will disclose his bid price. Have you violated the Anti-Kickback Act?

Most likely. These facts are similar to a case where the United States charged the defendant with violating the Anti-Kickback Act on two counts: (1) the defendant allegedly gave 500,000 deutsche marks to a competing bidder to obtain information concerning the competing bid and to ensure that the defendant

INFLUENCING GOVERNMENT ACTIONS § 7:46

was awarded the contract (Kickback Violation #1), and (2) as part of the defendant's payoff, the competing bidder apparently became a subcontractor to the defendant's contract (Kickback Violation #2).[1]

D. COMPLIANCE INITIATIVES

§ 7:45 Generally

Because a kickback violation can result in substantial sanctions against your company and your employees, it is important that you establish procedures to minimize the possibility that you may be accused of illegal kickback activity. Neither the Anti-Kickback Act nor the implementing regulations require that you adopt specific procedures to comply with the Act so long as you have in place "reasonable procedures designed to prevent and detect violations" of the Act. Nevertheless, the implementation of certain policies and procedures will minimize the risk that your company or employees will be accused of violating the Anti-Kickback Act.

Investigation of suspected kickbacks has become one of the top investigative priorities for many agencies, particularly DOD. You can expect this trend to continue, and you should be very cautious about any activity that might be viewed as a kickback scheme.

The three critical control points in your company are upper management, procurement personnel (including contracting, sales, and marketing), and internal auditors and accountants. The activities of the personnel in each of these groups will heavily influence whether your company can successfully avoid kickbacks.

§ 7:46 Establish policies & procedures

You must first decide as matter of policy the types of compliance tools that are most appropriate for your company. These may include the following:

(a) Providing a *training program* to educate employees about the company policies.

(b) Requiring subcontractors and/or employees to *certify* compliance with the Act, regulations, and company policies.

(c) Establishing specific procurement and audit *procedures*.

(d) Establishing *reporting* procedures both within the company and to law enforcement agencies.

(e) Establishing *screening* procedures for employment

[Section 7:44]

[1]*Haustechnik v. U.S.*, 34 Fed. Cl. 740 (1996).

§ 7:46   GOVERNMENT CONTRACT COMPLIANCE HANDBOOK

applicants.

Your most important duties are educating your employees as to what constitutes prohibited kickback activity, setting up policies to prevent kickbacks, and enforcing those policies. Your company policy should clearly state that the solicitation, offer, and acceptance of kickbacks are strictly prohibited, and that anyone violating the policy will be disciplined. You should also consider an education program for your *subcontractors*, detailing the definition, penalties, and steps they should take if they suspect a kickback or attempted kickback.

Develop a *policy manual* to be given to each employee and subcontractor, which discusses the indicators of kickbacks as well as company rules and procedures for handling kickback situations. You should require that your employees read this manual and sign a *certification* that they have read, understood, and agree to comply with the policy.

Make sure that all employees are aware of the potential for becoming involved, even inadvertently, in a kickback situation. Many activities that are acceptable in a commercial setting are illegal in the context of Government procurement.

Finally, when you are informed about kickbacks or kickback attempts, you must have procedures to ensure that the allegations are properly *investigated*. If there are "reasonable grounds" to believe the allegations have substance, you must *report* the kickback allegations to the proper authorities and *cooperate* with them in their investigation.

§ 7:47   Develop policies for auditors & accountants

You should develop a policy and procedure manual for all internal auditors and accountants to ensure that they understand the types of behavior that are improper and to establish a working, traceable system to detect kickbacks.

Auditors and accountants should review awards of subcontracts and purchase orders that appear to be priced higher than other bids. They should look for situations where a low bidder or subcontractor changes his bid, especially where the change keeps him as low bidder but at a smaller margin below the second lowest bidder.

Furthermore, auditors and accountants should carefully *monitor* department *funds* to determine if there are funds missing or unaccounted for and report any suspected kickback to the appropriate company officials.

§ 7:48   Recommendations

(a) Establish an in-house *education program* for *employees* and *subcontractors* that explain what kickbacks are and how to detect them, the company policies and procedures with respect to kickbacks, and the penalties that will be imposed for violating kickback laws. Have your employees sign a *certification* that they understand and agree to comply with the company policy. Administer periodic training sessions to educate employees in sensitive positions about the scope of their responsibilities and have internal auditors perform *testing* to ensure that the policies and procedures are being followed.

(b) Establish an in-house *ethics committee* to oversee suspected kickback activity and establish a "company hotline" or other means by which suspected kickback violations can be reported anonymously by employees.

(c) Be prepared to report to the agency Inspector General any *reasonable suspicion* of kickbacks and to cooperate fully with federal agencies when they conduct kickback investigations.

Chapter 8

Conflicts of Interest

I. OVERVIEW
§ 8:1 Scope note

II. PERSONAL CONFLICTS

A. PROCUREMENT INTEGRITY ACT
§ 8:2 Generally
§ 8:3 One-year ban on hiring former agency officials
§ 8:4 Restrictions on employment discussions
§ 8:5 Penalties
§ 8:6 Frequently asked questions

B. ETHICS REFORM ACT
§ 8:7 Generally
§ 8:8 Communications and appearances with intent to influence, generally
§ 8:9 Lifetime ban on communications and appearances
§ 8:10 Two-year ban on communications and appearances
§ 8:11 One-year ban on communications and appearances
§ 8:12 Penalties

C. CRIMINAL "REVOLVING-DOOR" STATUTES
§ 8:13 Generally

III. ORGANIZATIONAL CONFLICTS
§ 8:14 Generally
§ 8:15 Government responsibilities
§ 8:16 Contractor responsibilities
§ 8:17 Frequently asked questions

IV. HOW TO RECOGNIZE THE PROBLEM

A. PERSONAL CONFLICTS
§ 8:18 Generally
§ 8:19 Examples

B. ORGANIZATIONAL CONFLICTS

§ 8:20 Generally
§ 8:21 Examples

V. COMPLIANCE INITIATIVES

A. PERSONAL CONFLICTS

§ 8:22 Generally
§ 8:23 Recommendations

B. ORGANIZATIONAL CONFLICTS

§ 8:24 Generally
§ 8:25 Recommendations

KeyCite®: Cases and other legal materials listed in KeyCite Scope can be researched through the KeyCite service on Westlaw®. Use KeyCite to check citations for form, parallel references, prior and later history, and comprehensive citator information, including citations to other decisions and secondary materials.

I. OVERVIEW

§ 8:1 Scope note

In 2004, the former senior career civilian procurement official for the Air Force admitted to steering contracts to a large defense contractor while negotiating employment for her daughter, her future son-in-law, and herself.[1] She served nine months in prison, the contractor's Chief Financial Officer, with whom she negotiated, served four months, and the contracts in question had to be recompeted.[2] Additionally, the company's Chief Executive Officer resigned due to fallout from the scandal. These events illustrate the problems that can arise when your company fails to comply with conflicts of interest law.

The term "conflict of interest" typically refers to the clash between the interests of the public and the private pecuniary interests of an individual. The term is most often used to refer to *personal* conflicts of interest—the relationship of Government officials and employees to matters of private interest or personal gain. Personal conflicts of interest frequently arise when a

---

[Section 8:1]

[1]*See generally* Branstetter, Darleen Druyun: An Evolving Case Study in Corruption, Power, and Procurement, 34 Pub. Cont. L.J. 443 (Spring 2005).

[2]*See* Lockheed Martin Corp., B-295402, 2005 CPD 24 (February 18, 2005); Lockheed Martin Corp. et al., B-295401, 2005 CPD 41 (February 24, 2005).

Government employee is seeking employment in the private sector. The concern is that a Government employee may use his decision-making authority in the Government to benefit a future employer in the private sector. Two key laws place post-Government-employment restrictions on former and current Government officials and employees to prevent conflicts of interest: the Procurement Integrity Act[3] and the Ethics Reform Act.[4] Both laws are implemented by complex regulations requiring strict compliance to avoid administrative, civil, and criminal sanctions. These laws and regulations sanction not only actual conflicts of interest, but also the *appearance* of improprieties in the acquisition process.[5]

The acquisition regulations also limit *organizational* conflicts of interest.[6] An "organizational conflict of interest" means that because of other activities or relationships with other persons, a person is unable or potentially unable to render *impartial assistance* or *advice* to the Government, or the person's objectivity in performing the contract work is or might otherwise be impaired, or a contractor has an *unfair competitive advantage* for future contracts because of the performance of current Government contracts.[7] An organizational conflict of interest can develop, for example, when your company is currently performing a contract to create the statement of work for a future contract, and your company later bids on that future contract. In an effort to limit organizational conflicts, the Government has promulgated complex regulations designed to prevent the existence of conflicting roles that might bias a contractor's judgment and create an unfair competitive advantage.

II. PERSONAL CONFLICTS

A. PROCUREMENT INTEGRITY ACT

§ 8:2 Generally

The Procurement Integrity Act regulates the relationship between Government employees involved in the procurement process and contractors competing for federal contracts. The Act is implemented in the Federal Acquisition Regulation in subpart 3.104. The Act's restrictions on *acceptance of employment* by former agency officials from Government contractors and on *employ-*

---

[3]*See, generally*, FAR 3.104, et seq.

[4]P.L. 101-194, implemented at 5 C.F.R. §§ 2635.2634 to 2635.2641.

[5]41 U.S.C.A. § 423(c); 18 U.S.C.A. § 207; FAR 3.104, et.seq.; 5 C.F.R. Pts. 2637, 2641. *See NKF Engineering, Inc. v. U.S.*, 805 F.2d 372 (Fed. Cir. 1986).

[6]FAR 9.5, et. seq.

[7]FAR 9.501.

ment contacts between agency officials and Government contractors are discussed below. (For a discussion of the Procurement Integrity Act's restrictions on the disclosure or obtaining of procurement information, see §§ 6:1 et seq.).

§ 8:3 One-year ban on hiring former agency officials

Under the Act, designated former agency officials involved in a procurement *over $10 million* are prohibited from accepting compensation from the awardee as an employee, officer, director, or consultant of the contractor for *one year*.[1] The starting date for the one-year prohibition on employment of such officials is calculated from the date on which the official last acted in connection with the procurement or contract.[2]

Agency officials are subject to the employment ban if they served in one of the following capacities:[3]

(1) The procuring Contracting Officer, the source selection authority, a member of the source selection evaluation board, or the chief of a financial or technical evaluation team in a procurement in which the contractor was selected for award of a contract in excess of $10 million.

(2) The program manager, deputy program manager, or administrative Contracting Officer on a contract in excess of $10 million awarded to the contractor.

(3) An official who personally made a decision to award a contract, subcontract, modification, or task or delivery order over $10 million to the contractor, to establish overhead or other rates applicable to a contract or contracts of the contractor in excess of $10 million, to approve a contract payment or payments over $10 million to the contractor, or to pay or settle a claim over $10 million to the contractor.

The Procurement Integrity Act provides an exception for employment with contractor *divisions or affiliates* in certain circumstances. The Act does not prohibit a former agency official from accepting compensation from a division or affiliate of a contractor that does not produce the same or similar products or services as those involved in the $10-million procurement.[4]

§ 8:4 Restrictions on employment discussions

Under the Procurement Integrity Act, if an agency official, who

---

[Section 8:3]

[1] 41 U.S.C.A. § 2104(a); FAR 3.104-3(d).
[2] FAR 3.104-3(d)(2).
[3] 41 U.S.C.A. § 2104(a); FAR 3.104-3(d)(1).
[4] 41 U.S.C.A. § 2104(b); FAR 3.104-3(d)(3).

§ 8:4

is participating *personally and substantially* in a competitive federal agency procurement in excess of $150,000, *contacts* or is *contacted by* a bidder or offeror on that procurement regarding nonfederal employment, the agency official must:[1]

(1) Report the contact to his or her supervisor and the designated agency ethics official immediately.

(2) Promptly reject the employment opportunity or disqualify himself or herself from further participation in the procurement until formally authorized by the agency to resume participation in the procurement on the grounds that; (a) the bidder or offeror is no longer a bidder or offeror in that procurement, or (b) all discussions with the bidder or offeror regarding possible employment have terminated without an employment agreement or arrangement.

If your company contacts a Government employee about employment opportunities, the responsibility for reporting employment contacts by your company is on the Government employee.

Under the Act, these restrictions on offers of employment apply only to federal procurements using *competitive procedures* in excess of $150,000 (the simplified acquisition threshold).[2] The restrictions do not apply to sole-source contracts and contract modifications. In addition, the restrictions apply only to firms competing in a particular procurement. Thus, they do not apply to employment discussions between Government officials and subcontractors or companies that decide not to compete in the procurement. (However, contractors should be aware that other restrictions on discussions with agency officials with regard to future employment are contained in federal criminal law; see § 8:13 below.)

Although the Government official is given a great deal of discretion in deciding whether to reject the offer of employment or to disqualify him or herself from continuing to participate in the procurement, he or she may be subject to agency administrative action if disqualification from participation in a particular procurement interferes substantially with the individual's ability to perform assigned duties.[3] Similarly, a bidder or offeror that continues employment discussions with an agency employee knowing that the employee has not complied with the above reporting requirements is subject to penalties and to administra-

---

[Section 8:4]

[1]41 U.S.C.A. § 2103(a); FAR 3.104-3(c).

[2]41 U.S.C.A. § 2103(a); FAR 3.104-1.

[3]FAR 3.104-8(c).

tive sanctions.[4]

§ 8:5 Penalties

The Procurement Integrity Act provides the following *administrative sanctions* for violations of the Act: (1) cancellation of the procurement if a contract has not yet been awarded; (2) rescission of the contract; (3) suspension or debarment of the contractor from award and performance of Government contracts and subcontracts; and (4) initiation of adverse personnel action against a Government employee.[1] If the Government rescinds a contract for a violation, the Government also may recover, in addition to any penalty, the amount expended under the contract.

Any employee of your company and any Government employee who violates the Act are subject to a *civil fine* of not more than $50,000 for each violation, plus the amount of compensation that the individual offered or received for the prohibited conduct. If your company violates the Act, it will be subject to a fine of not more than $500,000 for the violation, plus twice the amount of compensation which your company received or offered for the prohibited conduct.[2]

No *criminal penalties* are imposed for violation of the hiring ban or employment contact provisions of the Procurement Integrity Act. The criminal penalties under the Act apply only to violations of the parts of the Act prohibiting the disclosure or obtaining of procurement information (see §§ 6:1 et seq.).[3]

§ 8:6 Frequently asked questions

Question 1: Who are the "former agency officials" prohibited by the Procurement Integrity Act from accepting compensation from contractors for one year after leaving Government employment?

Answer 1: The one-year prohibition against a "former official" accepting compensation from a contractor awarded a contract for more than $10 million applies to any official who: (a) served, at the time of the contract award, as the procurement contracting officer, the source selection authority, a member of the source selection evaluation board, or the chief of the financial or technical evaluation team; or (b) served as the program manager, deputy program manager, or administrative contracting officer; or (c) personally made the decision to award the contract or subcontract

---

[4]41 U.S.C.A. § 423(c)(4); FAR 3.104-8(b).

[Section 8:5]

[1]41 U.S.C.A. § 2105(c)(1).
[2]41 U.S.C.A. § 2105(b).
[3]41 U.S.C.A. § 2105(a).

CONFLICTS OF INTEREST § 8:6

to that contractor, to establish overhead or other rates, to award or approve issuance of a contract payment in excess of $10 million, or to pay or settle a claim in excess of $10 million.

Question 2: Is it possible for a non-Government employee to be an "agency official"?

Answer 2: Yes. A private contractor, subcontractor, consultant, expert, or advisor acting on behalf of, or providing advice to, a federal agency regarding a procurement at issue may qualify as an "agency official" under the Procurement Integrity Act.

Question 3: May an individual in private industry become an "agency official" simply by serving on a Government advisory board?

Answer 3: No. Individuals who serve on federal advisory committees or agency-level boards or panels will normally not be considered agency officials unless they participate "personally and substantially" in a federal agency procurement.

Question 4: If, instead of paying a commission directly to a former federal agency official for services, a contractor donates money to that individual's favorite charity or public interest group, will the donation be considered "compensation" for purposes of the Procurement Integrity Act?

Answer 4: Yes. The term "compensation" includes wages, salaries, honoraria, commissions, professional fees, and any other form of compensation, provided directly or indirectly for services rendered. Compensation is provided indirectly if it is paid to an entity other than the individual specifically in exchange for services provided by the individual.[1]

Question 5: May a contractor who is participating in a $5 million procurement employ a former federal agency official involved in the procurement within one year of the date the former official last acted on the contract?

Answer 5: Yes. The Procurement Integrity Act's one-year bar on employment of former federal agency officials pertains only to procurements valued at more than $10 million.

Question 6: Which "agency officials" are subject to the rules and procedures set forth in the Procurement Integrity Act if they are contacted by bidders or offerors regarding future employment?

Answer 6: The Act's employment contact restrictions apply to any "agency official who is participating personally and substantially in a Federal agency procurement for a contract in excess of the simplified acquisition threshold" (currently $150,000). Participating "personally and substantially" in a federal agency

---

[Section 8:6]
[1] FAR 3.104-1.

§ 8:6　Government Contract Compliance Handbook

procurement is defined as having "significant involvement" in activities related to that procurement such as drafting, reviewing, or approving the specification or statement of work for the procurement; preparing or developing the solicitation; evaluating bids or proposals or selecting a source; negotiating price or terms and conditions of contract; and reviewing and approving the award of the contract.[2]

An individual will generally not be considered to have participated personally and substantially in a procurement solely because that individual: (1) participated in reviewing and evaluating program milestones and making recommendations regarding alternative technologies or approaches for satisfying broad agency-level objectives; (2) performed general, technical, engineering, or scientific effort having broad application not directly associated with a particular procurement; (3) performed clerical functions supporting the conduct of the particular procurement; or (4) participated in management studies, preparation of in-house cost estimates and "most efficient organization" analyses, or furnishing data or technical support to be used by others.[3]

Question 7: May a contractor that is not participating in a specific procurement conduct future employment discussions with a federal agency official involved in that procurement?

Answer 7: Yes. The Procurement Integrity Act limits the prohibition on future employment discussions to bidders and offerors that are participating in the procurement.

Question 8: May a contractor that is competing in a procurement conduct future employment discussions with a federal agency official through an intermediary such as a subcontractor or a company that is not participating in the procurement?

Answer 8: No. Under the Procurement Integrity Act, third parties who are acting on behalf of a bidder or offeror in a procurement are prohibited from conducting future employment discussions with a federal agency official involved in the procurement.

Question 9: What is the time limit under the Procurement Integrity Act on former Government employees' accepting "compensation" from a contractor?

Answer 9: The time limit on the restriction against accepting compensation from a contractor is one year from the date the former Government employee last acted or made a decision on the contract.

Question 10: Under the Procurement Integrity Act, can my

---
[2]FAR 3.104-1.
[3]FAR 3.104-1.

CONFLICTS OF INTEREST § 8:6

company hire one of the designated Government employees, such as a Program Manager, and place the employee in a position unrelated to his or her Government duties as a Program Manager?

Answer 10: The Act prohibits certain Government employees holding designated source selection and contracting positions, including a Program Manager, from accepting "compensation" from a contractor, whether doing work unrelated or related to the former Government employee's official duties. Therefore, if your company division was involved in a procurement or contract over $10 million, you cannot hire such an employee and place the employee in that division doing unrelated duties to those performed by him or her in the former Government job. The Act and regulations provide for an exception, however, for the former Government employee accepting compensation from an *unrelated division or affiliate* of the contractor, as long as the products or services produced by that division or affiliate are different from those on the procurement or contract.

Question 11: Can my company be subject to penalties for "paying compensation" to a Government employee under the Procurement Integrity Act? It seems that the Act just applies to the Government employee "accepting compensation" from a contractor.

Answer 11: Yes. The Act also penalizes any contractor who *knowingly* employs a former Government employee who is prohibited from accepting compensation from your company.

Question 12: What if the former Government employee is not sure if he or she can accept employment with your company?

Answer 12: A former or current Government employee who is unsure if he or she is precluded by the Procurement Integrity Act from accepting a job with your company may request in writing advice from his or her agency ethics official before accepting the job. The employee is required to submit all relevant information, including information about your company and a description of your company's products or services.[4] You should request that the employee provide you with a copy of the request submitted to the ethics official and the written response from the ethics official. You should review these documents for accuracy and make an independent determination whether there are any potential violations of the Act before proceeding with further job discussions.

In addition to the response to this question provided in the principal text, DoD published an interim rule at 74 Fed. Reg. 2408 on January 15, 2009, to implement section 847 of the National Defense Authorization Act for Fiscal Year 2008 (Pub. L. No. 110-181). Section 847 requires that a DoD official, who has

---

[4]FAR 3.104-6.

participated personally and substantially in a DoD acquisition exceeding $10 million or who has held a key acquisition position, must request a written opinion from a DoD ethics counselor before accepting compensation from a DoD contractor within two years after leaving DoD service. In addition, section 847 prohibits a DoD contractor from providing compensation to such a DoD official without first determining that the official has received or appropriately requested a post-employment ethics opinion. This rule was made final on November 19, 2009, at 74 Fed. Reg. 59,913 and is implemented at DFARS 203.171, 209.406-2, and 252.203-7000.

Subsequently, DoD has concluded that it is not able to fully track whether Government officials covered by Section 847 are obtaining a written opinion from a DoD ethics counselor or whether contractors are verifying that the official has done this before hiring that person. Accordingly, DoD requires contractors to certify that all "covered officials" employed by the contractor are presently in compliance with DFARS 203.171-3. and DFARS 252.203-7000 and with other post-employment restrictions covered by 18 USCA § 207. The proposed regulations, which apply to all contracts, do not describe what steps the contractor is expected to take in order to verify compliance.

Question 13: If a former or current Government employee receives advice from the agency ethics official that accepting the position with your company will not violate the Procurement Integrity Act, can the employee still be prosecuted for a violation of the Act?

Answer 13: If the former or current Government employee is advised in a written opinion by the agency ethics official that he or she may accept a job with your company, and does so in good faith reliance on that advice, then neither the employee nor your company would be found to have *knowingly* violated the Act. However, if the Government employee or your company has actual knowledge or reason to believe that the opinion is based on fraudulent, misleading, or otherwise incorrect information, the employee's and your company's reliance on the ethics official's advice will be considered to be in bad faith.[5]

Question 14: Do the Procurement Integrity Act's restrictions on accepting "compensation" from a contractor apply only to competitive procurements?

Answer 14: No. Although the Act's restrictions on "employment contacts" apply only to competitive procurements, the Act's restrictions on accepting "compensation" from a contractor apply to both competitive and noncompetitive acquisitions.

---

[5]FAR 3.104-6(d)(3).

CONFLICTS OF INTEREST § 8:6

Question 15: Do the Procurement Integrity Act's restrictions on employment contacts apply to all federal competitive procurements?

Answer 15: No. The restrictions apply only to a competitive procurement for a contract in excess of the simplified acquisition threshold (currently $150,000). Noncompetitive procurements, such as a sole-source contract award or a modification to an existing contract, are excluded. Although procurements for less than the simplified acquisition threshold amount are not covered by the Act, you still could be in violation of revolving-door statutes and regulations for engaging in employment discussions or negotiations when competing for such procurements, however (see § 8:13 below).[6]

Question 16: Under what circumstances is my company subject to the Act's prohibitions on employment contacts to agency officials?

Answer 16: When your company is a bidder or offeror on a competitive procurement and your company makes a contact regarding future employment with your company.

Question 17: Does the Procurement Integrity Act apply to my company's subcontractors?

Answer 17: The Act applies only to "bidders or offerors," and these terms are not defined by the Act or the FAR. Provided your subcontractor does not act as an "intermediary," the Act will probably not apply to your company's subcontractors.

Question 18: What kind of "contacts" are prohibited by the Procurement Integrity Act?

Answer 18: The Act applies to any contact made by a Government employee and any contact made by you to a Government employee regarding nonfederal employment.

Question 19: Will my company be in violation of the Procurement Integrity Act for contacting a Government employee who is involved personally and substantially in a competitive procurement for which we are an offeror to discuss future employment, knowing the Government employee has failed to make the required reports of the contact to his/her supervisor and the agency ethics official?

Answer 19: Yes. An offeror in this situation who engages in employment discussions with such an employee *knowing* that the employee may be in violation of the Act is subject to penalties.[7] Likewise, a Government employee who refuses to terminate

---

[6]18 U.S.C.A. § 208; 5 C.F.R. § 2635, Subpt. F, "Seeking Other Employment."

[7]FAR 3.104-8(b).

§ 8:6   GOVERNMENT CONTRACT COMPLIANCE HANDBOOK

employment discussions is subject to administrative action.[8]

Question 20: What if we were not aware that a Government employee who we contacted for future employment was "personally and substantially" involved in a procurement for which we were competing?

Answer 20: The Procurement Integrity Act requires a violation to be *"knowing."* If you can show that you did not know the Government employee was involved in a competitive procurement, you would not be in violation of the Act. Because of the risk of possible violation of the Act, however, when you contact *any* Government employee to discuss possible future employment, you should first determine whether the employee is involved in a procurement for which you are competing. If so, you should immediately cease discussions with the Government employee.

Question 21: I understand that the Troubled Asset Relief Program (TARP) has its own "personal conflict of interest" provisions. What do they require?

Answer: 21: For the background of the TARP program and a discussion of the key definitions in the new TARP conflict of interest regulations, which are set forth at 31 C.F.R. §§ 31.1 et seq., see § 8:15, *infra*, dealing with organizational conflicts of interest. Those regulations define a personal conflict of interest (PCI) as:

> . . . a personal, business, or financial interest of an individual, his or her spouse, minor child, or other family member with whom the individual has a close personal relationship, that could adversely affect the individual's ability to perform under the arrangement, his or her objectivity or judgment in such performance, or his or her ability to represent the interests of the treasury.

Before commencing work, a contractor must obtain from management officials and key individuals information in writing about their personal, business, and financial relationships, as well as those of their spouses, minor children, and other family members with whom the individuals have a close personal relationship that would cause a reasonable person with knowledge of the relevant facts to question the individual's ability to perform, his or her objectivity or judgment in such performance, or his or her ability to represent the interests of the Treasury. The retained entity must certify within 10 days of the effective date of the arrangement that all of its management officials and key individuals performing services have no personal conflicts of interest or are subject to a mitigation plan or waiver approved by Treasury.

Also, the regulations prohibit potential TARP contractors from

---

[8]FAR 3.104-8(c).

CONFLICTS OF INTEREST § 8:7

directly or indirectly discussing or offering future employment or business opportunities with any Treasury employee with personal or direct responsibility for that procurement. Similarly, a potential contractor is prohibited from directly or indirectly soliciting or obtaining any non-public information that was prepared for use by Treasury for the purpose of evaluating a proposal for work. And, of course, a contractor is prohibited under the regulations from directly or indirectly offering a gratuity or anything of value to a Treasury employee, except as permitted by Government-Wide Ethics Rules. Before entering into any arrangement or accepting a modification to an existing arrangement, the contractor must certify that it is aware of these prohibitions and that to the best of its knowledge after making a reasonable inquiry, the entity has no information concerning a possible violation. Lastly, and very significantly, each officer, employee, and representative of the retained entity who participated personally and substantially in preparing and submitting a proposal must certify that he or she (1) is familiar with and will comply with these prohibitions and (2) has no information of any possible violations and will report immediately to the entity any subsequently gained information concerning a possible violation. Thus, these rules mirror to some degree the new requirement to disclose a possible violation of Federal criminal law and the civil FCA contained in FAR 52.203-13, entitled "Contractor Code of Business Ethics and Conduct (DEC 2007)" and discussed above in § 4:1.

B. ETHICS REFORM ACT

§ 8:7 Generally

The integrity of the Government acquisition process requires the complete independence and loyalty of Government decisionmakers. The prospect of a future job with a Government contractor may compromise and conflict with the independence and loyalty required of a Government official. Even when there is no intent by you or your company to influence a Government employee in the award or performance of a Government contract, there may be an *appearance* that his or her independence has been compromised when you enter into discussions with a current or former employee regarding a job or business opportunity with your company.

In addition to the Procurement Integrity Act provisions that regulate the hiring of Government employees, discussed above in §§ 8:2 to 8:6, you should be aware of certain criminal laws known as "revolving-door" statutes. These statutes serve to implement the principle that a public servant owes "undivided loyalty" to the Government. The objective of these laws is to prevent Government officials from "switching sides" on matters that come before

§ 8:7   Government Contract Compliance Handbook

them in their official capacities, while at the same time to ensure that the Government attracts highly-skilled professionals from the private sector into public service.[1]

The key revolving-door statute is the Ethics Reform Act of 1989,[2] which is a criminal statute that places restrictions on the tasks certain former Government employees may perform after leaving Government service. The restrictions vary both in scope and duration depending on the employee's position and responsibilities while in the Government. The length of the restriction on post-employment activities range from a permanent ban to one or two years after leaving Government employment. This law also establishes conflict-of-interest rules that must be followed by you and the Government employee when you are considering offering a job to the employee. See also § 8:13 below.

Violations of this law may result in criminal and civil fines, and administrative sanctions against your company, the former Government employee, and other company employees.

§ 8:8 Communications and appearances with intent to influence, generally

The Ethics Reform Act and its implementing regulations prohibit communications to or appearances before an agency "made with the intent to influence."[1] "Communications" apply to oral statements but also may include telephone calls, letters, or other types of correspondence.[2] "Appearances" may be formal or informal.[3] Because contractors and former Government employees must avoid even an appearance of a conflict or impropriety, a former Government employee's mere attendance at a meeting or delivery of a proposal to the employee's former agency may be seen as an attempt to influence the former agency on behalf of the contractor.[4]

§ 8:9 Lifetime ban on communications and appearances

The Ethics Reform Act places a permanent restriction on former Government employees from making certain communica-

---

[Section 8:7]

    [1]*U.S. v. Medico Industries, Inc.*, 784 F.2d 840, 843 (7th Cir. 1986).

    [2]Pub. L. No. 101-194, 103 Stat. 1716 (1989) (codified at 18 U.S.C.A. § 207(a) to (e)).

[Section 8:8]

    [1]18 U.S.C.A. § 207(a).

    [2]5 C.F.R. § 2641.201(d).

    [3]5 C.F.R. § 2641.201(d)(2).

    [4]*U.S. v. Schaltenbrand*, 930 F.2d 1554 (11th Cir. 1991).

§ 8:9

tions with and appearances before Government departments, agencies, and courts on behalf of another person in a particular matter in which the former employee participated *personally and substantially* in the matter while employed by the Government. A violation occurs where the former employee *knowingly* communicated with or appeared before the Government department, agency, or court, and the former Government employee's communication was made with *intent to influence* an officer or employee of a Government department, agency, or court on behalf of any person.

A key requirement is that the former Government employee must have participated "personally and substantially" in the transaction in question. It is not sufficient that the matter was one that was pending under the Government employee's official responsibility.

To violate this section of the Ethics Reform Act (and the section discussed below which provides for a two-year ban on a former Government employee's activities) the former Government employee's actions must involve the "same particular issue" the employee worked on during the course of his Government employment. The definition of this phrase suggests that the prohibition applies only when the parties, facts, and subject matter are the same. However, the definition is not so narrow as to remove persons from liability when minor changes in the facts or subject matter occur. For example, in one instance, a court found that a modification to a contract being performed by one contractor and the original contract performed by another contractor were the "same contract" for purposes of applying the revolving-door statute to a former Army Contracting Officer who had formed a consulting firm. The court concluded that both contracts concerned the same artillery shells and the modification only increased the number of shells to be produced.[1]

The determination of what constitutes "personal and substantial" involvement and "particular matter" are very fact specific. In *CNA Corp. v. U.S.*, 81 Fed. Cl. 722 (2008), the court rejected a decision by the Department of Health and Human Services to exclude a contractor from the current and presumably future competitions because its proposed "principal investigator" was barred from participating under 18 U.S.C.A § 207(a). The contract in question, which covered Montgomery County, Maryland, was one of approximately 80 that were to be awarded during 2007 and 2008 as part of a 20 year program to assess the effect of environmental exposures on children's health and development

---

[Section 8:9]

[1] *U.S. v. Medico Industries, Inc.*, 784 F.2d 840 (7th Cir. 1986).

from before birth to age 21. The agency contended that the principal investigator's previous role as a team leader of a working group assisting in making recommendations for the protocol for one facet of the overall program made her ineligible to participate in contracts that were awarded to carry out that program. The court noted that the statute prohibited a person from attempting to influence an agency with respect to a "particular matter" in which the person had been "personally and substantially" involved as a Government employee. It then questioned whether a single contract, which constituted a very small part of a multi-contract, 20-year program, was a "particular matter" within the meaning of the statute. Furthermore, the court found that there had been 22 separate working groups comprised of over 200 scientists and 2500 other personnel that had provided input during the planning phase of the project and that the individual in question had only worked on the planning phase on a part-time basis. In light of this, the court concluded that the individual had not been "substantially" involved in the project while a Government employee and that that the permanent restrictions under 18 U.S.C.A. § 207(a) did not apply.

Compliance with the Ethics in Government Act will keep federal employees and contractors from violating the "revolving door" statutory prohibition. However, compliance with 18 U.S.C. § 207 is not dispositive of the possible existence of an organizational conflict of interest. A contractor may be excluded from a competition under the "organizational conflicts of interest" rules in FAR 9.5 even though the individual employee has not violated 18 U.S.C.A. § 207. In *KAR Contracting, LLC, B-310454, B-310537*, 2007 CPD 226 (Comp. Gen. 2007), GAO stated:

> In our view, the restrictions of 18 U.S.C.A. § 207 do not set the outer boundaries for a CO's reasonable exercise of discretion about whether the award of a contract will create the appearance of impropriety. Specifically, even if KAR can argue that the facts here would not support a criminal conviction for violation of the post-employment restrictions, that would not mean there was no reasonable basis for concluding that KAR was ineligible for award.

§ 8:10 Two-year ban on communications and appearances

Former Government employees who had *official responsibility* for a matter while in Government service are prohibited for two years after leaving Government employment from making the same type of appearances and communications regarding that matter before a court or agency on behalf of another person. This prohibition covers matters that the former employee "*knows* or *reasonably should know* was actually pending under his or her official responsibility" as part of his or her Government

CONFLICTS OF INTEREST § 8:11

employment.[1] The law focuses on particular matters that were the responsibility of the former Government employee during the last year of employment.

For example, in one case, a former General Services Administration (GSA) leasing branch chief contracted to assist a bidding company with a lease project that had come across her desk while employed at GSA. The branch chief was found not to have violated the statute because the Government failed to prove that she had *knowledge* of her prior association with the project. The only evidence of her involvement in the project were documents that bore her signature. Since the branch chief signed 50 or more such documents each day, these documents were of a routine, ministerial nature. Her signature alone on these documents was found to be insufficient to prove that she knew, or reasonably should have known, that these matters were under her official responsibility.[2]

The Joint Ethics Regulation provides an example of a matter which fell under the official's responsibility while employed with the government.

> A division director at the Food and Drug Administration disqualified himself from participating in the review of a drug for Alzheimer's disease, in accordance with subpart E of 5 CFR part 2635, because his brother headed the private sector team which developed the drug. The matter was instead assigned to the division director's deputy. The director continues to have official responsibility for review of the drug. The division director also would have retained official responsibility for the matter had he either asked his supervisor or another division director to oversee the matter.[3]

§ 8:11 One-year ban on communications and appearances

The Ethics Reform Act restricts *all* Government employees (except employees who have minor or administrative roles) for one year following Government service from *aiding* or *advising* any person concerning ongoing *trade or treaty* negotiations in which the employee *personally and substantially* participated and had access to protected information. Thus, this restriction applies to former Government employees of the executive and legislative branch who participated in and had access to nonpublic information concerning trade or treaty negotiations, and who later seek to work in the private sector. If their participation in those negotiations were *personal* and *substantial,*

[Section 8:10]
[1] 18 U.S.C.A. § 207(a)(2)(B) (emphasis added); 5 C.F.R. § 2641.202(a).
[2] Katie M. Arguello, GSBCA 10158-E, 90-2 BCA 22920.
[3] 5 C.F.R. § 2641.202(j)(7) and example 8 to paragraph (j).

§ 8:11

these former Government employees are prohibited from aiding or advising another party to the negotiations within one year after leaving Government employment.[1]

The Act also imposes a one-year ban on the post-employment activities of specified *senior* employees and *very senior* employees of the executive branch and independent agencies who seek to work in the private sector. A very senior employee is defined to include the Vice-President and certain Presidential or Vice-Presidential appointees, including Cabinet members. The law restricts communications with and appearances before the former agency or designated executive branch appointees on behalf of another person concerning a particular matter. The former senior and very senior officials are prohibited from *knowingly* making any such communication or appearance.[2]

The Office of Government Ethics (OGE) has granted waivers of the restrictions on former senior employees to numerous Government agencies, including the Department of Defense and the military departments. The OGE has determined that these restrictions would create an undue hardship on the department in obtaining qualified personnel to fill certain positions, and a grant of a waiver does not create the potential for use of undue influence or unfair advantage.[3] Eligible senior employees who fall under these waivers are permitted to communicate to or appear before components of their former department after they leave the Government.

The Honest Leadership and Open Government Act of 2007,[4] increased the ban on post-employment activities of specified *very senior* employees of the executive branch and independent agencies from one to two years.

§ 8:12 Penalties

Former Government officials and employees convicted of violating the "revolving-door" prohibitions of the Ethics Reform Act are subject to both civil and criminal penalties. Individuals are subject to imprisonment for one year and up to five years for a "willful" violation. Both individuals and companies are subject to criminal and civil fines and penalties. Any person violating this law is subject to a civil penalty of not more than $50,000 for each

---

[Section 8:11]

[1] 18 U.S.C.A. § 207(b).

[2] 18 U.S.C.A. § 207(c), (d).

[3] *See* 5 C.F.R. Pt. 2641, App. A (list of agencies exempt from 18 U.S.C.A. § 207(c)).

[4] Pub. L No. 110-81, 121 Stat. 735, enacted September 14, 2007.

C. CRIMINAL "REVOLVING-DOOR" STATUTES

§ 8:13 Generally

Federal criminal law provides that no Government employee may participate personally and substantially in a matter affecting the financial interests of any person or organization with whom the employee is negotiating employment opportunities or has any arrangement concerning prospective employment.[1] Courts have construed this law broadly, finding that even preliminary discussions between a company and a Government employee, where the ultimate objective is to reach some sort of agreement, may violate the statute's restrictions.[2] Violations may subject the Government employee, as well as contractor employees who knowingly violate the law, to civil and criminal penalties, including imprisonment.[3]

The former Air Force procurement official discussed in this chapter's introduction pleaded guilty to 18 U.S.C.A. § 208. Her extensive employment negotiations with the contractor's CFO, without recusing herself from negotiations regarding Government contracts, resulted in jail sentences for both the company official and the procurement official.[4]

In addition, the senior official had extensive employment discussions with at least two contractors who were seeking contracts for Air Force work and failing to recuse herself from her position as Source Selection Authority for those contracts. In a follow-up, a court held that an unsuccessful offeror on one of those procurements had a cause of action for the recovery of its bid and proposal costs against the Government based on the al-

---

[Section 8:12]

[1]18 U.S.C.A. § 216(b).

[Section 8:13]

[1]18 U.S.C.A. § 208.

[2]*See U.S. v. Conlon*, 628 F.2d 150 (D.C. Cir. 1980); *U.S. v. Hedges*, 912 F.2d 1397 (11th Cir. 1990).

[3]18 U.S.C.A. § 216; 28 C.F.R. § 85.3(c) (2006).

[4]Branstetter, Darleen Druyun: An Evolving Case Study in Corruption, Power, and Procurement, 34 Pub. Cont. L.J. 443 (Spring 2005).

§ 8:13   GOVERNMENT CONTRACT COMPLIANCE HANDBOOK

leged bad faith of the procurement official in the selection process.[5]

III. ORGANIZATIONAL CONFLICTS

§ 8:14 Generally

The objective of Government contracting rules relating to organizational conflicts of interest is to ensure that the Government receives *impartial assistance and advice* from contractors and that contractors do not gain an *unfair competitive advantage* when competing for a new contract.[1] Organizational conflicts of interest often occur if you perform contracts involving management support services, consultant and professional services, technical assistance, and systems engineering and technical direction work when you do not have overall contractual responsibility for development or production.

An understanding of the organizational conflict-of-interest rules are particularly important to you if your company has been involved in a merger and acquisition, which have occurred with increasing frequency due to the consolidation of portions of the defense industry. There is an increased likelihood that an organizational conflict will occur if your company is part of a business combination. In that case, you will need to review and analyze past and current contracts of all your company business units to ensure compliance with these rules.

The FAR prescribes responsibilities, general rules, and procedures for identifying, evaluating, and resolving organizational conflicts of interest.[2]

§ 8:15 Government responsibilities

The Contracting Officer is primarily responsible for identifying, evaluating, and resolving potential organizational conflicts of interest. The regulations are designed to place limitations on contracting to avoid, neutralize, or mitigate organizational conflicts of interest. There are two underlying principles at work: (1) preventing the existence of conflicting roles that might bias a contractor's judgment; and (2) preventing an unfair competitive

---

[5]*L-3 Communications Integrated Systems, L.P. vs. United States*, 79 Fed.Cl. 453 (November 26, 2007).

[Section 8:14]

[1]*See generally* Gordon, Organizational Conflicts of Interest: A Growing Integrity Challenge, 35 Pub. Cont. L.J. 25 (Fall 2005).

[2]FAR 9.5, eq. seq.

advantage.[1]

In the past, "organizational conflicts of interest"—while recognized as a problem that could undermine competition—were relatively infrequent and captured few headlines. A number of factors contributed to this. First, the Government's customary practice was to rely on full-time employees in conducting procurement activities. Also, because of the level of available technology, a company's involvement with its products often stopped once that product had been delivered to the customer. As a consequence, contractors were not typically concerned that their competitors might have participated in defining the Government's requirements or the structure of the procurement itself, let alone that a competitor might be actively involved in the review and evaluation of their proposals and related proprietary data.

Now, much of this has changed due to government "outsourcing" and the increased reliance on the private sector for specialized services and technical support. A number of reasons account for this: limitations on the number of authorized full-time employees, the unavailability of certain capabilities among federal employees, the need for operational flexibility, and the need for "surge capacity." Thus, it is not uncommon for a contractor to find an employee of one of its competitors providing technical support to the program office developing the requirements or acting as "advisors" to a source selection evaluation board. The companies who sell a complex system to the Government are now very often the same companies who are, at least initially, hired to install and maintain that system and to assist in the planning for the next generation of equipment.

The problems stemming from the increased use of private contractors have been compounded by the fact that many OCI issues do not surface until after contract award. While FAR 9.504 places primary responsibility for identifying OCIs at the earliest possible date and taking steps to avoid, neutralize or mitigate those conflicts before contract award, the FAR provides little guidance on how to accomplish this. As a consequence, the amount of litigation in which a disappointed offeror challenges the award of a contract to its competitor on the basis that the awardee has an impermissible conflict of interest has grown significantly in recent years. Concerns over the occurrence and adverse consequences of organizational conflicts of interest have also led to new Congressional and administrative scrutiny. Thus, for Government contractors, identifying and mitigating actual or potential OCIs will be an increasingly important aspect of their

---

[Section 8:15]
[1]FAR 9.505.

§ 8:15

compliance programs.²

The regulations provide that an organizational conflict of interest can occur in two situations. First, under a current contract being performed by your company, an organizational conflict of interest may result when factors create an actual or potential conflict of interest. Second, an organizational conflict of interest may develop when the nature of the required contract work your company is performing creates such a conflict on a future acquisition. In the latter instance, the FAR requires that the Contracting Officer place restrictions on your company's future activities.³

If the Contracting Officer determines that a *significant* potential organizational conflict of interest exists, the Contracting Officer, before issuing a solicitation, must submit for approval to the chief of the contracting office (unless a higher level is designated) a written analysis, including a recommended course of action to avoid, neutralize, or mitigate the conflict.⁴ The approving official is required to review the Contracting Officer's analysis and recommended course of action, including the proposed draft contract clause providing for any restraints. He or she may approve, modify, or reject those recommendations.⁵

If the Contracting Officer's recommendations and clause are approved, the Government will proceed with the acquisition and issue a solicitation stating the nature of the potential conflict and the proposed restraint on future contracting activities. Depending on the nature of the acquisition, the Contracting Officer will state whether the clause providing for restraints is subject to negotiation.⁶

If, as a condition of award, a contractor's eligibility for future prime contract or subcontract awards is to be restricted or requires some other restraint, the solicitation will include a proposed clause that specifies the nature and duration of the proposed restraint. Before contract award, the Contracting Officer will negotiate the final terms of the clause with the successful offeror.⁷

If you are the apparent successful offeror, the Contracting Of-

---

²Gordon, Organizational Conflicts of Interest: A Growing Integrity Challenge, 35 Pub. Cont. L.J. 25 (Fall 2005) and Szeliga, Conflict and Intrigue in Government Contracts: A Guide to Identifying and Mitigating Organizational Conflicts of Interest, 35 Pub. Cont. L.J. (Summer 2006).

³FAR 9.502(c).
⁴FAR 9.506(b)(1).
⁵FAR 9.506(c).
⁶FAR 9.507-1.
⁷FAR 9.507-2(a).

§ 8:15

ficer is required to award you the contract unless he or she determines a conflict of interest exists that cannot be avoided or mitigated. If the Contracting Officer determines to withhold award from you based on a conflict of interest, the contracting office must notify you and provide the reasons for the withholding and give you a reasonable opportunity to respond.[8] Also, the FAR authorizes the Government agency head or designee to waive the conflict-of-interest rules when it is determined to be in the best interests of the Government.[9] Therefore, when you provide a response to the Contracting Officer, you may request that a waiver be granted regarding any potential or actual conflict.

If your company is a successful offeror in such situations, you should try to limit the duration of the restraint to the shortest possible period. For example, if your company drafts specifications for nondevelopmental equipment, you will be eliminated from competing for the production contract that uses the specifications. However, you should seek to limit this restraint to the end of the first production contract. In some instances, the Government may seek to impose a restraint on you through the entire life of a system. You should try to avoid such a restraint, particularly when you can demonstrate that the specifications you drafted will materially change over the life of the system.

Conceptually, OCI cases tend to fall into three factual settings. "Biased ground rules" arise when a Government contractor has set the ground rules for another Government contractor by, for example, writing the statement of work. "Impaired objectivity" involves cases where a Government contractor's work under one contract could entail its evaluating itself, either through an assessment of performance under another contract or an evaluation of proposals. "Unequal access to information" covers situations where a contractor in some fashion gains access to nonpublic information concerning the Government's needs. Significantly, "Incumbent status by itself is insufficient to create an OCI" for purposes of a claim of "unequal access."[10] Likewise, there is no "unequal access to information" OCI where both competitors have access to that information or where the Government had a right to disclose it to a competitor pursuant to a Government Purpose License agreement.[11]

The Government Accountability Office (GAO) has been the

---

[8] FAR 9.504(e).

[9] FAR 9.503.

[10] *Alabama Aircraft Industries, Inc.—Birmingham v. U.S.*, 83 Fed. Cl. 666 (2008), See also *PAI Corp. v. U.S.*, 2009 WL 3049213 (Fed. Cl. 2009), aff'd 2010 WL 3064174 (Fed. Cir. 2010) (offeror's plan to subcontract portion of work to incumbent contractor did not, by itself, raise an OCI issue).

[11] *ITT Corporation-Electronic Systems*, B-402808, 2010 WL 3201245 (Comp.

§ 8:15   GOVERNMENT CONTRACT COMPLIANCE HANDBOOK

traditional forum for challenging the award of a contract on the basis of an OCI. Generally, GAO will not overturn a contracting officer's determination regarding an OCI unless it is shown to be unreasonable. For example, in a case where a subcontractor to the successful offeror had served as an evaluator for the agency in connection with a previous procurement, the contracting officer determined that the subcontractor did not aid the awardee in preparing its proposal other than by submitting a subcontract proposal. Furthermore, GAO found that the contracting officer had reasonably concluded that any potential for conflict of interest was mitigated because the subcontractor had signed a non-disclosure agreement in connection with her performance as an evaluator. Thus, GAO denied the protest.[12] Other recent GAO protests involving similar facts have reached the same result.[13]

Gen. 2010).

[12]*Maden Technologies*, B-298543.2, 2006 CPD 167 (Comp. Gen. 2006).

[13]*See, e.g., Leader Communications Inc.*, B-298734, B-298734.2, 2006 CPD 192 (Comp. Gen. 2006) (no conflict because "[contractor] had no opportunity to participate in the acquisition planning, drafting of specification, work statements or any other facet of the [current] acquisition"); *OK Produce; Coast Citrus Distributors*, B-299058, B-299058.2, 2007 CPD 31 (Comp. Gen. 2007) (protest alleging unfair competitive advantage by hiring former Government employee who had served as a technical evaluator for a previous procurement denied where record showed the individual did not assist in the preparation of the solicitation and there was no reason to believe inside information was shared with awardee); *Operational Resource Consultants, Inc.*, B-299131.1, B-299131.2, 2007 CPD 38 (Comp. Gen. 2007) (protest that award was tainted by organizational conflicts of interest was denied where the record did not support allegations that the awardee participated in the drafting of the statement of work or had access to non-public information that would have provided a competitive advantage); *Chenega Federal Systems, LLC*, B-299310.2, 2007 CPD 196 (Comp. Gen. 2007) (protester presented no evidence to challenge results of agency investigation finding that a former contracting officer's technical representative performed only low-level administrative functions and thus had no access to sensitive data that would have given the protestor's competitor an unfair advantage); *KAR Contracting, LLC*, B-310454, B-310537, 2007 CPD 226 (Comp. Gen. 2007) (contracting officer reasonably concluded that contractor was ineligible for award of two construction contracts because contractor was previously a COTR on the projects and had participated in the preparation of the construction drawings); *Karrar Systems Corporation*, B-310661, B-310661.2, 2008 CPD 51 (Comp. Gen. 2008) (protest denied where contracting officer reasonably concluded that OCI issues had been resolved when competitor advised that it was withdrawing from all teaming arrangements with another contractor who had major responsibilities for the overall project); *Karrar Systems Corporation*, B-310661.3, B-310661.4, 2008 CPD 55 (Comp. Gen. 2008) (contracting officer reasonably concluded that no OCI existed as a result of contractor's proposal to mitigate effects of tight job market at new location of the project by recruiting spouses of Government personnel who were transferred there because there was no evidence contractor knew identity of source selection board and the recruitment proposal was only one of 15 elements of the mitigation plan); *Detica*, B-400523, B-400523.2, 2008 CPD 217 (Comp. Gen. 2008) (protest that success-

CONFLICTS OF INTEREST § 8:15

A contracting officer may properly exclude a contractor even though no actual conflict is shown to exist; a reasonably based judgment that a situation conveys the "appearance of impropriety" is sufficient. In *Asia Resource Partners K.K., B-4004552*, 2008 CPD 201 (Comp. Gen. 2008) the agency excluded the proposal of a company whose majority shareholder was married to a contracting officer in the same contracting organization. Although the spouse was in a different *group* from the one that was conducting the procurement, she had access to the files of that group by virtue of a shared computer network. The contractor contended it would be a simple matter to prevent computer access to those files, but the contracting officer noted that FAR 3.601 prohibited the award of a contract to a Government employee and that here, the spouse's majority ownership in the company would be imputed to the spouse. GAO noted that under FAR 3.101-1, an award should not be made in cases in which there was even the appearance of impropriety. GAO denied the protest, stating:

> [Under FAR 3.101-1] [a]n agency may exclude an offeror from a procurement to protect the integrity of the federal procurement system, even if no actual impropriety can be shown, provided that the agency's determination is based on fact, and not mere innuendo and suspicion. Accordingly, an agency can reasonably reject a proposal to avoid even the appearance of an impropriety.[14]

On the other hand, a protest will be granted if it is shown that

---

ful vendor has an impermissible "biased ground rules" type of organizational conflict of interest is denied, where record shows that, contrary to protester's assertion, former agency official working for successful vendor did not participate in planning the acquisition or preparing the solicitation). See also, *Overlook Systems Technologies, Inc., B-298099.4, B-298099.5*, 2006 CPD 185 (Comp. Gen. 2006) (protest denied where agency acknowledged there was a "slight potential" for a conflict during the course of the protest and took "corrective action" to mitigate the problem); PCCP Constructors, JV; *Bechtel Infrastructure Corporation, B- 405036, B- 405036.2, B- 405036.3, B- 405036.4, B- 405036.5, B- 405036.6*, 2011 CPD P 156, 2011 WL 3510746 (August 4, 2011) (protest sustained where only the awardee knew it could bid below an RFP's $700 million design-build ceiling).

[14]*See also, VRC, Inc., B-310100*, 2007 CPD 202 (Comp. Gen. 2007) (contracting officer acted reasonably in rejecting offeror's proposal after learning that its proposed subcontractor was partly owned by another firm who was providing an employee under a separate contract to assist in evaluation of proposals, even though there was no "hard evidence" that the offeror obtained any source selection information from that employee); *Energy Systems Group, B-402324*, 2010 CPD 73, (Comp. Gen. 2010) (contracting officer properly excluded contractor on basis of "biased ground rules" OCI even though, at the time the contractor prepared a feasibility study, the Government had not made a decision to use the contractor-prepared materials in a competitive procurement) and *McTech Corp., B-406100*, 2012 CPD 97 (Comp. Gen. 2012) (firm excluded based on OCI appearance stemming from mentor-protégé relationship).

§ 8:15   GOVERNMENT CONTRACT COMPLIANCE HANDBOOK

the contracting officer failed to make a reasonable evaluation of the possibility of an OCI and a contractor's plan to mitigate its effects. For example, GAO sustained the protest of an award where the agency unreasonably failed to determine the extent of an offeror's organizational conflict of interest and unreasonably concluded that the offeror's mitigation plan was acceptable, where it did not avoid, mitigate, or neutralize the OCI, and instead relied on agency's existing process that made government responsible for final decisions.[15]

In *C2C Solutions, Inc., B-401106.5*, 2010 CPD 38, (Comp. Gen. 2010) GAO concluded: "In contrast to the contracting officer's initial, deliberate evaluation of the conflicts posed by award to AdvanceMed and mitigation strategies, the record reflects a seemingly last-minute and hasty acceptance of AdvanceMed's "amended" mitigation strategy, which itself comprised a single sentence. The contracting officer's immediate acceptance of this revised mitigation approach is defective in several respects." After the agency took corrective action by re-negotiating the mitigation plan with the "apparent awardee," a second protest followed alleging that the FAR did not allow for the discussion of deficiencies (the mitigation plan) after award. GAO disagreed. "There is nothing in FAR sect. 9.504(e) to suggest that an offeror's status as either the apparent or actual awardee has any bearing on how the agency should engage the offeror regarding its OCI mitigation strategy. In any event, in this case, because CMS's award decision is now in flux as a consequence of its decision to take corrective action, AdvanceMed is in essentially the same position as that of an "apparent" awardee. In sum, we see no basis to conclude that the agency's proposed corrective action is precluded by FAR sect. 9.504(e)."

Section 207 of the Weapons System Acquisition Reform Act of 2009[16] required DoD to revise the DFARS to provide uniform guidance and tighten existing requirements for organizational conflicts of interest (OCIs) by contractors in major defense acquisition programs. As discussed below, DoD has issued a final rule implementing this provision.[17]

In *Celadon Laboratories, Inc., B-298533*, 2006 CPD 158 (Comp. Gen. 2006) GAO found that even though the contractor had documented its concerns prior to the evaluation of its proposal, the agency conducted no independent investigation, but relied on a routine "self-assessment" by each evaluator as a basis for concluding there was no conflict. GAO did not decide whether

---

[15]*Nortel Government Solutions, Inc., B-299522.5, B-299522.6*, 2009 CPD 10 (Comp. Gen. 2008).

[16]Pub. L. No. 111-23, 123 STAT. 1704 (May 22, 2009).

[17]75 Fed. Reg. 81908.

§ 8:15

there was, in fact, a conflict or whether the disappointed offeror was prejudiced as a result. Instead, it emphasized that the regulations focused on both actual and *apparent* conflicts and that where there was such a conflict, "to maintain the integrity of the procurement process, [GAO] will presume that the protester was prejudiced, unless the record establishes the absence of prejudice." In *The Analysis Group, LLC, B-401726*, 2009 CPD § 237 (Comp. Gen. 2009) GAO sustained a protest that the successful vendor had an "impaired objectivity" OCI where record demonstrated that the successful vendor's advice could lead to agency's procurement of other products and services offered by that vendor and that there was no indication the agency adequately considered the possibility of an OCI or whether such a potential OCI could be avoided, neutralized or mitigated. GAO sustained a protest of an information technology services procurement on two separate grounds in *L-3 Services, Inc., B-400134.11*, 2009 CPD 171 (Comp. Gen. 2009). First it found the agency had unreasonably determined that the awardee did not have a "biased ground rules" OCI where the record showed that the awardee's subcontractor provided procurement development services to the Government that put it in a position to affect the subsequent competition in its favor. GAO also found that the agency unreasonably determined that the awardee did not have an "unequal access to information" OCI because the record also indicated that the subcontractor had access to competitively useful, non-public information, and the drafts of the mitigation plans intended to prevent the disclosure of that information were not furnished to the agency until after the conclusion of the performance of the work covered by those plans.

In the reverse situation, an agency cannot exclude a contractor from the competition where it improperly failed to consider the OCI mitigation plan included in its proposal; unreasonably concluded that the firm would evaluate its own products, given that the agency did not subscribe to the firm's network which described its products and services; and improperly failed to give the contractor notice of and an opportunity to respond to the agency's OCI concerns before being disqualified.[18] GAO sustained a protest stemming from an allegation that each of the evaluators was "employed by a firm whose 'economic lifeblood' was directly competitive with the technology proposed by the [offeror]."[19]

If the basis of the protest comes to light after the contract has

---

[18]*AT & T Government Solutions, Inc., B-400216*, 2008 CPD 170 (Comp. Gen. 2008).

[19]*See also Superlative Technologies, Inc., B-310489, B-310489.2*, 2008 CPD 12 (Comp. Gen. 2008) (decision to cancel solicitation based on potential OCI and

§ 8:15   GOVERNMENT CONTRACT COMPLIANCE HANDBOOK

been awarded, GAO will sustain the protest and direct the contracting officer to review the matter consistent with his obligations under FAR 3.101-1. *Health Net Federal Services, LLC, B-401652.3*, 2009 CPD 220 (Comp. Gen. 2009) (protest that awardee's use of a former high-level government employee in preparing its proposal created an appearance of impropriety based on the unfair competitive advantage stemming from the individual's access to non-public proprietary and source selection sensitive information was sustained where the contracting officer had never considered the matter because the awardee did not bring it to his attention prior to award).

FAR 9.503 and 9.504 authorize the agency head or designee to waive OCIs. Assuming the contracting officer follows the specified procedures, GAO will not review that decision.[20]

In the past, litigation of OCI issues in the federal courts has been relatively limited. Recent signs indicate that all of that is about to change. In *Axiom Resource Management, Inc. v. U.S.*, 78 Fed. Cl. 576 (2007), the United States Court of Federal Claims signaled that it anticipates substantial litigation over this issue in the future. The opening paragraph of that decision contained this rather remarkable statement:

> The federal government's increased use of and dependence on outside contractors to perform essential government functions often entails providing these contractors with governmental, business proprietary, and otherwise private information to perform their duties. This has increased potential and actual conflicts of interest regarding how, and the extent to which, such information is utilized in performing contract services and otherwise. *See* Ralph C. Nash, *Organizational Conflicts of Interest: An Increasing Problem*, 20 No. 5 NASH & CIBINIC; REPORT 24 (May 2006). Establishing the parameters of access to and use of this information will be among the most important decisions that the United States Court of Federal Claims and the United States Court of Appeals for the Federal Circuit will make in the next few years—not only for

---

procurement integrity issues involving a particular company was unreasonable as record indicated agency took no steps to investigate or remedy supposed problems before issuing sole-source contract to an 8(a) who used that same company as its principal subcontractor and where record indicated true reason for cancellation was to avoid those issues and potential of a bid protest). In order to exclude a firm based on the appearance of impropriety, the procuring agency must be able to point to "hard facts" giving rise to the appearance. *See*, *VSE Corporation, B-404833.4*, 2011 CPD 268 (Comp. Gen. 2011 (award cancellation based on misinterpretation of relevant statutes and contracting officer determinations not supported by evidence). See also, *NikSoft Systems Corp., B-406179*, 2012 CPD 104 (Comp. Gen. 2012); 54 GC 121 (Agency concluded without explanation that information vendor received was competitively useful.).

[20]*ITT Corporation-Electronic Systems, B-401954.2*, 2010 WL 3422053 (Comp. Gen. 2010). *See generally*, Daniel A. Cantu, Organizational Conflicts Of Interest IV, Briefing Papers 06-12, Thomson/West (2006).

government contract jurisprudence, but to maintain competition in this growing segment of the economy.

As with GAO, the COFC protest will be granted if it is shown that the contracting officer failed to make a reasonable evaluation of the possibility of an OCI and a contractor's plan to mitigate its effects. *Jacobs Technology v. U.S.*, 2011 WL 3555595 (Fed. Cl. July 29, 2011) (court found contracting officer improperly failed to investigate potential OCI given findings by GAO in an earlier protest).

However, as is also the case at GAO, if the court finds that the contracting officer did perform a thorough investigation of the OCI allegations, it will not second-guess the results of that analysis. For example, *Masai Technologies Corp. v. U.S.*, 79 Fed. Cl. 433 (2007) involved a procurement for computer and technical support for the Army's new medical logistics information system known as "TEWLS." Masai contended that its competitor had an unfair advantage because two of its proposed subcontractors had been involved in earlier contracts for systems engineering work relating to the creation of TEWLS. However, the court found that the contracting officer had performed a thorough analysis in reaching the conclusion that the systems engineering work performed by the subcontractors was narrow in scope and did not affect the content of the solicitation and that the subcontractors had not gained access to non-public data as part of their earlier work that would give them an unfair advantage in preparing their proposals for the current procurement.[21]

However, the court will enjoin performance where the contracting officer fails to consider that the successful offeror was performing services for the agency that plainly raised serious questions regarding its participation in other procurements by that same office. *Netstar-1 Government Consulting, Inc. v. U.S.*, 2011 WL 2307659 (Fed. Cl. June 13, 2011) (contracting officer failed to require a mitigation plan prior to award even thought contractor had access to fully loaded labor rates of its competitor and access to agency's budget plans for current contract).

Contractors can challenge adverse GAO decisions in the United

---

[21] *See also e.g., Alion Science and Technology Corp. v. U.S.*, 74 Fed. Cl. 372 (2006) (application for restraining order denied where agency made a thorough review and analysis of the contractor's proposed OCI mitigation plan before making award); *Axiom Resource Management, Inc. v. U.S.*, 564 F.3d 1374 (Fed. Cir. 2009) (proper standard for evaluating reasonableness of contracting officer's decision is the "arbitrary and capricious" standard set forth in the Administrative Procedures Act, 5 U.S.C.A. § 706(2)(A), and should generally be based on the administrative record that existed at the time the decision was made), and *PAI Corp. v. U.S.*, 2009 WL 3049213 (Fed. Cl. 2009), aff'd 2010 WL 3064174 (Fed. Cir. 2010) (contracting officer "fully complied" with FAR requirements for identifying OCIs as early as possible in the acquisition process).

§ 8:15

States Court of Federal Claims. In doing so, the COFC does not conduct a *de novo* assessment, but rather evaluates whether the GAO decision, and thus the agency's decision to follow it, had a rational basis. *Centect Grp. v. U.S.*, 554 F.3d 1029 (Fed.Cir. 2009) In *Turner Construction Co., Inc. v. U.S.*, 94 Fed.Cl. 561, (Fed. Cl. 2010), aff'd 645 F.3d 1377 (Fed. Cir. 2011), GAO sustained "unequal access to information" and "biased ground rules" protests where a company that provided design and proposal evaluation services to the Government in connection with the construction of a hospital and a design firm who acted as a subcontractor to the awardee were both owned by the same parent company. Based on this decision, the Army terminated the construction contract. The awardee then filed suit in the court contending that the agency's action in terminating the contractor was arbitrary and capricious because the GAO decision was itself irrational. The court agreed, finding that GAO did not have a rational basis for sustaining either protest because it improperly conducted a *de novo* review of the record without giving the contracting agency evaluation the deference it was due and because GAO did not point to any "hard facts" that would demonstrate even the appearance of impropriety. The court then granted a permanent injunction directing the agency to restore the contract to the original awardee.

Recently, both Congress and GAO questioned whether additional regulations are needed to deal with conflicts arising from outsourcing. Significantly, the Government's increased use of contractor personnel in the procurement process has given rise not only to concern over *organizational* conflicts of interest, but *personal* conflicts as well. In 2007, the Acquisition Advisory Panel, (AAP) which was created by Congress in the Services Acquisition Reform Act, addressed the appropriate role of contractors who provide support to the Government. The AAP found that the use of contractor employees to perform functions previously performed by government employees combined with consolidation in many sectors of the contractor community has increased the potential for OCIs. It recommended that Government acquisition personnel receive additional training to identify and deal with OCIs. Likewise, it recommended that the FAR Council consider developing a standard OCI clause, or a set of standard clauses, for inclusion in solicitations and contracts that set forth the contractor's responsibility to assure its employees, and those of its subcontractors, partners, and any other affiliated organization, complied with OCI requirements. With respect to *personal* conflicts, the AAP found that contractor personnel who were supporting Government activities generally were not subject to the same laws and regulations that are designed to prevent personal conflicts of interest among federal employees. It recommended that the FAR Council evaluate the need for financial disclosure statements by contractor employees and the need for regulations detailing prohibited relationships and transactions by those employees. Relevant portions of the final report of the AAP are located at http://acquisition.gov/comp/aap/documents/Chapter6.pdf.

Subsequently, GAO conducted its own review of the personal conflict of interest issue. In a lengthy report that focused on 21 DOD offices, GAO (as had AAP) noted that generally the laws and regulations regarding personal conflicts of interest by federal employees did not apply to contractor personnel. GAO found that 19 of the 21 offices used safeguards such as contract clauses to prevent personal conflicts of interest for contractor personnel who were *directly* involved in the source selection process, but only six of those offices used similar clauses for other sensitive areas such as requirements development, cost estimating, and test and evaluation work. In addition, GAO determined that only a small number of contractors performing work for these offices had policies that directly required their employees to disclose potential personal conflicts of interest with respect to their work at DOD so that the conflicts could be identified and mitigated. Consequently, GAO recommended that DOD develop department wide personal conflict of interest safeguards for contractor employees who provide the type of services that affect Governmental decisions, similar to those required of DOD's federal employees.[22] In a similar vein, GAO also recently expressed concern over the extensive use of contractor personnel in the role of "contract specialists," finding that the line separating contractor from government personnel was "blurry" and that the work performed by contractor employees contained elements of personal services contracts which are generally prohibited under the FAR.[23]

As a consequence of these concerns and the statutory mandate of section 841(a) of the Duncan Hunter National Defense Authorization Act for Fiscal Year 2009, Pub. L. No. 110-417, to tighten the rules on personal conflicts of interest, the FAR Council has amended the Federal Acquisition Regulation to address "personal conflicts of interest" by employees of Government contractors performing acquisition functions "closely associated with inherently governmental functions" for or on behalf of a Federal agency or department. See FAR Subpart 3.11; FAR 52.203-16.

---

[22]*See* "Additional Personal Conflict of Interest Safeguards Needed for Certain DOD Contractor Employees" (GAO-08-169, March 7, 2008), available at http://www.gao.gov/new.items/d08169.pdf.

[23]*See*, "Defense Contracting: Army Case Study Delineates Concerns with Use of Contractors as Contract Specialists" (GAO-08-360, March 26, 2008), available at http://www.gao.gov/assets/280/274007.pdf.

§ 8:15

"Personal conflict of interest" is defined as a situation in which a covered employee has a financial interest, personal activity, or relationship that could impair the employee's ability to act impartially and in the best interest of the Government when performing under the contract. Among the sources of personal conflicts of interest are:
- Financial interests of the covered employee, of close family members, or of other members of the household,
- Other employment or financial relationships (including seeking or negotiating for prospective employment or business), and
- Gifts, including travel.

The proposed regulation states that "financial interests" may arise from:
- Compensation, including wages, salaries, commissions, professional fees, or fees for business referrals,
- Consulting relationships (including commercial and professional consulting and service arrangements, scientific and technical advisory board memberships, or serving as an expert witness in litigation),
- Services provided in exchange for honorariums or travel expense reimbursements,
- Research funding or other forms of research support,
- Investment in the form of stock or bond ownership or partnership interest (excluding diversified mutual fund investments),
- Real estate investments,
- Patents, copyrights, and other intellectual property interests, or
- Business ownership and investment interests.

Acquisition tasks that are "closely associated with inherently governmental functions" include:
- Planning acquisitions,
- Determining what supplies or services are to be acquired by the Government, including developing statements of work,
- Developing or approving any contractual documents, to include documents defining requirements, incentive plans, and evaluation criteria,
- Evaluating contract proposals,
- Awarding Government contracts,
- Administering contracts (including ordering changes or giving technical direction in contract performance or contract quantities, evaluating contractor performance, and accepting or rejecting contractor products or services),
- Terminating contracts, and
- Determining whether contract costs are reasonable, allocable, and allowable.

§ 8:15

The contracting officer shall require each contractor whose employees perform acquisition functions closely associated with inherently Government functions to:

- Have procedures in place to screen covered employees for potential personal conflicts of interest including (i) obtaining and maintaining a financial disclosure statement from each covered employee when the employee is initially assigned to the task under the contract, (ii) ensuring that the disclosure statements are updated by the covered employees at least on an annual basis, and (iii) requiring each covered employee to update the disclosure statement whenever a new personal conflict of interest occurs,
- Take steps for each covered employee to (i) prevent personal conflicts of interest, including not assigning or allowing a covered employee to perform any task under the contract if the contractor has identified a personal conflict of interest for the employee that the contractor or employee cannot satisfactorily prevent or mitigate in consultation with the contracting agency, (ii) prohibit use of non-public Government information for personal gain, and (iii) obtain a signed non-disclosure agreement to prohibit disclosure of non-public Government information,
- Inform covered employees of their obligation (i) to disclose changes in personal or financial circumstances and prevent personal conflicts of interest, (ii) not to use non-public Government information for personal gain, and (iii) to avoid even the appearance of personal conflicts of interest,
- Maintain effective oversight to verify compliance with personal conflict-of-interest safeguards,
- Take appropriate disciplinary action in the case of covered employees who fail to comply with policies established pursuant to this section, and
- Report to the contracting officer any personal conflict-of-interest violation by a covered employee as soon as identified. This report shall include a description of the violation and the actions taken by the contractor in response to the violation.

If a contractor reports a personal conflict-of-interest violation to the contracting officer, the contracting officer shall:

- Review the actions taken by the contractor,
- Decide whether the contractor has resolved the violation satisfactorily, and
- Take any other appropriate action in consultation with agency legal counsel.

Potential remedies available to the contracting officer include:

- Suspension of contract payments or loss of award fee, consistent with the award fee plan, for the performance period in which the Government determined contractor non-compliance,

§ 8:15 GOVERNMENT CONTRACT COMPLIANCE HANDBOOK

- Termination of the contract for default or cause,
- Disqualification of the contractor from subsequent related contractual efforts, or
- Suspension or debarment.

Finally, the regulation requires that the contract clause implementing these requirements be flowed down in subcontracts that exceed $150,000 and in which subcontractor employees may perform acquisition functions closely associated with inherently governmental functions. FAR 3.1106.

The TARP program, which was created by the Emergency Economic Stabilization Act of 2008 (EESA), authorized the Treasury Department "to purchase, and to make and fund commitments to purchase, troubled assets from any financial institution, on such terms and conditions as are determined by the Secretary, and in accordance with this Act and the policies and procedures developed and published by the Secretary." The TARP program contemplated that Treasury would award contracts to private concerns to support the TARP effort. EESA provided that those contracts would not necessarily be subject to FAR:

> For purposes of this Act, the Secretary may waive specific provisions of the Federal Acquisition Regulation upon a determination that urgent and compelling circumstances make compliance with such provisions contrary to the public interest.

Section 108 of ESSA specifically required Treasury to issue regulations to prohibit conflicts of interest, including post employment restrictions on employees:

> (a) STANDARDS REQUIRED.—The Secretary shall issue regulations or guidelines necessary to address and manage or to prohibit conflicts of interest that may arise in connection with the administration and execution of the authorities provided under this Act, including—
>
> (1) conflicts arising in the selection or hiring of contractors or advisors, including asset managers;
>
> (2) the purchase of troubled assets;
>
> (3) the management of the troubled assets held;
>
> (4) post-employment restrictions on employees; and
>
> (5) any other potential conflict of interest, as the Secretary deems necessary or appropriate in the public interest.

Treasury issued interim regulations on January 21, 2009, to implement earlier guidance that had been announced on October 6, 2008.[24] The rule applies to a "retained entity" which is defined as an "individual or entity" seeking or having an "arrangement" with the Treasury, but excluding "special government employees" who are employed by the Government for no more than 130 days

---

[24]*See* 74 Fed. Reg. 3431 and 31 C.F.R. §§ 31.1 et seq.

per year. The definition includes subcontractors and consultants hired by the entity to perform TARP services. The regulations define an OCI as:

> . . . a situation in which the retained entity has an interest or relationship that could cause a reasonable person with knowledge of the relevant facts to question the retained entity's objectivity or judgment to perform under the arrangement or its ability to represent the Treasury.

The regulations describe five factual scenarios that could amount to an OCI, including permitting a retained entity to obtain an unfair competitive advantage in obtaining work, being involved in litigation as an adverse party to Treasury in connection with the EESA, providing the same services to Treasury at the same time it is providing those services to itself or other companies, obtaining an unfair competitive advantage through access to inside information, and having a financial interest that could be affected by its performance of its arrangement. Under the regulations the retained entity is prohibited from maintaining an OCI unless the conflict has been disclosed to Treasury and mitigated under a plan approved by Treasury or unless Treasury has waived the conflict. Furthermore, for arrangements for the acquisition, valuation, management, or disposition of troubled assets, the retained entity must maintain a compliance program designed to detect and prevent violation of federal securities laws and organizational conflicts of interest. The retained entity must provide detailed information regarding its ownership of any troubled assets; information concerning all other business or financial interest of the retained entity, its proposed subcontractors, or its related entities which could conflict with the retained entity's obligations to the Treasury; a description of all actual and potential conflicts of interest; and a written detailed plan to mitigate those conflicts. The retained entity must certify that the information is complete and accurate "in all material respects."

Congress expressed its concern over one aspect of the OCI issue in Section 807 of the National Defense Authorization Act for Fiscal Year 2007,[25] by providing that no entity performing lead system integrator (LSI) functions in the acquisition of a major system by DOD may have any direct financial interest in the development or construction of any individual system or element of any system of systems. The Act contains an exception where the Secretary of Defense certifies that the contractor was selected on the basis of competition and that DOD took appropriate steps to prevent any organizational conflict of interest in the selection process. Also, the Act exempts the LSI if it is selected by a

---

[25]Pub. L. No. 109-364, 120 Stat. 2083 (Oct. 17, 2006).

§ 8:15 GOVERNMENT CONTRACT COMPLIANCE HANDBOOK

subcontractor to do lower tier subcontract work as long as the LSI exercised no control in the selection process. DoD implemented these provisions in the DFARS on January 10, 2008.[26] This rule was made final on January 20, 2010.[27] The Department of Homeland Security issued an interim rule placing similar restrictions on LSIs.[28]

More recently, § 207 of the Weapons System Acquisition Reform Act of 2009,[29] requires DoD to revise the DFARS to provide uniform guidance and tighten existing requirements for organizational conflicts of interest (OCIs) by contractors in major defense acquisition programs. In response, DoD has *proposed* amending the DFARS by adding a new subpart 203.12 that would contain comprehensive guidance for the treatment of OCIs in major weapons systems programs.[30] That proposed rule was comprehensive and covered topics beyond what was required by § 207 of the act. For example, it would have applied to contracts (including task or delivery orders) and modifications to contracts with both profit and nonprofit organizations, including nonprofit organizations created largely or wholly with Government funds and to contracts for commercial products, except commercial off-the-shelf items. However, the recently issued final rule, which applies only to major defense acquisition programs, backed off from the proposed rule considerably.[31] Basically, the new regulations, which are set out in DFARS Subpart 209.571, provide simply that if the contract is for the performance of systems engineering and technical assistance for a major defense acquisition program or a pre-major defense acquisition program, the contractor or any of its affiliates is prohibited from participating as a prime contractor or major subcontractor in the development or production of a weapons system in the follow-on program. A "major subcontractor" is a party who is awarded a subcontract whose value exceeds either (1) both the cost or pricing data threshold and 10 percent of the contract price under which it was awarded or (2) $50 million. However, this prohibition does not apply if the contractor or major subcontractor has submitted an acceptable mitigation plan. The mitigation plan, which is to be incorporated into the contract, is a "material requirement" of the contract and if the contractor fails to adhere to that plan it may be excluded from the follow-on procurement. Of course, the contractor may also

---

[26]73 Fed. Reg. 1823.
[27]See 75 Fed. Reg. 3178.
[28]75 Fed. Reg. 41097.
[29]Pub. L. No. 111-23, 123 Stat. 1704 (May 22, 2009).
[30]75 Fed. Reg. 20954.
[31]75 Fed. Reg. 81908.

face potential liability under the civil False Claims Act (FCA) as well.[32]

Following close on the heels of the new DFARS requirements, the FAR Councils published *proposed* revisions to the OCI regulations in the FAR.[33] As noted above, conceptually, OCI cases have tended to fall into three factual settings. "Biased ground rules" arise when a Government contractor has set the ground rules for another Government contract by, for example, writing the statement of work. "Impaired objectivity" involves cases where a Government contractor's work under one contract could entail its evaluating itself, either through an assessment of performance under another contract or an evaluation of proposals. "Unequal access to information" covers situations where a contractor in some fashion gains access to nonpublic information concerning the Government's needs. The proposed regulations recognized these factual settings, but only treat the first two—biased ground rules and impaired objectivity—as true OCI situations. However, the Councils recognized that "unequal access" issues do not actually involve conflicts of interest at all, and may arise from circumstances unrelated to a OCI, such as where a former Government employee who has had access to competitively useful nonpublic information has been hired by a vendor. Accordingly, the proposed regulations treat the "true" OCI issues as an "improper business practice" and would transfer coverage from FAR Subpart 9.5 to a new Subpart 3.12. The proposed regulations treat unequal access issues as a Government administrative matter and transfer its coverage to FAR Subpart 3.12.

The proposed OCI regulations, which would appear in FAR Subpart 3.12, would apply to contracts and subcontracts with both profit and nonprofit organizations, including contracts for commercial items and COTS items. Conceptually, the regulations identify two concerns posed by OCIs: (1) a threat to the integrity of the acquisition process and (2) a threat to the Government's business interest. The regulations stress that the contracting officer must address OCIs on a case-by-case basis and consider both the specific facts and circumstances of the situation and the nature and potential extent of the risks associated with an OCI when determining what method or methods of addressing the conflict will be appropriate. If an OCI is such that it risks impairing the integrity of the competitive acquisition process, then the contracting officer must take action to substantially reduce or eliminate this risk. If the only risk created by an OCI is a performance risk relating to the Government's business interests, then

---

[32]*See U.S. v. Science Applications Intern. Corp.*, 653 F. Supp. 2d 87 (D.D.C. 2009) rev'd on other grounds 626 F.3d 1257 (D.C. Cir. 2010) discussed in § 8:16.

[33]76 Fed. Reg. 23236.

the contracting officer has broad discretion to select the appropriate method of addressing the conflict, including the discretion to conclude that the Government can accept some or all of the performance risk.

The proposed regulations indicate that there are four possible methods of addressing OCIs. First, is "avoidance," *i.e.* taking actions to prevent an OCI from arising in a *future* procurement. These include drafting the SOW to exclude tasks that require contractors to make recommendations, provide analysis, and prepare solicitation and contract documents. Second, requiring the contractor to implement structural barriers and internal controls to forestall future OCIs. Third, a limitation on future contracting that allows the contractor to perform on the instant contract but precludes it from acting as a prime or subcontractor on future contracts. The final method, which applies where a potential OCI already exists, is to require a Government approved mitigation plan. An acceptable mitigation plan might include having a non-conflicted subcontractor perform the portion of the work impacted by the prime's OCI or requiring the contractor to implement suitable structural and internal controls. These controls might include requiring a nondisclosure agreement between the contractor and all of its affiliates, requiring that the board of directors include a member who had no prior relationship with the company, and the creation of a corporate OCI compliance official. If the OCI risk relates *only* to the business interests of the Government and if the potential harm to the Government is outweighed by the benefit of having the conflicted contractor, the contracting officer has the discretion to accept the performance risk even though the mitigation plan does not remove all vestiges of the OCI.

The proposed regulations require the contracting officer to make an initial assessment of the nature of the work to decide whether performance may create an OCI. If so, he should assess whether this can be avoided by careful drafting of the scope of work. If the perceived risk affects only the Government's business interests he can take this into account by including an evaluation factor in the technical rating.

The proposed regulations include solicitation provisions and contract clauses which (1) inform the contractor that the contracting officer believes there may be a potential OCI issue and requires the offeror to disclose any relevant information and to explain how it proposes to deal with the issue; (2) requires the contractor to disclose potential OCIs that arise during contract performance; (3) incorporates the contractor's mitigation plan into the contract; and (4) identifies any limitation on future contracting that results from the OCI.

With regard to controlling contractor access to nonpublic infor-

CONFLICTS OF INTEREST § 8:16

mation, the proposed regulations permit access only where it is necessary for performance of the contract and only for persons who require access to that information to perform the contract. This policy would be implemented through three solicitation and contract provisions. The first requires that (1) the contractor protect the data and use it only for authorized purposes, (2) it indemnifies the Government for losses resulting from the contractor's misuse of protected data, (3) the owner of the data is a third-party beneficiary of the contractor's obligations under the clause, (4) the contractor obtain nondisclosure agreements from each person who has access to the data, and (5) the contractor report violations of its duties under the clause. An alternate clause adds a provision allowing the contracting officer to require the contractor to execute nondisclosure agreements directly with the owners of the data. Finally, two other provisions advise contractors that the data contained in their proposals or generated in the resulting contract may be provided to other contractors who have agreed to the obligations and restrictions in the clause summarized above.

These proposed regulations are bound to provoke controversy and likely will be revised in their final form. Nonetheless, they reflect the Government's concern of the impact of outsourcing to private contractors for many technical services that were traditionally performed by Government employees. From a compliance perspective, contractors need to be extremely careful to avoid (or properly deal with) OCIs or gaining improper access to third party data. Knowingly violating existing or proposed requirements in this area could lead to liability under the FCA or other statutes.

§ 8:16 Contractor responsibilities

The FAR lists four types of contractor activities that may result in an organizational conflict of interest. These occur where your company may have had some prior involvement in a contract or program and the participation related to: (1) systems engineering and technical direction; (2) development of specifications and work statements; (3) technical evaluation or assistance services; or (4) access to proprietary information. The four activities and their related rules are discussed below.

Systems engineering and technical direction: If you provide systems engineering and technical direction for a system (even though you do not have overall contractual responsibility for its development, integration, assembly and checkout, or production) you cannot be awarded a contract to supply the system or any of its major components or be a subcontractor or consultant to a

§ 8:16   Government Contract Compliance Handbook

supplier of the system or any of its major components.[1]

Development of specifications and work statements: If you prepare the complete specifications covering nondevelopmental items to be used in a competitive procurement, you cannot furnish these items, either as a prime contractor or as a subcontractor, for a reasonable period of time including, at least, the duration of the initial production contract. This rule does not apply if you furnish specifications or product data at Government request, even though the specifications or data may have been paid for separately, or if you act as one of several industry representatives in helping the Government prepare, refine, or coordinate specifications, regardless of source, provided the assistance is supervised and controlled by Government representatives.[2]

Evaluation services: Generally, you may not receive contracts involving evaluations of other contractors' offers for products or services if you will be evaluating or advising the Government concerning your own products or activities or those of a competitor, without proper safeguards to ensure your objectivity and to protect the Government's interests. This rule protects competitors' proprietary information submitted to the Government in connection with proposals or bids.[3]

Access to proprietary information: If you obtain access to a competitor's proprietary information in performing advisory services for the Government, you must negotiate an agreement with your competitor under which you obligate your company to protect the information from unauthorized use or disclosure for as long as it remains proprietary and refrain from using the information for any purpose other than that for which it was furnished. The Contracting Officer is responsible for your proper adherence to these agreements.[4] Nevertheless, you should establish company procedures to ensure that a competitor's proprietary information is protected and not used in a manner that would result in an organizational conflict of interest.

As explained above, if the Contracting Officer determines that a significant organizational conflict of interest may exist, he or she must include a provision in the solicitation stating the nature of the conflict, the nature of the proposed restraint on future contracting activities, and whether these terms are subject to negotiation. If you are awarded the contract, you must abide by the terms of this provision and the future contracting restraints

---

[Section 8:16]

[1] FAR 9.505-1.
[2] FAR 9.505-2.
[3] FAR 9.505-3.
[4] FAR 9.505-4.

specified. Generally, the restraints are for a fixed term of reasonable duration and specify termination either by a specific date or on the occurrence of an identifiable event. Failure to abide by these terms may prompt a criminal prosecution of you and your company based on a false statement (see §§ 1:1 et seq.) and could result in severe administrative, civil, and criminal penalties.

If you use a "marketing consultant," you must make certain that the use of the consultant does not create a conflict of interest based on the knowledge of the consultant. A "marketing consultant" is defined as any independent contractor who furnishes advice, information, direction, or assistance to an offeror or any other contractor in support of the preparation or submission of an offer for a Government contract by that offeror.[5]

A contractor must comply with all contractual provisions aimed at eliminating or neutralizing potential OCIs and the failure to do so can lead to a potential violation of the False Claims Act. For example, the Nuclear Regulatory Commission awarded two contracts to SAIC calling for the development of options and potential standards for the recycling and reuse of radioactive material by the private sector. The court found that in both contracts SAIC represented that it would disclose any relationships which might compromise its neutrality under the contracts. The Government brought suit under the FCA after learning that SAIC failed to disclose that it sponsored a trade association that advocated reusing radioactive and contaminated materials. The court denied SAIC's motion to dismiss, stating "By directly working with a trade association whose aim was to advocate in favor of recycling and reusing radioactive materials, SAIC's ability to provide impartial assistance to the NRC as was required under the contracts could easily be called into question." A jury found SAIC guilty of making false claims in connection with these events.[6]

§ 8:17 Frequently asked questions

Question 1: Our company is a systems engineering firm primarily engaged in defense contracts providing engineering and technical services. We recently completed a Navy contract that provided for delivery of a statement of work for a radar system. Our company is being acquired by a large defense contractor that produces radar equipment for the military services. If the acquiring defense contractor plans to submit a proposal on a solicitation that uses a portion of the statement of work we provided to the Navy, is there a potential organizational conflict of interest

---

[5]FAR 9.501.

[6]*U.S. v. Science Applications Intern. Corp.*, 653 F. Supp. 2d 87 (D.D.C. 2009) rev'd on other grounds 626 F.3d 1257 (D.C. Cir. 2010).

§ 8:17   GOVERNMENT CONTRACT COMPLIANCE HANDBOOK

problem?

Answer 1: Yes. The acquisition of your firm by the large defense contractor creates a potential conflict of interest on future Government contracts for which your firm provided system engineering or technical direction as defined in the regulations. However, the acquiring company may be able to avoid or mitigate the potential conflict of interest by preparing and submitting to the Contracting Officer a comprehensive conflict avoidance plan. The plan should clearly specify mechanisms for identifying, avoiding, and mitigating the potential conflicts.

Question 2: What are the elements of a good conflict avoidance plan?

Answer 2: Generally, a company's conflict avoidance plan should establish clear procedures for identifying and avoiding conflicts and, for those potential or actual conflicts identified, the steps your company will take to mitigate the effects of the conflicts. In instances of a merger or acquisition, a detailed review should be done of each company's contracts and their statements of work. When actual or potential conflicts are identified, clear procedures must be established to avoid and mitigate the conflicts.

Question 3: If an *actual* organizational conflict is identified and it is clear the conflict cannot be avoided or mitigated, is there any way a contractor can still receive a contract?

Answer 3: Yes. The FAR establishes a "waiver" procedure.[1] Your company may submit to the Contracting Officer a written request for waiver which must be approved by the agency head or designee. In no case may the designee be lower than the head of the contracting activity. Your written request should identify the actual conflict and provide a strong rationale as to why it is in the Government's best interest to grant the waiver and award the contract to your company.

Question 4: A consultant for our company has come across some proposal information of a competitor on a current procurement for which we are submitting a proposal to the Government. The consultant has informed us that the proprietary legend placed on the cover sheet is just another example of our competitor claiming proprietary rights in information it does not own. Should we use this information in connection with submitting our competing proposal?

Answer 4: No. You should not use proprietary information of a competitor when preparing your company proposal. If you use

---

[Section 8:17]
   [1]FAR 9.503.

the information, you risk being eliminated from the competition. The FAR cautions contractors about obtaining proprietary or source selection information from marketing consultants, and admonishes contractors to inquire as to the source of such information to ensure no unfair competitive advantage is gained.[2] If any company personnel working on your proposal reviewed the information, you should relieve them from working on the proposal effort to avoid allegations that an unfair competitive advantage was gained by reviewing the information.

Question 5: Our company wishes to compete for a new contract on an Air Force program for which we originally provided certain development work under a prime contract. Are we prohibited from competing for this program because of an organizational conflict of interest?

Answer 5: Probably not. You should review the prime contract terms to determine whether any restraints were placed on your company. The FAR recognizes that while a development contractor has a competitive advantage, it is an unavoidable one that will not be considered to be unfair, and generally no prohibitions will be imposed on the original development contractor.[3]

IV. HOW TO RECOGNIZE THE PROBLEM
A. PERSONAL CONFLICTS
§ 8:18 Generally

Vigilance alone will not identify all personal conflicts of interest. You must be aware of the specific statutes and regulations that identify relationships that may constitute personal conflicts of interest. These statutes and regulations govern the way that you can contact a Government employee to discuss employment opportunities, provide compensation to former Government employees, or assign responsibilities to a former Government employee currently working for your company. Furthermore, you must keep in mind that the Government may find that you have violated these statutes and regulations either by specific action or by the mere appearance of impropriety.

---

[2]FAR 9.505-4.

[3]FAR 9.505-2(a)(3). "In development work, it is normal to select firms that have done the most advanced work in the field. These firms can be expected to design and develop around their own prior knowledge. Development contractors can frequently start production earlier and more knowledgeably than firms that did not participate in the development, and this can affect the time and quality of production, both of which are important to the Government. In many instances the Government may have financed the development. Thus, while the development contractor has a competitive advantage, it is an unavoidable one that is not considered unfair; hence no prohibition should be imposed."

§ 8:19 Examples

The following examples will help you recognize the types of activities that may be considered personal conflicts of interest or that may create the appearance of a personal conflict of interest. Some of the examples were taken from the facts of decisions interpreting earlier provisions of the Procurement Integrity Act[1] and the revolving-door statutes. However, the examples continue to be helpful in identifying potential conflicts of interest under current laws.

Contact current Government employee: Assume you are a major defense contractor contemplating hiring Mr. Q, the current Government Program Manager for the ground radar system program for which your company is the prime contractor, and you are currently competing for a follow-on contract award. You plan to contact him after the next program status briefing to discuss possible employment as your company's deputy program manager for the ground radar system program. You should not contact Mr. Q for employment discussions. The Procurement Integrity Act prohibits any contact by a bidder or offeror to an agency official regarding nonfederal employment. The Act applies to your company since you are competing for the follow-on contract.

If you contact Mr. Q regarding future employment, he must report the contact in writing to both his supervisor and the agency ethics official. Also, he must reject the possibility of any employment with your company or disqualify himself from further personal and substantial participation in the procurement. Finally, if the contract is valued at $10 million or more, Mr. Q is prohibited from accepting compensation from the division of your company that produces the ground radar (or from any other division or affiliate that produces the same or similar products) for one year after his Government service, even if such employment would be unrelated to the ground radar system program. If the Act is violated, both Mr. Q and your company are subject to administrative, civil, and criminal penalties.

Source selection authority: General G, an Air Force officer, served as the Source Selection Authority (SSA) for a space communications system contract awarded to your company. On retirement, General G accepts a position with your company in which she represents your company and negotiates several modifications to the contract for which she was the SSA. General G may have violated the Procurement Integrity and Ethics Reform Acts

---

[Section 8:19]

[1] 41 U.S.C.A. §§ 2101 et seq.

§ 8:19

and be subject to criminal and civil penalties. In addition, your company may have violated the Procurement Integrity Act by providing compensation to a former federal official who served during a source selection as the SSA in which you received a contract of more than $10 million. Thus, you and your company may be subject to civil penalties of $500,000 for each violation by the company plus twice the amount of illegal compensation received by General G.

Inside information: A federal court held in one case that the delivery of a contractor's bid to the Naval Sea Systems Command (NAVSEA) by a former employee of NAVSEA was not an "appearance" as a representative of the bidder within the meaning of the Ethics Reform Act and that the former NAVSEA employee's use of "inside information" while preparing the successful bidder's proposal did not result in an unfair competitive advantage. Thus, the contract was not required to be set aside. The "inside information" was found not to have resulted in an unfair competitive advantage because; (a) it consisted of documents that had become public in the solicitation before the date the contractor hired the former NAVSEA employee, and (b) the Navy offered compelling testimony that undisclosed information that the former NAVSEA employee had access to would not provide the contractor with a competitive advantage. This undisclosed information included technical and schedule risk identification, potential contractors in the draft Acquisition Strategy, the names of the Technical Award Review Panel members, and certain classified information in the draft letter of Operational Requirements.[2]

Development of work statement or source selection plan: A prospective subcontractor employed a former Government employee who had participated in the initial development of the performance work statement and source selection plan for a procurement for medical services. The GAO decided that although the former Government employee was a procurement official, that fact did not create an improper conflict of interest. The former Government employee's involvement in the procurement ended more than three months before the solicitation was issued and long before any proposals were submitted. Thus, the former employee had no opportunity to influence the evaluation of proposals. Neither the work statement nor the selection plan were in final form when the former employee terminated his or her participation in the procurement; therefore, the former employee had no information regarding the procurement that could give the subcontractor a competitive advantage over other offerors. In ad-

---

[2]*Robert E. Derecktor of Rhode Island, Inc. v. U.S.*, 762 F. Supp. 1019 (D.R.I. 1991).

§ 8:19   Government Contract Compliance Handbook

dition, the former Government employee was not hired by the subcontractor to work on the contract. In these circumstances, the GAO decided that no conflict of interest existed.[3]

Contract forfeiture: The Chief of the Plant Branch for the Corps of Engineers "assisted" a company in procuring three bulkhead rehabilitation contracts in exchange for payments ranging from 5% of the contract price to 25% of the contract's profits. The Corps' official also supervised the contract work, tolerated unsatisfactory work, and recommended that the Corps make additional payments to the contractor. This Corps' official eventually pleaded guilty to violation of the conflict-of-interest statute. The Claims Court held that the conflict of interest permitted the Government to recover from the contractor the amounts previously paid under all three contracts, two of which were completed.[4] While the facts of this case seem extreme, the lesson is clear: conflicts of interest may lead to criminal penalties, including fines, but they also expose you to the risk of *forfeiture* of all contract payments made under tainted contracts.

Inside information: A contractor appeared to have won the award of a communications system until a competitor asserted that the agency's Chief of Telecommunications had left the agency, gone to work for one of the awardee's subcontractors, and worked on the telecommunications proposal preparation team. Furthermore, the former Government employee discussed the proposal with Government officials and advised the company regarding the Government's requirements and capabilities on certain procurement-related issues. The GSA Board of Contract Appeals held that, as a former supervisory employee, the individual violated the conflict-of-interest statute by communicating with the Government within the one-year restricted period with the intent to influence the Government's actions.[5] The board noted that the Contracting Officer could void a contract for an actual *or* apparent conflict of interest. The board, as a result, directed the award of the contract to a competitor.

New Government employees: Five executives of a large aerospace contractor resigned or took early retirement to accept important positions with the Government. In an effort to mitigate the substantial financial losses the employees expected to suffer by changing employment, the contractor made unconditional lump sum payments to each departing employee before the formation of their employment relationships with the Government. The Government later asserted that the payments constituted at-

---

[3]*FHC Options*, Comp. Gen. Dec. B-246793.3, 92-1 CPD 336.

[4]*K & R Engineering Co., Inc. v. U. S.*, 222 Ct. Cl. 340, 616 F.2d 469 (1980).

[5]*United Telephone Co. of the Northwest*, GSBCA 10031-P, 89-3 BCA 22108.

tempts to supplement the individuals' compensation as federal employees and, therefore, created a conflict of interest that breached the fiduciary duty of undivided loyalty employees owe to the Government. The Government sought payment from the contractor of the amount paid to the former employees, as well as imposition of a constructive trust on the money received by the individuals.

In reviewing this case, the Supreme Court distinguished unconditional pre-employment severance payments from ongoing payments and found that to constitute a statutory violation, *the payments must be made while the individuals serve as Government employees.* Since the payments at issue were made before the start of Government employment, the Court held that the payments did not violate the statute. However, the Court went to great lengths to explain that this strict construction of a *criminal* statute did not extinguish the appearance of a potential conflict.[6]

Access to proprietary information: A bidder on a Government contract challenged the Contracting Officer's decision to disqualify it from the bidding process. The Contracting Officer disqualified the bidder from obtaining, or attempting to obtain, proprietary information from a competitor which may have given the bidder an unfair competitive advantage, even though obtaining the information violated no law or regulation. The Claims Court held that the Contracting Officer has the authority to disqualify a bidder based solely on the appearance of impropriety when, in the Contracting Officer's honest judgment, it is necessary to do so to protect the integrity of the procurement process.[7]

Access to proprietary information: An aerospace contractor had its launch division suspended from the federal procurement process for nearly two years when the Government discovered that the contractor possessed thousands of pages of documents divulging proprietary information of its major competitor. The launch division's remaining contracts were awarded to the competitor.[8]

Payments to future federal official: Officers of a corporation made payments to the defendant in anticipation of his or her becoming a federal official and agreeing to lobby on behalf of the corporation. The defendant never became a federal official. The U.S. Court of Appeals for the Second Circuit held, however, that one who is not and never becomes a public official may nevertheless be convicted of conspiracy to violate the revolving-door stat-

---

[6]*Crandon v. U.S.*, 494 U.S. 152, 110 S. Ct. 997, 108 L. Ed. 2d 132 (1990).

[7]*Compliance Corp. v. U.S.*, 22 Cl. Ct. 193, (1990), aff'd, 960 F.2d 157 (Fed. Cir. 1992).

[8]*See* "Air Force Lifts Boeing Suspension," March 4, 2005, available at: http://www.washingtonpost.com/wp-dyn/articles/A48241-2004Nov13.html.

ute that prohibits the receipt of or the agreement to receive any compensation for services to be rendered in relation to any proceeding, application, request for ruling or other determination, contract, claim, or matter in which the United States is a party or has a direct and substantial interest, at a time when the intended recipient is an officer of the United States. The relevant question in such a case, the court said, is whether the alleged conspirators subjectively believed that the conditions necessary for attaining the objective were likely to be fulfilled.[9]

Shareholder Government official: The GAO held that the Army properly rejected the bid of a firm whose president was a Government employee where the Army reasonably concluded that the Government employee, as president and 20% shareholder, substantially controlled the firm's business, and, thus, a conflict of interest existed.[10]

Spouse of bidder is Government employee: The GAO held that the Army properly excluded a firm from participating in the procurement where the spouse of the firm's president was the supervisor of the Contracting Officer who had access to the Government estimate for the procurement, and where the spouse failed to state her relationship to the firm on her financial disclosure form.[11]

Hiring a former Government official: You learn that the commanding officer of an organization in the Air Force with whom you regularly do business has recently retired. The retired general directly supervised most activities in the organization, but contracting activities were supervised by a related command located at another base. You hire the retired general, and he assists you in preparing a proposal. Have you violated the Procurement Integrity Act?

No. The retired general is not a federal agency official for the purposes of the Act because he did not act or advise his agency with regard to a federal procurement. Since the retired general did not have access to source selection or bid or proposal information, his participation in helping you prepare your proposal would not have given you an unfair competitive advantage.[12]

B. ORGANIZATIONAL CONFLICTS

§ 8:20 Generally

Recognizing organizational conflicts of interest requires a

---

[9]*U.S. v. Wallach*, 935 F.2d 445, 33 Fed. R. Evid. Serv. 1 (2d Cir. 1991).

[10]*KSR, Inc.*, Comp. Gen. Dec. B-250160, 93-1 CPD 37 (January 13, 1993).

[11]*Applied Resources Corp.*, Comp. Gen. Dec. B-249258, 92-2 CPD 272, (October 22, 1992), reconsideration denied, 93-1 CPD 180 (February 26, 1993).

[12]*PRC, Inc.*, Comp. Gen. Dec. B-274698, 97-1 CPD 115.

detailed analysis of the facts and circumstances of each case. Your focus in identifying organizational conflicts will be the *nature* of the *contract* and the *work* that you may have done on related items—particularly research and development work and the development of specifications for future solicitations—for the same agency.

§ 8:21 Examples

The following are examples of the types of activities or relationships that may create an organizational conflict of interest. Some of the examples are based on examples set forth in the FAR to help Contracting Officers apply the FAR rules; others are based on the facts of actual cases.

Development of specifications: A company entered into a contract with the Defense Information System Agency to supply electromagnetic-spectrum engineering-support services to the Agency's Defense Spectrum Office. The contract required the company to analyze and evaluate matters that would affect both the Agency and the contractor's competitors. GAO found that this situation presented an unacceptable risk of impaired objectivity.[1]

Continuing Financial Interests: The Department of Housing and Urban Development entered into a contract with a company to manage and market HUD-acquired properties. Because it was the firm's responsibility to oversee closing agents, HUD required the contractor to sell its portion of business that served as a closing agent contractor for another HUD property. The contractor did so, but significant weekly payments were to be received well into the contract term. GAO found an unacceptable risk of OCI existed where the contractor had a financial interest in the continued viability of the company which it was overseeing.[2]

FAR examples:[3]

(1) Your company agrees to provide systems engineering and technical direction for the Navy on the System X power plant for a group of submarines (i.e., turbines, drive shafts, and propellers). As a result, you should not be allowed to supply any power plant components. You can, however, supply components of the submarine unrelated to the power plant (for example, fire control and navigation). The "system" is the power plant, not the submarine, and the ban on supplying components

---

[Section 8:21]

[1]*Alion Science & Tech. Corp.*, Comp. Gen. Dec. B-297342, 2006 CPD 1.

[2]*Greenleaf Constr. Co., Inc.*, B-293105.18, B-293105.19, 2006 CPD 19, (Comp. Gen. 2006).

[3]FAR 9.508(a) to (i).

§ 8:21   GOVERNMENT CONTRACT COMPLIANCE HANDBOOK

applies only to the system.

(2) If your company is the systems engineering and technical direction contractor for the System X power plant, however, and, after some progress but before completion the system (your contract) is canceled, you may avoid an organizational conflict. If later, power plant System Y is developed to achieve the same purposes as System X, but in a fundamentally different fashion, and another company is the systems engineering and technical direction contractor for system Y, your company may supply System Y or its components.

(3) Your company develops new electronic equipment and, as a result of this development, prepares specifications. Your company may supply the equipment.

(4) XYZ Tool Company and PQR Machinery Company, representing the American Tool Institute, work under Government supervision and control to refine specifications or to clarify the requirements of a specific acquisition. These companies may supply the item.

(5) Before an automatic data processing (ADP) equipment acquisition is conducted, your company receives a contract to prepare data system specifications and equipment performance criteria to be used as the basis for the equipment competition. Because the specifications form the basis for selection of commercial hardware, a potential conflict of interest exists. Your company should be excluded from the initial follow-on ADP hardware acquisition.

(6) Your company receives a contract to define the detailed performance characteristics an agency will require for purchasing rocket fuels. You have not developed the particular fuels. When the contract is awarded, it becomes clear that the agency will use your performance characteristics to choose a contractor competitively to develop or produce the fuels. Your company cannot receive this follow-on contract.

(7) Your company received a contract to prepare a detailed plan for scientific and technical training of an agency's personnel. You suggest a curriculum that the agency endorses and incorporates in its request for proposals to establish and conduct the training. You cannot be awarded a contract to conduct this training.

(8) Your company is selected to study the use of lasers in communications. The agency intends to ask that firms doing research in the field make proprietary information available to you. The contract must require your company to enter into agreements with these firms to protect any proprietary information they provide and refrain from using the information in supplying lasers to the Government or for any purpose other than that for which it was intended.

§ 8:21

(9) An agency that regulates an industry wishes to develop a system for evaluating and processing license applications. Your company helps develop the system to process the applications. You are prohibited from acting as a consultant to any of the applicants during your period of contract performance and for a reasonable period thereafter.

Unequal footing: In 1979, the Navy issued three sole-source contracts to different contractors, each of which produced a major hardware component of an electronic support system for ships and submarines. Contractor A received a contract to integrate the components and later received contracts to produce four systems. Contractor B produced one system under a separate contract. Contractor C chose not to compete for further production. Contractor A later received contracts to provide technical support services to the Navy in evaluating problems with the system and related services in response to task orders on a time-and-materials basis.

In subsequent procurements, Contractor B protested Contractor A's right to compete for further production contracts or field change or upgrade kits for the systems. Contractor B asserted that Contractor A provided systems engineering and technical direction for the system even though it did not have overall responsibility for development, integration, assembly, or production and, as a result, should not be awarded the contract to supply the system.

In ruling on Contractor B's protest, the GAO first noted that exclusion of Contractor A from further production work would create a sole-source position for Contractor B. Furthermore, the Navy consistently asserted that Navy personnel created the statements of work without assistance from Contractor A. The Navy made sure that all information earlier made available to Contractor A was made available to Contractor B. The GAO concluded that although Contractor A may have gained an advantage, the Navy had no obligation to equalize a competitive advantage that one contractor may enjoy because of its particular business circumstances or because it gained experience under prior contracts, unless the advantage results from a preference or an unfair action by the contracting agency.[4]

Unequal footing: The Government issued a solicitation for systems engineering, installation, and integration of local area networks. You are familiar with the Government's needs as a result of your previous contracts for the equipment called for in the solicitation. Also, you possess proprietary technical informa-

---

[4]*S.T. Research Corp.*, Comp. Gen. Dec. B-233309, 89-1 CPD 223 (March 2, 1989); *S.T. Research Corp.*, Comp. Gen. Dec. B-233115.2, 89-1 CPD 332 (March 30, 1989).

§ 8:21   GOVERNMENT CONTRACT COMPLIANCE HANDBOOK

tion and literature concerning the same equipment under a prior contract. The Government's evaluation of proposals was based on a system that you had designed and installed under an earlier contract. The Contracting Officer, without giving notice to all offerors of any potential or actual organizational conflict of interest and without requiring you to submit a mitigation plan, awards you the new contract.

You gained an unfair advantage when you were allowed to offer products from your prior contract to fulfill the requirements of the new acquisition. The Government may be required to terminate your new contract, revise the solicitation, and resolicit because the organizational conflict of interest gave you an unfair advantage.[5]

Unequal footing: Under similar facts as above; the Government issued a solicitation for IT engineering services. However, the incumbent now has possession of what you believe to be your company's proprietary information (though not marked as such) which was submitted to the Government for use on a previous contract.

You do not have a successful "unequal access to information" OCI claim because unless the technical data was marked as proprietary, the Government does not have a limit on its use.[6]

Narrowing the scope of involvement: The National Cancer Institute (NCI) awarded Contractor P a contract to evaluate certain cancer communications programs including programs that Contractor P developed or was developing under separate contracts. NCI explained that safeguards in place would prevent biased evaluations. NCI required Contractor P to produce raw data with its reports which would be reviewed to ensure that the contractor's interpretation was sound. Furthermore, NCI planned to review all research designs, surveys, and questionnaires designed by Contractor P, and the agency's project officer would work closely with Contractor P to monitor and review Contractor P's performance. Finally, the agency structured the contract work on a task order basis so that the agency could exercise control over the scope of Contractor P's work to ensure that the contractor did not evaluate a program in which it was heavily involved. In considering a protest alleging the existence of organizational conflict of interest, the GAO concluded that NCI's procedures prevented the impairment of Contractor P's objectivity and that

---

[5]*Network Solutions, Inc. v. Department of the Air Force*, GSBCA 11498-P et al., 92-3 BCA 25083 (April 30, 1992)(redacted opinion).

[6]*Snell Enters., Inc.*, Comp. Gen. Dec. B-290113, 2002 CPD 115 (June 10, 2002).

CONFLICTS OF INTEREST § 8:21

contract award to Contractor P was proper.[7]

Waiving the conflict: The Navy issued a solicitation for services to repair and alter a guided missile cruiser. One of the competitors had information regarding the procurement prior to others. While this might typically constitute an OCI, the Navy followed proper FAR 9.503 procedures and executed a waiver, determining it was in the Navy's best interest to allow the contractor to compete.[8]

Consultant's dual employment: A consultant was hired by the U.S. Postal Service (USPS) to assist in software development, to assist offerors during the testing process, and to help evaluate proposals for the procurement of mail-handling equipment. This same consultant, unbeknownst to you, was simultaneously working for your company as a software consultant on the same procurement. The dual employment of a consultant with the USPS and your company tainted the procurement. There was a conflict of interest because the consultant participated personally and substantially as a USPS consultant in the same matter in which your company and he had a financial interest. The consultant's dual relationships place any competing offeror at a competitive disadvantage.[9]

Conflict-of-interest avoidance plan: You have just won a $2.5 billion contract for managed health care services. A subsidiary of your subcontractor, who was to receive $183 million subcontract from your company, was responsible for assisting the Government in evaluating the proposals for this contract. Your proposal identified that this subcontractor would receive the $183 million subcontract. However, your conflict-of-interest avoidance plan failed to reveal the extent of the conflict. A competing offeror protests to GAO the award of this contract to you.

The GAO ruled that the contract had to be terminated for convenience and that award be made to the disappointed offeror. An organizational conflict of interest existed because a subsidiary of the subcontractor was in a position to evaluate the proposals for the Government. GAO has authority to determine whether an awardee's conflict avoidance plan is adequate; actual bias and/or prejudice from possible conflict need not be shown.[10]

---

[7]*D.K. Shifflet & Assocs., Inc.*, Comp. Gen. Dec. B-234251, 89-1 CPD 419 (May 2, 1989).

[8]*Knights' Piping, Inc.*, Comp. Gen. Dec. B-280398.2, 98-2 CPD 91 (October 9, 1998).

[9]Martin Marietta Technologies, Inc. v. U.S. Postal Serv., Arbitration Decision of the USPS Arbitration Panel (Nov. 9, 1994), reconsideration denied (Dec. 23, 1994).

[10]*Aetna Govt. Health Plans, Inc.*, B- 254397, B- 254397.15, B- 254397.16, B-

V. COMPLIANCE INITIATIVES
A. PERSONAL CONFLICTS
§ 8:22 Generally

To avoid violations of the civil and criminal personal conflict-of-interest laws involving the employment of current and former Federal Government employees, your human resources department must be familiar with the relevant laws and regulations. Your company should develop sound internal procedures *in writing* for handling these situations. You should ensure that all employees understand the pitfalls of *contacting* current Government employees to discuss job opportunities with your company. Employees must also be made aware of the prohibitions against certain designated former source selection and contracting employees *accepting compensation* from your company as an employee, officer, director, or consultant. You should also establish procedures to remind former federal employees of their obligation to abstain from dealing directly in matters in which they participated *personally and substantially* while employed with the Government.

§ 8:23 Recommendations

(a) Require your human resources department to become familiar with all Government-wide and agency-specific laws and regulations concerning personal conflicts of interest.

(b) Implement a *training program* for company employees that provide training and updates on the Procurement Integrity Act and the "revolving-door" statutes. The program should address the importance of identifying conflicts on a timely basis, methods for avoiding conflicts, and procedures for mitigating the effects of potential or actual conflicts.

(c) Establish *written procedures* for identifying and addressing personal conflict-of-interest situations.

(d) *Before* offering employment to a former Government employee who may be subject to federal conflict-of-interest laws and rules, require that the prospective employee provide you with an *opinion letter* from the designated agency ethics official that no personal conflict of interest exists.

(e) Remember that in dealing with personal conflicts of interest, the mere *appearance* of a conflict may prove as damaging to

---

254397.17, B- 254397.18, B- 254397.19, 95-2 CPD P 129 (July 27, 1995); Foundation Health Fed. Servs., Inc., Comp. Gen. B-254397.15 et al., 95-2 CPD 129 (July 27, 1995). *See also Washington Utility Group*, Comp. Gen. Dec. B-266333, 96-1 CPD 27 (January 29, 1996)(GAO denied a protest filed by an offeror who failed to propose a meaningful conflict avoidance plan).

your company as an actual conflict of interest, and may result in the loss of a contract award.

(f) Prepare and maintain a comprehensive *conflict-avoidance plan* and review the plan on a regular basis in connection with planned business strategies and bid and proposal activities. The plan should identify all potential conflicts of company business units, require timely notice to senior management and other appropriate managers of such conflicts, and establish procedures for avoiding and mitigating such conflicts.

B. ORGANIZATIONAL CONFLICTS

§ 8:24 Generally

The onus of complying with the regulations governing organizational conflicts of interest lies primarily with the Contracting Officer. However, you must ensure that your company complies with any *restrictive contract clauses* included in your contracts regarding conflicts. You should consider establishing a company-wide *data base* that will alert your company managers and employees of potential organizational conflicts of interest. Depending on the size of your company, you may want to establish a focal point to receive information regarding the nature of all contract work, identify potential organizational conflicts of interest, and assist units in developing mitigation plans.

Your contracts department should be responsible for tracking any restrictive clauses in your contracts and advising your company with the assistance of your legal counsel, about the nature and duration of the imposed restraints. If your company prepares a proposal for a contract on which you are ineligible to compete due to a prior restrictive contract clause, the money and time would be wasted. Therefore, your company employees responsible for submitting proposals should maintain open lines of communication with your contracts department.

At the inception of a Government procurement, the Contracting Officer, with the assistance of legal and technical counsel, must identify any potential organizational conflicts to avoid, neutralize, or mitigate such conflicts *before* contract award. Furthermore, the Government must *notify* you that the organizational conflict-of-interest rules will be applied and must explain the extent of any restrictions that may be imposed in a future acquisition. The Government does this through use of a solicitation notice and a proposed contract clause.

§ 8:25 Recommendations

(a) When you agree to assist the Government in preparing specifications or providing technical advice, evaluate the impact this work will have on all your company business units' ability to compete for future *related* procurements.

(b) Become familiar with any *restrictive contract clauses* that prohibit your involvement in follow-on contracts. However, you should not simply accept the clause that the Government offers. Ensure that the clause you negotiate with the Contracting Officer is reasonable in nature and duration. Furthermore, if you have previously negotiated contracts of a similar nature that do not have restrictive clauses, you should oppose the insertion of such a clause in the new contract.

(c) Be alert to the possibility that, in assisting the Government in developing a procurement, you may provide proprietary information. Clearly *identify* any *proprietary information* you provide and make certain that the Government protects your interest in this data by requiring other contractors with access to it to enter into *agreements* regarding its *protection*. Likewise, if you obtain proprietary information from another contractor, you will be required to enter into a written agreement with that contractor that prohibits you from using or disclosing the proprietary information without authorization from its owner. This agreement may specify sanctions against you if you violate it. You should provide a copy of this agreement to the Contracting Officer.

(d) You may also attempt to negotiate a *"task order" contract*. A task order contract would give you the opportunity to "opt out" of tasks that would call for application of the restrictive rules. This agreement would allow you to avoid organizational conflicts of interest by not performing tasks under your contract that would force you to forgo participation in follow-on contracts or put you in the role of violating the organizational conflict-of-interest regulations.

(e) Although the onus of identifying organizational conflicts of interest is on the Contracting Officer, be aware of any potential organizational conflicts of interest when you decide to compete for a contract or *follow-on award*. Also, be aware of any *clauses* in your existing contracts that may *restrict* your ability to participate in the competition for follow-on contracts.

(f) Implement a *training program* for your employees on organizational conflict-of-interest rules addressing the importance of identification of conflicts on a timely basis, methods for avoiding conflicts, and procedures for mitigating the effects of potential or actual conflicts.

Chapter 9

Defective Pricing

I. OVERVIEW
§ 9:1   Background

II. CURRENT REQUIREMENTS

A. TRUTH IN NEGOTIATIONS ACT

§ 9:2   Generally
§ 9:3   Applicability
§ 9:4   Defining "cost or pricing data"
§ 9:5   Submission of data
§ 9:6   Certification of data
§ 9:7   Exceptions & waiver
§ 9:8   —Adequate price competition
§ 9:9   —Prices set by law or regulation
§ 9:10 —Commercial item acquisitions
§ 9:11 —"Exceptional case" waiver
§ 9:12 —Modifications
§ 9:13 Information other than cost or pricing data
§ 9:14 Subcontractor data
§ 9:15 Price adjustment for defective pricing
§ 9:16 —Burden of proof
§ 9:17 —Measure of government's recovery
§ 9:18 —Your defenses
§ 9:19 —Offset
§ 9:20 Other penalties
§ 9:21 —Civil fraud
§ 9:22 —Criminal fraud
§ 9:23 —Suspension & debarment

B. FREQUENTLY ASKED QUESTIONS

§ 9:24 Questions & answers

C. ADDITIONAL DOD REQUIREMENTS: ESTIMATING SYSTEMS

§ 9:25 Generally
§ 9:26 Applicability

§ 9:27   Disclosure & government review
§ 9:28   Correction of deficiencies

III. HOW TO RECOGNIZE THE PROBLEM
§ 9:29   Generally
§ 9:30   Examples

IV. COMPLIANCE INITIATIVES
§ 9:31   Generally
§ 9:32   Recommendations

> **KeyCite®:** Cases and other legal materials listed in KeyCite Scope can be researched through the KeyCite service on Westlaw®. Use KeyCite to check citations for form, parallel references, prior and later history, and comprehensive citator information, including citations to other decisions and secondary materials.

I. OVERVIEW

§ 9:1 Background

The Government procures goods and services in predominantly two ways: (1) through comparison of sealed bids submitted in response to an advertised solicitation; and (2) through negotiations with offerors who submit proposals. When the acquisition is made through submission of *sealed bids*, the Government makes a contract award by (a) verifying which bidders are responsible, (b) determining which bids are responsive to the specifications set forth in the solicitation, and (c) evaluating the proposed prices, and in some cases, other elements in the bid. In sealed bids, contractors must offer prices that will be low enough to ensure award because they may not negotiate with the Government and have no idea of the price their competitors will bid. In theory at least, the sealed-bid approach assures the Government that the marketplace will produce reasonable prices for the goods and services the Government acquires.

The Government has less assurance that market forces produce reasonable prices when it makes a purchase by *negotiation*. In a negotiated procurement, offerors can present their own individual approaches to meeting the Government's needs, at substantially different prices. Therefore, because approaches may differ, a comparison of the prices will not necessarily reveal which price is low, or whether any of the prices offered are reasonable. When the Government negotiates for goods, it evaluates the merits of different proposals.

The Government enters the negotiation process in a substan-

§ 9:1

tially inferior bargaining position because the contractor, in theory at least, is in the best position to estimate its expected costs for providing the goods or services the Government seeks. To put the Government on a more equal footing with contractors, the law has required—since 1962 when the Truth in Negotiations Act (TINA)[1] was enacted—that contractors provide the Government all the cost or pricing information *a reasonable person* would think relevant to the expected costs of contract performance. Once in possession of this contractor *"cost or pricing data,"* the Government will be able to negotiate on the basis of *equal information* regarding the reasonableness of the costs the contract is proposing.

Since the Government uses and relies on the data you submit when it evaluates your proposal, the slightest defect or omission in your cost or pricing data—*even if innocent or unintentional*—may lead to a *reduction in the contract price* or even a *fraud investigation* with potentially serious consequences for both your company and the individual employees involved. If the Government launches an investigation of your company, it will probably begin by searching for TINA violations.

The Government recognizes, however, that requiring contractors to submit cost or pricing data can slow the acquisition process, and in some cases (where the reasonableness of an offer can be easily determined or assumed) needlessly waste contractor and Government resources.[2] As a consequence, in the mid-1990s, legislative initiatives eliminated or relaxed a number of requirements concerning the submission of contractor cost or pricing data.

Because the liability you may incur for submitting defective cost or pricing data to the Government could be substantial, you should be familiar with all of the current rules that govern this area of Government contracting. This chapter provides guidance on how to comply with the "defective pricing" laws and rules.

[Section 9:1]

[1] Pub. L. No. 87-653, 76 Stat. 528 (1962) (currently codified at 10 U.S.C.A. § 2306a and 31 U.S.C.A. § 3501.

[2] *See* FAR 15.402(a)(3).

§ 9:2　Government Contract Compliance Handbook

II. CURRENT REQUIREMENTS
A. TRUTH IN NEGOTIATIONS ACT

§ 9:2　Generally

TINA and its implementing regulations in the FAR[1] set forth the rules that you must follow when submitting cost or pricing data to the Government.

§ 9:3　Applicability

TINA generally requires the submission of certified cost or pricing data before the award of any prime contract, subcontract, or modification to any contract that is expected to *exceed $700,000*.[1] The head of the contracting activity, however, can authorize the Contracting Officer (CO) to obtain cost or pricing data for contract actions over the simplified acquisition threshold (currently $150,000) if the data are necessary to determine whether the offered contract or modification price is fair and reasonable.[2] The dollar threshold for application of TINA may be adjusted every five years to account for inflation.

The general requirement to provide the Government with cost or pricing data on contract actions over $700,000 does not apply in all situations. In addition to contracts, subcontracts, and contract modifications of less than $700,000 TINA, as implemented in the FAR, provides other exceptions from the Act's requirements. Cost or pricing data "shall not" be required:[3]

(1) When the CO determines that the price negotiated is based on (a) adequate price competition, or (b) set by law or regulation.

(2) When a "commercial item" is being acquired.

(3) When a waiver has been granted by the head of the contracting activity.

(4) When modifying a contract or subcontract for commercial items, a contract that was originally exempt because of adequate price competition, or a contract that was originally exempt because the price was set by law or regulation.

[Section 9:2]

[1]Section 807 of the Ronald W. Reagan National Defense Authorization Act for Fiscal Year 2005, P. L. 108-375, requires an adjustment every five years of acquisition related thresholds for inflation. Accordingly, effective October 1, 2010, the threshold for application of TINA was raised to $700,000. 75 Fed. Reg. 53129.

[Section 9:3]

[1]FAR 15.403-4.
[2]*See* FAR 15.403-4(a)(2).
[3]*See* FAR 15.403-1, 15.403-2.

Defective Pricing § 9:4

(5) When exercising an option at the price established at contract award or initial negotiation did not require submission of cost or pricing data.

(6) When submitting proposals used solely for overrun funding or interim billing price adjustments.

(7) For acquisitions at or below the simplified acquisition threshold (currently $150,000).

These exceptions, which are mandatory, are discussed in greater detail below in § 9:7.

You should be aware, however, that despite these exceptions, the CO "may require" information *other than* cost or pricing data to support a determination of price reasonableness.[4] This may happen particularly if the value of your contract is below the dollar threshold for the application of TINA.

§ 9:4 Defining "cost or pricing data"

The first step to ensuring TINA compliance is understanding what constitutes "cost or pricing data." "Cost or pricing data" is defined in the FAR as follows:[1]

> [A]ll facts that, as of the date of price agreement, or, if applicable, an earlier date agreed upon between the parties that is as close as practicable to the date of agreement on price, prudent buyers and sellers would reasonably expect to affect price negotiations significantly. Cost or pricing data are factual, not judgmental; and are verifiable.

Essentially, in seeking to verify the reasonableness of your proposed price, the Government wants as much information as possible relating to the past and future costs of your product, supply, or service. Therefore, cost or pricing data "are more than historical accounting data; they are all the facts that can be reasonably expected to contribute to the soundness of estimates of future costs and to the validity of determinations of costs already incurred."[2]

The kinds of information that typically comprise cost or pricing data are historical accounting data, vendor quotations, nonrecurring costs, information on changes in production methods, changes in production or purchasing volume, data underlying projections of business prospects and objectives, unit cost trends, make-or-buy decisions, and information on management deci-

---

[4]FAR 15.403-1, 15.403-3.

[Section 9:4]

[1]FAR 2.101. *See* 10 U.S.C.A. § 2306a(h)(1); 41 U.S.C.A. § 3501(a)(2).
[2]FAR 2.101.

§ 9:4　　Government Contract Compliance Handbook

sions that could have a significant bearing on costs.³

It may be difficult to determine what information to submit concerning your future cost estimates. TINA expressly states that "judgmental information" is *not* cost or pricing data. However, the factual information from which the judgment was derived *is* cost or pricing data.⁴ Case law and TINA's legislative history provide some examples of the differences between business judgments concerning future costs (which are not cost or pricing data) and the factual information from which these judgments were derived (which is cost or pricing data):

(1) *Labor rates*: A decision to *negotiate* a new labor wage rate structure is not cost or pricing data; however, if the company has *offered* a new rate, the details and status of the offer are cost or pricing data and should be disclosed to the Government.⁵ Estimated Standard Labor Hour reports may be considered cost or pricing data depending on how the estimates were created.⁶

(2) *Significant management decisions*: Plans that management intends to institute that may affect the costs of providing a certain product or service also may have to be disclosed to the CO. For example, one board of contract appeals has held that a plan to offer dealer discounts on products, although not implemented, should be disclosed to the Government.⁷ Another board has held that collective bargaining plans may have to be disclosed if senior management approved their use or knew about them.⁸

(3) *Corporate restructuring*: A 1996 Defense Contract Audit Agency (DCAA) memorandum states that decisions to institute corporate restructuring are cost or pricing data under TINA because the restructuring may affect some of the cost elements in contract proposals.⁹

Unfortunately, because the line between judgment and fact is

---

³FAR 2.101. *See also Aerojet Solid Propulsion Company v. White*, 291 F.3d 1328 (Fed. Cir. 2002), reh'g en banc denied, (Aug. 20, 2002) (the existence of a subcontractor proposal lockbox containing vendor quotes was cost or pricing data that prime contractor should have disclosed to the Government, even though prime contractor's policy prohibited lockbox access at the time of price agreement with the Government).

⁴*See* 10 U.S.C.A. § 2306a(h)(1).

⁵*See* H. Conf. Rep. No. 99-1001, 2d Sess. (1986).

⁶*Compare Appeal of Litton Systems, Inc.*, 96-1 B.C.A. 28201, (ASBCA. 1996), *with Appeal of Litton Systems, Inc., Amecom Div.*, 92-2 B.C.A. 24842, (ASBCA 1992).

⁷*See Appeal of Millipore Corp.*, 91-1 B.C.A. 23345 (GSBCA, 1990).

⁸*See Appeals of Lockheed Corp.*, 95-2 B.C.A. 27722 (ASBCA, 1995).

⁹*See* DCAA Memorandum, "Audit Guidance on Restructuring Cost and Savings Proposals" (Aug. 28, 1996), Govt. Cont. Rep. (CCH) 99998.68 (Jan. 21,

DEFECTIVE PRICING § 9:5

not always clear, it may not be easy to identify what is cost or pricing data. In addition, you should be mindful that the facts and verifiable data that typically are cost or pricing data may be so *intertwined* with judgments that the judgments must be disclosed to make the facts or data *meaningful*.

In *U.S. ex rel. Campbell v. Lockheed Martin Corp.*, 282 F. Supp. 2d 1324 (M.D. Fla. 2003), the Government awarded a letter contract to the contractor for a number of targeting and navigation devices used on military aircraft. The contractor had produced a large quantity of these devices over the years at its Orlando plant, but advised the Government that portions of the work under the new contract would be performed at its Ocala facility and that this move would lead to higher per unit costs than might have been achieved in Orlando. Negotiation of the definitive contract lasted more than a year, during which time the contractor produced a few units at the Ocala plant. Apparently, the actual cost data for these units indicated the incurred manhours for production units were less than the estimates contained in the contractor's proposal. However, the contractor did not disclose this data to the Government during the course of the negotiations. The contractor contended this did not constitute "cost or pricing data" because it was "unreliable" in that it reflected the easiest part of the work that had been performed over a relatively short period of eight months and had been performed in part by engineers rather than the usual "touch laborers." The court found that this data was "factual" and that the contractor was obligated to furnish it to the Government and *then* to make its case that the data was not significant.

§ 9:5 Submission of data

Unless otherwise specified by the CO, you generally must "submit" cost or pricing data to the Government in conformance with FAR Table 15-2 as part of your formal proposal submission.[1] (The FAR Table 15-2 instructions for submitting cost/price proposals when cost or pricing data are required are set forth in Appendix J to this Handbook.) The CO may, however, specify an alternative format or allow you to use your own format.[2] If the CO requests information *other than* cost or pricing data to establish price reasonableness, you can present the requested data in any format unless the CO requires in the solicitation that your

---

1997).

[Section 9:5]
   [1]*See* FAR 15.403-5(b)(1).
   [2]*See* FAR 15.403-5(b)(1).

§ 9:5

non-cost or pricing data should be submitted in a particular form.[3]

You satisfy your obligations to submit cost or pricing data when all data *reasonably available* to you have been furnished to the Government as of the *date of agreement* on contract price or another time *agreed upon* between you and the CO.[4] The regulations governing the submission of cost or pricing data are very strict and heavily favor the Government. The fact that you may make data "available" or give the Government "access" to the data is not necessarily sufficient to comply with your obligations under TINA. In certain instances, you may not only have to submit the data, but you may also be required to call information specifically to the attention of the Government negotiators.

The regulations warn of the difference between "submitting" data and merely "making it available."[5] You have a responsibility to the Government to identify the relevant cost or pricing data early and, if necessary, make the *significance* of the relevant data known to the Government.[6] One case suggests that TINA disclosure obligations stop short of requiring you to analyze the certified cost or pricing data that you deliver to the Government.[7] Furthermore, TINA does *not* require you to modify your cost accounting systems to develop documents that will make it easier for the Government to analyze prices.[8] Nevertheless, you cannot provide the Government with data inferior to what you actually have if to do so would put the Government at a significant disadvantage in estimating price.[9] For example, submitting quotations to support material costs will not suffice if you also have current purchase histories for these parts at the time of negotiations.

You must disclose the relevant data to the proper Government official. Submission of data to a Government representative not involved in the negotiation or not designated by the appropriate CO may not constitute proper submission. The Armed Services Board of Contract Appeals has held, however, that you may not be required to deliver cost or pricing data to the Government negotiator if you have provided the information to the appropri-

---

[3]*See* FAR 15.403-3(a)(2), 15.403-5(b)(2).

[4]*See* FAR 15.408, Table 15-2, n.1.

[5]*See* FAR 15.408, Table 15-2, n.1.

[6]*See M-R-S Mfg. Co. v. U. S.*, 203 Ct. Cl. 551, 492 F.2d 835 (1974); *Sylvania Elec. Products, Inc. v. U. S.*, 202 Ct. Cl. 16,479 F.2d 1342, 24 A.L.R. Fed. 304 (1973); *Sperry Univac Div., Sperry Rand Corp.*, DOTCAB 1144, 82-2 BCA 15182.

[7]*See Appeal of Hughes Aircraft Co.*, 90-2 B.C.A. 22847, related reference, 91-2 B.C.A. 23867, related reference, 93-1 B.C.A. 25379, (ASBCA, 1992).

[8]*See Appeal of Rosemount, Inc.*, 95-2 B.C.A. 27770 (ASBCA, 1995).

[9]*See Appeals of Grumman Aerospace Corp.*, 90-2 B.C.A. 22842 (ASBCA, 1990).

ate officials at the DCAA.[10]

If the Government, through an appropriate Government representative, has *actual knowledge* of specific cost or pricing data, your company may be deemed to have sufficiently disclosed the data. However, the Government has no duty to seek out the relevant data. The Government does have the burden, however, of showing that your company failed to disclose the relevant data in a meaningful fashion.

It is important to note that the determination of what qualifies as an adequate submission of cost or pricing data is fact-specific. It is difficult to make generalizations regarding what is or is not an adequate submission of data. The *only* safe course of action is to disclose to the CO *all* relevant data in a manner that enables the Government to conduct its own analysis of the data if it so desires. Anything less puts you in jeopardy.

The Department of Defense December 2, 2011, *proposed* a new rule requiring offerors to complete a "Proposal Adequacy Checklist" and submit with any proposal requiring the submission of certified cost or pricing data. This checklist, as *proposed*, will require offerors to identify the specific location of various cost elements in their proposals, and to provide explanation if an element is absent.[11]

§ 9:6 Certification of data

When submitting cost or pricing data to the Government, you must also submit a "Certificate of Current Cost or Pricing Data" stating that, "to the best of my knowledge and belief," the cost or pricing data submitted "are accurate, complete, and current" as of the price agreement date.[1] (Please be aware, however, that you are *not* required to certify information *other than* cost or pricing data that you may be requested to submit; see § 9:13 below.)

The regulations require that you submit only one "Certificate" for a procurement as soon as practicable after agreement on price. The effective date on which cost or pricing data must be accurate, complete, and current is the "handshake date" (or another time agreed upon) rather than the date of actual execution of the "Certificate" or the contract execution date.

It is often difficult to ensure that all most-current data are

---

[10]*Appeal of Hughes Aircraft Co.*, 90-2 B.C.A. 22847, related reference, 91-2 B.C.A. P 23867, related reference, 93-1 B.C.A. 25379, (ASBCA, 1992). *See also Appeal of Litton Systems, inc., Amecon Div.*, 93-2 B.C.A. 25707, Appeal of Texas Instruments, Inc., 87-3 B.C.A. 20195, (ASBCA, 1987).

[11]*See* 76 Fed. Reg. 75512, now located at DFARS 252.215-7009.

[Section 9:6]

[1]*See* FAR 15.403-4(b), 15.406-2.

§ 9:6   GOVERNMENT CONTRACT COMPLIANCE HANDBOOK

provided to your contract team negotiating with the Government, particularly in a large industrial organization. In this regard, the regulations provide some limited flexibility. The regulations regarding certification set forth a basic standard of "reasonableness." The certification requirement extends only to data "reasonably available."[2] The concept of "reasonable availability" is addressed in some detail in the regulations.

For example, since some data may not be reasonably available before the normal periodic closing date of your books of account, you must *update* the data to the *latest closing date* for which information is available before agreement is reached on price. Also, data existing within your organization on matters significant to management and to the Government are always treated as being "reasonably available."[3] What is "significant" depends on the circumstances of each acquisition.

Finally, you should note that failure to actually sign a "Certificate of Current Cost or Pricing Data" is not a defense to a charge of defective pricing. The requirement for contractors to submit accurate, current, and complete cost or pricing data is based on the statute and applies *as a matter of law* when the contract or modification being negotiated is covered by TINA.[4]

§ 9:7 Exceptions & waiver

Although the Government seeks contractor cost or pricing data to assist it in leveling the negotiation playing field, the Government also recognizes that requiring cost or pricing data "leads to increased proposal preparation costs, generally extends acquisition lead time, and consumes additional contractor and Government resources."[1] As a result, the Government has established exceptions to the cost or pricing data requirement for contracts in which sufficient price information is otherwise available or can be obtained from other sources. Whether an exception applies to a specific procurement action used to be a matter of the CO's discretion,[2] however, TINA and its implementing regulations now prohibit contracting agencies from requiring certified cost or pricing data when an exception applies.[3] Therefore, if you think you may qualify for one of the following TINA exceptions, you should

---

[2]*See* FAR 15.408, Table 15-2, n.1. *See also* FAR 15.406-2(b), (c).
[3]*See* FAR 15.406-2(c).
[4]*See* 10 U.S.C.A. § 2306a(e)(3)(D).

[Section 9:7]
[1]*See* FAR 15.402(a)(3).
[2]*E.g., Sperry Flight Systems v. U. S.*, 212 Ct. Cl. 329, 548 F.2d 915 (1977).
[3]10 U.S.C.A. § 2306a(b)(1); 41 U.S.C.A. § 3502(a); FAR 15.403-1.

DEFECTIVE PRICING § 9:8

request exemption from the requirement to supply certified cost or pricing data to the CO.

Although it is not addressed specifically in the regulations, in certain circumstances the contracting agency may grant a *partial exemption* from TINA requirements by requiring you to submit cost or pricing data for only those components of a procurement that do *not* qualify for the exemption. For Department of Defense (DOD) procurements, a DOD memorandum notes that the policy of avoiding unnecessary data submission requirements applies to contracts and subcontracts where some *line items* qualify for exemption and others do not. The monetary threshold criteria for application of TINA are applied only to the part of the contract that is not exempt.[4]

§ 9:8 Exceptions & waiver—Adequate price competition

TINA embodies the common sense view that where there is adequate price competition, the Government has no need for cost or pricing data, and thus, asking for such data and reviewing it would be a waste of time and resources.[1] The CO determines whether there is adequate price competition. Adequate price competition generally exists in three different situations:[2]

(1) *Two or more offers*: The FAR provides that a price is based on adequate price competition if (a) two or more responsible offerors, competing independently, submit priced offers that satisfy the Government's expressed requirements, and (b) award will be made to the offeror whose proposal represents the "best value" to the Government (where price is a substantial factor in source selection) and there is no finding that the price of the successful offeror is otherwise unreasonable.[3]

Be mindful, however, that just because two contractors submit proposals, adequate price competition may not exist. For example, if the CO determines that one of the two offers is technically nonresponsive to the requirements of the solicitation, the CO might find that adequate price competition does not exist.[4]

In 2012, the DFARS was amended to require, in certain cir-

---

[4]*See* Memorandum for Directors of Defense Agencies (May 29, 1992), 57 Fed. Cont. Rep. (BNA) 890 (June 8, 1992).

[Section 9:8]

[1]*See* FAR 15.402(a)(2)(i).
[2]*See* FAR 15.403-1(c)(1).
[3]FAR 15.403-1(c)(1)(i).
[4]*See Appeal of Litton Systems, Inc.*, 96-1 B.C.A. (CCH) P 28201, 1996 WL 69568 (Armed Serv. B.C.A. 1996).

§ 9:8　Government Contract Compliance Handbook

cumstances, that a CO obtain certified cost and pricing data if competitive procedures were used and only one offer was received. If only one offer is received, the CO can still use this exception if he can determine that the prices are fair and reasonable, with approval at a higher level. However, in the absence of such approval, the CO should obtain certified cost or pricing data.[5]

(2) *One offer submitted in expectation of competition*: Adequate price competition may also exist where only one offer is received from a responsible, responsive offeror provided the contracting agency had "a reasonable expectation, based on market research or other assessment, that two or more responsible offerors, competing independently, would submit priced offers," and the CO can reasonably conclude that the offer was submitted with the expectation of competition.[6][7]

(3) *One offer that is clearly reasonable*: Adequate price competition is also deemed to exist when price analysis "clearly demonstrates that the proposal price is reasonable in comparison with current or recent prices for the same or similar items" purchased in comparable quantities under comparable terms and conditions under contracts that resulted from adequate price competition.[8]

§ 9:9　Exceptions & waiver—Prices set by law or regulation

A price is set by law or regulation, and hence exempt from the cost or pricing data submission requirements, if the price is set by "a governmental body."[1] Examples are utility rates and the like.

§ 9:10　Exceptions & waiver—Commercial item acquisitions

To make it easier for commercial vendors to contract with the Federal Government, TINA exempts "commercial item" procure-

---

[5]DFARS 215.371, et. seq.

[6]FAR 15.403-1(c)(1)(ii).

[7]But see DFARS 252.215-7008(a), Only One Offer (Oct 2013) ("After initial submission of offers, the Offeror agrees to submit any subsequently requested additional cost or pricing data if the Contracting Officer notifies the offeror that—(1) Only one offer was received; and (2) Additional cost or pricing data is required in order to determine whether the price is fair and reasonable or to comply with the statutory requirement for certified cost or pricing data (10 U.S.C.A. § 2306a and FAR 15.403-3)."

[8]FAR 15.403-1(c)(1)(iii).

[Section 9:9]

[1]*See* FAR 15.403-1(c)(2).

DEFECTIVE PRICING § 9:11

ments from the cost or pricing data submission requirements of TINA.[1] Remember, however, that if an agency procures a commercial item, a CO can nevertheless request the submission of information *other than* certified cost or pricing data to the extent necessary to determine the reasonableness of the price of the contract, subcontract, or modification.[2]

The term "commercial item" is defined in FAR 2.101 and essentially includes items (supplies and services) that have been sold in the commercial marketplace, items that have been introduced in the commercial marketplace but not yet sold, and items that have not yet been introduced in the commercial marketplace but will be available when Government deliveries commence. For a more detailed discussion of the commercial item exception. (See §§ 10:1 et seq.)

The FAR Council has issued an interim rule which allows services which are "of a type offered and sold competitively in substantial quantities in the commercial marketplace" to be considered "commercial services" for purposes of the commercial services exemption to TINA even though they have not been offered and sold competitively in substantial quantities "if the contracting officer determines in writing that the offeror has submitted sufficient information to evaluate, through price analysis, the reasonableness of the price of such services." 74 Fed. Reg. 52852.[3]

§ 9:11 Exceptions & waiver—"Exceptional case" waiver

If one of the above three exceptions does not apply to your procurement, you still may avoid submitting cost or pricing data. TINA provides that "in an exceptional case," the head of the contracting activity may waive the cost or pricing data submission requirement if the Government can establish price reasonableness through other available information.[1] In fact, the DCAA has stated that the use of waivers when data other than cost or pricing are available to determine price reasonableness is DOD's preferred pricing process.[2] Some of the alternative information that you may be allowed to submit before being required to dis-

---

[Section 9:10]

[1] *See* 10 U.S.C.A. § 2306a(b)(1)(B); 41 U.S.C.A. § 3503(a)(3).
[2] *See* FAR 15.403-3.
[3] FAR 15.403-1(c)(3)(ii).

[Section 9:11]

[1] 10 U.S.C.A. § 2306a(b)(1)(C); 41 U.S.C.A. § 3503(a)(3); FAR 15.403-1(b)(4), 15.403-4(a)(1).
[2] *See* 67 Fed. Cont. Rep. (BNA) 189 (Feb. 2, 1997).

close cost or pricing data includes information related to prices (i.e., catalog or market prices) or information other than cost or pricing data.[3]

§ 9:12 Exceptions & waiver—Modifications

Where the original contract or subcontract was for the acquisition of a "commercial item" and therefore was exempt from the requirement to submit certified cost or pricing data based on the commercial item exception, the pricing of any modification of that contract or subcontract is also exempt. The regulations are clear, however, that if your modification to a commercial item contract changes the nature of the work under the contract either by a change to the commercial item or by the addition of other noncommercial work, the CO may obtain cost or pricing data.[1]

You also may be exempt from submitting cost or pricing data under this exception if the price of your proposed modification is set by law or regulation.[2]

§ 9:13 Information other than cost or pricing data

Under TINA, even if an exception to the cost or pricing data requirements applies, the CO may obtain information other than certified cost or pricing data "to the extent necessary to determine the reasonableness of the price of the contract."[1] The regulations provide that information other than cost or pricing data may also be required to determine "cost realism."[2] If the CO determines that adequate price competition exists, no additional information generally is required for the CO to determine the reasonableness of the price.[3] If the solicitation involves commercial items, the CO may request that you provide sales data relating to your product or information you regularly maintained during your commercial operations. Other information that a CO may seek includes catalog listings, market prices or publications, or sales receipts for your goods.[4] When a CO requests information that is "other than cost or pricing data," you may present the information in

---

[3]See FAR 15.402(a)(2).

[Section 9:12]

[1]See FAR 15.403-1(b)(5).

[2]See FAR 52.215-21, para. (a)(1)(i).

[Section 9:13]

[1]10 U.S.C.A. § 2306a(d)(1); 41 U.S.C.A. § 3505(a).

[2]FAR 15.403-3(a)(1)(ii). See also FAR 15.401(cost realism "means that the costs in an offeror's proposal are realistic for the work to be performed").

[3]See FAR 15.403-3(b).

[4]See FAR 15.403-3(c), 52.215-20.

DEFECTIVE PRICING § 9:13

your own format unless the CO decides that use of a specific format is "essential."[5]

If you submit information other than cost or pricing data to the CO, the information does not have to be certified as accurate, complete, and current and should be limited to the minimum necessary to determine the reasonableness of the contract price.[6] Nevertheless, if you submit any information to the Government that is false, you always face potential criminal or civil liability.

Under TINA, even if an exception applies the contracting officer may obtain data other than certified cost or pricing data "to the extent necessary to determine the reasonableness of the price for the contract." FAR implemented this concept by permitting the contracting officer to request "information other than cost or pricing data." The FAR defined this phrase as meaning "any type of information that is not required to be certified . . . ." The FAR Councils believed that definition and its use throughout FAR 15 created an ambiguity in that it suggested that in such situations, the *type* of data that could be requested was different from (and excluded) the sort of data that must be submitted and certified if there were no applicable exemption. The Councils were apparently concerned that this has led contracting officers to hesitate to require sufficiently detailed data from contractors to support the reasonableness of their cost estimates. According to the Councils:

> The apparent misunderstanding leads to confusion over what information can be obtained under "information other than cost or pricing data." The Councils believe that the terminology should be changed because they believe that it should be clear that the contracting officer should be free to ask for any information necessary to determine the price to be fair and reasonable. This could include any cost data or pricing data that would support price reasonableness even though certification is not required.[7]

Accordingly, the FAR Councils issued a final rule that deleted the phrase "Information other than cost or pricing data" and substituted "Data other than certified cost or pricing data" to make clear that even though there was no certification requirement, the contracting officer could request data that might otherwise be subject to certification in evaluating price reasonableness.[8] The final rule also amended various provisions in FAR 15.4 to reflect this new terminology. The new definition at FAR 2.101(b)(2) now reads:

---

[5]*See* FAR 15.403-5(b)(2).
[6]FAR 15.403-3(a).
[7]72 Fed. Reg. 20092 (Apr. 23, 2007).
[8]75 Fed. Reg. 53135.

§ 9:13   GOVERNMENT CONTRACT COMPLIANCE HANDBOOK

Data other than certified cost or pricing data means pricing data, cost data, and judgmental information necessary for the contracting officer to determine a fair and reasonable price or to determine cost realism. Such data may include the identical types of data as certified cost or pricing data, consistent with Table 15-2 of 15.408, but without the certification. The data may also include, for example, sales data and any information reasonably required to explain the offeror's estimating process, including, but not limited to—

(1) The judgmental factors applied and the mathematical or other methods used in the estimate, including those used in projecting from known data; and

(2) The nature and amount of any contingencies included in the proposed price.

There was concern, presumably from the contractor sector, that this definition expanded the scope of information that the contracting officer could request even where certification was not required and encouraged contracting officers to seek as much data as possible, especially judgmental data, in every case. The Councils tried to dispel these concerns by noting that FAR 15.502(a)(2) and (a)(3) outlined an "order of preference" in requesting data and cautioned against requesting more data than was reasonably required while at the same time reiterating that obtaining "judgmental data" might in some cases be necessary and could be required to supplement other cost and pricing data that was required to be certified:

This rule neither expands nor diminishes the existing rights of contracting officers to request cost or pricing data (whether certified or other than certified) or other information, or the existing responsibilities of the offeror to submit such data or other information. Similarly, the rule does not require, encourage, or authorize contracting officers to obtain cost or pricing data or other information unless it is needed to determine that prices offered are fair and reasonable, which may include the request for such data in connection with a cost realism analysis. As the rule explains, requiring contractors to submit more data than what is needed can "lead to increased proposal preparation costs, generally extend acquisition lead time, and consume additional contractor and Government resources."

* * *

The current FAR, as well as the proposed and final rule, protect against [automatically requesting all available data]. Contracting officers must generally follow the order of preference at FAR 15.402, and are required by that section to "obtain the type and quantity of data necessary to establish a fair and reasonable price, but not more data than is necessary." In theory, this could include all of the elements prescribed under FAR 15.408, Table 15-2. However, in most cases the data necessary for a contracting officer to determine cost fairness and reasonableness, or cost realism, will fall short of this level of data. The rule should not result in contracting officers requiring contractors to submit full cost or pricing data as if certification will be required when it is not necessary.

* * *

Data used to support an offer will necessarily contain some information that is non-factual, i.e., judgmental information. Due to its nature, judgmental information cannot be certified. Even in situations where "certified cost or pricing data" are required, judgmental information is not certified, and it is part of "data other than certified cost or pricing data" that supplements certified cost or pricing data.

Notwithstanding the Councils' comments, if the motivating concern was that contracting officers were not requesting as much data as permitted under FAR, then it seems contractors will likely be required to provide more data than in the past during price negotiations with the Government. While it may not be necessary to certify this data under TINA, contractors must still take care to assure the data is accurate and is not misleading to avoid potential civil or criminal liability. See § 9:16 for a discussion of the potential liability for failing to accurately describe estimating and pricing practices, even those the contract is not subject to TINA.

§ 9:14 Subcontractor data

If you are a prime contractor, not only are you potentially responsible for submitting your own certified cost or pricing data to the Government, you also may be responsible for submitting your *subcontractors'* cost or pricing data. The Government requires any contractor that submitted cost or pricing data to *obtain and analyze* its subcontractors' cost or pricing data before awarding any subcontract, change, or modification expected to exceed the cost or pricing data threshold (currently $700,000).[1] Please note that if you were granted an "exceptional case" waiver to the requirement to submit cost and pricing data, the regulations consider you as having been required to submit cost or pricing data; consequently, award of any lower-tier subcontract expected to exceed the cost or pricing data threshold requires the submission of cost or pricing data unless an exception otherwise applies to the subcontract or the waiver specifically includes that subcontract.[2]

The regulations further require your *prospective* subcontractors to provide cost or pricing data *to the Government* in support of *your* own proposal if a proposed subcontract is for $12,500,000 or

---

[Section 9:14]

[1]*See* FAR 15.403-4(a)(1)(ii), 15.404-3(c).

[2]*See* FAR 15.403-1(c)(4).

§ 9:14   GOVERNMENT CONTRACT COMPLIANCE HANDBOOK

more or the subcontract is for more than the cost or pricing data threshold and greater than 10% of your own proposed price. A CO can also demand to see your subcontractor's cost or pricing data, regardless of the monetary threshold, if the CO considers the data necessary to price your prime or higher-tier subcontract.[3]

Your liability to the Government for the defective data of prospective or actual subcontractors is virtually *absolute*. You are responsible for (1) ensuring that your subcontractor data are current, accurate, and complete as of the date of your price agreement with the Government, and (2) certifying to the data's accuracy on *your* cost or pricing data Certificate.[4] Therefore, you are liable to the extent that defective subcontractor data causes an increase in price, costs, or fee to the Government. In most circumstances, you will be held liable even if you did not know about the subcontractor's price data or if the subcontractor's data became available just before the end of the closing or cutoff date on price agreement.[5] Accordingly, it is advisable for your company to include an *indemnification clause* in pertinent subcontracts holding the subcontractor liable for price reductions caused by subcontractor defective data.

§ 9:15   Price adjustment for defective pricing

TINA requires contracts to contain a provision that permits the Government to adjust the contract price to exclude any significant amount by which the contract price was increased because of the submission of defective (inaccurate, incomplete, or noncurrent) cost or pricing data.[1] Therefore, every contract that requires the submission of certified cost or pricing data includes, or will be deemed to include, a "Price Reduction for Defective Cost or Pricing Data" clause.[2] The "Price Reduction" clause provides remedies to the Government for defective cost or pricing data submit-

---

[3]*See* FAR 15.404-3(c)(1) to (3).

[4]*See* FAR 15.404-3(c)(4).

[5]*See, e.g., Appeal of McDonnell Aircraft Co.*, 97-1 B.C.A. 28977, (ASBCA, 1977), related reference, Appeal of Motorola, Inc., 96-2 B.C.A. 28465 (ASBCA, 1996), aff'd, 125 F.3d 1470 (Fed. Cir. 1997), reh'g denied, (Oct. 16, 1997) and related reference, Appeal of Martin Marietta Corp., 96-2 B.C.A. 28270 (ASBCA, 1996), related reference, Martin Marietta Corp., 98-1 B.C.A. 29592 (ASBCA, 1998), Martin Marietta, 98-1 B.C.A. 88026 (ASBCA, 1998), reconsideration denied, 98-2 B.C.A. 29741, Appeals of Arral Industries, Inc., 96-1 B.C.A. 28030 (ASBCA, 1995).

[Section 9:15]

[1]10 U.S.C.A. § 2306a(e); 41 U.S.C.A. § 3506(a)(1).

[2]*See* FAR 15.407-1(b), 15.408(b), 52.215-10. *See also Appeal of University of California*, 97-1 B.C.A. 28642, related reference, V.A.B.C.A. No. 4661.

ted by contractors.[3]

To determine whether you have submitted defective certified cost or pricing data, for *three years* after final payment on the contract the Government has a right to *audit* all your books, records, documents, and other data "related to" the negotiation, pricing, or performance of your contract.[4] This audit right does not extend, however, to the right to audit "other than" certified cost or pricing data for accuracy.[5]

Although the Government is entitled, under a contract's "Price Reduction" clause, to reduce the contract price if the Government finds that incomplete, inaccurate, or noncurrent cost or pricing data caused an increase in that price, if the Government has *already* paid you for performance and later finds that you submitted defective cost or pricing data, the price reduction penalties can be particularly expensive. The discovery of defective pricing after payment entitles the Government to recover the price adjustment amount, interest on the overpayments paid, and penalties up to the amount of the overpayments if you *knowingly* submitted defective data.[6]

§ 9:16 Price adjustment for defective pricing—Burden of proof

The Government has the burden of proof in a defective pricing case. Generally, courts and boards of contract appeals have found that the Government must prove three elements to recover on a defective pricing claim:[1]

(1) The information alleged to be defective is "cost or pricing data" within the meaning of TINA.

(2) Such cost or pricing data were not disclosed, or not meaningfully disclosed, to a proper Government representative.

(3) The Government relied on the defective data and can show by some reasonable method the amount by which the final negotiated contract price was overstated.

---

[3]*See* FAR 15.407-1(b).

[4]*See* FAR 15.209(b), 52.215-2, para. (f).

[5]10 U.S.C.A. § 2306a(g); 41 U.S.C.A. § 3508.

[6]*See* 10 U.S.C.A. § 2306a(f); 41 U.S.C.A. § 3507; FAR 15.407-1(b)(7)(i), (iii); FAR 52.215-10 (d)(2).

[Section 9:16]

[1]*See, e.g., Sylvania Elec. Products, Inc. v. U. S.*, 202 Ct. Cl. 16, 479 F.2d 1342, 24 A.L.R. Fed. 304 (1973); *Appeal of Hughes Aircraft Co.*, 97-1 B.C.A. 28972, (1997); *Appeal of Martin Marietta Corp.*, 96-2 B.C.A. 28270, (1996), related reference, 98-1 B.C.A. 29592, 98-1 B.C.A. 88026, reconsideration denied, 98-2 B.C.A. (CCH) P 29741, Appeal of Limpiezas Corona S.A., 96-1 B.C.A. 28137, Appeal of Rosemount, Inc., 95-2 B.C.A. 27770, Appeal of Boeing Co., 92-1 B.C.A. 24414, (ASBCA 1991), on reconsideration, ASBCA 33881(ASBCA 1991).

§ 9:16 GOVERNMENT CONTRACT COMPLIANCE HANDBOOK

"Cost or pricing data" under TINA includes "all facts that, as of the date of price agreement or, if applicable, an earlier date agreed upon between the parties that is as close as practicable to the date of agreement on price, prudent buyers and sellers would reasonably expect to affect price negotiations significantly." In *U.S. ex rel. Sanders v. Allison Engine Co., Inc.*, 471 F.3d 610, vacated and remanded on other grounds, 128 S. Ct. 2123, 170 L. Ed. 2d 1030, 37 A.L.R. Fed. 2d 773 (2008), the shipbuilder and its first-tier subcontractor, who manufactured ship-board generator sets, discussed the possibility of reducing the cost of generators installed on Navy ships through a re-design of the existing model. In November 1993, the parties modified an existing contract to substitute the new design at no change in contract price. Thirteen months later, the first-tier contractor negotiated a $74,000 per unit reduction with its existing subcontractor who provided key components of the new design. The court found that while the first-tier contractor hoped to achieve cost savings, there had been no discussions, let alone an agreement, with its subcontractor as to potential savings when first-tier subcontractor had reached price agreement with the shipbuilder on the new design. The court found that the contractor's "hopes" and "expectations" were not "facts" within the meaning of TINA and thus there had been no violation of either TINA or the False Claims Act.

Although the Government in theory bears the burden of proving defective pricing, courts and boards presume, absent evidence to the contrary, that the defective pricing resulted in an increase in the contract price.[2] Therefore, the contractor really has the burden of rebutting this presumption. You must show, by evidence presented to the CO, board, or court that your defective data did *not* cause the price to be increased.[3] This is a heavy burden to bear, since it requires that your company reconstruct in a hypothetical manner what the results of the negotiations would have been if the pricing data submitted to the Government had been different.

Under TINA, there is a presumption that the natural and probable consequence of defective cost or pricing data is to cause an overstated price. However, a contractor can rebut this presumption by showing that the Government did not "rely" on the allegedly defective data. In the largest defective pricing action ever litigated—involving almost $300 million—the contractor successfully demonstrated that neither DCAA, the Government's price analyst, the contracting officer, nor the cost panel had ever

---

[2]*Appeal of EDO Corp.*, 93-3 B.C.A. 26135 (June 1993).

[3]*Wynne v. United Technologies Corp.*, 463 F.3d 1261 (Fed. Cir. 2006). *See also* Bodenheimer, Feature Comment, "Government's Defective Pricing Claim in the Great Engine War Flames Out at the Federal Circuit," 48 GC 338.

DEFECTIVE PRICING § 9:17

reviewed the cost and pricing data that the contractor had submitted with its FPR. Since the Government had not relied on the data, there was no liability under TINA. *See Wynne v. United Technologies Corp.*, 463 F.3d 1261 (Fed. Cir. 2006). That decision, however, did not end the matter. The Government filed a separate action alleging that the contractor had submitted false claims in connection with the final four option years of the contract. The FCA suit focused on the truth of statements that the contractor made in its FPR rather that the accuracy or completeness of the underlying cost and pricing data. The court found that the contractor's explanation of how it had calculated price reductions that might be achieved during negotiation of its subcontracts, the cost impact of expected inflation, and the price of certain parts was false. The court noted that "[w]hile Pratt was not obliged to utilize any particular means of predicting of decrements, inflation, or part prices, once it proclaimed to the Government that it had used some particular method, it was obliged to have done so." The court rejected the contractor's argument that there could be no liability since the ASBCA had previously held that the Government had not "relied" on the actual cost data that formed the basis of the statements in the FPR, finding that the FCA did not require a showing of "reliance." The court also concluded that the false statements were "material" because the "natural tendency" of the statements had the potential effect of causing a false claim to be paid, and that the contractor was thus liable under the FCA. The court then assessed the $10,000 statutory penalty then in effect, for each of 709 invoices that the contractor submitted over the four-year period, for a total penalty of $7,090,000. *U.S. v. United Technologies Corp.*, 2008 WL 3007997 (S.D. Ohio 2008) rev'd on other grounds, 626 F.3d 313 (6th Cir. Nov. 18, 2010). *See also, U.S. ex rel. Longhi v. Lithium Power Technologies, Inc.*, 530 F. Supp. 2d 888 (S.D. Tex. 2008), aff'd, 575 F.3d 458 (5th Cir. 2009) (exaggerating or overstating one's experience and resources in a proposal constituted false claims based on a "fraud in the inducement theory"). From a compliance perspective, the fact a contractor has a legitimate defense to a defective pricing action does not preclude the possibility of a parallel FCA action based on essentially the same facts. More broadly, these cases emphasizes that contractors must make certain that all of the statements and representations in a proposal are completely accurate.

§ 9:17 Price adjustment for defective pricing—Measure of government's recovery

The Government's remedy for defective pricing under the "Price Reduction" clause is a reduction in the contract price measured as the difference between the actual contract price based on the

§ 9:17   GOVERNMENT CONTRACT COMPLIANCE HANDBOOK

defective data and the price that would have been negotiated had accurate, complete, and current data been disclosed. Generally, under the decisions of courts and boards of contract appeals—and consistent with the requirements of the DOD FAR Supplement—the Government will receive this dollar-for-dollar reduction in the contract price as a matter of course unless the contractor presents evidence that the defective data did not have such an impact on the negotiated price.[1] Thus, although, as noted above, the Government ostensibly has the burden of proving that the defective data caused an increase in price, case law has effectively shifted the burden to the contractor.

Usually, the price adjustment is calculated by finding the difference between the pricing data the contractor failed to disclose and the most recent data the contractor actually disclosed to the Government. One decision handed down by the U.S. Court of Appeals for the Federal Circuit, however, has added a significant degree of uncertainty to determining contractor liability for defective pricing under TINA. In this case, the court measured the difference between the nondisclosed data and the data the Government used to establish its *prenegotiation* position.[2] This method of computing a price reduction is a clear departure from precedent in which the contractor's liability for defective pricing has been limited to the data for which the contractor was directly responsible. If you are ever charged with defective pricing you should be particularly alert to how the Government measures the price adjustment.

TINA further provides that once the Government establishes that an overpayment has been made to your company because of defective cost or pricing data, then you must pay *interest* to the Government on the overpayment at the Treasury rate for "the period beginning on the date the overpayment was made to the contractor and ending on the date the contractor repays the amount of such overpayment to the United States."[3] The Act further provides that if you submit the defective data *knowingly*, then an *additional amount* equal to the amount of the overstate-

---

[Section 9:17]

[1]*See, e.g., Appeal of Aydin Monitor Systems*, 84-2 B.C.A. 17297 (1984); *Appeal of Muncie Gear Works, Inc.*, 75-2 B.C.A. 11380 (1975).

[2]*See Unisys Corp. v. U.S.*, 888 F.2d 841 (Fed. Cir. 1989), suggestion for reh'g en banc declined, (Jan. 25, 1990). Also see, In *Lockheed Martin Aeronautics Co.*, 13-1 BCA 35220 (2013), the Board found the Air Force was not entitled to an adjustment for defective pricing because the undisclosed subcontract prices were both unrelated to the contract and would have resulted in a higher contract price.

[3]*See* 10 U.S.C.A. § 2306a(b)(3); 41 U.S.C.A. § 3506(c)(1)(A).

DEFECTIVE PRICING § 9:18

ment will be levied as a penalty.[4]

§ 9:18 Price adjustment for defective pricing—Your defenses

Possible defenses to allegations that the certified cost or pricing data you submitted to the Government are defective include the following:

(a) No cost or pricing data were required to be submitted.

(b) Cost or pricing data were not reasonably available to you prior to agreement on price.[1]

(c) You in fact submitted the data.

(d) The Government had actual knowledge of the data.

(e) The Government did not rely on your data (i.e., the data did not cause an increase in the contract price).[2]

Under TINA, there are certain defenses that are not available to contractors, however. For example, you cannot successfully argue that the contract price would not have been modified because your company was the sole source for the property or services or was in a superior bargaining position.[3] Also, the defense of "constructive notice" is no longer available. Thus, you cannot argue that the Government "should have known" the data was defective despite your failure to make affirmative disclosure.[4] Neither is it a defense that your contract was based on an agreement as to total price and that no agreement existed as to each cost element in the contract.[5] Remember also, as noted above, failure to submit a "Certificate of Current Cost or Pricing Data" does not relieve your company of liability for defective pricing.[6]

In addition, loss contracts or inadequate proposal preparation time are not defenses to defective pricing. Furthermore, final payment of a contract does not bar a defective pricing action by the Government because neither the regulations nor the contract's

---

[4]*See* 10 U.S.C.A. § 2306a(f); 41 U.S.C.A. § 3507.

[Section 9:18]

[1]*See Appeal of Boeing Co.*, 92-1 B.C.A. 24414, (1991), on reconsideration, A.S.B.C.A. No. 33881, (1991).

[2]*See Appeal of Boeing Co.*, 92-1 B.C.A. 24414, (1991), on reconsideration, ASBCA No. 33881, 1991 WL 165710. (ASBCA 1991); *Appeal of General Dynamics Corp.*, 93-1 B.C.A. 25378 (ASBCA 1992).

[3]FAR 15.407-1(b). *See* 10 U.S.C.A. § 2306a(e)(3)(A); 41 U.S.C.A. § 3506(c)(1)(A).

[4]FAR 15.407-1(b). *See* 10 U.S.C.A. § 2306a(e)(3)(B); 41 U.S.C.A. § 3506(c)(2).

[5]FAR 15.407-1(b). *See* 10 U.S.C.A. § 2306a(e)(3)(C); 41 U.S.C.A. § 3506(c)(3).

[6]FAR 15.407-1(b). *See* 10 U.S.C.A. § 2306a(e)(3)(D); 41 U.S.C.A. § 3506(c)(4).

§ 9:18   GOVERNMENT CONTRACT COMPLIANCE HANDBOOK

"Disputes" clause place time limits on such claims.

The Contract Disputes Act requires that, with the exception of cases involving fraud, the Government must submit claims against a contractor relating to a contract within six years of the "accrual of the claim." In *Mcdonnell Douglas Services, Inc.*, 10-1 BCA 34325 (2009), the contractor successfully contended that this statute of limitations barred the Government's defective pricing claim. The Board stated:

> Here, we do not need to determine a precise date on which the government was on notice of, was aware of, or should have been aware of, its potential defective pricing claim against the contractor because the undisputed and incontrovertible facts demonstrate that the government had established the basis for its defective pricing claim against the prime contractor well before, and definitely no later than, 14 May 2002, more than six years before the COs' June 2008 decisions issued.

Since the government's claim was time barred, the contracting officer's final decision was a nullity and the Board lacked jurisdiction to consider it.

§ 9:19   Price adjustment for defective pricing—Offset

In certain circumstances, you can reduce your liability for defective data that increased the contract price by the amount of any other defective data that actually *decreased* the contract price. Under TINA, offsets are permitted where your company certifies entitlement and proves that the data were available before the date of price agreement but were not submitted.[1] Offsets are prohibited, however, where you knew about the defective data before signing a "Certificate," or where the Government proves that the price would not have been decreased as a result of the proper submission of the offset data.[2]

In calculating the amount of any price reduction, the FAR directs the CO to take into account any understated cost or pricing data submitted with respect to the same pricing action.[3] It is important to keep the following points in mind with regard to offsets:

(1) The understatements of cost or pricing data must relate to the *same pricing action*. For example, if the initial contract price is at issue, you cannot claim offsets from an underpriced modification to the same contract.

[Section 9:19]

[1]*See* 10 U.S.C.A. § 2306a(e)(4)(A); 41 U.S.C.A. § 3506(d)(1).

[2]*See* 10 U.S.C.A. § 2306a(e)(4)(B); 41 U.S.C.A. § 3506(d)(2).

[3]*See* FAR 15.407-1(b)(4).

Defective Pricing § 9:21

(2) The understatement must relate to cost or pricing data submitted *at the time of the proposal* in question. An "overrun" in labor, material, or overhead that cannot be traced back to understated cost or pricing data does not qualify for offset. The cost or pricing data must be shown to be defective (understated) just as the Government's claim requires that the data be shown to be defective (overstated).

(3) If these first two conditions are met, then *any* offset is to be considered in reduction or elimination of the Government's claim. For example, the Government's claim may be based on overstated material costs, but the offset can be in labor or overhead as well as in material.

(4) You *cannot* turn an offset into an *affirmative* claim against the Government. An offset is usable only up to the amount of the Government's claim, or in other words, you cannot turn an offset into a higher contract price.

Although the regulations direct the CO to take all qualifying offsets into account, for your own protection you should find and calculate each qualifying offset and prepare and present the back-up data that will convince the Government to allow the offsets.

§ 9:20 Other penalties

In addition to liability under TINA for a contract price adjustment for submitting defective cost or pricing data to the Government, if you *knowingly* or *intentionally* submitted the data to the Government, you may also be liable for a variety of civil or criminal penalties, including fines, imprisonment, and suspension and debarment from contracting with the Government. In fact, contractors that violate TINA are often charged with violations of other federal statutes.[1]

§ 9:21 Other penalties—Civil fraud

If you supply the Government with defective cost or pricing data, you also may be liable under the civil False Claims Act

---

[Section 9:20]

[1]*See, e.g., U.S. ex rel. Thistlethwaite v. Dowty Woodville Polymer, Ltd.*, 110 F.3d 861 (2d Cir. 1997), on remand to, 976 F. Supp. 207 (S.D. N.Y. 1997), related reference, 6 F. Supp. 2d 263 (S.D. N.Y. 1998); *U.S. v. Broderson*, 67 F.3d 452 (2d Cir. 1995) abrogation recognized by, *U.S. v. Bracciale*, 374 F.3d 998 (11th Cir. 2004)); Communications Equipment and Contracting Co., Inc. v. U.S., 37 Cont. Cas.Fed. (CCH) P 76,195 (1991).

§ 9:21   GOVERNMENT CONTRACT COMPLIANCE HANDBOOK

(FCA)[1] (see §§ 1:1 et seq.). The civil FCA makes clear that *no proof of fraudulent intent* is required for civil liability to attach to the submission of a false claim. The only requirement for a finding of liability under the civil FCA is proof that the contractor presented the cost or pricing data *knowing* it was false or with *reckless disregard* for or in deliberate ignorance of its truth or falsity.

The line between an honest mistake and a dishonest claim is rather narrow—at least as to the matters that the Government must prove to establish a civil false claim offense. The ramifications for you and your company are significant, however. The remedies for violation of the civil FCA include treble damages and penalties for each false claim. Because a "claim" has in effect been defined as any request for payment submitted to the Government, the possibilities exist for liability in huge amounts.[2]

Falsely claiming an exemption to TINA can potentially lead to liability under the False Claims Act. In *U.S. ex rel. Ubl v. IIF Data Solutions*, 2007 WL 2220586 (E.D. Va. 2007) a whistleblower alleged that his employer had falsely claimed that it qualified for the commercial item exemption in FAR 15.403-1(b)(3) and that the prices paid by the Government were substantially higher than they would have been had the contractor submitted cost and pricing data as required by TINA. The court found that these allegations, if true, would support liability under the False Claims Act.

§ 9:22   Other penalties—Criminal fraud

If you knowingly submit defective data to the Government, you may be liable under the criminal False Claims Act.[1] The criminal FCA provides for substantial fines and imprisonment up to five years (see §§ 1:1 et seq.). As with the civil FCA, a specific intent to defraud the United States is not a necessary element to establish a violation of the criminal FCA. Neither must the Government sustain monetary damages as a result of the false claim for criminal liability to attach.

A contractor who knowingly submits a false "Certificate of Current Cost or Pricing Data" with the intent to deceive the Government may also be criminally liable under the False Statements

---

[Section 9:21]
    [1]*See* 31 U.S.C.A. §§ 3729 to 3733.
    [2]*See,* 31 U.S.C.A. § 3729(a).

[Section 9:22]
    [1]*See,* 18 U.S.C.A. § 287.

DEFECTIVE PRICING § 9:24

statute[2] (see §§ 1:1 et seq.). The statute requires that the false statement be material, but the Government need not prove either that it relied on the false statement or suffered damages as a result of the statement. A violation of the False Statements statute may result in criminal monetary penalties as well as imprisonment.

One case suggests that liability under the False Statements statute for defective pricing may be quite broad. In that case, a contractor failed to submit *all* of its cost or pricing data for a particular project, which led the Government into negotiating the contract at a higher price. Although the cost or pricing data that the contractor did submit were accurate and current, the contractor neglected to supply other cost or pricing data to the Government that would have reduced the contract price. The court found that the omitted relevant cost or pricing data rendered the contractor's "Certificate of Current Cost or Pricing Data" (and the data actually submitted) equivalent to a false statement.[3]

§ 9:23 Other penalties—Suspension & debarment

A risk to your company that is potentially greater than the threat of civil or criminal penalties for submitting defective cost or pricing data to the Government is the possibility of suspension or debarment from Government contracting. Contractors are routinely suspended when merely *indicted* for fraud, even though they may be acquitted at trial or the charges later dropped. Accordingly, it is of paramount importance that you resolve defective pricing disputes as early as possible to avoid the harsh consequences of an indictment.

B. FREQUENTLY ASKED QUESTIONS

§ 9:24 Questions & answers

Question 1: Are exceptions from TINA's requirements granted automatically by the CO or must I specifically request an exception?

Answer 1: For an exception based on adequate price competition, the CO will determine if your proposal is exempt from the requirements to submit cost or pricing data. However, if you are offering a commercial item or a product priced by law or regulation, or if you are seeking a general TINA waiver, you have the obligation to submit a written request to the CO for an exception from the cost or pricing data requirements. In these instances, you should be prepared to supply the CO with information other

---

[2]*See,* 18 U.S.C.A. § 1001.

[3]*U.S. v. Poarch*, 878 F.2d 1355 (11th Cir. 1989).

§ 9:24   GOVERNMENT CONTRACT COMPLIANCE HANDBOOK

than cost or pricing data that can establish the reasonableness of your contract price.[1] You benefit the most from any exception, and it is in your best interest to make sure the CO recognizes and grants any exception to which you believe yourself entitled.

Question 2: If I know that cost or pricing data on my product will be available around the time of the cut-off (handshake) date, is there anything I can do to ensure that the Government will not think that I defrauded it if the data actually became available right after the cut-off date?

Answer 2: Yes. First, you should inform the CO that you expect the data to be available near the cut-off date but that you are not sure of the exact time it will be available. You then should request that the cut-off date be pushed back to accommodate for last-minute price negotiations. You do not want the Government to allege that you violated TINA in that you agreed to a cut-off date knowing that relevant cost or pricing data would be available right after that date.

Question 3: If I find out that my company should have, but failed to supply the Government with certified cost or pricing data, what should I do?

Answer 3: This is often a difficult question. In many cases, for a number of reasons, you should inform the CO of the cost or pricing data omission immediately. First, if you inform the CO of the mistake right away, there is less likelihood that the Government will penalize you for knowingly submitting defective pricing. Second, because interest accrues on any payments that the Government has made to you under an inflated contract price, you want to settle any price adjustments as soon as possible. Third, and perhaps most important, your immediate disclosure should help reduce your liability in case the Government decides to pursue civil or criminal remedies against you for defective pricing.

C. ADDITIONAL DOD REQUIREMENTS: ESTIMATING SYSTEMS

§ 9:25   Generally

In an effort to ensure the reasonableness and accuracy of defense contractor cost and pricing estimates, DOD has promulgated special regulations to govern the large business contractors with which it does business. These DOD regulations apply to defense contracts *only* and require certain defense contractors to establish estimating systems that enable more efficient and

---

[Section 9:24]

[1] *See* FAR 52.215-20.

DEFECTIVE PRICING § 9:27

methodological review of large contractor cost data. These regulations are independent of and *in addition to* TINA's cost or pricing data disclosure requirements for any specific contract action. You do not satisfy the DOD's estimating system requirements by merely supplying the Government with complete "cost or pricing data" on a specific contract.

§ 9:26 Applicability

If your company had at least $50 million worth of negotiated prime and subcontracts in the previous fiscal year requiring the submission of certified cost or pricing data, the DOD estimating system regulations apply to your DOD contracts. The Government may, at its discretion, apply the estimating system regulation to your company if you had at least $10 million in DOD contracts in the previous year for which cost or pricing data were required and the CO determines that it is in the Government's best interest to apply the system to your company.[1]

§ 9:27 Disclosure & government review

The DOD regulations require that contractors establish, maintain, and use an adequate estimating system and disclose the system to the Government in writing. An "estimating system" is simply a contractor's "policies, procedures, and practices for generating estimates of costs and other data included in proposals submitted to customers in the expectation of receiving contract awards."[1] It includes the contractor's organizational structure, established lines of authority and responsibility, internal controls and management reviews, estimating methods and techniques (including accumulation of historical costs), and the analyses used to generate the estimates.[2] An estimating system will be considered adequate if it provides a consistent estimating approach using appropriate source data and sound estimating techniques and adheres to established policies and procedures.[3]

Disclosure of the estimating system to the Government must be sufficiently detailed to permit evaluation, and changes in the

---

[Section 9:26]
   [1]*See* DFARS 215.407-5-70.

[Section 9:27]
   [1]*See* DFARS 252.215-7002, para. (a).
   [2]*See* DFARS 252.215-7002, para. (a).
   [3]*See* DFARS 215.407-5-70(c)(2)(ii).

§ 9:27

system must be disclosed in a "timely" fashion.[4]

If your company is required to disclose its estimating system, the regulations require that the Government conduct a "system review" at least every three years.[5] System reviews may be conducted more or less frequently if the auditor and CO determine that the system subjects the Government either to a high or low risk.[6] DCAA auditors conduct the system reviews and, after holding an exit conference, prepare and provide a report to the contractor.[7]

§ 9:28 Correction of deficiencies

If your company is notified of any "significant estimating deficiencies," you have 45 days to respond or submit a plan of action to correct any identified deficiencies.[1] If you disagree with the report, the Government will evaluate your response to determine whether there are, in fact, deficiencies that need correction, notify you of its intent to disapprove your company's system, and give your company 45 days to submit an acceptable corrective action plan.[2]

If the Government is negotiating a contract with your company during the period between initial notification of "significant deficiencies" and the 45-day correction notice, the Government may do the following:[3]

(a) Allow time for your company to correct the deficiency and submit a corrected proposal.

(b) Consider use of another type of contract—for example, fixed-price or incentive-fixed-price.

(c) Perform an additional cost analysis on your proposal.

(d) Segregate the questionable cost area as a cost-reimbursable line item.

(e) Reduce the negotiation objective for profit or fee.

(f) Include a contract clause that provides for adjustment of the contract amount after award ("reopener" clause).

During the 45-day correction period, the Government may reduce progress payments on your existing contracts and recom-

---

[4]*See* DFARS 215.407-5-70(f).

[5]*See* DCMA Guidance, section (3) (http://guidebook.dcma.mil/47).

[6]DCMA Guidance, section (3) (http://guidebook.dcma.mil/47).

[7]See footnote (5) above.

[Section 9:28]

[1]DFARS 215.407-5-70(f).

[2]*See* DCMA Guidance, section 5.1.2.1 (http://guidebook.dcma.mi./47/).

[3]*See* DFARS 242.7000.

DEFECTIVE PRICING § 9:29

mend against award of future contracts to your company.[4] If your company has not corrected the significant deficiency after the 45-day correction period, the Government may continue reduction of your progress payments and disapprove all or part of your company's estimating system for future contracts, which could lead to a finding that your company is not a responsible contractor.[5]

III. HOW TO RECOGNIZE THE PROBLEM

§ 9:29 Generally

Your company always wants to avoid a defective pricing investigation because allegations of defective pricing could result in substantial criminal and civil penalties. The *appearance* of a defective pricing problem alone can result in a full-scale investigation. Therefore, you need to be able to spot any evidence of defective pricing early and correct it before it comes to the attention of a Government official. The best way to identify a potential problem is to study the "indicators" of fraud on which the Government auditors will focus.

One of the most important areas of inquiry regarding fraud-indeed a key area from the point of view of DOD—is contract pricing. A major section of the DOD Inspector General's biannual reports is devoted to fraud in contract pricing. Moreover, the Inspector General has emphasized that auditors should "think fraud" when conducting postaward reviews and should regard defective pricing, when identified, as an "indicator of fraud."

The DOD Inspector General has issued a number of defective pricing manuals and publications to provide guidance to its auditors on how to detect defective pricing.[1] These manuals provide a number of "scenarios" intended to alert auditors to defective pricing. Although most of the following scenarios do not alone constitute defective pricing, they are considered to be possible "indicators of defective pricing":

(1) Use of a vendor other than the one proposed.
(2) Intentional failure to update cost or pricing data.
(3) Selective disclosure of pricing data such as labor hours or labor rates.

---

[4]DFARS 242.7000.
[5]DFARS 242.7000.

[Section 9:29]

[1]*See, e.g.,* the following DOD Inspector General publications: "Truth in Negotiations Act (TINA) Handbook" (1993), "Handbook on Fraud Indicators for Contract Auditors" (1993), "Criminal Defective Pricing and the Truth in Negotiations Act" (1988), "Handbook on Scenarios of Potential Defective Pricing Fraud" (1986), "Indicators of Fraud in Department of Defense Procurement" (1986).

§ 9:29   GOVERNMENT CONTRACT COMPLIANCE HANDBOOK

(4) Undated negotiations memoranda or dates on quotes changed from before date of price agreement to after date of price agreement.

(5) Lost records, such as labor records or time cards of previous contracts.

(6) Lack of data support for proposal cost items, or data not maintained.

(7) Change in make-versus-buy status of certain contract items.

(8) No production break as represented in proposal, where management is aware of production scheduling.

(9) Failure to disclose material and labor cost savings from combining purchases of material requirements.

The Inspector General also alerts auditors to the following indicators of defective pricing schemes:

(a) Intentionally eliminating support to increase the proposal prices.

(b) Including inflated rates in the proposal such as insurance or workers compensation.

(c) Intentionally duplicating costs by proposing them as both direct and indirect.

(d) Proposing obsolete items that are not needed.

(e) Continually failing to provide requested data.

(f) Not disclosing an excess material inventory that is used in later contracts.

(g) Refusing to provide data that are requested for elements of proposed costs.

(h) Failing to disclose actuals for follow-on contracts.

(i) Knowingly using intercompany divisions to perform part of the contract but proposing purchase, or vice versa.

(j) Ignoring established estimating practices.

(k) Suppressing studies that do not support the proposed costs.

(l) Commingling work orders with other work orders to hide productivity improvements.

You should view the above "indicators" not only as a signal of a potential defective pricing problem but as a tool for evaluating your own pricing procedures. You might consider incorporating these indicators into your own internal review processes to assist in contract pricing and to ensure that there is not even an appearance of fraud.

In addition, the DOD Inspector General has instructed COs, DCAA auditors, and others involved in the procurement process to refer defective pricing cases to the proper *investigative agencies* when the following "indicators of fraud" are found:

(1) Persistent defective pricing.

(2) Repeated defective pricing involving similar patterns or

conditions.

(3) Failure to correct known system deficiencies.

(4) Failure to update cost or pricing data with knowledge that past activity showed that prices have decreased.

(5) Specific contractor knowledge that is not disclosed regarding significant cost issues that will reduce proposal costs.

(6) Denial by responsible contractor employees of the existence of historical records that are subsequently found.

(7) Utilization of unqualified personnel to develop cost or pricing data used in the estimating process.

(8) Indications of falsification or alteration of supporting data.

(9) Distortion of the overhead accounts or base information by the transfer of charges or accounts that have a material impact on Government contracts.

(10) Failure to make complete disclosure of data known to responsible contractor personnel.

(11) Protracted delay in release of data to the Government to preclude possible price reductions.

(12) Employment of people known to have previously perpetrated fraud against the Government.

Your company should ensure that employees involved with estimating and contract pricing are thoroughly familiar with the DOD Inspector General's "indicators" listed above. Your employees should be alerted to the fact that the existence of one or more of the "indicators" in your company, albeit unintentionally, may expose the company to investigation for criminal or civil fraud.

The above list is not meant to be exhaustive. Remember that Congress amends and enacts new laws with regularity, and the Government continuously amends its regulations. In addition, rules can change as courts and boards of contract appeals decide new cases. As with other areas of Government procurement, you need to be alert to any changes in the law of defective pricing. Remember, ignorance of the law is no defense, you will be held accountable regardless of your knowledge.

§ 9:30 Examples

Poor data collection: Your company, a small manufacturer of high-grade plastics for industrial use, recently decided to enter the Government contracts market. Your only experience in Government contracting has been several training seminars attended by personnel from your sales, engineering, and legal departments. Notwithstanding your inexperience with Government contract law, when you learned that the Army was soliciting bids for the production of lightweight, bulletproof field shelters for its infantry, you determined to obtain the award. You

§ 9:30

submitted your proposal and, after a month of negotiations, the Army awarded you the contract for 400 shelters at a total price of $50 million.

Unable to qualify for a TINA exception, you prepared cost or pricing data which you disclosed to the Army at the commencement of negotiations, and which you later certified as accurate, current, and complete as of the date of agreement on price. During negotiations, and unbeknownst to your negotiating team or the Army, however, your procuring agents had begun to acquire a new type of resin used in the manufacturing of plastic at prices considerably lower than those reflected in your cost or pricing data. You subsequently use the new resin during performance of the contract, significantly decreasing your costs and increasing your profits. Could you be liable under TINA even though your negotiating team did not know of the new resin?

Yes. The nondisclosure of the lower price for resin was improper under TINA, which requires that prices be current at the time of the "handshake date." You are not excused from liability just because your negotiating team was unaware of your company's recent shift to a new, less expensive resin. If your company had a systematic compliance program in place that required regular monitoring of cost information by your negotiating team, you could have avoided this misfortune. If the DCAA discovers this price differential in a post-award audit, you not only will be liable under TINA, you could be subject to a civil and criminal investigation.

Spare parts: Assume your company has been asked to rebuild an entire fleet of military tanks that after years of use needs extensive maintenance. You submit a proposal to the Government and win the award, partly because of your well-received performance under a separate contract that required you to build an entirely new set of tanks from scratch. During negotiations, you submit cost or pricing data for the tank repairs and replacements that essentially mimic the cost or pricing data from the other tank contract. The Government accepts your data without comment. However, you decide to use some leftover parts from your previous tank project that were in your inventory. You never told the Government about the spare parts. Do you face any potential liability under TINA?

Yes. A failure to disclose inventory data that could have led the Government to negotiate a lower contract price can constitute defective pricing. In this case, the spare parts left over from the other contract were presumably already paid for by the Government, and the nondisclosure of the inventory information conceivably led to a final negotiated contract price that was overstated.

§ 9:30

Volume discounts: Assume that the United States recently decided to sell new computer-assisted radar systems to several of its Mideast allies in accordance with the United States' policy to deter military aggression in that region. These improvements require the procurement of new computer hardware and software. The United States entered into a sole-source contract with you for production of the hardware and software packages.

Your proposal stated that each system required one X-type memory unit, one Y-type memory unit, or one Y-type expansion kit. X-type units have two times the capacity of Y-type units. Although the computer system requires the memory capacity of an X-type unit, it can function on either one X-unit or two Y-units. By using a Y-type memory configuration, however, you could purchase more Y-type units from your vendor and receive a discount for the increased quantity and thereby reduce your overall production costs.

You disclosed and certified your cost or pricing data but did not specifically inform the Government that by reconfiguring X-type memory with two units of Y-type memory, and by combining quantities of units to be furnished under this contract with quantities to be furnished under an imminent contract from the same agency, you would be able to obtain the components at a discount. Have you done anything wrong?

You are potentially liable for defective pricing in connection with the memory unit data. Your failure to present the data in a manner that would indicate your intention to reconfigure the X-type memories and avail yourself of a lower cost through acquisition of more Y-type units rendered your cost or pricing data defective. The Government most likely would testify that if it had known of the subcontract discount rate, the Government would have obtained a lower contract price. Remember that when a contractor furnishes cost or pricing data to the Government, it must present the data in such a manner that Government personnel may grasp the significance of the data. In this case, your data were defective because they included only the undiscounted costs of component parts.

Settlement offer: The United States entered into a contract with your company on June 1 for the production of several dozen boilers. During the course of your negotiations with the Government, you encountered a dispute with Atlas Steel Corporation, your chief supplier of steel for the boiler production operation. The dispute related to Atlas' revocation of a discount price for special steel that you had used to produce boilers under a prior contract with the United States.

Before completion of price negotiations on the June 1 contract, Atlas made an offer to settle the dispute by offering a reduced

§ 9:30   GOVERNMENT CONTRACT COMPLIANCE HANDBOOK

quantity of the discounted steel. Although the Government was aware of the dispute, you never disclosed Atlas' settlement offer during negotiations even though some of the steel subject to this dispute potentially could have been used in performance of the June 1 contract. Negotiations were concluded, the contract was awarded on June 1, and you settled your dispute shortly thereafter based on Atlas' original offer. You then used some of the discounted steel on the prior contract and canceled the remainder. None of the discounted steel was used in performance of the June 1 contract. Have you done anything wrong?

Possibly, yes. Although you have not yet accepted the settlement offer, the mere existence of a pending settlement might be considered to be cost or pricing data that should be disclosed to the Government. In that case, if the Government had known of the pending settlement, it might have postponed reaching final agreement on price until this issue was resolved.

Subcontractor data: Your company has been negotiating for a contract to supply the Navy with specialized night vision binoculars. Your company produces the binoculars' titanium casing and specially compressed silicon lenses. You subcontract with a company named NiteWar for the night vision, infra-red technology to be used in the binocular lenses. Although your contract with the Government exceeds the dollar threshold for submission of cost or pricing data, the CO granted your request for an "exceptional case" cost or pricing data waiver because you submitted enough other information to the CO for a price reasonableness determination. Your subcontract with NiteWar also exceeds the cost or pricing data threshold, and NiteWar has informed you that it will be switching to new, cheaper night vision technology. Because a TINA waiver has been granted, do you have to disclose NiteWar's change to new technology to the CO?

Yes. Despite the "exceptional case" waiver for the prime contract, the regulations are clear that a subcontractor must nevertheless submit cost or pricing data if the subcontract is over the cost or pricing data dollar threshold. In this situation, NiteWar's decision to use new night vision technology is cost or pricing data that must be disclosed.

Undisclosed purchase orders: Your company manufactures machine guns that are purchased by several foreign countries. Recently, the U.S. Army decided to equip several thousand of its troops with machine guns like those you manufacture, and you respond to the Government's solicitation for machine gun proposals. You obtain price quotations from your vendors and provide the Government with a proposal for its DCAA prenegotiation audit. DCAA accepts all of your proposed costs.

Negotiations begin a month later and last for three weeks.

When you and the Army reach agreement, you present your "Certificate of Current Cost or Pricing Data." After the contract is completed, the Government conducts an audit during which the auditors note that you disclosed vendor price quotations as your pricing data in connection with your special machine tool cost elements. The auditors then discover that you had actually purchased these machine tools *before* final agreement on price but had not disclosed the attendant purchase orders—which were lower than the vendor price quotations—as part of your cost or pricing data. Is the Government entitled to a price reduction?

Yes. Your failure to disclose the purchase orders is a violation of TINA. Purchase orders are facts that provide a more certain basis than vendor quotes for estimating costs and are therefore facts that prudent buyers and sellers would expect to have a significant effect on price negotiations. The special machine tool data were not complete, accurate, and current as of the certification date because the purchase orders had not been disclosed. The Government would be entitled to a price reduction equal to the amount of the difference between the proposed costs for the contract items and the costs reflected in the undisclosed purchase orders.

IV. COMPLIANCE INITIATIVES

§ 9:31 Generally

The requirement for submission of certified cost or pricing data can set up a dangerous trap for the honest but unwary contractor. To obtain a price reduction, the Government need prove only that your defective data caused an increase in the contract price, not that your company was out to deceive the Government. Contractor honesty and integrity are not defenses to a defective pricing claim. The regulations favor the Government with regard to defective pricing. Moreover, as discussed above, if there is any question that your nondisclosure was knowing or intentional, the consequences may be far worse than liability for a price adjustment.

Although all your employees should be aware of the liabilities that may arise from defective pricing, there are certain target groups within your company that are more directly involved with contract pricing and, thus, with cost or pricing data. These groups include upper management, financial managers, contract managers, negotiators and salesmen, and the law department.

Personnel in these groups are all susceptible to creating a defective pricing and fraud situation by their actions or inactions. For example, *upper management's* failure to educate employees regarding the requirements for submitting cost or pricing data, or failure to implement control mechanisms and policies that ensure compliance with data submission requirements, could result in defective pricing charges and a fraud investigation by the Government with potentially catastrophic effects for your company.

Your *financial managers* and accountants must be made aware of the need for accumulating accurate and current pricing data that are timely disclosed to your negotiators for submission to the Government. Otherwise, your company faces the possibility of charges of false claims and false statements, and suspension or debarment from Government contracting.

Your *contract managers*, *negotiators*, and *salesmen* are the contact points between your company and the Government customer. Failure of this group to realize the seriousness and complexities of the cost or pricing data requirements, to submit the proper data in a timely fashion to the proper Government authority, or to obtain a firm data submission cut-off date could result in liability for defective pricing. Similarly, if your contract negotiator seeks the advice of your *law department* regarding the need to disclose certain information, and the law department is unaware of the legal requirements for data submission, incorrect advice given the negotiator could result in defective pricing and a potentially damaging fraud investigation.

All employees in these target groups must be familiar with the legal and practical requirements for submission of cost or pricing data to the Government customer. Set forth below are some practical recommendations to ensure that your company avoids liability for defective pricing.

§ 9:32 Recommendations

(a) Upper management should create and enforce a *written company policy* making compliance with cost or pricing data submission requirements a top priority for all employees involved in the submission process. This corporate policy should include written requirements that middle management and contract negotiating teams follow company guidelines on submission of data.

(b) One person on the negotiation team should be specifically charged with *central responsibility and authority* with respect to cost or pricing data. It should be his or her job to canvass all of the other members and all parts of the organization to see to it that the latest cost or pricing data are provided to the Government.

(c) Make sure to obtain an *agreement on data reporting cut-off dates*. At the time you submit your proposal to the Government, you should already have listed all of the periodic reports that are relevant to the proposal and their issuance or cut-off dates. A

Defective Pricing § 9:32

listing of these should be provided to the Government negotiators with a request *in writing* for agreement on the cut-off dates to be used.

(d) Make sure you submit all cost or pricing data to the *Government official with the proper authority*. It is often preferable to submit all data to *one* Government official to avoid miscommunications or misunderstandings.

(e) Just before or at the *time of agreement on price*, you should once more *check all departments within your organization* for any new cost or pricing data. For example, your production engineering department may be on the verge of providing the production department with a new technique that will save labor hours. If your production engineering department knows about the technique and it is significant, it may constitute cost or pricing data whether or not the production or estimating departments even know it exists.

(f) After an agreement is reached on price but *before* signing the "Certificate of Cost or Pricing Data," make a *final check* of all departments within your organization once again looking for any possible changes in your cost or pricing data or new developments.

(g) Make sure to *document your efforts*. Each time you ask your organization for new cost or pricing data, you should make a written record of all data submitted and the corresponding dates of submittal for inclusion in the negotiation file. This may be extremely important later in distinguishing an "innocent mistake" from something worse. Consider using "internal certifications" to be executed by all departments or cost centers furnishing original or updated cost data.

(h) Your documentation should include a *record of negotiations*. You should very carefully document all the events and conversations that take place during negotiations. The Government makes a meticulous record of negotiations and may attempt to use it against you later. The only sure defense is to keep your own record of what happened and make sure the record is accurate. You may even consider taping negotiations and meetings subject to the Government's approval.

(i) Always *err on the side of disclosure*. When there is any doubt as to whether data must be disclosed, you should err on the side of disclosure. At the negotiation stage, disclosure can do you no real harm, although it may place an additional burden on you with regard to conduct of the negotiation. You can adhere to your pricing position regardless of what the data shows, and you can explain the data to real trouble later on. The potentially harsh fines and punishments that accompany violations of TINA and other federal statutes could be devastating to your business. Therefore, remember: *When in doubt, disclose your data.*

(j) *Disclose your mistakes.* If, after contract award, data turns up that were reasonably available prior to the cut-off date and were not disclosed, consider bringing such data to the attention of the Government as soon as possible. Similarly, if, subsequent to award, you realize you made a material mistake in your data submittal, consider bringing it to the attention of the Government as soon as possible.

Chapter 10

Selling Commercial Items

I. OVERVIEW

§ 10:1 Scope note

II. COMMERCIAL ITEM ACQUISITIONS

§ 10:2 Generally
§ 10:3 Defining commercial items
§ 10:4 Defining commercial services

A. EXEMPTION FROM STATUTORY COMPLIANCE

§ 10:5 Generally
§ 10:6 Exemptions for prime contracts
§ 10:7 Exemption for subcontracts
§ 10:8 Other exemptions
§ 10:9 Application of the Truth in Negotiations Act

B. COMMERCIAL ITEM CONTRACT CLAUSES AND DATA RIGHTS

§ 10:10 Contract terms and conditions
§ 10:11 Implementation of statutes and executive orders
§ 10:12 Representations and certifications
§ 10:13 Subcontract clauses
§ 10:14 Rights in technical data & computer software

C. FREQUENTLY ASKED QUESTIONS

§ 10:15 Questions & answers

III. SPECIAL CONTRACTING METHODS

A. GSA'S MAS PROGRAM

§ 10:16 Generally
§ 10:17 MAS pricing
§ 10:18 Contract price reductions
§ 10:19 Industrial funding fee
§ 10:20 Competition requirements

B. SMALL PURCHASES

§ 10:21   Generally
§ 10:22   Laws inapplicable to simplified acquisitions

IV. HOW TO RECOGNIZE THE PROBLEM

§ 10:23   Generally
§ 10:24   Examples

V. COMPLIANCE INITIATIVES

§ 10:25   Generally
§ 10:26   Gratuities
§ 10:27   Access to information
§ 10:28   Recommendations

KeyCite®: Cases and other legal materials listed in KeyCite Scope can be researched through the KeyCite service on Westlaw®. Use KeyCite to check citations for form, parallel references, prior and later history, and comprehensive citator information, including citations to other decisions and secondary materials.

I. OVERVIEW

§ 10:1 Scope note

For more than two decades, the Federal Government has sought to simplify the acquisition process by purchasing supplies and services that have been accepted in the commercial marketplace.[1] In the Federal Acquisition Streamlining Act of 1994 (FASA),[2] Congress recognized several advantages in purchasing commercial items: elimination of the need for research and development, reduction of acquisition lead time, and reduction of the need for detailed design specifications and expensive testing. Thus, under FASA, Congress directed agencies to acquire commercial items where suitable or nondevelopmental items

---

[Section 10:1]

[1] *See,* Pub. L. No. 98-369, div. B, title VII, Sec. 2721, 98 Stat. 1185 (providing that federal agencies "promote the use of commercial products whenever practicable"), Competition in Contracting Act of 1984, 41 U.S.C.A. §§ 3301 et seq. and 10 U.S.C.A. §§ 2304 et seq. *See also,* Defense Procurement Reform Act of 1984, Pub. L. No. 98-525, § 1202, 98 Stat. 2588, 2589 (requiring Secretary of Defense to direct that standard or commercial parts be used "whenever such use is technically acceptable or cost effective").

[2] Pub. L. No. 103-355, 108 Stat. 3243.

(NDIs) when commercial items would not meet an agency's needs.[3] FASA also encouraged agencies to purchase commercially available off-the-shelf (COTS) items.

The Clinger-Cohen Act of 1996 provided an additional statutory basis for facilitating the Government's purchase of commercial items.[4] Together, these statutes and the Federal Acquisition Regulation (FAR) provisions implementing them have eliminated many of the Government-unique rules and policies that apply to purchasing commercial items, completely reforming federal agency commercial item procurements.

Since these legislative and regulatory reforms, contractors' sales of commercial items to the Government more closely resemble sales to commercial customers, but distinctions remain.[5] Commercial vendors selling to the Federal Government must still use caution to comply with the remaining *special requirements* Government contracts impose. In addition, selling to the Federal Government presents significant risks for companies that have previously sold only in the commercial marketplace and to companies that sell to both Federal Government and commercial customers.

Despite the newer, relaxed procedures for the purchase of commercial items, contractor conduct generally tolerated in commercial sales can sometimes appear fraudulent or criminal in sales of these same items to the Government. Therefore, you must ensure that your contract administration, financial, and sales personnel understand the significant differences between selling commercial products in the general marketplace and selling the same products to the Federal Government.

II. COMMERCIAL ITEM ACQUISITIONS

§ 10:2 Generally

Contractors competing for commercial item contracts must offer products or services that not only meet the technical requirements of the solicitation but also meet the regulatory definition of a commercial item. This imposes additional obligations on contractors whose focus has been limited to either the commercial or the government contract arena because they now must meet requirements that apply to both.

---

[3]10 U.S.C.A. § 2377; 41 U.S.C.A. § 3307.

[4]Pub. L. No. 104-106, § 4201, 110 Stat. 186.

[5]FAR 12.000 ("This part . . . implements the Federal Government's preference for the acquisition of commercial items . . . by establishing acquisition policies more closely resembling those of the commercial marketplace and encouraging the acquisition of commercial items and components.").

§ 10:3 Defining commercial items

(1) *Commercial item*: The definition of a commercial item in FASA, as implemented by the FAR, is as follows:[1]

"Commercial item" means—

(1) Any item, other than real property, that is of a type customarily used by the general public or by non-governmental entities for purposes other than governmental purposes, and—

   (i) Has been sold, leased, or licensed to the general public; or

   (ii) Has been offered for sale, lease, or license to the general public;

(2) Any item that evolved from an item described in paragraph (1) of this definition through advances in technology or performance and that is not yet available in the commercial marketplace, but will be available in the commercial marketplace in time to satisfy the delivery requirements under a Government solicitation;

(3) Any item that would satisfy a criterion expressed in paragraphs (1) or (2) of this definition, but for—

   (i) Modifications of a type customarily available in the commercial marketplace; or

   (ii) Minor modifications of a type not customarily available in the commercial marketplace made to meet Federal Government requirements. Minor modifications mean modifications that do not significantly alter the nongovernmental function or essential physical characteristics of an item or component, or change the purpose of a process. Factors to be considered in determining whether a modification is minor include the value and size of the modification and the comparative value and size of the final product. Dollar values and percentages may be used as guideposts, but are not conclusive evidence that a modification is minor;

(4) Any combination of items meeting the requirements of paragraphs (1), (2), (3), or (5) of this definition that are of a type customarily combined and sold in combination to the general public;

(5) Installation services, maintenance services, repair services, training services, and other services if—

   (i) Such services are procured for support of an item referred to in paragraph (1), (2), (3), or (4) of this definition, regardless of whether such services are provided by the same source or at the same time as the item; and

   (ii) The source of such services provides similar services

---

[Section 10:3]

[1] FAR 2.101.

contemporaneously to the general public under terms and conditions similar to those offered to the Federal Government;

(6) Services of a type offered and sold competitively in substantial quantities in the commercial marketplace based on established catalog or market prices for specific tasks performed or specific outcomes to be achieved and under standard commercial terms and conditions. This does not include services that are sold based on hourly rates without an established catalog or market price for a specific service performed or a specific outcome to be achieved. For purposes of these services—

(i) "Catalog price" means a price included in a catalog, price list, schedule, or other form that is regularly maintained by the manufacturer or vendor, is either published or otherwise available for inspection by customers, and states prices at which sales are currently, or were last, made to a significant number of buyers constituting the general public; and

(ii) "Market prices" means current prices that are established in the course of ordinary trade between buyers and sellers free to bargain and that can be substantiated through competition or from sources independent of the offerors.

(7) Any item, combination of items, or service referred to in paragraphs (1) through (6) of this definition, notwithstanding the fact that the item, combination of items, or service is transferred between or among separate divisions, subsidiaries, or affiliates of a contractor; or

(8) A nondevelopmental item, if the procuring agency determines the item was developed exclusively at private expense and sold in substantial quantities, on a competitive basis, to multiple State and local governments.

"Nondevelopmental item" means—

(1) Any previously developed item of supply used exclusively for governmental purposes by a Federal agency, a State or local government, or a foreign government with which the United States has a mutual defense cooperation agreement;

(2) Any item described in paragraph (1) of this definition that requires only minor modification or modifications of a type customarily available in the commercial marketplace in order to meet the requirements of the procuring department or agency; or

(3) Any item of supply being produced that does not meet the requirements of paragraphs (1) or (2) solely because the item is not yet in use.

Commercially available off-the-shelf items (COTS): —

(1) Means any item or supply (including construction material) that is –

(i) A commercial item (as defined in paragraph (1) of the definition in this section);

(ii) Sold in substantial quantities in the commercial marketplace; and

(iii) Offered to the Government, under a contract or subcontract at any tier, without modification, in the same form in which it is sold in the commercial marketplace; and

(2) Does not include bulk cargo, as defined in 46 U.S.C. 40102(4), such as agricultural products and petroleum products. Solicitations frequently call for "commercially available off-the-shelf" items. COTS items are commercial products or services sold in substantial quantities in the commercial marketplace that are offered to the Government in the same form in which they are sold in the commercial marketplace.[2] COTS items are, thus, a subset of "commercial items" described above.[3]

§ 10:4 Defining commercial services

As noted above, commercial items include both products and services. Initially, the Government used commercial item acquisitions as vehicles for purchasing off-the-shelf products, such as computers and office furnishings. Increasingly, however, the Government also has been using commercial item acquisitions to obtain services. For example, the Department of Defense established a pilot program for acquiring utilities and housekeeping services, education and training services, and medical services through commercial item acquisitions.[1] Commercial services are defined as follows:[2]

(6) Services of a type offered and sold competitively in substantial

---

[2]Pub. L. No. 104-106, § 4203, 110 Stat. 186.

[3]*See,* Allen and Yukins, Feature Comment: An Analysis of FY 1996 Defense Authorization Act Procurement Reform Measures, 38 Govt. Contractor 69 (Feb. 14, 1996).

[Section 10:4]

[1]Section 814 of the National Defense Authorization Act for Fiscal Year 2000, PL 106-65, 113 Stat 512.

[2]A final rule implementing provisions of the National Defense Authorization Act for FY 1999, P. L. No. 105-261,112 Stat 1920 and the National Defense Authorization Act for FY 2000, P. L. No. 106-65, 113 Stat 512 amended the definition of "commercial item" in FAR 2.101 and the clause at FAR 52.202-1 to clarify that a commercial item must be of a type used by the general public or by nongovernmental entities for purposes other than governmental purposes. FAR 12.102 was revised to explain that the phrase "purposes other than governmental purposes" means "purposes that are not unique to the government." The provision regarding services ancillary to a commercial item were amended to clarify that the services need not be provided by the same vendor or at the same time as the item.

FAC 2001-01, 66 Fed. Reg. 53,478, 53,483.

SELLING COMMERCIAL ITEMS § 10:5

quantities in the commercial marketplace based on established catalog or market prices for specific tasks performed or specific outcomes to be achieved and under standard commercial terms and conditions. This does not include services that are sold based on hourly rates without an established catalog or market price for a specific service performed or a specific outcome to be achieved.

The Government's interest in using commercial item acquisitions to obtain services has resulted in disputes regarding what constitutes a commercial service. For example, GAO has held that international moving services meet the FAR definition of a commercial service.[3] However, in another case, GAO held that helicopter maintenance services were not commercial services because the Government required custom-tailored services that would not normally be provided to commercial customers.[4]

In addition, the FAR Council issued an interim rule which allows services which are "of a type offered and sold competitively in substantial quantities in the commercial marketplace" to be considered "commercial services" for purposes of the commercial services exemption to TINA even though they have not been offered and sold competitively in substantial quantities "if the contracting officer determines in writing that the offeror has submitted sufficient information to evaluate, through price analysis, the reasonableness of the price of such services."[5] The interim rule has been implemented in the FAR.[6][7]

A. EXEMPTION FROM STATUTORY COMPLIANCE

§ 10:5 Generally

Federal contracts generally impose socioeconomic requirements on contractors that do not exist in the commercial marketplace. These include meeting small business and small disadvantaged business subcontracting goals,[1] complying with laws and regulations that govern wages and benefits paid to employees,[2] and

---

[3]*Aalco Forwarding, Inc.*, Comp Gen. Dec. B-277241.8, 97-2 CPD 110 (October 21, 1997).

[4]*Crescent Helicopters*, Comp. Gen. Dec. B-284706, 2000 CPD 90 (May 30, 2000).

[5]74 Fed. Reg. 52853.

[6]FAR 15.403-1(c)(3)(ii)(A).

[7]In February 2012, the Far Councils issued a final rule amending the FAR to ensure that time and material and labor hour contracts are used to acquire commercial services only if no other suitable contract type is appropriate. See, 77 Fed. Reg. 194.

[Section 10:5]

[1]1 See, FAR Part 19, "Small Business Programs."

[2]Contract Work Hours and Safety Standards Act, 40 U.S.C.A. §§ 3701 to

§ 10:5   GOVERNMENT CONTRACT COMPLIANCE HANDBOOK

meeting certain workforce hiring criteria.[3]

FASA and the Clinger-Cohen Act exempted commercial item procurements from many Government procurement laws, rules, certifications, and contract clauses that would otherwise apply to Government procurements. These changes have reduced the administrative burden and costs imposed on companies that sell commercial products to the Government, and have made it easier for the Government to buy commercial items.[4]

Accordingly, the FAR directs that contracts for the acquisition of commercial items "shall, to the maximum extent practicable," include only those clauses (1) required to implement laws or Executive Orders applicable to the acquisition, or (2) determined to be consistent with customary commercial practice."[5]

§ 10:6   Exemptions for prime contracts

Contractors who supply commercial items to the Government are exempt from complying with many of the Government-unique socioeconomic statutes and regulations.[1] The FAR provides that the following eight laws (and their implementing contract clauses) do not apply to *prime contracts* for the acquisition of commercial items:[2]

    (1) Contingent fees restrictions [41 U.S.C.A. § 3901(b)(1); 10 U.S.C.A. § 2306(b)]

    (2) Minimum Response Time for Offers (41 U.S.C.A. § 1708)

    (3) Drug-Free Workplace Act (41 U.S.C.A. §§ 8102 to 8106)

    (4) Veterans Employment Reporting Requirements, 31

3708, and implementing regulations; FAR Part 22.3; Service Contract Act of 1965, 41 U.S.C.A. §§ 6701 to 6707, and implementing regulations; FAR Part 22.10.

    [3]Executive Order 11246 (Sept. 24, 1965) (requires all Government contracting agencies to ensure compliance by contractors with prescribed Department of Labor regulations mandating equal employment opportunity for all persons regardless of race, color, religion, sex, or national origin); FAR Parts 22.8, 22.9, 22.13, and 22.14 (prescribing policies and procedures pertaining to nondiscrimination in employment by Government contractors and subcontractors).

    [4]The Secretary of Defense is authorized to prevent serious impairment to DOD's mission under FASA § 833 to (c) deem any item or service to be a commercial item for purposes of federal procurement laws, and (d) make purchases of property or services not exceeding $7.5 million if the contracting officer reasonably expects only commercial items will be offered.

    [5]FAR 12.301(a).

[Section 10:6]

    [1]Federal Acquisition Streamlining Act) (FASA), Pub. L. No. 103-355, §§ 8105, 8301, 108 Stat. 3243; Clinger-Cohen Act of 1996, Pub. L. No. 104-106, § 4204, 110 Stat. 186.

    [2]FAR 12.503(a).

SELLING COMMERCIAL ITEMS   § 10:7

U.S.C.A. 1354(a)

(5) Contracts for Materials, Supplies, Articles, and Equipment Exceeding $10,000 (41 U.S.C.A., Chapter 65)

(6) Payment Protections for Subcontractors and Suppliers, Section 806(a)(3) of P.L. 102-190, 105 Stat 1290, as amended by sections 2091 and 8105 of P.L. 103-355, 108 Stat 3243 (10 U.S.C.A. § 2302 note)

(7) GAO Access to Contractor Employees, 41 U.S.C.A. § 4706(d)(1); 10 U.S.C.A. § 2313(c)(1)

(8) Policy on Personal Conflicts of Interest by Contractor Employees, 41 U.S.C.A. § 2303(b)

"Certain requirements of the following laws are not applicable to executive agency contracts for the acquisition of commercial items":[3]

(1) 40 U.S.C.A. chapter 31, Requirement for a certificate and clause under the Contract Work Hours and Safety Standards statute.[4]

(2) 41 U.S.C.A §§ 8703 and 8704, Requirement for a clause and certain other requirements related to kickbacks.[5]

(3) 49 U.S.C.A. 40118, Requirement for a clause under the Fly American provisions (see 47.405).[6]

The applicability of the following laws have been modified in regards to Executive agency contracts for the acquisition of commercial items:[7]

(1) 41 U.S.C.A. § 4704 and 10 U.S.C. § 2402, Prohibition on Limiting Subcontractor Direct Sales to the United States

(2) 41 U.S.C.A. chapter 35, Truthful Cost or Pricing Data, and 10 U.S.C. § 2306a, Truth in Negotiations[8]

(3) 41 U.S.C. chapter 15, Cost Accounting Standards (48 CFR chapter 99)[9]

§ 10:7 Exemption for subcontracts

The FAR also lists 12 laws that do not apply to *subcontracts* for the acquisition of commercial items:[1]

(1) Transportation of Supplies by Sea [except for the types of

---

[3]FAR 12.503(b).
[4]FAR 22.305.
[5]FAR 3.502.
[6]FAR 4.705.
[7]FAR 12.503(c).
[8]FAR 15.403.
[9]FAR 12.214.

[Section 10:7]
[1]FAR 12.504(a).

§ 10:7   Government Contract Compliance Handbook

subcontracts listed at 47.504(d)], 10 U.S.C.A. § 2631

(2) Requirements relative to labor surplus areas under the Small Business Act (see Subpart 19.2); 15 U.S.C.A. § 644(d)

(3) Contracts for Materials, Supplies, Articles and Equipment Exceeding $10,000, 41 U.S.C. § 6505[2]

(4) Validation of Proprietary Data Restrictions, 41 U.S.C.A. § 4703[3]

(5) Contingent Fees, 41 U.S.C.A. § 3901(b) and 10 U.S.C.A. § 2306(b)[4]

(6) Examination of Records of Contractor, when a subcontractor is not required to provide cost or pricing data, 41 U.S.C. § 4706 and 10 U.S.C.A. § 2313(c)[5]

(7) Minimum Response Time for Offers under Office of Federal Procurement Policy Act, 41 U.S.C.A. § 1708 (see Subpart 5.2)

(8) Rights in Technical Data, 41 U.S.C.A. § 2302[6]

(9) Drug-Free Workplace Act of 1988, 41 U.S.C.A. §§ 8102 et seq.[7]

(10) Transportation in American Vessels of Government Personnel and Certain Cargo, 46 U.S.C.A. §§ 55301 et seq., [except for the types of subcontracts listed at 47.504(d)][8]

(11) Fly American provisions, 49 U.S.C.A. § 40118[9]

(12) Minimum Response Time for Offers, 41 U.S.C.A. § 1708(e)(3)[10]

(13) Payment Protections for Subcontractors and Suppliers, Section 806(a)(3) of Pub. L. 102-190, 105 Stat 1290, as amended by Sections 2091 and 8105 of Pub. L. 103-355, 108 Stat 3243 (10 U.S.C.A. § 2302 note)[11]

§ 10:8   Other exemptions

The Department of Defense FAR Supplement (DFARS) also lists additional laws that, in whole or in part, do not apply to

---

[2]FAR subpart 22.6.
[3]FAR subpart 27.4.
[4]FAR subpart 3.4.
[5]FAR 15.209.
[6]FAR subpart 27.4.
[7]FAR Subpart 23.5.
[8]FAR subpart 47.5.
[9]FAR subpart 47.4.
[10]FAR subpart 5.2.
[11]FAR 28.106-6.

SELLING COMMERCIAL ITEMS § 10:8

defense prime contracts and subcontracts for commercial items.¹
   (1) Prohibition on Contingent Fees, 10 U.S.C.A. § 2306(b)
   (2) Allowable Costs Under Defense Contracts, 10 U.S.C.A. § 2324
   (3) Requirement to Identify Suppliers, 10 U.S.C.A. § 2384(b)
   (4) Reports by Employees or Former Employees of Defense Contractors, 10 U.S.C.A § 2397(a)(1)
   (5) Limits on Employment for Former DoD Officials, 10 U.S.C. 2397b(f)
   (6) Defense Contractor Requirements Concerning Former DoD Officials, 10 U.S.C.A § 2397c
   (7) Prohibition on Persons Convicted of Defense Related Felonies, 10 U.S.C. 2408(a)
   (8) Contractor Inventory Accounting System Standards, 10 U.S.C.A. § 2410b, (see DFARS 252.242-7004)
   (9) Reporting Requirement Regarding Dealings with Terrorist Countries, (Section 843(a), P.L. 103-160, 107 Stat 1720)
   (10) Domestic Content Restrictions in the National Defense Appropriations Acts for Fiscal Years 1996 and Subsequent Years, unless the restriction specifically applies to commercial items. For the restriction that specifically applies to commercial ball or roller bearings as end items, see DFARS 225.7009-3 (section 8065 of Pub. L. 107-117, 115 Stat 2230)
   (11) Section 8116 of the Defense Appropriations Act for Fiscal Year 2010 (Pub. L. 111-118, 123 Stat 3409) and similar sections in subsequent DoD appropriations acts

The following statutes and clauses are not applicable to "subcontracts at any tier for the acquisition of commercial items or commercial components."²
   (1) Prohibition on Contingent Fees, 10 U.S.C.A. § 2306(b)
   (2) Examination of Records of a Contractor, 10 U.S.C.A. § 2313(c)
   (3) Allowable Costs Under Defense Contracts, 10 U.S.C.A. § 2324
   (4) Reporting Requirement Regarding Dealings with Terrorist Countries, 10 U.S.C.A. § 2327,
   (5) Requirement to Identify Suppliers, 10 U.S.C.A. § 2384(b)
   (6) Notification of Substantial Impact on Employment, 10 U.S.C.A. § 2391 note
   (7) Prohibition Against Doing Business with Certain Offerors or Contractors 10 U.S.C.A. § 2393
   (8) Reports by Employees or Former Employees of Defense

[Section 10:8]
   ¹DFARS 212.503(a).
   ²DFARS 212.504(a).

§ 10:8   Government Contract Compliance Handbook

Contractors 10 U.S.C.A. § 2397(a)(1)

(9) Limits on Employment for Former DoD Officials, 10 U.S.C.A. 2397b(f)

(10) 10 U.S.C. 2397c, Defense Contractor Requirements Concerning Former DoD Officials

(10) Prohibition on Persons Convicted of Defense Related Felonies, 10 U.S.C.A. § 2408(a)

(11) Contractor Inventory Accounting System Standards, 10 U.S.C.A. § 2410b

(12) Notification of Proposed Program Termination, 10 U.S.C.A. § 2501 note

(13) Miscellaneous Limitations on the Procurement of Goods Other Than United States Goods, 10 U.S.C.A. § 2534

(14) Transportation of Supplies by Sea (except as provided in the DFARS clause at 252.247-7023, Transportation of Supplies by Sea) 10 U.S.C. § 2631

(15) Domestic Content Restrictions in the National Defense Appropriations Acts for Fiscal Years 1996 and Subsequent Years, unless the restriction specifically applies to commercial items. For the restriction that specifically applies to commercial ball or roller bearings as end items, see DFARS 225.7009-3 (section 8065 of P. L. 107-117, 115 Stat 2230)

(16) Section 8116 of the Defense Appropriations Act for Fiscal Year 2010 (Pub. L. 111-118, 123 Stat 3409) and similar sections in subsequent DoD appropriations acts.

Certain requirements of the following laws have been eliminated for subcontracts at any tier for the acquisition of commercial items or commercial components:

(1) Subcontractor Reports Under Prohibition Against Doing Business with Certain Offerors, 10 U.S.C.A. § 2393(d), (see FAR 52.209-6)

(2) Prohibition on Limiting Subcontractor Direct Sales to the United States, 10 U.S.C.A. § 2402 (see FAR 3.503 and 52.203-6).

Under the Clinger-Cohen Act, "commercially available off-the-shelf items," as defined above in § 10:3, are also exempt from a wide range of federal procurement laws.[3] The Act directs the Office of Federal Procurement Policy to designate laws that will not apply to COTS items procurements.[4] "Section 12.505 lists the laws that are not applicable to COTS items (in addition to 12.503 and 12.504)."[5]

(1) The portion of 41 U.S.C.A. § 8302(a)(1) that reads

---

[3]Pub. L. No. 104-106, § 4203(a), 110 Stat. 186.
[4]79 Fed. Reg. 24192-02.
[5]79 Fed. Reg. 24192-02.

344

"substantially all from articles, materials, or supplies mined, produced, or manufactured in the United States," Buy American—Supplies, component test (see 52.225-1 and 52.225-3)

(2) The portion of 41 U.S.C.A. § 8303(a)(2) that reads "substantially all from articles, materials, or supplies mined, produced, or manufactured in the Unites States," Buy American—Construction Materials, component test (see 52.225-9 and 52.225-11)

(3) Certification and Estimate of Percentage of Recovered Material, 42 U.S.C.A. § 6962(c)(3)(A)[6]

(4) "Clinger-Cohen provides that if a provision of law contains criminal or civil penalties, or if the Administrator for Federal Procurement Policy makes a written determination that it is not in the best interest of the Federal Government to exempt COTS item contracts, the provision of law will apply."[7]

The FAR also provides that *certifications* or *contract clauses* relating to the following laws have been eliminated for both commercial item prime contracts and subcontracts:[8]

(1) Contract Work Hours and Safety Standards Act, 40 U.S.C.A. §§ 3701 to 3708

(2) Anti-Kickback Act 41 U.S.C.A. §§ 8703 et seq. (prime contracts only)

(3) Fly American provisions 49 U.S.C.A. § 40118

Although commercial item contractors and subcontractors are no longer required to execute these certifications, the underlying statutory obligations and requirements still apply.

Finally, the FAR identifies three laws whose coverage has been *modified* with respect to commercial item prime contracts and subcontracts:[9]

(a) Prohibition on Limiting Subcontractor Direct Sales to the United States 41 U.S.C.A. § 4704; 10 U.S.C.A. § 2402

(b) Truth in Negotiations Act 10 U.S.C.A. § 2306a

(c) Cost Accounting Standards, 41 U.S.C.A. § 1502

§ 10:9 Application of the Truth in Negotiations Act

As discussed in §§ 9:1 et seq., the Truth in Negotiations Act (TINA) exempts commercial item contractors from the requirement to provide certified cost or pricing data in certain large negotiated procurements. The Clinger-Cohen Act, as implemented by the FAR, provides that a CO "shall not" require submission of

---

[6]FAR 12.505.
[7]74 Fed. Reg. 14633-01.
[8]FAR 12.503(b), 12.504(b).
[9]FAR 12.503(c), 12.504(c).

cost or pricing data when acquiring commercial items.[1] Thus, as long as the acquisition is for a product or service that meets the FAR definition of "commercial item," the offeror cannot be required to submit cost or pricing data.[2] The exemption extends to any modification of the original contract or subcontract for a commercial item if the modification does not change the nature of the item or service from commercial to noncommercial.[3]

On August 30, 2010, the FAR Council issued a final rule aimed at making clear that even where a procurement is not subject to the Truth In Negotiation Act, the contracting officer may still request ". . . any data, including cost or pricing data and judgmental information" in order to evaluate the reasonableness of the proposed price. This rule will have a significant impact on commercial item acquisitions since commercial contractors have generally been unwilling to provide detailed cost and pricing data which, in a non-commercial procurement, would have to be certified. See 75 Fed. Reg. 53135. For a discussion of this rule, see the commentary at § 9:13, supra.

Although there is an *unqualified* exemption under TINA for contracts and subcontracts "for the acquisition of a commercial item," COs may still request "information other than certified cost or pricing data" from the offeror to "the extent necessary to determine the reasonableness of the price." Such data "shall include, at minimum, appropriate information on the prices at which the same or similar items have previously been sold, adequate for determining the reasonableness of the price."[4] There are limitations on the types of information that the CO may require when buying commercial items, however, as follows:[5]

(1) Requests for sales data relating to commercial items shall be limited to data for the same or similar items during a relevant time period.

(2) The contracting officer shall, to the maximum extent practicable, limit the scope of the request for information relating to commercial items to include only information that is in the form regularly maintained by the offeror as part of its commercial operations.

(3) Information obtained relating to commercial items that is exempt from disclosure under . . . the Freedom of Information Act . . . shall not be disclosed outside the Government.

[Section 10:9]

[1]FAR 15.403-1(b). *See,* Pub. L. No. 104-106, § 4201, 110 Stat. 186.
[2]FAR 15.403-1(c)(3).
[3]FAR 15.403-1(c)(3).
[4]FAR 15.403-3(a).
[5]FAR 15.403-3(c).

SELLING COMMERCIAL ITEMS § 10:11

As when supplying any information or making any representation to the Government, a contractor must be able to show that any supporting information it has provided is accurate and verifiable from its established and regularly-maintained records. A contractor's failure to provide accurate information will subject it, and its responsible individual employees, to sanctions under federal civil and criminal laws.

B. COMMERCIAL ITEM CONTRACT CLAUSES AND DATA RIGHTS

§ 10:10 Contract terms and conditions

The FAR provides a standard clause—"Contract Terms and Conditions-Commercial Items"—for inclusion in Government commercial item prime contracts.[1] This clause sets forth the terms and conditions that apply to commercial item contracts, such as changes, disputes, excusable delay, limitation of liability, and terminations. Contracting Officers may tailor the provisions of this clause to be consistent with customary commercial practices.[2]

The Contract Terms and Conditions clause also requires commercial item contractors to comply with certain statutes:[3]

(a) Limitations on the use of appropriated funds to influence certain federal contracts (31 U.S.C.A. § 1352, the "Byrd Amendment")

(b) "Officials not to benefit" provisions (18 U.S.C.A. § 431)

(c) Contract Work Hours and Safety Standards Act (40 U.S.C.A. §§ 3701 et seq.)

(d) Anti-Kickback Act (41 U.S.C.A. §§ 8703 to 8707)

(e) Whistleblower protections (41 U.S.C.A. § 4712 and 10 U.S.C.A. 2409)

(f) Fly American provisions (49 U.S.C.A. § 40118)

(g) Procurement Integrity (41 U.S.C.A. § 2101 et seq.)

The CO does not have discretion to alter or tailor many of these provisions, but may supplement these mandatory clauses to implement agency statutes that apply to the procurement.[4]

§ 10:11 Implementation of statutes and executive orders

Commercial item contracts also include the clause "Contract Terms and Conditions Required to Implement Statutes or Execu-

---

[Section 10:10]

[1]FAR 52.212-4.
[2]FAR 12.302.
[3]FAR 52.212-4, para. (r).
[4]FAR 12.301(f).

tive Orders-Commercial Items" clause. This clause lists the FAR clauses that are either mandatory in the commercial item contracts or are optional at the discretion of the CO.[1] The three mandatory clauses are "Combating Trafficking in Persons (FAR 52.222-50), "Applicable Law for Breach of Contract Claim" (FAR 52.233-4)[2] and "Protest After Award" (FAR 233-3).[3] The CO has discretion to include any of the 35 optional clauses depending upon whether they apply to the specific procurement.

The Contract Terms and Conditions clause also requires that for negotiated commercial items contracts, the contractor must agree to permit the Government *access* to and the right to *examine* its "directly pertinent" records involving transactions related to this contract for three years after final payment on the contract.[4]

§ 10:12 Representations and certifications

Finally, commercial item prime contractors must complete certain representations and certifications of compliance with socioeconomic requirements that apply to commercial item contracts.[1] These include small business subcontracting, equal employment opportunity, country of origin and other requirements, to the extent these provisions apply to the procurement.[2] The CO is not permitted to tailor these representations and certification clauses.

§ 10:13 Subcontract clauses

Government prime contractors are required to "flow down" the following FAR clauses to subcontractors:

(1) 52.203-13, Contractor Code of Business Ethics and Conduct (APR 2010).[1]

(2) 52.219-8, Utilization of Small Business Concerns (JUL 2013) in all subcontracts that offer further subcontracting opportunities. If the subcontract (except subcontracts to small

---

[Section 10:11]

[1] FAR 52.212-5.
[2] Pub. L. No. 108-77, 108-78 (Oct. 2004).
[3] 31 U.S.C.A. § 3553.
[4] FAR 52.212-5, para. (a).

[Section 10:12]

[1] FAR 52.212-3.
[2] FAR 52.212-3.

[Section 10:13]

[1] Pub. L. No. 110-252, Title VI, Chapter 1 (41 U.S.C.A. § 3509).

business concerns) exceeds $650,000 ($1.5 million for construction of any public facility), the subcontractor must include 52.219-8 in lower tier subcontracts that offer subcontracting opportunities.

(3) 52.222-26, Equal Opportunity (MAR 2007).[2]

(4) 52.222-35, Equal Opportunity for Veterans (SEP 2010).[3]

(5) 52.222-36, Affirmative Action for Workers with Disabilities (October 2010).[4]

(6) 52.222-40, Notification of Employee Rights Under the National Labor Relations Act (DEC 2010).[5] Flow down required in accordance with paragraph (f) of the clause.

(7) 52.222-41, Service Contract Act of 1965, (Nov 2007).[6][7]

(8) 52.222-50, Combating Trafficking in Persons (FEB 2009).[8]

(9) 52.222-51, Exemption from Application of the Service Contract Act to Contracts for Maintenance, Calibration, or Repair of Certain Equipment—Requirements (NOV 2007).[9]

(10) 52.222-53, Exemption from Application of the Service Contract Act to Contracts for Certain Services—Requirements (FEB 2009).[10]

(11) 52.222-54, Employment Eligibility Verification (AUG 2013).

(12) 52.226-6, Promoting Excess Food Donation to Nonprofit Organizations. (MAR 2009).[11]

(13) 52.247-64, Preference for Privately Owned U.S.-Flag Commercial Vessels (February 2006).[12]

CO's may supplement these flow-down provisions by including other clauses implementing agency-specific statutes.[13]

§ 10:14 Rights in technical data & computer software

The FAR expressly provides that in commercial item acquisi-

---

[2] E.O. 11246.

[3] 38 U.S.C.A. § 4212.

[4] 29 U.S.C.A. § 793.

[5] E.O. 13496.

[6] 41 U.S.C.A. §§ 6702 et seq.

[7] The Service Contract Act and FAR clause are only applicable in service contracts where there are "non-exempt" contractor employees.

[8] 22 U.S.C.A. § 7104(g), Alternate I (AUG 2007) of 52.222-50 (22 U.S.C. 7104(g)).

[9] 41 U.S.C.A. §§ 6701 to 6707.

[10] 41 U.S.C.A. § 6702(b).

[11] Flow down required in accordance with paragraph (e) of the clause.

[12] 46 U.S.C.A. 53105 and 10 U.S.C.A. § 2631. Flow down required in accordance with paragraph (d) of the clause.

[13] FAR 44.402(c).

§ 10:14   Government Contract Compliance Handbook

tions, the Government normally will obtain only minimal rights in technical data or computer software.[1] Essentially, the Government obtains only the same rights as any commercial customer unless it explicitly negotiates additional rights and pays for them. With regard to commercial technical data, the FAR provides: "Except as provided by agency-specific statutes, the Government shall acquire only the technical data and the rights in that data customarily provided to the public with a commercial item or process."[2] The FAR also provides that the software and documentation "shall be acquired under licenses customarily provided to the public to the extent such licenses are consistent with Federal law and otherwise satisfy the Government's needs."[3]

DOD has different, but comparable regulations that apply to commercial defense contracts with the following underlying policy: "DoD shall acquire only the technical data customarily provided to the public with a commercial item or process [with limited explicit exceptions]."[4] For commercial computer software and its documentation, the DFARS provides: "Commercial computer software and commercial computer software documentation shall be acquired under the licenses customarily provided to the public unless such licenses are inconsistent with Federal procurement law or do not otherwise satisfy user needs."[5] Thus, the Government "shall have only the rights specified in the license under which the commercial computer software or commercial computer software documentation was obtained."[6]

The Department of Defense effective September 20, 2011,

[Section 10:14]

[1]FAR pt. 12. The term "technical data" as used in the FAR and DFARS does not include computer software. In the FAR, "computer software" includes the software documentation; in the DFARS, software documentation is considered technical data. FAR 27.401; DFARS 252.227-7013.

[2]FAR 12.211.

[3]FAR 12.212.

[4]DFARS 227.7102-1 provides that,

(a) DoD shall acquire only the technical data customarily provided to the public with a commercial item or process, except technical data that—

(1) Are form, fit, or function data;

(2) Are required for repair or maintenance of commercial items or processes, or for the proper installation, operating, or handling of a commercial item, either as a standalone unit or as a part of a military system, when such data are not customarily provided to commercial users or the data provided to commercial users is not sufficient for military purposes;

(3) Describe the modifications made at Government expense to a commercial item or process in order to meet the requirements of a Government solicitation.

[5]DFARS 227.7202-1(a).

[6]DFARS 227.7202-3.

implemented a final rule amending the DFARS such that technical data and software related to major weapon systems are presumed to have not been developed at private expense. See 76 Fed. Reg. 58144. The rule makes an exception for Commercial Off-The-Shelf (COTS) items, but companies with non-COTS commercial items developed at private expense will now need to assert ownership.

C. FREQUENTLY ASKED QUESTIONS

§ 10:15 Questions & answers

Question 1: Can an item that a contractor has developed specifically for the Government ever be considered a commercial item?

Answer 1: Yes. If the item is a nondevelopmental item that qualifies as a commercial item under FAR 2.101, and was sold to multiple state or local Governments on a competitive basis.

Question 2: Does a product have to be in existence when the Government issues a solicitation in order for the product to be considered a commercial item?

Answer 2: No. The FAR recognizes that technology is rapidly changing. So long as the product is available in the commercial marketplace "in time to satisfy the delivery requirements" of the contract it will be considered a commercial item.[1]

Question 3: Are services required for the installation of a commercial item considered to be commercial services?

Answer 3: Yes. Such services would be considered to be a commercial item so long as the contractor provides these services to the general public under terms and conditions similar to those offered to the federal Government.

Question 4: FAR 2.101(1) requires that an item must have been "offered for sale, lease, or licensed to the general public" in order to qualify as a commercial product. What does "offered for sale" mean?

Answer 4: "Offer" is not synonymous with the contractual term "offer" defined in FAR 2.101 as "a response to a solicitation that, if accepted, would bind the offeror to perform the resultant contract." Rather the term requires only a showing that a contractor has made an effort to sell the product. In *Precision Lift, Inc. v. U.S.*, 83 Fed. Cl. 661 (2008), the court found that the contractor had conducted various and apparently unsuccessful advertising and marketing efforts to sell a helicopter maintenance platform to the general public and thus the product met the definition of a commercial item. But, the court went on to say:

[Section 10:15]
[1]FAR 2.101.

However, this is not to say that the statute is clear. The definition is broad, unclear, and will be interpreted as setting the "commercial item" standard very low. If the Federal Acquisition Regulations are intended to use the term in a very limiting way, its plain language does not communicate that intent.

III. SPECIAL CONTRACTING METHODS

A. GSA'S MAS PROGRAM

§ 10:16 Generally

The Multiple Award Schedule (MAS) program, administered by the General Services Administration (GSA), provides Government agencies with a streamlined process for purchasing commercial products and services using commercial buying practices. Under the MAS program, GSA negotiates contracts with multiple suppliers for the delivery of commercial items which the Government commonly uses. Individual agencies then select from among the products and services offered by thousands of competing suppliers who have contracted with GSA.

§ 10:17 MAS pricing

Under the MAS program, GSA seeks to negotiate "best customer" pricing under terms and conditions that are similar to those in vendors' commercial contracts. To accomplish this, the CO must determine that an offeror's prices are fair and reasonable and that the award is otherwise in the Government's best interest.[1] To determine whether an offeror's prices are fair and reasonable, the CO will consider the following factors:[2]

(1) Aggregate volume of anticipated purchases.

(2) The purchase of a minimum quantity or a pattern of historic purchases.

(3) Any combination of discounts and concessions offered to commercial customers.

(4) Length of the contract period.

(5) Warranties, training, and/or maintenance included in the purchase price or provided at additional cost to the product prices.

(6) Ordering and delivery practices.

(7) Any other relevant information.

To obtain a GSA MAS contract, your company must disclose sales and discount information to GSA in a "Commercial Sales Practices" chart contained in the solicitation as part of its offer.

[Section 10:17]

[1] GSAR 538.270(d).

[2] GSAR 538.270(c).

SELLING COMMERCIAL ITEMS § 10:18

You must state whether the discounts and concessions you are offering to the Government are equal to, or better than, your best price to any customer acquiring the same items regardless of quantity or terms and condition.

"Discount" means a "reduction to catalog prices," whether published or not. Discounts include "rebates, quantity discounts, purchase option credits, and any other terms or conditions" that reduce the price the customer pays for the goods or services purchased. Any net price that is lower than the list price is a "discount." The amount of the discount is calculated by comparing the percent difference between the net sale price and the list price.[3]

If you do not offer the Government your best discount, you must justify the prices you are offering to GSA by identifying and explaining any difference between GSA's terms and conditions and the terms and conditions that apply to when you offer your best price, i.e., your "most favored customer" price.[4] You are also required to identify a "customer or category of customer," i.e., a "benchmark customer," to whom you offer your best discounts under similar terms and conditions to those in the GSA contract.[5] MAS contractors must continue to monitor their sales after GSA awards the MAS contract to insure that the relationship between the price offered to GSA and the price offered to the benchmark customer is maintained during contract performance.[6]

§ 10:18 Contract price reductions

MAS contracts include two "Price Reduction" clauses. The first clause, "Price Adjustment-Failure to Provide Accurate Information," gives the Government the right to reduce the GSA price *retroactively* for items it has paid for under the contract if, during contract performance, the CO determines that the contract price was increased because the contractor misrepresented or failed to provide accurate information during contract negotiations.[1]

(a) The Government, at its election, may reduce the price of

---

[3]GSAR 552.238-75.
[4]GSAR 538.270(c)(7).
[5]GSAR 515.408.
[6]GSAR 552.215-72.

[Section 10:18]

[1]United States ex rel. Hicks v. Oracle Corp., No. 03-CV-422, settlement announced (D. Md. Oct. 10, 2006). Oracle Corp. agreed to pay $98.5 million to resolve false claims allegations that PeopleSoft Inc, a firm that Oracle acquired in 2004, had failed to disclose to the Government during the negotiation of an MAS contract that it offered commercial customers more favorable pricing than it was proposing to the Government. The qui tam relator reportedly received more than $17 million of the settlement amount according to the Department of

§ 10:18   Government Contract Compliance Handbook

this contract or contract modification if the Contracting Officer determines after award of this contract or contract modification that the price negotiated was increased by a significant amount because the contractor failed to:

    (1) provide information required by this solicitation/contract or otherwise requested by the Government; or

    (2) submit information that was current, accurate, and complete; or

    (3) disclose changes in the contractor's commercial pricelist(s), discounts or discounting policies which occurred after the original submission and prior to the completion of negotiations.

* * *

    (e) In addition to the remedy in paragraph (a) of this clause, the Government may terminate this contract for default. The rights and remedies of the Government specified herein are not exclusive, and are in addition to any other rights and remedies provided by law or under this contract.

The second clause, "Price Reductions," requires that during contract performance the contractor must report any price reductions it offers to the benchmark customer, and must reduce its price to GSA accordingly.[2] Such price reductions include the following:[3]

    (1) Revisions to the commercial catalog, price list, schedule, or other document on which the MAS contract was predicated to reduce prices.

    (2) More favorable discounts or terms and conditions than those in the price list or catalog on which the MAS contract was predicated.

    (3) Discounts to the applicable customer or category of customers that was the basis of award that "disturbs the price/discount relationship of the Government to the customer (or category of customers) that was the basis of award."

When any of these three situations occur, the contractor must notify the Government of the price reduction as soon as possible, but not later than 15 calendar days after its effective date, and then the contractor must offer Government customers a similar price reduction.[4]

Certain instances do not trigger price reductions under this clause. They include: (a) sales to commercial customers under firm, fixed-price definite quantity contracts with specified delivery

---

Justice.
    [2]GSAR 552.238-75, para. (b).
    [3]GSAR 552.238-75.
    [4]GSAR 552.238-75, para. (f).

in excess of the maximum order amount specified in the MAS contract, (b) sales to federal Government agencies (contractors may extend price reductions to the Government at any time during the contract period),[5] and (c) sales resulting from a quotation or billing error, if the contractor can adequately document the mistake to the CO.[6] GSA has certain access-to-records and audit rights both before making a contract award and for three years after final payment under the contract was made, so as to enforce these price reductions clauses.[7]

§ 10:19 Industrial funding fee

GSA finances administration of the MAS program by charging contractors an "Industrial Funding Fee" (IFF) on sales they make under their GSA contracts.[1] Contractors must report MAS sales to GSA quarterly, and then must remit an IFF, which is currently a fee of 0.75%, on their total sales volume under the contract for the previous quarter. This clause imposes significant burdens on the MAS contractor because failure to submit sales reports, falsification of sales reports, and/or failure to pay the IFF in a timely manner may result in termination or cancellation of the contract or could result in civil and criminal false claims.

§ 10:20 Competition requirements

It is not necessary for agencies to allow MAS contractors to compete for the award of a task or delivery order under a GSA MAS contract, because GSA has already determined that contractors' prices are fair and reasonable when it awarded the MAS contract. Thus, awards of task or delivery orders under a MAS contract are generally not subject to a bid protest. However, if an agency issues a solicitation or requests quotes for a requirement from GSA contractors in order to obtain prices that are lower than their GSA prices, GAO will entertain a protest to ensure that the competition is fair, reasonable, and consistent with the terms of the solicitation or request for quotes. For example, GAO has held that when an agency solicits quotes or offers from GSA contractors, the agency must give contractors sufficient detail in

---

[5]GSAR 552.238-75, para. (e).
[6]GSAR 552.238-75, para. (d).
[7]*See*, GSAR 552.215-70.

[Section 10:19]
[1]GSAR 552.238-74.

§ 10:20   Government Contract Compliance Handbook

the solicitation to allow them to compete intelligently and fairly.[1]

B. SMALL PURCHASES

§ 10:21 Generally

FASA established special procedures for small purchases and exempted two types of small purchases from the detailed "full and open" competition procedures and other contractor recordkeeping and certification requirements established by statute. One, the "simplified acquisition threshold," applies to procurements of supplies and services (including, but not limited to, commercial items) not exceeding $150,000.[1] The other is the "micro-purchase threshold," which is currently $3,000, and thus applies to procurements of $3,000 or less. The streamlined procurement procedures that apply to these types of procurements are set forth in the FAR.[2]

The Clinger-Cohen Act, as implemented by the FAR, authorizes a test program to permit agencies to use simplified acquisition procedures to acquire property or services with a purchase value not to exceed $6.5 million ($12 million for acquisitions to facilitate defense against nuclear, biological, or chemical attack) when the CO reasonably expects that offerors will respond with only commercial items.[3]

§ 10:22 Laws inapplicable to simplified acquisitions

The following laws (and their implementing contract clauses) do not apply, in whole or in part, to contracts and subcontracts at or below the simplified acquisition threshold:[1]

(1) Certain provisions of the Anti-Kickback Act of 1986 (41 U.S.C.A. § 8703(a) and (b), specifically the requirement for the incorporation of the contractor procedures for the prevention and detection of violations and the contractual requirement for contractor cooperation in investigations

(2) Miller Act (40 U.S.C.A. § 3131) (alternative forms of payment protection for suppliers of labor and material are still required if the contract exceeds $100,000)

(3) Contract Work Hours and Safety Standards Act (40

[Section 10:20]

[1]*Draeger Safety, Inc., B-285366 et al.*, 2000 CPD 139.

[Section 10:21]

[1]Pub. L. No. 103-355, §§ 4001 to 4404, 108 Stat. 3243.
[2]FAR pt. 13.
[3]Pub. L. No. 104-106, § 4202, 110 Stat. 186; FAR subpt. 13.5.

[Section 10:22]

[1]FAR 13.005.

SELLING COMMERCIAL ITEMS § 10:23

U.S.C.A. §§ 3701 to 3708)

(4) Drug Free Workplace Act (41 U.S.C.A. § 8102) except for the provisions that apply to individuals

(5) Certain provisions of the Solid Waste Disposal Act (42 U.S.C.A. § 6962; specifically the requirement for providing the estimate of recovered material utilized in the performance of the contract)

(6) Contract clause regarding contingent fees (10 U.S.C.A. § 2306(b); 41 U.S.C.A. §§ 3901, 3905 and 3906)

(7) Authority to examine books and records of contractors (10 U.S.C.A. § 2313; 41 U.S.C.A. §§ 3901, 3905 and 3906)

(8) Prohibition on limiting subcontractor direct sales to the United States (10 U.S.C.A. § 2402; 41 U.S.C.A. § 4704)

(9) The HUBZone Act of 1997 (15 U.S.C.A. § 631) except for 15 U.S.C.A. § 657a(b)(2)(B) which is optional for the agencies

(10) Veterans employment reporting requirements (31 U.S.C.A. § 1354(a))

In addition, the following FAR clauses do not apply to contracts and subcontracts at or below the simplified acquisition threshold:[2]

(a) 52.203-5, Covenant against Contingent Fees.

(b) 52.203-6, Restrictions on Subcontractor Sales to the Government.

(c) 52.203-7, Anti-Kickback Procedures.

(d) 52.215-2, Audits and Records—Negotiation.

(e) 52.222-4, Contract Work Hours and Safety Standards Act—Overtime Compensation.

(f) 52.223-6, Drug-Free Workplace, except for individuals.

(g) 52.223-9, Estimate of Percentage of Recovered Material Content for EPA-Designated Products.

IV. HOW TO RECOGNIZE THE PROBLEM

§ 10:23 Generally

A company that sells to both commercial customers and Government customers must be careful to distinguish between the types of conduct and operational methods appropriate for commercial sales and those appropriate for Government sales, even when the same items are being sold. Although sales of commercial items and services to the Government have been exempted from the application of many of the laws and rules that apply to other Government procurements, contractors still must comply with a number of Government-unique terms and conditions that apply to the sale of commercial items. For example, although a contractor need not submit certified cost or pricing data to the Government in a negotiated commercial item procurement,

---

[2]FAR 13.006.

the CO may nevertheless require submission of price-related "information other than cost or pricing data." If you supply information that is inaccurate, incomplete, or is not current, you could face allegations of making false statements or claims to the Government.

Moreover, when selling a combination of commercial and noncommercial items to the Government—some of which are exempt from Government-unique requirements (because they are "commercial items") and others which are not—you must pay attention to problems arising from mixed operations. In such cases, you will need to take care to establish adequate procedures and controls to assure compliance with all Government requirements.

The following examples provide guidance in recognizing where trouble may arise when selling commercial items to the Government.

§ 10:24 Examples

(a) *Refurbished equipment*: Your company operates a single commercial assembly line for computer equipment sold both to commercial customers and to the Federal Government. Some components used to produce the equipment are refurbished, remanufactured, or simply recovered from returned products. The end items are then warehoused and later sold from inventory to Government or commercial customers.

In several high technology industries, such as the computer industry, using recovered parts is a common practice. Certain nonmechanical components are believed equally reliable whether brand-new or not. For example, some experts claim that a "burned-in" computer board is superior to a new one. Procurement regulations used to mandate that most Government solicitations for supply contracts require that all components of a product sold to the Government be new. Failure to provide exclusively new supplies or components, thus, violated the "Material Requirements" clause.[1] However, current regulations direct COs that, when acquiring commercial items, they must "consider the customary practices in the industry for the item being acquired."[2]

(b) *MAS contract/incomplete sales data*: Assume your company sells computer equipment and software and provides related maintenance and training services in the U.S. and overseas. You have a sales force consisting of hundreds of field sales representatives here and abroad. Your company maintains a centralized

---

[Section 10:24]
[1]*See* FAR 52.211-5.
[2]FAR 11.302(c).

billing system, designed to record and monitor sales volume, classes of customers, and terms and conditions of sales for all items and services, including any special terms or discounts granted to customers.

Your company competes for a MAS contract for certain computer hardware, software, and maintenance services, and in that process, it submits data on the volume and terms of sale of all relevant items covered by the contract. After award, you learn that one of your company's regional offices has offered substantially deeper discounts to a commercial customer on certain items and services you offered or disclosed to GSA in your MAS proposal. As a result, those commercial customers enjoy prices considerably below the contract prices you negotiated with the Government. You are concerned about the possible consequences of these inconsistent pricing actions.

Under the terms of the MAS contract, if the commercial customer involved was an "applicable," i.e. benchmark customer, you must report the discount to the Government, with an explanation of the conditions under which the reduced price was made, within 15 calendar days after the reduction becomes effective. If the lower price disturbs the relationship between the price offered to the benchmark customer and your GSA price, you must reduce your GSA price accordingly. Failure to report a price reduction within the prescribed period and to reduce your GSA price accordingly if necessary, can result in civil liability for false claims. If the customer was not an "applicable" customer, you do not need to report this information immediately, however, you must maintain this information and disclose it to GSA at the time of contract extension or renewal.

Even if you are able to collect all of the appropriate pricing and discount data required to accompany your proposal and to monitor this data during contract performance, the database that you compile is no better than the accuracy (and honesty) of the individuals in your company who provide this information. Therefore, you must carefully train your sales staff, accounting personnel, and others responsible for collecting the raw data on the importance of maintaining current, accurate, and complete information. Problems traditionally arise in the area of "completeness," where sales staff neglects to include special sales or discounts granted to certain customers. This potential problem is exacerbated where sales representatives are offered incentives for increasing their sales volumes, regardless of the discounts given to customers. To avoid such problems, many companies develop screens as part of their order entry data processing systems that prohibit the processing of sales of items on the GSA contract at below the GSA price to certain categories of customers. This approach will minimize the possibility of making sales at

§ 10:24

prices that will have a negative impact on GSA MAS contracts.

(c) *Modified products*: In response to a solicitation requiring offerors to propose computer equipment, your company, which is also the incumbent contractor, proposes equipment that is functionally enhanced but substantially equivalent to the basic equipment now being used to perform the contract. After the Government makes a new award to your company, another offeror protests the award on the ground that your company's enhanced equipment fails to meet the commerciality requirements contained in the solicitation.

If you submit a commercial item to the Government, you may modify that item to meet the specifications set forth in the solicitation. As noted earlier in this chapter, minor modification of a commercial product will not destroy "commerciality," while a major modification of a commercial item may jeopardize its "commerciality." What constitutes a "major" modification must be determined on a case-by-case basis. Thus, you should consider very carefully making any modification beyond an obviously minor one to avoid a challenge to the commerciality of the product you offer.

V. COMPLIANCE INITIATIVES

§ 10:25 Generally

Although the Government waives many requirements for contractors supplying "commercial items," the process of conducting "hybrid" (part commercial, part federal) operations can sometimes raise more complications and dangers than conducting a fully Government business. Simultaneously conducting commercial and federal sales creates many problems that do not exist in a purely federal sales environment.

For example, in a company selling to both commercial and Government customers, sales and administrative personnel are often confused by the rules that cover Government contracts. Personnel responsible for commercial contracting generally do not face the same internal controls on costs, discount policies, sales techniques, gratuities, or timekeeping as those responsible for Government contracting. Employees selling to federal customers may naturally follow the commercial practices of fellow employees selling to commercial customers. However, the inclination to follow commercially acceptable conduct when selling to the Government can prove hazardous. At worst, it may lead to charges of fraud, defective pricing, or illegal gratuities, as well as the suspension or debarment of your firm from doing business with the Government. However, companies that institute robust compliance programs can maintain greater control over sales and may find that such programs assist in generating greater profits.

Integrating a commercial and federal business requires *organizing your company* to do both Government and commercial business and *properly training* your sales force to handle both types of sales. Sales personnel tend to apply the same code of conduct in Government sales that is widely accepted in the commercial sales world.

§ 10:26 Gratuities

Your sales force for Government contracts must operate with more care than your commercial sales force. For example, gratuities laws prohibit the giving of virtually anything of value (with the exception of nominal promotional items such as pens, key chains, and similar objects) to a federal employee (see §§ 7:1 et seq.). Although guarding against providing gratuities may be natural for companies that sell exclusively to the Federal Government, when a company sells to *both* the Government and commercial customers, compliance with the rules governing gratuities can be a challenge.

In addition, under the Anti-Kickback Act, the Government's general prohibition against providing gratuities to Government employees also applies to the provision of gratuities in transactions between purely commercial entities such as prime and subcontractors (see §§ 7:1 et seq.). Commercial companies traditionally have networks of suppliers for various parts, raw materials, and services. These suppliers may exchange gratuities in accordance with normal commercial practice. These practices may be perfectly acceptable until the prime contractor sells its products to the Government. Although the standard for an unlawful "kickback" has proven to be more pragmatic than the standard for gratuities made to Government employees, the language of the Anti-Kickback Act nevertheless remains very broad—prohibiting the gift of "anything of value."

§ 10:27 Access to information

Another difference between Government and commercial sales is that your Government sales force must comply with strict rules on access to proprietary or source selection Government information (see §§ 6:1 et seq.). Certain types of access are strictly prohibited by law and, if detected, may result in a criminal investigation and prosecution. Similarly, the business expenses your sales force incurs, their access to Government personnel and data, and common sales "puffery" may all create problems when your sales force is selling to Government contracts. Your sales representatives are your front line in dealing with federal customers. They must conduct themselves in a manner very different from accepted methods of selling to commercial customers.

§ 10:28 Recommendations

(a) Be aware of and comply with unique Government requirements imposed on contractors who supply commercial products to the Government.

(b) Alert your employees responsible for soliciting contract opportunities and preparing proposals for the Government that they should take note of any *"most favored customer"* provisions that may be included in Government solicitations. MFC provisions generally require the contractor to represent that the Government will receive the contractor's lowest price under similar contract terms and conditions to those offered to the contractor's most favored customer. You will bear the burden of establishing that these criteria have been met. For example, a computer business seeking to justify lower prices offered to a dealer must bear the burden of identifying and quantifying any special services the dealer provides or special terms and conditions in its contracts with the dealer that justify charging the Government a higher price for the same commercial items.

(c) If you run a hybrid commercial/Federal Government business, you must *segregate* commercial and noncommercial work areas and *train* both commercial and noncommercial employees adequately regarding the differences between sales to the general public and sales to the Government. Both commercial and noncommercial employees must be educated about the internal controls and recordkeeping requirements imposed on Government contractors relating to, among other things, cost charging, discount policies, materials control, country-of-origin rules, socioeconomic requirements, sales techniques, quality controls, and timekeeping.

(d) Train your sales force to be aware of the differing standards of conduct and acceptable *sales techniques* involved in selling to the federal Government as opposed to selling to commercial customers. To help protect against unwitting yet improper conduct by your sales force in dealing with Government personnel, formulate a *written policy*, distribute to all employees, concerning acceptable sales practices, restrictions on offering gratuities or gifts to Government employees, and other Government-specific rules discussed above.

Part III

CONTRACT PERFORMANCE

Chapter 11

Cost Allowability

I. OVERVIEW
§ 11:1 Scope note

II. CURRENT REQUIREMENTS
A. FAR COST PRINCIPLES
§ 11:2 Generally
§ 11:3 Coverage
§ 11:4 "Allowable" costs
§ 11:5 Specific unallowable & restricted costs
§ 11:6 Apportioning costs
§ 11:7 Accounting rules

B. LIABILITY FOR UNALLOWABLE COSTS
§ 11:8 Disallowance of unallowable costs
§ 11:9 Certificate of final indirect costs
§ 11:10 "Penalties for unallowable costs" clause
§ 11:11 Referral of fraud cases

C. FREQUENTLY ASKED QUESTIONS
§ 11:12 Questions & answers

III. HOW TO RECOGNIZE THE PROBLEM
§ 11:13 Generally
§ 11:14 Examples

IV. COMPLIANCE INITIATIVES
§ 11:15 Generally
§ 11:16 Upper management
§ 11:17 Supervisors & middle management

§ 11:18   Nonsupervisory employees
§ 11:19   Accounting department
§ 11:20   Recommendations

> **KeyCite®:** Cases and other legal materials listed in KeyCite Scope can be researched through the KeyCite service on Westlaw®. Use KeyCite to check citations for form, parallel references, prior and later history, and comprehensive citator information, including citations to other decisions and secondary materials.

I. OVERVIEW

§ 11:1 Scope note

Assume you are the president of a fast growing high-tech Government contracts firm located in South Dakota. To continue your company's rapid growth and remain on the leading edge of technology, you need to entice some of the country's best young engineering talent to join your company. While many of the potential recruits are excited by your company's work, they do not like the remoteness of South Dakota. To overcome their reluctance to relocate, you offer these engineers a $10,000 moving bonus as an incentive. This tactic is successful, and you hire a number of these engineers.

While you may have solved your personnel problems, you may have created a Government contract cost problem. The cost regulations set forth in the Federal Acquisition Regulation (FAR) restrict the types and amounts of costs you may allocate to a Government contract. Is the moving bonus an allowable compensation cost, an unallowable relocation expense, or an allowable recruitment cost? This is a difficult question to answer and an important one, because if you include an unallowable cost in your cost pools, you may be faced with Government allegations of wrongdoing.

Cost allowability questions are often difficult to resolve because two or more conflicting FAR cost principles may appear to apply to the cost in question. The cost may be allowable under one cost principle and unallowable under another cost principle. Moreover, the allowability of a cost has nothing to do with its "legitimacy." For instance, interest, although clearly a legitimate business expense, is an unallowable cost under Government contracts—that is, a cost the Government, as a matter of policy, has chosen not to pay.[1] Thus, some legitimate business expenses

---

[Section 11:1]

[1]FAR 31.205-20.

are not necessarily reimbursable costs under your Government contracts.

Moreover, federal statutes require contractors to *certify*, under penalty of perjury, that their interim and final indirect cost proposals submitted to the Government for certain types of contracts do not contain any unallowable costs.[2] Filing a false or erroneous certification may subject the contractor to substantial penalties.

II. CURRENT REQUIREMENTS

A. FAR COST PRINCIPLES

§ 11:2 Generally

FAR Part 31, which is referred to generally as the "cost principles," sets forth restrictions on the type or amount of costs that may be included as an element of a negotiated contract price or paid by the Government to a contractor during the course of contract performance.[1]

§ 11:3 Coverage

The cost principles apply generally to contracts awarded by both civilian agencies and the Department of Defense.[1] The first step in understanding the rules governing the recovery of costs under Government contracts is determining whether the cost principles apply at all. With respect to commercial organizations, the FAR provides that the cost principles apply to seven different types of contracts or transactions:[2]

(1) *Pricing* of a *negotiated contract* whenever a cost analysis of an offeror's proposal is performed.

(2) Determining *reimbursable costs* under a cost-reimbursement contract or subcontract.

(3) Negotiating *indirect cost rates*, including those for interim and final billing rates and progress payment rates.

(4) Proposing, negotiating, or determining costs where the contract has been *terminated* (except where the contract is

---

[2]10 U.S.C.A. § 2324(h)(1); 41 U.S.C.A. § 4308.

[Section 11:2]

[1]*See generally* Manos, 2 Government Contract Costs & Pricing §§ 6–59; Arnavas, Government Contract Cost Recovery, Briefing Papers No. 01-6 (May 2001).

[Section 11:3]

[1]*See also* DFARS pt. 231.
[2]FAR 31.102, 31.103.

for a commercial item).[3]
(5) *Revising* the price of a *fixed-price incentive* contract.
(6) *Redetermining* the price under a *price redetermination* contract.
(7) *Pricing* changes and other *contract modifications*.

The only contract type *not* directly covered by the cost principles is a *firm-fixed-price* contract awarded on the basis of sealed bids or price competition. Even then, however, any modification to that contract would most likely be subject to the cost principles.[4]

§ 11:4 "Allowable" costs

The cost principles provide that only "allowable" costs may be considered in the costing and pricing functions described in the preceding section. For example, in negotiating a contract, the Contracting Officer (CO) may only consider and agree to negotiate on the basis of costs that are "allowable" within the meaning of FAR Part 31. For a cost to be allowable, it must meet five basic requirements.[1]

First, the cost must be *"reasonable."*[2] Under the FAR, a cost is considered to be reasonable "if, in its nature and amount, it does not exceed that which would be incurred by a prudent person in the conduct of competitive business."[3] There is no presumption of reasonableness with respect to a contractor's incurred cost, and the burden of establishing reasonableness is on the contractor when a CO challenges the reasonableness of a cost.[4]

Second, the cost must be *allocable to the contract* in question.[5] The FAR states that a cost is allocable to a contract if it (a) is incurred specifically for the contract, (b) benefits more than one contract and can be distributed to them in reasonable proportion to the benefits received, or (c) is necessary to the overall operation of the business even though a direct relationship to any particular contract cannot be shown.[6]

Third, for certain contracts, the treatment of the cost must be in accordance with the *Cost Accounting Standards*. Otherwise,

---

[3]FAR 12.403(d)(ii).
[4]FAR 31.102; *see* DFARS 252.243-7001.

[Section 11:4]
[1]FAR 31.201-2(a).
[2]FAR 31.201-2(a)(1).
[3]FAR 31.201-3(a).
[4]FAR 31.201-3(a).
[5]FAR 31.201-2(a)(2).
[6]FAR 31.201-4.

COST ALLOWABILITY § 11:5

the treatment of the cost must be in accordance with generally accepted accounting principles.[7] (See §§ 12:1 et seq.)

Fourth, the cost must be in accordance with the *terms of the contract*.[8] For example, if the parties agree in the contract to limit the amount of a cost that will be allowed—even though the amount is not otherwise limited by the regulations—the courts and boards of contract appeals will enforce the provision. The CO could not, however, agree to reimburse a contractor for a cost that otherwise is expressly unallowable.

Fifth, the allowability of a cost is subject to "any limitations set forth in this subpart."[9] This refers to the limitations applicable to over 50 items of *selected costs* that are set forth in detail in FAR Part 31 (and discussed below in the following section).[10]

§ 11:5 Specific unallowable & restricted costs

Examples of costs that are unallowable or have restrictions on their allowability include the following:

(1) *Public relations and advertising costs* are generally unallowable. However, the regulation does contain certain significant exceptions. Thus, advertising costs incurred in acquiring scarce items for contract performance and costs incurred in promoting the export of products normally sold to the Government are allowable. Likewise, examples of allowable public relations costs include the cost of communicating with the public, press, and stockholders and the costs of participating in community service activities.[1]

(2) *Bad debts* are unallowable.[2]

(3) *Compensation for personal services*[3] is generally allowable if reasonable, when it is based upon and conforms to an established compensation plan, and is related to services performed during the period of contract performance, except as follows: (a) costs that are unallowable under other paragraphs of the cost principles are unallowable as compensation for personal services;[4] (b) severance pay is

---

[7]FAR 31.201-2(a)(3).
[8]FAR 31.201-2(a)(4).
[9]FAR 31.201-2(a)(5).
[10]FAR 31.205.

[Section 11:5]
[1]FAR 31.205-1.
[2]FAR 31.205-3.
[3]FAR 31.205-6.
[4]FAR 31.205-6(a)(5).

only allowable under certain conditions;[5] (c) backpay as compensation for services *not* performed is unallowable;[6] (d) compensation incidental to business acquisitions is unallowable;[7] (e) that portion of the cost of company-furnished automobiles that relates to personal use by employees is unallowable;[8] (f) employee rebate and discount plans are unallowable;[9] and (g) senior management (the chief executive officer plus the five most highly compensated employees in management positions at each home office and each segment of the contractor) wages and deferred compensation in excess of the benchmark compensation amount are unallowable.[10]

(4) *Contingencies* are generally unallowable except for estimating future costs arising from a known and existing condition, the effects of which are foreseeable within reasonable limits of accuracy.[11]

(5) *Contributions or donations*[12] are unallowable except to the extent allowable as a cost of "participation in community service activities (e.g., blood bank drives, charity drives, savings bond drives, disaster assistance, etc.)."[13]

(6) *Economic planning costs* are generally allowable.[14]

(7) *Employee morale, health, welfare, food service, and dormitory costs and credits*[15] are generally allowable except for gifts,[16] costs of recreation except company-sponsored sports teams,[17] and losses from operating food and dormitory services unless the objective is to operate such services on a break-even basis.[18]

(8) *Entertainment costs*, including costs of membership in

---

[5] FAR 31.205-6(g).
[6] FAR 31.205-6(h).
[7] FAR 31.205-6(l).
[8] FAR 31.205-6(m)(2).
[9] FAR 31.205-6(n).
[10] FAR 31.205-6(p). *See generally* Manos, Allowability of Executive Compensation Costs, Briefing Papers No. 97-13 (Dec. 1997).
[11] FAR 31.205-7.
[12] FAR 31.205-8.
[13] FAR 31.205-1(e)(3).
[14] FAR 31.205-12.
[15] FAR 31.205-13.
[16] FAR 31.205-13(b).
[17] FAR 31.205-13(c).
[18] FAR 31.205-13(d).

social, dining, or country clubs, are unallowable.[19]
(9) *Fines, penalties, and mischarging costs* are unallowable except when incurred as a result of compliance with specific terms of the contract or written instructions from the CO.[20]
(10) *Idle capacity costs* are generally allowable, but *idle facilities costs* are unallowable unless the facilities are necessary to meet fluctuation in workload or were necessary when acquired and are now idle "because of changes in requirements, production economies, reorganization, termination, or other causes which could not have been reasonably foreseen." Such costs are allowable for a reasonable period, ordinarily not to exceed one year.[21]
(11) *Independent research and development and bid and proposal costs* are generally allowable subject to restrictions and ceilings.[22]
(12) *Insurance and indemnification* costs are generally allowable except that costs for business interruption or similar insurance must be limited to exclude coverage of profit. Also, the "cost of insurance to protect the contractor against the costs of correcting its own defects in materials or workmanship is unallowable," but "insurance costs to cover fortuitous or casualty losses resulting from defects in materials or workmanship are allowable as a normal business expense."[23]
(13) *Interest and other financial costs* are unallowable.[24]
(14) *Lobbying and political activity costs* are generally unallowable.[25]
(15) *Losses on other contracts* are unallowable.[26]
(16) *Organization costs* are generally unallowable.[27]
(17) *Patent costs* incurred as requirements of a Government contract are allowable, but patent costs not required by

---

[19] FAR 31.205-14.

[20] FAR 31.205-15.

[21] FAR 31.205-17.

[22] FAR 31.205-18. *See generally* Manos, FAR 31.205-18, Independent Research & Development & Bid & Proposal Costs, Briefing Papers No. 03-12 (Nov. 2003).

[23] FAR 31.205-19.

[24] FAR 31.205-20. *See generally* Hanson & Jackson, Interest In & On Claims, Briefing Papers No. 06-4 (Mar. 2006).

[25] FAR 31.205-22.

[26] FAR 31.205-23.

[27] FAR 31.205-27.

§ 11:5   GOVERNMENT CONTRACT COMPLIANCE HANDBOOK

the contract are unallowable.[28]

(18) *Plant reconversion costs* are generally unallowable in the absence of an advance agreement except for the cost of removal of Government property and restoration costs caused by such removal.[29]

(19) *Professional and consultant service costs* are generally allowable except where services are for an improper purpose or incurred in connection with an activity whose costs are unallowable under other cost principles.[30]

(20) *Recruitment costs* are generally allowable except where the advertisement (a) does not describe specific positions or classes of positions, or (b) includes material not relevant to recruitment purposes.[31]

(21) *Relocation costs* are generally allowable with certain limitations.[32] The following costs are unallowable: (a) loss on sale of home, (b) costs incident to acquiring a home in a new location, (c) continuing mortgage principal payments on residence being sold, and (d) costs incident to furnishing equity or nonequity loans to employees or making arrangements with lenders for employees to obtain lower-than-market-rate mortgage loans.[33] Note, however, that where relocation costs are included as direct or allocable indirect cost on a Government contract, and the employee resigns within 12 months for reasons within the control of the employee, the contractor must refund or credit the relocation costs to the Government.[34]

(22) *Rental costs* are generally allowable, but rental costs under a sale and leaseback are allowable only up to the amount the contractor would be allowed if the contractor retained title.[35]

(23) The following *taxes* are unallowable: (a) federal income and excess profits taxes, (b) taxes in connection with financing, refinancing, refunding operations, or reorganizations, (c) taxes from which exemptions are available to the contractor, (d) special assessments on land that represent capital improvements, and (e) taxes on real or personal property used exclusively in connection with

---

[28]FAR 31.205-30.
[29]FAR 31.205-31.
[30]FAR 31.205-33.
[31]FAR 31.205-34.
[32]FAR 31.205-35.
[33]FAR 31.205-35(c)(1) to (c)(4).
[34]FAR 31.205-35(d).
[35]FAR 31.205-36.

work other than on Government contracts.[36]

(24) *Travel costs* have limited allowability.[37] Airfare, with some narrow exceptions, is basically limited to the lowest customary fare offered during normal business hours.[38] Cost of travel by company-owned, -leased, or -chartered aircraft is limited to commercial standard airfare unless subject to an advance agreement or approval by the CO.[39]

(25) *Costs related to legal and other proceedings* are generally unallowable where incurred (a) in a proceeding brought against the contractor for a violation of law and the result is unfavorable, (b) in defense against a Federal Government claim or appeal or in prosecution of a claim or appeal against the Government, (c) in organization or reorganization activities, (d) in defense of an antitrust suit, (e) in connection with litigation between prime and subcontractors arising under a teaming agreement, (f) in patent infringement litigation, (g) in representation of groups or individuals that the contractor is not legally bound to provide, where the participant was convicted or found liable in a criminal, civil, or administrative proceeding, and (h) in protests or defense of protests of Federal Government solicitations or contract awards unless pursuant to a written request from the cognizant CO.[40]

(26) *Deferred research and development costs* are generally unallowable.[41]

(27) *Goodwill* is unallowable.[42]

(28) *Costs of alcoholic beverages* are unallowable.[43]

§ 11:6 Apportioning costs

The FAR recognizes that situations will arise in which more than one of the cost principles' "selected costs" rules will apply to a specific cost. It provides that, in this instance, you should *apportion* the costs among the appropriate cost principles where possible, and that a determination of allowability should be made on each cost in accordance with the guidelines of the relevant

---

[36]FAR 31.205-41.
[37]FAR 31.205-46.
[38]*See* FAR 31.205-46(b).
[39]*See* FAR 31.205-46(c).
[40]FAR 31.205-47. *See generally* Manos, Allowability of Legal Costs, Briefing Papers No. 05-5 (Apr. 2005).
[41]FAR 31.205-48.
[42]FAR 31.205-49.
[43]FAR 31.205-51.

§ 11:6   GOVERNMENT CONTRACT COMPLIANCE HANDBOOK

subsection.[1]

In some cases, costs may not be apportionable, notwithstanding that more than one subsection of the FAR is relevant. In such instances, the FAR states that the determination of allowability shall be based on the guidance contained in the subsection "that most specifically deals with, or best captures the essential nature of, the cost at issue."[2]

The effect of the regulations is to establish a two-step analysis for dealing with cases where more than one cost principle arguably applies to an expenditure. First, you must determine what is the nature of the cost. In other words, you must determine what is the *principal apparent purpose* of the transaction that gave rise to the cost. Second, once you have correctly identified the nature of the cost, you must determine whether that cost satisfies all the requirements of allowability. Merely falling under one of the cost principles specifying allowability is not enough. The cost must satisfy all of the *general allowability requirements* of the cost principles.

You must apportion costs correctly. Where costs are easily apportionable between two cost principles, such as where the bill for an employee picnic includes amounts for both the cost of the food and the cost of alcoholic beverages, apportioning the costs should not present a problem. The real difficulty arises in determining how to treat a cost that could easily fit within two or more cost categories. Particularly where an item is allowable under one cost principle but would be *unallowable* (or its allowability would be limited) under another cost principle, it becomes important to determine which type of cost the item more nearly resembles. If an item more closely resembles the unallowable type of cost, then that item cannot be "made" allowable by saying it also could qualify as another type of cost.

In other words, it is an "either/or" situation. Either the item constitutes a type of cost that is allowable, or it constitutes one that is not. It cannot be viewed as falling equally within both categories so as to avoid the limitation on allowability that exists under one of the two cost principles.

It is up to *you* to classify costs. You should make the determination *at the time the expenditure is incurred* because determining the "essential nature of the cost"[3] is more clearly seen at that point than in hindsight. Nevertheless, even a contemporaneous

---

[Section 11:6]
  [1]FAR 31.204(d).
  [2]FAR 31.204(d).
  [3]FAR 31.204(d).

determination can be difficult in many cases.

§ 11:7 Accounting rules

Where the FAR and Cost Accounting Standard 405, "Accounting for Unallowable Costs,"[1] apply, you must *identify* expressly unallowable costs and *exclude* them from any billing, claim, or proposal to which the cost principles apply.[2] (See §§ 12:1 et seq.) You must also exclude any "directly associated cost," but *only if* it is "material" as defined in the regulation.[3] Moreover, unallowable costs must bear their proportionate share of indirect costs. For example, if a total cost input base is used for allocated general and administrative (G&A) costs, all items that are properly part of the cost input base, whether allowable or unallowable, must be included in the base and bear their pro rata share of G&A costs.[4]

B. LIABILITY FOR UNALLOWABLE COSTS

§ 11:8 Disallowance of unallowable costs

At any time during the performance of a cost-reimbursement contract, a fixed-price incentive contract, or a contract providing for price redetermination, the cognizant CO may issue a notice of intent to disallow costs incurred or planned for incurrence under the contract that have been determined not to be allowable under the contract terms.[1] The contractor is provided an opportunity to make a written response to the CO justifying the allowability of the costs. The CO must then either withdraw the notice or issue a written decision disallowing the costs that the contractor may appeal under the "Disputes" clause of the contract.[2]

Where the costs at issue have already been incurred, an auditor may initiate the disallowance process by issuing a notice of contract costs suspended and/or disapproved.[3] The notice used for this purpose is often a Defense Contract Audit Agency (DCAA) Form 1.[4] The costs disallowed by the notice are deducted by the CO from any payment vouchers submitted by the contractor. If

---

[Section 11:7]

[1] 48 C.F.R. § 9903.405. *See generally* Manos, 2 Government Contract Costs & Pricing § 66.

[2] FAR 31.201-6(a).

[3] FAR 31.201-6(e).

[4] FAR 31.203(d).

[Section 11:8]

[1] FAR 42.801.

[2] FAR 42.801(f); *see* FAR 52.233-1.

[3] FAR 42.803(b)(2).

[4] DFARS 242.705-2.

the contractor disagrees with the deduction from current payments, the contractor may submit a request to the cognizant CO to consider whether the unreimbursed costs should be paid, file a claim under the "Disputes" clause of the contract, or both.[5] (DCAA Form 1, "Notice of Contract Costs Suspended and/or Disapproved," appears as Appendix K to this Compliance Handbook.)

§ 11:9 Certificate of final indirect costs

The FAR implements the statutory requirement that a contractor's final indirect cost rate proposal "shall not be accepted and no agreement shall be made to establish indirect cost rates unless the costs have been certified by the contractor."[1] The "Certificate of Final Indirect Costs" must be signed by an individual of the contractor's organization at a level not lower than a vice president or chief financial officer of the business segment of the contractor that submits the proposal.[2] The individual executing the "Certificate" on behalf of the contractor certifies that he or she has *reviewed* the proposal and that, to the best of his or her *knowledge and belief,* the costs included to establish the final indirect cost rates are allowable under the cost principles and the proposal does not include any costs that are expressly unallowable under the cost principles.[3] (The "Certificate" is set forth in Appendix L.)

§ 11:10 "Penalties for unallowable costs" clause

Solicitations and contracts over $650,000, except fixed-price contracts without cost incentives or any firm-fixed-price contract for the purchase of commercial items, must include the "Penalties for Unallowable Costs" clause.[1] (See Appendix M.) Under the terms of the clause, if the CO determines that a cost submitted by the contractor in its proposal is expressly unallowable under a cost principle, the contractor "shall be assessed" a penalty equal to the amount of the disallowed cost plus Treasury rate interest on the amount paid to the contractor, including progress payments, in excess of the amount to which the contractor was

---

[5]FAR 42.803(b)(3).

[Section 11:9]

[1]FAR 42.703-2; see 10 U.S.C.A. § 2324(h); 41 U.S.C.A. § 256(h).
[2]FAR 52.242-4, para. (a)(3).
[3]FAR 52.242-4, para. (c).

[Section 11:10]

[1]FAR 42.709-6; see FAR 52.242-3.

Cost Allowability § 11:10

entitled.[2] Moreover, if the CO determines that a cost submitted by the contractor in a proposal contains a cost previously determined to be unallowable for that contractor, then the contractor will be assessed a penalty equal to *two* times the amount of the disallowed cost allocated to the contract.[3] The CO's assessments of penalties under the clause are final decisions subject to appeal by the contractor under the "Disputes" clause.[4]

The CO is authorized to *waive* the penalties for unallowable indirect costs when (1) the contractor withdraws the proposal before the Government formally initiates an audit and submits a revised proposal, (2) the amount of the unallowable costs is $10,000 or less, or (3) the contractor demonstrates that it had in place an adequate internal control process for excluding unallowable costs and that the costs were inadvertently incorporated into the proposal.[5]

Cases & Commentary: In one case, the contracting officer disallowed several categories of costs under various cost-reimbursement contracts. Furthermore, the contracting officer claimed that the costs were "expressly unallowable" under the FAR cost principles and assessed a penalty equal to 100% of the amount of the disallowed costs (a so-called "level 1 penalty") pursuant to the "Penalties For Unallowable Costs" clause included in certain of those contracts.[6] The Armed Services Board of Contract Appeals reaffirmed an earlier decision that the Government has the burden of proof in justifying the penalties.[7] Furthermore, quoting from the earlier decision, the Board stated that in order to prove that a disputed cost was "expressly unallowable," the Government needed to show that there were no circumstances under which a contractor could reasonably conclude that the costs would be allowable:

> The FAR and CAS definitions of "expressly unallowable" point to the need to examine the particular principle involved in light of the surrounding circumstances. Moreover, since Congress adopted the "expressly unallowable" standard to make it clear that a penalty should not be assessed where there were reasonable differences of opinion about the allowability of costs, we think the Government must show that it was unreasonable under all the circumstances

---

[2] FAR 52.242-3, para. (d).

[3] FAR 52.242-3, para. (e).

[4] FAR 52.242-3, para. (f).

[5] FAR 42.709-5.

[6] *See Appeal of Fiber Materials, Inc.*, A.S.B.C.A. No. 53616, 07-1 B.C.A. (CCH) ¶ 33563, 2007 WL 1252481 (Armed Serv. B.C.A. 2007).

[7] *See In re General Dynamics Corp.*, A.S.B.C.A. No. 49372, 02-2 B.C.A. (CCH) ¶ 31888, 2002 WL 1307491 (Armed Serv. B.C.A. 2002), rev'd in part on other grounds, 365 F.3d 1380 (Fed. Cir. 2004).

§ 11:10　　　Government Contract Compliance Handbook

for a person in the contractor's position to conclude that the costs were allowable. The scope of the inquiry will vary with the clarity and complexity of the particular cost principle and the circumstances involved.

Also, the amount of the disallowance for a particular item cost that was allocable to a specific contract was in several cases less than $10,000. The Board noted that although the "Penalties For Unallowable Costs" clause provided that the contracting offer "may" waive penalties pursuant to the criteria in FAR 42.709-5, that regulation provided that the contracting officer "shall" waive them if the costs that are subject to the penalties are $10,000 or less. Thus, the contracting officer was required to waive them in all such cases.

§ 11:11　Referral of fraud cases

Both the CO and the contract auditor are tasked with responsibility to refer matters to the appropriate criminal investigative organization if there is any evidence that the contractor "knowingly" submitted unallowable costs.[1] The regulations do not attempt to define the term "knowingly." However, the impetus is placed on the contractor to show that any submission of unallowable costs was inadvertent. The best way for a contractor to avoid the problem is to establish an internal control and review system to identify unallowable costs and preclude them from being included in final indirect cost rate proposals.

C. FREQUENTLY ASKED QUESTIONS

§ 11:12　Questions & answers

Question 1: For a cost to be allowable it must be reasonable, allocable, allowable under the cost principles and the terms of the contract, and consistent with the Cost Accounting Standards, if applicable, or generally accepted accounting principles. What is the test for whether a cost is "reasonable?"

Answer 1: Under the regulations, a cost is "reasonable" if, in its nature and amount, it does not exceed that which would be incurred by a prudent person in the conduct of competitive business.[1] What is reasonable depends on a variety of factors, including whether the cost (a) is of the type generally recognized as ordinary and necessary for the conduct of the contractor's business or performance of the contract, (b) comports with gener-

---

[Section 11:11]
　[1]FAR 42.709-2(a)(3), (b)(3).
[Section 11:12]
　[1]FAR 31.201-3(a).

ally accepted sound business practices, arm's-length bargaining, and federal and state laws and regulations, (c) is consistent with the contractor's responsibilities to the Government, its other customers, its owners and employees, and the public at large, and (d) deviates significantly from the contractor's established practices.[2] In short, whether or not a cost is reasonable is largely a factual question. If you intend to incur a cost that is significant in amount and is unusual based on your past practices, you would be well advised to document fully the reasons why the incurrence of such a cost makes sound business judgment. This documentation can take the form of board minutes, cost approval reports, or any other writing that can be preserved in the ordinary course of business.

Question 2: Must a cost directly benefit the Government to be allocable under a Government contract?

Answer 2: There are three separate tests for allocability under a Government contract. A cost is allocable to a Government contract if it (a) is incurred specifically for the contract, (b) benefits both the contract and other work and can be distributed to them in reasonable proportion to the benefits received, or (c) is necessary to the overall operation of the business, although a direct relationship cannot be shown.[3] A cost that meets *any* of these three tests is allocable. It is not necessary that a cost be a *direct* benefit to a Government contract to meet the last test, i.e., necessary to the overall business.[4] For example, costs that are a prerequisite for doing business, such as franchise taxes, meet the third test even though they have no direct benefit to a Government contract. Furthermore, costs incurred by a contractor to obtain commercial business and remain a viable commercial enterprise may be allocable to Government contracts even though the benefit is indirect.

Question 3: Do the cost principles apply to contracts for commercial items?

Answer 3: Contracts for commercial items generally must be firm-fixed-price contracts or fixed-price contracts with economic

---

[2]FAR 31.201-3(b).

[3]FAR 31.201-4.

[4]*See Boeing North American, Inc. v. Roche*, 298 F.3d 1274 (Fed. Cir. 2002) (involving the allocability of legal fees incurred in defending a shareholder derivative suit and holding that the word "benefit" is an accounting concept that describes the nexus required between the cost and the contract to which it is allocated and cautioning that that the requirement of a "benefit" to the Government was not "designed to permit contracting officers, the [board of contract appeals], or this court to embark on an amorphous inquiry into whether a particular cost sufficiently 'benefits' the government so that the cost should recoverable from the government"). *See generally* Manos, Allowability of Legal Costs, Briefing Papers No. 05-5 (Apr. 2005).

§ 11:12   GOVERNMENT CONTRACT COMPLIANCE HANDBOOK

price adjustment, which are primarily awarded based on sealed bids or negotiated based on price analysis.[5] Therefore, the cost principles do not apply to the initial pricing of a commercial item contract. Moreover, the cost principles do not apply in determining the amount to be paid a contractor when the Government terminates a commercial item contract for convenience.[6]

However, with regard to pricing *modifications* to commercial item contracts, the regulations do not expressly exempt such modifications from application of the cost principles and, in fact, provide that commercial item procurements are subject to the policies set forth in other parts of the FAR to the extent that they are not inconsistent with the policies in FAR Part 12, "Acquisition of Commercial Items."[7] Despite this ambiguity, as a practical matter, the cost principles probably do not apply to pricing of modifications in commercial item contracts. Under the "Commercial Items" contract clause, any changes to a commercial item contract must be bilateral.[8] Therefore, if the contractor does not agree to the modification price, the change cannot be issued unilaterally by the CO as is the case under noncommercial item contracts. (Commercial item acquisitions are discussed in §§ 10:1 et seq.)

Question 4: If a type of cost is not specifically listed in the FAR cost principles, is it allowable or unallowable?

Answer 4: The FAR cost principles do not cover every element of cost. The fact that a cost is not identified in the cost principles does not imply that it is either allowable or unallowable. The determination of allowability is based on whether the cost is reasonable, allocable, consistent with contract terms, and in accordance with either the Cost Accounting Standards, if applicable, or with generally accepted accounting principles and on the treatment of similar or related items that are expressly covered.[9]

Question 5: If a type of cost is identified as allowable under the cost principles, does that mean that it is automatically allowable under a Government contract?

Answer 5: No. Even if a cost is specifically identified as allowable under the cost principles, it still must meet the other tests for allowability, i.e., reasonableness, allocability, and consistency with the Cost Accounting Standards or generally accepted ac-

---

[5] FAR 12.207.
[6] FAR 12.403(d)(1)(ii).
[7] FAR 12.102(c).
[8] FAR 52.212-4, para. (c).
[9] FAR 31.204(d).

§ 11:12

counting principles.[10] Moreover, even if a cost meets all of these requirements, it still may be unallowable based on a specific contractual provision.[11] For example, a cost-reimbursement contract may establish a ceiling on the amount of indirect costs, such as overhead or G&A costs, which may be recovered by the contractor. Such a provision is enforceable and may result in a cost being unallowable even though it meets all of the other tests of allowability.

Question 6: It is sometimes difficult to determine the exact nature of a cost. To what extent can the parties define that cost in the terms of the contract?

Answer 6: If a cost is plainly unallowable, the Contracting Officer cannot simply agree to make it allowable. On the other hand, the parties can enter into an advance agreement with respect to the reasonableness or allocability of a cost or to the allowability of a cost to the extent such treatment is not inconsistent with the specific cost principles.[12] In the absence of an advance agreement, the intent of the parties may be determinative. For example in one case, the contractor entered into a commercial contract for the production and delivery of a new rocket motor. The contract specifically stated that that it did not include the initial engineering work needed to develop the motor and the contract price did not include any amounts for this effort. The Government challenged the contractor's treatment of the initial development costs as an "independent research and development" expense on the basis that that engineering work was a necessary prerequisite of the production of the motor, whereas the independent research and development cost principle specifically excluded the cost of effort "required in the performance of a contract."[13] The court found that since the parties had clearly expressed their intention to exclude the development work from the contract, completion of the development of the motor was not, in a legal sense, "required in the performance of [the] contract" even though in a physical sense it was an undeniable prerequisite to the production of the motor.[14]

Question 7: The FAR requires that contracts that provide for establishment of final indirect cost rates must include a clause

---

[10]FAR 31.204, 31.201-2(a).

[11]FAR 31.201-2(a)(4).

[12]FAR 31.109.

[13]FAR 31.205-18(a).

[14]*ATK Thiokol, Inc. v. U.S.*, 68 Fed. Cl. 612 (2005), 48 GC 8. *See generally* Burgett, Feature Comment: Decision on Accounting for IR&D Costs Has Important Implications for Intellectual Property Rights of Government Contractors, 48 GC 12 (Jan. 18, 2006); Manos, Postscript: Independent Research and Development Costs, 20 Nash & Cibinic Rep. (Jan. 2006).

§ 11:12   GOVERNMENT CONTRACT COMPLIANCE HANDBOOK

requiring the contractor to sign a "Certificate of Final Indirect Costs."[15] Does a contractor, through this certification, guarantee that there are no unallowable costs in its final indirect costs rate proposal?

Answer 7: The clause requires that the person who executes the "Certificate" must be, at a minimum, a vice president or chief financial officer of the company and must certify that he has reviewed the proposal and that, "to the best of my knowledge and belief," the representations that the costs included to establish the final indirect cost rates are allowable under the cost principles and that the proposal does not include any expressly unallowable costs.[16] It is likely that the person who executes the "Certificate" is not, through his signature, "guaranteeing" that the statements are true. The individual is simply certifying in good faith that he believes them to be true. Thus, including a cost in the proposal that could *reasonably* be argued is allowable would probably not violate the "Certificate."

Question 8: Does the Government have to show that a contractor intentionally included a unallowable cost in its final indirect costs rate proposal for there to be a breach of the "Certificate of Final Indirect Costs"?

Answer 8: You may make a false certification when you include an "expressly" unallowable cost in your proposal through either *oversight or inadvertence*. This is because the "Certificate" states that you "have reviewed this proposal." Therefore, accidentally including even one item that is unallowable could, in theory, be viewed as an automatic violation of the "Certificate" because the Government could allege that you were required to review each and every item for allowability, and had you performed such a review you undoubtedly would have discovered the unallowable item. In short, there is no explicit "excuse" for your inclusion of an "expressly" unallowable item.

The obvious response would be that the required "review" is simply that: a review and not a line-by-line analysis of each item of cost contained in the proposal. You would contend that you must maintain "adequate" accounting procedures, not procedures that guarantee the total absence of errors. Therefore, as long as appropriate procedures are in place, you could certify to the best of your "knowledge and belief" that all costs in the proposal are properly allowable. Obviously, this argument makes more sense in light of practical realities. However, there is no guarantee that the Government will embrace this approach and even if does, questions remain—for example, what is an acceptable level of er-

---

[15]FAR 42.703-2, 52.242-4.
[16]FAR 52.242-4.

Cost Allowability § 11:12

ror inherent in an accounting system?

In recognition of the fact that a line-by-line review is not a realistic solution, the FAR permits contractors to use statistical sampling to identify and exclude unallowable costs from their proposals. Sampling is permitted if it results in an unbiased sample that is a reasonable representation of the sampling universe, if large- dollar-value or high-risk transactions are separately reviewed, and if the process permits audit verification. The regulation further recommends that the sampling methods should be the subject of an advance agreement between the contractor and the Government.[17]

Using sampling techniques, especially when they are covered by an advance agreement, goes a long way to eliminating the uncertainty inherent in executing the "Certificate of Final Indirect Costs." *However, it is still important to review your indirect cost proposals carefully.* Doing this will have two effects: (1) it may disclose at least some of the unallowable items that may have crept in, and (2) it will provide a stronger basis for you to contend that the certification was in fact "to the best of my knowledge and belief."

Question 9: What is a contractor's liability for a false certification of final indirect costs?

Answer 9: It is likely that if you include false information in your "Certificate of Final Indirect Costs," the Government would proceed against you under the False Claims Act or false statements statute.[18] The Government could also pursue you under the Program Fraud Civil Remedies Act of 1986 and its implementing regulations, which authorize the Government to proceed administratively against you in certain cases and to assess civil penalties.[19] (See §§ 1:1 et seq.)

Question 10: What are the ramifications if the contractor refuses to sign the "Certificate of Final Indirect Costs"?

Answer 10: The FAR states that "a proposal shall not be accepted and no agreement shall be made to establish indirect cost rates unless the costs have been certified by the contractor."[20] The regulations provide, however, that the agency head or designee may waive the certification requirement when it is determined to be in interests of the United States, and, where a waiver is not appropriate, the CO may unilaterally establish the

---

[17]FAR 31.201-6(c).
[18]18 U.S.C.A. §§ 287, 1001; 31 U.S.C.A. §§ 3729 to 3733.
[19]31 U.S.C.A. §§ 3801 to 3812.
[20]FAR 42.703-2(a).

§ 11:12   GOVERNMENT CONTRACT COMPLIANCE HANDBOOK

rates.[21] In establishing the rate, the regulations caution COs to set it sufficiently low "to ensure that unallowable costs will not be reimbursed."[22]

Question 11: If a contractor includes in its final indirect cost rate proposal a cost that is expressly unallowable under a cost principle, will the contractor be assessed the double penalty provided for in the "Penalties for Unallowable Costs" clause?

Answer 11: The FAR provides that where a contractor includes in its final indirect cost rate proposal or final statement of costs indirect costs that were determined to be unallowable *before* the proposal submission, the CO *shall* assess a penalty in the amount of two times the amount of the disallowed costs.[23] The regulations identify four situations that evidence "prior determinations of unallowability":[24] (1) a DCAA Form 1, "Notice of Contract Costs Suspended and/or Disapproved," or similar notice was issued but was not appealed or withdrawn; (2) a CO's final decision disallowing costs was issued but was not appealed; (3) a prior board or court decision upheld a cost disallowance involving your contracts; and (4) a determination of unallowability existed under the FAR provision "Accounting for Unallowable Costs."[25]

Question 12: Do the penalties for unallowable costs[26] include the amount of the unallowable costs themselves?

Answer 12: No. Payment by the contractor of any penalty assessed pursuant to the regulations does not constitute repayment of any unallowable cost that has been paid by the Government to the contractor.[27]

III. HOW TO RECOGNIZE THE PROBLEM

§ 11:13 Generally

Because costs are continually charged to ongoing contracts, complying with the cost regulations is a continuing process during contract performance. Thus, you must determine whether costs are allowable *as they are being charged*. However, it is especially critical that you closely review the costs charged to your indirect cost pools before you submit proposals for billing rates and final indirect cost rates, as well as before you submit progress payment requests. (See §§ 14:1 et seq.)

---

[21]FAR 42.703-2(b), (c).
[22]FAR 42.703-2(c)(2)(ii).
[23]FAR 42.709-1(a)(2).
[24]FAR 42.709-3(b).
[25]FAR 31.201-6.
[26]*See* FAR 42.709-1.
[27]FAR 52.242-3, para. (h).

Although you must always be careful in charging costs on your Government contracts, you should be aware of certain situations in which problems with unallowable costs almost always occur. For example, anytime you realize that a cost would be *unallowable* under one cost principle but potentially *allowable* under another cost principle, you must examine that expenditure carefully to determine the essential nature or primary purpose of the expenditure or apportion the cost between two or more categories of cost if appropriate.[1] Similarly, when you see that a cost has been *reclassified* in your system, especially where the cost has been reclassified as an allowable cost, you must examine that cost carefully to ensure that reclassification was appropriate. Finally, certain *types* of costs require special attention. For example, when a cost relates to a company event at which alcoholic beverages are provided, you should take particular care to ensure that you do not charge the Government for any of the alcoholic beverages costs.[2] Similarly, you should be particularly wary when charging an expense that may include interest as one of its elements to ensure that you do not charge the Government for any part of the interest cost.[3]

§ 11:14 Examples

Promotional, recruitment, or training costs: Assume that you make a film that depicts your company in glowing terms. You show this film to potential employees at job fairs, as well as to all new employees as part of their training. In addition, when a public group or school requests that someone from your company speak to them about the company, the film is shown during these presentations. Is the cost of making the film allowable under your Government contract?

This is a classic example of a cost that may be governed by a number of different cost principles. Under the FAR cost principle for public relations and advertising costs, the cost of promotional material is unallowable.[1] However, under separate cost principles, certain types of recruitment costs are allowable[2] and training

---

[Section 11:13]
[1] FAR 31.204(d).
[2] FAR 31.205-51.
[3] FAR 31.205-1(f)(5).

[Section 11:14]
[1] FAR 31.205-20.
[2] FAR 31.205-34.

costs are generally allowable.[3] Thus, the cost for a film that could be shown to active recruits, new employees, or the public at large could be *either* an allowable training or recruitment cost *or* an unallowable promotional cost.

You must determine the essential nature of the cost to determine how to handle the cost. In this example, it appears that the primary purpose of making the film was for recruitment and training and not for general public promotional purposes, and, thus, if the cost satisfies all the additional tests for allowability, it probably would be allowable. However, if the film had been made to show to public groups, the cost would be unallowable.

This case demonstrates the importance of classifying the cost *at the time the cost is incurred* rather than later. If you made the film to show to the general public but you did not classify the cost until your company recognized a secondary training function for the film, you may be tempted to include the cost as an allowable training cost, which could subject your company to liability.

Alcoholic beverages costs and employee morale costs: To enhance employee morale, your company holds an annual employee awards dinner at which alcoholic beverages are served. The caterer presents you with an itemized bill showing food, alcoholic beverages, and other miscellaneous charges. Is the cost of the entire dinner or any portion of it allowable?

This is a classic instance where costs should be *apportioned*. The cost principle for employee morale, health, welfare, food service, and dormitory costs and credits provides that employee morale costs are generally allowable.[4] The cost principle for alcoholic beverage costs unqualifiedly provides that such costs are unallowable.[5] Accordingly, the cost of alcoholic beverages needs to be segregated from the rest of the dinner costs and put into an unallowable cost category. Generally, the rest of the dinner costs would constitute allowable employee morale costs.

If the employee in charge of the awards dinner was unaware of the alcoholic beverages cost prohibition and failed to ask the catering company to identify and segregate the alcoholic beverages cost, and, as a result, the entire award dinner cost is placed in an allowable cost pool, your company could face stiff penalties. Although the employee did not know that what the employee was doing was wrong, liability might still be imposed on the theory that your company failed to implement policies to avoid the inclusion of this type of unallowable cost in your charges or that your

---

[3] FAR 31.205-44.
[4] FAR 31.205-13.
[5] FAR 31.205-51.

company failed to bring such policies to the attention of the employee. Although at the time of signing the "Certificate of Final Indirect Costs" your chief financial officer may have had no knowledge that the cost of the dinner included the alcoholic beverages, he arguably should have known that the company's existing accounting procedures were inadequate in this regard. Similarly, if the DCAA had cautioned you by letter after last year's employee awards dinner that it expected you to amend your procedures to segregate alcoholic beverages charges from all future "company morale" expenses, and you did not take appropriate action, you could be assessed penalties.

In contrast, even if you had established clear guidelines regarding the unallowability of alcoholic beverages costs, your employee may have chosen to disregard the guidelines when the caterer refused to prepare a breakdown of the alcoholic beverages costs. This is a difficult area. Your policies were obviously "deliberately" violated. Yet there was no reason for the chief financial officer to have known this. Arguably, both the certification and (even more likely) the penalty provisions have been violated. This situation demonstrates that, in the real world, guidelines, diligent monitoring, elaborate sampling, and other compliance techniques cannot provide *absolute* assurance that an unallowable cost will not creep into your system. In the final analysis, you may have to rely on the good faith and understanding of the DCAA auditor and the CO. Keep in mind, though, that the CO's discretion under the "Penalties for Unallowable Costs" clause appears to be very limited and the imposition of a penalty appears to be *mandatory* if your proposal includes a clearly unallowable cost.

Employee morale or entertainment costs: Your company has an annual Fourth of July athletic outing and dinner at the local country club. The club charges your company $40 per person for the day. In addition to your company's employees, you invite a number of customers. Are any of these costs allowable? Are any unallowable?

Here you have a situation where costs can be apportioned between employees and customers. The costs associated with employee attendance are arguably allowable employee morale costs,[6] while the costs associated with customer attendance are unallowable entertainment costs.[7] Assuming that your accounting staff makes the proper apportionment and includes only the allowable employee morale costs (excluding costs for alcoholic beverages) there should be no problem. However, the "athletic outing" portion of the activity may be deemed to be recreation that is unal-

---

[6] FAR 31.205-13.
[7] FAR 31.205-14.

§ 11:14   GOVERNMENT CONTRACT COMPLIANCE HANDBOOK

lowable even if it is for employee morale purposes.[8] Accordingly, under this scenario only the cost of the employees' dinners (exclusive of alcoholic beverages) would be an allowable cost. This points out the importance of itemized billing that permits separation and segregation of allowable from unallowable costs.

Company-sponsored blood drive: Your company sponsors a Red Cross blood drive in your facility and allows each of your employees two hours of compensated time to give blood. Are these labor costs allowable?

Here you have a conflict between two cost principles. One provides that contributions and donations are unallowable,[9] while the other provides that allowable public relations costs include participation in community service activities such as blood bank drives.[10] Here, the rule that the *specific takes precedence over the general* would apply. In this instance, the specific reference in cost principle for public relations costs to the allowability of the costs of participation in a blood drive[11] would take priority over the general limitation in the cost principle for contributions or donations regarding the unallowability of contributions.[12]

Complying with the Cost Accounting Standards: A portion of the home office expense allocated to your division represents the cost of staff support for the division's engineering department. The engineering department is largely engaged in developing new commercial products. The DCAA contends that under Cost Accounting Standard 410, "Allocation of Business Unit General and Administrative Expenses to Final Cost Objectives,"[13] these costs should have been included in the division's engineering overhead account rather than in home office G&A expense. The DCAA concludes that your company is not in compliance with Cost Accounting Standard 410, disallows the added cost from the final indirect cost rate proposal, and persuades the CO to assess a 100% penalty under the "Penalties for Unallowable Costs" clause.[14]

To be "allowable," a cost must not only be consistent with the requirements of the cost principles[15] but must also be reasonable and allocable and comply with the Cost Accounting Standards or

---

[8] FAR 31.205-13(c).

[9] FAR 31.205-8.

[10] FAR 31.205-1(e)(3).

[11] FAR 31.205-1(e)(3).

[12] FAR 31.205-8.

[13] 44 C.F.R. § 9904.410. *See generally* Manos, 2 Government Contract Costs & Pricing § 71.

[14] FAR 52.242-3.

[15] FAR 31.205.

generally accepted accounting principles and with any specific terms of the contract.[16] Thus, if it is determined that a cost has not been allocated consistent with the Cost Accounting Standards, it will be unallowable.

IV. COMPLIANCE INITIATIVES

§ 11:15 Generally

As noted earlier in this chapter, your ability to classify costs correctly depends on a two-step analysis: (1) determining the essential nature or primary purpose of the cost; and (2) determining whether the cost satisfies all of the regulatory requirements to constitute an allowable cost. Your ability to perform this analysis will require the efforts of upper management, supervisors and middle management, nonsupervisory labor personnel, and accounting department personnel.

§ 11:16 Upper management

Upper management should establish the *criteria* to follow when determining the essential nature of a cost for classification purposes on Government contracts. Upper management may even decide how *specific* questionable costs will be treated.

Upper management has essentially three major tasks to accomplish to help ensure that unallowable costs are excluded from proposals and other transactions that are subject to the cost principles. First, upper management must *communicate* to employees the importance of correctly identifying the nature of costs that are incurred and must provide those employees with sufficiently *detailed guidelines* to permit them to make that determination. Upper management's task is to establish procedures that give employees and supervisors *little or no discretion* in determining the nature of a cost and thus reduce the chance that mistakes will be made.

Second, upper management must also implement effective *internal audit procedures*. Internal cost principles compliance audits should be conducted frequently. These audits should cover the same tests customarily performed by the DCAA and should include a sampling of charges for each department and conversations with employees regarding their understanding of the company's charging guidelines and whether they have experienced difficulty in implementing the guidelines.

Third, upper management must be aware that certain items of expense fall into *"gray" areas*—they may or may not be allowable. The "gray" areas can involve single items of substantial expense

---

[16]FAR 31.201-2(a).

§ 11:16   GOVERNMENT CONTRACT COMPLIANCE HANDBOOK

or a continuing number of relatively small items. The company's procedures must *identify those areas* and provide steps that will ensure that the classification of such costs is brought to the attention of upper management for final determination.

§ 11:17   Supervisors & middle management

Middle management has the task of implementing upper management's cost-charging criteria. Middle management plays a key role in successfully identifying unallowable costs because it is this group that initiates many of the activities that generate controversial costs, such as activities involving selling and marketing,[1] independent research and development and bids and proposals,[2] employee morale and health,[3] entertainment,[4] public relations and advertising,[5] and travel.[6]

The first and perhaps most important point at which a supervisor has immediate control of a cost is at the time the supervisor authorizes the incurrence of the charge. Thus, your company's procedures should not only define the criteria for charging the various cost codes but should also require that the classification of the cost be identified *at the time it is authorized*. This will reduce the chance that the nature of the activity will be mischaracterized later and after its true cost is known.

Second, your procedures should require that middle management review not only the time cards of nonsupervisory employees but the *charges to overhead accounts* as well. This may not disclose individual instances in which a specific cost item was incorrectly characterized, but it should provide an indication of where a pattern of such activity has developed.

Third, your procedures must require that middle management *document* any *subsequent changes* in the charging of an item. For example, if certain costs are transferred from a selling or marketing expense account to a bid and proposal account, the justification should be clearly documented to avoid any later suggestion that possibly unallowable costs were recharacterized as allowable.

§ 11:18   Nonsupervisory employees

Nonsupervisory employees' role in complying with the cost

[Section 11:17]

[1]*See* FAR 31.205-38.
[2]*See* FAR 31.205-18.
[3]*See* FAR 31.205-13.
[4]*See* FAR 31.205-14.
[5]*See* FAR 31.205-1.
[6]*See* FAR 31.205-46.

principles is generally limited and may involve only the treatment of reimbursable expenses. Thus, where management has implemented effective procedures, nonsupervisory labor should have essentially a mechanical recording function to perform with *limited discretion* for determining the essential nature of the cost.

An important exception, however, involves employees engaged in independent research and development/bid and proposal work. Those individuals may, as part of filling out time cards, be required to determine whether their work constitutes independent research and development, bid and proposal, or one of the various types of selling and marketing costs. In these cases, there is a substantial risk of mischaracterizing the nature of the activity, thus, making the existence of clear guidelines extremely crucial.

At the nonsupervisory employee level, there should be the least chance for mischaracterization of a cost. If your company enforces well-drafted guidelines for identifying (and distinguishing between) different types of costs, and if the charging of costs is reviewed by middle management on a routine basis, most inadvertent errors by employees should be detected and eliminated.

§ 11:19 Accounting department

Finally, you cannot reduce the risk that an unallowable cost will be included in any proposal or transaction subject to the Government's cost principles unless you have established effective controls in the accounting department. Generally, the accounting department is responsible for preparing wage and indirect cost rates to be used in contract proposals and other transactions that are subject to the cost principles. However, in view of the provisions requiring that the chief financial officer or vice president *certify* that interim and final billing rates and requests for progress payments do not include unallowable costs, it has become even more crucial that the accounting department establish and adhere to procedures designed to screen out unallowable costs.

Your company's accounting department performs three different functions in ensuring compliance with the cost principles. First, it is responsible for *drafting the guidelines* that are to be used by others. This is not something that can be done in isolation. It is important that accounting personnel understand the nature of the company's operations and be aware of the practical difficulties that can arise in determining exactly how a given item is to be charged. Thus, development of effective guidelines requires consultation with others, including those in the middle management group. This is especially true for costs that fall into the "gray" areas. If this effort still does not produce satisfactory guidelines, the accounting department should consider entering into an *advance agreement* with the Government regarding difficult items of cost.

Second, your accounting department is responsible for *accumulating and allocating costs* in accordance with the cost principles. In other words, it is one thing to establish a guideline to be used by middle management in identifying marketing costs as distinct from independent research and development expenses; it is another thing to ensure that those costs are allocated in accordance with the cost principles, Cost Accounting Standards, and generally accepted accounting principles. This requires a professional accounting staff committed to keeping abreast of current developments in the areas of accounting and Government contract regulations.

The third task is the preparation of the accounting information that will be used in contract proposals or in billing rates and progress payment requests. The certification requirements and the contract penalties relating to indirect cost proposals—not to mention the potential exposure to charges of fraud in any transaction subject to the cost principles—require that the accounting department *review each of the company's proposals* far more thoroughly than perhaps has been done in the past. In particular, it should consider an item-by-item review of a statistically significant number of charges to verify their allowability.

§ 11:20 Recommendations

Remember that regardless of the steps you may take to eliminate your liability for unallowable costs, it is possible only to *minimize*, not totally avoid, the risks. Accounting systems were never intended to be foolproof, and no accounting system can absolutely guarantee that all unallowable costs will be excluded. However, you can minimize the instances in which unallowable costs occur. Taking positive steps to control the frequency and magnitude of the occurrences should substantially reduce the possibility of incurring administrative, civil, or criminal penalties. The major steps you should take include the following:

(a) *Communicate* to employees the importance of correctly identifying the nature of costs that are incurred and provide those employees with sufficiently *detailed guidelines* to permit them to make the proper determinations.

(b) Implement effective *internal audit procedures*. This includes ensuring that questions about costs in *"gray" areas* are brought to the attention of the appropriate level of management for resolution.

(c) Define the nature of an expense *at the time it is authorized*, not afterward.

(d) Establish procedures that require that middle management review not only the time cards of nonsupervisory employees but also the *charges to overhead accounts*.

(e) Establish procedures that require that middle management *document* any *changes* in the charging of an item.

(f) *Work with others* to develop effective cost guidelines. Development of effective guidelines cannot be done in isolation; it requires a thorough knowledge of the operation of the company and consultation with others, including those in middle management.

(g) *Know the cost principles*. The accumulation and allocation of costs in accordance with the Government's cost principles requires a thorough knowledge of the regulations and a commitment to keeping abreast of current developments in the field.

(h) *Review each cost proposal thoroughly*. The certification requirements and the contract penalties relating to indirect cost proposals, not to mention the potential exposure to charges of fraud in any transaction subject to the cost principles, make it mandatory that your accounting department thoroughly review each proposal to be submitted to the Government and document that review.

Chapter 12

Cost Accounting

I. OVERVIEW
§ 12:1 Scope note

II. CURRENT REQUIREMENTS

A. COST ACCOUNTING STANDARDS
§ 12:2 Background
§ 12:3 Do the CAS apply to your company?
§ 12:4 —Exempt contracts
§ 12:5 —Waiver
§ 12:6 —Full CAS coverage
§ 12:7 —Modified CAS coverage
§ 12:8 CAS contract clauses
§ 12:9 Disclosure statement
§ 12:10 Educational institutions
§ 12:11 Accounting changes & contract adjustments

B. CFAO COMPLIANCE DETERMINATIONS
§ 12:12 Generally
§ 12:13 Types of noncompliance
§ 12:14 Initial finding of noncompliance
§ 12:15 Agreement with CFAO's initial finding
§ 12:16 Disagreement with CFAO's initial finding
§ 12:17 Unilateral accounting changes

C. COST ACCOUNTING STANDARDS VS. COST PRINCIPLES
§ 12:18 Generally

D. CONTRACTOR LIABILITY

1. Liability For False Statements
§ 12:19 Generally
§ 12:20 Solicitation representations & certifications
§ 12:21 Proposals where cost or pricing data are required
§ 12:22 Disclosure statements

§ 12:23   Overhead or final indirect cost certifications
§ 12:24   Cost impact proposals

2. Liability For False Claims

§ 12:25   Generally
§ 12:26   Errors in progress payment billings
§ 12:27   Overbilling on cost contracts & invoices

E. FREQUENTLY ASKED QUESTIONS

§ 12:28   Questions & answers

III. HOW TO RECOGNIZE THE PROBLEM

§ 12:29   Generally
§ 12:30   Examples

IV. COMPLIANCE INITIATIVES

§ 12:31   Generally
§ 12:32   Develop a system of internal controls
§ 12:33   Employ CAS-qualified personnel
§ 12:34   Educate your employees
§ 12:35   Recommendations

KeyCite®: Cases and other legal materials listed in KeyCite Scope can be researched through the KeyCite service on Westlaw®. Use KeyCite to check citations for form, parallel references, prior and later history, and comprehensive citator information, including citations to other decisions and secondary materials.

I. OVERVIEW

§ 12:1   Scope note

Assume you are a senior manager, comptroller, or contract administrator of a large Government contractor. You normally allocate and charge the cost of your Print Shop to your contracts as an indirect cost and have previously disclosed this accounting practice to the Government. You have just received a $12 million cost-reimbursement contract with the Army, which you proposed in accordance with your normal practices. Because performance of the contract will require the creation and production of a large number of operation and maintenance manuals, your contract administrator hires extra Print Shop personnel specifically to accomplish this task and instructs your accounting department to bill these labor charges directly to the new contract in the next payment voucher to the Army. The accounting department complies with the request. The Defense Contract Audit Agency

(DCAA) conducts an audit of the payment request, cites your company for a violation of Cost Accounting Standard (CAS) 401, and forwards your case to the Defense Department Inspector General for criminal investigation under the false claims and false statements statutes.

Ridiculous? Perhaps. Impossible? Not in today's contracting environment. The Government is conducting criminal investigations of this nature daily. The risk of committing fraud in CAS-related activities is very real. Nevertheless, because of the complexity of the CAS, the potential for liability is usually not as apparent to contractors as in other areas. Therefore, you must take great care to disclose your cost accounting practices accurately to the Government and to ensure compliance with the Standards if you are to avoid this kind of civil and criminal risk.

This chapter explains some of the key rules relating to the CAS and recommends steps you can take to ensure that you comply with them. The CAS are a complex subject that concerns only certain individuals within your company—managers, sales personnel, comptrollers, and contract administrators. As a result, the discussion that follows is specifically addressed to these officials.

II. CURRENT REQUIREMENTS

A. COST ACCOUNTING STANDARDS

§ 12:2 Background

In 1968, Congress directed the then General Accounting Office—now the Government Accountability Office (GAO)—to study the feasibility of applying cost accounting standards to negotiated defense contracts of $100,000 or more.[1] Cost accounting standards are now applied to defense contracts over $700,000, and will automatically increase to match the Truth In Negotiation Act threshold.[2] GAO issued a report in January 1970, identifying numerous benefits of applying cost accounting standards to the negotiation and performance of Government contracts. These benefits included; (1) providing a common framework for developing both prospective and actual costs by supplying guidance, support, and coordination for more consistent cost estimates and subsequent reports of actual costs, (2) facilitating the preparation, reporting, and auditing of cost data, and (3) providing guidance to ensure that incurred cost elements on a given contract are reported consistently and are comparable

---

[Section 12:2]

[1] Pub. L. No. 90-370, 82 Stat. 279.

[2] 41 U.S.C.A. § 1502(b)(1)(B); *see also* 76 Fed. Reg. 79545.

§ 12:2   GOVERNMENT CONTRACT COMPLIANCE HANDBOOK

to originally proposed costs as well as to costs presented in change orders, claims for reimbursement, and termination claims.[3]

Relying on the GAO's findings, in August 1970, Congress created the Cost Accounting Standards Board as a legislative agency.[4] The CAS Board was authorized to establish Cost Accounting Standards designed to achieve uniformity and consistency in cost accounting practices used by defense contractors and subcontractors. On September 30, 1980, the first CAS Board was dissolved when Congress failed to appropriate funds for its operation. Although the first CAS Board went out of existence, the 19 Standards that it promulgated in its almost 10 years of operation continue to have the force and effect of law.[5]

On November 17, 1988, the President signed the Office of Federal Procurement Policy (OFPP) Act Amendments of 1988. One of the provisions of the statute established an independent CAS Board within the OFPP.[6] The new Board, thus, resumed the functions of the first CAS Board.

Congress has given the Board "the exclusive authority to prescribe, amend, and rescind" the Cost Accounting Standards and related interpretations. All existing Standards that the previous CAS Board promulgated, thus, remain in effect until superseded or changed.[7] Once new Standards are promulgated, their use is mandatory by all executive agencies, both civilian and military, and by contractors and subcontractors for all negotiated prime contracts and subcontracts with the U.S. that exceed $500,000 (increased from the $100,000 threshold under the first Board's rules). However, although there were attempts to grant the CAS Board authority to promulgate rules covering the allowability of costs currently covered by Federal Acquisition Regulation (FAR) Part 31, the authority of the Board is limited to establishing rules regarding *allocation*, not allowability, of costs.[8]

Before promulgating new Standards and interpretations, the CAS Board must take into account, after consultation and discussions with the Comptroller General, professional accounting organizations, contractors, and other interested parties: the probable cost of implementation; advantages, disadvantages and

---

[3]GAO, "Feasibility Of Applying Uniform Cost-Accounting Standards To Negotiated Defense Contracts" (1970).

[4]Pub. L. No. 91-379, 84 Stat. 796.

[5]*See Boeing Co. v. U. S.*, 230 Ct. Cl. 663, 680 F.2d 132 (1982).

[6]OFPP Act § 26, as added by OFPP Act Amendments of 1988, Pub. L. No. 100-679, 102 Stat. 4059, § 5(a) (codified at 41 U.S.C.A. § 1502).

[7]41 U.S.C.A. § 1502(a)(1).

[8]41 U.S.C.A. § 1502(a)(1); *see generally* Manos, Government Contract Costs & Pricing; Arnavas, Government Contract Cost Recovery, Briefing Papers No. 01-6 (May 2001).

COST ACCOUNTING § 12:4

improvements anticipated in the pricing, administration, and settlement of disputes under Government contracts; and possible acceptable alternatives to a CAS change.[9] Any new or modified Standards and interpretations must be published in the *Federal Register* for comment before they become final and acquire the force and effect of law.[10]

The CAS Board may also exempt classes or categories of contractors and subcontractors from CAS requirements and establish procedures for the waiver of requirements with respect to individual contractors or subcontractors.[11] Finally, the Board is directed to prescribe regulations in the FAR to implement the CAS and any modifications or amendments.[12]

§ 12:3 Do the CAS apply to your company?

The first step in recognizing whether you have a CAS compliance problem is determining whether you are required to conform your cost accounting practices to the CAS. The CAS apply only to certain categories of Government contracts and subcontracts. Moreover, depending on whether certain criteria are met, your CAS-covered contract or subcontract may be exempt from compliance with all Standards except four, CAS 401, 402, 405, 406. You may find it difficult, however, to determine whether the CAS apply, in whole or in part, to your accounting practices since the rules can be complicated.

§ 12:4 Do the CAS apply to your company?—Exempt contracts

Basically, all prime and subcontracts are subject to CAS except for the following:[1]

(1) Sealed bid contracts.
(2) Negotiated contracts and subcontracts not in excess of the TINA threshold ($700,000). For purposes of this exception, an order issued by one segment to another segment of that company shall be treated as a subcontract.[2]
(3) Contracts and subcontracts with small businesses. The CAS adopt the definition of "small business" set forth in

---

[9]41 U.S.C.A. § 1502(c)(1).
[10]41 U.S.C.A. § 1502(c)(3).
[11]41 U.S.C.A. § 1502(b)(3).
[12]41 U.S.C.A. § 1502(f).

[Section 12:4]

[1]48 C.F.R. § 9903.201-1(b); *see generally* Manos, 2 Government Contract Costs & Pricing § 60.

[2]48 C.F.R. § 9903.201-1(b)(2).

§ 12:4   GOVERNMENT CONTRACT COMPLIANCE HANDBOOK

the Small Business Act and the rules and regulations of the Small Business Administration.[3]

(4) Contracts or subcontracts awarded to foreign governments or their agents or instrumentalities or, insofar as the requirements of CAS other than CAS 401, 402 are concerned, any contract or subcontract awarded to a foreign concern.[4]

(5) Contracts and subcontracts where the price is set by law or regulation.[5]

(6) Firm-fixed-price and fixed-price with economic price adjustment provisions (provided that the price adjustment is not based on actual costs incurred), time-and-materials, and labor-hour contracts and subcontracts for the acquisition of commercial items.[6]

(7) Contracts or subcontracts of less than $7.5 million, provided that, at the time of award, the business unit of the contractor or subcontractor is not currently performing any CAS-covered contracts or subcontracts valued at $7.5 million or greater.[7]

(8) Subcontracts under the NATO PHM Ship program to be performed outside the U.S. by a foreign concern.[8]

(9) Contracts and subcontracts executed and performed entirely outside the U.S., its territories, and possessions.[9]

(10) Firm-fixed-price contracts and subcontracts awarded on the basis of adequate price competition without the submission of cost or pricing data.[10]

Cases & Commentary:

Effective October 11, 2011, the CAS Board issued a final rule eliminating the exemption at 48 C.F.R. 9903-201(b)(14) from the Cost Accounting Standards for contracts executed and performed entirely outside the United States, its territories, and

---

[3] 15 U.S.C.A. § 637(b)(6); 48 C.F.R. § 9903.301.

[4] 48 C.F.R. § 9903.201-1(b)(4).

[5] 48 C.F.R. § 9903.201-1(b)(5).

[6] 48 C.F.R. § 9903.201-1(b)(6). Effective February 12, 2007, FAR was amended to add Time & Material and Labor Hour contracts as an acceptable contract type for acquiring commercial items to implement § 1432 of the National Defense Authorization Act for Fiscal Year 2004, Pub. L. No. 108-136. In light of that, the CAS Board determined that there was no significant benefit in applying CAS to T&M/LH contracts for commercial items. Thus, effective July 3, 2007, 48 C.F.R. § 9903-201-1(b) was revised to exclude such contracts and subcontracts from coverage.

[7] 48 C.F.R. § 9903.201-1(b)(7).

[8] 48 C.F.R. § 9903.201-1(b)(13).

[9] 48 C.F.R. § 9903.201-1(b)(14).

[10] 48 C.F.R. § 9903.201-1(b)(15).

possessions.[11] However, all other exemptions continue to be available to foreign concerns including 9903-201(b)(4).

Thus, even if other exemptions did not apply, foreign concerns would only be required to comply with CAS 401 and 402.

§ 12:5 Do the CAS apply to your company?—Waiver

The CAS Board is authorized to waive the CAS requirements and to establish procedures for the granting of waivers.[1] The head of an executive agency is authorized to waive the requirements of the CAS for contractors primarily engaged in commercial work if the contract or subcontract is valued at less than $15 million and certain other criteria are met.[2] An agency may also grant a waiver "under exceptional circumstances where necessary to meet the needs of the agency."[3] In addition, an agency may request that the CAS Board waive the requirements when a contractor or subcontractor refuses to accept a contract that contains the CAS clause and no other source is available to provide the necessary supplies or services on a timely basis.[4]

§ 12:6 Do the CAS apply to your company?—Full CAS coverage

The extent or degree to which you are subject to the CAS regulation depends on the value of your CAS-covered contracts and when you receive them. If your Government contract meets any of the criteria set forth below, your company is subject to "full" CAS coverage, i.e., you must comply with *all* of the Cost Accounting Standards:[1]

(1) You receive a single CAS-covered contract (that is, a contract that does not qualify under any of the exemptions) of $50 million or more during the current cost accounting period (typically your fiscal year).

(2) You received $50 million or more in net CAS-covered contract awards during the preceding cost accounting period.

---

[11]76 Fed. Reg. 49365.

[Section 12:5]

[1]41 U.S.C.A. § 1502(b)(2).
[2]48 C.F.R. § 9903.201-5.
[3]48 C.F.R. § 9903.201-5.
[4]48 C.F.R. § 9903.201-5.

[Section 12:6]

[1]48 C.F.R. § 9903.201-2(a).

§ 12:7 Do the CAS apply to your company?—Modified CAS coverage

However, if you have not received a single CAS-covered contract of $50 million or more in the current cost accounting period and you received less than $50 million in covered contracts in the preceding period, you are only subject to "modified CAS coverage." Modified coverage requires that you follow *only* CAS 401, "Consistency in Estimating, Accumulating, and Reporting Costs," CAS 402, "Consistency in Allocating Costs Incurred for the Same Purpose," CAS 405, "Accounting for Unallowable Costs," and CAS 406, "Cost Accounting Period."[1]

If any one contract is awarded to you with modified CAS coverage, all CAS-covered contracts awarded to you during that cost accounting period must also have modified coverage. However, once you receive a single CAS-covered contract of $50 million or more, that contract and any covered contracts awarded to you thereafter will be subject to full CAS coverage.[2]

§ 12:8 CAS contract clauses

All contracts subject to the CAS must include one of two clauses—a full coverage clause or a modified coverage clause—which impose certain obligations on your company. Unless a contract is exempt from the CAS or is eligible for modified coverage, the *full* coverage "Cost Accounting Standards" clause must be included in the contract.[1] This clause requires you to do the following:

(a) Disclose your cost accounting practices, in writing, through the submission to the Government of a Disclosure Statement if the criteria for filing the Statement are otherwise met.

(b) Follow your cost accounting practices consistently in accumulating and reporting contract performance cost data.

(c) Comply with all CAS in effect either on your contract award date or the date of your signed "Certificate of Current Cost or Pricing Data" (see §§ 9:1 et seq.).

(d) Comply with all CAS that become applicable to your prime contract or subcontract after award, subject to an equitable adjustment in the contract price if the change causes an

---

[Section 12:7]
[1] 48 C.F.R. § 9903.201-2(b)(1).
[2] 48 C.F.R. § 9903.201-2(b)(2).

[Section 12:8]
[1] 48 C.F.R. § 9903.201-4(a).

increase in your cost.

(e) Agree to an equitable adjustment for any unilateral change in your cost accounting practices, providing that no agreement may increase the costs paid by the United States.

(f) Negotiate an equitable adjustment when the parties agree that a change in cost accounting practice is desirable and not detrimental to the interests of the United States.[2]

(g) Agree to a contract price or cost adjustment for any failure to comply with an applicable CAS or to follow any cost accounting practice disclosed in your Disclosure Statement.

(h) Agree that if you disagree with the Government on a contract adjustment or disagree on the question of CAS compliance, the disagreement shall constitute a dispute pursuant to the "Disputes" clause of the contract.

(i) Permit authorized officials (i.e., DCAA) to examine and make copies of your documents or records relating to compliance with the CAS.

(j) Include the "CAS" clause in all negotiated subcontracts in excess of $700,000 and not otherwise exempt from CAS coverage.

If your contract meets the conditions for *modified* CAS coverage, you are only required to comply with the modified CAS clause, entitled "Disclosure and Consistency of Cost Accounting Practices."[3] This clause requires you to do the following:

(a) Comply with CAS 401, CAS 402, CAS 405, CAS 406.

(b) Follow your cost accounting practices consistently.

(c) Describe your cost accounting practices through submission of a Disclosure Statement if the criteria for filing the Statement are otherwise met.

(d) Negotiate an equitable adjustment in the contract price for any unilateral change in your cost accounting practices to which you and the Government both agree.

(e) Negotiate an equitable adjustment in the contract price when the parties agree that a change in cost accounting practice is desirable and not detrimental to the interests of the United States.

(f) Agree to an adjustment of contract price or cost for any failure to comply with applicable CAS or disclosed cost accounting practices.

(g) Agree that disagreements are subject to the "Disputes"

---

[2]Effective March 31, 2008, FAR 30.604(h)(4) was revised to indicate that the Changes clause is to be used to negotiate equitable adjustments related to "required" or "desirable" changes in the contractor's cost accounting practices. *See* 73 Fed. Reg. 10964.

[3]48 C.F.R. § 9903.201-4(c).

§ 12:8   Government Contract Compliance Handbook

        clause of the contract.
- (h) Permit authorized officials to examine and copy documents and records relating to CAS compliance.
- (i) Include the modified "CAS" clause or full "CAS" clause, as appropriate, in all negotiated subcontracts in excess of $700,000, except those otherwise exempt.

Contracts subject to either full or modified CAS coverage must also contain the "Administration of Cost Accounting Standards" clause which specifies the rules for administering CAS requirements and procedures to be followed in cases of failure to comply.[4]

§ 12:9   Disclosure statement

Once you determine that you are subject to full or modified CAS coverage, there are many rules you must follow. CAS regulations require that in certain cases you must disclose your cost accounting practices in writing and follow them consistently. For this, the CAS Board developed a detailed Disclosure Statement form (Form CASB-DS-1) (see Appendix N to this Compliance Handbook). The requirements for determining whether you must file a Disclosure Statement are set forth in the regulations[1] and are stated in terms of the whole company (a company together with its segments or divisions), a business unit, a segment, and a corporate or home office. Completed Disclosure Statements must be filed by the following:

- (a) Any *business unit* which itself receives a CAS-covered contract or subcontract of $50 million or more.
- (b) Any *company* which, together with its *segments*, received net awards of negotiated prime contracts and subcontracts subject to the CAS totaling $50 million or more in its most recent cost accounting period.
- (c) When a Disclosure Statement is required, a separate Disclosure Statement must be submitted for each segment whose costs were included in the total price of any CAS covered contract or subcontract exceeding $700,000 unless the contract or subcontract is otherwise exempt or unless the segment's CAS-covered awards in the preceding cost accounting period are less than 30% of the total sales of that segment and total sales for that segment are less than $10 million.
- (d) Each corporate or other *home office* that allocates costs to any segment performing CAS-covered contracts (Part VIII

---

[4]FAR 30.201-4(d); FAR 52.230-6.

[Section 12:9]

[1]48 C.F.R. § 9903.202-1(b).

of the Disclosure Statement only).

Your Disclosure Statement must be *amended* whenever you change any of your disclosed cost accounting practices.[2] It makes no difference whether the practices are changed to comply with new Cost Accounting Standards or are self-initiated for business reasons. Amendments are submitted to the same office that received your original Disclosure Statement and apply prospectively to all CAS-covered contracts and subcontracts and to all contracts and subcontracts currently being performed.

In response to industry concerns, the first CAS Board promulgated a *confidentiality* regulation, which provides that if you desire to protect the information in your Disclosure Statement, you should place a restrictive legend on the Statement indicating that it contains trade secrets and commercial or financial information that you regard as privileged and confidential.[3] A subcontractor that wishes to protect its confidential information from disclosure to the prime contractor may submit its Disclosure Statement directly to the Government.[4]

You should emphasize to your employees the importance of submitting a complete and accurate Disclosure Statement to the Government. If you knowingly or willfully falsify or conceal a material fact in the Disclosure Statement, you may be subject to fines, imprisonment, or both under the civil and criminal fraud statutes.

§ 12:10 Educational institutions

Originally, educational institutions were exempt from CAS requirements. However, effective January 1995, the CAS Board withdrew this exemption. In doing so, however, the Board recognized the unique nature and structure of these institutions and established separate regulations for them.[1]

Under the current regulations, if an educational institution or segment of an educational institution receives a negotiated CAS-covered contract in excess of $700,000, except for CAS-covered contracts awarded to Federally Funded Research and Development Centers (FFRDCs) that are operated by an educational institution, that institution must comply with a separate series of four Standards that essentially parallel the four Standards

---

[2] 48 C.F.R. § 9903.202-3.
[3] 48 C.F.R. § 9903.202-4.
[4] 48 C.F.R. § 9903.202-8(c)(1).

[Section 12:10]

[1] *See* 48 C.F.R. §§ 9903.201-2(c), 9903.201-4(e), 9903.202-1(f), and 9905; *see also* Kenney and Mason, Federal Research Compliance: Financial & Administrative Issues, Briefing Papers No. 01-11 (Oct. 2001).

§ 12:10

included in the "modified coverage" that applies to certain commercial contractors.[2] (Negotiated contracts awarded to FFRDCs run by educational institutions were already subject to the same rules covering full and modified CAS coverage discussed above and, therefore, were not affected by the 1995 rule change.)[3] In addition, contracts with educational institutions must include a clause—"Cost Accounting Standards-Educational Institutions"— that imposes obligations similar to those required in contracts subject to modified CAS coverage discussed above.[4] Thus, in essence, the CAS Board has applied modified CAS coverage to contracts with educational institutions.

CAS regulations also require that in certain cases educational institutions must disclose their cost accounting practices in writing to the Government and must follow them consistently. For this, the CAS Board developed a Disclosure Statement form (Form CASB-DS-2) specifically for those organizations.[5] The following entities must file completed Disclosure Statements:[6]

(a) Any business unit of an educational institution listed in Exhibit A of Office of Management and Budget (OMB) Circular A-21 that receives a CAS-covered contract or subcontract in excess of $700,000 unless the entity received less than $25 million in federal contracts and financial assistance awards in the preceding cost accounting period.

(b) Any business unit that receives a contract or subcontract of $25 million or more.

(c) Any educational institution which, together with its segments, received net awards of negotiated prime and subcontracts subject to the CAS totaling $25 million or more in its most recent cost accounting period, of which at least one award exceeded $1 million.

Independently, in May 1996, OMB modified Circular A-21 to make applicable to all *federally sponsored agreements* received by educational institutions the four CAS and CAS Disclosure Statement requirements that apply to educational institutions.[7] A "sponsored agreement" is any grant, contract, or other agreement between the institution and the Federal Government.

Thus, many educational institutions that do business with the Government, like many commercial contractors, are now subject to a complex set of obligations regarding the methods and

---

[2]48 C.F.R. §§ 9905, 9903.201-2(c)(3).
[3]48 C.F.R. § 9903.201-2(c)(4).
[4]48 C.F.R. § 9903.201-4(e).
[5]48 C.F.R. § 9903.202-10.
[6]48 C.F.R. § 9903.202-1(f)(2).
[7]61 Fed. Reg. 20880.

COST ACCOUNTING § 12:11

techniques they employ for the accumulation and allocation of costs. These educational institutions will need to exercise diligent oversight in implementing these highly technical rules and in assuring continued compliance with them to avoid future allegations of mischarging, overbilling, and fraud.

§ 12:11 Accounting changes & contract adjustments

As noted above, the CAS contract clauses for both "full" and "modified" coverage require you to follow your disclosed or established cost accounting practices *consistently*. A "cost accounting practice" is defined as "any disclosed or established accounting method or technique which is used for allocation of cost to cost objectives, assignment of cost to cost accounting periods, or measurement of cost."[1]

The clauses also specify the contractual consequences of changing or deviating from disclosed or established practices. For example, as discussed previously, you may unilaterally change your cost accounting practice, but the change may not result in the Government paying increased costs unless the conditions for an equitable adjustment are first met. If you fail to follow your disclosed or established practices, and that failure results in an increased cost to the Government, you must pay the increased costs through a contract adjustment, together with interest. The severity of these consequences points out the need for you to understand what constitutes a "change to a cost accounting practice."

For example, under a firm-fixed-price contract, increased costs would result if, during the accumulating and reporting process, the contractor adopted accounting practices that *decreased* the cost allocated to the Government compared with the cost allocation the contractor used during the contract estimating process. In other words, the Government would contend that there had been "increased costs" within the meaning of the CAS regulations if an accounting change results in *fewer* costs being charged to a contract (and a corresponding increase in profit) even though it only paid the "fixed price" specified in the contract. Any such increase in costs is measured by the difference between the estimated cost to complete the work using the changed practice and the estimated cost using the current (original) accounting practice.[2]

Although some contractors may not be required to file a

[Section 12:11]
[1] 48 C.F.R. § 9903.302-1.
[2] FAR 30.604(h)(3).

§ 12:11   Government Contract Compliance Handbook

Disclosure Statement identifying their cost accounting practices, all contractors have "established" cost accounting practices. To accommodate both situations, the regulations define the term "change to a cost accounting practice" as "any alteration in a cost accounting practice . . . whether or not such practices are covered by a Disclosure Statement," thereby including *both* disclosed and established cost accounting practices.[3]

The regulations that provide "illustrations" of what does and does not constitute a "change to a cost accounting practice" are relatively clear.[4] However, determining whether a specific event constitutes a change to a cost accounting practice is more difficult. Some Government Administrative Contracting Officers (ACOs) and auditors take a very expansive view of "change"—to include, for example, the disposal of a division or consolidation of two divisions. The Government contractor community takes a more narrow view. Ultimately, the courts and the boards of contract appeals will decide, unless the CAS Board decides to intervene.

B. CFAO COMPLIANCE DETERMINATIONS

§ 12:12 Generally

The agency will assign a Cognizant Federal Agency Official (CFAO) to administer CAS.[1] Usually this will be the ACO. DCAA is responsible for reviewing your cost accounting practices for compliance with the CAS and serves as an advisor to the CFAO on all accounting matters relating to CAS compliance or noncompliance.[2] The CFAO is required to request and consider auditor advice as appropriate when performing CAS administration.[3] The FAR prescribes detailed procedures that your CFAO must follow in making decisions regarding your compliance or noncompliance with the CAS.[4]

§ 12:13 Types of noncompliance

There are three general types of CAS noncompliance:

(1) The cost accounting practices disclosed in your Disclosure Statement or your established practices do not comply with the CAS.

(2) Your actual practices of estimating costs do not comply

---

[3] 48 C.F.R. § 9903.302-2.

[4] 48 C.F.R. §§ 9903.302-3, 9903.302-4.

[Section 12:12]

[1] FAR 30.601.

[2] DCAA Contract Audit Manual 7640.1, 8-104.1 (October 2013).

[3] FAR 30.601(c).

[4] FAR subpt. 30.6.

with the CAS.

(3) Your actual practices of accumulating or reporting costs do not comply with the CAS.

DCAA will look for CAS noncompliances in your disclosed or established cost accounting practices during review of your initial Disclosure Statement, during review of changes in your disclosed or established practices, and during audits of your price proposals and final overhead cost proposals. DCAA reviews of your estimating practices for CAS compliance will occur during proposal evaluations or as part of an estimating system survey. DCAA audits of your cost accumulation and reporting practices for CAS compliance will occur during routine audits of your actual costs or final annual overhead reviews.

If DCAA determines that any of your cost accounting practices do not comply with the CAS, the responsible auditor will issue an audit report to your CFAO. Generally, you will be given an opportunity to comment on the draft DCAA report before it is submitted to the CFAO. In such instances, you should carefully examine the cost accounting practices in issue and clearly explain your position in writing to the auditor with a copy to your CFAO. Your goal should be to convince DCAA and the CFAO as early as possible that your practices comply with the CAS.

§ 12:14 Initial finding of noncompliance

Within 15 days of receiving a report from DCAA of alleged CAS noncompliance, your CFAO must make an initial finding of your compliance and advise DCAA of this finding.[1] If the CFAO determines your practices comply with the CAS, then the audit findings are resolved and closed.

If, however, the CFAO concludes that your practices do not comply with the CAS and that the cost impact will be "material," he or she will immediately notify you in writing of the specific nature of the noncompliance and give you 60 days within which to agree to the noncompliance or to submit reasons why you deem the cost accounting practices at issue to be in compliance. This finding by the CFAO is referred to as an "initial finding of noncompliance" and is a first step in a very complex procedure that could lead to withholding a portion of contract payments and to a dispute that must be resolved under the Contract Disputes Act.[2] At this point, you should review the cost accounting prac-

---

[Section 12:14]

[1]FAR 30.605(b).

[2]FAR 30.605(i); FAR 30.604(i); *see also* Feldman, Government Contract Guidebook §§ 21–24.

§ 12:14   GOVERNMENT CONTRACT COMPLIANCE HANDBOOK

tices the CFAO questioned and the applicable Cost Accounting Standards. Depending on the complexity of the issues raised and your in-house CAS expertise, you may want to seek legal and accounting advice to assist you in formulating your response to the CFAO's initial finding of noncompliance.

§ 12:15 Agreement with CFAO's initial finding

If, after completing your analysis, you conclude that the CFAO is correct in the initial finding of CAS noncompliance, you must submit a complete description of any corrective cost accounting change.[1] If you can demonstrate that there is no material increase in costs to the Government as a result of the noncompliance, there will be no requirement for a contract cost or price adjustment to the CAS-covered contracts and subcontracts.[2]

Once the CFAO receives your proposed corrective cost accounting change, the CFAO, with the assistance and advice of DCAA, will review the accounting change for adequacy and CAS compliance. If the change is adequate and complies with the CAS, the CFAO will notify you and request a cost impact proposal.[3] The regulations define two types of costs estimates: a "general dollar magnitude" estimate, which can be based on an analysis of a representative sample of affected CAS-covered contracts and subcontracts, or a "detailed cost-impact" proposal, which analyzes the impact on each CAS-covered contract and subcontract.[4] If the contractor is required to submit a Detailed Cost Impact proposal, the CFAO "shall promptly evaluate the DCI proposal" as part of negotiating and resolving the impact of the noncompliance.[5] The cost impact of a *single* instance of noncompliance that affects both cost estimating and cost accumulation shall be determined by combining the separate cost impacts of both the cost estimating and cost accumulation noncompliances.[6]

The CFAO, with the assistance of DCAA, will review the pro-

[Section 12:15]

[1]FAR 30.605(c).
[2]FAR 30.605(c).
[3]FAR 30.605(c).
[4]FAR 30.605 (d), (f).
[5]FAR 30.605(f).
[6]FAR 30.605(f); In its comments on March 2008 revisions to FAR 30.605(f), the CAS Board restated its previous view that where the individual cost impact of *two* or more noncompliances or unilateral changes is an increase in costs in the aggregate, the noncompliance and change may be combined for administrative ease in resolving the total cost impact. However, the CAS Board also made clear that if any of the individual noncompliances or unilateral changes resulted in decreased costs, they could not be combined to determine the total cost impact. In essence, the CAS Board was stating that allowing a

posal and then proceed to negotiate the contract price adjustments on behalf of all Government agencies. When the adjustment of the price of any contract or subcontract is increased or decreased by $100,000 or more, the CFAO will coordinate with the affected Procuring Contracting Officer(s) to participate in the negotiations.[7] When the parties agree on the cost impact of the CAS noncompliance, the CFAO will execute supplemental agreements to the individual contracts to reflect the contract adjustments.[8]

§ 12:16 Disagreement with CFAO's initial finding

If you disagree with the CFAO's initial finding of CAS noncompliance, you should advise the CFAO accordingly, explaining in writing the reasons why you consider your practices to be in compliance.[1] The CFAO will then review your written position and make a determination of compliance or noncompliance.

If the CFAO agrees that you are in compliance, the CFAO will notify you in writing and send a copy to DCAA.[2] If, however, the CFAO still considers your cost accounting practice to be in noncompliance with the CAS, the CFAO will require the contractor to submit within 60 days a description of any cost accounting practice change that is needed to correct the compliance.[3] The CFAO, with the assistance of the auditor will then review the proposed change to determine whether it corrects the noncompliance. If it does, the CFAO will then request that you submit a "general dollar magnitude" cost proposal.[4] If you refuse to provide a cost impact proposal, the CFAO has discretion to withhold an amount not to exceed 10% of each subsequent payment you request on individual CAS-covered contracts until a cost impact proposal is furnished to the CFAO.[5] After evaluating this proposal, the CFAO will conduct negotiations in an effort to reach an adjustment in the prices of the affected contracts. If the parties do eventually reach agreement, the prices of the affected

---

contractor to "offset" cost increases against cost decreases would not comply with the statutory requirement that the Government recover the increased costs in the aggregate for each unilateral change/noncompliance. *See* 73 Fed. Reg. 10,964.

[7]FAR 30.606 (a).
[8]FAR 30.606(c)(6).

[Section 12:16]
[1]FAR 30.605(b)(2).
[2]FAR 30.605(b)(3).
[3]FAR 30.605(c).
[4]FAR 30.605(c).
[5]FAR 30.604(i).

§ 12:16   Government Contract Compliance Handbook

contracts will be modified accordingly.[6] However, if agreement is not possible, the regulations authorize the CFAO to unilaterally establish the amount of the price adjustment by issuing a Final Decision under the "Disputes" clause of one of the affected contracts.[7] In addition, the CFAO has discretion to take action under the contract debt provisions of the FAR.[8]

If the CFAO determines that the noncompliance will result in no material increase in costs to the Government, and you decide not to take any corrective action, the CFAO will notify you in writing that he or she still considers your practices to be in noncompliance with CAS, request again that you take corrective action, and advise you that if the noncompliance later results in materially increased costs, the applicable contractual remedies will be enforced.[9]

§ 12:17 Unilateral accounting changes

You have the right to establish your own cost accounting practices provided they comply with the CAS. The regulations recognize that from time to time you will make unilateral changes in your disclosed or established cost accounting practices for business reasons independent of the CAS.[1]

If, at any time, you decide to make such a change, you should notify your CFAO by submitting, not less than 60 days before the proposed implementation date, a description of the proposed accounting change.[2] After receipt of your unilateral change submission, the CFAO will, with the assistance and advice of DCAA, review the change for adequacy and compliance. If the CFAO determines the change to be both adequate and CAS compliant, he or she will notify you and request that you submit a cost impact proposal identifying all CAS-covered contracts and subcontracts and the cost impact of the proposed change on each affected contract and subcontract.[3]

On receipt of your cost impact proposal, the CFAO, with the assistance of DCAA, will analyze the proposal to determine whether the proposed change will result in increased costs being paid by the Government. Even when the CFAO determines that

---

[6]FAR 30.606(c)(6).
[7]FAR 30.606(c)(6).
[8]FAR subpt. 32.6.
[9]FAR 30.605(b)(4).

[Section 12:17]
[1]FAR 30.603-2(a).
[2]FAR 30.603-2(c).
[3]FAR 30.604(b)(1).

the proposed change will result in increased costs to the Government, the change is permissible if the CFAO determines that the change is desirable and not detrimental to the Government.[4]

If you fail to submit a cost impact proposal as required, or if you are unable to reach agreement with the CFAO as to the cost impact of the proposed change, the CFAO, with DCAA's assistance, will estimate the cost impact on CAS-covered contracts and subcontracts and will unilaterally implement that price adjustment by issuing a Final Decision under the "Disputes" clause.[5] The CFAO may also take action under the FAR contract debt provisions.[6]

Cases & Commentary: The requirement that the CFAO "shall promptly evaluate the DCI proposal" was also made applicable to the resolution of unilateral changes in accounting practices by revisions to FAR 30.604(g) which became effective on March 31, 2008.[7] Note also § 12:15 regarding the combining of multiple unilateral changes in determining the total cost impact of those changes. Combining multiple changes is permissible if each individual change resulted in *increased* costs to the Government. However if any change resulted in *decreased* costs, the cost impact must be individually determined for each unilateral change.

FAR 30.604 provides that the CFAO "shall consider all of the contractor's affected CAS-covered contracts" to determine whether a proposed change in accounting practice will result in increased costs being paid by the Government. FAR 30.001 defines an "affected CAS-covered contract for which a contractor (1) used one cost accounting practice to estimate costs and a changed practice to accumulate and report costs or (2) used a noncompliant practice for purposes of estimating or accumulating and reporting costs under a contract. In one U.S. Court of Appeals for the Federal Circuit case, the Government and the contractor were engaged in re-pricing major portions of the F-22 contract at the same time the contractor was implementing a change in accounting practice with regard to certain categories of labor. The court affirmed a decision by the ASBCA that the F-22 contract was not an "affected" contract that needed to be taken into account in evaluating the cost impact of the changed practice. The court noted that the contractor used its changed practices when re-pricing a portion of the contract and that the Government was aware of this. The court agreed with the Board that a

---

[4]FAR 30.604(c).
[5]FAR 30.604(i).
[6]FAR subpt. 32.6.
[7]*See* 73 Fed. Reg. 10,964.

contract is not "affected" as long as each contract cost is estimated and reported using the same accounting methods, even if some of the costs are estimated and reported using one practice and other costs are estimated and reported using a different practice.[8]

C. COST ACCOUNTING STANDARDS VS. COST PRINCIPLES

§ 12:18 Generally

The CAS address fundamental issues of cost *allocability* and establishing accounting systems to facilitate cost allocation. Put another way, the purpose of the CAS is to instruct you on how to set up an accounting system that will result in costs trickling down to "cost objectives" in a certain way. The purpose of the FAR cost principles, on the other hand, is fundamentally different (see §§ 11:1 et seq.) FAR Part 31, which contains the cost principles, is concerned primarily with defining cost *allowability* under Government contracts. To analogize, the CAS establish a "piping system" for costs, and FAR Part 31 governs the "on and off valves" determining whether the costs may properly be paid into the pipes. This is, of course, an oversimplification, but it is worth keeping in mind as a basic difference between the CAS and the cost principles.

This distinction blurs somewhat when FAR Part 31 incorporates one of the Cost Accounting Standards. When this occurs, it means either that the Standards have gotten close to addressing issues of cost "allowability" or the FAR is dealing with a matter of cost "allocation." For example, CAS 405 directs contractors to set up an accounting system to segregate unallowable costs, i.e., costs that will not be reimbursed under Government contracts. The FAR requires that unallowable costs be separately identified and excluded from any billing, claim, or proposal applicable to a Government contract.[1] Thus, in addition to disallowing these costs, the FAR also requires that they be separately accounted for, a function more generally left to the Cost Accounting Standards. Conversely, CAS 405 requires the identification of costs that will not be paid by the Government, a role the FAR Part 31 cost provisions typically assume.

As another example, there is overlap in the CAS and the FAR regarding the treatment of the cost of money. CAS 414 establishes criteria for measuring and allocating the cost of money as a contract cost of capital committed to facilities. The FAR cost principles incorporate CAS 414 and apply the requirements to all

---

[8]*See Donley v. Lockheed Martin Corp.*, 608 F.3d 1348 (Fed Cir. 2010).

[Section 12:18]

[1]FAR 31.201-6.

Government contracts whether or not they are subject to the CAS.[2] Thus, the FAR expands into CAS areas of allowability.

D. CONTRACTOR LIABILITY

1. Liability For False Statements

§ 12:19 Generally

At each stage of the procurement process, from submitting a proposal to closing out a contract, you will be required to complete and sign a multitude of Government-specified forms. Each time you execute one of these forms, you are making legal representations to the Government. Errors, whether deliberate or inadvertent, can have serious consequences for you, including fines and imprisonment for submitting a false statement to the Government (see §§ 1:1 et seq.) Some of these Government contract forms involve representations concerning your compliance with the CAS.

§ 12:20 Solicitation representations & certifications

When you respond to a Government solicitation, you must complete a standard form—Standard Form 33—including "Section K" of the form, which is a litany of contractor representations, certifications, and other statements. Typically, completing these certifications involves selecting and checking off appropriate boxes representing your assurances and guarantees to the Government.

The form includes certifications relating to the Cost Accounting Standards.[1] To complete this section accurately, your certifying company official must be familiar with all applicable CAS regulations. The solicitation requires that you make the following certifications, where appropriate, by checking the appropriate boxes:

(a) That a CAS Disclosure Statement has been submitted concurrently with the proposal.

(b) That your company qualifies for an exemption from the Disclosure Statement requirement because of the value of its Government contract(s).

(c) That your company qualifies for an interim exemption because you first exceeded the monetary exemption for disclosure in the cost accounting period immediately preceding the one in which this proposal was submitted.

(d) That you have submitted a previous Disclosure Statement

---

[2]FAR 31.205-10.

[Section 12:20]

[1]FAR 52.230-1.

to the Government and that your accounting practices have not changed.
(e) That the contract is totally exempt from CAS coverage.
(f) That the contract qualifies for modified CAS coverage.
(g) That award of the contract will (or will not) require a change in your established cost accounting practices affecting existing contracts and subcontracts.

§ 12:21 Proposals where cost or pricing data are required

For negotiated procurements that require the contractor to prepare a contract pricing proposal where cost or pricing data are required, the FAR sets forth several questions that the contractor must respond to regarding its compliance with the CAS.[1] These questions include; (1) whether your organization is subject to CAS, (2) whether your organization has submitted a CAS Disclosure Statement and if it has been determined to be adequate, (3) whether you have you been notified that you are or may be in noncompliance with your Disclosure Statement or with the CAS and, if yes, whether any aspect of the proposal is inconsistent with your disclosed practices or with the applicable CAS, and (4) whether the proposal is consistent with your established estimating and accounting procedures and the cost principles in FAR Part 31.

§ 12:22 Disclosure statements

As discussed earlier in this chapter, CAS regulations require that you disclose to the Government, in writing, your cost accounting practices and follow them consistently. To monitor compliance with these requirements, the CAS Board developed a detailed Disclosure Statement form (set forth in Appendix N). Form CASB-DS-1 consists of a cover sheet and eight sections requiring statements and certifications about your company and its accounting practices. A brief description of each section follows.

Cover Sheet: On this sheet you identify your company or reporting unit, your address, and the company official to contact regarding the Statement. An authorized signatory of your company must certify the completeness and accuracy of the Statement. The cover sheet specifically cautions the company that "the penalty for making a false statement in this disclosure is prescribed in 18 U.S.C.A. § 1001" (the False Statements Statute).

[Section 12:21]
[1]FAR 15.408 (Table 15-2, "General Instructions").

COST ACCOUNTING § 12:23

Part I: General Information: This part includes information about your reporting unit, annual Government and total sales, types of products or services sold, type of cost system, and extent of integration of the cost system with the general accounts.

Part II: Direct Costs: In this part, you define the elements of cost that you treat as direct labor, direct materials, or other direct costs, and the circumstances and timing of charging each type of direct cost to contracts. If you use a standard cost system, you must explain what is included in the standard cost; variance accumulation and disposition must be described in detail. Your cost accounting policies for contract cost credits and interorganizational transfers must also be explained.

Part III: Direct vs. Indirect Costs: Here, you must designate how various functions, cost elements, and transactions are treated, and, if indirect, what aggregating pools are used.

Part IV: Indirect Costs: This section inquires about the manner in which service center costs, general and administrative expenses, and manufacturing overhead are pooled. You must also describe and identify the allocation bases for all indirect cost pools.

Part V: Depreciation and Capitalization Practices: You must specify the criteria for capitalization, the methods of depreciation used, the treatment of gains and losses from disposition, and the basis for determining useful life in this portion of the Disclosure Statement.

Part VI: Other Costs and Credits: In this part, you must describe the method of charging and crediting vacation, sick pay, holiday, and other employee benefits such as supplemental unemployment and severance.

Part VII: Deferred Compensation and Insurance Cost: This section requires description of your pension plans and the determination of pension costs, as well as certain types of deferred compensation and insurance costs.

Part VIII: Home Office Expenses: In this part, you describe the expenses or pools of expenses accumulated at the segment or home office level. You also describe whether such expenses are directly chargeable or separately allocated to segments and your methods for direct charging and allocation. The Form CASB-DS-1 also allows home office preparation of Parts V, VI, and VII where the home office incurs and allocates these costs or establishes the cost accounting practices. When a home office completes part of the form, however, the segment should review the home office cost accounting practices to determine whether any compliance issues exist.

§ 12:23 Overhead or final indirect cost certifications

When you submit a proposal for settlement of final indirect

§ 12:23

costs to the Government, you must certify that all indirect costs included in your settlement proposal are allowable.[1] The "Certification of Final Indirect Costs" (see Appendix L and §§ 11:1 et seq.), which must be signed by your corporate vice-president or chief financial officer, states that the signatory declares that; (1) he or she has reviewed the proposal to establish final indirect cost rates and, "to the best of my knowledge and belief," (2) all costs included in the proposal are allowable in accordance with the FAR cost principles, and (3) the proposal does not include any expressly unallowable costs.

To execute this "Certification" properly, your corporate official must be able to rely on your company's basic compliance with applicable CAS provisions relating to accounting for unallowable costs (CAS 405), allocation of general and administrative expenses (CAS 410), and allocation of direct and indirect costs (CAS 418). Other Cost Accounting Standards may also be involved.

§ 12:24 Cost impact proposals

As discussed earlier in this chapter, the regulations require that you report to the Government any change in your cost accounting practices, unilateral or otherwise, as well as all failures by your company to abide by an applicable Cost Accounting Standard. The regulations also indicate that the CFAO may require you to conduct a cost impact study and submit a detailed proposal regarding the impact of the change or noncompliance on costs being paid by the Government.[1] The "Administration of Cost Accounting Standards" clause requires that detailed cost impact proposals submitted regarding a change in cost accounting practices shall show the calculation of the cost impact and show the estimated increase or decrease in cost accumulations for each affected contract, as agreed upon by you and the CFAO.[2] As you might expect, preparation of this proposal is an extremely rigorous process and involves a great deal of "number crunching." It is a job for one of your company's CAS experts.

When you submit a cost impact proposal to the CFAO, you are attesting to the correctness of the representations contained in it. Errors or misstatements can lead to charges of false statements or false claims. For example, if, as a result of a change in your cost accounting practices, costs are shifted in a manner that

---

[Section 12:23]

[1]FAR 52.242-4.

[Section 12:24]

[1]FAR 30.605(c), 52.230-6.

[2]FAR 52.230-6, para. (e).

results in the company owing the Government money, this must be reported in the cost impact proposal. Deliberate failure to do so could be construed as a criminal or civil false claim. Therefore, it is critical that you prepare any cost impact proposal carefully.

  2. Liability For False Claims

§ 12:25 Generally

The "Cost Accounting Standards" contract clauses discussed earlier in this chapter require adjustments in the contract price when you fail to comply with an applicable CAS or to follow the cost accounting practices disclosed in your Disclosure Statement. While not to be taken lightly, these are "garden variety" Government contract issues that are routinely encountered and handled every day. In most cases, the outer limit of this type of risk is the payment of money or possibly a termination of the contract for default.

However, much more significantly, this same failure to adhere to disclosed practices or applicable CAS can also lead to criminal or civil liability for submitting false claims to the Government, exposing your company to penalties and suspension or debarment from contracting with the Government. In addition to potential false claims charges arising from errors in your cost impact proposal, false claims may also arise in the following situations.

§ 12:26 Errors in progress payment billings

As discussed in § 14, progress payments you receive in the course of performance of certain Government contracts are a type of interest-free loan to your company from the Government. The amount of the payments is determined in its most basic sense by what you have spent on the contract—i.e., your incurred costs. Your accounting system should tell you what resources have been devoted to the contract at any particular point in time. However, if this system is inaccurate as a result of CAS noncompliances in your accounting practices, then the figure you use to bill the Government for progress payments could be inflated. If you know of this problem but nonetheless submit erroneous requests to the Government for progress payments, you could possibly be prosecuted for submitting a false claim to the Government.

§ 12:27 Overbilling on cost contracts & invoices

In a cost-type contract with the Government, you bill and receive payments based on your actual incurred costs. In the same manner as progress payment billings, if these costs are overstated because of a CAS-noncompliant accounting system,

§ 12:27   GOVERNMENT CONTRACT COMPLIANCE HANDBOOK

you could be prosecuted under the false claims statutes. Similarly, you could be overbilling the Government every time you submit an invoice on the contract. Should you know of this situation, you may be liable for submitting false claims to the Government.

E. FREQUENTLY ASKED QUESTIONS

§ 12:28   Questions & answers

Question 1: We are reorganizing our company and under the new management structure the marketing department will report directly to the Corporate Vice President for the sector. Under the previous structure, the marketing department reported to the General Manager of the sector. Under the new structure, the costs of the marketing department will continue to be included in the sector's general and administrative expense pool. Is the reorganization an accounting change that requires an amendment to our CAS Disclosure Statement?

Answer 1: An organizational change that results in "a change to a cost accounting practice" is determined on a case-by-case basis. For example, a change to a cost accounting practice would likely occur if an organizational change resulted in transferring an ongoing function to a new or different indirect cost group that used a different allocation basis. In contrast, the U.S. Court of Appeals for the Federal Circuit has ruled that an organizational change that involved regrouping five business segments did not—in itself—constitute a change in cost accounting practice because it did not result in a change in the measurement, assignment, or allocation of costs.[1] In this instance, although you have modified the organizational structure of your company, you have not changed the accounting treatment of the marketing department costs, so there is no change in accounting practices.

The issue of when a contractor's organizational change constitutes a change to a cost accounting practice has engendered considerable controversy in recent years. Some within the Government have taken an expansive view, contending, for example, that corporate reorganizations could constitute such a change. Government contractors, understandably, view the matter much more narrowly.

Question 2: We recently changed the interest rate used in the actuarial assumptions we use to compute pension costs we allocate to the Government under our CAS-covered contracts. Is this an accounting change that requires an amendment to our CAS Disclosure Statement?

[Section 12:28]

[1]*Perry v. Martin Marietta Corp.*, 47 F.3d 1134 (Fed. Cir. 1995).

§ 12:28

Answer 2: No. Adopting an increase or decrease in the interest rate used in actuarial assumptions is not a cost accounting change.

Question 3: Normally, we treat marketing costs as an indirect expense and allocate the costs on the basis of direct labor. Last year, we aggressively marketed a new product to the Government and were successful in obtaining a fixed-price production contract. The cost of the marketing effort was substantial, accounting for the bulk of our total marketing expense for the year, yet the value of the contract we received was fairly small. Are we required to pull this cost out of our indirect pool and charge it directly to the contract because of its relative size?

Answer 3: Probably not. In a decision involving similar facts, the Federal Circuit held that a specific item of cost in an indirect pool could not be "singled out" for special treatment just because it might be disproportionately large as long as it had been incurred for the same purpose and under like circumstances as the other costs in the pool.[2] However, you may be required to change the basis of allocation for all costs within that pool, especially if you continue to experience situations in which these costs appear large in relation to the size of the resulting contract.

Question 4: In a recent fixed-price procurement, the Contracting Officer asked us to provide him with certain cost information regarding material costs and engineering and production manhours from an earlier contract. We provided the data on an "informal" basis since the Truth in Negotiations Act did not apply to the procurement. Furthermore, the data were only used by the Contracting Officer to check for mistakes or omissions in our proposal and not as a basis for price negotiations. Can we maintain that this contract is exempt from complying with CAS requirements since the contract was a firm-fixed-price contract "awarded without submission of any cost data?"[3]

Answer 4: No. In the same case noted above in Question 3, the Federal Circuit held that the phrase "any cost data" must be read broadly to include *all* types of cost data, not simply the "cost or pricing data" that might be required under the Truth in Negotiations Act.[4] This meant that even though the contractor provided the information "informally," it could not claim the resulting contract was exempt from CAS requirements. Contractors should thus be alert to the fact that if they submit any cost data during the award process, they run the risk of not being able to rely on this CAS exemption.

---

[2] *Aydin Corp. v. Widnall*, 61 F.3d 1571 (Fed. Cir. 1995).
[3] 48 C.F.R. § 9903.201-1(b)(15).
[4] *See Aydin Corp. v. Widnall*, 61 F.3d 1571 (Fed. Cir. 1995).

§ 12:28   GOVERNMENT CONTRACT COMPLIANCE HANDBOOK

Question 5: Our company submitted cost or pricing data as part of its negotiation of a CAS-covered contract. When we submitted the data, we did not include information about planned accounting changes related to the restructuring of our company which increased the Government's costs under the contract. We also failed to include information on our planned accounting change in our most recent CAS Disclosure Statement. Have we violated the CAS, are we liable for defective pricing, or both?

Answer 5: You may be liable for both. Under the CAS, you are required to report unilateral changes to your cost accounting practices to the Government, and you will be liable for any increased costs to the Government as a result of these changes. In addition, under the "Defective Pricing" clause of your contract, you may be liable to the Government for any increased costs the Government has paid as a result of your failure to provide current, accurate, and complete cost or pricing data when you submitted your proposal (see §§ 9:1 et seq.).

Question 6: For many years, our company has valued certain assets at a useful life of 10 years. Because of changes in technology, we have now determined that these assets have a useful life of only seven years. Is this an accounting change that requires an amendment to our CAS Disclosure Statement?

Answer 6: No. A change in the estimated useful life of an asset is not an accounting change. You are not changing the method you use to determine the value of the asset, you are only changing the estimated life of the asset.

Question 7: We recently hired a new comptroller who has suggested changing the company's method for computing depreciation on certain assets from a straight-line to an accelerated depreciation method. Is this an accounting change under the CAS?

Answer 7: Yes. The change in the method of depreciation you use will affect the cost accounting periods to which the depreciation is allocated. This constitutes a change in accounting practices, which requires that you amend your CAS Disclosure Statement.

III. HOW TO RECOGNIZE THE PROBLEM

§ 12:29   Generally

The CAS Board has promulgated 19 Cost Accounting Standards during its life. This section summarizes the requirements and compliance issues relating to four of those Standards, which we use as examples below. Our purpose is not to try to give a detailed course on the CAS, but to illustrate the complexity of the Standards and the difficulty of assuring compliance with them.

As previously discussed, contractors violating the CAS can face civil and criminal liability under the fraud statutes. A description of this risk is included for each of the illustrations discussed below. It is important to remember that you may be vulnerable to prosecution under the false claims or false statements statutes for violating any of the Standards whenever the violation can be tied into a claim for money or a statement to the Government.

§ 12:30 Examples

CAS 401: This Standard, entitled "Consistency in Estimating, Accumulating and Reporting Costs," requires that in submitting proposals to the Government, your company use practices in estimating costs that are consistent with the cost accounting practices the company uses in accumulating and reporting *actual* costs. More specifically, the Standard requires consistency in; (a) the classification of elements or functions of cost as direct or indirect, (b) the indirect cost pools to which costs are charged or proposed to be charged, and (c) your method of allocating indirect costs to the contract.[1] Consistency is intended to ensure better financial control over costs during contract performance and aid in establishing accountability for costs in the manner agreed to by both parties at the time of contracting.[2] It allows you and the Government to check estimates against actuals in a meaningful way throughout contract performance.

CAS 401 allows grouping of homogeneous costs in cases where it is not practicable to estimate contract costs by individual cost element or function. Estimated costs, however, must be presented in such detail that any significant cost can be compared with the actual cost accumulated and reported. The following example illustrates cost accounting practices that are deemed to be *consistent* under CAS 401:[3]

> Estimating: You estimate an average direct labor rate for manufacturing direct labor by labor category or function.
>
> Accumulating & Reporting: You record manufacturing direct labor based on your actual cost for each individual and collect such costs by labor category or function.

[Section 12:30]

[1]*See Texas Instruments, Inc.*, ASBCA No. 18621, 79-1 BCA 13800, aff'd. on reconsideration, 79-2 BCA ¶ 14184 (CAS 401 does not require costs to be estimated, accumulated, and reported by contract where job order costing is not consistent with the nature of the contractor's operation, contractor's practice of estimating average unit product line costs was consistent with practice of accumulating, and reporting costs by product line).

[2]48 C.F.R. § 9904.401.

[3]48 C.F.R. § 9904.401-60(a).

The following example illustrates *noncompliance* with CAS 401:[4]

Estimating: You estimate a total dollar amount for engineering labor which includes disparate and significant elements or functions of engineering labor. You do not provide supporting data reconciling this amount to the estimates for the same engineering labor costs functions for which you will separately account in contract performance.

Accumulating & Reporting: You account for engineering labor by cost function, i.e., drafting, designing, production engineering, etc.

If your company violates CAS 401 in your estimating practices, the Government may later be able to argue that your contract price was artificially inflated. When you later bill under the contract for acceptable finished products, you may be open to a civil or criminal false claim charge resulting in fines, penalties, damages and possibly prison sentences. Whether fraud sanctions apply will, of course, depend on your state of mind at the time you submitted the billings. Similarly, any representation you make to the Government that you are in compliance with CAS 401 constitutes an official statement to the Government. If the statement is wrong and you know it to be wrong, you may be subject to liability under the criminal False Statements Statute. (See §§ 1:1 et seq.)

Let us assume that after you have secured a contract you suddenly change some of your methods of accumulating actual costs. Again, you are in violation of CAS 401. Worse, if you now submit a progress payment request based on your incurred cost, you may be vulnerable to a civil or criminal false claim charge because the Government can argue that the progress payment was artificially inflated because of the CAS 401 violation.

CAS 402: CAS 402, "Consistency in Allocating Costs Incurred for the Same Purpose," requires that you allocate each type of cost only once and on only one basis to any contract or other cost objective. The criteria for determining the allocation of costs to a product, contract, or other cost objective should be the same for all similar objectives. The intent is to protect against "double counting" which most frequently occurs when some cost items are allocated directly to a cost objective without eliminating similar cost items from indirect cost pools that are also allocated to that cost objective.[5] Illustrations of "double counting" include the following:

(1) Charging some travel expenses directly to a Government contract and accumulating other travel expenses in an indirect cost pool that is allocated to all contracts, includ-

---

[4]48 C.F.R. § 9904.401-60(b).
[5]48 C.F.R. § 9904.402.

§ 12:30

ing the Government contract.

(2) Charging inspection costs directly to a Government contract and at the same time including other but similar inspection costs in an overhead pool that is allocated to all cost objectives, including the Government contract.

However, where your special tooling costs are normally allocated directly to contracts, and the costs of general purpose tooling are normally included in the indirect cost pool that is allocated to all contracts, CAS 402 is not violated if both practices were disclosed to the Government and the costs were not incurred for the same purpose.[6]

Violation of CAS 402 exposes your company to possible liability under the false statements and false claims statutes. For example, the Government may argue that your final product invoices were inflated because the CAS 402 violation (double counting) caused the final price of the contract to be higher that it should. Alternatively, the Government may argue that the progress payment invoices you submitted to the Government were inflated because of the CAS 402 violations. Finally, a false statement charge may be based on your representation that you comply with CAS 402 when in fact you do not.

CAS 405: "Accounting for Unallowable Costs" (CAS 405) is intended to facilitate the negotiation, audit, administration, and settlement of contracts by establishing guidelines for identification of costs specifically described as unallowable and the cost accounting treatment to be accorded such identified unallowable costs to promote consistent application of sound cost accounting principles covering all incurred costs.[7] CAS 405 does not provide criteria for determining the allowability of costs. That function remains with the appropriate procurement authority.[8]

Under CAS 405, you must identify and exclude from any Government contract proposal, billing, or claim any costs expressly unallowable (costs that are unallowable by law, regulation, or contract) including directly associated costs. You must also exclude costs and directly associated costs that specifically become designated as unallowable as a result of a written decision furnished by a Contracting Officer pursuant to contract disputes procedures.[9]

Your company must maintain records in sufficient detail to establish and maintain visibility of identified unallowable costs, their accounting status in terms of allocability to contract cost

---

[6] 48 C.F.R. § 9904.402-60(b)(1).
[7] 48 C.F.R. § 9904.405.
[8] 48 C.F.R. § 9904.405-40(b).
[9] 48 C.F.R. § 9904.405-40(c).

§ 12:30   GOVERNMENT CONTRACT COMPLIANCE HANDBOOK

objectives, and the cost accounting treatment that you have accorded such costs.[10] The visibility requirement is satisfied by any form of cost identification that is adequate for purposes of contract cost determination and verification, and includes such alternative practices as segregating unallowable costs in regular books of account or developing and maintaining separate accounting records or work papers.[11]

CAS 405 also provides that all unallowable costs shall be subject to the same cost accounting principles governing cost allocability as allowable costs. Thus, where unallowable costs would normally be part of your regular indirect cost allocation base or bases, they must remain in such base or bases.[12]

Your failure to identify and exclude unallowable costs from any billings or price proposals submitted to the Government constitutes a violation of CAS 405. The violation could also lead to civil and criminal liability for submitting false statements and false claims to the Government. For example, if you fail to identify and remove unallowable costs from your manufacturing overhead and then include those costs in some of your cost or progress payment billings, you may have submitted a false claim to the Government. The same may be true if you fail to retain the unallowable costs in your base for allocation of general and administrative expenses. The general and administrative rate will be higher as a result, and the Government may charge you with making false claims. Similarly, if you represented that your cost accounting practices were CAS compliant, the Government could try to prosecute you under the False Statements Statute.

CAS 407: This Standard, "Use of Standard Costs for Direct Material and Direct Labor," governs the use of standard cost systems in estimating, accumulating, and reporting costs of direct material and direct labor. CAS 407 also provides criteria relating to the establishment of standards and the accumulation and disposition of variances from standard costs.[13]

Under CAS 407, you may use standard costs for estimating, accumulating, and reporting costs of direct material and labor only when the following criteria are met:[14]

(1) Standard costs are entered into your books of account.
(2) Standard costs and related variances (the difference between a pre-established measure and an actual measure) are appropriately accounted for at the level of the produc-

---
[10] 48 C.F.R. § 9904.405-50.
[11] 48 C.F.R. § 9904.405-50(b).
[12] 48 C.F.R. § 9904.405-60(b).
[13] 48 C.F.R. § 9904.407-20.
[14] 48 C.F.R. § 9904.407-40.

tion unit, which is defined as "a grouping of activities which either uses homogeneous inputs of direct material and direct labor or yields homogeneous outputs such that the costs or statistics related to these homogeneous inputs or outputs are appropriate as bases for allocating variances."

(3) Your practices with respect to the setting and revising of standards, use of standard costs, and disposition of variances are stated in writing and consistently followed.

Your company's written statement of practices with respect to standards must include the bases and criteria you use in setting and revising standards, the period during which standards remain effective, the level at which you set material quantity standards and labor-time standards, and conditions that material price standards and labor-rate standards are designed to reflect.

If you manipulate your material or labor standards or use standards in violation of CAS 407 and submit a price proposal, product invoice, or progress payment request to the Government based on those standards, you may face civil and criminal prosecution under the false statements and false claims statutes. The pricing documents and billings could possibly constitute both a false statement and false claim within the meaning of these statutes.

For example, assume that you normally use a standard cost system. In a current proposal, you price the bill of materials with quotations rather than with material price standards. Your written statement of practices, prepared to comply with CAS 407, states that material price standards are revised effective January 1, each year and remain in effect until the end of the calendar year. The proposed contract will be performed in the current calendar year.

The use of quotations to price the bill of materials violates CAS 401 because it is inconsistent with your practice of measuring direct material cost by standards and variances. In addition, this practice violates CAS 407 because the bill of materials should be priced using the material price standards currently in effect. Because of these CAS violations, you could be subject to prosecution under the False Statements Statute for falsely representing that your cost accounting practices were CAS-compliant. More significantly, this practice may also violate the false claims statute. For example, there could be a significant difference between the prices of your bill of materials estimated by standards and your prices billed to the Government (through progress payment or final product invoices) through use of quotations. The Government billings could be viewed as inflated if, for example, quotations are for the quantities required for the proposed contract and standards are based on economic order quantities for all of your business. Should this be the case, the Government

§ 12:30   Government Contract Compliance Handbook

could seek civil or criminal penalties for submission of a false claim.

IV. COMPLIANCE INITIATIVES

§ 12:31   Generally

Careful planning and monitoring will help your company reduce the risk of a Government fraud investigation for violations of the Cost Accounting Standards. Some of the more basic measures that you should consider implementing to ensure CAS compliance are discussed below.

§ 12:32   Develop a system of internal controls

Initial responsibility to ensure that your company's accounting practices comply with the Cost Accounting Standards lies with upper management. An important first step is to establish a system of internal controls to evaluate and monitor CAS compliance. This system must include written, well-defined policies and procedures which are communicated to the right people in the organization. Once the internal controls are in place, management must also develop a mechanism to audit the system both for continued compliance with the CAS regulations and to identify necessary adjustments to the company's cost accounting practices. You should consider the participation of both internal and outside independent auditors in monitoring the system.

§ 12:33   Employ CAS-qualified personnel

CAS rules and regulations are extremely complicated and require familiarity and expertise. Even the most sophisticated internal system to monitor compliance will fail unless it is designed and implemented by personnel well-versed in the CAS. Your company must ensure that you have such CAS-qualified people on board. Of course, you can train personnel from within your organization. Given the complexity of this area, you may conclude that this goal can best be met by hiring people with CAS expertise from outside. For smaller companies, using the services of an experienced outside accounting/consulting firm may be an attractive and effective solution.

§ 12:34   Educate your employees

Once your company has implemented a system of internal controls to monitor compliance with the CAS, you should also establish a program to educate key employees regarding your policies and procedures. The program should be simple, straightforward, and supplemented with easy-to-follow written materials. Not every employee needs to know about CAS. You need to target the groups that do.

§ 12:35 Recommendations

You have now seen the importance of maintaining cost accounting practices that comply with each of the Cost Accounting Standards. Your and your company's exposure for civil or criminal sanctions for fraud arising from CAS violations under the fraud statutes is all too real in today's environment. The following are specific recommendations for CAS compliance.

(a) Establish and maintain a system of *internal controls* to evaluate and monitor CAS compliance, including *written policies and procedures* for complying with the CAS. Make sure your CAS compliance program is tailored to your company's particular needs.

(b) *Employ CAS-qualified people*. CAS issues should be entrusted only to CAS experts. Ensure that *all financial personnel* are trained in CAS requirements to the extent necessary for them to carry out their duties properly. Most importantly, ensure each employee understands that if he or she is not a CAS expert, he or she should not try to make decisions on CAS-related issues. Leave these decisions to people with CAS expertise.

(c) Use *outside consultants* to audit your cost accounting system for CAS compliance on a periodic basis.

(d) Monitor employee adherence to procedures through *internal audits* or otherwise. Make sure all CAS-involved employees *understand the procedures* and the potential for *civil and criminal liability* for violating CAS.

(e) *Do not change your cost accounting practices* without full consultation with your CAS experts.

(f) As an employer, do not permit Government contract *certifications* to be signed in ignorance. As an employee, never execute CAS certifications or representations unless you are sure of what you are doing.

Chapter 13

Time Charging

I. OVERVIEW
§ 13:1   Scope note

II. CURRENT REQUIREMENTS
§ 13:2   Generally
§ 13:3   Administrative requirements
§ 13:4   Certifications
§ 13:5   Penalties for mischarging for companies
§ 13:6   Penalties for mischarging for individuals
§ 13:7   Frequently asked questions

III. HOW TO RECOGNIZE THE PROBLEM
§ 13:8   Generally
§ 13:9   Dramatic changes in time charging
§ 13:10 Lack of change over extended period
§ 13:11 Adjustments in recorded time entries
§ 13:12 Clear undercharging to a visible account
§ 13:13 Reclassification of employees by labor category
§ 13:14 Charging patterns that affect your CAS disclosure statement
§ 13:15 Unexplained adjustments in labor standards
§ 13:16 Overly rigid budgetary controls
§ 13:17 Contract provisions that limit costs
§ 13:18 Contract definition contracts
§ 13:19 Examples

IV. COMPLIANCE INITIATIVES

A. SYSTEM OF ACCUMULATING & REPORTING LABOR COSTS
§ 13:20 Generally

B. UPPER MANAGEMENT
§ 13:21 Establish policies & procedures
§ 13:22 Cost allocation policy
§ 13:23 Education of employees

§ 13:24 Enforcement through internal audits

C. MIDDLE MANAGEMENT

§ 13:25 Review all charges carefully
§ 13:26 Assignment of work
§ 13:27 Review & approval of time cards
§ 13:28 Review of transfers of labor charges

D. NONSUPERVISORY EMPLOYEES

§ 13:29 Submit accurate time cards

E. ACCOUNTING DEPARTMENT

§ 13:30 Screen for invalid charges
§ 13:31 Effective designation of project numbers
§ 13:32 Maximum automation of systems
§ 13:33 Control of invalid labor charges

F. AVOIDING PROBLEMS

§ 13:34 Recommendations

KeyCite®: Cases and other legal materials listed in KeyCite Scope can be researched through the KeyCite service on Westlaw®. Use KeyCite to check citations for form, parallel references, prior and later history, and comprehensive citator information, including citations to other decisions and secondary materials.

I. OVERVIEW

§ 13:1 Scope note

As discussed in §§ 11:1 et seq., the Government scrutinizes how contractors charge their costs to Government cost contracts to "deter, identify and address fraud, abuse, mismanagement, and waste of taxpayer funds."[1] Because labor is often a contractor's single largest category of cost, labor mischarging has been a top priority in the Government's investigation of fraud. Government contractors have been forced to pay millions of dollars in civil, criminal, and administrative penalties due to improper time-charging practices.[2]

The purpose of this chapter is to alert you to the possible "ir-

---

[Section 13:1]

[1] Mission Statement of Department of Homeland Security Inspector General, at http://www.oig.dhs.gov/.

[2] *See, e.g., Jana, Inc. v. U.S.*, 41 Fed. Cl. 735 (1998) (contractor allegedly

regularities" that may arise in charging labor costs under Government contracts and to suggest some controls that can be implemented to minimize, and hopefully eliminate, mischarging. This chapter does not focus specifically on technical cost allowability issues (which are addressed in §§ 11:1 et seq.); rather, the chapter concentrates on avoiding the problems that can arise in the use of specific time-charging mechanisms. The focus here is to alert you to some of the practices that you can implement to ensure that once you have made a decision regarding where a particular cost should be charged, your time and cost distribution system accurately reflects your intention.

II. CURRENT REQUIREMENTS

§ 13:2 Generally

As a contractor doing business with the Government, you must accurately record and charge the costs you incur in performing your contracts. Often, your right to payment depends on your ability to charge costs to the proper account. At other times, the price the Government is willing to negotiate for a contract may depend on the costs you have recently incurred for labor hours in certain categories. In addition, if you improperly record your costs or improperly alter your cost records, you may subject yourself to administrative, civil, or criminal liability.

§ 13:3 Administrative requirements

The requirement that contractors properly charge and report their labor costs to the Government applies essentially to all types of Government contracts. The Federal Acquisition Regulation (FAR) provisions on *cost-reimbursement* contracts provide that a contractor may be reimbursed for only those costs that are both *allowable* and properly *allocable* to the contract.[1] Similarly, in the case of price-redeterminable contracts, the FAR provides that the price will be redetermined only on the basis of the *allow-*

---

altered time cards submitted to the Navy under its time-and-materials contract); see also 18 Andrews Gov't Cont. Litig. Rep. 1 (Nov. 8, 2004) (discussing a $1.9 million settlement between Department of Justice and Photon Research Associates for allegedly submitting invoices containing inflated labor costs); 46 GC ¶ 32 (Jan. 21, 2004) (discussing charges brought against two employees of Ogilvy & Mather who allegedly submitted time cards with intentionally inflated labor hours); 36 GC ¶ 50 (Jan. 26, 1994) (discussing the settlement of Curtiss-Wright subsidiary, Target Rock Corp., where the contractor paid $17.5 million to settle allegations of labor mischarging and the submission of false and inflated invoices and expense vouchers).

[Section 13:3]
[1]FAR 16.307, subpt. 31.2, 52.216-7.

§ 13:3   GOVERNMENT CONTRACT COMPLIANCE HANDBOOK

able costs properly *allocable* to the contract.[2] Contractors must also track labor hours accurately in performing *fixed-price* contracts, where those contracts are negotiated on the basis of cost or pricing data or where the Government makes progress payments based on cost.

The determination of what costs are allowable and to which contract(s) they may be allocated is governed primarily by the cost principles of the FAR (see §§ 11:1 et seq.),[3] the Cost Accounting Standards (CAS) (see §§ 12:1 et seq.),[4] and generally accepted accounting practices. Your CAS Disclosure Statement is important because it can obligate you to observe specific rules relating to how you account for and charge labor and other costs under your Government contracts.[5] (See §§ 12:1 et seq.) Other requirements may arise as a result of conditions imposed by the Defense Contract Audit Agency (DCAA) in its assessment of the reliability of a specific contractor's accounting system.

Together, these requirements govern which costs are allowable and allocable when you are seeking recovery under cost-reimbursement or price-redeterminable contracts or progress payments under fixed-price contracts. If your employees are not properly recording their time, you cannot ensure that the costs charged to a particular Government contract are both allowable and allocable.

§ 13:4   Certifications

The Truth in Negotiations Act (TINA)[1] requires contractors to supply the Government with accurate, complete, and current cost or pricing data when they negotiate any contract, subcontract, or contract modification expected to exceed $700,000, unless otherwise excepted.[2] You must update the data so as to maintain, accuracy, completeness, and currency up to the time you and the Government reach agreement on price. At that point, you will be required to *certify* the accuracy, completeness, and currency of the data.[3] (TINA is discussed in greater detail in §§ 9:1 et seq.)

Similarly, the Contract Disputes Act requires contractors who submit claims against the United States of more than $100,000

---

[2]FAR 16.205-4, 16.206-4, 52.216-5, 52.216-6.
[3]FAR pt. 31.
[4]FAR pt. 30; 48 C.F.R. ch. 99.
[5]FAR 30.202-1; 48 C.F.R. § 9903.202-1.

[Section 13:4]

[1]10 U.S.C.A. § 2306a; 41 U.S.C.A. §§ 3501 et seq.
[2]FAR 15.403-4.
[3]10 U.S.C.A. § 2306a(a)(2); 41 U.S.C.A. § 3502(b); *see* FAR 15.406-2.

TIME CHARGING § 13:6

to *certify* that the claim is made in good faith and that the supporting data for the claim are accurate and complete.[4] (See §§ 16:1 et seq.)

If you have not instituted procedures to ensure that employee labor costs are properly reflected in your company's records, you cannot make the certifications noted above with any degree of confidence.

§ 13:5 Penalties for mischarging for companies

If your company mischarges labor costs to the Government, it will have to reimburse the Government for the mischarged costs. However, you may also be subject to a number of criminal, civil, or administrative penalties. A host of criminal statutes may be invoked to punish mischargers, including the False Claims Act, the false statements statute, the Major Fraud Act of 1988, the mail and wire fraud statutes, the Racketeer Influenced and Corrupt Organizations Act, and various conspiracy statutes. (See §§ 1:1 et seq.)

The Government has not been reluctant to use any or all of these statutes to punish violators. For example, the Government brought a criminal suit against a contractor for allegedly creating false and inaccurate time records for work performed on a Government contract and thereafter destroying the actual time records in furtherance of its scheme to submit inflated requests for payment.[1] The Government has also been willing to intervene in False Claims Act qui tam suits alleging labor mischarging.[2] (See §§ 1:1 et seq.) In another example, the Government sued a shipbuilder constructing military transport vessels, claiming that the shipbuilder violated the False Claims Act by charging time for developing commercial transport vessels to an indirect independent research and development (IR&D) cost account allocable to all of the contractor's Government contracts, rather than as a direct charge to commercial vessel contracts.[3]

§ 13:6 Penalties for mischarging for individuals

Liability for mischarging labor costs reaches beyond the

---

[4]41 U.S.C.A. § 7103(b).

[Section 13:5]

[1]*U.S. v. Frequency Electronics*, 862 F. Supp. 834 (E.D. N.Y. 1994).

[2]*See, e.g., U.S. ex rel. O'Keefe v. McDonnell Douglas Corp.*, 918 F. Supp. 1338 (E.D. Mo. 1996) (Government intervened in qui tam suit alleging that contractor intentionally inflated labor costs by $11 million and instructed employees to charge labor hours to unrelated Government contracts).

[3]*U.S. v. Newport News Shipbuilding, Inc.*, 276 F. Supp. 2d 539 (E.D. Va. 2003).

§ 13:6 GOVERNMENT CONTRACT COMPLIANCE HANDBOOK

corporate structure. Employees and management personnel who have been involved in mischarging, even sometimes inadvertently, may also be *individually* subject to civil and criminal penalties under common law and the statutes cited above. In fact, when prosecuting a company for labor mischarging, the Government will typically also prosecute the employees who engaged in the mischarging or who *supervised* the employees who mischarged. For example, in one case where a contractor was forced to pay almost $900,000 to the Government for mischarging labor costs, the company's chief executive officer agreed to pay $500,000 to settle personal allegations against him.[1] Two employees of another contractor who were involved in falsifying time records were indicted and convicted of making false statements to Government officials, submitting false claims, and committing mail fraud.[2] Similarly, where a company president and vice president altered employee time cards to make it appear that work done under commercial contracts had been charged to Government contracts, the two were indicted and convicted of making false statements to Government officials and conspiring to defraud the United States.[3]

An employee who has engaged in improper charging of time and expenses may also, of course, be disciplined by the company. Such discipline may include dismissal, suspension without pay, or reassignment.

§ 13:7 Frequently asked questions

Question 1: What if my time-charging procedures are simply "sloppy"? Can I be liable to the Government even if I have no specific intent to submit inaccurate costs to receive increase payments under federal contracts?

Answer 1: Yes. Assume that your company was performing numerous Government and commercial contracts and permitted employees to alter their time cards without restriction, to replace the time cards at will, and to sign the cards in blank in advance of performing work. Your company also permitted invoices, receipts, and travel vouchers to be indiscriminately altered and

---

[Section 13:6]

[1]DOD Inspector General, Semiannual Report to the Congress for April 1, 1996 to September 30, 1996, at 26.

[2]*U.S. v. Systems Architects, Inc.*, 757 F.2d 373, 17 Fed. R. Evid. Serv. 705 (1st Cir. 1985).

[3]*U.S. v. Martel*, 792 F.2d 630, 20 Fed. R. Evid. Serv. 1104 (7th Cir. 1986); see also *U.S. v. EER Systems Corp.*, 950 F. Supp. 130 (D. Md. 1996) (Government sued contractor and its president and vice president for, among other things, mischarging direct labor time incurred on fixed-price contracts to overhead accounts under cost-reimbursement contracts).

signed in blank. This method of timekeeping inevitably led to the shifting of labor costs from Government cost-ceiling contracts, where the ceiling had been reached, to other Government or commercial contracts. You decide to assert that your organization was merely sloppy and that any mischarging that occurred was unintentional.

In a similar case, notwithstanding its "negligence" defense, a contractor was found guilty under the False Claims Act.[1] As discussed more fully below, the problem of "excessive sloppiness" could have been avoided by implementing and enforcing rules for time card preparation.

Question 2: If I only perform fixed-price contracts, why does the Government care how I allocate my labor costs?

Answer 2: The Government cares because contractors may submit applications for progress payments based on their actual costs incurred, and the Government is concerned that misallocated or unallowable labor costs will be submitted in a progress payment invoice. (See §§ 14:1 et seq. for a discussion of progress payments.) In addition, where the contractor submits cost or pricing data to the Government when negotiating the contract price, such data ultimately affect the both direct and indirect elements of the contract price. Thus, if the cost or pricing data are inflated, the Government will overpay the contractor for the work.

Question 3: As a manager, how can I be sure that every employee is accurately charging the employee's time on each contract?

Answer 3: There is, in short, no simple answer. However, you can take steps to ensure that employees are aware of and follow proper procedures for recording their time. These procedures, as well as management and accounting initiatives to avoid time-charging irregularities, are discussed below.

III. HOW TO RECOGNIZE THE PROBLEM

§ 13:8 Generally

On many contracts, labor is the single largest category of cost charged to the Government. Consequently, the cost of labor at many contractor locations is the most sensitive cost element that the Government is required to audit. It is therefore essential that you understand how the Government will monitor and audit your time-charging practices.

Your accounting staff and, perhaps, other cost personnel should

---

[Section 13:7]

[1]*United States v. Bradford Nat'l Corp.*, Crim. No. 81 Cr. 870 (S.D. N.Y., Dec. 24, 1981).

§ 13:8

have access to the current DCAA *Contract Audit Manual,* which is a comprehensive, two-volume publication used by the DCAA in performing contract audits.[1] The *Manual* provides detailed instructions to auditors on virtually all aspects of performing a Government contract audit. The *Manual* also makes clear that the DCAA places a great deal of emphasis on a contractor's ability to track labor costs accurately. Significantly, the *Manual,* as well as the DOD Inspector General's *Handbook on Fraud Indicators for Contract Auditors,*[2] and the GSA Inspector General's *Procurement Fraud Handbook,*[3] discusses some of the most common indicators of labor mischarging and advises Government auditors how to recognize and pursue those indicators. You would do well to structure your internal control program to minimize the number and occurrence of such indicators in your time distribution system. Some of the indicators that the Government considers to be most prominent are discussed in the sections below.

§ 13:9 Dramatic changes in time charging

A certain way to draw the attention of Government auditors or investigators is to permit significant, unexplained changes in time-charging patterns or distributions within your system to occur. It is often much less important how or where the change occurs within your system than that there is a significant change. The changes can be in labor category (for example, engineering to marketing), program category (for example, IR&D to bid and proposal (B&P), or direct to indirect) or program cost category (for example, fixed-price contract to cost-type contract). Any significant reduction or increase of labor hours in a particular category is likely to draw attention. A critical element of your internal audit system must be the identification of surges and drops of hours by various labor categories. Where such surges and drops are unavoidable, you must *document* the *causes* for the fluctuations.

You must be particularly sensitive to sudden reductions in hours charged to projects or cost pools that have reached their fixed *ceilings.* An alarm should sound within your system when such reductions are accompanied by simultaneous surges in hours

---

[Section 13:8]

[1]*See also* DCAA, Guidelines for a Comprehensive Audit of Labor Costs (designed for field auditors conducting comprehensive labor audits of Government contractors).

[2]DOD Inspector General, Handbook on Fraud Indicators for Contract Auditors (Mar. 31, 1993).

[3]U.S. GSA Inspector General, Procurement Fraud Handbook (Dec. 2012).

TIME CHARGING § 13:12

charged to cost-type projects or cost pools that do not have ceilings. Mid-level supervisors must be instructed to consult with higher-level managers when they find the need to shift one or more employees who have been performing substantial amounts of work on a fixed-price contract to work on a cost-type contract. Similarly, sudden cessation of IR&D and B&P charges near the end of your fiscal year will likely draw attention from Government auditors.

§ 13:10 Lack of change over extended period

Just as significant reductions or increases in labor hours in certain categories often draw the attention of the Government, so too will noticeable lack of change in labor hours over extended periods. It is to be expected that labor hours by category will fluctuate to some degree as the mix and stage of the work changes. In this regard, it is the *extraordinary consistency* of the charging that draws attention. Suspicion of time-charging manipulation often arises where an employee charges the same amount of time for a number of projects over an extended period of time (for example, where the employee's time card consistently reads, 1 hr.-project X, 2 hrs.-project Y, 5 hrs.-project Z).

§ 13:11 Adjustments in recorded time entries

You should be particularly careful to implement controls over changing or transferring time entries already recorded by employees. Most contractor accounting systems are designed to accommodate the transfer of labor charges from one account to another through journal entries. Prudent contractors make certain that journal transfers cannot be made without both *explanation* and *verification* by appropriate personnel. The DCAA *Contract Audit Manual* instructs auditors that they should look for adequate rationale and documentation to support all significant labor transfers. If significant movements appear to involve more than normal corrections, the Government's risk and vulnerability is deemed to be high and the costs will be reviewed by auditors.[1]

§ 13:12 Clear undercharging to a visible account

By their nature or prominence, certain projects or cost pools automatically draw the attention of Government auditors. The greater the project's or pool's visibility within your organization, the greater the scrutiny. For example, you may decide to compete

---

[Section 13:11]
[1]DCAA Contract Audit Manual ¶¶ 5-913, 6-404.6.b(6).

§ 13:12   Government Contract Compliance Handbook

for a highly publicized program, and this intention may be widely discussed within the company, with the result that Government auditors and program personnel also hear of your intent to compete for the program. They know the program is important to you and they are curious how much effort you are devoting to preparing the proposal. The auditors examine your most recent B&P charges and discover that you are charging substantially less time to the proposal effort than would appear to be warranted. Employee interviews may confirm what appears to be organized mischarging. In short, you should pay particularly close attention to highly visible programs and accounts, regardless of type.

§ 13:13   Reclassification of employees by labor category

"Reclassification of employees by labor category" is perhaps a variation of the "dramatic changes in time charging" indicator discussed above. However, this activity manifests itself through a very specific, noticeable change in your operations. The "indicator" arises when you actually change an employee's (or group of employees') labor category and not merely issue temporary instructions on how the employee is to charge the employee's time. Reclassification occurs, for example, where you decide to redesignate a group of employees as technical marketers that had previously been designated as engineers. Depending on your business mix and disclosed accounting practices, this redesignation could have a dramatic impact on how the time of the employees is charged and distributed. This in turn could invite allegations that you have violated the description of your cost accounting practices set forth in your CAS Disclosure Statement (see §§ 12:1 et seq.) and illegally manipulated time charges.

§ 13:14   Charging patterns that affect your CAS disclosure statement

Your company's internal auditors should be familiar with your CAS Disclosure Statement. Government auditors will undoubtedly be aware of the contents of your Disclosure Statement, and certain time-charging practices will automatically lead the auditors to compare the charging practices to the Disclosure Statement. For example, Government auditors often examine how a contractor is instructing its employees to charge warranty work. The auditors look to confirm that employees are not charging warranty work on fixed-price contracts to indirect cost pools while charging warranty work on cost-type contracts directly to the contracts.

§ 13:15   Unexplained adjustments in labor standards

Many contractors develop one or more sets of labor standards that prove useful in tracking labor efficiencies, preparing proposals, or administering contracts. The standards typically represent model times for performing certain tasks by labor category. Although Government auditors frequently suspect that significant adjustments in such standards may constitute defective pricing, such adjustments can also lead to allegations of labor mischarging. As with any significant adjustment reflecting labor recording, you must be prepared to explain any significant adjustments made in labor standards.

§ 13:16 Overly rigid budgetary controls

Many contractors understandably have management systems that require strict adherence to budgetary controls. If those budgetary controls are too inflexible, however, auditors realize that labor charges may have a tendency to follow the identical track of budgeted amounts, which may result in "predetermined" labor charges by the contractor. This risk may be especially high where managers' bonuses or incentives are tied to a particular fixed budget.

§ 13:17 Contract provisions that limit costs

A contract provision or modification may contain language that increases the incentive for labor mischarging. For example, a provision may put ceilings on certain costs or labor rates, or even require the contractor to deliver goods or services at no cost to the Government. These restrictions prevent a contractor from recovering costs incurred above the preset limits. If the contractor incurs costs above these ceilings, the auditor will likely look for possible improper cost transfers (discussed in § 13:11).

§ 13:18 Contract definition contracts

Contract Definition (CD) contracts are generally short-term, fixed-price contracts that are awarded to several contractors that will compete for a major follow-on prime contract. The Government will use the results delivered under the CD contracts to prepare the request for proposals. Because a contractor's performance under the CD contract will have a direct bearing on its chance of winning the prime contract, there may be a tendency to spend more than the value of the CD contract. Consequently, the DCAA believes that CD contracts are "highly susceptible" to labor mischarging and instructs auditors to review them to make sure

§ 13:18   Government Contract Compliance Handbook

all allocable effort is being charged.[1]

§ 13:19   Examples

Transfer of precontract labor costs: Suppose that you have historically performed only commercial work and have developed a practice of beginning work under your contracts before the contracts are formally activated. Your customers have reacted favorably to the responsive and enthusiastic way that you pursued your new orders. After obtaining a Government contract to produce a variant of one of your commercial products, you begin—consistent with your commercial practice and without the Government's approval—performing the Government contract before the effective date of the contract. Under the terms of the contract, you are to be paid based on the number of hours spent in performing the contract. However, you are aware that, absent a special agreement, you may not charge labor costs to a Government contract that are incurred before the effective date of the contract.

To recover your precontract labor costs, your president and vice president direct the manager of accounting to shift time entries to make it appear that work done under commercial contracts had actually been performed under the Government contract. You contend that the transferred costs were intended to approximate the precontract costs you incurred in performing the Government contract. Have you done anything wrong?

Yes. Notwithstanding your contention, the transfer of labor costs from the commercial to the Government contract was illegal. The company, along with the president and vice president, could be convicted of making false statements to the Government and conspiring to defraud the United States.[1]

When fraud is committed at the highest levels of a company, even the implementation of effective compliance procedures may not be enough to prevent wrongdoing. Nevertheless, even in this case, implementation of certain procedures would have reduced the likelihood that the fraud could have gone undetected within your company. For example, the mischarging might have been avoided had your company's procedures required that any change to an employee time card must be initialed by the employee. It might likewise have been avoided had your company's procedures required middle management to review the cost status of

---

[Section 13:18]

[1]DCAA Contract Audit Manual ¶ 6-404.6.b(8).

[Section 13:19]

[1]*U.S. v. Martel*, 792 F.2d 630, 20 Fed. R. Evid. Serv. 1104 (7th Cir. 1986).

TIME CHARGING § 13:19

contracts periodically. A review of the costs of the commercial and Government contracts would have revealed cost discrepancies indicating the mischarging.

Labor transfers resulting in defective pricing: Assume you are performing two Government contracts: the first is a fixed-price contract for the rehabilitation of aircraft, the second is a fixed-price level-of-effort contract for the rewiring of wing sections. Under the second contract, you are paid a fixed price for each hour spent in rewiring the wing sections. Meanwhile, you are expecting the Government to offer a follow-on contract to rewire additional wing sections at a fixed price. Your contract administrator suspects that the fixed price the Government would be willing to negotiate would be based on the number of hours you spent in rewiring the wing sections under your existing contract. To make the number of hours spent in rewiring the existing wing sections appear larger, your contract administrator instructed employees working on both the rehabilitation and rewiring contracts to charge their time to the rewiring contract. The employees charged their time in accordance with your contract administrator's instructions. The mischarged time was later reflected in cost or pricing data submitted to the Government in negotiation of the follow-on rewiring contract. Does your company face any liability for these actions?

Yes. On the Government's discovery of the mischarging, your contract administrator could be indicted and possibly convicted of making false statements to Government officials and conspiring to defraud the United States.[2]

An effective system of accumulating and reporting costs might have prevented this mischarging. Your company's procedures should have impressed on the contract administrator and the employees the importance of charging time accurately. The mischarging might also have been avoided if middle management had regularly reviewed the cost reports of the two contracts. A review would have revealed an abnormally low number of hours on the rehabilitation contract and an abnormally high number of hours on the rewiring contract. This would have indicated the possibility of mischarging.

Labor transfers to manipulate cost ceilings: Assume you are the owner and president of a new laundry and cleaning service that won its first Government contract six months ago. The contract, which was awarded by the General Services Administration (GSA) as a cost-reimbursement contract, contains fairly low indirect cost rate ceilings to ensure that the Government did not pay for potentially high overhead costs.

---

[2]*U.S. v. Poarch*, 878 F.2d 1355 (11th Cir. 1989).

§ 13:19   GOVERNMENT CONTRACT COMPLIANCE HANDBOOK

Just recently, you won your second Government contract based on a proposal submitted to the Department of Housing and Urban Development (HUD). The HUD contract, which is basically similar to your GSA contract, contains an indirect cost rate that is higher than the rate contained in your GSA agreement. Your program manager, who is responsible for overseeing your new Government contracts business, notices that you can recover more overhead costs by charging labor incurred in performing the GSA contract to the HUD contract. Is there a problem with shifting these labor charges?

Yes. The shifting of labor costs is improper. Although the laundry and cleaning work was done for the GSA, your shifting of labor hours to the HUD contract inappropriately increased the direct costs from which your overhead reimbursement was based. In this case, proper company procedures—such as requiring the program manager to document the reasons for the transfer of labor costs—would have gone a long way towards alerting your program manager that the transfer was clearly improper.

IV. COMPLIANCE INITIATIVES

A. SYSTEM OF ACCUMULATING & REPORTING LABOR COSTS

§ 13:20   Generally

A well-conceived, well-implemented system of accumulating and reporting labor costs will minimize the possibility of labor mischarging. It will also provide checks that alert management to any cases of possible mischarging. To be effective, a system of accumulating and reporting labor costs must at least do the following:

(a) Provide *clear direction to employees* regarding what costs should be charged to various accounts.
(b) Place *responsibility* for the proper charging of the employee's time on the *employee* performing the effort.
(c) Provide for *internal checks* on the accuracy of the system.
(d) Provide *periodic review* of the reported costs.

Implementing such a system requires the support and involvement of at least four groups within the company: (1) upper management, (2) middle management and employee supervisors, (3) nonsupervisory employees, and (4) accounting personnel.

B. UPPER MANAGEMENT

§ 13:21   Establish policies & procedures

Upper management is primarily responsible for deciding how various types of costs should be treated and communicating these

TIME CHARGING § 13:23

decisions to various groups within the organization. "Upper management" includes the president, vice presidents, controller or vice president of finance, general counsel or other in-house lead attorney, and critical program and technical managers for the company's larger programs. Upper management has three major tasks in attempting to ensure that labor mischarging does not occur:

(1) *Policymaking*: Determine how certain major types of labor costs are to be billed to the Government.
(2) *Education*: Communicate effectively to all employees the obligation to record time accurately and the company's obligation to reflect these charges accurately in billings to the Government.
(3) *Enforcement*: Ensure that the company institutes effective internal audit mechanisms to test compliance with its directives.

§ 13:22 Cost allocation policy

The determination of what costs are allowable and the contract(s) to which costs are properly allocable is governed principally by the FAR cost principles and the Cost Accounting Standards. These regulations and Standards allow contractors some flexibility in structuring their cost accounting systems and, to a limited extent, in determining cost treatment. Upper management's first responsibility is to exercise its prerogatives in accordance with legal requirements and the company's goals.

For example, upper management may decide to undertake a substantial computer upgrade program to enhance the company's competitive position on several major programs. The management group will have to decide whether the effort is to be treated as an IR&D cost, a technical engineering overhead cost, or a direct charge to one or more specific contracts or accounts. If upper management has ensured that detailed procedures for treatment of Government contract costs are in place and being followed, its own range of choice in this instance will already have been restricted. Effective procedures and a carefully crafted CAS Disclosure Statement (where required) will provide guidelines for distinguishing an IR&D effort from a direct contract effort. Such procedures and the Disclosure Statement would provide guidance as to how the computer enhancement costs should be treated.

§ 13:23 Education of employees

Having overseen the establishment of the company's accounting practices and policies, upper management must then ensure that employees are educated about the practices and their obligation to follow them. Upper management can satisfy this obligation by directing that the company publish detailed policies governing employee time charging and proper distribution of time charges within the accounting system. Upper management should also communicate directly with employees through periodic memoranda. For larger companies, video presentations may be appropriate.

The DCAA states that companies should establish time-charging awareness programs with orientation training for new employees and refresher courses for existing employees.[1] At a minimum, company procedures should be in place to inform employees at every level as to how they are to record time. The objective in all cases is to structure procedures that *limit employee and supervisor discretion* as to how labor is charged to the contractor's Government and commercial contracts.

§ 13:24 Enforcement through internal audits

Upper management can limit the risk that mischarging will occur by implementing an effective internal audit program. Most large Government contractors have an internal audit function that assesses and monitors employee compliance with the company's time-charging procedures. For larger companies, it is often advisable to employ a *second* internal audit function at a local or divisional level. Internal audits of compliance with time-charging procedures should be conducted with sufficient frequency and detail to cover the same tests that are performed by the Government in its floor checks and comprehensive labor audits.

Your internal auditors should regularly conduct the following two tests to assess employee compliance with company time-charging procedures. These tests correspond roughly to those that the DCAA performs in reviewing employee time cards: (a) an "attribute test" that assesses an employee's compliance with company procedures by examining the employee's time card at the end of each week after the card has been submitted for approval; and (b) regular "floor checks" to determine, at any point in time, the aggregate level of employee compliance with company time-charging procedures.

(1) *Attribute test*: The attribute test ensures that each time card that has been submitted complies with the company's time-charging procedures. The attribute test is conducted by collecting the time cards of a preestablished percentage of all employees for a designated period. The cards showing nonconformance with company procedures are recorded and the employees involved are

---

[Section 13:23]

[1]DCAA Contract Audit Manual ¶ 5-907.

TIME CHARGING § 13:24

contacted and required to correct or explain the irregularities.

In most cases, it is appropriate to conduct the attribute test before the time cards are transmitted to the accounting department for input into the company's cost records. It is difficult, if not impossible, to perform a meaningful attribute test with copies of time cards. Therefore, the review process must be extremely efficient and streamlined so as to avoid interruption of the normal time-recording process. Some companies perform the process by grouping supervisors under key administrators who are in positions to ensure that the time cards are collected, analyzed, corrected, and returned promptly. (See Appendix O for a sample of a time card attribute test analysis sheet.)

(2) *Floor checks*: The second test, commonly called the "floor check," involves physical observation of how an employee spends the employee's time and how that time is recorded at the employee's work station. This process is designed to monitor aspects of employee compliance with company time-charging procedures that cannot be verified once a time card has been completed and submitted.

For example, a floor check can determine whether employees are filling out time cards in advance or are waiting to make entries on their time cards until the end of the week, neither of which can be detected when a time card is analyzed after the fact. The company's internal audit floor check procedures should match the floor check procedures that the DCAA is likely to perform at your facility.

The DCAA *Contract Audit Manual* states that the following procedures should be employed by auditors in reviewing a contractor's timekeeping controls during a floor check: (a) observe and evaluate the specific method for recording time at various work areas; (b) determine whether employee attendance is controlled by clock cards, time cards, or other suitable means and review the procedure for employees arriving late and leaving early; (c) review and evaluate the means by which time records are controlled at each station, including the assignment of task numbers for jobs performed; (d) determine whether hours on time tickets are periodically reconciled with attendance records and payroll; (e) determine whether there is a division of responsibility for personnel in charge of preparation of time records and those responsible for payroll; (f) determine whether there is a division of responsibility for personnel in charge of preparation of time records and those responsible for operating within budgets; (g) determine the procedures for recording idle time; (h) determine whether records of piecework and work performed under wage incentive plans are checked and controlled independently as to production counts, approvals for allowances, and other opera-

§ 13:24   Government Contract Compliance Handbook

tions; (i) perform independent floor checks to test employee attendance and accuracy in recording work performed; (j) when appropriate, ask representatives of the Contracting Officer to accompany the auditor on floor checks; (k) scan batches of labor distribution documents for obvious errors and arbitrary allocations of time to contracts; and (l) determine if the contractor has an employee work-at-home program and assess the materiality of the costs incurred by employees in the program.[1]

C. MIDDLE MANAGEMENT

§ 13:25 Review all charges carefully

Middle management has a number of responsibilities. These include assisting upper management in deciding how various types of costs should be treated within the system and communicating these decisions to nonsupervisory employees, reviewing reports of actual costs to identify possible instances of noncompliance, and controlling nonsupervisory employees to ensure that they accurately record their time in accordance with management directives. In performing each of these tasks, middle management can serve as an internal check on the accuracy of the system.

"Middle management" includes supervisors who direct time charging as well as project administrators and program managers. It is at this level that actions and omissions generate the greatest risk of mischarging.[1] Your supervisors and project administrators probably have more control over how time is charged and billed to your contracts than any other group of employees. There are three critical control points relating to time charging at this level: (1) the assignment of work, (2) the review and approval of time cards, and (3) the review and revision of transfers of labor charges.

§ 13:26 Assignment of work

As noted above, you must institute procedures that *minimize* the *discretion* of supervisors and employees to determine how time will be charged to company projects. While the discretion of supervisors and employees should be limited, your time-charging system must not be so inflexible as to prevent the exercise of

---

[Section 13:24]

[1]DCAA Contract Audit Manual ¶ 6-405.2.

[Section 13:25]

[1]*See* DOD Inspector General, Handbook on Fraud Indicators for Contract Auditors II-3 (Mar. 31, 1993) (noting that company pressures to satisfy performance goals may on occasion motivate project administrators to manipulate time charges).

TIME CHARGING § 13:27

discretion even when clearly appropriate, however. For example, the system must allow employees who are assigned to a specific new B&P project but who normally charge their time to other indirect pools to charge their time directly to their new B&P assignment.

Procedures should require that documents accompany each task or project whenever possible. This serves two important functions: (1) it reduces the risk of manipulation of labor charges by supervisors; and (2) it reduces the number of situations in which a charge cannot be substantiated through documentation if questioned by Government auditors.

When documents travel with a project or assignment, employees know exactly what project number to charge. This also reduces the possibility of supervisor manipulation of employee time cards since each project number to be charged appears on the applicable work assignment or work order. For assembly-line laborers, a "travel" or work order can often accompany an item under process. Similarly, a work order or request for engineering services can often be sent with an engineering assignment.

There are, of course, instances when it is not possible to send documents with work assignments. For example, when an employee performs work that benefits a number of cost objectives, it is often impossible or extremely burdensome to require that a specific work order accompany each task that is to be performed. (See Appendix P, which is a copy of an actual time card that was submitted by an employee who worked on a number of projects simultaneously.) In such cases, a supervisor should draft a memorandum describing how the employee should allocate the employee's time among the projects.

Supervisors and project managers should prepare *detailed documentation* of sustained changes in personnel use or project utilization. For instance, when a supervisor determines that all work being performed by a particular employee should be charged to an indirect rather than direct pool, the supervisor should document the rationale for directing the employee to change how the employee is charging time. As noted above, the DOD Inspector General views unexplained reclassification of employees as a primary indicator of fraud.[1]

§ 13:27 Review & approval of time cards

In most companies, employees must submit their time cards to

[Section 13:26]

[1]*See* DOD Inspector General, Handbook on Fraud Indicators for Contract Auditors II-8 (Mar. 31, 1993) (cautioning auditors to review situations in which a work order is discontinued, but employees continue to perform similar work under a new work order).

§ 13:27   GOVERNMENT CONTRACT COMPLIANCE HANDBOOK

their supervisors for approval before the cards are submitted to the accounting department. The supervisor reviews the time card and, if it is properly completed by the employee, approves and signs the time card. Nearly all companies have published procedures that forbid supervisors from making *any* changes on employee time cards. However, such procedures are not always enforced. In some instances, supervisors have been permitted to make changes directly on employee time cards. Needless to say, such practices invite allegations of fraud. In this regard, the DOD recommends that each employee's time card should remain exclusively under the employee's control at all times and that the employee should initial any changes made to the time card.

Supervisors should not handle time cards at all except as specifically provided for in the company's time distribution procedures. Supervisors should conduct daily compliance checks with as many employees as possible to ensure that all employees are completing time cards in ink on a daily basis and are not signing the time cards in advance.

Where procedures requiring documentation of work assignments have been implemented, supervisors should find little if any need to handle employee time cards or to request that employees change their time cards. Moreover, a supervisor will not feel comfortable manipulating time on an employee's time card when the supervisor knows that there may be a document that indicates that the employee did not work on the project to which the supervisor has recorded the employee's time.

§ 13:28   Review of transfers of labor charges

Transfers of labor charges should be limited and monitored, and procedures governing such transfers should include specific steps that supervisors, administrators, and accounting department personnel must observe.

In most companies, a labor transfer is effected through a journal voucher or a memorandum requesting that the accounting department issue a journal voucher. A journal voucher is an accounting ledger sheet that records the transfer of a cost from one project or job order to another. In the past, it was not uncommon to find that a company imposed virtually no limitations on how its project managers or administrators could transfer labor charges among projects, and there were often no limitations imposed regarding when such transfers could be made. In one instance, project administrators could move virtually any amount of labor charges out of their own projects and into projects over which they did not even have responsibility. Such transfers could be made without the signature or approval of the administrator whose project was to receive the transferred labor charges. Obviously, this permitted project administrators to move time from their overrun projects to projects that were not even within their own purview, all without the knowledge of the administrator whose project was to receive the transferred labor charges. In some instances, labor transfers were made more than a year after the time was initially recorded. The DOD Inspector General and the DCAA view transfers of labor charges as a significant risk area for mischarging.[1]

Make sure you adopt labor charge *transfer procedures* that at a minimum require the following:

(a) The concurrence and signatures of *both* the administrator making the transfer and the administrator whose project will receive the transfer together with a *written statement* of the reason for the transfer.

(b) Special supervisory *approval* for labor transfers that are proposed more than a set time period after the labor is recorded (for example, three months).

(c) Issuance of specific *guidance to the accounting department*, including at a minimum (1) *notice* of the rules referenced in items a and b above, (2) *verification* that both of the projects or job orders involved in the transfer are valid project numbers, and (3) special attention to transfers from *fixed-price* contracts to *cost-type* contracts or into or out of IR&D or B&P or *indirect charge* projects.

D. NONSUPERVISORY EMPLOYEES

§ 13:29 Submit accurate time cards

The cornerstone of any system of accumulating and reporting labor costs is the time card of the individual employee. It is on this document that the employee records the employee's time in performing specific tasks. These costs are entered "into the system" and eventually reported and billed to the Government. The employee's role in the system is to record accurately the employee's time in accordance with management directives. The proper treatment of specific types of costs is generally outside the purview of the nonsupervisory employee's responsibility. That is more properly the province of management.

Implementation of a well-conceived set of time-charging procedures will greatly reduce the possibility that mischarging can occur as a result of actions taken at the nonsupervisory employee level. Mischarging is usually the result of inadvertence,

---

[Section 13:28]

[1]DOD Inspector General, Handbook on Fraud Indicators for Contract Auditors II-10 (Mar. 31, 1993); DCAA Contract Audit Manual ¶ 6-404.6.b(6).

§ 13:29   Government Contract Compliance Handbook

sloppiness, or compliance with erroneous supervisory instructions. Nonsupervisory employees have little or no incentive to engage in mischarging. In most instances where mischarging is suspected, the suspicion would never have arisen had the employee followed company time-charging procedures. Thus, there really need be only one short directive to employees regarding time-charging procedures: FOLLOW THE RULES.

For most companies, there are only a few mechanical rules that need to be articulated to employees completing time cards. These rules correspond with the areas that are of the greatest interest to Government auditors.

Nonsupervisory employees often believe that it is more important to submit a *neat* time card than to make changes in accordance with company rules that might result in a sloppy-looking time card. Therefore, the company rules should include procedures that must be followed regarding how to make changes even if the result is a card that is less neat than would otherwise be desired. (See Appendix Q for a sample time card that exhibits a number of violations of a company's time-charging rules.)

E. ACCOUNTING DEPARTMENT

§ 13:30   Screen for invalid charges

All time charges generated within your company that eventually find their way to the Government flow through your accounting department. Implementation of effective controls within your accounting department can significantly reduce the likelihood of mischarging. No Government contractor can avoid mischarging unless it has instituted efficient accounting controls specifically designed to track and test cost treatment by discrete category. The sections set forth below do not attempt to discuss all of the controls that can be implemented to reduce the risk of mischarging, but they do offer a few suggestions regarding a number of controls that can prove particularly effective in reducing that risk.

§ 13:31   Effective designation of project numbers

Although the designation of project numbers is usually the responsibility of a company's contracts department and not the accounting department, ineffective or sloppy designation of project numbers can contribute to accounting problems which, in turn, can lead to mischarging. In many instances, a company's contracts department may use the same basic project number for time charging that is used to designate the proposal effort that led to the award of the contract. For example, when a proposal effort is initiated, a project number is usually assigned. When employees charge time to the proposal effort, they are often instructed to charge their time to the new project number along with a two- (or more) digit number in the job order or code column of the time card. The two-digit code is the company's standard accounting code indicating proposal effort. When a contract is awarded pursuant to the proposal effort, employees are instructed to record the project number without the two-digit code that designated the proposal effort.

This practice may invite problems if your time-charging procedures do not direct your accounting department to close the proposal numbers (the project number with the two-digit code following) promptly after contracts are awarded. Otherwise, employees may continue to charge time to the proposal project rather than the new contract by including the two-digit number. If the accounting department has not closed the proposal number, labor that should be charged to the new contract may improperly find its way into your B&P pool. Instituting the following two procedures will eliminate this risk:

(1) When a contract is awarded, the contracts department should assign a new project number to the contract that is *different* from the number for the corresponding proposal effort.
(2) The accounting department and contracts department should *close out* a proposal project number once the proposal effort is completed to prevent the possibility that employees may continue to charge the obsolete proposal number.

§ 13:32 Maximum automation of systems

To limit the possibility of the occurrence of fraud or serious mistakes, your financial management operations should be automated to the maximum possible extent. Manual systems create far greater opportunities for mistakes and manipulation of labor charges than automated systems. Time cards should be read electronically if at all possible. This may require installation of special equipment that allows employees to place their time cards into machines that can print the numbers on the time cards each day. These numbers can then be read by an optical scanner. Many companies have even replaced proposal time card systems with completely computerized systems that permit employees to input their time data directly into the appropriate data bases.

§ 13:33 Control of invalid labor charges

Most accounting systems automatically reject time that can be readily identified as improperly charged by employees. Such systems automatically reject time charged to a project number that has been closed out, time for which an employee has

§ 13:33

misrecorded a project number, or time for which an employee has recorded a project number that is inappropriate for the location or job function of the employee. In these instances, the accounting department's computer system rejects the time and collects it in a special suspense pool. Typically, these charges are then sent back to the appropriate supervisors for correction or clarification. Such charges are commonly referred to as "invalid labor charges."

Sloppy handling of invalid labor charges can itself result in mischarging. This may occur, for example, if you allow invalid labor charges to remain on the books before they are resolved. The likelihood that the charges will ultimately be accurately recorded decreases with the passage of time.

Some companies even retain invalid labor charges in overhead pools on the assumption that the charges are valid costs that may be charged to the Government. The companies reason, erroneously, that the uncertain labor charges probably were legitimate labor charges entered by the employees working on Government contracts and, therefore, are allocable in some way to the company's Government contracts. You should ensure that your accounting procedures provide for the earliest possible resolution of invalid labor charges and that such resolution does not merely amount to dumping the charges into available overhead pools.

F. AVOIDING PROBLEMS

§ 13:34 Recommendations

(a) Promulgate and distribute to all employees explicit time-charging procedures that *limit employee discretion* regarding how they record and charge their time.

(b) Require all employees to follow the rules and *sanction* supervisors for failing to enforce the rules.

(c) Institute effective *internal audit procedures*.

(d) Institute procedures requiring that *documentation accompany assignments of work* whenever possible.

(e) Require supervisors and administrators to *document changes* in assignment of personnel or project utilization.

(f) Do *not* permit supervisors to handle nonsupervisory *employee time cards*.

(g) Issue specific procedures *limiting* the use of *labor cost transfers*.

(h) Tighten procedures for issuing *project numbers*.

(i) *Automate* the financial management system to the extent possible.

(j) Require *prompt resolution* of invalid labor charges.

Chapter 14

Progress Payments

I. OVERVIEW
§ 14:1   Scope note

II. CURRENT REQUIREMENTS

A.   OVERVIEW
§ 14:2   Generally

B.   PROGRESS PAYMENT REQUESTS
§ 14:3   Generally
§ 14:4   Submission of accounting data
§ 14:5   Certification

C.   PROGRESS PAYMENT RATE
§ 14:6   Generally

D.   CALCULATING PROGRESS PAYMENTS
§ 14:7   Generally
§ 14:8   Cumulative total costs
§ 14:9   Progress payments to subcontractors
§ 14:10 Allowable, reasonable, and allocable costs

E.   LIQUIDATION OF PROGRESS PAYMENTS
§ 14:11 Generally
§ 14:12 Subcontractor progress payments

F.   TREATMENT OF "LOSS CONTRACTS"
§ 14:13 Generally

G.   TITLE TO PROPERTY
§ 14:14 Generally

H.   SUSPENSION & REDUCTION OF PROGRESS PAYMENTS
§ 14:15 Generally

§ 14:16 Failure to comply with material contract requirement
§ 14:17 Failure to make progress or unsatisfactory financial condition
§ 14:18 Excessive inventory
§ 14:19 Delinquency in paying costs of performance
§ 14:20 Unliquidated payments exceed fair value of work
§ 14:21 Actual profit less than estimated
§ 14:22 Substantial evidence of fraud
§ 14:23 Setoff

I. FREQUENTLY ASKED QUESTIONS

§ 14:24 Questions & answers

III. HOW TO RECOGNIZE THE PROBLEM

§ 14:25 Generally
§ 14:26 Examples

IV. COMPLIANCE INITIATIVES

A. OVERVIEW

§ 14:27 Generally

B. UPPER MANAGEMENT

§ 14:28 Generally
§ 14:29 Segregate subcontractor progress payments
§ 14:30 Establish cut-off dates for accumulation of costs
§ 14:31 Segregate allowable from unallowable costs
§ 14:32 Monitor contract performance
§ 14:33 Retain accounting records

C. ACCOUNTING DEPARTMENT

§ 14:34 Compliance with company's procedures

D. INTERNAL AUDITORS

§ 14:35 System oversight

E. AVOIDING PROBLEMS

§ 14:36 Recommendations

PROGRESS PAYMENTS § 14:1

> **KeyCite®:** Cases and other legal materials listed in KeyCite Scope can be researched through the KeyCite service on Westlaw®. Use KeyCite to check citations for form, parallel references, prior and later history, and comprehensive citator information, including citations to other decisions and secondary materials.

I. OVERVIEW

§ 14:1 Scope note

Government contracts frequently are large in scale, both in terms of their dollar value and the length of performance. Financing the cost of performance over an extended period can impose a difficult burden on businesses regardless of their size. The Government's preference is for contractors to finance their contracts from private sources without the need for Government guarantees.[1] However, FAR also recognizes that private financing may only be available at unreasonable terms and that financing by the Government can be a useful working tool in the acquisition process.[2]

FAR Part 32 splits the subject of Government financing into two major categories with regard to goods and services: commercial item and non-commercial item financing. The available methods of financing a commercial item procurement include advance payments, interim payments; delivery payments, and installment payments.[3] The financing of non-commercial item procurements is accomplished through progress payments, performance-based payments, advance payments, and loan guarantees.[4]

The focus of this chapter is on one specific type of financing: progress payments based on costs in a non-commercial item procurement.[5] This method of financing raises the most serious compliance issues for a contractor because, as the phrase suggests, the Government makes periodic payments based not on the physical degree of completion of the work, but principally on the amount of costs incurred by the contractor while work is

---

[Section 14:1]

[1]FAR 32.106(a).

[2]FAR 32.106(a); FAR 32.104(a).

[3]FAR 32.202-2, FAR 32.206(g).

[4]FAR 32.102.

[5]For a complete discussion of the various types of Government financing for both commercial and non-commercial items, see Chierichella & Gallacher, Financing Government Contracts / Edition II—Part I, Briefing Papers No. 04-12 (Nov. 2004); Chierichella & Gallacher, Financing Government Contracts / Edition II—Part II, Briefing Papers No. 04-13 (Dec. 2004).

§ 14:1   GOVERNMENT CONTRACT COMPLIANCE HANDBOOK

underway.

Cost-based progress payments can be ideal. They are payments made by the Government to you in *advance* of delivery of items that require long production lead-time and substantial expenditure of costs before product delivery.[6] Progress payments are a form of interest-free contract financing provided directly by the Government. The Government periodically reimburses you for a percentage of certain paid and incurred costs in advance of delivery of the contract items. Progress payments thus help prevent the depletion of a contractor's working capital. Although FAR states a preference for performance-based payments (when the Government finds they are practical and the contractor agrees to their use), in terms of both frequency of use and total dollar amount, progress payments continue to be one of the most prevalent forms of Government contract financing.[7]

Before you begin to believe that progress payments are too good to be true, you should be aware that contractor requests for progress payments are subject to stringent procedural requirements. In general, only costs actually paid and incurred within established time frames may form the basis for progress payment requests. If you fail to comply with any of the procedural requirements, the Government can reduce or even stop progress payments. Moreover, the Government can prosecute you for progress payment fraud, which could expose you to fines, imprisonment, and other harsh consequences. The Department of Defense (DOD) Inspector General treats improper requests for progress payments as a significant indicator of fraud and advises Contracting Officers (COs), auditors, and other Government investigators to be on the lookout for such practices.[8]

II. CURRENT REQUIREMENTS

A. OVERVIEW

§ 14:2 **Generally**

For most contracts, progress payments are based on costs accumulated by the contractor as work progresses under the contract. Progress payments are generally available to large business concerns only on procurements in excess of $2,500,000.[1] Each payment request must be for $2,500 or more, unless agency

---

[6]FAR 32.104(a)(1), (d)(1)(i).

[7]FAR 32.1001(a).

[8]DOD Inspector General, "Indicators of Fraud in Department of Defense Procurement," 14–15 (June 1987).

[Section 14:2]

[1]FAR 32.104(d)(2)(i).

procedures authorize a lower amount.[2] The standard "Progress Payments" contract clause and the regulations governing progress payment policies and procedures are set forth in the Federal Acquisition Regulation (FAR).[3] Deviations from the specified frequency of payment, standard rates, and specified method of liquidation result in "unusual progress payments," which require special approvals.[4]

B. PROGRESS PAYMENT REQUESTS

§ 14:3 Generally

You are required to request progress payments on Standard Form 1443, "Contractor's Request for Progress Payment."[1] (See Appendix R to this Handbook for a copy of the form.) You may not use your own invoice in lieu of Standard Form 1443 to request progress payments.

§ 14:4 Submission of accounting data

The Government is entitled to request that your company submit supporting data with your Standard Form 1443.[1] As a general matter, you will be required to provide cost data on a contract-by-contract basis. In certain circumstances, however, the Government may request that you accumulate and segregate your costs on a line-item or similarly more detailed basis.

Under Paragraph (g) of the standard "Progress Payments" clause, you must provide the Government with financial data, as reasonably requested, as well as the opportunity to examine and verify your books and records.[2] You may be liable for fraud if you support your request for progress payments with inaccurate data. The FAR provides for periodic post-payment reviews or audits of progress payments by the CO to determine the validity of payments already made or expected to be made.[3]

§ 14:5 Certification

When you submit your Standard Form 1443, you must certify

---

[2]FAR 52.232-16(a)(8).
[3]FAR 52.232-16; FAR subpt. 32.5. *See also* DFARS subpt. 232.5.
[4]FAR 32.501-2.

[Section 14:3]
[1]FAR 52.232-16(g)(3)(i), 53.301-1443.

[Section 14:4]
[1]FAR 52.232-16(g)(3)(ii).
[2]FAR 52.232-16 (g).
[3]FAR 32.503-5.

§ 14:5   GOVERNMENT CONTRACT COMPLIANCE HANDBOOK

to the best of your knowledge and belief that (1) the progress payment request was prepared from your books and records in accordance with the instructions, (2) the costs included have been paid or will be paid in the ordinary course of business, (3) the work has been performed, (4) the quantities and amounts involved are consistent with contract requirements, (5) there are no encumbrances against property that would impair the Government's rights, (6) there has been no material adverse change in your financial condition, (7) compliance with any contract provision limiting progress payments pending first article approval, and (8) following the payment reflected by the request, the unliquidated progress payments will not exceed the maximum unliquidated progress payments permitted by the contract.[1] False statements with respect to any of these items could expose you to criminal liability under the False Statements Statute and civil or criminal liability under the False Claims Act.

C. PROGRESS PAYMENT RATE

§ 14:6 Generally

The Government pays your company at periodic intervals, not more frequently than monthly, a stated percentage of the costs incurred and paid by your company in performance of the contract. The percentage of the costs the Government pays is called the "progress payment rate."

The standard progress payment rate for most contracts is 80% of total costs for large businesses and 85% for small businesses.[1] The DOD customary rate applied to ordinary DOD contracts and to contracts under the DOD Foreign Military Sales program is also 80% of total costs for large businesses, but 90% for small business concerns, and 95% for small disadvantaged business concerns.[2] The Government adjusts these rates periodically to reflect national economic conditions.

D. CALCULATING PROGRESS PAYMENTS

§ 14:7 Generally

You are entitled to a percentage of costs paid during the particular period, which includes paid costs and selected incurred costs, plus 100% of progress payments paid to subcontractors. The Standard Form 1443, "Contractor's Request for Progress Payment," is

---

[Section 14:5]
   [1]FAR 53.301-1443.

[Section 14:6]
   [1]FAR 32.501-1.
   [2]DFARS 232.501-1.

designed to enable you to determine how much the Government should pay you based on a running total of includable costs less progress payments already paid. Each progress payment equals 80% of the contractor's "cumulative total costs," plus 100% of certain progress payments made to subcontractors less the sum of all previous payments.[1] Thus, the basic components of a progress payment are *cumulative total costs* and *subcontractor progress payments*. In addition, total costs eligible for progress payments are limited to *allowable, reasonable, and allocable costs*. Each of these components is discussed below.

§ 14:8 Cumulative total costs

Historically, both FAR and Standard Form 1443 considered that your company's "cumulative total costs" consisted of two basic types of costs: "paid" costs (previously included on Line 9 of the 1443) and "incurred" costs (previously listed on Line 10). Paid costs included those items of work for which payment has already been made, whereas incurred costs included those items for which the contractor was obligated, but had not yet paid. The distinction was important because some categories of incurred (but unpaid) costs, particularly the cost of completed subcontractor work, were not eligible for progress payments. Thus, a contractor was required to identify paid and incurred costs separately. This was referred to as the "paid cost" rule.

However, in 2000 and 2002, the Government amended FAR to eliminate the paid cost rule.[1] Thus, incurred costs are eligible as long as they are paid in accordance with the terms and conditions of the subcontract or invoice and ordinarily within 30 days of the submission of the contractor's payment request.[2] Accrued pension contributions may be included if the contractor's practice is to actually make contributions to the retirement fund on at least quarterly basis and the payment is made within 30 days of the end of that period.[3]

Standard Form 1443 has since been revised, and both lines 9 and 10 are marked 'RESERVED,' so no entry should be made on these lines. Thus, line 11 should include total costs incurred, whether or not actually paid, plus financing payments to

---

[Section 14:7]
[1]*See* FAR 52.232-16 (a)(1).

[Section 14:8]
[1]*See* 67 Fed. Reg. 70,520; 65 Fed. Reg. 16,274.
[2]FAR 52.232-16 (a)(2).
[3]FAR 52.232-16 (a)(3).

subcontractors.[4]

The "Progress Payments" clause requires that the following costs must be *excluded* from "cumulative total costs" regardless of whether the contractor has merely incurred the cost or actually made payment:[5]

(1) Costs incurred by subcontractors or suppliers.

(2) Any payments made or amounts payable to subcontractors or suppliers, except for completed work, including partial deliveries, to which your company has acquired title.

(3) Any costs ordinarily capitalized and subject to depreciation or amortization, except for the properly amortized or depreciated portion of such costs.

In sum, with the exceptions noted above, both your *paid* and *incurred* costs comprise the "total costs" eligible for progress payments. These total costs are included on Line 11 of Standard Form 1443 and are eligible for Government reimbursement at the standard rate.

§ 14:9 Progress payments to subcontractors

Progress payments requested by subcontractors constitute the second element in your cost base for computing progress payments. Subcontracts may include either performance-based payments or progress payments.[1] The Government will reimburse you for the total amount of subcontractor progress payments so long as the provisions in the subcontract relating to progress payments are (a) substantially similar to the provisions in the standard "Progress Payments" prime contract clause, (b) at least as favorable to the Government as the terms of the clause, and (c) not more favorable to the subcontractor than are the terms of the standard clause to your company.[2]

Progress payments to subcontractors are included on Line 14 of Standard Form 1443. Your requests for progress payments may include the full amount of commercial item purchase financing payments, performance-based payments, or progress payments to a subcontractor, whether paid or unpaid, provided that the unpaid amounts are limited to amounts determined due and that the contractor will pay within 30 days of the submission of the

---

[4]FAR 52.232-16(a)(1) to (4).

[5]FAR 52.232-16 (a)(4)(ii), (iii), (iv).

[Section 14:9]

[1]FAR 32.504(a).

[2]FAR 52.232-16 (j)(3).

progress payment request.[3] The progress payment rate used in the subcontract should be the customary rate applied by the contracting agency.[4] Unlike your paid and incurred costs, you are entitled to *100% reimbursement* of progress payments made to subcontractors.

The amount requested on Line 14 is limited to *progress payments* to subcontractors—that is, your payment to your subcontractors of a percentage of paid and selected incurred costs prior to completion or delivery. Only subcontractor progress payments are entitled to 100% reimbursement. If the payment to your subcontractor is, in fact, payment for completed supplies or services, it must be included on Line 11 and is eligible only for customary progress payment rate reimbursement. (See § 14:8).

§ 14:10 Allowable, reasonable, and allocable costs

The total costs eligible for progress payments must be "reasonable, allocable to the contract, consistent with sound and generally accepted accounting principles and practices, and . . . not otherwise excluded by the contract."[1] Although Standard Form 1443 does not expressly require a contractor to include only costs that are "allowable" in accordance with FAR Part 31, you can avoid potential controversy if you limit your submitted costs to allowable costs.[2]

The regulations set forth five factors to be considered in determining the *allowability* of any cost: (1) reasonableness, (2) allocability, (3) standards promulgated by the Cost Accounting Standards Board, if applicable; otherwise, the generally accepted accounting principles and practices appropriate to the circumstances, (4) the terms of the contract, and (5) any limitations set forth in the FAR cost principles.[3] A cost is *reasonable* if, "in its nature and amount, it does not exceed that which would be incurred by a prudent person in the conduct of competitive business."[4] Whether a cost is reasonable depends on a variety of considerations and circumstances involving both the nature and amount of the cost in question including, among other things, whether it is the type of cost "generally recognized as ordinary and necessary for the conduct of the contractor's business or the

---

[3]FAR 32.504(b). *See also* FAR 52.232-16 paras. (j)(3) to (5).

[4]FAR 52.232-16(j)(6).

[Section 14:10]

[1]FAR 52.232-16 (a)(4)(i).

[2]*See* FAR 31.201-6(a) ("Costs that are expressly unallowable . . . shall be . . . excluded from any billing, claim, or proposal . . . .").

[3]FAR 31.201-2.

[4]FAR 31.201-3(a).

§ 14:10   GOVERNMENT CONTRACT COMPLIANCE HANDBOOK

contract performance," and such factors as "generally accepted sound business practices."[5]

A cost is *allocable* if "it is assignable or chargeable to one or more cost objectives on the basis of relative benefits received or other equitable relationships."[6] A cost is allocable if it (a) is incurred specifically for the contract; (b) benefits both the contract and other work and can be distributed to them in reasonable proportion to the benefits received; or (c) is necessary to the overall operation of the business, although a direct relationship to any particular cost objective cannot be shown.[7]

Under the above definition, any allowable direct cost is clearly allocable to a contract. Allowable indirect costs are allocable to a contract if such costs *either* benefit that contract *or* are necessary to the overall operation of the business. (See §§ 11:1 et seq. for a more detailed discussion of the FAR cost principles.)

E. LIQUIDATION OF PROGRESS PAYMENTS

§ 14:11 Generally

Progress payments are interest-free Government loans to contractors to finance work-in-process. As such, progress payments must be repaid. This repayment is called "liquidation."

Liquidation is accomplished by deducting a stated percentage of the *invoiced* price due your company when you deliver a contract end item. The amount deducted is credited to your outstanding progress payment "loan" balance. The percentage deducted from contract invoices to liquidate outstanding progress payments is called the "liquidation rate." You may use one of two methods for liquidating your progress payments: (1) the "ordinary" method of liquidation in which the liquidation rate equals the applicable standard progress payment rate,[1] or (2) the "alternate" method of liquidation in which a special rate is negotiated with the Government reflecting your earned profit on the contract.[2]

The "ordinary" method of liquidation is the *only* method that may be used at the inception of a contract. The "alternate" method will apply only if the CO adjusts the liquidation rate upward or

---

[5]FAR 31.201-3(b).
[6]FAR 31.201-4.
[7]FAR 31.201-4.

[Section 14:11]
[1]FAR 32.503-8.
[2]*See* FAR 32.503-9.

downward.[3] The Government has the right unilaterally to change from the ordinary liquidation rate to the alternate rate when deemed appropriate for proper contract financing. The Government typically exercises this right to raise the liquidation rate above the standard rate to prevent underliquidation of progress payments.[4]

At your company's request, the CO may *reduce* the liquidation rate in circumstances in which you are experiencing a significant profit on the contract and your "loan" can safely be repaid at a lower rate.[5]

§ 14:12 Subcontractor progress payments

You liquidate your subcontractors' progress payments in much the same way the Government liquidates yours. When a subcontractor delivers an end item to you, you deduct a certain percentage of the invoiced price and credit it to the outstanding progress payment balance. The amount of liquidated progress payments is included on Line 14b of your Standard Form 1443 and subtracted from Line 14a ("Progress Payments Paid to Subcontractors").

Amounts you paid to subcontractors on receipt of delivered items are included on Line 11. (See § 14:8) These consist of the liquidated subcontractor progress payments included on Line 14b plus any other payments you make to your subcontractors for each delivery. Your Standard Form 1443 will be inflated if you fail to deduct the liquidated subcontractor progress payments from the total of progress payments made to your subcontractors. Deduct the liquidated payments from Line 14a to exclude them from costs entitled to 100% reimbursement. Include this amount, plus any other payments to your subcontractors, on Line 11 for customary rate reimbursement. (See § 14:8).

F. TREATMENT OF "LOSS CONTRACTS"

§ 14:13 Generally

You must treat "loss contracts" differently from contracts on which you expect to earn a profit. A "loss contract" occurs when the contract price is less than the sum of (a) total costs incurred to date in performance of the contract and (b) the estimated additional costs to complete the contract.[1] In a loss contract situation, all further progress payments must be adjusted according to

---

[3]*See* FAR 32.503-9.
[4]FAR 32.503-9(b)(1).
[5]FAR 32.503-9(a).

[Section 14:13]
[1]FAR 32.503-6(g).

§ 14:13   GOVERNMENT CONTRACT COMPLIANCE HANDBOOK

a "Loss Ratio Factor" to exclude the percentage of loss. Instructions for calculating the "Loss Ratio Factor" and computing progress payments under loss contracts are set forth in the FAR and summarized briefly below.[2]

The "Loss Ratio Factor" equals the revised contract price *divided by* the sum of the total costs incurred to date plus the estimated costs to complete the contract. The "Revised Contract Price" is simply the contract price used in progress payment computations, plus any unpriced change orders or other contract actions, to the extent funds for such actions have been obligated.[3]

Once the "Revised Contract Price" has been calculated, it should be entered on Line 5 ("Contract Price") of Standard Form 1443. The "Loss Ratio Factor" is used to compute the "Recognized Costs for Progress Payments." The "Recognized Costs for Progress Payments" are simply the contractor's "Total Costs Eligible for Progress Payments" adjusted by the "Loss Ratio Factor." An example of such a calculation is set forth below.

(1) *Revised Contract Price*

Contract price	$950,000
Change orders and unpaid orders to extent obligated	$50,000
REVISED CONTRACT PRICE	$1,000,000

(2) *Total Costs Incurred to Date & Estimated Costs of Completion*

Total costs incurred to date	$900,000
Estimated additional costs to complete	$300,000
TOTAL	$1,200,000

(3) *Loss Ratio Factors*

Loss Ratio Factor = $\frac{\text{(a) (1,000,000)}}{\text{(b) (1,200,000)}}$ = 83.3%

Total costs eligible for progress payments	$900,000
Loss Ratio Factor	×83.3%
RECOGNIZED COSTS FOR PROGRESS PAYMENTS	$749,700

Once calculated, the amount of "Recognized Costs for Progress

---

[2] FAR 32.503-6(g).
[3] FAR 32.503-6(g)(1)(i).

Payments" is entered on Line 11 of Standard Form 1443 in lieu of the amount of "Total Costs Eligible for Progress Payments."

Cases & Commentary: Form 1443 and the related regulations make it clear that the contractor's progress payments are to be reduced in proportion to any loss the contractor expects to incur at completion of the contract. Currently, line 12.b of Form 1443 requires the contractor to state the additional amount of costs it expects to incur at completion. Contractors are required to furnish their "best estimate" of the remaining costs to the Government and that the estimate be in sufficient detail to allow the Government to verify it. The contractor certifies the accuracy of this estimate at completion figure when it signs the progress payment request. Although contractors face liability under the current clause for including false information in Form 1443, the reference to "best estimate" and the requirement that the estimate be prepared in sufficient detail to allow verification and be submitted as part of the progress payment request emphasize the importance of preparing an estimate that accurately reflects the total cost the contractor expects to incur.[4]

G. TITLE TO PROPERTY

§ 14:14 Generally

To assure some security for the progress payments made, the "Progress Payments" clause provides that the Government has title to all property "allocable or properly chargeable" to the contract.[1] This includes, for example, parts, materials, inventories, work-in-process, special tooling and testing equipment, and other nondurable items necessary to perform the contract.[2] You should note that the "title" provisions of the clause have resulted in conflicting judicial decisions on the scope of the Government's interest in contractor property in bankruptcy and other proceedings, with some courts holding that the Government holds title to the property and other courts finding that the Government acquires only a lien interest in the property.[3]

Although title vests in the Government, you bear the risk of

---

[4]See 74 Fed. Reg. 28,430.

[Section 14:14]

[1]FAR 52.232-16 (d)(1).

[2]FAR 52.232-16 (d)(2).

[3]*Compare, e.g., U.S. v. Hartec Enterprises*, 967 F.2d 130 (5th Cir. 1992) (Government had only lien interest in contractor property financed by progress payments; therefore, defendants could not be convicted for theft of Government property where it sold the property for scrap), and *U.S. v. Dominicci*, 899 F. Supp. 42 (D.P.R. 1995) (same) *with American Pouch Foods, Inc. v. U.S.*, 769 F.2d 1190 (7th Cir. 1985) (Government obtains title to contractor property financed by progress payments).

§ 14:14

loss of such property before delivery to the Government, except to the extent that the Government expressly assumes that risk.[4] Title to any property remaining after contract performance will revert to you on completion of the contract and liquidation of all progress payments.[5]

You cannot dispose of any property to which the Government retains title without the advance approval of the CO. If you dispose of Government property without the consent of the Government, you may subject yourself to fines and other penalties under the so-called "theft of Government property statute" (see §§ 6:1 et seq.).[6] If the Government authorizes the transaction, you must exclude the allocable costs of the property from the costs of contract performance and repay any unliquidated progress payments allocable to the property.[7]

Government-owned property must remain unencumbered during performance of your contract and until you have liquidated all of the progress payments. Unless there is reason to believe otherwise, the Contracting Officer should accept your certification that the property remains unencumbered. However, if you fail to disclose existing encumbrances, the Government is entitled to reduce or suspend progress payments for breach of a material contract requirement. (See § 14:16) You could also be found civilly and criminally liable for submission of a false claim.[8]

H. SUSPENSION & REDUCTION OF PROGRESS PAYMENTS

§ 14:15 Generally

Paragraph (c) of the standard "Progress Payments" clause identifies six circumstances where the Government may reduce or suspend progress payments to a contractor or liquidate the payments at a rate higher than the rate established in the contract. In addition, the Government may reduce or suspend progress payments when there is substantial evidence that a progress payment request is based on fraud.[1] The following discussion addresses each of these circumstances.

---

[4]FAR 32.503-16, 52.232-16 (e).
[5]FAR 52.232-16, para. (d)(6).
[6]18 U.S.C.A. § 641.
[7]FAR 52.232-16, para. (d)(5).
[8]FAR 32.503-14.

[Section 14:15]

[1]National Defense Authorization Act for Fiscal Year 1991, Pub. L. No. 101-510, § 836, 104 Stat. 1485, 1615 (codified at 10 U.S.C.A. § 2307(h)); Federal Acquisition Streamlining Act of 1994, Pub. L. No. 103-355, § 2051(e), 108 Stat. 3243 (codified at 41 U.S.C.A. § 4506(b)).

§ 14:16 Failure to comply with material contract requirement

Your failure to comply with the terms of your contract will justify a suspension or reduction in progress payments only if you violate a "material" contract requirement—that is, one that is significant or essential to the contract. For example, the regulations identify as material the contract requirement to maintain an efficient and reliable *accounting system* and *controls* adequate for proper administration of progress payments. If you fail to maintain such a system, the regulations direct the CO to suspend progress payments until you have made the changes to your accounting system necessary for the proper administration of progress payments.[1]

Your failure to comply with a material contract requirement will not justify suspension or reduction of progress payments by the Government, however (other than to correct overpayments or obtain amounts due from you), where the failure resulted *solely* from causes beyond your control and without your fault and negligence.[2]

§ 14:17 Failure to make progress or unsatisfactory financial condition

If you so fail to make progress or are in such unsatisfactory financial condition as to *endanger contract performance*, the Government may be justified in reducing or suspending your progress payments. Since the suspension of payments could force you out of business, the Government normally will not reduce or suspend your progress payments on these grounds without first requiring you to make additional operating or financial arrangements that reasonably ensure contract completion without loss to

---

[Section 14:16]

[1]FAR 32.503-6(b). *See also* DFARS 209.104-1 (requiring that contractors' accounting systems must reasonably establish that the contractors' cost data are reliable); *Flight Refueling, Inc.*, ASBCA 46846 et al., 97-2 BCA ¶ 29000 (Government's refusal to make progress payments was proper and not a breach of contract in light of the inadequacy of the contractor's accounting system and controls); *Vinyl Technology, Inc.*, ASBCA 47767 et al., 97-2 BCA ¶ 29235 (declining to grant summary judgment in appeal of CO's decision terminating contract for default and decision to stop making progress payments based on inadequacy of contractor's accounting system). Any special requirement that a CO places on a contractor's accounting system, however, is a contractual matter that if not included in the original contract may constitute a compensable change, *see, e.g., Aydin Corp. (West) v. Secretary of the Air Force*, 61 F.3d 1571 (Fed. Cir. 1995) (holding that the CO's directive, which required the contractor to modify its accounting system and change its billing of progress payments, was a constructive change for which the contractor was entitled to compensation).

[2]FAR 32.503-6(b)(2).

the Government.[1]

§ 14:18 Excessive inventory

If the inventory you have allocated to the contract exceeds reasonable requirements, the Government may reduce or suspend progress payments to correct the overallocation. The apparent rationale is to prevent you from applying Government financing to nonGovernment work.[1] Thus, if you are producing a product for the Government and also marketing that product commercially, you may not include costs incurred in commercial production as part of the costs used to compute progress payments under the Government contract.

§ 14:19 Delinquency in paying costs of performance

If you are delinquent in paying costs of contract performance in the ordinary course of business, the Government may be justified in reducing or suspending progress payments. Your failure to pay your suppliers, subcontractors, or others in a timely fashion may result in reduction or suspension of progress payments.[1]

Payments are not considered delinquent if subcontractors and suppliers claim them but you *dispute* them in good faith. However, such payments will be considered delinquent if and when they have been judged to be due through litigation or arbitration. The disputed amounts cannot be included in your progress payment cost base until and unless paid.[2]

§ 14:20 Unliquidated payments exceed fair value of work

If you have failed to make progress so that the unliquidated progress payments exceed the fair value of the work accomplished on the uncompleted portion of the contract, the Government may reduce or suspend progress payments. The fair value of the work

---

[Section 14:17]

[1]FAR 32.503-6(c)(1).

[Section 14:18]

[1]FAR 32.503-6(d).

[Section 14:19]

[1]FAR 32.503-6(e).

[2]FAR 32.503-6(e)(2). However, this rule does not apply to small business prime contractors. See FAR 52.232-16, alt. I; *Southwest Marine*, ASBCA 47621, 96-2 BCA ¶ 28601 (holding that progress payments paid to small business prime contractor were not subject to recoupment based on alleged failure to pay debts owed to subcontractors because small business progress payment clause allows for progress payments to be computed as a percentage of total costs incurred, "whether or not actually paid").

is the lesser of (1) the contract price of the undelivered work minus the estimated costs required for completing contract performance, or (2) the incurred costs applicable to the undelivered items.[1]

In determining the fair value of undelivered work, the CO is required to give full consideration to the degree of completion of contract performance, the quality and amount of work performed on the undelivered portion of the contract, the amount of work remaining to be done and the estimated costs of completion of the contract, and the unpaid amount remaining under the contract.[2]

§ 14:21 Actual profit less than estimated

If you are using the alternate method of liquidation and you are realizing less profit than the estimated profit used to establish the alternate rate, the Government may reduce or suspend progress payments to correct any past underliquidation. Normally, the Government will simultaneously raise the liquidation rate to prevent future underliquidation.

§ 14:22 Substantial evidence of fraud

The National Defense Authorization Act for Fiscal Year 1991 and the Federal Acquisition Streamlining Act of 1994 direct agency heads to reduce or suspend progress payments when there is substantial evidence the contractor has submitted a fraudulent progress payment request.[1] Such a reduction will be commensurate with the anticipated loss to the United States resulting from the fraud.[2] The statutes and implementing regulations, however, entitle a contractor to written notice of a proposed reduction and an opportunity to submit supporting documentation to the agency head before his decision on the proposed reduction.[3] The Government must periodically review the suspen-

---

[Section 14:20]

[1]FAR 32.503-6(f)(1).

[2]FAR 32.503-6(f)(2).

[Section 14:22]

[1]National Defense Authorization Act for Fiscal Year 1991, Pub. L. No. 101-510, § 863(a), 104 Stat. 1485, 1615 (codified at 10 U.S.C.A. § 2307(h)); Federal Acquisition Streamlining Act of 1994, Pub. L. No. 103-355, § 2051(e), 108 Stat. 3243 (codified at 41 U.S.C.A. § 4056(b) and implemented by FAR 32.006, DFARS 232.006).

[2]10 U.S.C.A. § 2307(h)(3); 41 U.S.C.A. § 4056(d) (implemented by FAR 32.006-4(c)).

[3]10 U.S.C.A. § 2307(h)(5); 41 U.S.C.A. § 4056(f) (implemented by FAR 32.006-4(e)).

§ 14:22   GOVERNMENT CONTRACT COMPLIANCE HANDBOOK

sion and determine whether the suspension should continue.[4]

§ 14:23   Setoff

The Government can also reduce or withhold progress payments by exercising its common law right of set-off. For example, in one case a court approved the Government's setting off of liquidated damages that were allegedly due because of the late completion of the work against an otherwise undisputed progress payment.[1] The court found that the common law right of set-off was well established and could only be defeated by explicit statutory or contractual language.

I. FREQUENTLY ASKED QUESTIONS

§ 14:24   Questions & answers

Question 1: If the Government pays me an excess amount in progress payments, do I have to pay them back? If so, when?

Answer 1: Yes. If the Government has mistakenly overpaid your progress payments, you should *promptly* repay the excessive amount because the Government may be entitled to interest on the overpayments.[1]

Question 2: Does the Government gain title to all the property or material that I use or produce in performing a contract funded by progress payments?

Answer 2: Not necessarily. There are conflicting judicial decisions on this issue. As noted above in § 14:14, some courts hold that the Government acquires title to property obtained in connection with a contract financed by progress payments, while other courts hold that the Government obtains only a lien interest in such property. Of course, a contractor that successfully completes performance of a fixed-price contract retains title to any excess material purchased for purposes of the contract even where the contract is financed by Government progress payments.[2]

Question 3: If I experience some delays in contract performance will the Government automatically suspend my progress payments?

Answer 3: Not usually. As long as you are making progress on

---

[4]10 U.S.C.A. § 2307(h)(6); 41 U.S.C.A. § 4056(g) (implemented by FAR 32.006-4(h)).

[Section 14:23]

[1]*See Johnson v. All-State Construction, Inc.*, 329 F.3d 848 (Fed. Cir. 2003).

[Section 14:24]

[1]*See Electronics & Space Corp.*, ASBCA 47539, 95-2 BCA ¶ 27768.

[2]FAR 52.232-16 (d)(6).

PROGRESS PAYMENTS § 14:26

the contract, your progress payments usually should not be in jeopardy. However, the Government can always reduce your payments or liquidate at a higher rate if it deems your progress on the contract less than satisfactory.[3]

III. HOW TO RECOGNIZE THE PROBLEM

§ 14:25 Generally

You must be able to identify potential progress payment compliance problems. The Government's primary interest is in preventing you from including in progress payment requests costs to which you are not entitled. This can occur when you include costs that you have not incurred and therefore will not pay, or you have paid but for which you have not accepted completed work or delivery.

Failure to comply with progress payment technicalities could result in a reduction or suspension of progress payments and civil and criminal prosecution under the False Claims Act and the False Statements Statute.[1] (See §§ 1:1 et seq.) The complicated rules in this area make progress payments fertile ground for experienced Government auditors and investigators on the lookout for contractor fraud.

§ 14:26 Examples

Subcontractor payments for completed items: Assume you have a large firm-fixed-price Government contract for systems integration. In conjunction with this contract, on April 2 you order 1,000 color monitors to be installed in workstations at your plant. Two weeks later the supplier advises that they will ready for delivery on May 1. Because your work space is small, you tell your supplier to deliver 500 monitors as planned, but defer delivery of the remaining 500 units by two weeks. However, you pay the supplier in full for the 1,000 monitors on May 1. You need the money so you include the entire amount in the progress payment request that you submit to the Government on May 3. Have you done anything wrong?

Yes. Even though you have made actual payment for the entire quantity before submitting your payment request on May 3, you could not bill for the second 500 units. You can only bill for completed items if you have both received delivery and accepted title to the goods as of the date of the request.

Subcontractor payments: You are a large business performing a

---

[3]*See, e.g., Florida Dept. of Ins. v. U.S.*, 81 F.3d 1093 (Fed. Cir. 1996).

[Section 14:25]

[1]31 U.S.C.A. §§ 3729 to 3733; 18 U.S.C.A. §§ 287, 1001.

§ 14:26   GOVERNMENT CONTRACT COMPLIANCE HANDBOOK

fixed-price contract to supply helicopters to the Government. You have subcontracted the avionics system to ABC Avionics and the airframe to Airframe, Inc., both under fixed-price contracts. Airframe's contract contains a "Progress Payments" clause under which you agree to pay Airframe 99% of its cumulative costs.

You receive requests for payment from both ABC and Airframe on the first of each month. ABC's request includes costs incurred but not paid beyond those permitted by the "Progress Payments" clause. You pay them on the 15th. You submit your request for progress payments to the Government on the 10th. You include your payments to both ABC and Airframe in your request to the Government. You have paid Airframe by that date. Do you face any liability for requesting these progress payments from the Government?

Most likely, yes. You may have committed progress payment fraud. First, you cannot include the payment to ABC *at all* because it includes cost that the *subcontractor* has incurred but not yet paid. While you may request reimbursement for progress payments to subcontracts before actually making payment (due to the elimination of the "paid cost" rule), you must still *exclude* from your request any amount representing a subcontractor's *incurred* cost. You cannot include all of Airframe's progress payments because Airframe has more favorable progress payment terms than you do in your prime contract (i.e., 99% of cumulative costs rather than 80% as required by the regulations).

The check is not in the mail: You have a contract with the Government to deliver heavy-duty laundry equipment for a veterans' hospital. You purchase and receive a quantity of sheet metal to begin the fabrication. Your accounting department receives and approves the invoice for the sheet metal on September 1. The check is prepared and dated September 2. The check is sent to the mailroom where it is batched and mailed on September 5. You include the sheet metal payment in your request to the Government for progress payments dated September 3. Is your progress payment request improper?

No. Due to the elimination of the "paid cost" rule, a contractor may include incurred, but unpaid, costs for subcontractor products. However, the contractor must make payment in accordance with the terms and conditions of the subcontract or invoice and ordinarily within 30 days of the submission of the contractor's payment request to the Government.

Loss contracts: Assume you are performing at a loss under your fixed-price contract for fabrication of air conditioning units. You know that if you advise the Government of your status, your progress payments will be reduced. You need the money to complete the contract. You submit your request for progress payments without using the formula required for loss contracts. Do you face any liability for not using the loss formula?

Yes. Once again you would have committed progress payment fraud. A Government contractor faces sanctions for failing to disclose a loss situation when submitting progress payment requests.

Payments to affiliates: You have a major contract with the Government for sophisticated communications systems. To manufacture these systems, you purchase special wiring equipment from your wholly-owned subsidiary, XYZ Company. You do not pay XYZ progress payments but rather 100% of the invoice amount on delivery. You then include this payment on Line 14 of Standard Form 1443 for 100% reimbursement from the Government. Have you acted appropriately?

No. You have submitted a false claim to the Government. Your affiliates must be treated as any other subcontractor and be paid either progress payments or regular payments.[1] If you pay your affiliate progress payments, you are entitled to 100% reimbursement for those payments on Line 14 of your Standard Form 1443. On the other hand, if you make regular payments to your affiliate, you are required to account for such payments on Line 11 for 80% reimbursement by the Government. (See § 14:8).

You may also create problems by failing to treat your affiliate *consistently*. You may not pay your affiliate 100% of its costs and then include those costs on Line 14 for 100% reimbursement from the Government. You may *either* (a) pay your affiliate 80% of its costs through progress payments and obtain from the Government 100% reimbursement for those payments, *or* (b) pay your affiliate 100% of its costs through regular payments and obtain from the Government 80% reimbursement for those payments. Thus, under the above facts, you should have included your payment to your affiliate on Line 11 for 80% reimbursement.

Costs incurred for an alternate contract: You have two contracts with the Government to provide computer systems. One is with the Air Force (AF) and the other is with the Social Security Administration (SSA). The AF contract calls for a state-of-the-art system which is secured against intrusion. The system for the SSA is also state-of-the-art but does not require security features. You find yourself short of capital on the AF contract because the security system is more difficult than expected to install. You include some of the cumulative costs from the SSA contract in your request for progress payments on the AF contract in order to increase your payments applicable to that contract. Can you

---

[Section 14:26]

[1]*See* FAR 31.205-26(e) (governing interdivisional transfers).

distribute your costs in this manner?

No. You have not only mischarged against the contract but have also committed progress payment fraud because your Standard Form 1443 includes costs that were not associated with that contract. This type of fraud has been severely punished. In one case, a major defense contractor pleaded guilty to making these types of false statements in its Standard Form 1443. The problem occurred when lower-level employees completed time cards (approved by their supervisors) which showed that they had worked on one contract when in fact they had worked on another. As a result, the Standard Form 1443 contained false information. The contractor paid the Government $650,000 as double damages, $167,000 in interest, and $30,000 in criminal fines.

Failure to deduct liquidated payments: You have a contract with the Government to develop and build a tactical fighter simulator. You subcontract the optical system to XYZ Company. You pay XYZ progress payments, and XYZ delivers a contract end item and invoices you for the full amount of the system. You pay XYZ's invoice, less progress payment liquidation, but include the full amount of the invoice on Line 11 of your Standard Form 1443. You fail to deduct the liquidated progress payments from Line 14b of your Standard Form 1443. Are there consequences for not deducting the liquidated progress payments from Standard Form 1443?

Yes. You may have committed progress payment fraud. You must liquidate your subcontractor's progress payments and reflect that liquidation on Line 14b of your Standard Form 1443. After deducting the liquidated amounts from Line 14, you must include that amount plus any other payments you make to your subcontractor for that delivery on Line 11 of your Standard Form 1443.

Encumbering Government title to property: You are trying to expand your business and you need additional capital. The bank asks you for a security interest in all of your work-in-progress. You agree. Some of the work-in-progress is under a Government contract for which you are receiving progress payments. You submit your next request for progress payments without mentioning the bank's lien on the work-in-progress. Is your omission of the lien from the progress payments form improper?

Yes. You may have committed progress payment fraud. The Government has title to all work-in-progress until contract completion and full progress payment liquidation. You cannot encumber the Government's title without the express approval of the CO. The FAR provides that where the Government discovers that a contractor is not disclosing encumbrances against property to which the Government has title, the CO should consult with legal counsel concerning the contractor's possible violations of the

False Claims Act.[2]

IV. COMPLIANCE INITIATIVES
A. OVERVIEW
§ 14:27 Generally

It is critical that the following departments within your company be knowledgeable about Government contract financing rules: (1) upper management, (2) the accounting staff, and (3) internal auditors and the financial department. The decisions, actions, and inactions of each of these groups will determine whether your progress payment requests are properly computed and submitted. Some procedures to safeguard against progress payment fraud are discussed below.

B. UPPER MANAGEMENT
§ 14:28 Generally

The greatest danger that you face with respect to progress payments is that, either intentionally or unintentionally, your employees will prepare inaccurate progress payment requests, certify such requests, and submit them to the Government. This action will expose your company and its individual employees to criminal and civil liability under the fraud statutes and cause the Government to suspend your progress payments. This could effectively shut your company down.

Progress payment requests are inaccurate if they include costs that should not be included. For example, while the "paid cost" rule has been eliminated, your Standard Form 1443 would be inaccurate if it included incurred costs, but you did not make payment in accordance with the terms and conditions of the subcontract or invoice or did not ordinarily make payment within 30 days of the submission of the contractor's payment request to the Government.

It is the responsibility of upper management to *develop procedures* for calculating, documenting, and submitting progress payment requests on Standard Form 1443, to *communicate* these procedures and train accounting, bookkeeping, and auditing personnel to follow them, and to develop controls to *enforce* the procedures. Legal counsel or outside accountants experienced in Government contracts should review your progress payment procedures to verify that they comply with Government requirements.

The most important step for ensuring against progress pay-

---

[2]FAR 32.503-14(c).

ment fraud is to establish an adequate accounting system and controls. An accounting system is adequate for progress payment purposes if it *segregates and accumulates* costs accurately. Your system for proper segregation and accumulation of costs should, at a minimum, include the following procedures.

§ 14:29 Segregate subcontractor progress payments

You may be liable for false claims if your accounting system fails to segregate your progress payments to subcontractors and suppliers from your other paid and incurred costs. Progress payments to subcontractors are entitled to 100% reimbursement while paid and incurred costs are entitled to only 80% reimbursement. A false claim could result if you include paid or incurred costs in your claim for 100% reimbursement for progress payments made to subcontractors.

§ 14:30 Establish cut-off dates for accumulation of costs

To avoid false claims, you must establish one cut-off date per month for all incurred costs reported on Standard Form 1443. You should use this cut-off date to prepare cost reports that accumulate labor, material, and other eligible costs for that month. The same cut-off date must be used for all costs incurred for which you seek payment from the Government.

The particular cut-off date for incurred costs must be designated in the heading of "Section II" of Standard Form 1443. The instructions for Standard Form 1443 provide that the "Section II date" represents the "date through which costs have been accumulated from inception for inclusion in this request" and "is applicable to item entries in Sections II and III."

The "Section II date" is different from the "date of the request" in Line 8B of Standard Form 1443. The date in Line 8B is the date you send the completed Standard Form 1443 to the Government. Depending on how long it takes you to prepare the Standard Form 1443, the "Section II date" may be anywhere from a few days to a few weeks earlier than the Line 8B date. To avoid false claims, your accounting system must ensure that you include in the current Standard Form 1443 only costs incurred as of the earlier cut-off date, not the later date of the request.

§ 14:31 Segregate allowable from unallowable costs

You may submit a false claim unless your accounting system excludes unallowable costs from your cost base for computing progress payments. The types of costs that are unallowable are set forth in the FAR and discussed in greater detail in this Handbook in §§ 11:1 et seq. In addition, as set forth in the standard "Progress Payments" clause, your cost base must exclude costs ordinarily capitalized and subject to depreciation or amortization, except for the properly depreciated or amortized portion of such costs.[1]

§ 14:32 Monitor contract performance

You could submit a false claim if your contract is in a loss position and you employ the standard formula for computing progress payments. As discussed earlier, loss contracts require the use of a different formula. Accordingly, you should monitor contract performance to ensure that you use the proper method for calculating your progress payments. Remember that under certain circumstances the Government is entitled to reduce or suspend progress payments and liquidate them at a higher rate.

§ 14:33 Retain accounting records

You are required to provide the Government with financial data and an opportunity to examine and verify your books and records. You must maintain accurate and thorough records of the data used to prepare your Standard Form 1443. You must also retain these records after submission of the forms and until the document disposal date established by your contract. The Government is entitled to audit your records and withhold progress payments pending the audit if there is (1) reason to question the reliability or accuracy of your certification or (2) reason to believe that the contract will involve a loss.[1] You must be able to produce adequate records to challenge any potential withholding by the Government.

C. ACCOUNTING DEPARTMENT

§ 14:34 Compliance with company's procedures

Your company accountants' most important responsibility is to follow your company's progress payment procedures *precisely*. No exceptions or changes to the procedures should be made without specific written approval from upper management. If you can *automate* the system and prevent it from being tampered with, so much the better.

In any event, your accountants should develop and rely on a *checklist* to ensure compliance with every procedure. At a mini-

---

[Section 14:31]
    [1]FAR 52.232-16 (a)(4)(iii).
[Section 14:33]
    [1]FAR 32.503-4(b).

mum, the checklist should require verification of the following elements of your Standard Form 1443:

(1) The amounts of all incurred costs included on Line 11 to ensure that they will be paid in the ordinary course of business.
(2) The dates of all incurred costs included on Line 11 to ensure that the costs were incurred as of the cut-off date.
(3) The amounts of all progress payments made or to be made to subcontractors included on Line 14.
(4) The status of your contract to determine whether it is in a loss position.
(5) The mathematical accuracy of all computations on your Standard Form 1443.

Verification should be performed by at least *two* employees who were *not* involved in the preparation of your Standard Form 1443. These employees should initial and date each step of their review of the Standard Form 1443.

D. INTERNAL AUDITORS

§ 14:35 System oversight

One risk that you face is failure to detect that employees in your organization are preparing inaccurate or insupportable progress payment requests. It is the job of your internal auditors and financial department to ensure that *each* element in your company's Standard Form 1443 is capable of being verified by a *documented* audit trail. You should (a) develop procedures to ensure that all data included in the Standard Form 1443 can be tied to cost reports, payment vouchers, or similar documentation and (b) perform random periodic audits of your company's Standard Forms 1443 to verify that all data included in the forms can in fact be tied to such reports and vouchers.

Your auditors and financial analysts must verify compliance with your company's progress payment procedures. In the event instances of noncompliance are discovered, your auditors and financial analysts should *notify* upper management and recommend immediate corrective action.

E. AVOIDING PROBLEMS

§ 14:36 Recommendations

While the elimination of the "paid cost" rule has somewhat simplified the preparation of a payment request, you should still be thoroughly familiar with the procedural requirements associated with requesting progress payments and comply precisely with those requirements. Here are some simple guidelines for properly requesting and administering progress payments under

PROGRESS PAYMENTS § 14:36

your Government contracts:

(a) Make sure all *incurred* costs included on Line 11 of your Standard Form 1443 have been incurred as of the "Section II date" of Standard Form 1443.

(b) Remember that *all* costs included on Standard Form 1443 must be allowable, reasonable, and allocable to your contract.

(c) If you make progress payments to any of your *subcontractors* or *affiliates*, you should (1) make them on the same terms under which you receive progress payments from the Government, (2) include the amount of the progress payments to your subcontractors or affiliates on Line 14 of Standard Form 1443 for 100% reimbursement from the Government, and (3) include the appropriate portion of liquidation of those progress payments on Line 11 of your Standard Form 1443 for 80% reimbursement from the Government. (See § 14:8).

(d) If you do *not* make progress payments to your *subcontractors* or *affiliates*, you must include on Line 11 of your Standard Form 1443 only costs paid to those subcontractors or affiliates for *completed and delivered* items. (See § 14:8).

(e) *Monitor contract performance* to avoid circumstances that could lead to reduction or suspension of progress payments. If your profit is more or less than anticipated, evaluate whether the liquidation rate should be *changed* to prevent underliquidation or overliquidation of your progress payments. If you have a *loss contract*, you must follow different rules for application of the liquidation rate.

(f) *Do not encumber* any of the property to which the Government has title under the "Progress Payments" clause without the CO's express approval.

(g) *Maintain adequate records* to support the data in your Standard Form 1443.

(h) *Cooperate with Government auditors* in the event of an audit. Remember that these auditors can recommend suspension of your progress payments to the CO, which could shut your company down.

Chapter 15

Product Substitution

I. OVERVIEW
§ 15:1 Scope note

II. CURRENT REQUIREMENTS
A. CONTRACT QUALITY REQUIREMENTS
§ 15:2 Contractor's responsibilities for quality control
§ 15:3 Types of contract quality requirements
§ 15:4 Contractor inspection requirements for commercial item contracts
§ 15:5 Contractor inspection requirements for small contracts
§ 15:6 Standard inspection requirements
§ 15:7 Higher-level quality requirements

B. PENALTIES
§ 15:8 Generally
§ 15:9 Penalties for individuals
§ 15:10 Penalties for companies

C. FREQUENTLY ASKED QUESTIONS
§ 15:11 Questions & answers

III. HOW TO RECOGNIZE THE PROBLEM
§ 15:12 Examples

IV. COMPLIANCE INITIATIVES
§ 15:13 Upper management
§ 15:14 Middle management
§ 15:15 Quality assurance personnel
§ 15:16 Recommendations

GOVERNMENT CONTRACT COMPLIANCE HANDBOOK

> **KeyCite®:** Cases and other legal materials listed in KeyCite Scope can be researched through the KeyCite service on Westlaw®. Use KeyCite to check citations for form, parallel references, prior and later history, and comprehensive citator information, including citations to other decisions and secondary materials.

I. OVERVIEW

§ 15:1 Scope note

The Government has the right to insist on strict compliance with contract specifications.[1] According to the Government, product substitution occurs where a contractor delivers goods or services that do not conform in every respect to contract requirements while seeking payment based on the alleged delivery of conforming products or services.[2]

Product substitution may occur where contractors provide products that are *different* from those required by the contract (by using, for example, raw materials other than those specified, providing components from nonapproved sources, furnishing defective parts, or otherwise failing to meet technical specification requirements). Product substitution may also occur where the contractor *fails to test or inspect* products as required by the contract *regardless* of whether the products are in fact *deficient*.

As procurement budgets of federal agencies decline and competition for Government contracts increases, there are ever-growing concerns about contractors cutting corners, skipping required tests, and fabricating inspection reports and test results. In 1991, based on a survey of 22 federal agencies, a presidential council reported that 85% of Government employees who perform quality assurance/quality control functions or use/receive products furnished under Government contracts are aware of product substitution problems.[3] In 1996, the General Accounting Office (since renamed the Government Accountability Office) (GAO) concluded that, next to contract mischarging, product substitution is the most frequent type of procurement fraud reported under the Department of Defense (DOD) voluntary disclosure

---

[Section 15:1]

[1]*Valenzuela Engineering, Inc.*, ASBCA No. 53608, 04–1 BCA ¶ 32517.

[2]*See* DOD Office of Inspector General, Indicators of Fraud in Department of Defense Procurement § 6-1 (June 1987) (*see* Appendix T to this Compliance Handbook); *see also* GAO, Briefing Report to the U.S. Senate, "DOD Fraud Investigations: Characteristics, Sanctions and Prevention" 23 (Jan. 1988) (*see* Appendix S).

[3]*See* Office of Federal Procurement Policy, "Reporting Nonconforming Products and Materials," 56 Fed. Reg. 4112 (1991) (citing a July 1990 survey by the President's Council on Integrity and Efficiency).

PRODUCT SUBSTITUTION § 15:1

program. (See §§ 4:1 et seq.)[4]

Often contractors ignore or simply fail to understand the dangers and consequences of product substitution. This is commonly the case where contractors believe that the substituted goods/services are as good as *or better than* what the contract requires, and that, therefore, the substitution causes no harm to the Government. The DOD Inspector General (IG) has pointed out several fallacies of this argument:[5]

(a) The substituted product is usually not as good as the item or service specified, often inferior in quality or workmanship. This inferiority may have a serious and detrimental impact on the safety of DOD personnel and the accomplishment of important missions.

(b) Even if any immediate harm that the substitute product might cause is sometimes difficult to determine, the introduction of the substituted item into Government supply channels undermines the reliability of the entire supply system. If, for example, a nonspecified part is surreptitiously incorporated into a military end item that fails, the failure might not be easily traced to the inferior quality of that part.

(c) Even if the substitute item is as good as the product called for in the contract, acceptance impairs the integrity of the competitive procurement process, which is based on all competitors offering to furnish the item precisely described in the specifications. Permitting each offeror to substitute its own judgment as to the quality of the item proposed undermines the fundamental principle of common basis bidding.

Product substitution often seems to be a subtle problem, encompassing actions—seemingly innocent—that lead to delivery of a product that does not comply *in each and every respect* with the item specified in the contract documents. The penalties for noncompliance, however, may be far from subtle. This has been a painful lessen to learn for many contractors, as numerous investigations and prosecutions for product substitution have led to multimillion-dollar civil judgments and criminal fines, prison terms for corporate officers, and suspension and debarment from Government contracting. (See generally Appendices S and T to this Compliance Handbook.)

---

[4]GAO, Report to the Senate Judiciary Comm., Subcomm. on Administrative Oversight and the Courts, "DoD Procurement—Use and Administration of DoD's Voluntary Disclosure Program" (Feb. 6, 1996).

[5]DOD Inspector General, Indicators of Fraud in Department of Defense Procurements § 6-1(c) (June 1987) (*see* Appendix T in this Handbook).

483

II. CURRENT REQUIREMENTS

A. CONTRACT QUALITY REQUIREMENTS

§ 15:2 Contractor's responsibilities for quality control

For a contractor, the key to avoiding product substitution problems is to comply with contract quality requirements and develop an effective quality assurance program. Your primary quality assurance obligations are set forth in Part 46 of the Federal Acquisition Regulation (FAR) and Part 246 of the DOD FAR Supplement (DFARS). The FAR states that the contractor is responsible for the following:[1]

(1) *Controlling the quality* of supplies or services tendered to the Government.

(2) Tendering to the Government for acceptance only supplies or services that *conform to contract requirements*.

(3) Ensuring that *suppliers* of raw materials, parts, components, and subassemblies have an acceptable quality control system.

(4) If required by the contract, maintaining *substantiating evidence* that the supplies or services conform to contract quality requirements and furnishing such information to the Government as required.

(5) If required by the contract, providing and maintaining an inspection system or program for quality control that is acceptable to the Government. (See §§ 15:3 to 15:7.)

Responsibility for control of quality may extend to (a) manufacturing processes, (b) drawings, specifications, and engineering changes, (c) testing and inspection, (d) reliability and maintainability assessment (e.g., life, endurance, and continued readiness of the product/system), (e) fabrication and delivery of products to ensure only conforming products are tendered to the Government, (f) technical documentation, (g) preservation, packaging, packing, and marking, and (h) procedures and processes to ensure that services meet contract performance requirements.[2] In addition, the contractor is responsible for performing all inspections and tests required by the contract except those specifically reserved for performance by the Government.[3]

§ 15:3 Types of contract quality requirements

The type of quality assurance procedures you must use depends

---

[Section 15:2]

[1]FAR 46.105(a), (b).
[2]FAR 46.105(c).
[3]FAR 46.105(d).

on the type of procurement involved. For example, the Government generally relies on inspection only by the contractor during performance when purchasing commercial items[1] but may require the contractor to comply with a Government-approved quality control system when purchasing complex or safety-critical items.[2] The FAR describes three levels of quality assurance: (1) inspection only by the contractor; (2) standard inspection; and (3) higher-level quality inspection.[3] With the current emphasis on discouraging the use of Government-unique specifications and standards in favor of encouraging the use of commercial practices, however (see §§ 10:1 et seq.), the Government less frequently uses higher-level quality assurance requirements in solicitations in favor of reliance on the use of commercial quality systems.

§ 15:4 Contractor inspection requirements for commercial item contracts

If you are providing "commercial items" to the Government, under the streamlined rules for commercial item acquisitions incorporated in the FAR, you may rely on your *existing* quality assurance system as a substitute for Government inspection and testing before you tender items to the Government for acceptance, regardless of the value of the contract.[1] Put simply, you may rely on the *same* quality assurance system that you use when selling these same products to commercial customers, provided that your quality assurance system comports with customary practice in the commercial marketplace.

Under the streamlined rules for commercial item acquisitions, the Government has no right to conduct any in-process inspection—that is, it has no right to inspect until the items are ready for final acceptance—unless in-process inspections are a customary commercial practice for the items to be acquired. However, even if customary, the Government must conduct such in-process inspections in a manner consistent with commercial practice.[2]

§ 15:5 Contractor inspection requirements for small contracts

The FAR provides special "simplified acquisition procedures"

[Section 15:3]
　[1]FAR 46.202-1.
　[2]FAR 46.202-4.
　[3]FAR 46.202.

[Section 15:4]
　[1]FAR 12.208, 46.202-1.
　[2]FAR 12.208, 46.202-1.

§ 15:5   GOVERNMENT CONTRACT COMPLIANCE HANDBOOK

for the acquisition of supplies and services (including construction, research and development, and commercial items) where the contract award does not exceed the "simplified acquisition threshold" (currently $100,000).[1] Generally, for purchases at or below the simplified acquisition threshold, during the performance of contract work, the Government will *not* conduct inspection or testing but will rely *solely on the contractor* to perform all inspection and testing needed to ensure that the supplies or services acquired conform to contract requirements.[2]

There are, however, certain situations where the Government may decide to conduct its own inspection and testing of supplies or services before they are tendered for acceptance or to pass judgment on the adequacy of the contractor's internal work processes. In making this determination, the Contracting Officer (CO) must take into consideration the following factors: (a) the nature of the supplies and services being purchased and their intended use; (b) potential losses in the event of defects; (c) the likelihood of uncontested replacement or correction of defective work; and (d) the cost of detailed Government inspection.[3]

§ 15:6   Standard inspection requirements

If your Government contract is not for the acquisition of commercial items, and the amount of the award exceeds $150,000, the contract will probably contain a standard FAR "Inspection" clause describing the contract's quality assurance requirements. For example, the standard FAR "Inspection" clause for fixed-price supply contracts sets forth the following contractor obligations and Government rights:[1]

(1) The contractor shall *maintain an inspection system that is acceptable to the Government*.
(2) The contractor shall tender to the Government for acceptance only supplies that *have been inspected* in accordance with that inspection system and found by the contractor to *conform* with contract requirements.
(3) The contractor shall *keep complete records* of all inspections and results thereof, which shall be made available to the Government for review.

[Section 15:5]

    [1]FAR pt. 13, 2.101.
    [2]FAR 46.202-2.
    [3]FAR 46.202-2.

[Section 15:6]

    [1]FAR 52.246-2 ("Inspection of Supplies-Fixed-Price" clause), paras. (b), (c), (d).

(4) The Government has the right to *test or inspect all supplies at any time during contract performance*, including the right to perform in-process inspections as long as they are performed in a manner that does not unduly interfere with performance.
(5) Although the Government has the right to test and inspect, the *Government has no duty* to do so, and the performance of any testing or inspections by the Government does not relieve the contractor of any of its quality assurance obligations.
(6) In the event that the Government does perform inspection or testing on the contractor's premises, the *contractor shall furnish*, at no increase in contract price, all reasonable *facilities and assistance* for the safe and convenient performance thereof.

Similar requirements exist under the standard FAR "Inspection" clauses for fixed-price service contracts and construction contracts.[2]

§ 15:7 Higher-level quality requirements

Higher-level quality requirements may be appropriate where the products or services being acquired by the Government are *complex* or they have a *critical* application to a Government mission.[1] According to the FAR, "[c]omplex items have quality characteristics, not wholly visible in the end item, for which contractual conformance must be established progressively through precise measurements, tests, and controls applied during purchasing, manufacturing, performance, assembly, and functional operation."[2] Items are defined in the FAR as *critical* in their application if "the failure of the item could injure personnel or jeopardize a vital agency mission."[3]

Where, for example, a defense contractor supplies the U.S. military with complex items or items critical in their application, the contract may include the FAR's "Higher-Level Contract Quality Requirement (Government Specification)" clause.[4] This clause requires the contractor to comply with a Government-specified inspection system, quality control system, or quality program.

The DOD policy provisions on quality assurance state that

---

[2]*See* FAR 52.246-4 ("Inspection of Services-Fixed-Price" clause) and FAR 52.246-12 ("Inspection of Construction" clause).

[Section 15:7]

[1]*See* FAR 46.202-4.
[2]FAR 46.203(b).
[3]FAR 46.203(c).
[4]FAR 52.246-11.

§ 15:7   GOVERNMENT CONTRACT COMPLIANCE HANDBOOK

DOD departments and agencies shall provide contractors "the maximum flexibility in establishing efficient and effective quality programs to meet contractual requirements," and that contractor quality programs "may be modeled on military, commercial, national, or international quality standards."[5] In addition, the FAR provisions on higher-level contract quality requirements reflect the Government's preference for commercial contract quality requirements over military or federal specifications.[6]

DOD places heightened scrutiny on counterfeit electronic parts, and contractors subject to the Cost Accounting Standards are required to establish and maintain a Government-accepted counterfeit electronic part detection and avoidance system, or risk disapproval of their purchasing system and payment withholds.[7] An acceptable counterfeit electronic part detection and avoidance system must address the following areas:[8]

(1) Personnel training.
(2) Electronic parts inspection and testing.
(3) Processes to abolish counterfeit parts proliferation.
(4) Processes for maintaining electronic part traceability.
(5) Use of original manufacturers, or sources authorized by the original manufacturer.
(6) Reporting and quarantining of counterfeit and suspected counterfeit electronic parts.
(7) Methodologies to identify suspect counterfeit electronic parts and to quickly determine if it is counterfeit.
(8) Design, operation, and maintenance of systems to deterc and avoid counterfeit electronic parts.
(9) Flow down of counterfeit detection and avoidance requirements to suppliers.
(10) Process for continued learning on counterfeit information and trends.
(11) Process for screening the Government-Industry Data Exchange Program (GIDEP) reports and other credible information sources.
(12) Control of obsolete electronic parts in order to maximize availability of authentic, qualified parts.

B. PENALTIES

§ 15:8 Generally

Product substitution is like any other fraud perpetrated against

---
[5]DFARS 246.102(4).
[6]FAR 46.202-4(b).
[7]DFARS 246.870-2(a).
[8]DFARS 246.870-2(b).

the Government, and, as such, it subjects the contractor to potentially severe criminal and civil penalties under a whole panoply of federal statutes such as (among others) the civil and criminal False Claims Acts, the false statements statute, and the federal conspiracy statute.[1] In addition, the Government may impose administrative sanctions such as suspension and debarment from doing business with the Government.[2] (See §§ 1:1 et seq.)

§ 15:9 Penalties for individuals

A DOD IG report revealed that, although product substitution cases were the top law enforcement priority of DOD criminal investigative organizations, individuals convicted in such cases often received short prison sentences (less than 18 months) or were never incarcerated.[1] Concerned that such punishment was not of significant deterrent value, the DOD and the Department of Justice increased their emphasis on prosecuting individuals and securing longer prison sentences in cases of product substitution.[2]

In addition to civil and criminal fines and imprisonment, the Government debars individuals involved in product substitution from participation in further federal contracting. Although, under the FAR, the period of debarment for product substitution generally does not exceed three years,[3] in some circumstances it may be possible for the Government to effectively debar individuals for a more extended time period. Additionally, a federal appeals court has held that the Government is not prohibited from debarring an individual more than once for multiple product substitution activities that occur during the same period.[4] However, federal courts, in debarment cases, have also increased the Government's burden of proving that the individual actually *knew* of the product substitution. Under the FAR, an individual may be

---

[Section 15:8]

[1] 31 U.S.C.A. §§ 3729 to 3733; 18 U.S.C.A. §§ 287, 1001, 371.

[2] *See* FAR subpt. 9.4. *See generally* West, Hatch, Brennan & VanDyke, Suspension & Debarment, Briefing Papers No. 06-9 (Aug. 2006).

[Section 15:9]

[1] DOD Office of Inspector General, Review of Significant Product Substitution Cases Within the Department of Defense (Sept. 1987).

[2] *See, e.g.,* 61 Fed. Cont. Rep. (BNA) 258–59 (Feb. 21, 1994).

[3] FAR 9.406-4; *see also* DFARS 203.570-2, 252.203-7001 (anyone convicted of product substitution fraud may be prohibited from working for a Government contractor as a consultant, agent, or representative for five years from the date of his/her conviction).

[4] *See, e.g., Wellham v. Cheney,* 934 F.2d 305 (11th Cir. 1991); FAR 9.406-4.

§ 15:9   GOVERNMENT CONTRACT COMPLIANCE HANDBOOK

debarred if the individual actually knew or had "reason to know" of his or her company's product substitution while it was occurring.[5] In one case, the U.S. Court of Appeals for the District of Columbia Circuit voided the Government's debarment of an individual who failed to stop product substitution of which he "should have known" because individual liability for product substitution cannot be based on a "duty to inquire." It held instead that individual liability exists under the "reason to know" standard only if the individual in question actually had information from which "a person of ordinary intelligence would infer" either (1) product substitution was occurring, or (2) such a substantial chance of product substitution existed that an individual exercising reasonable care would take action.[6] However, an individual cannot afford to ignore suspicions about product substitution; an individual will be held accountable if the individual learns of facts that would lead to an inference of product substitution but does nothing to stop it.

Cases & Commentary: A laboratory employee for a NASA contractor was sentenced to one year of probation and a $1,000 fine after pleading guilty to charges she had falsified tests to conceal the fact that batteries intended for use on astronauts' suits failed to meet contract requirements.[7]

§ 15:10 Penalties for companies

Companies may receive substantial fines if their employees engage in product substitution. For example, in January 1995, a supplier of gearboxes for a Navy fighter aircraft and the Army's multiple launch rocket system admitted to falsifying quality records, selling nonconforming parts to the Government, using faulty test equipment, and making unauthorized repairs. The supplier pleaded guilty to submitting false statements to the Government and paid an $18.5 million criminal fine.[1]

Courts will impose liability on your company if your employees' product substitution somehow benefited the company.[2] In fact, some courts hold the company responsible even if the company

---

[5]FAR 9.406-5(b).

[6]*Novicki v. Cook*, 946 F.2d 938 (D.C. Cir. 1991).

[7]United States Attorney's Office District of Connecticut Press Release (Feb. 1, 2007).

[Section 15:10]

[1]*See* DOD Inspector General, Semiannual Report to Congress for October 1, 1994 to March 31, 1995, at 3-4 to 3-5.

[2]*Grand Union Co. v. U.S.*, 696 F.2d 888 (11th Cir. 1983).

received no benefit whatsoever from the product substitution.[3] In extreme cases, the fines can put the company out of business. You should also be aware that under the U.S. Sentencing Guidelines for organizations (see §§ 1:1 et seq.), courts can *increase* the sentences and fines imposed on companies convicted of product substitution *above* those suggested in the Guidelines where the product substitution resulted in a "foreseeable risk of death or bodily injury." The amount of the increase will depend on "the nature of the harm" and the "extent to which the harm was intended or knowingly risked."[4]

Moreover, a company can be *debarred* from Government contracting if any company employee engages in product substitution.[5] The Government can also *suspend* your company from federal contracting during the pendency of its investigation of alleged product substitution and before any convictions have been obtained.[6]

At a minimum, the Government can *terminate* your contract for default on discovering improper product substitution.[7] Even with this minimal penalty, your company can suffer substantial financial damage for product substitution.[8]

In addition to all of the damages, penalties, and sanctions discussed above, a company that engages in product substitution may also have to bear the cost of *reinspecting* or *retesting* finished products, *correcting* defects, refitting equipment in the field, and otherwise undoing the harm caused by the product substitution.

Allegations of product substitution against companies often arise in False Claims Act cases filed by contractor employees and

---

[3]*U.S. v. O'Connell*, 890 F.2d 563, 29 Fed. R. Evid. Serv. 422, 15 Fed. R. Serv. 3d 197, 107 A.L.R. Fed. 653 (1st Cir. 1989).

[4]U.S. Sentencing Comm'n, Sentencing Guidelines Manual § 8C4.2 (2005).

[5]*See, e.g.*, 59 Fed. Cont. Rep. (BNA) 545 (Apr. 19, 1993); 61 Fed. Cont. Rep. (BNA) 6 (Jan. 10, 1994) (one-year Government-wide debarment of a contractor that pleaded guilty to falsifying test results of electronic switches used in weapon systems, but the Government lifted the debarment eight months later claiming that it was no longer required to protect the Government's business interests; the contractor had established a company-wide ethics program, offered to make restitution to the Government, and retained an independent auditor to monitor its integrity program); *see also* FAR 9.406.

[6]*See, e.g., Medical Devices of Fall River, Inc.*, GSBCA No. 6534–5, 82-2 BCA ¶ 15804; *see also* FAR 9.407.

[7]*AAR Corp.*, ASBCA No. 16311 et al., 74-1 BCA ¶ 10607.

[8]*See, e.g.*, Daff, Trustee in *Daff v. U.S.*, 31 Fed. Cl. 682 (1994), judgment aff'd, 78 F.3d 1566 (Fed. Cir. 1996) (court sustained default termination and ordered the return of approximately $5.6 million of progress payments and payment under the False Claims Act's treble damages provision of an additional $600,000 to the Government, three times the $200,000 in actual damages the Government incurred as a result of the contractor's fraud).

former employees under the Act's qui tam provisions (see §§ 1:1 et seq.). For example, a 1998 qui tam suit resulted in a jury verdict of $390 million (later reduced to $90 million) against a contractor that falsely reported that its amphibious fighting vehicle had been thoroughly tested for swim operations when it actually leaked water.[9]

Cases & Commentary: The Government continues to seek stiff penalties under the False Claims Act and other statutes from companies in cases of product substitution. For example, a manufacturer of military combat vehicles agreed to pay $1.8 million to settle a suit claiming that the vehicles built by the company did not comply with military specifications, contained substandard parts and had known defects in their operating systems.[10] In another case, a maker of military insignia agreed to pay the Government $251,000 to settle charges that it supplied products made from zinc rather than brass as required by the contract.[11]

ATK Launch Systems Inc. April 23, 2012 agreed to a $36,967,160 settlement with the Department of Justice to resolve allegations that ATK sold dangerous and defective illumination flares to the Army and the Air Force. According to the Government, from 2000 to 2006, ATK delivered illuminating para-flares to the Defense Department that were incapable of withstanding a 10-foot drop test without exploding or igniting, as required by specifications, and that ATK was aware of this when it submitted claims for payment.[12]

C. FREQUENTLY ASKED QUESTIONS

§ 15:11 Questions & answers

Question 1: Can product substitution occur when products tendered for delivery fail to conform to specifications but the deviation is not substantial, and the items are manufactured in accordance with best commercial practice and are just as good as

---

[9]*United States ex rel. Boisvert v. FMC Corp.*, No. C-86-20163 (N.D. Cal. 1998); *see also* 64 Fed. Cont. Rep. (BNA) 307-08 (Oct. 9, 1995) (former machinist employed by the supplier of gearboxes to the Army and Navy filed a qui tam lawsuit against the company for failure to properly test military aircraft parts and knowingly shipping defective parts to the U.S. military; the company agreed to pay approximately $88 million to settle the lawsuit, including more than $19 million for the qui tam relator); Wall St. J., Oct. 2, 1995, at B6.

[10]*United States ex. rel. Chomyn v. force Protection Inc.*, No. 05-CV-1906, settlement announced (D.S.C. Aug. 30, 2006).

[11]*United States ex rel. Ira Green Inc. v. Hillborn Hamburger Inc.*, No. 04-CV-2507, settlement approved (D.N.J. May 30, 2007).

[12]Dept. of Justice Press Release 12-520 (Apr. 23, 2012), *available at* http://www.justice.gov/opa/pr/2012/April/12-civ-520.html.

§ 15:11 PRODUCT SUBSTITUTION

the required items?

Answer 1: Yes. Product substitution occurs where a Government contractor delivers goods or services that do not conform to contract requirements, and the contractor fails to inform the Government of the discrepancies and seeks payment based on alleged delivery of conforming products or services. Absent unusual facts and circumstances, the Government is entitled to insist on strict compliance with all contract provisions. Therefore, it is no defense to charges of product substitution fraud that known deviations from the specifications are minor or that the nonconforming products are manufactured in accordance with best commercial practices. Furthermore, it is no defense even that the nonconforming products or services are as good *or better than* those called for by the contract, or that the same items have been supplied under prior procurements and used by the Government without complaint. Similarly, it is no defense even that the contractor can demonstrate that the nonconforming products have never been known to fail.

Question 2: Can a contractor be charged with product substitution fraud where parts, components, or raw materials used in performing a Government contract are provided by a source other than a Government-approved source (where required by the contract), and the use of the nonapproved source saves the Government money and the delivered product functions perfectly?

Answer 2: Yes. Product substitution encompasses attempts by prime contractors and subcontractors to deliver products integrating components from a source other than an approved source, as required by contract. For example, suppose you have a contract with the Air Force requiring you to deliver valves from a Government-approved source for the ejection system of a fighter plane. You contact the approved source initially but decide you can produce valves of the same quality at a lower cost and in less time. Because contract performance is running behind schedule and over budget, and because you believe that valves produced in-house will be just as good as those provided by the approved source, you decide to produce the valves yourself but do not clear this decision with the CO before delivery. Even if you can show that every valve delivered to the Air Force meets the Air Force's safety and quality requirements, your risk of liability for fraud is very real.[1]

Question 3: Can product substitution occur where products tendered for delivery strictly comply with every design and performance requirement in the specifications/drawings, but the

---

[Section 15:11]

[1]*See U.S. v. Aerodex, Inc.*, 469 F.2d 1003 (5th Cir. 1972).

§ 15:11

products have not been inspected or tested as required by the contract?

Answer 3: Yes. You engage in prohibited product substitution if you fail to test products that your contract requires to be tested, *regardless* of whether the untested products are actually deficient. For example, assume that you have a contract to produce breach bolts for Army machine guns. Your contract requires you to test-fire the parts with Government-supplied equipment and to perform magnetic particle inspections of each part after firing to ensure an absence of defects. Because your company is running behind in production, you deliver the products to the Government without performing the required tests. However, you certify that the tests have been conducted and that the test results conform to contract specifications. Even if subsequent testing of the parts confirms that the parts contain no defects, you will still be liable for product substitution because your contract required you to supply products that were pretested.[2]

Question 4: In a services contract, can a contractor be charged with product substitution fraud where all services are satisfactorily performed but the contractor has used less qualified personnel than those specified in the contract?

Answer 4: Yes. The DOD IG has noted that product substitution encompasses not only the substitution of goods but also *worker substitution*.[3] For example, assume you are awarded a contract for the maintenance of military aircraft. The contract requires that the persons you employ to service certain types of aircraft must have technical certifications that are higher than usual for technicians that usually work on those types of aircraft. You are unable to locate and hire a sufficient number of workers with the required certification at a reasonable cost. As a result, you are forced to hire technicians who you believe are competent and sufficiently trained for the work under the contract but who do not meet the contract's certification requirements. By engaging in such a course of conduct, your company will be exposed to a significant risk of liability for product substitution fraud.

Question 5: Assume you are a contractor that is faced with an instance where the product you manufacture for the Government does not conform to all requirements in your contract. Aside from not tendering the nonconforming item for delivery and engaging in expensive rework, do you have any other viable option?

Answer 5: You may be able to tender nonconforming goods or services to the Government provided you notify the Government

---

[2] *U.S. v. Genii Research, Inc.,* Crim. No. 85-2795 (E.D. N.Y. 1986).

[3] DOD Inspector General, Indicators of Fraud in Department of Defense Procurements § 6-2 (June 1987) (*see* Appendix T).

PRODUCT SUBSTITUTION § 15:12

in advance and request a deviation or waiver from the specifications, and the Government *approves*. A "deviation" is an authorization, *before manufacture*, to depart from a design requirement. A "waiver" is an authorization to *accept a tendered item* containing a departure from design requirements.[4] This Government approval usually is at some cost to you (such as a downward adjustment in contract price).

Question 6: Are there limitations on the Government's inspection rights?

Answer 6: As set forth above, limitations on the Government's rights to inspect will depend on the type of procurement involved. For example, if you are providing commercial items in an acquisition conducted under FAR Part 12 (see §§ 10:1 et seq.), the Government generally may not conduct any inspection until after the completion of manufacturing when the items are tendered for delivery (i.e., no in-process inspections unless customary in the commercial marketplace). Even where the Government has a contractual right to inspect all supplies at any time during contract performance, however, there are still limitations on the Government's inspection rights. For example, the Government has the right to insist on strict compliance with specifications, but the contractor is only required to meet standards prescribed in the contract and is not required to furnish a product to higher performance standards. Accordingly, although the Government may be entitled to conduct tests not specified in the contract, the Government cannot use the inspection process to impose on the contractor higher quality standards or more stringent performance requirements than those prescribed in the contract. Any attempt by the CO to do so constitutes a constructive change for which the contractor may be entitled to an equitable adjustment in contract price and/or delivery schedule. Furthermore, in every contract, the Government has an implied duty to cooperate. Accordingly, if Government inspectors unreasonably interfere in the performance of contract work (through, for example, excessive supervision, unreasonable delay in performance of inspections, or wrongful refusal to inspect) the contractor may be entitled to an extension of time and recovery of increased costs.

III. HOW TO RECOGNIZE THE PROBLEM

§ 15:12 Examples

The following examples—many of which are taken from actual cases—may assist you in understanding the sometimes subtle obligations regarding compliance with specification and quality assurance requirements and thus help you to recognize instances

---

[4]*Canadian Commercial Corp.*, ASBCA No. 17187, 76-2 BCA ¶ 12145.

§ 15:12   GOVERNMENT CONTRACT COMPLIANCE HANDBOOK

in which liability for product substitution may occur.

(a) *Substandard raw materials*: Assume you have a DOD contract to supply springs to be used in CH-47 helicopters, cruise missiles, F-18 fighters, and B-1 bombers. In your proposal, you state that you will make the springs from a certain type and grade of steel. Your proposal forms part of the contract. The cost of that type of steel increases substantially during contract performance. You determine that another type of steel will produce springs of a similar quality. You switch to the second type of steel but fail to inform the Government of this change. Under these facts, which are based on an actual case, the court sentenced the president of the company to seven months' confinement, five years' probation, a monetary fine, and 400 hours of community service.[1]

(b) *Brand name or equal*: You are awarded an Army contract to supply 6,600 motor vehicle generator regulators. The contract requires Delco-Remy, General Motors, or International Harvester regulators "*or equal*." You did not state that you were providing an "equal" in your bid. When you find that you cannot obtain regulators from the listed manufacturers at the price included in your bid, you manufacture your own regulators that are "equal" in all respects to the regulators specified. However, you affix pirated "Delco-Remy" labels to the regulators to simplify the acceptance process and deliver the regulators to the Army. The Army discovers the mislabeling, tests the regulators, and finds that they work properly. It directs you to deliver the remaining units and pays the full contract price for all units. Government criminal investigators thereafter bring an action against you for violation of the False Claims Act, and the court finds that each of the eight vouchers you submitted for payment before the discovery of the scheme constituted a false claim.[2]

(c) *Switching products after inspection*: You have a contract to deliver rifle barrels for M-14 and M-21 weapons to the DOD. Because of an employee strike, you are far behind your production schedule. Although you have just settled the strike, it has complicated existing financial problems in your company and seriously threatened the company's financial stability. The Government is threatening to terminate your contract for default if you do not speed up delivery of the rifle barrels and will charge you with the costs of the delay and of reprocurement, which could bankrupt your company. You cannot gear up your production line

---

[Section 15:12]

[1]*See U.S. v. Spring Works, Inc.*, Crim. No. 86-1112-WMB (C.D. Cal., Apr. 6, 1987).

[2]*See U.S. v. National Wholesalers*, 236 F.2d 944 (9th Cir. 1956).

quickly enough to produce the number of barrels that must be delivered. However, you are able to manufacture a small number of rifle barrels that meet specifications. You show these acceptable barrels to DOD inspectors during quality assurance checks but then substitute in their place other barrels from your existing stockpile of rejects and ship them to DOD depots. You then show the previously viewed acceptable barrels to DOD at the next quality assurance check. In this actual case, the company was fined $400,000 and debarred from Government contracting.[3]

(d) *Newly manufactured vs. used equipment*: Your subcontract requires you to supply newly manufactured parts for installation on Air Force F-4 and F-104 fighters. The prime contractor has a very tight schedule, and you are under constant pressure to make your deliveries. You have a slowdown in production because of several mechanical failures on your production line. You have numerous parts that you have previously manufactured and that you could refurbish or recondition to satisfy the Government's requirements, a process permitted on your other Air Force contracts. Because of the cost and time savings, you deliver refurbished parts. The Air Force subsequently discovers that some of the parts you supplied to the prime were not newly manufactured but refurbished. You never informed the Air Force that you were submitting anything to your prime other than new parts. In this actual case, the company was convicted of conspiracy and of submitting false statements to the Government and was ordered to pay $1 million in fines. The company's president and vice president were fined and sentenced to prison terms.[4]

(e) *False test data*: You have a Government contract that requires you to test the paint you supply for use on roads and airstrips by air-drying painted panels at various temperatures and degrees of humidity. Your laboratory is set up to test paint in accordance with established trade practice in your state but not as required by your federal contract. Although you modify your testing procedures to accommodate your contract requirements, the tests are not always consistently performed in accordance with contract requirements. Even if all of your paint passes the tests as conducted by your lab, you are potentially liable for product substitution fraud if you certify that your products were tested pursuant to contract requirements.[5]

(f) *Failure to test*: Your company manufactures, tests, and delivers pressure transducers to the Navy and the Coast Guard that assist in measuring and controlling the altitude of a high-

---

[3]*See* DOD Inspector General, Indicators of Fraud in Department of Defense Procurements § 6-3 (June 1987) (*see* Appendix T).

[4]*See* L.A. Times, Aug. 16, 1988, § 2, at 1.

[5]*See Pervo Paint Co.*, GSBCA No. 8220 et al., 87-1 BCA. ¶ 19409.

§ 15:12						Government Contract Compliance Handbook

speed antiradar missile during flight. You have produced, tested, and delivered several lots of transducers and have never had any serious problems. You have no problems during production that would lead you to believe any products are defective. After you test a few of the transducers and find no defects, you see no reason to continue testing all the transducers required to be tested by the contract, given the expense and time that you will incur for the testing. You do not tell the Government that you have not completed testing. Following the Government's investigation in this actual case, three company executives pleaded guilty to conspiracy and to making false statements to the Government.[6]

(g) *Misrepresentations to avoid inspection*: You represent to the Government that you possess new, unused surplus aircraft parts that are former Government-owned material manufactured by another company, and the Government agrees to purchase the "surplus." In actuality, you have manufactured the parts yourself. The Government applies a lesser inspection standard to the surplus parts, believing that they have already been inspected by the Government and determined to meet certain "milspec" standards when they were produced at the other company. Since you produced the parts yourself without Government supervision, however, the parts have not been inspected before. In this actual case, the company and several executives were convicted of conspiracy to defraud the United States and of making false statements in connection with contracts for surplus aircraft parts.[7]

(h) *Buy American Act compliance*: Your contract for the supply of hacksaw blades includes a FAR "Buy American Act" clause, which requires your blades to be "domestic end products," with the cost of components mined, produced, or manufactured in the United States exceeding 50% of the cost of all components. (See §§ 17:1 et seq. for a discussion of domestic preference rules.) Your production process starts with hacksaw "blanks," which constitute a component of the blades. During manufacture of the blades, the cost of the blanks more than doubles. You locate blanks from Swedish and Japanese sources at much lower prices, and you purchase and incorporate these blanks into your process. However, in delivering your blades, you certify that they comply with the Buy American Act's requirements. The Government subsequently discovers that the hacksaw blanks were manufactured abroad and comprise more than 50% of the cost of all the blade's components. In this actual case, the court assessed penalties of $604,000—a $2,000 penalty for each false certification of Buy American Act compliance—even though the total contract

---

[6]*See* L.A. Times, Nov. 8, 1988, § 2, at 1.
[7]*See U.S. v. Allred*, 867 F.2d 856 (5th Cir. 1989).

PRODUCT SUBSTITUTION § 15:14

price was just $1.3 million.[8]

(i) *Use of non-OEM parts*: Your contract with the Air Force to build computer equipment requires that certain equipment be produced by the original equipment manufacturer (OEM). Although you originally plan to use OEM equipment, you learn you can acquire equipment that is identical in all respects to the OEM equipment and of the same quality but costs substantially less. You supply this non-OEM equipment to the Government without informing the Government of the change in manufacturer. According to the DOD IG's Office, you and your company would be liable for product substitution fraud.[9]

IV. COMPLIANCE INITIATIVES

§ 15:13 Upper management

Your compliance program to avoid product substitution fraud will only succeed if upper management is fully engaged in the program. If management only pays lip service to the problem, the company may well end up paying the consequences. If management is serious about compliance in this area, it should consider taking the following steps:

(a) Make sure that the company *Code of Conduct* forbids falsification of any records or documents.
(b) Establish a corporate commitment that any conduct even bordering on product substitution *will not be tolerated*. Make sure this commitment is communicated to all employees at all levels in the company.
(c) Establish an education and *training program* for mid-level management that delineates Government contracting quality requirements and the type of conduct expected in response to problems.
(d) Consider establishing an organizational structure that provides *independence* for quality assurance and inspection personnel under separate authority from the program manager's authority.
(e) Establish a program of *compliance audits* to ensure that tests required by your contracts are being performed and that records of the tests are accurate.

§ 15:14 Middle management

Once corporate upper management has set the expectations of the company and put in place mechanisms to ensure compliance,

---

[8]*See U.S. v. Rule Industries, Inc.*, 878 F.2d 535 (1st Cir. 1989).

[9]*See* DOD Inspector General, Indicators of Fraud in Department of Defense Procurements § 6-1 (June 1987) (*see* Appendix T).

§ 15:14   GOVERNMENT CONTRACT COMPLIANCE HANDBOOK

much of the task of achieving compliance devolves on middle management. Mid-level management should do the following:

(a) Provide *training* to ensure that all employees—but particularly engineers and technical personnel—understand that products or services delivered must strictly comply with contract requirements. In particular, make sure that employees understand that it is not their prerogative to substitute their judgment as to whether components or designs are "better than" or "equal to" those required by specifications. Similarly, it is not their job to determine that nonconforming products nevertheless pass some kind of "form, fit, or function" standard and can be tendered to the Government.

(b) Strongly *discourage* negotiation tactics or business practices that make use of "half truths" or concealment. Allowing a Government official to proceed under an expressed mistaken judgment of fact can cause as many problems as actively misleading the official.

(c) Emphasize the need to *document* all discussions with Government representatives that involve *deviations* from or *waivers* of contract requirements—even if such deviations or waivers appear relatively minor.

(d) Maintain complete records supporting quality assurance activities and establish a procedure to *control changes* (by outlawing erasures, "white-outs," or the like) on quality assurance *records*.

(e) Institute careful *disciplinary rules* covering employee infractions in the product substitution area.

§ 15:15 Quality assurance personnel

Corporate quality assurance personnel remain the first line of defense against product substitution. They should have the highest possible level of professional training and ethics. In addition, they should do the following:

(a) Review the contract specification "tree" thoroughly at the outset of a new contract. Be sure that the company is working with the *latest revision* of the specification documents and that it fully understands the interrelationship of the specification documents as they relate to contract tasks.

(b) Ensure that quality assurance documentation is *not altered* (through erasures, "white-outs," or the like). Follow company policy regarding documentation.

(c) Carry out approved quality assurance procedures *precisely* with respect to every item to be reviewed or tested.

(d) *Report immediately* any suspected problem with the quality assurance process to a supervisor or through the company

hotline.
(e) Avoid reliance on the oral direction of a Government representative to alter approved quality assurance procedures. Request appropriate *written* confirmation from the CO or the CO's authorized representative.
(f) Notify a supervisor immediately of any suspected discrepancy in *vendor* or *subcontractor* quality assurance procedures.

§ 15:16 Recommendations

As a contractor, it is unrealistic to expect that you will never encounter problems meeting contract specification requirements. Therefore, you should understand what to do if you cannot tender conforming goods or services.

(a) Do not *certify* in any form that the goods/services tendered conform with contract requirements. False certification will subject you to civil and criminal liability as well as possible debarment from Government contracting. The consequences of failure to deliver or late delivery are not as serious as the consequences of false certification of product conformance.

(b) At a minimum, do *not* knowingly deliver any noncompliant products without first *informing* the Government. It may be possible to inform the Government of the noncompliance problem in *advance* and to obtain a contract modification or waiver that relaxes the specification requirement in issue.

(c) Be aware of, understand, and implement *all* of your contract's *quality assurance provisions* relating to inspection, acceptance, and warranties. In addition, if higher-level quality requirements are included in the contract, be sure to comply with the procedures and requirements contained therein. Be familiar with the quality assurance provisions in FAR Part 46, which set forth regulatory obligations for both you and the Government.

(d) Make sure your *compliance program* extends to and adequately covers the product quality area, including policies, procedures, a hotline, a training program, and an audit program.

Part IV
SPECIAL PROBLEMS

Chapter 16
Contract Claims

I. OVERVIEW

§ 16:1   Scope note

II. CERTIFYING & PRICING CONTRACT "CLAIMS"

§ 16:2   Definition of "claim"
§ 16:3   Certification
§ 16:4   —Effect of defective certification
§ 16:5   —Certification language
§ 16:6   —Who must certify?
§ 16:7   —Defense contracts
§ 16:8   Pricing methods
§ 16:9   Pricing CDA claims or requests for equitable adjustment
§ 16:10   Fraud liability
§ 16:11   Frequently asked questions

III. HOW TO RECOGNIZE THE PROBLEM

§ 16:12   Generally
§ 16:13   Examples

IV. COMPLIANCE INITIATIVES

§ 16:14   Establish a claims team
§ 16:15   Maintain records
§ 16:16   Corroborate & document the facts
§ 16:17   Claim negotiation
§ 16:18   Claim litigation
§ 16:19   Recommendations

> **KeyCite®:** Cases and other legal materials listed in KeyCite Scope can be researched through the KeyCite service on Westlaw®. Use KeyCite to check citations for form, parallel references, prior and later history, and comprehensive citator information, including citations to other decisions and secondary materials.

I. OVERVIEW

§ 16:1 Scope note

Although most Government contracts are performed and paid for in satisfactory fashion, serious disagreements between the parties occasionally arise over, for example, added or delayed work. If the parties are unable to resolve their disagreement, the contract contains a mechanism—the "Disputes" clause—that allows the contract work to continue while a settlement of the dispute is sought. If a mutually acceptable settlement cannot be attained, the parties must turn to the Contract Disputes Act (CDA)[1] procedures to resolve their differences. Under the CDA, the Contracting Officer (CO) has the power to decide the issue unilaterally, and, if the contractor disagrees with the CO's decision, it has the option to litigate the matter before the appropriate agency board of contract appeals or the Court of Federal Claims.

If you have a claim against the Government relating to a contract, you should be aware that if you seriously mishandle the procedures set forth in the CDA for resolving your claim you may not only fail to recover the amounts the Government owes you, but, even worse, if the claim can be construed as containing any "false" elements or "false" statements, you may find yourself defending against criminal or civil allegations of fraud. The Government is aggressively prosecuting companies and individuals that submit false claims to the Government for payment. The Government has available an array of criminal and civil sanctions that it may impose against you if you err, whether innocently or knowingly, in the claim preparation and submittal process (see §§ 1:1 et seq.). Therefore, your understanding of the potential trouble spots in preparing, submitting, and negotiating claims is imperative to the continued well being of your business as a whole.

Employees of Government contractors will also find this subject important from a personal standpoint. In certain situations, employees may be held *individually liable* for submission of false

---

[Section 16:1]

[1]Pub. L. 95-563, 92 Stat. 2383 (Nov. 1, 1978) (codified at 41 U.S.C.A. §§ 601 to 613). *See also Medina Const., Ltd. v. U.S.*, 43 Fed. Cl. 537 (1999).

claims to the Government. Managers often certify or sign claims as well as set policies for the preparation and submission of claims. Members of the contracts department may sign certifications, as well as invoices, progress payment requests, etc., and may assist in developing claims and requests for equitable adjustments. Financial personnel put together the numbers for invoices and progress payment requests and may price equitable adjustment claims. Many of these employees could be charged with fraud under federal law if they submit false information or statements to the Government.

II. CERTIFYING & PRICING CONTRACT "CLAIMS"

§ 16:2 Definition of "claim"

The first step in the Government contract "disputes" process is the submission (usually by the contractor) of a "claim" to the CO for decision. Under the CDA, "claim" is a legal term, and the statute and implementing Federal Acquisition Regulation (FAR) provisions set forth the requirements for and definition of the term. The CDA does not define "claim," but it does specify that (1) all claims by a contractor "shall be in writing and submitted to the contracting officer for a decision," and (2) all contractor claims over $100,000 must be certified.[1] The FAR defines a claim as "a written demand or written assertion by one of the contracting parties seeking, as a matter of right, the payment of money in a sum certain, the adjustment or interpretation of contract terms, or other relief arising under or relating to the contract."[2] The FAR admonishes that a "voucher, invoice, or other routine request for payment that is not in dispute when submitted is not a claim."[3] The U.S. Court of Appeals for the Federal Circuit has held that the FAR only "explicitly excludes from the definition of a 'claim' those 'routine request[s] for payment' that are not in dispute when submitted to the CO"; therefore, by implication, other written demands intended to obtain a CO's decision regarding payment as a matter or right are 'claims,' whether already in dispute or not.[4]

Determining whether a submission constitutes a "claim" within

---

[Section 16:2]

[1] 41 U.S.C.A. §§ 605(a), 605(c)(1); *see generally* Feldman, Government Contract Guidebook 4 § 22.

[2] FAR 2.201. See *Appeal of—Precision Standard, Inc.*, A.S.B.C.A. No. 55865, 11-1 B.C.A. (CCH) ¶ 34669, 2011 WL 310613 (Armed Serv. B.C.A. 2011) (appeal dismissed where contractor seeking "at least" $151,749.06 in damages did not state a sum certain).

[3] FAR 2.201.

[4] *Reflectone, Inc. v. Dalton*, 60 F.3d 1572, 1576 (Fed. Cir. 1995); *but see*

§ 16:2

the meaning of the CDA is important. The CDA provides for (1) interest on a claim from the date of submission, (2) a 60-day period in which the CO (if the claim is under $100,000) must decide the claim or (if it is over $100,000) must either decide the claim or notify the contractor of the date a decision will be made, and (3) jurisdictional grounds for access to an agency board of contract appeals or the Court of Federal Claims.

If the submission does not meet the formal definition of a "claim," none of the CDA provisions come into effect and the Government has no duty to take any action on that submission.

§ 16:3 Certification

The FAR states that for claims seeking $100,000 or more, the contractor must provide the following certification:[1]

> I certify that the claim is made in good faith; that the supporting data are accurate and complete to the best of my knowledge and belief; that the amount requested accurately reflects the contract adjustment for which the contractor believes the Government is liable; and that I am duly authorized to certify the claim on behalf of the contractor.

You should note that the Truth in Negotiations Act certification regarding cost or pricing data (see §§ 9:1 et seq.) is in addition to and not the same as CDA claim certification. You should also be aware that federal law requires you to certify a request for an equitable adjustment on a Department of Defense (DOD) contract.[2] This certification is also separate and distinct from that required by the CDA. See below.

§ 16:4 Certification—Effect of defective certification

Until 1992, a valid certification was a nonwaivable "jurisdictional" prerequisite to initiating a suit or appeal on a contract claim over the threshold statutory amount. An improperly certified claim deprived a board or court of jurisdiction under the CDA because there was no "claim" that had been properly

---

James M. Ellett Constr. Co. v. U.S., 93 F.3d 1537, 1544 (Fed. Cir. 1996) (finding a termination settlement proposal was a negotiation tool, not a request for the CO's decision). See also *Parsons Global Services, Inc. ex rel. Odell Intern., Inc. v. McHugh*, 677 F.3d 1166 (Fed. Cir. 2012); 54 GC ¶ 144 (where contractor's submissions for overhead costs mistakenly omitted from previous bills were found to be "routine requests for payment" and not claims).

See *URS Energy & Const., Inc. v. Dept. of Energy*, CBCA No. 2589, 12-1 BCA ¶ 35,055 (certification defective for not indicating a good faith submission or identifying the signor as having authorization to certify).

[Section 16:3]

[1] FAR 33.207(c).

[2] 10 U.S.C.A. § 2410(a).

§ 16:5 CONTRACT CLAIMS

"submitted." Therefore, if the certification was defective, the CO was neither required nor authorized to render a decision, the time periods for issuance of a CO decision could not commence, and interest would not begin to run on the claim.

In response to industry complaints that the courts and boards had superimposed overly technical rules on the CDA certification requirement—especially regarding who could properly certify claims for a contractor[1]—Congress passed the Federal Courts Administration Act of 1992 (FCAA).[2] The FCAA amended the CDA to state that a "defect in the certification of a claim shall not deprive a court or agency board of contract appeals of jurisdiction over that claim."[3] Now, although a proper certification of a claim is still required, the merits of the claim and the validity of the certification can be decided independently.

§ 16:5 Certification—Certification language

Although it is the safest course to certify your claim using the certification language set forth in the FAR (see above), failure to use the exact words prescribed by the regulation will not deprive the court or board of jurisdiction, though the certification must be corrected prior to the tribunal's decision.[1] For example, in one case, the U.S. Claims Court held that a contractor's certification that the "claim is made in good faith, with accurate supporting data and to the best of our knowledge is complete" substantially complied with the CDA certification requirement, even though the certification did not recite verbatim all operative words in the statute. The court ruled that this omission was not determinative because the standard for certification is "substantial compliance" with the statutory requirements.[2]

The extent to which your certification language may vary from the statutory language set forth in the FAR remains uncertain. However, the certification must be complete, unqualified, and unequivocal.[3] It does not do any good for an otherwise inadequate certification to state that it is intended to comply with the CDA

[Section 16:4]

[1]*See generally* Ivey, Claim Certification, Briefing Papers No. 91-11 (Oct. 1991), 9 Briefing Papers 489; Nash, Postscript: Contractor Certification of Claims, 6 Nash & Cibinic Rep. ¶ 49 (Aug. 1992).

[2]Pub. L. 102-572, 106 Stat. 4506 (Oct. 29, 1992).

[3]*See also* FAR 33.207(f).

[Section 16:5]

[1]*See JSA Health Care Corp.*, ASBCA No. 482962, 97-2 BCA ¶ 29126.

[2]*Alcan Elec. & Engineering Co., Inc. v. U.S.*, 24 Cl. Ct. 704 (1992). *See also Medina Const., Ltd. v. U.S.*, 43 Fed. Cl. 537 (1999).

[3]*E.g., Cochran Constr. Co.*, ASBCA No. 34378, 87-3 BCA ¶ 1993.

certification requirement, for a certification that does not substantially comply with the FAR will be held to be a failure to certify and thus not only deprive the court or board of jurisdiction, but eliminate any accrued interest as well.[4] Further, a failure to sign the certificate will be held as a failure to certify.[5]

Regarding the $100,000 threshold for claim certification, you should also be aware that claims arising from one incident cannot be split into separate claims each amounting to claims for less than $100,000 to avoid the certification requirement. Only truly separate claims—that is, those that arise from different causative events and different facts—may be submitted separately.[6]

§ 16:6 Certification—Who must certify?

The FAR states that "the certification may be executed by any person duly authorized to bind the contractor with respect to the claim."[1] The prescribed FAR certification form includes a statement that the certifying individual is, in fact, "duly authorized to certify the claim on behalf of the contractor."[2]

The person who certifies a contract claim must have knowledge of the basis of the claim, knowledge of the accuracy and completeness of the supporting data, and knowledge of the claim.[3] The certifier need not have firsthand involvement in the events giving rise to the claim but may base his or her "knowledge" on a review of company records. If a prime contractor is certifying on behalf of a subcontractor, the prime need only believe that there is "good ground" to support the claim of the sub.[4] In other words, the prime must believe the claim is made in good faith and is not frivolous.

Finally, the person signing the certificate on behalf of a joint venture is important. A representative for each contractor in a joint venture must sign unless the joint venture agreement states otherwise.[5] If your company changes names, it must sign under its new name.

---

[4]*Chester P. Schwartz*, VABCA No. 2856, 89-2 BCA ¶ 21681.

[5]*See Hawaii CyberSpace*, ASBCA No. 54065, 04-1 BCA ¶ 32455.

[6]*See, e.g., Engineered Demolition, Inc. v. U.S.*, 60 Fed. Cl. 822 (2004).

[Section 16:6]

[1]41 U.S.C.A. § 605(c)(7); FAR 33.207(e).

[2]FAR 33.207(c).

[3]41 U.S.C.A. § 605(c)(1). *See also* FAR 33.207(c).

[4]*See Christie-Willamette*, NASA BCA No. 1182-16, 85-1 BCA ¶ 17930.

[5]*Stradedile/Aegis JV*, ASBCA No. 39318, 95-1 BCA ¶ 27397.

§ 16:7 Certification—Defense contracts

If your company does not wish to submit its "claim" under the CDA, it can choose to have it treated as a "request for equitable adjustment," more commonly referred to as an "REA." The essential difference between an REA and a CDA "claim" is the contractor forgoes the benefits of the CDA (i.e., interest on the claim from the date of submission, the right to a final decision, and the right to appeal to an agency board or the Court of Federal Claims). Nonetheless, there are certain requirements that a non-CDA request for equitable adjustment must meet.

The DOD specifically requires certification of REAs and requests for extraordinary contractual relief under Public Law 85-804 that exceed $100,000. This "Requests for Equitable Adjustment" contract clause requires the contractor to certify "that the request is made in good faith, and that the supporting data are accurate and complete" to the best of the contractor's "knowledge and belief."[1] The CDA certification language (quoted above) is broader and requires additional representations. Defense contractors should be aware that because the briefer language of the DOD certification does not contain all of the representations required by the CDA, a certification of an REA that satisfies DOD requirements may not, if the contractor decides to convert the REA into a CDA "claim," satisfy the CDA claim certification requirements.

§ 16:8 Pricing methods

You should give careful consideration to the method you use to price your contract claim. The Government may challenge not only your entitlement to recover on the claim but the way in which you calculated the amount (often called "quantum") you believe is due. Therefore, when you first encounter new, changed, or prolonged work, and you believe the Government bears the responsibility for the added work and cost, you should consider *how* best to price and calculate the increased costs. There are three primary methods of pricing and calculating the quantum of your claim.

The favored method for determining claim quantum is the *direct calculation of costs incurred* due to the actions or inactions of the Government that caused a change in the contract work and/or delayed your performance. Sometimes, you will find that it is difficult to identify specifically the Government actions or inactions that form the bases for your claim and to calculate the related

---

[Section 16:7]

[1]DFARS 252.243-7002.

§ 16:8

claim amount. Under these circumstances, it may be necessary to use another method. Two methods contractors frequently used are the total cost method and the modified total cost method.

Under the *total cost* method, you subtract the cost of the contract work as originally bid or proposed from the total cost incurred on your contract. Because this method presumes that the original contract bid or proposed cost is reasonable, and because it ignores your inefficiencies during contract performance, the method is looked on with disfavor by the courts and boards and recovery on this basis is sharply restricted.[1] The total cost method is permitted only when no other means of fixing the amount of the claim is available and the reliability of the supporting data is fully substantiated.[2] Because contractors tend to use the total cost approach in situations in which it is difficult to clearly demonstrate the exact extent to which the Government "caused," the added costs, using this method increases the likelihood that the Government may allege your claim is false or fraudulently made.

If the contractor determines that it must use this pricing technique, it is vitally important that the contractor take into account—that is, eliminate from the claim—any costs for which it is responsible. These include the effect of an "underbid," and any inefficiencies during performance for which the Government is not liable. See the discussion at § 5, infra, for the consequences of failing to identify and eliminate such costs when preparing a claim on a "total cost" basis.

Although the *modified total cost* method is also not favored by the courts and boards, it is an acceptable method for quantifying your claim.[3] Under this approach, you analyze your incurred costs in those cost areas where reliable *direct* cost data are available. Also, you present detailed evidence of the factors that caused your company to incur added costs and the reasonableness of those costs, and you subtract any amounts that clearly were not incurred through the fault of the Government. If you take the appropriate steps, your modified total cost claim will likely be accepted and will reduce the likelihood that the Government will view your claim to include any false or fraudulent costs.

§ 16:9 Pricing CDA claims or requests for equitable adjustment

A CDA claim or a request for equitable adjustment seeks

[Section 16:8]

[1]*ECC Intl. Corp.*, ASBCA No. 39044 et al., 94-2 BCA ¶ 26639, p. 132,502.

[2]*See Hi-Shear Technology Corp. v. U.S.*, 356 F.3d 1372 (Fed. Cir. 2004).

[3]*Raytheon Co. v. White*, 305 F.3d 1354 (Fed. Cir. 2002).

§ 16:9 CONTRACT CLAIMS

recovery on a claim against the Government under the contract—typically under the contract's "Changes" clause.[1] An equitable adjustment is the corrective measure used by the Government to modify your contract unilaterally. Your company's finance department and pricing personnel can cause serious problems for your company if they ignore or fail to recognize the rules for pricing claims for equitable adjustments. Your costs must be allowable, reasonable, and allocable as set forth in the FAR.

The FAR Part 31 cost principles provide the following factors in determining the *allowability* of any cost: (1) the cost is reasonable; (2) the cost is allocable to the contract; (3) if governed by the Cost Accounting Standards, the costs are accumulated and allocated in accordance with your Cost Accounting Standards Board Disclosure Statement and the Cost Accounting Standards (see §§ 12:1 et seq.); (4) the costs do not contravene any terms of the contract; and (5) the costs meet the limitations set forth in the FAR.[2] The FAR also lists specific major allowable and unallowable costs.[3] (See §§ 11:1 et seq. for a discussion of contract cost allowability.)

What is *reasonable* depends on a variety of considerations and circumstances involving both the nature and amount of the cost in question including, among other things, whether it is the type of cost "generally recognized as ordinary and necessary for the conduct of the contractor's business or the contract performance," and such factors as "generally accepted sound business practices."[4] The FAR provides that "[n]o presumption of reasonableness shall be attached to the incurrence of costs by a contractor."[5] In fact, if the CO challenges a specific incurred cost, the burden is on the contractor to establish its reasonableness.

A cost is *allocable* if it (a) is incurred specifically for the contract, (b) benefits both the contract and other work and can be distributed to them in reasonable proportion to the benefits received, or (c) is necessary to the overall operation of the business, even though a direct relationship to any particular cost objective cannot be shown.[6] Under this definition of allocability, any direct cost of contract performance is allocable to a contract. Indirect costs are allocable to a contract if such costs *either* benefit the contract *or* are necessary to the overall operation of the

---

[Section 16:9]
[1] *See* FAR 52.243-1.
[2] FAR 31.201-2.
[3] FAR 31.205.
[4] FAR 31.201-3.
[5] FAR 31.201-3(a).
[6] FAR 31.201-4.

§ 16:9   GOVERNMENT CONTRACT COMPLIANCE HANDBOOK

business.

You must also be aware of the special pricing rules when your claim seeks an "equitable adjustment" in the contract price. The basic rule is that a contractor is entitled to the difference between the cost of the new or added work and what the deleted work *would have cost*. You must be wary of using the bid price in determining the cost of the deleted work. Such a theory of computation has been rejected as it would allow a contractor that underbid a contract and that would otherwise expect to take a loss on the contract to be made whole through adjustments to the contract. If the estimated cost of performance is greater than the contract price for the items, you must continue to suffer that loss. By the same token, though, if you can demonstrate that the cost of the deleted work would have been *less than* your bid price (and would have thus resulted in a larger profit had the work not been changed), you are entitled to use this figure in calculating the amount of the equitable adjustment, thereby permitting you to retain this added profit. In other words, the goal in pricing an equitable adjustment is not to allow the contractor to "get well" after an improvident bid nor to deprive it of any increased profit that it may have realized had the contract not been "changed." Rather, from a profit perspective, it is to leave the contractor in exactly the same position it would have been in the absence of the change. Any pricing scenario that produces a different result is open to challenge and potentially to an allegation of fraud.

§ 16:10 Fraud liability

Miscertification by a contractor of the accuracy of any claim statement, facts, or data under the CDA (or other statute or regulation) could be considered a "false claim" or "false statement" under federal criminal and civil law, resulting in fines, forfeiture of the claim, and even imprisonment.[1] In addition, the CDA itself provides additional civil sanctions for miscertification. Under the Act, a contractor may be civilly liable for fraud or "misrepresentation of fact," which is defined in the CDA as "a false statement of substantive fact, or any conduct which leads to a belief of a substantive fact material to proper understanding of the matter in hand, made with intent to deceive or mislead."[2] The contractor who submits a fraudulent claim may be held liable under the CDA for "an amount equal to such unsupported part of

---

[Section 16:10]

[1]*E.g.*, civil False Claims Act, 31 U.S.C.A. §§ 3729 to 3733; Forfeiture of Claims statute, 28 U.S.C.A. § 2514; criminal False Statements Statute, 18 U.S.C.A. § 1001.

[2]41 U.S.C.A. §§ 604, 601(7).

§ 16:10

the claim in addition to all costs to the Government attributable to the cost of reviewing said part of his claim."[3]

Submitting a false or fictitious *claim* also exposes you to significant risk under the criminal and civil statutes. For example, inflated costs in a contractor write-up of a request for equitable adjustment could lead to prosecution under the false claims and false statements statutes.[4] Similarly, a false claim sent through the mail could constitute mail fraud. In short, the Government has many remedies available for fraud in connection with contract claims (see §§ 1:1 et seq.).

Recent cases demonstrate that the Government will pursue all available remedies when it believes a contractor's claim for added costs is tainted by fraud, *even though the amount at issue is relatively small*. The Government denied a certified claim for $277,844 for added costs allegedly incurred by the contractor in replacing aggregate that formed the base course for an asphalt road. In the litigation that followed, the Government filed counterclaims alleging violations of the False Claims Act, the anti-fraud provisions of the Contract Disputes Act, and the Forfeiture of Fraudulent Claims Act.[5] Significant from the perspective of Government contract compliance is that the amount challenged by the Government was only $63,000. The court denied the contractor's request that these counterclaims be summarily denied, thus likely forcing the contractor into lengthy and costly litigation in pursuit of a relatively small claim.

One of the principal areas of concern in contract claims is the contractor's failure to review the contract and related documents and correspondence in order to verify the reasonableness of it claims. In *Trafalgar House Const., Inc. v. U.S.*, 77 Fed. Cl. 48 (2007), aff'd, 274 Fed. Appx. 898 (Fed. Cir. 2008), the contractor submitted a "Type I" differing site condition claim in which it contended that the amount of "fill" that was available at the site was less than indicated in the contract. The Government argued that this was a "false claim" because the contract did not indicate a precise quantity that would be available. The court found that while the *exact* quantities were not specified, the contract did indicate that *some* amount of fill would be available. The court then concluded that although the contractor's estimate of that

---

[3] 41 U.S.C.A. § 604.

[4] In *Daewoo Engineering and Const. Co., Ltd. v. U.S.*, 73 Fed.Cl. 547 (2006), the court found that the contractor's CDA certification was fraudulent because it had "submitted false records and made false statements in preparing, certifying, and pursuing its claim . . . ." As a consequence, the court imposed a $50.6 million penalty under the fraudulent claims provisions of the CDA and a $10,000 fine under the civil False Claims Act.

[5] *M.A. DeAtley Const., Inc. v. U.S.*, 75 Fed. Cl. 812 (2007).

§ 16:10   GOVERNMENT CONTRACT COMPLIANCE HANDBOOK

amount was incorrect, it was not "so unreasonable, given the information in the contract documents, as to rise to the level of a false claim." In reaching this conclusion, the court emphasized "At a minimum, a contractor is required to examine records to ensure they are consistent with the submitted claim." The court contrasted this case with the decision in *Commercial Contractors, Inc. v. U.S.*, 154 F.3d 1357 (Fed. Cir. 1998), where the court found that the contractor's claim that it expected there would be a five-foot clearance between the work site and a retaining wall was fraudulent because the contract plans clearly showed the distance was only about three feet.

In another case, a contractor had submitted a claim totaling almost $64 million for added costs in constructing a road on a remote island in the Republic of Palau.[6] The contractor claimed that over $13 million of added cost had already been incurred and that the remaining $50.6 million would be incurred in completing the project. During the course of the trial at the Court of Federal Claims, the Department of Justice filed counterclaims pursuant to the False Claims Act, the Forfeiture of Claims statute, and the penalty provisions of the Contract Disputes Act alleging that the portion of the claim relating to future costs was fraudulent. The court agreed, finding that the calculation assumed that the Government was responsible for each day of additional performance beyond the original 1080-day contract period, without even considering whether there was any contractor-caused delay or delay for which the government was not responsible. The calculation then simply assumed that the contractor's current daily expenditures represented costs for which the Government was responsible. The contractor apparently used no outside experts to make its certified claim calculation, and at trial made no real effort to justify the accuracy of the claim for future costs or even to explain how it was prepared. Furthermore, The contractor's damages experts at trial treated the certified claim computation as essentially worthless, did not utilize it, and did not even bother to understand it. The Court of Federal Claims pointed out that the contractor's claim preparation witnesses inconsistently referred to and interchanged actual, future, estimated, calculated and planned costs. The court found that the contractor's main witness, who certified the claim, gave false testimony. The court also found that the testimony of another witness regarding the calculation of the contractor's certified claim "left no doubt that [the contractor's] case was unsupportable and was pursued by [the contractor] with fraudulent intent." The court ultimately concluded that the claim for future

---

[6]*Daewoo Engineering and Const. Co., Ltd. v. U.S.*, 73 Fed. Cl. 547 (2006), cert. den., 130 S. Ct. 490 (2009).

CONTRACT CLAIMS § 16:10

costs was just a "negotiating tactic":

> [T]he extra $50 million claim was a means to get the Government's attention, and to show the Government what would happen if it did not approve the new compaction method that plaintiff wanted. [the contractor] did not file that part of the claim in good faith; it was not an amount to which plaintiff honestly believed it was entitled. Whether [the contractor] wanted the money or wanted the Government's attention, $64 million was not an amount the Government owed plaintiff at the time of certification, and plaintiff knew it.

Based on this, the court found that $50.6 million of the total claim was fraudulent and in accordance with the CDA assessed a penalty "in an amount equal to such unsupported part of the claim," i.e., $50.6 million. In addition the court found the contractor liable under the Forfeiture of Claims statute, thereby forfeiting the remaining $13 million of its claim. The court also assessed a $10,000 penalty for violation of the civil False Claims Act. The Federal Circuit affirmed the lower court decision in its entirety.

In another case, The Court of Federal Claims penalized the contractor $347,050 based on the Forfeiture of Fraudulent Claims Act and the False Claims Act.[7] The contractor had filed a $3.8 million claim for costs incurred on a Federal Emergency Management Agency (FEMA) contract to deactivate temporary housing in Mississippi for Hurricane Katrina victims. COFC found that the contractor acted with "specific intent to deceive FEMA with regard to the dates on which inspections were performed and a reckless indifference to the hundreds of duplicate inspections that were billed to FEMA." The Court found these actions amounted to fraud. The contractor's $3.8 million claim was forfeit and the company was penalized for the fraudulent invoices. The lesson from these cases is plain: in order to minimize the chance of a Government accusation of fraud regarding a claim, it is essential that contractors implement the compliance initiatives outlined in Section IV of this chapter, including staffing a claims team with experience personnel from a range of disciplines, maintaining all records relating to the project, and perhaps most important, making certain you have support and corroboration for all elements of your claim. You should be extremely careful when pricing your claim on a "total cost/total time" basis as was done in the Daewoo case. There is nothing inherently wrong in using this technique, but as emphasized in Daewoo, a contractor must make a special effort to exclude any costs that might be its own responsibility from the amounts being claimed against the Government. Above all, do not fall into the trap of submitting an

---

[7]*Alcatec, LLC v. U.S.*, 100 Fed. Cl. 502 (2011), aff'd, 2012 WL 2826946 (Fed. Cir. 2012).

§ 16:10 GOVERNMENT CONTRACT COMPLIANCE HANDBOOK

inflated claim just "to get the Government's attention."

§ 16:11 Frequently asked questions

Question 1: Our company believes that we are entitled to an equitable adjustment in the contract price due to changes in the work ordered by the Government. Should we make a simple demand for payment to the CO by submitting a request for equitable adjustment or filing a certified claim under the CDA? Are there any advantages to filing a certified CDA claim at this time?

Answer 1: One clear advantage to submitting a certified CDA claim is that the Government must pay interest on any amount found due and unpaid from the date the contractor's certified claim was received by the CO. However, the ability to accrue interest on the claim should be weighed against the possible inability to seek reimbursement for your claim preparation costs once the certified claim is submitted. Generally, for contracts subject to the FAR cost principles, the FAR permits the contractor to recover the costs of professional and consultant services, including legal and accounting fees, to the extent these costs are incurred in connection with the contract performance or contract administration.[1] Such costs include negotiating an uncertified demand for payment.[2] One the other hand, costs associated with "defense against Federal Government claims or appeals or the prosecution of claims or appeals against the Federal Government" are expressly unallowable under the FAR cost principles.[3] Therefore, the costs of preparing and pursuing a certified CDA "claim"—or even negotiating resolution on a matter in litigation—would not be allowable contract administration costs. Depending on the complexity of your request for equitable adjustment, your legal and administrative costs associated with the negotiation of an uncertified demand for payment may be significantly greater than any interest you would accrue through early certification of your "request" as a "claim." If you think the matter will ultimately be settled through negotiations, then waiting to certify the claim may be the better choice.

If negotiations are unsuccessful, you can then convert the request for equitable adjustment into a CDA "claim" by executing the required certification and (assuming the REA meets the other technical requirements for a "claim") request that the contracting officer resolve it in accordance with the CDA.

[Section 16:11]

[1] FAR 31.205-33.

[2] *Bill Strong Enterprises, Inc. v. Shannon*, 49 F.3d 1541 (Fed. Cir. 1995) (overruled by, *Reflectone, Inc. v. Dalton*, 60 F.3d 1572 (Fed. Cir. 1995)).

[3] FAR 31.205-47(f)(1).

CONTRACT CLAIMS § 16:12

Question 2: We have received direction from a member of the Government's program office asking that we make a modification to the design of our product. This person is not the CO but we believe that he may be acting under her authority. How should we accommodate the design request while protecting ourselves in the event that we have to submit a claim for an equitable adjustment in the contract price or schedule?

Answer 2: To protect yourself in case you eventually need to submit a claim to the Government, you need to consider both the need to prove that you are *entitled* to compensation and the need to prove the *amount* (quantum) owed to you. If the Government employee that asked you to do the additional work does not have authority to make the request or is not working as an agent of the CO, the Government will not be obligated to compensate you for any additional design work. At this point, you should send a letter to the CO describing the situation. Typically, the contract's "Changes" clause requires that you inform the CO of additional work within 30 days of being directed to perform new or changed work. The letter should identify the individual asking for the design change, the nature of the change as you perceive it, and it should seek clarification as to whether or not the individual is authorized to give direction to the contractor.

Assuming the individual has authority to bind the Government, you need to determine if this individual was *asking* for design changes or *directing* you to make design changes. Even if this individual has authority to change the scope of work, it is unclear that the requested design changes are *required* to be made. If not, and you do the work, the Government may argue that you *volunteered* the extra work.

Measuring the quantum of the claim after the design change has been completed can be a difficult task. You should establish a separate costs account for the changed work early on and instruct employees performing the extra work to assign the costs associated with extra work to this account. You also need to ensure that the employees are able to distinguish between work associated with existing contract requirements and work that is new. Unless a contractor can explain why it was not possible to identify and document its added costs while performing the work, the failure to support the claim with customary cost records will seriously jeopardize recovery of the added costs.[4]

III. HOW TO RECOGNIZE THE PROBLEM

§ 16:12 Generally

Even honest, law-abiding people can be accused of committing

---

[4]*See HOF Constr., Inc. v. Gen. Servs. Admin.*, GSBCA No. 13317, 96-2 BCA ¶ 28406.

fraud in the preparation, negotiation, submission, and litigation of claims. Such allegations of fraud often occur due to inadvertent mistakes in claim preparation, but they nonetheless occur. Set forth below are examples of how honest people can be accused of making false contract claims to the Government.

§ 16:13 Examples

Item replacement in claim pricing: Assume your company enters into a contract with the Government to supply a turn-key computer system. The CO directs you to supply hardware different from that for which you originally contracted. Therefore, you eliminate from your design several pieces of hardware and replace them with new hardware. In pricing your claim to the Government for the increased costs you have incurred, you account only for the effort associated with the new work. You forget to deduct the labor and material that was to have been spent on the original hardware. The company certifies and submits its claim containing this accidental, innocent error.

In pricing a claim where one item is substituted for another, especially when you are still working from a drawing, you must deduct the cost of the replaced item. Your failure to deduct the cost of the original item could result in the Government paying for both items while only receiving one. By failing to take the deleted work into account, you are claiming more money than you are entitled to. The Government could and would allege that you have submitted a false claim in this instance and falsely certified the claim as well.

Failure to check all facts: Your company has a contract with the Government to develop and manufacture a state-of-the-art high-definition television system. The Government directs you to do additional work during contract performance, which work you consider to be greater than required under the existing contract. The company appoints you, a member of the contracts department, to prepare a claim. You prepare the claim basically on the testimony of one engineer who was involved with the entire program. This employee provides you with supporting documents involving the added work. You check no files, and you fail to talk to any other personnel before certifying and submitting the claim. Subsequently, you discover that the company's files contained numerous documents that contradict the documents you submitted in support of the claim. Further, interviews with other engineers result in a story quite different from what the first individual told you. Due to your actions, false statements and claims may have been made to the Government. Your actions have placed the company and certain individuals in serious jeopardy of a Government investigation.

Claims made in bad faith: Your company has brought claims against the Government arising out of a contract with the Corps of Engineers for a dam. You have submitted 10 separate claims that are being negotiated as a package. The company certified its claims under the Contract Disputes Act. Bob Talker, who is leading your company's negotiating team, realizes that the company can reach an amicable settlement with the Government if it throws out three claims that the Government believes are completely unfounded. Talker agrees to this saying that "one claim was a bargaining chip, another was a throw-away, and the last a negotiating tool." The parties then agree to a total-dollar settlement that is substantially less that the claimed amount. Talker signs a "memorandum of agreement" which states that this dollar amount "accurately reflects the actual costs of the changes in this contract." Subsequently, the Government indicts your company and Talker for submitting false claims and false statements, alleging that the three withdrawn claims were fraudulently prepared.

The company and Talker could be facing some serious problems. Talker forgot that the CDA certification requirements were designed to prevent "padded" claims. Further, the company certified that all its claims were made in good faith, that the supporting data were complete and accurate to the best of its knowledge and belief, and that the amount requested accurately reflected the contract adjustment for which the company believed the Government to be liable. Talker's words in calling certified claims "throw-aways," "negotiating tools," and "bargaining chips" provide the Government with evidence that the claim you certified was not made in good faith. The fact that claims were not included in the final settlement does not eliminate this problem. Talker's signature on the "memorandum of agreement" adds further support for the Government's argument. Talker failed to realize that the Justice Department may prosecute you for a criminal violation *even if the contracting agency has settled the claim.*

Use of cost estimates: Your company has brought claims against the Government arising out of a swimming pool maintenance service contract with the General Services Administration (GSA). You are claiming that the GSA required you to perform work in excess of the contract requirement when it required you to send maintenance personnel throughout the country and world. However, instead of using actual accounting records in pricing your claims for increased costs, you simply estimate the travel and subsistence costs of the personnel. You do not refer to the actual records because they are in storage.

In auditing the claims, the Government reviews all the travel and subsistence records. Unfortunately, your estimated costs are twice as high as the actual costs. The Government may allege that you have submitted a false claim. The moral of this example is *if the records exist, use them*.

Product substitution: Your company has a contract with the Government to supply automobiles. The Government directs you to use a more powerful, more expensive engine. You obtain a price quote for the engine, which is the amount you include in your claim for an equitable adjustment to the contract price. In fact, when your company actually orders this engine, there is a shortage and you can not obtain it. However, the engine manufacturer offers you a similar engine at a substantially lower price. Your company uses these engines in assembling the cars. The person pricing the claim did not know of this change, and due to his lack of knowledge, he includes the price of the more expensive engine in the claim you submit to the Government. You may be liable for making a false claim to the Government. Depending on how you wrote the claim, you may also have made false statements. The moral of this example is, in pricing claims, *do not assume* that because your company considered using a particular product or process that it actually used that product or process. *Make sure.*

IV. COMPLIANCE INITIATIVES

§ 16:14 Establish a claims team

To perform claim preparation work efficiently with minimal risk of incurring any liability, you ought to form a claims team consisting of members from the following categories:

(1) A member of the *contracts department* familiar with all of the elements and stages of the contract.
(2) A member of the company's *program office* familiar with the basic contract documents, as well as the technical and management aspects of the contract work, and who was present during the events giving rise to the claim.
(3) Someone with *technical expertise*. This person must be able to communicate complex technical problems in terms that are understandable to a layperson.
(4) Someone with *pricing experience*. This person needs to understand the structure of the initial bid or proposal, as well as your company's incurrence of costs under the contract, including details of your company's procedures for accumulating and reporting costs.
(5) *Legal counsel*. All claims should be reviewed by counsel before being submitted to the Government. This is especially true in light of the Government's increased alertness to situations that indicate contractor fraud.

Your claims team must be composed of competent, intelligent, hard-working people. Remember: if your claim is not successful, the extra costs you incurred will come out of the profit dollars you expected to earn on the contract. Thus, it is important that you staff the claim effort with motivated, competent people.

§ 16:15 Maintain records

Your company's finance and contracts departments must take primary responsibility for recordkeeping. Claim preparation is much easier if complete records are kept. Historically, there are certain areas in which contractors do not do their best when maintaining records. A particular area of neglect by contractors and their employees is that of oral communications. If you have not done so already, you should develop specific forms for *recording oral communications*. These forms should require, at a minimum,

(1) the name of the person who is preparing the memorandum and his or her title,
(2) the date and place of the communication,
(3) the names of the people with whom the communication took place and any other parties who participated in the communication,
(4) the substance of the communication, and
(5) a summary of the impact of the communication, if any, on contract performance.

A related area of importance is documenting *constructive changes*. All too often the Government orally directs you to do work that you believe is in excess of what is required by the contract. Although you may argue with the Government over the work, all too often you establish no paper trail to document the disagreement and grudgingly you do the work. In this situation, you face a real danger that you may have failed properly to establish that the Government directed you to perform the changed work. In that case, you are entitled to nothing for your efforts. To protect yourself in this situation, you should always send a letter to the Government objecting to the work as being beyond existing contract requirements, and you should *demand written direction* from the Government before proceeding with the work.

§ 16:16 Corroborate & document the facts

A key to claims preparation is the physical documentation and corroboration of facts. It is imperative that you develop a claim based on an accurate and consistent set of facts. Facts need to be corroborated by the company's employees, and there must be as much supporting evidence for your claim as possible. If you are the person charged with preparing the claim, at some point you

§ 16:16

will want to speak with a knowledgeable person from each affected area.

In the claim you submit to the Government, you must be certain that you have *support* for each and every statement made and that your claim can withstand intense scrutiny. It is not advisable to rely on the testimony of only one witness without obtaining corroboration. One person could be recalling events inaccurately, thus possibly exposing the company to numerous legal problems and potential criminal liabilities. The corroboration can come from another person. Obviously, it is better to talk with this person before he or she and the first witness speak, so that you receive an unbiased recollection of the events. Support or corroboration also can come from documents—memoranda, letters, telexes, notes of a meeting, notes of a telephone conversation, a purchase order for material, and so forth. Generally, it is preferable to have *documentary* evidence in support of your claim.

This brings us to a very important point. To ensure that your claim can withstand analysis by potentially hostile reviewers, you must examine *all* the records, not just the records that appear to support your claim. You must make sure that your facts are correct and that your statements about them are logical. When reviewing the facts, ask yourself if these facts make sense or if there are internal inconsistencies.

Pricing the claim is also an area potentially full of pitfalls for the careless contractor. You have to be certain that your accounting system is correct and proper from a Government contracting standpoint, and you must make sure that you have accounting records that will support your claims. Your pricing must be done consistently and in accordance with your Cost Accounting Standards Disclosure Statement and/or with generally accepted accounting practices. Do not use a method other than the method that you normally employ in pricing proposals unless you have professional legal and accounting help. Make sure in your calculations that you take into account the effect of any of your own deficiencies or decreases in work. For example, if the Government causes you to add a new system but addition of the new requirement allows you to delete a specified part, you must make sure that you delete the cost of that part in determining the impact of the change.

§ 16:17 Claim negotiation

The same major concerns apply to the negotiation of the claim as applied to the preparation of the claim. You must be on the lookout for misrepresentations and overstatements that could be construed as false claims and false statements. You must be cautious in how you state the facts. Finally, you must also be conscious of what you say during negotiations.

The CDA claim certification requirements discussed earlier in this chapter were designed to prevent "padded" claims. Be aware that the Government may choose to examine a claim *already settled* for evidence that you padded your original claim. Thus, you should avoid taking a position during settlement negotiations that could be interpreted as indicating that the original claim was inaccurate. You should avoid characterizing conceded items as "bargaining chips," "padding," or "throw-aways."

In addition, you should not execute *settlement documents* that proclaim the settlement figures as the "accurate" or real claim amount. Your signature on such documents may lead Government investigators and prosecutors to infer that the original claim was inaccurate or was overstated. If you do compromise your claim, you should affirm in writing that the lower recovered dollar amount was agreed to only for the purposes of settlement. In fact, language to this effect ought to be included in every settlement modification.

§ 16:18 Claim litigation

As in preparing and negotiating a claim, you must be concerned with misstatements, overstatements, false claims, and false statements in litigating a claim. If your claim is denied by the CO and you appeal that denial to a board of contract appeals or file a complaint on the denied claim at the Court of Federal Claims, you should be aware that the notice of appeal or complaint is *itself* a claim. If the complaint or notice of appeal is overstated in terms of amount, the Government could determine that your claim is fraudulent. Not only your company's law department but also any employees in your company who may have to participate in the litigation during discovery or at a hearing or trial must be aware of the potential dangers. For example, you could face sanctions under the fraud statutes if you withhold requested documents while informing the Government that the documents you are providing respond to the Government's discovery request. Your false testimony during a deposition certainly could be considered a false statement as well as perjury. This is also true of your trial testimony. At all times, you must be aware of the potential consequences of your story and not make inaccurate or false statements or exaggerate the cost impact of your claim.

It is becoming increasingly common for the Government to raise allegations of fraud for the first time during the course of a hearing or trial. See the discussion in § 16:10, *supra*, of recent cases in which DoJ filed counterclaims pursuant to the False Claims Act, the Forfeiture of Claims statute, and the penalty provisions of the Contract Disputes Act during litigation at the Court

§ 16:18

of Federal Claims. However, the Contract Disputes Act does not give the Civilian Board of Contract Appeal or the Armed Services Board of Contract Appeals jurisdiction to decide issues of fraud. Thus, if the Government raises a question of fraud in a case pending at either the CBCA or the ASBCA, those boards will often suspend proceedings pending resolution of the those issues. The decision will be based on a number of considerations including (1) the similarity of facts, issues, and witnesses between the contract claim and the allegation of fraud, (2) whether proceeding with the board action might compromise an ongoing investigation, (3) the prejudice to the contractor's case, and (4) the reasonableness of the length of the requested stay.[1]

§ 16:19 Recommendations

(a) Recall that the definition of a "claim" can be very broad, encompassing *any* written demand for payment of money or transfer of property.

(b) The certification of a CDA claim should not be taken lightly, as any *improper certification* can result in civil and criminal false claims allegations affecting the company as well as on the certifier individually.

(c) When preparing a claim, management should establish a *claims team*. This team will be enormously helpful in identifying, gathering, and analyzing the supporting documentation for claims.

(d) Remember that the two keys to preparing a successful claim are establishing the facts in a logical manner and *supporting by corroboration or documentation* every statement in the claim relating to both entitlement and pricing. The individual writing the claim (often a member of the contracts or law department) and the person pricing the claim (often an individual from the finance department) must be particularly conscientious in ensuring that adequate documentation or corroboration exists.

(e) Remember that your claim will be subject to intense scrutiny, so you must be able to support *every statement* in the claim.

(f) *Contemporaneous recordkeeping* will eliminate numerous potential trouble spots when it comes time to prepare your claim.

(g) Include all direct and indirect costs and profit in your claim to which you are entitled but do not abandon or modify your

---

[Section 16:18]

[1]See *In re Palm Springs General Trading and Contracting Establishment*, A.S.B.C.A. No. 56290, 08-2 B.C.A. (CCH) ¶ 34007, 2008 WL 4924800 (Armed Serv. B.C.A. 2008).

§ 16:19

normal accounting procedures so as to price a claim in a manner that yields a more favorable recovery. If you have a pricing problem, obtain professional accounting advice.

(h) Before submitting a claim to the Government, make sure that legal counsel reviews your claim submission. Verify that, if it is required, the certification uses the *exact language* required by the Contract Disputes Act and set forth in the FAR. Finally, be sure that the certification is *signed* by the *proper company official*.

(i) *Document all claim negotiations*, including telephone conferences and meetings. A member of your claims team should be designated to take minutes of negotiation sessions, including the names and positions of attendees, offers, counter-offers, and keep a list of all documents provided to the Government.

(j) Be careful what you *say* during the negotiation and the trial preparation process. Thoughtless statements may come back to haunt you.

Chapter 17

Domestic & Foreign Product Acquisition Preferences

I. OVERVIEW
§ 17:1   Scope note

II. PRINCIPAL LAWS & RULES

A. TREATIES, STATUTES & RULES
§ 17:2   Generally
§ 17:3   BAA requirements
§ 17:4   The Berry Amendment
§ 17:5   TAA (WTO GPA) requirements
§ 17:6   Free trade agreements

B. OTHER EXCEPTIONS
§ 17:7   Generally
§ 17:8   BAA exceptions
§ 17:9   TAA exceptions

C. IDENTIFYING END PRODUCTS
§ 17:10 Generally

D. DETERMINING COUNTRY OF ORIGIN
§ 17:11 Generally
§ 17:12 BAA—"Domestic" end products
§ 17:13 —"Qualifying country" (DOD) end products
§ 17:14 TAA—Designated country end products
§ 17:15 U.S.-made end products
§ 17:16 NAFTA marking rules—FAR vs. Customs

E. PENALTIES
§ 17:17 BAA penalties
§ 17:18 TAA penalties

F. FREQUENTLY ASKED QUESTIONS
§ 17:19 Questions & answers

III. "MADE IN USA" LABELS

§ 17:20　Generally
§ 17:21　FTC requirements
§ 17:22　Penalties
§ 17:23　Frequently asked questions

IV. HOW TO RECOGNIZE THE PROBLEM

§ 17:24　Generally
§ 17:25　Offers to supply products
§ 17:26　Postaward activities & contract performance
§ 17:27　Examples

V. COMPLIANCE INITIATIVES

§ 17:28　Generally
§ 17:29　Create a "history" of end products & their components
§ 17:30　Keep inventories separate
§ 17:31　Establish a compliance monitor & oversight procedures
§ 17:32　Plan ahead
§ 17:33　On-site review
§ 17:34　Recommendations

KeyCite®: Cases and other legal materials listed in KeyCite Scope can be researched through the KeyCite service on Westlaw®. Use KeyCite to check citations for form, parallel references, prior and later history, and comprehensive citator information, including citations to other decisions and secondary materials.

I. OVERVIEW

§ 17:1　Scope note

Protectionism versus free trade is a perennial issue of debate in American politics. Notwithstanding the debate, since the end of World War II, the significant trend in American politics is toward freer trade. The Buy American Act ("BAA") and the Trade Agreements Act ("TAA") serve as bookends to the debate. Enacted in 1933 in the throes of the Great Depression, the BAA seeks to protect United States industry by giving it a price preference over foreign industry competing for United States Government contracts.[1] The BAA is the protectionist bookend.

Enacted in 1979, the TAA, and the trade agreements negotiated under the TAA, provides for non-discriminatory treatment between United States and foreign industries competing for United States Government contracts on the promise that the foreign government(s) will similarly not discriminate against United States industry in their own procurements.[2] The TAA is the free trade bookend.

Key to both the BAA and the TAA is determining if the proposed products or services are "domestic," that is, United States products or services (and, in the case of the TAA, products or services of reciprocating countries). That determination can be difficult in the increasingly globalized economy in which many Government contractors now operate. That determination is, however, critical both to ensuring that you can best position your company to compete for Government contracts, and in ensuring your company's compliance with regard to contracts awarded to it.

This chapter addresses the more important of the laws and regulations that impose preferences or limitations on the national origin of products and services acquired in non-construction federal procurements.

II. PRINCIPAL LAWS & RULES

A. TREATIES, STATUTES & RULES

§ 17:2 Generally

The BAA and the TAA, and the various trade agreements negotiated thereunder, are the primary statutes and agreements that apply to the acquisition of foreign items by the Government. The BAA directs Government officials to give preference generally to contractors that offer to provide domestic end products.

The BAA and the TAA interact with each other. The TAA waives the BAA preference for domestic end products by permitting the Government to acquire end products from countries agreeing not to discriminate against United States products in their own government procurement or from certain less developed countries (so called "designated country" end products). Designated country end products are end products from a World Trade Organization Government Procurement Agreement (WTO GPA)

[Section 17:1]
[1]See 41 U.S.C.A. §§ 8301 to 8305 and FAR 25.105.
[2]19 U.S.C.A. §§ 2501 to 2581; FAR 25.402(a)(1).

§ 17:2

country,[1] a Free Trade Agreement (FTA) country,[2] a least developed country,[3] or a Caribbean Basin[4] country.[5] Where a Government procurement is subject to the TAA, the Government is prohibited from acquiring end products from nonsignatory countries when the value of the procurement exceeds a certain dollar threshold.

You are responsible for certifying that your supplies are TAA compliant.[6] You must ensure that your products are either *domestic, or designated, (including FTA, Caribbean Basin, or qualifying country)* end products not only at the time you submit the certification, but throughout your performance of the contract. (The term "designated country" refers to countries with which the United States has negotiated free trade agreements. The term "qualifying" country refers to countries with which the United States has negotiated free trade agreements in military items.) This is often an area that contractors fail to adequately monitor, which is a major mistake given the fact that sources of supply, or even locations where companies manufacture, change rapidly in the growing world economy. Failure to carefully monitor this point has resulted in a growing number of successful False Claims Act prosecutions brought either by qui tam relators

---

[Section 17:2]

[1] Members of the WTO GPA are Armenia, Austria, Canada, Belgium, Bulgaria, China, Chinese Taipei, Croatia, Cyprus, Czech Republic, Estonia, Denmark, Finland, France, Germany, Greece, Hong Kong, Hungary, Iceland, Ireland, Israel, Italy, Japan, Korea, Latvia, Liechtenstein, Lithuania, Luxembourg, Malta, Netherlands, Norway, Poland, Portugal, Romania, Singapore, Slovak Republic, Slovenia, Spain, Sweden, Switzerland and the United Kingdom; http://www.wto.org/english/tratop_e/gproc_e/memobs_e.htm.

[2] The United States has signed FTAs with Australia, Bahrain, Canada, Chile, Columbia, Costa Rica, Dominican Republic, El Salvador, Guatemala, Honduras, Israel, Korea, Mexico, Morocco, Nicaragua, Oman, Panama, Peru, and Singapore; FAR 25.402.

[3] Least Developed Countries are Afghanistan, Angola, Bangladesh, Benin, Bhutan, Burkina Faso, Burundi, Cambodia, Central African Republic, Chad, Comoros, Democratic Republic of Congo, Djibouti, Equatorial Guinea, Eritrea, Ethiopia, Gambia, Guinea, Guinea-Bissau, Haiti, Kiribati, Laos, Lesotho, Liberia, Madagascar, Malawi, Mali, Mauritania, Mozambique, Nepal, Niger, Rwanda, Samoa, Sao Tome and Principe, Senegal, Sierra Leone, Solomon Islands, Somalia, South Sudan, Tanzania, Timor-L'este, Togo, Tuvalu, Uganda, Vanuatu, Yemen, and Zambia; FAR 25.003.

[4] Caribbean Basin nations benefiting from the trade initiative are Antigua and Barbuda, Aruba, Bahamas, Barbados, Belize, Bonaire, British Virgin Islands, Curacao, Dominica, Grenada, Guyana, Haiti, Jamaica, Montserrat, Saba, St. Kitts and Nevis, St. Lucia, St. Vincent and the Grenadines, Sint Eusstatius, Sint Maarten, and Trinidad and Tobago; FAR 25.003.

[5] FAR 52.225-5.

[6] See FAR 52.225-4.

or the Department of Justice.

The Federal Acquisition Regulation (FAR) and the Department of Defense (DOD) FAR Supplement (DFARS) set forth most of the rules implementing these statutes.[7] The TAA, is the most prominent of these country of origin statutes.[8] In addition, you should be aware that several other statutes, regulations, and agreements, e.g., the Caribbean Basin Trade Initiative,[9] the North American Free Trade Agreement,[10] DOD Memoranda of Understanding,[11] and the U.S.—Israel Free Trade Act[12] among others, impose further country of origin requirements and preferences, making application of country of origin rules somewhat complicated.

§ 17:3 BAA requirements

The BAA essentially requires the Government to give preference to domestic end products over all foreign products in its acquisition of supplies for use inside the U.S. While the BAA covers "contracts for services that involve the furnishing of supplies," services are not subject to the preferences of the BAA. The BAA applies to contracts above the micro-purchase threshold, which is currently $3,000.[1] The BAA does not apply to acquisitions of information technology commercial items.[2]

While the BAA appears to prohibit the purchase of certain foreign products, in reality, the BAA operates only as an *evaluation preference* for domestic end products. The FAR essentially directs Contracting Officers (COs) to attach an (evaluation penalty (6% if the domestic offer is from a large business; 12% if the domestic offer is from a small business) to the price of any contractor's proposal to supply foreign end products. The adjusted price of the foreign goods is then compared to the price of proposals offering to supply domestic products in order to determine contract award. If the adjusted price of the foreign end product is *lower* than the price offered for the domestic item, the domestic price is deemed to be unreasonable and award will be made to

---

[7]See FAR pt. 25; DFARS pt. 225.
[8]See 19 U.S.C.A. §§ 2511 to 2518.
[9]19 U.S.C.A. §§ 2701 to 2707.
[10]Pub. L. No. 103-182.
[11]DFARS 225.872.
[12]19 U.S.C.A. § 2112 note.

[Section 17:3]
[1]See FAR 25.100(b)(1), 2.101.
[2]See FAR 25.103(e).

the offer of foreign material.[3] This evaluation process is easily applied in sealed bid procurements, but it is more complicated to apply in negotiated best value procurements.

Although the BAA is not an absolute bar to the procurement of goods manufactured in foreign countries, you should be aware that currently transactions involving Cuba, Iran or Sudan are prohibited, as are most imports from Burma or North Korea.[4]

DOD has slightly modified the FAR's BAA requirements to fit its own procurement needs. Under the DFARS, DOD will give preference to offers of domestic or qualifying country end products.[5] The term "qualifying country" means a country that has Memorandum of Understanding or international agreement with the United States to procure defense items reciprocally.[6] (A list of current DOD qualifying countries is set forth as Appendix U to this Compliance Handbook.)

Unlike the FAR, the DFARS attaches an evaluation penalty of 50% to all offers of nonqualifying country end products.[7] However, when the application of the 50% penalty will not result in a domestic product award, the DFARS directs that the evaluation penalty should not be applied to the nonqualifying country offer.[8] Some statutes and regulations may require the acquisition of only domestic products in certain DOD procurements.[9] In these circumstances, you should ensure that you *offer* and *supply* domestic end products.

The BAA relies on a system of self-certification; in other words, you are solely responsible for ensuring that your products are either *domestic end products* or *qualifying country end products* (for DOD procurements).[10] While the furnishing of foreign end products is not absolutely prohibited in a BAA procurement, if a contractor does not identify an end product in its BAA certification as a foreign end product, the contractor is required to provide a domestic end product.

§ 17:4 The Berry Amendment

To protect U.S. industry during wartime, in 1941, Congress

---

[3]See FAR 25.105.

[4]See FAR 25.701(b).

[5]See DFARS 225.502(b).

[6]See DFARS 225.003; DFARS 252.225-7001 (defining "qualifying country"); DFARS 225.872-1 (listing qualifying countries).

[7]See DFARS 225.105(b).

[8]See DFARS 225.502(c)(ii)(E)(2).

[9]See, e.g., 10 U.S.C.A. § 2534(a); DFARS subpt. 225.70.

[10]See FAR 25.1101(a)(2).

§ 17:4

passed what later became known as the Berry Amendment.[1] The Berry Amendment requires the Department of Defense to procure food, clothing, fabrics, specialty metals, and hand tools from domestic sources. Unlike the BAA, which only applies to contracts performed within the U.S., the Berry Amendment also applies to contracts performed overseas.[2] Additionally, while the BAA allows for a finished product to contain up to 49% foreign components, the Berry Amendment requires the item to be *entirely* domestic in origin.[3] The procuring agency has a duty to go beyond your company's self-certification regarding Berry Amendment requirements if it has reason to believe you will not provide compliant products.[4]

There are several exceptions to the Berry Amendment. The Berry Amendment only applies to defense contracts above the simplified acquisition threshold, which is currently $150,000.[5] In addition, the Berry Amendment restrictions can be waived if the Secretary of Defense (or a few, select DOD officials) determines, after an analysis of alternatives, that the items cannot be obtained when needed in a satisfactory quality and sufficient quantity at U.S. market prices.[6]

Despite its original purpose, the Berry Amendment no longer applies to acquisitions outside the U.S. in support of combat operations or acquisitions of food, specialty metals, or hand tools in support of contingency operations or in times of unusual and compelling urgency.[7] Emergency procurements by activities located outside the U.S. are also exempt from the Berry Amendment restrictions.[8] Components of a finished product containing natural fibers (i.e. cotton, wool, etc. . . .) of foreign origin are exempt from the Berry Amendment provided the fibers do not constitute more than 10% of the total price of the end product

---

[Section 17:4]

[1] 10 U.S.C.A. § 2533a.

[2] See Valerie Bailey Grasso "The Berry Amendment: Requiring Defense Procurement to Come from Domestic Sources," CRS Report for Congress (Apr. 21, 2005).

[3] See Valerie Bailey Grasso, "The Berry Amendment: Requiring Defense Procurement to Come from Domestic Sources," CRS Report for Congress (Apr. 21, 2005).

[4] See *MMI-Federal Marketing Service Corp.*, Comp. Gen. Dec. B-297537, 2006 CPD ¶ 38.

[5] DFARS 225.7002-2(a); FAR 2.101.

[6] DFARS 225.7002-2(b).

[7] DFARS 225.7002-2(d) to (f).

[8] DFARS 225.7002-2(g).

§ 17:4   Government Contract Compliance Handbook

and they do not exceed the simplified acquisition threshold.[9]

With the exception of seafood, food may be of foreign origin provided it is manufactured or processed in the U.S.[10]

§ 17:5   TAA (WTO GPA) requirements

When the TAA (WTO GPA) applies to a procurement, implementing regulations and the case law create an *absolute prohibition* on agency procurement of items from foreign countries *other than* qualifying countries (for DOD procurements), and designated countries.[1] Thus, currently when the TAA (WTO GPA) applies to a procurement, a contractor may not supply end products from nondesignated countries. The FAR's absolute prohibition is intended to encourage additional countries to become parties to the WTO Government Procurement Agreement.

The TAA (WTO GPA) applies to acquisitions of end products listed under certain North American Industrial Class System (NAICS) codes, where the value of the acquisition is equal to or above the WTO GPA dollar threshold ($204,000 as of June 2014). When the TAA (WTO GPA) applies to a procurement, the regulations essentially treat products that are substantially transformed in certain foreign countries, referred to as "eligible products" as if they were the same as items that satisfy the BAA's definition of "domestic end products" (i.e., without adding any price evaluation penalty).[2]

The FAR defines "eligible products" to include products of the designate countries under the TAA (specifically the signatory countries to the WTO GPA) and end products from a country identified by the FAR as a least developed country.[3] However, the term "eligible products" also extends to end products from FTA countries and countries designated under the Caribbean Basin Trade Initiative.[4] Therefore, when a procurement is subject to the WTO GPA's dollar threshold, the Government will exempt products from over 100 countries from any evaluation penalty. When the value of the acquisition is below the relevant TAA threshold, however, all products manufactured in foreign

---

[9]DFARS 225.7002-2(j).
[10]DFARS 225.7002-2(l).

[Section 17:5]

[1]See 19 U.S.C.A. § 2512(a); FAR 25.402(c); *Data Transformation Corp.*, GSBCA No. 8982-P, 87-3 BCA ¶ 20017; *Marbex, Inc.*, Comp. Gen. Dec. B-225799, 87-1 CPD ¶ 468; *Jewett-Cameron Lumber Corp.*, Comp. Gen. Dec. B-223779.2, 87-2 CPD ¶ 433.

[2]See FAR 25.402(a)(1).
[3]See FAR 25.404.
[4]See FAR 25.400.

countries are treated as foreign end products, and no consideration is generally given to whether the product was manufactured in a designated or nondesignated country (subject to the lower dollar threshold requirements of NAFTA and the U.S.-Israel Free Trade Agreement (see § 17:6)).

The DFARS again has a slightly different version of the FAR's TAA (WTO GPA) requirements. For DOD supply procurements over the TAA dollar threshold, end products from designated, NAFTA, or Caribbean Basin countries will be entitled to a waiver of the DOD's 50% price evaluation penalty only if the offered end products are in one of the Federal Supply Groups (FSGs) listed in the DFARS.[5] If the solicited end products are not in DOD-listed FSGs, the TAA will not apply to the DOD procurement and the solicitation will be subject to the DOD's BAA requirements.

§ 17:6 Free trade agreements

The U.S. Trade Representative (USTR) has waived BAA restrictions for procurements coming from countries that have signed an FTA with the U.S.[1] These countries are identified in Section 17.2 above. Thus, in federal acquisitions, the Government must treat goods, services, and suppliers from these countries as if they were domestic.

The threshold for application of the FTA is significantly lower than the GPA threshold of $204,000 for supplies or services.[2] For Canada, the threshold currently is $25,000 for supplies and $79,507 for services, and for Mexico, Chile, Singapore, and Australia, the threshold currently is $79,507 for both supplies as well as services.

As with other trade agreements, there are exceptions that render FTAs inapplicable. For instance, if the procuring agency has set the acquisition aside for small business, FTAs do not apply.[3] Additionally, acquisitions necessary for national security or national defense (i.e. arms and ammunition) are exempt from FTAs.

Furthermore, the U.S.-Israel Free Trade Agreement provides for a waiver of the price evaluation penalty on Israeli end products when the estimated value of the supplied end products equals or exceeds $50,000. Note, however, that this waiver for Israeli end products does not apply to the DOD, the Department

---

[5]*See* DFARS 225.401-70.

[Section 17:6]

[1]See FAR 25.402(a)(1).
[2]See FAR 25.402(b).
[3]FAR 25.401(a)(1).

§ 17:6   GOVERNMENT CONTRACT COMPLIANCE HANDBOOK

of Energy, the Department of Transportation, the Bureau of Reclamation of the Department of the Interior, the Federal Housing Finance Board, and the Office of Thrift Supervision.[4]

B. OTHER EXCEPTIONS

§ 17:7 Generally

Both the BAA and TAA contain numerous exceptions to their requirements which may allow you to avoid the BAA's price evaluation penalty or the TAA's prohibition against acquiring end products from nondesignated countries. Many of these exceptions are listed and discussed below. You should consult with your CO, however, before you offer any foreign end product that may not be allowed or excepted under the BAA or TAA.

§ 17:8 BAA exceptions

(1) *Use Outside the United States*: The statute, implementing regulations, and case law provide for an exception to the BAA's price evaluation penalty if the solicitation calls for end products or materials that will be used outside of the United States.[1]

(2) *Nonavailability Determination:* The BAA does not apply when items to be procured are not mined, produced, or manufactured in the United States in sufficient and reasonably available commercial quantities, of a satisfactory quality.[2] The FAR contains an extensive list of over 100 items that are considered domestically unavailable and exempt from the BAA's price evaluation penalty.[3]

(3) *Postaward Waiver*: Although compliance with the BAA must be certified at the time of contract award, the FAR addresses the possibility of obtaining a waiver of the BAA's requirements after a contract for construction materials has been awarded.[4] Typically, the determination of domestic end product price unreasonableness (through the addition of an evaluation penalty on the price of offered foreign end products) is made before the contract award. Suppliers of BAA-compliant products, however, may encounter situations where the quoted prices of the supplies

---

[4]*See* FAR 25.406.

[Section 17:8]

[1]*See* 41 U.S.C.A. § 8302(a)(2); FAR 25.001(a)(1); *Systems & Defense Services Intl.*, Comp. Gen. Dec. B-254254.2, 94-1 CPD ¶ 91.

[2]*See* FAR 25.103(b).

[3]FAR 25.104.

[4]*See* FAR 25.205.

unforeseeably rise after award is granted.[5] In these situations, a contractor may be able to request a postaward waiver of the BAA's requirement that the contractor supply domestic end product unless another exception applies.[6]

§ 17:9 TAA exceptions

(1) *Certain Purchases*: The TAA's requirement that offers of end products be restricted to designated country end products (eligible products) does not apply to the purchase of arms, ammunition or war materials, or purchases indispensable for national security or for national defense purposes (as determined by the DOD or the United States Trade Representative).[1] The TAA's requirements also do not extend to Small Business set-asides and contracts for the resale of items.[2] However, it should be noted that procurements of goods set aside for small business generally require the small business to furnish a product manufactured by a small business in the United States.[3]

(2) *Insufficiency of TAA-Compliant Products*: The TAA does not apply to a procurement if offers of domestic end products or eligible products are either not received or are insufficient to fulfill the Government's requirements.[4] However, insufficiency or nonavailability of a product is established by the contracting officer not receiving offers of compliant product at all or in a sufficient quantity to satisfy the Government. Generally, there is no process for waiver on these grounds prior to receipt of proposals.

(3) *Waiver*: In acquisitions covered by the WTO GPA, the TAA allows for waiver of the TAA's requirements in certain defense procurement situations where reciprocal competitive Government procurement opportunities are available for United States products and suppliers of those products.[5] The TAA allows the Secretary of Defense to waive the TAA's rules for offers of products from a country with which the DOD has its own recipro-

---

[5]*See, e.g., John C. Grimberg Co. v. U.S.*, 869 F.2d 1475 (Fed. Cir. 1989).

[6]*But see C. Sanchez & Son, Inc. v. U.S.*, 6 F.3d 1539, 1545–1546 (Fed. Cir. 1993) (finding that a contractor's failure to make a timely waiver request to supply nondomestic wire barred contractor's claims for equitable adjustment); *LoSasso Elec. Co.*, ASBCA No. 49407, 96-2 BCA ¶ 28392 (finding that a contractor, which unknowingly offered a foreign end product instead of a domestic end product for a solicitation, would not be entitled to a postaward BAA waiver).

[Section 17:9]

[1]*See* FAR 25.401(a)(2).
[2]*See* FAR 25.401(a)(1), (a)(3).
[3]*See* FAR 19.001, 25.101(b).
[4]*See* FAR 25.403(c)(1).
[5]*See* 19 U.S.C. § 2512(b); FAR 25.403(c)(2).

cal procurement agreement or memorandum of understanding (MOU).

C. IDENTIFYING END PRODUCTS

§ 17:10 Generally

One of the most important steps in complying with BAA or TAA requirements is discerning which solicitation items constitute *end products* for BAA or TAA application. The FAR defines "end products" as "articles, materials, and supplies to be acquired for public use."[1] In most cases, each contract line item or subcontract line item constitutes a *separate* end product.[2] However, COs have discretion in identifying a solicitation's end products, and a CO may decide that a solicited item constitutes an end product subject to the BAA or TAA even if the item is not a separate line item. For example, in procurements of information technology, the Government may treat certain articles contained within a system contract line item (i.e., the computer box, keyboard, monitor, and pointing device) as separate end products, each of which must be BAA or TAA compliant.[3]

Determining a solicitation's end products is not always easy. Sometimes the solicitation clearly defines the end products. Other times you should request this information from your CO during the question-and-answer phase of a procurement.

D. DETERMINING COUNTRY OF ORIGIN

§ 17:11 Generally

The purpose behind the BAA and TAA is to promote the acquisition of end products from domestic or privileged foreign sources and deter the procurement of goods from disfavored countries. Therefore, the Government does not react favorably to contractors who fraudulently, or even mistakenly, certify an end product's country of origin. As discussed below (see §§ 17:17, 17:18), penalties for violations of a BAA or TAA certification can result in termination of contracts, suspension and debarment of contractors, as well as civil fines *and* imprisonment. Therefore, when you offer end products to the Government and certify to the products' country of origin, you should be very careful to ensure that all of your country-of-origin representations are as true and accurate as possible. The following discussion is intended to

---

[Section 17:10]

[1]*See* FAR 25.003.

[2]*See Data Transformation Corp.*, GSBCA No. 8982-P, 87-3 BCA ¶ 20017.

[3]*See Laptop Falls Church, Inc.*, GSBCA No. 12953-P, 95-1 BCA ¶ 27311; *CompuAdd Corp. v. Department of the Air Force*, GSBCA No. 12021-P et al., 93-2 BCA ¶ 25811.

DOMESTIC & FOREIGN PRODUCT ACQUISITION PREFERENCES § 17:12

familiarize you with the tests and standards used to determine an end product's country of origin.

§ 17:12 BAA—"Domestic" end products

Under the BAA, the Government gives preference to procuring *domestic end products*. As defined in part in the FAR:[1]

> "Domestic end product"... means (1) an unmanufactured end product mined or produced in the United States, or (2) an end product manufactured in the United States, if the cost of its components mined, produced, or manufactured in the United States exceeds 50 percent of the cost of all its components.

Most of the items that you will supply to the Government, whether commercial items or items specifically tailored for an agency procurement, will be manufactured products. For a manufactured item to be considered a domestic end product (definition (2) above), the FAR requires two elements: (1) that the end product be manufactured in the United States; *and* (2) that the cost of the end product's *domestic* components exceeds 50% of the cost of all the product's components.[2] These two prerequisites are further explained below.

(1) *End Product Manufactured in the United States:* The determination of whether an end product is manufactured in the United States is made on a case-by-case basis. The assembly of an end product's components in the United States, as long as it is more than simple assembly, will constitute domestic manufacture in many (but not all) cases. Mere re-assembly of foreign components will not constitute domestic manufacture.[3] Further, work on components that does not in some way alter the form or use of the components does not necessarily constitute manufacturing. For example, in one case, the Comptroller General determined that the sterilization of foreign-made surgeon's gloves did not materially alter the form of the gloves but merely involved the "treatment of the finished product." The Comptroller General found, therefore, that the glove treatment did not constitute a separate manufacturing operation for BAA purposes.[4]

(2) *Cost of Domestic Components Exceeds 50% of Product's Cost:* The FAR defines components, for the purpose of Part 25 (Foreign Acquisitions), as "an article, material, and supply incorporated

---

[Section 17:12]

[1] FAR 25.003.

[2] *See* FAR 25.003; see also DFARS 252.225-7001(a)(2).

[3] *See Rolm Corp.*, Comp. Gen. Dec. B-200995, 81-2 CPD ¶ 106.

[4] *See Marbex, Inc.*, Comp. Gen. Dec. B-225799, 87-1 CPD ¶ 468.

§ 17:12   GOVERNMENT CONTRACT COMPLIANCE HANDBOOK

directly into an end product or construction material."[5] The country where the component is mined, produced, or manufactured becomes the component's country of origin for purposes of the 50% domestic component cost test. There is no subcomponent cost test for determining a component's country of origin. Manufacture of domestic subcomponents into foreign components, however, can change the domestic cost percentage. This is the primary area where many sophisticated Government contractors with a detailed understanding of the BAA will make production decisions that will allow them to comply with the law while minimizing their production costs. The cost of any component purchased by the contractor includes transportation costs to the place of incorporation into the end product and any applicable duty.[6] For components manufactured by the contractor, all costs associated with the manufacture of the component, including transportation cost, plus allocable overhead costs, but excluding profit are included in determining the cost of the component.[7] However, cost of components does not include any costs associated with the manufacture of the end product.[8]

§ 17:13   BAA—"Qualifying country" (DOD) end products

The DFARS definition for "qualifying country end product" is similar to the FAR's definition of "domestic end product"—

(i) An unmanufactured end product mined or produced in a qualifying country; or

(ii) An end product manufactured in a qualifying country if the cost of the following types of components exceeds 50% of the cost of all its components:

    (A) Components mined, produced, or manufactured in a qualifying country.

    (B) Components mined, produced, or manufactured in the United States.

    (C) Components of foreign origin of a class or kind for which the Government has determined that sufficient and reasonably available commercial quantities of a satisfactory quality are not mined, produced, or manufactured in the United States.

Thus, a qualifying country end product must be manufactured in a *qualifying country* as defined in the DFARS, and the product's qualifying country or domestic components must cost more

---

[5]FAR 25.003.

[6]FAR 25.003. *See also Specialty Plastic Prods., Inc.*, ASBCA No. 42085 et al., 95-2 BCA ¶ 27895 (applying 50% component cost test).

[7]FAR 52.225-1(a)(2).

[8]FAR 52.225-1(a)(2).

than 50% of all the product's components.[1]

§ 17:14 TAA—Designated country end products

As stated previously, if the TAA clause applies to a procurement, instead of offering domestic end products, you may generally offer products from a designated country and be considered for contract award. The FAR provisions defining end products from these countries state that an eligible product (a) is wholly the growth, product, or manufacture of a particular eligible country, or (b) in the case of an article that consists in whole or in part of materials from another country or instrumentality, has been substantially transformed in the eligible country into a new and different article of commerce with a name, character, or use distinct from that of the article or articles from which it was so transformed.[1] Unlike with the BAA, the TAA does not establish a foreign product's country of origin through a component cost percentage test. The difference in the standard for determining the country of origin under the BAA and TAA arises from the fact that the TAA reflects international trade agreements. Most foreign countries use the transformation test - and so, the United States, in its trade agreements, adopted this same standard.

To ensure TAA compliance, it is essential that you understand the concept of *substantial transformation*. Courts, boards of contract appeals, and particularly the U.S. Customs Service (Customs) have addressed the issue of what constitutes substantial transformation. In fact, Customs has statutory and regulatory authority to make substantial transformation decisions for TAA purposes.[2] Since Customs is the agency responsible for country-of-origin determinations (and because boards of contract appeals have given great weight to Customs' substantial transformation rulings),[3] the following discussion focuses primarily on Customs' rulings concerning substantial transformation.

To determine if an article has been substantially transformed in a particular country, Customs considers whether the product was subject to a manufacturing process in that country which resulted in a "new and different" article of commerce-bearing a

---

[Section 17:13]

[1]DFARS 252.225-7001(a) ("Buy American Act and Balance of Payments Program" clause).

[Section 17:14]

[1]*See* FAR 25.003.

[2]*See* 19 U.S.C.A. § 2515; 19 C.F.R. pt. 134.

[3]*See, e.g., CompuAdd Corp. v. Department of the Air Force,* GSBCA No. 12301-P et al., 93-3 BCA ¶ 26123.

§ 17:14   Government Contract Compliance Handbook

new name, character, or use.[4] Customs looks to five general characteristics of manufacturing operations when deciding whether a manufacturing process caused a substantial transformation in a product:

(1) *The complexity of the manufacturing process:* A manufacturing process that is complex and involves many steps to produce a finished article is more likely substantially to transform a product than a relatively simple manufacturing technique.
(2) *Technical skill:* A manufacturing operation that requires skilled employees to perform the accompanying work is more likely to cause a substantial transformation in a product than a relatively simple manufacturing process.
(3) *Expense entailed/value added:* Processes that cost a lot of money to perform on a product or add considerable value to a product are more likely substantially to transform a product than manufacturing techniques that are inexpensive and do not add much value to the end product.
(4) *Essential character of the finished article:* If the end product's essential character stems from the processing method, not the product's imported components or materials, the manufacturing operation may be considered as the catalyst for the substantial transformation.
(5) *Change in tariff classification:* Customs will often perform an analysis to determine whether the manufacturing process converting components into an end product results in a change in tariff classification under Customs' law. Customs is more likely to find that a manufacturing process results in a substantial transformation if it also results in goods undergoing a change in tariff classification.

The substantial transformation test can be very subjective and inconsistently applied. Therefore, a variety of Customs rulings and court opinions are summarized below to familiarize you with the concept of substantial transformation.

(a) Customs held that a blank computer diskette is substantially transformed when a software program is copied on it.[5] However, the mere reformatting of a computer diskette does not result in a substantial transformation.
(b) Customs ruled that the populating of blank printed circuit boards (PCBs) with various electronic components substan-

---

[4]*See* U.S. Intl. Trade Commn., Investigation No. 332-366, "Country-of-Origin Marking: Review of Laws, Regulations, and Practices," pp. 2-4 to 2-5 (1996) (summarizing Customs Service use of "substantial transformation" test).

[5]HQ 735409 (May 27, 1994); HQ 735281 (Feb. 24, 1994); HQ 732087 (Feb. 7, 1990).

tially transformed the blank PCBs.[6]
(c) Customs found that the conversion of a computer monitor into a "touch screen" monitor substantially transformed the computer monitor.[7]
(d) The Court of Federal Claims found that assembly of pots and pans by attaching handles to the pans and covers did not constitute a substantial transformation of the cookware.[8]
(e) A federal court located in Wisconsin determined that the "pointing" of fluted drill blanks (the process by which a drill bit is formed to be capable of drilling into a surface) substantially transformed the drill blanks.[9]

Remember that the determination of whether a process substantially transforms an article is inherently subjective. If you are uncertain whether a manufacturing technique has substantially transformed your end products, you should request a ruling from the Customs Service. (See §§ 17:6, 17:19.)

§ 17:15 U.S.-made end products

Consider the following scenario: your multinational company wants to offer computers to the Government in a procurement that is subject to the TAA. The components for the computers are all manufactured overseas, but they are assembled and substantially transformed into computers in the United States. How will the Government treat your offer?

You should recall that for a manufactured end product to be a domestic end product, the article must be manufactured in the United States and satisfy the 50% domestic component cost test. Clearly, your computer does not satisfy the domestic component cost criteria because all of the parts are from overseas. Moreover, for your computer to qualify as an eligible foreign end product, the computer must be substantially transformed in a designated country, and the United States is not identified as a designated country. While at one time end items substantially transformed in the United States were in a definitional no man's land, the FAR now specifically provides that a contractor can supply a U.S.-made end product.[1] Therefore, your computer will be

---

[6]HQ 733690 (Feb. 22, 1991).

[7]HQ 734213 (Feb. 20, 1992).

[8]*Ran-Paige Co. v. U.S.*, 35 Fed. Cl. 117 (1996).

[9]*In re Property Seized From ICS Cutting Tools, Inc.*, 163 F.R.D. 292 (E.D. Wis. 1995).

[Section 17:15]

[1]*See e.g.*, FAR 52.225-5.

§ 17:15   Government Contract Compliance Handbook

considered an eligible product that the Government may acquire in a TAA procurement.

§ 17:16   NAFTA marking rules—FAR vs. Customs

An issue that you should not overlook is the differing treatment that the FAR and the U.S. Customs Service give to NAFTA country-of-origin determinations. Particularly if your company does business in NAFTA countries (Canada and Mexico), you want to make sure that you have properly certified the origin of the end products that you supply to the Federal Government.

As stated earlier, the FAR uses a "substantial transformation" test to determine the country of origin of products alleged to come from Mexico and Canada (NAFTA countries).[1] Although the Customs Service generally uses a "substantial transformation" test to determine the country of origin of imports, the Customs Service uses a different set of standards for NAFTA country-of-origin determinations that may not coincide with the FAR's "substantial transformation" test. Customs Service regulations list a hierarchy of tests that are used in NAFTA country-of-origin decisions[2]-none of these tests, however, involve the classic subjective "substantial transformation" test used for purposes of the TAA. (See § 17:14.)

Instead, for products that do not originate exclusively in a NAFTA country, Customs uses a *change in tariff classification* test to determine whether an end product has a NAFTA country of origin. Specifically, this test provides in most, but not all, instances that an end product's country of origin will be the last place that all of the foreign components underwent a change in tariff classification.

If you supply NAFTA products to the Government, you must be careful to ensure that your product's country of origin is determined by a "substantial transformation" standard and not solely by the "tariff shift" test that Customs uses to determine whether a product has a NAFTA country of origin. If you rely on a Customs Service country-of-origin determination for a NAFTA product, you may unknowingly supply the Government with a product that does not meet the FAR's "NAFTA country end product" definition. Although the results under the "substantial transformation" and "tariff shift" tests often are the same, the change in tariff classification test occasionally leads to an end product being classified as originating in a NAFTA country when

---

[Section 17:16]

   [1]*See* FAR 25.003.

   [2]19 C.F.R. § 102, subpt. B.

DOMESTIC & FOREIGN PRODUCT ACQUISITION PREFERENCES   § 17:17

the substantial transformation test would not.

E. PENALTIES

§ 17:17 BAA penalties

If you certify to the CO that you will supply "domestic end products" during contract performance, any violation of your BAA certificate can carry potentially heavy penalties. Before award, a false certification risks the removal of your contract from the competitive range.[1] If you supply foreign end products instead of domestic end products during contract performance, the Government may demand that you furnish domestically made materials.[2] Any increased costs of this postaward compliance with the BAA will likely be borne by you.[3] Even if the Government decides to allow you to continue supplying the foreign end products, the Government would most likely reduce your contract price (assuming that the foreign end products are cheaper to buy than domestic end products).[4]

It must be emphasized that the Government has the right to choose its remedy, and the scenarios discussed above are the best that you could hope for in the event of your failure to comply with your BAA certification. What is more likely is that the Government would terminate your contract for default if you inappropriately supply foreign end products.[5] Even worse, if your noncompliance with the BAA is sufficiently serious, you may be debarred, suspended, or otherwise rendered ineligible from competing for Government contracts.[6] If your contract involves construction or construction materials, you risk additional liability under a special statute that provides for suspension for up to three years from any public construction contracting for you, your subcontractors, materialmen, or affiliated suppliers for fail-

---

[Section 17:17]

[1]*See University Sys., Inc. v. Department of Health & Human Servs.*, GSBCA No. 12039-P, 93-2 BCA ¶ 25646.

[2]*See, e.g.*, FAR 25.206(c)(2); *S.J. Amoroso Constr. Co. v. U.S.*, 12 F.3d 1072 (Fed. Cir. 1993); *C. Sanchez & Son, Inc. v. U.S.*, 6 F.3d 1539 (Fed. Cir. 1993); *Ran-Paige Co. v. U.S.*, 35 Fed. Cl. 117 (1996).

[3]*See S.J. Amoroso Constr. Co. v. U.S.*, 12 F.3d 1072, 1077-1078 (Fed. Cir. 1993); *C. Sanchez & Son, Inc. v. U.S.*, 6 F.3d 1539, 1546 (Fed. Cir. 1993).

[4]FAR 25.206(c)(3).

[5]FAR 25.206(c)(3). See also *Ran-Paige Co. v. U.S.*, 35 Fed. Cl. 117, 119 (1996).

[6]FAR 25.206(c)(4). *Ali v. U.S.*, 932 F. Supp. 1206 (N.D. Cal. 1996); *Strand Hunt Constr., Inc.*, ASBCA No. 48690, 96-1 BCA ¶ 28080.

ure to comply with BAA requirements.[7]

Fraudulent noncompliance with the BAA may subject you to statutory civil and criminal penalties. You may be liable under the False Claims Act, as well as for criminal false statements for any intentional misrepresentation of a product's country of origin on your BAA certificate (see §§ 1:1 et seq.).[8] Furthermore, if you alter or attempt to alter any country-of-origin markings on foreign products, the customs laws impose monetary fines up to $250,000 and allow for imprisonment up to one year for any intent to conceal the actual country of origin of your end products.[9] For example, in one case, a subcontractor certified to the Government that it was supplying BAA-compliant electrical tape to DOD. The electrical tape was manufactured entirely in Mexico, however, and the subcontractor was removing the foreign manufacturing labels before sending the tape to the DOD. The subcontractor was indicted for violations of the False Claims Act and the Tariff Act and was sentenced to 10 months in prison and a $10,000 fine.[10]

§ 17:18 TAA penalties

The penalties that attach to violations of your TAA certificate are generally the same as the penalties for BAA noncompliance (i.e., removal from the competitive range, default termination, suspension and debarment, or criminal and civil penalties). Because submitting a false BAA or TAA certification to the Government can be harmful to your future as a Government contractor, you must deliver the items that you certify under the contract.

F. FREQUENTLY ASKED QUESTIONS

§ 17:19 Questions & answers

Because of the numerous BAA and TAA regulations, contract clauses, and exceptions, as well as the country-of-origin issues that almost always arise in deciding how to certify your product's country of origin, you may have many questions concerning the applicability of the BAA or TAA to a particular procurement. Some of the more frequently raised questions are discussed below.

Question 1: If a solicitation calls for multiple line items, how do I determine whether the BAA or TAA will apply to the products

---

[7]41 U.S.C.A. § 8303(c).

[8]See, e.g. *U.S. ex rel Crennen v. Dell Marketing L.P.*, 711 F. Supp. 2d 157 (D.Mass 2010); *U.S. ex rel Schweizer v. Oce, N.V.*, 681 F. Supp. 2d 64 (D.D.C. 2010).

[9]19 U.S.C.A. § 1304(k).

[10]*U.S. v. Thomas*, 13 F.3d 151 (5th Cir. 1994).

§ 17:19

that I offer-does the value of the *total procurement* have to exceed the TAA dollar threshold, or does the price of *each line item* have to be greater than the TAA threshold for the TAA to apply?

Answer 1: What appears to be the most likely answer is that the application of the BAA or TAA to your offer of end products will be determined on a *line-item-by-line-item* basis. In other words, line items under the TAA dollar threshold will be subject to the BAA's requirements while line items priced above the TAA dollar threshold will be subject to the TAA's rules.[1] Nevertheless, you always should ask your CO how the contracting agency intends to apply the TAA to your particular procurement. There have been instances where the CO determined that once the TAA threshold was passed, all items offered under the solicitation must be TAA compliant, regardless of whether individual line items are under the threshold.

Question 2: If a solicitation requires postdelivery services associated with an end product (or line-item), such as installation, testing, and personnel training, or creation of instruction manuals for end product use, will these postdelivery costs be included when the BAA price evaluation penalty is attached if I supply a foreign end product?

Answer 2: In general, no. Many postdelivery costs are not included in an end-product or line-item evaluation. However, you should be aware that if design, administrative, or other costs are associated with the delivery of the end product itself, these probably will be included in the BAA cost component.[2]

Question 3: How can I be more sure of my product's country of origin?

Answer 3: You can request a final determination or an advisory ruling from the Customs Service with respect to the country of origin of your foreign product. Customs has detailed regulations on how to obtain these rulings and final determinations.[3] Customs will give first priority to requests that relate to a Government procurement. A final determination is a binding, judicially reviewable decision. However, there is no agency tasked with providing guidance in advance of an offer as to whether a product satisfies

---

[Section 17:19]

[1] *See* FAR 25.501. *See generally Laptops Falls Church, Inc. v. Department of Justice,* GSBCA No. 12953-P, 95-1 BCA ¶ 27311; *Data Transformation Corp.,* GSBCA No. 8982-P, 87-3 BCA ¶ 20017 (determining TAA applicability on an item-by-item basis).

[2] *See Dynatest Consulting, Inc.,* Comp. Gen. Dec. B-257822.4, 95-1 CPD ¶ 167 (citing court and board decisions concerning pre- and postdelivery costs associated with end products).

[3] 19 C.F.R. pt. 177, subpt. B.

§ 17:19   Government Contract Compliance Handbook

the requirements for a domestic end product.

Question 4: Is the CO or the contracting agency responsible for ascertaining before award any defects in my BAA or TAA certification?

Answer 4: If, before an award, an agency has reason to believe that you will not deliver compliant end products, the agency should investigate your certification. However, when the agency does not have any information before award that your product might not comply with your own certification, the agency may rely on your certification without any further investigation.[4] In any event, it is not a defense to an award protest or to a subsequent Government investigation to argue that the Government should have known that you were not going to supply a domestic end product notwithstanding a positive affirmation to the contrary in your certification.

III. "MADE IN USA" LABELS

§ 17:20   Generally

Suppose that in response to a solicitation you offer to supply DOD with a domestic end product or U.S.-made end product (see § 17:15). You win the contract award and, because you want to represent proudly the fact that your goods come primarily from the United States, you decide to attach a "Made in USA" label on your end products. Can you do this without facing any potential liability?

Suppose further that you simultaneously sell overseas the same domestic end products that you offer to the Government. The foreign countries have import marking regulations that require a "Made in USA" label on your exports. Can you supply your labeled exports to the Federal Government without suffering any repercussions?

Many Americans buy products that they believe are "homegrown" and many domestic businesses rely on the American consumer's preference for truly domestic products. Accordingly, the Government (through the Federal Trade Commission (FTC)) for many years has considered it an unfair or deceptive trade practice to label products "Made in USA" unless the products satisfy very strict domestic sourcing requirements. Unfortunately for Government contractors, the FTC's "Made in USA" standards are different and significantly more difficult to satisfy than the Government's "domestic end product" preferences or other countries' import marking requirements (which often use a

---

[4]*See Bridgeport Machines, Inc.*, Comp. Gen. Dec. B-265616, 95-2 CPD ¶ 249; *E.D.I., Inc.*, Comp. Gen. Dec. B-251750 et al., 93-1 CPD ¶ 364.

"substantial transformation" test). Furthermore, legislative and regulatory initiatives have strengthened or added penalties for noncompliant FTC "Made in USA" labeling. For you, all of these regulations mean additional standards that you must meet if you want to supply the Government with a "Made in USA"-labeled product.

§ 17:21 FTC requirements

The Federal Trade Commission Act provides that any person who "introduces, sells, advertises, or offers for sale in commerce a product with a 'Made in the USA' or 'Made in America' label" shall ensure that the label conforms with the FTC's decisions and orders concerning its "Made in USA" labeling requirements.[1]

In the past, the FTC has issued advisory opinions and staff opinion letters that discuss the standards applicable to using a "Made in USA" label. Generally, an affirmative representation that a product is "Made in the USA" means that the product in its entirety is domestic. According to the FTC, the applicable standard is "that a product advertised as 'Made in USA' be 'all or virtually all' made in the United States, i.e., that all or virtually all of the parts are made in the U.S. and all or virtually all of the labor is performed in the U.S.A."[2]

The FTC has determined, for example, that it would be improper for a computer company to use the "Made in the USA" designation in labeling or advertising a computer of which 23% of the factory cost was accounted for by imported parts and 77% was accounted for by domestically produced parts, assembly, and factory testing in the United States. While the system for advisory opinions is still in place, the FTC has not issued any new opinions since 1999 and is instead relying on agency guidelines.

In addition to place of assembly, the Commission considers other factors "such as how much of the product's total manufacturing costs can be assigned to U.S. parts and processing, and how far removed any foreign content is from the finished product."[3] An example presented by the FTC: A company produces a propane barbecue grill in Nevada. The grill's major components include the gas valve, burner and aluminum housing, all of which are made in the U.S. The knobs and tubing, however, are made in Mexico. A "Made in the USA" label would not be deceptive because the knobs and tubing make up a

---

[Section 17:21]

[1]*See* 15 U.S.C.A. § 45a.

[2]62 Fed. Reg. 25020.

[3]"Complying with the Made in the USA Standard" available at http://www.ftc.gov/bcp/conline/pubs/buspubs/madeusa.htm.

negligible portion of the product's total manufacturing costs and are insignificant parts of the final product.[4]

The FTC has also stated that foreign content incorporated early in the manufacturing process will frequently be less significant to consumers than content that is a direct component of the finished product. For example, the steel used to make a single component of a computer's floppy drive is an early input into the computer's manufacture, and is likely to constitute a very small portion of the final product's total cost.[5] Although, if a pharmaceutical company manufactures a drug in the U.S. which contains an active ingredient of partially foreign origin, a "Made in USA" label would be deceptive.[6]

§ 17:22 Penalties

The penalties for attaching an inappropriate "Made in USA" label to your products can be substantial. On notice of an improper labeling claim, the FTC will issue a cease and desist (C&D) order requesting you to stop affixing the "Made in USA" label to your products. If you fail to comply with the C&D order, the FTC most likely will pursue an injunction against your labeling practices. If an injunction is issued by a court and you fail thereafter to comply with the court orders, you can be found civilly liable up to $10,000 for each instance of noncompliance.[1] The FTC can also seize improperly marked goods.

Although the FTC enforcement may occur over a period of time, federal procurement suspension and debarment authorities can take swift remedial action. Under the FAR, if you intentionally affix a fraudulent "Made in USA" label on products sold in or shipped to the United States, you can be immediately debarred or suspended from contracting with the Government.[2] The DFARS provides for its own debarment proceedings if you are criminally convicted of intentionally affixing a fraudulent "Made in America" label to your products.[3]

---

[4]"Complying with the Made in the USA Standard" available at http://www.ftc.gov/bcp/conline/pubs/buspubs/madeusa.htm.

[5]"Complying with the Made in the USA Standard" available at http://www.ftc.gov/bcp/conline/pubs/buspubs/madeusa.htm.

[6]See "Five Manufacturers of Over-the-Counter Analgesic Products Agree to Settle Charges of Mislabeling Certain Products as 'Made in USA'" available at http://www.ftc.gov/opa/2001/11/musa.htm.

[Section 17:22]

[1]15 U.S.C.A. § 45(l).

[2]See FAR 9.406-2(a)(4), 9.407-2(a)(5).

[3]See DFARS 209.406-2(a) (implementing 10 U.S.C.A. § 2410f).

§ 17:23 Frequently asked questions

Question 1: Under the FTC's current rules, can I provide any kind of reference to my product's domestic components if I do not satisfy the FTC's "Made in USA" standards?

Answer 1: Yes. The FTC currently allows you to label your products as "Made in (or Assembled in) USA of USA and _____ *(country or countries) components*" if your product's last substantial transformation occurred in the United States and more than 50% of the total cost of the finished product is added in the United States.[1]

Question 2: Can I request an FTC labeling determination similar to a Customs Service country-of-origin ruling?

Answer 2: Yes, but you are unlikely to get a response. The FTC has a procedure in place under which you can request advice about how to label your product.[2] However, hypotheticals generally will not be considered, and you must identify yourself to the FTC. This is potentially dangerous because that may put the FTC on alert about a product of yours that may be inappropriately labeled.

IV. HOW TO RECOGNIZE THE PROBLEM

§ 17:24 Generally

The maze of regulations and exceptions concerning the Government's solicitation of domestic and foreign goods requires that, if at any time during the procurement process you make a change to an end product that you offer and supply to the Government, that product may become noncompliant with BAA or TAA restrictions. If you keep in mind, however, the following general considerations as you go through the various stages of contract performance, you will more easily catch noncompliance with the BAA and TAA if, and when, it happens.

§ 17:25 Offers to supply products

(a) *End products*: When you are first confronted with a solicitation, you must make sure that you understand what end products the Government is seeking. If you erroneously believe, for example, that a desktop computer system is the end product when the Government considers the computer's parts (i.e., computer box, monitor, keyboard, and pointing device) to be separate

---

[Section 17:23]

[1] *See* 62 Fed. Reg. 25045 (qualified U.S. origin claims); 62 Fed. Reg. 63769 ("Enforcement Policy Statement on U.S. Origin Claims; Section V").

[2] 16 C.F.R. §§ 1.2 to 1.4.

§ 17:25   Government Contract Compliance Handbook

end products, you may find that the products you offer the Government do not comply with the BAA and TAA requirements.

(b) *Applicable rules*: You must determine what laws and regulations apply to the procurement. Remember that in a multiple-line-item acquisition, some end products may be subject to the BAA while other line items are subject to the TAA clause. Familiarity with the various rules will allow you to know which products from which countries are eligible for contract award.

(c) *Determine country of origin*: You must take particular care before completing any contract certifications that you have made a good faith effort to discern an offered end product's country of origin. You should detail all of an end product's components and where they originated. Be wary of "manufacturing processes" that do not alter or materially change a product. Furthermore, remember that country-of-origin determinations may be different under the Customs Service rules and under the FAR rules. Finally, you should keep in mind, especially if your company trades in many countries, that United States' marking laws and origin determinations may differ from what other countries require of their imports and exports.

§ 17:26   Postaward activities & contract performance

(a) *Product variations*: Be careful to ensure that the items that you previously certified to supply to the Government are sufficiently available and still produced in the same manner as when you originally certified them in your offer. Changes in component vendors or manufacturing locations and processes may render an end product noncompliant with BAA or TAA requirements as well as with your certification to the Government.

(b) *Monitoring*: Perhaps most importantly, you should monitor and check that the supplies you offered to the Government are actually used during contract performance. Improper shipments, misplaced orders, and poor management or organization can cause noncompliant supplies to be sent from the wrong warehouse or factory and subsequently used in the contract work or supplied to the Government.

§ 17:27   Examples

Following are examples of situations in which your company may encounter potentially serious trouble for failure to comply with BAA and TAA requirements.

"Made in USA" labels and U.S.-made end products: Suppose that you recently became the sales representative for a Southern Texas office supply manufacturer. Your company produces desk lamps that it sells commercially in Canada, Western Europe, and

the United States for approximately $30 each. More than half of the components that are incorporated into the lamp are produced in the United States; the rest are manufactured in Mexico and the Caribbean. The lamp itself is assembled in your Texas factory because of a specialized lamp molding process that your company uses. After the finished product is complete, your company ships the desk lamps that it will send to other countries to your warehouse in New York. At this warehouse, a "Made in USA" stamp is placed on all of the desk lamps that will be exported. All other lamps are sent to your warehouse in Arkansas.

You recently responded to a Federal Government solicitation for 2,000 desk lamps needed for a new federal office building in New York, and you offer to supply your company's lamps. Because you know that the lamp ultimately is manufactured in the United States and has many American components, you certify in your offer that the lamp is a domestic end product. In addition, for your company's convenience and to save the Government the cost of shipping your lamps from Arkansas, you offer to supply the New York warehouse's "Made in USA"-stamped lamps. You win the contract award. Do you face any potential liability?

Yes. Assuming that your offer must meet BAA requirements because the acquisition amount ($30 × 2,000 lamps = $60,000) would be for less than the TAA dollar threshold (currently $204,000), your desk lamp might not satisfy the BAA's "domestic end product" definition. Remember that the BAA's definition of domestic end product requires that (1) the end product must be manufactured in the United States, *and* (2) the *cost* of the domestic components must exceed 50% of the costs of all the components. Clearly, your lamp is manufactured in the United States. You must find out, however, if the cost of the lamp's American components exceeds 50% of the cost of all of the lamp's components. Before certifying that your lamp is a domestic end product, therefore, you would need to conduct a component cost analysis to see if your lamp satisfies the BAA's "domestic end product" definition.

Furthermore, if you supply the Government with your New York warehouse's "Made in USA"-stamped lamps, you may risk suspension or debarment for fraudulently submitting a product with a "Made in USA" label to the Government. You also may be held liable for unfair or deceptive trade practices under the FTC's rules. The lamps in the New York warehouse are intended for export to other countries. As stated earlier, the United States' marking requirements for "Made in USA" labels are different and more difficult to satisfy than many of the country-of-origin marking requirements that other countries place on United States imports. Although your lamps might be "substantially transformed" in the United States for the purposes of export marking

§ 17:27   GOVERNMENT CONTRACT COMPLIANCE HANDBOOK

requirements, substantial transformation is not the test for determining whether products sold in the United States are "Made in the USA." These lamps clearly would not satisfy the FTC's requirements for a product to be labeled "Made in USA."

The BAA and U.S.-made end products: Using the same facts stated in the example above, suppose now that another Government agency solicited shipment of 10,000 desk lamps and you offer the lamps stored in your Arkansas warehouse (the lamps without the "Made in USA" label). Assuming that your lamps do not satisfy the BAA's domestic end product test, will your offer even be considered?

Most likely. Since this solicitation most likely would be subject to the TAA clause ($30 × 10,000 = $300,000), under the FAR you would need to supply the Government with designated country, or U.S.-made end products. Mexico falls within the definition of designated country and so do many, but not all Caribbean countries.

V. COMPLIANCE INITIATIVES

§ 17:28   Generally

There are many effective procedures and initiatives that you can develop to reduce the risk of BAA or TAA noncompliance in your business dealings with the Government, some of which are set forth below. Remember that complicated issues often arise regarding the domestic preference requirements that, if handled improperly, could subject you to loss of contract award, or worse, serious fines and penalties. Ask the CO for guidance when appropriate and seek legal guidance before making decisions that could ultimately subject your company to significant liabilities.

§ 17:29   Create a "history" of end products & their components

Keep track of the manufacturing or other processes that your company applies to its products. Your manufacturing records should contain information on the location of any manufacturing processes, the particular production steps involved in making your products, and the components used in building the products. You should also detail the technical skill involved in accomplishing these production tasks.

Try to maintain similar records on all components incorporated into your end products. These records may help establish your products' countries of origin if disputes or concerns about BAA or TAA applicability ever arise.

For *vendors'* products, make sure to question your vendors about the production methods involved in developing the components or materials you buy from them. Request documentation on manufacture location, processing techniques, etc., that will help you determine the country of origin of your vendor's products.

§ 17:30 Keep inventories separate

Consider maintaining a *separate stock* of the end products that you will sell to the Government, particularly if your company sells products internationally or commercially that would not satisfy BAA requirements for domestic end products or the TAA's definition of a designated country end product. Because the materials that you export or sell commercially may be marked in a manner that is inconsistent with your BAA/TAA certification, you want to ensure that inventories sent to the Government are not pulled from noncompliant inventories. Furthermore, if you employ different manufacturing techniques for the products that you supply to the Government and for the products that you market commercially, you need to be careful to send to the Government the product that was developed with the Government procurement in mind.

§ 17:31 Establish a compliance monitor & oversight procedures

Consider training a current employee or hiring someone to handle all of your BAA and TAA administration questions. A BAA/TAA compliance monitor can review all of your product manufacturing documentation and check that the end product that you will supply to the Government satisfies the BAA and TAA regulations. A compliance monitor also could assist in ensuring that the Government receives its end products from the appropriate inventories.

Create a chain-of-command for your compliance monitor in case he or she is having trouble settling a difficult BAA or TAA issue. Make sure that certain managers or senior-level officials are consulted before the compliance monitor decides on a course of action concerning the certification of a particular product. If the compliance monitor's concerns still are not adequately addressed after discussions with management, consider discussing the compliance issues with your CO or requesting a Customs Service country-of-origin ruling.

§ 17:32 Plan ahead

Make sure that you have enough, or can produce enough, BAA/TAA-compliant products to fulfill your contract obligations to the Government. You risk losing a contract award, suffering a default

§ 17:32   GOVERNMENT CONTRACT COMPLIANCE HANDBOOK

termination of the contract, or otherwise suffering a monetary loss if you cannot find BAA/TAA-compliant materials to substitute for your diminished stock.

Similarly, establish plans of action if you find the products that you certified to the Government as BAA/TAA compliant cannot be supplied. For example, if you certify that you will supply a designated country end product under a TAA procurement, make sure to canvass the market after award and be prepared to substitute another TAA-compliant product if you cannot fulfill your original offer.

§ 17:33   On-site review

Send someone to the contract site or have somebody monitor your shipments to the Government to ensure that you are sending the correct products to the Government.

§ 17:34   Recommendations

Failure to understand and comply with the complex rules concerning the Government's acquisition of goods from domestic and foreign sources can lead to fairly severe criminal and civil penalties. In addition to following the compliance initiatives set forth above, you should always keep in mind the following two suggestions when you supply the Government with a product that is not entirely made or produced in the United States:

(a) *Never* supply a product to the Government or certify its origin status unless you are *sure* that the product's country of origin for BAA/TAA purposes is *accurate and truthful*. When in doubt, seek advice from the CO, the Customs Service, or legal counsel.

(b) Remember that country-of-origin determinations and product labeling requirements *vary according to the purpose for which the product is being marked.* Do not just supply the Government with a product appropriately marked for one purpose but not appropriately marked under the Government's procurement regulations.

Chapter 18

Acquisitions & Mergers

I. OVERVIEW
§ 18:1   Scope note

II. PLANNING & EXECUTING THE ACQUISITION OR MERGER

A. COST ISSUES
§ 18:2   Generally
§ 18:3   Planning & execution costs
§ 18:4   Financing costs
§ 18:5   Depreciation of the combined assets
§ 18:6   Cost of money
§ 18:7   Restructuring costs: defense contracts
§ 18:8   Adjustment of prices of contracts subject to CAS

B. NOVATION AGREEMENTS
§ 18:9   Generally
§ 18:10   Requirements
§ 18:11   Failure to execute a novation agreement

III. SPECIAL CONCERNS FOR THE RESULTING COMPANY
§ 18:12   Organizational conflicts of interest
§ 18:13   Small-business size status
§ 18:14   Responsibility to perform contracts
§ 18:15   Facilities that violate environmental requirements
§ 18:16   Liability for acquired company's prior actions

IV. FOREIGN ACQUISITIONS OF U.S. COMPANIES
§ 18:17   Generally
§ 18:18   Restrictions on ownership
§ 18:19   Restrictions on access to classified information
§ 18:20   Methods to protect classified information

V. DUE DILIGENCE REVIEW
§ 18:21   Generally

§ 18:22   Due diligence checklist

> **KeyCite®:** Cases and other legal materials listed in KeyCite Scope can be researched through the KeyCite service on Westlaw®. Use KeyCite to check citations for form, parallel references, prior and later history, and comprehensive citator information, including citations to other decisions and secondary materials.

I. OVERVIEW

§ 18:1   Scope note

In recent years, there have been a significant number of acquisitions and mergers among Government contractors, resulting in substantial consolidation, especially in the defense industry. The combining of companies always requires a significant due diligence review, but the merger or acquisition of a Government contractor requires even greater effort because many unique rules apply to companies doing business with the Government. These special rules have a major impact on the rights and obligations of the buyers and sellers.

II. PLANNING & EXECUTING THE ACQUISITION OR MERGER

A. COST ISSUES

§ 18:2   Generally

Federal procurement regulations limit or disallow various costs associated with business combinations in all pricing actions subject to the cost principles. (The topic of cost allowability is discussed at greater length in Chapter 11.) Contractors may not pass such costs along to the Government, but must instead absorb them. Therefore, the attractiveness of any business combination will depend, at least in part, on the relative amount of such costs.

§ 18:3   Planning & execution costs

The costs you incur while considering the general advisability of a business combination may be *allowable* under the Federal Acquisition Regulation (FAR) cost principles as *long-range economic planning costs*. Allowable costs include, for example, the "costs of generalized long-range management planning that is concerned with the future overall development of the contractor's business."[1] At the same time, however, the costs you incur in *actually planning for and executing* an acquisition or merger are generally *not* allowable. Thus, the cost principles do not allow costs incurred in connection with "(1) planning or executing the organization or reorganization of the corporate structure of a business, including mergers and acquisitions, (2) resisting or planning to resist the reorganization of the corporate structure of a business or a change in the controlling interest in the ownership of a business, and (3) raising capital."[2]

There is no bright line separating allowable costs for generalized long-range planning from the unallowable costs of planning an acquisition. Therefore, you need to analyze carefully and fully the allowability of all costs associated with an acquisition or a merger.

§ 18:4 Financing costs

Financing is generally a significant cost in all acquisitions and mergers. This is especially true where the transaction will be financed with cash or debt instruments instead of stock. Unfortunately, the costs that contractors incur when raising capital to finance a business combination are usually *not* allowable under the cost principles. This is true regardless of the form the financing takes. The FAR cost principles disallow the costs of "[i]nterest on borrowings (however represented), bond discounts, costs of financing and refinancing capital . . ., legal and professional fees paid in connection with preparing prospectuses, costs of preparing and issuing stock rights, and directly associated costs."[1]

Therefore, you cannot pass the costs of financing the combination on to the Government. Instead, you must absorb such costs.

§ 18:5 Depreciation of the combined assets

Depreciation charges are a significant cost factor for many Government contractors. Financial accounting standards identify the purchase method as the method to be used when accounting for business combinations.[1] Under the purchase method, the combined company records the cost basis of the assets at their

---

[Section 18:3]

[1]FAR 31.205-12.

[2]FAR 31.205-27(a).

[Section 18:4]

[1]FAR 31.205-20. *See also* FAR 31.205-27.

[Section 18:5]

[1]Statement of Financial Accounting Standards No. 141.

fair market value (generally the cost at which the assets were acquired as part of the combination).[2]

In recent years, the market value of assets has generally exceeded their book value. As a result, financial accounting standards usually dictate that the combined company step-up the cost basis of, and thus the depreciation charges against, the acquired assets. Unfortunately, the cost principles generally prohibit contractors from using this stepped-up cost basis in pricing contracts. In other words, the resulting company may formally step-up the cost basis of the acquired assets, however, the allowable depreciation will be limited to that based on the cost basis of the assets as recorded by the companies prior to the combination.

Under financial accounting principles, in a business combination implemented via the purchase method where the amount paid is less than the precombination book value of the assets, the company would typically step down the cost basis of the assets to reflect their market value, thus reducing the allowable depreciation charges.[3] Although the FAR limitations previously applied only to step up adjustments, the FAR now implements a general "no step down" rule as well.[4] As with all of the costs incurred in connection with an acquisition or merger, you need to consider the impact of these rules carefully before proceeding with any business combination.

§ 18:6 Cost of money

Under FAR 31.205-10, the cost of money is an imputed cost that contractors may charge the Government. It is based, in part, on the book value of the company's facilities. As with depreciation, the FAR cost principles and the CAS generally require that cost of money charges be based on the net book value of assets at the time of the acquisition or merger transaction.[1] Again, it is important that you assess the impact of this rule before proceeding with any planned acquisition.

§ 18:7 Restructuring costs: defense contracts

For contracts with the Department of Defense (DOD), additional restrictions apply to the allowability of costs incurred in restructuring operations following a business combination. Restructuring costs are disallowed unless the savings resulting

---

[2]Statement of Financial Accounting Standards No. 141.

[3]*See* DCAA Contract Audit Manual 7-1705.3(b) (Apr. 2014).

[4]*See* FAR 31.205-52.

[Section 18:6]

[1]FAR 31.205-52(a); 48 C.F.R. § 9904.404-50(d)(1).

from the restructuring are at least twice the costs of the restructuring. In cases where the business combination preserves a critical military or other capability that might otherwise be lost, however, projected savings need only be equal to the costs of restructuring to be allowed.[1]

While these restrictions may not be significant for some companies, they are extremely important in the case of combinations of companies holding many DOD contracts. This is especially true where significant restructuring is expected. Therefore, you need to assess the likely impact of these restrictions on any proposed business combination where you expect to incur significant restructuring costs.

§ 18:8 Adjustment of prices of contracts subject to CAS

If your company or the company that you are acquiring holds contracts subject to the CAS, you must be aware of the requirements to adjust the prices of those contracts to reflect any changes to either company's cost accounting practices. It is not unusual for companies over time to change their cost accounting practices to reflect an acquisition or merger. Companies not subject to the CAS are free to make such changes without regard to any federal contracts they hold. Companies subject to the CAS are likewise free to make such changes, but they must ensure that the Government does not suffer the consequences of such a change (for example, through higher contract costs being charged to the Government). The regulations require companies to notify the Government of any changes to their cost accounting practices and provide it with an estimate of the cost impact of such changes. If the effect of the change is "material," you must adjust the price of your contracts subject to the CAS such that the Government is not charged higher costs resulting from the change.[1] (See §§ 12:1 et seq. for a more detailed discussion of the CAS.)

The attractiveness of an acquisition or merger will depend, in part, on the dollar value of the contracts subject to the CAS and the likely impact of any changes in either company's cost accounting practices expected to result from the acquisition or merger. It is, therefore, important that you consider the impact of the Cost Accounting Standards and related regulations before effecting any acquisition or merger.

[Section 18:7]

[1]*See* DFARS 231.205-70.

[Section 18:8]

[1]FAR 30.602. *See also* FAR 52.230-6.

B. NOVATION AGREEMENTS

§ 18:9 Generally

Federal law prohibits the assignment of Government contracts without the Government's approval. For example, federal contracts cannot be transferred from an acquired company to the acquiring or merged company without the Government's approval.[1] The Government will, however, generally approve a transfer where the successor contractor's interest in the contract arises out of the transfer of: (1) all of the contractor's assets; or (2) the entire portion of the assets involved in performing the contract, and where the transfer is in the Government's best interest.[2] A novation agreement is unnecessary when there is a change in ownership of a contractor as a result of a stock purchase, with no legal change in the contracting party, and when that contracting party remains in control of the assets and is the party performing the contract.[3]

However, even if the contract is "novated," the transferor continues to be liable for the performance of all obligations that were assumed by the transferee.[4] Thus, it is important to the seller that the party to whom the contract is transferred have the financial and technical ability to complete performance.

§ 18:10 Requirements

Before approving the transfer of a contract, the Government requires significant information from the parties, including the document describing the proposed transaction necessitating the transfer (e.g., the acquisition or merger), a list of all affected contracts between the transferor and the Government, and evidence of the transferee's capability to perform the contracts.[1] The approval itself will be evidenced by a novation agreement, the terms of which are set forth in the FAR.[2]

In addition, the terms of the novation agreement provide that the Government is not obligated to pay or reimburse either the transferor or transferee for any cost, taxes, or other expenses arising out of or resulting from the novation, other than what it

---

[Section 18:9]
 [1]FAR 42.1204(a).
 [2]FAR 42.1204(a).
 [3]FAR 42.1204(b).
 [4]FAR 42.1204(i), para. (b)(8).

[Section 18:10]
 [1]FAR 42.1204(e).
 [2]FAR 42.1204(h).

would otherwise have been obligated to pay under the contract.[3] Thus, for example, in a cost contract, this provision would prohibit the transferee from recovering any increased overhead costs that might have resulted from the reorganization of the acquired company.[4]

§ 18:11 Failure to execute a novation agreement

In the absence of a novation agreement, the original contracting party's failure to perform the contract may be grounds for the Government to terminate the contract for default.[1] It could also bar any claims the company might have against the Government in the future.[2] Therefore, it is imperative that you obtain the Government's consent to the transfer of any contracts before effecting the acquisition or merger. Your failure to do so could result in the termination of the affected contracts for default, impairing your present operations and possibly your ability to compete for future Government contracts.

III. SPECIAL CONCERNS FOR THE RESULTING COMPANY

§ 18:12 Organizational conflicts of interest

The ability of a postcombination company to compete for future Government contracts may depend upon whether the company encounters organizational conflicts of interest. To provide companies with an equal opportunity to bid for federal contracts, companies are prohibited from bidding on contracts when their prior federal contracting experience may give them an unfair competitive advantage over other companies. The FAR identifies four general types of contract activity that may create such organizational conflicts of interest. These include situations where a contractor has (1) provided to the Government systems engineering and technical direction, (2) prepared specifications or work statements for the Government, (3) provided technical evaluation of offers or advisory and assistance services to the Government, and (4) acquired proprietary information from other

---

[3]FAR 42.1204(i).

[4]*Appeal of ITT Gilfillan, Inc.*, 68-2 B.C.A. (CCH) ¶ 7086, 1968 WL 611 (Armed Serv. B.C.A. 1968), related reference, 200 Ct. Cl. 367, 471 F.2d 1382 (1973).

[Section 18:11]

[1]FAR 42.1204(c).

[2]*See Westinghouse Elec. Co. v. U.S.*, 56 Fed. Cl. 564 (2003), aff'd, 97 Fed. Appx. 931 (Fed. Cir. 2004).

§ 18:12   GOVERNMENT CONTRACT COMPLIANCE HANDBOOK

companies to perform a Government contract.[1] (See §§ 8:14 et seq. for a discussion of organizational conflicts of interest.)

In sum, organizational conflicts of interest can seriously limit the federal contracts for which companies may compete. Especially since GAO has recently focused a great deal of attention on OCI disputes,[2] it is important that, before implementing any business combination, you review the past and current contracting activities of all companies involved in the combination, along with any proposal activity, to determine what organizational conflicts, if any, exist that might impact the business prospects of the combined company.

§ 18:13 Small-business size status

A company's status as a small business can significantly affect both its ability to compete for, and the profitability of, federal contracts. For example, small businesses may enjoy preferences in the award of competitive procurements,[1] compete for procurements set aside for award only to small businesses,[2] receive preferential financing,[3] secure patent rights under contracts performed as a prime and subcontractor,[4] enjoy exemption from compliance with federal Cost Accounting Standards, and be sought after by large businesses that are seeking to meet their own small-business subcontracting goals.[5]

A company's status as a small business is normally determined either by its number of employees or its annual receipts.[6] In determining the number of employees or annual receipts, the Government considers not only the company itself but also any affiliated company.[7] Thus, in the case of a business combination, the size status of the resulting company will likely be determined by consideration of the number of employees (or annual receipts) of all of the participating companies. It is, therefore, common

---

[Section 18:12]

[1]FAR 9.505-1 to 9.505-4.

[2]*See e.g., Greenleaf Constr. Co., Inc.*, Comp. Gen. Dec. B-293105.18, *et al.*, 2006 CPD ¶ 19,; *Alion Science & Technology Corporation*, Comp. Gen. Dec. B-297022.3, et al., 2006 CPD ¶ 2, related reference, 74 Fed. Cl. 372 (2006).

[Section 18:13]

[1]FAR 19.202-3, 25.105(b)(2).

[2]*See generally* FAR subpt. 19.5.

[3]FAR 32.104(b) and (d)(3), 32.403(g), 32.501-1(a), 52.216-7, para. (c).

[4]FAR 27.306, 52.227-11, para. (g).

[5]FAR 30.000.

[6]FAR 19.001.

[7]FAR 19.001.

that an acquisition or merger involving a small business will result in the loss of small business status, along with the loss of the benefits accruing to such status.

Additionally, various socio-economic programs have been established for qualifying small businesses. Acquisition of participants in the 8(a) Program,[8] a small disadvantaged business concern,[9] a participant in the Historically Underutilized Business Zone (HUBZone) program,[10] a service-disabled veteran-owned small business,[11] or a women-owned small business[12] will often terminate the preferential treatment these businesses receive in Government contracting. For this reason, before undertaking a business combination, you must consider the effect of the transaction on the size and ownership status of the resulting company and the effect the loss of small-business status may have on the company's business.

§ 18:14 Responsibility to perform contracts

Federal contracts may generally be awarded only to companies having a satisfactory history of performance on prior contracts and a satisfactory history of integrity and business ethics.[1] The past performance of companies prior to an acquisition or merger may impact the responsibility of the resulting company and, thus, its prospects for receiving further Government contracts. The regulations recognize that the performance of a particular company may not necessarily taint its affiliates. The regulation provides that "[a]ffiliated concerns . . . are normally considered separate entities in determining whether the concern that is to perform the contract meets the applicable standards of responsibility."[2] Nonetheless, the past performance of affiliated companies may be considered, where "the affiliate's past performance and integrity . . . may adversely affect the prospective contractor's responsibility."[3] Thus, it is important that you consider the past performance and integrity of each company participating in the merger or acquisition and identify methods by which you might isolate any adverse conduct such that it does

---

[8]FAR subpt. 19.8.
[9]FAR subpt. 19.11.
[10]FAR subpt. 19.13.
[11]FAR subpt. 19.14.
[12]FAR subpt. 19.15.

[Section 18:14]
[1]FAR 9.103, 9.104-1(c), (d).
[2]FAR 9.104-3(c).
[3]FAR 9.104-3(c).

§ 18:14

not impact the responsibility of the resulting company.

§ 18:15 Facilities that violate environmental requirements

Federal contracts generally will not be awarded to companies planning to use facilities in the performance of the contract that have been listed by the Environmental Protection Agency as violating the Clean Air Act or Clean Water Act.[1] Therefore, you must review the facilities of all companies participating in an acquisition or merger to determine their compliance with these two acts and to ensure that, if the facilities are not compliant, there are no plans to use those specific facilities in performing Government contracts. Your failure to identify and exclude from your proposals the noncompliant facilities could result in your being forced to expend potentially significant sums to bring the facilities into compliance or to maintain idle facilities.

§ 18:16 Liability for acquired company's prior actions

Generally, successor companies in acquisitions or mergers assume the liabilities of the predecessor companies. In the case of Government contractors, these liabilities can include such matters as reimbursements due the Government for violations of the Truth in Negotiations Act[1] (see Chapter 9), contractual requirements pertaining to the Buy American Act and various Trade Agreements (see Chapter 17), responsibility for Government property furnished to the companies,[2] and, most significantly, responsibility for violations of the False Claims Act and False Statements Statute[3] (see §§ 1:1 et seq.). These requirements unique to Government contractors are of significant importance in evaluating any proposed acquisition or merger involving Government contractors. Thus, it is important that you conduct a *due diligence review* to uncover such potential liabilities before agreeing to the acquisition or merger. It is also important that you include appropriate representations and warranties in the purchase or merger agreement and include sufficient indemnification provisions so that if a situation arises post-closing, the buyer has potential remedies. The checklist of items set forth below in

---

[Section 18:15]

[1]*See* 64 FR 72414 (Dec. 1999).

[Section 18:16]

[1]10 U.S.C.A. § 2306a(e); 41 U.S.C.A. § 3506; FAR 15.407.

[2]FAR 45.103.

[3]31 U.S.C.A. §§ 3729 to 3733 (civil False Claims Act); 18 U.S.C.A. § 287 (criminal False Claims Act); 18 U.S.C.A. § 1001 (False Statements Statute).

Section V should serve as a guide in conducting such reviews.

Cases & Commentary: The importance of conducting a thorough "due diligence" review was emphasized by Oracle Corp.'s agreement to pay $98.5 million to resolve false claims allegations that PeopleSoft Inc, a firm that Oracle acquired in 2004, had failed to disclose to the Government during the negotiation of a multiple award schedule contract that it offered commercial customers more favorable pricing than it was proposing to the Government.[4]

IV. FOREIGN ACQUISITIONS OF U.S. COMPANIES

§ 18:17 Generally

Foreign investment in U.S. companies has many economic, political, and social ramifications. The effect of foreign investment in the United States is of special concern when a foreign investor chooses to invest in a U.S. company that does business with the Federal Government. There is even a greater concern when the U.S. company is a defense contractor.[1]

§ 18:18 Restrictions on ownership

U.S. laws and regulations are generally receptive to foreign investors. However, they may prohibit foreign ownership in certain industries and place restrictions on foreign ownership in others, particularly where the foreign acquisition is of a U.S. company whose production is important to national security.

Under the so-called "Exon-Florio Provisions," the United States may block any acquisition or merger of U.S. companies by or with foreign interests when, in the view of the President, the foreign interest exercising control over the U.S. entity might take action that threatens to impair the national security.[1] Unlike the export control laws and industrial security regulations (i.e., regarding

---

[4]United States ex re. Hicks v. Oracle Corp., No. 03-CV-422, settlement announced (D. Md. Oct. 10, 2006).

[Section 18:17]

[1]Although this section of the chapter focuses on foreign investment and ownership of U.S. companies, the growth of mergers, acquisitions, and other types of business relationships between United States defense companies and foreign firms in general has created some conflict within DOD regarding the need to protect national security and the need to recognize the trend toward a globalized economy. *See* The Business Combinations Desk Book, available at http://www.acq.osd.mil/ip/docs/business_combinations_desk_book.pdf.

[Section 18:18]

[1]31 C.F.R. § 800.101, implementing Defense Production Act of 1950, tit. VII, § 721, as amended by the Foreign Investment and National Security Act of 2007, Pub. L. No. 110-49, 121 Stat. 246.

§ 18:18　　　　　　Government Contract Compliance Handbook

restrictions on access to classified information), the Exon-Florio Provisions are not aimed at preventing the unauthorized disclosure of sensitive information. Rather, the provisions are aimed at maintaining control over the U.S. industrial base necessary to national security.[2]

The Exon-Florio Provisions rely on *voluntary notification* for their enforcement. Parties to a foreign acquisition of a U.S. business may voluntarily notify the Committee on Foreign Investment in the United States (CFIUS) of the acquisition.[3] But should CFIUS determine a transaction for which no voluntary notice has been filed may raise national security concerns, CFIUS may request notice be filed.[4] Based on the information provided, CFIUS reviews the acquisition and may permit the transaction, if the committee deems appropriate.[5] If the committee feels the transaction should be prohibited, cannot reach an decision, or requests the President make the determination, CFIUS shall submit a report to the President detailing the committee's findings.[6] The President then determines the action he will take.[7]

While there is no requirement that parties to a foreign acquisition notify CFIUS of the transaction, given the current emphasis on national security concerns, as a matter of due diligence, legal practitioners generally advise parties to notify CFIUS of all foreign acquisitions because the "cost" of miscalculating the President's reaction (ordering divestment, for example) is rather significant. For example, on September 28, 2012, the President ordered a company to divest interests in four wind farm companies in Oregon. The President determined evidence was sufficiently credible that the acquisition by the company, which was ultimately controlled by citizens of the People's Republic of China, threatened to impair US national security.[8] Note that CFIUS approval does not ensure that the transaction can be completed. Thus, for example, in 2006 a United Arab Emirate company's proposed acquisition of a firm that ran operations at six of the largest U.S. ports, which CFIUS had approved, was so severely criticized by Congress that the transaction was never completed.

Should you submit a notification to CFIUS, or if you are providing information in response to a CFIUS investigation, you will be

---

[2]31 C.F.R. § 800.224.
[3]31 C.F.R. § 800.401(a).
[4]31 C.F.R. § 800.401(b).
[5]31 C.F.R. §§ 800.504, 800.506(d).
[6]31 C.F.R. § 800.506.
[7]31 C.F.R. § 800.601.
[8]See Presidential Order "Regarding the Acquisition of Four U.S. Wind Farm Project Companies by Ralls Corporation," September 28, 2012.

required to certify the information is accurate and complete.[9] Note that any matieral misstatement or omission in a notice or false certification—either intentionally or through gross negligence—exposes your company to a $250,000 civil penalty for each violation.[10]

§ 18:19 Restrictions on access to classified information

Acquiring a company that has or requires access to classified information raises potentially significant problems, as access to classified information is denied to all persons, including U.S. citizens, unless and until they have been granted a personal security clearance, and the facility at which the classified information will be used has been granted a facility security clearance (FCL).[1] When a parent-subsidiary relationship exists between two companies, the parent company must have an FCL of the same or higher classification as the subsidiary unless formal action is taken by the parent's board of directors or similar executive body to exclude the parent from all access to either (a) classified information held by the subsidiary, or (b) classified information held by the subsidiary that is of a higher security clearance level than the parent's FCL.[2]

Foreign access to U.S. classified information is severely restricted. Special procedures must be implemented in the case of a foreign acquisition of a U.S. company doing classified work to ensure that the foreign interests neither have access to nor control over the classified information involved. The same rules regarding parent-subsidiary relationships apply to foreign interests acquiring U.S. companies, with the added complexity that foreign persons are generally prohibited from being granted either personal or facility security clearances.[3] Thus, foreign interests acquiring U.S. companies doing classified work will generally be prohibited from having access to, or control over, classified information involved in such work. Rather, the parties are required to implement special procedures to ensure that the foreign interests do not have such access.

§ 18:20 Methods to protect classified information

DOD, the agency generally responsible for protecting classified

---

[9] 31 C.F.R. §§ 800.202, 800.402(l), 800.701(c).

[10] 31 C.F.R. § 800.801(a).

[Section 18:19]

[1] National Industrial Security Program Operating Manual 2-100 and 2-200(a) (Feb. 2006).

[2] National Industrial Security Program Operating Manual 2-109.

[3] National Industrial Security Program Operating Manual 2-209.

§ 18:20   GOVERNMENT CONTRACT COMPLIANCE HANDBOOK

information, recognizes five methods by which a company can ensure that classified information is protected from foreign access. These are (1) a board resolution, (2) a voting trust agreement, (3) a proxy agreement, (4) a reciprocal security agreement, and (5) a special security agreement.

1. *Board Resolution.* The easiest method of controlling access is via a resolution by the company's board of directors certifying that the foreign interests will not have access to classified information or occupy positions that would enable foreign owners to influence company policies and practices in the performance of classified contracts.[1] While a board resolution is usually the easiest method of controlling access, its use is limited to cases where the foreign person does not own voting interests sufficient to elect, or otherwise is not entitled to representation on the U.S. company's governing board. In the board resolution to control access to classified information, the board shall (1) identify the foreign shareholder and describe the type and number of foreign-owned shares, (2) acknowledge the company's obligation to comply with all industrial security program and export control requirements, (3) certify that the foreign shareholder can be effectively precluded from unauthorized access to all classified information and will not be permitted to hold positions that may enable it to influence the performance of classified contracts, and (4) provide for an annual certification acknowledging the continued effectiveness of the resolution.[2]

2. *Voting Trust Agreement & Proxy Agreement.* The voting trust agreement and proxy agreement are arrangements whereby the foreign owner relinquishes most rights associated with ownership of the company to cleared U.S. citizens approved by the Federal Government. Unlike the board resolution, these methods are acceptable even where a foreign interest owns a majority of the voting stock of the firm or the foreign stockholders are in a position to control, or have the dominant influence over, the business management of the firm.

Under a voting trust or proxy agreement, the foreign stockholders transfer their stock voting rights to the trustees or proxy holders, all of whom must become directors of the cleared company's board. The agreements must unequivocally provide for the exercise of all prerogatives of ownership by the trustees or proxy holders "with complete freedom to act independently from

---

[Section 18:20]

[1]National Industrial Security Program Operating Manual 2-303(a).
[2]National Industrial Security Program Operating Manual 2-303(a).

the foreign owners."[3] However, the trustees or proxy holders are not prohibited from consulting with the foreign stockholders or vice versa, where otherwise consistent with U.S. laws, regulations, and the terms of the voting trust or proxy agreement.

The voting trustees or proxy holders must assume full responsibility for the voting interests in such a way as to ensure that the foreign owners are insulated from the cleared company and are placed solely in the status of beneficiaries. The company must organize and finance itself so as to be capable of operating as a viable business entity independent of the foreign owners.[4]

3. *Limited FCL Under Reciprocal Security Agreement.* While the United States generally denies personal and facility clearances to non-U.S. persons, limited clearances may be available to foreign-owned U.S. companies where the foreign country has a reciprocal industrial security agreement with the United States. The United States has entered into reciprocal agreements with several countries that permit FCLs to be granted to companies under ownership by nationals of the countries party to such agreements. Access limitations are inherent in the granting of limited FCLs.[5]

A limited FCL may be granted on satisfaction of the following criteria: (1) there is an Industrial Security Agreement with the foreign government of the country from which the foreign ownership is derived, and (2) release of classified information conforms with the U.S. National Disclosure Policy.[6] Where these criteria cannot be satisfied, a limited FCL may be granted where there is a compelling national security need to do so.[7] The main advantage of this method for the foreign investor is that, unlike the case with voting trusts and proxy agreements, the investor is able to maintain control over the management of the U.S. company.

4. *Special Security Agreement.* As its name implies, the use of a special security agreement as a means of addressing the security concerns of foreign ownership and control of a U.S. company is tailored to the specific situation. Thus, a special security agreement may be used when a foreign interest owns a majority of a U.S. company and a voting trust or proxy agreement is inappropriate for some reason. A special security agreement imposes substantial industrial security and export control measures within the corporate practices and procedures, requires active involvement of senior managers and board members in security

---

[3] National Industrial Security Program Operating Manual 2-303(b)(1).
[4] National Industrial Security Program Operating Manual 2-303(b)(2).
[5] National Industrial Security Program Operating Manual 2-309.
[6] National Industrial Security Program Operating Manual 2-309(a).
[7] National Industrial Security Program Operating Manual 2-309(b).

§ 18:20   Government Contract Compliance Handbook

matters, provides for the establishment of a Government Security Committee to oversee classified matters, and preserves the foreign shareholder's right to a direct voice in the management of the company while denying unauthorized access to classified information.[8]

V. DUE DILIGENCE REVIEW

§ 18:21 Generally

A "due diligence review" is an organized investigation, analysis, and resolution of the principal issues likely to be of importance in a business combination. Prudence dictates that if you are contemplating acquiring or merging with a Government contractor, you will need to consider more than simply the assets, personnel, liabilities, and business prospects of the companies in question. Your due diligence review of the transaction must consider matters that are peculiar to Government contracting. Experience has shown that any acquisition or merger that takes place without a focused and specific due diligence assessment of possible Government contracts problems invites trouble for the resulting company or companies.

A due diligence review usually requires a visit to the company that is to be acquired. The visit may be as short as a day or may last for a week or more. The review may be conducted by your personnel, by outside experts, or by a combination of both. The key is to make sure that you have a checklist summarizing what to look for and that you have sufficient expertise to spot potential problems and bring them to management's attention.

§ 18:22 Due diligence checklist

A prudent due diligence review takes a combination of sound common sense and Government contracting expertise. The following checklist highlights issues that should be considered in any acquisition or merger involving Government contractors.

1. *Experience of key personnel*
   a. Government contracts expertise?
   b. Quality control expertise?
   c. Accounting expertise?
   d. Estimating expertise?
   e. Cost Accounting Standards expertise?
   f. What are the training procedures for each type of employee?
   g. What is the availability of legal and accounting advice?

---

[8]National Industrial Security Program Operating Manual 2-303(c).

ACQUISITIONS & MERGERS   § 18:22

  h. Are there hotlines for such advice? For any other type of problems?
  i. Have there been any reports of misconduct?
 2. *Company Organization*
  a. Is the compliance function independent from the marketing function?
  b. Who controls marketing?
  c. Who has the final say regarding all decisions of the contractor?
  d. Is there undue pressure on employees to meet sales quotas?
  e. Does the contractor grant authority to any agents or representatives to bind the company?
 3. *Government & customer relations*
  a. What are the contractor's relations with the Government agency's Administrative Contracting Officer?
  b. Does the contractor have good relations with the agency's auditing personnel?
  c. Are there good relations between contractor personnel and the Procuring Contracting Officer who actually awards the contracts?
  d. Is the agency Inspector General involved in any investigations of the company?
  e. Does the contractor maintain good relations with the people from the agency who monitor Government property (property owned by the Government but in the possession of the contractor, whether acquired under a contract or otherwise)?
  f. Are there good relations between the prime contractor and subcontractors?
  g. What are the outstanding or open issues with each of these groups?
 4. *Gratuities & kickbacks*
  a. Does the company have written compliance procedures or an employee code of conduct, and are all employees aware of these rules?
  b. What are the contractor's policies, and have those policies been articulated adequately to all employees?
  c. Does the contractor perform any compliance audits or seek to control this problem in any other way?
  d. Are there any outstanding issues? What is being done about them?
 5. *Internal audits*
  Do audits for the past five years raise any red flags?

6. *Cost accounting & estimating*
   a. Is the contractor's system for estimating costs adequate?
   b. Are unallowable costs excluded from billings, etc.?
   c. Are travel costs within limits?
   d. Does the contractor comply with all Cost Accounting Standards?
   e. Is the contractor's Cost Accounting Standards Disclosure Statement accurate? Is it up-to-date? Has it been approved by the Government agency?
   f. Have any accounting changes by the contractor been reported to the Government agency? What impact will they have?
   g. Have independent research and development and bid and proposal costs that are not required by contract been accounted for properly?
7. *Cost or pricing data system*
   a. Are there written procedures under which the contractor submits the data it has used in determining cost or price?
   b. Has the contractor complied with the written procedures?
   c. Do the procedures comply with the statutory requirements of the Truth in Negotiations Act and federal regulations?
   d. Does the contractor perform internal audits to ensure the accuracy of its cost or pricing data?
   e. Are there any defective pricing disputes with the Government pending?
8. *Commercial products*
   a. If the contractor sells to both the Federal Government and to commercial customers, does it adequately segregate its commercial and noncommercial work?
   b. Has the contractor claimed an exemption from the requirements of the Truth in Negotiations Act based on its sales of commercial items?
9. *Progress payments*
   a. Are the procedures used by the contractor to receive progress payments adequate and legal?
   b. Does the contractor's billing system exclude unallowable costs?
10. *Status of indirect cost-rate settlement*
    a. For what years has the company negotiated final indirect cost-rate settlements with the Government?

b. Are any audits completed or underway?
c. Approximately how much money in indirect costs is in dispute?
11. *GSA schedule*
   a. How was the customer of comparison established?
   b. How does the company track sales to ensure that it is in compliance with most favored customer and price reduction provisions?
12. *Quality assurance system*
   a. What is the scope of the contractor's written procedures for assuring quality?
   b. Has a Government agency rejected any items or suspended its acceptance of any items for quality assurance reasons?
   c. Are there any outstanding disputes with the Government regarding quality assurance?
   d. Are quality assurance problems covered by the contractor's warranties?
   e. Does the contractor have a system under which it audits its own quality of production?
13. *Material controls*
   a. Is there an adequate inventory system to keep track of all property belonging to the Government, whether acquired under the contract or otherwise?
   b. How does the company track ongoing compliance with Buy American Act and Trade Agreements Act requirements?
14. *Security* (where classified contracts are involved)
   a. What is the status of security at all of the contractor's facilities?
   b. Has anyone ever conducted an audit of the contractor's security system? What were the results?
   c. Are there any outstanding security violations?
   d. Is the contractor currently performing contracts with specific security clearance requirements? If so, will the merger or acquisition jeopardize those contracts?
15. *Environmental audits*
   a. Has the contractor ever been cited for any environmental regulation violations?
   b. Does the contractor have written procedures in place to address environmental issues inherent to its business?
   c. Are pertinent contractor employees aware of and familiar with these procedures?

d. Does the contractor perform periodic self-audits in this area?
16. *Contract claims*
    a. Are there any existing disputes with the Government regarding the payment of money or the interpretation of contract terms?
    b. What is the status of those disputes?
    c. Does the contractor have a system for preparing and verifying claims that arise from the disputes? What is that system?
17. *Review of sample contract files*
    a. Are contract files accessible and in good order?
    b. Does the review of a random selection of three or four contract files reveal any disputes or other outstanding issues?

Chapter 19

International Sales

I. OVERVIEW
§ 19:1   Scope note

II. EXPORT REGULATIONS

A. INTERNATIONAL TRAFFIC IN ARMS REGULATIONS

§ 19:2   Exports
§ 19:3   Deemed Exports
§ 19:4   Re-exports
§ 19:5   Significant Military Equipment
§ 19:6   Brokering
§ 19:7   Registration
§ 19:8   Temporary imports
§ 19:9   Penalties

B. EXPORT ADMINISTRATION REGULATIONS

§ 19:10   Exports
§ 19:11   Deemed Exports
§ 19:12   Re-exports
§ 19:13   Non-Country Specific Restrictions
§ 19:14   Other
§ 19:15   Penalties
§ 19:16   Office of Foreign Assets Control Regulations
§ 19:17   How To Recognize The Problem

C. COMPLIANCE INITIATIVES

§ 19:18   Both the DDTC and the BIS provide guidance regarding the initiatives that companies might undertake to ensure their compliance with U.S. export control laws. Briefly, companies should:

III. FOREIGN CORRUPT PRACTICES ACT

A. ANTI-BRIBERY PROVISIONS

§ 19:19   Prohibited Payments

§ 19:20   Permitted Payments
§ 19:21   Your Affirmative Defenses
§ 19:22   Penalties
§ 19:23   International Initiatives

B. ACCOUNTING PROVISIONS

§ 19:24   Required Records And Controls
§ 19:25   Penalties

C. HOW TO RECOGNIZE THE PROBLEM

§ 19:26   Generally
§ 19:27   Examples

D. COMPLIANCE INITIATIVES

§ 19:28   Educate your employees
§ 19:29   Beware of misconduct
§ 19:30   Seek an advisory opinion from the government
§ 19:31   Implement adequate recordkeeping

IV. ANTIBOYCOTT PROVISIONS.

A. EXPORT ADMINISTRATION REGULATIONS

§ 19:32   Prohibitions
§ 19:33   Penalties

B. INTERNAL REVENUE ADMINISTRATION

§ 19:34   Generally

C. HOW TO RECOGNIZE THE PROBLEM

§ 19:35   Generally
§ 19:36   Examples

D. COMPLIANCE INITIATIVES

§ 19:37   Educate your marketing staff
§ 19:38   Review contract documents carefully
§ 19:39   Refuse to supply boycott-related information
§ 19:40   Monitor your agents' and partners' actions
§ 19:41   Report boycott requests

V. RESTRICTIONS ON AGENTS & REPRESENTATIVES.

§ 19:42   Generally
§ 19:43   How to recognize the problem

INTERNATIONAL SALES § 19:2

§ 19:44 Examples
§ 19:45 Compliance initiatives
§ 19:46 Recommendations

> **KeyCite®:** Cases and other legal materials listed in KeyCite Scope can be researched through the KeyCite service on Westlaw®. Use KeyCite to check citations for form, parallel references, prior and later history, and comprehensive citator information, including citations to other decisions and secondary materials.

I. OVERVIEW

§ 19:1 Scope note

Many companies are currently marketing their products and services overseas. With the prospect of greater trade with an expanded European Union, China, and East Asia, there will be increased opportunities for international sales in the future.

Sales by American companies outside of the U.S. are governed by a complex set of rules and regulations. For example, if your company intends to export any military supply or service, your company will be subject to several separate sets of specific rules that apply to such transactions. In addition, you will be subject to the rules that apply to foreign sales generally, such as U.S. export regulations, the Foreign Corrupt Practices Act, the antiboycott provisions, and the restrictions on use of agents and representatives. This chapter will discuss both the requirements and restrictions on the sale of military-related items, and those that apply to foreign sales generally. The next chapter discusses the rules that apply to sales under the Foreign Military Sales program.

II. EXPORT REGULATIONS

A. INTERNATIONAL TRAFFIC IN ARMS REGULATIONS

§ 19:2 Exports

Exports from the United States are regulated, for the most part, by the International Traffic In Arms Regulations ("ITAR")[1] or the Export Administration Regulations.[2] As its name implies, the ITAR regulates the export of defense related items. The ITAR is administered by the Directorate of Defense Trade Controls

---

[Section 19:2]
[1] 22 C.F.R. §§ 120 to 130.
[2] 15 C.F.R. §§ 732 to 774.

579

§ 19:2   GOVERNMENT CONTRACT COMPLIANCE HANDBOOK

("DDTC") of the United States Department of State.

The ITAR regulatory scheme is simple. The ITAR requires, with very limited exceptions, that one obtain the approval of the DDTC before exporting any defense related article, technical data or service.[3] The very limited exceptions apply primarily to exports to Canada.

Articles subject to the ITAR are listed on the United States Munitions List ("USML").[4] The List includes twenty-one categories of articles. DDTC places articles on the USML based on whether the item provides a critical military or intelligence advantage,[5] and whether the item has properties peculiarly responsible for achieving or exceeding controlled performance levels, characteristics or functions referenced on the USML.[6] Items will also be treated as being listed on the USML if the item provides the equivalent performance capabilities of an item that is listed.[7] The DDTC has, in recent years, revised the USML to be more specific and descriptive so that one can determine whether any particular item is, or is, not a defense article simply by reviewing the USML. As the preceding sentences indicate, however, there is still a matter of judgment involved in determining whether any particular item is, or is not, a defense article. One should, therefore, be cautious about concluding that an item with defense applications is not a defense article simply because it is not specifically referenced on the USML.

"Technical data" and "services" are defined with reference to defense articles. "Technical data" is defined as "[i]nformation . . . which is required for the design, development, production, manufacture, assembly, operation, repair, testing, maintenance or modification of defense articles."[8] "Technical data" also includes any classified information related to defense articles.[9] "Technical data" does not include, however, information which is in the public domain.[10]

"Defense services" are defined as the furnishing of assistance to foreign persons in the design, development, engineering, manufacture, production, assembly, testing, repair, maintenance, modification, operation, demilitarization, destruction, processing

---

[3]22 C.F.R. §§ 123.1(a), 124.1 and 125.2 and 125.3.
[4]22 C.F.R. § 120.6.
[5]22 C.F.R. § 120.3(b).
[6]22 C.F.R. § 120.41(a)(1).
[7]22 C.F.R. § 120.3(a)(2).
[8]22 C.F.R. § 120.10(a)(1).
[9]22 C.F.R. § 120.10(a)(2).
[10]22 C.F.R. § 120.10(b).

or use of defense articles.[11] As with technical data, the furnishing of defense services constitutes an "export" regardless of where the assistance is furnished.[12] "Defense services" also include military training of foreign persons, again whether in the United States or abroad.[13]

Perhaps the most common method of obtaining DDTC approval to export is via an application for an export license. Form DSP-5 is the license application for the permanent export of unclassified defense items.[14] Form DSP-85 is the license application for the permanent export of classified defense items.[15]

Oftentimes, United States exporters will want to do more than simply export a defense article. Oftentimes, the United States exporter will want to provide the recipient with technical assistance and/or license the recipient to manufacture a defense article abroad. Approval of such activities is obtained via a Technical Assistance Agreement or Manufacturing License and Technical Assistance Agreement.[16] Despite their use of the word "agreement," Technical Assistance Agreements and Manufacturing Licenses and Technical Assistance Agreements are licenses. The ITAR dictates the terms of the "Agreements."[17] Business arrangements between the United States exporter and the recipient are set forth in separate agreements between the exporter and the recipient.

Once the DDTC approves the Agreement, the United States exporter may export technical data referenced in the Agreement without need for any further license approval from the DDTC.[18] The United States exporter must, however, separately obtain approval to export hardware associated with the Agreement.

The ITAR also provides for distribution licenses allowing the United States exporter to export defense articles to warehouses abroad for further distribution within a defined territory and to defined end-users.[19] Such licenses obviate the need separately to obtain DSP-5 licenses for the repeat export of articles to the same end-users.

---

[11] 22 C.F.R. § 120.9(a)(1).
[12] 22 C.F.R. § 120.9(a)(1).
[13] 22 C.F.R. § 120.9(a)(3).
[14] 22 C.F.R. § 123.1(a)(1).
[15] 22 C.F.R. § 123.1(a)(4).
[16] 22 C.F.R. § 124.1.
[17] 22 C.F.R. §§ 124.7 and 124.8.
[18] 22 C.F.R. § 124.3(a) and (b).
[19] 22 C.F.R. § 124.14.

§ 19:3 Deemed Exports

The ITAR defines "exports" with respect to technical data to include not only sending technical data outside of the United States but also disclosing technical data to persons who are not citizens or permanent residents of the United States (or protected refugees) regardless of where the disclosure takes place. Thus, disclosing, in the United States, technical data to a person who is not a citizen or permanent resident of the United States (or a protected refugee) constitutes an export of that data with the country of destination taken to be the country of citizenship of such person. This is the so-called "deemed export" rule.

Deemed exports can arise in a variety of settings. Engaging foreign persons as employees, technical meetings attended by foreign persons and plant tours by foreign persons can all implicate the deemed export rule.

§ 19:4 Re-exports

The ITAR regulates not only the export of defense articles, technical data and services. It also regulates the re-export of such items. With limited exceptions, the recipient of United States defense articles or technical data cannot re-export - i.e. cannot transfer such articles or data to others - without the prior approval of the DDTC.[1] This requirement merits special note inasmuch as, unlike the United States, most nations do not regulate re-exports from their countries. Foreign recipients of United States exports are, therefore, likely not to be aware of this requirement. Accordingly, the United States exporter should take measures to advise the recipients of its items that they cannot re-export those items without the approval of the DDTC. In fact, the ITAR requires the United States exporter to advise the recipient of the restrictions on re-exporting and prescribes language that the United States exporter must include in its shipping, or similar, documents advising the recipient of the same.[2]

The ITAR does provide for limited exceptions to the requirement that the recipient obtain the approval of the DDTC before re-exporting items. Thus, recipients may, without the prior approval of the DDTC, re-export United States origin components incorporated into foreign defense articles to NATO, NATO agencies, the government of a NATO country, Australia, Israel, Japan,

---

[Section 19:4]

[1]22 C.F.R. § 123.9(a).

[2]22 C.F.R. § 123.9(b)(1).

INTERNATIONAL SALES § 19:6

New Zealand or the Republic of Korea.[3] This exception is not available, however, if the United States origin components are significant military equipment or major defense articles.

§ 19:5 Significant Military Equipment

"Significant military equipment" are articles for which special export controls are warranted because of their capacity for substantial military utility or capability.[1] The ITAR identifies articles of significant military equipment by marking them with an asterisk on the USML. Among those special controls, a person intending to export significant military equipment must not only obtain the approval of the DDTC, he must also have the recipient execute a DSP-83 Form, Non-Transfer and Use Certificate by which the recipient warrants that it will not transfer or use the significant military equipment otherwise than as set forth in the license.[2]

Similarly, the exceptions noted above for the re-export of Untied States orgin defense items to NATO, Australia, Israel, Japan, New Zealand or the Republic of Korea are not available in the case of significant military equipment valued at over $25 million.[3]

Finally, the DDTC is required to notify Congress before approving any Manufacturing License Agreement calling for the manufacture abroad of significant military equipment.[4]

§ 19:6 Brokering

The ITAR regulates not only the export of defense related items. It also regulates brokering in such items. The ITAR requires that persons obtain the approval of the DDTC before brokering the transfer of specified defense related items.[1] The specified items are ones of special military significance.

"Brokering" is broadly defined to include "any action on behalf of another to facilitate the manufacture, export, permanent import, transfer, reexport or retransfer of a U.S. or foreign

---

[3]22 C.F.R. § 123.9(a).

[Section 19:5]

[1]22 C.F.R. § 120.7.
[2]22 C.F.R. § 123.(b)(5).
[3]22 C.F.R. § 123.9(e).
[4]22 C.F.R. § 124.11(a).

[Section 19:6]

[1]22 C.F.R. § 129.4(a).

§ 19:6

defense article or service regardless of its origin."[2] The applicability of the brokering requirements are likewise broad. The requirements apply to: (i) any United States person, (ii) any foreign person located in the United States, and (iii) any foreign person located outside of the United States where the foreign person is owned or controlled by a United States person.[3]

There are certain exceptions. The phrase "on behalf of another" operates to except persons brokering defense articles or services on behalf of themselves. The most common situation is an employee brokering the manufacture or transfer of its employer's defense articles or services. Employees are not required to obtain approval to broker their employer's products. Nor is approval required for brokering the manufacture or transfer of defense articles or services wholly within or destined exclusively for NATO, any NATO country, Australia, Israel, Japan, New Zealand or the Republic of Korea.[4]

§ 19:7 Registration

In addition to regulating the export of defense related items, the ITAR requires that persons engaged in the business of manufacturing, exporting or temporarily importing defense items register with the DDTC.[1] It is worth noting that manufacturers are required to register regardless of whether or not they are involved in exporting.

Similarly, the ITAR requires that persons subject to the ITAR's brokering requirements register with the DDTC.[2] However, persons who are already registered with the DDTC as a manufacturer or exporter of defense items need not separately register as a broker. They can note their brokering activity on their manufacturer or exporter registration.[3]

§ 19:8 Temporary imports

In addition to regulating the export of defense related items, the ITAR also regulates the temporary import of defense related items. With a number of exceptions, the ITAR requires that one obtain the approval of the DDTC before temporarily importing

---

[2]22 C.F.R. § 129.2(b).
[3]22 C.F.R. § 129.2(a).
[4]22 C.F.R. § 129.5(b).

[Section 19:7]
[1]22 C.F.R. § 122.1(a).
[2]22 C.F.R. § 129.3(a).
[3]22 C.F.R. § 129.3(d).

any defense item.[1] The permanent import of defense items into the United States is regulated by the Bureau of Alcohol, Tobacco, Firearms and Explosives of the Department of Justice.

§ 19:9 Penalties

Significant penalties can be imposed for violations of the ITAR. Violators are subject to fines of up to $1 million and imprisonment for up to twenty years.[1] The defense items involved in any violation are also subject to be seized.[2] Perhaps the most significant penalty, at least for companies involved in exporting, is that the violator may be debarred - i.e. such person will not be permitted to export defense items for the length of the debarment.[3] Debarment essentially closes down the violator's export business for the length of the debarment.

Violators are well advised to consider voluntarily reporting their violations to the DDTC. The ITAR provides that voluntary disclosure is a mitigating factor that the DDTC will consider in determining what penalties, if any, to pursue.[4] Experience shows that the DDTC is more interested in fostering compliance than in imposing penalties. The DDTC will often forgo pursuing penalties - at least where the violation was innocent and the violator demonstrates a commitment to future compliance.

B. EXPORT ADMINISTRATION REGULATIONS

§ 19:10 Exports

With the exception of certain nuclear items, whose export is regulated by the Department of Energy, the Export Administration Regulations ("EAR") regulate the export of all non-defense related articles, technology and services. That is, the EAR regulates the export of all items whose export is not regulated by the ITAR. The EAR is administered by the Bureau of Industry and Security ("BIS") of the Department of Commerce.

Regulating a wider spectrum of items than the ITAR does, the EAR's licensing scheme is more complex than the ITAR scheme. Unlike the ITAR for which approval to export is always required, the EAR may, or may not, require that one obtain the prior approval of the BIS before exporting a non-defense related article,

---

[Section 19:8]

[1]22 C.F.R. § 123.3(a).

[Section 19:9]

[1]22 C.F.R. § 127.3; 22 U.S.C.A. § 2778(c).
[2]22 C.F.R. § 127.6.
[3]22 C.F.R. § 127.7.
[4]22 C.F.R. § 127.12(a).

§ 19:10   GOVERNMENT CONTRACT COMPLIANCE HANDBOOK

technology or service depending on the nature of the item and the country of destination. Generally, the less sophisticated the item and the more friendly the country of destination is to United States' interests, the more likely it is that one can export the item without approval. Conversely, the more sophisticated the item and the less friendly the country of destination is to the United States' interests, the more likely it is that approval to export is required.

To determine whether the approval of BIS is required, one must review the Commerce Control List and the Commerce Country Chart.[1] The Commerce Control List lists various products and technology organized in ten major categories.[2] Within each major category are a number of subcategories titled Export Control Classification Number ("ECCN"). Each ECCN describes the item(s) falling under the ECCN and the reason(s) for which the export of such items is controlled. The first step in determining whether approval to export is required is to identify the ECCN covering the item in question and the reason(s) for which the export of the item is controlled. Knowing the reason(s) for which export of the item is controlled, one can then review the Commerce Country Chart to determine if approval is required to export items controlled for that reason(s) to the country in question.[3]

If approval is required, the EAR prohibits one from exporting the item without the prior approval of the BIS. The typical method of approval is via an export license application.

Note that we speak above of "technology." The EAR does not use the phrase "technical data." It uses the word technology." The EAR defines "technology," however, in much the same way that the ITAR defines "technical data."[4]

§ 19:11 Deemed Exports

Like the ITAR, the EAR defines exports of technology to include disclosing technology to persons who are not citizens or permanent residents of the United States (or protected refugees) regardless of where the disclosure takes place.[1] Thus, disclosing technology within the United States to a person not a citizen or

---

[Section 19:10]

[1]15 C.F.R. § 774, Supp. 1.
[2]15 C.F.R. § 738.2(a).
[3]15 C.F.R. § 738.4.
[4]15 C.F.R. § 772.1.

[Section 19:11]

[1]15 C.F.R. § 734.2(b).

permanent resident of the United States (or a protected refugee) constitutes an export of the technology with the country of citizenship being taken as the country of destination. If the EAR requires that one obtain the approval of BIS before exporting the technology in question to the country of destination, the EAR requires that one obtain the approval of BIS before disclosing the technology to the foreign country's citizens within the United States.

§ 19:12 Re-exports

Like the ITAR, the EAR regulates the re-export of non-defense related items. Unlike the ITAR, however, approval to re-export is not required if the re-exported item contains only *de minimis* amounts of controlled United States' content.[1] If export of the item from the United States to the foreign country in question would require approval, the re-export of the item will require approval unless the re-exported items contains only *de minimis* amounts of controlled United States content.

The amount of controlled United States content that is considered to be *de minimis* depends on the country to which the item is to be re-exported. A foreign recipient of controlled United States content can combine the United States content with foreign content and re-export the combined item to countries friendly to United States' interests without BIS approval if the controlled content is less than twenty-five percent of the combined item.[2] In the case of countries less friendly to United States' interests, the foreign recipient must obtain BIS approval before re-exporting controlled United States content if such controlled content accounts for more than ten percent of the combined item.[3] The EAR lists the specific countries that qualify for the twenty-five percent *de minimis* rules. The *de minimis* rules do not apply to certain highly controlled items.[4] The re-export of any amount of United States content of such items requires approval.

The preceding paragraphs speak of "controlled" United States content. If the EAR would allow the export of the United States item to the country of destination without BIS approval, the foreign recipient can re-export the United States item to that country without BIS approval.

[Section 19:12]

[1] 15 C.F.R. § 736.2(b)(2).
[2] 15 C.F.R. § 734.4(d).
[3] 15 C.F.R. § 734.4(c).
[4] 15 C.F.R. § 734.4(a) and (b).

§ 19:13 Non-Country Specific Restrictions

The EAR may also restrict exports based on reasons other than the country of destination. Thus, the EAR identifies a number of persons and organizations to which one is prohibited from exporting.[1] These generally are persons or organizations who are suspected of being involved in supporting terrorism or narcotics trafficking or who have been found guilty of past violations of the EAR.

The EAR also prohibits one from exporting in defiance of a specific BIS directive prohibiting the same.[2] Such directives are generally aimed at specified persons or organizations. Similarly, the EAR prohibits proceeding with an export transaction while knowing that it is being carried out in violation of the EAR.[3]

§ 19:14 Other

Unlike the ITAR, the EAR provides for a number of standard exceptions allowing persons to export without BIS approval where, without the exception, approval would be required. The ECCN identifies the exceptions that are applicable to the items falling under the ECCN.

Unlike the ITAR, the EAR does not require persons to register with the EAR. Nor does the EAR regulate brokering of the manufacture or transfer of non-defense related items, or the temporary, or permanent, import of non-defense related items.

§ 19:15 Penalties

As with the ITAR, significant penalties can be imposed for violations of the EAR. Violators are subject to fines of up to 5 times the value of the export involved or $1 million whichever is greater, and imprisonment for up to ten years.[1] And as with the ITAR, violators can be debarred - i.e. they can be denied the right to export.[2]

Finally, as with the ITAR, the EAR encourages that persons voluntarily report suspected violations. Voluntary disclosure is a mitigating factor that the BIS will consider in determining what

---

[Section 19:13]

[1] 15 C.F.R. § 736.2(b)(5).
[2] 15 C.F.R. § 736.(2)(4).
[3] 15 C.F.R. § 736.2(b)(10).

[Section 19:15]

[1] 15 C.F.R. § 764.3(a)(2).
[2] 15 C.F.R. § 764.3(a)(2).

INTERNATIONAL SALES § 19:16

penalties, if any, to pursue.³ As with the DDTC, experience shows that the BIS is more interested in fostering compliance than in imposing penalties. The BIS will often forgo pursuing penalties - at least where the violation was innocent and the violator demonstrates a commitment to future compliance.

§ 19:16 Office of Foreign Assets Control Regulations

The Office of Foreign Assets Control ("OFAC") of the Department of the Treasury implements United States embargos. The embargos, and the OFAC regulations implementing them, are country specific. Some of the embargos are more comprehensive than others. There is a separate set of regulations for each embargoed country.[1]

Typically, however, the OFAC regulations will restrict exports to the embargoed country and further restrict United States persons' dealings with the embargoed country. The restrictions on dealings with embargoed countries apply irrespective of the nature of the dealings. Thus, the regulations will typically prohibit, for example, United States persons from assisting in business dealings between non-United States persons and the embargoed country. The OFAC export restrictions are repeated in the ITAR and EAR. Thus, if one complies with the ITAR and EAR export regulations, one will necessarily comply with the OFAC export restrictions. The OFAC restrictions on the activities of United States persons vis-à-vis the embargoed country have no counterpart in other regulations. One must review the OFAC regulations for the country in question to identify the restrictions.

In addition to implementing United States embargos against countries, the OFAC regulations also implement embargos against specified organizations, persons and activities. Thus, there are currently OFAC restrictions on Untied States persons' dealings with transnational criminal organizations,[2] with persons suspected of supporting terrorism[3] and with trade in rough diamonds.[4]

Formally, the OFAC regulations typically state that United States persons can engage in otherwise restricted activities after obtaining license approval from the OFAC do to so. However,

---

[3]15 C.F.R. § 764.5.

[Section 19:16]
[1]31 C.F.R. Parts 510 to 588.
[2]31 C.F.R. Part 590.
[3]31 C.F.R. Parts 594, 595 and 596.
[4]31 C.F.R. Part 592.

§ 19:16   GOVERNMENT CONTRACT COMPLIANCE HANDBOOK

OFAC seldom approves licenses for activities other than those recognized in the regulations.

As with the ITAR and the EAR, significant penalties can be imposed for violations of the OFAC regulations.

§ 19:17 How To Recognize The Problem

a. Generally.

Recognizing your export control obligations is relatively easy if you are exporting a tangible item to a foreign person. You can check the CCL and Munitions List to see if the item you intend to export requires an export license or other official approval. If your item is not restricted, you simply determine if an export license is required by checking the regulations. Many exports are not, however, so easy to categorize. Discussed below are some examples of the many situations in which an innocent act may run afoul of the export regulations.

b. Release of technical data.

A difficult problem arises when you are disclosing technical data to a foreign person. There are many common business situations that may involve the export of U.S. "know-how."

A disclosure of technical data can occur during an ordinary conversation or a preliminary sales pitch, it can occur visually through the demonstration of equipment or during a plant tour, or it can even happen when you permit a prospective foreign customer to view a specification list.[1] Further, the release of technical data need not occur outside of the U.S. to implicate export regulations. If you think in terms of disclosing U.S. "know-how," you will be able to recognize most situations that implicate the export regulations.

c. Examples.

The following are examples of situations in which a release of technical data can occur.

Carrying data abroad: Assume your company sells military hardware to a NATO country and you have planned a trip abroad to see the customer. Before you leave, the customer calls you to ask if you would bring some technical data on another one of your products for him to consider. You put the data package in your briefcase and fly to Europe. With just such an innocent act, you may have violated U.S. export regulations and subjected yourself and your company to criminal and administrative penal-

---

[Section 19:17]

[1] 22 C.F.R. § 120.17(a)(4); 15 C.F.R. § 770.3.

ties, seizure and forfeiture of the technical data, and suspension or debarment from future exporting.

Hiring foreign citizens: You are expanding your production facility as a result of a new contract you have been awarded for delivery of a telecommunications system to an Eastern European country. The export of your end product and the operational technical data to be delivered with the product have already been approved for export. You hire an individual who is a foreign citizen to assist in the design and development of a new component. You may have violated U.S. export regulations. The hiring of a foreign national to assist in the development and design of U.S. technology creates an export regulation issue. Any communication with a foreign national may be considered an export of U.S. "know-how" unless the required authorizations have been obtained.

Plant tour: You have just completed negotiations with a foreign customer and were careful to follow all the export regulations regarding the release of technical data during the preliminary negotiations. Your customer asks for a tour of your plant and you agree. While on the plant tour, your customer talks with some of your technical operators about another product you manufacture. The chances are good that both your plant tour and your technical expert's conversation have violated export regulations. Plant tours nearly always implicate export controls.

C. COMPLIANCE INITIATIVES

§ 19:18 Both the DDTC and the BIS provide guidance regarding the initiatives that companies might undertake to ensure their compliance with U.S. export control laws. Briefly, companies should:

i. Review their products, technical data and services and determine if their export is controlled by the ITAR or the EAR, and the appropriate USML category or ECCN applicable to each. Maintain a list of your determinations for each product and piece of technical data. This will both ensure that the company deliberately considers the regulations applicable to each product, piece of technical data or service, and facilitates the determination of what license approvals, if any, are required to export the product, technical data or service.

Request the DDTC to issue a commodity jurisdiction decision regarding any product or technical data of which you are unsure if it is regulated by the ITAR or the EAR. The BIS will also issue commodity jurisdiction decisions. However, because the DDTC is more conservative than the BIS, it is advisable to request commodity jurisdiction requests from the DDTC. Aeroflex, Inc, in 2014, settled charges of exporting products in violation of the

§ 19:18   GOVERNMENT CONTRACT COMPLIANCE HANDBOOK

ITAR, paying a civil penalty of $20 million, notwithstanding that Aeroflex had obtained commodity jurisdiction decisions from the BIS stating that the products were subject to the EAR not the ITAR. While the DDTC recognized the mitigating impact of Aeroflex having obtained jurisdiction decisions from the BIS, DDTC brought the charges noting that, regardless of the BIS' views, the products were subject to the ITAR and were exported in violation of the ITAR.[1]

ii. Mark technical data subject to the ITAR with legends indicating that the data cannot be exported or disclosed to foreign persons without the prior approval of the DDTC. Mark technical data subject to the EAR with legends indicating that the data may not be able to be exported to, or disclosed to foreign persons or citizens of, certain countries without the prior approval of the BIS.

iii. Adopt policies and procedures for ensuring the company's compliance with the ITAR and EAR. Distribute copies of the policies and procedures to employees involved in the export of such items, international marketing employees and employees travelling overseas.

iv. Periodically audit the company's compliance with its policies and procedures for ensuring compliance with the ITAR and EAR.

v. Establish a hotline by which employees can anonymously report suspected violations of the ITAR or EAR.

vi. Investigate any reports of suspected violations of the ITAR or EAR. Maintain records of the investigation and the company's conclusions.

vi. Consider reporting any violations of the ITAR or EAR to the DDTC or the BIS.

vii. Providing periodic training to all employees involved in exporting or coming into contact with foreign persons.

ix. Maintain records required by the ITAR and EAR.

x. Register with the DDTC if your company engages in the manufacturing or exporting of items subject to the ITAR.

It is critical, of course, that a company make reasonable efforts to follow its compliance policies and procedures. It is not sufficient simply that a company established policies and procedures. To this point, Raytheon Company, in 2013, paid a civil penalty of $8 million to settle charges of violations of the ITAR. There was no question that Raytheon had acceptable policies and procedures.

[Section 19:18]

[1](CITE) www.pmddtc.state.gov/compliance/consent_agreements/pdf/Aeroflex%20executed%20order.pdf.

It was rather that Raytheon did not make sufficient efforts to ensure that it employees followed them.[2]

III. FOREIGN CORRUPT PRACTICES ACT
A. ANTI-BRIBERY PROVISIONS
§ 19:19 Prohibited Payments

Enacted in 1977, the Foreign Corrupt Practices Act ("FCPA") has become a staple of international business transactions. At its heart, the FCPA is simple. It prohibits bribery of foreign officials in the conduct of business. The FCPA consists of two parts. The one part, the so-called anti-bribery provisions, prohibit the bribing of foreign officials.[1] The second part, the so-called books and records provisions, requires one to maintain books and records accurately reflecting the company's business - that is, the company cannot set up secret accounts from which bribes can be paid.

The anti-bribery provisions provide that it shall be unlawful for any "domestic concern":

> To make use of the mails or other instrumentality of interstate commerce corruptly in further of an offer, payment, promise to pay, or authorization of the payment of any money, or offer, gift, promise to give or authorization of the giving of anything of value to . . . any foreign official for the purposes of . . . influencing any act or decision of such foreign official in his official capacity . . . in order to assist the domestic concern in obtaining or retaining business. . . .[2]

The reference to use of the mails and instrumentalities of interstate commerce are intended to provide a constitutional basis for Congressional action. Corruptly refers to the idea that one makes the offer, etc. with the intention of influencing the government official. Note that no bribe need be paid to find a violation of the FCPA. It is sufficient if a bribe was offered.

Foreign officials include not only foreign government officials, but officials of foreign political parties as well. The idea here is that in many foreign countries party officials play a larger role in

---

[2](CITE) www.pmddtc.state.gov/compliance/consent_agreements/pdf/raytheon_order.13.pdf.

[Section 19:19]

[1]There are, in fact, three separate statutory sections with mirror provisions aimed at prohibiting bribery by companies having classes of stock registered pursuant to the Securities and Exchange Act (15 U.S.C.A. § 78dd-2), "domestic concerns" (i.e. United States persons) (15 U.S.C.A. § 78dd-2) and persons subject to the jurisdiction of the United States (15 U.S.C.A. § 78dd-3). We reference here 15 U.S.C.A. § 78dd-2.

[2]15 U.S.C.A. § 78dd-2(a).

§ 19:19

government than they do in the United States. Thus, one may well be able to influence government officials via party officials. And as noted above, the courts have interpreted the phrase "obtaining or retaining business" broadly to include anything that might affect a company's business.

"Domestic concern" is defined as any citizen or resident of the United States or any company organized under the laws of the United States, or with its principal place of business in the United States.[3] That said, related provisions likewise prohibit bribery by any company registered with the United States Security and Exchange Commission and by any person physically in the United States.[4]

Significantly, the FCPA prohibits the indirect bribing of foreign government officials as well as direct bribing. That is, the FCPA prohibits one from offering or giving anything of value to a person while knowing that such person will use such thing of value to bribe a foreign official.[5] "Knowing" does not require absolute knowledge. It rather is a defined term and includes "being aware of a high probability" that the person will use the thing of value to bribe a foreign official.[6]

The typical situation here is where one engages an agent on a contingent basis to assist one in securing foreign business. Oftentimes, the agent is paid a lucrative commission - and, thus, has the money to pay a bribe and, because he/she is not paid the commission unless the business is consummated, the agent has some incentive to bribe officials to secure the business.

§ 19:20 Permitted Payments

The FCPA expressly allows one to pay "any facilitating or expediting payment to a foreign official, political party or party official the purpose of which is to expedite or to secure the performance of a routine governmental action. . . ."[1] These are commonly referred to as "grease, or facilitating payments." As the Department of Justice and Securities and Exchange Commission Resource Guide to the Foreign Corrupt Practices Act ("Resource Guide") notes, however, this exception applies only to "routine governmental action" which "does [not] involve non-discretionary

---

[3]15 U.S.C.A. § 78dd-2(h)(1).
[4]15 U.S.C.A. § 78dd-1 and 78dd-3.
[5]15 U.S.C.A. § 78dd-2(a)((3).
[6]15 U.S.C.A. § 78dd-2(h)(3).

[Section 19:20]

[1]15 U.S.C.A. § 78dd-2(b).

act."[2] For example, the Resource Guide states:

> Examples of "routine government action" include processing of visas, providing police protection or mail service, and supplying utilities like phone service, power, and water.[3]

The Resource Guide continues on to note that

> Routine government action does not include a decision to award new business or to continue business with a particular group. Nor does it include acts that are within an official's discretion or that would constitute misuse of an official's office.[4]

And while the exception does not depend "on the size of the payment" the size of the payment can be telling. A "large payment is more suggestive of corrupt intent. . . ."[5]

And as a word of caution, even though a payment may qualify as a facilitating payment under the FCPA, it may, nonetheless, be against the local law in the country in which the payment is made.

§ 19:21 Your Affirmative Defenses

Similarly, the FCPA permits, as affirmatives defense to a charge of violating the Act, the fact that the payment "was lawful under the written laws . . . of the foreign official's . . . country," or that the payment "was a reasonable and bona fide expenditure . . . ." The first of these two defense may be more apparent than real inasmuch as the Department of Justice and the Securities and Exchange Commission - the two organizations principally charged with enforcing the FCPA - note that "the written laws and regulations of countries rarely, if ever, permit corrupt payments" of their governmental officials.[1] It is not sufficient that the local law simply does not prohibit corrupt payments. The local law must affirmatively permit such payments.[2] Nor is it sufficient that, as a practical matter, "bribes may not be prosecuted under local law."[3]

The defense that the payment was a bona fide expenditure is more widely available. The FCPA itself gives the example of payment of "travel and lodging expenses . . . of a foreign official . . .

---

[2]Resource Guide to U.S. FCPA, pg. 25.
[3]Resource Guide to U.S. FCPA, pg. 24.
[4]Resource Guide to U.S. FCPA, pg. 24.
[5]Resource Guide to U.S. FCPA, pg. 24.

[Section 19:21]
[1]Resource Guide to U.S. FCPA, pg. 23.
[2]Resource Guide to U.S. FCPA, pg. 23.
[3]Resource Guide to U.S. FCPA, pg. 23

that [is] directly related to . . . the promotion, demonstration, or explanation of [the payor's] products or services," or the "execution or performance of a contract with a foreign government. . . . ."[4] The Resource Guide offers further guidance of steps that one may take to help ensure that the defense will cover the expenditure, including refraining from "select[ing] the particular official who will participate in the . . . proposed trip," "pay[ing] all costs directly to the travel and lodging vendors," and "ensur[ing] that the expenditures are transparent."[5]

§ 19:22 Penalties

Penalties for violations of the FCPA can be severe. Natural persons can be fined up to $100,000 and/or imprisoned for up to five years for each violation.[1] Non-natural persons can be fined up to $2 million.[2]

§ 19:23 International Initiatives

The United States long stood alone in prohibiting bribery of foreign government officials. In 1997, however, the Organization for Economic Cooperation and Development adopted a resolution calling for its member states to enact domestic legislation similar to the FCPA.[1] They have, and today many of the industrialized countries of the world have their own equivalent of the FCPA.

This international effort has had two important compliance related impacts. One, international companies and persons working in multiple countries may find themselves subject to a host of FCPA-like laws. Two, local authorities are increasingly cooperating across country lines to investigate and prosecute bribery. This has led to increased enforcement both in the United States and in foreign countries.

B. ACCOUNTING PROVISIONS

§ 19:24 Required Records And Controls

The accounting provisions of the FCPA serve as a complement to the anti-bribery provisions prohibiting companies from establishing hidden accounts from which bribes might be paid.

---

[4]15 U.S.C.A. § 78dd-2(c)(2).

[5]Resource Guide to U.S. FCPA, pg. 24.

[Section 19:22]

[1]15 U.S.C.A. § 78dd-2(g) and 78dd-3(e).

[2]15 U.S.C.A. § 78dd-2(g) and 78dd-3(e).

[Section 19:23]

[1]See Treaty Doc. 105-43, 105th Cong., 2nd Sess.

INTERNATIONAL SALES § 19:25

Specifically, the accounting provisions require that companies "make and keep books, records, and accounts which, in reasonable detail, accurately and fairly reflect the transactions and dispositions of the [company's] assets."[1] Companies are further required to "maintain a system of internal accounting controls sufficient to provide reasonable assurances that [among other things] transactions are executed in accordance with management's general or specific authorizations [and] permit preparation of financial statements in conformity with generally accepted accounting principles. . . ."[2] "Reasonable detail" and "reasonable assurances" are defined to mean "such level of detail and degree of assurance as would satisfy prudent officials in the conduct of their affairs."[3] Given that the accounting provisions are located within United States securities laws, one should expect that the expected standard is high.

Companies are responsible for ensuring the compliance not only of their own books and records but also those of any subsidiary company. Where, however, the company owns less than fifty percent of the stock of the subsidiary, the company is required only to act in "good faith to use its influence to the extent reasonable . . . to cause the [subsidiary] to devise and maintain a system of internal accounting controls" as set forth above.[4] Obviously, as the percentage ownership declines one might expect the parent's influence to decrease accordingly.

Unlike the anti-bribery provisions which apply to all persons subject to the jurisdiction of the United States, the accounting provisions apply only to companies issuing securities pursuant to the regulations of the United States Securities and Exchange Commission.[5]

§ 19:25 Penalties

The Accounting Provisions of the FCPA are part and parcel of the record-keeping requirements required by the Securities and Exchange Act of 1934. The penalties applicable to any violation are those applicable to violations of the Act and can include fines

---

[Section 19:24]
[1] 15 U.S.C.A. § 78m(b)(2).
[2] 15 U.S.C.A. § 78m(b)(2).
[3] 15 U.S.C.A. § 78m(b)(7).
[4] 15 U.S.C.A. § 78m(b)(6).
[5] 15 U.S.C.A. § 78m(b)(2).

§ 19:25   GOVERNMENT CONTRACT COMPLIANCE HANDBOOK

and imprisonment for willful violations.[1]

C. HOW TO RECOGNIZE THE PROBLEM

§ 19:26 Generally

If you are an issuer of securities, you may encounter compliance problems under both the accounting provisions[1] and the antibribery provisions[2] of the FCPA. If you are a domestic concern or individual subject to the FCPA, but not an issuer you need comply only with the antibribery provisions of the Act.[3]

A compliance problem may arise under the accounting provisions if you are not following accounting procedures that allow you to *track all payments* made to *foreign agents* or through *foreign bank accounts*. The FCPA accounting provisions attempt to prevent bribery of foreign officials by requiring issuers to maintain adequate records of financial transactions and transfers of funds and to make these accounts available for review through financial disclosures and periodic audits. The intent of this disclosure and recordkeeping requirement is to prevent creation and use of off-the-books accounts or slush funds for corrupt purposes.

A compliance problem may also arise if you have an *affiliate or subsidiary* in which you hold less than 50% of the voting stock. The same may be true with respect to joint ventures or teaming partners. You should have a policy of informing your foreign partners and affiliates of the FCPA's requirements and requiring them to comply.

Avoiding compliance problems under the Act also requires you to be aware of the actions of your officers, employees, and agents, as well as subsidiaries under your control. If any person is making payments to a foreign official *on your behalf*, you may have a compliance problem. Although certain grease payments to foreign government officials are allowed, *any* payment to a foreign official should be subject to scrutiny.

Remember that the antibribery provisions of the Act prohibit bribes paid to foreign officials to "obtain or retain" business.[4] Accordingly, if you encounter circumstances that are out of the ordinary accompanying your retention or acquisition of business,

---

[Section 19:25]

[1] 15 U.S.C.A. § 78m(u).

[Section 19:26]

[1] 15 U.S.C.A. § 78m(b).
[2] 15 U.S.C.A. § 78dd-1.
[3] 15 U.S.C.A. §§ 78dd-2, 78dd-3.
[4] 15 U.S.C.A. §§ 78dd-1, 78dd-2.

INTERNATIONAL SALES § 19:27

you may have a compliance problem. Such circumstances may be present when you acquire business in a foreign country that has routinely rejected American companies. Likewise, if a newly-hired agent is pulling in a great deal of business in a territory where others have failed continually, his practices may be suspect.

§ 19:27 Examples

Affiliate's accounting practices: Assume you are an issuer of securities registered under the Securities Exchange Act of 1934. Your foreign subsidiary, of which you own 49% of the voting stock, sells industrial equipment to various foreign countries. Your subsidiary is a German corporation, Rising Star, with its principal place of business in Berlin. You have painstakingly revamped your own internal accounting controls, and your assets are all carefully accounted for so as to meet the requirements of the recordkeeping provisions of the FCPA. You have no company policy dealing with the accounting practices of your subsidiaries, however, and you have not, to your knowledge, broached the subject with your subsidiary, Rising Star. You have long suspected that your subsidiary follows shoddy accounting procedures, yet your management insists there is nothing you can do about it since you do not control Rising Star.

An investigation of Rising Star uncovers secret accounts that were not reflected in its books. Funds from these accounts were used by agents and employees of Rising Star to bribe foreign officials to obtain business. Moreover, it was discovered that basic accounting methods would have uncovered the secret accounts which had been in existence for years. When approached by authorities, Rising Star's officials claim they were not aware of the accounting provisions of the FCPA because nobody had told them or, worse yet, they were aware but ignored the requirement to continue business as usual in Germany. The SEC then brings an action against you for violation of the accounting provisions of the Act.

You may be liable in this situation for *failure to use your influence* to cause your subsidiary to conform to the accounting provisions of the Act. Even though you do not control your subsidiary, you have a great deal of influence because of your ownership of 49% of the voting stock. If you can demonstrate a *good faith effort* to encourage your subsidiary to conform, you will have no liability in this type of situation. At a minimum, a good faith effort requires a policy that implements adequate accounting practices.

Payments for discretionary acts: You are a domestic concern operating in foreign country X. You sell computer hardware, and X controls the prices in your market. Your agent makes payments to the official in X who is responsible for authorizing price increases in the computer hardware market. You know that your agent makes the described payments, and you believe they are legitimate grease payments under the antibribery provisions of the FCPA.

You may be liable for a violation of the Act in this situation. The authorization of price increases requires an *exercise of discretion* by X's official. Remember that payments for acts that require the exercise of discretion by a foreign official are not permitted where the exercise of discretion is the functional equivalent of *obtaining or retaining business for you*. Because the price controls affect your participation in the computer hardware market of X, it may be that the actions of X's official are the functional equivalent of keeping you in business. Also, since there is no question that you *knew* your agent was making the payments, you will be liable for his corrupt payments.

Willful ignorance: You are a Delaware corporation attempting to enter a particular foreign market. To this end, you hire an agent in the foreign country after completing an exhaustive background check. You carefully draft your agent's agreement and require your agent to conform with the antibribery provisions of the FCPA. Your agent says "Don't you worry, I've never had problems with that before—I'm too smart for that."

Your agent's success is unbelievable and you are more than happy to pay his high fees in cash. Later, one of your competitors approaches you with circumstantial evidence of corrupt activity by your agent. The evidence includes photographs of your agent and high government officials together in various locations. You noticed such photographs yourself in your agent's office but were not overly concerned. Subsequently, it is discovered that your agent was bribing foreign government officials to obtain business for you. You disclaim liability for his actions, however, because you knew of no illegality.

You may be liable under the antibribery provisions of the FCPA. Although the Act makes you liable only if you knew of the bribes, you may be found to have willfully blinded yourself to the facts. The standard is far from clear, but it is certain that you may have knowledge of the improper conduct based on something *less than* concrete proof of your agent's impropriety. The thing to do in this situation is to be sensitive to your agent's actions, exercise due diligence, and follow up on your suspicions.

D. COMPLIANCE INITIATIVES

§ 19:28 Educate your employees

To comply with the FCPA, you must not allow your employees or agents to make corrupt payments to foreign officials to obtain or retain business. Accordingly, you must educate your employees and agents about the prohibitions in the FCPA.

You should establish a *written company policy* prohibiting all types of improper payments and formulate guidelines based on that policy and other ethical considerations. Distribute this written material to all officers and to any employee who may deal with foreign officials and be certain that the material is understood. You should also *train* your employees and agents regarding your policy and the differences between acceptable grease payments and improper bribes. Make sure the differences between acceptable payments and prohibited payments are understood.

§ 19:29 Beware of misconduct

You must not ignore the indicia of corrupt payments by your employees, agents, or third parties. As discussed above, you are liable under the FCPA for the acts of third parties if you *know* they are making bribes or even if you do *not* have actual knowledge of the misdeed but you *consciously disregard* the situation. To avoid potential problems, you should exercise due diligence and *investigate* appearances of impropriety.

§ 19:30 Seek an advisory opinion from the government

Perhaps the most important precaution available to you is the review procedure of the Department of Justice. While it may not be advisable to pursue this procedure in all cases, this procedure entitles you to request a statement from the Department about its present enforcement intentions under the antibribery provisions of the FCPA regarding any proposed business conduct. The FCPA requires the Attorney General to issue an opinion in response to specific inquiries within 30 days of receipt of all necessary information supporting the request. If the Department's opinion states that your conduct conforms with its current policy, there is a rebuttable presumption that your conduct conforms with the requirements of the Act.[1]

DOJ and US Securities and Exchange Commission November 14, 2012 released "A Resource Guide to the U.S. Foreign Corrupt Practices Act" which provides detailed information about the FCPA, its provisions and enforcement and presents hypotheticals, enforcement action examples, case law summaries, and DOJ opinion releases. If you intend to conduct work abroad, it is strongly encouraged that you consult this resource guide when

---

[Section 19:30]

[1]15 U.S.C.A. §§ 78dd-1(e)(1), 78dd-2(f)(1), 78dd-3.

§ 19:30 GOVERNMENT CONTRACT COMPLIANCE HANDBOOK

establishing your compliance program. The guide is available at http://www.justice.gov/criminal/fraud/fcpa/guide.pdf.

§ 19:31 Implement adequate recordkeeping

Compliance with the accounting provisions of the FCPA requires you to work with your accountant to implement an adequate system of recordkeeping. Of course, you cannot falsify records nor can you knowingly circumvent the accounting procedures you devise. The procedures you follow should satisfy you as a reasonable business person that no violations are occurring.

Instruct your subsidiaries in proper recordkeeping requirements under the Act and make a *good faith effort* to satisfy yourself that they are being met. Maintain copies of correspondence to your subsidiaries concerning compliance with the FCPA accounting provisions. These copies may help you establish that you made a good faith effort to encourage your subsidiary to comply with the Act.

IV. ANTIBOYCOTT PROVISIONS.
A. EXPORT ADMINISTRATION REGULATIONS
§ 19:32 Prohibitions

When one speaks of the "antiboycott provisions" one is generally referring to the antiboycott provisions of the Export Administration Regulations.[1] While addressing any boycott not authorized by the United States, the regulations were implemented in response to the Arab Boycott of Israel and are perhaps best explained in relation to the Arab Boycott.

The Arab Boycott of Israel was instituted soon after the founding of the State of Israel in 1948. The boycott is documented in[2] __ to which a number of Arab countries have, from time-to-time subscribed. The boycott might be thought of as operating on three levels. On the primary level, the boycotting countries refuse to deal with Israel, including government units and companies, or in Israeli goods. On the secondary level, the boycotting countries refuse to deal with persons dealing with Israel or in Israeli goods. And on the tertiary level, the boycotting countries refuse to deal with persons dealing with persons dealing with Israel or in Israeli goods.

[Section 19:32]

[1]15 C.F.R. Part 760.

[2]"The Arab Boycott Regulations," 3 Pa. Y.B. Int'l. Law 189 (1986) and "Unified Boycott of Israel: Law as Approved by the Council of the League of Arab States in its Twenty-Second Session Dated 11 December 1954," 4 Pal. Y.B. Int'l. Law 359 (1987-88).

§ 19:32

The refusals are typically implemented via questionnaires that the boycotting countries require contracting parties to complete. The questionnaires ask the contracting party to identify various information regarding the transaction in question, as well as the contracting party's dealings with Israel or in Israeli goods, etc. and to agree to adhere to the principles of the Arab Boycott of Israel. The boycotting country may request the same information and the same agreement via the contract, letters of credit, certificates of origin, etc.

The Antiboycott Provisions generally permit United States persons to comply with the primary level of an unauthorized boycott, but prohibit compliance with the secondary or tertiary levels of the boycott. Thus, one can, consistent with the Antiboycott Provisions agree not to deliver Israeli goods.[3] One cannot, however, agree not to deal generally with Israel or in Israeli goods - the secondary level. And one cannot agree not to deal with persons dealing with Israel or in Israeli goods - the tertiary level.[4]

In complying with the primary level of an unauthorized boycott, the Provisions require that one speak affirmatively, not negatively.[5] Thus, one can state, for example, that one will be delivering goods originating in a particular country or countries. One cannot, however, state that one will not deliver goods originating in Israel.

In related provisions, the Antiboycott Provisions prohibit United States persons from discriminating against other United States persons on the basis of race, religion, sex or national origin.[6]

In order to track the rigor with which unauthorized boycotts are being pursued and to aid in enforcement, the Provisions require United States persons to report any request to comply with an unauthorized boycott to the Office of Antiboycott Compliance of the United States Department of Commerce.[7] While one might report requests with respect to which one does not comply, as one might expect, companies complying with boycott related requests generally do not report the request and their violation. And, of course, one complying with a boycott request will provide the requesting country with information regarding such person's compliance with the request. It is, thus, typically the case that where the United States charges one with violations of the

---

[3]15 U.S.C.A. § 760.2(a)(1) and 760.3(a).
[4]15 U.S.C.A. § 760.2(a)(1).
[5]15 U.S.C.A. § 760.3(a), Example (ii).
[6]15 U.S.C.A. § 760.2(b)(1).
[7]15 U.S.C.A. § 760.5(a) and (b)(4).

§ 19:32   GOVERNMENT CONTRACT COMPLIANCE HANDBOOK

antiboycott provisions it also charges such persons with failing to report the boycott request and with providing information to the boycotting country as well. (*See, for example*, the Department of Commerce's settlement 2013 orders with *TMX Shipping, Inc.*,[8] *Digi-Key Corporation*,[9] *BAC Florida Bank*,[10] and *Baker Eastern, S.A.*[11])

Finally, the Antiboycott Provisions follow the rule that "silence is golden." That is, if there is a request to comply with an unauthorized boycott, the Provisions prohibit United States persons from advising whether they will, or will not comply.[12] Generally, all that one can respond is that one will deliver goods of a specified country. Similarly, United States persons are prohibited from providing, in response to an unauthorized boycott request, any information regarding the race, religion, sex or national origin of any United States person.[13]

§ 19:33 Penalties

The Antiboycott Provisions are part of the Export Administration Regulations. As such, the penalties for violations of the Antiboycott Provisions mirror those for the violation of the export control regulations. Violators are subject to fines of up to 5 times the value of the export involved or $1 million whichever is greater, and imprisonment for up to ten years.[1] And as with violations of the export control regulations, violators can be debarred - i.e. they can be denied the right to export.[2]

---

[8](CITE) efoia.bis.doc.gov/index.php/component/docman/doc_download/897-a737?Itemid

[9](CITE) www.expertprac.com/nt/a/getdocumentaction/i/53595

[10](CITE) efoia.bis.doc.gov/index.php/component/docman/doc_download/861-a731?Itemid

[11](CITE) efoia.bis.doc.gov/index.php/component/docman/doc_download/860-a732?Itemid

[12]15 U.S.C.A. § 760.2(d)(1).

[13]15 U.S.C.A. § 760(c)(1).

[Section 19:33]

[1]15 C.F.R. § 764.3(a)(2).

[2]15 C.F.R. § 764.3(a)(2).

INTERNATIONAL SALES § 19:35

B. INTERNAL REVENUE ADMINISTRATION

§ 19:34 Generally

The Internal Revenue Code ("IRC") contains its own set of antiboycott regulations.[1] Unlike the Department of Commerce's regulations, the IRC regulations are not generally applicable. They are rather aimed at persons claiming the tax benefits of the foreign tax credit and foreign sales corporations. To the extent that one is willing to forgo these benefits, one generally need not concern themselves with the IRC's provisions.

While there are differences between the requirements of the Department of Commerce and the IRC, conduct which violates the Commerce regulations will typically also violate the IRC provisions.

C. HOW TO RECOGNIZE THE PROBLEM

§ 19:35 Generally

To avoid liability under the antiboycott laws, you and your employees must become sensitive to boycott-related requests. Be on the lookout for anyone asking that you *refuse to deal* with particular countries, companies, or individuals or that you get your suppliers, subcontractors, or other companies to do the same. Beware of any *requests for information* concerning business dealings with specific countries or specific companies. Closely scan all contracts and *letters of credit* for these types of requests. If appropriate, *report* any such requests to the Commerce Department and report the same information to the Internal Revenue Service when you file your tax forms.

Antiboycott compliance problems usually involve Arab League countries. The Treasury Department publishes a quarterly list in the *Federal Register* of countries that may require cooperation with international boycotts.[1] When you conduct business with any of these countries or their nationals be especially sensitive to boycott-related requests. However, problems may arise in dealings in any country. A third party who is not from an Arab League country may nevertheless be complying with the boycott and make boycott-related requests. In particular, beware of special requests concerning Israel, Israeli companies or nationals, or members of the Jewish faith.

[Section 19:34]

[1]26 U.S.C.A. § 999.

[Section 19:35]

[1]*See* 26 U.S.C.A. § 999(a)(3).

§ 19:36 Examples

Certificate of origin: Assume that the government of a boycotting country contracts with your company for delivery of certain goods. The boycotter requires a certificate stating that (a) the goods did not originate in Israel, (b) the goods were not supplied by blacklisted persons, (c) the goods are not insured by blacklisted persons, (d) the goods were not shipped on a blacklisted carrier, and (e) the vessel carrying the goods did not call at a port in Israel. If you simply respond "no" to all questions, you have violated the EAA. You can, however, respond by listing specifically the names of the countries where the goods originated, the suppliers, the insurer, the carrier, and the ports where the carrier stopped.

Requests to boycott: Your company normally purchases automobile parts from a company that does business in Israel. You want to expand your nonautomobile operations into a boycotting country. So, in anticipation of a request from the boycotting country that you refuse to deal with companies doing business in Israel, you switch to a different parts manufacturer. Although you did not act in response to a boycott request, you acted for boycott reasons. Therefore, you violated the EAA.

You do not violate the EAA by complying with boycott-related requests that involve the sovereignty or territoriality of the boycotting country. For example, suppose your company receives an order from a boycotting country for a product that normally contains component parts made in Israel. You *can* substitute component parts from another country for the Israeli parts. You may comply with the boycotter's import prohibitions, even if the prohibitions are boycott-related.

Transfer of personnel: Your company receives a request from an Arab League country for a product that is normally made at a plant supervised by a Jewish manager. If you transfer another manager into the plant to replace the Jewish manager, you have violated EAA antiboycott restrictions on discriminating against a United States person on the basis of race, religion, sex, or national origin.

Agreement to refuse to do business: Your company receives an offer to bid on a contract in a boycotting country. The tender states that you must agree not to deal with companies on the boycotting country's blacklist. You do not know which companies are on the blacklist, and your bid makes no commitment regarding refusals to deal. Nonetheless, at the point that the boycotting country accepts your bid, you have violated the EAA because the terms of the tender are part of the contract.

D. COMPLIANCE INITIATIVES

§ 19:37 Educate your marketing staff

Your commercial dealings with foreign countries sponsoring or supporting boycott activities often begin with your marketing staff. Therefore, if you currently do business with foreign governments, your marketing staff must be aware of the unique restrictions imposed by the EAA.

The natural tendency of someone who is trying to make a sale is to give the customer what it wants. When doing business with boycotting countries, that attitude is extremely dangerous. The marketing representative, whether an employee of your company or an outside agent, must understand that information concerning foreign affiliations or relating to race, religion, or national origin is suspect and must not be provided to the foreign customer without careful consideration of the customer's boycott motives. Your representatives must not make commitments regarding terms of the proposed contract or letter of credit that directly or indirectly support boycott activities. In addition, your marketing representatives must report suspected boycott requests to responsible management officials for evaluation and appropriate action.

§ 19:38 Review contract documents carefully

Once you receive an order or contract from a foreign entity, review it carefully for boycott-related terms. Such terms may be included even though no reference was made to such requirements during the sales presentations or contract negotiations. Your careful review must extend to contract *supporting* documents, such as the letter of credit, shipping instructions, or requirements for processing visas for in-country delivery or training.

§ 19:39 Refuse to supply boycott-related information

Requests for boycott-related information may take several forms. For example, the customer may make requests during sales presentations concerning subcontracts with companies the foreign customer considers inappropriate. Likewise, the contract itself may require a list of company personnel responsible for in-country activities, including installation and training. The procedures or forms for requesting approval of personnel or for visas may solicit information concerning race, religion, or national origin. You must *not* supply *any* information that appears to be boycott motivated.

§ 19:40 Monitor your agents' and partners' actions

You or your company may be liable for antiboycott violations based on the actions of others. This liability includes violations by your employees, sales agents, and possibly subsidiaries, teaming partners, or joint venture partners. Liability stems either from traditional notions of the vicarious liability of a principal for the acts of his or her agent, or from statutory and regulatory obligations administered by the Commerce Department.

In either case, the essence of the liability is your ability to control the actions of the party who violated the antiboycott restrictions. This concept assumes that if you control the actions of the other person or company, you could prevent them from violating the law. Therefore, to comply with the law and the implementing regulations, you must be able to demonstrate that you make the effort to *oversee* the actions of the other parties to prevent violations.

§ 19:41 Report boycott requests

You must report to the Commerce Department all requests to comply with an international boycott. To satisfy this requirement, you, in turn, must impose a reporting obligation on those inside or outside your company who are likely to receive boycott-related requests.

Once information of a possible boycott-related request is received, you must investigate it sufficiently to enable you to determine whether it is significant enough to report to the Commerce Department. These decisions should be made with the advice of legal counsel.

V. RESTRICTIONS ON AGENTS & REPRESENTATIVES.

§ 19:42 Generally

It is common that companies seeking to market abroad engage agents to assist them. Oftentimes, the companies compensate the agents via fees contingent on the culmination of a sale. Engaging agents presents special concerns for compliance. Engaging agents on a contingent fee basis presents even more concern. That is not to say that one should not engage agents on a contingent fee basis. Rather it is to say that companies doing so need to make further compliance efforts to ensure that the agent does not act improperly (of if he or she does, the company is insulated from such improper activity).

The primary concern is with regard to the FCPA. The agent's fee being contingent on the culmination of the sale, the agent has a great interest in seeing the sale culminated. The concern is that if he or she believes that he or she must bribe a foreign official to have the sale culminated, he or she will do so. However innocent was the United States person engaging the agent, the

United States person will nonetheless come under suspicion. It is incumbent then on the United States person to be able to show that they had no reason to know that the agent might bribe a foreign official.

§ 19:43 How to recognize the problem

Liability for your agent's actions is indirect because it is his or her actions that give rise to the liability, not your actions. Therefore, you must be able to recognize the danger signs that suggest improper actions taken by your agents.

Be wary of any agent who *guarantees results*. This may be a sign that your agent will resort to any means necessary to fulfill his guarantee. Similarly, avoid using an agent whose reputation is questionable or who is known to have engaged in corrupt practices in the past.

If your agent proposes payment terms that are out of the ordinary, it may suggest that he or she engages in corrupt practices. Examples of *suspicious payment terms* include payment to a Swiss bank account, payment through a third country, payment in a fictitious name, or large, up-front payments in cash. By hiring a reputable agent and being sensitive to warning signs such as those mentioned above, you may avoid future compliance problems.

§ 19:44 Examples

Payment of expenses: You retain an agent in a foreign country and negotiate an agreement that merely specifies how the commission may be earned and calculated and that you will pay all reasonable expenses. All payments are to be made to a bank account in a third country in the name of a holding company created for tax purposes. Almost immediately, the vouchers for payment of expenses begin arriving in your office, and you pay them. Before you can even ask your agent about these questionable expenses, he calls to advise you that he obtained a large order from the Ministry of Defense. You decide not to spoil your relationship by questioning the expenses.

Your agent may have violated the FCPA, and your company may be held liable for the violation. You must limit the authority of your agent under the agency agreement to actions in compliance with U.S. and local laws. You must make the agreement and the obligation to pay commissions *contingent on* that compliance. You also must question all unjustified or excessive requests made under unusual circumstances for payment of expenses, commissions, or advances.

Guaranteed results: You are looking for an agent in a foreign

§ 19:44   GOVERNMENT CONTRACT COMPLIANCE HANDBOOK

country. As chance would have it, you are contacted by a person wishing to serve in this capacity. His resume indicates past contacts with important government officials. He guarantees quick results and asks for a relatively large retainer.

There may be nothing wrong with this arrangement, but it raises important questions. The agent should provide references in addition to the resume. You should check these through the Department of Commerce and with other companies doing business in the area. Do a complete background check to verify the information and the reputation of your potential agent. Finally, make sure your agency agreement protects your interests as well as the agent's.

§ 19:45   Compliance initiatives

Conduct Background Investigations: To guard against liability for your agents' illegal actions, you should investigate carefully the background of any agent before entering into an agency agreement. You can take several specific steps to determine whether you should engage a particular agent.

First, always require the prospective agent to provide you with *references*. Check the references and inquire into the agent's character through *independent sources* such as the U.S. Embassy or Consulate or other companies doing business in the area. One indication that an agent is legitimate is that his business is conducted in the agency name and is characterized by the conduct of regular business. You can generally gain adequate information through your contacts in the local business community.

Next, you should attempt to determine whether the agent has any *prior arrests or convictions* for bribery or a general reputation for dishonesty. Beware of any agent who guarantees success. There are no guarantees in sales, and such promises may hinge on improper influence and bribery. Cease discussions immediately with any agent who suggests that he can get business for you through improper means.

Negotiating & Drafting The Agency Agreement: Proper negotiation and drafting of the agency agreement may help you avoid liability for improper actions of your agent. When negotiating contract terms, you should carefully question the reasons for any *payment terms* that are out of the ordinary. Such payment terms suggest business practices that may be improper and that the agent is attempting to hide. You should determine whether the agent's fees are reasonable by obtaining as much information as you can on fees and costs of other agents in the area.

Any agreement with an agent should be *in writing*. You should include in your agreement the clauses that characterize a bona fide agency within the meaning of the procurement regulations.

You must make sure that (a) the fee is not inequitable, (b) your agent has adequate knowledge of your product, and (c) that he or she will not use improper influence to obtain business for you. You should limit the scope of the agency agreement as appropriate. When drafting payment provisions, establish method, time, and amount of payments, and do not include any payment terms that suggest improper business methods.

When drafting an international agent agreement, make absolutely clear what *type of relationship* is being created—that is, whether the agent will be an *employee* of your company or an independent contractor. Whether the agent is an employee can affect crucial issues such as the benefits you must provide, the liability you have for the agent's actions, what notice of termination is required, and the compensation that must be paid on termination.[1]

The important differences between independent agents and company employees should be included in your agreement. The indicia of an agent include the following:

(1) The agent's income comes from *commissions* on each sale paid by the selling company.

(2) The agent usually has the authority to *bind* a company on contracts. (However, you should define carefully in the agency agreement the *scope of authority* your agent has to make contracts.)

(3) The agent's employment conditions generally are *not* subject to *local labor laws*.

If the relationship requires a hybrid agency-employment status and you are in doubt as to your agent's status as an employee, you should draft a no-employment-relationship-created provision so that your agent's employment conditions will not be subject to local labor laws.

The agency agreement should delineate the agent's *sales territory* with precision and provide for a mutually-acceptable *dispute settlement procedure*. Do *not* allow the assignment of your agent's contract, the appointment of subagents for all or part of the obligations of the contract, or a change of ownership or control of your agent. You should specify that none of these actions may be taken without your *written consent*.

Have your agent *certify* that he or she will not use undue influence in obtaining contracts for you, and make the contract *voidable* at your discretion if the agent does use improper influence. It is a good idea also to include a clause that requires your agent

---

[Section 19:45]

[1]Lewis, "Drafting International Sales and Agent/Distributor Agreements," Commerce Dept. Speaks (Legal Aspects of Intl. Trade) 9 (1990).

§ 19:45   GOVERNMENT CONTRACT COMPLIANCE HANDBOOK

to comply with all of the statutes and regulations of the United States.

Always try to retain control over the drafting of the agreement. After negotiations and when a final agreement is drawn up, make sure that you *carefully review* it before execution. For further advice on finding, evaluating, and negotiating with agents, you may contact the nearest office of the Department of Commerce's International Trade Administration.

§ 19:46   Recommendations

In order to ensure that your company does not expose itself to liability for the actions of rogue agents, you should:

(a) Make sure that your employees involved in international marketing and sales are aware that *you are liable* for any acts that your agents perform in the course of conducting your business.

(b) Be *wary* of any agent who guarantees results, whose reputation is questionable, or who proposes unusual payment terms.

(c) Understand the U.S. *procurement regulations* that apply to bona fide agents who are involved in foreign military sales.

(d) Be cognizant of any *local rules* governing agents of foreign countries.

(e) Investigate carefully the *background* of any agent before entering into an agreement.

(f) In negotiating a contract, carefully question any *payment terms* that are out of the ordinary.

(g) Take care in drafting any *agreement* with an agent. Be sure the agreement (a) describes a bona fide agency (as defined in the regulations), (b) distinguishes the agent from a company employee, (c) defines the scope of the agent's territory, and (d) specifies that the agent will not use undue influence in making sales.

(h) Make your obligation to *pay* the agent's fees or commissions expressly conditioned on *compliance* by the agent with U.S. and local laws.

Chapter 20

Foreign Military Sales

I. OVERVIEW
§ 20:1   Scope note

II. CURRENT REQUIREMENTS

A. FMS SALES

§ 20:2   Statutory Basis
§ 20:3   Mechanics of the sale
§ 20:4   Types of government-to-government FMS case sales
§ 20:5   Pricing the FMS Sale
§ 20:6   FMS commissions and "bona fide" agent contingent fees

B. DIRECT COMMERCIAL SALES

§ 20:7   Generally
§ 20:8   FMS credit-financed (FMF) sales
§ 20:9   —Credit guidelines
§ 20:10 —Certification
§ 20:11 —FMF commissions and contingent fees
§ 20:12 "Pseudo" FMS Cases

C. NONRECURRING COSTS RECOUPMENT

§ 20:13 History of recoupment policy
§ 20:14 Current policy
§ 20:15 Waiver of recoupment charges

D. OFFSET ARRANGEMENTS

§ 20:16 Generally
§ 20:17 Reporting requirements
§ 20:18 FMS offsets
§ 20:19 FMF offsets

III. HOW TO RECOGNIZE THE PROBLEM

§ 20:20 Generally
§ 20:21 Examples

GOVERNMENT CONTRACT COMPLIANCE HANDBOOK

IV. COMPLIANCE INITIATIVES
§ 20:22 Generally
§ 20:23 FMS and direct commercial sales
§ 20:24 FMS credit-financed (FMF) sales
§ 20:25 Recommendations

> **KeyCite®:** Cases and other legal materials listed in KeyCite Scope can be researched through the KeyCite service on Westlaw®. Use KeyCite to check citations for form, parallel references, prior and later history, and comprehensive citator information, including citations to other decisions and secondary materials.

I. OVERVIEW

§ 20:1 Scope note

This chapter examines the procedures for and restrictions on sales of defense articles or services to foreign governments under the Foreign Military Sales (FMS) program and through U.S. Government-financed Foreign Military Financing (FMF) transactions.

Military export sales can be conducted by either of two methods: (1) through the FMS program, consisting of a procurement by the U.S. Government followed by a government-to-government (U.S. Government to foreign government) sale; or (2) through a direct commercial sale by you, the contractor, to a foreign government purchaser. A direct commercial sale can be financed either by foreign government funds or by U.S. Security Assistance funds appropriated by Congress. Requirements for direct commercial sales financed by U.S. Security Assistance funds (FMF sales) are discussed in this chapter.

II. CURRENT REQUIREMENTS

A. FMS SALES

§ 20:2 Statutory Basis

The statutory basis for the FMS program is the Arms Export Control Act (AECA).[1] The AECA recognizes two types of military export sales. These are government-to-government sales of defense equipment, known as FMS case sales, and contractor-to-government sales, known as direct commercial sales.

Military export sales are governed by the AECA, as imple-

[Section 20:2]
[1] 22 U.S.C.A. §§ 2751 to 2799aa-2.

mented by the International Traffic in Arms Regulations,[2] the Federal Acquisition Regulation (FAR), the DOD FAR Supplement (DFARS),[3] and the DOD *Security Assistance Management Manual* (SAMM).[4] Different regulations and procedures apply to FMS sales, direct commercial sales, and FMS credit-financed direct commercial sales.

§ 20:3 Mechanics of the sale

In a government-to-government sale, the U.S. Government negotiates a Letter of Offer and Acceptance (LOA) with a foreign government for the sale of defense articles or services. Even though the U.S. Department of State has primary authority under the AECA, the DOD has been delegated responsibility for many steps in the processing of government-to-government sales. The Defense Security Cooperation Agency (DSCA) is the DOD component primarily charged with management of FMS sales.

After an LOA is signed, one of the DOD Military Departments (the Army, Air Force, or Navy) procures the articles or services specified in the LOA from a U.S. contractor for resale to the foreign government. The contractor is paid by the DOD with funds provided by the foreign government purchaser to a special Trust Account at the Security Assistance Accounting Center, which is part of the U.S. Treasury.

Because the contractor's customer is, from a strictly legal perspective, an agency of the DOD, the FAR and DFARS apply to procurements for FMS transfer.[1] However, even though a contractor selling a military item to the U.S. Government for an FMS sale must comply with the same requirements as for any other sale to the U.S. Government, there are a few differences between these sales.

Among these differences is a special *exception* to rules governing *competitive solicitations*. Although the FAR's general requirement for competition applies to procurements by the DOD for FMS sales, sole-source procurements are permitted at the request of the foreign government.[2] However, if the requesting government does not designate a source, it may not influence the com-

---

[2] 22 C.F.R. §§ 120 to 130.

[3] DFARS 225.7300 to 225.7307.

[4] DOD Directive 5105.38-M (Oct. 1998) [SAMM]. Reissued under DOD Directive 5105.65 (Oct. 2000). Website reference http://www.samm.dsca.mil/.

[Section 20:3]

[1] DFARS 225.7300; SAMM section 5.4.3.

[2] DFARS 225.7304(a).

§ 20:3   GOVERNMENT CONTRACT COMPLIANCE HANDBOOK

petitive solicitation process in any way.[3] Similarly, the foreign government is prohibited from directing awards of subcontracts by the prime contractor unless it has initially designated the prime contractor as a sole source.[4]

This has become an issue with some nations whose import laws now prohibit the designations of a particular contractor, even though there is only one source available (e.g., Army helicopters, such as the Boeing Longbow Apache. In such cases, the CO may use the FAR exception to full and open competition found at FAR 6.302-1, Only One Responsible Source and No Other Supplies or Services Will Satisfy Agency Requirements. In addition, if the foreign government requests a specific product, by brand name only, and there is only one manufacturer who produces items using that name, then use of FAR 6.302-4, International Agreements, is "equivalent" to the foreign government designating a particular contractor. "We are unwilling to decide, however, that the Army's impropriety, which the Army attempted to correct, operates to deny Egypt or other FMS customers of the prerogative to request brand name items in subsequent procurements, unless it is shown that the Army has acted in bad faith in those procurements to preclude JRL from competing." We believe that our taking exception to this procurement simply would penalize the FMS customer for the Army's deficiency, notwithstanding the Army's attempts to rectify the error. *Julie Research Laboratories, Inc. Reconsideration, B- 218244, B- 218108, B- 216312, B- 218108.2, B- 218244.2, B- 216312.2,* 85-1 CPD P 672 (June 12, 1985).

§ 20:4 Types of government-to-government FMS case sales

There are three types of government-to-government FMS case sales: Defined Order Cases, Blanket Order Cases, and Cooperative Logistics Supply Support Arrangements.[1]

A *Defined Order Case* is used to provide Significant Military Equipment (SME), including Major Defense Equipment (MDE) and the related initial support package; explosives, including munitions; specific services; and Technical Data Packages (TDPs). The LOA explicitly states the items, services, training, or data to be provided to the foreign purchaser.[2]

A *Blanket Order Case* is used for the sale of relatively minor,

---

[3]DFARS 225.7304(b).
[4]DFARS 225.7304(b).

[Section 20:4]

[1]SAMM C5.4.3.
[2]SAMM C5.4.3.1.

§ 20:4

non-SME items that do not require intensive by-item control. The Blanket Order Case operates as an indefinite quantities contract, with the LOA describing item categories and setting forth a dollar ceiling against which the foreign customer may purchase items under the agreement. A Blanket Order Case allows the foreign purchaser to submit requests for articles or services without needing to prepare a defined LOA for each article or service required. A Blanket Order can be used to procure items such as publications, support equipment, supplies, maintenance services, technical assistance services, training services, training aids, and spare parts. However, in contrast to a Cooperative Logistics Supply Support Arrangement (discussed below), the foreign purchaser does not have access to the DOD inventory. Parts purchased through a Blanket Order are subject to normal procurement lead-time conditions.[3]

The *Cooperative Logistics Supply Support Arrangement* (CLSSA) is used to provide peacetime military logistics support for U.S.-origin military equipment in the possession of foreign governments. A CLSSA reflects support for end items with no definitive listing of items or quantities, although items and quantities may be negotiated with the foreign purchaser as part of the CLSSA management process. There are two types of CLSSA LOAs: FMSO I and FMSO II. The scope of a CLSSA is limited by the LOA description of end items to be supported and the dollar values of the FMSOs I and II that make up each CLSSA. These dollar values are based on the cost of forecasted requirements for the anticipated period of support.[4]

FMSO I LOAs provide for purchases from the DOD inventory normally equal to 17 months of projected recurring demand. The FMSO I normally provides for an equity investment (capitalization) in five months of on-hand and 12 months of on-order DOD components.[5]

The FMSO II complements the FMSO I FMS case and allows the foreign purchaser to withdraw stocks from DOD inventories and deposit funds for routine FMSO I replenishment. The FMSO II does not identify specific items in quantities, but states a dollar amount for the estimated use of FMSO I stock. FMSO II case requisitions received before receipt of augmentation stock are normally placed on back order pending maturity of the FMSO I. As augmentation stocks become available, requisitions received under the FMSO II can be filled from stock. FMSO II cases are undefined in terms of items and quantities, reflecting instead the

---

[3]SAMM C5.4.3.2.
[4]SAMM C5.4.3.3.
[5]SAMM C5.4.3.3.

§ 20:4   Government Contract Compliance Handbook

value of material that the country is expected to requisition during the agreed-on ordering period covered by the case, plus the appropriate accessorial, administrative, and asset use-of charges.

§ 20:5   Pricing the FMS Sale

When the DOD undertakes purchasing defense articles or services for a foreign country that has committed itself to bear the cost of the acquisition, the DOD assumes responsibility for ensuring that no more than a fair price is paid for the acquisition. Accordingly, FMS contracts are priced on the same principles and with the same care as defense contracts for U.S. military forces' needs.[1]

This requirement does not mean that prices charged under domestic defense contracts for an item automatically apply to FMS contracts for the same item. On the contrary, application to FMS contracts of the pricing principles established by FAR Part 15 ("Contracting by Negotiation") and FAR Part 31 ("Contract Cost Principles and Procedures") may require pricing that differs from domestic defense contract prices for the same item. Certain kinds of costs may reasonably arise in different amounts for FMS contracts than for the domestic defense contracts. For this reason, known FMS requirements should be separately identified in solicitations for U.S. Government contracts with combined FMS and non-FMS requirements.

If you have made sales of an item to foreign customers under comparable conditions, including quantity and delivery, the pricing of FMS contracts must be in accordance with FAR Part 15, including the requirement that there be consistency in accounting and to some extent in pricing.[2] In pricing FMS contracts, recognition is given to costs of doing business with a foreign government or international organization. Guidelines provide that such costs are allowable whenever comparable costs of doing business with the United States would be recognized in pricing domestic defense contracts. Thus, recognition should be given to reasonable and allocable costs, even though such costs might not be recognized in the same amounts in pricing domestic defense contracts. Examples of such costs include, but are not limited to, the following: selling expenses, product support and post-delivery service expenses, costs associated with the implementation of DOD offset arrangements, and costs that are the subject of

---

[Section 20:5]

[1]DFARS 225.7303; SAMM C6.3.
[2]DFARS 225.7303-1.

§ 20:5

advance understanding.[3]

Finally, sales commissions and contingent fees paid in connection with a government-to-government sale are allowable costs. However, such costs are allowable only if the fees are paid to a "bona fide" agent or an established commercial or selling agency maintained for the purpose of securing such business (see § 20:6). The allowability of the cost of the sales commission and contingent fees in an FMS contract is limited to $50,000.[4] Nothing in excess of that amount may be included in the contract price; therefore, any agent fees in excess of the $50,000 limitation must be paid from other company funds.

The U.S. Government will notify the foreign government purchaser in the LOA of the name and address of the agent, the fee arrangement, and the U.S. Government position as to the fairness and reasonableness of the proposed fee.[5] Some foreign governments will not sanction reimbursement of agent fees. Therefore, care must be taken to ascertain the allowability of agent fees or commissions on a case-by-case basis.

A contractor need not submit cost or pricing data to the U.S. Government for an FMS acquisition if the foreign government has conducted a competition resulting in adequate price competition.[6] Potential U.S. suppliers should consult with the foreign government regarding FAR 15.403-1(b)(1) for determining whether adequate price competition has been obtained. There can be adequate price competition in some circumstances, for example, where there is only one offeror. The CO will consult with the foreign government through security assistance personnel to determine if "adequate" price competition has occurred.

Contractors may not inflate prices in an FMS sale simply because another government is paying. In one case, the defendant contracted with the Government to produce certain infrared systems for sale to Saudi Arabia, Greece, and Bahrain under the Arms Export Control Act. The defendant sought summary judgment on the ground that because the AECA states that foreign military sales shall result in "no loss" to the Government, the defendant could not incur liability under the False Claims Act (FCA). The court concluded that the "fact that the Government might, by some unrelated means, ultimately be protected against

---

[3]DFARS 225.7303-2(a).

[4]DFARS 225.7303-4; SAMM C6.3.7.2.2. For a number of countries, payment of contingent fees in any amount is prohibited "unless the contractor identifies the payments and the foreign customer approves the payment in writing before contract award [(DFARS 225.7303-4(b)]." Otherwise, contingent fees exceeding $50,000 is prohibited.

[5]SAMM C6.3.7

[6]DFARS 225.7303(b).

loss" did not mean that no claim is made against the U.S. Treasury in the first instance. Moreover, "there is no privity of contract between the defendant and the foreign countries" and, therefore, the defendant could not escape FCA liability based on the "mere fortuity" that the systems were later to be resold by the United States to foreign countries through an entirely separate transaction.[7]

§ 20:6 FMS commissions and "bona fide" agent contingent fees

In an FMS case sale, you act essentially as a subcontractor to the U.S. Government in its sale to a foreign government. Therefore, you must comply with the federal procurement statutes and FAR and DFARS provisions concerning agents.[1] You are prohibited from paying an agent a contingent fee unless the agency is "bona fide" within the meaning of the law.[2] An agent is "bona fide" if it is an established, commercial selling agency that you maintain for the purpose of securing business, and it neither exerts nor proposes to exert improper influence to solicit or obtain Government contracts nor holds itself out as being able to obtain any Government contracts through improper influence.[3]

The contracting officer will look at your *relationship* with your agent to determine whether the agent is bona fide. Although each arrangement is evaluated in light of the attendant circumstances, the following considerations generally apply:

(1) The fee should not be inequitable or exorbitant when compared to the services performed or to customary fees for similar services related to commercial business.

(2) The agent should have adequate knowledge of your business and products as well as any other qualifications necessary to sell your products or services on the merits.

(3) You and your agent should have a continuing relationship or, in newly formed relationships, should contemplate future continuity.

(4) The agency should be an established concern that has existed for a considerable period or be a newly established going concern likely to continue in the future. The business of the agency should be conducted in the agency name and characterized by the customary indicia of conduct of regular business.

---

[7]*U.S. ex rel. Campbell v. Lockheed Martin Corp.*, 282 F. Supp. 2d 1324 (M.D. Fla. 2003).

[Section 20:6]

[1]DFARS 225.7303-4. *See* SAMM C6.3.7.

[2]10 U.S.C.A. § 2306(b); 41 U.S.C.A. § 3901(b).

[3]FAR 3.401.

(5) Although an agency that confines its selling activities to Government contracts is not disqualified, the fact that the agent represents you in both Government and commercial sales should receive favorable consideration.

While it is the policy of the U.S. Government to deal directly with the foreign government, an agent also may be appointed by the foreign government for the legitimate purpose of accomplishing the FMS transaction. A form letter set forth in the SAMM is to be used for this purpose (see Appendix W to this Handbook). This letter, which designates the agent of the foreign government, should be signed at the Minister or Deputy Minister of Defense level.

Regardless of your arrangement with the agent, the agent is not bona fide if it proposes to exert or exerts improper influence in obtaining contracts. The regulations define "improper influence" as "any influence that induces or tends to induce a Government employee or officer to give consideration or to act regarding a Government contract on any basis other than the merits of the matter."[4]

Contracts for noncommercial items in excess of the simplified acquisition threshold (currently $150,000) contain the FAR "Covenant against Contingent Fees" clause. Under this provision, you, as the contractor, warrant that no person (other than a bona fide agent or employee) has received a contingent fee. Breach of this warranty entitles the Government to annul the contract or to otherwise recover the amount of the contingent fee from you.[5]

Again, you should also be aware of foreign government limitations and restrictions on the allowability of bona fide agent commission costs for FMS transactions involving the foreign government.[6] Some countries refuse to pay for commission costs.

B. DIRECT COMMERCIAL SALES

§ 20:7 Generally

Unlike FMS case sales through an agency of the DOD, in a direct commercial sale, a defense contractor sells directly to a foreign government without the U.S. Government acting as middleman. Therefore, the FAR and DFARS do not apply to direct commercial sales, unless incorporated by reference. The contractor, however, must comply with the export control regulations, the anti-boycott rules, and the Foreign Corrupt Practices Act, as discussed in §§ 19:1 et seq.

Some foreign governments and some defense contractors prefer

---

[4]FAR 3.401.
[5]FAR 52.203-5.
[6]DFARS 225.7303-4; SAMM, Table C6.T1.

§ 20:7   GOVERNMENT CONTRACT COMPLIANCE HANDBOOK

to avoid the special restrictions of FMS case sale transactions. A U.S. defense contractor can apply to the DOD for a *direct sales preference* if it is the sole U.S. supplier of a certain defense article or service, and if it prefers not to participate in a government-to-government acquisition via the FMS procedure. Theoretically, the DOD has no preference with respect to Foreign Military Sales or direct commercial sales as a means of providing defense articles or services.[1]

You are not prohibited or restrained from marketing to, negotiating with, or selling to foreign governments directly, even absent a DOD direct sales preference.[2] However, such marketing transactions are governed by the AECA requirements regarding the need for export licenses before disclosing technical data or other technical information and before making an offer to sell "significant military equipment" items. These limitations are discussed in §§ 19:1 et seq.

§ 20:8   FMS credit-financed (FMF) sales

In an FMS credit-financed sale (FMF), you sell directly to a foreign government, but the sale is financed with U.S. Security Assistance funds appropriated by Congress and managed by the DOD. As a consequence, this type of transaction combines elements common to a direct commercial sale with some of the more restrictive regulations applicable to FMS case sales. Like direct commercial sales, FMF sales are subject to export control regulations, the anti-boycott rules, and the Foreign Corrupt Practices Act (see §§ 19:1 et seq.). In addition, because these sales are financed with DOD funds, they are subject to specific guidelines set forth in the SAMM.

§ 20:9   FMS credit-financed (FMF) sales—Credit guidelines

The Defense Security Cooperation Agency issued revised guidelines for FMF Direct Commercial Contracts (DCCs) to be followed by all eligible countries (see Appendix X).[1] Also, DSCA issued separate FMF guidelines for the Government of Israel effective the same date. The key requirements established by the guidelines are as follows:

(1) DCCs are not authorized for standard DOD items, and

[Section 20:7]
    [1]SAMM, C4.3.6.
    [2]SAMM, C4.3.6.

[Section 20:9]
    [1]SAMM, C9.7.3.

generally these items must be purchased under FMS procedures. Standard DOD items are those that have national stock numbers. However, DSCA will grant exceptions to this rule when the purchasing country provides sufficient written justification explaining why the requirement should be obtained through a DCC. In such instances, the items or services purchased must be manufactured and assembled in the United States, purchased from U.S. firms, and composed of U.S.-origin components and services.

(2) DCCs are authorized for procurement of nonstandard items (items that do not have national stock numbers).

(3) The DSCA will permit the use of FMF direct commercial contracts for the development and procurement of major country-unique systems. However, the purchaser should consult with the DSCA and receive approval before proceeding with contract negotiations. Written justification for such use of a funded DCC should be provided to DSCA as far in advance as possible but not less than 60 days before solicitation of offers or negotiation of the contract.

(4) Purchases must be from U.S.-incorporated firms licensed to do business in the U.S.

(5) The items and services purchased must be manufactured and assembled in the U.S., purchased from U.S. firms, and composed of U.S.-origin components and services. DSCA will consider an exception to this requirement for those items originally manufactured in the U.S. and purchased by a U.S. contractor from foreign sources. In the event that the purchase of a U.S. end item consists of both U.S. and non-U.S. components or services, only the value of U.S. components and services normally will be financed.

(6) Only DCCs having a minimum contract value of $100,000 will be eligible for FMF.

(7) FMF is discouraged for purchases containing offset provisions.

(8) Commissions or contingent fees to agents will not be funded under FMF contracts and will be treated as unallowable costs. However, when commissions or contingent fees are to be paid by the purchaser with other funds, the contractor must notify DSCA at the time the contract is presented for funding approval. Also, the contractor must maintain a cost accounting system sufficient to show that no commission or contingent fee is funded by FMF.

(9) Purchases should be made directly from the prime manufacturer of the article or service.

(10) A DOD preaward survey may be required to verify the contractor's statements and determine its capacity to perform as a condition of FMF approval. Such preaward surveys

normally are not required for firms with previous DOD contracting experience.

(11) DOD requires 60 days to make an FMF determination. A pre-award survey of a contractor who does not regularly sell to the U.S. requires at least another 30 days for U.S. Government representatives to conduct the survey.

(12) FMF will not be approved for financing of direct letters of credit which provide direct payment to suppliers on presentation of documents. Contracts that include supplier performance bonds or other forms of letters of guarantee require the use of a bank or financial institution chartered or incorporated in and doing business in the United States.

(13) No payments will be made with FMF for transportation by other than U.S. carriers.

(14) Contractor payments for travel, per diem, accommodations, lodging, car rental, personal expenses, entertainment, or other similar expenses of purchasing country personnel in connection with a direct commercial contract will not be approved for FMF. Although these types of expenses may be included in the direct commercial contract, the expenses must be expressly identified and paid by the purchasing country with national funds.

(15) Any purchase agreement that provides for a refund, penalty, liquidated damages, bonding provisions, or any other form of financial reimbursement to the purchasing country must be structured to ensure that such payment is made by the contractor or designated agent (including contractor's commercial bank) directly and without undue delay, from the payor to the U.S. Government. Should the foreign purchaser exercise a draw down on a U.S. private letter of credit, it must ensure that the funds are transferred directly from the payor to the U.S. Treasury.

In addition to complying with these restrictions, to obtain FMF, the contract between the foreign government and the U.S. contractor must include certain basic information identifying the seller, the purchaser, the items being sold, the quantity, the prices, and other details of the sale.

The DSCA guidelines for Israel provide that the Government of Israel may request that DSCA approve the use of FMF for contracts between Israeli prime contractors and U.S. subcontractors. In such cases, the Government of Israel is required to obtain from the U.S. subcontractor a signed Contractor's Certification and Agreement with DSCA (see § 20:10). FMF in these cases is limited to subcontracts of $500,000 or more. The restrictions outlined above also apply to these subcontracts, including the oversight and audit controls.

§ 20:10 FMS credit-financed (FMF) sales—Certification

Before an FMF is approved, you, as the prime contractor, must execute a "Certification and Agreement" with DSCA.[1] In signing this "Certification and Agreement," you certify and agree that you have complied with the "Guidelines for FMS Financing of Direct Commercial Contracts." (The "Certification and Agreement" is set forth as Appendix Y to this Handbook.)

The "Certification and Agreement" requires you to "certify" two major aspects of your conduct-*compliance* with the "Guidelines" and the *accuracy* of information provided to the Government. As a contractor, you also "agree" to comply with requirements or limitations governing future conduct. This portion of the form is contractual in nature, and a future breach of these terms would subject a contractor to a potential action for breach of contract. False statements contained in the signed Certification also raise issues under the False Statements Statute and the False Claims Act (see §§ 1:1 et seq.).[2]

A U.S. District Court in Minnesota cited ambiguities in the DSCA guidelines concerning procurement of United States manufactured items in dismissing indictments against a contractor charged with falsely certifying the country of manufacture of FMF items.[3] Existing guidelines generally limited FMF to items, including their components, manufactured in the United States. Contractors must certify their compliance with this requirement and list any items of non-United States manufacture. The company sold spare military parts, financed with FMF funds, to the Government of Turkey. The company obtained the parts from, among others, dealers in Israel and Canada, although the parts were originally manufactured in the United States. In connection with the FMF, the company certified that the spare parts were "predominantly of U.S. manufacture."

The company was subsequently charged with violating the False Claims Act in submitting claims for parts that were not of United States manufacture. The Government argued that the DSCA guidelines were intended to prohibit use of FMF for foreign purchases regardless of the original country of manufacture. The company argued for a literal reading of the guidelines which spoke not of "foreign purchases" but of "foreign manufacture." The company argued that because its spare parts were originally manufactured in the United States, the claims were not false.

[Section 20:10]

[1]SAMM section C9.7.3.

[2]18 U.S.C.A. § 1001; 18 U.S.C.A. § 287; 31 U.S.C.A. §§ 3729 to 3733.

[3]*U.S. v. Napco Intern., Inc.*, 835 F. Supp. 493 (D. Minn. 1993).

§ 20:10   GOVERNMENT CONTRACT COMPLIANCE HANDBOOK

The court agreed with the company, dismissing the indictments, and stating that the DSCA guidelines were "clearly ambiguous" and did not clearly distinguish between originally- and newly-manufactured United States items.

A contractor official (a vice-president or more senior official) responsible for the making of the contract is required to sign the Certification "under penalty of perjury" to the best of his/her knowledge that the representations made are true and correct, and that he/she has "exercised personal due diligence" to ascertain that the statements made are true and correct. Thus, to avoid allegations of false statements and claims, the company official signing your Certification should carefully review the representations made and use due diligence to ensure the statements are accurate.

Paragraphs 6 through 8 of the "Certification and Agreement" place specific requirements on your *subcontractors* involved in the FMF transaction. These terms include the following:[4]

(a) The prime contractor shall "flow down" a provision in all lower-tiered subcontracts or purchase orders of $10,000 or more (with limited exceptions) notifying the subcontractors that the U.S. Government shall have the right to examine all books, documents, papers, or other records for a period of three years following final payment by DSCA to the prime contractor.

(b) The prime contractor agrees that all provisions of the Certification apply to all subcontractors; and the prime contractor agrees to obtain the written compliance with the guidelines from first- and second-tier subcontractors.

(c) The subcontracts shall contain a "prominently displayed" statement that United States Government funds will be used to finance the subcontract and that acceptance of the subcontract order constitutes acknowledgment that the subcontractor is notified of U.S. Government financing.

§ 20:11 FMS credit-financed (FMF) sales—FMF commissions and contingent fees

The DSCA prohibits the use of FMF funds for commissions or contingent fees.[1] Further, you will be required to certify that no commissions or contingent fees were paid with DSCA funds. If such fees are to be paid by you to a bona fide agent (see § 20:6) with funds other than the FMF provided by the U.S. Government, you must advise the DSCA of these fees at the time the

---

[4]http://www.dsca.mil/sites/default/files/contractor_certificationv4_0.pdf.

[Section 20:11]

[1]SAMM, 9.7.3.

contract is presented for funding approval.[2]

§ 20:12 "Pseudo" FMS Cases

During the Iraq and Afghanistan wars, "pseudo" FMS cases have been prominent in financing military equipment purchased by those governments, as well as the Pakistani government. A "pseudo" FMS case uses funds appropriated by Congress to the DoD rather than to the country's FMS Trust Fund. Unlike traditional FMS Trust Fund appropriations that are funded as part of the U.S. State Department security assistance program which are generally "permanent, indefinite, no-year authority funds,"[1] "pseudo" FMS case funds are expiring appropriations with limited periods of availability, generally one or two years. These funds, like those made available to federal government agencies, will expire if not used within the period of availability. If the funds are properly put on contract, the disbursements must be made within five years of the date that availability ends. If not disbursed, they are cancelled and are no longer available for any purpose.[2]

The FMS procedures, authorities and responsibilities are used to purchase military equipment for these governments, after consultation on their needs with the U.S. Central Command. Cases are then processed through the government-to-government FMS procedures described above.

C. NONRECURRING COSTS RECOUPMENT

§ 20:13 History of recoupment policy

In the early 1960s, the Pentagon was concerned that the United States was "footing the bill" for foreign governments that purchased defense equipment from U.S. Government contractors at prices that did not reflect the DOD investment in developing and producing these products.[1] To address that concern, the DOD implemented a policy that required foreign governments who bought defense equipment from U.S. manufacturers to pay a fair

---

[2]SAMM, 9.7.3.

[Section 20:12]

[1]http://www.samm.dsca.mil/policy-memoranda/dsca-11-06.

[2]http://www.samm.dsca.mil/policy-memoranda/dsca-11-06. *See*, Pub. L. No. 112-81, 125 Stat. 1298, section 1533, Availability of Funds in Afghanistan Security Forces Fund.

[Section 20:13]

[1]DoD Directive 2140.2, Recoupment of Nonrecurring Costs (NCs) on Sales of U.S. Items.

§ 20:13   GOVERNMENT CONTRACT COMPLIANCE HANDBOOK

share of the cost of developing the equipment.[2] The Government's recovery of its investment in those products is termed "recoupment."

In 1969, the policy was incorporated into the Armed Services Procurement Regulation.[3] In 1974, DOD expanded the recoupment requirement to include foreign direct commercial sales and domestic commercial sales. In 1976, the practice of recouping DOD nonrecurring cost investment from Foreign Military Sales was mandated by Congress in the Arms Export Control Act.[4]

In June 1992, the Bush Administration moved to abolish recoupment fees on FMS transactions, except for sales of Major Defense Equipment. MDE is defined as "any item of significant military equipment" on the U.S. Munitions List having a nonrecurring research and development cost of more than $50 million or a total production cost of more than $200 million.[5] On October 7, 1992, a DOD memorandum directed removal from DOD contracts of any requirement for the recoupment of nonrecurring costs with respect to sales of U.S. products and technologies on or after October 7, 1992, except as expressly required by statute. In 1993, DOD Directive 2140.2, "Recoupment of Nonrecurring Costs on Sales of U S. Items," was revised.[6] The rule eliminates recoupment of nonrecurring costs on all commercial sales, including MDE, sold on or after January 13, 1993. The 1993 Directive, along with the 1992 memorandum, eliminate all nonstatutory recoupment requirements from existing and new DOD contracts.[7]

§ 20:14   Current policy

The AECA still requires that the DOD collect recoupment fees on sales of MDE under the FMS program. Letters of offer for the sale of defense articles or for the sale of defense services issued pursuant to certain sections of the Arms Export Control Act shall include charges for a proportionate amount of any nonrecurring costs of research, development, and production of MDE (except

---

[2]DoD Directive 2140.2, Recoupment of Nonrecurring Costs (NCs) on Sales of U.S. Items.

[3]ASPR 7-104.64.

[4]22 U.S.C.A. § 2761.

[5]22 U.S.C.A. § 2794(6).

[6]DoD Directive 2140.2, Recoupment of Nonrecurring Costs (NCs) on Sales of U.S. Items

[7]35 No. 37 GOVTCONT ¶ 594.

FOREIGN MILITARY SALES § 20:16

for equipment wholly paid for from certain funds).[1] Recoupment will be determined directly by DOD and its FMS customer.[2]

§ 20:15 Waiver of recoupment charges

The President is authorized to waive MDE recoupment charges if imposition of the charge would likely result in loss of the sale, or if the resulting sale provides a reduction in overall unit costs to U.S. Armed Forces which substantially offset the forgone recoupment fee.[1]

Generally, DOD will agree to waive MDE recoupment charges when it concludes that the waiver will be in the best interests of the U.S. Government. A waiver from the charges required under the recoupment policy must be requested and approved *before* a sale is consummated, unless the acceptance is made conditional on approval of the waiver.[2] Requests for waivers associated with *foreign sales* should originate from the foreign government and be submitted to the Director of the Defense Security Cooperation Agency.[3] Waiver requests are evaluated on a case-by-case basis, and blanket waivers are not available.

D. OFFSET ARRANGEMENTS

§ 20:16 Generally

An offset arrangement is an agreement whereby the U.S. Government agrees to purchase goods or services from the foreign government as part of the FMS transaction, or where the contractor agrees to purchase goods or services from the foreign government or within the foreign country as part of the direct commercial sale. U.S. export law requires that offset transactions be reported to the U.S. Government by the U.S. company making the foreign sale. However, as a general rule, offsets between the U.S. Government and the foreign government will not be permitted as an element of an FMS transaction. While offset arrangements are more common with commercial transactions, the DSCA will not directly fund offsets in FMF transactions. If a direct commercial sale is funded by Security Assistance funds, the FMF transaction involving offsets must comply with SAMM guidelines.

[Section 20:14]

[1] 22 U.S.C.A. §§ 2761, 2762.

[2] 22 U.S.C.A. § 2761(e).

[Section 20:15]

[1] Pub. L. No. 104-106, Div. D, § 4303 (codified at 22 U.S.C.A. § 2761(e)(2)). *See also* 38 GOVTCONT ¶ 439.

[2] DOD Directive 2140.2 (March 15, 1967).

[3] DOD Directive 2140.2 (March 15, 1967).

§ 20:17 Reporting requirements

U.S. firms may be subject to offset reporting requirements. These provisions apply to U.S. firms entering an offset arrangement in excess of $5 million for the sale of defense articles or equipment to a foreign country or firm. These provisions also apply to offset transactions completed in performance of existing offset commitments for which an offset credit of $250,000 or more has been claimed by the foreign representative.[1]

Part 701 of Title 15 of the Code of Federal Regulations describes offset reporting requirements. Reports are to be made only by the prime contractor to avoid double accounting of offsets. Thus, the prime contractor must report all offset transactions involving the foreign customer, even those offset provisions involving subcontractors. Reports are to be submitted yearly and cover offset transactions occurring during the previous calendar year. Reports should be delivered to the Offsets Program Manager in the Commerce Department's Bureau of Export Administration.[2]

The offset reporting requirements apply to FMS, FMF transactions, direct commercial sales, and sales of defense articles or services to foreign governments.

§ 20:18 FMS offsets

The President has directed that DOD not encourage, enter directly into, or commit U.S. firms to any FMS offset arrangements. The DFARS leaves the decision to engage in and negotiate offset arrangements with the companies involved in the transaction.[1]

§ 20:19 FMF offsets

FMF guidelines do not permit the use of Security Assistance funds to pay for the direct costs or administrative costs associated with offsets. However, offset administration costs can be paid with repayable FMS credits or foreign purchaser funds.[1]

[Section 20:17]

[1]15 C.F.R. Pt. 701.3.

[2]15 C.F.R. § 701.4.

[Section 20:18]

[1]DFARS 225.7306.

[Section 20:19]

[1]DFARS 225.7303-2(a)(3); *also see* http://www.samm.dsca.mil/policy-memorandum/dsca-02-16, subject: "SAMM E-Change 31 – Inclusion of Offset Costs and Related Statements in Letters of Offer and Acceptance (LOAs)(DSCA 02-

III. HOW TO RECOGNIZE THE PROBLEM

§ 20:20 Generally

Assume you have a competitive solicitation for a contract with the U.S. Army. The solicitation indicates that part of the contract deliveries are for requirements of an allied government in the Middle East. Deliveries for the FMS quantities are to be made directly to a point in the Middle East. You have a marketing agent in the country of the foreign customer. You would prefer to deal directly with the foreign government through your agent. Regardless of how the transaction eventually takes place, you have important compliance issues to face.

If you *bid for the contract* with the Army, the contract will be covered by the FAR and DFARS. Your price will be set by the competitive bid process. However, it costs more to sell to foreign customers. You must cover the costs of the foreign sales office and the foreign agent. Can you include these costs in your bid for this contract? The short answer is that you may include some portion of these foreign selling costs in the price offered for the FMS requirements, but you may not include any portion of these costs in the price for the requirements of the U.S. Army. Depending on the size of the FMS portion of the deliveries, the solicitation may not provide for separate pricing.

If you attempt to *sell directly* to the foreign government, your company could be designated as a desired sole source for the FMS requirements. In the alternative, you could convince the foreign government to buy from your company through a direct commercial sale for these requirements rather than through the FMS program. Either of these alternatives would have a direct impact on the competitive solicitation for the U.S. Army. The Army contracting officials may resist the sole-source designation or the decision to purchase through a direct commercial sale by persuading the foreign government that it can get a better price through competitive bidding. This is allowable, even though DOD, as a matter of policy, should have no preference for FMS case sales over direct commercial sales.

If you do convince the foreign government to buy your products under a direct commercial transaction, the foreign government may wish to finance the purchase using U.S. Security Assistance FMF funds. In that case, the contract with the foreign customer must be reviewed by DSCA before the use of the funds for the contract will be approved. You must sign a "Certification and Agreement" directly with DSCA, which will impose a number of surprising requirements on your otherwise totally commercial

---

16).

§ 20:20

transaction with the foreign customer. In most cases, the foreign government will back away from the commercial contract unless DSCA approves the use of the FMF for payment of the contract price.

As you can see, any foreign military export transaction involves myriad choices and pitfalls for a contractor. Below are a few more examples of how trouble can arise in selling defense equipment to foreign governments.

§ 20:21 Examples

Sales commission ceiling: Assume you have contracted with the U.S. Government to sell it certain items that it will sell to a foreign government. You have paid a marketing and selling agency over $65,000 to help you obtain the contract. You include this cost in the contract price. You have probably violated the DFARS. Only up to $50,000 of sales commission and contingent fee costs may be included as part of the contract price.

Sale of non-U.S. components: You have contracted to sell to a foreign government a product that contains a mechanism you purchased from a company incorporated in the United States. You assume that because you bought the mechanism from a U.S. manufacturer, all the components are also manufactured in the United States. Thus, you do not identify in the contract any non-U.S. components. Furthermore, you state in your "Certification and Agreement" that your product is entirely of U.S. origin. If it turns out that some of the components are, in fact, of foreign origin, DOD may refuse to finance the sale. In addition, you probably have violated your "Certification and Agreement" and the DFARS requirements for FMF direct commercial sales.

IV. COMPLIANCE INITIATIVES

§ 20:22 Generally

The steps your company should take to ensure compliance in this area depend, in part, on whether (1) you are involved in an FMS sale or direct commercial sale, (2) you are involved in an FMF direct commercial sale, and (3) the sale item was developed or produced under a U.S. Government contract.

§ 20:23 FMS and direct commercial sales

If your company is involved in an FMS sale, your customer is one of the U.S. military departments, and you must take the same steps to ensure compliance with procurement laws and rules as you would take for any other sale to the U.S. Government. You must also comply with special FMS laws and rules (see above). If your company is involved in a direct commercial sale, you must comply with the export control regulations, the anti-boycott rules, and the Foreign Corrupt Practices Act (see §§ 19:1 et seq.).

§ 20:24 FMS credit-financed (FMF) sales

If your company is involved in an FMF direct commercial sale, you must comply with all the laws and rules governing a direct commercial sale. In addition, you must comply with the policies and procedures set out in the SAMM (see above). More specifically, you must ensure the accuracy of information supplied as part of the *certifications* made on the "Certification and Agreement." Therefore, you need to develop policies and procedures to *verify* that the material or component provided is of U.S. manufacture, unless otherwise specified, and to ensure proper identification of all non-U.S. origin items, components, and services. In addition, you must ensure that your vendors or suppliers identify non-U.S. origin items and components.

You will need to institute specific procedures for *accounting* for FMF funds. You must be sure that no FMF funds are used to compensate foreign companies and individuals who are not residents of the United States unless the transaction has been disclosed to DSCA in advance. You should verify and track all sales commissions and contingent fees. You should establish an accounting system that maintains a clear audit trail of the use of FMF funds. You will need to verify and keep track of personnel support costs, such as costs of transportation, lodging, and meals incurred by or on behalf of the foreign purchaser's personnel that are paid by your company and ensure that these costs are *not* financed with FMF funds.

§ 20:25 Recommendations

(a) Make sure that any *agent* you engage for soliciting military export sales is a "bona fide" agent and that the *fee is limited* to $50,000 or paid from other than contract funds.

(b) If the sale is financed with FMF funds, verify that the material or components are *manufactured in the U.S.* and composed of U.S.-manufactured and U.S.-assembled items, components, and services.

(c) If the sale is financed with FMF funds, make sure that you comply with all the *certifications* in the "Certification and Agreement."

(d) Obtain the required *export licenses* and approvals for any military articles or services that you are exporting under a direct commercial sale or FMF sale and be aware of the prohibitions of the Foreign Corrupt Practices Act and anti-boycott rules.

APPENDICES

Appendix A. Summary of Criminal and Civil Statutes Applicable to Procurement Matters
Appendix B. Representations and Certifications Chart
Appendix C. Sentencing Guidelines for Organizations
Appendix D. List of the Federal Inspectors General
Appendix E. Sample Code of Business Ethics and Conduct
Appendix F. DoD Hotline Poster
Appendix G. Sample Company Policy Statement on Bribery and Gratuities
Appendix H. FAR 52.203-2: "Certificate of Independent Price Determination" Clause
Appendix I. Department of the Army Memorandum, Procurement Fraud Indicators, SELCE-LG-JA (27-10i) (Feb. 20, 1990)
Appendix J. FAR Table 15-2: Instructions for Submitting Cost/Price Proposals When Cost or Pricing Data are Required
Appendix K. DCAA Form 1: "Notice of Contract Costs Suspended and/or Disapproved"
Appendix L. FAR 52.242-4: "Certification of Final Indirect Costs"
Appendix M. FAR 52.242-3: "Penalties for Unallowable Costs Clause"
Appendix N. Form CASB-DS-1: "Cost Accounting Standards Board Disclosure Statement"
Appendix O. Time Card Analysis Attribute Test
Appendix P. Sample Time Card
Appendix Q. Sample Time Cards Which Exhibit Violations
Appendix R. Standard Form 1443: "Contractor's Request for Progress Payment"
Appendix S. GAO, "DOD Fraud Invesgitations: Characteristics, Sanctions and Prevention" (Jan. 1988)
Appendix T. DOD Office of Inspector General, "Indicators of Fraud in DOD Procurement" (June 1987)
Appendix U. DFARS 225.872-1: List of Current DOD Qualifying Countries
Appendix V. FAR 25.003: List of Designated Countries

Appendix W. DOD Security Assistance Management Manual Form Letter

Appendix X. Defense Security Cooperation Agency, "Guidelines for Foreign Military Financing of Direct Commercial Contracts"

Appendix Y. Contractor's Certificiation and Agreement with Defense Security Cooperation Agency

APPENDIX A

Summary of Criminal and Civil Statutes Applicable to Procurement Matters

Provision	Title	Act	Intent	Standard of Proof	Maximum Penalty Per Count
18 U.S.C.A. §§ 1341 and 1343	Mail and Wire Fraud Statutes	You devised or participated in a scheme or artifice to defraud or to obtain money or property by means of false or fraudulent pretenses, representations, or promises. You used or caused to be used the United States mails/wires in furtherance of the execution of that scheme.	You did so knowingly, willfully or recklessly, and with intent to defraud.	Beyond a reasonable doubt.	18 U.S.C.A. § 3571 "Sentence of Fine" penalties and/or five years imprisonment. If violation affects financial institution then fine up to $1 million and/or 30 years imprisonment.
18 U.S.C.A. § 1031	Major Fraud Act	You executed, or attempted to execute, a scheme or artifice. You did so in a procurement of property or services where you were a prime contractor, subcontractor, or supplier on a contract with the Unites States. The value of the contract, subcontract, or any constituent part thereof for property or services was $1 million or more.	You did so knowingly and with the intent to defraud the United States, or to obtain money or property by means of false or fraudulent pretenses, representations or promises.	Beyond a reasonable doubt.	$1 million fine and 10 years imprisonment. $5 million fine if: (1) gross loss to the Government or gross gain to a defendant was $500,000 or greater; or (2) the offense involved a conscious or reckless risk of serious personal injury. $10 million fine for multiple counts under this section.

Appendix A

Provision	Title	Act	Intent	Standard of Proof	Maximum Penalty Per Count
18 U.S.C.A. § 287	Criminal False Claims Statute	You made or presented a claim to a Government official or to a Government department or agency. The claim was asserted against the United States or its agencies or departments. The claim was false, fictitious or fraudulent when presented.	You knew the claim was false, fictitious or fraudulent when presented.	Beyond a reasonable doubt.	5 years imprisonment and/or 18 U.S.C.A. § 3571 "Sentence of Fine" penalties; $1 million fine for false claims relating to DOD contracts.
— Corruption Offenses —					
41 U.S.C.A. § 8707	Criminal Anti-Kickback Statute	You provided, attempted to provide, or offered to provide a kickback; you solicited, accepted, or attempted to accept a kickback; or you included the amount of the kickback in the contract price. A kickback is compensation to a contractor or subcontractor for the purpose of improperly obtaining or rewarding favorable treatment in connection with a Government contract.	You did so knowingly and willfully.	Beyond a reasonable doubt.	18 U.S.C.A. § 3571 "Sentence of Fine" penalties and/or 10 years imprisonment.

Provision	Title	Act	Intent	Standard of Proof	Maximum Penalty Per Count
41 U.S.C.A. § 8706(a)(1)	Civil Anti-Kickback Act	You provided, attempted to provide, or offered to provide a kickback; you solicited, accepted, or attempted to accept a kickback; or you included the amount of a kickback in a contract price.	You did so knowingly.	Preponderance of evidence.	2 times the amount of the kickback, plus $10,000, for each kickback.
41 U.S.C.A. § 8706(a)(2)		An employee, subcontractor or subcontractor employee of yours provided, accepted or charged a kickback.	Vicarious liability.	Preponderance of evidence.	The amount of the kickback.
18 U.S.C.A. § 201(b)	Bribery Statute	You directly or indirectly gave, offered, or promised to a public official anything of value for the public official or any other person or entity. (Note: this statute also applies to the person who was bribed.)	You acted corruptly. You acted with the intent to influence an official act of the public official, or to influence the public official to allow a fraud on the United States.	Beyond a reasonable doubt.	15 years imprisonment; 3 times the bribe; disqualification; and/or 18 U.S.C.A. § 3571 "Sentence of Fine" penalties.

APPENDIX A

Provision	Title	Act	Intent	Standard of Proof	Maximum Penalty Per Count
18 U.S.C.A. § 201(c)	Illegal Gratuities Statute	You directly or indirectly gave, offered or promised to a public official or former public official anything of value. (Note: This statute also applies to the person who received the gratuity.)	You did so for or because of an official act performed or to be performed by the public official.	Beyond a reasonable doubt.	18 U.S.C.A. § 3571 "Sentence of Fine" penalties and/or 2 years imprisonment.

Provision	Title	Act	Intent	Standard of Proof	Maximum Penalty Per Count
31 U.S.C.A. § 3729	Civil False Claims Act	You knowingly presented or caused to be presented to a Government official a false or fraudulent claim for payment or approval; or You knowingly made, used, or caused to be made or used a false record or statement to get a false or fraudulent claim paid or approved; or You conspired to defraud the Government by getting a false or fraudulent claim allowed or paid; or You knowingly made, used, or caused to be made or used, a false record or statement to conceal, avoid, or decrease an obligation to pay or transmit money or property to the Government. (Note: Either the Government or a private party on behalf of the Government may initiate an action.)	You knew the claim or statement material to the claim was false, fictitious, or fraudulent when presented, or you presented the claim with reckless disregard for in deliberate ignorance of its truth or falsity. No specific intent to defraud is required.	Preponderance of evidence.	$5,500–$11,000 civil fine; 3 times the damage to the Government; and costs of prosecution. Reduced penalties of not more than 2 times the damage for disclosure and cooperation.

APPENDIX A

Provision	Title	Act	Intent	Standard of Proof	Maximum Penalty Per Count
18 U.S.C.A. § 1001	False Statements Statute	You made a false, fictitious, or fraudulent statement or used a document knowing the same to contain any false, fictitious, or fraudulent statement or entry. The statement concerned a matter within the jurisdiction of an agency or department of the United States. The statement was false, fictitious or fraudulent. The statement was material.	You made the statement willfully, and with knowledge that it was false, fictitious or fraudulent.	Beyond a reasonable doubt.	5 years imprisonment; and/or 18 U.S.C.A. § 3571 "Sentence of Fine" penalties.
31 U.S.C.A. §§ 3801 to 3812	Program Fraud Civil Remedies Act	For elements, see False Claims and False Statements. This Act applies to false claims under $150,000 and to certified false statements.	You knew the claim was false, fictitious, or fraudulent when presented, or presented the claim with reckless disregard for or in deliberate ignorance of its truth or falsity. No specific intent to defraud is required.	Preponderance of evidence.	$5,500 civil fine; 2 times the amount of the false claim if the Government has paid on the claim.

App. A — GOVERNMENT CONTRACT COMPLIANCE HANDBOOK

Provision	Title	Act	Intent	Standard of Proof	Maximum Penalty Per Count
18 U.S.C.A. § 207(a)(1)	Ethics Reform Act	You are a former Government employee. You made a communication to or appearance before a Government agency or court in connection with a particular matter in which the United States was a party or had a direct and substantial interest; in which you participated personally and substantially as an officer or employee; and which involved a specific party or parties at the time of such participation.	You did so knowingly and with the intent to influence.	Beyond a reasonable doubt.	18 U.S.C.A. § 3571 "Sentence of Fine" penalties and 1 year imprisonment (or 5 years imprisonment for willful violations); $50,000, or amount of compensation received illegally, whichever is greater.

APPENDIX A

Provision	Title	Act	Intent	Standard of Proof	Maximum Penalty Per Count
18 U.S.C.A. § 207(a)(2)		You are a former Government employee within 2 years of Government service. You made a communication to or appearance before a Government agency or court in connection with a particular matter in which the United States was a party or had a direct and substantial interest; the matter was actually pending under your official responsibility as an employee within a period of one year before termination of your Government service; and the matter involved a specific party or parties at the time it was so pending.	You knew, or reasonably should have known, that the matter was actually pending under your responsibility, and you made the communication or appearance knowingly and with the intent to influence.	Beyond a reasonable doubt.	18 U.S.C.A. § 3571 "Sentence of Fine" penalties and 1 year imprisonment (or 5 years imprisonment for willful violations); $50,000, or amount of compensation received illegally, whichever is greater.

Provision	Title	Act	Intent	Standard of Proof	Maximum Penalty Per Count
41 U.S.C.A. §§ 2101 to 2107	Procurement Integrity Provisions	You solicited or accepted, from a competing contractor, future employment, a business opportunity, or a gratuity. You disclosed proprietary or source selection information regarding a procurement to an unauthorized person. You participated in negotiations leading to award of a contract or participated personally and substantially on behalf of the competing contractor, within two years of when you last participated substantially in the conduct of such a procurement.	You did so knowingly, or you made certifications that were false, fictitious, or fraudulent.	Varies with penalty.	1. Criminal: Five years imprisonment; and/or 18 U.S.C.A. § 3571 "Sentence of Fine" penalties; suspension or debarment; termination for default; denial of profits. 2. Civil: $50,000 for each violation (a)individual—plus 2 times the amount received or offered for the prohibited conduct. (b)organization—$500,000 for each violation plus 2 times the amount received or offered for the prohibited conduct. 3. Administrative: cancellation of procurement; suspension and debarment, return of money obtained from procurement.

Appendix A

Provision	Title	Act	Intent	Standard of Proof	Maximum Penalty Per Count
31 U.S.C.A. § 1352	Limitation on use of appropriated funds to influence certain Federal contracting and financial transactions ("Byrd Amendment")	You expended appropriated funds to influence or attempt to influence a Government or congressional employee in connection with the award of a Federal contract or the making of a grant, loan, or cooperative arrangement.	No specific intent required.	Preponderance of the evidence.	$100,000 for each expenditure; $100,000 for each failure to file a declaration.
2 U.S.C.A. §§ 1601 to 1612	Lobbying Disclosure Act	You failed to make a proper Lobbying Disclosure Act filing.	"Knowing violation."	Preponderance of the evidence.	$50,000 civil fine.

— Improper Access To Government Property & Documents —

App. A — Government Contract Compliance Handbook

Provision	Title	Act	Intent	Standard of Proof	Maximum Penalty Per Count
18 U.S.C.A. § 793(d)	Communication of Classified Documents	You lawfully had a document or information relating to the national defense. You transmitted the document or information to someone not entitled to receive it.	You did so willfully and with reason to believe that the information could be used to the injury of the United States or to the advantage of any foreign nation.	Beyond a reasonable doubt.	10 years imprisonment; and/or 18 U.S.C.A. § 3571 "Sentence of Fine" penalties.
18 U.S.C.A. § 793(f)(1)	Loss of Classified Documents	You permitted a document or information relating to the national defense in your lawful possession to be removed, lost, stolen, abstracted, destroyed, or delivered to anyone in violation of your trust.	You did so through gross negligence.	Beyond a reasonable doubt.	10 years imprisonment; and/or 18 U.S.C.A. § 3571 "Sentence of Fine" penalties.
18 U.S.C.A. § 793(f)(2)	Failure to Report Loss of Classified Documents	You failed promptly to report the loss, theft, or destruction of a document or information relating to the national defense in your lawful possession.	You knew that the document or information was illegally removed, lost, stolen, or destroyed.	Beyond a reasonable doubt.	10 years imprisonment; and/or 18 U.S.C.A. § 3571 "Sentence of Fine" Penalties.

APPENDIX A

Provision	Title	Act	Intent	Standard of Proof	Maximum Penalty Per Count
18 U.S.C.A. § 641	Theft of Government Property Statute	You embezzled, stole, purloined, or converted to your use or the use of another, or you without authority sold, conveyed, or disposed of a record, voucher, money, or thing of value of the United States, or any property made or being made under contract for the United States; or you received, concealed, or retained with the intent to convert to your use or gain Government property that you knew was embezzled, stolen, purloined, or converted.	Intent depends on specific charge.	Beyond a reasonable doubt.	18 U.S.C.A. § 3571 and/or 10 years imprisonment (for property more than $1,000). 1 year imprisonment and/or 18 U.S.C.A. § 3571 "Sentence of Fine" penalties (for property $1,000 or less).
— Obstruction of Justice Offenses —					
18 U.S.C.A. § 1516	Obstruction of a Federal Audit Statue	You tried to influence, obstruct, or impede a Federal auditor in the performance of his or her official duties. The official's duties related to a person receiving more than $100,000 in any one year under a Government contract or subcontract.	You did so with the intent to deceive or defraud the United States.	Beyond a reasonable doubt.	18 U.S.C.A. § 3571 "Sentence of Fine" penalties; 5 years imprisonment.

App. A   GOVERNMENT CONTRACT COMPLIANCE HANDBOOK

Provision	Title	Act	Intent	Standard of Proof	Maximum Penalty Per Count
18 U.S.C.A. § 1503	Obstruction of Justice Statute	You endeavored to influence, intimidate, or impeded any grand or trial juror or court official; or you influenced, obstructed, or impeded, or endeavored to influence, obstruct, or impede the due administration of justice.	You did so corruptly or by threats of force, or by any threatening communication.	Beyond a reasonable doubt.	5 years imprisonment; and/or 18 U.S.C.A. § 3571 "Sentence of Fine" penalties.
18 U.S.C.A. § 1512(b)	Witness Tampering Statute	You used or attempted to use intimidation, physical force, threats, or misleading conduct toward another person with the intent to influence, delay, or prevent that person's testimony in an official proceeding; to cause or induce that person to withhold testimony, documents, or physical evidence from a proceeding; or to hinder, delay, or prevent the communication of information relating to the commission or possible commission of a Federal offense to a law enforcement officer or judge.	You did so knowingly.	Beyond a reasonable doubt.	10 years imprisonment; and/or 18 U.S.C.A. § 3571 "Sentence of Fine" penalties.

App. A-14

Appendix A

Provision	Title	Act	Intent	Standard of Proof	Maximum Penalty Per Count
18 U.S.C.A. § 1512(c)		You harassed another person and thereby hindered, delayed, prevented, or dissuaded the person from attending or testifying in an official proceeding or reporting to a law enforcement officer or judge the commission or possible commission of a Federal offense.	You did so intentionally.	Beyond a reasonable doubt.	One year imprisonment; and/or 18 U.S.C.A. § 3571 "Sentence of Fine" penalties.
18 U.S.C.A. § 1505	Obstruction of Administrative Proceedings Statute	You influenced, obstructed, impeded, or endeavored to influence, obstruct, or impede the due and proper administration of the law under which any pending proceeding was being had before any department or agency of the United States.	You did so corruptly or by threats of force, or by any threatening communication.	Beyond a reasonable doubt.	5 years imprisonment; and/or 18 U.S.C.A. § 3571 "Sentence of Fine" penalties.

Provision	Title	Act	Intent	Standard of Proof	Maximum Penalty Per Count
18 U.S.C.A. § 1621	Perjury Statute	You took an oath to testify truly before a competent tribunal, officer, or person or made a declaration under such oath or under penalty of perjury. The law of the United States authorized an oath to be administered in such a case. Contrary to your oath, you stated or subscribed to a material matter that you did not believe to be true.	You did so willfully.	Beyond a reasonable doubt.	5 years imprisonment; and/or 18 U.S.C.A. § 3571 "Sentence of Fine" penalties.
18 U.S.C.A. § 1623	False Declarations Statute	You took an oath or made a declaration under penalty of perjury in any proceeding before or ancillary to any court or grand jury. You made a declaration or made or used any other information. The declaration or information was materially false.	You did so knowing that the declaration or information was false.	Beyond a reasonable doubt.	5 years imprisonment; and/or 18 U.S.C.A. § 3571 "Sentence of Fine" penalties.

— Conspiracy Offenses —

Appendix A

Provision	Title	Act	Intent	Standard of Proof	Maximum Penalty Per Count
18 U.S.C.A. § 371	Conspiracy Statute	You agreed with one or more other person to commit any offense against the United States or to defraud the United States. One conspirator took an overt act in furtherance of the conspiracy.	You knowingly became a member of the conspiracy. The conspirator who committed the overt act did so knowingly.	Beyond a reasonable doubt.	5 years imprisonment; and/or 18 U.S.C.A. § 3571 "Sentence of Fine" penalties.
— RICO —
18 U.S.C.A. §§ 1961 to 1968	Racketeer Influenced & Corrupt Organizations Act (RICO)	You were employed or associated with an enterprise which affected interstate or foreign commerce. You participated in the affairs of the enterprise through a pattern of racketeering activity, i.e., you committed two predicate crimes.	Depends on predicate crimes.	Beyond a reasonable doubt.	18 U.S.C.A. § 3571 "Sentence of Fine" penalties; Life imprisonment if violation is for racketeering activity for which maximum penalty includes life imprisonment, 20 years imprisonment; forfeiture. (Civil penalties are treble damages, costs, and attorney fees.)
— Antitrust Offenses —

App. A

Provision	Title	Act	Intent	Standard of Proof	Maximum Penalty Per Count
15 U.S.C.A. §§ 1 et seq.	Sherman Antitrust Act	The conspiracy to accomplish an unlawful purpose in which you are charged with participating during the time alleged in the indictment. The conspiracy concerned goods or services in interstate or foreign commerce.	You knowingly joined the conspiracy. You joined the conspiracy with the intent unreasonably to restrain competition.	Beyond a reasonable doubt.	$350,000 and 3 years imprisonment for an individual; $10 million fine for a corporation; and/or 18 U.S.C.A. § 3571 "Sentence of Fine" penalties.

APPENDIX B
Representations and Certifications Chart

REPRESENTATIONS AND CERTIFICATIONS CHART

FIXED-PRICE-SUPPLY CONTRACTS[1]

FAR Clause	FAR Implementing Section		Title
52.203-2	3.103-1		"Certificate of Independent Price Determination"
		Why:	To prevent collusion between contractors when submitting bid or proposal prices because collusive bidding adversely affects competition.
		How:	You must certify that prices were not disclosed to or discussed with other offerors or competitors. This certification applies not only to discussions that were intended to be part of a collusive effort, but also to seemingly innocent discussions in which prices were discussed but in which no collusion was intended.
		Remedies:	Contractual: rejection of bid or proposal if certificate is not signed; cancellation of contract. Criminal: bid-rigging and antitrust statutes may apply if your certification is false; false statements statute; False Claims Act; conspiracy statutes.
52.203-3	3.202		"Gratuities"
		Why:	To prevent the exercise of improper influence on Government officials involved in the procurement process.

---

[1] The Representations and Certifications provisions listed in this chart include the provisions that are "required" for use in Fixed Price Supply contracts and the more significant of those that are to be used "when applicable."

FAR Clause	FAR Implementing Section			Title
		How:		Prescribes Government remedies if you offer any gratuity to an employee of the United States that is intended to elicit favorable treatment under a contract. You must be aware that even providing minor items may be considered to be a gratuity.
		Remedies:		Civil/Contractual: termination of the contract; debarment/suspension; exemplary damages in cases involving defense contracts; False Claims Act if the gratuity is included in a claim for payment to the Government. Criminal: Federal gratuities law; False Claims Act.
52.203-5	3.404			**"Covenant Against Contingent Fees"**
		Why:		To enable the Government to review and thereby prohibit contingent fee arrangements that might lead to the exercise of improper influence on Government officials by parties attempting to obtain Government contracts in order to collect their contingent fees.
		How:		You must warrant that no contingent fees exist, except as between the contractor and its "bona fide" employees or agents.
		Remedies:		Civil /Contractual: cancellation of contract, deduction from the contract price of the amount of the contingent fee; False Claims Act if the amount of the contingent fee is passed on to the Government. Criminal: false statements statute; False Claims Act; conspiracy statutes; fraud; bribery; other statutes dealing with improper influence.

APPENDIX B

FAR Clause	FAR Implementing Section		Title
52.203-6	3.503-2		**"Restrictions on Subcontractor Sales to the Government"**
		Why:	To prevent subcontract provision that would improperly restrict a subcontractor's ability to make direct sales to the Government; thereby limiting competition for those products.
		How:	You must agree not to enter into any agreement with either actual or prospective subcontractors that would improperly restrict the subcontractor in making direct sales to the Government for items to be supplied to the Government by the prime contractor or pursuant to any follow-on contract.
		Remedies:	Civil/Contractual: breach of contract or termination of contract for default if certification is false; cancellation of contract if the agreement precludes competition. Criminal: antitrust violation; false statements statute.
52.203-7	3.502-3		**"Anti-Kickback Procedures"**
		Why:	To prevent the giving of kickbacks to prime or subcontractors for the purpose of obtaining favorable treatment in connection with a particular contract. This provision is designed to ensure fair and equal competition among both prime and subcontractors.
		How:	Makes illegal the giving, attempting to give, accepting, or attempting to accept kickbacks. Also makes illegal the inclusion of the kickbacks in the contract price. You must report reasonable suspicions of kickbacks and install procedures to detect kickbacks.

FAR Clause	FAR Implementing Section		Title
		Remedies:	Civil/Contractual: offset the amount of the kickback against moneys owed by the Government to the contractor; direct the prime contractor to withhold payments to its subcontractors; False Claims Act; suspension/debarment; cancellation of contract. Criminal: Anti-Kickback Act; conspiracy statutes; False Claims Act.
52.203-8	3.104-9(a)		**"Cancellation, Rescission, & Delivery of Funds for Illegal or Improper Activity"**
		Why:	To prevent violations of the procurement integrity statutes, which are intended to prevent unfair competition in the solicitation and award process.
		How:	Prescribes various penalties that can be levied if you attempt to or obtain illegally another contractor bid, proposal, or source selection information.
		Remedies:	Contractual: Cancellation of awarded contract; rescission of awarded contract and recovery of any amounts paid to you under contract. Civil: Substantial monetary penalties. Criminal: Imprisoned for up to five years and/or criminal monetary penalties for violation of the Procurement Integrity Act.
52.203-10	3.104-9(b)		**"Price or Fee Adjustment for Illegal or Improper Activity"**
		Why:	To prevent violations of the Procurement Integrity Act and implement the regulations. The procurement integrity provisions operate to prevent unfair competition in the solicitation and award process.

APPENDIX B

FAR Clause	FAR Implementing Section		Title
		How:	Prescribes various penalties that can be levied if you attempt to or obtain illegally another contractor bid, proposal, or source selection information.
		Remedies:	Contractual: Adjustment (reduction) in payment by the Government for your contract price or cost. Civil: Substantial monetary penalties. Criminal: Imprisoned for up to five years and/or criminal monetary penalties for violation of the OFPP Act (41 U.S.C. § 423).
52.203-11	3.808		**"Certification & Disclosure Regarding Payments to Influence Certain Federal Transactions"**
		Why:	To prohibit the use of appropriated funds to pay or influence members of Congress or Government employees in the award of Government contracts.
		How:	You must certify that no appropriated funds were used to influence a member of Congress or a Government employee; you must disclose whether nonappropriated funds were used to influence a member of Congress or other Government employee; you must "flow down" certification and disclosure requirements in subcontracts over $100,000.
		Remedies:	Civil penalties between $10,000 and $100,000 for each violation of the disclosure/certification requirements.

FAR Clause	FAR Implementing Section		Title
52.203-12	3.808		"Limitation on Payments to Influence Certain Federal Transactions"
		Why:	To prevent violations of the Byrd Amendment, which prohibits contractors from using appropriated funds to pay someone to influence certain federal transactions.
		How:	Prescribes civil monetary penalties for violations of the Byrd Amendment. Also requires disclosure of non-appropriated funds paid to someone for influencing federal transactions.
		Remedies:	Contractual: cancellation of contract. Civil penalties between $10,000 and $100,000 for each violation of the disclosure/certification requirements.
52.204-3	4.905		"Taxpayer Identification"
		Why:	To require reporting of certain information in conformity with the Internal Revenue Code.
		How:	You must report taxpayer information and corporate status data.
		Remedies:	Government may withhold up to 20 percent of payments due under the contract.
52.204-5	4.603(b)		"Women-Owned Business (Other Than Small Business)"
		Why:	To encourage contracting with women-owned businesses that do not qualify as small businesses.
		How:	You must represent that you are a women-owned non-small business concern.

APPENDIX B

FAR Clause	FAR Implementing Section		Title
		Remedies:	Civil/Contractual: cancellation of contract; suspension/debarment. Criminal: false statements statute.
52.204-7	4.1104		"Central Contractor Registration"
		Why:	To provide identifying information on the contractor to the Government.
		How:	You must register contractor information in the CCR database prior to contract award.
		Remedies:	Liability for the Government's reliance on inaccurate or incomplete data.
52.209-5	9.409(a)		"Certification Regarding Debarment, Suspension, Proposed Debarment & Other Responsibility Matters"
		Why:	To require contractors to certify that they are in good standing and that they are responsible offerors..
		How:	You must certify that you have or have not been suspended or debarred, indicted, convicted, or found liable for certain enumerated civil and criminal violation sin the last three years, or had a contract terminated for default in the last three years.
		Remedies:	Liability for the Government's reliance on inaccurate or incomplete data.
52.212-3	12.301(b)(2)		"Offeror Representations and Certifications—Commercial Items"
		Why:	To incorporate a streamlined list of representations and certifications in commercial item contracts.
		How:	You must represent and certify to the clauses included in the streamlined list of representations and certifications.

FAR Clause	FAR Implementing Section		Title
		Remedies:	Civil/Contractual: cancellation of contract; suspension/debarment. Criminal: false statements statute, False Claims Act.
15.406-2	15.406-2		**"Certificate of Current Cost or Pricing Data"**
			To enable the Government and the contractor to negotiate a fair and reasonable price for items purchased under negotiated contracts.
		How:	Requires that with certain exceptions, in all negotiated contracts expected to exceed $650,000 or modification to any sealed bid or negotiated contract involving a price adjustment over $650,000, you must supply the Government with all cost or pricing data that a prudent seller would reasonably expect to affect price negotiations. You must also certify that the data are current, accurate, and complete to the best of your knowledge.
		Remedies:	Civil/Contractual: price reduction in contract if cost or pricing data are not accurate, current, or complete; breach of contract; common law fraud; False Claims Act; suspension/debarment. Criminal: False Claims Act; false statements statute; conspiracy statutes if contractor intentionally tries to mischarge the Government using false cost or pricing data.
52.215-10	15.408(b)		**"Price Reduction for Defective Cost or Pricing Data"**
		Why	To ensure that the prices charged to the Government are fair and reasonable

APPENDIX B

FAR Clause	FAR Implementing Section		Title	
		How	Price Government paid will be adjusted to reflect amounts Government overpaid as a result of the defective cost or pricing data the contractor provided to the Government during contract negotiations.	
		Remedies	Civil/Contractual: price reduction in contract if cost or pricing data are not accurate, current, or complete; breach of contract; common law fraud; False Claims Act; suspension/debarment. Criminal: False Claims Act; false statements statute; conspiracy statutes if contractor intentionally tries to mischarge the Government using false cost or pricing data.	
52.215-11	15.408(c)		**"Price Reduction for Defective Cost or Pricing Data - Modifications"**	
		Why	To ensure that the prices charged to the Government as a result of contract modifications involving price adjustments are fair and reasonable	
		How	Price Government paid will be adjusted to reflect amounts Government overpaid because the contractor supplied defective cost or pricing data during negotiation of the modification.	
		Remedies	Civil/Contractual: price reduction if cost or pricing data are not accurate, current, or complete; breach of contract; common law fraud; False Claims Act; suspension/debarment. Criminal: False Claims Act; false statements statute; conspiracy statutes if contractor intentionally tries to mischarge the Government using false cost or pricing data.	

FAR Clause	FAR Implementing Section		Title
52.215-12, -13	15.408(d)(e)		"Subcontractor Cost or Pricing Data, - Modifications"
		Why	To ensure that subcontractor costs that are charged to the Government are fair and reasonable
		How	Prime contractor agrees that where the prime contractor must submit cost or pricing data, that have subcontracts over $650,000, or modifications to subcontracts over $650,000, the subcontractor must certify that cost or pricing data are current, accurate, and complete.
		Remedies	Civil/Contractual: price reduction if cost or pricing data are not accurate, current, or complete; breach of contract; common law fraud; False Claims Act; suspension/debarment. Criminal: False Claims Act; false statements statute; conspiracy statutes if subcontractor intentionally tries to mischarge the Government using false subcontract cost or pricing data.
52-219-1	19.304(a)		"Small Business Program Representation"
		Why:	To determine whether an offeror is a small business and therefore eligible for the preferences provided to small businesses. Certification of status enables the Government to make such a determination without having to undertake its own investigation.

Appendix B

FAR Clause	FAR Implementing Section		Title
		How:	You must ensure that your company meets the detailed definition of a small business that applies to its industry as set out in the Small size standards (FAR 19.1). You cannot assume that because of your relatively small size your company meets those standards.
		Remedies:	Civil/Contractual: bid may be rejected if the representation is incorrect or false; common law fraud for obtaining payment under false pretenses of being a small business; False Claims Act if payment is obtained as a result of a contract award being made under false pretenses; cancellation of contract. If contract is under $150,000, Program Fraud Civil Remedies Act may apply. Criminal: false statements statute, False Claims Act.
52.219-8	19.708(a)		"Utilization of Small Business Concerns"
		Why:	To promote the award of subcontracts under Government prime contracts to small business firms.
		How:	You agree to award subcontracts to small businesses to the fullest extent consistent with efficient contract performance.
		Remedies:	Civil/Contractual: breach of contract; common law fraud. Criminal: false statements statute.
52.219-9	19.708(b)		"Small Business Subcontracting Plan"
		Why:	To promote the award of subcontracts under Government prime contracts to small business firms.

FAR Clause	FAR Implementing Section		Title
		How:	For contracts valued at $500,000 or more ($100,000 or more for construction), you are required to submit a subcontracting plan that sets forth goals for awarding subcontracts to small businesses. This subcontracting plan will impose a contract obligation on your company to adhere to that plan.
		Remedies:	Civil/Contractual: rejection of bid/proposal if plan is not submitted or if the plan is defective; breach of contract if plan is not carried out; common law fraud. Criminal: false statements statute.
52.222-4	22.305		"Contract Work Hours & Safety Standard Act -- Overtime Compensation"
		Why:	To ensure that all laborers and mechanics on Government contracts receive fair and equitable compensation.
		How:	Requires that you pay all laborers and mechanics who work more than 40 hours in any workweek 1 and ½ times the basic rate of pay for each hour worked over 40 hours. You must maintain records of hourly rates paid for three years after completion of the contract and must grant access to those records to the Government.
		Remedies:	Civil/Contractual: Government may withhold money payable under the contract to ensure payment of unpaid wages; breach of contract. Criminal: fine and/or imprisonment.
52.222-19	22.1505(b)		"Child Labor-Cooperation with Authorities and Remedies"
		Why	To ensure that the Government does not purchase items produced with child labor.

APPENDIX B

FAR Clause	FAR Implementing Section		Title	
		How	You must agree to cooperate fully with authorized officials of the contracting agency, the Department of the treasury, or the Department of Justice by providing reasonable access to records, documents, persons, or premises upon reasonable request by authorized officials investigating child labor allegations.	
		Remedies	Termination of the contract, suspension/debarment of the contractor.	
52.222-20	22.610		**"Walsh-Healey Public Contracts Act"**	
		Why:	To ensure fair and equitable treatment of all laborers on Government contracts who are employed by "manufacturers" or "regular dealers."	
		How:	You must represent that your company is or is not a manufacturer or regular dealer of the supplies offered under the contract. You also must represent that, if your company is a manufacturer or regular dealer, it will pay all employees the minimum wage as prescribed by the Secretary of Labor. You must refer to the statutory definitions in making this determination.	
		Remedies:	Civil/Contractual: termination of the contract; Government may fulfill its needs through open-market purchases and may charge the contractor for any increased costs; debarment/suspension. Criminal: false statements statute.	
52.222-21	22.810(a)(1)		**"Certification of Nonsegregated Facilities"**	
		Why:	To prevent the award of a contract to a firm that discriminates by ensuring that neither the offeror nor any of its proposed subcontractors operate segregated facilities.	

FAR Clause	FAR Implementing Section		Title
		How:	You must certify that you do not and will not maintain segregated facilities for your employees and further agree to obtain identical certifications from proposed subcontractors.
		Remedies:	Civil /Contractual: bid may be rejected if representation is false; suspension /debarment by the Secretary of Labor is also possible as well as civil penalties under the Program Fraud Civil Remedies Act. Individual civil actions under civil rights statutes could also be brought. Criminal: false statements statute; civil rights statutes.
52.222-22	22.810(a)(2)		**"Previous Contracts & Compliance Reports"**
		Why:	To determine whether you and proposed subcontractors have equal opportunity compliance reports on file with the Government so as to enable the Government to review those reports before contract award.
		How:	You must represent that you have, or have not, participated in previous contracts or subcontracts that are subject to an equal opportunity clause.
		Remedies:	Civil /Contractual: rejection of bid if no representation is made; debarment/ suspension if representation is false. Criminal: false statements statute.
52.222-25	22.810(d)		**"Affirmative Action Compliance"**
		Why:	To determine whether you and proposed subcontractors have an affirmative action plan on file as evidence that the contractor has an affirmative action program.

Appendix B

FAR Clause	FAR Implementing Section		Title
		How:	You must represent that you have, or have not, developed an affirmative action plan have it on file.
		Remedies:	Civil /Contractual: rejection of bid if no representation is made; debarment/ suspension if representation is false. Criminal: false statements statute.
52.222-26	22.810(e)		"Equal Opportunity"
		Why:	To promote the national policy against discrimination and to prevent the award of Government contracts to contractors that discriminate.
		How:	You must agree that, during performance of the contract, you will not discriminate in employment as to race, sex, color, religion, or national origin. You must agree to take affirmative steps to ensure nondiscrimination, including the posting of notices to inform employees who to contact in cases of discrimination. You must also agree to comply with Executive Order 11246 and to grant the Government access to your records to help it determine contractor compliance.
		Remedies:	Civil/ Contractual: cancellation of contract; suspension/debarment; civil monetary penalties under Executive Order 11246; publication of names of the noncomplying contractors. Criminal: Department of Justice and Equal Employment Opportunity Commission may institute criminal actions.
52.223-3	23.303		"Hazardous Material Identification and Material Safety Data"
		Why	To ensure that the Government has notice of any hazardous materials that will be used in contract performance.

FAR Clause	FAR Implementing Section		Title
		How	You must identify any hazardous materials that will be used in performing the contract.
		Remedies	Civil /Contractual: rejection of bid/offer if no certification is made; suspension/ debarment if certification is false. Criminal: false statements statute.
52.223-4	23.405		**"Recovered Material Certification"**
		Why:	To ensure that you will use "recovered materials" (defined in FAR 23.402 to include materials recovered from solid waste) to the maximum extent possible.
		How:	You must certify that recovered materials will be used as required by the applicable specifications.
		Remedies:	Civil /Contractual: rejection of bid if no certification is made; suspension /debarment if certification is false. Criminal: false statements statute.
52.223-6	23.505		**"Drug-Free Workplace"**
		Why:	To ensure that contractors maintain a drug-free workplace.
		How:	You must make a good faith effort to maintain a drug-free workplace, publish a statement that it is unlawful to use, possess, or distribute controlled substances in the workplace, establish an awareness program, condition employment on adherence to your anti-drug policies, and notify the Contracting Officer of employees' drug convictions.
		Remedies:	Suspension of contract payments; termination for default; suspension or debarment.

Appendix B

FAR Clause	FAR Implementing Section		Title
52.225-2	25.1101(a)(2)		"Buy American Certificate"
		Why:	To ensure that, in contracts for the acquisition of supplies, or for services involving the furnishing of supplies, for use in the United States, you will comply with the Buy American Act requiring that a preference be given to domestic end products.
		How:	You must certify that each product, except those you specifically list, is a domestic end product, that the offeror has considered components of unknown origin to have been mined, produced, or manufactured outside the United States.
		Remedies:	Civil/Contractual: rejection of bid or proposal; imposition of civil sanctions under the Buy American Act; common law fraud; cancellation of contract. Criminal: false statements statute.
52.225-4	25.1101(b)(2)(i)		"Buy American Act – Free Trade Agreements- Israeli Trade Act Certificate"
		Why:	To ensure that, in contracts for the acquisition of supplies, or for services involving the furnishing of supplies, for use inside the United States, preference will be given to domestic end-products, Free Trade Agreement country end products, and Israeli end products.
		How:	You must certify that each product, except those you specifically list, is a domestic end product, Free Trade Agreement Country end product, or Israeli end product.

FAR Clause	FAR Implementing Section		Title
		Remedies:	Civil/Contractual: rejection of bid or proposal; common law fraud; cancellation of contract. Criminal: false statements statute. Criminal: false statements statute.
52.225-6	25.1101(c)(2)		**"Trade Agreements Certificate"**
		Why	To ensure that, in contracts for the acquisition of supplies, or for services involving the furnishing of supplies the supplies are U.S.-made, designated country end products, Caribbean Basin country, or Free Trade Agreements country end-products.
		How	You must certify that each product you supply, except those you specifically list, is a U.S.-made, designated country, Caribbean Basin country, or Free Trade Agreements country end-product.
		Remedies	Civil/Contractual: rejection of bid or proposal; common law fraud; cancellation of contract. Criminal: false statements statute; False Claims Act.
52.227-14	27.409(a)		**"Rights in Data – General"**
		Why	To allocate rights in technical data used to perform the contract between the Government and the contractor
		How	You must identify any data to be provided to the Government with "limited rights" or computer software that is to be provided with "restricted rights."
		Remedies	You may lose your ability to protect "limited rights" data and "restricted rights" data.

APPENDIX B

FAR Clause	FAR Implementing Section		Title
52.230-1, -2	30.201-3, -4		"Cost Accounting Standards"
		Why:	To require offerors to disclose their cost accounting practices and procedures under certain circumstances.
		How:	You certify that you have submitted or will submit a written Disclosure Statement describing your cost accounting practices and that your practices are consistent with those described in your Disclosure Statement; alternatively, you certify that you are exempt from such a filing.
		Remedies:	Contractual: Price adjustment or disallowance of costs. Possible suspension or debarment. Civil: False Claims Act. Criminal: False Claims Act; false statements statute.
52.246-15	46.315		"Certificate of Conformance"
		Why:	To provide for a more efficient and convenient way for the Government to accept goods without having to inspect those goods.
		How:	The Government may permit the contractor to ship goods, which would otherwise require Government inspection, with a Certificate of Conformance, certifying that the shipped goods satisfy the requirements of the contract. The Certificate is authorized where your reputation and past performance are such as to provide the Government with reasonable assurance that the goods will be acceptable.

FAR Clause	FAR Implementing Section		Title
		Remedies:	Civil/Contractual: Government may still inspect and reject goods within a reasonable time after delivery and the contractor must cure defects within a reasonable time at his own expense; False Claims Act; debarment/suspension. Criminal: false statements statute; False Claims Act.
52.247-64	47.507(a)		**"Preference for Privately Owned U.S. Flag Commercial Vessels**
		Why	To ensure that sea transportation associated with contract performance is via U.S. flag commercial vessels
		How	You must represent that you will use privately owned U.S.-flag commercial vessels to ship at least 50 percent of the gross tonnage involved under the contract.
		Remedies	Contractural: Price adjustment or disallowance of costs for transportation; suspension/debarment. Civil: False Claims Act penalties. Criminal: False Claims Act; false statements statute.

APPENDIX C
Sentencing Guidelines for Organizations

CHAPTER EIGHT - SENTENCING OF ORGANIZATIONS

Introductory Commentary

The guidelines and policy statements in this chapter apply when the convicted defendant is an organization. Organizations can act only through agents and, under federal criminal law, generally are vicariously liable for offenses committed by their agents. At the same time, individual agents are responsible for their own criminal conduct. Federal prosecutions of organizations therefore frequently involve individual and organizational co-defendants. Convicted individual agents of organizations are sentenced in accordance with the guidelines and policy statements in the preceding chapters. This chapter is designed so that the sanctions imposed upon organizations and their agents, taken together, will provide just punishment, adequate deterrence, and incentives for organizations to maintain internal mechanisms for preventing, detecting, and reporting criminal conduct.

This chapter reflects the following general principles:

First, the court must, whenever practicable, order the organization to remedy any harm caused by the offense. The resources expended to remedy the harm should not be viewed as punishment, but rather as a means of making victims whole for the harm caused.

Second, if the organization operated primarily for a criminal purpose or primarily by criminal means, the fine should be set sufficiently high to divest the organization of all its assets.

Third, the fine range for any other organization should be based on the seriousness of the offense and the culpability of the organization. The seriousness of the offense generally will be reflected by the greatest of the pecuniary gain, the pecuniary loss, or the amount in a guideline offense level fine table. Culpability generally will be determined by six factors that the sentencing court must consider. The four factors that increase the ultimate punishment of an organization are: (i) the involvement in or tolerance of criminal activity; (ii) the prior history of the organization; (iii) the violation of an order; and (iv) the obstruction of justice. The two factors that mitigate the ultimate punishment of an organization are: (i) the existence of an effective compliance and ethics program; and (ii) self-reporting, cooperation, or acceptance of responsibility.

Fourth, probation is an appropriate sentence for an organizational defendant when needed to ensure that another sanction will be fully implemented, or to ensure that steps will be taken within the organization to reduce the likelihood of future criminal conduct.

These guidelines offer incentives to organizations to reduce and ultimately eliminate criminal conduct by providing a structural foundation from which an organization may self-police its own conduct through an effective compliance and ethics program. The prevention and detection of criminal conduct, as facilitated by an effective compliance and ethics program, will assist an organization in encouraging ethical conduct and in complying fully with all applicable laws.

Historical Note: Effective November 1, 1991 (see Appendix C, amendment 422). Amended effective November 1, 2004 (see Appendix C, amendment 673).

App. C GOVERNMENT CONTRACT COMPLIANCE HANDBOOK

PART A - GENERAL APPLICATION PRINCIPLES

§8A1.1.   Applicability of Chapter Eight

This chapter applies to the sentencing of all organizations for felony and Class A misdemeanor offenses.

Commentary

Application Notes:

1. "Organization" means "a person other than an individual." 18 U.S.C. § 18. The term includes corporations, partnerships, associations, joint-stock companies, unions, trusts, pension funds, unincorporated organizations, governments and political subdivisions thereof, and non-profit organizations.

2. The fine guidelines in §§8C2.2 through 8C2.9 apply only to specified types of offenses. The other provisions of this chapter apply to the sentencing of all organizations for all felony and Class A misdemeanor offenses. For example, the restitution and probation provisions in Parts B and D of this chapter apply to the sentencing of an organization, even if the fine guidelines in §§8C2.2 through 8C2.9 do not apply.

Historical Note: Effective November 1, 1991 (see Appendix C, amendment 422).

§8A1.2.   Application Instructions - Organizations

(a) Determine from Part B, Subpart 1 (Remedying Harm from Criminal Conduct) the sentencing requirements and options relating to restitution, remedial orders, community service, and notice to victims.

(b) Determine from Part C (Fines) the sentencing requirements and options relating to fines:

   (1) If the organization operated primarily for a criminal purpose or primarily by criminal means, apply §8C1.1 (Determining the Fine - Criminal Purpose Organizations).

   (2) Otherwise, apply §8C2.1 (Applicability of Fine Guidelines) to identify the counts for which the provisions of §§8C2.2 through 8C2.9 apply. For such counts:

   (A) Refer to §8C2.2 (Preliminary Determination of Inability to Pay Fine) to determine whether an abbreviated determination of the guideline fine range may be warranted.

   (B) Apply §8C2.3 (Offense Level) to determine the offense level from Chapter Two (Offense Conduct) and Chapter Three, Part D (Multiple Counts).

APPENDIX C

(C) Apply §8C2.4 (Base Fine) to determine the base fine.

(D) Apply §8C2.5 (Culpability Score) to determine the culpability score. To determine whether the organization had an effective compliance and ethics program for purposes of §8C2.5(f), apply §8B2.1 (Effective Compliance and Ethics Program).

(E) Apply §8C2.6 (Minimum and Maximum Multipliers) to determine the minimum and maximum multipliers corresponding to the culpability score.

(F) Apply §8C2.7 (Guideline Fine Range - Organizations) to determine the minimum and maximum of the guideline fine range.

(G) Refer to §8C2.8 (Determining the Fine Within the Range) to determine the amount of the fine within the applicable guideline range.

(H) Apply §8C2.9 (Disgorgement) to determine whether an increase to the fine is required.

For any count or counts not covered under §8C2.1 (Applicability of Fine Guidelines), apply §8C2.10 (Determining the Fine for Other Counts).

(3) Apply the provisions relating to the implementation of the sentence of a fine in Part C, Subpart 3 (Implementing the Sentence of a Fine).

(4) For grounds for departure from the applicable guideline fine range, refer to Part C, Subpart 4 (Departures from the Guideline Fine Range).

(c) Determine from Part D (Organizational Probation) the sentencing requirements and options relating to probation.

(d) Determine from Part E (Special Assessments, Forfeitures, and Costs) the sentencing requirements relating to special assessments, forfeitures, and costs.

Commentary

Application Notes:

1. *Determinations under this chapter are to be based upon the facts and information specified in the applicable guideline. Determinations that reference other chapters are to be made under the standards applicable to determinations under those chapters.*

2. *The definitions in the Commentary to §1B1.1 (Application Instructions) and the guidelines and commentary in §§1B1.2 through 1B1.8 apply to determinations under this chapter unless otherwise specified. The adjustments in Chapter Three, Parts A (Victim-Related Adjustments), B (Role in the Offense), C (Obstruction and Related Adjustments), and E (Acceptance of Responsibility) do not apply. The provisions of Chapter Six (Sentencing Procedures, Plea Agreements, and Crime Victims' Rights) apply to proceedings in which the defendant is an organization. Guidelines and policy statements not referenced in this chapter, directly or*

indirectly, do not apply when the defendant is an organization; _e.g._, the policy statements in Chapter Seven (Violations of Probation and Supervised Release) do not apply to organizations.

3. The following are definitions of terms used frequently in this chapter:

   (A) "Offense" means the offense of conviction and all relevant conduct under §1B1.3 (Relevant Conduct) unless a different meaning is specified or is otherwise clear from the context. The term "instant" is used in connection with "offense," "federal offense," or "offense of conviction," as the case may be, to distinguish the violation for which the defendant is being sentenced from a prior or subsequent offense, or from an offense before another court (_e.g._, an offense before a state court involving the same underlying conduct).

   (B) "High-level personnel of the organization" means individuals who have substantial control over the organization or who have a substantial role in the making of policy within the organization. The term includes: a director; an executive officer; an individual in charge of a major business or functional unit of the organization, such as sales, administration, or finance; and an individual with a substantial ownership interest. "High-level personnel of a unit of the organization" is defined in the Commentary to §8C2.5 (Culpability Score).

   (C) "Substantial authority personnel" means individuals who within the scope of their authority exercise a substantial measure of discretion in acting on behalf of an organization. The term includes high-level personnel of the organization, individuals who exercise substantial supervisory authority (_e.g._, a plant manager, a sales manager), and any other individuals who, although not a part of an organization's management, nevertheless exercise substantial discretion when acting within the scope of their authority (_e.g._, an individual with authority in an organization to negotiate or set price levels or an individual authorized to negotiate or approve significant contracts). Whether an individual falls within this category must be determined on a case-by-case basis.

   (D) "Agent" means any individual, including a director, an officer, an employee, or an independent contractor, authorized to act on behalf of the organization.

   (E) An individual "condoned" an offense if the individual knew of the offense and did not take reasonable steps to prevent or terminate the offense.

   (F) "Similar misconduct" means prior conduct that is similar in nature to the conduct underlying the instant offense, without regard to whether or not such conduct violated the same statutory provision. For example, prior Medicare fraud would be misconduct similar to an instant offense involving another type of fraud.

   (G) "Prior criminal adjudication" means conviction by trial, plea of guilty (including an Alford plea), or plea of nolo contendere.

   (H) "Pecuniary gain" is derived from 18 U.S.C. § 3571(d) and means the additional before-tax profit to the defendant resulting from the relevant conduct of the offense. Gain can result from either additional revenue or cost savings. For example, an offense involving

APPENDIX C   App. C

odometer tampering can produce additional revenue. In such a case, the pecuniary gain is the additional revenue received because the automobiles appeared to have less mileage, i.e., the difference between the price received or expected for the automobiles with the apparent mileage and the fair market value of the automobiles with the actual mileage. An offense involving defense procurement fraud related to defective product testing can produce pecuniary gain resulting from cost savings. In such a case, the pecuniary gain is the amount saved because the product was not tested in the required manner.

(I) *"Pecuniary loss" is derived from 18 U.S.C. § 3571(d) and is equivalent to the term "loss" as used in Chapter Two (Offense Conduct). See Commentary to §2B1.1 (Theft, Property Destruction, and Fraud), and definitions of "tax loss" in Chapter Two, Part T (Offenses Involving Taxation).*

(J) *An individual was "willfully ignorant of the offense" if the individual did not investigate the possible occurrence of unlawful conduct despite knowledge of circumstances that would lead a reasonable person to investigate whether unlawful conduct had occurred.*

Historical Note: Effective November 1, 1991 (see Appendix C, amendment 422); November 1, 1997 (see Appendix C, amendment 546); November 1, 2001 (see Appendix C, amendment 617); November 1, 2004 (see Appendix C, amendment 673); November 1, 2010 (see Appendix C, amendment 747); November 1, 2011 (see Appendix C, amendment 758).

App. C GOVERNMENT CONTRACT COMPLIANCE HANDBOOK

PART B - REMEDYING HARM FROM CRIMINAL CONDUCT, AND EFFECTIVE COMPLIANCE AND ETHICS PROGRAM

Historical Note: Effective November 1, 1991 (see Appendix C, amendment 422). Amended effective November 1, 2004 (see Appendix C, amendment 673).

1. REMEDYING HARM FROM CRIMINAL CONDUCT

Historical Note: Effective November 1, 2004 (see Appendix C, amendment 673).

Introductory Commentary

As a general principle, the court should require that the organization take all appropriate steps to provide compensation to victims and otherwise remedy the harm caused or threatened by the offense. A restitution order or an order of probation requiring restitution can be used to compensate identifiable victims of the offense. A remedial order or an order of probation requiring community service can be used to reduce or eliminate the harm threatened, or to repair the harm caused by the offense, when that harm or threatened harm would otherwise not be remedied. An order of notice to victims can be used to notify unidentified victims of the offense.

Historical Note: Effective November 1, 1991 (see Appendix C, amendment 422).

§8B1.1. Restitution - Organizations

    (a)   In the case of an identifiable victim, the court shall—

        (1)   enter a restitution order for the full amount of the victim's loss, if such order is authorized under 18 U.S.C. § 2248, § 2259, § 2264, § 2327, § 3663, or § 3663A; or

        (2)   impose a term of probation or supervised release with a condition requiring restitution for the full amount of the victim's loss, if the offense is not an offense for which restitution is authorized under 18 U.S.C. § 3663(a)(1) but otherwise meets the criteria for an order of restitution under that section.

    (b)   *Provided*, that the provisions of subsection (a) do not apply—

        (1)   when full restitution has been made; or

        (2)   in the case of a restitution order under § 3663; a restitution order under 18 U.S.C. § 3663A that pertains to an offense against property described in 18 U.S.C. § 3663A(c)(1)(A)(ii); or a condition of restitution imposed pursuant to subsection (a)(2) above, to the extent the court finds, from facts on the record, that (A) the number of identifiable victims is so large as to make restitution impracticable; or (B) determining complex issues of fact related to the cause or amount of the victim's losses would complicate or prolong the sentencing process to a degree that the need to provide restitution to any victim is outweighed by the burden on the sentencing process.

APPENDIX C

(c) If a defendant is ordered to make restitution to an identifiable victim and to pay a fine, the court shall order that any money paid by the defendant shall first be applied to satisfy the order of restitution.

(d) A restitution order may direct the defendant to make a single, lump sum payment, partial payments at specified intervals, in-kind payments, or a combination of payments at specified intervals and in-kind payments. See 18 U.S.C. § 3664(f)(3)(A). An in-kind payment may be in the form of (1) return of property; (2) replacement of property; or (3) if the victim agrees, services rendered to the victim or to a person or organization other than the victim. See 18 U.S.C. § 3664(f)(4).

(e) A restitution order may direct the defendant to make nominal periodic payments if the court finds from facts on the record that the economic circumstances of the defendant do not allow the payment of any amount of a restitution order, and do not allow for the payment of the full amount of a restitution order in the foreseeable future under any reasonable schedule of payments.

(f) Special Instruction

(1) This guideline applies only to a defendant convicted of an offense committed on or after November 1, 1997. Notwithstanding the provisions of §1B1.11 (Use of Guidelines Manual in Effect on Date of Sentencing), use the former §8B1.1 (set forth in Appendix C, amendment 571) in lieu of this guideline in any other case.

Commentary

Background: Section 3553(a)(7) of Title 18, United States Code, requires the court, "in determining the particular sentence to be imposed," to consider "the need to provide restitution to any victims of the offense." Orders of restitution are authorized under 18 U.S.C. §§ 2248, 2259, 2264, 2327, 3663, and 3663A. For offenses for which an order of restitution is not authorized, restitution may be imposed as a condition of probation.

Historical Note: Effective November 1, 1991 (see Appendix C, amendment 422); November 1, 1997 (see Appendix C, amendment 571).

§8B1.2. **Remedial Orders - Organizations (Policy Statement)**

(a) To the extent not addressed under §8B1.1 (Restitution - Organizations), a remedial order imposed as a condition of probation may require the organization to remedy the harm caused by the offense and to eliminate or reduce the risk that the instant offense will cause future harm.

(b) If the magnitude of expected future harm can be reasonably estimated, the court may require the organization to create a trust fund sufficient to address that expected harm.

Commentary

<u>Background</u>: *The purposes of a remedial order are to remedy harm that has already occurred and to prevent future harm. A remedial order requiring corrective action by the organization may be necessary to prevent future injury from the instant offense, <u>e.g.</u>, a product recall for a food and drug violation or a clean-up order for an environmental violation. In some cases in which a remedial order potentially may be appropriate, a governmental regulatory agency, <u>e.g.</u>, the Environmental Protection Agency or the Food and Drug Administration, may have authority to order remedial measures. In such cases, a remedial order by the court may not be necessary. If a remedial order is entered, it should be coordinated with any administrative or civil actions taken by the appropriate governmental regulatory agency.*

<u>Historical Note</u>: Effective November 1, 1991 (<u>see</u> Appendix C, amendment 422).

§8B1.3. Community Service - Organizations (Policy Statement)

Community service may be ordered as a condition of probation where such community service is reasonably designed to repair the harm caused by the offense.

Commentary

<u>Background</u>: *An organization can perform community service only by employing its resources or paying its employees or others to do so. Consequently, an order that an organization perform community service is essentially an indirect monetary sanction, and therefore generally less desirable than a direct monetary sanction. However, where the convicted organization possesses knowledge, facilities, or skills that uniquely qualify it to repair damage caused by the offense, community service directed at repairing damage may provide an efficient means of remedying harm caused.*

In the past, some forms of community service imposed on organizations have not been related to the purposes of sentencing. Requiring a defendant to endow a chair at a university or to contribute to a local charity would not be consistent with this section unless such community service provided a means for preventive or corrective action directly related to the offense and therefore served one of the purposes of sentencing set forth in 18 U.S.C. § 3553(a).

<u>Historical Note</u>: Effective November 1, 1991 (<u>see</u> Appendix C, amendment 422).

§8B1.4. Order of Notice to Victims - Organizations

Apply §5F1.4 (Order of Notice to Victims).

<u>Historical Note</u>: Effective November 1, 1991 (<u>see</u> Appendix C, amendment 422).

* * * * *

APPENDIX C

2. EFFECTIVE COMPLIANCE AND ETHICS PROGRAM

Historical Note: Effective November 1, 2004 (see Appendix C, amendment 673).

§8B2.1. Effective Compliance and Ethics Program

(a) To have an effective compliance and ethics program, for purposes of subsection (f) of §8C2.5 (Culpability Score) and subsection (b)(1) of §8D1.4 (Recommended Conditions of Probation - Organizations), an organization shall—

   (1) exercise due diligence to prevent and detect criminal conduct; and

   (2) otherwise promote an organizational culture that encourages ethical conduct and a commitment to compliance with the law.

Such compliance and ethics program shall be reasonably designed, implemented, and enforced so that the program is generally effective in preventing and detecting criminal conduct. The failure to prevent or detect the instant offense does not necessarily mean that the program is not generally effective in preventing and detecting criminal conduct.

(b) Due diligence and the promotion of an organizational culture that encourages ethical conduct and a commitment to compliance with the law within the meaning of subsection (a) minimally require the following:

   (1) The organization shall establish standards and procedures to prevent and detect criminal conduct.

   (2) (A) The organization's governing authority shall be knowledgeable about the content and operation of the compliance and ethics program and shall exercise reasonable oversight with respect to the implementation and effectiveness of the compliance and ethics program.

   (B) High-level personnel of the organization shall ensure that the organization has an effective compliance and ethics program, as described in this guideline. Specific individual(s) within high-level personnel shall be assigned overall responsibility for the compliance and ethics program.

   (C) Specific individual(s) within the organization shall be delegated day-to-day operational responsibility for the compliance and ethics program. Individual(s) with operational responsibility shall report periodically to high-level personnel and, as appropriate, to the governing authority, or an appropriate subgroup of the governing authority, on the effectiveness of the compliance and ethics program. To carry out such operational responsibility, such individual(s) shall be given adequate resources, appropriate authority, and direct access to the governing authority or an appropriate subgroup of the governing authority.

(3) The organization shall use reasonable efforts not to include within the substantial authority personnel of the organization any individual whom the organization knew, or should have known through the exercise of due diligence, has engaged in illegal activities or other conduct inconsistent with an effective compliance and ethics program.

(4) (A) The organization shall take reasonable steps to communicate periodically and in a practical manner its standards and procedures, and other aspects of the compliance and ethics program, to the individuals referred to in subparagraph (B) by conducting effective training programs and otherwise disseminating information appropriate to such individuals' respective roles and responsibilities.

(B) The individuals referred to in subparagraph (A) are the members of the governing authority, high-level personnel, substantial authority personnel, the organization's employees, and, as appropriate, the organization's agents.

(5) The organization shall take reasonable steps—

(A) to ensure that the organization's compliance and ethics program is followed, including monitoring and auditing to detect criminal conduct;

(B) to evaluate periodically the effectiveness of the organization's compliance and ethics program; and

(C) to have and publicize a system, which may include mechanisms that allow for anonymity or confidentiality, whereby the organization's employees and agents may report or seek guidance regarding potential or actual criminal conduct without fear of retaliation.

(6) The organization's compliance and ethics program shall be promoted and enforced consistently throughout the organization through (A) appropriate incentives to perform in accordance with the compliance and ethics program; and (B) appropriate disciplinary measures for engaging in criminal conduct and for failing to take reasonable steps to prevent or detect criminal conduct.

(7) After criminal conduct has been detected, the organization shall take reasonable steps to respond appropriately to the criminal conduct and to prevent further similar criminal conduct, including making any necessary modifications to the organization's compliance and ethics program.

(c) In implementing subsection (b), the organization shall periodically assess the risk of criminal conduct and shall take appropriate steps to design, implement, or modify each requirement set forth in subsection (b) to reduce the risk of criminal conduct identified through this process.

APPENDIX C

Commentary

Application Notes:

1. *Definitions.*—For purposes of this guideline:

    "Compliance and ethics program" means a program designed to prevent and detect criminal conduct.

    "Governing authority" means the (A) the Board of Directors; or (B) if the organization does not have a Board of Directors, the highest-level governing body of the organization.

    "High-level personnel of the organization" and "substantial authority personnel" have the meaning given those terms in the Commentary to §8A1.2 (Application Instructions - Organizations).

    "Standards and procedures" means standards of conduct and internal controls that are reasonably capable of reducing the likelihood of criminal conduct.

2. *Factors to Consider in Meeting Requirements of this Guideline.*—

    (A) *In General.*—Each of the requirements set forth in this guideline shall be met by an organization; however, in determining what specific actions are necessary to meet those requirements, factors that shall be considered include: (i) applicable industry practice or the standards called for by any applicable governmental regulation; (ii) the size of the organization; and (iii) similar misconduct.

    (B) *Applicable Governmental Regulation and Industry Practice.*—An organization's failure to incorporate and follow applicable industry practice or the standards called for by any applicable governmental regulation weighs against a finding of an effective compliance and ethics program.

    (C) *The Size of the Organization.*—

    (i) *In General.*—The formality and scope of actions that an organization shall take to meet the requirements of this guideline, including the necessary features of the organization's standards and procedures, depend on the size of the organization.

    (ii) *Large Organizations.*—A large organization generally shall devote more formal operations and greater resources in meeting the requirements of this guideline than shall a small organization. As appropriate, a large organization should encourage small organizations (especially those that have, or seek to have, a business relationship with the large organization) to implement effective compliance and ethics programs.

    (iii) *Small Organizations.*—In meeting the requirements of this guideline, small organizations shall demonstrate the same degree of commitment to ethical conduct and compliance with the law as large organizations. However, a small organization may meet the requirements of this guideline with less formality and fewer resources than would be expected of large organizations. In appropriate circumstances, reliance on existing resources and simple systems can demonstrate a degree of commitment that, for a large organization, would only be demonstrated through more formally planned and implemented systems.

Examples of the informality and use of fewer resources with which a small organization may meet the requirements of this guideline include the following: (I) the governing authority's discharge of its responsibility for oversight of the compliance and ethics program by directly managing the organization's compliance and ethics efforts; (II) training employees through informal staff meetings, and monitoring through regular "walk-arounds" or continuous observation while managing the organization; (III) using available personnel, rather than employing separate staff, to carry out the compliance and ethics program; and (IV) modeling its own compliance and ethics program on existing, well-regarded compliance and ethics programs and best practices of other similar organizations.

(D) *Recurrence of Similar Misconduct.*—Recurrence of similar misconduct creates doubt regarding whether the organization took reasonable steps to meet the requirements of this guideline. For purposes of this subparagraph, "similar misconduct" has the meaning given that term in the Commentary to §8A1.2 (Application Instructions - Organizations).

3. *Application of Subsection (b)(2).*—High-level personnel and substantial authority personnel of the organization shall be knowledgeable about the content and operation of the compliance and ethics program, shall perform their assigned duties consistent with the exercise of due diligence, and shall promote an organizational culture that encourages ethical conduct and a commitment to compliance with the law.

If the specific individual(s) assigned overall responsibility for the compliance and ethics program does not have day-to-day operational responsibility for the program, then the individual(s) with day-to-day operational responsibility for the program typically should, no less than annually, give the governing authority or an appropriate subgroup thereof information on the implementation and effectiveness of the compliance and ethics program.

4. *Application of Subsection (b)(3).*—

   (A) *Consistency with Other Law.*—Nothing in subsection (b)(3) is intended to require conduct inconsistent with any Federal, State, or local law, including any law governing employment or hiring practices.

   (B) *Implementation.*—In implementing subsection (b)(3), the organization shall hire and promote individuals so as to ensure that all individuals within the high-level personnel and substantial authority personnel of the organization will perform their assigned duties in a manner consistent with the exercise of due diligence and the promotion of an organizational culture that encourages ethical conduct and a commitment to compliance with the law under subsection (a). With respect to the hiring or promotion of such individuals, an organization shall consider the relatedness of the individual's illegal activities and other misconduct (*i.e.*, other conduct inconsistent with an effective compliance and ethics program) to the specific responsibilities the individual is anticipated to be assigned and other factors such as: (i) the recency of the individual's

APPENDIX C

illegal activities and other misconduct; and (ii) whether the individual has engaged in other such illegal activities and other such misconduct.

5. *Application of Subsection (b)(6).—Adequate discipline of individuals responsible for an offense is a necessary component of enforcement; however, the form of discipline that will be appropriate will be case specific.*

6. *Application of Subsection (b)(7).—Subsection (b)(7) has two aspects.*

   First, the organization should respond appropriately to the criminal conduct. The organization should take reasonable steps, as warranted under the circumstances, to remedy the harm resulting from the criminal conduct. These steps may include, where appropriate, providing restitution to identifiable victims, as well as other forms of remediation. Other reasonable steps to respond appropriately to the criminal conduct may include self-reporting and cooperation with authorities.

   Second, the organization should act appropriately to prevent further similar criminal conduct, including assessing the compliance and ethics program and making modifications necessary to ensure the program is effective. The steps taken should be consistent with subsections (b)(5) and (c) and may include the use of an outside professional advisor to ensure adequate assessment and implementation of any modifications.

7. *Application of Subsection (c).—To meet the requirements of subsection (c), an organization shall:*

   (A) Assess periodically the risk that criminal conduct will occur, including assessing the following:

   (i) The nature and seriousness of such criminal conduct.

   (ii) The likelihood that certain criminal conduct may occur because of the nature of the organization's business. If, because of the nature of an organization's business, there is a substantial risk that certain types of criminal conduct may occur, the organization shall take reasonable steps to prevent and detect that type of criminal conduct. For example, an organization that, due to the nature of its business, employs sales personnel who have flexibility to set prices shall establish standards and procedures designed to prevent and detect price-fixing. An organization that, due to the nature of its business, employs sales personnel who have flexibility to represent the material characteristics of a product shall establish standards and procedures designed to prevent and detect fraud.

   (iii) The prior history of the organization. The prior history of an organization may indicate types of criminal conduct that it shall take actions to prevent and detect.

   (B) Prioritize periodically, as appropriate, the actions taken pursuant to any requirement set forth in subsection (b), in order to focus on preventing and detecting the criminal conduct identified under subparagraph (A) of this note as most serious, and most likely, to occur.

App. C GOVERNMENT CONTRACT COMPLIANCE HANDBOOK

(C) Modify, as appropriate, the actions taken pursuant to any requirement set forth in subsection (b) to reduce the risk of criminal conduct identified under subparagraph (A) of this note as most serious, and most likely, to occur.

<u>Background</u>: This section sets forth the requirements for an effective compliance and ethics program. This section responds to section 805(a)(5) of the Sarbanes-Oxley Act of 2002, Public Law 107–204, which directed the Commission to review and amend, as appropriate, the guidelines and related policy statements to ensure that the guidelines that apply to organizations in this chapter "are sufficient to deter and punish organizational criminal misconduct."

The requirements set forth in this guideline are intended to achieve reasonable prevention and detection of criminal conduct for which the organization would be vicariously liable. The prior diligence of an organization in seeking to prevent and detect criminal conduct has a direct bearing on the appropriate penalties and probation terms for the organization if it is convicted and sentenced for a criminal offense.

<u>Historical Note</u>: Effective November 1, 2004 (<u>see</u> Appendix C, amendment 673). Amended effective November 1, 2010 (<u>see</u> Appendix C, amendment 744); November 1, 2011 (<u>see</u> Appendix C, amendment 758); November 1, 2013 (<u>see</u> Appendix C, amendment 778).

APPENDIX C   App. C

PART C - FINES

1. DETERMINING THE FINE - CRIMINAL PURPOSE ORGANIZATIONS

§8C1.1.   Determining the Fine - Criminal Purpose Organizations

If, upon consideration of the nature and circumstances of the offense and the history and characteristics of the organization, the court determines that the organization operated primarily for a criminal purpose or primarily by criminal means, the fine shall be set at an amount (subject to the statutory maximum) sufficient to divest the organization of all its net assets. When this section applies, Subpart 2 (Determining the Fine - Other Organizations) and §8C3.4 (Fines Paid by Owners of Closely Held Organizations) do not apply.

Commentary

Application Note:

1. *"Net assets," as used in this section, means the assets remaining after payment of all legitimate claims against assets by known innocent bona fide creditors.*

<u>Background</u>: *This guideline addresses the case in which the court, based upon an examination of the nature and circumstances of the offense and the history and characteristics of the organization, determines that the organization was operated primarily for a criminal purpose (e.g., a front for a scheme that was designed to commit fraud; an organization established to participate in the illegal manufacture, importation, or distribution of a controlled substance) or operated primarily by criminal means (e.g., a hazardous waste disposal business that had no legitimate means of disposing of hazardous waste). In such a case, the fine shall be set at an amount sufficient to remove all of the organization's net assets. If the extent of the assets of the organization is unknown, the maximum fine authorized by statute should be imposed, absent innocent bona fide creditors.*

Historical Note: Effective November 1, 1991 (see Appendix C, amendment 422).

* * * * *

2. DETERMINING THE FINE - OTHER ORGANIZATIONS

§8C2.1.   Applicability of Fine Guidelines

The provisions of §§8C2.2 through 8C2.9 apply to each count for which the applicable guideline offense level is determined under:

(a)   §§2B1.1, 2B1.4, 2B2.3, 2B4.1, 2B5.3, 2B6.1;
       §§2C1.1, 2C1.2, 2C1.6;
       §§2D1.7, 2D3.1, 2D3.2;
       §§2E3.1, 2E4.1, 2E5.1, 2E5.3;
       §2G3.1;

§§2K1.1, 2K2.1;
§2L1.1;
§2N3.1;
§2R1.1;
§§2S1.1, 2S1.3;
§§2T1.1, 2T1.4, 2T1.6, 2T1.7, 2T1.8, 2T1.9, 2T2.1, 2T2.2, 2T3.1; or

(b) §§2E1.1, 2X1.1, 2X2.1, 2X3.1, 2X4.1, with respect to cases in which the offense level for the underlying offense is determined under one of the guideline sections listed in subsection (a) above.

Commentary

Application Notes:

1. *If the Chapter Two offense guideline for a count is listed in subsection (a) or (b) above, and the applicable guideline results in the determination of the offense level by use of one of the listed guidelines, apply the provisions of §§8C2.2 through 8C2.9 to that count. For example, §§8C2.2 through 8C2.9 apply to an offense under §2K2.1 (an offense guideline listed in subsection (a)), unless the cross reference in that guideline requires the offense level to be determined under an offense guideline section not listed in subsection (a).*

2. *If the Chapter Two offense guideline for a count is not listed in subsection (a) or (b) above, but the applicable guideline results in the determination of the offense level by use of a listed guideline, apply the provisions of §§8C2.2 through 8C2.9 to that count. For example, where the conduct set forth in a count of conviction ordinarily referenced to §2N2.1 (an offense guideline not listed in subsection (a)) establishes §2B1.1 (Theft, Property Destruction, and Fraud) as the applicable offense guideline (an offense guideline listed in subsection (a)), §§8C2.2 through 8C2.9 would apply because the actual offense level is determined under §2B1.1 (Theft, Property Destruction, and Fraud).*

Background: *The fine guidelines of this subpart apply only to offenses covered by the guideline sections set forth in subsection (a) above. For example, the provisions of §§8C2.2 through 8C2.9 do not apply to counts for which the applicable guideline offense level is determined under Chapter Two, Part Q (Offenses Involving the Environment). For such cases, §8C2.10 (Determining the Fine for Other Counts) is applicable.*

Historical Note: Effective November 1, 1991 (see Appendix C, amendment 422). Amended effective November 1, 1992 (see Appendix C, amendment 453); November 1, 1993 (see Appendix C, amendment 496); November 1, 2001 (see Appendix C, amendments 617, 619, and 634); November 1, 2005 (see Appendix C, amendment 679).

§8C2.2. Preliminary Determination of Inability to Pay Fine

(a) Where it is readily ascertainable that the organization cannot and is not likely to become able (even on an installment schedule) to pay restitution required under §8B1.1 (Restitution - Organizations), a determination of the guideline fine range is unnecessary because, pursuant to §8C3.3(a), no fine would be imposed.

(b) Where it is readily ascertainable through a preliminary determination of the minimum of the guideline fine range (see §§8C2.3 through 8C2.7) that the organization cannot and is not likely to become able (even on an installment schedule) to pay such minimum guideline fine, a further determination of the guideline fine range is unnecessary. Instead, the court may use the preliminary determination and impose the fine that would result from the application of §8C3.3 (Reduction of Fine Based on Inability to Pay).

Commentary

Application Notes:

1. In a case of a determination under subsection (a), a statement that "the guideline fine range was not determined because it is readily ascertainable that the defendant cannot and is not likely to become able to pay restitution" is recommended.

2. In a case of a determination under subsection (b), a statement that "no precise determination of the guideline fine range is required because it is readily ascertainable that the defendant cannot and is not likely to become able to pay the minimum of the guideline fine range" is recommended.

Background: Many organizational defendants lack the ability to pay restitution. In addition, many organizational defendants who may be able to pay restitution lack the ability to pay the minimum fine called for by §8C2.7(a). In such cases, a complete determination of the guideline fine range may be a needless exercise. This section provides for an abbreviated determination of the guideline fine range that can be applied where it is readily ascertainable that the fine within the guideline fine range determined under §8C2.7 (Guideline Fine Range - Organizations) would be reduced under §8C3.3 (Reduction of Fine Based on Inability to Pay).

Historical Note: Effective November 1, 1991 (see Appendix C, amendment 422).

§8C2.3. Offense Level

(a) For each count covered by §8C2.1 (Applicability of Fine Guidelines), use the applicable Chapter Two guideline to determine the base offense level and apply, in the order listed, any appropriate adjustments contained in that guideline.

(b) Where there is more than one such count, apply Chapter Three, Part D (Multiple Counts) to determine the combined offense level.

Commentary

Application Notes:

1. In determining the offense level under this section, "defendant," as used in Chapter Two, includes any agent of the organization for whose conduct the organization is criminally responsible.

App. C   GOVERNMENT CONTRACT COMPLIANCE HANDBOOK

2. *In determining the offense level under this section, apply the provisions of §§1B1.2 through 1B1.8. Do not apply the adjustments in Chapter Three, Parts A (Victim-Related Adjustments), B (Role in the Offense), C (Obstruction and Related Adjustments), and E (Acceptance of Responsibility).*

Historical Note: Effective November 1, 1991 (see Appendix C, amendment 422). Amended effective November 1, 2011 (see Appendix C, amendment 758).

§8C2.4. Base Fine

(a) The base fine is the greatest of:

 (1) the amount from the table in subsection (d) below corresponding to the offense level determined under §8C2.3 (Offense Level); or

 (2) the pecuniary gain to the organization from the offense; or

 (3) the pecuniary loss from the offense caused by the organization, to the extent the loss was caused intentionally, knowingly, or recklessly.

(b) *Provided*, that if the applicable offense guideline in Chapter Two includes a special instruction for organizational fines, that special instruction shall be applied, as appropriate.

(c) *Provided, further,* that to the extent the calculation of either pecuniary gain or pecuniary loss would unduly complicate or prolong the sentencing process, that amount, i.e., gain or loss as appropriate, shall not be used for the determination of the base fine.

(d) Offense Level Fine Table

Offense Level	Amount
6 or less	$5,000
7	$7,500
8	$10,000
9	$15,000
10	$20,000
11	$30,000
12	$40,000
13	$60,000
14	$85,000
15	$125,000
16	$175,000
17	$250,000
18	$350,000
19	$500,000
20	$650,000

APPENDIX C   App. C

21	$910,000
22	$1,200,000
23	$1,600,000
24	$2,100,000
25	$2,800,000
26	$3,700,000
27	$4,800,000
28	$6,300,000
29	$8,100,000
30	$10,500,000
31	$13,500,000
32	$17,500,000
33	$22,000,000
34	$28,500,000
35	$36,000,000
36	$45,500,000
37	$57,500,000
38 or more	$72,500,000

Commentary

Application Notes:

1. *"Pecuniary gain," "pecuniary loss," and "offense" are defined in the Commentary to §8A1.2 (Application Instructions - Organizations). Note that subsections (a)(2) and (a)(3) contain certain limitations as to the use of pecuniary gain and pecuniary loss in determining the base fine. Under subsection (a)(2), the pecuniary gain used to determine the base fine is the pecuniary gain to the organization from the offense. Under subsection (a)(3), the pecuniary loss used to determine the base fine is the pecuniary loss from the offense caused by the organization, to the extent that such loss was caused intentionally, knowingly, or recklessly.*

2. *Under 18 U.S.C. § 3571(d), the court is not required to calculate pecuniary loss or pecuniary gain to the extent that determination of loss or gain would unduly complicate or prolong the sentencing process. Nevertheless, the court may need to approximate loss in order to calculate offense levels under Chapter Two. See Commentary to §2B1.1 (Theft, Property Destruction, and Fraud). If loss is approximated for purposes of determining the applicable offense level, the court should use that approximation as the starting point for calculating pecuniary loss under this section.*

3. *In a case of an attempted offense or a conspiracy to commit an offense, pecuniary loss and pecuniary gain are to be determined in accordance with the principles stated in §2X1.1 (Attempt, Solicitation, or Conspiracy).*

4. *In a case involving multiple participants (i.e., multiple organizations, or the organization and individual(s) unassociated with the organization), the applicable offense level is to be determined without regard to apportionment of the gain from or loss caused by the offense. See §1B1.3 (Relevant Conduct). However, if the base fine is determined under subsections (a)(2) or (a)(3), the court may, as appropriate, apportion gain or loss considering the defendant's relative culpability and other pertinent factors. Note also that under §2R1.1(d)(1),*

App. C GOVERNMENT CONTRACT COMPLIANCE HANDBOOK

the volume of commerce, which is used in determining a proxy for loss under §8C2.4(a)(3), is limited to the volume of commerce attributable to the defendant.

5. Special instructions regarding the determination of the base fine are contained in §§2B4.1 (Bribery in Procurement of Bank Loan and Other Commercial Bribery); 2C1.1 (Offering, Giving, Soliciting, or Receiving a Bribe; Extortion Under Color of Official Right; Fraud Involving the Deprivation of the Intangible Right to Honest Services of Public Officials; Conspiracy to Defraud by Interference with Governmental Functions); 2C1.2 (Offering, Giving, Soliciting, or Receiving a Gratuity); 2E5.1 (Offering, Accepting, or Soliciting a Bribe or Gratuity Affecting the Operation of an Employee Welfare or Pension Benefit Plan; Prohibited Payments or Lending of Money by Employer or Agent to Employees, Representatives, or Labor Organizations); and 2R1.1 (Bid-Rigging, Price-Fixing or Market-Allocation Agreements Among Competitors).

Background: Under this section, the base fine is determined in one of three ways: (1) by the amount, based on the offense level, from the table in subsection (d); (2) by the pecuniary gain to the organization from the offense; and (3) by the pecuniary loss caused by the organization, to the extent that such loss was caused intentionally, knowingly, or recklessly. In certain cases, special instructions for determining the loss or offense level amount apply. As a general rule, the base fine measures the seriousness of the offense. The determinants of the base fine are selected so that, in conjunction with the multipliers derived from the culpability score in §8C2.5 (Culpability Score), they will result in guideline fine ranges appropriate to deter organizational criminal conduct and to provide incentives for organizations to maintain internal mechanisms for preventing, detecting, and reporting criminal conduct. In order to deter organizations from seeking to obtain financial reward through criminal conduct, this section provides that, when greatest, pecuniary gain to the organization is used to determine the base fine. In order to ensure that organizations will seek to prevent losses intentionally, knowingly, or recklessly caused by their agents, this section provides that, when greatest, pecuniary loss is used to determine the base fine in such circumstances. Chapter Two provides special instructions for fines that include specific rules for determining the base fine in connection with certain types of offenses in which the calculation of loss or gain is difficult, e.g., price-fixing. For these offenses, the special instructions tailor the base fine to circumstances that occur in connection with such offenses and that generally relate to the magnitude of loss or gain resulting from such offenses.

Historical Note: Effective November 1, 1991 (see Appendix C, amendment 422). Amended effective November 1, 1993 (see Appendix C, amendment 496); November 1, 1995 (see Appendix C, amendment 534); November 1, 2001 (see Appendix C, amendment 634); November 1, 2004 (see Appendix C, amendments 666 and 673).

§8C2.5. Culpability Score

(a) Start with 5 points and apply subsections (b) through (g) below.

(b) Involvement in or Tolerance of Criminal Activity

If more than one applies, use the greatest:

(1) If—

(A) the organization had 5,000 or more employees and

– 508 –

App. C-20

APPENDIX C

        (i)   an individual within high-level personnel of the organization participated in, condoned, or was willfully ignorant of the offense; or

        (ii)   tolerance of the offense by substantial authority personnel was pervasive throughout the organization; or

   (B)   the unit of the organization within which the offense was committed had 5,000 or more employees and

        (i)   an individual within high-level personnel of the unit participated in, condoned, or was willfully ignorant of the offense; or

        (ii)   tolerance of the offense by substantial authority personnel was pervasive throughout such unit,

add **5** points; or

(2)   If—

   (A)   the organization had 1,000 or more employees and

        (i)   an individual within high-level personnel of the organization participated in, condoned, or was willfully ignorant of the offense; or

        (ii)   tolerance of the offense by substantial authority personnel was pervasive throughout the organization; or

   (B)   the unit of the organization within which the offense was committed had 1,000 or more employees and

        (i)   an individual within high-level personnel of the unit participated in, condoned, or was willfully ignorant of the offense; or

        (ii)   tolerance of the offense by substantial authority personnel was pervasive throughout such unit,

add **4** points; or

(3)   If—

   (A)   the organization had 200 or more employees and

        (i)   an individual within high-level personnel of the organization participated in, condoned, or was willfully ignorant of the offense; or

        (ii)   tolerance of the offense by substantial authority personnel was pervasive throughout the organization; or

(B) the unit of the organization within which the offense was committed had 200 or more employees and

   (i) an individual within high-level personnel of the unit participated in, condoned, or was willfully ignorant of the offense; or

   (ii) tolerance of the offense by substantial authority personnel was pervasive throughout such unit,

add **3** points; or

(4) If the organization had 50 or more employees and an individual within substantial authority personnel participated in, condoned, or was willfully ignorant of the offense, add **2** points; or

(5) If the organization had 10 or more employees and an individual within substantial authority personnel participated in, condoned, or was willfully ignorant of the offense, add **1** point.

(c) <u>Prior History</u>

If more than one applies, use the greater:

(1) If the organization (or separately managed line of business) committed any part of the instant offense less than 10 years after (A) a criminal adjudication based on similar misconduct; or (B) civil or administrative adjudication(s) based on two or more separate instances of similar misconduct, add **1** point; or

(2) If the organization (or separately managed line of business) committed any part of the instant offense less than 5 years after (A) a criminal adjudication based on similar misconduct; or (B) civil or administrative adjudication(s) based on two or more separate instances of similar misconduct, add **2** points.

(d) <u>Violation of an Order</u>

If more than one applies, use the greater:

(1) (A) If the commission of the instant offense violated a judicial order or injunction, other than a violation of a condition of probation; or (B) if the organization (or separately managed line of business) violated a condition of probation by engaging in similar misconduct, i.e., misconduct similar to that for which it was placed on probation, add **2** points; or

(2) If the commission of the instant offense violated a condition of probation, add **1** point.

APPENDIX C

(e) Obstruction of Justice

If the organization willfully obstructed or impeded, attempted to obstruct or impede, or aided, abetted, or encouraged obstruction of justice during the investigation, prosecution, or sentencing of the instant offense, or, with knowledge thereof, failed to take reasonable steps to prevent such obstruction or impedance or attempted obstruction or impedance, add **3** points.

(f) Effective Compliance and Ethics Program

    (1) If the offense occurred even though the organization had in place at the time of the offense an effective compliance and ethics program, as provided in §8B2.1 (Effective Compliance and Ethics Program), subtract **3** points.

    (2) Subsection (f)(1) shall not apply if, after becoming aware of an offense, the organization unreasonably delayed reporting the offense to appropriate governmental authorities.

    (3) (A) Except as provided in subparagraphs (B) and (C), subsection (f)(1) shall not apply if an individual within high-level personnel of the organization, a person within high-level personnel of the unit of the organization within which the offense was committed where the unit had 200 or more employees, or an individual described in §8B2.1(b)(2)(B) or (C), participated in, condoned, or was willfully ignorant of the offense.

        (B) There is a rebuttable presumption, for purposes of subsection (f)(1), that the organization did not have an effective compliance and ethics program if an individual—

            (i) within high-level personnel of a small organization; or

            (ii) within substantial authority personnel, but not within high-level personnel, of any organization,

        participated in, condoned, or was willfully ignorant of, the offense.

        (C) Subparagraphs (A) and (B) shall not apply if—

            (i) the individual or individuals with operational responsibility for the compliance and ethics program (see §8B2.1(b)(2)(C)) have direct reporting obligations to the governing authority or an appropriate subgroup thereof (e.g., an audit committee of the board of directors);

            (ii) the compliance and ethics program detected the offense before discovery outside the organization or before such discovery was reasonably likely;

(iii) the organization promptly reported the offense to appropriate governmental authorities; and

(iv) no individual with operational responsibility for the compliance and ethics program participated in, condoned, or was willfully ignorant of the offense.

(g) Self-Reporting, Cooperation, and Acceptance of Responsibility

If more than one applies, use the greatest:

(1) If the organization (A) prior to an imminent threat of disclosure or government investigation; and (B) within a reasonably prompt time after becoming aware of the offense, reported the offense to appropriate governmental authorities, fully cooperated in the investigation, and clearly demonstrated recognition and affirmative acceptance of responsibility for its criminal conduct, subtract **5** points; or

(2) If the organization fully cooperated in the investigation and clearly demonstrated recognition and affirmative acceptance of responsibility for its criminal conduct, subtract **2** points; or

(3) If the organization clearly demonstrated recognition and affirmative acceptance of responsibility for its criminal conduct, subtract **1** point.

Commentary

Application Notes:

1. *Definitions.*—For purposes of this guideline, "condoned", "prior criminal adjudication", "similar misconduct", "substantial authority personnel", and "willfully ignorant of the offense" have the meaning given those terms in Application Note 3 of the Commentary to §8A1.2 (Application Instructions - Organizations).

   "Small Organization", for purposes of subsection (f)(3), means an organization that, at the time of the instant offense, had fewer than 200 employees.

2. For purposes of subsection (b), "unit of the organization" means any reasonably distinct operational component of the organization. For example, a large organization may have several large units such as divisions or subsidiaries, as well as many smaller units such as specialized manufacturing, marketing, or accounting operations within these larger units. For purposes of this definition, all of these types of units are encompassed within the term "unit of the organization."

3. "High-level personnel of the organization" is defined in the Commentary to §8A1.2 (Application Instructions - Organizations). With respect to a unit with 200 or more employees, "high-level personnel of a unit of the organization" means agents within the unit who set the policy for or control that unit. For example, if the managing agent of a unit with 200 employees participated in an offense, three points would be added under subsection (b)(3); if that organization had 1,000 employees and the managing agent of the unit with 200 employees

APPENDIX C

were also within high-level personnel of the organization in its entirety, four points (rather than three) would be added under subsection (b)(2).

4. Pervasiveness under subsection (b) will be case specific and depend on the number, and degree of responsibility, of individuals within substantial authority personnel who participated in, condoned, or were willfully ignorant of the offense. Fewer individuals need to be involved for a finding of pervasiveness if those individuals exercised a relatively high degree of authority. Pervasiveness can occur either within an organization as a whole or within a unit of an organization. For example, if an offense were committed in an organization with 1,000 employees but the tolerance of the offense was pervasive only within a unit of the organization with 200 employees (and no high-level personnel of the organization participated in, condoned, or was willfully ignorant of the offense), three points would be added under subsection (b)(3). If, in the same organization, tolerance of the offense was pervasive throughout the organization as a whole, or an individual within high-level personnel of the organization participated in the offense, four points (rather than three) would be added under subsection (b)(2).

5. A "separately managed line of business," as used in subsections (c) and (d), is a subpart of a for-profit organization that has its own management, has a high degree of autonomy from higher managerial authority, and maintains its own separate books of account. Corporate subsidiaries and divisions frequently are separately managed lines of business. Under subsection (c), in determining the prior history of an organization with separately managed lines of business, only the prior conduct or criminal record of the separately managed line of business involved in the instant offense is to be used. Under subsection (d), in the context of an organization with separately managed lines of business, in making the determination whether a violation of a condition of probation involved engaging in similar misconduct, only the prior misconduct of the separately managed line of business involved in the instant offense is to be considered.

6. Under subsection (c), in determining the prior history of an organization or separately managed line of business, the conduct of the underlying economic entity shall be considered without regard to its legal structure or ownership. For example, if two companies merged and became separate divisions and separately managed lines of business within the merged company, each division would retain the prior history of its predecessor company. If a company reorganized and became a new legal entity, the new company would retain the prior history of the predecessor company. In contrast, if one company purchased the physical assets but not the ongoing business of another company, the prior history of the company selling the physical assets would not be transferred to the company purchasing the assets. However, if an organization is acquired by another organization in response to solicitations by appropriate federal government officials, the prior history of the acquired organization shall not be attributed to the acquiring organization.

7. Under subsections (c)(1)(B) and (c)(2)(B), the civil or administrative adjudication(s) must have occurred within the specified period (ten or five years) of the instant offense.

8. Adjust the culpability score for the factors listed in subsection (e) whether or not the offense guideline incorporates that factor, or that factor is inherent in the offense.

9. Subsection (e) applies where the obstruction is committed on behalf of the organization; it does not apply where an individual or individuals have attempted to conceal their misconduct

from the organization. The Commentary to §3C1.1 (Obstructing or Impeding the Administration of Justice) provides guidance regarding the types of conduct that constitute obstruction.

10. *Subsection (f)(2) contemplates that the organization will be allowed a reasonable period of time to conduct an internal investigation. In addition, no reporting is required by subsection (f)(2) or (f)(3)(C)(iii) if the organization reasonably concluded, based on the information then available, that no offense had been committed.*

11. *For purposes of subsection (f)(3)(C)(i), an individual has "direct reporting obligations" to the governing authority or an appropriate subgroup thereof if the individual has express authority to communicate personally to the governing authority or appropriate subgroup thereof (A) promptly on any matter involving criminal conduct or potential criminal conduct, and (B) no less than annually on the implementation and effectiveness of the compliance and ethics program.*

12. *"Appropriate governmental authorities," as used in subsections (f) and (g)(1), means the federal or state law enforcement, regulatory, or program officials having jurisdiction over such matter. To qualify for a reduction under subsection (g)(1), the report to appropriate governmental authorities must be made under the direction of the organization.*

13. *To qualify for a reduction under subsection (g)(1) or (g)(2), cooperation must be both timely and thorough. To be timely, the cooperation must begin essentially at the same time as the organization is officially notified of a criminal investigation. To be thorough, the cooperation should include the disclosure of all pertinent information known by the organization. A prime test of whether the organization has disclosed all pertinent information is whether the information is sufficient for law enforcement personnel to identify the nature and extent of the offense and the individual(s) responsible for the criminal conduct. However, the cooperation to be measured is the cooperation of the organization itself, not the cooperation of individuals within the organization. If, because of the lack of cooperation of particular individual(s), neither the organization nor law enforcement personnel are able to identify the culpable individual(s) within the organization despite the organization's efforts to cooperate fully, the organization may still be given credit for full cooperation.*

14. *Entry of a plea of guilty prior to the commencement of trial combined with truthful admission of involvement in the offense and related conduct ordinarily will constitute significant evidence of affirmative acceptance of responsibility under subsection (g), unless outweighed by conduct of the organization that is inconsistent with such acceptance of responsibility. This adjustment is not intended to apply to an organization that puts the government to its burden of proof at trial by denying the essential factual elements of guilt, is convicted, and only then admits guilt and expresses remorse. Conviction by trial, however, does not automatically preclude an organization from consideration for such a reduction. In rare situations, an organization may clearly demonstrate an acceptance of responsibility for its criminal conduct even though it exercises its constitutional right to a trial. This may occur, for example, where an organization goes to trial to assert and preserve issues that do not relate to factual guilt (e.g., to make a constitutional challenge to a statute or a challenge to the applicability of a statute to its conduct). In each such instance, however, a determination that an organization has accepted responsibility will be based primarily upon pretrial statements and conduct.*

15. *In making a determination with respect to subsection (g), the court may determine that the chief executive officer or highest ranking employee of an organization should appear at*

– 514 –

APPENDIX C

sentencing in order to signify that the organization has clearly demonstrated recognition and affirmative acceptance of responsibility.

<u>Background</u>: *The increased culpability scores under subsection (b) are based on three interrelated principles. First, an organization is more culpable when individuals who manage the organization or who have substantial discretion in acting for the organization participate in, condone, or are willfully ignorant of criminal conduct. Second, as organizations become larger and their managements become more professional, participation in, condonation of, or willful ignorance of criminal conduct by such management is increasingly a breach of trust or abuse of position. Third, as organizations increase in size, the risk of criminal conduct beyond that reflected in the instant offense also increases whenever management's tolerance of that offense is pervasive. Because of the continuum of sizes of organizations and professionalization of management, subsection (b) gradually increases the culpability score based upon the size of the organization and the level and extent of the substantial authority personnel involvement.*

<u>Historical Note</u>: Effective November 1, 1991 (<u>see</u> Appendix C, amendment 422). Amended effective November 1, 2004 (<u>see</u> Appendix C, amendment 673); November 1, 2006 (<u>see</u> Appendix C, amendment 695); November 1, 2010 (<u>see</u> Appendix C, amendment 744).

§8C2.6. Minimum and Maximum Multipliers

Using the culpability score from §8C2.5 (Culpability Score) and applying any applicable special instruction for fines in Chapter Two, determine the applicable minimum and maximum fine multipliers from the table below.

Culpability Score	Minimum Multiplier	Maximum Multiplier
10 or more	2.00	4.00
9	1.80	3.60
8	1.60	3.20
7	1.40	2.80
6	1.20	2.40
5	1.00	2.00
4	0.80	1.60
3	0.60	1.20
2	0.40	0.80
1	0.20	0.40
0 or less	0.05	0.20

<u>Commentary</u>

Application Note:

1. *A special instruction for fines in §2R1.1 (Bid-Rigging, Price-Fixing or Market-Allocation Agreements Among Competitors) sets a floor for minimum and maximum multipliers in cases covered by that guideline.*

<u>Historical Note</u>: Effective November 1, 1991 (<u>see</u> Appendix C, amendment 422).

§8C2.7. Guideline Fine Range - Organizations

(a) The minimum of the guideline fine range is determined by multiplying the base fine determined under §8C2.4 (Base Fine) by the applicable minimum multiplier determined under §8C2.6 (Minimum and Maximum Multipliers).

(b) The maximum of the guideline fine range is determined by multiplying the base fine determined under §8C2.4 (Base Fine) by the applicable maximum multiplier determined under §8C2.6 (Minimum and Maximum Multipliers).

Historical Note: Effective November 1, 1991 (see Appendix C, amendment 422).

§8C2.8. Determining the Fine Within the Range (Policy Statement)

(a) In determining the amount of the fine within the applicable guideline range, the court should consider:

(1) the need for the sentence to reflect the seriousness of the offense, promote respect for the law, provide just punishment, afford adequate deterrence, and protect the public from further crimes of the organization;

(2) the organization's role in the offense;

(3) any collateral consequences of conviction, including civil obligations arising from the organization's conduct;

(4) any nonpecuniary loss caused or threatened by the offense;

(5) whether the offense involved a vulnerable victim;

(6) any prior criminal record of an individual within high-level personnel of the organization or high-level personnel of a unit of the organization who participated in, condoned, or was willfully ignorant of the criminal conduct;

(7) any prior civil or criminal misconduct by the organization other than that counted under §8C2.5(c);

(8) any culpability score under §8C2.5 (Culpability Score) higher than 10 or lower than 0;

(9) partial but incomplete satisfaction of the conditions for one or more of the mitigating or aggravating factors set forth in §8C2.5 (Culpability Score);

(10) any factor listed in 18 U.S.C. § 3572(a); and

(11) whether the organization failed to have, at the time of the instant offense, an effective compliance and ethics program within the meaning of §8B2.1 (Effective Compliance and Ethics Program).

APPENDIX C   **App. C**

    (b)   In addition, the court may consider the relative importance of any factor used to determine the range, including the pecuniary loss caused by the offense, the pecuniary gain from the offense, any specific offense characteristic used to determine the offense level, and any aggravating or mitigating factor used to determine the culpability score.

Commentary

Application Notes:

1. Subsection (a)(2) provides that the court, in setting the fine within the guideline fine range, should consider the organization's role in the offense. This consideration is particularly appropriate if the guideline fine range does not take the organization's role in the offense into account. For example, the guideline fine range in an antitrust case does not take into consideration whether the organization was an organizer or leader of the conspiracy. A higher fine within the guideline fine range ordinarily will be appropriate for an organization that takes a leading role in such an offense.

2. Subsection (a)(3) provides that the court, in setting the fine within the guideline fine range, should consider any collateral consequences of conviction, including civil obligations arising from the organization's conduct. As a general rule, collateral consequences that merely make victims whole provide no basis for reducing the fine within the guideline range. If criminal and civil sanctions are unlikely to make victims whole, this may provide a basis for a higher fine within the guideline fine range. If punitive collateral sanctions have been or will be imposed on the organization, this may provide a basis for a lower fine within the guideline fine range.

3. Subsection (a)(4) provides that the court, in setting the fine within the guideline fine range, should consider any nonpecuniary loss caused or threatened by the offense. To the extent that nonpecuniary loss caused or threatened (*e.g.*, loss of or threat to human life; psychological injury; threat to national security) by the offense is not adequately considered in setting the guideline fine range, this factor provides a basis for a higher fine within the range. This factor is more likely to be applicable where the guideline fine range is determined by pecuniary loss or gain, rather than by offense level, because the Chapter Two offense levels frequently take actual or threatened nonpecuniary loss into account.

4. Subsection (a)(6) provides that the court, in setting the fine within the guideline fine range, should consider any prior criminal record of an individual within high-level personnel of the organization or within high-level personnel of a unit of the organization. Since an individual within high-level personnel either exercises substantial control over the organization or a unit of the organization or has a substantial role in the making of policy within the organization or a unit of the organization, any prior criminal misconduct of such an individual may be relevant to the determination of the appropriate fine for the organization.

5. Subsection (a)(7) provides that the court, in setting the fine within the guideline fine range, should consider any prior civil or criminal misconduct by the organization other than that counted under §8C2.5(c). The civil and criminal misconduct counted under §8C2.5(c) increases the guideline fine range. Civil or criminal misconduct other than that counted under §8C2.5(c) may provide a basis for a higher fine within the range. In a case involving a pattern of illegality, an upward departure may be warranted.

6. Subsection (a)(8) provides that the court, in setting the fine within the guideline fine range, should consider any culpability score higher than ten or lower than zero. As the culpability score increases above ten, this may provide a basis for a higher fine within the range. Similarly, as the culpability score decreases below zero, this may provide a basis for a lower fine within the range.

7. Under subsection (b), the court, in determining the fine within the range, may consider any factor that it considered in determining the range. This allows for courts to differentiate between cases that have the same offense level but differ in seriousness (*e.g.*, two fraud cases at offense level 12, one resulting in a loss of $21,000, the other $40,000). Similarly, this allows for courts to differentiate between two cases that have the same aggravating factors, but in which those factors vary in their intensity (*e.g.*, two cases with upward adjustments to the culpability score under §8C2.5(c)(2) (prior criminal adjudications within 5 years of the commencement of the instant offense, one involving a single conviction, the other involving two or more convictions).

Background: Subsection (a) includes factors that the court is required to consider under 18 U.S.C. §§ 3553(a) and 3572(a) as well as additional factors that the Commission has determined may be relevant in a particular case. A number of factors required for consideration under 18 U.S.C. § 3572(a) (*e.g.*, pecuniary loss, the size of the organization) are used under the fine guidelines in this subpart to determine the fine range, and therefore are not specifically set out again in subsection (a) of this guideline. In unusual cases, factors listed in this section may provide a basis for departure.

Historical Note: Effective November 1, 1991 (see Appendix C, amendment 422). Amended effective November 1, 2004 (see Appendix C, amendment 673).

§8C2.9. Disgorgement

The court shall add to the fine determined under §8C2.8 (Determining the Fine Within the Range) any gain to the organization from the offense that has not and will not be paid as restitution or by way of other remedial measures.

Commentary

Application Note:

1. This section is designed to ensure that the amount of any gain that has not and will not be taken from the organization for remedial purposes will be added to the fine. This section typically will apply in cases in which the organization has received gain from an offense but restitution or remedial efforts will not be required because the offense did not result in harm to identifiable victims, *e.g.*, money laundering, obscenity, and regulatory reporting offenses. Money spent or to be spent to remedy the adverse effects of the offense, *e.g.*, the cost to retrofit defective products, should be considered as disgorged gain. If the cost of remedial efforts made or to be made by the organization equals or exceeds the gain from the offense, this section will not apply.

Historical Note: Effective November 1, 1991 (see Appendix C, amendment 422).

APPENDIX C

§8C2.10. Determining the Fine for Other Counts

For any count or counts not covered under §8C2.1 (Applicability of Fine Guidelines), the court should determine an appropriate fine by applying the provisions of 18 U.S.C. §§ 3553 and 3572. The court should determine the appropriate fine amount, if any, to be imposed in addition to any fine determined under §8C2.8 (Determining the Fine Within the Range) and §8C2.9 (Disgorgement).

Commentary

Background: The Commission has not promulgated guidelines governing the setting of fines for counts not covered by §8C2.1 (Applicability of Fine Guidelines). For such counts, the court should determine the appropriate fine based on the general statutory provisions governing sentencing. In cases that have a count or counts not covered by the guidelines in addition to a count or counts covered by the guidelines, the court shall apply the fine guidelines for the count(s) covered by the guidelines, and add any additional amount to the fine, as appropriate, for the count(s) not covered by the guidelines.

Historical Note: Effective November 1, 1991 (see Appendix C, amendment 422).

* * * * *

3. IMPLEMENTING THE SENTENCE OF A FINE

§8C3.1. Imposing a Fine

(a) Except to the extent restricted by the maximum fine authorized by statute or any minimum fine required by statute, the fine or fine range shall be that determined under §8C1.1 (Determining the Fine - Criminal Purpose Organizations); §8C2.7 (Guideline Fine Range - Organizations) and §8C2.9 (Disgorgement); or §8C2.10 (Determining the Fine for Other Counts), as appropriate.

(b) Where the minimum guideline fine is greater than the maximum fine authorized by statute, the maximum fine authorized by statute shall be the guideline fine.

(c) Where the maximum guideline fine is less than a minimum fine required by statute, the minimum fine required by statute shall be the guideline fine.

Commentary

Background: This section sets forth the interaction of the fines or fine ranges determined under this chapter with the maximum fine authorized by statute and any minimum fine required by statute for the count or counts of conviction. The general statutory provisions governing a sentence of a fine are set forth in 18 U.S.C. § 3571.

When the organization is convicted of multiple counts, the maximum fine authorized by statute may increase. For example, in the case of an organization convicted of three felony counts related to a $200,000 fraud, the maximum fine authorized by statute will be $500,000 on each count, for an aggregate maximum authorized fine of $1,500,000.

Historical Note: Effective November 1, 1991 (see Appendix C, amendment 422).

§8C3.2. Payment of the Fine - Organizations

(a) If the defendant operated primarily for a criminal purpose or primarily by criminal means, immediate payment of the fine shall be required.

(b) In any other case, immediate payment of the fine shall be required unless the court finds that the organization is financially unable to make immediate payment or that such payment would pose an undue burden on the organization. If the court permits other than immediate payment, it shall require full payment at the earliest possible date, either by requiring payment on a date certain or by establishing an installment schedule.

Commentary

Application Note:

1. When the court permits other than immediate payment, the period provided for payment shall in no event exceed five years. 18 U.S.C. § 3572(d).

Historical Note: Effective November 1, 1991 (see Appendix C, amendment 422).

§8C3.3. Reduction of Fine Based on Inability to Pay

(a) The court shall reduce the fine below that otherwise required by §8C1.1 (Determining the Fine - Criminal Purpose Organizations), or §8C2.7 (Guideline Fine Range - Organizations) and §8C2.9 (Disgorgement), to the extent that imposition of such fine would impair its ability to make restitution to victims.

(b) The court may impose a fine below that otherwise required by §8C2.7 (Guideline Fine Range - Organizations) and §8C2.9 (Disgorgement) if the court finds that the organization is not able and, even with the use of a reasonable installment schedule, is not likely to become able to pay the minimum fine required by §8C2.7 (Guideline Fine Range - Organizations) and §8C2.9 (Disgorgement).

Provided, that the reduction under this subsection shall not be more than necessary to avoid substantially jeopardizing the continued viability of the organization.

APPENDIX C App. C

Commentary

Application Note:

1. *For purposes of this section, an organization is not able to pay the minimum fine if, even with an installment schedule under §8C3.2 (Payment of the Fine - Organizations), the payment of that fine would substantially jeopardize the continued existence of the organization.*

Background: Subsection (a) carries out the requirement in 18 U.S.C. § 3572(b) that the court impose a fine or other monetary penalty only to the extent that such fine or penalty will not impair the ability of the organization to make restitution for the offense; however, this section does not authorize a criminal purpose organization to remain in business in order to pay restitution.

Historical Note: Effective November 1, 1991 (see Appendix C, amendment 422).

§8C3.4.   **Fines Paid by Owners of Closely Held Organizations**

The court may offset the fine imposed upon a closely held organization when one or more individuals, each of whom owns at least a 5 percent interest in the organization, has been fined in a federal criminal proceeding for the same offense conduct for which the organization is being sentenced. The amount of such offset shall not exceed the amount resulting from multiplying the total fines imposed on those individuals by those individuals' total percentage interest in the organization.

Commentary

Application Notes:

1. *For purposes of this section, an organization is closely held, regardless of its size, when relatively few individuals own it. In order for an organization to be closely held, ownership and management need not completely overlap.*

2. *This section does not apply to a fine imposed upon an individual that arises out of offense conduct different from that for which the organization is being sentenced.*

Background: For practical purposes, most closely held organizations are the alter egos of their owner-managers. In the case of criminal conduct by a closely held corporation, the organization and the culpable individual(s) both may be convicted. As a general rule in such cases, appropriate punishment may be achieved by offsetting the fine imposed upon the organization by an amount that reflects the percentage ownership interest of the sentenced individuals and the magnitude of the fines imposed upon those individuals. For example, an organization is owned by five individuals, each of whom has a twenty percent interest; three of the individuals are convicted; and the combined fines imposed on those three equals $100,000. In this example, the fine imposed upon the organization may be offset by up to 60 percent of their combined fine amounts, i.e., by $60,000.

Historical Note: Effective November 1, 1991 (see Appendix C, amendment 422).

* * * * *

4. DEPARTURES FROM THE GUIDELINE FINE RANGE

Introductory Commentary

The statutory provisions governing departures are set forth in 18 U.S.C. § 3553(b). Departure may be warranted if the court finds "that there exists an aggravating or mitigating circumstance of a kind, or to a degree, not adequately taken into consideration by the Sentencing Commission in formulating the guidelines that should result in a sentence different from that described." This subpart sets forth certain factors that, in connection with certain offenses, may not have been adequately taken into consideration by the guidelines. In deciding whether departure is warranted, the court should consider the extent to which that factor is adequately taken into consideration by the guidelines and the relative importance or substantiality of that factor in the particular case.

To the extent that any policy statement from Chapter Five, Part K (Departures) is relevant to the organization, a departure from the applicable guideline fine range may be warranted. Some factors listed in Chapter Five, Part K that are particularly applicable to organizations are listed in this subpart. Other factors listed in Chapter Five, Part K may be applicable in particular cases. While this subpart lists factors that the Commission believes may constitute grounds for departure, the list is not exhaustive.

Historical Note: Effective November 1, 1991 (see Appendix C, amendment 422).

§8C4.1. Substantial Assistance to Authorities - Organizations (Policy Statement)

(a) Upon motion of the government stating that the defendant has provided substantial assistance in the investigation or prosecution of another organization that has committed an offense, or in the investigation or prosecution of an individual not directly affiliated with the defendant who has committed an offense, the court may depart from the guidelines.

(b) The appropriate reduction shall be determined by the court for reasons stated on the record that may include, but are not limited to, consideration of the following:

(1) the court's evaluation of the significance and usefulness of the organization's assistance, taking into consideration the government's evaluation of the assistance rendered;

(2) the nature and extent of the organization's assistance; and

(3) the timeliness of the organization's assistance.

Commentary

Application Note:

1. *Departure under this section is intended for cases in which substantial assistance is provided in the investigation or prosecution of crimes committed by individuals not directly affiliated*

– 522 –

APPENDIX C

with the organization or by other organizations. It is not intended for assistance in the investigation or prosecution of the agents of the organization responsible for the offense for which the organization is being sentenced.

Historical Note: Effective November 1, 1991 (see Appendix C, amendment 422).

§8C4.2. Risk of Death or Bodily Injury (Policy Statement)

If the offense resulted in death or bodily injury, or involved a foreseeable risk of death or bodily injury, an upward departure may be warranted. The extent of any such departure should depend, among other factors, on the nature of the harm and the extent to which the harm was intended or knowingly risked, and the extent to which such harm or risk is taken into account within the applicable guideline fine range.

Historical Note: Effective November 1, 1991 (see Appendix C, amendment 422).

§8C4.3. Threat to National Security (Policy Statement)

If the offense constituted a threat to national security, an upward departure may be warranted.

Historical Note: Effective November 1, 1991 (see Appendix C, amendment 422).

§8C4.4. Threat to the Environment (Policy Statement)

If the offense presented a threat to the environment, an upward departure may be warranted.

Historical Note: Effective November 1, 1991 (see Appendix C, amendment 422).

§8C4.5. Threat to a Market (Policy Statement)

If the offense presented a risk to the integrity or continued existence of a market, an upward departure may be warranted. This section is applicable to both private markets (e.g., a financial market, a commodities market, or a market for consumer goods) and public markets (e.g., government contracting).

Historical Note: Effective November 1, 1991 (see Appendix C, amendment 422).

§8C4.6. Official Corruption (Policy Statement)

If the organization, in connection with the offense, bribed or unlawfully gave a gratuity to a public official, or attempted or conspired to bribe or unlawfully give a gratuity to a public official, an upward departure may be warranted.

Historical Note: Effective November 1, 1991 (see Appendix C, amendment 422).

§8C4.7. Public Entity (Policy Statement)

If the organization is a public entity, a downward departure may be warranted.

Historical Note: Effective November 1, 1991 (see Appendix C, amendment 422).

§8C4.8. Members or Beneficiaries of the Organization as Victims (Policy Statement)

If the members or beneficiaries, other than shareholders, of the organization are direct victims of the offense, a downward departure may be warranted. If the members or beneficiaries of an organization are direct victims of the offense, imposing a fine upon the organization may increase the burden upon the victims of the offense without achieving a deterrent effect. In such cases, a fine may not be appropriate. For example, departure may be appropriate if a labor union is convicted of embezzlement of pension funds.

Historical Note: Effective November 1, 1991 (see Appendix C, amendment 422).

§8C4.9. Remedial Costs that Greatly Exceed Gain (Policy Statement)

If the organization has paid or has agreed to pay remedial costs arising from the offense that greatly exceed the gain that the organization received from the offense, a downward departure may be warranted. In such a case, a substantial fine may not be necessary in order to achieve adequate punishment and deterrence. In deciding whether departure is appropriate, the court should consider the level and extent of substantial authority personnel involvement in the offense and the degree to which the loss exceeds the gain. If an individual within high-level personnel was involved in the offense, a departure would not be appropriate under this section. The lower the level and the more limited the extent of substantial authority personnel involvement in the offense, and the greater the degree to which remedial costs exceeded or will exceed gain, the less will be the need for a substantial fine to achieve adequate punishment and deterrence.

Historical Note: Effective November 1, 1991 (see Appendix C, amendment 422).

§8C4.10. Mandatory Programs to Prevent and Detect Violations of Law (Policy Statement)

If the organization's culpability score is reduced under §8C2.5(f) (Effective Compliance and Ethics Program) and the organization had implemented its program in response to a court order or administrative order specifically directed at the organization, an upward departure may be warranted to offset, in part or in whole, such reduction.

Similarly, if, at the time of the instant offense, the organization was required by law to have an effective compliance and ethics program, but the organization did not have such a program, an upward departure may be warranted.

Historical Note: Effective November 1, 1991 (see Appendix C, amendment 422). Amended effective November 1, 2004 (see Appendix C, amendment 673).

§8C4.11. Exceptional Organizational Culpability (Policy Statement)

If the organization's culpability score is greater than 10, an upward departure may be appropriate.

If no individual within substantial authority personnel participated in, condoned, or was willfully ignorant of the offense; the organization at the time of the offense had an effective program to prevent and detect violations of law; and the base fine is determined under §8C2.4(a)(1), §8C2.4(a)(3), or a special instruction for fines in Chapter Two (Offense Conduct), a downward departure may be warranted. In a case meeting these criteria, the court may find that the organization had exceptionally low culpability and therefore a fine based on loss, offense level, or a special Chapter Two instruction results in a guideline fine range higher than necessary to achieve the purposes of sentencing. Nevertheless, such fine should not be lower than if determined under §8C2.4(a)(2).

Historical Note: Effective November 1, 1991 (see Appendix C, amendment 422).

App. C GOVERNMENT CONTRACT COMPLIANCE HANDBOOK

PART D - ORGANIZATIONAL PROBATION

Introductory Commentary

Section 8D1.1 sets forth the circumstances under which a sentence to a term of probation is required. Sections 8D1.2 through 8D1.4, and 8F1.1, address the length of the probation term, conditions of probation, and violations of probation conditions.

Historical Note: Effective November 1, 1991 (see Appendix C, amendment 422). Amended effective November 1, 2004 (see Appendix C, amendment 673).

§8D1.1.　Imposition of Probation - Organizations

(a) The court shall order a term of probation:

    (1) if such sentence is necessary to secure payment of restitution (§8B1.1), enforce a remedial order (§8B1.2), or ensure completion of community service (§8B1.3);

    (2) if the organization is sentenced to pay a monetary penalty (e.g., restitution, fine, or special assessment), the penalty is not paid in full at the time of sentencing, and restrictions are necessary to safeguard the organization's ability to make payments;

    (3) if, at the time of sentencing, (A) the organization (i) has 50 or more employees, or (ii) was otherwise required under law to have an effective compliance and ethics program; and (B) the organization does not have such a program;

    (4) if the organization within five years prior to sentencing engaged in similar misconduct, as determined by a prior criminal adjudication, and any part of the misconduct underlying the instant offense occurred after that adjudication;

    (5) if an individual within high-level personnel of the organization or the unit of the organization within which the instant offense was committed participated in the misconduct underlying the instant offense and that individual within five years prior to sentencing engaged in similar misconduct, as determined by a prior criminal adjudication, and any part of the misconduct underlying the instant offense occurred after that adjudication;

    (6) if such sentence is necessary to ensure that changes are made within the organization to reduce the likelihood of future criminal conduct;

    (7) if the sentence imposed upon the organization does not include a fine; or

    (8) if necessary to accomplish one or more of the purposes of sentencing set forth in 18 U.S.C. § 3553(a)(2).

APPENDIX C

Commentary

<u>Background</u>: *Under 18 U.S.C. § 3561(a), an organization may be sentenced to a term of probation. Under 18 U.S.C. § 3551(c), imposition of a term of probation is required if the sentence imposed upon the organization does not include a fine.*

<u>Historical Note</u>: Effective November 1, 1991 (<u>see</u> Appendix C, amendment 422). Amended effective November 1, 2004 (<u>see</u> Appendix C, amendment 673).

§8D1.2.   Term of Probation - Organizations

    (a)   When a sentence of probation is imposed—

          (1)   In the case of a felony, the term of probation shall be at least one year but not more than five years.

          (2)   In any other case, the term of probation shall be not more than five years.

Commentary

Application Note:

1. *Within the limits set by the guidelines, the term of probation should be sufficient, but not more than necessary, to accomplish the court's specific objectives in imposing the term of probation. The terms of probation set forth in this section are those provided in 18 U.S.C. § 3561(c).*

<u>Historical Note</u>: Effective November 1, 1991 (<u>see</u> Appendix C, amendment 422). Amended effective November 1, 2013 (<u>see</u> Appendix C, amendment 778).

§8D1.3.   Conditions of Probation - Organizations

    (a)   Pursuant to 18 U.S.C. § 3563(a)(1), any sentence of probation shall include the condition that the organization not commit another federal, state, or local crime during the term of probation.

    (b)   Pursuant to 18 U.S.C. § 3563(a)(2), if a sentence of probation is imposed for a felony, the court shall impose as a condition of probation at least one of the following: (1) restitution or (2) community service, unless the court has imposed a fine, or unless the court finds on the record that extraordinary circumstances exist that would make such condition plainly unreasonable, in which event the court shall impose one or more other conditions set forth in 18 U.S.C. § 3563(b).

    (c)   The court may impose other conditions that (1) are reasonably related to the nature and circumstances of the offense or the history and characteristics of the organization; and (2) involve only such deprivations of liberty or property as are necessary to effect the purposes of sentencing.

<u>Historical Note</u>: Effective November 1, 1991 (<u>see</u> Appendix C, amendment 422). Amended effective November 1, 1997 (<u>see</u> Appendix C, amendment 569); November 1, 2009 (<u>see</u> Appendix C, amendment 733).

§8D1.4. Recommended Conditions of Probation - Organizations (Policy Statement)

(a) The court may order the organization, at its expense and in the format and media specified by the court, to publicize the nature of the offense committed, the fact of conviction, the nature of the punishment imposed, and the steps that will be taken to prevent the recurrence of similar offenses.

(b) If probation is imposed under §8D1.1, the following conditions may be appropriate:

(1) The organization shall develop and submit to the court an effective compliance and ethics program consistent with §8B2.1 (Effective Compliance and Ethics Program). The organization shall include in its submission a schedule for implementation of the compliance and ethics program.

(2) Upon approval by the court of a program referred to in paragraph (1), the organization shall notify its employees and shareholders of its criminal behavior and its program referred to in paragraph (1). Such notice shall be in a form prescribed by the court.

(3) The organization shall make periodic submissions to the court or probation officer, at intervals specified by the court, (A) reporting on the organization's financial condition and results of business operations, and accounting for the disposition of all funds received, and (B) reporting on the organization's progress in implementing the program referred to in paragraph (1). Among other things, reports under subparagraph (B) shall disclose any criminal prosecution, civil litigation, or administrative proceeding commenced against the organization, or any investigation or formal inquiry by governmental authorities of which the organization learned since its last report.

(4) The organization shall notify the court or probation officer immediately upon learning of (A) any material adverse change in its business or financial condition or prospects, or (B) the commencement of any bankruptcy proceeding, major civil litigation, criminal prosecution, or administrative proceeding against the organization, or any investigation or formal inquiry by governmental authorities regarding the organization.

(5) The organization shall submit to: (A) a reasonable number of regular or unannounced examinations of its books and records at appropriate business premises by the probation officer or experts engaged by the court; and (B) interrogation of knowledgeable individuals within the organization. Compensation to and costs of any experts engaged by the court shall be paid by the organization.

(6) The organization shall make periodic payments, as specified by the court, in the following priority: (A) restitution; (B) fine; and (C) any other monetary sanction.

APPENDIX C

Commentary

Application Note:

1. *In determining the conditions to be imposed when probation is ordered under §8D1.1, the court should consider the views of any governmental regulatory body that oversees conduct of the organization relating to the instant offense. To assess the efficacy of a compliance and ethics program submitted by the organization, the court may employ appropriate experts who shall be afforded access to all material possessed by the organization that is necessary for a comprehensive assessment of the proposed program. The court should approve any program that appears reasonably calculated to prevent and detect criminal conduct, as long as it is consistent with §8B2.1 (Effective Compliance and Ethics Program), and any applicable statutory and regulatory requirements.*

   Periodic reports submitted in accordance with subsection (b)(3) should be provided to any governmental regulatory body that oversees conduct of the organization relating to the instant offense.

Historical Note: Effective November 1, 1991 (see Appendix C, amendment 422). Amended effective November 1, 2004 (see Appendix C, amendment 673); November 1, 2010 (see Appendix C, amendment 744).

§8D1.5. [Deleted]

Historical Note: Effective November 1, 1991 (see Appendix C, amendment 422); was moved to §8F1.1 effective November 1, 2004 (see Appendix C, amendment 673).

App. C   GOVERNMENT CONTRACT COMPLIANCE HANDBOOK

PART E - SPECIAL ASSESSMENTS, FORFEITURES, AND COSTS

§8E1.1.   <u>Special Assessments - Organizations</u>

A special assessment must be imposed on an organization in the amount prescribed by statute.

Commentary

Application Notes:

1. This guideline applies if the defendant is an organization. It does not apply if the defendant is an individual. <u>See</u> §5E1.3 for special assessments applicable to individuals.

2. The following special assessments are provided by statute (<u>see</u> 18 U.S.C. § 3013):

   <u>For Offenses Committed By Organizations On Or After April 24, 1996:</u>

   (A) $400, if convicted of a felony;
   (B) $125, if convicted of a Class A misdemeanor;
   (C) $50, if convicted of a Class B misdemeanor; or
   (D) $25, if convicted of a Class C misdemeanor or an infraction.

   <u>For Offenses Committed By Organizations On Or After November 18, 1988 But Prior To April 24, 1996:</u>

   (E) $200, if convicted of a felony;
   (F) $125, if convicted of a Class A misdemeanor;
   (G) $50, if convicted of a Class B misdemeanor; or
   (H) $25, if convicted of a Class C misdemeanor or an infraction.

   <u>For Offenses Committed By Organizations Prior To November 18, 1988:</u>

   (I) $200, if convicted of a felony;
   (J) $100, if convicted of a misdemeanor.

3. A special assessment is required by statute for each count of conviction.

<u>Background</u>: Section 3013 of Title 18, United States Code, added by The Victims of Crimes Act of 1984, Pub. L. No. 98-473, Title II, Chap. XIV, requires courts to impose special assessments on convicted defendants for the purpose of funding the Crime Victims Fund established by the same legislation.

<u>Historical Note</u>: Effective November 1, 1991 (<u>see</u> Appendix C, amendment 422); November 1, 1997 (<u>see</u> Appendix C, amendment 573).

APPENDIX C

§8E1.2. **Forfeiture - Organizations**

Apply §5E1.4 (Forfeiture).

Historical Note: Effective November 1, 1991 (see Appendix C, amendment 422).

§8E1.3. **Assessment of Costs - Organizations**

As provided in 28 U.S.C. § 1918, the court may order the organization to pay the costs of prosecution. In addition, specific statutory provisions mandate assessment of costs.

Historical Note: Effective November 1, 1991 (see Appendix C, amendment 422).

PART F - VIOLATIONS OF PROBATION - ORGANIZATIONS

Historical Note: Effective November 1, 2004 (see Appendix C, amendment 673).

§8F1.1. Violations of Conditions of Probation - Organizations (Policy Statement)

Upon a finding of a violation of a condition of probation, the court may extend the term of probation, impose more restrictive conditions of probation, or revoke probation and resentence the organization.

Commentary

Application Notes:

1. *Appointment of Master or Trustee.*—In the event of repeated violations of conditions of probation, the appointment of a master or trustee may be appropriate to ensure compliance with court orders.

2. *Conditions of Probation.*—Mandatory and recommended conditions of probation are specified in §§8D1.3 *(Conditions of Probation - Organizations)* and 8D1.4 *(Recommended Conditions of Probation - Organizations)*.

Historical Note: Effective November 1, 2004 (see Appendix C, amendment 673).

APPENDIX D

List of the Federal Inspectors General

Appendix D

List of the Federal Inspectors General

FEDERAL INSPECTORS GENERAL

The entities of the Federal Government with Inspectors General Include:

Agency for International Development
Agriculture, Department of
Amtrak
Appalachian Regional Commission
Architect of the Capitol
U.S. Capitol Police
Central Intelligence Agency
Commerce, Department of
Commodity Futures Trading Commission
Consumer Product Safety Commission
Corporation for National and Community Service
Corporation for Public Broadcasting
Defense, Department of
Defense Intelligence Agency
Denali Commission
Education, Department of
U.S. Election Assistance Commission
Energy, Department of
Environmental Protection Agency
Equal Employment Opportunity Commission
Export-Import Bank of the United States
Farm Credit Administration
Federal Communications Commission
Federal Deposit Insurance Corporation
Federal Election Commission
Federal Housing Finance Agency
Federal Labor Relations Authority
Federal Maritime Commission
Federal Reserve Board/Bureau of Consumer Financial Protection
Federal Trade Commission
General Services Administration
Government Accountability Office
Government Printing Office
Health and Human Services, Department of
Homeland Security, Department of
Housing and Urban Development, Department of
Interior, Department of
U.S. International Trade Commission
Justice, Department of
Labor, Department of
Legal Services Corporation
Library of Congress
National Aeronautics and Space Administration
National Archives
National Credit Union Administration
National Endowment for the Arts
National Endowment for the Humanities
National Geospatial-Intelligence Agency
National Labor Relations Board
National Reconnaissance Office
National Security Agency
National Science Foundation
Nuclear Regulatory Commission
Office of Inspector General of the Intelligence Community
Office of Personnel Management
Peace Corps
Pension Benefit Guaranty Corporation
Postal Regulatory Commission
U.S. Postal Service
Railroad Retirement Board
Securities and Exchange Commission
Small Business Administration
Smithsonian Institution
Social Security Administration
Special Inspector General for Afghanistan Reconstruction
State, Department of
Tennessee Valley Authority
Transportation, Department of
Treasury, Department of
Treasury Inspector General for Tax Administration
Veterans Affairs, Department of

APPENDIX E

Sample Code of Business Ethics and Conduct

SAMPLE CODE OF BUSINESS ETHICS AND CONDUCT

Introduction

It is the policy of our company to comply with all laws governing our domestic and foreign operations and to conduct our affairs in keeping with the highest moral, legal, and ethical standards.

Compliance with the law means not only following the law, but conducting our business so that we will deserve and receive recognition as good and law-abiding citizens, alert to our responsibilities in all areas of good citizenship. Even where the law does not apply, certain standards of ethics and morality relate to our activities and require the same diligence and attention to good conduct and citizenship.

There is both a management and an individual obligation to fulfill the intent of this policy. Any clear infraction of applicable laws or of prevailing business ethics will subject an employee to *disciplinary action*, which may include reprimand, probation, suspension, reduction in salary, demotion, or dismissal—depending on the seriousness of the offense.

Moreover, disciplinary measures will apply to any supervisor who directs or approves of such actions, or has knowledge of them and does not move promptly to correct them. Appropriate disciplinary measures also will apply to any supervisor who fails to carry out the management responsibility to ensure that employees are informed about this policy.

The following pages contain a number of specific directives regarding our company's Code of Business Ethics and Conduct. We urge you to review these on a regular basis so that you may incorporate them into your daily practices. If you need guidance on particular circumstances that may arise, contact the Law Department for assistance.

I. Product Quality & Safety

We are committed to producing quality products that meet all contractual obligations and our own quality standards. The products we deliver must:
(1) Be made from the quality of materials ordered.

(2) Be properly tested.
(3) Be properly identified as to foreign-origin.
(4) Meet contract specifications.
(5) Be safe for their normally intended uses, and be accompanied by proper instructions.
(6) Meet all applicable laws and regulations and industry standards.

II. Competing Fairly

- **Bid Practices**

The antitrust laws are designed to ensure competition and preserve the free enterprise system. They apply to all domestic and some foreign transactions by United States businesses. Some of the most common antitrust issues with which an employee may be confronted are in the areas of pricing, boycotts, and trade association activity.

The following actions constitute violations of law and must *not* be engaged in under any circumstances.
(1) An agreement with one or more competitors to fix prices at any level or other terms and conditions of sale; to allocate customers or markets; to fix levels of production or production quotas; or to boycott a supplier or customer.
(2) Any form of bid rigging.
(3) An agreement with a customer to fix a resale price.

Because the antitrust laws are complex, employees are instructed to take special care in this area. This Code of Business Ethics and Conduct is not a substitute for legal advice. Any questions on the interpretation of the antitrust laws should be referred promptly to the Law Department.

- **Contract Negotiation**

In negotiating contracts, be accurate and complete in all representations. The submission to a U.S. Government customer of a proposal, quotation, or other document or statement that is false, incomplete, or misleading can result in civil

APPENDIX E

and criminal liability for the company, the involved employee, and any supervisors who condone such a practice. In negotiating contracts with the U.S. Government, we have an affirmative duty to disclose current, accurate, and complete cost or pricing data where such data are required under appropriate law or regulation.

III. Maintaining Accurate Records

- **Charging Of Costs/Timecard Reporting**

Employees who file timecards must be particularly careful to do so in a complete, accurate and timely manner. Employees performing U.S. Government contracts must be particularly careful to ensure that hours worked and costs are applied to the account for which they were in fact incurred. No cost may be charged or allocated to a Government contract if the cost is unallowable by regulation or contract provision or is otherwise improper.

Employees are required to sign their own timecards. Your signature on a timecard is your representation that the timecard accurately reflects the number of hours worked on the specified project or job order. The supervisor's signature is a representation that the timecard has been reviewed and that steps have been taken to verify the validity of the hours reported and the correctness of the allocation of the hours. Supervisors must avoid placing pressure on subordinates that could lead them to believe that deviations from appropriate charging practices will be condoned.

- **Financial Records**

The records of our company are maintained in a manner that provides for an accurate and auditable record of all financial transactions in conformity with generally accepted accounting principles. No false or deceptive entries may be made, and all entries must contain an appropriate description of the underlying transaction. All company funds must be retained in corporate bank accounts and no undisclosed or unrecorded fund or asset shall be established for any purpose. All reports, vouchers, bills, invoices, payroll and service records, and other essential data must be prepared with care and honesty.

IV. Employment Practices

• Equal Opportunity

Our company recognizes that its continued success depends on the development and utilization of the full range of human resources. At the foundation of this precept is equal employment opportunity.

It is the continuing policy of this company to afford equal employment opportunity to qualified individuals regardless of their race, color, religion, sex, national origin, age, or physical or mental handicap, and to conform to applicable laws and regulations.

This policy of equal opportunity pertains to all aspects of the employment relationship, including application and initial employment, promotion and transfer, selection for training opportunity, wage and salary administration, and the application of service, retirement, seniority, and employee benefit plan policies.

It is also the policy of this company to provide employees a workplace free from any form of sexual harassment. Sexual harassment in any manner or form is expressly prohibited.

• Hiring Of Federal Employees

Complex rules govern the recruitment and employment of U.S. Government employees in private industry. Prior clearance to discuss possible employment with, make offers to, or hire (as an employee or consultant) any current or former Government employee (military or civilian) must be obtained from the Human Resources Department.

V. Proper Use Of Company Resources

• Providing Business Courtesies To Customers

Our success in the marketplace results from providing superior products and services at competitive prices. Our company does not seek to gain improper advantage by offering business courtesies such as entertainment, meals,

Appendix E

transportation, or lodging to our customers. Employees should never offer *any* type of business courtesy to a customer for the purpose of obtaining favorable treatment or advantage.

To avoid even the appearance of impropriety, do not provide any customer with gifts or promotional items (for example, pens or calendars) of more than nominal value.

Except for additional restrictions that apply to U.S. Government customers and are noted below, you may pay for reasonable meal, refreshment, or entertainment expenses for customers that are incurred only occasionally, are not required or solicited by the recipient, and are not intended to or likely to affect the recipient's business decisions with respect to our company. You may provide or pay for a customer's travel or lodging expenses only with the advance approval of the corporate officer responsible for your unit or group, or his designee, and the additional approval of the Law Department if the travel or lodging is not for a directly business-related purpose.

With regard to *U.S. Government customers*, you may *not* provide or pay for *any* meal, refreshment, entertainment, travel, or lodging expenses for a U.S. Government employee without the advance written approval of the Law Department. There may also restrictions on providing business courtesies, including meals and refreshments, to state, local, or foreign customers which you must observe. If you do business with these authorities, you are expected to know and respect all such restrictions

- **Supplier Relationships**

When dealing with or making decisions affecting suppliers, employees shall be careful not inadvertently to obligate either themselves or the company to a supplier. In conducting business with suppliers, employees are also expected to act fairly and objectively and in the best interests of the company.

(1) *Gifts*—Employees may not accept gifts or gratuities from suppliers, with the exception of advertising novelties of a nominal value marked with the donor's company name. Gifts received that are unacceptable according to this policy must be

returned to the donors. You should also notify the company of such gifts and of their return.

(2) *Entertainment*—Employees may not accept purely social entertainment offered or sponsored by suppliers. Entertainment is not construed to mean an occasional business meal or a function where the company stands to benefit from the supplier association.

(3) *Reimbursement*—Employees may not accept reimbursement from suppliers for travel and hotel expenses, for speaker's fees or honoraria for addresses or papers given before supplier audiences, or for consulting services or advice they may render. Likewise, employees shall not request or accept monetary loans or personal services from suppliers, nor shall they enter contests sponsored by suppliers.

(4) *Kickbacks*—Federal laws prohibit the offering, soliciting, or accepting of any kickback, as well as the including of any amount of a kickback in a contract with the United States. A kickback is defined as any money, fee, commission, credit, gift, gratuity, thing of value, or compensation of any kind that is provided for the purpose of improperly obtaining or rewarding favorable treatment in connection with a contract with the United States. In addition, the "Anti-Kickback Act of 1986" requires each prime contractor or subcontractor promptly to report a violation of the kickback laws to the appropriate Federal agency Inspector General or the Department of Justice if the contractor has reasonable grounds to believe that a violation exists.

- **Dealing With Foreign Officials**

Do not promise, offer, or make any payments in money, products, or services to any foreign official, either directly or indirectly, in exchange for or to induce favorable business treatment or to affect any government decision. In some foreign countries, the law may permit minor payments to clerical personnel to expedite performance of their duties. Such minor payments may be made only with the express approval of the country general manager on advice of the Law Department, must never exceed $50 per payment, and must never be made to gain or retain business.

APPENDIX E

- **Political Activities**

Our company believes strongly in the democratic political process and encourages employees to participate personally on their own time in that process. A corporation's activities, however, are limited significantly by law. For this reason, no political contribution of corporate funds or use of corporate property, services, or other assets may be made without the written approval of the Law Department.

In this connection, indirect expenditures on behalf of a candidate or elected official, such as travel on corporate aircraft or use of telephones and other corporate equipment, may be considered as contributions. Any questions should be referred to the Law Department. In no event may an employee be reimbursed in any manner for political activities.

VI. Maintaining Your Position Of Trust

We expect you to devote your full working time and efforts to the company's interests and to avoid any activity that might detract from or conflict with those interests. In particular, you must be aware of certain situations that might compromise your position of trust.

- **Conflicts Of Interest**

You may not have any employment, consulting, or other business relationship with a competitor, customer, or supplier of the company, or invest in any competitor, customer, or supplier (except for moderate holdings of publicly-traded securities) unless you have the advance written permission of the corporate officer responsible for your unit or group, after consultation with the Law Department.

Outside employment may also constitute a conflict of interest if it places an employee in the position of appearing to represent the company, involves providing goods or services substantially similar to those the company provides or is considering making available, or lessens the efficiency, alertness, or productivity normally expected of employees on their jobs. All outside employment that raises any question in this regard must be approved in advance by the employee's immediate supervisor and Human Resources representative who shall consult the Law Department.

You must notify the company of all benefits you obtain from third parties because of your position, and must pay over to the company all such benefits that are capable of being transferred. Benefits subject to notification include, for example, interest-free or low-interest loans.

- **Insider Trading**

Do not trade in the securities of the company or any other company, or buy or sell any property or assets, on the basis of non-public information you have acquired through your employment at the company whether such information comes from the company or from another company with which the company has a confidential relationship.

- **Restricted Company Information**

Do not disclose to any outside party—except as specifically authorized by management pursuant to established policy and procedures—any non-public business, financial, personnel, or technological information, plans, or data that you have acquired during your employment at the company. On termination of employment, you may not copy, take, or retain any documents containing restricted information.

The prohibition against disclosing restricted information extends indefinitely beyond your period of employment. Your agreement to protect the confidentiality of such information in perpetuity is considered an important condition of your employment at the company.

- **Government Classified & Proprietary Information**

We have special obligations to comply with laws and regulations that protect classified information. Employees with valid security clearances who have access to classified information must ensure that the information is handled in accordance with pertinent Federal procedures. These restrictions apply to any form of information, whether in written or electronic form.

APPENDIX E

The company does not solicit nor will it receive any sensitive proprietary internal Government information, including budgetary or program information, before it is available through normal processes.

VII. Reporting Violations

Employees are expected to report any suspected violations of this Code of Business Ethics and Conduct or other irregularities to their supervisor, the general auditor, or the Law Department. Employees of units doing business with the U.S. Government may also report suspected violations or irregularities to the U.S. Government sector Ombudsman (who can be reached at 1-800-__-__). No adverse action or retribution of any kind will be taken against an employee because he or she reports a suspected violation of this Code or other irregularity. Such reports shall be treated confidentially to the maximum extent consistent with fair and rigorous enforcement of the Code.

Conclusion

Each of us has an obligation to behave at all times with honesty and propriety because such behavior is morally and legally right and because our business success and reputation for integrity depends on the actions of each employee. This Code of Business Ethics and Conduct outlines your major obligations. Be certain to read, understand, and adhere to this Code as you carry out your daily activities. For clarification or guidance on any point in the code, please contact the Law Department for assistance.

APPENDIX F
DoD Hotline Poster

APPENDIX G

Sample Company Policy Statement on Bribery and Gratuities

**SAMPLE COMPANY POLICY STATEMENT
ON BRIBERY AND GRATUITIES**

Your company Policy Statement concerning bribery of or gratuities offered to Government personnel should include terms such as the following:

(a) No employees shall give, offer, or discuss offering a gift, favor, entertainment, transportation, loan, hospitality, future employment with (name of company), or any other tangible or intangible item, regardless of value, to any employee or representative of the United States Government, except as stated below.

(b) Designated employees may provide Government representatives items such as pens, note pads, etc., which promote (name of company) only after it has been determined by (name of company) and division management that (i) the retail value of any particular promotional item proposed for distribution to Government representatives is less than $20, (ii) the distribution of the item in question is not for the purpose of influencing a Government representative in the discharge of his or her duties, and (iii) it is highly unlikely that the item will be perceived as being offered for such purpose.

(c) Employees shall not attend any meeting or function other than approved public or industry association events when it is known that (i) Government representative (s) will be present at the meeting or function, and (ii) no provision has been made for the Government people to pay or share in the payment for meals, prizes, and other arrangements incident to the meeting or function, unless the meeting or function is essentially a civic or community activity (such as a Little League luncheon or garden club meeting) or a trade or industry function (such as a conference, trade show,. or seminar) and is clearly open to the public generally or to the members of a broadly-defined class (such as manufacturers of aerospace products or parents of little league participants).

(d) If any employee determines that it is clearly impracticable for him to avoid providing a Government representative transportation, meals, or lodging in connection with official business, the employee shall notify division management. Under no circumstances shall an employee offer to provide transportation, meals, or lodging to a Government representative until appropriate division management has authorized the offer. Under no circumstances shall the division management authorize payment for transportation, meals, or lodging for a Government representative until it is determined that the Government representative has undertaken to explain the unusual circumstances to his or her superiors and to seek authorization from his or her superiors to accept the items offered. An employee requesting authorization for payment of transportation, meals, or lodging for a Government representative must request such authorization as soon as the employee becomes aware that the transportation, meals, or lodging will be required.

(e) When it is determined by division management that it is necessary or desirable for attendance of Government representatives at a function sponsored by (name of company), the employee responsible for organizing the function shall coordinate the invitation of Government representatives with the Ethics Officer for the Government activity employing the Government representatives to be invited. The Ethics Officer should be informed of any meal, transportation, or other amenity that will be provided at the function and the approximate value of same, as well as the identity of attendees and specifics regarding the agenda of any program to be presented at the function.

(f) If Government representatives are expected to attend a function sponsored by (name of company) where it has been impossible or impractical for the employee responsible for organizing the function to coordinate arrangements for the attendance of the Government representatives with the appropriate Government Ethics Officer or other official, the employee shall ensure that a collection basket is discreetly displayed in the reception area for the function with a notice informing the Government attendees of the approximate value of any refreshment or meals provided at the function and inviting contribution from the Government representatives if appropriate.

(g) Unless an employee has consulted with the company's Law Department and obtained permission to do so, no employee shall discuss the prospect of future employment at (name of company) or one of its divisions with individuals employed by any Government activity with which a division has a contract or can reasonably be expected to submit a proposal for a contract in the near future.

(h) Violation of the laws and regulations discussed above could result in criminal and civil sanctions including imprisonment and fines of up to $500,000. Violation by an employee of any portion of this Policy Statement will result in disciplinary action, including suspension, transfer, dismissal of the responsible employee, deductions and set-offs from employee compensation, and institution of other appropriate disciplinary action.

APPENDIX H

FAR 52.203-2: "Certificate of Independent Price Determination" Clause

52.203-2 Certificate of Independent Price Determination.

As prescribed in 3.103-1, insert the following provision. If the solicitation is a Request for Quotations, the terms "Quotation" and "Quoter" may be substituted for "Offer" and "Offeror."

CERTIFICATE OF INDEPENDENT PRICE DETERMINATION
(APR 1985)

(a) The offeror certifies that—

(1) The prices in this offer have been arrived at independently, without, for the purpose of restricting competition, any consultation, communication, or agreement with any other offeror or competitor relating to—

(i) Those prices;

(ii) The intention to submit an offer;, or

(iii) The methods or factors used to calculate the prices offered.

(2) The prices in this offer have not been and will not be knowingly disclosed by the offeror, directly or indirectly, to any other offeror or competitor before bid opening (in the case of a sealed bid solicitation) or contract award (in the case of a negotiated solicitation) unless otherwise required by law; and

(3) No attempt has been made or will be made by the offeror to induce any other concern to submit or not to submit an offer for the purpose of restricting competition.

(b) Each signature on the offer is considered to be a certification by the signatory that the signatory—

(1) Is the person in the offeror's organization responsible for determining the prices being offered in this bid or proposal, and that the signatory has not participated and will not participate in any action contrary to subparagraphs (a)(1) through (a)(3) of this provision; or

(2)(i) Has been authorized, in writing, to act as agent for the following principals in certifying that those principals have not participated, and will not participate in any action contrary to subparagraphs (a)(1) through (a)(3) of this provision _____ *[insert full name of person(s) in the offeror's organization responsible for determining the prices offered in this bid or proposal, and the title of his or her position in the offeror's organization]*;

(ii) As an authorized agent, does certify that the principals named in subdivision (b)(2)(i) of this provision have not participated, and will not participate, in any action contrary to subparagraphs (a)(1) through (a)(3) of this provision; and

(iii) As an agent, has not personally participated, and will not participate, in any action contrary to subparagraphs (a)(1) through (a)(3) of this provision.

(c) If the offeror deletes or modifies subparagraph (a)(2) of this provision, the offeror must furnish with its offer a signed statement setting forth in detail the circumstances of the disclosure.

(End of provision)

APPENDIX I

Department of the Army Memorandum, Procurement Fraud Indicators, SELCE-LG-JA (27-10i) (Feb. 20, 1990)

DEPARTMENT OF THE ARMY

SELCE-LG-JA (27-10i)

MEMORANDUM FOR: See Distribution

SUBJECT: Procurement Fraud Indicators

1. Provided for your information is a list of indicators of Procurement Fraud. While there is no precise formula for determining how many or how few indicators need be present before a fraud investigation is initiated, I recommend that even the presence of one indicator be discussed with your supervisors. Information obtained from alert employees often provides criminal investigators the key pieces necessary to complete the puzzle.

2. Cases of suspected procurement fraud should be reported to the Procurement Fraud Advisor, CPT Christopher N. Patterson, (703) 349-5257/5258, Autovon 229-5257/5258. While these reports are routinely made through supervisory channels or after coordination with supervisory personnel, all Vint Hill Farms Station personnel are authorized to communicate directly and confidentially with CID or the Procurement Fraud Advisor in appropriate cases.

3. <u>FRAUD INDICATORS IN IDENTIFICATION OF GOVERNMENT'S REQUIREMENTS</u>:

  - Requiring excessively high stock levels.

  - Declaring items which are serviceable as excess or selling them as surplus while continuing to purchase similar items.

  - Purchasing items, services or research projects in response to aggressive marketing efforts.

  - Failing to develop "second-sources" for items, spare parts, and services being continually purchased from a single source.

  - A needs assessment is not adequately or accurately developed or when an agency continually changes its mind about what it wants.

  - Government identifies the need to purchase proprietary, trade secret or other technical information without making reasonable attempts to determine if that information is already owned by the Government.

4. <u>FRAUD INDICATORS IN PRE-SOLICITATION PHASE</u>:

  - Placing any restrictions in the solicitation documents which would tend to restrict competition.

  - Unnecessary sole source/noncompetitive procurement justifications.

App. I   GOVERNMENT CONTRACT COMPLIANCE HANDBOOK

SELCE-LG-JA
SUBJECT: Procurement Fraud Indicators

- Providing contractors any advice, advance information, or release of information concerning requirements or pending purchases on a preferential or selective basis.

- Using statements of work, specifications, or sole source justifications developed by or in consultation with a contractor who will be permitted to compete in the procurement.

- Permit contractors that participated in the development of statements of work, specifications or the preparation of the invitations for bids or request for proposals, to bid on or be involved with the prime contract or any subcontracts.

- Splitting requirements so that small purchase procedures can be utilized or to avoid required levels of review or approval.

- Bid specifications or statements of work which are not consistent with the need determination.

5. **FRAUD INDICATORS IN THE SOLICITATION PHASE:**

- Procurements which are restricted to exclude or hamper any qualified contractor.

- Limiting the time for the submission of bids.

- Technical or contracting personnel revealing information about the procurement to one contractor which is not revealed to all.

- Failure to amend a solicitation to include necessary changes or clarifications.

- Failure to assure that a sufficient number of potential competitors are aware of the solicitation.

- Special assistance to any contractor in preparing its bid or proposal.

- "Referring" a contractor to a specific subcontractor, expert, or source of supply.

- Improper communication with contractors at trade or professional meetings or improper social contact with contractor representatives.

- Government personnel or their families acquiring stock or financial interest in contractor or subcontractor.

Appendix I

SELCE-LG-JA
SUBJECT: Procurement Fraud Indicators

- Government personnel discussing possible employment with a contractor or subcontractor.

- Improper acceptance of a late bid.

- Falsification of documents or receipts to get a late bid accepted.

- Change in a bid after another bidders' prices are known.

- Withdrawal of the low bidder who later becomes a subcontractor to the higher bidder who gets the contract.

- Any indication of collusion or bid rigging between bidders.

- False certification by contractor.

- Falsification of information concerning contractor qualifications, financial capacity, facilities, ownership of equipment and supplies, qualifications of personnel and successful performances of previous jobs, etc.

6. **FRAUD INDICATORS IN THE AWARD PHASE**:

- Deliberately discarding or "losing" the bid or proposal of an "outsider" who wants to participate.

- Improperly disqualifying the bid or proposal of a contractor.

- Disqualification of any qualified bidder.

- Accepting nonresponsive bids from preferred contractors.

- Seemingly unnecessary contacts with contractor personnel by persons other than the contracting officer during the solicitation, evaluation, and negotiation process.

- Any unauthorized release of information to a contractor or other person.

- Any exercise of favoritism toward a particular contractor during the evaluation process.

- Using biased evaluation criteria or using biased individuals on the evaluation panel.

- Award of a contract to a contractor who is not the lowest responsible, responsive bidder.

3

SELCE-LG-JA
SUBJECT: Procurement Fraud Indicators

- Allowing a low bidder to withdraw without justification.

- Failure to forfeit bid bonds when a contractor withdraws improperly.

- Material changes in the contract shortly after award.

- Awards made to contractors with an apparent history of poor performance.

- Awards made to the lowest of a very few bidders without readvertising considerations or without adequate publicity.

- Awards made that include items other than those contained in bid specifications.

- Awards made without adequate documentation of all preaward and postaward actions, including all understanding or oral agreements.

- Release of advance information concerning the award of a major contract.

- Inadequate evaluation of contractor's present responsibility, including ignoring or failing to obtain information regarding a contractor's record of business ethics and integrity.

7. **FRAUD INDICATORS IN THE NEGOTIATION PHASE**:

- Back-dated or after-the-fact justifications in the contract file.

- Disclosure of information to one contractor which is not given to others.

- Improper release of information.

- Any indications that a contractor has provided false cost or pricing data.

- Failure of Government personnel to obtain or rely on a Certificate of Current Cost or Pricing Data.

- Approval of less than full and open competition by an unauthorized person or for an improper reason.

- Inadequate evaluation of contractor's present responsibility, including ignoring or failing to obtain information regarding a contractor's record of business ethics and integrity.

APPENDIX I

SELCE-LG-JA
SUBJECT: Procurement Fraud Indicators

8. **DEFECTIVE PRICING FRAUD INDICATORS:**

   - Indicators of falsification or alteration of supporting data.

   - Failure to update cost or pricing data even though it is known that past activity showed that costs or prices have decreased.

   - Failure to make complete disclosure of data known to responsible contractor personnel.

   - Distortion of the overhead accounts or base line information by transferring changes or accounts that have material impact on Government contracts.

   - Failure to correct known system deficiencies which lead to defective pricing.

   - Protracted delay by contractor employees of the existence in discovering historical records that are subsequently found.

9. **ANTITRUST INDICATORS:**

   - Agreements to adhere to published price lists.

   - Agreements to raise prices by a specified increment.

   - Agreements to establish, adhere to, or eliminate discounts.

   - Agreement not to advertise prices.

   - Agreements to maintain specified price differentials based on quantity, type, or size of product.

10. **FRAUD INDICATORS OF COLLUSIVE BIDDING AND PRICE FIXING:**

    - Bidders who are qualified and capable of performing but who fail to bid, with no apparent reason.

    - Certain contractors always bid against each other or, conversely, certain contractors do not bid against one another.

    - The successful bidder repeatedly subcontracts work to companies that submitted higher bids or to companies that picked up bid packages and could have bid as prime contractor but did not.

SELCE-LG-JA
SUBJECT: Procurement Fraud Indicators

- Different groups of contractors appear to specialize in federal, state, or local jobs exclusively.

- There is an apparent pattern of low bids regularly recurring, such as corporation "x" always being the low bidder in a certain geographical area or in a fixed rotation with other bidders.

- Failure of original bidders to rebid, or an identical ranking of the same bidders upon rebidding, when original bids were rejected as being too far over the Government estimate.

- A certain company appears to be bidding substantially higher on some bids than on other bids with no logical cost difference to account for the increase.

- Bidders that ship their product a short distance bid more than those who must incur greater expense by shipping their product long distance.

- Identical bid amounts on a contract line item by two or more contractors.

- Bidders frequently change prices at about the same time and to the same extent.

- Joint venture bids where either contractor could have bid individually as a prime.

- Any incidents suggesting direct collusion among competitors, such as the appearance of identical calculation or spelling errors in two or more competitive bids.

- Competitors regularly socialize or appear to hold meetings, or otherwise get together in the vicinity of procurement offices shortly before bid filing deadlines.

- Assertions by employees, former employees, or competitors that an agreement to fix bids and prices or otherwise restrain trade exists.

- Bid prices appear to drop whenever a new or frequent bidder submits a bid.

- Competitors exchange any form of price information among themselves.

Appendix I

SELCE-LG-JA
SUBJECT: Procurement Fraud Indicators

- Any reference by bidders to "association price schedules", "industry price schedules", "industry suggested prices", "industry wide prices", or "market-wide prices".

- A bidder's justification for a bid or terms, offered because they follow the industry or industry leader's pricing or terms, may include a reference to following a named competitors pricing or terms.

- Any statements by a representative of a contractor that his company "does not sell in a particular area" or that "only a particular firm sells in that area".

- Statements by a bidder that it is not their turn to receive a job or, conversely, that it is another bidder's turn.

11. PRODUCT SUBSTITUTION FRAUD INDICATORS:

- The provision of inferior quality raw materials.

- Materials that have not been tested as required by the contract specifications.

- Providing foreign made products where domestic products were required.

- Providing untrained workers when skilled technicians were required.

12. INDICATORS IN OTHER AREAS:

- Progress Payment Fraud.

- Cost Mischarging/Labor Mischarging.

- Fast Pay Fraud.

- Bribery, Gratuities, and Conflicts of Interest.

- Violations of the Anti-Kickback Enforcement Act.

SELCE-LG-JA
SUBJECT: Procurement Fraud Indicators

13. This list is by no means exhaustive. Only the imagination of contractors limits the ways fraud might be perpetrated against the Government. If it looks suspicious, report it!

14. As a Total Quality Management initiative, this office offers Fraud Awareness classes for any interested parties.

CHRISTOPHER N. PATTERSON
CPT, JA
Installation Judge Advocate

DISTRIBUTION: E

APPENDIX J

FAR Table 15-2: Instructions for Submitting Cost/Price Proposals When Cost or Pricing Data are Required

TABLE 15-2—INSTRUCTIONS FOR SUBMITTING COST/PRICE PROPOSALS WHEN COST OR PRICING DATA ARE REQUIRED
(FAR 15.408)

This document provides instructions for preparing a contract pricing proposal when cost or pricing data are required.

Note 1. There is a clear distinction between submitting cost or pricing data and merely making available books, records, and other documents without identification. The requirement for submission of cost or pricing data is met when all accurate cost or pricing data reasonably available to the offeror have been submitted, either actually or by specific identification, to the Contracting Officer or an authorized representative. As later information comes into your possession, it should be submitted promptly to the Contracting Officer in a manner that clearly shows how the information relates to the offeror's price proposal. The requirement for submission of cost or pricing data continues up to the time of agreement on price, or an earlier date agreed upon between the parties if applicable.

Note 2. By submitting your proposal, you grant the Contracting Officer or an authorized representative the right to examine records that formed the basis for the pricing proposal. That examination can take place at any time before award. It may include those books, records, documents, and other types of factual information (regardless of form or whether the information is specifically referenced or included in the proposal as the basis for pricing) that will permit an adequate evaluation of the proposed price.

I. General Instructions

A. You must provide the following information on the first page of your pricing proposal:

(1) Solicitation, contract, and/or modification number;

(2) Name and address of offeror;

(3) Name and telephone number of point of contact;

(4) Name of contract administration office (if available);

(5) Type of contract action (that is, new contract, change order, price revision/redetermination, letter contract, unpressed order, or other);

(6) Proposed cost; profit or fee; and total;

(7) Whether you will require the use of Government property in the performance of the contract, and, if so, what property;

(8) Whether your organization is subject to cost accounting standards; whether your organization has submitted a CASB Disclosure Statement, and if it has been determined adequate; whether you have been notified that you are or may be in noncompliance with your Disclosure Statement

App. J GOVERNMENT CONTRACT COMPLIANCE HANDBOOK

or CAS (other than a noncompliance that the cognizant Federal agency official has determined to have an immaterial cost impact), and, if yes, an explanation; whether any aspect of this proposal is inconsistent with your disclosed practices or applicable CAS, and, if so, an explanation; and whether the proposal is consistent with your established estimating and accounting principles and procedures and FAR Part 31, Cost Principles, and, if not, an explanation;

(9) The following statement:

This proposal reflects our estimates and/or actual costs as of this date and conforms with the instructions in FAR 15.403-5(b)(1) and Table 15-2. By submitting this proposal, we grant the Contracting Officer and authorized representative(s) the right to examine, at any time before award, those records, which include books, documents, accounting procedures and practices, and other data, regardless of type and form or whether such supporting information is specifically referenced or included in the proposal as the basis for pricing, that will permit an adequate evaluation of the proposed price.

(10) Date of submission; and

(11) Name, title, and signature of authorized representative.

B. In submitting your proposal, you must include an index, appropriately referenced, of all the cost or pricing data and information accompanying or identified in the proposal. In addition, you must annotate any future additions and/or revisions, up to the date of agreement on price, or an earlier date agreed upon by the parties, on a supplemental index.

C. As part of the specific information required, you must submit, with your proposal, cost or pricing data (that is, data that are verifiable and factual and otherwise as defined at FAR 2.101). You must clearly identify on your cover sheet that cost or pricing data are included as part of the proposal. In addition, you must submit with your proposal any information reasonably required to explain your estimating process, including—

(1) The judgmental factors applied and the mathematical or other methods used in the estimate, including those used in projecting from known data; and

(2) The nature and amount of any contingencies included in the proposed price.

D. You must show the relationship between contract line item prices and the total contract price. You must attach cost-element breakdowns for each proposed line item, using the appropriate format prescribed in the "Formats for Submission of Line Item Summaries" section of this table. You must furnish supporting breakdowns for each cost element, consistent with your cost accounting system.

E. When more than one contract line item is proposed, you must also provide summary total amounts covering all line items for each element of cost.

F. Whenever you have incurred costs for work performed before submission of a proposal, you must identify those costs in your cost/price proposal.

G. If you have reached an agreement with Government representatives on use of forward pricing rates/factors, identify the agreement, include a copy, and describe its nature.

H. As soon as practicable after final agreement on price or an earlier date agreed to by the parties, but before the award resulting from the proposal, you must, under the conditions stated in FAR 15.406-2, submit a Certificate of Current Cost or Pricing Data.

II. Cost Elements

Depending on your system, you must provide breakdowns for the following basic cost elements, as applicable:

A. *Materials and services*. Provide a consolidated priced summary of individual material quantities included in the various tasks, orders, or contract line items being proposed and the basis for pricing (vendor quotes, invoice prices, etc.). Include raw materials, parts, components, assemblies, and services to be produced or performed by others. For all items proposed, identify the item and show the source, quantity, and price. Conduct price analyses of all subcontractor proposals. Conduct cost analyses for all subcontracts when cost or pricing data are submitted by the subcontractor. Include these analyses as part of your own cost or pricing data submissions for subcontracts expected to exceed the appropriate threshold in FAR 15.403-4. Submit the subcontractor cost or pricing data as part of your own cost or pricing data as required in paragraph IIA(2) of this table. These requirements also apply to all subcontractors if required to submit cost or pricing data.

(1) Adequate Price Competition. Provide data showing the degree of competition and the basis for establishing the source and reasonableness of price for those acquisitions (such as subcontracts, purchase orders, material order, etc.) exceeding, or expected to exceed, the appropriate threshold set forth at FAR 15.403-4 priced on the basis of adequate price competition. For interorganizational transfers priced at other than the cost of comparable competitive commercial work of the division, subsidiary, or affiliate of the contractor, explain the pricing method (see FAR 31.205-26(e)).

(2) All Other. Obtain cost or pricing data from prospective sources for those acquisitions (such as subcontracts, purchase orders, material order, etc.) exceeding the threshold set forth in FAR 15.403-4 and not otherwise exempt, in accordance with FAR_15.403-1(b) (*i.e.*, adequate price competition, commercial items, prices set by law or regulation or waiver). Also provide data showing the basis for establishing source and reasonableness of price. In addition, provide a summary of your cost analysis and a copy of cost or pricing data submitted by the prospective

source in support of each subcontract, or purchase order that is the lower of either $11.5 million or more, or both more than the pertinent cost or pricing data threshold and more than 10 percent of the prime contractor's proposed price. The Contracting Officer may require you to submit cost or pricing data in support of proposals in lower amounts. Subcontractor cost or pricing data must be accurate, complete and current as of the date of final price agreement, or an earlier date agreed upon by the parties, given on the prime contractor's Certificate of Current Cost or Pricing Data. The prime contractor is responsible for updating a prospective subcontractor's data. For standard commercial items fabricated by the offeror that are generally stocked in inventory, provide a separate cost breakdown, if priced based on cost. For interorganizational transfers priced at cost, provide a separate breakdown of cost elements. Analyze the cost or pricing data and submit the results of your analysis of the prospective source's proposal. When submission of a prospective source's cost or pricing data is required as described in this paragraph, it must be included along with your own cost or pricing data submission, as part of your own cost or pricing data. You must also submit any other cost or pricing data obtained from a subcontractor, either actually or by specific identification, along with the results of any analysis performed on that data.

B. *Direct Labor*. Provide a time-phased (*e.g.,* monthly, quarterly, etc.) breakdown of labor hours, rates, and cost by appropriate category, and furnish bases for estimates.

C. *Indirect Costs*. Indicate how you have computed and applied your indirect costs, including cost breakdowns. Show trends and budgetary data to provide a basis for evaluating the reasonableness of proposed rates. Indicate the rates used and provide an appropriate explanation.

D. *Other Costs*. List all other costs not otherwise included in the categories described above (*e.g.*, special tooling, travel, computer and consultant services, preservation, packaging and packing, spoilage and rework, and Federal excise tax on finished articles) and provide bases for pricing.

E. *Royalties*. If royalties exceed $1,500, you must provide the following information on a separate page for each separate royalty or license fee:

(1) Name and address of licensor.

(2) Date of license agreement.

(3) Patent numbers.

(4) Patent application serial numbers, or other basis on which the royalty is payable.

(5) Brief description (including any part or model numbers of each contract item or component on which the royalty is payable)

(6) Percentage or dollar rate of royalty per unit.

APPENDIX J

(7) Unit price of contract item.

(8) Number of units.

(9) Total dollar amount of royalties.

(10) If specifically requested by the Contracting Officer, a copy of the current license agreement and identification of applicable claims of specific patents (see FAR 27.204 and 31.205-37).

F. *Facilities Capital Cost of Money.* When you elect to claim facilities capital cost of money as an allowable cost, you must submit Form CASB-CMF and show the calculation of the proposed amount (see FAR 31.205-10).

III. Formats for Submission of Line Item Summaries

A. *New Contracts (including letter contracts).*

COST ELEMENTS	PROPOSED CONTRACT ESTIMATE—TOTAL COST	PROPOSED CONTRACT ESTIMATE—UNIT COST	REFERENCE
(1)	(2)	(3)	(4)

Column and Instruction

(1) Enter appropriate cost elements.

(2) Enter those necessary and reasonable costs that, in your judgment, will properly be incurred in efficient contract performance. When any of the costs in this column have already been incurred (*e.g.,* under a letter contract), describe them on an attached supporting page. When preproduction or startup costs are significant, or when specifically requested to do so by the Contracting Officer, provide a full identification and explanation of them.

(3) Optional, unless required by the Contracting Officer.

(4) Identify the attachment in which the information supporting the specific cost element may be found.

(Attach separate pages as necessary.)

B. *Change Orders, Modifications, and Claims.*

Cost Elements	Estimated Cost of All Work Deleted	Cost of Deleted Work Already Performed	Net Cost To Be Deleted	Cost of Work Added	Net Cost of Change	Reference
(1)	(2)	(3)	(4)	(5)	(6)	(7)

	Column and Instruction
(1)	Enter appropriate cost elements.
(2)	Include the current estimates of what the cost would have been to complete the deleted work not yet performed (not the original proposal estimates), and the cost of deleted work already performed.
(3)	Include the incurred cost of deleted work already performed, using actuals incurred if possible, or, if actuals are not available, estimates from your accounting records. Attach a detailed inventory of work, materials, parts, components, and hardware already purchased, manufactured, or performed and deleted by the change, indicating the cost and proposed disposition of each line item. Also, if you desire to retain these items or any portion of them, indicate the amount offered for them.
(4)	Enter the net cost to be deleted, which is the estimated cost of all deleted work less the cost of deleted work already performed. Column (2) minus Column (3) equals Column (4).
(5)	Enter your estimate for cost of work added by the change. When nonrecurring costs are significant, or when specifically requested to do so by the Contracting Officer, provide a full identification and explanation of them. When any of the costs in this column have already been incurred, describe them on an attached supporting schedule.
(6)	Enter the net cost of change, which is the cost of work added, less the net cost to be deleted. Column (5) minus Column (4) equals Column (6). When this result is negative, place the amount in parentheses.
(7)	Identify the attachment in which the information supporting the specific cost element may be found.

(Attach separate pages as necessary.)

Appendix J

C. *Price Revision/Redetermination.*

Cutoff Date	Number of Units Completed	Number of Units To Be Completed	Contract Amount	Redetermination Proposal Amount	Difference
(1)	(2)	(3)	(4)	(5)	(6)

Cost Elements	Incurred Cost— Preproduction	Incurred Cost— Completed Units	Incurred Cost— Work in Progress	Total Incurred Cost	Estimated Cost to Complete	Estimated Total Cost	Reference
(7)	(8)	(9)	(10)	(11)	(12)	(13)	(14)

(Use as applicable)

Column and Instruction

(1) Enter the cutoff date required by the contract, if applicable.

(2) Enter the number of units completed during the period for which experienced costs of production are being submitted.

(3) Enter the number of units remaining to be completed under the contract.

(4) Enter the cumulative contract amount.

(5) Enter your redetermination proposal amount.

(6) Enter the difference between the contract amount and the redetermination proposal amount. When this result is negative, place the amount in parentheses. Column (4) minus Column (5) equals Column (6).

(7) Enter appropriate cost elements. When residual inventory exists, the final costs established under fixed-price-incentive and fixed-price-redeterminable arrangements should be net of the fair market value of such inventory. In support of subcontract costs, submit a listing of all subcontracts subject to repricing action, annotated as to their status.

(8) Enter all costs incurred under the contract before starting production and other nonrecurring costs (usually referred to as startup costs) from your books and records as of the cutoff date. These include such costs as preproduction engineering, special plant rearrangement, training program, and any identifiable nonrecurring costs such as initial rework,

App. J-7

App. J   GOVERNMENT CONTRACT COMPLIANCE HANDBOOK

spoilage, pilot runs, etc. In the event the amounts are not segregated in or otherwise available from your records, enter in this column your best estimates. Explain the basis for each estimate and how the costs are charged on your accounting records (*e.g.,* included in production costs as direct engineering labor, charged to manufacturing overhead). Also show how the costs would be allocated to the units at their various stages of contract completion.

(9)   Enter in Column (9) the production costs from your books and records (exclusive of preproduction costs reported in Column (8)) of the units completed as of the cutoff date.

(10)   Enter in Column (10) the costs of work in process as determined from your records or inventories at the cutoff date. When the amounts for work in process are not available in your records but reliable estimates for them can be made, enter the estimated amounts in Column (10) and enter in column (9) the differences between the total incurred costs (exclusive of preproduction costs) as of the cutoff date and these estimates. Explain the basis for the estimates, including identification of any provision for experienced or anticipated allowances, such as shrinkage, rework, design changes, etc. Furnish experienced unit or lot costs (or labor hours) from inception of contract to the cutoff date, improvement curves, and any other available production cost history pertaining to the item(s) to which your proposal relates.

(11)   Enter total incurred costs (Total of Columns (8), (9), and (10)).

(12)   Enter those necessary and reasonable costs that in your judgment will properly be incurred in completing the remaining work to be performed under the contract with respect to the item(s) to which your proposal relates.

(13)   Enter total estimated cost (Total of Columns (11) and (12)).

(14)   Identify the attachment in which the information supporting the specific cost element may be found.

(Attach separate pages as necessary.)

APPENDIX K

DCAA Form 1: "Notice of Contract Costs Suspended and/or Disapproved"

February 24, 2014

6185
Figure 6-9-1

Figure 6-9-1
DCAA Form 1

App. K GOVERNMENT CONTRACT COMPLIANCE HANDBOOK

6186
Figure 6-9-1

February 24, 2014

**Figure 6-9-1
DCAA Form 1 (cont.)**

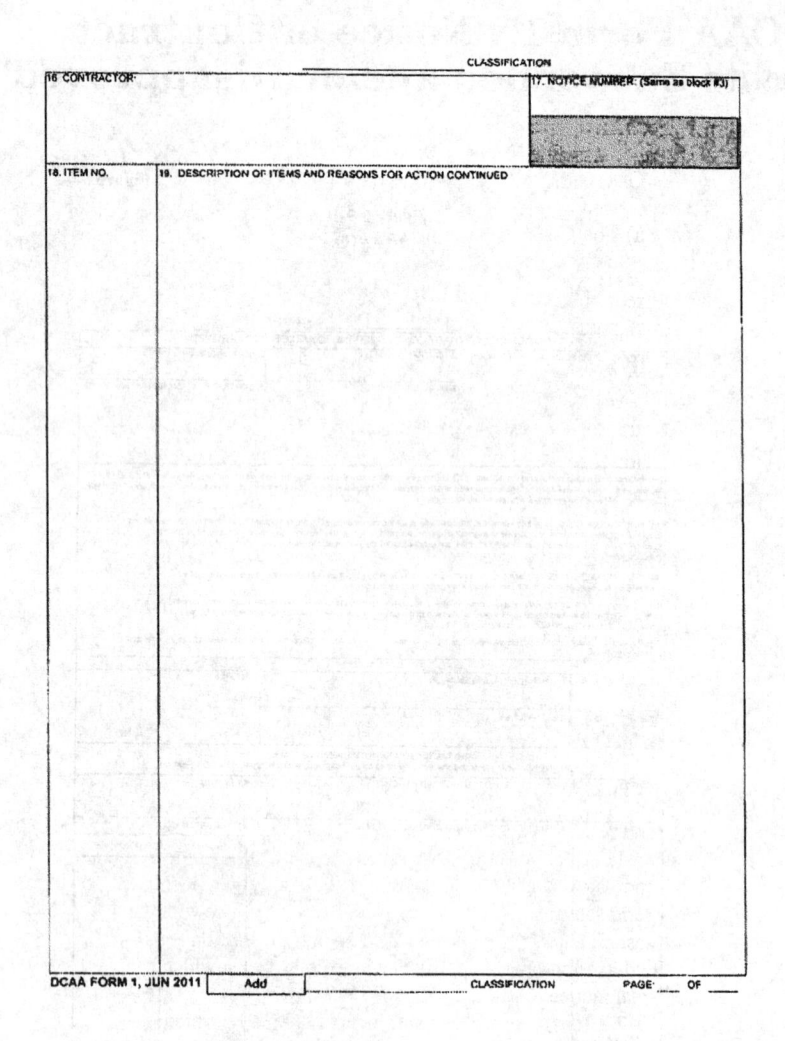

DCAA Contract Audit Manual

App. K-2

APPENDIX L

FAR 52.242-4: "Certification of Final Indirect Costs"

CERTIFICATION OF FINAL INDIRECT COSTS (JAN 1997)

(a) The Contractor shall—

(1) Certify any proposal to establish or modify final indirect cost rates;

(2) Use the format in paragraph (c) of this clause to certify; and

(3) Have the certificate signed by an individual of the Contractor's organization at a level no lower than a vice president or chief financial officer of the business segment of the Contractor that submits the proposal.

(b) Failure by the Contractor to submit a signed certificate, as described in this clause, may result in final indirect costs at rates unilaterally established by the Contracting Officer.

(c) The certificate of final indirect costs shall read as follows:

CERTIFICATE OF FINAL INDIRECT COSTS

This is to certify that I have reviewed this proposal to establish final indirect cost rates and to the best of my knowledge and belief:

1. All costs included in this proposal (identify proposal and date) to establish final indirect cost rates for (identify period covered by rate) are allowable in accordance with the cost principles of the Federal Acquisition Regulation (FAR) and its supplements applicable to the contracts to which the final indirect cost rates will apply; and

2. This proposal does not include any costs which are expressly unallowable under applicable cost principles of the FAR or its supplements.

Firm: _____
Signature: _____
Name of Certifying Official: _____
Title: _____
Date of Execution: _____

(End of clause)

(e) If the Contracting Officer determines that a cost submitted by the Contractor in its proposal includes a cost previously determined to be unallowable for that Contractor, then the Contractor will be assessed a penalty in an amount equal to two times the amount of the disallowed cost allocated to this contract.

(f) Determinations under paragraphs (d) and (e) of this clause are final decisions within the meaning of the Contract Disputes Act of 1978 (41 U.S.C. 601, *et seq.*).

(g) Pursuant to the criteria in FAR 42.709-5, the Contracting Officer may waive the penalties in paragraph (d) or (e) of this clause.

(h) Payment by the Contractor of any penalty assessed under this clause does not constitute repayment to the Government of any unallowable cost which has been paid by the Government to the Contractor.

(End of clause)

APPENDIX M

FAR 52.242-3: "Penalties for Unallowable Costs Clause"

52.242-3 Penalties for Unallowable Costs.

As prescribed in 42.709-6, use the following clause:

Penalties for Unallowable Costs (Mar 2001)

(a) *Definition.* "Proposal," as used in this clause, means either—

(1) A final indirect cost rate proposal submitted by the Contractor after the expiration of its fiscal year which—

(i) Relates to any payment made on the basis of billing rates; or

(ii) Will be used in negotiating the final contract price; or

(2) The final statement of costs incurred and estimated to be incurred under the Incentive Price Revision clause (if applicable), which is used to establish the final contract price.

(b) Contractors which include allowable indirect costs in a proposal may be subject to penalties. The penalties are prescribed in 10 U.S.C. 2324 or 41 U.S.C. 256, as applicable, which is implemented in Section 42.709 of the Federal Acquisition Regulation (FAR).

(c) The Contractor shall not include in any proposal any cost that is unallowable, as defined in Subpart 2.1 of the FAR, or an executive agency supplement to the FAR.

(d) If the Contracting Officer determines that a cost submitted by the Contractor in its proposal is expressly unallowable under a cost principle in the FAR, or an executive agency supplement to the FAR, that defines the allowability of specific selected costs, the Contractor shall be assessed a penalty equal to—

(1) The amount of the disallowed cost allocated to this contract; plus

(2) Simple interest, to be compounded—

(i) On the amount the Contractor was paid (whether as a progress or billing payment) in excess of the amount to which the Contractor was entitled; and

(ii) Using the applicable rate effective for each six-month interval prescribed by the Secretary of the Treasury pursuant to Pub. L. 92-41 (85 Stat. 97).

APPENDIX N

Form CASB-DS-1: "Cost Accounting Standards Board Disclosure Statement"

FAR Appendix—CAS Regulation
FORM APPROVED OMB NUMBER
0348-0051

COST ACCOUNTING STANDARDS BOARD DISCLOSURE STATEMENT REQUIRED BY PUBLIC LAW 100-679	INDEX

Page

GENERAL INSTRUCTIONS			(1)
COVER SHEET AND CERTIFICATION			C-1
PART I	-	General Information	I-1
PART II	-	Direct Costs	II-1
PART III	-	Direct vs. Indirect Costs	III-1
PART IV	-	Indirect Costs	IV-1
PART V	-	Depreciation and Capitalization Practices	V-1
PART VI	-	Other Costs and Credits	VI-1
PART VII	-	Deferred Compensation and Insurance Cost	VII-1
PART VIII	-	Home Office Expenses	VIII-1

COST ACCOUNTING STANDARDS BOARD DISCLOSURE STATEMENT REQUIRED BY PUBLIC LAW 100-679	GENERAL INSTRUCTIONS

1. This Disclosure Statement has been designed to meet the requirements of Public Law 100-679, and persons completing it are to describe the contractor and its contract cost accounting practices. For complete regulations, instructions and timing requirements concerning submission of the Disclosure Statement, refer to Section 9903.202 of Chapter 99 Of Title 48 CFR (48 CFR 9903.202).

2. Part I of the Statement provides general information concerning each reporting unit (e.g., segment, Corporate or other intermediate level home office, or a business unit). Parts II through VII pertain to the types of costs generally incurred by the segment or business unit directly performing Federal contracts or similar cost objectives. Part VIII pertains to the types of costs that are generally incurred by a Home office and are allocated to one or more segments performing Federal contracts. For a definition of the term "home office", see 48 CFR 9904.403.

3. Each segment or business unit required to disclose its cost accounting practices should complete the Cover Sheet, the Certification, and Parts I through VII.

4. Each home office required to disclose its cost accounting practices for measuring, assigning and allocating its costs to segments performing Federal contracts or similar cost objectives shall complete the Cover Sheet, the Certification, Part I and Part VIII of the Disclosure Statement. Where a home office either establishes practices or procedures for the types of costs covered by Parts V, VI and VII, or incurs and then allocates these types of cost to its segments, the home office may complete Parts V, VI and VII to be included in the Disclosure Statement submitted by its segments. While a home office may have more than one segment submitting Disclosure Statements, only one Statement needs to be submitted to cover the home office operations.

5. The Statement must be signed by an authorized signatory of the reporting unit.

6. The Disclosure Statement should be answered by marking the appropriate line or inserting the applicable letter code which describes the segment's (reporting unit's) cost accounting practices.

7. A number of questions in this Statement may need narrative answers requiring more space than is provided. In such instances, the reporting unit should use the attached continuation sheet provided. The continuation sheet may be reproduced locally as needed. The number of the question involved should be indicated and the same coding required to answer the questions in the Statement should be used in presenting the answer on the continuation sheet. Continuation sheets should be inserted at the end of the pertinent Part of the Statement. On each continuation sheet, the reporting unit should enter the next sequential page number for that Part and, on the last continuation sheet used, the words "End of Part" should be inserted after the last entry.

8. Where the cost accounting practice being disclosed is clearly set forth in the contractor's existing written accounting policies and procedures, such documents may be cited on a continuation sheet and incorporated by reference at the option of the contractor. In such cases, the contractor should provide the date of issuance and effective date for each accounting policy and/or procedures document cited. Alternatively, copies of the relevant parts of such documents may be attached as appendices to the pertinent Disclosure Statement Part. Such continuation sheets and appendices should be labeled and cross-referenced with the applicable Disclosure Statement number and follow the page number specified in paragraph 7. Any supplementary comments needed to adequately describe the cost accounting practice being disclosed should also be provided.

9. Disclosure Statements must be amended when cost accounting practices are changed to comply with a new CAS or when practices are changed with or without knowledge of the Government (Also see 48 CFR 9903.202-3).

COST ACCOUNTING STANDARDS BOARD DISCLOSURE STATEMENT REQUIRED BY PUBLIC LAW 100-679	GENERAL INSTRUCTIONS

10. Amendments shall be submitted to the same offices to which submission would have been made were an original Disclosure Statement filed.

11. Each amendment, or set of amendments should be accompanied by an amended cover sheet (indicating revision number and effective date of the change) and a signed certification. For all resubmissions, on each page, insert "Revision Number ___" and "Effective Date ___" in the Item Description block; and, insert a revision mark (e.g., "R") in the right hand margin of any line that is revised. Completely resubmitted Disclosure Statements must be accompanied by similar notations identifying the items which have been changed.

12. Use of this Disclosure Statement, amended February 1996, shall be phased in as follows:

A. <u>New Contractors</u>. This form shall be used by new contractors when they are initially required to disclose their cost accounting practices pursuant to 9903.202-1.

B. <u>Existing Contractors</u>. If a contractor has disclosed its cost accounting practices on a prior edition of the Disclosure Statement (CASB DS-1), such disclosure shall remain in effect until the contractor amends or revises a significant portion of the Disclosure Statement in accordance with CAS 9903.202-3. Minor amendments to an existing DS-1 may continue to be made using the prior form. However, when a substantive change is made, a complete Disclosure Statement must be filed using this form. In any event, all contractors and subcontractors must submit a new Disclosure Statement (this version of the CASB DS-1) not later than the beginning of the contractor's next full fiscal year after December 31, 1998.

ATTACHMENT - Blank Continuation Sheet

COST ACCOUNTING STANDARDS BOARD DISCLOSURE STATEMENT REQUIRED BY PUBLIC LAW 100-679	CONTINUATION SHEET
	NAME OF REPORTING UNIT

Item No.	Item description

FORM CASB DS-1 (REV 2/96)

APPENDIX N

COST ACCOUNTING STANDARDS BOARD DISCLOSURE STATEMENT REQUIRED BY PUBLIC LAW 100-679	COVER SHEET AND CERTIFICATION

0.1 **Company or Reporting Unit.**

    Name

    Street Address

    City, State, & Zip Code

    Division or Subsidiary of (if applicable)

0.2 **Reporting Unit:** (Mark one.)

    A. ____ Business Unit comprising an entire business organization which is not divided into segments.
    B.1. ____ Corporate Home Office
       2. ____ Intermediate Level Home Office
       3. ____ Segment or business unit reporting directly to a home office.

0.3 **Official to Contact Concerning this Statement.**

    Name and Title

    Phone number (including area code and extension)

0.4 **Statement Type and Effective Date:**

    A. (Mark type of submission. If a revision, enter number)
       (a)____ Original Statement
       (b)____ Revised Statement; Revision No.____

    B. Effective Date of this Statement/Revision:____

0.5 **Statement Submitted To** (Provide office name, location and telephone number, include area code and extension):

    (a) Cognizant Federal Agency: _____
    (b) Cognizant Federal Auditor:_____

CERTIFICATION

I certify that to the best of my knowledge and belief this Statement, as amended in the case of a revision, is the complete and accurate disclosure as of the above date by the above-named organization of its cost accounting practices, as required by the Disclosure Regulation (48 CFR 9903.202) of the Cost Accounting Standards Board under P.L. 100-679.

_____
(Name)

_____
(Title)

THE PENALTY FOR MAKING A FALSE STATEMENT IN THIS DISCLOSURE IS PRESCRIBED IN 18 U.S.C. § 1001

FORM CASB DS-1 (REV 2/96)   C-1

COST ACCOUNTING STANDARDS BOARD DISCLOSURE STATEMENT REQUIRED BY PUBLIC LAW 100-679	PART I - GENERAL INFORMATION
	NAME OF REPORTING UNIT

Item No.	Item description

Part I Instructions

Sales data for this part should cover the most recently completed fiscal year of the reporting unit. "Government CAS Covered Sales" includes sales under both prime contracts and subcontracts. "Annual CAS Covered Sales" includes intracorporate transactions.

1.1.0 Type of Business Entity of Which the Reporting Unit is a Part. (Mark one.)

- A. ____ Corporation
- B. ____ Partnership
- C. ____ Proprietorship
- D. ____ Not-for-profit organization
- E. ____ Joint Venture
- F. ____ Federally Funded Research and Development Center (FFRDC)
- Y. ____ Other (Specify) _____

1.2.0 Predominant Type of Government Sales. (Mark one.) 1/

- A. ____ Manufacturing
- B. ____ Research and Development
- C. ____ Construction
- D. ____ Services
- Y. ____ Other (Specify) _____

1.3.0 Annual CAS Covered Government Sales as Percentage of Total Sales (Government and Commercial). (Mark one. An estimate is permitted for this section.) 1/

- A. ____ Less than 10%
- B. ____ 10%-50%
- C. ____ 51%-80%
- D. ____ 81% - 95%
- E. ____ Over 95%

1.4.0 Description of Your Cost Accounting System for Government Contracts and Subcontracts. (Mark the appropriate line(s) and if more than one is marked, explain on a continuation sheet.) 1/

- A. ____ Standard costs - Job order
- B. ____ Standard costs - Process
- C. ____ Actual costs - Job order
- D. ____ Actual costs - Process
- Y. ____ Other(s) 2/

1/ Do not complete when Part I is filed in conjunction with Part VIII.
2/ Describe on a Continuation Sheet.

FORM CASB DS-1 (REV 2/96)   I - 1

APPENDIX N

COST ACCOUNTING STANDARDS BOARD DISCLOSURE STATEMENT REQUIRED BY PUBLIC LAW 100-679	PART I - GENERAL INFORMATION
	NAME OF REPORTING UNIT

Item No.	Item description
1.5.0	**Identification of Differences Between Contract Cost Accounting and Financial Accounting Records.**
	List on a continuation sheet, the types of costs charged to Federal contracts that are supported by memorandum records and identify the method used to reconcile with the entity's financial accounting records.
1.6.0	**Unallowable Costs.** Costs that are not reimbursable as allowable costs under the terms and conditions of Federal awards are identified as follows: (Mark all that apply and if more than one is marked, describe on a continuation sheet the major cost groupings, organizations, or other criteria for using each marked technique.)
1.6.1	Incurred costs.
	A. ____ Specifically identified and recorded separately in the formal financial accounting records.
	B. ____ Identified in separately maintained accounting records or workpapers.
	C. ____ Identifiable through use of less formal accounting techniques that permit audit verification.
	D. ____ Determinable by other means. 1/
1.6.2	Estimated costs.
	A. ____ By designation and description (in backup data, workpapers, etc) which have specifically been identified and recognized in making estimates.
	B. ____ By description of any other estimating technique employed to provide appropriate recognition of any unallowable amounts pertinent to the estimates.
	C. ____ Other. 1/
1.7.0	**Fiscal Year:** _____ (Specify twelve month period used for financial accounting and reporting purposes, e.g., 1/1 to 12/31.)
1.7.1	**Cost Accounting Period:** _____ (Specify period. If the cost accounting period used for the accumulation and reporting of costs under Federal contracts is other than the fiscal year identified in Item 1.7.0, explain circumstances on a continuation sheet.)
	1/ Describe on a Continuation Sheet.

FORM CASB DS-1 (REV 2/96)   I - 2

COST ACCOUNTING STANDARDS BOARD DISCLOSURE STATEMENT REQUIRED BY PUBLIC LAW 100-679	PART II - DIRECT COSTS
	NAME OF REPORTING UNIT

Item No.	Item description

Part II Instructions

This part covers the three major categories of direct costs, i.e., Direct Material, Direct Labor, and Other Direct Costs.

It is not the intent here to spell out or define the three elements of direct costs. Rather, each contractor should disclose practices based on its own definitions of what costs are, or will be, charged directly to Federal contracts or similar cost objectives as Direct Material, Direct Labor, or Other Direct Costs. For example, a contractor may charge or classify purchased labor of a direct nature as "Direct Material" for purposes of pricing proposals, requests for progress payments, claims for cost reimbursement, etc.; some other contractor may classify the same cost as "Direct Labor," and still another as "Other Direct Costs." In these circumstances, it is expected that each contractor will disclose practices consistent with its own classifications of Direct Material, Direct Labor, and Other Direct Costs.

2.1.0 **Description of Direct Material.** Direct material as used here is not limited to those items of material actually incorporated into the end product; they also include material, consumable supplies, and other costs when charged to Federal contracts or similar cost objectives as Direct Material. (Describe on a continuation sheet the principal classes or types of material and services which are charged as direct material; group the material and service costs by those which are incorporated in an end product and those which are not.)

2.2.0 **Method of Charging Direct Material.**

2.2.1 **Direct Charge Not Through an Inventory Account at:** (Mark the appropriate line(s) and if more than one is marked, explain on a continuation sheet.)

    A. ____ Standard costs (Describe the type of standards used.) 1/
    B. ____ Actual Costs
    Y. ____ Other(s) 1/
    Z. ____ Not applicable

2.2.2 **Charged Direct from a Contractor-owned Inventory Account at:** (Mark the appropriate line(s) and if more than one is marked, explain on a continuation sheet.)

    A. ____ Standard costs 1/
    B. ____ Average Costs 1/
    C. ____ First in, first out
    D. ____ Last in, first out
    Y. ____ Other(s) 1/
    Z. ____ Not applicable

1/ Describe on a Continuation Sheet.

FORM CASB DS-1 (REV 2/96)   II - 1

APPENDIX N

COST ACCOUNTING STANDARDS BOARD DISCLOSURE STATEMENT REQUIRED BY PUBLIC LAW 100-679	PART II - DIRECT COSTS
	NAME OF REPORTING UNIT

Item No.	Item description
2.3.0	**Timing of Charging Direct Material.** (Mark the appropriate line(s) to indicate the point in time at which direct material are charged to Federal contracts or similar cost objectives, and if more than one line is marked, explain on a continuation sheet.) A. ____ When orders are placed B. ____ When both the material and invoice are received C. ____ When material is issued or released to a process, batch, or similar intermediate cost objective D. ____ When material is issued or released to a final cost objective E. ____ When invoices are paid Y. ____ Other(s) 1/ Z. ____ Not applicable
2.4.0	**Variances from Standard Costs for Direct Material.** (Do not complete this item unless you use a standard cost method, i.e., you have marked Line A of Item 2.2.1, or 2.2.2. Mark the appropriate line(s) in Items 2.4.1, 2.4.2, and 2.4.4, and if more than one line is marked, explain on a continuation sheet.)
2.4.1	**Type of Variance.** A. ____ Price B. ____ Usage C. ____ Combined (A and B) Y. ____ Other(s) 1/
2.4.2	**Level of Production Unit used to Accumulate Variance.** Indicate which level of production unit is used as a basis for accumulating material variances. A. ____ Plant-wide Basis B. ____ By Department C. ____ By Product or Product Line Y. ____ Other(s) 1/
2.4.3	**Method of Disposing of Variance.** Describe on a continuation sheet the basis for, and the frequency of, the disposition of the variance.
2.4.4	**Revisions.** Standard costs for direct materials are revised: A. ____ Semiannually B. ____ Annually C. ____ Revised as needed, but at least once annually Y. ____ Other(s) 1/

1/ Describe on a Continuation Sheet.

FORM CASB DS-1 (REV 2/96)

App. N — Government Contract Compliance Handbook

FAR Appendix—CAS Regulation

COST ACCOUNTING STANDARDS BOARD DISCLOSURE STATEMENT REQUIRED BY PUBLIC LAW 100-679	PART II - DIRECT COSTS NAME OF REPORTING UNIT

Item No.	Item description

2.5.0 Method of Charging Direct Labor: (Mark the appropriate line(s) for each Direct Labor Category to show how such labor is charged to Federal contracts or similar cost objectives, and if more than one line is marked, explain on a continuation sheet. Also describe on a continuation sheet the principal classes of labor rates that are, or will be applied to Manufacturing Labor, Engineering Labor, and Other Direct Labor, in order to develop direct labor costs.

	Direct Labor Category		
	Manufacturing	Engineering	Other Direct
A. Individual/actual rates	___	___	___
B. Average rates — uncompensated overtime hours included in computation 1/	___	___	___
C. Average rates — uncompensated overtime hours excluded from computation	___	___	___
D. Standard costs/rates 1/	___	___	___
Y. Other(s) 1/	___	___	___
Z. Labor category is not applicable	___	___	___

2.6.0 Variances from Standard Costs for Direct Labor. (Do not complete this item unless you use a standard costs/rate method, i.e., you have marked Line D of Item 2.5.0 for any direct labor category. Mark the appropriate line(s) in each column of Items 2.6.1, 2.6.2, and 2.6.4. If more than one is marked, explain on a continuation sheet.)

2.6.1 Type of Variance.

	Direct Labor Category		
	Manufacturing	Engineering	Other Direct
A. Rate	___	___	___
B. Efficiency	___	___	___
C. Combined (A and B)	___	___	___
Y. Other(s) 1/	___	___	___
Z. Labor category is not applicable	___	___	___

1/ Describe on a Continuation Sheet.

FORM CASB DS-1 (REV 2/96)   II - 3

COST ACCOUNTING STANDARDS BOARD DISCLOSURE STATEMENT REQUIRED BY PUBLIC LAW 100-679	PART II - DIRECT COSTS
	NAME OF REPORTING UNIT

Item No.	Item description
2.6.2	**Level of Production Unit used to Accumulate Variance.** Indicate which level of production unit is used as a basis for accumulating the labor variances.

	Direct Labor Category		
	Manufacturing	Engineering	Other Direct
A. Plant-wide basis	____	____	____
B. By department	____	____	____
C. By product or product line	____	____	____
Y. Other(s) 1/	____	____	____
Z. Labor category is not applicable	____	____	____

2.6.3 **Method of Disposing of Variance.** Describe on a continuation sheet the basis for, and the frequency of, the disposition of the variance.

2.6.4 **Revisions.** Standard costs for direct labor are revised:

- A. ____ Semiannually
- B. ____ Annually
- C. ____ Revised as needed, but at least once annually
- Y. ____ Other(s) 1/

2.7.0 **Description of Other Direct Costs.** Other significant items of cost directly identified with Federal contracts or other final cost objectives. Describe on a continuation sheet the principal classes of other costs that are always charged directly, that is, identified specifically with final cost objectives, e.g., fringe benefits, travel costs, services, subcontracts, etc.

2.7.1 When Employee Travel Expenses for lodging and subsistence are charged direct to Federal contracts or similar cost objectives the charge is based on:

- A. ____ Actual Costs
- B. ____ Per Diem Rates
- C. ____ Lodging at actual costs and subsistence at per diem
- Y. ____ Other Method 1/
- Z. ____ Not Applicable

2.8.0 **Credits to Contract Costs.** When Federal contracts or similar cost objectives are credited for the following circumstances, are the rates of direct labor, direct materials, other direct costs and applicable indirect costs always the same as those for the original charges? (Mark one line for each circumstance, and for each "No" answer, explain on a continuation sheet how the credit differs from the original charge.)

Circumstance	A. Yes	B. No	Z. Not Applicable
(a) Transfers to other jobs/contracts	____	____	____
(b) Unused or excess materials remaining upon completion of contract	____	____	____

1/ Describe on a Continuation Sheet.

FORM CASB DS-1 (REV 2/96) II - 4

App. N   GOVERNMENT CONTRACT COMPLIANCE HANDBOOK

FAR APPENDIX—CAS REGULATION

COST ACCOUNTING STANDARDS BOARD DISCLOSURE STATEMENT REQUIRED BY PUBLIC LAW 100-679	PART III - DIRECT VS. INDIRECT COSTS
	NAME OF REPORTING UNIT

Item No.	Item description
3.1.0	**Criteria for Determining How Costs are Charged to Federal Contracts Or Similar Cost Objectives.** Describe on a continuation sheet your criteria for determining when costs incurred for the same purpose, in like circumstances, are treated either as direct costs only or as indirect costs only with respect to final cost objectives.
3.2.0	**Treatment of Costs of Specified Functions, Elements of Cost, or Transactions.** (For each of the functions, elements of cost or transactions listed in Items 3.2.1, 3.2.2, and 3.2.3, enter one of the Codes A through F, or Y, to indicate how the item is treated. Enter Code Z in those lines that are not applicable to you. Also, specify the name(s) of the indirect pool(s) (as listed in 4.1.0, 4.2.0 and 4.3.0) for each function, element of cost, or transaction coded E or F. If Code E, Sometimes direct/Sometimes indirect, is used, explain on a continuation sheet the circumstances under which both direct and indirect allocations are made.)

Treatment Code

A. Direct material
B. Direct labor
C. Direct material and labor
D. Other direct costs
E. Sometimes direct/Sometimes indirect
F. Indirect only
Y. Other(s) 1/
Z. Not applicable

3.2.1	**Functions, Elements of Cost, or Transactions Related to Direct Material**	Treatment Code	Name of Pool(s)
	(a) Cash Discounts on Purchases	____	_____
	(b) Freight in	____	_____
	(c) Income from Sale of Scrap	____	_____
	(d) Income from Sale of Salvage	____	_____
	(e) Incoming Material Inspection (receiving)	____	_____
	(f) Inventory adjustment	____	_____
	(g) Purchasing	____	_____
	(h) Trade Discounts, Refunds, Rebates, and Allowances on Purchases	____	_____

1/ Describe on a Continuation Sheet.

FORM CASB DS-1 (REV 2/96)   III - 1

APPENDIX N

App. N

FAR APPENDIX—CAS REGULATION

COST ACCOUNTING STANDARDS BOARD DISCLOSURE STATEMENT REQUIRED BY PUBLIC LAW 100-679	PART III - DIRECT VS. INDIRECT COSTS NAME OF REPORTING UNIT

Item No.	Item description		
3.2.2	**Functions, Elements of Cost, or Transactions Related to Direct Labor**	Treatment Code	Name of Pool(s)
	(a) Incentive Compensation	_____	_____
	(b) Holiday Differential (Premium Pay)	_____	_____
	(c) Vacation Pay	_____	_____
	(d) Overtime Premium Pay	_____	_____
	(e) Shift Premium Pay	_____	_____
	(f) Pension Costs	_____	_____
	(g) Post Retirement Benefits Other Than Pensions	_____	_____
	(h) Health Insurance	_____	_____
	(i) Life Insurance	_____	_____
	(j) Other Deferred Compensation 1/	_____	_____
	(k) Training	_____	_____
	(l) Sick Leave	_____	_____

1/ Describe on a Continuation Sheet.

FORM CASB DS-1 (REV 2/96)   III - 2

App. N   GOVERNMENT CONTRACT COMPLIANCE HANDBOOK

FAR APPENDIX—CAS REGULATION

COST ACCOUNTING STANDARDS BOARD DISCLOSURE STATEMENT REQUIRED BY PUBLIC LAW 100-679	PART III - DIRECT VS. INDIRECT COSTS
	NAME OF REPORTING UNIT

Item No.	Item description			
3.2.3	**Functions, Elements of Cost, or Transactions - Miscellaneous**		Treatment Code	Name of Pool(s)
	(a)	Design Engineering (in-house)	___	_____
	(b)	Drafting (in-house)	___	_____
	(c)	Computer Operations (in-house)	___	_____
	(d)	Contract Administration	___	_____
	(e)	Subcontract Administration Costs	___	_____
	(f)	Freight Out (finished product)	___	_____
	(g)	Line (or production) Inspection	___	_____
	(h)	Packaging and Preservation	___	_____
	(i)	Preproduction Costs and Start-up Costs	___	_____
	(j)	Departmental Supervision	___	_____
	(k)	Professional Services (consultant fees)	___	_____
	(l)	Purchased Labor of Direct Nature (on premises)	___	_____
	(m)	Purchased Labor of Direct Nature (off premises)	___	_____
	(n)	Rearrangement Costs	___	_____
	(o)	Rework Costs	___	_____
	(p)	Royalties	___	_____
	(q)	Scrap Work	___	_____
	(r)	Special Test Equipment	___	_____
	(s)	Special Tooling	___	_____
	(t)	Warranty Costs	___	_____
	(u)	Rental Costs	___	_____
	(v)	Travel and Subsistence	___	_____
	(w)	Employee Severance Pay	___	_____
	(x)	Security Guards	___	_____

FORM CASB DS-1 (REV 2/96)   III - 3

APPENDIX N

COST ACCOUNTING STANDARDS BOARD DISCLOSURE STATEMENT REQUIRED BY PUBLIC LAW 100-679	PART IV - INDIRECT COSTS
	NAME OF REPORTING UNIT

Item No.	Item description

Part IV Instructions

For the purpose of this part, indirect costs have been divided into three categories: (i) manufacturing, engineering, and comparable indirect costs, (ii) general and administrative (G&A) expenses, and (iii) service center and expense pool costs, as defined in Item 4.3.0. The term "overhead," as used in this part, refers only to the first category of indirect costs.

The following Allocation Base Codes are provided for use in connection with Items 4.1.0, 4.2.0 and 4.3.0.

A. Sales
B. Cost of sales
C. Total Cost input (direct material, direct labor, other direct costs and applicable overhead)
D. Value-added cost input (total cost input less direct material and subcontract costs)
E. Total cost incurred (total cost input plus G&A expenses)
F. Prime cost (direct material, direct labor and other direct cost)
G. Processing or conversion cost (direct labor and applicable overhead)

H. Direct labor dollars
I. Direct labor hours
J. Machine hours
K. Usage
L. Unit of production
M. Direct material cost
N. Total payroll dollars (direct and indirect employees)
O. Headcount or number of employees (direct and indirect employees)
P. Square feet
Y. Other(s), or more than one basis (Describe on a continuation sheet.)
Z. Pool not applicable

4.1.0 <u>Overhead Pools.</u> List all the overhead pools, i.e., pools of indirect costs, other than general and administrative (G&A) expenses, that are allocated to final cost objectives without any intermediate allocations. A segment or business unit may have only a single pool encompassing all of its overhead costs or alternatively it may have several pools such as manufacturing overhead, engineering overhead, material handling overhead, etc. For each pool listed indicate the base used for allocating such pooled expenses to Federal contracts or similar cost objectives. Also, for each of the pools indicate (a) the major functions, activities, and elements of cost included, and (b) the make up of the allocation base. Use a continuation sheet if additional space is required.

Allocation
Base Code

1. _____   ____

   (a) Major functions, activities, and elements of cost included:
   _____
   _____

   (b) Description/Make up of the allocation base:
   _____
   _____

FORM CASB DS-1 (REV 2/96) IV - 1

App. N   GOVERNMENT CONTRACT COMPLIANCE HANDBOOK

FAR APPENDIX—CAS REGULATION

COST ACCOUNTING STANDARDS BOARD DISCLOSURE STATEMENT REQUIRED BY PUBLIC LAW 100-679	PART IV - INDIRECT COSTS
	NAME OF REPORTING UNIT

Item No.	Item description
4.1.0	Continued. *Allocation Base Code* 2. _____ ___ (a) Major functions, activities, and elements of cost included: _____ _____ (b) Description/Make up of the allocation base: _____ _____
4.2.0	**General and Administrative (G&A) Expense Pool(s).** Select among the three categories of pools below that describe(s) the manner in which G&A expenses are allocated. For each category of pool(s) selected indicate the base(s) used for allocating such pooled expenses to Federal contracts or similar cost objectives. Also, for each category of pool(s) selected, indicate (a) the major functions, activities, and elements of cost included, and (b) the make up of the allocation base(s). For example, if direct labor dollars are used, are fringe benefits included? If a total cost input base is used, is the imputed cost of capital included? Use a continuation sheet if additional space is required. *Allocation Base Code* **Single Pool Containing G&A Expenses Only** _____ ___ (a) Major functions, activities, and elements of cost included: _____ _____ (b) Description/Make up of the allocation base: _____ _____

FORM CASB DS-1 (REV 2/96)   IV - 2

| COST ACCOUNTING STANDARDS BOARD DISCLOSURE STATEMENT REQUIRED BY PUBLIC LAW 100-679 | PART IV - INDIRECT COSTS |
| | NAME OF REPORTING UNIT |

Item No.	Item description	
4.2.0	Continued.	
	Single Pool Containing Both G&A and Non-G&A Expenses	Allocation Base Code
	_____	____
	(a) Major functions, activities, and elements of cost included:	
	_____	
	_____	
	(b) Description/Make up of the allocation base:	
	_____	
	_____	
	Special Allocations	Allocation Base Code
	1. _____	____
	(a) Major functions, activities, and elements of cost included:	
	_____	
	_____	
	(b) Description/Make up of the allocation base:	
	_____	
	_____	
	2. _____	____
	(a) Major functions, activities, and elements of cost included:	
	_____	
	_____	
	(b) Description/Make up of the allocation base:	
	_____	
	_____	

FORM CASB DS-1 (REV 2/96) IV - 3

COST ACCOUNTING STANDARDS BOARD DISCLOSURE STATEMENT REQUIRED BY PUBLIC LAW 100-679	PART IV - INDIRECT COSTS
	NAME OF REPORTING UNIT

Item No.	Item description
4.3.0	**Service Center and Expense Pool Allocation Bases.**

Service centers are departments or other functional units which perform specific technical and/or administrative services primarily for the benefit of other units within a reporting unit. Expense pools are pools of indirect costs that are allocated primarily to other units within a reporting unit. Examples of service centers are data processing centers, reproduction services and communications services. Examples of expense pools are use and occupancy pools and fringe benefit pools.

Category Code

Generally, costs incurred by such centers or pools are, or can be, charged or allocated (i) partially to specific final cost objectives as direct costs and partially to other indirect cost pools (such as a manufacturing overhead pool) for subsequent reallocation to several final cost objectives, referred to herein as Category "A", and (ii) only to several other indirect cost pools (such as a manufacturing overhead pool, engineering overhead pool and G&A expense pool) for subsequent reallocation to several final cost objectives, referred to herein as Category "B".

Rate Code

Some service centers or expense pools may use predetermined billing or costing rates to charge or allocate the costs (Rate Code A) while others may charge or allocate on an actual basis (Rate Code B).

List all the service centers and expense pools and enter in column (1) Code A or B to indicate the category of pool. Enter in Column (2) one of the Allocation Base Codes A through P, or Y, listed on Page ___, to indicate the base used for charging or allocating service center or expense pool costs. Enter in Column (3) Rate Code A or B to describe the costing method used. Also, for each of the centers and pools indicate (a) the major functions, activities, and elements of cost included, and (b) the make up of the allocation base. Use a continuation sheet if additional space is required.

	Service Center or Expense Pool	Category Code (1)	Allocation Base Code (2)	Rate Code (3)
1.	_____	___	___	___
	(a) Major functions, activities, and elements of cost included: _____			
	(b) Description/Make up of the allocation base: _____			
2.	_____	___	___	___
	(a) Major functions, activities, and elements of cost included: _____			
	(b) Description/Make up of the allocation base: _____			

FORM CASB DS-1 (REV 2/96)   IV - 4

APPENDIX N

App. N

FAR APPENDIX—CAS REGULATION

COST ACCOUNTING STANDARDS BOARD DISCLOSURE STATEMENT REQUIRED BY PUBLIC LAW 100-679	PART IV - INDIRECT COSTS
	NAME OF REPORTING UNIT

Item No.	Item description

4.4.0	**Treatment of Variances from Actual Cost (Underabsorption or Overabsorption).** Where predetermined billing or costing rates are used to charge costs of service centers and expense pools to Federal contracts or other indirect cost pools (Rate Code A in Column (3) of Item 4.3.0), variances from actual costs are: (Mark the appropriate line(s) and if more than one is marked, explain on a continuation sheet.)
	
	    A. _____ Prorated to users on the basis of charges made, at least once annually
	    B. _____ All charged or credited to indirect cost pool(s) at least once annually
	    Y. _____ Other(s) 1/
	    Z. _____ Service center is not applicable to reporting unit

4.5.0	**Application of Overhead and G&A Rates to Specified Transactions or Costs.**
	
	This item is directed to ascertaining your practice in special situations where, in lieu of establishing a separate indirect cost pool, allocation is made from an established overhead or G&A pool at a rate other than the normal full rate for that pool. In the case of such a special allocation, the terms "less than full rate" or "more than full rate" should be used to describe the practice. The terms do **not** apply to situations where, as in some cases of off-site activities, etc., a separate indirect cost pool and base are used and the rate for such activities is lower than the "in-house" rate.
	
	For each of the transactions or costs listed below, enter one of the following codes to indicate your indirect cost allocation practice with respect to that transaction or cost. If Code A, full rate, is entered, identify on a continuation sheet the pool(s) reported under items 4.1.0, 4.2.0, and 4.3.0, which are applicable. If Codes B or C, less than or more than the full rate, is entered, describe on a continuation sheet the major types of expenses that are covered by such a rate.
	
	                            Rate Code
	
	    A. Full rate C. Special allocation at more than full rate
	    B. Special allocation at less than full rate D. No overhead or G&A is applied
	            Z. Transaction or cost is not applicable to reporting unit
	
	Transaction or Cost to Which Rate
	Indirect Costs May be Allocated Code
	
	    (a) Subcontract costs _____
	    (b) Purchased Labor _____
	    (c) Government-furnished materials _____
	    (d) Self-constructed depreciable assets _____
	    (e) Labor on installation of assets _____
	    (f) Off-site work _____
	    (g) Interorganizational transfers out _____
	    (h) Interorganizational transfers in (Also indicate on a continuation sheet the basis used by you as transferee to charge the cost or price of interorganizational transfers to Federal contracts or similar cost objectives. If the charge is based on cost, indicate whether the transferor's G&A expenses are included.) _____
	    (i) Other transactions or costs (Enter Code B or C on this line if there are other transactions or costs to which either less than full rate or more than full rate is applied. List such transactions or costs on a continuation sheet, and for each describe the major types of expenses covered by such a rate. If there are no other such transactions or costs, enter code Z.) _____

1/ Describe on a Continuation Sheet.

FORM CASB DS-1 (REV 2/96)   IV - 5

COST ACCOUNTING STANDARDS BOARD DISCLOSURE STATEMENT REQUIRED BY PUBLIC LAW 100-679	PART IV - INDIRECT COSTS
	NAME OF REPORTING UNIT

Item No.	Item description
4.6.0	<u>Independent Research and Development (IR&D) and Bid and Proposal (B&P) Costs.</u> Definitions of and requirements for the allocation of IR&D and B&P costs are contained in 48 CFR 9904.420. The full rate of all allocable manufacturing, engineering, and/or other overhead is applied to IR&D and B&P costs as if IR&D and B&P projects were under contract, and the "burdened" IR&D and B&P costs are: (Mark appropriate line(s).)
	A. ____ Allocated to Federal contracts or similar cost objectives by means of a composite pool with G&A expenses.
	B. ____ Allocated to Federal contracts or similar cost objectives by means of a separate pool.
	C. ____ Transferred to the corporate or home office level for reallocation to the benefiting segments.
	Y. ____ Other 1/
	Z. ____ Not applicable
4.7.0	<u>Cost of Capital Committed to Facilities.</u> In accordance with instructions for Form CASB-CMF, undistributed facilities capital items are allocated to overhead and G&A expense pools: (Mark one.)
	A. ____ On a basis identical to that used to absorb the actual depreciation or amortization from these facilities; <u>land is assigned in the same manner as the facilities to which it relates</u>.
	B. ____ On a basis not identical to that used to absorb the actual depreciation or amortization from these facilities. (Describe on a continuation sheet the difference for each step of the allocation process.)
	C. ____ By the "alternative allocation process" described in instructions for Form CASB-CMF.
	Z. ____ Not applicable.

1/ Describe on a Continuation Sheet.

APPENDIX N

App. N

FAR APPENDIX—CAS REGULATION

COST ACCOUNTING STANDARDS BOARD DISCLOSURE STATEMENT REQUIRED BY PUBLIC LAW 100-679	PART V - DEPRECIATION AND CAPITALIZATION PRACTICES
	NAME OF REPORTING UNIT

Item No.	Item description
	Part V Instructions
	Where a home office either establishes practices or procedures for the types of costs covered in this Part or incurs and then allocates these costs to its segments, the home office may complete this Part to be included in the submission by the segment as indicated on page (i) 4., General Instructions.
5.1.0	**Depreciating Tangible Assets for Government Contract Costing.** (For each of the asset categories listed on Page ___, enter a code from A through H in Column (1) describing the method of depreciation (Code F for assets that are expensed); a code from A through C in Column (2) describing the basis for determining useful life; a code from A through C in Column (3) describing how depreciation methods or use charges are applied to property units; and a Code A, B or C in Column (4) indicating whether or not residual value is deducted from the total cost of depreciable assets. Enter Code Y in each column of an asset category where another or more than one method applies. Enter Code Z in Column (1) only, if an asset category is not applicable.)

Column (1)—Depreciation Method Code

A. Straight Line
B. Declining balance
C. Sum-of-the years digits
D. Machine hours
E. Unit of production
F. Expensed at acquisition
G. Use charge
H. Method of depreciation used under the applicable Internal Revenue Procedures
Y. Other or more than one method 1/
Z. Asset category is not applicable

Column (2)—Useful Life Code

A. Replacement experience adjusted by expected changes in periods of usefulness
B. Term of Lease
C. Estimated on the basis of Asset Guidelines under Internal Revenue Procedures
Y. Other, or more than one method 1/

Column (3)—Property Units Code

A. Individual units are accounted for separately
B. Applied to groups of assets with similar service lives
C. Applied to groups of assets with varying service lives
Y. Other or more than one method 1/

Column (4)—Residual Value Code

A. Residual value is estimated and deducted
B. Residual value is covered by the depreciation method (e.g., declining balance)
C. Residual value is estimated but not deducted in accordance with the provisions of 48 CFR 9904.409 1/
Y. Other or more than one method 1/

1/ Describe on a Continuation Sheet.

FORM CASB DS-1 (REV 2/96)   V - 1

App. N GOVERNMENT CONTRACT COMPLIANCE HANDBOOK

FAR APPENDIX—CAS REGULATION

COST ACCOUNTING STANDARDS BOARD DISCLOSURE STATEMENT REQUIRED BY PUBLIC LAW 100-679	PART V - DEPRECIATION AND CAPITALIZATION PRACTICES
	NAME OF REPORTING UNIT

Item No.	Item description
5.1.0	Continued.

Asset Category	Depreciation Method Code (1)	Useful Life Code (2)	Property Units Code (3)	Residual Value Code (4)
(a) Land improvements	___	___	___	___
(b) Building	___	___	___	___
(c) Building improvements	___	___	___	___
(d) Leasehold improvements	___	___	___	___
(e) Machinery and equipment	___	___	___	___
(f) Furniture and fixtures	___	___	___	___
(g) Automobiles and trucks	___	___	___	___
(h) Data processing equipment	___	___	___	___
(i) Programming/reprogramming costs	___	___	___	___
(j) Patterns and dies	___	___	___	___
(k) Tools	___	___	___	___
(l) Other depreciable asset categories (Enter Code Y on this line if other asset categories are used and enumerate on a continuation sheet each such asset category and the applicable codes. Otherwise enter Code Z.)	___	___	___	___

5.2.0 <u>Depreciation Practices for Costing, Financial Accounting, and Income Tax.</u> Are depreciation practices the same for costing Federal contracts as for financial accounting and income tax? (Mark either (A) or (B) on each line under Financial Accounting and Income Tax. Not-for-profit organizations need not complete this item.)

<u>Financial Accounting</u>   A. <u>Yes</u>   B. <u>No</u>

(a) Methods   ___   ___
(b) Useful lives   ___   ___
(c) Property units   ___   ___
(d) Residual values   ___   ___

<u>Income Tax</u>   A. <u>Yes</u>   B. <u>No</u>

(e) Methods   ___   ___
(f) Useful lives   ___   ___
(g) Property units   ___   ___
(h) Residual values   ___   ___

FORM CASB DS-1 (REV 2/96)   V - 2

App. N-22

APPENDIX N

App. N

FAR APPENDIX—CAS REGULATION

COST ACCOUNTING STANDARDS BOARD DISCLOSURE STATEMENT REQUIRED BY PUBLIC LAW 100-679	PART V - DEPRECIATION AND CAPITALIZATION PRACTICES
	NAME OF REPORTING UNIT

Item No.	Item description
5.3.0	**Fully Depreciated Assets.** Is a usage charge for fully depreciated assets charged to Federal contracts? (Mark one.) A. ___ Yes 1/ B. ___ No Z. ___ Not applicable
5.4.0	**Treatment of Gains and Losses on Disposition of Depreciable Property.** Gains and losses are: (Mark the appropriate line(s) and if more than one is marked, explain on a continuation sheet.) A. ___ Credited or charged currently to the same overhead or G&A pools to which the depreciation of the assets was charged B. ___ Taken into consideration in the depreciation cost basis of the new items, where trade-in is involved C. ___ Not accounted for separately, but reflected in the depreciation reserve account Y. ___ Other(s) 1/ Z. ___ Not applicable
5.5.0	**Capitalization or Expensing of Specified Costs.** (Mark one line on each item to indicate your practices regarding capitalization or expensing of specified costs incurred in connection with capital assets. If the same specified cost is sometimes expensed and sometimes capitalized, mark both lines and describe on a continuation sheet the circumstances when each method is used.) Cost A. _Expensed_ B. _Capitalized_ (a) Freight-in ____ ____ (b) Sales taxes ____ ____ (c) Excise taxes ____ ____ (d) Architect-engineer fees ____ ____ (e) Overhauls (extraordinary repairs) ____ ____

1/ Describe on a Continuation Sheet.

FORM CASB DS-1 (REV 2/96)   V - 3

COST ACCOUNTING STANDARDS BOARD DISCLOSURE STATEMENT REQUIRED BY PUBLIC LAW 100-679	PART V - DEPRECIATION AND CAPITALIZATION PRACTICES
	NAME OF REPORTING UNIT

Item No.	Item description

5.6.0	**Criteria for Capitalization.** Enter (a) the minimum dollar amount of acquisition cost or expenditures for addition, alteration and improvement of depreciable assets capitalized, and (b) the minimum number of expected life years of capitalized assets.
	
	If more than one dollar amount or number applies, show the information for the majority of your depreciable assets, and enumerate on a continuation sheet the dollar amounts and/or number of years for each category or subcategory of assets involved which differ from those for the majority of assets.
	
	    (a) Minimum dollar amount capitalized _____
	
	    (b) Minimum service life years _____

5.7.0	**Group or Mass Purchase.** Are group or mass purchases (original complement) of low cost equipment, which individually are less than the capitalization amount indicated above, capitalized? (Mark one. If Yes is marked, provide the minimum aggregate dollar amount capitalized.)
	
	    A. ____ Yes
	
	    _____ Minimum aggregate dollar amount capitalized
	
	    B. ____ No

FORM CASB DS-1 (REV 2/96)

APPENDIX N

COST ACCOUNTING STANDARDS BOARD DISCLOSURE STATEMENT REQUIRED BY PUBLIC LAW 100-679	PART VI - OTHER COSTS AND CREDITS
	NAME OF REPORTING UNIT

Item No.	Item description

Part VI Instructions

Where a home office either establishes practices or procedures for the types of costs covered in this Part or incurs and then allocates these costs to its segments, the home office may complete this Part to be included in the submission by the segment as indicated on page (ii) 4., <u>General Instructions</u>.

6.1.0 <u>Method of Charging and Crediting Vacation, Holiday, and Sick Pay.</u> (Mark the appropriate line(s) in each column of Items 6.1.1, 6.1.2, 6.1.3 and 6.1.4 to indicate the method used to charge, or credit any unused or unpaid vacation, holiday, or sick pay. If more than one method is marked, explain on a continuation sheet.)

			Salaried	
		Hourly (1)	Non-exempt 1/ (2)	Exempt 1/ (3)

6.1.1 Charges for Vacation Pay

    A. When Accrued (earned)
    B. When Taken
    Y. Other(s) 2/

6.1.2 Charges for Holiday Pay

    A. When Accrued (earned)
    B. When Taken
    Y. Other(s) 2/

6.1.3 Charges for Sick Pay

    A. When Accrued (earned)
    B. When Taken
    Y. Other(s) 2/

6.1.4 Credits for Unused or Unpaid Vacation, Holiday, or Sick Pay

    A. Credited to Accounts Originally charged at Least Once Annually
    B. Credited to Indirect Cost Pools at Least Once Annually
    C. Carried Over to Future Cost Accounting Periods 2/
    Y. Other(s) 2/
    Z. Not Applicable

1/ For the definition of Non-exempt and Exempt salaries, see the Fair Labor Standards Act, 29 U.S.C. 206.
2/ Describe on a Continuation Sheet.

FORM CASB DS-1 (REV 2/96)   VI - 1

COST ACCOUNTING STANDARDS BOARD DISCLOSURE STATEMENT REQUIRED BY PUBLIC LAW 100-679	PART VI - OTHER COSTS AND CREDITS
	NAME OF REPORTING UNIT

Item No.	Item description

6.2.0 **Supplemental Unemployment (Extended Layoff) Benefit Plans.** Costs of such plans are charged to Federal contracts: (Mark the appropriate line(s) and if more than one is marked, explain on a continuation sheet.)

    A. ____ When actual payments are made directly to employees
    B. ____ When accrued (book accrual or funds set aside but no trust fund involved)
    C. ____ When contributions are made to a nonforfeitable trust fund
    D. ____ Not charged
    Y. ____ Other(s) 1/
    Z. ____ Not applicable

6.3.0 **Severance Pay and Early Retirement.** Costs of normal turnover severance pay and early retirement incentive plans, as defined in FAR 31.2 or other pertinent procurement regulations, which are charged directly or indirectly to Federal contracts, are based on: (Mark the appropriate line(s) and if more than one is marked, explain on a continuation sheet.)

    A. ____ Actual payments made
    B. ____ Accrued amounts on the basis of past experience
    C. ____ Not charged
    Y. ____ Other(s) 1/
    Z. ____ Not applicable

6.4.0 **Incidental Receipts.** (Mark the appropriate line(s) to indicate the method used to account for incidental or miscellaneous receipts, such as revenues from renting real and personal property or selling services, when related costs have been allocated to Federal contracts. If more than one is marked, explain on a continuation sheet.)

    A. ____ The entire amount of the receipt is credited to the same indirect cost pools to which related costs have been charged
    B. ____ Where the amount of the receipt includes an allowance for profit, the cost-related part of the receipt is credited to the same indirect cost pools to which related costs have been charged; the profits are credited to Other (Miscellaneous) Income
    C. ____ The entire amount of the receipt is credited directly to Other (Miscellaneous) Income
    Y. ____ Other(s) 1/
    Z. ____ Not applicable

1/ Describe on a Continuation Sheet.

FORM CASB DS-1 (REV 2/96)

APPENDIX N

COST ACCOUNTING STANDARDS BOARD DISCLOSURE STATEMENT REQUIRED BY PUBLIC LAW 100-679	PART VI - OTHER COSTS AND CREDITS
	NAME OF REPORTING UNIT

Item No.	Item description
6.5.0	**Proceeds from Employee Welfare Activities.** Employee welfare activities include all of those activities set forth in FAR 31.2. (Mark the appropriate line(s) to indicate the practice followed in accounting for the proceeds from such activities. If more than one is marked, explain on a continuation sheet.) A. ___ Proceeds are turned over to an employee-welfare organization or fund; such proceeds are reduced by all applicable costs such as depreciation, heat, light and power B. ___ Same as above, except the proceeds are not reduced by all applicable costs C. ___ Proceeds are credited at least once annually to the appropriate cost pools to which costs have been charged D. ___ Proceeds are credited to Other (Miscellaneous) Income Y. ___ Other(s) 1/ Z. ___ Not applicable

1/ Describe on a Continuation Sheet.

FORM CASB DS-1 (REV 2/96) VI - 3

COST ACCOUNTING STANDARDS BOARD DISCLOSURE STATEMENT REQUIRED BY PUBLIC LAW 100-679	PART VII - DEFERRED COMPENSATION AND INSURANCE COST
	NAME OF REPORTING UNIT

Item No.	Item description
	Part VII Instructions
	This part covers the measurement and assignment of costs for employee pensions, post retirement benefits other than pensions (including post retirement health benefits), certain other types of deferred compensation, and insurance. Some organizations may incur all of these costs at the corporate or home office level, while others may incur them at subordinate organizational levels. Still others may incur a portion of these costs at the corporate level and the balance at subordinate organizational levels.
	Where the segment (reporting unit) does not directly incur such costs, the segment should, on a continuation sheet, identify the organizational entity that incurs and records such costs, and should require that entity to complete the applicable portions of this Part VII. Each such entity is to fully disclose the methods and techniques used to measure, assign, and allocate such costs to the segment(s) performing Federal contracts or similar cost objectives. Necessary explanations required to achieve that objective should be provided by the entity on a continuation sheet.
	Where a home office either establishes practices or procedures for the types of costs covered in this Part VII or incurs and then allocates those costs to its segments, the home office may complete this Part to be included in the submission by the segment as indicated on page (i) 4., General Instructions.
7.1.0	**Pension Plans with Costs Charged to Federal Contracts.** Identify the types and number of pension plans whose costs are charged to Federal contracts or similar cost objectives: (Mark applicable line(s) and enter number of plans.)

Type of Pension Plan	Number of Plans
A. Defined-Contribution Plan (Other than ESOPs (see 7.5.0))	
1. Non-Qualified	___
2. Qualified	___
B. Defined-Benefit Plan	
1. Non-Qualified	
a. Costs are measured and assigned on accrual basis	___
b. Costs are measured and assigned on cash (pay-as-you-go) basis	___
2. Qualified	
a. Trusteed (Subject to ERISA's minimum funding requirements)	___
b. Fully-insured plan (Exempt from ERISA's minimum funding requirements) treated as a defined-contribution plan	___
c. Collectively bargained plan treated as a defined-contribution plan	___
Y. ___ Other 1/	___
Z. ___ Not Applicable (Proceed to Item 7.2.0)	

1/ Describe on a Continuation Sheet.

FORM CASB DS-1 (REV 2/96)   VII - 1

APPENDIX N   App. N

FAR APPENDIX—CAS REGULATION

COST ACCOUNTING STANDARDS BOARD DISCLOSURE STATEMENT REQUIRED BY PUBLIC LAW 100-679	PART VII - DEFERRED COMPENSATION AND INSURANCE COST NAME OF REPORTING UNIT

Item No.	Item description

7.1.1	**General Plan Information.** On a continuation sheet for each plan identified in Item 7.1.0, provide the following information:
	   A. The plan name
	   B. The Employer Identification Number (EIN) of the plan sponsor as reported on IRS Form 5500, if any
	   C. The plan number as reported on IRS Form 5500, if any
	   D. Is there a funding agency established for the plan?
	   E. Indicate where costs are accumulated:
	      (1) Home Office
	      (2) Segment
	   F. If the plan provides supplemental benefits to any other plan, identify the other plan(s).

7.1.2	**Defined-Contribution Plan(s) and Certain Defined-Benefit Plans treated as Defined-Contribution Plans.** Where numerous plans are listed under 7.1.0.A., 7.1.0.B.2.b., or 7.1.0.B.2.c., for those plans which represent the largest dollar amounts of costs charged to Federal contracts, or similar cost objectives, describe on a continuation sheet the basis for the contribution (including treatment of dividends, credits, and forfeitures) required for each fiscal year. (If there are not more than three plans, provide information for all the plans. If there are more than three plans, information should be provided for those plans that in the aggregate account for at least 80 percent of those defined-contribution plan costs allocable to this segment or business unit.) Z. ____ Not applicable. (Proceed to Item 7.1.3)

7.1.3	**Defined-Benefit Plan(s).** Where numerous plans are listed under 7.1.0.B. (excluding certain defined-benefit plans treated as defined-contribution plans reported under 7.1.0.B.2.b. and 7.1.0.B.2.c.), for those plans which represent the largest dollar amounts of costs charged to Federal contracts, provide the information requested below on a continuation sheet. (If there are not more than three plans, provide information for all the plans. If there are more than three plans, information should be provided for those plans that in the aggregate account for at least 80 percent of those defined-benefit plan costs allocable to this segment or business unit.):
	   A. <u>Actuarial Cost Method.</u> Identify the actuarial cost method used, including the cost method(s) used to value ancillary benefits, for each plan. Include the method used to determine the actuarial value of assets. Also, if applicable, include whether normal cost is developed as a level dollar amount or as a level percent of salary. For plans listed under 7.1.0.B.1.b., enter "pay-as-you-go".
	   B. <u>Actuarial Assumptions.</u> Describe the events or conditions for which significant actuarial assumptions are made for each plan. Do not include the current numeric values of the assumptions, but provide a description of the basis used for determining these numeric values. Also, describe the criteria used to evaluate the validity of an actuarial assumption. For plans listed under 7.1.0.B.1.b., enter "not applicable".
	   C. <u>Market Value of Funding Agency Assets.</u> Indicate if all assets of the funding agency are valued on the basis of a readily determinable market price. If yes, indicate the basis for the market value. If no, describe how the market values are determined for those assets that do not have a readily determinable market price. For plans listed under 7.1.0.B.1.b., enter "not applicable".
	   D. <u>Basis for Cost Computation.</u> Indicate whether the cost for the segment is determined as:
	      1. An allocated portion of the total pension plan cost.
	      2. A separately computed pension cost for one or more segments. If so, identify those segments.
	   Z. ____ Not applicable, proceed to Item 7.2.0.

FORM CASB DS-1 (REV 2/96)   VII - 2

App. N-29

App. N GOVERNMENT CONTRACT COMPLIANCE HANDBOOK

FAR APPENDIX—CAS REGULATION

INSERT CASB DS-1 DEFERRED COMPENSATION AND INSURANCE COSTS (PG. VII-3)

COST ACCOUNTING STANDARDS BOARD DISCLOSURE STATEMENT REQUIRED BY PUBLIC LAW 100-679	PART VII - DEFERRED COMPENSATION AND INSURANCE COST
	NAME OF REPORTING UNIT

Item No.	Item description
7.2.0	**Post-retirement Benefits (PRBs) Other than Pensions (including post-retirement health care benefits) Charged to Federal Contracts.** Identify the accounting method used to determine the costs and the number of PRB plans whose costs are charged to Federal contracts or similar cost objectives. Where retiree benefits are provided as an integral part of an employee group insurance plan that covers active employees, report that plan under 7.3.0. (Mark applicable line(s) and enter number of plans.)

      Method Used to Determine Costs   Number of Plans

- A. Accrual Accounting
- B. Cash (pay-as-you-go) Accounting
- C. Purchased Insurance from unrelated Insurer
- D. Purchased Insurance from Captive Insurer
- E. Self-Insurance (including insurance obtained through Captive Insurer)
- F. Terminal Funding
- Y. Other 1/
- Z. ____ Not Applicable (Proceed to Item 7.3.0)

7.2.1 General PRB Plan Information. On a continuation sheet for each plan identified in item 7.2.0, provide the following information grouped by method used to determine costs:

    A. The plan name

    B. The Employer Identification Number (EIN) of the plan sponsor as reported on IRS Form 5500, if any

    C. The plan number as reported on IRS Form 5500, if any

    D. Is there a funding agency or funded reserve established for the plan?

    E. Indicate where costs are accumulated:
      (1) Home Office
      (2) Segment

    F. Are benefits provided pursuant to a written plan or an established practice? If established practice, briefly describe.

    G. If this PRB plan is listed under 7.2.0.C., 7.2.0.D., or 7.2.0.E., indicate whether the plan is operated as an employee group insurance program. If this PRB plan is listed under 7.2.0.Y., indicate whether the plan is operated as a group insurance program. If the plan is operated as an employee group insurance program, report this plan under 7.3.0. and 7.3.1., as appropriate. If no, report the plan under 7.2.2.

1/ Describe on a Continuation Sheet.

FORM CASB DS-1 (REV 2/96)   VII - 3

APPENDIX N

COST ACCOUNTING STANDARDS BOARD DISCLOSURE STATEMENT REQUIRED BY PUBLIC LAW 100-679	PART VII - DEFERRED COMPENSATION AND INSURANCE COST
	NAME OF REPORTING UNIT

Item No.	Item description

7.2.2	PRB Plan(s). Where numerous plans are listed under 7.2.0, for those plans which represent the largest dollar amounts of costs charged to Federal contracts, or other similar cost objectives, provide the information below on a continuation sheet. (If there are not more than three plans, provide information for all the plans. If there are more than three plans, information should be provided for those plans that in the aggregate account for at least 80 percent of those PRB costs allocable to this segment or business unit.)
	
	    A. <u>Actuarial Cost Method.</u> Identify the actuarial cost method used for each plan or each benefit, as appropriate. Include the method used to determine the actuarial value of assets. Identify the amortization methods and periods used, if any. For plans listed under 7.2.0.B., enter "cash accounting". For plans listed under 7.2.0.F., enter "terminal funding" and identify the amortization methods and periods used, if any.
	
	    B. <u>Actuarial Assumptions.</u> Describe the events or conditions for which significant actuarial assumptions are made for each plan. Do not include the current numeric values of the assumptions, but provide a description of the basis used for determining these numeric values. Also, describe the criteria used to evaluate the validity of an actuarial assumption. For plans under 7.2.0.B. or 7.2.0.F., enter "not applicable".
	
	    C. <u>Funding.</u> Provide the following information on the funding practice for the costs of the plan: (For plans under 7.2.0.B. or 7.2.0.F., enter "not applicable".)
	        1. Describe the criteria for or practice of funding the measured and assigned cost; e.g., full funding of the accrual, funding is made pursuant to VEBA or 401(h) rules.
	        2. Briefly describe the funding arrangement.
	        3. Are all assets valued on the basis of a readily determinable market price? If yes, indicate the basis used for the market value. If no, describe how the market value is determined for those assets that are not valued on the basis of a readily determinable market price.
	
	    D. <u>Basis for Cost Computation.</u> Indicate whether the cost for the segment is determined as:
	        1. An allocated portion of the total PRB plan cost
	        2. A separately computed PRB cost for one or more segments. If so, identify those segments.
	
	    E. <u>Forfeitability.</u> Does each participant have a non-forfeitable contractual right to their benefit or account balance? If no, explain.
	
	    Z. ____ Not applicable, proceed to Item 7.3.0.

COST ACCOUNTING STANDARDS BOARD DISCLOSURE STATEMENT REQUIRED BY PUBLIC LAW 100-679	PART VII - DEFERRED COMPENSATION AND INSURANCE COST
	NAME OF REPORTING UNIT

Item No.	Item description
7.3.0	**Employee Group Insurance Charged to Federal Contracts or Similar Cost Objectives.** Does your organization provide group insurance coverage to its employees? (Includes coverage for life, hospital, surgical, medical, disability, accident, and similar plans for both active and retired employees, even if the coverage was previously described in 7.2.0.) A. ____ Yes (Complete Item 7.3.1) B. ____ No (Proceed to Item 7.4.0)
7.3.1	Employee Group Insurance Programs. For each program that covers a category of insured risk (e.g., life, hospital, surgical, medical, disability, accident, and similar programs for both active and retired employees), provide the information below on a continuation sheet, using the codes described below: (If there are not more than three policies or self-insurance plans that comprise the program, provide information for all the policies and self-insurance plans. If there are more that three policies or self-insurance plans, information should be provided for those policies and self-insurance plans that in the aggregate account for at least 80 percent of the costs allocable to this segment or business unit for the program that covers each category of insured risk identified.) Description of Employee Group Insurance Program: _____ | Policy or Self-Insurance Plan	Cost Accumulation (1)	Cost Basis (2)	Includes Retirees (3)	Purchased Insurance Rating Basis (4)	Self-Insurance Projected Average Loss (5)	Self-Insurance Insurance Administrative Expenses (6) | Column (1) -- <u>Cost Accumulation</u> Enter Code A, B, or Y, as appropriate. A. Costs are accumulated at the Home Office. B. Costs are accumulated at Segment Y. Other 1/ Column (2) -- <u>Cost Basis</u> Enter code A, B, C, or Y, as appropriate. A. Purchased Insurance from unrelated third party B. Self-insurance C. Purchased Insurance from a captive insurer Y. Other 1/

1/ Describe on a Continuation Sheet.

FORM CASB DS-1 (REV 2/96)

COST ACCOUNTING STANDARDS BOARD DISCLOSURE STATEMENT REQUIRED BY PUBLIC LAW 100-679	PART VII - DEFERRED COMPENSATION AND INSURANCE COST
	NAME OF REPORTING UNIT

Item No.	Item description
7.3.1	Continued.

Column (3) – Includes Retirees

Enter code A, B, C, or Y, as appropriate.

- A. No, does not include benefits for retirees.
- B. Yes, PRB benefits for retirees that are a part of a policy or coverage for both active employees and retirees are reported here instead of 7.2.0.
- C. Yes, PRB benefits for retirees are a part of a PRB plan previously reported under 7.2.0.
- Y. Other 1/

Column (4) – Purchased Insurance Rating Basis

For each plan listed enter code A, B, C, Y, or Z, as appropriate.

- A. Retrospective Rating (also called experience rating plan or retention plan).
- B. Manually Rated
- C. Community Rated
- Y. Other, or more than one type 1/
- Z. Not applicable

Column (5) – Projected Average Loss

For each self-insured group plan, or the self-insured portion of purchased insurance, enter code A, B, C, Y, or Z, as appropriate.

- A. Self-insurance costs represent the projected average loss for the period estimated on the basis of the cost of comparable purchased insurance.
- B. Self-insurance costs are based on the contractor's experience, relevant industry experience, and anticipated conditions in accordance with accepted actuarial principles.
- C. Actual payments are considered to represent the projected average loss for the period.
- Y. Other, or more than one method 1/
- Z. Not applicable

Column (6) – Insurance Administration Expenses

For each self-insured group plan, or the self-insured portion of purchased insurance, enter code A, B, C, D, Y, or Z, as appropriate, to indicate how administrative costs are treated.

- A. Separately identified and accumulated in indirect cost pool(s).
- B. Separately identified, accumulated, and allocated to cost objectives either at the segment and/or home office level (Describe allocation method on a Continuation Sheet).
- C. Not separately identified, but included in indirect cost pool(s). (Describe pool(s) on a Continuation Sheet)
- D. Incurred by an insurance carrier or third party (Describe accumulation and allocation process on a Continuation Sheet).
- Y. Other 1/
- Z. Not applicable

1/ Describe on a Continuation Sheet.

FORM CASB DS-1 (REV 2/96)   VII - 6

COST ACCOUNTING STANDARDS BOARD DISCLOSURE STATEMENT REQUIRED BY PUBLIC LAW 100-679	PART VII - DEFERRED COMPENSATION AND INSURANCE COST
	NAME OF REPORTING UNIT

Item No.	Item description
7.4.0	<u>Deferred Compensation, as defined in CAS 9904.415.</u> Does your organization award deferred compensation, other than ESOPs, which is charged to Federal contracts or similar cost objectives? (Mark one.) A. ____ Yes (Complete Item 7.4.1.) B. ____ No (Proceed to Item 7.5.0.)

7.4.1	General Plan Information. On a continuation sheet for all deferred compensation plans, as defined by CAS 9904.415, provide the following information:
	
	 A. The plan name
	
	 B. The Employer Identification Number (EIN) of the plan sponsor as reported on IRS Form 5500, if any
	
	 C. The plan number as reported on IRS Form 5500, if any
	
	 D. Indicate where costs are accumulated:
	  (1) Home office
	  (2) Segment
	
	 E. Are benefits provided pursuant to a written plan or an established practice? If established practice, briefly describe.

7.4.2	Deferred Compensation Plans. Where numerous plans are listed under 7.4.1, for those plans which represent the largest dollar amounts of costs charged to Federal contracts, or other similar cost objectives, provide the information below on a continuation sheet. (If there are not more than three plans, provide information for all the plans. If there are more than three plans, information should be provided for those plans that in the aggregate account for at least 80% of these deferred compensation costs allocable to this segment or business unit):
	
	 A. Description of Plan.
	  1. Stock Options
	  2. Stock Appreciation Rights
	  3. Cash Incentive
	  4. Other (explain)
	
	 B. Method of Charging Costs to Federal Contracts or Similar Cost Objectives.
	  1. Costs charged when accrued and the accrual is fully funded
	  2. Costs charged when accrued and the accrual is partially funded or not funded
	  3. Costs charged when paid to employee (pay-as-you-go)
	  4. Other (explain)

FORM CASB DS-1 (REV 2/96)   VII - 7

APPENDIX N

App. N

FAR APPENDIX—CAS REGULATION

COST ACCOUNTING STANDARDS BOARD DISCLOSURE STATEMENT REQUIRED BY PUBLIC LAW 100-679	PART VII - DEFERRED COMPENSATION AND INSURANCE COST
	NAME OF REPORTING UNIT

Item No.	Item description
7.5.0	**Employee Stock Ownership Plans (ESOPs).** Does your organization make contributions to fund ESOPs that are charged directly or indirectly to Federal contracts or similar cost objectives? (Mark one) A. ____ Yes (Proceed to Item 7.5.1) B. ____ No (Proceed to Item 7.6.0)
7.5.1	General Plan Information. On a continuation sheet, for all ESOPs provide the following information: A. The plan name B. The Employer Identification Number (EIN) of the plan sponsor as reported on IRS Form 5500, if any C. The plan number as reported on IRS Form 5500, if any D. Indicate where costs are accumulated: (1) Home office (2) Segment E. Are benefits provided pursuant to a written plan or an established practice? If established practice, briefly describe. F. Indicate whether the ESOP plan is a defined-contribution plan subject to CAS 9904.412. (Answer Yes or No). G. Indicate whether the ESOP is leveraged or nonleveraged. H. **Valuation of Stock or Non-Cash Assets.** Are the plan assets valued on the basis of a readily determinable market price? If yes, indicate the basis for the market value. If no, indicate how the market value is determined for those assets that do not have a readily determinable market price. I. **Forfeitures and Dividends.** Describe the accounting treatment for forfeitures and dividends, on both allocated and unallocated shares, in the measurement of ESOP costs charged directly or indirectly to Federal contracts or similar cost objectives for each plan identified. J. **Administrative Costs.** Describe how the costs of administration of each plan listed are identified, grouped, and accumulated.

FORM CASB DS-1 (REV 2/96)   VII - 8

COST ACCOUNTING STANDARDS BOARD DISCLOSURE STATEMENT REQUIRED BY PUBLIC LAW 100-679	PART VII - DEFERRED COMPENSATION AND INSURANCE COST
	NAME OF REPORTING UNIT

Item No.	Item description
7.6.0	**Worker's Compensation, Liability, and Property Insurance.** Does your organization have insurance coverage regarding worker's compensation, liability and property insurance? A. ____ Yes (Complete Item 7.6.1.) B. ____ No (Proceed to Part VIII)
7.6.1	Worker's Compensation, Liability and Property Insurance Coverage. For each line of insurance that covers a category of insured risk (e.g., worker's compensation, fire and similar perils, automobile liability and property damage, general liability), provide the information below on a continuation sheet using the codes described below: (If there are not more than three policies or self-insurance plans that are applicable to the line of insurance, provide information for all the policies and self-insurance plans. If there are more than three policies or insurance plans, information should be provided for those policies and self-insurance plans that in the aggregate account for at least 80 percent of the costs allocable to this segment or business unit for each line of insurance identified.) Description of Line of Insurance Coverage: _____

Policy or Self-Insurance Plan	Cost Accumulation (1)	Cost Basis (2)	Crediting of Dividends and Earned Refunds (3)	Self-Insurance Projected Average Loss (4)	Insurance Administrative Expenses (5)

Column (1) – Cost Accumulation

Enter code A, B, or Y, as appropriate.

A. Costs are accumulated at the Home Office.
B. Costs are accumulated at Segment
Y. Other 1/

Column (2) – Cost Basis

Enter code A, B, C, or Y, as appropriate.

A. Purchased Insurance from unrelated third party
B. Self-Insurance
C. Purchased Insurance from a captive insurer
Y. Other 1/

1/ Describe on a Continuation Sheet.

FORM CASB DS-1 (REV 2/96) VII - 9

APPENDIX N

COST ACCOUNTING STANDARDS BOARD DISCLOSURE STATEMENT REQUIRED BY PUBLIC LAW 100-679	PART VII - DEFERRED COMPENSATION AND INSURANCE COST
	NAME OF REPORTING UNIT

Item No.	Item description
7.6.1	Continued. **Column (3) – Crediting of Dividends and Earned Refunds** For each line of coverage listed, enter code A, B, C, D, E, Y, or Z, as appropriate. A. Credited directly or indirectly to Federal contracts or similar cost objectives in the year earned B. Credited directly or indirectly to Federal contracts or similar cost objectives in the year received, not necessarily in the year earned C. Accrued each year, as applicable, to currently reflect the net annual cost of the insurance D. Not credited or refunded to the contractor but retained by the carriers as reserves in accordance with 48 CFR 9904.416-50(a)(1)(iv) E. Manually Rated - not applicable Y. Other, or more than one 1/ Z. Not applicable **Column (4) – Projected Average Loss** For each self-insured group plan, or the self-insured portion of purchased insurance, enter code A, B, C, Y, or Z, as appropriate. A. Costs that represent the projected average loss for the period estimated on the basis of the cost of comparable purchased insurance. B. Costs that are based on the contractor's experience, relevant industry experience, and anticipated conditions in accordance with generally accepted actuarial principles and practices. C. The actual amount of losses are considered to represent the projected average loss for the period. Y. Other, or more than one method. 1/ Z. Not applicable **Column (5) – Insurance Administration Expenses** For each self-insured group plan, or the self-insured portion of purchased insurance, enter code A, B, C, D, Y, or Z, as appropriate, to indicate how administrative costs are treated. A. Separately identified and accumulated in indirect cost pool(s). B. Separately identified, accumulated, and allocated to cost objectives either at the segment and/or home office level (Describe allocation method on a Continuation Sheet). C. Not separately identified, but included in indirect cost pool(s). (Describe pool(s) on a Continuation Sheet). D. Incurred by an insurance carrier or third party. (Describe accumulation and allocation process on a Continuation Sheet). Y. Other 1/ Z. Not applicable 1/ Describe on a Continuation Sheet.

FORM CASB DS-1 (REV 2/96) VII - 10

COST ACCOUNTING STANDARDS BOARD DISCLOSURE STATEMENT REQUIRED BY PUBLIC LAW 100-679	PART VIII - HOME OFFICE EXPENSES
	NAME OF REPORTING UNIT

Item No.	Item description
	Part VIII Instructions
	<u>FOR HOME OFFICE, AS APPLICABLE</u> (includes home office type operations of subsidiaries, joint ventures, partnerships, etc.). 1/
	This part should be completed <u>only</u> by the office of a corporation or other business entity where such an office is responsible for administering two or more segments, where it allocates its costs to such segments and where at least one of the segments is required to file Parts I through VII of the Disclosure Statement.
	Data for this part should cover the reporting unit's (corporate or other intermediate level home office's) most recently completed fiscal year. For a corporate (home) office, such data should cover the entire corporation. For a intermediate level home office, they should cover the subordinate organizations administered by that group office.
8.1.0	<u>Organizational Structure.</u>
	On a continuation sheet, provide the following information:
	1. In column (1) list segments and other intermediate level home offices reporting to this home office,
	2. In column (2) insert "yes" or "no" to indicate if reporting units have recorded any CAS-covered Government Sales, and
	3. In column (3) provide the percentage of annual CAS-covered Government Sales as a Percentage of Total Sales (Government and Commercial), if applicable, as follows:
	A. Less than 10% B. 10%-50% C. 51%-80% D. 81%-95% E. Over 95%
	Segment or CAS Covered Government Sales as a Other Intermediary Home Office Government Sales Percentage of Total Sales (1) (2) (3)
8.2.0	<u>Other Applicable Disclosure Statement Parts.</u> (Refer to page (i) 4., <u>General Instructions</u>, and Parts V, VI and VII of the Disclosure Statement. Indicate below the parts that the reporting unit has completed concurrently with Parts I and VIII.)
	A. ____ Part V - Depreciation and Capitalization Practices B. ____ Part VI - Other Costs and Credits C. ____ Part VII - Deferred Compensation and Insurance Costs Z. ____ Not Applicable
	1/ For definition of home office see 48 CFR 9904.403.

FORM CASB DS-1 (REV 2/96)   VIII - 1

APPENDIX N

App. N

FAR APPENDIX—CAS REGULATION

COST ACCOUNTING STANDARDS BOARD DISCLOSURE STATEMENT REQUIRED BY PUBLIC LAW 100-679	PART VIII - HOME OFFICE EXPENSES NAME OF REPORTING UNIT

Item No.	Item description
8.3.0	**Expenses or Pools of Expenses and Methods of Allocation.** For classification purposes, three methods of allocation, defined as follows, are to be used: (i) Directly Allocated—those expenses that are charged to specific corporate segments or other intermediate level home offices based on a specific identification of costs incurred, as described in 9904.403; (ii) Homogeneous Expense Pools—those individual or groups of expenses which are allocated using a base which reflects beneficial or causal relationships, as described in 9904.403; and (iii) Residual Expense—the remaining expenses which are allocated to all segments by means of a base representative of the total activity of such segments. **Allocation Base Codes** A. Sales B. Cost of Sales C. Total Cost Input (Direct Material, Direct Labor, Other Direct Costs, and Applicable Overhead) D. Total Cost Incurred (Total Cost Input Plus G&A Expenses) E. Prime Cost (Direct Material, Direct Labor, and Other Direct Costs) F. Three factor formula (CAS 9904.403-50(c)) G. Processing or Conversion Cost (Direct Labor and Applicable Overhead) H. Direct Labor Dollars I. Direct Labor Hours J. Machine Hours K. Usage L. Unit of Production M. Direct Material Cost N. Total Payroll Dollars (Direct and Indirect Employees) O. Headcount or Number of employees (Direct and Indirect Employees) P. Square Feet Q. Value Added Y. Other, or More than One Basis 1/ (On a continuation sheet, under each of the headings 8.3.1, 8.3.2, and 8.3.3 enter the type of expenses or the name of the expense pool(s). For each of the types of expense or expense pools listed, also indicate as item (a) the major functions, activities, and elements of cost included. In addition, for items listed under 8.3.2 and 8.3.3 enter one of the Allocation Base Codes A through Q, or Y, to indicate the basis of allocation and describe as item (b) the make up of the base(s). For example, if direct labor dollars are used, are overtime premiums, fringe benefits, etc. included? For items listed under 8.3.2 and 8.3.3, if a pool is not allocated to all reporting units listed under 8.1.0, then list those reporting units either receiving or not receiving an allocation. Also identify special allocations of residual expenses and/or fixed mangement charges (see 9904.403-40(c)(3)). 1/ Describe on a Continuation Sheet.

COST ACCOUNTING STANDARDS BOARD DISCLOSURE STATEMENT REQUIRED BY PUBLIC LAW 100-679	PART VIII - HOME OFFICE EXPENSES
	NAME OF REPORTING UNIT

Item No.	Item description
	Type of Expenses or Name of Pool of Expenses
8.3.1	**Directly Allocated**
	1. _____
	(a) Major functions, activities, and elements of cost include:
	_____
	_____
	2. _____
	(a) Major functions, activities, and elements of cost include:
	_____
	_____
8.3.2	**Homogeneous Expense Pools** **Allocation Base Code**
	1. _____ _____
	(a) Major functions, activities, and elements of cost include:
	_____
	_____
	(b) Description/Make up of the allocation base:
	_____
	_____
	2. _____ _____
	(a) Major functions, activities, and elements of cost include:
	_____
	_____
	(b) Description/Make up of the allocation base:
	_____
	_____

FORM CASB DS-1 (REV 2/96)   VIII - 3

	COST ACCOUNTING STANDARDS BOARD DISCLOSURE STATEMENT REQUIRED BY PUBLIC LAW 100-679	PART VIII - HOME OFFICE EXPENSES
		NAME OF REPORTING UNIT
Item No.	Item description	
8.3.3	<u>Residual Expenses</u> <u>Allocation Base Code</u> (a) Major functions, activities, and elements of cost include: (b) Description/Make up of the allocation base:	
8.4.0	<u>Transfer of Expenses.</u> If there are normally transfers of expenses from reporting units to this home office, identify on a continuation sheet the classification of the expense and the name of the reporting unit incurring the expense.	

FORM CASB DS-1 (REV 2/96)   VIII - 4

APPENDIX O

Time Card Analysis Attribute Test

Time Card Analysis (Exceptions)
Attribute Test

Location Code # _____
Title _____
W/E _____
Date of Analysis _____
Analyst Signature _____

NAME OF EMPLOYEE & LIFE #	1	2	3	4	5	6	COMMENTS
Totals							

1. Time card not prepared in blue or black ink.
2. Time card had improper alteration.
3. Time card had erasure.
4. Time card had white out.
5. Time card had a "write-over".
6. Other (i.e. appears Employee/Supervisors signature by same person) explain in comments section.

Results of Analysis

Number of Employees
Checked _____ Having One or More Exceptions _____ % of Exceptions _____

APPENDIX P

Sample Time Card

SAMPLE TIME CARD

CHARGE				DAILY HOURS TO NEAREST TENTH							ACCOUNTING USE ONLY	
	PROJECT	JOB	CODE	MON.	TUE.	WED.	THURS.	FRI.	SAT.	SUN.	STRAIGHT TIME	OVERTIME
8	H	21	39	2.0	2.0	2.0	2.0	1.0	1.0		10	4.5
7	G	40										
6	F	42		2.2	2.0	2.0	2.2	1.2				
5	E	89	39	2.0	2.0	2.0	2.0	1.0	1.0		10	.5
4	D	28	39	1.0	1.0	1.0	1.0	1.0	1.0		6	.5
3	C	21	39	1.0	1.0	1.0	1.0	1.0	1.0		6	.5
2	B	10	39	2.0	2.0	2.0	2.0	2.0	1.0		11	.5
1	A			2.0	2.0	2.0	2.0	2.0			10	
	TOTAL HOURS INCLUDING OVERTIME			10.0	10.0	10.0	10.0	8.0	5.0		53	6.5
											40	19.5

APPENDIX Q

Sample Time Cards Which Exhibit Violations

SAMPLE TIME
CARDS WHICH
EXHIBIT VIOLATIONS

APPENDIX R

Standard Form 1443: "Contractor's Request for Progress Payment"

App. R — GOVERNMENT CONTRACT COMPLIANCE HANDBOOK

INSTRUCTIONS

GENERAL - All dollar amounts must be shown in whole dollars, rounded using a consistent methodology (e.g., always round up, always round down, always round to the nearest dollar). All line item numbers not included in the instructions below are self-explanatory.

SECTION I - IDENTIFICATION INFORMATION. Complete items 1 through 8b in accordance with the following instructions.

Item 1. TO - Enter the name and address of the cognizant Contract Administration Office (the office administering the contract).
PAYING OFFICE - Enter the designation of the paying office, as indicated on the contract.

Item 2. FROM - CONTRACTOR'S NAME AND ADDRESS/ZIP CODE - Enter the name and mailing address of the contractor. If applicable, the division of the company performing the contract should be entered immediately following the contractor's name.

Item 3. Enter an "X" in the appropriate block to indicate whether or not the contractor is a small business concern.

Item 4. Enter the contract number, including the task or delivery order number if applicable. Progress payment requests under individual orders shall be submitted as if the order constituted a separate contract, unless otherwise specified in this contract (FAR 52.232-16(m)).

Item 5. Enter the total contract price in accordance with the following (See FAR 32.501-3):
(1) Under firm-fixed-price contracts, the contract price is the current amount fixed by the contract plus the not-to-exceed amount for any unpriced modifications.
(2) If the contract is redeterminable or subject to economic price adjustment, the contract price is the initial price until modified.
(3) Under a fixed-price incentive contract, the contract price is the target price plus the not-to-exceed amount for any unpriced modifications. However, if the contractor's properly incurred costs exceed the target price, the contracting officer may provisionally increase the price up to the ceiling or maximum price.
(4) Under a letter contract, the contract price is the maximum amount obligated by the contract as modified.
(5) Under an unpriced order issued against a basic ordering agreement, the contract price is the maximum amount obligated by the order, as modified.
(6) Any portion of the contract specifically providing for reimbursement of costs only shall be excluded from the contract price.

Item 6A. PROGRESS PAYMENT RATES - Enter the 2-digit progress payment percentage rate shown in paragraph (a) (1) of the progress payment clause.

Item 6B. LIQUIDATED RATE - Enter the current progress payment liquidation rate prescribed in the contract (FAR 52.232-16(b)) using three digits - Example: show 80% as 800 - show 72.3% as 723. Decimals between tenths must be rounded up to the next highest tenth (not necessarily the nearest tenth), since rounding down would produce a rate below the minimum rate calculated (FAR 32.503-10(b) (4)).

Item 7. DATE OF INITIAL AWARD - Enter the four digit calendar year. Use two digits to indicate the month. Example: Show January 2005 as 2005/01.

Item 8A. PROGRESS PAYMENT REQUEST NUMBER - Enter the number assigned to this request. All requests under a single contract must be numbered consecutively, beginning with 1. Each subsequent request under the same contract must continue in sequence, using the same series of numbers without omission.

Item 8B. Enter the date of the request.

SECTION II - STATEMENT OF COSTS UNDER THIS CONTRACT.
Date. In the space provided in the heading enter the date through which costs have been accumulated from inception for inclusion in this request. This date is applicable to item entries in Sections II and III.

Cost Basis. In accordance with FAR 52.232-16 (a) (1), the basis for progress payments is the contractor's total costs incurred under this contract, whether or not actually paid, plus financing payments to subcontractors (computed in accordance with FAR 52.232-16(j)), less the sum of all previous progress payments made by the Government under this contract.

Item 11. Costs eligible for progress payments under the progress payments clause. Compute the eligible costs in accordance with the requirements at FAR 52.232-16(a)(1) through (4). First articles: Before first article approval, the acquisition of materials or components for, or the commencement of production of, the balance of the contract quantity is at the sole risk of the contractor. Before the first article approval, the costs thereof shall not be allowable for purposes of progress payments. (See FAR 52.209-3(g) and FAR 52.209-4(h)).

Item 12a. Enter the total contract costs incurred to date; if the actual amount is not known, enter the best possible estimate. If an estimate is used, enter (E) after the amount.

Item 12b. Enter the estimated cost to complete the contract. The contractor shall furnish estimates to complete that have been developed or updated within six months of the date of the progress payment request. The estimates to complete shall represent the contractor's best estimate of total costs to complete all remaining contract work required under the contract. The estimates shall include sufficient detail to permit Government verification.

Items 14a through 14e. Include only financing payments (progress payments, performance-based payments, and commercial item financing) on subcontracts which are in accordance with the requirements of FAR 52.232-16(j). Do not include interim payments under a cost reimbursement contract.

Item 14a. Enter only financing payments actually paid.

Item 14b. Enter total financing payments recouped from subcontractors.

Item 14d. Include the amount of unpaid subcontract progress payment billings which have been approved by the contractor for the current payment in the ordinary course of business.

SECTION III - ADVANCE PAYMENTS/ACCEPTED ITEMS. This Section must be completed only if the contractor has received advance payments against this contract, or if the items have been delivered, invoiced and accepted as of the date indicated in the heading of Section II above.
EXCEPTION: Item 27 must be completed for all progress payment requests where the line 12c amount exceeds the amount on Line 5.

Item 20a. Of the costs reported in Item 11, compute and enter only costs which are properly allocable to items delivered, invoiced and accepted to the applicable date. In order of preference, these costs are to be computed on the basis of one of the following: (a) The actual unit cost of items delivered, giving proper consideration to the deferment of the starting load costs or (b) projected unit costs (based on experienced costs plus the estimated cost to complete the contract), where the contractor maintains cost data which will clearly establish the reliability of such estimates.

Item 23. Enter total progress payments liquidated (monies recouped from the contractor on prior billings) and those to be liquidated from billings submitted but not yet paid (monies to be recouped from the contractor on submitted but unpaid billings).

CERTIFICATION
Paragraph (f). If no financial information has been provided previously in connection with this contract, insert "N/A" in the submission date block and the financial information date block. Otherwise, insert respectively, the "as of" date of the financial information submitted last and the date of the last submission.

STANDARD FORM 1443 (REV. 7/2009) BACK

APPENDIX S

GAO, "DOD Fraud Invesgitations: Characteristics, Sanctions and Prevention" (Jan. 1988)

GAO	United States General Accounting Office Briefing Report to the Honorable William V. Roth, Jr., U.S. Senate

January 1988	**DOD FRAUD INVESTIGATIONS** Characteristics, Sanctions, and Prevention

GAO/AFMD-88-5BR

App. S-1

App. S   GOVERNMENT CONTRACT COMPLIANCE HANDBOOK

GAO United States
General Accounting Office
Washington, D.C. 20548

Accounting and Financial
Management Division

B-224759

January 20, 1988

The Honorable William V. Roth, Jr.
United States Senate

Dear Senator Roth:

At your request, we reviewed fraud investigations that the Department of Defense (DOD) referred to the Department of Justice or state and local authorities for prosecution. As agreed with your office, we conducted detailed reviews at the Departments of Health and Human Services (specifically the Medicare and Medicaid programs), Agriculture, Labor, and Defense and the General Services Administration. On July 7, 1987, we briefed your staff on Medicare and Medicaid fraud and subsequently issued a report[1] on the results of our review. On January 20, 1988, we briefed your staff on the results of our work at DOD. This report is a written version of that briefing. We will brief you or your staff on our work at the other agencies later.

The purpose of this review was to identify (1) the characteristics of fraud, including theft, being referred for prosecution by the DOD Inspector General (IG) and the military services, in terms of the most prevalent types and the functions or activities most affected, (2) actions taken against those who have been caught defrauding the government, and (3) whether DOD's investigative agencies determine the underlying causes of detected fraud and provide this information to program officials so that action can be taken to reduce vulnerabilities.

In conducting this review, we used information in the DOD Office of Inspector General (OIG) Defense Investigative Management Information System data base on fiscal year 1984 and 1985 investigations involving losses of $1,000 or more

---

[1] Health Care Fraud: Characteristics, Sanctions, and Prevention (GAO/AFMD-87-29BR, July 15, 1987).

APPENDIX S

B-224759

conducted by DOD's four investigative agencies: the Defense Criminal Investigative Service (located within the DOD Inspector General's office), the Army Criminal Investigation Command, the Naval Security and Investigative Service, and the Air Force Office of Special Investigations. At the time we began our review, which was conducted primarily from May 1986 through December 1986, cases from this time period represented the most current readily available data on closed DOD fraud referrals for prosecution. In order to make our analysis as current as possible, we updated selected information during the period June through August 1987. We also identified trends in investigative activity over a 4-year period, fiscal years 1983-86, in terms of the (1) functions (such as procurement and pay and allowances) in which investigations occurred and (2) punitive actions that were taken. Our focus was on aggregate data, and, accordingly, we did not evaluate the quality of any particular investigation.

We also talked with officials in each of the agencies about the characteristics of fraud they investigated, trends in investigations, and initiatives to identify and report underlying causes of fraud. In addition, we identified the number of referrals of suspected procurement fraud made by the Defense Contract Audit Agency (DCAA). Further details about our scope and methodology and the results of our work are in appendix I.

FRAUD CHARACTERISTICS IN DOD

DOD investigated 794 cases of fraud which had losses of $1,000 or more and had been referred for prosecution and were closed during fiscal years 1984 and 1985, according to the most readily available information from the DOD OIG data base. We did not look at smaller cases. DOD data shows that losses totaled $66.2 million from the 794 cases during the 2-year period that we reviewed. DOD data also shows that fines and recoveries in these cases totaled about $39 million.

Our review found that theft was the most prevalent type of DOD case, accounting for about one-third of DOD's referrals. However, the second most prevalent type—procurement fraud, which accounted for 29 percent—was responsible for about 81 percent of the dollar losses.

Our review also found that 55 percent of fraud cases, with losses totaling $44 million, resulted in legal and/or administrative action against those who were caught

B-224759

defraulding the government. These actions included 376 criminal convictions. Other actions taken included restitutions, job terminations, and contractor suspensions and debarments. All the actions taken on this group of cases resulted in fines and recoveries totaling about $33 million.

In 45 percent of the cases referred for prosecution, with losses totaling $22 million, DOD records show the cases were declined for prosecution and that no action was taken against the subjects investigated. The most common reason for declination of prosecution was that the cases were "below a U.S. Attorney's dollar threshold for prosecution or the case involved a minimal federal interest." Nevertheless, DOD recouped about $6 million in these cases through recoveries made during investigations. In some future cases, DOD will be able to apply new authority provided by the Program Fraud Civil Remedies Act of 1986 which provides for administrative penalties and recoveries in certain cases even though they may be declined for prosecution. Under the act, administrative proceedings can be brought, with approval of the Attorney General, against persons who make, present, or submit false claims and statements involving up to $150,000. If the subject is found liable, a civil penalty of not more than $5,000 can be assessed for each false claim or statement, plus double any amount of such claim the government paid.

RECENT INVESTIGATION TRENDS

We noted that DOD investigators more than doubled the number of procurement fraud investigations in fiscal year 1986 (1,919 investigations) compared to fiscal year 1983 (870 investigations). In addition, investigations of suspected fraud in nonappropriated fund and pay and allowance activities have decreased substantially. In this regard, nonappropriated fund investigations decreased from 1,300 in fiscal year 1983 to 688 in fiscal year 1986, while pay and allowance investigations decreased from 3,186 to 1,661 over the same period. DOD OIG officials attribute these changes to investigator efforts to focus on more significant cases as recommended in an earlier GAO report.[2] Another reason for the increase is additional referrals for

---

[2] DOD Can Combat Fraud Better By Strengthening Its Investigative Agencies (GAO/AFMD-83-33, March 21, 1983).

3

APPENDIX S

B-224759

investigation from DCAA auditors—up to 325 referrals in fiscal year 1986 from 60 in fiscal year 1983. DOD OIG officials told us that many of these cases were very significant and that the number of cases had increased dramatically just prior to our review. Therefore, we reviewed the most significant cases under investigation in the 1-year period ending March 31, 1986, in order to see how DOD's emphasis has shifted to procurement fraud. Many of these cases had been referred for investigation by DCAA. In total, 173 cases were being investigated that the DOD OIG characterized as significant because estimated losses were $50,000 or more and/or for other reasons. Most of the cases (86 percent) involved procurement fraud. These procurement cases involved losses totaling almost $400 million, or 97 percent of the estimated losses associated with the 173 cases. One case alone involved estimated losses over $100 million because a contractor allegedly mischarged for spare parts over a 6-year period. As of August 12, 1987, this case was still pending. We were told it will be presented to a grand jury.

The increase in referrals of alleged procurement fraud for investigations has prompted the DOD OIG to adopt a best case selection strategy. Because many of DOD's largest contractors faced multiple cost mischarging/defective pricing cases, the DOD OIG directed that only the best one or two cases (those most likely to result in criminal prosecution) against any one DOD contractor be investigated. As part of the DOD OIG strategy, the cases not pursued criminally will be handled with civil and administrative remedies. We also noted that DOD has increasingly used debarments and suspensions to keep troublesome contractors from conducting business with the government. From fiscal year 1983 to fiscal year 1987, suspensions and debarments more than tripled from 280 to 898.

Currently, the highest priority is given to the investigation and prosecution of product substitution procurement fraud because malfunctioning defective parts in weapon systems can jeopardize DOD missions and personnel.

DOD OIG ACTIONS TO IDENTIFY AND REPORT
UNDERLYING CAUSES OF FRAUD

We found that the DOD OIG has initiated both short-term and long-term efforts to use information developed during criminal investigations of internal control or management weaknesses that allowed or contributed to fraud. The

4

B-224759

short-term efforts include two special studies for which teams were formed to review closed criminal investigations involving product substitution and the illegal diversion and exportation of DOD property. These studies identified control weaknesses that allowed such activities to occur. The weaknesses were reported to DOD management so that corrective action could be initiated. The long-term effort includes a DOD IG requirement that the DOD investigative agencies identify underlying causes of fraud and provide this information to appropriate managers so that corrective action can be taken to protect DOD resources. At the time of our review, the investigative agencies were in the early stages of planning their implementation of this initiative.

In our opinion, it is too soon to determine the effectiveness of the long-term initiative. We believe that, if properly carried out, it could be an important step in the prevention of fraud.

<u>AGENCY COMMENTS</u>

We obtained official written comments from the DOD Inspector General in December 1987. She essentially agreed with the report and provided more current data which we included where appropriate. A copy of her comments is included in appendix V.

We would be pleased to discuss this information with you at your convenience. Unless you publicly announce the contents of this report earlier, we will not distribute it until 30 days from its date. At that time, we will send copies to the Director of the Office of Management and Budget, the Secretaries of Defense, the Army, Navy, and Air Force, and interested congressional committees. We will make copies available to others on request. If you or members of your staff have any questions about the results of our work, please call me on 275-9359.

Sincerely yours,

John J. Adair
Associate Director

5

Appendix S

Contents

APPENDIX		Page
I	INTRODUCTION AND BACKGROUND	8
	Objectives	12
	Scope and Methodology	14
II	CHARACTERISTICS OF DOD FRAUD CASES REFERRED FOR PROSECUTION	18
	Defective Pricing	22
	Cost/Labor Mischarging	22
	Product Substitution	23
	Theft	23
	Recent Investigation Trends	25
III	ACTIONS TAKEN AGAINST SUBJECTS REFERRED FOR PROSECUTION	32
	Legal Actions	33
	Administrative Actions	35
	Punitive Actions Are Increasing	37
	Reasons for Declinations	38
IV	DOD OIG EFFORTS TO IDENTIFY AND REPORT WEAKNESSES THAT CONTRIBUTE TO FRAUD	42
	Special Short-Term Studies	43
	Long-Term Efforts	44
V	COMMENTS FROM THE DEPARTMENT OF DEFENSE	46

FIGURES

II.1	Closed DOD Fraud Cases Referred for Prosecution, by Activity, Fiscal Years 1984 and 1985	19
II.2	Dollar Losses by Type of Closed DOD Fraud Cases Referred for Prosecution, Fiscal Years 1984 and 1985	20
II.3	Dollar Losses by Type of Closed DOD Procurement Fraud Cases Referred for Prosecution, Fiscal Years 1984 and 1985	21

II.4	Dollar Losses by Type of Theft Cases Referred for Prosecution, Fiscal Years 1984 and 1985	24
III.1	Administrative Actions Taken Against DOD Employees	36
III.2	Administrative Actions Taken Against Contractors/Vendors	37
III.3	Reasons Justice Declined 433 Subjects of Fraud Cases	39

TABLES

I.1	Staffing Levels and Operating Cost of DOD Criminal Investigative Agencies as of September 30, 1987	9
I.2	Number of DOD Agents Trained in Fraud Investigations, Fiscal Year 1982 and 1987	10
II.1	Types of Open Procurement Cases Reported to the Secretary of Defense (April 1, 1985, Through March 31, 1986)	28
III.1	Prison Sentences	34
III.2	Suspended Sentences	34
III.3	Probation Periods	35
III.4	Selected Punitive Actions Taken Against Those Who Defrauded DOD Programs, Fiscal Years 1983-87	38

ABBREVIATIONS

AFOSI	Air Force Office of Special Investigations
CIDC	Army Criminal Investigation Command
DCAA	Defense Contract Audit Agency
DCIS	Defense Criminal Investigative Service
DOD	Department of Defense
IG	inspector general
NIS	Naval Security and Investigative Command
OIG	Office of Inspector General

APPENDIX I

INTRODUCTION AND BACKGROUND

Senator William V. Roth, Jr., requested that we review fraud investigations that statutory inspectors general (IG) referred to the Department of Justice for prosecution. Specifically, he asked us to analyze fraud investigations referred by the IGs at the Departments of Agriculture, Defense, and Labor and the General Services Administration as well as the Department of Health and Human Services for those cases involving the Medicare and Medicaid programs. This briefing report presents the results of our examination of Department of Defense (DOD) fraud investigations that were referred to Justice or state and local authorities for prosecution.

In order to upgrade DOD-level audit, investigation, and inspection activities, the Congress established a statutory IG in the Department of Defense Authorization Act of 1983. The DOD OIG was patterned after the civilian agency IG offices created by the Inspector General Act of 1978 (Public Law 95-452). The Authorization Act also combined several existing DOD-level audit and investigative organizations under the DOD IG. The DOD IG performs audits, conducts criminal investigations of fraud throughout DOD, recommends action to the appropriate management levels to correct program deficiencies, and reports the status of actions being taken to correct these deficiencies. The DOD IG is also responsible for providing policy guidance and oversight of the Army, Navy, and Air Force audit and investigative agencies. Resource levels as of September 30, 1987, for the investigative agencies are shown in table I.1.

APPENDIX I   APPENDIX I

Table I.1: **Staffing Levels and Operating Costs of DOD Criminal Investigative Agencies as of September 30, 1987**

	Investigative professionals[a] on board	Total operating costs
DOD OIG Defense Criminal Investigative Service (DCIS)	270	$ 18,506,000
Army Criminal Investigation Command (CIDC)	1,085	72,218,000
Naval Security And Investigative Command (NIS)	1,173	94,184,000
Air Force Office of Special Investigations (AFOSI)	1,558	86,678,000
Total	4,086	$271,586,000

[a] With the exception of the DOD IG investigative function, which is totally civilian, professionals include both military and civilian personnel.

While DCIS investigators are dedicated to criminal fraud investigations involving major theft, fraud, and corruption in the procurement process, the military investigative agencies have other responsibilities in addition to criminal fraud investigations. The three military investigative agencies also investigate other types of crime including homicide, assault, and drug violations. Also, NIS and AFOSI conduct counterintelligence investigations.

According to DOD IG officials, the number of agents fully trained to conduct fraud investigations has increased dramatically since fiscal year 1982. Table I.2 shows that the number of trained fraud agents has increased by about 150 percent.

APPENDIX I

Table I.2: **Number of DOD Agents Trained In Fraud Investigations, Fiscal Years 1982 and 1987**

	Number of fraud agents	
	Fiscal year 1982	Fiscal year 1987
DCIS	110	279
Army CIDC	60	226
NIS	38	135
AFOSI	167	291
Total	375	931

APPENDIX I   APPENDIX I

OBJECTIVES

IDENTIFY CHARACTERISTICS OF FRAUD

IDENTIFY PUNITIVE ACTIONS

DETERMINE WHETHER INVESTIGATORS IDENTIFY AND REPORT UNDERLYING CAUSES OF FRAUD TO PROGRAM MANAGERS SO THAT ACTIONS CAN BE TAKEN TO PREVENT FUTURE FRAUD

APPENDIX I

OBJECTIVES

The objectives of this review were to identify (1) the characteristics of fraud being referred for prosecution by the DOD OIG and the military services in terms of the most prevalent types and the functions or activities most affected, (2) the types of punitive actions taken against those referred for prosecution, and (3) whether the DOD investigative agencies identified and reported the underlying causes of fraud to program officials so that actions could be taken to reduce vulnerabilities. In addition, we identified trends in investigative activities in terms of the types of DOD functions in which investigations occurred and the actions taken against those who commit fraud. We focused on aggregate data and, accordingly, did not evaluate the quality of any particular investigation or the rationale for Department of Justice prosecutorial decisions.

APPENDIX I

SCOPE AND METHODOLOGY

ANALYZED DATA ON 794 FISCAL YEAR 1984 AND 1985 CLOSED FRAUD CASES WITH DOLLAR LOSSES OF $1,000 OR MORE

REVIEWED CASE FILES FOR 208 OF 794 INVESTIGATIONS

REVIEWED DOD OIG FISCAL YEAR 1983-86 SEMIANNUAL REPORTS ON ALL CASES INVESTIGATED TO IDENTIFY TRENDS IN (1) FUNCTIONS AFFECTED BY FRAUD AND (2) PUNITIVE ACTIONS TAKEN

REVIEWED SUMMARIES OF 173 SIGNIFICANT OPEN FRAUD CASES

IDENTIFIED MECHANISMS USED BY INVESTIGATORS TO IDENTIFY UNDERLYING CAUSES OF REPORTED FRAUD

APPENDIX I   APPENDIX I

SCOPE AND METHODOLOGY

   In order to identify the characteristics of fraud and theft
cases referred for prosecution and determine the type of action
taken against those investigated, we obtained information on 794
cases that had been referred for prosecution and were closed during
fiscal years 1984 and 1985, each of which had losses of $1,000 or
more. These cases were referred for prosecution by DOD's four
investigative agencies.[3] We obtained this information from the
Defense Investigative Management Information System data base which
is maintained by the DOD OIG. The 794 cases included 235 cases
investigated by the Army's CIDC, 154 investigated by the Air
Force's Office of Special Investigations, 211 cases investigated by
the Navy's NIS, and 194 cases investigated by the DOD OIG's DCIS.
We used this information because at the time we began our review it
was the most current readily available information on closed DOD
fraud referrals for prosecution. Using DOD OIG definitions, we
analyzed this information to determine the types of fraud and
activities most affected, as well as the outcome of cases in terms
of prosecution results and/or any other action taken.

   In order for us to more clearly understand the types of fraud
referred for prosecution, as well as how fraud affects DOD
functions, we reviewed the case files for 208 of the 794 cases
referred for prosecution. We judgmentally selected cases for
review with the greatest weight on large dollar losses and the most
prevalent types of fraud. This review of 208 case files identified
missing information and numerous inaccuracies in the DOD OIG data
base. We pointed out these problems to the OIG staff, who
corrected the problems we identified as well as others they had
identified as part of their ongoing efforts to improve the accuracy
of the management information system. We then used printouts of
the corrected data to analyze totals as to type of fraud,
disposition, and dollar losses.

   Furthermore, because of a significant increase in the volume
of procurement fraud investigations during our review, we examined
summaries of 173 open fraud cases which had been reported to the
Secretary of Defense during the last half of fiscal year 1985 and
the first half of fiscal year 1986. Many of these involved
suspected procurement fraud referred for investigation by the

---

[3]Out of the 794 cases, 38 cases were referred to state and/or local
governments.

APPENDIX I

Defense Contract Audit Agency (DCAA). These cases included indications of fraud which were still under active investigation. They were reported to the Secretary of Defense because of their significance in that they involved (1) potential losses of at least $50,000,[4] (2) high-ranking DOD officials, and/or (3) extensive media coverage. Of the 173 significant cases, 148 involved alleged procurement fraud.

To identify patterns of DOD fraud, investigative trends, and punitive actions taken, we analyzed but did not verify information submitted to the DOD OIG for the semiannual report on all fiscal year 1983-86 fraud cases investigated and closed by the four investigative agencies. This information included aggregate totals on types of fraud investigated, functional areas affected, and sanctions taken against those investigated, regardless of value associated with the case or whether it was referred for prosecution.

In order to determine whether the investigative agencies identified the underlying causes of fraud and provided this information to program managers so that corrective action could be taken to protect DOD resources, we (1) reviewed and discussed guidance and requirements for investigators with responsible officials and (2) identified mechanisms used to notify program managers of vulnerabilities to fraud and abuse discovered during criminal investigations.

We also talked with officials in each of the agencies about the characteristics of fraud they investigated, trends in investigations, and initiatives to determine and correct underlying causes of fraud. In addition, we identified statistics on referrals of suspected procurement fraud made by DCAA.

Our work was conducted from May through December 1986 at the DOD IG headquarters as well as the headquarters of each service's investigative agency. We also updated selected information during June through August 1987 in order to make our analysis as current as possible.

---

[4]Since our review, the $50,000 threshold has been increased to $100,000.

APPENDIX S — App. S

APPENDIX II — APPENDIX II

CHARACTERISTICS OF DOD FRAUD
REFERRED FOR PROSECUTION

THEFT IS MOST PREVALENT TYPE OF FRAUD (ABOUT 33 PERCENT OF CASES)

PROCUREMENT FRAUD IS MOST COSTLY (81 PERCENT OF TOTAL LOSSES)

    -- **DEFECTIVE PRICING VIOLATIONS ACCOUNTED FOR THE HIGHEST PROCUREMENT LOSSES**

DETECTION OF SUSPECTED PROCUREMENT FRAUD IS INCREASING

EMPHASIS INCREASED ON INVESTIGATING MORE SIGNIFICANT FRAUD

APPENDIX II   APPENDIX II

CHARACTERISTICS OF DOD FRAUD CASES REFERRED FOR PROSECUTION

As shown in figure II.1, theft cases (property theft/larceny/embezzlement) accounted for the largest percentage (32.5) of cases with losses of $1,000 or more that were referred for prosecution. Procurement and procurement related fraud cases made up 29 percent of the cases, pay and allowance fraud cases which include travel fraud accounted for 13.5 percent, and nonappropriated fund activities fraud cases such as alleged fraud against military exchanges or morale, welfare, and recreation programs accounted for 9 percent of the fraud cases. Other areas, including fraud in the Civilian Health and Medical Program of the Uniformed Services and commissary/subsistence activity fraud, made up 16 percent of the cases.

Figure II.1: Closed DOD Fraud Cases Referred for Prosecution, by Activity, Fiscal Years 1984 and 1985[a]

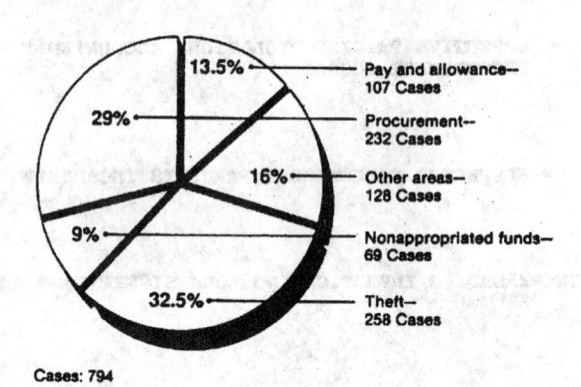

- 13.5% — Pay and allowance — 107 Cases
- 29% — Procurement — 232 Cases
- 16% — Other areas — 128 Cases
- 9% — Nonappropriated funds — 69 Cases
- 32.5% — Theft — 258 Cases

Cases: 794

[a]Data on closed DOD fraud cases referred for prosecution for fiscal years 1986 and 1987, provided by the DOD OIG in its comments on this report, showed that of 789 closed cases during that period, 43.5 percent were procurement; 22.9 percent, theft; 14.7 percent, pay and allowance; 4.2 percent, nonappropriated funds; and 14.7 percent, other areas. Thus, the theft category has decreased the most as a percentage, while procurement has increased the most.

APPENDIX II

Figure II.2 shows, for the cases we reviewed, the amount of reported losses by type of fraud for fiscal years 1984 and 1985.

Figure II.2: Dollar Losses by Type of Closed DOD Fraud Cases Referred for Prosecution, Fiscal Years 1984 and 1985[a]

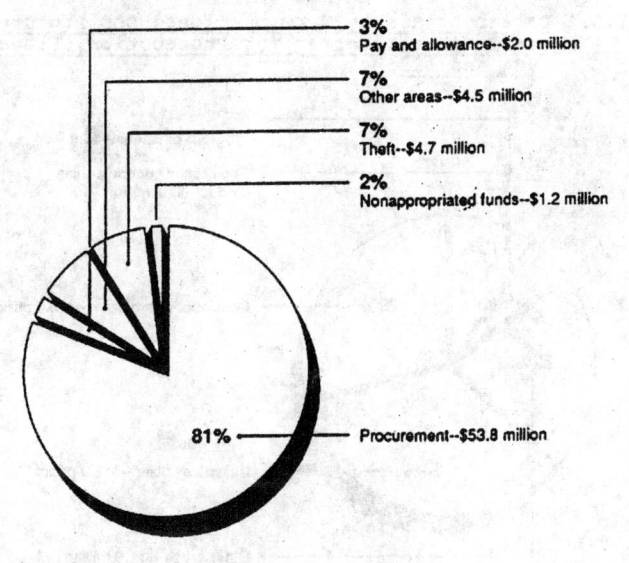

3%
Pay and allowance--$2.0 million

7%
Other areas--$4.5 million

7%
Theft--$4.7 million

2%
Nonappropriated funds--$1.2 million

81% — Procurement--$53.8 million

Cases: 794
Losses: $66.2 million

[a] Data for fiscal years 1986 and 1987 provided by the DOD OIG showed that losses of $134.5 million were 73.7 percent from procurement; 13.1 percent, pay and allowances; 5.6 percent, theft; 0.1 percent, nonappropriated funds; and 7.5 percent, other areas. Thus, since the data we analyzed for fiscal years 1984 and 1985, procurement losses have decreased as a percentage of losses and those for pay and allowances have increased. The total losses of $134.5 million for the 789 cases in fiscal years 1986 and 1987 are substantially larger than the $66.2 million reported for about the same number of cases in fiscal years 1984 and 1985.

App. S GOVERNMENT CONTRACT COMPLIANCE HANDBOOK

APPENDIX II   APPENDIX I

Figure II.3, breaks down the procurement cases investigated. Examples of the major categories follow. ("Other areas" includes bribery, conflict of interest, kickbacks, undelivered products, fast pay program claims, misuse/diversion of government-furnished material, false statements, mail fraud, false claims, antitrust violations, and misrepresentations.)

Figure II.3: Dollar Losses by Type of Closed DOD Procurement Fraud Cases Referred for Prosecution, Fiscal Years 1984 and 1985[a]

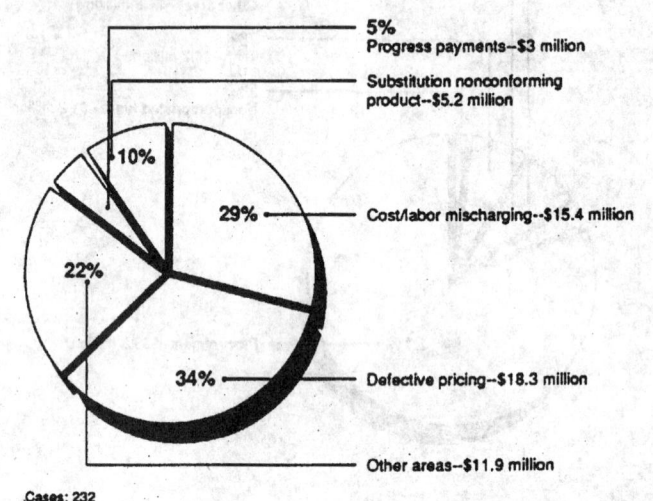

- 5% Progress payments--$3 million
- 10% Substitution nonconforming product--$5.2 million
- 29% Cost/labor mischarging--$15.4 million
- 34% Defective pricing--$18.3 million
- 22% Other areas--$11.9 million

Cases: 232
Losses: $53.8 million

[a]For fiscal years 1986 and 1987, DOD informed us that there were 343 procurement cases involving total losses of $99.1 million. The percentage of dollar losses was 30.4 percent for substitution/nonconforming product; 26.3 percent, cost/labor mischarging; 18.5 percent, defective pricing; 4.3 percent, progress payments; and 20.5 percent, all other areas. Thus, the percentage for the substitution/nonconforming product category has increased substantially, while that of the defective pricing category has gone down.

APPENDIX S   App. S

APPENDIX II   APPENDIX II

DEFECTIVE PRICING

Under the Truth in Negotiations Act (Public Law 87-653), defense contractors generally are required to submit cost or pricing data and certify that such data are accurate, complete, and current. Fraud associated with defective pricing involves the deliberate concealment or misrepresentation of significant cost elements. This includes falsification or alteration of supporting data and/or submission of inaccurate, incomplete, or noncurrent cost or pricing data.

In one DOD defective pricing procurement case investigated jointly by the Federal Bureau of Investigation and DCIS, a contractor was found to have inflated the cost of spare parts for diesel heaters and air compressors, resulting in overpayments in excess of $1.7 million on 33 separate contracts. For one part, the contractor paid $60.62 per unit and submitted a pricing proposal showing $166.40 per unit. For another, the proposal showed a cost of $1,074 when the contractor had paid only $444. In still another instance, the contractor charged DOD $58 per unit for an item that cost 41 cents. The largest overcharge, $236,151, occurred when the contractor sold over 4,500 ignition boxes costing $43.49 each to the government over a 2-year period, charging as high as $123 each. According to the case file, the defective pricing was discovered when an administrative contracting officer began reviewing small details of the pricing proposals and found indications of false pricing support documents. An officer of the contractor was sentenced to five consecutive 2-year prison terms. Also, criminal fines and penalties amounted to $3 million, and a civil judgment was ordered that enables DCAA and DCIS to maintain strict oversight of the contractor's pricing policies and claims under future awards.

COST/LABOR MISCHARGING

Cost and/or labor mischarging occurs whenever a contractor charges the government for costs which are not allowable, not reasonable, or which cannot be directly or indirectly allocated to the contract. In one DOD cost/labor mischarging procurement case, a contractor involved in missile targeting processes mischarged labor costs, travel costs, and related expenses resulting in a loss of about $325,000 to the government. For example, some of the contractor's employees falsified the time distribution on their time cards, but their supervisor certified them as being correct. The contractor pleaded guilty to three counts of false statements and was ordered to pay $650,000 (for double the amount of damages), $167,000 in interest, and a fine of $30,000.

App. S-23

APPENDIX II

APPENDIX II

PRODUCT SUBSTITUTION

Product substitution refers to attempts by contractors to deliver goods or services which do not conform to contract requirements. Contractors do not inform DOD of the discrepancies and seek reimbursement based upon delivery of conforming products or services.

One of DOD's product substitution investigations involved a contractor who allegedly supplied almost 2 million yards of substandard parachute suspension cord resulting in an estimated loss of about $685,000. The contractor submitted false laboratory test reports to government inspectors showing the cord had met contract specifications. After he presented quality assurance inspectors a cord that met specifications, the contractor shipped DOD another cord that was 25 years old. The fraud was discovered after an allegation was received. According to the case file, very serious neck and back injuries could occur if shock were absorbed by the neck and back instead of by the parachute cord. The firm's owner pleaded guilty to two counts of mail fraud and received a 2-year prison sentence, was ordered to perform 200 hours of community service, and was fined $7,000. The vice president pleaded guilty to making false statements and received a 1-month jail sentence. In addition, the vice president was placed on probation for 4 years and 9 months and was ordered to perform 800 hours of community service. The firm was fined $26,000 and was ordered to pay a $225,000 restitution.

THEFT

As noted previously, the largest number of cases referred for prosecution involved theft. Figure II.4 shows the dollar losses by types of theft. Examples of the major theft categories are in succeeding paragraphs. "Other areas" includes weapon systems hardware, computer hardware and software, and computerized data. The services/benefits category includes such items as medical benefits.

23

APPENDIX II

Figure II.4: <u>Dollar Losses by Type of Theft Cases Referred for Prosecution, Fiscal Years 1984 and 1985</u>

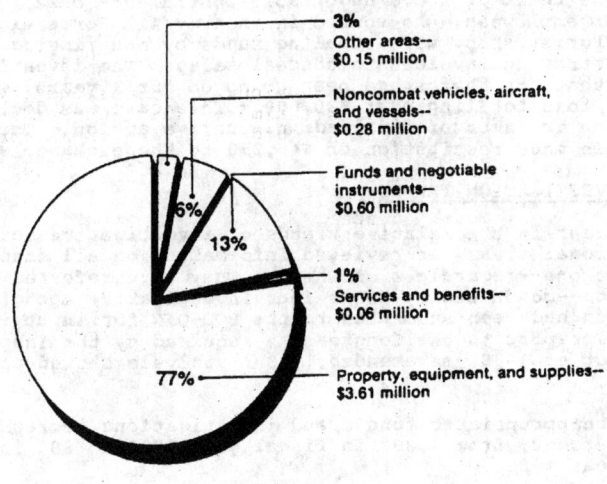

- 3% Other areas-- $0.15 million
- Noncombat vehicles, aircraft, and vessels-- $0.28 million
- 6%
- 13% Funds and negotiable instruments-- $0.60 million
- 1% Services and benefits-- $0.06 million
- 77% Property, equipment, and supplies-- $3.61 million

Cases: 258
Losses: $4.7 million

An example of a theft of government supplies involved employees of a company that delivered copier paper to 53 DOD facilities. The individuals stole almost 900 cases of paper valued at about $30,000 by removing the paper from various facilities without authorization in some instances and shorting deliveries in others. Four individuals pleaded guilty to the theft. Their sentences included fines and restitutions of $4,764 and various probation and community service terms.

Another example involved four individuals who stole about $43,000 worth of aluminum landing mats from firing ranges and sold the items to a steel company for almost $6,000. This case was declined for prosecution due to weak or insufficient evidence. The case file did not include evidence of any action taken.

A theft in the noncombat vehicle category occurred when a youth entered an unsecured office, stole athletic uniforms and the keys to a van, and drove off in the van. He was later stopped by

APPENDIX II   APPENDIX II

the police for improper driving, leading to the recovery of the van
and uniforms. The juvenile was placed on indefinite probation and
enrolled in a residential treatment and training program.

In one theft of funds/negotiable instruments case, four
contractor employees, who worked in an Army/Air Force exchange
service florist shop, were stealing funds by not ringing up sales
and by destroying invoices to conceal sales. The investigation
revealed that the thefts had been going on for 3 years, with an
estimated loss totaling over $30,000. This case was declined for
prosecution in favor of civil/administrative action. The
individuals made restitution of $45,270 to the exchange service.

RECENT INVESTIGATION TRENDS

To identify the relative trends of investigative activities in
DOD functional areas, we reviewed information on all fraud
investigations--regardless of whether they were referred for
prosecution--conducted by DOD's four investigative agencies. (This
information had been submitted to the DOD OIG for input into the
semiannual report to the Congress as required by the Inspector
General Act of 1978, as amended.) Our analysis showed the
following.

-- Nonappropriated fund fraud investigations decreased 47
   percent, from 1,300 in fiscal year 1983 to 688 in fiscal
   year 1986.

-- Pay and allowances fraud investigations decreased about 48
   percent, from 3,186 in fiscal year 1983 to 1,661 in fiscal
   year 1986.

-- Overall theft of government property fraud investigations
   decreased about 8 percent, from 6,453 in fiscal year 1983
   to 5,960 in fiscal year 1986.

-- Procurement fraud investigations increased about 121
   percent, from 870 in fiscal year 1983 to 1,919 in fiscal
   year 1986.

Most (76 percent) of the decrease in nonappropriated fund
fraud investigations occurred in the Army's CIDC. According to a
CIDC official, this decrease resulted because in 1985 CIDC began
investigating only nonappropriated fund fraud allegations involving
losses of $1,000 or more, whereas before that time CIDC
investigated all cases with losses totaling $250 or more. (The
Army's military police now investigate nonappropriated fund fraud
allegations under $1,000.) Also, initiatives to identify
fraudulent activity decreased in retail areas such as

APPENDIX S   App. S

APPENDIX II   APPENDIX II

nonappropriated funds. Currently, CIDC is focusing more on areas that affect combat readiness--major contract fraud and supply diversion.

A large portion (85 percent) of the decrease in the number of fraud investigations in the pay and allowance area is attributable to the Air Force and Navy investigative agencies. According to AFOSI and NIS officials, pay and allowance investigations have decreased because their investigative agencies have established agreements with their respective accounting and finance offices whereby the offices handle the smaller dollar cases and only refer the most significant cases for criminal investigation.

The emphasis on investigating more significant fraud cases is due to a response to a report we issued in 1983--<u>DOD Can Combat Fraud Better By Strengthening Its Investigative Agencies</u> (GAO/AFMD-83-33, March 21, 1983)--which indicated that Army, Navy, and Air Force fraud cases often involve relatively minor allegations. The report stated that minor fraud allegations may be more appropriately handled by commanding officers, military inspectors general, or the military police because courts-martial or Department of Justice prosecutions are unlikely and the matters can be dealt with administratively. We recommended that the DOD IG issue guidelines to the Department's criminal investigators that require them to investigate only fraud allegations that will (1) probably result in prosecutions if substantiated, (2) meet a minimum dollar loss, or (3) indicate larger or systemic problems that must be investigated and refer the remaining allegations to commanding officers, military inspectors general, or military police for investigation.

In response to this recommendation, DOD issued Instruction 5505.2, entitled "Criminal Investigations of Fraud Offenses," which requires that the military departments (1) establish procedures providing for the investigation of less significant fraud allegations by alternative investigative resources, including military or security police or command authorities and (2) ensure that all allegations of significant fraud are referred promptly for investigation to the appropriate DOD criminal investigative organization.

DOD OIG officials also cited numerous publications developed by their office and the services that are distributed to quality assurance representatives and contracting officials that (1) identify conditions that have been indicators of fraud and abuse in the contracting process and (2) emphasize reporting such indications of suspected irregularities to investigative agencies.

APPENDIX II   APPENDIX II

The OIG officials also told us that procurement fraud referrals from DCAA to the DOD investigative agencies have increased substantially. Such referrals more than quintupled, from 60 in fiscal year 1983 to 325 in fiscal year 1986. When we discussed this increase with a DCAA official, especially the dramatic increase between fiscal years 1985 and 1986 (from 154 to 325), we were told that the increase was due to (1) better education of DCAA employees as to what should be referred and (2) new procedures designed to ensure that all suspected fraud or other irregularities are reported directly to the appropriate investigative authority. He cited an August 29, 1985, DCAA Office of General Counsel memorandum to all employees which outlined procedures for reporting suspected fraud and stipulated that no delays in referrals are allowed.

Most of the referrals from DCAA involve suspected cost mischarging and defective pricing. DOD OIG officials told us that these types of cases were very significant and had increased dramatically just prior to our review. Therefore, we reviewed case summaries for 173 cases under investigation that had been reported to the Secretary of Defense during the last half of fiscal year 1985 and the first half of fiscal year 1986. Many of these investigations resulted from DCAA referrals. The DOD OIG's procedures include reporting significant open cases to the secretary. Significant cases are defined as those cases that involve (1) potential losses of at least $50,000[5], (2) high ranking DOD officials, and/or (3) extensive media coverage. We found that most of these open cases (148, or 86 percent) involved procurement matters. In addition, procurement cases accounted for almost $400 million or 97 percent of the total estimated dollar losses in this group of cases. As shown in table II.1, cost/labor mischarging is the most prevalent type of case, accounting for more than a third of the procurement cases and about 72 percent of the procurement losses from this set of cases.

---

[5]Since our review, the $50,000 threshold has been increased to $100,000.

27

APPENDIX II

Table II.1: Type of Open Procurement Cases Reported to the Secretary of Defense (April 1, 1985, Through March 31, 1986

Type	Number of cases	Percentage	Estimated dollar loss	Percentage
Cost and/or Labor mischarging	50	33.8	$278,632,831	71.9
Defective pricing	21	14.2	56,554,202	14.6
Product substitution nonconforming product	32	21.6	32,068,222	8.3
Progress payment claims	15	10.1	11,549,000	3.0
Contractor kickbacks	6	4.1	3,650,000	.9
Bribery/solicitation of bribe	11	7.4	1,000,000	.3
Undelivered product	3	2.0	486,240	.1
Conflict of interest	5	3.4	400,000	.1
Other procurement cases	5	3.4	3,056,504	.8
Total	148	100.0	$387,396,999	100.0

In one of the cost and/or labor mischarging open cases, a DCAA audit uncovered suspected cost escalations on over 300 spare parts in 3,200 contracts, resulting in an estimated loss of over $100 million. The contractor had allegedly been manipulating cost transfers from one contract to another over a 6-year period. As of August 12, 1987, the case was pending and will be presented before a grand jury.

In one of the defective pricing open cases, a subcontractor was allegedly overpricing spare parts for a missile warning system contract. Based on the subcontractor's overpricing, the contractor was charging from 70 percent to 2,472 percent more than the Federal Supply Schedule prices, resulting in an estimated loss to the government of $2 million.

APPENDIX II   APPENDIX II

   Recently, the DOD IG established the investigation and prosecution of product substitution procurement fraud as its number one priority because malfunctioning defective parts in critical components of weapons systems can jeopardize both DOD missions and personnel. According to DOD IG officials, since January 1986, DCIS product substitution fraud investigations have resulted in 85 indictments. In addition, as of October 1987, DCIS was investigating 231 fraud cases involving product substitution. One open case involved a contractor who provided portable bridge kits for military tanks. The case summary indicated that an investigation ensued after a former contractor employee alleged that the contractor provided 144 defective kits to DOD, resulting in an estimated loss of $14.2 million. According to the summary, five former employees indicated that steel was not preheated as required, certification documents for inspection and stress reaction were falsified, rust was not cleaned from steel prior to welding, joints were improperly fitted, welding was accomplished with substandard wire, and holes in hydraulics were covered to hide them from government inspectors.

   During our review, 55 of the DOD's top 100 contractors, those that received the largest dollar volume of defense contract awards, were being investigated in 274 cases of alleged procurement fraud. The majority of these cases involved alleged fraud for cost mischarging (133 cases), defective pricing (57 cases), and product substitution (25 cases).

   The increase in referrals of alleged procurement fraud for investigations involving contractors has prompted the DOD OIG to adopt a best case selection strategy. In this regard, because many of DOD's largest contractors faced multiple cost mischarging/defective pricing cases, the DOD OIG directed that the best use of investigative resources included choosing the best one or two cases--those most likely to result in criminal prosecution--against any single DOD contractor and devoting investigative resources only to those cases. As part of the DOD OIG strategy, the remaining cases not pursued criminally will be handled with civil and administrative remedies.

   As discussed earlier, information furnished by the DOD OIG in commenting on this report demonstrates the increased emphasis on investigating and referring for prosecution suspected procurement fraud. DOD IG data on 789 closed fiscal year 1986 and 1987 cases with losses of $1,000 or more that were referred for prosecution showed that

-- procurement cases made up a higher percentage of fraud referrals (about 44 percent for this period vs. 29 percent of fiscal year 1984 and 1985 cases);

APPENDIX II

-- theft cases referred decreased from almost one-third of fiscal year 1984 and 1985 cases referred to 23 percent in 1986 and 1987.

Moreover, DOD OIG's data for the fiscal year 1986 and 1987 cases referred for prosecution also showed a significant increase in dollar losses--$134.5 million for 789 fiscal year 1986 and 1987 cases versus about $66 million for 794 fiscal year 1984 and 1985 cases referred. Procurement losses continued to make up the largest portion of the losses in the later cases (about 74 percent). The data also reflected DOD's concentration on its number one investigative priority--suspected product substitution fraud. Losses identified in these types of procurement fraud cases had increased to $30.1 million or 30 percent of total procurement losses versus $5.2 million or 10 percent of total losses in fiscal year 1984 and 1985 cases.

APPENDIX III

ACTIONS TAKEN AGAINST SUBJECTS
REFERRED FOR PROSECUTION

LEGAL AND/OR ADMINISTRATIVE ACTION TAKEN AGAINST THOSE REFERRED FOR PROSECUTION IN 435, OR 55 PERCENT, OF THE CASES

- -- 418 LEGAL ACTIONS TAKEN ON DOD REFERRALS FOR PROSECUTION

- -- 434 ADMINISTRATIVE ACTIONS TAKEN ON DOD FRAUD REFERRALS

NO ACTION REPORTED TAKEN AGAINST THOSE REFERRED FOR PROSECUTION IN 359, OR 45 PERCENT, OF THE CASES

LEGAL AND ADMINISTRATIVE ACTIONS HAVE INCREASED FROM FISCAL YEAR 1983 TO FISCAL YEAR 1987

APPENDIX III   APPENDIX III

ACTIONS TAKEN AGAINST SUBJECTS REFERRED FOR PROSECUTION

Fraud cases that are referred for prosecution are either accepted or declined. If the case is accepted, legal action, such as criminal prosecution or civil proceedings, may be taken against individuals or organizations. If subjects are found guilty of criminal fraud, sentences can include court imposed monetary assessments, imprisonment, and/or probation. According to a DOD OIG official, civil actions may be pursued by Justice in some DOD cases where financial loss has been incurred and/or civil penalties can be levied for false claims against the government or for other fraud. In civil cases, a person cannot be sent to prison as in a criminal case. DOD may also take administrative action against subjects of fraud investigations in addition to any criminal prosecutions and civil actions. If prosecution is declined, administrative action may be taken. These administrative actions include requiring repayment of losses, suspensions or termination of employment, and suspension or debarment of contractors from participating in the DOD procurement process. As discussed on pages 39 and 40, the range of administrative options should soon increase as DOD implements the Program Fraud Civil Remedies Act of 1986, which authorizes recoupment of the government's losses and administrative fines for certain cases.

The 794 cases that were referred for prosecution involved 1,353 subjects. We found that action was taken against 707 subjects in 435, or 55 percent of these cases. Reported losses in these cases totaled $44 million and actions taken in these cases resulted in fines and recoveries of about $33 million. In the 435 cases, 852 actions were taken, including 418 legal actions and 434 administrative actions.

LEGAL ACTIONS

We found that 418 legal actions, criminal or civil, were taken in 313 cases. These actions resulted in 376 criminal convictions, 13 civil actions, and 29 pretrial diversions. In the latter, the subject and prosecutor signed an agreement that diverted the subject from traditional criminal justice processing into a program of supervision for a specified period. If the subject successfully completes the established requirements, prosecution is declined. If not, prosecution can be initiated.

An individual convicted of fraud against the government may or may not be sentenced to prison. In addition, if a prison sentence is levied, all or part of it may be suspended. Moreover, an

33

APPENDIX S

APPENDIX III

individual may be sentenced to probation in addition to prison or probation without prison. Of the 376 criminal convictions, we found that

— 254 individuals received prison sentences,

— 151 individuals had all or part of their sentences suspended, and

— 273 individuals were placed on probation, either in addition to a prison sentence or as the only sentence.

The following three tables show the length of punishment received by defendants as well as other relevant data.

Table III.1: Prison Sentences

Length	Number of individuals	Percentage of individuals
6 months or less	64	25
7 months to 1 year	50	20
13 months to 2 years	55	22
25 months to 3 years	34	13
More than 3 years	51	20
Total	254	100

Table III.2: Suspended Sentences

Length	Number of individuals	Percentage of individuals
6 months or less	26	17
7 months to 1 year	33	22
13 months to 2 years	40	26
25 months to 3 years	30	20
More than 3 years	22	15
Total	151	100

APPENDIX III   APPENDIX III

Table III.3: Probation Periods

Length	Number of individuals	Percentage of individuals
6 months or less	12	4
7 months to 1 year	41	15
13 months to 2 years	67	25
25 months to 3 years	77	28
More than 3 years	76	28
Total	273	100

The 313 cases in which legal action was taken had reported losses of about $41 million. As a result of criminal penalties, 304 subjects were assessed fines and restitutions of about $25.4 million, about $8.5 million of which included civil actions taken against 13 subjects. In addition to the above $25.4 million in assessments, investigative recoveries and seizures for these cases totaled $3.2 million. Thus, the government recovered $28.6 million of its $41 million in losses in this group of cases where legal action was taken.

ADMINISTRATIVE ACTIONS

Administrative actions were taken against subjects referred for prosecution in 235, or 30 percent, of the cases. In total, 434 administrative actions were taken against 388 subjects in our study period. These actions included those taken against individuals as shown in figure III.1 and those taken against DOD contractors and vendors as shown in figure III.2. Dollar recoveries resulting from administrative actions totaled $4.1 million.

APPENDIX III

Figure III.1: <u>Administrative Actions Taken Against DOD Employees (232 Actions)</u>

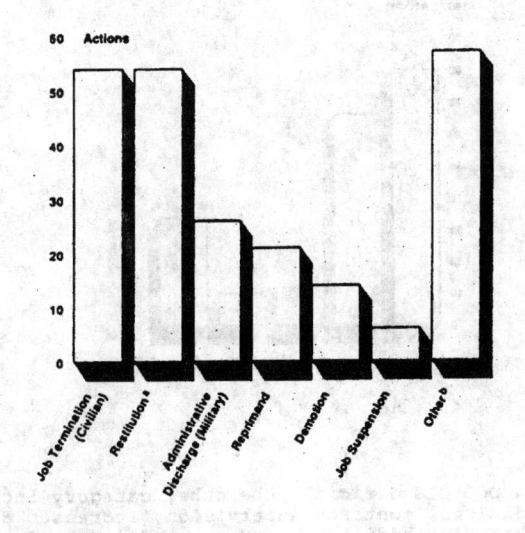

[Bar chart showing number of actions (0-60 scale) for categories: Job Termination (Civilian) ~54, Restitution[a] ~54, Administrative Discharge (Military) ~26, Reprimand ~22, Demotion ~15, Job Suspension ~7, Other[b] ~57]

[a]Includes garnishment of wages.

[b]"Other" includes such things as increased supervision and being temporarily transferred to another job.

APPENDIX III

APPENDIX III

Figure III.2: **Administrative Actions Taken Against Contractors/ Vendors (202 Actions)**

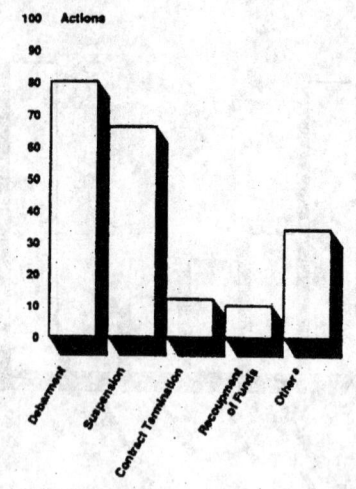

[Bar chart showing: Debarment ~80, Suspension ~65, Contract Termination ~12, Recoupment of Funds ~10, Other[a] ~33]

[a]According to a DOD OIG official, the other category includes such actions as additional contract supervision, increased audit activity, withholding additional orders, and in the future holding the contractor/vendor as a nonresponsible bidder.

PUNITIVE ACTIONS ARE INCREASING

As discussed previously, for our fiscal year 1984 and 1985 study period of closed cases with losses totaling $1,000 or more, there were 376 criminal convictions, 66 suspensions of DOD contractors, and 80 debarments of DOD contractors. Our analysis of these activities resulting from all cases regardless of dollar loss for a 5-year period (fiscal years 1983-87) showed that these types of punitive actions have increased significantly. Table III.4 shows that over this time period, criminal convictions by the Department of Justice increased almost 50 percent from 207 in fiscal year 1983 to 307 in fiscal year 1987. In addition, DOD's total suspensions and debarments of contractors totaled 898 in fiscal year 1987, over three times the 280 such actions taken in fiscal year 1983.

37

APPENDIX S

APPENDIX III

Table III.4: Selected Punitive Actions Taken Against Those Who Defrauded DOD Programs, Fiscal Years 1983-87

Fiscal year	Suspensions	Debarments	Total suspensions and debarments	Justice criminal convictions
1983	195	85	280	207
1984	134	260	394	192
1985	225	357	582	333
1986	470	415	885	344
1987	393	505	898	307
Total	1,417	1,622	3,039	1,383

DOD OIG officials told us that suspensions and debarments have increased because of the high-level emphasis placed on using those actions as an administrative tool to protect the government against fraudulent or irresponsible contractors and because more fraudulent contractors are being prosecuted by the Department of Justice.

DOD is also implementing a coordinated fraud remedies program to ensure that all fraud cases related to procurement are referred for action and that all appropriate remedies, including suspensions and debarments, are pursued. The program calls for DOD components to monitor all investigations of procurement fraud that involved alleged losses of $50,000 or more and all procurement corruption cases that involve bribery, gratuities, or conflicts of interest to ensure that all possible criminal, civil, administrative, and contractual remedies are identified and that the cases are referred to appropriate officials and pursued promptly.

REASONS FOR DECLINATIONS

For the 794 closed fiscal year 1984 and 1985 fraud cases, a total of 710 subjects in 393[6] cases were declined for prosecution by Justice. We were able to determine Justice's reasons for the declinations for 433 subjects. The reasons are shown in figure III.3. The "other" category in the figure included reasons such as the offender's age, health, personal history, or other personal circumstances.

---

[6]The 393 cases include all cases where at least one subject was declined for prosecution. Other subjects within these cases could have been accepted for prosecution.

App. S   GOVERNMENT CONTRACT COMPLIANCE HANDBOOK

APPENDIX III   APPENDIX III

Figure III.3: Reasons Justice Declined 433 Subjects of Fraud Cases

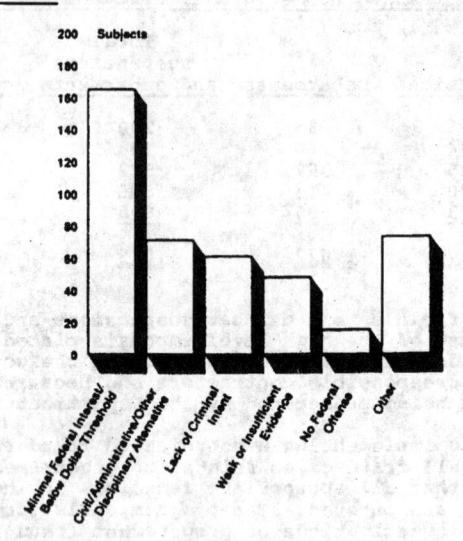

[Bar chart showing number of subjects (0-200) by reason: Minimal Federal Interest/Below Dollar Threshold; Civil/Administrative/Other Disciplinary Alternative; Lack of Criminal Intent; Weak or Insufficient Evidence; No Federal Offense; Other]

We found that in many of the cases that were declined for criminal prosecution, little or no action was taken against the subjects investigated. In 359, or 45 percent of the cases, no legal or administrative action was taken against those referred for prosecution. Reported losses in these cases totaled $22 million, while recoveries made during investigations totaled about $6 million. We believe that in the future, DOD will have more authority to act in such cases because of the Program Fraud Civil Remedies Act of 1986, especially in those instances where cases are declined because the loss involved is below a U.S. attorney dollar threshold. This act, which was passed in October 1986 (while our review was ongoing) as Section 6103 of the Omnibus Budget Reconciliation Act of 1986, provides federal agencies with an administrative remedy for recouping losses by assessing penalties on those who knowingly submit false claims and/or statements. Under the act, administrative proceedings can be brought, with the approval of the Attorney General, against persons who make, present, or submit false claims and statements. For false claims and false statement cases involving up to $150,000 that the Department of Justice has declined to prosecute, the act has

App. S-40

APPENDIX III

established an administrative remedy. If the person is found liable, a civil penalty of not more than $5,000 can be assessed for each false claim or statement, plus double any amount of such claim the government paid.

In passing the act, the congressional conferees noted that while judicial remedies are available to penalize and deter fraud against the government, the cost of litigation often exceeds the amount recovered, thus making it economically impractical for the Justice Department to go to court. Before the new law was enacted, the government was frequently left without a practical remedy for the small dollar cases.

OIG officials also informed us that recent legislation amending the Truth in Negotiations Act will provide another tool for deterring wrongdoing. In this regard, the act was amended by the National Defense Authorization Act for Fiscal Year 1987 to prevent unearned and excessive contractor profits. The amendments made contractors liable for double the amount paid by the government when an overpayment was based on the intentional submission of defective cost or pricing data. The double damage penalty for the intentional wrongdoing was not part of the original Truth in Negotiations Act.

APPENDIX IV

APPENDIX IV

**DOD IG EFFORTS TO IDENTIFY AND REPORT
WEAKNESSES THAT CONTRIBUTE TO FRAUD**

DOD IG HAS INITIATED BOTH SHORT-TERM AND LONG-TERM EFFORTS TO
IDENTIFY AND REPORT INTERNAL CONTROL WEAKNESSES THAT ALLOW OR
CONTRIBUTE TO FRAUD

TWO 1986 SPECIAL STUDIES, BY REVIEWING CLOSED FRAUD CASES,
IDENTIFIED CAUSES OF PRODUCT SUBSTITUTION FRAUD AS WELL AS ILLEGAL
DIVERSION AND EXPORTATION OF DOD PROPERTY

RECENT DOD IG INITIATIVE REQUIRES INVESTIGATIVE AGENCIES TO
(1) ROUTINELY IDENTIFY WEAKNESSES THAT ALLOW FRAUD TO OCCUR AND
(2) REPORT THEM TO MANAGERS

42

APPENDIX IV

APPENDIX IV

DOD OIG EFFORTS TO IDENTIFY AND REPORT
WEAKNESSES THAT CONTRIBUTE TO FRAUD

In keeping with the DOD IG's legislative mandate to make recommendations that will prevent fraud and other illegal activity, the DOD IG has initiated both short-term and long-term efforts to identify and report to managers information developed during criminal investigations concerning internal control or management weaknesses that allowed or contributed to fraudulent activity.

SPECIAL SHORT-TERM STUDIES

Using internal control weakness information developed in criminal investigations, the DOD IG conducted two studies in 1986 that identified underlying causes of fraud in two areas. In the first study, the DOD OIG was concerned about whether criminal investigations involving contractor product substitution practices pointed to systemic weaknesses in DOD's quality assurance. Thus, an audit team reviewed selected criminal investigations that substantiated the substitution and delivery of nonconforming products. The team found poor quality assurance practices that had contributed to fraud. These conditions included (1) government quality assurance representatives relying on documents falsified by contractors as to the adequacy of quality assurance, (2) prescribed quality assurance procedures not being followed during inspections and testing, and (3) contractors shipping rejected or uninspected items. For example, in 58 percent of the cases, the team found that government quality assurance personnel had relied on documents falsified by contractors to verify the adequacy of quality assurance. The contractors provided government quality assurance personnel (1) false documents to conceal the substitution of inferior and foreign-made parts and (2) falsified parts lists, certificates of conformance, test procedures and records, welding certifications, drawings, purchase orders, and invoices.

Because the quality assurance representatives were not required to systematically verify the contractors' records, the representatives did not detect inferior products the contractors introduced into the DOD supply system. According to the study report, in each case, additional verification and control of documentation could have permitted early detection of problems. In one case cited as an example, the contractor submitted test reports showing that required testing of microcircuit devices had been done. However, had the quality assurance representative checked the test logs, he would have found that the testing required by the contract specifications was not done. Consequently, millions of improperly tested and potentially faulty microcircuits were accepted by the government.

43

App. S-44

APPENDIX IV

A report depicting indicators and conditions conducive to unauthorized quality assurance practices was provided to DOD management in order to highlight a category of weaknesses conducive to potential fraud. The team found that the Defense Logistics Agency was actively pursuing several actions to identify and reduce the number of nonconforming products entering the DOD supply system. In addition, the military departments and Defense Logistics Agency were training DOD quality assurance personnel to identify and report for investigation indicators of product substitution.

In the second special study conducted in 1986, a joint DOD OIG and Customs Service team was formed to investigate and develop recommendations to curtail the illegal diversion and exportation of DOD disposal material to prohibited countries. In its review of closed fraud investigations and audit and inspection reports, it found, among other things, weaknesses in controls over items requiring export licenses and inadequate procedures for tracking munition items and ensuring required demilitarization of controlled items so that they cannot be sold as usable items. The deputy IG reported these problems to the Secretary of Defense and indicated that actions were underway to correct the problems and to strengthen internal controls and accountability for Defense disposal material.

LONG-TERM EFFORTS

In still another effort to correct the underlying causes of fraud, the DOD IG directed the establishment of a comprehensive DOD crime analysis program in April 1986. The program requires each DOD investigative organization to establish an organizational capability to (1) perform criminal fraud analysis, (2) identify from their investigations, systemic weaknesses and vulnerabilities which allow fraudulent activity and loss to occur, and (3) provide this information to appropriate managers so that they can implement measures to protect DOD resources. The investigative agencies are also required to develop computerized systems to collect and use these data for trend analyses and identifying systemic weaknesses.

As of August 6, 1987, the four DOD investigative agencies were in the process of implementing this requirement. According to the DOD IG project director, all four had agreed to accept the responsibility to fulfill this requirement. They had established organizational entities responsible for implementing such a program and were working out the details of how to meet the requirement. We believe that this program, if carried out properly, can be an important step in the prevention of fraud.

APPENDIX V

COMMENTS FROM THE DEPARTMENT OF DEFENSE

Note: GAO comments supplementing those in the report text appear at the end of this appendix.

INSPECTOR GENERAL
DEPARTMENT OF DEFENSE
400 ARMY NAVY DRIVE
ARLINGTON, VIRGINIA 22202

DEC 4 1987

Mr. Frederick D. Wolf
Director
Accounting and Financial
  Management Division
U.S. General Accounting Office
Washington, D.C. 20548

Dear Mr. Wolf:

This is the Department of Defense (DoD) response to the General Accounting Office (GAO) Draft Report, "DoD FRAUD INVESTIGATIONS: Characteristics, Sanctions, and Prevention," dated October 19, 1987 (GAO Code 911589/OSD Case 7435). It generally confirms the information provided at the November 3 meeting with the GAO staff.

DOD IG appendixes are not included here but were considered in finalizing this report. They are available from us upon request.

The Department has no substantial objection to any portion of the report. There are, however, a few additions and corrections at Appendix A that would add to the overall report. In addition, more current data than was available to the GAO during its review would be useful, as follows:

See page 38.
See comment 1.
See comment 2.
See page 10.
See page 38.

Appendix B - Convictions--FY 1982-FY 1987
Appendix C - Overall Monetary Outcomes--
  FY 1982-FY 1987
Appendix D - Criminal Fines and Restitutions--
  FY 1982-FY 1987
Appendix E - Fraud Agent Strength--FY 1982-FY 1987
Appendix F - Suspensions and Debarments--
  FY 1984-FY 1987

In addition, a brief narrative is included at Appendix G (with statistics and examples), outlining the progress made, since 1986, with respect to the top DoD law enforcement priority--i.e., the investigation and prosecution of product substitution cases. The statistics reflect a current emphasis not discernible from the cases reviewed as part of the report.

See pages 4 and 29.

The report incorrectly described an antitrust case at pages 22-23, which was not actually prosecuted as such. The GAO reliance on the case resulted from an inaccurate case description in the DoD data base that was only recently discovered. As a

See comment 3.

APPENDIX V

susbstitute example of the DoD antitrust effort, a summary of antitrust cases involving dredging contractors is provided at Appendix H. Also included are recent statistics reflecting the level of effort within the Office of the Inspector General relative to antitrust cases.

See pages 20 and 21.

Updated and corrected charts are also provided for those appearing as Figures II.2 and II.3 in the GAO draft report. The revisions (included at Appendices I and J, respectively) are necessary due to a change regarding an erroneously reported $15.2 million loss (which should have been $152,000) and the change of one case involving a $15 million loss from antitrust to cost mischarging.

The inclusion of the updated data available for FY 1986 and FY 1987 would emphasize the increased DoD efforts that are outlined in the report. The updated data are provided, as follows:

See page 19 and comment 4.

Appendix K - Closed DoD Fraud Cases Referred for Prosecution, by Activity, FY 1985 and FY 1986

See page 20.

Appendix L - Dollar Losses by Type of Closed DoD Fraud Cases Referred for Prosecution, FY 1986 and FY 1987

See page 21.

Appendix M - Dollar Losses by Type of Closed DoD Procurement Fraud Cases Referred for Prosecution, FY 1986 and FY 1987

See comment 5.

Appendix N - Comparison of Fraud Data, FY 1984-FY 1985 and FY 1986-FY 1987

The Department appreciates the opportunity to comment on the draft report.

Sincerely,

June Gibbs Brown
Inspector General

Enclosures
(Appendices A-N)

47

APPENDIX V

The following are GAO's comments on the Department of Defense letter dated December 4, 1987.

<u>GAO COMMENTS</u>

1. We did not include this data because it includes monetary outcomes on all cases whether or not they were referred for prosecution.

2. We did not include this information in our report because it does not specifically relate to the cases included in our review.

3. An example of antitrust fraud case is no longer needed because--due to DOD IG's erroneous classification of an antitrust fraud case--this category of fraud is no longer one of the largest for fiscal year 1984 and 1985 fraud referred for prosecution.

4. The information actually provided by the DOD IG was for fiscal years 1986 and 1987.

5. We did not include this data in our report because it repeats information already provided and also includes information not within the scope of our review.

(911618)

APPENDIX T

DOD Office of Inspector General, "Indicators of Fraud in DOD Procurement" (June 1987)

IG, DoD 4075.1-H

DEPARTMENT OF DEFENSE

Office of Inspector General

Indicators of Fraud in DoD Procurement

JUNE 1987

App. T   GOVERNMENT CONTRACT COMPLIANCE HANDBOOK

PREFACE

Fraud in Department of Defense Procurement

This is the first complete revision of our procurement fraud indicators handbook. The Department of Defense (DoD) has made great strides in less than five years in detecting various forms of contract fraud and responding to such fraud with a variety of innovative criminal, civil, administrative, and contractual remedies.

Since 1982, when the Inspector General, DoD, was created, there has been a marked increase in the number of contract fraud cases identified and resolved. For example, convictions have risen from 102 to 258 last year; suspension and debarment actions have risen from 163 in 1982 to 676 in 1986.

The increases are directly attributable to the sensitivity by DoD procurement personnel to indicators of contract fraud. This Handbook is designed to provide information of possible fraudulent practices by DoD contractors. The indicators, by themselves, are not an absolute identification of fraud, but should cause DoD procurement personnel to ask more questions regarding the contractor and to refer the matter to an appropriate Defense criminal investigative organization.

The revised Handbook contains new sections; for example, there is an entirely new section relating to contractor kickbacks which explains the new provisions of the Anti-kickback Enforcement Act of 1986 (Chapter 10). There is also a discussion of the DoD coordination of remedies program (Chapter 11), as well as an explanation of the DoD voluntary disclosure program that encourages and creates self policing by DoD contractors (Chapter 12).

Preventing and detecting contract fraud is a responsibility of all DoD personnel. In order to fulfill that responsibility, we must remain alert to the presence of fraudulent practices and exercise sound judgment in the expenditure of public funds. The Handbook is designed to provide practical advice and guidance in this area. I encourage you to study the guidance carefully and utilize it.

Derek J. Vander Schaaf
Deputy Inspector General

APPENDIX T

OFFICE OF INSPECTOR GENERAL
DEPARTMENT OF DEFENSE

INDICATORS OF FRAUD IN
DEPARTMENT OF DEFENSE PROCUREMENT

GOVERNMENT CONTRACT COMPLIANCE HANDBOOK

TABLE OF CONTENTS

Introduction

Chapter 1. Crimes Involved in Contract Fraud.

1-1. Introduction

1-2. False Statements, 18 U.S.C. 1001

1-3. False Claims, 18 U.S.C. 287

1-4. Mail Fraud, 18 U.S.C. 1341, and Wire Fraud, 18 U.S.C. 1343

1-5. Bribery, Gratuities, and Conflicts of Interest, Generally 18 U.S.C. 201-208

1-6. Trade Secrets Act, 18 U.S.C. 1905

1-7. Theft, Embezzlement, or Destruction of Public Money, Property, or Records, 18 U.S.C. 641

1-8. Anti-kickback Act, 41 U.S.C. 54

1-9. Sherman Antitrust Act, 15 U.S.C. 1

1-10. Conspiracy, 18 U.S.C. 371

Chapter 2. Fraud in Government Contracts.

2-1. Fraud in the identification of the Government's need for goods or services

2-2. Fraud in the pre-solicitation phase

2-3. Fraud in the solicitation phase

2-4. Fraud in the award of the contract

2-5. Fraud in the negotiation of a contract

Chapter 3. Defective Pricing.

3-1. Introduction: The Truth in Negotiations Act

3-2. Cost or Pricing Data Provision: 10 U.S.C. 2306(a)

3-3. Regulatory Requirements: Federal Acquisition Regulation (FAR)

3-4. Defective Pricing Indicators

Chapter 4. Antitrust Violations: Collusive Bidding and Price Fixing.

4-1. Introduction

4-2. Impact on the procurement process

4-3. Indicators of collusive bidding and price fixing

4-4. Collusive bidding and price fixing examples

Chapter 5. Cost Mischarging.

5-1. Introduction

5-2. Allowable Costs

5-3. Accounting Mischarges

5-4. Material Cost Mischarges

5-5. Labor Mischarges

5-6. Cost Mischarging Examples

Chapter 6. Product Substitution.

6-1. Introduction

6-2. Fraud potential

6-3. Product substitution examples

Chapter 7. Progress Payment Fraud.

7-1. Introduction

7-2. Progress payment fraud indicators

7-3. Progress payment fraud examples

Chapter 8. Fast Pay Fraud.

8-1. Introduction

8-2. Fast pay fraud indicators

8-3. Fast pay fraud examples

Chapter 9. Bribery, Gratuities, and Conflicts of Interest.

9-1. Introduction

9-2. Bribery and Integrity Awareness

9-3. Gratuities

9-4. Conflicts of Interest

Chapter 10. Commercial Bribery and Kickbacks.

10-1. Introduction

10-2. Anti-kickback Enforcement Act of 1986

10-3. Other Considerations

10-4. Kickback Case Examples

Chapter 11. Civil, Contractual, and Administrative Remedies for Fraud.

11-1. Introduction

11-2. Coordinated Approach to Remedies

11-3. Available Remedies

11-4. Personnel Actions

Chapter 12. Voluntary Disclosure of Fraud.

12-1. Introduction

Appendix A. Voluntary Disclosure Program Announcement.

Appendix B. Department of Justice Letter lnre: DoD Voluntary Disclosure Program.

Appendix T

Introduction.

a. Fraud is characterized by acts of guile, deceit, trickery, concealment or breach of confidence which are used to gain some unfair or dishonest advantage. The objective may be to obtain money, property or services; to avoid the payment or loss of money, property or services; or to secure business or personal advantage. Fraud may occur at any stage of the Government contracting process. As discussed in Chapters I and II, fraud may have criminal, civil, contractual, and administrative ramifications.

b. This chapter discusses factors which may indicate the presence of, or enhanced potential for, fraud at various stages in the procurement process. The indicators included in this chapter are not intended, each taken by themselves, to establish the existence of fraud. Rather, the presence of any of the indicators, when taken in the context of the particular procurement action being conducted, should cause DoD employees to be alert to the possibility of impropriety and take appropriate actions to ensure the integrity of the process. Three later chapters will discuss in more detail the concepts of (1) collusive bidding and price fixing; (2) defective pricing; and (3) bribery, gratuities and conflicts of interest. These activities are present in some of the indicators presented in this chapter and should be considered in light of the later explanations.

c. The motives and methods for fraud in the contract award process are varied. There are many instances where fraud is perpetrated to obtain a contract in order to create the opportunity to later engage in such activities as theft or embezzlement, product substitution, cost mischarging, fast pay or progress payment fraud. In some instances the fraud is perpetrated to obtain a contract at a higher price or with better terms than would have occurred in an award untainted by fraud. Still others commit fraud merely to obtain Government contracts because they need the business to keep their companies in operation when private sector activity is low.

d. Another factor to be considered is that frauds are sometimes committed by or with the help of DoD employees. The possibility should not be overlooked that a DoD employee has solicited or accepted bribes or gratuities or has a financial interest in a contractor. There have even been instances of DoD employees creating or participating in the ownership of outside businesses for the purpose of committing fraud through their ability to impact on or control the award process.

Chapter 1
Crimes Involved in Contract Fraud

1-1. Introduction.

When the Government and its programs have been defrauded or corrupted, Federal investigators and prosecutors will usually find that one or more Federal statutes have been violated. It is their job to develop conclusive evidence that each of the elements of a specific crime exists. This chapter discusses some of the most frequently violated statutes. The criminal penalties for violation of these statutes can result in up to 10 years imprisonment and a $1 million fine.

1-2. False Statements, 18 U.S.C. 1001.

a. This statute makes it illegal to engage in any of three types of activity in any matter within the jurisdiction of any department or agency of the United States.

(1) Falsifying, concealing, or covering up a material fact by any trick, scheme, or device;

(2) Making false, fictitious, or fraudulent statements or representations; or

(3) Making or using any false document or writing.

Any certification in a DoD contract which contains false, fictitious, or fraudulent information may be a violation of this statute.

b. The following is a typical scheme which resulted in convictions for violations of this statute. A contractor was required to provide test certifications to DoD for parts it supplied for use in the breech mechanism of a 105mm cannon. The test certifications provided by the contractor contained false representations because the tests had not been performed. The contractor was convicted of making false statements in violation of 18 U.S.C. 1001 for that conduct. It is significant to note that the contractor was prohibited from introducing evidence that the parts would have passed the tests if they were performed. The only relevant issue was whether the tests had been performed at the time the contractor made its certification. The crime is complete upon the submission of the statement to the Government. It is not necessary to prove that the Government relied on or was harmed by the false statement.

1-3. False Claims, 18 U.S.C. 287.

a. This statute makes it illegal to present or make any false, fictitious, or fraudulent claim against any agency or department of the United States. The crime is also complete when the claim is presented. Payment of the claim is not an element of the offense and need not be proven to obtain a conviction. (In a related civil statute, 31 U.S.C. 3729, the United States can recover treble damages, plus the cost of the civil action, plus a forfeiture of $5,000 to $10,000 per false claim for any false claims against the DoD. See Chapter 11.)

b. The following scheme is typical of false claims violations which result in convictions. A contractor altered subcontractor invoices to show inflated prices on purchases made from a subcontractor. The inflated prices were then charged to the Government resulting in a monetary loss of over $1 million. The company paid a total of $3 million in fines, penalties, and restitution. The executive vice president was sentenced to five consecutive two year prison terms.

c. Any claim for a cost which has been declared unallowable by statute or regulation is a criminal and civil violation of the False Claims Act under the Defense Procurement Improvement Act of 1985 (10 U.S.C. 2324(i)) (See Chapter 11).

d. In addition, 18 U.S.C. 286 makes it a crime for two or more persons to agree or conspire to defraud the United States by obtaining or aiding in obtaining payment or allowance of any false, fictitious or fraudulent claim.

1-4. Mail Fraud, 18 U.S.C. 1341, and Wire Fraud, 18 U.S.C. 1343.

a. These statutes make it illegal to engage in any scheme to defraud in which the mails or wire communications are utilized. Utilization of the mails or wire communications includes sending or receiving any matter through the use of these mediums. As an example, they cover receiving payment from the Government which has been sent through the mail or by wire when such occurs in connection with a scheme to defraud.

b. A Virginia based contractor defrauded the Navy in performing a contract awarded and administered in California. The scheme to defraud involved the mailing of false claims (based on false and inflated costs for direct labor and employee benefits) to the Navy. The scheme also involved cost mischarging in an attempt to recover cost overruns on a fixed price contract by concealing the costs in later claims. The corporation and its president were convicted of violating the false claims, false statements, and mail

App. T-5

fraud statutes. The president was sentenced to five years in prison on two charges and received a five year suspended sentence and five years probation on a third charge. In addition, the president was ordered to perform 2,500 hours of community service. The corporation was fined $22,000 and ordered to make restitution in the amount of $185,000.

1-5. Bribery, Gratuities, and Conflicts of Interest, Generally, 18 U.S.C. 201-208.

a. These statutes prohibit a broad range of activities which can be described generally as corruption. Such activities include giving or receiving a bribe or gratuity, as well as engaging in a conflict of interest. (See Chapter 9) (New authority delegated by the President in November 1983, under 18 U.S.C. 218, permits agencies to rescind any contract tainted by bribery, graft, or conflict of interest after conviction for such activity. See Chapter 11.)

(1) Bribery includes giving a Government employee something of value for the purpose of influencing the performance of an official duty.

(2) Gratuities include giving a Government employee something of value because of his official position. There is no requirement for the Government to prove that the gratuity was given for the purpose of influencing any official act.

(3) Conflicts of interest include those situations where a Government employee engages in activities which create a conflict between his personal interests and his duty to protect and serve the interests of the Government.

b. The following schemes are typical of these violations:

(1) *Bribery* - A base laundry, dry cleaning and clothing repair contractor offered a quality assurance inspector (QAI) a bribe in return for approval of monthly service costs to the Air Force. The QAI notified the Air Force Office of Special Investigations (AFOSI) and cooperated in an undercover investigation during which the contractor provided money, food, hotel accommodations, liquor, and other gifts to the QAI. The contractor was found guilty on two counts of bribery and two counts of false claims. He was sentenced to three years in jail, given three years probation, and fined $5,000.

(2) *Gratuities* - A GS-12 contracting officer's technical representative (COTR) admitted soliciting and receiving gratuities from a contractor for which he had responsibility. The gratuities consisted of video equipment, meals, and use of an automobile and a beach condominium over the course of one year. There was no evidence that the COTR did anything in return for these gratuities. The COTR was convicted of receiving gratuities in violation of 18 U.S.C. 201 (g). and was sentenced to one year in jail which was suspended and two years probation. He resigned from Federal service while removal action was pending.

(3) *Conflicts of Interest* - A military member used the authority of his position to direct the award of a contract to a subcontracting firm. The subcontractor, in turn, was to further subcontract to a firm which was wholly owned by the military member. The estimated loss to the Government was $45,500. The member pled guilty to two counts of bribery and one count of acts affecting personal financial interests (conflict of interest). He was sentenced to two years in prison on each of the three counts. He was confined for six months and received supervised probation for two years. He was also fined $2,000 for each count.

1-6. Trade Secrets Act, 18 U.S.C. 1905.

a. This statute prohibits unauthorized release of any information relating to trade secrets or confidential business data by a Federal employee who receives such information in the course of his employment. Such information includes advance procurement information, prices, technical proposals, proprietary information, income information, etc. (A conviction for violating this statute requires mandatory removal from employment.)

b. Criminal prosecutions under the statute are not brought frequently because it is only a misdemeanor; instead, prosecutors frequently choose to prosecute under the theft statute (see Section 1-7).

1-7. Theft, Embezzlement, or Destruction of Public Money, Property, or Records, 18 U.S.C. 641.

a. This statute prohibits intentional and unauthorized taking, destruction, or use of Government property or records. It also prohibits receiving or concealing such property or records.

b. The following is a typical case involving the theft of Government records pertaining to an upcoming solicitation. A quality assurance representative (QAR) solicited a bribe from a major electronics contractor and promised to return inside information on an upcoming bid solicitation. The QAR delivered the bid information in exchange for a $2,500 bribe. The QAR suggested a second transaction in exchange for payment of $30,000. A second meeting was scheduled and the QAR was arrested after asking for the payment again. The QAR was indicted on two counts of theft of Government property and two counts of bribery. The QAR pled guilty on the bribery counts in exchange for full cooperation with the prosecutor. The cooperation resulted in the indictment of a co-conspirator who was charged with theft of Government property and conspiracy. The QAR received a five year sentence, and the second defendant is awaiting trial.

1-8. Anti-kickback Act, 41 U.S.C. 54.

a. This Act makes it a crime for any person to provide, attempt to provide or offer any fee, commission, compensation, gift or gratuity to a prime contractor or any higher tier subcontractor, or an employee of one of these, for the purpose of improperly obtaining favorable treatment under a Government Contract (See Chapter 10).

b. A buyer for a major DoD contractor entered into an agreement with certain machine shops which provided that they would pay him an amount equal to five percent of the value on all contracts which he awarded to them. The Government identified $14,000 in such kickbacks to him. He was convicted on one count each of tax fraud, mail fraud, and violations of the Anti-kickback Act, and was sentenced to six months in jail and a $14,000 fine.

1-9. Sherman Antitrust Act, 15 U.S.C. 1.

a. This Act prohibits competitors from entering into any agreement to restrain trade in interstate commerce, including price fixing, bid rigging, and bid rotation schemes. (See Chapter 4)

b. The following is typical of the type of antitrust violations that can occur in connection with DoD contracts. A contractor entered into an agreement with a number of its competitors to divide the available Army Corps of Engineers dredging contracts between them. The scheme was carried out through meetings during which the competitors decided who among them would submit the low bid on any given solicitation. The president of the company was convicted for violating the Sherman Antitrust Act in connection with his activities in this regard, and was sentenced to three years in prison. The company was fined $325,000 and ordered to pay civil damages of $250,000.

1-10. Conspiracy, 18 U.S.C. 371.

a. This statute prohibits any agreement between two or more persons to defraud the United States or to violate any Federal law or regulation when at least one act is taken in furtherance of the agreement.

b. The president and vice president of a subcontractor conspired to provide defective aluminum castings for use by prime contractors in manufacturing the Navy Phoenix missile, the Air Force mobile radio tower, and the cockpit display of the F-16. The officials agreed to and did make concerted efforts to ensure that the prime contractors and the Government were deceived regarding the defective nature of the parts. This involved instructing company employees who conducted random tests of the parts to test additional parts, whenever one or more of the originally selected parts failed, until the required number of parts passed the tests. In addition, the officials instructed shipping employees to conceal obviously defective parts by stacking conforming parts on top of them. The officials pled guilty to one count of conspiracy each after being charged with three counts of conspiracy and four counts of false claims. They were sentenced to imprisonment and required to pay substantial fines.

Chapter 2
Fraud in Government Contracts

2-1. Fraud in the identification of the Government's need for goods or services.

a. Normally, procurement actions are initiated after a formal or informal determination of general requirements. The requirements consist of a brief description of the types and amounts of goods and services needed together with a justification for the need. Fraud occurring during this stage of the procurement process may result in decisions to buy goods and services in excess of those actually needed or possibly not needed at all. As an example, need determinations for items that have scheduled disposal and reprocurement or reorder levels can be manipulated by including false information. In recent cases, this type of manipulation has resulted in excessive purchases of items such as drugs or auto parts. Further examination of the cases also disclosed indications of other criminal activity such as theft or diversion of the items.

b. With respect to fraud in defining requirements and stock levels, fraud indicators include:

(1) Requiring excessively high stock levels and inventory requirements to justify continued purchasing activity from certain contractors.

(2) Declaring items which are serviceable as excess or selling them as surplus while continuing to purchase similar items. (One documented scheme involved repurchasing the same items being sold as surplus on a recurring basis.)

(3) Purchasing items, services or research projects in response to aggressive marketing efforts (and possible favors, bribes or gratuities) by contractors rather than in response to valid requirements.

(4) Defining needs improperly in ways that can be met only by certain contractors.

(5) Failing to develop "second-sources" for items, spare parts, and services being continually purchased from a single source.

c. In addition to the fraud indicators listed above certain types of activity create a greater vulnerability to fraud and may enhance the potential for fraud to occur.

(1) Such a situation can occur when a needs assessment is not adequately or accurately developed or when an agency continually changes its mind about what it wants. This provides an opportunity for the unscrupulous to try and recoup losses for which they could not otherwise be compensated by falsely characterizing them as increased costs due to Government mandated changes or defective specifications.

(2) Another situation that increases the potential for fraud exists when the Government identifies the need to purchase proprietary, trade secret or other technical information without making reasonable attempts to determine if that information is already owned by the Government.

2-2. Fraud in the pre-solicitation phase.

a. Bid specifications and statements of work detailing the types and amounts of goods or services to be provided are prepared to assist in the selection process. They are intended to provide both potential bidders and the selecting officials with a firm basis for making and accepting bids. A well-written contract will have specifications, standards and statements of work which make it clear what the Government is entitled to. Sloppy or carelessly written specifications make it easy for a contractor to claim that it is entitled to more money for what the Government later defines as what it really wants. Sometimes, there is deliberate collusion between Government personnel and the contractor to write vague specifications. At other times there is an agreement to amend the contract to increase the price immediately after the award. One contractor actually developed a "cost enhancement plan," identifying all of the changes he would make in order to double the cost of the contract, before it was even signed.

b. Fraud indicators include:

(1) Placing any restrictions in the solicitation documents which would tend to restrict competition.

(a) Defining statements of work and specifications to fit the products or capabilities of a single contractor.

(b) Designing "prequalification" standards or specifications to exclude otherwise qualified contractors or their products.

(2) Unnecessary sole source/noncompetitive procurement justifications:

(a) Based on falsified statements.

(b) Which are signed by unauthorized officials.

(c) For which required levels of review were deliberately bypassed.

(3) Providing contractors any advice, advance information, or release of information concerning requirements or pending purchases on a preferential or selective basis. (Applies equally, whether committed by Government personnel, consultants or contractors.)

(4) Using statements of work, specifications, or sole source justifications developed by or in consultation with a contractor who will be permitted to compete in the procurement. (Institutional conflict of interest.)

(5) Permitting contractors (architect engineers, design engineers, other firms or individuals) that participated in the development of statements of work, specifications or the preparation of the invitations for bids or request for proposals, to bid on or be involved with the prime contract or any subcontracts.

(6) Splitting requirements so that small purchase procedures can be utilized or to avoid required levels of review or approval, e.g., to keep each within the contracting authority of a particular person or activity.

c. Bid specifications or statements of work which are not consistent with the need determination, if unexplained, may indicate an attempt to steer a procurement to a preferred contractor.

(1) Splitting requirements so contractors each get a "fair share" may increase the potential for collusive bidding. (See Chapter 4)

(2) Vague specifications may inhibit the reasonable comparison of bids or proposals and facilitate steering a contract to a favored contractor.

2-3. Fraud in the solicitation phase.

a. Contractors are offered an opportunity to submit bids or proposals for the provision of goods or services that will meet the Government's needs as set forth in specifications or statements of work. This process is intended generally to maximize the use of competition and to ensure that the Government obtains goods and services which meet its needs at the best possible price.

b. Fraud indicators in this phase include:

(1) Procurements which are restricted to exclude or hamper any qualified contractor.

(2) Limiting the time for the submission of bids, thereby creating a situation where only those with advance information have an adequate time to prepare bids or proposals.

(3) Technical or contracting personnel revealing information about the procurement to one contractor which is not revealed to all. Examples of the types of information found to have been illegally disclosed in prior cases include competitor's cost or pricing data; competitor's trade secrets or proprietary information; the results of Government technical evaluations; and Government estimates.

(4) Failure to amend a solicitation to include necessary changes or clarifications. (Telling one contractor of changes that can be made afterward.)

(5) Bid solicitation which is vague as to time, place, or other requirements for submitting acceptable bids.

(6) Failure to assure that a sufficient number of potential competitors are aware of the solicitation. (Use of obscure publications, publishing in holiday seasons, providing a vague or inadequate synopsis to Commerce Business Daily, etc.)

(7) Special assistance to any contractor in preparing its bid or proposal.

(8) "Referring" a contractor to a specific subcontractor, expert, or source of supply. (Express or implied that if you use the referred business, you will be more likely to get the contract.)

(9) Improper communication with contractors at trade or professional meetings or improper social contact with contractor representatives.

(10) Government personnel or their families acquiring stock or a financial interest in a contractor or subcontractor.

(11) Government personnel discussing possible employment with a contractor or subcontractor for themselves or a family member.

(12) Improper acceptance of a late bid.

(13) Falsification of documents or receipts to get a late bid accepted.

(14) Change in a bid after other bidders prices are known. This is sometimes done by mistakes deliberately "planted" in a bid.

(15) Withdrawal of the low bidder who later becomes a subcontractor to the higher bidder who gets the contract.

(16) Any indication of collusion or bid rigging between bidders. (See Chapter 4)

(17) False certifications by contractor.
(a) Small business certification.
(b) Minority business certification.
(c) Information provided to other agencies to support special status.
(d) Certification of independent price determination. (See Chapter 3)
(e) Buy American Act certification.

(18) Falsification of information concerning contractor qualifications, financial capability, facilities, ownership of equipment and supplies, qualifications of personnel and successful performance of previous jobs, etc.

2-4. Fraud in the award of the contract.

a. Government contracts are awarded based on the evaluation of contractor's bids and proposals. The evaluation process encompasses many factors, including price, responsiveness, and responsibility.

b. Fraud indicators during the evaluation and award process include:

(1) Deliberately discarding or "losing" the bid or proposal of an "outsider" who wants to participate. (May be part of a conspiracy between a Government official and a select contractor or group of contractors.)

(2) Improperly disqualifying the bid or proposal of a contractor.

(3) Disqualification of any qualified bidder.

(4) Accepting nonresponsive bids from preferred contractors.

(5) Seemingly unnecessary contacts with contractor personnel by persons other than the contracting officer during the solicitation, evaluation, and negotiation processes.

(6) Any unauthorized release of information to a contractor or other person.

(7) Any exercise of favoritism toward a particular contractor during the evaluation process.

(8) Using biased evaluation criteria or using biased individuals on the evaluation panel.

(9) Award of a contract to a contractor who is not the lowest responsible, responsive bidder.

(10) Allowing a low bidder to withdraw without justification.

(11) Failure to forfeit bid bonds when a contractor withdraws improperly.

(12) Material changes in the contract shortly after award.

(13) Awards made to contractors with an apparent history of poor performance.

(14) Awards made to the lowest of a very few bidders without readvertising considerations or without adequate publicity.

(15) Awards made that include items other than those contained in bid specifications.

(16) Awards made without adequate documentation of all preaward and postaward actions, including all understandings or oral agreements.

(17) Release of advance information concerning the award of a major contract. Such a release increases the potential illegal insider trading in the stock of both winning and losing contractors.

(18) Inadequate evaluation of contractor's present responsibility, including ignoring or failing to obtain information regarding a contractor's record of business ethics and integrity.

2-5. Fraud in the negotiation of a contract.

a. Negotiation occurs whenever the Government contracts without formal advertising. Negotiating permits bargaining and affords offerors an opportunity to revise their offers before award of a contract (Federal Acquisition Regulation (FAR) 15.102).

b. There are a number of abuses that can occur in the negotiation of a contract. The first stems from the assumption of many personnel that once it has been determined that negotiated procurement procedures can be used, that procurement on a sole source basis has also been justified. It is clear, however, that the FAR requires negotiated contracts to be awarded on a competitive basis unless less than full and open competition is authorized by an exception (FAR 6.301 and 15.105).

c. Fraud indicators involving negotiated contracts include:

(1) Back-dated or after-the-fact justifications in the contract file.

(2) Disclosure of information to one contractor which is not given to others, thereby giving that contractor an unfair competitive advantage.

(3) Improper release of information (e.g., prices, technical data, identity, or rank of competing proposals, proprietary data or trade secrets, or Government price estimates).

(4) Any indications that a contractor has provided false cost or pricing data. (See Chapter 3)

(5) Failure of Government personnel to obtain or rely on a Certificate of Current Cost or Pricing Data.

(6) Approval of less than full and open competition by an unauthorized person or for an improper reason (a reason other than one of the authorized exceptions to the requirement for full and open competition).

(7) Inadequate evaluation of contractor's present responsibility, including ignoring or failing to obtain information regarding a contractor's record of business ethics and integrity.

Chapter 3
Defective Pricing

3-1. Introduction: The Truth in Negotiations Act.

In the 1950s and early 1960s, the General Accounting Office (GAO) discovered numerous instances of "overpricing" by Government contractors on negotiated contracts. That is, costs quoted to the Government as those which would be incurred by the contractor in performing the work were found to be higher than the actual expenditures. At the time, however, the Government had no legal redress to reprice the contracts unless it could show fraud or deliberate misrepresentation by the contractor. In 1959, the DoD adopted regulations requiring the contractor to provide data reflecting the costs it would incur in performing the contract, called "cost and pricing data." However, GAO later found that the data were not being required or examined by the Military Departments. Consequently, in 1962, Congress passed the Truth in Negotiations Act. The Act required, among other things, submission of complete and current cost and pricing data to the Government during pre-award negotiations for all contracts valued at more than $100,000, and thereby ensured that the Government had the information necessary to determine the reasonableness of the contractor's bid price. The law also provided Government access to contractor records for purposes of assessing the costs of the contract. When a contractor's data submission is "defective," the Act permitted the Government to reduce contract payments by the amount attributable to the defective data.

3-2. Cost or Pricing Data Provision: 10 U.S.C. 2306(a).

a. The cost or pricing data provisions of the Truth in Negotiations Act are contained in 10 U.S.C. 2306 (a). That section provides, in part, that a prime or subcontractor *shall* be required to submit cost or pricing data, and *shall* be required to certify that, to the best of his knowledge and belief, the data submitted is accurate, complete, and current, under the following circumstances:

(1) Prior to the award of any contract other than one using sealed-bid procedures where the price is expected to exceed $100,000.

(2) Prior to pricing a change or modification of *any* contract if the price adjustment is expected to exceed $100,000, or any lesser amount if so prescribed by the agency head.

(3) Prior to the award of a subcontract when the subcontract price is expected to exceed $100,000 *and* the prime contractor and each higher tier subcontractor was required, under the contract, to submit cost or pricing data.

(4) Prior to pricing a change or modification to a subcontract covered by paragraph (3), above, for which the price adjustment is expected to exceed $100,000, or any lesser amount if so prescribed by the agency head.

The certifications are to be made to the Government contracting officer in the case of prime contractors and to the prime contractor in the case of subcontractors. The exceptions to certification of data include contracts or subcontracts for which the price is based on "adequate price competition," "established catalog or market prices of commercial items sold in substantial quantities to the general public," "prices set by law or regulation," or, in exceptional cases, when waived by the head of the agency. Conversely, despite the above-noted provisions, the head of any agency can require submission of data if it is determined necessary for the evaluation of the reasonableness of the price of the contract or subcontract.

b. The Act also requires that each contract that falls under the Truth in Negotiations provisions contain a clause for allowing for a price reduction based on the amount of any overpricing due to defective data submissions by either the prime or any subcontractors. The reduction would include profits and fees. The Act does state, however, that if the contractor can show the Government did not rely on the data submitted, that fact can be a defense in any price reduction action.

c. As part of the 1986 Defense Authorization Act (PL 99-661), a penalty in an amount equal to the overpayment can be assessed against a contractor who knowingly submits defective cost data. In any case of overpricing, the Government is entitled to recover interest on the amount of the overpayment for the period beginning on the date of the overpayment until repayment of the sum owed (10 U.S.C. 2306a(e) - See Chapter 11).

3-3. Regulatory Requirements: Federal Acquisition Regulation (FAR).

a. Section 15.801 of the FAR defines cost or pricing data and specifies the form and language for the certificate of current cost or pricing data. Price reduction rights of the Government are found in clauses at FAR 52.214-217, 52.215-22, and 52.215-23.

b. Cost or pricing data are submitted to the DoD on DD633, Contracting Pricing Proposal Cover Sheet. Along with that form, the contractor (or offeror, if no contract award has yet been made) is required to provide a breakdown of his costs, and submit supporting documentation such as invoices or firm price quotes from his suppliers. In addition, the contractor must submit the certification as soon as practicable after agreement is reached on the contract or modification price. The certification references FAR15.801 to specifically include vendor quotes as "cost or pricing data." A knowingly false or inaccurate certification by a contractor can lead to criminal prosecution for submission of false statements in violation of 18 U.S.C. 1001. A claim which is subsequently paid based on the false statement is a false claim which can be criminally prosecuted under 18 U.S.C. 287, and can result in civil liability under the civil False Claims Act (31 U.S.C. 3729). In addition, a false statement via certification can be penalized administratively under the Program Fraud Civil Remedies Act of 1986, Chapter 38 of Title 31, U.S.C. (See Chapter 11).

3-4. Defective Pricing Indicators.

a. In September 1983, the Director of the Defense Contract Audit Agency (DCAA) issued a memorandum to DCAA auditors stating guidance in the area of defective pricing where certain conditions exist which might indicate fraud. Auditors were instructed that when indications of fraud are found, the case will be referred to the proper investigative agency. Some of the most significant indicators include:

(1) Indications of falsification or alteration of supporting data.

(2) Failure to update cost or pricing data even though it is known that past activity showed that costs or prices have decreased.

(3) Failure to make complete disclosure of data known to responsible contractor personnel.

(4) Distortion of the overhead accounts or base line information by transferring changes or accounts that have a material impact on Government contracts.

(5) Failure to correct known system deficiencies which lead to defective pricing.

(6) Protracted delay in release of data to the Government to preclude possible price reductions.

(7) Repeated denial by the responsible contractor employees of the existence of historical records that are subsequently found.

b. As a result of increased emphasis on detection and referral of defective pricing cases, the Government, in 1986, prosecuted a major contractor and exacted the largest fraud penalty in DoD history. In July 1986, a Federal grand jury returned a 325 count indictment charging a major Defense contractor and two corporate officers, with engaging in a scheme to defraud the DoD of approximately $6,300,000 in connection with the bidding and award of 45 prime and subcontracts between 1975 and 1984. The charges, all relating to defective pricing, included concealing and covering up material facts, racketeering, mail fraud, conspiracy, and false statements. The indictment charged that the defendants submitted false and fraudulent cost and pricing data, representing to the DoD that the contractor would be paying more for material than the company would in fact pay. The inflated submissions became known as "chicken fat" among the conspirators and were accomplished by various means, including the use of blank quotation forms obtained from material vendors, and obtaining quotations at book or catalog prices which were higher than the actual costs known to the contractor. One defendant was also charged with failing to disclose to the Government the rebates the company received from vendors on purchases, and that he also lied to an auditor from the DCAA. The contractor agreed to plead guilty to all counts set forth in the indictment and to pay approximately $15 million to the Government in criminal and civil penalties and restitution. The individual defendants likewise pled guilty and were sentenced to imprisonment (suspended in one case), five years probation, and fines of $10,000 and $10,500.

c. The fraud indicators should be used by contracting officers as well as auditors and investigators. Particular note should be made of "intent" indicators in defective pricing cases. These are critical to a determination of whether a criminal act occurred. The deliberate concealment or misrepresentation of a single significant cost element could constitute a prosecutable crime.

Chapter 4
Antitrust Violations: Collusive Bidding and Price Fixing

4-1. Introduction.

a. Collusive bidding, price fixing, or bid rigging are commonly used interchangeable terms that describe many forms of illegal anticompetitive activity. The common thread throughout all of the anticompetitive activities is that they involve any agreements or informal arrangements among independent competitors which limit competition. Schemes that allocate contracts and limit competition can take many forms and are only limited by the imagination of the parties. Common schemes, which will be discussed in more detail later, include bid suppression or limiting, complementary bidding, bid rotation, and market division.

b. The essential elements of a criminal antitrust offense are (1) the formulation of a contract, combination, agreement, or conspiracy, and (2) the restraint of trade or commerce among the several states. With regard to the first element, the agreement must be between two or more real competitors. The evidence must establish that the competitors had a common plan, understanding, arrangement, or agreement to fix or stabilize prices, allocate customers, or allocate territories or markets. In regard to the second element, to satisfy the interstate commerce element of the offense, the evidence must establish that the conspiracy involved goods or funds traveling in the flow of interstate commerce, e.g., materials shipped by common carrier interstate, or affected interstate commerce, e.g., Federal funds involved in the procurement. There are certain agreements or business practices that by statute are *per se* violations. These agreements or practices, because of their previous effect on competition and lack of any redeeming virtue, are conclusively presumed to be unreasonable and thus illegal. These types of agreements among competitors which would violate the law include, but are not limited to, the following:

(1) Agreements to adhere to published price lists.

(2) Agreements to raise prices by a specified increment.

(3) Agreements to establish, adhere to, or eliminate discounts.

(4) Agreements not to advertise prices.

(5) Agreements to maintain specified price differentials based on quantity, type, or size of product.

c. The Antitrust Division, Department of Justice (DOJ), has primary prosecutive jurisdiction on all Federal antitrust violations. Responsible antitrust attorneys are located at the seven field office locations: Atlanta, Chicago, Cleveland, Dallas, Philadelphia, New York City, and San Francisco. The Antitrust Division has successfully prosecuted defendants who have fixed prices or rigged bids in conjunction with the award of contracts for the following types of commodities and services widely used by DoD: asphalt paving; electrical equipment; shipment of household goods; wholesale produce; retail gasoline; waste disposal; bread; milk; dredging; roofing; lumber; cigarettes; coal; and building construction. Prosecution of Sherman Antitrust Act offenses present in Defense procurement is a high priority within the DOJ Antitrust Division.

4-2. Impact on the procurement process.

a. One of the cornerstones of the Federal procurement system is the requirement that Government contracts should be awarded, to the greatest extent possible, on the basis of free and open competition. The preference for competition in the procurement of goods or services on

Appendix T

behalf of the United States was first set by statute in 1890. That preference still remains and has been specifically expressed in statutes concerning DoD purchases and contracts. Title 10, U.S. Code, Section 2304(a), sets forth a specific requirement that, "Purchase of and contracts for property and services covered by this chapter shall be made by formal advertising, and shall be awarded on a competitive bid basis to the lowest responsible bidder, in all cases in which the use of such method is feasible and practicable under existing conditions and circumstances." In addition, 10 U.S.C 2304(g) requires that, except in certain limited circumstances, competition must also be obtained in negotiated procurements. The requirements are also contained in DoD policy regarding competition as outlined in FAR 14.103.

b. Further evidence of the importance of competition in the DoD procurement process is provided by the requirement for "Certification of Independent Price Determination," FAR 3.103-1. The regulation requires contractors to certify that they have not engaged in certain specific activities which constitute what can generally be described as collusive bidding or price fixing.

c. It should be obvious that collusive bidding or price fixing among competitors completely undermines the Government efforts to use competitive purchasing and contracting methods. The harm in this situation, however, is not limited to the mere circumvention of the important Government policies that encourage free and open competition. In fact, collusive bidding and price fixing result in increased costs, destroy public confidence in the country's economy, and undermine our system of free enterprise. To illustrate the impact of the activities on DoD procurement, consider just a few recent cases:

(1) A 1983 prosecution in the Southeastern United States resulted in the conviction and incarceration of an electrical subcontractor. Plea negotiations culminated with the defendant pleading guilty to a criminal information charging a violation of 15 U.S.C. 1 (Sherman Antitrust Act). The subcontractor was sentenced to a six and one-half month prison term for his part in a conspiracy to "...fix, raise, and maintain electrical subcontract work on a $455,049 Army Corps of Engineers contract...."

(2) In 1983, two household goods moving and storage companies and their respective presidents, entered guilty pleas to charges of price fixing in a Federal district court in South Carolina. The contractors, serving the Army base at FortJackson, South Carolina, were indicted for "...conspiring to fix, raise, maintain, and establish the rates charged for providing non-temporary storage of household goods owned by military personnel...." The two companies received respective fines of $100,000 and $25,000, and were debarred from bidding on Government contracts. The individual defendants were each fined $25,000 and $5,000, and personally debarred.

(3) A 1985 prosecution in the Southeastern United States yielded the first of several significant convictions of Army Corps of Engineers dredging contractors for bid rigging. Following a guilty plea to a criminal information alleging a conspiracy to rig bids on a $1.4 million contract, a Virginia dredging company and its president received substantial sentences in a Federal district court. The company was ordered to pay a criminal fine of $200,000. The president received a two year suspended sentence and was ordered to pay a $50,000 fine. A separate administrative/civil settlement with the Army Corps of Engineers and the DOJ resulted in the payment of a $235,000 civil fine.

d. It has been demonstrated that collusive bidding and price fixing schemes cause the DoD to pay much more for goods or services than it would have if true competition existed. Even though this is the case, the bids may appear to be fair and reasonable because the Government estimate may be too high. The appearance of reasonable prices should therefore not mistakenly be construed as proof that collusive bidding and price fixing are not occurring or that a violation of law does not exist because the harm in terms of monetary loss is not apparent. In fact, when such conduct is criminally prosecuted, the defendants are prohibited from introducing any evidence to justify their conduct or to demonstrate its reasonableness.

4-3. Indicators of collusive bidding and price fixing.

a. The list of indicators below is intended to facilitate recognition of those situations which may involve collusive bidding or price fixing. In and of themselves these indicators will not prove that illegal anticompetitive activity is occurring. They are, however, sufficient to warrant referral to appropriate authorities for investigation. Use of indicators such as these to identify possible anticompetitive activity is important because schemes to restrict competition are by their very nature secret and their exact nature is not readily visible.

b. Practices or events that may evidence collusive bidding or price fixing are:

(1) Bidders who are qualified and capable of performing but who fail to bid, with no apparent reason. A situation where fewer competitors than normal submit bids typifies this situation. (This could indicate a deliberate scheme to withhold bids.)

(2) Certain contractors always bid against each other or, conversely, certain contractors do not bid against one another.

(3) The successful bidder repeatedly subcontracts work to companies that submitted higher bids or to companies that picked up bid packages and could have bid as prime contractors but did not.

(4) Different groups of contractors appear to specialize in Federal, state, or local jobs exclusively. (This might indicate a market division by class of customer.)

(5) There is an apparent pattern of low bids regularly recurring, such as corporation "x" always being the low bidder in a certain geographical area or in a fixed rotation with other bidders.

(6) Failure of original bidders to rebid, or an identical ranking of the same bidders upon rebidding, when original bids were rejected as being too far over the Government estimate.

(7) A certain company appears to be bidding substantially higher on some bids than on other bids with no logical cost difference to account for the increase, i.e., a local company is bidding higher prices for an item to be delivered locally than for delivery to points farther away.

(8) Bidders that ship their product a short distance bid more than those who must incur greater expense by shipping their product long distances.

(9) Identical bid amounts on a contract line item by two or more contractors. Some instances of identical line item bids are explainable, as suppliers often quote the same prices to several bidders. But a large number of identical bids on any service-related item should be viewed critically.

(10) Bidders frequently change prices at about the same time and to the same extent.

(11) Joint venture bids where either contractor could have bid individually as a prime. (Both had technical capability and production capacity.)

(12) Any incidents suggesting direct collusion among competitors, such as the appearance of identical calculation or spelling errors in two or more competi-

tive bids, or the submission by one firm of bids for other firms.

(13) Competitors regularly socialize or appear to hold meetings, or otherwise get together in the vicinity of procurement offices shortly before bid filing deadlines.

(14) Assertions by employees, former employees, or competitors that an agreement to fix bids and prices or otherwise restrain trade exists.

(15) Bid prices appear to drop whenever a new or infrequent bidder submits a bid.

(16) Competitors exchange any form of price information among themselves. This may result from the existence of an "industry price list" or "price agreement" to which contractors refer in formulating their bids, or it may take other subtler forms such as discussions of the "right price."

(17) Any reference by bidders to "association price schedules," "industry price schedules," "industry suggested prices," "industry-wide prices," or "market-wide prices."

(18) A bidder's justification for a bid price or terms, offered because they follow the industry or industry leader's pricing or terms, may include a reference to following a named competitors pricing or terms.

(19) Any statements by a representative of a contractor that his company "does not sell in a particular area" or that "only a particular firm sells in that area."

(20) Statements by a bidder that it is not their turn to receive a job or, conversely, that it is another bidders' turn.

4-4. Collusive bidding and price fixing examples.

Common collusive bidding and price fixing schemes that DoD personnel may be able to recognize are discussed below. The schemes relate to one another and overlap. Frequently, an agreement by competitors to rig bids will involve more than one of the schemes.

a. Bid suppression or limiting. In this type of scheme, one or more competitors agree with at least one other competitor to refrain from bidding or agrees to withdraw a previously submitted bid so that another competitor's bid will be accepted. Other forms of this activity involve agreements by competitors to fabricate bid protests or to coerce suppliers and subcontractors not to deal with nonconspirators who submit bids.

b. Complementary bidding. Complementary bidding (also known as "protective" or "shadow" bidding) occurs when competitors submit token bids that are too high to be accepted (or if competitive in price, then on special terms that will not be acceptable). Such bids are not intended to secure the buyer's acceptance, but are merely designed to give the appearance of genuine bidding.

c. Bid rotation. In bid rotation, all vendors participating in the scheme submit bids, but by agreement take turns being the low bidder. In its most basic form, bid rotation will consist of a cyclical pattern for submitting the low bid on certain contracts. The rotation may not be as obvious as might be expected if it is coupled with a scheme for awarding subcontracts to losing bidders, to take turns according to the size of the contract, or one of the other market division schemes explained below.

d. Market division. Market division schemes are agreements to refrain from competing in a designated portion of a market. Division of a market for this purpose may be accomplished based on the customer or geographic area involved. The result of such a division is that competing firms will not bid or will submit only complementary bids when a solicitation for bids is made by a customer or in an area not assigned to them.

Chapter 5
Cost Mischarging

5-1. Introduction.

a. One of the most common of abuses found in the procurement system is cost mischarging. This is due in large part to the fact that most high-dollar Government research and development and production contracts are awarded as cost type contracts. Because such contracts are paid on the basis of incurred costs, the contractor may increase profits by mischarging. It is important to recognize that the impact of such mischarging is almost always far greater than the basic costs which were falsified. For example, a single hour of labor which is mischarged may result in payments of as much as three times the labor hour rate due to indirect cost allowances which are added based on that hour.

b. Mischarging can occur in a number of situations, with a variety of results. It can involve charging labor hours from one contract to another, charging at higher than allowed rates, charging to indirect accounts those charges which should be direct, or viceversa, as well as other schemes. In all cases, mischarging is a serious matter. Even when unintentional or without a fraudulent motive, it undermines confidence in the contractor's accounting and control systems and should raise questions as to the validity of other submissions.

c. The issue of whether a mischarge was a "mistake" or a crime usually turns on the intent of the maker. Investigators should examine the issue of intent. Because intentional false submissions themselves are criminal, prosecutors may pursue those cases even though no substantial loss occurs, particularly where the contractor has actively sought to conceal costs. Additionally, to overlook situations such as mischarging from one Government contract to another on the theory that it is merely a case of "robbing Peter to pay Paul" is to ignore the serious consequences of such a scheme. Because cost estimates for future procurements rely in large part on accurate historical cost figures from similar work, the estimates for later work will be tainted by false accounting. Further, moving costs from a Government job which is tight on budget to one which is "fat" could prevent an overrun in the case of the former and thus make the contractor appear more efficient than he actually is. This could result in awarding incentive fees or follow-on contracts which would not be appropriate were the true costs known.

d. Under cost type contracts, the Government reimburses the contractor's costs which are allowable, allocable to the contract, and reasonable. Those types of contracts include cost plus fixed fee, cost plus incentive fee, cost plus award fee, cost reimbursable, and cost sharing contracts. In addition, contract changes and equitable adjustments to contracts are reimbursed on the basis of incurred costs even on fixed price contracts. Cost mischarging occurs whenever the contractor charges the Government for costs which are not allowable, not reasonable, or which cannot be directly or indirectly allocated to the contract.

5-2. Allowable Costs.

a. The FAR 31-205 identifies costs which are allowable and those which cannot be charged to Government contracts. Such costs may be direct costs, such as labor and materials used on one contract and no other, or indirect costs, which contribute to a number of different contracts. Indirect costs are placed in "cost pools" which are then allocated to contracts on some agreed basis (such as total cost or

Appendix T

labor hours). Title 10, U.S.C., Section 2324, specifically identifies certain unallowable costs for covered DoD contracts and requires the Secretary of Defense to prescribe regulations to clarify the allowability for certain other costs. The statute also requires that a proposal for settlement of indirect costs applicable to a covered contract include a certification by a contractor official that, to the best of his knowledge, all indirect costs submitted are allowable.

b. Unallowable costs include:

(1) Advertising costs (except to obtain workers or scarce materials for a contract, or to sell surplus or byproduct materials).

(2) Bid and proposal costs in excess of a set limit.

(3) Stock options and some forms of deferred compensation.

(4) Contingencies.

(5) Contributions and donations.

(6) Entertainment costs.

(7) Costs of idle facilities except in limited circumstances.

(8) Interest.

(9) Losses on other contracts.

(10) Long-term leases of property or equipment and leases from related parties are limited to the costs of ownership.

(11) Independent research and development costs beyond set limits.

(12) Legal costs related to a contractor's defense of any civil or criminal fraud proceeding or similar proceeding (including false certifications) brought by the Government when the contractor is found liable or has pled nolocontendre.

(13) Payments of fines and penalties resulting from violations of, or failure to comply with, Federal, state, local, or foreign laws and regulations, except in cases where authorized in writing by the contracting officer or by adherence to contract specifications.

(14) Costs incurred to influence (directly or indirectly) legislative action on any matter pending before Congress or a state legislature.

(15) Costs of membership in any social, dining, or country club or organization.

(16) Costs of alcoholic beverages.

(17) Costs of promotional items and memorabilia, including models, gifts, and souvenirs.

(18) Costs for travel by commercial aircraft which exceed the amount of the standard commercial fare.

5-3. Accounting Mischarges.

a. The mischarging most frequenty encountered by DCAA auditors is called an accounting mischarge. A fraudulent accounting mischarge involves knowingly charging unallowable costs to the Government, concealing or misrepresenting them as allowable costs, or hiding them in accounts (such as office supplies) which are not audited closely. Another common fraud variation involves intentionally charging types of costs which have reached their limits (such as bid and proposal costs or independent research and development costs) to other cost categories.

5-4. Material Cost Mischarges.

a. Material is physical inventory and component deliverables. Material includes raw material, purchased parts, as well as subcontractor and intercompany transfers. Like labor, material costs are sometimes mischarged, both as to their reasonableness and allocability. Numerous cases have been discovered where Government-owned material was used on a similar commercial contract but the material accountability records showed that the material was used on a Government contract. There have also been cases where Government-owned materials were stolen and the thefts were concealed by showing the materials as being issued to and used on Government contracts.

b. Mischarges of materials are usually confined to situations involving raw material or interchangeable parts. Specialized material, such as a certain type gyroscope, cannot be easily mischarged and go undetected due to its character. For example, a gyroscope for a C-130 aircraft just will not fit on a KC-135 aircraft and would be easily detected as an improper billing. An excellent guide to detecting material mischarges, *Handbook on Fraud Indicators: Material*, was published in July 1986 by the Office of the Inspector General, DoD, and is available through the Assistant Inspector General for Audit Policy and Oversight.

5-5. Labor Mischarges.

a. Labor costs are more susceptible to mischarging than material costs because employees' labor can be readily shifted to any contract with the stroke of a pen on their time cards. The only absolute way to assure that labor costs are charged to the correct contract is to observe the actual work of each employee to determine which contract he is working on and then determine from the accounting records that the employee's cost is charged to the proper contract.

b. Contractors have devised a number of ways to mischarge labor costs. As in the case of material cost fraud vulnerability, the Assistant Inspector General for Audit Policy and Oversight has available a guide on the subject, titled, *Handbook on Labor Fraud Indicators*, dated August 1985. Labor mischarging schemes range from very crude to very sophisticated. Some of the common methods of mischarging are set forth below:

(1) *Transfer of Labor Cost.* This mischarge is usually made after the contractor realizes that he has suffered a loss on a fixed priced contract. To eliminate the loss, a journal entry is made to remove the labor cost from the fixed priced contract and put it on the cost type contract. This type of mischarge is very easy to detect but is difficult to prove. The contractor will contend that the labor charges to the fixed price contract were in error and the journal entry, transferring the cost to the cost type contract, was made to correct that error. Frequently the dollar amount of the transfer is estimated.

(2) *Time and Charges Do Not Agree with Contractor Billing to the Government.*

(a) This accounting mischarge method is probably the easiest to detect and prove. It is a simple matter of totaling the time and hours expended on the cost type contract and comparing them to the hours billed. For example, the time cards may show that 1,000 hours have been expended on the cost type contract when, in fact, the contractor has billed the Government for 2,000 hours of labor. The difference is obvious and the accounting records (time cards) will not support the billings.

(b) Contractor labor billings to the Government are normally supported by two accounting records. The source record is the individual employee time card. The other record is the labor distribution. The labor distribution is usually a computer printout that summarizes by contract the individual time card entries. The contractor will commonly use the labor distribution to support his Government billings. It is relatively easy to falsify a labor distribution but it is necessary to corrupt the entire work force to falsify the time cards. Hence, the individual time cards should be totaled and reconciled to the labor distribution at least on a test basis.

(3) *Original Time Cards are Destroyed or Hidden and New Time Cards are Prepared for the Auditor's Benefit.* This is a very successful method of concealing a labor mischarge. Mischarges of this nature are very difficult to detect. They are detected when:

(a) The hidden time cards are inadvertently given to the auditor.

(b) All of the old time cards are not destroyed and the auditor finds them.

(c) Employee signatures on the time cards are carbon copies because the employee's original signature has been traced.

(d) Time card entries are compared to time records maintained by individual employees (copies of time cards, logs, etc.).

(4) *Changes are Made to Individual Time Cards.* A frequent labor fraud encountered by the DCAA auditor involves improper changes to the original contract charge numbers on employee time cards. Some of the charges are so well done that it is difficult to tell that a change has been made. In one instance, the change was made so expertly that the auditor could not tell that a change had been made just from looking at the time sheet. The auditor detected the change by running his finger across the entry and noticed a difference in the "feel." Under magnification, the "white out" material used to cover the original entry could be seen. The auditors used a "light box" to determine what the original charge had been, i.e., by placing a light underneath the time sheet the auditor could read through the "white out" to determine the original charge. Just because changes are made on time cards, it does not necessarily mean that a fraud is being perpetrated. Many times innocent errors are made and corrected. In determining the possibility of fraudulent activity, one should:

(a) Determine the magnitude of the changes. If only a few changes have been made then, in all probability, the changes were made to correct errors. However, if a significant percentage of the charges have been changed, the probability of fraudulent activity is increased.

(b) A comparison of the original charge number to the revised charge number should be made. If the net effect of the changes is to increase the charges to cost reimbursable contracts, the likelihood of fraud is further increased.

(c) Make a review of the sequence of events. For example, in one case the tail number of the aircraft that the employee worked on was posted to the time card in addition to the contract charge number. The following discrepancies were noted:

1. The original contract charge number corresponded to the contract for which work was to be accomplished on a specified aircraft. The changed contract charge number was for work on another contract for an entirely different type of aircraft, i.e., the original charge was to the C-130 aircraft and the tail number was a C-130 aircraft, but the new charge was made to the KC-135 aircraft.

2. Based on the changed charge numbers, a ridiculous number of employees were working on the same aircraft during the same labor shift.

(d) Identify the employee who made the changes, find out why the changes were made and what was the employee's source of information for the changed charge number.

(5) *Time Card Charges are Made by Supervisors.* One should be especially skeptical of timekeeping systems where time card labor charges are posted by supervisors. Management can exert pressure and influence on supervisors to accomplish certain goals. The pressure may influence the supervisor to falsify time charges in order to keep higher level management satisfied with his performance. An even more serious situation occurs when senior level management requires the supervisor to record time charges in a manner most profitable to the company. Management might even go so far as to provide supervisors with "budgets" of how to charge the time for each job. However, if individual employees post their time cards it would be difficult to corrupt the entire work force.

(6) *Impact of labor mischarges.* When a labor cost is mischarged, so is the associated overhead and general and administrative (G&A) expenses. Overhead costs are allocated to labor costs based on an overhead rate or percentage. Overhead costs usually exceed 100 percent of the labor cost. Therefore, any mischarging on labor rates also impacts on overhead charges, which ultimately results in a greater than double loss to the Government. The same is true for G&A rates. In computing the dollar amount of the fraud, one must add the overhead and G&A cost because applied overhead and G&A will probably be more than the labor cost involved.

5-6. Cost Mischarging Examples.

a. An overhead audit conducted by DCAA disclosed substantial cost mischarging by a DoD accoustical research contractor. The mischarging principally involved shifting costs on both commercial and DoD contracts to the overhead category and then allocating the overhead to those contracts (principally DoD) which provided the best overhead rate. A thorough review of the audit work papers disclosed numerous examples of time sheets which had been altered by whiteouts. As a result of the audit and investigation, two senior company vice presidents were found guilty of violations of the Federal conspiracy statute and making false statements. Furthermore, the company was fined $706,000 and ordered to make restitution of approximately $2 million; the two senior vice presidents were fined $20,000 each and given six month sentences.

b. A major DoD contractor was found to have improperly shifted individual research and development costs (IR&D) to cost type contracts. The corporation was convicted and fined $50,000. An accompanying civil and administrative settlement resulted in the company paying an additional $720,000 to DoD. The corporation also agreed to major revisions in corporate contracting practices and to increased DoD audit access to contractor records. Additionally, $300,000 in legal costs were disallowed.

c. A company contracted by the Army to rewrite military technical manuals was convicted, as well as its president and vice president, of conspiracy to defraud and of submitting false statements after a seven-day jury trial which found the defendants had mischarged labor costs. The charges stemmed from a scheme where the company, whose contract with the Army was on a time and material basis of cost reimbursement, charged over $140,000 of commercial expenses against the DoD contract. The corporation was fined, and the officers were fined and sentenced to work-release and probation terms.

d. Based on information initially supplied by a Defense Logistics Agency employee who became suspicious of a price quote submitted by an Air Force parts supplier, a contractor was convicted of material mischarging and paid fines and recoveries amounting to $3 million. The contractor had altered documents to reflect greatly inflated costs of products of which it was then able to further inflate by adding on a percentage-of-cost overhead rate.

**Chapter 6
Product Substitution**

6-1. Introduction.

a. The term product substitution generally refers to attempts by contractors to deliver to the Government goods or services which do not conform to contract requirements, without informing the Government of the deficiency, while seeking reimbursement based on alleged delivery of conforming products or services.

Appendix T

It is the policy of the DoD that goods and services acquired must conform to the quality and quantity required in the contract. Goods or services which do not conform in all respects to contractual requirements are to be rejected. It is essential that this policy be strictly adhered to, as failure to do so can result in providing substandard, untested, and possibly defective material to our Armed Forces. Defective material can have a serious and detrimental impact on the safety of DoD personnel, as well as the accomplishment of important missions.

b. When a contract calls for delivery of an item produced by the original equipment manufacturer (OEM), then the contractor must furnish that item. The rule excludes even items that may be identical in all respects but are not produced by the OEM. If the contract requires the delivery of end products produced in the United States, then the contractor is obligated to supply items manufactured in the United States. This is required even though comparable or identical items are available from foreign sources at lower costs to the contractor. Further, if the contract requires that certain tests be conducted to ensure that an item is suitable for its intended use and can be relied upon to perform as expected, those tests must be conducted. The contractor's ability to produce an item that will perform within acceptable limits regardless of whether actually tested is not relevant.

c. Contractors frequently argue that substituted goods or services delivered to the Government were "just as good" as what was contracted for, even if specifications are not met, and that, therefore, no harm is done to the Government. There are several important fallacies to be noted when considering this argument. First and foremost, the substitute is usually not as good as what was contracted for. In cases of product substitution investigated to date, the substitute is usually one of inferior quality or the workmanship is extremely poor because it was done by lesser qualified and cheaper labor. Secondly, while the immediate harm that the substitute might cause or may have, in fact, caused is sometimes difficult to determine, its introduction into Defense supply channels undermines the reliability of the entire supply system. If, for example, a microchip were in use in larger components which failed, the cause of the failure might not be directly traceable to the inferior quality of the microchip. Third, even if the item is useable, there is harm to the integrity of the competitive procurement system which is based on all competitors offering to furnish the item precisely described in specifications.

6–2. Fraud potential.

a. There are a wide variety of fraudulent schemes that may involve product substitution. Many of the recent product substitution fraud allegations involve consumable or off-the-shelf items. Defense employees should be aware of similar problems that have arisen in component parts and materials used in weapon systems, ships, aircraft, and vehicles. Cases have included:

(1) The provision of inferior quality raw materials;

(2) Materials that have not been tested as required by the contract specifications;

(3) Providing foreign made products where domestic products were required; and

(4) Providing untrained workers when skilled technicians were required.

b. Product substitution cases sometimes involve Government employees. For example, gratuities and bribes have been paid to Government inspection personnel to accept items which do not conform to contract requirements.

c. The potential for a product substitution case is greatest where DoD relies on contractor integrity to ensure that the Government gets what it has paid for. For example, fast pay procedures apply to small purchases. The Government pays contractors for goods based on certification of shipment. Quality assurance is frequently limited in scope and is performed after payment has been made. Thus, small purchases are particularly susceptible to unscrupulous contractors.

d. In large dollar value procurements, Government quality personnel often rely on testing performed by the contractor. Falsification of the test documents may conceal the fact that a piece of equipment has not passed all the tests required by contract or has not been tested at all. False entries may also conceal the substitution of inferior or substandard materials in a product. When Government personnel actually witness or perform tests themselves, there is always the possibility that what they are seeing is a specifically prepared sample not representative of the contractor's actual production.

e. In August 1986, the OIG, DoD, issued a research report on Unauthorized Quality Assurance Practices by contractors. The project was conducted to identify possible systemic weaknesses in DoD quality assurance practices. The report determined Government reliance on contractor falsified documentation, inadequate Government inspection and testing, and the lack of adequate control over end items were three conditions conducive to unauthorized quality assurance practices by contractors. The report also concluded that in 22 of 24 DoD investigation cases studied, the contractors intentionally and knowingly delivered or planned to deliver products that were not in conformance with contract requirements. Related analysis in the report disclosed predominant issues that pertained to quality assurance practices. Some of the indicators of and conditions conducive to unauthorized quality assurance practices included a history of poor performance by the contractor; negative preaward survey; awards to unusually low bidders; misuse of fast pay contracts; Government quality assurance representatives reliance on contractor falsified documentation; and insufficient Government quality assurance practices.

f. Finally, the Buy American Act (41 U.S.C. 10) generally prohibits the use of foreign manufactured articles, materials, or supplies in Government contracts.

6–3. Product substitution examples.

a. A DoD contractor provided false certifications of quality testing for coating on aluminum troop backpack frames. The backpacks are intended for use by military ground troops, and the anodized coating on frames are dyed light fast olive drab to avoid enemy detection. Inferior anodizing could endanger the lives of U.S. military personnel through the exposure of reflective metal. Investigation disclosed that no testing was performed and a sample of completed units failed at a rate of 70 percent. The owner of the company, who entered a plea of guilty to false statements, was sentenced to 3 years supervised probation, fined $6,000, and required to perform 500 hours of community service.

b. A complainant alleged that a product manufacturer of parts for Army howitzers was submitting defective items which, if installed, could produce significant safety hazards. An investigation revealed that the testing certificates being submitted by the contractor were false. The investigation kept the defective parts from being installed in Army howitzers and kept howitzers from being sold under the Foreign Military Sales program. The corporate president pled guilty to making false statements to the U.S. Government and was sentenced to one year supervised probation; the company and its president have also been debarred from contracting with the Government.

c. An investigation was conducted concerning a company that had a Navy contract to install fire-retardant decorative plastic laminate throughout the enlisted dining area of a Navy ship. The contract required the company to provide certification that the laminate was a fire-retardant material. When the company installed laminate that was not fire retardant, it seriously jeopardized the lives of the ship's crew. The investigation determined and a Federal grand jury charged that the company substituted and installed laminate that was not fire retardant and that an officer and an employee of the company conspired to falsify a certification to the Navy that the material was fire retardant. As a result of the false claims, the company fraudulently received over $25,000. Both individuals pled guilty to making false statements and claims against the Government. The president was ordered to pay restitution, and the vice president was fined $1,000.

d. A DoD investigation established that a contractor had substituted inferior check valves with the potential to damage aircraft and jeopardize personnel safety. The contractor was asked to furnish specified valves manufactured by a particular company. The scheme was discovered when the contractor billed the Government for a progress payment and billed for more valves than had been delivered. A later inspection of the delivered valves found the substitute items. The president of the company was convicted of mail fraud and submitting false statements.

e. A DoD contractor devised a scheme to deliver nonconforming and defective rifle barrels for M-14 and M-21 weapons to the DoD. Under the contract, 1,800 rifle barrels were to be provided to the Department at a price of about $245,000. The DoD inspectors were shown acceptable rifle barrels during quality assurance checks. Then the contractor substituted nonconforming rifle barrels and shipped them to DoD depots. The contractor also allegedly violated contract provisions by selling rifle barrels made for the DoD to the general public. Some of the defective barrels exploded during user tests and could have caused serious injury. A joint investigation by the Army, DoD, and Department of Justice was conducted. The president and vice president were indicted on charges of racketeering, mail fraud, obstruction of justice, and perjury. The company has been fined $400,000 and suspended from receiving future contracts.

f. Three company officials pled guilty to charges of conspiracy and filing false statements on a contract after installing pipe flanges aboard nuclear submarines without making proper tests and certifications. The defective flanges, which have a critical application aboard submarines, have been removed. The corporate president and vice president were sentenced to two years imprisonment and fined $10,000 each, and a third corporate official was sentenced to six months imprisonment and ordered to perform 500 hours community service. The corporation was debarred.

g. An investigation resulted in guilty pleas by a DoD contractor to charges of submitting false claims on Government contracts to supply aircraft parts. The company was found to have either provided nonconforming parts or to have short shipped ordered parts. The company, its owner, and two other companies that participated in the fraud, in addition to other criminal sanctions and fines, including a prison term, were debarred from receiving future Government contracts.

h. A contractor provided defective foreign-made ammunition under a Foreign Military Sales contract. The contract required 15 million rounds of 5.56mm ammunition. The first shipment of approximately 2 million rounds was according to contract specifications. However, when subsequent ammunition received from the contractor caused rifles to misfire and jam, an investigation was initiated. It was determined that the defective ammunition was produced in a foreign country, and bribery payoffs were made to facilitate acceptance of the defective product. The corporate president, vice president, and a foreign national businessman who facilitated obtaining the contracts, all pled guilty to conspiracy to defraud the U.S. Government. The president and vice president were sentenced to two and three year sentences, respectively, and the foreign national businessman was sentenced to one year confinement and fined $10,000. The corporation has been recommended for debarment.

Chapter 7
Progress Payment Fraud

7-1. Introduction.

a. Progress payments are payments made as work progresses under a contract, based on the costs incurred, the percentage of work accomplished, or the attainment of a particular stage of completion. They do not include payments for partial deliveries accepted by the Government.

b. Fraud in progress payments occurs when a contractor submits a progress payment request based on falsified direct labor charges, on material costs for items not actually purchased, or on falsified certification of a stage of completion attained/work accomplished.

c. When a DoD contract contains one of the contract clauses in FAR 52.232.16, a contractor may submit monthly progress payment requests and is entitled to receive a contractually specified percentage of its total costs.

d. Requests for progress payments are made on Standard Form 1443 (FAR 53.301-1443). On the form, the contractor identifies its contract costs and certifies that the statement of costs has been prepared from the contractor's books and records and is correct. In addition, the contractor also makes a certification concerning encumbrances against the materials acquired for the contract.

e. The purpose of progress payments is to provide contractors with a continuing source of revenue throughout contract performance, and to ensure that a contractor will have the necessary financial resources to meet its contractual obligations. Although some progress payment requests are audited before payment, for the most part DoD relies solely on a contractor's integrity in making the payments. When a contractor requests payments for costs not actually incurred, the Government is harmed in the following ways:

(1) The contractor has the interest free use of money to which it is not entitled and which the Government itself may have had to borrow from the public.

(2) The Government may lose its advances if the contractor goes out of business and there are no materials or completed products against which the Government may assert an interest.

(3) Honest contractors lose their faith in the system and others, who are less scrupulous, are encouraged to take advantage of the system.

7-2. Progress payment fraud indicators.

a. Firms with cash flow problems are the most likely to request funds in advance of being entitled to them. Progress payments which do not appear to coincide with the contractor's plan and capability to perform the contract are suspicious. This could indicate the contractor is claiming payment for work not yet done.

b. Another type of contractor fraud in this area is to submit a progress payment claim for materials that have not been purchased. The contractor may be issuing a check to the supplier, then holding it until the Government progress payment arrives. One way to confirm the irregularity is to check the cancellation dates on the contractor's checks. If the bank received the check about the same time or later than the contractor received the progress payment, the check was probably held.

7-3. Progress payment fraud examples.

a. A contractor entered into an agreement with the Government to refurbish/overhaul heavy equipment vehicles. The contractor instructed its employees to work on the company's private commercial projects but to use a United States Government time card and punch that card as though working on a Government project. The contractor received large prepayment amounts from the Government in order to support its lagging private business. The Government's monies were then used for purposes other than to repair Government vehicles. Consequently, the Government vehicles either were not repaired or did receive a few repairs but not of the extent indicated on the Government repair documents and were returned to the Government as totally overhauled or refurbished equipment. The company president pled guilty to one count of making false statements, was placed on probation for two years, and fined $5,000. The company was fined $1,000. The company and its president were debarred from future business with the Government.

b. A contractor was awarded a contract to manufacture locking devices for trigger mechanisms valued at $87,000. The former president of the company allegedly submitted false invoices as proof of costs incurred, thus receiving progress payments. The president subsequently pled guilty and was sentenced to 5 years probation, fined $10,000, ordered to make restitution of $11,000, and ordered to serve 200 hours community service. The president and the company were debarred from bidding on Government contracts during his period of probation.

Chapter 8
Fast Pay Fraud

8-1. Introduction.

a. Fast pay is a special DoD procedure that allows certain contractors to be paid for contract work prior to receipt and inspection of the product by the Government. In general, the fast pay procedure is limited to contract orders that do not exceed $25,000. The fast payment procedure set forth in FAR 13.3 is designed to reduce delivery times and to improve DoD relations with certain suppliers by expediting contract payments. The procedure provides for payment based on the contractor's submission of an invoice. That invoice is a representation by the contractor that the supplies have been delivered to a post office, common carrier, or point of first receipt.

b. Fraud in fast pay occurs when a contractor submits an invoice requesting payment for supplies that have not been shipped or delivered to the Government. If the supplies are not in transit or actually delivered at the time the contractor submits his invoice, a criminal violation has occurred because the contractor submitted a false statement. It does not matter if the supplies are subsequently delivered to the Government.

c. There are specific DoD regulations regarding fast pay. Fast pay orders are usually issued on DD Form 1155. Regardless of the contract form used for the fast pay purchase, the contract will contain the following certification clause: "The Contractor agrees that the submission of an invoice to the Government for payment is a certification that the supplies for which the Government is being billed have been shipped or delivered in accordance with shipping instructions issued by the ordering officer, in the quantities shown on the invoice, and that such supplies are in the quantity and of the quality designated by the cited purchase order."

d. The fast pay procedure benefits both the contracting community and DoD. However, contractor integrity and honesty is essential. Payments are made before DoD is in a position to verify that it has received what it bargained for. In many cases, especially where overseas deliveries are involved, it may be weeks or even months before the DoD activity that actually issued the fast pay order is advised of either a nonconforming delivery or a nonreceipt. By that time, an unscrupulous contractor may have had an opportunity to defraud the Government of thousands of dollars and to drop out of sight. Because of the potential for large losses, and the effect that such losses could have on continued use of the fast pay procedure, immediate detection of those who have abused the system is necessary.

8-2. Fast pay fraud indicators.

a. How can DoD personnel dealing with fast pay identify possible fraud? The most obvious, and sometime most difficult, thing to do is check for the correlation between the claim for payment and the delivery of goods. Since the claim for payment and receipt of goods occurs at different locations, this will require communication between paying and receiving points. An employee who becomes suspicious should check with the receiving point to verify that the goods have arrived. Some important things to check for include: not receiving the goods at all, receiving the goods later than would be expected if they were mailed when claimed, and receiving nonconforming goods. The latter sometimes occurs because the contractor has lost the incentive to perform fully to contract specifications after it has been paid.

b. DoD personnel should also be alert for indications that the invoice submitted by the contractor is forged or altered in some way to make it appear that the goods were sent. Information on the invoice may raise questions such as shipment on a weekend or holiday.

8-3. Fast pay fraud examples.

a. A DoD supply center received a shipment of bricks instead of several electronic connection plugs allegedly shipped by the contractor. A review of 15 other contracts held by the contractor identified 8 for which payment had been made, but shipments were not received at various supply centers across the country. The value of the eight undelivered shipments was over $45,000. The contractor provided alleged proof of shipment and tracer documents which, on further investigation, were determined to be forgeries. The president of the company pled guilty to three counts each of mail fraud and false claims. He was sentenced to concurrent three year prison terms, ordered to pay $35,915 plus interest as restitution, and fined $3,000.

b. A contractor submitted fraudulent bills of lading to obtain payment for various quantities of hardware allegedly shipped to several DoD installations throughout the United States. The contractor was shipping the product at a date far after payment was received and, in

15

some instances, never shipped the product as indicated on the bills of lading. The company, through its president, pled guilty to 93 instances of violating the provisions of the fast pay clause. The company was fined $7,500 and ordered to pay restitution of $13,753.

Chapter 9
Bribery, Gratuities, and Conflicts of Interest

9-1. Introduction.

This chapter is dedicated to the discussion of integrity awareness. It will inform managers and employees about their responsibilities to be alert for bribe offers, to avoid the acceptance of gratuities and to recognize conflicts of interest. It also calls attention to the relationship and impact of these issues in the procurement process.

9-2. Bribery and Integrity Awareness.

Federal law prohibits both the giving or offering of anything of value to influence official actions and the acceptance of such items by Government officials. The crime is complete on making the offer to a Government employee. Acceptance of the bribe does not have to be proven. In addition to being a crime, contractors who resort to bribery and gratuities in their dealings with the Government also change the nature of their business relationships with the Government. Such unethical business practices certainly bear on the issue of contractor responsibility and possibly the retention of security clearances. Much of the Government procurement system relies on contractor integrity. The corruption of the procurement system by bribery is particularly damaging. Both Federal regulations and common sense dictate that the Government avoid business dealings with contractors who do not have a satisfactory record of integrity and business ethics.

a. Manager responsibilities.

(1) Managers have many responsibilities in the area of integrity awareness. They must set examples, not only of personal integrity and high ethical standards, but also of a willingness to participate in the referral and investigation process. Too often employees are discouraged from paying attention to or reporting possible bribe situations because it is thought that subsequent actions are time-consuming and disliked by managers because of the work involved. Instead of giving any impressions that they are unsympathetic to this process, managers should actively encourage their employees to be acutely aware of potential bribe overtures, encourage their employees to report bribe attempts immediately, and indicate to their employees that they will have full support from management in any efforts to assist investigators in obtaining evidence of the offense.

(2) The tendency to treat less blatant attempts at bribery as ordinary occupational hazards or as routine innuendos which can easily be ignored or dismissed is another reason that many bribes are not reported. Another reason might include the sentiment that refusal of a bribe offer is deterrent enough. It is part of a manager's job to ensure that these conditions are not impediments to rapid, timely, and efficient reporting of attempted bribes.

b. Employee responsibilities. There are some primary areas that should be focused on in discussing bribery awareness with employees. The areas of concern can be grouped into several questions.

(1) *What constitutes a bribe?* A bribe is an offer to employees of something of value to (a) do something they should not do, or (b) fail to do something they should do, in their official duties. The something of value need not be money, it can be anything of value.

(2) *When is a bribe being offered?*

(a) People who offer bribes are generally astute and aware individuals. A blatant offer is a rarity. Generally, the party offering a bribe will make subtle overtures in a conventional fashion. They may begin by discussing the employee's life style, family, or salary. They are looking for a vulnerable area where they can exploit the employee. They may seek to establish that the employee has college age children and begin discussing the high cost of education. They may learn that the employee is a new homeowner and discuss high mortgage payments and the expenses of fixing up a new home. If unable to detect an area in which the employee is particularly vulnerable, they may move to more glamorous and alluring areas; cash, cars, and travel. In summary, if the employee feels the individual is getting beyond mere civility and the professional purpose for the meeting, the employee should be alert to the possibility of a bribe attempt.

(b) The preliminary conversation may be an attempt to feel the employee out. The person attempting the bribe knows that bribe offers are illegal. They also know that an employee has an obligation to report the attempted bribe. Most importantly, the offeror of the bribe does not want to get caught. If the employee is not receptive to subtle overtures and alternative attempts fail, the person may not make any overt bribe offer. An employee has an obligation to determine the nature of the person's remarks. The very subtlety of preliminary overtures makes the employee's job of detecting a bribe a delicate one.

(3) *Why not accept a bribe?*

(a) The clear answer to this question is that the acceptance of a bribe is a criminal act that can result in prosecution, dismissal, fines, and embarrassment to the family and friends of the employee.

(b) In addition, accepting a bribe leaves one at the mercy of the person who paid it. There is no such thing as a one-time favor for one who accepts a bribe. Since the employee has committed a crime, the briber can ask anything later on under the threat of reporting the bribe, claiming it was solicited, and threatening exposure.

(4) *Why not just refuse a bribe without reporting it?*

(a) When an employee rejects a bribe, the offeror of the bribe may become concerned that the employee will report the attempt. He may decide that the best way to deal with the situation is to report that the employee tried to solicit a bribe and offer to cooperate in having the employee prosecuted or dismissed. If the employee has not reported the attempt, it would give credence to the offeror's allegation. Even though the employee has done nothing wrong, the allegation would have to be investigated and could cause undue problems and time to resolve.

(b) Furthermore, since the attempt to bribe a Government official is in itself a crime, failure to report an attempted bribe, as well as other crimes, leaves the employee open to possible prosecution.

(c) The failure to report a bribe attempt also leaves the offeror free to try again with another employee of the Government. The next employee may not be able to resist the offer. Further, there is no deterrent effect in refusal of an attempt. The offeror is free to try again without fear of the potential consequences. Investigation and prosecution of those who would try to corrupt our employees and our system of Government is the only way to deter others from believing that this is the way to do business with the DoD.

c. Bribes are a reality. As a demonstration that the foregoing discussion relates to a very real problem, a few examples of recent DoD bribery cases follow:

Appendix T

(1) A Navy contracting officer at a Navy supply depot was found guilty of conspiracy to defraud the Government in connection with his receipt of approximately $21,000 in cash and other gifts in exchange for awarding Navy contracts. He was sentenced to two years confinement and fined $10,000.

(2) An Army contracting officer's technical representative was sentenced to five years in prison and fined $20,000 in connection with his receipt of over $5,000 in bribes from a contractor performing in excess of $5 million in Army contracts.

(3) An Air Force inventory management specialist was fined $1,000 and required to pay $13,500 in restitution as a result of his pleading guilty to Federal charges relating to his receipt of bribes to assist a contractor in transporting material unrelated to Government contracts from the United States to a foreign country at Government expense. The contractor was also convicted of Federal charges, sentenced to six years in jail, and required to pay $40,000 in restitution.

(4) A corporate sales manager was sentenced to ten years in prison, fined $1,000, and ordered to make nearly $10,000 in restitution after conviction on multiple charges of bribing a DoD civilian employee relating to a scheme of false and inflated billings.

(5) A GS-4 file clerk was convicted of receiving approximately $50,000 in bribes from various contractors to provide them inside information used to enhance their bid packages.

9–3. Gratuities.

a. Gratuities are generally distinguished from bribery in that there is usually no request for specific improper action in exchange for what is being given. Gratuities are generally given to assist in enhancing the "relationship" between the offeror and the Government employee. This "more favorable atmosphere" in which to do business may later move the employee to "lean" in the contractor's favor if needed. Some contractors have actually gone so far in providing gratuities as to budget substantial sums (in excess of $150,000 for a project in one case) to create a favorable atmosphere for their dealings with Government employees.

b. Dealings with those who seek to and who do business with the Government should be conducted in an objective manner, above reproach, and avoiding even the appearance of favoritism or other impropriety. Acceptance of gratuities of any kind should be avoided in order to maintain both the form and the substance of objectivity in official dealings. It should also be remembered that the offer or acceptance of a gratuity is a felony. Furthermore, the provision of a gratuity is in violation of a standard clause in DoD contracts (FAR 52.203), and any claim by a contractor for reimbursement of expenses of a gratuity is a civil and criminal violation of the False Claims Act (10 U.S.C. 2324(i)).

c. An example of illegal gratuities can be seen in the case of a Navy commander who was responsible for keeping track of Navy flight hours used in support of the filming of a commercial movie. During the filming, the commander received over $5,500 from the movie company through the payment of a bogus invoice for set materials. Ultimately, the commander understated the number of hours flown in support of the movie, which resulted in over $600,000 in lost reimbursement from the movie company. The commander was later convicted of receiving an illegal gratuity, fined $5,000, and placed on three years probation. The commander and the movie company were sued in Federal court and later settled with the repayment of $400,000 in civil damages. It was also determined that the captain of the carrier had repeatedly accepted gratuities from the producer during filming of the movie. The gratuities included a $1,500 hang glider and over $400 in meals, accommodations, and transportation expenses for his family to watch the filming of the movie. The captain received a letter of caution and was required to repay all gratuities.

9–4. Conflicts of Interest.

Employees of DoD are generally prohibited by both criminal laws and Standards of Conduct requirements from taking official actions that deal with businesses in which they or their immediate families have a direct financial interest. In addition to the general prohibition, 10 U.S.C. 2397 (as amended by the DoD Authorization Act, PL 99–661), imposes other post employment restrictions on certain procurement officials, grades GS-13 or O-4 and above. Any DoD employee who is unsure of the conflict of interest statutes and their personal application should consult with their organization's ethics official for guidance.

In dealing with contractors, the Government may terminate for default any contract that was obtained as a result of a conflict of interest. Even the *appearance* of a conflict of interest, although not proven in court, has been held to be sufficient to disqualify an otherwise eligible bidder on a contract and, by extension, may be sufficient to terminate such a contract after award (See Chapter 11).

All DoD employees should be alert to situations in which they suspect a possible conflict of interest and report them to appropriate authorities. The following recent cases are reflective of situations to which all DoD employees should be sensitive.

a. A buyer with the Defense Electronics Supply Center (DESC), along with his wife and sister-in-law, formed a company to represent various electronics companies in their efforts to obtain contracts with DESC. On numerous occasions, the buyer, who was responsible for bid solicitation and price determination for a selected series of electronic items, recommended awards of Government contracts to those same companies. The buyer also used an affiliate of the company he had formed to sell solenoids to DESC under approximately 50 contracts with the Government. As a DESC employee, he personally participated in the award of the contracts to his own company. No disclosure of his interest in the company was made to DESC. The buyer charged DESC over $70,000 as a result of the contracts. Based on a complaint from a co-worker at DESC, the buyer was convicted under the Federal conflict of interest statute.

b. A senior medical officer, who served as a consultant to the Surgeon General of a Military Department, recommended that DoD procure an item of medical equipment on a sole source basis from one company. At no time did the officer disclose that he was a director and major stockholder in the company. When the Surgeon General agreed to the recommendation, the officer sought to recapitalize the company in anticipation of receiving a large amount of new orders. When the officer learned that he was suspected of conflict of interest, he denied his ownership in the company and had the company prepare false and backdated documents to show that he had no involvement with the company. In addition, the officer improperly received payments from various drug companies for drug tests performed at a military hospital, but failed to disclose to the hospital the receipt of that money. The allegations in this case were made by two doctors at the hospital who became aware of the medical officer's conflicts of interest. The medical officer was convicted of Federal violations of unlawfully supplementing his income.

17

Chapter 10
Commercial Bribery and Kickbacks

10-1. Introduction.

The payment of bribes and kickbacks by subcontractors to DoD prime contractors or higher tier subcontractors, in connection with work on Defense contracts, constitutes a serious problem. While it is similar in many ways to the bribery of a Government official, until recently commercial bribery had not had the focus of public attention and little had been done to address the problem. However, Congress recently addressed the problem, and through the passage of the Anti-Kickback Enforcement Act of 1986 has now strengthened the law in this area. The DoD is also focusing on the problem by conducting more aggressive investigations and by working with the business community for the establishment of effective company ethics programs. However, commercial bribery and kickbacks remain a problem which is not easily detected and controlled. The courts have established the presumption that the cost of any kickback activity is always passed on to the Government.

10-2. Anti-Kickback Enforcement Act of 1986.

a. With the passage of the Anti-Kickback Enforcement Act of 1986 (PL 99-634), it is illegal for any person to provide, attempt to provide, or offer any kickback to a Government contractor or contractor employee for the purpose of improperly obtaining any favorable treatment under a Government contract. The prohibition covers any money, commission, gratuity, or any other things of value, whether provided directly or indirectly, and applies equally to persons who solicit, accept, or attempt to accept kickbacks. The legislation further prohibits the inclusion of any kickback amounts in the contract price charged by a contractor.

b. In addition to providing criminal penalties, which include imprisonment for up to 10 years, the legislation also provides for civil action and administrative offsets when illegal kickbacks are involved. In a civil action, the United States may recover a penalty of twice the amount of the kickback plus $10,000 for each kickback payment. The Government contracting officer may also administratively offset the amount of any kickback against any moneys owed by the United States under the contract.

c. The Act also requires contractors to establish internal programs to detect and prevent kickback activity. Contractors are required to report any kickback activity to the Inspector General, DoD, and to cooperate fully in any investigation regarding kickbacks. Contractors are also required to allow the Inspector General, DoD, access to facilities and to audit books and records in order to determine compliance with the Act.

10-3. Other Considerations.

a. In addition to the Anti-Kickback Enforcement Act, instances of commercial bribery may also involve various other criminal statutes. The individuals paying and/or receiving the bribes may be in violation of the statute dealing with conspiracy to defraud the Government (18 U.S.C. 371), may have made false statements or certifications under the contract (18 U.S.C. 1001), or violated various other Federal or state statutes.

b. The illegal kickbacks not only affect the integrity of the procurement process and inflate Government costs, but, in some instances, the kickbacks paid may be so significant they affect the subcontractor's performance. In such cases, contract specifications may not be met or there are other performance failures due to underfunding, which results in deliveries being delayed or prevented and the ultimate user being deprived of the contracted items.

10-4. Kickback case examples.

A quick look at some case examples provides a clear picture of the extent to which the payments affect DoD contracts.

a. Six officials of a DoD subcontractor pled guilty to Federal charges in connection with kickback schemes involving an executive vice president of a major Defense prime contractor who, along with his assistant, received approximately $5 million in kickbacks. The corporate officer fled the country following his indictment and remains a fugitive from justice.

b. In another case, 26 people were convicted in connection with a kickback scheme operated within a major shipbuilding contractor. The scheme involved approximately $1 million in kickbacks.

c. A vice president of an advertising firm in New York City pled guilty to receiving illegal kickbacks of $60,000 in connection with the company's contract to provide national advertising for the United States Army.

d. In the aerospace industry, investigations have resulted in multiple convictions of prime contractor employees who have received kickbacks. The investigations, which developed evidence of over 70 companies where buyers for the prime contractor had received kickbacks, led the United States Attorney controlling the investigation to testify before Congress that, "It is my opinion that kickbacks on defense subcontracts are a pervasive long-standing practice which has corrupted the subcontracting process at most, if not all, defense contractors...."

Chapter 11
Civil, Contractual, and Administrative Remedies for Fraud

11-1. Introduction.

a. Traditionally, Government contracting officials have relied on the criminal justice system to police fraud by DoD contractors. The reliance included forbearance from certain administrative and contractual actions until the criminal case was completed. However, the reliance was often misplaced for a number of reasons.

b. First, criminal cases must be proven beyond a reasonable doubt. While there may be insufficient information to warrant a criminal conviction, contracting officials do not need that level of proof in order to take administrative and contractual actions.

c. Second, even if criminal action is taken, many cases are plea bargained to lesser offenses. This tends to mislead people into believing that a less serious offense was proven, or that less fraudulent activity took place than really did. An example of the confusion comes from one documented case in which four nonappropriated fund officials pled guilty to accepting bribes from a contractor. The contractor, however, pled guilty to only a misdemeanor for trespassing on a Federal reservation. Contracting officials, when confronted with the fact that the contractor had been convicted of only a misdemeanor, believed that the contractor's actions had not been very serious in nature. The facts showed the seriousness of the actions despite the plea to only a minor infraction of the law.

d. Third, many contracting officials are not aware of the fact that prosecutors must set priorities for the use of their resources, and, in doing so, they are not able to prosecute every case that is brought to their attention by investigators. The deci-

APPENDIX T

sion not to prosecute a case is not always based on the failure to establish that wrongdoing has taken place. There are instances when the investigators prove a crime took place, but the circumstances do not warrant taking judicial action at that time. When a case has been declined for prosecution, contracting officials should consider the facts established by the proof the investigator has gathered to determine whether alternative action is warranted by them.

e. Fourth, the criminal justice system does not have as one of its functions the recoupment of assets lost during a fraud, or the protection of the procurement system from future dealings with the contractors who practice deception. Although a company might be convicted of or plead guilty to a crime, this does not, without action by contracting officials, prevent the company from obtaining future contracts, recoup monies paid to the contractor due to fraud, or obtain the desired or intended performance under the contract.

f. Finally, DoD officials and not the DOJ are responsible for the integrity of the DoD contracting and procurement process. The FAR and DoD implementing regulations require contracting officials to take positive action on any evidence of contractor impropriety and nonresponsibility. Therefore, it is necessary for managers and contracting officials to be aware of and effectively use the civil, administrative, and contractual powers and remedies which are available to protect the Government, to prevent further loss to the Government, and to recover Government assets and funds lost through fraud.

11-2. Coordinated approach to remedies.

a. Officials of DoD are responsible for the integrity of DoD contracts and must be prepared to take immediate action to protect the Government. This often includes positive action while a criminal investigation is under way and before an indictment or conviction has been obtained. Criminal cases often take years to complete and DoD can take many contractual and administrative actions on evidence less than that necessary for a conviction. Timely action by a contracting official, such as pre-indictment suspension or a contract default termination, will aid the Government by precluding the contractor from continuing to benefit while an investigation is under way.

b. By taking a coordinated approach to criminal, civil, contractual, and administrative actions, the Government is often able to induce guilty contractors into pleading guilty more quickly. Simultaneous consideration of all remedies available to DoD and DOJ also enables the Government and the court to fashion a single comprehensive remedy package that will punish the contractor, protect the Government from further harm, and make the Government whole from any losses suffered.

c. Early action by contracting officials is important. The action must be coordinated with a variety of officials in both DoD and DOJ. The coordination is essential to ensure that none of the actions taken will adversely affect the ability of the Government to pursue any of the other actions available. An example of how the coordination of remedies process can work is demonstrated by a recent case involving a major DoD contractor who was investigated for engaging in product substitution, cost mischarging, and defective pricing. As a result of coordinated efforts by contracting officials, investigators, the DOJ, and other DoD officials, the following results were achieved:

(1) Suspension of the contractor during the investigation to prevent the award of additional or follow-on contracts (which would have required a finding of responsibility and putting additional funds at risk).

(2) Guilty plea by the contractor to numerous felonies, resulting in criminal fines of $380,000 being paid by the contractor.

(3) Agreement by the contractor to pay restitution of over $160,000 and civil damages of over $1.6 million.

(4) Agreement by the contractor to make significant changes in its cost accounting and quality assurance procedures.

(5) Dismissal of numerous employees by the contractor for their participation in the fraud, helping to assure the Government that a repeat of the fraud was unlikely.

d. The Secretary of Defense issued DoD Directive 7050.5, "Coordination of Remedies for Fraud and Corruption Related to Procurement Activities," dated June 28, 1985, to ensure that the type of coordination discussed above takes place. The Directive requires that each Military Department and Defense Agency establish a centralized point of coordination for criminal, civil, contractual, and administrative actions in contract fraud and corruption cases. The following are some of the centralized points of coordination established under that Directive:

(1) Army - Office of the Judge Advocate General, Procurement Fraud Division. (Army Regulation 27-21)

(2) Navy - Office of the Naval Inspector General, Investigative Oversight Division (NOP-81).

(3) Air Force - Office of the Inspector General of the Air Force, Office of Review and Oversight. (Air Force Regulation 125-2)

(4) Defense Logistics Agency - Office of the General Counsel, Associate Counsel Logistics Services.

e. The Directive mentioned above requires that the centralized points of coordination be informed by the Defense criminal investigative organizations each time they open a significant investigation involving fraud or corruption in procurement or procurement related activities. The centralized point of coordination is then responsible for ensuring that a remedies plan is prepared, and updated as needed, taking into account the available remedies and the timing of their use. The coordination will involve communication between the centralized point of coordination and various officials in the investigative, prosecutive, program, and procurement areas of concern to balance the needs of each and foster communication between them. Through this process, the Government will be able to use fully the variety of remedies available for fraud and do so in a more efficient and effective manner.

f. The following segments contain a brief discussion of the many remedies for fraud that can be used by the Government. A number of these remedies have been created or changed by recent legislative action.

11-3. Available remedies.

The Government has the right to take action against contractors who engage in fraudulent activities. The Government right is based on several statutory grounds. Many of the civil actions taken based on those statutes are filed by the DOJ and may be filed in conjunction with, after, or instead of a criminal prosecution.

Under contract law and principles, the Government has the right to insist on certain standards of responsibility and business integrity from its contractors. The violation of any of those principles gives the Government the right to take a variety of actions. These actions may also be taken in conjunction with, after, or instead of a criminal prosecution.

a. Civil False Claims Act.

(1) The submission of a false claim to the Government can make a contractor li-

able to the Government, both criminally and civilly. The Civil False Claims Act, 31 U.S.C. 3729-3731, establishes liability for false claims. The law provides for the Government to be able to recover penalties and damages for false claims in addition to or instead of any criminal sanctions. Through such actions, the Government can recover assets lost through fraud.

(2) The statute, as recently amended, provides for penalties of $5,000 to $10,000 per false claim (previously the penalty was $2,000 per claim). Each invoice submitted by a contractor could, under appropriate circumstances, be considered as a false claim for purposes of the statute. The Government can also recover treble damages (previously it was double damages) or three times the amount of a false claim. The Government must actually suffer monetary damages to collect under that portion of the statute but not to have the civil penalties assessed. The Government is precluded from intentionally paying a claim it knows is false merely to activate the damages portion of the statute.

(3) The Government must prove, by a preponderance of the evidence, that the contractor knowingly submitted a false claim. Knowing submission means actual knowledge or deliberate ignorance of the truth (failure to take reasonable steps to find out if the claim is truthful) or reckless disregard of the truth (failure to pursue indications of falsity to find out the truth). It is not necessary to show that the contractor acted with the specific intention to defraud the Government.

b. Program Fraud Civil Remedies Act.

(1) This recently enacted law allows Federal agencies to impose administratively penalties and damages for all false claims where the damages are under $150,000, and all false statements. Government agencies are, at this writing, in the process of establishing administrative procedures to implement the provisions of the law. The procedures will be designed to protect the interests and rights of both the contractors and the Government in the determination of liability and the amount of any penalties and damages assessed against a contractor.

(2) The law provides for a penalty of $5,000 per false claim or false statement. Damages for false claims are double the amount of the provable loss (rather than the treble damages of the Civil False Claims Act which requires judicial action to obtain). The standard of proof which must be met by the Government in establishing the liability of a contractor under this law is the same as that under the Civil False Claims Act, a knowing submission of the false claim or statement.

c. Contract Disputes Act. Under the Civil False Claims Act and the Program Fraud Civil Remedies Act, the Government may only recover damages when they have actually been suffered, e.g., when a false claim is paid. The Government is limited to the assertion of the appropriate penalty if an audit or investigation determines that a claim or statement is false and no payment is made. Under the Contract Disputes Act, 41 U.S.C. 604, a contractor is liable to the Government for the amount of any unsupported part of a claim plus the costs of reviewing the claim, if the claim is based even in part on fraud or misrepresentation of fact. The Government does not have to pay the claim in order to recover.

d. Forfeiture of Fraudulent Claims. The U.S. Court of Claims can, under 27 U.S.C. 2514, order the forfeiture of the entire amount of a claim in which it judges the proof, statement, establishment, or allowance thereof is based on a fraud or attempted fraud by a contractor. The Government does not have to pay a claim first for the statute to be operative. A contractor making a claim, which the contracting officer denies, risks losing the entire claim by going to the Court of Claims if the claim is based even in part on fraud.

e. Termination for Default.

(1) The submission of a false claim or statement on a contract is clear evidence of a contractor's nonresponsibility and failure to perform on a contract. The contracting officer has the right and obligation to terminate a contract for default under those circumstances. There is no requirement that a conviction take place for such a termination. Terminations for convenience are never appropriate when fraud is present on a contract.

(2) Furthermore, certain improper actions also give rise to a statutory right to terminate for default. The Government has the right to terminate a contract for default whenever a contractor offers a gratuity to a Government employee. The right is set forth in 10 U.S.C. 2207, and implemented in FAR 52.203-3 and DFAR Appendix D. The Government also has the right under those same provisions, in addition to all other default remedies, to penalize the contractor in the amount of three to ten times the value of the gratuity. The Navy recently convened an adhoc gratuities board and, using the procedures in DFAR Appendix D, assessed a penalty of over $650,000 against a major DoD contractor after it was established the contractor had paid over $65,000 in gratuities to Navy personnel.

f. Rescission of Contracts.

(1) Rescission is a common law remedy in contracts. The remedy allows for the return of both parties to their position before the contract; that is, the contract is void and treated as if it were so from the start. The remedy has been used by the Government and upheld by the courts most frequently when there is fraud or corruption involved in the obtaining or award stage of the contract.

(2) The Government also has a right under 18 U.S.C. 218 to rescind a contract administratively under certain circumstances. The statute allows the Government to administratively rescind a contract when there has been a final conviction for bribery, gratuities, or conflicts of interest in connection with the award of a contract. The provisions of FAR Subpart 3.7 set forth the procedures developed to accomplish the administrative voiding and rescission of contracts.

(3) A recent case serves to illustrate the use of the above provisions. The case involved a Government employee who had been awarding contracts to firms in which the employee held a financial interest. The financial interest was held in the names of aliases used by the employee to conceal any interest from audit officials reviewing the contractors. All of the contracts awarded to the contractors in which the employee held a financial interest were rescinded.

g. Denial of Claims. Contracting officials do not have the authority to pay claims where there is a reasonable suspicion that the claim is tainted by fraud. The Contract Disputes Act, at 41 U.S.C. 605, contains provisions under which DoD is not authorized to "...administer, settle, compromise or otherwise adjust any claim involving fraud." Therefore, whenever fraud is detected in a claim, contracting officials should not take any further action on any portion of the claim without coordination with DOJ. (FAR 33.009, 33.010)

h. Findings of Nonresponsibility. The provisions of the FAR at Subpart 9.1 state that contracts may only be awarded to responsible contractors. Contractors are required to demonstrate affirmatively their responsibility, including a satisfactory record of integrity and business ethics. Any evidence of fraud by a contractor is clearly a matter which should be considered by contracting officers in making responsibility determinations.

i. Suspension and Debarment.

(1) Contractors may be precluded from doing business with the Government

for the commission of fraud or for various other actions indicating a lack of business integrity. The procedures for accomplishing this are found in the FAR Subpart 9.4. The Government has never had a suspension or debarment action challenged successfully so long as those procedures are followed.

(2) Suspension is an interim measure, based on adequate evidence of fraud, designated to protect the Government while a criminal investigation or trial is under way and evidence of fraud is present. A contractor may be suspended for up to 18 months while an investigation is under way. Once an indictment or civil suit is filed, the contractor can remain suspended until the completion of all legal proceedings.

(3) Debarment is a final determination of a contractor's nonresponsibility. A contractor can be debarred, based on a conviction of a crime, or on sufficient evidence that a contractor has repeatedly failed to perform properly or has committed acts which indicate a lack of business integrity and honesty. Debarment can be in effect for up to three years. A contracting officer can recommend the debarment of companies and individuals, and can impute the conduct of certain key individuals in a company to that company in recommending its debarment.

(4) Contracting officers must forward reports of improper contractor activity to the suspension and debarment authority at the earliest opportunity in order for suspension and debarment to be effective. Reporting procedures are set forth in the DoD FAR Supplement Subsection 9.472.

(5) Each of the Military Departments and DLA require contractors to certify, as part of their bid or proposal package, that the contractor and its owners, officers, and directors are not on the suspended and debarred bidders list.

j. Disallowance of Legal Costs. Contractors who are found to have engaged in fraud on cost type contracts are not entitled, under FAR 31.205-5, to recover legal and administrative costs incurred in unsuccessfully defending against Government action. While an investigation is under way, it is important for contracting officers to take prompt action to require contractors to identify such costs as they are incurred. The contracting officer should then deny claims for such costs in all appropriate cases, which will be made easier by their earlier identification by the contractor.

k. Prohibition on Employment of Certain Felons. The employment of felons convicted of DoD contract related felonies is prohibited by 10 U.S.C. 2408. The statute states that any person convicted of a felony arising out of a Defense contract cannot work in a management or supervisory capacity on any Defense contract for a period of not less than one year from the date of conviction. Any contractor who knowingly employs such a person can be fined up to $500,000. Contracting officials should be alert to whether or not persons prohibited by the statute are involved in management or supervision of Defense contracts and report such instances through appropriate channels to the Defense criminal investigative organizations for action.

l. Contract Penalties for False Claims and Defective Pricing. Recently enacted Federal statutes allow for contract penalties for claims for unallowable costs and defective pricing. Under 10 U.S.C. 2324, a contractual penalty can be assessed whenever a contractor submits a claim for a direct or indirect cost, when such a cost is specifically ruled unallowable by either statute or regulation. (See also DFAR Supplement Subpart 31.70) Similarly, 10 U.S.C. 2306a(e) authorizes a penalty for the knowing submission of defective cost or pricing data. Because violations of those statutes may also be a violation of various criminal and civil fraud laws, contracting officer actions should be coordinated with the centralized points for coordination of procurement fraud remedies and the DOJ.

m. Administrative Penalties for Conflicts of Interest. Under the provisions of 10 U.S.C. Sections 2397b and c, major DoD contractors are prohibited from employing or paying any gift, gratuity, or other form of compensation over $250 to certain covered DoD officials for a period of two years after the DoD official leaves the Government. Those DoD officials are primarily persons in grades GS-13/O-4 and above who were employed as DoD procurement officials at sites or plants owned by the contractor. Contractors who knowingly pay such compensation are subject to a $500,000 civil fine and may also be required to pay up to $100,000 in liquidated damages. Major DoD contractors are also required to file an annual report with DoD which lists all compensation paid to all former employees for a period of two years after the employee leaves DoD. Failure to file an accurate a report can result in an administrative penalty of $10,000.

11-4. Personnel actions.

The Government has a variety of remedial actions it can take against employees who have colluded with contractors in fraudulent conduct or when an employee has engaged in improper actions (such as accepting or soliciting bribes or gratuities, or engaging in conflicts of interest). Some of these remedies include:

a. Termination. The receipt of a bribe or gratuity, or actions indicating a personal conflict of interest, can justify the immediate termination of a Federal employee. Managers should consider the gravity of the offense and its impact on the continued ability of the employee to carry out responsibilities of the position in deciding whether or not to retain employees found to have engaged in activities such as those discussed above.

b. Revocation of a Contracting Officer's Warrant. Contracting officers who engage in improper conduct can lose their right to contract on behalf of the Government. One contracting officer who knowingly accelerated the award of a contract to a company about to be suspended lost the authority to contract on behalf of the Government. Another contracting officer who engaged in a conspiracy to defraud the Government by preventing proper contract administration and approving false billings also lost the warrant given by the Government.

c. Recoupment of Funds Lost. Whenever a contractor gives a bribe or gratuity to a Government employee, both the contractor and the employee are jointly liable to the Government for an amount equal to the value of the bribe or gratuity. Action should be taken to deduct the value of any such bribe or gratuity from the pension contributions of the employee, prior to the termination of the employee (if termination action is taken). Similar actions can be taken against military personnel and retirees.

d. Administrative Penalties for Conflicts of Interest. Under the provisions of 10 U.S.C. 2397a and b, certain DoD procurement officials can face civil and administrative fines and penalties regarding improper negotiation regarding employment with DoD contractors, and the acceptance of compensation from such contractors. Generally, employees in grades GS-13/O-4 and above who are employed in a procurement function must immediately report any negotiations with a DoD contractor regarding future employment. Failure to report immediately the existence of negotiations, or failure to disqualify oneself from any official dealings with the contractor while such negotiations are under consideration can result in up to $20,000 in administrative penalties and a 10 year bar on employment with the contractor. Further restrictions apply to DoD employees, in grades GS-13/O-4 and above, who are engaged in a procurement function and are employed in plants owned or operated by a DoD contractor. Such employees are prohibited from accepting any employment, or any form of consideration over $250, from the contractor for a period of two years after leaving DoD. Acceptance of any form of compensation can result in a civil fine of up to $250,000.

Chapter 12
Voluntary Disclosure of Fraud

12-1. Introduction.

a. In July 1986, the Deputy Secretary of Defense announced a DoD program encouraging Defense contractors to disclose internally identified incidents involving problems affecting the acquisition process. The program encourages that disclosures of problems not involving fraud be made to the appropriate contracting officer or to DCAA. However, disclosures which involve potential criminal or civil fraud issues are to be directed to the Assistant Inspector General for Criminal Investigations Policy and Oversight, OIG, DoD.

b. The program does not provide the disclosing contractor with any guarantees that it will not be suspended or debarred by DoD, or that it will not be prosecuted by the Department of Justice. On the other hand, the program clearly intends that both Departments will recognize voluntary disclosure, accompanied by contractor cooperation, corrective action, and restitution, as significant factors in making decisions regarding appropriate remedies.

c. In making voluntary disclosures, contractors are advised that certain "key elements" should be included in their report to DoD. The elements are designed to require the revelation of all facts that will assist the DoD in conducting its own investigation, which will seek to verify the contractor's findings. The verification process will typically require DCAA auditors to test the cost conclusions of the report, and criminal investigators to analyze the issue of whether intent to defraud is present.

d. Appendix A contains a more detailed description of the DoD voluntary disclosure program and Appendix B states the Department of Justice policy on the program.

APPENDIX A

App. T   GOVERNMENT CONTRACT COMPLIANCE HANDBOOK

THE DEPUTY SECRETARY OF DEFENSE
WASHINGTON, D.C. 20301

24 JUL 1986

Dear

During the past few years, public and congressional interest in the Department of Defense management of its programs and operations has remained intense. This is nowhere more true than in the acquisition area. These issues continue to command our personal attention and involvement. Many of the problems in the acquisition area came to light because of audits and investigations conducted by the Department of Defense. We are committed to detecting and eliminating inefficiency and improper practices in our acquisition process; we believe that most Defense contractors have institutional commitments to these same goals.

To demonstrate this commitment, a number of major Defense contractors have adopted a policy of voluntarily disclosing problems affecting their corporate contractual relationship with the Department of Defense. These disclosures are made by the contractor, without an advance agreement regarding possible Department of Defense resolution of the matter. The contractors understand the Department's view that early voluntary disclosure, coupled with full cooperation and complete access to necessary records, are strong indications of an attitude of contractor integrity even in the wake of disclosures of potential criminal liability. We will consider such cooperation as an important factor in any decisions that the Department takes in the matter.

I encourage you to consider adopting a policy of voluntary disclosure as a central part of your corporate integrity program. Matters not involving potential criminal issues should be presented to the appropriate contracting officer or Defense Contract Audit Agency auditor. Matters involving potential criminal or civil fraud issues should be directed to the Deputy Inspector General, Department of Defense.

A-1

APPENDIX T

A description of the Department of Defense program for voluntary disclosures is enclosed herewith for your consideration.

I believe that your corporate commitment to complete and timely disclosures of irregularities, regardless of their magnitude, is essential to increasing confidence in our ability to provide for the national defense effectively and efficiently.

Sincerely,

William H. Taft, IV

Enclosure

Department of Defense Program for Voluntary Disclosures of Possible Fraud by Defense Contractors

Background

Officials within the Department of Defense (DoD) have been approached by a number of contractors to determine the conditions and agreements that might be structured with the Government if a contractor sought to disclose voluntarily information that might expose the contractor to liability under Federal statutes relating to criminal and civil fraud. From the Department's perspective, the voluntary disclosure of information otherwise unknown to the Government, and contractor cooperation in an ensuing investigation, offers a number of significant advantages:

- the Government is likely to recoup losses of which it might otherwise be unaware;

- limited detection assets within the Government are augmented by contractor resources;

- consideration of appropriate remedies can be expedited by both DoD and Department of Justice when adversarial tensions are relaxed;

- voluntary disclosure and cooperation are indicators of contractor integrity; and

- contractors engaging in voluntary disclosure are more likely to institute corrective actions to prevent recurrence of disclosed problems.

Requirements on Contractors

Department of Defense recognition of a contractor as a "volunteer" will depend on four key factors:

1. The disclosure must not be triggered by the contractor's recognition that the underlying facts are about to be discovered by the Government through audit, investigation, or contract administration efforts or reported to the Government by third parties.

2. The disclosure must be on behalf of the business entity, in contrast to admissions by individual officials or employees.

APPENDIX T

3. Prompt and complete corrective action, including disciplinary action and restitution to the Government where appropriate, must be taken by the contractor in response to the matters disclosed.

4. After disclosure, the contractor must cooperate fully with the Government in any ensuing investigation or audit.

Defining DoD expectations of "cooperation" in any situation will depend on the individual facts or circumstances underlying the disclosure. However, DoD may enter into a written agreement with any contractor seeking to make a voluntary disclosure where such an agreement will facilitate follow-on action without improperly limiting the responsibilities of the Government. This agreement, which may be coordinated with the Department of Justice, will describe the types of documents and evidence to be provided to DoD and will resolve any issues related to interviews, privileges, or other legal concerns which may affect the DoD ability to obtain all relevant facts in a timely manner.

Department of Defense Actions

If a contractor is recognized as a "volunteer" based on the preceding criteria, the DoD is prepared to undertake the following:

1. Identify one of the Military Departments or the Defense Logistics Agency as the cognizant DoD component to represent DoD for suspension/debarment purposes, i.e., to assess contractor integrity in light of the disclosures. Early identification of the appropriate DoD component will permit the contractor, from the outset of its cooperation, to provide relevant information relating to contractor integrity and management controls, e.g., internal controls, corrective measures, or disciplinary action taken as a result of the information disclosed.

2. The DoD, through the Office of the Inspector General and in cooperation with the Department of Justice, will seek to expedite the completion of any investigation and audit conducted in response to a voluntary disclosure, thereby minimizing the period of time necessary for identification of remedies deemed appropriate by the Government.

3. Advise the Department of Justice of the complete nature of the voluntary disclosure, the extent of contractor cooperation and the types of corrective action instituted by the contractor. As always, any determinations of appropriate criminal and civil fraud sanctions will be the ultimate prerogative of the Department of Justice.

Commencing a Voluntary Disclosure

Since initial judgments as to appropriate investigative and audit resources will be necessary in any voluntary disclosure involving possible fraud, the initial contact with the DoD on fraud-related disclosures should be with the Office of the Inspector General.

While the Office of the Inspector General will be the initial point of contact for fraud-related disclosures, other DoD components are expected to be advised or involved as circumstances warrant. Besides the Office of General Counsel, DoD, and the appropriate suspension/debarment authority, other DoD components that expectedly would be advised, or involved, in voluntary disclosures are the Office of the Assistant Secretary of Defense (Acquisition and Logistics) and the Defense Contract Audit Agency.

The Office of the Inspector General element that will serve as the initial point of contact is:

> Assistant Inspector General for Criminal Investigations
>   Policy and Oversight
> 400 Army Navy Drive
> Room 1037
> Arlington, Virginia 22202
> Telephone: 202-694-8958

APPENDIX B

Office of the Attorney General
Washington, D.C. 20530

February 5, 1987

Hon. William Howard Taft IV
Deputy Secretary of Defense
U.S. Department of Defense
The Pentagon
Washington, D.C. 20301

Dear Mr. ~~Taft~~ Will:

Thank you for your letter of 18 September 1986 describing the voluntary disclosure initiative of the Defense Department. You have my assurance that the Department of Justice fully supports this program and will work with the Department of Defense for its successful implementation.

I am encouraged that many defense contractors are adopting compliance programs and disclosing problems affecting defense contracts. The willingness of contractors to adopt self-policing programs may be regarded as a constructive product of our joint efforts in uncovering and successfully prosecuting, both criminally and civilly, major contract frauds over the past several years. Your voluntary disclosure program will further encourage corporate good citizenship.

You express the view that it would be helpful for the Department of Justice to provide guidance on voluntary disclosures. I agree that such guidance would be both useful and appropriate.

As you are undoubtedly aware, it is our practice to take into consideration factors relating to the integrity of a company in assessing whether to bring charges. A voluntary corporate disclosure of wrongdoing is rarely the sole basis for a decision not to prosecute; however, it is one of a number of factors we view as relevant to the charging decision. Others include the strength of the evidence, indicia of <u>scienter</u>, level of employee or management involved, pervasiveness of the conduct,

B-1

dollar impact on the taxpayers, the quality of cooperation during the investigation, the nature of the remedial actions taken in the wake of the discovery of misconduct, and the quality of the company's efforts to prevent misconduct in the first instance by a meaningful compliance program--implemented in fact, as well as recorded on paper.

Clearly, our objective is to bring prosecutions that will have a deterrent impact. At the same time we recognize the desirability of prosecutive judgments, whether at the charging stage, the plea stage, or the sentencing stage of the criminal justice process, which will encourage contractors to initiate compliance programs.

In prosecuting corporations, particularly defense contractors, deterrence is a most significant factor. Through criminal prosecution and punishment, other contractors are put on notice as to the requirements of law and encouraged to modify their behavior to conduct business in an honest and non-criminal manner. Prosecutions of contractor corporations create an incentive for management to establish preventive measures and establish clear standards of right and wrong for their employees.

On the other hand, contractors that make serious and responsible efforts to comply with the law and promptly disclose misconduct should not be discouraged from those practices by inflexible prosecutive policies. In some self-disclosure situations, criminal prosecution of the self-disclosing contractor could undermine our law enforcement objectives and would therefore be inappropriate.

With these general objectives in mind, we will be preparing guidance for our United States Attorneys in the form of a supplement to the United States Attorneys Manual. I will make sure you have a copy of the supplement as soon as it is issued.

On the civil side, the decision whether to pursue a False Claims Act case is governed by many of the same considerations I have just outlined. Of course, we are also interested in attempting to recover the actual funds defrauded from the Government, as well as using the "penalty" provisions of the Act to recover funds reflecting other losses to the Government, such as interest and the cost of investigations. As you know, the Congress recently passed and the President signed the False Claims Act Amendments of 1986, P.L. 99-562 (October 27, 1986). Those Amendments increase the damages the United States is entitled to recover from double damages to triple damages and the forfeiture amount from $2000 per false claim to not less than $5000 and not more than $10,000 per false claim. The Amendments specifically provide, however, that if prior to becoming aware of an ongoing investigation into a matter, a person provides appropriate investigating officials with all the information in their possession about the fraud within 30 days of discovery and fully cooperates with the Government's investigation, the court may reduce damages from triple to no less than double. Thus, on the civil side, we have a well defined statutory basis providing not only an incentive to your announced self-disclosure policy, but also appropriate treatment for persons or corporations that promptly disclose wrongdoing and cooperate with the Government.

Apart from the questions of prosecutorial judgment, I believe it is important that the Defense Department coordinate closely with the Justice Department in administering its voluntary disclosure program. Accordingly, we have provided each United States Attorney with a copy of your July 1986 release. In addition, to assure that coordination between our Departments is properly maintained, our Defense Procurement Fraud Unit in the Criminal Division will continue as the contact point to review all voluntary disclosure issues on behalf of the Department of Justice. To assure consistency of decision making, the Defense Procurement Fraud Unit will also have responsibility for making or reviewing prosecutive decisions in cases involving voluntary disclosure by defense contractors.

I hope these remarks provide some guidance for the voluntary disclosure initiative and will aid in a successful self-policing and self-disclosure program for the industry. We look forward to our continued cooperation and success in combatting fraud in defense procurement.

Sincerely,

Arnold I. Burns
Deputy Attorney General

APPENDIX U

DFARS 225.872-1: List of Current DOD Qualifying Countries

Appendix U

DFARS 225.872-1: List of Current DOD Qualifying Countries

225.872-1 General.

(a) As a result of memoranda of understanding and other international agreements, DoD has determined it inconsistent with the public interest to apply restrictions of the Buy American statute or the Balance of Payments Program to the acquisition of qualifying country end products from the following qualifying countries:

- Australia
- Belgium
- Canada
- Czech Republic
- Denmark
- Egypt
- Federal Republic of Germany
- Finland
- France
- Greece
- Israel
- Italy
- Luxembourg
- Netherlands
- Norway
- Poland
- Portugal
- Spain
- Sweden
- Switzerland
- Turkey
- United Kingdom of Great Britain and Northern Ireland

(b) Individual acquisitions of qualifying country end products from the following qualifying country may, on a purchase-by-purchase basis (see 225.872-4), be exempted from application of the Buy American statute and the Balance of Payments Program as inconsistent with the public interest:

    Austria

(c) The determination in paragraph (a) of this subsection does not limit the authority of the Secretary concerned to restrict acquisitions to domestic sources or reject an otherwise acceptable offer from a qualifying country source when considered necessary for national defense reasons.

APPENDIX V

FAR 25.003: List of Designated Countries

Appendix V

FAR 25.003: List of Designated Countries

FAR 25.003

"Designated country" means any of the following countries:

(1) A World Trade Organization Government Procurement Agreement country (Armenia, Aruba, Austria, Belgium, Bulgaria, Canada, Croatia, Cyprus, Czech Republic, Denmark, Estonia, Finland, France, Germany, Greece, Hong Kong, Hungary, Iceland, Ireland, Israel, Italy, Japan, Korea (Republic of), Latvia, Liechtenstein, Lithuania, Luxembourg, Malta, Netherlands, Norway, Poland, Portugal, Romania, Singapore, Slovak Republic, Slovenia, Spain, Sweden, Switzerland, Taiwan (known in the World Trade Organization as "the Separate Customs Territory of Taiwan, Penghu, Kinmen and Matsu" (Chinese Taipei)) or United Kingdom);

(2) A Free Trade Agreement country (Australia, Bahrain, Canada, Chile, Colombia, Costa Rica, Dominican Republic, El Salvador, Guatemala, Honduras, Korea (Republic of), Mexico, Morocco, Nicaragua, Oman, Panama, Peru, or Singapore);

(3) A least developed country (Afghanistan, Angola, Bangladesh, Benin, Bhutan, Burkina Faso, Burundi, Cambodia, Central African Republic, Chad, Comoros, Democratic Republic of Congo, Djibouti, Equatorial Guinea, Eritrea, Ethiopia, Gambia, Guinea, Guinea-Bissau, Haiti, Kiribati, Laos, Lesotho, Liberia, Madagascar, Malawi, Mali, Mauritania, Mozambique, Nepal, Niger, Rwanda, Samoa, Sao Tome and Principe, Senegal, Sierra Leone, Solomon Islands, Somalia, South Sudan, Tanzania, Timor-Leste, Togo, Tuvalu, Uganda, Vanuatu, Yemen, or Zambia); or

(4) A Caribbean Basin country (Antigua and Barbuda, Aruba, Bahamas, Barbados, Belize, Bonaire, British Virgin Islands, Curacao, Dominica, Grenada, Guyana, Haiti, Jamaica, Montserrat, Saba, St. Kitts and Nevis, St. Lucia, St. Vincent and the Grenadines, Sint Eustatius, Sint Maarten, or Trinidad and Tobago).

APPENDIX W

DOD Security Assistance Management Manual Form Letter

80104.B.   DOD 5105.38-M

B. <u>Form Letter.</u>

Director
Defense Security Assistance Agency
Room 4E837, The Pentagon
Washington, D.C. 20301-2800

Dear Sir:

       The Government of [country] hereby appoints [name] whose address is [address] as its Agent for the purpose of receiving deliveries of the following items: Above items will be used for the [manufacture/assembly/repair/ rehabilitation]* of the [program]. Said Agent is hereby authorized to sign in the name of the Government of [country] as its Agent for the receipt of these items as indicated by the shipping instructions contained in the LOA. The Government of [country] undertakes to instruct [name] as its Agent to maintain possession of the above specified items in accordance with the LOA until transferred by such Agent of the Government of [country].

                                                                Sincerely,

Such agency is acknowledged.

_____
        (Signature of Agent)

---

* Insert words describing the Agent's function.

APPENDIX X

Defense Security Cooperation Agency, "Guidelines for Foreign Military Financing of Direct Commercial Contracts"

DEFENSE SECURITY COOPERATION AGENCY

**GUIDELINES FOR FOREIGN MILITARY FINANCING
OF DIRECT COMMERCIAL CONTRACTS**

AUGUST 2009

DEFENSE SECURITY COOPERATION AGENCY
201 12TH STREET SOUTH, STE 203
ARLINGTON, VA 22202-5408

AUG 3 1 2009

MEMORANDUM FOR RECORD

SUBJECT: Revision to the Defense Security Cooperation Agency's Guidelines for Foreign Military Financing of Direct Commercial Contracts

The Defense Security Cooperation Agency (DSCA) revised its *Guidelines for Foreign Military Financing of Direct Commercial Contracts and Contractor's Certification and Agreement* with DSCA, both dated January 2005. The current editions of both documents are dated August 2009.

Full implementation of the August 2009 editions of both the *Guidelines for Foreign Military Financing of Direct Commercial Contracts and Contractor's Certification and Agreement with DSCA* is now in effect. Countries participating in the Foreign Military Financing of Direct Commercial Contracts program should complete their transition to the August 2009 editions not later than October 1, 2009.

We appreciate your continued interest and support of this important aspect of the Security Assistance Program, and look forward to working with you in the future.

Jeffrey A. Wieringa
Vice Admiral, USN
Director

APPENDIX X   **App. X**

**Direct Commercial Contracts Guidelines and Contractor's
Certification Revisions**

Summary of Changes

Note: **Summary of changes not all inclusive.** (*Paragraphs and page numbers have change).*

1. On page 2 of the Guidelines, paragraph 4, added the following: DSCA will forward the request to the appropriate MilDep which has the right of first refusal. If the MilDep agrees to process a sale as a FMS case, a request for a DCC will not be approved.

2. On page 4 of the Guidelines, added new paragraph 7C which reads: The non-U.S. content of spare parts that are acquired separately by the Purchaser in a stand-alone DCC, not as part of an end item or as part of a "system" procurement, will not be approved for FMF funding. Non-U.S. content of a spare part cannot be funded under the COTS items exception unless the same spare part meets the requirements for being considered a COTS item under paragraph 6C above.

3. On page 4 of the Guidelines, added new paragraph 8 which reads: Any license fee and/or royalty to be paid by the prime contractor or any of its second- or third-tier subcontractors to a non-U.S. entity (defined as any manufacturer or supplier not incorporated or licensed to do business in the United States or any non-U.S. governmental agency), must be identified as non-U.S. content. This non-U.S. content may be approved for funding if it falls within one of the exceptions in paragraph 6 above.

4. On page 4 of the Guidelines, added new paragraph 11 which reads: Warranty work, such as maintenance arrangements, to be performed in the host nation (defined as the Purchaser country eligible under U.S. law to establish a DCC funded with FMF and that has entered into the DCC with the prime contractor) or outside of the U.S., and by non-U.S. personnel (defined as neither U.S. citizens nor resident aliens in the U.S.) must be declared as non-U.S. content and will not be approved for FMF funding.

5. On page 5 of the Guidelines, added new paragraph 12 which reads: All host-nation content (defined as the value of any defense articles manufactured, assembled, or supplied by host nation manufacturers or suppliers or any services performed in the host nation by citizens or residents of the host nation) must be identified as non-U.S. content and will not be approved for FMF funding regardless of whether this non-U.S. content meets an exception under paragraph 6 above.

6. On page 8 of the Guidelines, under **Offset Provisions,** further clarifies offsets as follows: A.) Offsets are compensation practices required as a condition of purchase; B.) Direct offsets are contractual arrangements that involve articles and services being financed under the DCC. C.) An indirect offset is any other offset arrangement.

7. On page 10 of the Guidelines, under **Refunds, Penalties, Liquidated Damages, Performance Bonds, Remittances**, added new paragraph 26A, which reads as follows: This notification will include rationale for the draw down and acknowledgement that the prime contractor has been notified of the intended action. DSCA will provide written acknowledgment to Purchaser confirming receipt of Purchaser's letter of intent to draw down on the ILC. Purchaser will not draw upon any ILC until it has received DSCA acknowledgement in writing. At that time, DSCA will notify DFAS of Purchaser's intended action.

8. On page 12 of the Guidelines, added new paragraph 29 which reads as follows: DSCA will not approve a Defined Basic Ordering Agreement (DBOA) purchase order totaling $750,000 or more without a pricing review being conducted by DCMA. DCMA, with assistance as required from the Defense Contract Audit Agency (DCAA), will provide field-pricing support, at the Purchaser's expense, as a condition of FMF funding of the DBOA. The Purchaser must provide a copy of the offer to DCMA for its use in providing this support.

9. On page 17 of the Guidelines, **Enclosure 2 – Pricing Reviews**, provided clarification under paragraph 3 concerning "Field Support".

1. On page 1 of the **Contractor Certification and Agreement,** the paragraphs were renumbered to add a new paragraph 1 which reads as follows: Agrees the Contractor will comply in all respects with the "DSCA Guidelines for Foreign Military Financing of Direct Commercial Contracts" that **were** in effect when the contract **was** signed. Further, should a newer version of the Guidelines be published subsequent to contract award, the Contractor agrees to comply in all respects with the "DSCA Guidelines for Foreign Military Financing of Direct Commercial Contracts" that is in effect when any amendment or modification to such a contract is signed.

Appendix X

Overview

In 1984 the U.S. Department of Defense (DoD) established guidelines for the processing and review of commercial contracts for direct purchase of U.S. defense articles and services from U.S. firms to be financed with funds appropriated by the Congress. Since that time the program has been downscoped. Purchasers (defined as the foreign countries eligible by U.S. law to establish Direct Commercial Contracts (DCCs) funded with Foreign Military Financing (FMF)) are encouraged to use the Foreign Military Sales (FMS) system for their acquisition needs. These revised guidelines supersede the guidelines dated January 2005.

Direct commercial contracts are contracts to which the U.S. Government (USG) is not a party. Purchasers enter into DCCs directly with U.S. companies. FMF may be used to fund DCCs, when approved on a case-by-case basis by the Defense Security Cooperation Agency (DSCA), for the purchase of defense articles, defense services, and design and construction services. However, as indicated in the financing agreement to which the USG and the Purchaser foreign governments are parties, the USG is under no obligation to approve any specific DCC for FMF funding.

The financing of DCCs comes under the review and scrutiny of the General Accounting Office (GAO), the DoD Inspector General (DoD/IG), the Department of Justice (DOJ), and the Congress. Revisions of these guidelines, over time, reflect DoD's effort to minimize vulnerability to waste, fraud, and abuse, and where possible, maximize application of acquisition streamlining and reform principles.

The Security Assistance Management Manual (SAMM), DoD 5105.38-M, and the following guidelines explain DoD's policies and procedures for the use of FMF of DCCs between U.S. industry and Purchasers:

Contractor Eligibility

1. The prime contractor must be a U.S. supplier or manufacturer, incorporated or licensed to do business in the United States.

2. Purchase agreements should be made directly with the manufacturer of the defense article or service, if possible. The prime contractor is expected to add value to the product being sold.

A. Purchases of materiel should be made, to the maximum extent feasible, from the prime manufacturer, or assembler, or from a U.S.-based distributor of a manufacturer or assembler pursuant to a long-standing contractual or licensed relationship.

B. The prime contractor must demonstrate to the DSCA (through completion of a DoD preaward survey or other means) its capability -- including, e.g., expertise, experience, plant, and financial soundness -- to perform by itself a substantial portion of the work. Prior successful completion of recent DCCs financed with FMF funds or DoD contracts for the same or essentially similar items shall normally satisfy this requirement

C. When applicable, Purchasers should ensure that the items purchased demonstrate interoperability to enhance U.S. and allied nation compatibility and standardization.

D. Funding with FMF will not be considered for a procurement agent, broker, import-export firm or other intermediary unless justified by factors relating to specific country needs and the country's abilities to conduct commercial contracting. A request for exception will be considered if sufficient justification is provided by the Purchaser as to why the purchase is sought from a firm other than the prime manufacturer.

E. Prime contractors are required to ensure that all first and second tier suppliers and subcontractors are not excluded from federal programs (see paragraph 34). Prime contractors will maintain a list showing the names and addresses and materials/services procured of all first and second tier suppliers and subcontractors applicable to the DCC. The prime contractor must provide this list to DSCA on request.

Standard/Nonstandard Items

3. DCCs are intended for procurement of non-standard items, e.g., items that do not have a national stock number (NSN) and are not regularly procured through the U.S. supply system. Modified NSN items (items that have been altered from their normal/original NSN configuration) may not be procured under DCCs. Purchasers must demonstrate items are non-standard by providing catalog data or information received from the U.S. military department (MilDeps) or DoD components that the item cannot be procured through the U.S. supply system.

4. DCCs normally will not be permitted for items that are standard to DoD, e.g., items that have NSNs. However, the Purchaser may request exceptions from DSCA for the commercial procurement of standard DoD items. When doing so, the Purchaser must provide written justification to DSCA supporting its request. The justification should include the item description, required delivery date, and any other information that may be pertinent to the exception decision. In those instances where additional information regarding availability, performance, characteristics, releasability, etc. is required, DSCA will consult with the appropriate MilDep or DoD component. DSCA will forward the request to the appropriate MilDep which has the right of first refusal. If the MilDep agrees to process a sale as a FMS case, a request for a DCC will not be approved.

A. Purchaser representatives should allow approximately 45 days for DSCA to process an exception request and provide a written decision.

B. If DSCA has approved use of the DCC channel to meet the requirement, the Purchaser may then submit a contract to DSCA for consideration of FMF. When the

APPENDIX X

contract is submitted for review, the Purchaser must attach the exception letter (see Enclosure 1).

5. The use of FMF for DCCs is permissible for the development and/or procurement of articles and services in support of major country-unique programs. The Purchaser should consult with DSCA and receive approval prior to proceeding with contract negotiations on major unique systems. Written justification supporting the Purchaser's request to use FMF for a DCC should be provided to DSCA as far in advance as possible, but not less than 45 days before solicitation of offers or initiation of contract negotiations. This will allow sufficient time to evaluate the proposed acquisition and, if necessary, consult with the appropriate MilDep or DoD component. If justification is not provided to the DSCA prior to submission of a contract, processing of the request for funding approval may be delayed or the DCC may be returned without review.

U.S. and Non-U.S. Content

6. In order for a DCC to be approved for FMF funding, the defense articles purchased must be manufactured and assembled in the United States, or the defense services purchased must be performed by U.S. manufacturers and suppliers, purchased from U.S. manufacturers or suppliers, and composed of U.S.-origin materiel, components, goods, and services (hereafter "U.S. content"). Prime contractors must maintain and provide, if requested, supporting documentation for the value of both U.S. and non-U.S. origin content. In the event the purchase of a U.S. end item consists of both U.S. and non-U.S. origin content, only the value of the U.S. origin content will normally be financed.

A. An exception for FMF may be considered for items originally manufactured in the U.S. and purchased by a U.S. contractor from non-U.S. (foreign) sources.

B. An exception for FMF may be considered for non-U.S. content that is an integral part of end items manufactured and assembled in the United States when the USG has procured or is procuring the same end item from the same source. To allow this exception DSCA requires, as a minimum, identification of the non-U.S. content item, its value, and the corresponding USG contract number.

C. An exception for FMF may be considered for non-U.S. content that is an integral part of commercially available off-the-shelf (COTS) items. A COTS item is a commercial item sold in substantial quantities in the commercial marketplace and offered to the U.S. Government without modification and in the same form in which it is sold in the commercial marketplace (see 41 USC 431). COTS does not include bulk cargo such as agricultural products and petroleum products. A COTS item may be eligible for FMF if it is manufactured and assembled in the United States by a U.S. manufacturer or supplier and is composed of at least 51% U.S. origin content. To allow this exception DSCA requires, as a minimum, a detailed description of the COTS items and information about sales in the commercial marketplace. DSCA may require additional information to ensure that an item is COTS.

App. X GOVERNMENT CONTRACT COMPLIANCE HANDBOOK

7. Direct Commercial Contracts must specify all non-U.S. origin content. If not identified in the contract, non-U.S. content must be identified to DSCA by the Purchaser in supporting documents. To facilitate this:

A. The prime contractor is required to identify to the Purchaser any non-U.S. content, the corresponding value contained in the contract, and where applicable, supporting documentation to demonstrate that the USG has procured or is procuring the same non-U.S. content or non-U.S. origin items, components, or services from the same non-U.S. source for the same end item the USG has procured or is procuring. Supporting documentation should include the USG contract number(s) under which the non-U.S. content/item(s) was purchased, if appropriate, and any other pertinent information.

B. If raw materials, components, or items used in the manufacturing process are procured from both U.S. and non-U.S. sources, and are not segregated as to origin, and are incorporated on an interchangeable basis into the prime contractor's articles or services, the actual dollar value need not be identified. Instead, a non-U.S. content estimating methodology or system (for example, an annual survey) may be used by the prime contractor. The use of such a methodology must be approved by DSCA prior to DSCA processing the DCC.

C. The non-U.S. content of spare parts that are acquired separately by the Purchaser in a stand-alone DCC, not as part of an end item or as part of a "system" procurement, will not be approved for FMF funding. The non-U.S. content of a spare part cannot be funded under the COTS items exception unless the same spare part meets the requirement for being considered a COTS item under paragraph 6C above.

8. Any license fee and/or royalty to be paid by the prime contractor or any of its second- or third-tier subcontractors to a non-U.S. entity (defined as any manufacturer or supplier not incorporated or licensed to do business in the United States or any non-U.S. governmental agency), must be identified as non-U.S. content. This non-U.S. content may be approved for funding if it falls within one of the exceptions in paragraph 6 above.

9. Expenses incurred by non-U.S. (foreign) subsidiaries of U.S. prime contractors or their non-U.S. second- or third-tier subcontractors are considered to be non-U.S. content and must be declared. Reasonable expenses for support of U.S. contractor personnel (defined as U.S. citizen employees or U.S. resident alien employees of U.S. prime contractors) performing services temporarily in the host nation (purchaser country) are considered U.S. content and may be funded with FMF.

10. Profits to be earned and G&A expenses to be incurred, if any, by U.S. prime contractors and subcontractors are considered to be U.S. content and elements of the Purchase Agreement Price.

11. Warranty work, such as maintenance arrangements, to be performed in the host nation (defined as the Purchaser country eligible under U.S. law to establish a DCC

APPENDIX X

funded with FMF and that has entered into the DCC with the prime contractor) or outside of the U.S., and by non-U.S. personnel (defined as neither U.S. citizens nor resident aliens in the U.S.) must be declared as non-U.S. content and will not be approved for FMF funding.

12. All host-nation content (defined as the value of any defense articles manufactured, assembled, or supplied by host nation manufacturers or suppliers or any services performed in the host nation by citizens or residents of the host nation) must be identified as non-U.S. content and will not be approved for FMF funding regardless of whether this non-U.S. content meets an exception under paragraph 6 above.

Contract Dollar Threshold

13. Direct Commercial Contracts for less than $100,000 will not normally be approved for FMF.[1] All amendments and modifications to DCCs funded with FMF, including no cost amendments that do not change contract scope, must be submitted to DSCA for review and approval. Changes/amendments should be submitted in chronological order and numbered accordingly.

A. Any changes that add, delete, or substitute previously contracted articles or services must be accomplished through an amendment to the DCC. If the prime contractor has previously received payment for the articles or services deleted and not replaced, the prime contractor will be required to refund the amount of these payments. In any event, the DCC price will be reduced accordingly.

B. Changes to DCCs requiring additional FMF will not be approved for FMF funding later than five years from the date DSCA approved financing of the basic DCC. Requests for exception may be approved if the Purchaser provides sufficient justification to DSCA. Normally, the Purchaser will be required to enter into a new DCC if the Purchaser desires to continue purchasing the defense articles or services.

Competition Requirements

14. It is highly recommended that the Purchaser contact several U.S. companies or firms for solicitation of offers to meet its specific needs. All DCCs awarded on a competitive basis will require the Purchaser to identify, in writing, the various contractors solicited and the prices submitted. If the lowest offeror was not selected, the Purchaser must provide a written explanation of the basis for the contract award. If this information is not provided, the DCC will be returned to the Purchaser for inclusion of such data.

15. Sole source procurements shall be accompanied by sufficient justification; such as, but not limited to, urgent need, procurement history, standardization with Purchaser inventory, and Purchasers' own source selection process.

---

[1] Direct Commercial Contracts for the Government of Israel less than $30,000 will not normally be approved for FMF.

Contract Processing

16. Prime contractors and Purchaser representatives should plan for the time required by DoD to perform the processing necessary to determine the extent of FMF funding authorization. The processing time for DCCs that are in full compliance with these guidelines is approximately 20 calendar days. The Purchaser is responsible for providing copies of the DSCA Guidelines and the Contractor's Certification to the prime contractor. If the DCC is submitted without the required certification, the DCC will be returned to the Purchaser for inclusion of such data. When the prospective purchase is from a prime contractor that does not regularly sell to the U.S. Government, the Purchaser should set a commencement date for the DCC that allows at least an additional 30 days for the U.S. Government to conduct a preaward survey.

Contract Financing

17. The DCCs must clearly identify the amount of any financing payments and be in accordance with the following limitations:

A. The Purchaser is responsible for demonstrating the reasonableness and security of contract financing arrangements.

B. Advance payments for FMF-funded DCCs made before performance of work under the DCC shall not exceed 15 percent (15%) of the contract price. The Purchaser shall obtain adequate security for such payments in accordance with paragraph F below.

C. Financing arrangements for DCCs may provide for payments to be made on the basis of accomplishment of specific milestones detailed in the DCC, or other basis such as installments. Installments shall be payable no more frequently than quarterly.

D. Cumulative DCC financing shall not exceed 85 percent (85%) of the DCC price of undelivered items. See paragraph F below for security requirements.

E. Full payment for a DCC shall not be made until after complete performance of the DCC.

F. All unliquidated advance and interim financing payments made by the U.S. Government shall be secured by guarantee documents, such as Irrevocable Letters of Guarantee (ILOG), Irrevocable Letters of Credit (ILOC), or Irrevocable Performance Bonds (IPB). See paragraph 25). The security shall be at least equal to the amount of the unliquidated contract financing. Direct Commercial Contracts lacking adequate provisions to ensure prompt payment directly to the U.S. Government will not be accepted.

G. Purchasers may not assess charges to U.S. prime contractors for processing DCCs or invoices for payment. FMF will be withdrawn if such charges are determined to have been assessed or if the Purchaser representatives have solicited U.S. prime contractors to

APPENDIX X   App. X

provide free materiel, services, advertising, or other similar forms of benefits as a condition of award of a DCC or processing of invoices.

H. After validation of invoices, the Purchaser should submit them within 30 calendar days of receipt from the prime contractor to the Defense Finance and Accounting Service (DFAS) Indianapolis for payment.

Essential Elements of Contract

18. The Purchaser must submit complete copies of all DCCs and contract provisions to DSCA for FMF funding review. The Purchaser must also submit all subsequent modifications, amendments, side letters, or supplementary agreements that affect the contractual relationship between the Purchaser and the prime contractor.

A. Contracts should include, as a minimum, all essential contract elements outlined below:
(1) Purchaser Country.
(2) Complete identification of U.S. Prime Contractor to include name, address, and telephone number.
(3) Contract number.
(4) Complete nomenclature of defense articles and description of services to be provided.
(5) Complete description of quantities and prices.
(6) Complete description of financial arrangements:
   - Unit prices
   - Advance payment
   - Payment schedule (to include method of liquidating advance payment based on deliveries)
(7) Contract clauses for contract audit.
(8) Identification of shipment terms.
(9) Guarantee Documents (See paragraph 25). Identification of any guarantee documents or clauses that could result in a refund to the Purchaser, such as, but not limited to,:
   - Advance payment guarantee documents
   - Interim payment guarantee documents
   - Liquidated damages
(10) Acceptance (signature) by both parties.

B. In addition to the DCC, the following supporting documentation must be provided to DSCA for FMF funding approval:
(1) Identification of all non-U.S. origin content.
(2) Identification of offsets.
(3) Prime Contractor's Certification and Agreement with DSCA with original signatures.
(4) List of offerors and prices submitted on competitive procurements.
(5) Justification for selection of other than the lowest offeror on competitive contracts.
(6) Copy of Purchaser request for exception to use a DCC (if applicable e.g. to purchase an NSN item).

C. Undefined Basic Ordering Agreements (BOAs) are discouraged and will not be approved for FMF funding.

Contractor Disclosures & Certifications and Export Documentation

19. DSCA requires prime contractors to make disclosures and execute the Contractor's Certification and Agreement with DSCA, in the proposal and the contracting process. Full and accurate disclosures and certifications are prerequisites for DSCA approval of FMF funding. Export licenses documentation must be provided to DSCA and DFAS Indianapolis before FMF payments can be made.

A. For DCCs valued at $100,000 or more, the Contractor's Certification and Agreement must be signed by the prime contractor and be submitted by the Purchaser to DSCA when the DCC is provided for funding review. The date of the current Certification is August 2009. The Certification submitted to DSCA must have <u>original signatures of two</u> company officials other than those who signed the DCC.

B. Prime contractors who execute many DCCs for identical defense articles, services, or categories of such articles or services with the same Purchaser may request DSCA approve an annual Contractor's Certification and Agreement. To do so, prime contractors must demonstrate that their particular business operations promote the use of an annual Certification and that they have a sound estimating methodology to provide the information required by the Certification.

C. Prime contractors must provide copies of any or all export licenses related to the DCC (or alternatively, written documentation that confirms that an export license is not required) to "DFAS Indianapolis" and "DSCA OPS-ME/DCC".

Offset Provisions

20. Requesting FMF funding for DCCs containing offset provisions as a condition for securing the purchase is not encouraged. Grant FMF (nonrepayable FMF funds) will <u>not</u> be used to pay for any offsets, to include direct and indirect offsets, or the related costs of offset implementation. If the DCC is wholly financed with repayable FMF credit or a mix of repayable FMF credit and Purchaser funds, offset costs may be included in the DCC funding. However, if any nonrepayable FMF funds are used to fund a DCC, offset costs may only be paid if they are paid in full by repayable FMF credit or Purchaser's national funds. The amount of offset costs included in such DCCs must be disclosed to the USG.

A. Offsets are compensation practices required as a condition of purchase.

B. Direct offsets are contractual arrangements that involve articles and services being financed under the DCC

C. An indirect offset is any other offset arrangement.

APPENDIX X

Commissions or Contingent Fees

21. Commissions or contingent fees related to the DCC must be disclosed by the prime contractor during DCC negotiations and to DSCA at the time the DCC is presented for funding approval. The prime contractor shall maintain documents and records to demonstrate that commissions or contingent fees are not funded by the USG.

22. Commissions or contingent fees for the purpose of securing the DCC will not be included in the price of an FMF funded DCC, unless such payments have been identified and approved in writing by the Purchaser prior to contract award for payment in full with repayable FMF credit or Purchaser's national funds.[2]

Personnel Travel

23. FMF will not be approved for payments for travel, per diem, accommodations, lodging, car rental, personal expenses, entertainment, or other similar expenses incurred by or for Purchaser country personnel that relate directly or indirectly in any way with a DCC. The reasonable cost of business meals for prime contractor or subcontractor personnel is an allowable cost that may be incurred by the prime contractor.

Contracts with Transportation Requirements

24. The use of FMF will only be approved for the financing of transportation performed by U.S. carriers. Any waivers (general, security, or non-availability) will be in accordance with the Purchaser's agreement with DSCA. The waivers are described in the agreements and may apply to either specific shipments or for a specific period of financing. Prime contractors will include these requirements in all subcontracts for DCCs.

A. For ocean transportation of FMF shipments, the prime contractor and the Purchaser will use, or cause to be used, privately-owned U.S.-flag commercial vessels. For prime contractor-originated ocean shipments, the prime contractor will, within 20 days of loading, submit one legible copy of the rated on-board ocean bill of lading for each shipment to: US Maritime Administration, Office of Cargo Preference and Domestic Trade, Civilian Agencies Division, Mail Stop W23-453, 1200 New Jersey Avenue SE, Washington DC 20590. The bill of lading will identify: contract (DCC) number; name of vessel; flag of registry; date and port of loading; port of final discharge; description, weight, and value of cargo; and total ocean freight revenue.

B. No payments will be made to freight forwarders with FMF unless, prior to July 1, 1994, DSCA had authorized the Purchaser to use FMF-funded DCCs to procure freight forwarding services. Rated, on-board bills of lading or rated airway bills may be approved for direct payments to U.S. ocean or air carriers upon request.

---

[2] Neither Egypt nor Israel receive repayable FMF funds and the U.S. Congress has not currently appropriated repayable FMF funds to any other country.

App. X   GOVERNMENT CONTRACT COMPLIANCE HANDBOOK

Letters of Credit/Guarantee

25. FMF will not be approved for financing of commercial letters of credit or other guarantees which ensure payment to the prime contractor or subcontractor. FMF funding may be approved if the DCC requires irrevocable letters of credit, performance bonds, or other forms of performance guarantees from the prime contractor. They must be issued by a bank or financial institution licensed in and doing business in the United States. In addition, irrevocable letters of credit, performance bonds, or other forms of performance guarantees must be identified as a separate line item or clause within the DCC that states: "All irrevocable letters of credit, performance bonds, or other guarantees required by the Purchaser must provide for payment directly to the U.S. Government". (See paragraph 26).

A. Only federally-insured financial institutions licensed in and doing business in the United States, rated investment grade or higher shall issue or confirm an irrevocable letter of credit (ILC). Unless the financial institution issuing the ILC had letter of credit business of at least $25 million in the past year, ILCs over $5 million must be confirmed by another acceptable financial institution that had letter of credit business of at least $25 million in the past year and otherwise meets all of the requirements for issuing an ILC.

B. DFAS-IN will not disperse payments to prime contractors until it receives copies of all irrevocable letters of credit, bonding or guarantee documents applicable to the DCC. Copies must also be sent to DSCA/OPS-ME/DCC.

Refunds, Penalties, Liquidated Damages, Performance Bonds, Remittances

26. Any DCC that provides for a refund, penalty, liquidated damages, bonding provisions, or any other form of financial reimbursement to the Purchaser must be structured to ensure that such payment is made by the prime contractor or designated agent (including the prime contractor's commercial bank) directly and without undue delay, from the payor to the U.S. Government.

A. Should the Purchaser determine a draw on an irrevocable letter of credit is required, it must first notify DSCA/OPS-ME/DCC and the prime contractor in writing stating the exact reasons necessitating the draw down and the amount at least 15 calendar days prior to the draw down. This notification will include rationale for the draw down and acknowledgement that the prime contractor has been notified of the intended action. DSCA will provide written acknowledgment to Purchaser confirming receipt of Purchaser's letter of intent to draw down on the ILC. Purchaser will not draw upon any ILC until it has received DSCA acknowledgement in writing. At that time, DSCA will notify DFAS of Purchaser's intended action. It is the Purchaser's responsibility to ensure funds are transferred directly from the payor to the U.S. Government.

B. Bonding and guarantee documents, such as Performance Bonds, Irrevocable Letters of Guarantee, Irrevocable Letters of Credit, and any other such instruments that are established by the prime contractor or its agent pursuant to the DCC, must be sent to the

APPENDIX X   App. X

DFAS Indianapolis and DSCA/OPS-ME/DCC and made part of the DCC file. This is a prerequisite to disbursement of FMF funds to the prime contractor. Bonding and guarantee documents lacking adequate provisions to ensure prompt payment to the U.S. Government will not be accepted, and payments for the DCC will not be made until this requirement is satisfied.

C. Reimbursement payments must be remitted to the addresses noted below. These payments, when received by the DFAS Indianapolis, will be credited to the Purchaser's FMS trust fund account. Any reimbursement equal to or less than the FMF funds paid by the DSCA on the DCC may be applied to any FMS or commercial case approved for FMF. If a reimbursement exceeds the amount of FMF funds paid by the DSCA, the excess amount of may be applied as "cash" to any FMS case.

D. Remittances should be processed as follows:

(1) Payments by check must be accompanied by a letter, which identifies the Purchaser and the DSCA case identifier. The check must be made payable to the "United States Treasury" and mailed to:

Defense Finance and Accounting Service-Indianapolis Center
DFAS-IN/JAXBA (Credit Sales)
8899 E. 56th Street
Indianapolis, IN 46249-6300

(2) Payments by wire transfer should be transferred as follows:

United States Treasury
New York, New York
021-030-004
DFAS-IN/JAXBA
Agency Code 3801
Refund from: **(Name of Prime Contractor)**
For purchase made by the: Government of   **(Purchaser Country)**
DSCA case (Identifier)_____

Preaward Surveys

27. To verify the prime contractors' statements and determine its capability to perform under the DCC terms, a DoD preaward survey or verification of the prime contractor's Certification such as ISO 9000, may be required as a condition of FMF approval. Preaward surveys are not normally required for U.S. manufacturers or suppliers that are selling or have recently sold the same defense articles or services to DoD. Whether DSCA requires it or a Purchaser requests a preaward survey, the Purchaser will pay for this service under an FMS Letter of Offer and Acceptance (LOA) negotiated with Defense Contract Management Agency (DCMA).

App. X   GOVERNMENT CONTRACT COMPLIANCE HANDBOOK

Pricing Reviews

28. A pricing review is required prior to DCC award for all sole-source procurements of $750,000 or more. DCMA, with assistance as required from the Defense Contract Audit Agency (DCAA), will provide field-pricing support, at the Purchaser's expense, as a condition for FMF funding of the DCC. The Purchaser must provide a copy of the offer to DCMA for its use in providing this support.

A. DCMA, with DCAA assistance as required, will perform price reviews, and cost analyses and technical evaluations to determine price reasonableness of offers. The Purchaser should allow at least 45 calendar days for the U.S. Government representative to perform these functions and provide the subject reports to the Purchaser.

B. The Purchaser must include a copy of the pricing review as part of its justification submitted to DSCA in support of its request to use FMF to fund a DCC.

C. The Purchaser will be required to pay for this service under an FMS Letter of Offer and Acceptance (LOA) negotiated with DCMA.

D. On all amendments of $750,000 or more for DCCs previously approved for FMF funding the Purchaser will consult with DSCA to determine if a price review or cost analysis will be required.

E. The Purchaser is required to incorporate contract clauses consistent with the requirements detailed in Enclosure 2 into its requests for proposal on FMF-funded DCCs.

F. For sole source purchases of $750,000 or more of commercially available off-the-shelf (COTS) items that are sold pursuant to published catalog prices, DSCA will consider, on a case-by-case basis, the Purchaser's request for waiver of the DCMA field pricing analysis. All such requests must be accompanied by supporting documentation that demonstrates the reasonableness of the proposed price.

29. DSCA will not approve a Defined Basic Ordering Agreement (DBOA) purchase order totaling $750,000 or more without a pricing review being conducted by DCMA. DCMA, with assistance as required from the Defense Contract Audit Agency (DCAA), will provide field-pricing support, at the Purchaser's expense, as a condition of FMF funding of the DBOA. The Purchaser must provide a copy of the offer to DCMA for its use in providing this support.

Contract Administration/Audit Services

30. On all DCCs valued at $750,000 or more (sole source, DBOAs, or competitive awards) the Purchaser is required to contract with DCMA for contract audit services (CAS) using a DCMA FMS case. At a minimum, DCMA will arrange with DCAA to monitor the prime contractor's performance to ensure compliance with the DSCA Contractor's Certification throughout the life of the DCC. The Purchaser is required to

APPENDIX X

incorporate the following contract clause into its FMF-funded DCCs of $750,000 or more:

As a condition of FMF funding of the DCC, the prime contractor agrees that Defense Contract Audit Agency (DCAA) contract audit services will be performed to ensure that the prime contractor is in compliance with the Defense Security Cooperation Agency (DSCA) Contractor's Certification and Agreement. DCAA will perform contract audit services in accordance with the prime contractor's certification. To ensure prime contractor compliance DCAA contract audit services will be provided over the life of the DCC and will be coordinated with the Defense Contract Management Agency.

31. The Defense Contract Management Agency (DCMA) can perform quality assurance services if required by the DCC, if requested by the Purchaser, or if directed by DSCA.

A. The cost of DCMA quality assurance services may be provided in the DCC and paid to DFAS Indianapolis by the prime contractor on behalf of the Purchaser. However, the Purchaser is required to arrange for these services through an FMS agreement with the DCMA.

B. For some DCCs, DSCA may require DCMA quality assurance verification before delivery to ensure that the quality of the defense articles or services is in accordance with DCC contract terms. If DSCA determines such quality assurance verification is required as a condition for FMF funding, DSCA will notify the Purchaser. The Purchaser is obligated to notify the prime contractor. Generally, DoD quality assurance services are arranged by the Defense Contract Management Agency, International and Federal Business Team:

Defense Contract Management Agency
ATTN: DCMA-FBFR
6350 Walker Lane Suite 300
(703) 428-1327
(703) 428-1505 (Fax)
Alexandria, VA 22310-3266

U.S. Government Audits

32. All FMF-funded DCCs are subject to audit by the Defense Contract Audit Agency (DCAA). DCAA will perform audits, at the U.S. Government's expense, to ensure the prime contractor's compliance with these Guidelines and the requirements in the prime contractor's Certification. DCAA may initiate audits at any time up to three years following receipt of the final payment on the DCC by the prime contractor. The Purchaser is required to incorporate contract clauses consistent with the requirements detailed in Enclosure 3 into its requests for proposal on FMF-funded DCCs.

App. X GOVERNMENT CONTRACT COMPLIANCE HANDBOOK

Accounting Principles

33. Prime contractors must comply with generally accepted accounting principles and, if a prime contractor otherwise contracts with DoD, the prime contractor must comply with the applicable cost accounting standards. FMF may be disallowed for DCCs, which result in additional costs being transferred to the DoD. The DCAA has expressed concerns about the formation (by U.S. prime contractors) of separate corporate segments to conduct foreign sales. In some cases, when significant intracompany contracting is involved, the resulting allocations of costs are inconsistent with cost accounting standards and result unjustifiably in the allocation of additional costs to DoD contracts. If DoD prime contractors establish separate companies or other corporate segments for the purpose of conducting foreign sales and request FMF for sales by such segments, DSCA will request DCAA review of the transaction. FMF will be approved only upon confirmation by the DCAA that the arrangement is consistent with cost accounting standards and that there would be no unjustifiable additional cost on DoD contracts with the prime contractor.

Parties Excluded from FMF Funding

34. The Defense Contract Management Agency (DCMA) is the executive agency for debarment and suspension proceedings.

A. FMF funding will not be approved for DCCs with U.S. manufacturers, suppliers, or persons included on the U.S. General Services Administration List of Parties Excluded From Federal Procurement or Nonprocurement Programs; the U.S. Commerce List of Denial Orders Currently Affecting Export Privileges; or similar determinations in which the U.S. Department of State has made certain contractors ineligible to export material under the International Traffic in Arms Regulations (ITAR).

B. The applicable web site for the General Service Administration list is https://epls.gov; the Commerce Lists are found at http://www.bis.doc.gov/complianceandenforcement/liststocheck.htm; and the State Department list is http://www.pmddtc.state.gov/licensing/debar.html.

C. Before such DCCs can be considered for FMF funding, the U.S. prime contractor involved must take appropriate administrative or legal steps to remove the relevant organization or individual from the debarment/suspension list. Such action should be taken directly with the agency that has debarment responsibility. Proof of removal from such debarment or suspension lists must be provided to DSCA/OPS-ME/DCC.

Insurance Requirements

35. Use of a U.S. insurance firm is required if FMF funding is used to pay this cost.

APPENDIX X   App. X

Contract Dispute /Arbitration

36. Contract dispute resolution and/or arbitration, if the DCC includes an arbitration clause, must take place in either the United States or a mutually agreed third country, but not in the Purchaser's country. The arbitration clause shall provide that the arbitrator(s) shall determine the matters in dispute in accordance with the commercial law of the United States or of any state of the United States, as agreed by the parties and set forth in the DCC, notwithstanding that the rules of private international law (choice-of-law rules) might otherwise lead to the application of some other law.

DSCA Points of Contact

37. DCCs and supporting documentation should be submitted by the Purchaser to the following address:

Defense Security Cooperation Agency
ATTN: Director, OPS-ME/DCC
201 12th Street South, Suite 203
Arlington, VA 22202-5408

38. Inquiries concerning these policies and procedures or the DCC review process should be directed to the above address or by phone to (703) 601-3714 or (703) 604-6580.

39. A copy of these Guidelines and/or the Contractor's Certification and Agreement with DSCA, dated August, 2009 may be downloaded from the following internet address: http://www.dsca.mil.

Enclosures: As stated

ENCLOSURE 1

REQUESTS FOR EXCEPTIONS

Requests for exceptions for standard DoD items and/or justification for major-unique items to be funded with U.S. FMF funds must, at a minimum, include the following:

A. Purchaser Country:

B. Identification of Requirements:
   (1) U.S. Defense Items or Services (item description and NSN).
   (2) Quantity.
   (3) Estimated Purchase Agreement Value in U.S. Dollars.
   (4) Projected date of submission of contract to DSCA for funding approval.
   (5) Required delivery date.

C. Basis for requesting exception to allow FMF funding of a Direct Commercial Contract, including, but not limited to the following:
   (1) Statement as to why a DCC should be used instead of FMS.
   (2) Anticipated source of goods or services.
   (3) Documentation from MilDep or DoD component supporting FMF-DCC request.

APPENDIX X   App. X

ENCLOSURE 2

PRICING REVIEWS

1. As a condition of FMF funding of sole source contracts of $750,000 or more, or in other circumstances where such a pricing review is required by DSCA, the prime contractor must agree to the requirement for field pricing review. The Defense Contract Management Agency (DCMA) and the Defense Contract Audit Agency (DCAA) will conduct this review. It may include a technical and cost analysis of the contractor's proposal.

2. The Purchaser shall request field-pricing support through the DCMA International and Federal Business Team by emailing their request to mailbox, dodccp@dcma.mil. Field pricing support may include a review by the cognizant contract audit activity before concluding negotiation of the DCC or any modification. The prime contractor may be required to submit cost or pricing data in connection with pricing of the DCC or any modification to the DCC that affects the price of the DCC.

3. The U.S. Government field support is intended to give the Purchaser a detailed analysis of the proposal for use in contract negotiations to determine a fair and reasonable price prior to contract award. It normally would be a Defense Contract Audit Agency audit or procedure, appropriate to evaluate the contractor's proposal. It may also include a technical analysis by Defense Contract Management Agency, if required by the cognizant auditor. The field support may include any of the following:

A. A Cost audit of the individual cost elements:
   (1) Evaluation that that proposed costs are current, accurate, and complete, based on an adequate contractor proposal;
   (2) Comparison of costs proposed by the offeror to actual historical costs previously incurred by the same offeror;
   (3) Evaluation of forecasts or planned expenditures;
   (4) Verification of cost or pricing data and evaluation of the cost elements;
   (5) Analysis of the results of any make-or-buy program reviews in evaluating proposed subcontracts;
   (6) Independent evaluation of technical aspects of the contractor's estimates by appropriate Government technical specialists.

B. A Price review:
   (1) Establishment that the contractor's proposed supplies or services are eligible for commercial pricing status. Commercial items include any item of a type customarily used by the general public, or by nongovernmental entities, for purposes other than Government purposes that has been sold, leased, or licensed to the general public;
   (2) Comparison of the proposed prices to previously awarded Government and commercial contract prices for the same or similar items, if both the validity of the comparison and the reasonableness of the previous prices is established;

(3) Use of parametric estimating methods or other Cost Estimating Relationships (CERs);
(4) Comparison of the proposed prices to competitive published price lists, supplier's catalog, published market prices of commodities, similar indexes, and discount or rebate arrangements;
(5) Comparison of the proposed prices with prices obtained through market research;
(6) Analyzing any other pricing information provided by the offeror.

C. Verification that the offeror's cost/price submissions are in accordance with U.S. Federal Acquisition Regulations (FAR), Defense Federal Acquisition Regulations Supplement (DFARS), other contract cost principles and procedures, generally accepted accounting principles, and the requirements and procedures of the Cost Accounting Standards (CAS), as applicable.

D. A review to determine that all cost or pricing data necessary to make the contractor's proposal accurate, complete, and current has been either submitted or identified in writing by the contractor.

E. An analysis of the results of any make-or-buy program reviews, in evaluating subcontractor costs.

4. The technical analysis should include a review and assessment of: the quantities and kinds of material proposed; the need for the number and kinds of labor hours and the labor mix; any special tooling and facilities proposed; reasonableness of proposed scrap and spoilage factors; and any other data that may be pertinent to the cost or price analysis.

5. Non-competitively awarded subcontracts meeting the $750,000 or more threshold are subject to the same field pricing requirements as the prime contract.

Appendix X   App. X

ENCLOSURE 3

U.S. GOVERNMENT AUDITS

USG representatives shall have the right to examine and audit all the prime contractor's books, records, documents, and other data, related to proposing, negotiating, pricing, or performing the DCC, in order to evaluate the accuracy, completeness, and currency of the cost or pricing data. The right of examination shall extend to all documents necessary to permit adequate evaluation of the cost or pricing data submitted, along with the computations and projections used. The prime contractor shall make available at its office, at all reasonable times, the materials described above for examination, audit, or reproduction, until three (3) years after final payment under the DCC. General access to the prime contractor's books and financial records shall be limited to USG representatives. The USG representatives shall verbally notify the Purchaser immediately of data provided that is so deficient as to preclude review, or where the prime contractor has denied access to records or to cost or pricing data considered essential to the performance of a satisfactory review. This verbal notification shall be promptly confirmed in writing to the Purchaser describing the deficiency or the denial of access to data or records. A prime contractor's failure to provide adequate cost and pricing data may disqualify the DCC from consideration for FMF approval.

APPENDIX Y

Contractor's Certificiation and Agreement with Defense Security Cooperation Agency

**CONTRACTOR'S CERTIFICATION AND AGREEMENT
WITH
DEFENSE SECURITY COOPERATION AGENCY (DSCA)
AUGUST 2009**

Contractor's Name: _____

Contractor's Address: _____

Contractor POC and Phone #: _____

Purchaser: Government of _____

Contract Number: _____ Contract Date: _____

Amendment Number: _____ Amendment Date: _____

Intent of Contract (items/services to be provided): _____

Instructions: Read DSCA's Guidelines for Foreign Military Financing of Direct Commercial Contracts located at http://www.dsca.mil. Contractors must complete all sections; DSCA will not process Certifications with blank areas. Attach supporting documentation if necessary.

The Contractor named above, in entering into an agreement to sell defense articles, defense services, or design and construction services to the foreign government listed above as the Purchaser, hereby acknowledges that the sum to be claimed as due and owing under the contract or proforma invoice identified above (hereafter sometimes referred to as the "Purchase Agreement") is to be paid, in whole or in part, to the Contractor from U.S. Government funds made available to the foreign government under the provisions of the Arms Export Control Act, as amended. In consideration of the receipt of such sum, the Contractor certifies to and agrees with the U.S. Government, as represented by the Defense Security Cooperation Agency (DSCA), the following:

1. Agrees the Contractor will comply in all respects with the "DSCA Guidelines for Foreign Military Financing of Direct Commercial Contracts" that is in effect when the contract was signed. Further, should a newer version of the Guidelines be published subsequent to contract award, the Contractor agrees to comply in all respects with the "DSCA Guidelines for Foreign Military Financing of Direct Commercial Contracts" that is in effect when any amendment or modification to such a contract is signed.

2. Agrees that authorized representatives of the Department of Defense and the Government of the United States shall have access to and the right to examine any of the Contractor's directly pertinent books, documents, papers, or other records involving transactions related to this contract for a period of three years following receipt of the final payment made on this Purchase Agreement.

3. Agrees to permit Defense Contract Management Agency (DCMA) with support of Defense Contract Audit Agency (DCAA) to conduct pricing reviews at the Purchaser's expense on all sole source procurements of $750,000 or more as a condition for FMF funding of the contract.

4. Agrees to complete and accurate disclosure in connection with any and all pricing reviews accomplished by DCMA/DCAA in support of sole source procurements of $750,000 or more, or in other circumstances where such a pricing review is required by DSCA or the Purchaser. Acknowledges, that as a further condition of Foreign Military Financing (FMF) funding of the contract, findings as to the fairness and reasonableness of the price may be provided to the Purchaser.

5. Agrees to permit DCMA, with support from the DCAA, to perform contract administration and audit services on all contracts of $750,000 or more (sole source or competitive). Contract administration and audit services are at the Purchaser's expense.

6. Agrees to include in subcontracts under this contract, a clause to the effect that authorized representatives of the Government of the United States shall have access to and the right to examine, for a period of three (3) years following the final payment to the Contractor, any of the subcontractor's directly pertinent books, documents, papers, or other records involving transactions related to the subcontract.

The following subcontracts with suppliers are exempted from this provision [these items may be procured from both U.S. and foreign sources, and are subject to the non-U.S. origin disclosure requirement in paragraph 12]:

   a. Those orders equal to or less than $100,000 in value.
   b. Those orders in implementation of a Purchase Agreement awarded to the contractor on a competitive lowest responsive bid or best bid/best value basis.
   c. Those orders for common hardware[1] and/or raw materials[2].
   d. Those orders for commercially available U.S. off-the-shelf items[3].
   e. Those orders issued and effective prior to date of the Purchase Agreement identified above.

7. Agrees that it is the prime contractor's responsibility on all subcontracts (except those exempted under paragraph (6) to obtain written compliance from its first and second tier subcontractors to the certification signed by the prime contractor. Multi-year contracts must also meet this flow-down requirement. This includes cumulative contract amounts with all aggregate orders, modifications, and amendments under the Purchase Agreement.

8. Agrees to include in the written terms and conditions of every subcontract or order (except those exempted under paragraph 6e) a prominently displayed statement that United States

---

[1] Common hardware consists of commercially available, off-the-shelf items that do not require custom production or specific manufacture.
[2] Raw materials are items that are in a natural state, not subject to manufacturing, refining, or finishing processes, and routinely stored without accountability or segregation based on origin.
[3] Commercially available off-the-shelf item means a commercial item sold in substantial quantities in the commercial marketplace and offered to the U.S. Government without modification and in the same form in which it is sold in the commercial marketplace (see 41 USC 431). It does not include bulk cargo such as agricultural products and petroleum products.

Appendix Y

Government (USG) funds will be used to finance such subcontract, and that acceptance of the subcontract or order will constitute acknowledgment of such notification of USG financing.

9. Certifies and agrees that no bribes, rebates, gifts, kickbacks or gratuities have been or will be directly or indirectly offered or given, or have been or will be arranged with officers, officials, or employees of the Purchaser by the Contractor, its employees or agents to secure the Purchase Agreement or favorable treatment under the Purchase Agreement, or for any other purpose relating to the Purchase Agreement contrary to U.S. law or regulation.

10. Agrees to include in the written terms and conditions of every subcontract or order (except those exempted under paragraph 6e) a prominently displayed statement: Acceptance and implementation of the subcontract constitutes a declaration and agreement by the principal executive officers of the subcontractor that no bribes, rebates, gifts, kickbacks, or gratuities to secure the Purchase Agreement or the subcontract, or for favorable treatment under such agreements, or for any other purpose relating to the Purchase Agreement or the subcontract have been or will be directly or indirectly offered or given to, or have been or will be arranged with officers, officials or employees of the Purchaser by the subcontractor, its employees or agents.

11. Understands that it may not recover any offset costs under direct commercial sales financed with nonrepayable FMF funds (U.S. funds provided to a foreign government or international organization on a nonrepayable basis). To the extent the contractor seeks to recover such costs, it must be from the foreign Purchaser who must pay with its own funds or with repayable FMF credits.

Certifies that $_____ is the amount of offset costs included in the price of this Purchase Agreement.

12. Certifies that the materiel, components, goods, or services (hereafter "content") to be provided under the Purchase Agreement are of U.S. manufacture and/or origin. The dollar value of all non-U.S. content to be procured specifically for this Purchase Agreement is indicated below.

Certifies that $_____ is the current cumulative total dollar value of non-U.S. content in the Purchase Agreement identified above (including all amendments).

Further, certifies that of the above amount of non-U.S. content, $_____ is the current cumulative total dollar amount of Purchaser (host nation) content.

Certifies that $_____ is the current total dollar value of non-U.S. content in amendment # _____ to the Purchase Agreement identified above.

Further, certifies that of the above amount of non-U.S. content, $_____ is the current cumulative total dollar amount of Purchaser (host nation) content in amendment # _____ to the Purchase Agreement identified above.

   a. Agrees that regardless of whether DSCA approves financing of the total dollar value of non-U.S. content disclosed in this certification, or a lesser-specified dollar value of the disclosed non-U.S. content, or none of the disclosed non-U.S. content, the disclosed value will not be exceeded during the execution of said Purchase Agreement.

App. Y   GOVERNMENT CONTRACT COMPLIANCE HANDBOOK

    b. Agrees to promptly disclose to DSCA any change in value of non-U.S. content by submitting an amended original signed Contractor's Certification to DSCA-OPS-ME/DCC and a copy to the Purchaser country.

    c. Agrees that if FMF funds are denied either in whole or part, that the costs for which funding was denied will not be financed with funds received from the USG under the Purchase Agreement either directly or indirectly.

    d. Agrees to maintain and provide, if requested, supporting documentation for the value of both U.S. and non-U.S. origin content.

13. Certifies that USG funds received by the Contractor under the Purchase Agreement will not be used to purchase services, other than those disclosed in paragraph 12 above and approved by DSCA, from non-U.S. contractors or individuals that are not U.S. citizens or resident aliens of the United States, unless the financing of such services is expressly authorized by the DSCA.

14. Certifies that the recipient(s) and amount(s) of any commission, contingent fees, or similar compensation paid or to be paid in any way (to include payments to a bona fide employee or a bona fide commercial or selling agency), whether in cash or in kind, directly or indirectly related to the Purchase Agreement are fully disclosed below. This requirement does not apply to a purchase that is for an amount less than the simplified acquisition threshold or to a purchase of commercial items that are sold at catalog or published prices.

Recipient(s) of commissions, contingent fees, or compensation:

NAME and ADDRESS:

AGGREGATE AMOUNT PAID OR TO BE PAID: [4] _____
AGGREGATE AMOUNT INCLUDED IN PURCHASE AGREEMENT: [4] _____
RELATIONSHIP TO CONTRACTOR: _____
NATIONALITY: _____

    a. Certifies that the Purchase Agreement price does not include commissions, contingent fees, or similar compensation paid or promised to any person for the purpose of soliciting or securing the Purchase Agreement, unless such payments have been identified to and approved in writing by the Purchaser prior to contract award for payment with repayable FMF credit or with the Purchaser's national funds.

    b. Certifies that any commissions, contingent fees, or similar compensation paid or promised by the contractor to any person in relation to soliciting the Purchase Agreement were not in violation of U.S. law or regulations.

---

[4] N/A is not a proper response to this question. Certifying contractor must write zero or the amount paid in this space.

APPENDIX Y

App. Y

c. Agrees to include within every subcontract or order under the Purchase Agreement (except those exempted under paragraph 6) prominently displayed contract clause(s) requiring that the subcontractor provide the disclosures and certifications set forth in this paragraph 14 and 14(a and b).

15. Agrees to identify in its accounting records the full amount of any payment received under the Purchase Agreement as an advance payment, to apply these funds solely to the performance of obligations under this Purchase Agreement, and to provide a clear audit trail on the use of these funds. Agrees to certify on the invoice or request for any payment made before performance of work under the Purchase Agreement that it does not exceed 15 percent of the Purchase Agreement price.

16. Agrees that export transportation costs financed under terms of the Purchase Agreement will be paid only to steamship, barge, tug, and airline companies of United States registry unless such costs have been identified to and approved in writing by the Purchaser prior to contract award for payment with Purchaser's national funds. Agrees that amounts billed for such transportation shall be only the cost for shipping the defense articles provided under the terms of the Purchase Agreement. Freight forwarder services are not authorized for FMF funding unless specifically authorized and approved by DSCA.

17. Agrees that the cost of travel, per diem, accommodations, lodging, car rental, personal expenses, entertainment, or other similar expenses (except the reasonable cost of business meals) incurred by or for the purchasing country personnel, which relate directly or indirectly in any way to this contract, will not be paid by, be submitted, invoiced, or billed by the contractor for payment with FMF funds.

18. Certifies that the full extent of the contractual relationship between the Contractor and the purchasing government, as it pertains to this Purchase Agreement, consists of the contract and/or amendments identified on page one of this certification (provide/attach necessary documentation or correspondence, including purchase orders if necessary, to disclose the full extent of the agreement between the parties) and recognizes that the U.S. Government makes no commitment to finance any additional or subsequent agreements related to this Purchase Agreement.

19. Agrees to provide a copy of any or all export licenses related to this Purchase Agreement, or alternatively, written documentation that certifies that an export license is not required.

20. Agrees that invoices will be prepared in accordance with the relevant provisions of the Purchase Agreement and will be submitted through the Purchaser for presentation to the Defense Finance Accounting Service (DFAS) for payment, as follows:

    a. All Contractors' invoices must be submitted with the following certification:

The Contractor (   ) acknowledges U.S. Government funds are being used by the Government of _____ to finance this purchase and certifies that the invoice(s) submitted with respect thereto are free from any material false statement or misrepresentation and do not omit any material facts.

    b. If not already on file with DFAS and DSCA-OPS-MSA/DCC, all invoices or requests for reimbursement must be accompanied by a copy of the export license or documentation that certifies that an export license is not required.

c. All invoices should (as applicable) also:

    (1) Reflect the invoice date, Purchase Agreement number, DSCA case identifier, amount due, and payment due date
    (2) Specify whether the amount billed is an advance, interim, progress/milestone, or performance payment.
    (3) Provide description, quantity, unit of measure, unit price and extended price of the items and services delivered.
    (4) State the terms of any prompt payment discount, if offered.
    (5) Designate the name and address to where the payment should be sent.
    (6) Designate the FOB point and "ship to" address.
    (7) Indicate by a separate entry the transportation costs if not included in the item price.
    (8) Provide the name of the carrier(s) to be used from the U.S. Port of Embarkation whenever the amount being billed includes the "cost, insurance, and freight (CIF)" terms of delivery of invoiced items to a destination point outside the U.S.
    (9) Be supported by a stamped, dated and initialed copy of the freight bills, air way bills, or rated on-board bills-of-lading, fully accounting for the cost of inland and export transportation of the items covered by the invoice for which payment is requested.
    (10) Provide any other information or documentation required by the contract.
    (11) Provide name, title, and phone number of person to be contacted in event of questions. If the Contractor pays for the transportation, bills-of-lading or airway bills must be submitted with the invoice for which payment is requested, whether the transportation cost is included in the price of the item or billed separately to the Purchaser. A copy of the invoice for the cost of any insurance coverage on the shipment must also be submitted with the shipping documents.

d. If the contractor is not paying for the export transportation costs, the Contractor will submit a certification with the invoice as follows:

The Contractor (_____) acknowledges that U.S. Government funds are being used by the Government of _____ to finance this purchase and certifies that no shipping cost has been incurred by this firm for exporting this materiel from the United States and no shipping cost is included in the sales price or otherwise included in the invoiced amount for which payment is requested.

21. Agrees that any penalty payment, refund, or other reimbursement due to the Purchaser pursuant to this Purchase Agreement will be paid directly to the U.S. Government for credit to the FMS trust fund account of the Purchaser. Understands that DFAS will not disburse funds to contractors until it receives all copies of the bonding or guarantee documents applicable to the purchase agreement.

22. Certifies that neither the Contractor nor any of its employees are suspended or debarred from conducting business with any agency of the U.S. Government and that export privileges are not suspended or revoked. Further agrees that no suspended or debarred firms will be used as a source of supplies or as a subcontractor for this Purchase Agreement.

23. Agrees that the U.S. Government has the right, without accruing any liability, to suspend the financing of this Purchase Agreement on the instruction of the Purchaser or for any suspected or confirmed misrepresentation or violation of any certification or agreement provided by this Contractor to obtain FMF financing.

APPENDIX Y

24. For purposes of facilitating official U.S. Government inquiries to determine whether civil or criminal offenses may have been committed regarding the use, disbursement, or other disposition of funds made available under the U.S. Arms Export Control Act, to finance this Purchase Agreement, the Contractor agrees to provide to any requesting authorized U.S. government official, documents that demonstrate the cost and price elements for the final Purchase Agreement price, including total amounts and breakdowns for all cost and price elements.

25. In addition to the agreement in paragraphs 1 through 24 and for purposes of facilitating official U.S. Government inquiries to determine whether civil or criminal offenses may have been committed regarding the use, disbursement, or other disposition of funds made available under the U.S. Arms Export Control Act, to finance this Purchase Agreement, the Contractor agrees:

a. To identify and to consent to the disclosure of the following accounts to, and at the request of, the U.S. Department of Defense, the U.S. Department of Justice, or a U.S. Federal Grand Jury:

(1) Accounts wherever located in the name of such Contractor or any related corporate entities; and
(2) Accounts located outside the United States in the name of the principal executive officers of such Contractor (and any nominees) who have been personally and substantially involved in this Purchase Agreement, and

b. For these purposes to include in the written terms and conditions of each subcontract (other than those excepted under paragraph 6) applicable to this Purchase Agreement a statement that acceptance and implementation of the subcontract constitutes agreement by the subcontractor to identify and to consent to the disclosure of the following accounts to, and at the request of, the U.S. Department of Defense, or the U.S. Department of Justice, or a U.S. Federal Grand Jury:

(1) Accounts wherever located in the name of such subcontractor or supplier; and
(2) Accounts located outside the United States in the name of the principal executive officers of such subcontractor or supplier (and any nominees) who have been personally and substantially involved in this subcontract under the Purchase Agreement.

The term "consent to the disclosure" for purposes of sub-paragraphs (a) and (b) of this paragraph includes agreement to provide consent documents authorizing the disclosure of such information upon request.

26. By signature below, the named individuals hereby separately certify:

a. That he or she has actual authority to sign on behalf of the Contractor and to bind the Contractor with regard to all agreements and certifications contained hereon;

b. That this certification and agreement is being signed and submitted for the purpose of receiving payment under terms of the above listed Purchase Agreement to be financed by U.S. Government funds; and

c. That the information provided in this Certification and Agreement is complete and accurate to the best of each signatory's knowledge and belief after each has taken appropriate steps to verify the accuracy thereof. The person(s) signing the Purchase Agreement may not normally also sign this Certification and Agreement. In the event that the Contractor is a partnership, one general partner is required to sign this Certification and Agreement.

App. Y GOVERNMENT CONTRACT COMPLIANCE HANDBOOK

I certify under penalty of perjury that the foregoing certifications are complete and accurate to the best of my knowledge based upon: (1) written representation made to me by identifiable individuals within this company and which representations will be maintained for **six years** after receipt of the final payment made by DFAS on this Purchase Agreement; or (2) that I have exercised personal due diligence to ascertain that all statements in this certification are true and correct.

VICE PRESIDENT (OR OTHER SENIOR OFFICIAL) HAVING SUPERVISORY RESPONSIBILITIES OVER THE MAKING OF THIS PURCHASE AGREEMENT	TREASURER, COMPTROLLER, OR OTHER SENIOR FISCAL OFFICIAL
_____ (Signature)	_____ (Signature)
_____ (Typed name)	_____ (Typed name)
_____ (Title)	_____ (Title)
_____ (Date)	_____ (Date)

Table of Laws and Rules

UNITED STATES CONSTITUTION

Sec.
Amend V 1:36, 2:32

DEFENSE PRODUCTION ACT OF 1950

Sec.　　　　　　　　　　　　　Sec.
Title VII, § 721 .... 18:18

NATIONAL DEFENSE AUTHORIZATION ACT

Sec.	Sec.	Sec.	Sec.
815	1:53	846	1:20
842	1:20		

UNITED STATES CODE ANNOTATED

2 U.S.C.A. Sec.	Sec.
1601, et seq.	7:15
1601 to 1612	1:29, 7:13
1602(8)	7:16
1602(8)(a)(iii)	7:15
1602(8)(B)	7:16
1602(10)	7:16
1603	7:15
1603(a)(3)(A)	7:16
1604	7:15
1606	7:15

5 U.S.C.A. Sec.	Sec.
706(2)(A)	8:15
7351	7:1

5 U.S.C.A. App.	Sec.
3, § 2, 4	2:6
3, § 6(A)(4)	2:6
3, § 1 to 12	2:6

10 U.S.C.A. Sec.	Sec.
2207	7:1, 7:4
2302	10:6, 10:7
2304 et seq.	10:1
2306(b)	10:6, 10:7, 10:8, 10:22, 20:6
2306a	9:1, 9:8, 10:6, 10:8, 13:4
2306a(a)(2)	13:4
2306a(b)(1)	9:7
2306a(b)(1)(B)	9:10
2306a(b)(1)(C)	9:11
2306a(b)(3)	9:17
2306a(d)(1)	9:13
2306a(e)	9:15, 18:16
2306a(e)(3)(A)	9:18
2306a(e)(3)(B)	9:18
2306a(e)(3)(C)	9:18
2306a(e)(3)(D)	9:6, 9:18
2306a(e)(4)(A)	9:19
2306a(e)(4)(B)	9:19
2306a(f)	9:15, 9:17

UNITED STATES CODE ANNOTATED—Continued

10 U.S.C.A. Sec.	Sec.	15 U.S.C.A. Sec.	Sec.
2306a(g)	9:15	78m(b)	19:26
2306a(h)(1)	9:4	78m(b)(2)	19:24
2307(h)	14:15, 14:22	78m(b)(6)	19:24
2307(h)(3)	14:22	78m(b)(7)	19:24
2307(h)(5)	14:22	78m(u)	19:25
2307(h)(6)	14:22	78dd-1	1:28, 19:19, 19:26
2313	10:22	78dd-1(e)(1)	19:30
2313(c)	10:7, 10:8	78dd-2	1:28, 19:19, 19:26
2313(c)(1)	10:6	78dd-2(a)	19:19
2324	10:8	78dd-2(a)((3)	19:19
2324(h)	11:9	78dd-2(b)	19:20
2324(h)(1)	11:1	78dd-2(c)(2)	19:21
2327	10:8	78dd-2(f)(1)	19:30
2377	10:1	78dd-2(g)	19:22
2384(b)	10:8	78dd-2(h)(1)	19:19
2391	10:8	78dd-2(h)(3)	19:19
2393	10:8	78dd-3	19:19, 19:26, 19:30
2393(d)	10:8	78dd-3(e)	19:22
2397(a)(1)	10:8	631	10:22
2397b(f)	10:8	637(b)(6)	12:4
2397c	10:8	644(d)	10:7
2402	10:6, 10:8, 10:22	657a(b)(2)(B)	10:22
2408(a)	10:8	760(c)(1)	19:32
2409	1:20, 10:10	760.2(a)(1)	19:32
2410(a)	16:3	760.2(b)(1)	19:32
2410b	10:8	760.2(d)(1)	19:32
2410f	17:22	760.3(a)	19:32
2501	10:8	760.5(a)	19:32
2533a	17:4	760.5(b)(4)	19:32
2534	10:8		
2534(a)	17:3	**18 U.S.C.A. Sec.**	**Sec.**
2631	10:7, 10:8, 10:13	201	7:1
		201(b)	1:25, 7:3
12 U.S.C.A. Sec.	**Sec.**	201(c)	1:25, 7:4, 7:5
84	3:7	201(c)(1)(a)	7:5
375b	3:7	207	1:26, 8:1, 8:6, 8:9
		207(a) to (e)	8:7
15 U.S.C.A. Sec.	**Sec.**	207(a)	8:8, 8:9
1 to 7	1:29, 7:23	207(a)(2)(B)	8:10
1	3:13, 7:24	207(b)	8:11
12 to 27	1:29, 7:23, 7:25	207(c)	8:11
15(a)	7:25	207(d)	8:11
15a	7:25	208	8:6, 8:13
15c	7:25	216	8:13
26	7:25	216(b)	8:12
41 to 58	1:29, 7:23, 7:26	286	1:12
45(l)	17:22	287	1:10, 7:27, 9:22, 11:12, 14:25, 15:8, 18:16, 20:10
45a	17:21		

Table of Laws and Rules

UNITED STATES CODE ANNOTATED—Continued

18 U.S.C.A. Sec.	Sec.
371	1:12, 3:13, 7:27, 15:8
431	10:10
641	1:31, 6:12, 14:14
666	6:12
792 to 799	1:32
792	6:13
793(d)	6:13
793(f)	6:13
798(d)(1)	6:13
1001	1:3, 7:27, 9:22, 11:12, 12:22, 14:25, 15:8, 16:10, 18:16, 20:10
1014	1:5
1031	1:8
1031(g)	1:8
1031(h)	1:8
1341	1:6, 7:27
1343	1:6, 7:27
1346	1:6
1501 to 1518	2:23
1503	1:36, 1:39, 2:23
1505	1:39, 2:23
1512 to 1515	2:23
1512	1:38
1512(b)	1:38
1514A(a)(1)	1:20
1515(a)(3)	1:38
1516	1:34, 2:23
1621	1:40
1623	1:40
1623(e)	1:40
1961 to 1968	1:44, 7:27
1964	1:44
1964(a)	1:44
3559(a)(5)	7:3, 7:4
3571	1:43, 7:3, 7:4

19 U.S.C.A. Sec.	Sec.
1304(k)	17:17
2112	17:2
2501 to 2581	17:1
2511 to 2518	17:2
2512(a)	17:5
2512(b)	17:9
2515	17:14
2701 to 2707	17:2

22 U.S.C.A. Sec.	Sec.
2151 et seq.	1:22
2399b	1:22
2399b(a)	1:22, 1:51
2751 to 2799aa-2	20:2
2761	20:13, 20:14
2761(e)	20:14
2761(e)(2)	20:15
2762	20:14
2778(c)	19:9
2794(6)	20:13
7104(g)	10:13

26 U.S.C.A. Sec.	Sec.
999	19:34
999(a)(3)	19:35

28 U.S.C.A. Sec.	Sec.
530B	2:9
2461	1:15
2514	1:50, 16:10

29 U.S.C.A. Sec.	Sec.
793	10:13

31 U.S.C.A. Sec.	Sec.
1352	1:29, 7:13, 10:10
1352(a)(1)	7:14
1352(b)	7:14
1352(b)(4)	7:16
1352(c)(1)	7:14
1352(c)(2)	7:14
1352(d)(1)(A)	7:16
1352(d)(2)(B)	7:16
1354(a)	10:6, 10:22
3501	9:1
3553	10:11
3729 to 3733	2:20, 3:13, 4:2, 9:21, 11:12, 14:25, 15:8, 16:10, 18:16, 20:10
3729	1:15
3729(a)	1:15, 9:21
3729(a)(1)	1:15
3729(a)(1)(A)	1:15
3729(a)(1)(G)	1:15
3729(a)(2)	1:15
3729(a)(7)	1:20
3730(b)	1:17
3730(b)(1)	1:19, 1:21, 3:17
3730(b)(2)	1:19
3730(c)(1)	1:21

UNITED STATES CODE ANNOTATED—Continued

31 U.S.C.A. Sec.	Sec.
3730(d)(1)	1:21
3730(d)(2)	1:21
3730(e)	1:18, 5:16
3730(e)(3)	1:21
3730(e)(4)	1:18
3730(e)(4)(A)	1:18
3730(e)(4)(b)	1:18, 1:21
3730(h)	1:20, 2:20
3731(b)(2)	1:15
3801 to 3812	11:12
3801(a)(5)	1:23
3802(a)(1)	1:23
3802(a)(2)	1:23

38 U.S.C.A. Sec.	Sec.
4212	10:13

40 U.S.C.A. Sec.	Sec.
3131	10:22
3701 et seq.	10:10
3701 to 3708	10:5, 10:8, 10:22
Ch 31	10:6

41 U.S.C.A. Sec.	Sec.
51 to 58	1:27, 7:38
52(2)	7:39, 7:42
52(3)	7:39
53	7:39
54	7:41
55	7:41
55(a)(1)	7:41
55(a)(2)	7:41
56	7:41
56(b)	7:41
57	7:40
57(c)(1)	7:40
57(e)	7:40
256(h)	11:9
265	1:20
423	1:26, 1:30, 6:2
423(c)	8:1
423(c)(4)	8:4
601 to 613	7:32, 16:1
601(7)	16:10
604	16:10
605(a)	16:2
605(c)(1)	16:2, 16:6
605(c)(7)	16:6

41 U.S.C.A. Sec.	Sec.
609(d)	1:50
1502	10:8, 12:2
1502(a)(1)	12:2
1502(b)(1)(B)	12:2
1502(b)(2)	12:5
1502(b)(3)	12:2
1502(c)(1)	12:2
1502(c)(3)	12:2
1502(f)	12:2
1708	10:6, 10:7
1708(e)(3)	10:7
2101 et seq.	8:19, 10:10
2101 to 2107	6:2
2101(2)	6:3
2101(7)	6:3
2101(a)	6:3
2102	6:11
2102(a)	6:3
2102(b)	6:4, 6:11
2103(a)	6:5, 8:4
2104(a)	6:6, 8:3
2104(b)	8:3
2104(d)	6:7
2105(a)	6:7, 8:5
2105(b)	6:8, 8:5
2105(c)(1)	6:9, 8:5
2106	6:10
2107(2)	6:11
2302	10:7
2303(b)	10:6
3301 et seq.	10:1
3307	10:1
3501 et seq.	13:4
3501(a)(2)	9:4
3502(a)	9:7
3502(b)	13:4
3503(a)(3)	9:10, 9:11
3505(a)	9:13
3506	18:16
3506(a)(1)	9:15
3506(c)(1)(A)	9:17, 9:18
3506(c)(2)	9:18
3506(c)(3)	9:18
3506(c)(4)	9:18
3506(d)(1)	9:19
3506(d)(2)	9:19
3507	9:15, 9:17
3508	9:15

UNITED STATES CODE ANNOTATED—Continued

41 U.S.C.A. Sec.	Sec.	41 U.S.C.A. Sec.	Sec.
3509	10:13	8301 to 8305	17:1
3901	10:22	8302(a)(1)	10:8
3901(b)	10:7, 20:6	8302(a)(2)	17:8
3901(b)(1)	10:6	8303(a)(2)	10:8
3905	10:22	8303(c)	17:17
3906	10:22	8703 et seq.	10:8
4056(b)	14:22	8703 to 8707	10:10
4056(d)	14:22	8703	10:6
4056(f)	14:22	8703(a)	10:22
4056(g)	14:22	8703(b)	10:22
4308	11:1	8704	10:6
4506(b)	14:15	Ch 15	10:6
4703	10:7	Ch 35	10:6
4704	10:6, 10:8, 10:22	Ch 65	10:6
4706	10:7		
4706(d)(1)	10:6	**42 U.S.C.A. Sec.**	**Sec.**
4712	10:10	6962	10:22
6505	10:7	6962(c)(3)(A)	10:8
6701 to 6707	10:5, 10:13		
6702 et seq.	10:13	**46 U.S.C.A. Sec.**	**Sec.**
6702(b)	10:13	40102(4)	10:3
7101 to 7109	1:15	53105	10:13
7103(b)	13:4	55301 et seq.	10:7
8102 et seq.	10:7		
8102 to 8106	10:6	**49 U.S.C.A. Sec.**	**Sec.**
8102	10:22	40118	10:6, 10:7, 10:8, 10:10

UNITED STATES PUBLIC LAWS

Pub. L. No.	Sec.	Pub. L. No.	Sec.
11-350	6:2	102-572 (Oct. 29, 1992)	16:4
85-804	16:7	103-160, § 843(a)	10:8
87-653 (1962)	9:1	103-182	17:2
90-370	12:2	103-355	1:20, 10:1
91-379	12:2	103-355, § 2051(e)	14:15, 14:22
95-563 (Nov. 1, 1978)	16:1	103-355, § 2091	10:6, 10:7
98-369, § 2721	10:1	103-355, § 4001 to 4404	10:21
98-525, § 1202	10:1	103-355, § 8105	10:6, 10:7
99-509, § 6101 to 6104	1:23	103-355, § 8301	10:6
100-679, § 6 (1988)	6:2	104-65 (Dec. 19, 1995)	7:13
100-700, § 2(a)	1:8	104-106 (Feb. 10, 1996)	7:40
101-121, § 319	7:13	104-106, § 4201	10:1, 10:9
101-123, § 2(a)	1:8	104-106, § 4202	10:21
101-194	8:1, 8:7	104-106, § 4203	10:3
101-510, § 836	14:15	104-106, § 4203(a)	10:8
101-510, § 863(a)	14:22	104-106, § 4204	10:6
102-190, § 806(a)(3)	10:6, 10:7	104-106, § 4303	20:15

UNITED STATES PUBLIC LAWS—Continued

Pub. L. No.	Sec.
104-106, § 4304 (Feb. 10, 1996)	6:2
104-320 (Oct. 19, 1996)	3:13
104-410	1:15
105-261	10:4
105-315 (Oct. 30, 1998)	3:13
106-65	10:4
107-117, § 8065	10:8
108-77 (Oct. 2004)	10:11
108-78 (Oct. 2004)	10:11
108-136	12:4
108-237, § 215(a)	7:24
108-375	9:2
109-171, § 6031 to 6033	1:16
109-364 (Oct. 17, 2006)	8:15
110-49	18:18

Pub. L. No.	Sec.
110-81	7:15, 8:11
110-181	1:20, 8:6
110-252	10:13
110-417	1:20, 1:35, 2:3, 8:15
111-5	1:15, 1:20, 2:3
111-21	1:15
111-23 (May 22, 2009)	8:15
111-84	1:53
111-118	10:8
111-148	1:15
111-148, § 10104(j)(2)	1:18
111-203 (2010)	1:20
112-81, § 1533	20:12
112-199	1:20
112-239 (Jan. 2, 2013)	5:16

CODE OF FEDERAL REGULATIONS

5 C.F.R. Sec.	Sec.
Part 185	1:23
2635	7:1, 8:6
2635.202(b)	7:5
2635.203(b)	7:5
2635.203(b)(8)	7:5
2635.204	7:5
2635.204(a)	7:7
2635.204(b)	7:5
2635.204(g)(2)	7:7
2635.204(l)	7:5
2635.2634 to 2635.2641	8:1
Part 2637	8:1
Part 2641	8:1
Part 2641, Appx A	8:11
2641.201(d)	8:8
2641.201(d)(2)	8:8
2641.202(a)	8:10
2641.202(j)(7)	8:10
3601.103	7:5
2635.202 et. seq.	6:18

6 C.F.R. Sec.	Sec.
Part 13	1:23

7 C.F.R. Sec.	Sec.
Part 1	1:23

10 C.F.R. Sec.	Sec.
Part 13	1:23

10 C.F.R. Sec.	Sec.
Part 1013	1:23

15 C.F.R. Sec.	Sec.
Part 25	1:23
Part 701	20:17
Part 701.3	20:17
701.4	20:17
732 to 774	19:2
734.2(b)	19:11
734.4(a)	19:12
734.4(b)	19:12
734.4(c)	19:12
734.4(d)	19:12
736.(2)(4)	19:13
736.2(b)(2)	19:12
736.2(b)(5)	19:13
736.2(b)(10)	19:13
738.2(a)	19:10
738.4	19:10
Part 760	19:32
764.3(a)(2)	19:15, 19:33
764.5	19:15
770.3	19:17
772.1	19:10
Supp 1, § 774	19:10

16 C.F.R. Sec.	Sec.
1.2 to 1.4	17:23

TABLE OF LAWS AND RULES

CODE OF FEDERAL REGULATIONS—Continued

19 C.F.R.	Sec.
Subpart B, § 102	17:16
Part 134	17:14
Part 177, Subpart B	17:19

22 C.F.R.	Sec.
Part 35	1:23
120 to 130	19:2, 20:2
120.3(a)(2)	19:2
120.3(b)	19:2
120.6	19:2
120.7	19:5
120.9(a)(1)	19:2
120.9(a)(3)	19:2
120.10(a)(1)	19:2
120.10(a)(2)	19:2
120.10(b)	19:2
120.17(a)(4)	19:17
120.41(a)(1)	19:2
122.1(a)	19:7
123.(b)(5)	19:5
123.1(a)	19:2
123.1(a)(1)	19:2
123.1(a)(4)	19:2
123.3(a)	19:8
123.9(a)	19:4
123.9(b)(1)	19:4
123.9(e)	19:5
124.1	19:2
124.3(a)	19:2
124.3(b)	19:2
124.7	19:2
124.8	19:2
124.11(a)	19:5
124.14	19:2
125.2	19:2
125.3	19:2
127.3	19:9
127.6	19:9
127.7	19:9
127.12(a)	19:9
129.2(a)	19:6
129.2(b)	19:6
129.3(a)	19:7
129.3(d)	19:7
129.4(a)	19:6
129.5(b)	19:6
Part 224	1:23
Part 521	1:23

24 C.F.R.	Sec.
Part 28	1:23

28 C.F.R.	Sec.
Part 71	1:23
85.3(c)	8:13

29 C.F.R.	Sec.
Part 22	1:23

31 C.F.R.	Sec.
31.1 et seq.	8:6, 8:15
Part 136	1:23
Parts 510 to 588	19:16
Part 590	19:16
Part 592	19:16
Part 594	19:16
Part 595	19:16
Part 596	19:16
800.101	18:18
800.202	18:18
800.224	18:18
800.401(a)	18:18
800.401(b)	18:18
800.402(l)	18:18
800.504	18:18
800.506	18:18
800.506(d)	18:18
800.601	18:18
800.701(c)	18:18
800.801(a)	18:18

32 C.F.R.	Sec.
Part 516	7:33

34 C.F.R.	Sec.
Part 33	1:23

38 C.F.R.	Sec.
Part 42	1:23

39 C.F.R.	Sec.
Part 273	1:23

40 C.F.R.	Sec.
Part 27	1:23

43 C.F.R.	Sec.
Part 35	1:23

CODE OF FEDERAL REGULATIONS—Continued

44 C.F.R. Sec.	Sec.
9904.410	11:14

45 C.F.R. Sec.	Sec.
Part 79	1:23

48 C.F.R. Sec.	Sec.
9903-201(b)(14)	12:4
9903.201-1(b)	12:4
9903.201-1(b)(2)	12:4
9903.201-1(b)(4)	12:4
9903.201-1(b)(5)	12:4
9903.201-1(b)(6)	12:4
9903.201-1(b)(7)	12:4
9903.201-1(b)(13)	12:4
9903.201-1(b)(14)	12:4
9903.201-1(b)(15)	12:4, 12:28
9903.201-2(a)	12:6
9903.201-2(b)(1)	12:7
9903.201-2(b)(2)	12:7
9903.201-2(c)	12:10
9903.201-2(c)(3)	12:10
9903.201-2(c)(4)	12:10
9903.201-4(a)	12:8
9903.201-4(c)	12:8
9903.201-4(e)	12:10
9903.201-5	12:5
9903.202-1	13:3
9903.202-1(b)	12:9
9903.202-1(f)	12:10
9903.202-1(f)(2)	12:10

48 C.F.R. Sec.	Sec.
9903.202-3	12:9
9903.202-4	12:9
9903.202-8(c)(1)	12:9
9903.202-10	12:10
9903.301	12:4
9903.302-1	12:11
9903.302-2	12:11
9903.302-3	12:11
9903.302-4	12:11
9903.405	11:7
9904.401	12:30
9904.401-60(a)	12:30
9904.401-60(b)	12:30
9904.402	12:30
9904.402-60(b)(1)	12:30
9904.404-50(d)(1)	18:6
9904.405	12:30
9904.405-40(b)	12:30
9904.405-40(c)	12:30
9904.405-50	12:30
9904.405-50(b)	12:30
9904.405-60(b)	12:30
9904.407-20	12:30
9904.407-40	12:30
9905	12:10
Ch 99	10:6, 13:3

49 C.F.R. Sec.	Sec.
Part 31	1:23

FEDERAL RULES OF CIVIL PROCEDURE

Rule	Sec.	Rule	Sec.
9(b)	1:19, 1:21	26(c)	1:19

FEDERAL RULES OF CRIMINAL PROCEDURE

Rule	Sec.
17(c)	2:42

TABLE OF LAWS AND RULES

EXECUTIVE ORDER

No.	Sec.	No.	Sec.
11246 (Sept. 24, 1965)	10:5, 10:13	13496	10:13
12988	3:13		

FEDERAL ACQUISITION REGULATION

Sec.	Sec.	Sec.	Sec.
Part 12	10:14, 11:12, 15:11	3.104-8	6:7, 6:8
Part 13	10:21	3.104-8(a)	6:7
Part 13, § 2.101	15:5	3.104-8(b)	8:4, 8:6
Part 15	20:5	3.104-8(c)	8:4, 8:6
Part 19	10:5	3.202	7:4
Part 30	13:3	3.204(c)	7:4
Part 31	11:2, 11:4, 12:2, 12:18, 12:21, 13:3, 14:10, 16:9, 20:5	3.303	7:33
		3.401	20:6
Part 32	14:1	3.502	10:6
Part 46	15:2, 15:16	3.502-2	7:38
Part 22.3	10:5	3.502-2(i)	7:40
Part 22.8	10:5	3.502-2(i)(1)	7:42
Part 22.9	10:5	3.503	10:8
Part 22.10	10:5	3.601	8:15
Part 22.13	10:5	3.803	7:16, 7:20
Part 22.14	10:5	3.803(a)(2)(iii)	7:16
Part 16.307, Subpart 31.2	13:3	3.901 to 3.906	1:20
Subpart 9.7	7:31, 8:15, 10:7, 12:12, 12:16, 12:17, 13:3, 14:2, 15:8, 18:13	3.1002(a)	4:2
		3.1002(b)(2) to (3)	4:2
		3.1106	8:15
2.101	6:3, 6:11, 9:4, 9:10, 10:3, 10:4, 10:15, 17:3, 17:4	4.703(a)(1)	2:10
		4.705 to 4.705-3	2:10
2.101(1)	10:15	4.705	10:6
2.101(b)(2)	9:13	6.302-1	20:3
2.201	16:2	6.302-4	20:3
3.2	7:1	9.1	3:14
3.101-1	8:15	9.5	8:1, 8:9, 8:14
3.101-2	7:4	9.103	18:14
3.103-1	7:27	9.104-1(c), (d)	18:14
3.104, et seq.	8:1	9.104-3(c)	3:14, 18:14
3.104	6:1, 6:2, 8:1	9.405-2	1:53
3.104-1	6:3, 6:11, 8:4, 8:6	9.406	15:10
3.104-3(a)(1)	6:11	9.406-1	1:3
3.104-3(c)	8:4	9.406-1(a)	1:54, 3:18
3.104-3(d)	8:3	9.406-2	1:3, 1:54, 4:2, 7:27
3.104-3(d)(1)	8:3	9.406-2(a)(4)	17:22
3.104-3(d)(2)	8:3	9.406-3(b)(2)	1:55
3.104-3(d)(3)	8:3	9.406-3(c)	1:55
3.104-4	6:3	9.406-3(d)(2)	1:55
3.104-6	8:6	9.406-4	15:9
3.104-6(d)(3)	8:6	9.406-4(b)	1:54

Tbl of L&R-9

FEDERAL ACQUISITION REGULATION—Continued

Sec.	Sec.	Sec.	Sec.
9.406-5	7:32	12.403(d)(ii)	11:3
9.406-5(b)	15:9	12.503	2:3
9.407	15:10	12.503(a)	10:6
9.407-1(b)(2)	1:57	12.503(b)	10:6, 10:8
9.407-2	1:3, 4:2	12.503(c)	10:6, 10:8
9.407-2(a)	1:57	12.504(a)	10:7
9.407-2(a)(5)	17:22	12.504(b)	10:8
9.407-2(b)	1:57	12.504(c)	10:8
9.407-3	1:58	12.505	10:8
9.407-3(b)(2)	1:58	13.5	10:21, 10:22
9.407-3(b)(2)(d)	1:58	13.006	10:22
9.407-3(c)	1:58	15.4	9:13
9.407-4(a)	1:56	15.209	10:7
9.407-4(b)	1:56	Subpart 4.7, § 15.209(b)	2:10, 9:15
9.450(a)	1:53	15.401	9:13
9.501	8:1, 8:16	15.402(a)(2)	9:11
9.502(c)	8:15	15.402(a)(2)(i)	9:8
9.503	8:15, 8:17, 8:21	15.402(a)(3)	9:1, 9:7
9.504	8:15	15.403	10:6
9.504(e)	8:15	15.403-1	9:3, 9:7
9.505	8:15	15.403-1(b)	10:9
9.505-1 to 9.505-4	18:12	15.403-1(b)(1)	20:5
9.505-1	8:16	15.403-1(b)(3)	1:16, 9:21
9.505-2	8:16	15.403-1(b)(4)	9:11
9.505-2(a)(3)	8:17	15.403-1(b)(5)	9:12
9.505-3	8:16	15.403-1(c)(1)	9:8
9.505-4	8:16, 8:17	15.403-1(c)(1)(i)	9:8
9.506(b)(1)	8:15	15.403-1(c)(1)(ii)	9:8
9.506(c)	8:15	15.403-1(c)(1)(iii)	9:8
9.507-1	8:15	15.403-1(c)(2)	9:9
9.507-2(a)	8:15	15.403-1(c)(3)	10:9
9.508(a) to (i)	8:21	15.403-1(c)(3)(ii)	9:10
9.603	7:30	15.403-1(c)(3)(ii)(A)	10:4
9.701	7:31	15.403-1(c)(4)	9:14
9.703	7:31	15.403-2	9:3
11.302(c)	10:24	15.403-3	9:3, 9:8, 9:10
12.000	10:1	15.403-3(a)	9:13, 10:9
12.102	10:4	15.403-3(a)(1)(ii)	9:13
12.102(c)	11:12	15.403-3(a)(2)	9:5
12.207	11:12	15.403-3(b)	9:13
12.208	15:4	15.403-3(c)	9:13, 10:9
12.211	10:14	15.403-4	9:3, 13:4
12.212	10:14	15.403-4(a)(1)	9:11
12.214	10:6	15.403-4(a)(1)(ii)	9:14
12.301(a)	10:5	15.403-4(a)(2)	9:3
12.301(f)	10:10	15.403-4(b)	9:6
12.302	10:10	15.403-5(b)(1)	9:5
12.403(d)(1)(ii)	11:12	15.403-5(b)(2)	9:5, 9:13

TABLE OF LAWS AND RULES

FEDERAL ACQUISITION REGULATION—Continued

Sec.	Sec.	Sec.	Sec.
15.404-3(c)	9:14	25.1101(a)(2)	17:3
15.404-3(c)(1) to (3)	9:14	27.306	18:13
15.404-3(c)(4)	9:14	27.401	10:14
15.406-2	9:6, 13:4	28.106-6	10:7
15.406-2(b)	9:6	30.000	18:13
15.406-2(c)	9:6	30.001	12:17
15.407	18:16	30.201-4(d)	12:8
15.407-1(b)	9:15, 9:18	30.202-1	13:3
15.407-1(b)(4)	9:19	30.601	12:12
15.407-1(b)(7)(i)	9:15	30.601(c)	12:12
15.407-1(b)(7)(iii)	9:15	30.602	18:8
15.408	9:5, 9:6, 12:21	30.603-2(a)	12:17
15.408(b)	9:15	30.603-2(c)	12:17
15.502(a)(2)	9:13	30.604	12:17
15.502(a)(3)	9:13	30.604(b)(1)	12:17
16.205-4	13:3	30.604(c)	12:17
16.206-4	13:3	30.604(g)	12:17
19.001	17:9, 18:13	30.604(h)(3)	12:11
19.202-3	18:13	30.604(h)(4)	12:8
22.305	10:6	30.604(i)	12:14, 12:16, 12:17
25.001(a)(1)	17:8	30.605(b)	12:14
25.003	17:2, 17:10, 17:12, 17:14, 17:16	30.605(b)(2)	12:16
25.100(b)(1)	17:3	30.605(b)(3)	12:16
25.101(b)	17:9	30.605(b)(4)	12:16
25.103(b)	17:8	30.605(c)	12:15, 12:16, 12:24
25.103(e)	17:3	30.605(f)	12:15
25.104	17:8	30.605(i)	12:14
25.105	17:1, 17:3	30.606(a)	12:15
25.105(b)(2)	18:13	30.606(c)(6)	12:15, 12:16
25.205	17:8	31.102	11:3
25.206(c)(2)	17:17	31.103	11:3
25.206(c)(3)	17:17	31.109	11:12
25.206(c)(4)	17:17	31.201-2	14:10, 16:9
25.400	17:5	31.201-2(a)	11:4, 11:12, 11:14
25.401(a)(1)	17:6, 17:9	31.201-2(a)(1)	11:4
25.401(a)(2)	17:9	31.201-2(a)(2)	11:4
25.401(a)(3)	17:9	31.201-2(a)(3)	11:4
25.402	17:2	31.201-2(a)(4)	11:4, 11:12
25.402(a)(1)	17:1, 17:5, 17:6	31.201-2(a)(5)	11:4
25.402(b)	17:6	31.201-3	16:9
25.402(c)	17:5	31.201-3(a)	11:4, 11:12, 14:10, 16:9
25.403(c)(1)	17:9	31.201-3(b)	11:12, 14:10
25.403(c)(2)	17:9	31.201-4	11:4, 11:12, 14:10, 16:9
25.404	17:5	31.201-6	11:12, 12:18
25.406	17:6	31.201-6(a)	11:7, 14:10
25.501	17:19	31.201-6(c)	11:12
25.701(b)	17:3	31.201-6(e)	11:7
		31.203	4:8

FEDERAL ACQUISITION REGULATION—Continued

Sec.		Sec.	
31.203(d)	11:7	31.205-44	11:14
31.204	11:12	31.205-46	11:5, 11:17
31.204(d)	11:6, 11:12, 11:13	31.205-46(b)	11:5
31.205	11:4, 11:14, 16:9	31.205-46(c)	11:5
31.205-1	11:5, 11:17	31.205-47	2:35, 3:14, 4:8, 11:5
31.205-1(e)(3)	11:5, 11:14	31.205-47(f)(1)	16:11
31.205-1(f)(5)	11:13	31.205-48	11:5
31.205-3	11:5	31.205-49	11:5
31.205-6	11:5	31.205-51	11:5, 11:13, 11:14
31.205-6(a)(5)	11:5	31.205-52	18:5
31.205-6(g)	11:5	31.205-52(a)	18:6
31.205-6(h)	11:5	32.001	4:2
31.205-6(l)	11:5	32.006	14:22
31.205-6(m)(2)	11:5	32.006-4(c)	14:22
31.205-6(n)	11:5	32.006-4(e)	14:22
31.205-6(p)	11:5	32.006-4(h)	14:22
31.205-7	11:5	32.102	14:1
31.205-8	11:5, 11:14	32.104(a)	14:1
31.205-10	12:18, 18:6	32.104(a)(1)	14:1
31.205-12	11:5, 18:3	32.104(b)	18:13
31.205-13	11:5, 11:14, 11:17	32.104(d)(1)(i)	14:1
31.205-13(b)	11:5	32.104(d)(2)(i)	14:2
31.205-13(c)	11:5, 11:14	32.104(d)(3)	18:13
31.205-13(d)	11:5	32.106(a)	14:1
31.205-14	11:5, 11:14, 11:17	32.202-2	14:1
31.205-15	11:5	32.206(g)	14:1
31.205-17	11:5	32.403(g)	18:13
31.205-18	11:5, 11:17	32.501-1	14:6
31.205-18(a)	11:12	32.501-1(a)	18:13
31.205-19	11:5	32.501-2	14:2
31.205-20	11:1, 11:5, 11:14, 18:4	32.503-4(b)	14:33
31.205-22	11:5	32.503-5	14:4
31.205-23	11:5	32.503-6(b)	14:16
31.205-26(e)	14:26	32.503-6(b)(2)	14:16
31.205-27	11:5, 18:4	32.503-6(c)(1)	14:17
31.205-27(a)	18:3	32.503-6(d)	14:18
31.205-30	11:5	32.503-6(e)	14:19
31.205-31	11:5	32.503-6(e)(2)	14:19
31.205-33	11:5, 16:11	32.503-6(f)(1)	14:20
31.205-33(b)	4:8	32.503-6(f)(2)	14:20
31.205-33(d)	4:8	32.503-6(g)	14:13
31.205-34	11:5, 11:14	32.503-6(g)(1)(i)	14:13
31.205-35	11:5	32.503-8	14:11
31.205-35(c)(1) to (4)	11:5	32.503-9	14:11
31.205-35(d)	11:5	32.503-9(a)	14:11
31.205-36	11:5	32.503-9(b)(1)	14:11
31.205-38	11:17	32.503-14	14:14
31.205-41	11:5	32.503-14(c)	14:26

TABLE OF LAWS AND RULES

FEDERAL ACQUISITION REGULATION—Continued

Sec.		Sec.	
32.503-16	14:14	52.203-6	10:8
32.504(a)	14:9	52.203-7(c)(5)	7:40
32.504(b)	14:9	52.203-13	4:1, 4:2, 4:15, 8:6
32.1001(a)	14:1	52.203-13(b)	4:2
33.102(f)	6:10	52.203-13(c)	4:2
33.207(c)	16:3, 16:6	52.203-16	8:15
33.207(e)	16:6	52.204-2	4:12
33.207(f)	16:4	52.204-11	1:15
33.210	7:32	52.209-5	1:3
42.703-2	11:9, 11:12	52.209-6	1:53, 10:8
42.703-2(a)	11:12	52.211-5	10:24
42.703-2(b)	11:12	52.212-3	10:12
42.703-2(c)	11:12	52.212-4	10:10
42.703-2(c)(2)(ii)	11:12	52.212-4(c)	11:12
42.709-1	11:12	52.212-4(r)	10:10
42.709-1(a)(2)	11:12	52.212-5	10:11
42.709-2(a)(3)	11:11	52.212-5(a)	10:11
42.709-2(b)(3)	11:11	52.214-26	1:35
42.709-3(b)	11:12	52.215-2	1:35, 2:3, 2:10
42.709-5	11:10	52.215-2(f)	9:15
42.709-6	11:10	52.215-10	1:59, 9:15
42.801	11:8	52.215-10(d)(2)	9:15
42.801(f)	11:8	52.215-20	9:13, 9:24
42.803(b)(2)	11:8	52.215-21(a)(1)(i)	9:12
42.803(b)(3)	11:8	52.216-5	13:3
42.1204(a)	18:9	52.216-6	13:3
42.1204(b)	18:9	52.216-7(c)	18:13
42.1204(c)	18:11	52.222-50	10:11
42.1204(e)	18:10	52.225-1(a)(2)	17:12
42.1204(h)	18:10	52.225-4	17:2
42.1204(i)	18:9, 18:10	52.225-5	17:2, 17:15
44.402(c)	10:13	52.227-11(g)	18:13
45.103	18:16	52.230-1	12:20
46.105(a)	15:2	52.230-6	12:8, 12:24, 18:8
46.105(b)	15:2	52.232-16	14:2, 14:19
46.105(c)	15:2	52.232-16(a)(1) to (4)	14:8
46.105(d)	15:2	52.232-16(a)(8)	14:2
46.202	15:3	52.232-16(d)(5)	14:14
46.202-1	15:3, 15:4	52.232-16(d)(6)	14:14
46.202-2	15:5	52.232-16(g)(3)(i)	14:3
46.202-4	15:3, 15:7	52.232-16(g)(3)(ii)	14:4
46.202-4(b)	15:7	52.232-16(j)(6)	14:9
46.203(b)	15:7	52.232-16(j)(3) to (5)	14:9
46.203(c)	15:7	52.233-1	11:8
52.202-1	10:4	52.233-4	10:11
52.203-2	7:27	52.242-3	1:59, 11:10, 11:14
52.203-3	7:1, 7:4	52.242-3(d)	11:10
52.203-5	20:6	52.242-3(e)	11:10

FEDERAL ACQUISITION REGULATION—Continued

Sec.	Sec.	Sec.	Sec.
52.242-3(f)	11:10	52.246-2(b), (c), (d)	15:6
52.242-3(h)	11:12	52.246-4	15:6
52.242-4	11:12, 12:23	52.246-11	15:7
52.242-4(a)(3)	11:9	52.246-12	15:6
52.242-4(c)	11:9	53.301-1443	14:3, 14:5
52.243-1	16:9		

COST ACCOUNTING STANDARDS

No.	Sec.	No.	Sec.
401	12:1, 12:4, 12:7, 12:8, 12:30	407	12:30
401, 402	12:4	410	11:14, 12:23
402	12:7, 12:8, 12:30	414	12:18
405	11:7, 12:7, 12:8, 12:18, 12:23, 12:30	418	12:23
406	12:7, 12:8	401, 402, 405, 406	12:3

DEPARTMENT OF DEFENSE FEDERAL ACQUISITION REGULATION SUPPLEMENT

Sec.	Sec.	Sec.	Sec.
Part 231	11:3	225.7002-2(a)	17:4
Part 246	15:2	225.7002-2(b)	17:4
Subpart 209.571	8:15, 14:2	225.7002-2(d) to (f)	17:4
203.171	8:6	225.7002-2(g)	17:4
203.171-3	8:6	225.7002-2(j)	17:4
203.7001(a)	4:4	225.7002-2(l)	17:4
209.104-1	14:16	225.7009-3	10:8
209.406-1	1:54	225.7300	20:3
209.406-2	8:6	225.7303	20:5
209.406-2(a)	17:22	225.7303(b)	20:5
212.503(a)	10:8	225.7303-1	20:5
212.504(a)	10:8	225.7303-2(a)	20:5
215.371	9:8	225.7303-2(a)(3)	20:19
215.407-5-70	9:26	225.7303-4	20:5, 20:6
215.407-5-70(c)(2)(ii)	9:27	225.7303-4(b)	20:5
215.407-5-70(f)	9:27, 9:28	225.7304(a)	20:3
225.003	17:3	225.7304(b)	20:3
225.70	17:3	225.7306	20:18
225.105(b)	17:3	225.7300 to 225.7307	20:2
225.401-70	17:5	227.7102-1	10:14
225.502(b)	17:3	227.7202-1(a)	10:14
225.502(c)(ii)(E)(2)	17:3	227.7202-3	10:14
225.872	17:2	231.205-70	18:7
225.872-1	17:3	232.006	14:22

TABLE OF LAWS AND RULES

DEPARTMENT OF DEFENSE FEDERAL ACQUISITION REGULATION SUPPLEMENT—Continued

Sec.	Sec.
232.501-1 .... 14:6	252.215-7009 .... 9:5
242.705-2 .... 11:8	252.225-7001 .... 17:3
242.7000 .... 9:28	252.225-7001(a) 17:13
246.102(4) 15:7	252.225-7001(a)(2) 17:12
246.870-2(a) 15:7	252.227-7013 .... 10:14
246.870-2(b) 15:7	252.242-7004 .... 10:8
252.203-7000 .... 8:6	252.243-7002 .... 16:7
252.215-7002(a) 9:27	203.570-2, 252.203-7001 .... 15:9
252.215-7008(a) 9:8	

DOD DIRECTIVES REGULATIONS AND MANUALS

No.	Sec.
5220.22-M 4:12	

SECURITY ASSISTANCE MANAGEMENT MANUAL

No.	Sec.	No.	Sec.
C5.4.3 .... 20:4		C6.3 .... 20:5
C5.4.3.1 .... 20:4		C6.3.7 .... 20:5, 20:6
C5.4.3.2 .... 20:4		C6.3.7.2.2 .... 20:5
C5.4.3.3 .... 20:4		

U.S. GENERAL SERVICES ADMINISTRATION ACQUISITION REGULATION

Sec.	Sec.
552.238-76 .... 1:59	

UNITED STATES SENTENCING COMMISSION GUIDELINES MANUAL

Sec.	Sec.
5E.1.2 .... 1:47	8C4.2 .... 15:10
8C2.4 .... 1:48	Ch 2 .... 1:47
8C2.4(a) 1:48	Ch 3 .... 1:47
8C2.5 .... 1:48	Ch 5, Part A 1:47
8C2.5(f) 4:1	Ch 8 .... 1:48
8C2.6 .... 1:48	

FEDERAL REGISTER

56 Fed. Reg.	Sec.
4112	15:1

57 Fed. Reg.	Sec.
31852	7:33

61 Fed. Reg.	Sec.
4729	3:13
20880	12:10

62 Fed. Reg.	Sec.
224	6:2
22945	7:30
25020	17:21
25045	17:23
39250	3:13
63769	17:23

64 Fed. Reg.	Sec.
72414	18:15

65 Fed. Reg.	Sec.
16,274	14:8

66 Fed. Reg.	Sec.
53,478	10:4
53,483	10:4

67 Fed. Reg.	Sec.
70,520	14:8

72 Fed. Reg.	Sec.
20092	9:13

73 Fed. Reg.	Sec.
1823	8:15
10964	12:8, 12:15, 12:17

73 Fed. Reg.	Sec.
21791	1:3

74 Fed. Reg.	Sec.
2408	8:6
2410	1:20
3431	8:15
14634	1:20
18449	1:15
28,430	14:13
52851	1:35
52852	9:10
52853	10:4
59,913	8:6
59914	1:20
14633-01	10:8

75 Fed. Reg.	Sec.
3178	8:15
20954	8:15
41097	8:15
53129	9:2
53135	9:13, 10:9
81908	8:15

76 Fed. Reg.	Sec.
23236	8:15
39236	1:53
49365	12:4
58144	10:14
75512	9:5
79545	12:2

77 Fed. Reg.	Sec.
194	10:4

79 Fed. Reg.	Sec.
24192-02	10:8

HOUSE REPORTS

No.	Sec.
610	1:8

SENATE REPORTS

Sec.	Sec.	Sec.	Sec.
98-225	6:12	100-503, 100 Cong.	1:8
99-435	7:42		

Table of Cases

-- Kaman Precision Products, Inc., Appeals of, A.S.B.C.A. No. 56305, 2010 WL 2802406 (Armed Serv. B.C.A. 2010)—7:39

-- Palm Springs General Trading and Contracting Establishment, Appeals of, A.S.B.C.A. No. 56290, 2010 WL 1186022 (Armed Serv. B.C.A. 2010)—7:39

-- Precision Standard, Inc., Appeal of, A.S.B.C.A. No. 55865, 2011 WL 310613 (Armed Serv. B.C.A. 2011)—16:2

A

Aalco Forwarding, Inc., Comp Gen. Dec. B-277241.8—10:4

AAR Corp., ASBCA No. 16311 et al., 74-1 BCA ¶ 10607—15:10

Ab-Tech Const., Inc. v. U.S., 31 Fed. Cl. 429 (1994)—1:50

Accent Service Company, Inc., B-299888, 2007 CPD 169 (Comp. Gen. 2007)—6:3

Adamo Wrecking Co. v. Department of Housing and Urban Development, 414 F. Supp. 877 (D.D.C. 1976)—1:55

Aerojet Solid Propulsion Company v. White, 291 F.3d 1328 (Fed. Cir. 2002)—9:4

Aetna Govt. Health Plans, Inc., B- 254397, B- 254397.15, B- 254397.16, B- 254397.17, B- 254397.18, B- 254397.19, 95-2 CPD P 129 (July 27, 1995)—8:21

Alabama Aircraft Industries, Inc.-Birmingham v. U.S., 83 Fed. Cl. 666 (2008)—8:15

Alcan Elec. & Engineering Co., Inc. v. U.S., 24 Cl. Ct. 704, 1992 WL 4908 (1992)—16:5

Alcatec, LLC v. U.S., 100 Fed. Cl. 502 (2011)—1:50, 16:10

Ali v. U.S., 932 F. Supp. 1206 (N.D. Cal. 1996)—17:17

Alion Science & Tech. Corp., Comp. Gen. Dec. B-297342, 2006 CPD 1—8:21

Alion Science and Technology Corp. v. U.S., 74 Fed. Cl. 372 (2006)—8:15

Alion Science & Technology Corporation, Comp. Gen. Dec. B-297022.3—18:12

Allison Engine Co., Inc. v. U.S. ex rel. Sanders, 553 U.S. 662, 128 S. Ct. 2123, 170 L. Ed. 2d 1030, 37 A.L.R. Fed. 2d 773 (2008)—1:15

Applied Resources Corp., Comp. Gen. Dec. B-249258—8:19

Arizona v. Maricopa County Medical Soc., 457 U.S. 332, 102 S. Ct. 2466, 73 L. Ed. 2d 48 (1982)—7:29

Arthur Andersen LLP v. U.S., 544 U.S. 696, 125 S. Ct. 2129, 161 L. Ed. 2d 1008 (2005)—1:38

Asia Resource Partners K.K., B-4004552, 2008 CPD 201 (Comp. Gen. 2008)—8:15

Assessment and Training Solutions Consulting Corp. v. U.S., 92 Fed. Cl. 722 (2010)—6:3

AT & T Government Solutions, Inc., B-400216, 2008 CPD 170 (Comp. Gen. 2008)—8:15

ATK Thiokol, Inc. v. U.S., 68 Fed. Cl. 612 (2005)—11:12

Axiom Resource Management, Inc. v. U.S., 564 F.3d 1374 (Fed. Cir. 2009)—8:15

v. U.S., 78 Fed. Cl. 576 (2007)—8:15
Aydin Corp. v. Widnall, 61 F.3d 1571 (Fed. Cir. 1995)—12:28, 14:16
Aydin Monitor Systems, Appeal of, N.A.S.A.B.C.A. No. 381-1, 1984 WL 13307 (N.A.S.A.B.C.A. 1984)—9:17

B

Baird v. U.S., 76 Ct. Cl. 599, 1933 WL 1901 (1933)—1:50
Baxter v. Palmigiano, 425 U.S. 308, 96 S. Ct. 1551, 47 L. Ed. 2d 810 (1976)—2:32
Bechtel Infrastructure Corporation, B- 405036, B- 405036.2, B- 405036.3, B- 405036.4, B- 405036.5, B- 405036.6, 2011 CPD P 156, 2011 WL 3510746 (August 4, 2011)—8:15
Bill Strong Enterprises, Inc. v. Shannon, 49 F.3d 1541 (Fed. Cir. 1995)—16:11
BMY Combat Systems Div. of Harsco Corp. v. U.S., 38 Fed. Cl. 109 (1997)—3:5
Boeing Co. v. U. S., 230 Ct. Cl. 663, 680 F.2d 132 (1982)—12:2
Boeing Co., Appeal of, A.S.B.C.A. No. 33881, 1991 WL 185209 (Armed Serv. B.C.A. 1991)—9:18
Boeing North American, Inc. v. Roche, 298 F.3d 1274 (Fed. Cir. 2002)—11:12
Boston Auction Co., Ltd. v. Western Farm Credit Bank, 925 F. Supp. 1478 (D. Haw. 1996)—3:4
Bridgeport Machines, Inc., Comp. Gen. Dec. B-265616, 95-2 CPD ¶ 249—17:19
Bridges v. Omega World Travel, Inc., 2009 WL 5174283 (E.D. Ark. 2009)—1:15, 1:18
Brink's, Inc. v. City of New York, 539 F. Supp. 1139, 10 Fed. R. Evid. Serv. 1358 (S.D. N.Y. 1982)—2:32

C

Canadian Commercial Corp., AS-BCA No. 17187, 76-2 BCA ¶ 12145—15:11
Celadon Laboratories, Inc., B-298533, 2006 CPD 158 (Comp. Gen. 2006)—8:15
Cell Therapeutics, Inc. v. Lash Group, Inc., 586 F.3d 1204 (9th Cir. 2009)—1:21
Centech Group, Inc. v. U.S., 554 F.3d 1029 (Fed. Cir. 2009)—8:15
Chenega Federal Systems, LLC, B-299310.2, 2007 CPD 196 (Comp. Gen. 2007)—8:15
Chenega Management, LLC. v. U.S., 96 Fed. Cl. 556 (2010)—7:4
Childree v. UAP/GA CHEM, Inc., 92 F.3d 1140 (11th Cir. 1996)—1:20
CNA Corp. v. U.S., 81 Fed. Cl. 722 (2008)—8:9
Columbia/HCA Healthcare Corp. Billing Practices Litigation, In re, 293 F.3d 289, 58 Fed. R. Evid. Serv. 1451, 53 Fed. R. Serv. 3d 789, 2002 FED App. 0201P (6th Cir. 2002)—3:4
Commercial Contractors, Inc. v. U.S., 154 F.3d 1357 (Fed. Cir. 1998)—3:5, 16:10
Compact v. Metropolitan Government of Nashville & Davidson County, TN., 594 F. Supp. 1567 (M.D. Tenn. 1984)—7:30
Compliance Corp. v. U.S., 22 Cl. Ct. 193, 1990 WL 205528 (1990)—6:15, 8:19
CompuAdd Corp. v. Department of the Air Force, GSBCA No. 12301-P et al., 93-3 BCA ¶ 26123—17:14
v. Department of the Air Force, GSBCA No. 12021-P et al., 93-2 BCA ¶ 25811—17:10
Cook County, Ill. v. U.S. ex rel. Chandler, 538 U.S. 119, 123 S. Ct. 1239, 155 L. Ed. 2d 247 (2003)—1:15

Crandon v. U.S., 494 U.S. 152, 110 S. Ct. 997, 108 L. Ed. 2d 132 (1990)—8:19

Crescent Helicopters, Comp. Gen. Dec. B-284706, 2000 CPD 90 (May 30, 2000)—10:4

C. Sanchez and Son, Inc. v. U.S., 6 F.3d 1539 (Fed. Cir. 1993)—17:8, 17:17

C2C Solutions, Inc., B-401106.5, 2010 CPD 38, (Comp. Gen. 2010)—8:15

Curcio v. United States, 354 U.S. 118, 77 S. Ct. 1145, 1 L. Ed. 2d 1225 (1957)—2:32

D

Daewoo Engineering and Const. Co., Ltd. v. U.S., 557 F.3d 1332 (Fed. Cir. 2009)—1:50

v. U.S., 73 Fed. Cl. 547 (2006)—1:15, 16:10

Daff v. U.S., 31 Fed. Cl. 682 (1994)—15:10

Dantran, Inc. v. U.S. Dept. of Labor, 246 F.3d 36 (1st Cir. 2001)—3:10

Data Transformation Corp., GSBCA No. 8982-P, 87-3 BCA ¶ 20017—17:5, 17:10, 17:19

David I. Abse, B-174449, 1972 CPD 2, 51 Comp. Gen. 403 (January 12, 1972)—7:29

Detica, B-400523, B-400523.2, 2008 CPD 217 (Comp. Gen. 2008)—8:15

Diversified Industries, Inc. v. Meredith, 572 F.2d 596, 23 Fed. R. Serv. 2d 1473, 24 Fed. R. Serv. 2d 1201 (8th Cir. 1977)—3:4

D.K. Shifflet & Assocs., Inc., Comp. Gen. Dec. B-234251—8:21

Donley v. Lockheed Martin Corp., 608 F.3d 1348 (Fed. Cir. 2010)—12:17

Draeger Safety, Inc., B-285366 et al., 2000 CPD 139—10:20

Dynatest Consulting, Inc., Comp. Gen. Dec. B-257822.4, 95-1 CPD ¶ 167—17:19

E

E.D.I., Inc., Comp. Gen. Dec. B-251750—17:19

EDO Corp., Appeal of, A.S.B.C.A. No. 41448, 1993 WL 216057 (Armed Serv. B.C.A. 1993)—9:16

Electronics & Space Corp., ASBCA 47539, 95-2 BCA ¶ 27768—14:24

Energy Systems Group, B-402324, 2010 CPD 73, (Comp. Gen. 2010)—8:15

Engineered Demolition, Inc. v. U.S., 60 Fed. Cl. 822 (2004)—16:5

F

Facchiano Const. Co., Inc. v. U.S. Dept. of Labor, 987 F.2d 206 (3d Cir. 1993)—3:12

Fanslow v. Chicago Mfg. Center, Inc., 384 F.3d 469 (7th Cir. 2004)—1:20

Federal Recovery Services, Inc. v. U.S., 72 F.3d 447, 33 Fed. R. Serv. 3d 1264 (5th Cir. 1995)—1:18

FHC Options, Comp. Gen. Dec. B-246793.3—8:19

Fiber Materials, Inc., Appeal of, A.S.B.C.A. No. 53616, 2007 WL 1252481 (Armed Serv. B.C.A. 2007)—11:10

Fla., Dept. of Ins., State of v. U.S., 81 F.3d 1093 (Fed. Cir. 1996)—14:24

Flight Refueling, Inc., ASBCA 46846 et al., 97-2 BCA ¶ 29000—14:16

Fox v. California Sierra Financial Services, 120 F.R.D. 520 (N.D. Cal. 1988)—3:16

G

General Dynamics Corp., Appeal of, A.S.B.C.A. No. 32660, A.S.B.C.A. No. 32661, 1992 WL 215148 (Armed Serv. B.C.A. 1992)—9:18

General Dynamics Corp., In re, A.S.B.C.A. No. 49372, 2002 WL 1307491 (Armed Serv. B.C.A. 2002)—11:10

GEO Group, Inc. v. U.S., 100 Fed. Cl. 223 (2011)—6:4

Glaser v. Wound Care Consultants, Inc., 570 F.3d 907 (7th Cir. 2009)—1:18

Gonzalez v. Freeman, 334 F.2d 570 (D.C. Cir. 1964)—1:55

Graham v. Allis-Chalmers Mfg. Co., 41 Del. Ch. 78, 188 A.2d 125 (1963)—2:24

Graham County Soil & Water Conservation Dist. v. U.S. ex rel. Wilson, 545 U.S. 409, 125 S. Ct. 2444, 162 L. Ed. 2d 390 (2005)—1:20, 1:21

Grand Union Co. v. U.S., 696 F.2d 888 (11th Cir. 1983)—15:10

Grayson v. Advanced Management Technology, Inc., 221 F.3d 580 (4th Cir. 2000)—1:21

Greenleaf Constr. Co., Inc., Comp. Gen. Dec. B-293105.18—18:12

Greenleaf Constr. Co., Inc., B-293105.18, B-293105.19, 2006 CPD 19, (Comp. Gen. 2006)—8:21

Grumman Aerospace Corp., Appeals of, A.S.B.C.A. No. 35188, A.S.B.C.A. No. 35189, 1990 WL 42095 (Armed Serv. B.C.A. 1990)—9:5

H

Hale v. Henkel, 201 U.S. 43, 26 S. Ct. 370, 50 L. Ed. 652 (1906)—2:32

Harrison v. Westinghouse Savannah River Co., 176 F.3d 776 (4th Cir. 1999)—1:15, 1:21

Hartford Fire Ins. Co. v. Garvey, 109 F.R.D. 323 (N.D. Cal. 1985)—3:16

Haustechnik v. U.S., 34 Fed. Cl. 740 (1996)—7:44

Health Net Federal Services, LLC, B-401652.3, 2009 CPD 220, (Comp. Gen. 2009)—6:10, 8:15

Hi-Shear Technology Corp. v. U.S., 356 F.3d 1372 (Fed. Cir. 2004)—16:8

HOF Constr., Inc. v. Gen. Servs. Admin., GSBCA No. 13317, 96-2 BCA ¶ 28406—16:11

Honeywell Technology Solutions, Inc., B-400771, B-400771.2, 2009 CPD 49 (Comp. Gen. 2009)—6:10

Hooper v. Lockheed Martin Corp., 688 F.3d 1037, 89 Fed. R. Evid. Serv. 1 (9th Cir. 2012)—1:16

Hoyte v. American Nat. Red Cross, 518 F.3d 61 (D.C. Cir. 2008)—1:19, 1:20

Hudson v. U.S., 522 U.S. 93, 118 S. Ct. 488, 139 L. Ed. 2d 450, 162 A.L.R. Fed. 737 (1997)—3:7

Hughes Aircraft Co., Appeal of, A.S.B.C.A. No. 46321, 1997 WL 233993 (Armed Serv. B.C.A. 1997)—9:16

Hughes Aircraft Co., Appeal of, A.S.B.C.A. No. 30144, 1990 WL 42047 (Armed Serv. B.C.A. 1990)—9:5

I

In East West, Inc., B-400432.7, B-400325.7, B- 400325.8, 2010 CPD 187 (Comp. Gen. 2010)—6:3

ITT Gilfillan, Inc., Appeal of, 68-2 B.C.A. (CCH) ¶ 7086, 1968 WL 611 (Armed Serv. B.C.A. 1968)—18:10

J

Jacobs Technology Inc. v. U.S., 100 Fed. Cl. 198 (2011)—6:10, 8:15

James M. Ellett Const. Co., Inc. v. U.S., 93 F.3d 1537 (Fed. Cir. 1996)—16:2

Jana, Inc. v. U.S., 41 Fed. Cl. 735 (1998)—13:1

v. U.S., 34 Fed. Cl. 447 (1995)—1:15

Jewett-Cameron Lumber Corp.,

Comp. Gen. Dec. B-223779.2, 87-2 CPD ¶ 433—17:5

John C. Grimberg Co., Inc. v. U.S., 869 F.2d 1475 (Fed. Cir. 1989)—17:8

Johnson v. All-State Const., Inc., 329 F.3d 848 (Fed. Cir. 2003)—14:23

Jonathan Corp. v. Prime Computer, Inc., 114 F.R.D. 693 (E.D. Va. 1987)—3:16

Julie Research Laboratories, Inc. Reconsideration, B- 218244, B- 218108, B- 216312, B- 218108.2, B- 218244.2, B- 216312.2, 85-1 CPD P 672 (June 12, 1985)—20:3

K

K & R Engineering Co., Inc. v. U. S., 222 Ct. Cl. 340, 616 F.2d 469 (1980)—1:52, 8:19

KAR Contracting, LLC, B-310454, B-310537, 2007 CPD 226 (Comp. Gen. 2007)—8:9, 8:15

Karrar Systems Corporation, B-310661.3, B-310661.4, 2008 CPD 55 (Comp. Gen. 2008)—8:15

Karrar Systems Corporation, B-310661, B-310661.2, 2008 CPD 51 (Comp. Gen. 2008)—8:15

Kellogg Brown & Root Services, Inc. v. U.S., 99 Fed. Cl. 488 (2011)—1:16, 1:50

Kemron Environmental Services, Inc., B-299880, 2007 CPD 176 (Comp. Gen. 2007)—6:3

Knights' Piping, Inc., Comp. Gen. Dec. B-280398.2—8:21

KSR, Inc., Comp. Gen. Dec. B-250160—8:19

L

L-3 Communications Integrated Systems, L.P. v. U.S., 79 Fed. Cl. 453 (2007)—8:13

L-3 Services, Inc., B-400134.11, 2009 CPD 171 (Comp. Gen. 2009)—8:15

Laptop Falls Church, Inc., GSBCA No. 12953-P, 95-1 BCA ¶ 27311—17:10

Laptops Falls Church, Inc. v. Department of Justice, GSBCA No. 12953-P, 95-1 BCA ¶ 27311—17:19

Leader Communications Inc., B-298734, B-298734.2, 2006 CPD 192 (Comp. Gen. 2006)—8:15

Little v. Shell Exploration & Production Co., 690 F.3d 282 (5th Cir. 2012)—1:21

Litton Systems, Inc., Appeal of, A.S.B.C.A. No. 35914, 1996 WL 69568 (Armed Serv. B.C.A. 1996)—9:4

Litton Systems, Inc., Appeal of, 96-1 B.C.A. (CCH) P 28201, 1996 WL 69568 (Armed Serv. B.C.A. 1996)—9:8

Litton Systems, Inc., Amecom Div., Appeal of, A.S.B.C.A. No. 36509, 1992 WL 42752 (Armed Serv. B.C.A. 1992)—9:4

Litton Systems, inc., Amecon Div., Appeal of, A.S.B.C.A. No. 34435, A.S.B.C.A. No. 37615, A.S.B.C.A. No. 37616, 1992 WL 379288 (Armed Serv. B.C.A. 1992)—9:5

Lockheed Corp., Appeals of, A.S.B.C.A. No. 36420, A.S.B.C.A. No. 37495, A.S.B.C.A. No. 39195, 1995 WL 328854 (Armed Serv. B.C.A. 1995)—9:4

Lockheed Martin Aeronautics Co., 13-1 BCA 35220 (2013)—9:17

Long Island Sav. Bank, FSB v. U.S., 555 U.S. 812, 129 S. Ct. 38, 172 L. Ed. 2d 19 (2008)—1:52

Long Island Savings Bank, FSB v. U.S., 503 F.3d 1234 (Fed. Cir. 2007)—1:52

LoSasso Elec. Co., ASBCA No. 49407, 96-2 BCA ¶ 28392—17:8

Luckey v. Baxter Healthcare

Corp., 183 F.3d 730 (7th Cir. 1999)—1:15

M

M-R-S Mfg. Co. v. U. S., 203 Ct. Cl. 551, 492 F.2d 835 (1974)—9:5

M.A. DeAtley Const., Inc. v. U.S., 75 Fed. Cl. 812 (2007)—16:10

Maden Technologies, B-298543.2, 2006 CPD 167 (Comp. Gen. 2006)—8:15

Marbex, Inc., Comp. Gen. Dec. B-225799, 87-1 CPD ¶ 468—17:5, 17:12

Martin J. Simko Const., Inc. v. U.S., 852 F.2d 540 (Fed. Cir. 1988)—1:15

Martin Marietta Corp., Appeal of, A.S.B.C.A. No. 48223, 1996 WL 159053 (Armed Serv. B.C.A. 1996)—9:16

Martin Marietta Corp., In re, 856 F.2d 619 (4th Cir. 1988)—2:40, 3:4

Masai Technologies Corp. v. U.S., 79 Fed. Cl. 433 (2007)—8:15

McCormick v. U.S., 500 U.S. 257, 111 S. Ct. 1807, 114 L. Ed. 2d 307 (1991)—7:5

McDonnell Aircraft Co., Appeal of, A.S.B.C.A. No. 44504, 1997 WL 217389 (Armed Serv. B.C.A. 1997)—9:14

McDonnell Douglas Corp. v. U.S. E.E.O.C., 922 F. Supp. 235 (E.D. Mo. 1996)—3:4

McDonnell Douglas Services, Inc., Appeal of, A.S.B.C.A. No. 56568, 2009 WL 4774620 (Armed Serv. B.C.A. 2009)—9:18

McKing Consulting Corp. v. U.S., 78 Fed. Cl. 715 (2007)—6:3, 6:10

McMorgan & Co. v. First California Mortg. Co., 931 F. Supp. 703, 35 Fed. R. Serv. 3d 1170 (N.D. Cal. 1996)—3:4

McNally v. U.S., 483 U.S. 350, 107 S. Ct. 2875, 97 L. Ed. 2d 292 (1987)—1:6

McTech Corp., B-406100, 2012 CPD 97 (Comp. Gen. 2012)—8:15

Medical Devices of Fall River, Inc., GSBCA No. 6534-5, 82-2 BCA ¶ 15804—15:10

Medina Const., Ltd. v. U.S., 43 Fed. Cl. 537 (1999)—16:1, 16:5

Millipore Corp., Appeal of, G.S.B.C.A. No. 9453, 1990 WL 140514 (Gen. Services Admin. B.C.A. 1990)—9:4

Minnesota Ass'n of Nurse Anesthetists v. Allina Health System Corp., 276 F.3d 1032 (8th Cir. 2002)—1:21

MMI-Federal Marketing Service Corp., Comp. Gen. Dec. B-297537, 2006 CPD ¶ 38—17:4

Moore v. California Institute of Technology Jet Propulsion Laboratory, 275 F.3d 838, 160 Ed. Law Rep. 304 (9th Cir. 2002)—1:8, 1:20

Morse Diesel Intern., Inc. v. U.S., 79 Fed. Cl. 116 (2007)—1:50, 3:13, 7:41

v. U.S., 74 Fed. Cl. 601 (2007)—1:50, 3:13

Muncie Gear Works, Inc., Appeal of, A.S.B.C.A. No. 18184, 1975 WL 1714 (Armed Serv. B.C.A. 1975)—9:17

N

Natural Gas Royalties Qui Tam Litigation (CO2 Appeals), In re, 566 F.3d 956 (10th Cir. 2009)—1:19

NetStar-1 Government Consulting, Inc. v. U.S., 98 Fed. Cl. 729 (2011)—8:15

Network Solutions, Inc. v. Department of the Air Force, GSBCA 11498-P—8:21

Nevada ex rel. Steinke v. Merck & Co., Inc., 432 F. Supp. 2d 1082 (D. Nev. 2006)—1:16

NikSoft Systems Corp., B-406179, 2012 CPD 104 (Comp. Gen. 2012)—8:15

TABLE OF CASES

NKF Engineering, Inc. v. U.S., 805 F.2d 372 (Fed. Cir. 1986)—8:1

Nortel Government Solutions, Inc., B-299522.5, B-299522.6, 2009 CPD 10 (Comp. Gen. 2008)—8:15

Northern Pac. Ry. Co. v. U.S., 356 U.S. 1, 78 S. Ct. 514, 2 L. Ed. 2d 545 (1958)—7:32

Northrop Corp. v. McDonnell Douglas Corp., 705 F.2d 1030, 36 Fed. R. Serv. 2d 102 (9th Cir. 1983)—7:30

Novicki v. Cook, 946 F.2d 938 (D.C. Cir. 1991)—15:9

N.R. Acquisition Corp. v. U.S., 52 Fed. Cl. 490 (2002)—1:50

O

Ocean Ships Inc., B-401526.4, 2010 CPD 156 (Comp. Gen. 2010)—6:3

O'Connor v. Ortega, 480 U.S. 709, 107 S. Ct. 1492, 94 L. Ed. 2d 714 (1987)—2:31

OK Produce; Coast Citrus Distributors, B-299058, B-299058.2, 2007 CPD 31 (Comp. Gen. 2007)—8:15

Operational Resource Consultants, Inc., B-299131.1, B-299131.2, 2007 CPD 38 (Comp. Gen. 2007)—8:15

OSG Product Tankers LLC v. U.S., 82 Fed. Cl. 570 (2008)—3:14

Overlook Systems Technologies, Inc., B-298099.4, B-298099.5, 2006 CPD 185 (Comp. Gen. 2006)—8:15

P

PAI Corp. v. U.S., 2009 WL 3049213 (Ct. Fed. Cl. 2009)—8:15

Palm Springs General Trading and Contracting Establishment, In re, A.S.B.C.A. No. 56290, 2008 WL 4924800 (Armed Serv. B.C.A. 2008)—16:18

Parsons Global Services, Inc. ex rel. Odell Intern., Inc. v. McHugh, 677 F.3d 1166 (Fed. Cir. 2012)—16:2

Pentagen Technologies Intern., Ltd. v. CACI Intern. Inc., 1996 WL 435157 (S.D. N.Y. 1996)—1:9

Perry v. Martin Marietta Corp., 47 F.3d 1134 (Fed. Cir. 1995)—12:28

Pervo Paint Co., GSBCA No. 8220 et al., 87-1 BCA. ¶ 19409—15:12

Peter Kiewit Sons' Co. v. U. S. Army Corps of Engineers, 534 F. Supp. 1139 (D.D.C. 1982)—7:35

PRC, Inc., Comp. Gen. Dec. B-274698—8:19

Precision Lift, Inc. v. U.S., 83 Fed. Cl. 661 (2008)—10:15

Program Engineering, Inc. v. Triangle Publications, Inc., 634 F.2d 1188 (9th Cir. 1980)—7:25

Property Seized from ICS Cutting Tools, Inc., Matter of, 163 F.R.D. 292 (E.D. Wis. 1995)—17:14

Public Warehousing Co., Appeal of, A.S.B.C.A. No. 56116, 2008 WL 355060 (Armed Serv. B.C.A. 2008)—7:39

R

Rad Services, Inc. v. Aetna Cas. and Sur. Co., 808 F.2d 271, 22 Fed. R. Evid. Serv. 392 (3d Cir. 1986)—2:32

Ran-Paige Co., Inc. v. U.S., 35 Fed. Cl. 117 (1996)—17:14, 17:17

Raytheon Co. v. White, 305 F.3d 1354 (Fed. Cir. 2002)—16:8

Reflectone, Inc. v. Dalton, 60 F.3d 1572 (Fed. Cir. 1995)—16:2

Reiter v. Sonotone Corp., 442 U.S. 330, 99 S. Ct. 2326, 60 L. Ed. 2d 931, 27 Fed. R. Serv. 2d 653 (1979)—7:25

Riddle v. DynCorp Intern. Inc., 733 F. Supp. 2d 743 (N.D. Tex. 2010)—1:20

Ridenour v. Kaiser-Hill Co., L.L.C., 397 F.3d 925 (10th Cir. 2005)—1:19

Robert E. Derecktor of Rhode Island, Inc. v. U.S., 762 F. Supp. 1019 (D.R.I. 1991)—8:19

Rockwell Intern. Corp. v. U.S., 549 U.S. 457, 127 S. Ct. 1397, 167 L. Ed. 2d 190 (2007)—1:18

Rolm Corp., Comp. Gen. Dec. B-200995, 81-2 CPD ¶ 106—17:12

Rosemount, Inc., Appeal of, A.S.B.C.A. No. 37520, 1995 WL 373578 (Armed Serv. B.C.A. 1995)—9:5

S

Salmeron v. Enterprise Recovery Systems, Inc., 579 F.3d 787 (7th Cir. 2009)—1:21

Schindler Elevator Corp. v. U.S. ex rel. Kirk, 131 S. Ct. 1885, 179 L. Ed. 2d 825 (2011)—1:18

Seal 1 v. Seal A, 255 F.3d 1154 (9th Cir. 2001)—1:18

Searcy v. Philips Electronics North America Corp., 117 F.3d 154 (5th Cir. 1997)—1:21, 3:17

Securities and Exchange Commission v. Dresser Industries, Inc., 628 F.2d 1368 (D.C. Cir. 1980)—3:3

S.J. Amoroso Const. Co., Inc. v. U.S., 12 F.3d 1072 (Fed. Cir. 1993)—17:17

Skilling v. U.S., 561 U.S. 358,130—1:6

Snell Enters., Inc., Comp. Gen. Dec. B-290113, 2002 CPD 115 (June 10, 2002)—8:21

Southwest Marine, ASBCA 47621, 96-2 BCA ¶ 28601—14:19

Specialty Plastic Prods., Inc., ASBCA No. 42085 et al., 95-2 BCA ¶ 27895—17:12

Sperry Flight Systems v. U. S., 212 Ct. Cl. 329, 548 F.2d 915 (1977)—9:7

Sperry Univac Div., Sperry Rand Corp., DOTCAB 1144, 82-2 BCA 15182—9:5

Standard Oil Co. of New Jersey v. U.S., 221 U.S. 1, 31 S. Ct. 502, 55 L. Ed. 619 (1911)—7:32

Stoner v. Santa Clara County Office of Educ., 502 F.3d 1116, 225 Ed. Law Rep. 155 (9th Cir. 2007)—1:15

Strand Hunt Constr., Inc., ASBCA No. 48690, 96-1 BCA ¶ 28080—17:17

S.T. Research Corp., Comp. Gen. Dec. B-233115.2—8:21

S.T. Research Corp., Comp. Gen. Dec. B-233309—8:21

Superlative Technologies, Inc., B-310489.4, 2008 CPD 123 (Comp. Gen. 2008)—6:3

Superlative Technologies, Inc., B-310489, B-310489.2, 2008 CPD 12 (Comp. Gen. 2008)—6:3, 8:15

Supermex, Inc. v. U.S., 35 Fed. Cl. 29 (1996)—1:50, 7:7

Sylvania Elec. Products, Inc. v. U. S., 202 Ct. Cl. 16, 479 F.2d 1342, 24 A.L.R. Fed. 304 (1973)—9:16

v. U. S., 202 Ct. Cl. 16,479—9:5

Synetics, Inc. v. U.S., 45 Fed. Cl. 1 (1999)—6:15

Systems & Defense Services Intl., Comp. Gen. Dec. B-254254.2, 94-1 CPD ¶ 91—17:8

T

Tennier Indus., Inc., Comp. Gen. Dec. B-239025—7:16

Texas Instruments, Inc., ASBCA No. 18621, 79-1 BCA 13800—12:30

Tides v. The Boeing Co., 644 F.3d 809 (9th Cir. 2011)—1:20

Tower Air, Inc. v. Federal Exp. Corp., 956 F. Supp. 270 (E.D. N.Y. 1996)—7:30

Trafalgar House Const., Inc. v. U.S., 77 Fed. Cl. 48 (2007)—16:10

TABLE OF CASES

Turner v. DynMcDermott Petroleum Operations Co., 2010 WL 4633403 (E.D. La. 2010)—1:20
Turner Const. Co., Inc. v. U.S., 94 Fed. Cl. 561 (2010)—8:15

U

Unisys Corp. v. U.S., 888 F.2d 841 (Fed. Cir. 1989)—9:17
United States ex rel. Boisvert v. FMC Corp., No. C-86-20163 (N.D. Cal. 1998)—15:10
United Telephone Co. of the Northwest, GSBCA 10031-P, 89-3 BCA 22108—8:19
University of California, Appeal of, V.A.B.C.A. No. 4661, 1996 WL 681971 (Veterans Admin. B.C.A. 1996)—9:15
University Sys., Inc. v. Department of Health & Human Servs., GSBCA No. 12039-P, 93-2 BCA ¶ 25646—17:17
URS Energy & Const., Inc. v. Dept. of Energy, CBCA No. 2589, 12-1 BCA ¶ 35,055—16:2
U.S. v. Abrams, 427 F.2d 86 (2d Cir. 1970)—1:39
  v. Acme Process Equipment Co., 385 U.S. 138, 87 S. Ct. 350, 17 L. Ed. 2d 249 (1966)—1:52, 7:41
  v. Advance Tool Co., 86 F.3d 1159 (8th Cir. 1996)—1:16
  v. Aerodex, Inc., 469 F.2d 1003 (5th Cir. 1972)—15:11
  v. Agnello, 135 F. Supp. 2d 380 (E.D. N.Y. 2001)—2:29
  v. Aguilar, 515 U.S. 593, 115 S. Ct. 2357, 132 L. Ed. 2d 520 (1995)—1:36
  v. Allred, 867 F.2d 856 (5th Cir. 1989)—15:12
  v. Amdahl Corp., 786 F.2d 387 (Fed. Cir. 1986)—1:52
  v. Balsiger, 2011 WL 10879630 (E.D. Wis. 2011)—2:29
  v. The Baylor University Medical Center, 469 F.3d 263 (2d Cir. 2006)—1:17
  v. Bonanno Organized Crime Family of La Cosa Nostra, 879 F.2d 20 (2d Cir. 1989)—1:44
  v. Booker, 543 U.S. 220, 125 S. Ct. 738, 160 L. Ed. 2d 621 (2005)—1:46
  v. Broderson, 67 F.3d 452 (2d Cir. 1995)—9:20
  v. Brooks, 111 F.3d 365 (4th Cir. 1997)—1:36
  v. Browning, Inc., 572 F.2d 720 (10th Cir. 1978)—1:39
  v. Bustamante, 45 F.3d 933 (5th Cir. 1995)—7:5
  v. Caci Intern. Inc., 1997 WL 473549 (S.D. N.Y. 1997)—1:21
  v. Collins, 56 F.3d 1416 (D.C. Cir. 1995)—6:12
  v. Conlon, 628 F.2d 150 (D.C. Cir. 1980)—8:13
  v. Container Corp. of America, 393 U.S. 333, 89 S. Ct. 510, 21 L. Ed. 2d 526 (1969)—7:32
  v. Davis, 183 F.3d 231, 52 Fed. R. Evid. Serv. 732 (3d Cir. 1999)—1:36
  v. Dynamics Research Corp., 2008 WL 886035 (D. Mass. 2008)—7:39
  v. EER Systems Corp., 950 F. Supp. 130 (D. Md. 1996)—13:6
  v. Eghbal, 548 F.3d 1281 (9th Cir. 2008)—1:16
  v. Emergency Medical Associates of Illinois, Inc., 436 F.3d 726 (7th Cir. 2006)—1:21
  v. Eureka Laboratories, Inc., 103 F.3d 908 (9th Cir. 1996)—1:48
  v. Fairchild, 990 F.2d 1139 (9th Cir. 1993)—1:5
  v. Fowler, 932 F.2d 306, 33 Fed. R. Evid. Serv. 340 (4th Cir. 1991)—6:12
  v. Frequency Electronics, 862 F. Supp. 834 (E.D. N.Y. 1994)—13:5
  v. Fruchtman, 421 F.2d 1019, 8 A.L.R. Fed. 885 (6th Cir. 1970)—1:39
  v. Gaudin, 515 U.S. 506, 115 S.

Ct. 2310, 132 L. Ed. 2d 444 (1995)—1:5

v. Gold, 743 F.2d 800, 17 Fed. R. Evid. Serv. 669 (11th Cir. 1984)—1:15

v. Gosselin World Wide Moving, N.V., 411 F.3d 502 (4th Cir. 2005)—1:12

v. Hartec Enterprises, Inc., 967 F.2d 130 (5th Cir. 1992)—14:14

v. Harvey, 532 F.3d 326, 32 A.L.R. Fed. 2d 749 (4th Cir. 2008)—7:3

v. Health Possibilities, P.S.C., 207 F.3d 335, 2000 FED App. 0100P (6th Cir. 2000)—1:21

v. Hedges, 912 F.2d 1397 (11th Cir. 1990)—8:13

v. Higgins, 511 F. Supp. 453 (W.D. Ky. 1981)—1:39

v. Hobbs, 922 F.2d 848 (11th Cir. 1990)—1:39

v. Kenney, 185 F.3d 1217, 161 A.L.R. Fed. 765 (11th Cir. 1999)—7:5

v. Kordel, 397 U.S. 1, 90 S. Ct. 763, 25 L. Ed. 2d 1, 13 Fed. R. Serv. 2d 868 (1970)—1:58

v. Laurins, 857 F.2d 529, 26 Fed. R. Evid. Serv. 1346 (9th Cir. 1988)—1:39

v. Littleton, 76 F.3d 614 (4th Cir. 1996)—1:36

v. Mackby, 339 F.3d 1013 (9th Cir. 2003)—1:15

v. Martel, 792 F.2d 630, 20 Fed. R. Evid. Serv. 1104 (7th Cir. 1986)—13:6, 13:19

v. Massachusetts Institute of Technology, 957 F. Supp. 301, 37 Fed. R. Serv. 3d 711 (D. Mass. 1997)—3:4

v. Matzkin, 14 F.3d 1014 (4th Cir. 1994)—6:12

v. McAusland, 979 F.2d 970 (4th Cir. 1992)—6:12

v. McComb, 744 F.2d 555 (7th Cir. 1984)—1:36

v. Medico Industries, Inc., 784 F.2d 840 (7th Cir. 1986)—8:7, 8:9

v. Menominee Tribal Enterprises, 601 F. Supp. 2d 1061 (E.D. Wis. 2009)—1:15

v. Microsoft Corp., 253 F.3d 34 (D.C. Cir. 2001)—7:32

v. Miller, 600 F.2d 498, 4 Fed. R. Evid. Serv. 867 (5th Cir. 1979)—3:16

v. Mirikitani, 380 F.3d 1223 (9th Cir. 2004)—7:3

v. Muldoon, 931 F.2d 282 (4th Cir. 1991)—7:4, 7:5

v. Napco Intern., Inc., 835 F. Supp. 493 (D. Minn. 1993)—20:10

v. National Wholesalers, 236 F.2d 944 (9th Cir. 1956)—15:12

v. Nazon, 940 F.2d 255 (7th Cir. 1991)—1:15

v. Newport News Shipbuilding, Inc., 276 F. Supp. 2d 539 (E.D. Va. 2003)—13:5

v. Newson, 46 F.3d 730 (8th Cir. 1995)—2:40, 5:16

v. Northrop Corp., 59 F.3d 953 (9th Cir. 1995)—1:21

v. Northrop Corp., 5 F.3d 407 (9th Cir. 1993)—1:21

v. O'Connell, 890 F.2d 563, 29 Fed. R. Evid. Serv. 422, 15 Fed. R. Serv. 3d 197, 107 A.L.R. Fed. 653 (1st Cir. 1989)—15:10

v. Okwumabua, 828 F.2d 950, 23 Fed. R. Evid. Serv. 1048 (2d Cir. 1987)—2:21

v. Perry, 152 F.3d 900 (8th Cir. 1998)—3:7

v. Poarch, 878 F.2d 1355 (11th Cir. 1989)—9:22, 13:19

v. Quattrone, 441 F.3d 153 (2d Cir. 2006)—1:36

v. Raymond & Whitcomb Co., 53 F. Supp. 2d 436 (S.D. N.Y. 1999)—1:15

v. Reicher, 983 F.2d 168 (10th Cir. 1992)—7:34

Table of Cases

v. R. Enterprises, Inc., 498 U.S. 292, 111 S. Ct. 722, 112 L. Ed. 2d 795 (1991)—2:42

v. Ribas Dominicci, 899 F. Supp. 42 (D.P.R. 1995)—14:14

v. Risken, 788 F.2d 1361 (8th Cir. 1986)—1:38

v. Robie, 166 F.3d 444 (2d Cir. 1999)—6:12

v. Rule Industries, Inc., 878 F.2d 535 (1st Cir. 1989)—15:12

v. Sarno, 73 F.3d 1470 (9th Cir. 1995)—1:5

v. Schaltenbrand, 930 F.2d 1554 (11th Cir. 1991)—8:8

v. Science Applications Intern. Corp., 653 F. Supp. 2d 87 (D.D.C. 2009)—1:15, 8:15, 8:16

v. Secord, 726 F. Supp. 845 (D.D.C. 1989)—7:5

v. Shah, 44 F.3d 285 (5th Cir. 1995)—1:5

v. Smith & Nephew, Inc., 749 F. Supp. 2d 773 (W.D. Tenn. 2010)—2:40, 5:16

v. Southland Management Corp., 326 F.3d 669 (5th Cir. 2003)—1:15

v. Southland Management Corp., 288 F.3d 665 (5th Cir. 2002)—1:15

v. Standefer, 610 F.2d 1076 (3d Cir. 1979)—7:5

v. Sun-Diamond Growers of California, 526 U.S. 398, 119 S. Ct. 1402, 143 L. Ed. 2d 576 (1999)—7:5

v. Sun-Diamond Growers of California, 138 F.3d 961 (D.C. Cir. 1998)—7:5

v. Sun-Diamond Growers of California, 941 F. Supp. 1262 (D.D.C. 1996)—7:5

v. Systems Architects, Inc., 757 F.2d 373, 17 Fed. R. Evid. Serv. 705 (1st Cir. 1985)—13:6

v. Tadros, 310 F.3d 999 (7th Cir. 2002)—1:6

v. Tallant, 407 F. Supp. 878 (N.D. Ga. 1975)—1:39

v. TDC Management Corp., Inc., 24 F.3d 292 (D.C. Cir. 1994)—1:15

v. Tejada-Beltran, 50 F.3d 105 (1st Cir. 1995)—7:5

v. Thomas, 240 F.3d 445 (5th Cir. 2001)—7:5

v. Thomas, 13 F.3d 151 (5th Cir. 1994)—17:17

v. Tomblin, 46 F.3d 1369, 41 Fed. R. Evid. Serv. 964 (5th Cir. 1995)—7:5

v. United Technologies Corp., 2008 WL 3007997 (S.D. Ohio 2008)—1:16, 9:16

v. U.S. Gypsum Co., 438 U.S. 422, 98 S. Ct. 2864, 57 L. Ed. 2d 854 (1978)—7:32

v. Wallach, 935 F.2d 445, 33 Fed. R. Evid. Serv. 1 (2d Cir. 1991)—8:19

v. White, 322 U.S. 694, 64 S. Ct. 1248, 88 L. Ed. 1542, 152 A.L.R. 1202 (1944)—2:32

v. Whiteside, 285 F.3d 1345 (11th Cir. 2002)—1:3

v. Williams, 29 F. Supp. 2d 1 (D.D.C. 1998)—7:5

v. Wright, 704 F. Supp. 613 (D. Md. 1989)—1:39

USA ex rel. Barrett v. Johnson Controls, Inc., 2003-2 Trade Cas. (CCH) ¶ 74176, 2003 WL 21500400 (N.D. Tex. 2003)—1:18

U.S. Dept. of Transp. ex rel. Arnold v. CMC Engineering, 745 F. Supp. 2d 637 (W.D. Pa. 2010)—1:18

U.S. ex rel. A+ Homecare, Inc. v. Medshares Management Group, Inc., 400 F.3d 428, 2005 FED App. 0120P (6th Cir. 2005)—1:15

U.S. ex rel. Barajas v. U.S., 258 F.3d 1004 (9th Cir. 2001)—3:10

U.S. ex rel. Batiste v. SLM Corp., 659 F.3d 1204 (D.C. Cir. 2011)—1:19

U.S. ex rel. Berge v. Board of Trustees of the University of Alabama, 104 F.3d 1453, 115 Ed. Law Rep. 344 (4th Cir. 1997)—1:15

U.S. ex rel. Biddle v. Board of Trustees of Leland Stanford, Jr. University, 147 F.3d 821, 127 Ed. Law Rep. 596 (9th Cir. 1998)—1:21

U.S. ex rel. Bledsoe v. Community Health Systems, Inc., 342 F.3d 634, 56 Fed. R. Serv. 3d 1089, 2003 FED App. 0322P (6th Cir. 2003)—1:21

U.S. ex rel. Bondy v. Consumer Health Foundation, 28 Fed. Appx. 178 (4th Cir. 2001)—1:18

U.S. ex rel. Boothe v. Sun Healthcare Group, Inc., 496 F.3d 1169 (10th Cir. 2007)—1:18

U.S. ex rel. Branch Consultants v. Allstate Ins. Co., 560 F.3d 371 (5th Cir. 2009)—1:19

U.S. ex rel. Branch Consultants, L.L.C. v. Allstate Ins. Co., 782 F. Supp. 2d 248 (E.D. La. 2011)—1:18, 1:19

v. Allstate Ins. Co., 668 F. Supp. 2d 780 (E.D. La. 2009)—1:18

U.S. ex rel. Bunk v. Birkart Globistics GmbH & Co., 2012 WL 488256 (E.D. Va. 2012)—3:13

v. Birkart Globistics GMBH & Co., 2011-2 Trade Cas. (CCH) ¶ 77704, 2010 WL 4688977 (E.D. Va. 2010)—3:13

U.S. ex rel. Burns v. A.D. Roe Co., Inc., 919 F. Supp. 255 (W.D. Ky. 1996)—1:21

U.S. ex rel. Campbell v. Lockheed Martin Corp., 282 F. Supp. 2d 1324 (M.D. Fla. 2003)—9:4, 20:5

U.S. ex rel. Carter v. Halliburton Co., 2011 WL 2118227 (E.D. Va. 2011)—1:19

U.S. ex rel. Chovanec v. Apria Healthcare Group Inc., 606 F.3d 361 (7th Cir. 2010)—1:19

U.S. ex rel. Compton v. Circle B. Enterprises, Inc., 2011 WL 382758 (M.D. Ga. 2011)—7:39

U.S. ex rel. Costner v. U.S., 317 F.3d 883 (8th Cir. 2003)—1:15

U.S. ex rel. Crennen v. Dell Marketing L.P., 711 F. Supp. 2d 157 (D. Mass. 2010)—17:17

U.S. ex rel. Davis v. Prince, 766 F. Supp. 2d 679 (E.D. Va. 2011)—1:19

v. Prince, 753 F. Supp. 2d 569 (E.D. Va. 2011)—1:18

U.S. ex rel. Dekort v. Integrated Coast Guard Systems, 705 F. Supp. 2d 519 (N.D. Tex. 2010)—1:18

U.S. ex rel. DeKort v. Integrated Coast Guard Systems, LLC, 2010 WL 4363379 (N.D. Tex. 2010)—1:18

U.S. ex rel. Dick v. Long Island Lighting Co., 912 F.2d 13 (2d Cir. 1990)—1:21

U.S. ex rel. Doe v. John Doe Corp., 960 F.2d 318 (2d Cir. 1992)—1:21

v. X Corp., 862 F. Supp. 1502 (E.D. Va. 1994)—1:21

U.S. ex rel. DRC, Inc. v. Custer Battles, LLC, 2009 WL 3756343 (E.D. Va. 2009)—1:17

v. Custer Battles, LLC, 562 F.3d 295 (4th Cir. 2009)—1:15

v. Custer Battles, LLC, 472 F. Supp. 2d 787 (E.D. Va. 2007)—1:16

U.S. ex rel. Dyer v Raytheon Co., 2011 WL 3244489 (D. Mass. July 29, 2011)—1:20

U.S. ex rel. Eisenstein v. City of New York, New York, 556 U.S. 928, 129 S. Ct. 2230, 173 L. Ed. 2d 1255, 73 Fed. R. Serv. 3d 1132 (2009)—1:19

U.S. ex rel. Estate of Botnick v. Cathedral Healthcare System, Inc., 352 F. Supp. 2d 530 (D.N.J. 2005)—1:21

U.S. ex rel. Findley v. FPC-Boron

TABLE OF CASES

Employees' Club, 105 F.3d 675 (D.C. Cir. 1997)—1:21
U.S. ex rel. Fine v. Advanced Sciences, Inc., 99 F.3d 1000 (10th Cir. 1996)—1:21
  v. Advanced Sciences, Inc., 879 F. Supp. 1092 (D.N.M. 1995)—1:21
  v. Chevron, U.S.A., Inc., 72 F.3d 740, 105 Ed. Law Rep. 885 (9th Cir. 1995)—1:21
  v. MK-Ferguson Co., 861 F. Supp. 1544 (D.N.M. 1994)—1:21
U.S. ex rel. Folliard v. CDW Technology Services, Inc., 722 F. Supp. 2d 37 (D.D.C. 2010)—1:19
  v. Synnex Corp., 798 F. Supp. 2d 66 (D.D.C. 2011)—1:19
U.S. ex rel. Garrison v. Crown Roofing Services, Inc., 2011 WL 1005062 (S.D. Tex. 2011)—7:39
U.S. ex rel. Gebert v. Transport Administrative Services, 260 F.3d 909 (8th Cir. 2001)—1:21
U.S. ex rel. Hafter D.O.v. Spectrum Emergency Care, Inc., 190 F.3d 1156 (10th Cir. 1999)—1:21
U.S. ex rel. Haight v. Catholic Healthcare West, 602 F.3d 949 (9th Cir. 2010)—1:19
U.S. ex rel. Hall v. Teledyne Wah Chang Albany, 104 F.3d 230 (9th Cir. 1997)—1:21
U.S. ex rel. Hampton v. Columbia/ HCA Healthcare Corp., 318 F.3d 214 (D.C. Cir. 2003)—1:19
U.S. ex rel. Health Outcomes Technologies v. Hallmark Health System, Inc., 349 F. Supp. 2d 170 (D. Mass. 2004)—1:19
U.S., ex rel. Howard v. Urban Investment Trust, Inc., 30 I.E.R. Cas. (BNA) 918, 2010 WL 832294 (N.D. Ill. 2010)—1:20
U.S. ex rel. Jamison v. McKesson Corp., Medicare & Medicaid P 303329, 2010 WL 1276712 (N.D. Miss. 2010)—1:18
U.S., ex rel. Joseph Piacentile v. Sanofi Synthelabo, Inc., 2010 WL 5466043 (D.N.J. 2010)—1:19
U.S. ex rel. Karvelas v. Melrose-Wakefield Hosp., 360 F.3d 220, 57 Fed. R. Serv. 3d 1262 (1st Cir. 2004)—1:15, 1:20
U.S. ex rel. Killingsworth v. Northrop Corp., 25 F.3d 715, 28 Fed. R. Serv. 3d 1522 (9th Cir. 1994)—1:21, 3:17
U.S., ex rel. Laird v. Lockheed Martin Engineering & Science Services Co., 491 F.3d 254 (5th Cir. 2007)—1:16
U.S. ex rel. Laird v. Lockheed Martin Engineering and Science Services Co., 336 F.3d 346 (5th Cir. 2003)—1:18, 1:21
U.S. ex rel. Lam v. Tenet Healthcare Corp., 287 Fed. Appx. 396 (5th Cir. 2008)—1:18
U.S. ex rel. LeBlanc v. Raytheon Co., Inc., 913 F.2d 17 (1st Cir. 1990)—1:21
U.S. ex rel. Lockhart v. General Dynamics Corp., 529 F. Supp. 2d 1335 (N.D. Fla. 2007)—2:40, 5:16
U.S. ex rel. Longhi v. Lithium Power Technologies, Inc., 530 F. Supp. 2d 888 (S.D. Tex. 2008)—1:16, 9:16
U.S. ex rel. Lujan v. Hughes Aircraft Co., 67 F.3d 242 (9th Cir. 1995)—1:19
U.S. ex rel. Lusby v. Rolls-Royce Corp., 570 F.3d 849 (7th Cir. 2009)—1:19
U.S. ex rel. Marlar v. BWXT Y-12, L.L.C., 525 F.3d 439 (6th Cir. 2008)—1:20
U.S. ex rel. Maxwell v. Kerr-McGee Oil & Gas Corp., 2010 WL 3730894 (D. Colo. 2010)—1:15
U.S. ex rel. Mayman v. Martin

Marietta Corp., 886 F. Supp. 1243 (D. Md. 1995)—3:4

U.S. ex rel. McKenzie v. BellSouth Telecommunications, Inc., 123 F.3d 935, 1997 FED App. 0257P (6th Cir. 1997)—1:18, 1:21

U.S. ex rel Mistick PBT v. Housing Authority of City of Pittsburgh, 186 F.3d 376 (3d Cir. 1999)—1:21

U.S. ex rel. O'Keefe v. McDonnell Douglas Corp., 918 F. Supp. 1338 (E.D. Mo. 1996)—13:5

U.S. ex rel. Oliver v. Parsons Co., 195 F.3d 457 (9th Cir. 1999)—1:3

U.S. ex rel. Owens v. First Kuwaiti General Trading & Contracting Co., 612 F.3d 724 (4th Cir. 2010)—1:20

U.S. ex rel. Putnam v. Eastern Idaho Regional Medical Center, Medicare & Medicaid P 303116, 2009 WL 2901233 (D. Idaho 2009)—1:18

U.S., ex rel. Ramadoss v. Caremark Inc., 586 F. Supp. 2d 668 (W.D. Tex. 2008)—1:15, 1:17

U.S. ex rel. Rost v. Pfizer, Inc., 507 F.3d 720 (1st Cir. 2007)—2:40, 5:16

U.S., ex rel. Rostholder v. Omnicare, Inc., 799 F. Supp. 2d 547 (D. Md. 2011)—1:19

U.S. ex rel. Sanders v. Allison Engine Co., Inc., 471 F.3d 610, 2006 FED App. 0463P (6th Cir. 2006)—9:16

v. North American Bus Industries, Inc., 546 F.3d 288 (4th Cir. 2008)—1:17

U.S. ex rel. Schweizer v. Oce, N.V., 681 F. Supp. 2d 64 (D.D.C. 2010)—1:19, 17:17

U.S. ex rel. Siller v. Becton Dickinson & Co. By and Through Microbiology Systems Div., 21 F.3d 1339 (4th Cir. 1994)—1:19, 1:21

U.S. ex rel. Springfield Terminal Ry. Co. v. Quinn, 14 F.3d 645 (D.C. Cir. 1994)—1:18, 1:21

U.S. ex rel. St. John LaCorte v. Merck & Co., Inc., 2008 WL 818982 (E.D. La. 2008)—1:16

U.S. ex rel. Summers v. LHC Group, Inc., 2009 WL 1651503 (M.D. Tenn. 2009)—1:19

U.S. ex rel. Thistlethwaite v. Dowty Woodville Polymer, Ltd., 110 F.3d 861 (2d Cir. 1997)—9:20

U.S. ex rel. Totten v. Bombardier Corp., 380 F.3d 488 (D.C. Cir. 2004)—1:15

U.S. ex rel. Ubl v. IIF Data Solutions, 2009 WL 1254704 (E.D. Va. 2009)—1:19

v. IIF Data Solutions, 2007 WL 2220586 (E.D. Va. 2007)—1:16, 9:21

U.S. ex rel. Wickliffe v. EMC Corp., 2009 WL 911037 (D. Utah 2009)—1:19

U.S. ex rel. Wildhirt v. AARS Forever, Inc., Medicare & Medicaid P 303756, 2011 WL 1303390 (N.D. Ill. 2011)—1:21

U.S. ex rel. Wilson v. Kellogg Brown & Root, Inc., 525 F.3d 370 (4th Cir. 2008)—1:15

U.S. ex rel. Yannacopolous v. General Dynamics, 457 F. Supp. 2d 854 (N.D. Ill. 2006)—1:19

U.S. ex rel. Yesudian v. Howard University, 153 F.3d 731, 128 Ed. Law Rep. 1030 (D.C. Cir. 1998)—1:20

U.S. v. Spring Works, Inc., Crim. No. 86-1112-WMB (C.D. Cal., Apr. 6, 1987)—15:12

V

Valenzuela Engineering, Inc., ASBCA No. 53608, 04–1 BCA ¶ 32517—15:1

Veridyne Corp. v. U.S., 86 Fed. Cl. 668 (2009)—1:15

v. U.S., 83 Fed. Cl. 575 (2008)—1:50, 1:52

TABLE OF CASES

Vermont Agency of Natural Resources v. U.S. ex rel. Stevens, 529 U.S. 765, 120 S. Ct. 1858, 146 L. Ed. 2d 836 (2000)—1:15, 1:21
Vinyl Technology, Inc., ASBCA 47767 et al., 97-2 BCA ¶ 29235—14:16
VRC, Inc., B-310100, 2007 CPD 202 (Comp. Gen. 2007)—8:15
VSE Corporation, B-404833.4, 2011 CPD 268—8:15

W

Walburn v. Lockheed Martin Corp., 431 F.3d 966, 2005 FED App. 0479P (6th Cir. 2005)—1:21
Washington Utility Group, Comp. Gen. Dec. B-266333—8:21
Watts-Healy Tibbitts A JV v. U.S., 84 Fed. Cl. 253 (2008)—1:3
Wellham v. Cheney, 934 F.2d 305 (11th Cir. 1991)—15:9
Westinghouse Elec. Co. v. U.S., 56 Fed. Cl. 564 (2003)—18:11
Westinghouse Elec. Corp. v. Republic of Philippines, 951 F.2d 1414, 35 Fed. R. Evid. Serv. 1070, 22 Fed. R. Serv. 3d 377 (3d Cir. 1991)—3:4
Wilkins v. St. Louis Housing Authority, 314 F.3d 927 (8th Cir. 2002)—1:20
Wilson v. U.S., 221 U.S. 361, 31 S. Ct. 538, 55 L. Ed. 771 (1911)—2:32
Wynne v. United Technologies Corp., 463 F.3d 1261 (Fed. Cir. 2006)—9:16

Y

Young-Montenay, Inc. v. U.S., 15 F.3d 1040 (Fed. Cir. 1994)—1:50
Yuhasz v. Brush Wellman, Inc., 341 F.3d 559, 57 Fed. R. Serv. 3d 342, 2003 FED App. 0297P (6th Cir. 2003)—1:20

Index

ACCESS TO GOVERNMENT PROPERTY AND INFORMATION
Commercial items, § 10:27
Espionage, § 1:32, 6:13
Foreign acquisitions of United States companies, access to classified information, § 18:19, 18:20
Procurement Integrity Act (this index)
Theft of government property, § 1:31, 6:12

ACCOUNTING DEPARTMENT
Cost allowability, compliance initiatives, § 11:19
Progress payments, compliance initiatives, § 14:34
Time Charging (this index)

ACCOUNTS AND ACCOUNTING
Audits (this index)
Cost Accounting Standards (CAS) (this index)
Cost allowability, § 11:7
Foreign Corrupt Practices Act (this index)
Progress Payments (this index)

ACQUISITIONS
Mergers and Acquisitions (this index)

ACTIONS AND REMEDIES
Antiboycott Provisions (this index)
Contract claims, litigation of, § 16:18
Mergers and acquisitions, prior actions of acquired company, § 18:16
Parallel Proceedings (this index)

ADJUSTMENTS
Cost accounting standards (CAS), contract adjustments, § 12:11
Pricing, Defective (this index)

ADJUSTMENTS—Cont'd
Time Charging (this index)

ADMINISTRATIVE LAW
Antiboycott Provisions (this index)
Debarment (this index)
Export Regulations (this index)
Fines and Penalties (this index)
Obstruction of pending administrative proceedings, § 1:39
Suspension (this index)
Time charging, administrative requirements, § 13:3

ADVICE
Foreign Corrupt Practices Act, advisory government opinions, § 19:29

AFFILIATES
Collusive bidding, § 7:29

AGENCIES
Government Agencies (this index)

AGENTS AND REPRESENTATIVES
Foreign Military Sales (FMS) (this index)
International Sales (this index)

ALLOCATION OF COSTS
Apportionment and Allocation of Costs (this index)

ANTIBOYCOTT PROVISIONS
Generally, § 19:36-19:51
Actions and remedies
antitrust actions, § 19:34
Administrative law. Export Administration Act, below
Compliance initiatives
generally, § 19:37-19:51
document review, § 19:37
education of employees, § 19:37

ANTIBOYCOTT PROVISIONS—Cont'd
Compliance initiatives—Cont'd
  information related to boycott, refusal to supply, § 19:39
  monitoring agents and partners, § 19:40
  reporting requirements, § 19:41
Document review, § 19:38
Education of employees, § 19:37
Export Administration Act
  generally, § 19:36-19:51
  penalties, § 19:43
  prohibitions, § 19:32
Information related to boycott, refusal to supply, § 19:39
Internal Revenue Code, § 19:47
Monitoring agents and partners, § 19:40
Recognition of problem, § 19:35, 19:36
Reporting boycott requests, § 19:41

ANTITRUST
Collusive bidding, § 7:24

APPORTIONMENT AND ALLOCATION OF COSTS
Fair cost principles, § 11:6
Time charging, compliance initiatives, § 13:22

ARMS DEALERS
Defense Contractors (this index)

ASSISTANCE
Foreign Assistance Act (this index)
Security assistance management manual form letter of Defense Department, § Appx W

ATTORNEYS
Investigations (this index)

AUDITS
Compliance Audits (this index)
Federal Audits (this index)
Kickbacks, policies for auditors, § 7:47
Progress payments, internal auditors, § 14:35

AUDITS—Cont'd
Time charging, internal audits, § 13:24

AUTOMATION OF SYSTEMS
Time charging, compliance initiatives, § 13:32

BAA REQUIREMENTS
Domestic and Foreign Products (this index)

BERRY AMENDMENT
Domestic and foreign products, § 17:4

BIDDING
Collusive Bidding (this index)

BOYCOTTS
Antiboycott Provisions (this index)

BRIBERY AND ILLEGAL GRATUITIES
Generally, § 1:25, 7:1-7:12
Commercial items, § 10:26
Compliance initiatives
  generally, § 7:8-7:12
  employment, below
  policies and procedures, below
  recommendations, § 7:12
Employment
  government employees, requirement to pay, § 7:11
  monitoring employee activities, § 7:10
Foreign Corrupt Practices Act (this index)
Frequently asked questions, § 7:5
Government employees, requirement to pay, § 7:11
Monitoring employee activities, § 7:10
Policies and procedures
  generally, § 7:9
  sample company policy statement, § Appx G
Procurement Integrity Act, prohibition on official's acceptance of compensation, § 6:6
Recognition of problem, § 7:6, 7:7
Recommendations, § 7:12

BRIBERY AND ILLEGAL GRATUITIES—Cont'd
Statutory provisions, § 7:2-7:4

BROKERING
Export regulations, § 19:6
International traffic in arms regulations, § 19:6

BUDGETS
Time charging, overly rigid budgetary controls, § 13:16

BURDEN OF PROOF
Defective pricing, adjustments for, § 9:16

BURDENSOME LITIGATION
Parallel proceedings, § 3:5

BYRD AMENDMENT
Lobbying Restrictions (this index)

CAS
Cost Accounting Standards (CAS) (this index)

CDA CLAIMS
Pricing, § 16:9

CERTIFICATION
Chart of representations and certifications, § Appx B
Commercial items, § 10:12
Contract Claims (this index)
Costs (this index)
Defense Contractors (this index)
Foreign military sales (FMS), certification of credit-financed (FMF) sales, § 20:10
Pricing, Defective (this index)
Progress payments, requests for, § 14:5
Time charging, § 13:4

CFAO
Cost Accounting Standards (CAS) (this index)

CLAIMS
Contract Claims (this index)

CLASSIFIED INFORMATION
Foreign acquisitions of United States companies, § 18:19, 18:20

CLAYTON ACT
Collusive bidding, § 7:25

COLLUSIVE BIDDING
Generally, § 1:29, 7:23-7:36
Affiliates, § 7:29
Antitrust, § 7:24
Clayton Act, § 7:25
Compliance initiatives
  generally, § 7:35
  recommendations, § 7:36
Defense production pools, § 7:31
Federal Trade Commission (FTC), § 7:26
Frequently asked questions, § 7:32
Joint ventures, § 7:30
Monopolies, § 7:24
Recognition of problem, § 7:33, 7:34
Recommendations, § 7:36
Sherman Antitrust Act, § 7:24
Statutory provisions, § 7:23-7:31
Teaming agreements, § 7:30

COMMERCIAL ITEMS
Generally, § 10:1-10:28
Access to information, § 10:27
Bribery and illegal gratuities, § 10:26
Certifications, § 10:12
Competition, MAS program, § 10:20
Compliance initiatives
  generally, § 10:25-10:28
  access to information, § 10:27
  gratuities, § 10:26
  recommendations, § 10:28
Computer software, rights in, § 10:14
Contracts
  generally, § 10:10
  certifications, § 10:12
  executive orders, implementation of, § 10:11
  MAS program, below
  representations, § 10:12
  small contracts, below
  statutes, implementation of, § 10:11

COMMERCIAL ITEMS—Cont'd
Contracts—Cont'd
subcontracts, below
Definitions, § 10:3, 10:4
Executive orders, implementation of, § 10:11
Exemptions
generally, § 10:5-10:9
prime contracts, § 10:6
subcontracts, § 10:7
Truth in Negotiations Act, § 9:10, 10:9
Frequently asked questions, § 10:15
Gratuities, § 10:26
GSA. MAS program, below
Industrial funding fee, MAS program, § 10:19
MAS program
generally, § 10:16-10:20
competition, § 10:20
contract price reductions, § 10:18
industrial funding fee, § 10:19
pricing, § 10:17, 10:18
Pricing
MAS program, § 10:17, 10:18
Truth in Negotiations Act, § 9:10, 10:9
Prime contracts, § 10:6
Quality control, contractor inspection requirements, § 15:4
Recognition of problem, § 10:23, 10:24
Recommendations, § 10:28
Representations, § 10:12
Small contracts
generally, § 10:21, 10:22
quality control, contractor inspection requirements, § 15:5
Special contracting methods
MAS program, above
small purchases, § 10:21, 10:22
Statutes, implementation of, § 10:11
Subcontracts
clauses, § 10:13
exemption, § 10:7
Technical data rights, § 10:14
Truth in Negotiations Act, § 9:10, 10:9

COMMISSIONS
Foreign Military Sales (FMS) (this index)

COMMUNICATIONS
Conflicts of Interest (this index)
Investigations, communications with prosecutor, § 2:39

COMPANY HOTLINES
Compliance programs, § 4:12
Investigations, § 2:19

COMPETITION
Commercial items, MAS program, § 10:20
Price competition, Truth in Negotiations Act, § 9:8

COMPLIANCE AUDITS
Generally, § 4:13, 5:1-5:16
Controls, testing, § 5:9
Corrective action, § 5:14
Deliverables, development of, § 5:5
Documentation of audits, § 5:11
Employee interviews, § 5:8
Existing policies and procedures, review of, § 5:7
Follow-up, § 5:15
Formation of audit team, § 5:2
Implementation of audit results
generally, § 5:12-5:15
corrective action, § 5:14
follow-up, § 5:15
key steps, § 5:12
recommendations for improvement, § 5:13
Interviews of employees, § 5:8
Major tasks, § 5:6
Performance of audits
generally, § 5:6-5:11
employee interviews, § 5:8
existing policies and procedures, review of, § 5:7
major tasks, § 5:6
Planning audit
generally, § 5:2-5:5
deliverables, development of, § 5:5
formation of audit team, § 5:2
scope of audit, § 5:3

COMPLIANCE AUDITS—Cont'd
Planning audit—Cont'd
work programs for audit, § 5:4
Policies and procedures, review of, § 5:7
Recommendations for improvement, § 5:13
Reports of audit results to government, § 5:16
Review of existing policies and procedures, § 5:7
Sampling transactions, § 5:10
Scope of audit, § 5:3
Testing controls, § 5:9
Time charging, § 13:24
Work programs for audit, § 5:4

COMPLIANCE PROGRAMS
Generally, § 4:1-4:18
Antiboycott Provisions (this index)
Audits. **Compliance Audits** (this index)
Collusive Bidding (this index)
Commercial Items (this index)
Compliance book, § 4:3
Compliance officer, § 4:11
Conflicts of Interest (this index)
Contract Claims (this index)
Cooperation with government investigations, § 4:16
Cost Accounting Standards (CAS) (this index)
Cost Allowability (this index)
Costs of compliance, recovery of, § 4:8
Defense contractors, § 4:4
Development of compliance programs
generally, § 4:2-4:7
compliance book, § 4:3
defense contractors, § 4:4
employee screening, § 4:7
future modifications, § 4:6
settlement agreements, § 4:5
Disciplinary action, § 4:14
Domestic and Foreign Products (this index)
Education and training of employees, § 4:17

COMPLIANCE PROGRAMS —Cont'd
Employment
education and training of employees, § 4:17
screening of employees, § 4:7
Ethics, corporate code of, § 4:9
FAR compliance requirements, § 4:2
Foreign Corrupt Practices Act (this index)
Foreign Military Sales (FMS) (this index)
Future modifications of compliance programs, § 4:6
Hotlines, § 4:12
International Sales (this index)
Investigations
generally, § 4:13
government investigations, cooperation with, § 4:16
Kickbacks (this index)
Lobbying Restrictions (this index)
Modifications of compliance programs, § 4:6
Officer, compliance, § 4:11
Policies and procedures
generally, § 4:10
Bribery and Illegal Gratuities (this index)
compliance audits, review of existing policies and procedures, § 5:7
domestic and foreign products, § 17:31
kickbacks, § 7:46, 7:47
procurement information, § 6:17
time charging, § 13:21, 13:22
Pricing, Defective (this index)
Procurement Information (this index)
Progress Payments (this index)
Recommendations
bribery and illegal gratuities, § 7:12
collusive bidding, § 7:36
commercial items, § 10:28
compliance audits, § 5:13
Conflicts of Interest (this index)
contract claims, § 16:19

**COMPLIANCE PROGRAMS
—Cont'd**
Recommendations—Cont'd
cost accounting standards (CAS),
§ 12:35
cost allowability, § 11:20
domestic and foreign products,
§ 17:34
foreign military sales (FMS),
§ 20:25
kickbacks, § 7:48
lobbying restrictions, § 7:22
pricing, defective, § 9:32
procurement information, § 6:20
product substitution, § 15:16
progress payments, § 14:36
time charging, § 13:34
Reporting violations to government,
§ 4:15
Settlement agreements, § 4:5
Time Charging (this index)
Training of employees, § 4:17
Updating, § 4:18
Violations, reporting to government,
§ 4:15

**COMPROMISE AND
SETTLEMENT**
Compliance programs, § 4:5
Global Settlements (this index)

COMPUTER SOFTWARE
Commercial items, data rights,
§ 10:14

CONFLICTS OF INTEREST
Generally, § 1:26, 8:1-8:25
Communications and appearances.
Ethics Reform Act, below
Compliance initiatives
organizational conflicts, § 8:24,
8:25
personal conflicts, § 8:22, 8:23
Contractor responsibilities as to
organizational conflicts, § 8:16
Employment discussions, restrictions
on, § 8:4
Ethics Reform Act
generally, § 8:7-8:12
fines and penalties, § 8:12

**CONFLICTS OF INTEREST
—Cont'd**
Ethics Reform Act—Cont'd
intent to influence, communications and appearances with,
§ 8:8
lifetime ban on communications
and appearances, § 8:9
one-year ban on communications
and appearances, § 8:11
two-year ban on communications
and appearances, § 8:10
Fines and penalties
Ethics Reform Act, § 8:12
Procurement Integrity Act, § 8:5
Former agency officials, one-year ban
on hiring, § 8:3
Frequently asked questions
organizational conflicts, § 8:17
Procurement Integrity Act, § 8:6
Government responsibilities as to
organizational conflicts, § 8:15
Intent to influence, communications
and appearances with, § 8:8
Mergers and acquisitions,
organizational conflicts, § 18:12
Organizational conflicts
generally, § 8:14-8:17
compliance initiatives, § 8:24,
8:25
contractor responsibilities, § 8:16
frequently asked questions, § 8:17
government responsibilities, § 8:15
mergers and acquisitions, § 18:12
recognition of problem, § 8:20,
8:21
recommendations, § 8:25
Personal conflicts
generally, § 8:2-8:13
compliance initiatives, § 8:22,
8:23
Ethics Reform Act, above
Procurement Integrity Act, below
recognition of problem, § 8:18,
8:19
recommendations, § 8:23
revolving-door statutes, § 8:13
Procurement Integrity Act
generally, § 8:2-8:6

CONFLICTS OF INTEREST —Cont'd
Procurement Integrity Act—Cont'd
employment discussions, restrictions on, § 8:4
fines and penalties, § 8:5
former agency officials, one-year ban on hiring, § 8:3
frequently asked questions, § 8:6
Recognition of problem
organizational conflicts, § 8:20, 8:21
personal conflicts, § 8:18, 8:19
Recommendations
organizational conflicts, § 8:25
personal conflicts, § 8:23
Revolving-door statutes, § 8:13

CONSISTENCY
Parallel proceedings, inconsistent defenses, § 3:6

CONSPIRACY
Generally, § 1:12, 1:13

CONSTITUTIONAL LAW
Investigations (this index)

CONTINGENT FEES
Foreign Military Sales (FMS) (this index)

CONTRACT CLAIMS
Generally, § 16:1-16:19
CDA claims, pricing, § 16:9
Certification
generally, § 16:3-16:7
defective certification, § 16:4
defense contracts, § 16:7
language of certification, § 16:5
persons who must certify, § 16:6
Compliance initiatives
generally, § 16:14-16:19
claims team, establishment of, § 16:14
corroboration of facts, § 16:16
documentation of facts, § 16:16
litigation, § 16:18
negotiations, § 16:17
recommendations, § 16:19
recordkeeping, § 16:15

CONTRACT CLAIMS—Cont'd
Corroboration of contract claims, § 16:16
Defective certification, § 16:4
Definition, § 16:2
Documentation of contract claims, § 16:16
Equitable adjustment, requests for pricing, § 16:9
False Claims (this index)
Fraud and deceit, § 16:10
Frequently asked questions, § 16:11
Litigation of contract claims, § 16:18
Negotiations, § 16:17
Pricing claims
generally, § 16:8
CDA claims, pricing, § 16:9
equitable adjustment, requests for, § 16:9
Recognition of problem, § 16:12, 16:13
Recommendations, § 16:19
Records and recording, compliance initiatives, § 16:15

CONTRACTS
Claims. **Contract Claims** (this index)
Commercial Items (this index)
Cost Accounting Standards (CAS) (this index)
Fines and Penalties (this index)
Investigations, allegations by contracting officers, § 2:16
Performance of Contracts (this index)
Progress Payments (this index)
Time charging, § 13:17, 13:18

CONTROLS
Compliance audits, testing controls, § 5:9
Cost accounting standards (CAS), internal controls, § 12:32
Time charging, overly rigid budgetary controls, § 13:16

CORRECTION
Compliance audits, § 5:14
Pricing, defective, § 9:28

CORROBORATION
Contract claims, corroboration of, § 16:16

CORRUPTION
Generally, § 1:25-1:29
Bidding. **Collusive Bidding** (this index)
Bribery and Illegal Gratuities (this index)
Collusive Bidding (this index)
Conflicts of Interest (this index)
Foreign Corrupt Practices Act (this index)
Gratuities. **Bribery and Illegal Gratuities** (this index)
Kickbacks (this index)
Lobbying Restrictions (this index)

COST ACCOUNTING STANDARDS (CAS)
Generally, § 12:1-12:35
Accounting changes
generally, § 12:11
CFAO compliance determinations, unilateral accounting changes, § 12:16
Adjustments, contract, § 12:11
Applicability, § 12:3-12:7
Background, § 12:2
CFAO compliance determinations
generally, § 12:12-12:17
findings. Initial finding of noncompliance, below in this group
initial finding of noncompliance
generally, § 12:14
agreement with initial finding, § 12:15
disagreement with initial finding, § 12:15
types of noncompliance, § 12:13
unilateral accounting changes, § 12:16
Changes. Accounting changes, above
Compliance initiatives
generally, § 12:31-12:35
education of employees, § 12:34
employees, CAS-qualified, § 12:33

COST ACCOUNTING STANDARDS (CAS)—Cont'd
Compliance initiatives—Cont'd
internal controls, § 12:32
recommendations, § 12:35
Contract adjustments, § 12:11
Contract clauses, § 12:8
Cost principles compared, § 12:18
Disclosure statements
generally, § 12:9
false statements by contractors, § 12:22
text of Cost Accounting Standards Board disclosure statement, § Appx N
time charging, § 13:14
Educational institutions, § 12:10
Education of employees, § 12:34
Employees, CAS-qualified, § 12:33
Exempt contracts, § 12:4
False claims by contractors
generally, § 12:25-12:27
overbilling on cost contracts and invoices, § 12:27
progress payment billings, errors in, § 12:26
False statements by contractors
generally, § 12:19-12:24
cost impact proposals, § 12:24
cost or pricing data, proposals containing, § 12:21
disclosure statements, § 12:22
final indirect cost certifications, § 12:23
overhead cost certifications, § 12:23
proposals, § 12:21, 12:24
solicitation representations and certifications, § 12:20
Final indirect cost certifications, § 12:23
Findings. CFAO compliance determinations, above
Frequently asked questions, § 12:28
Full CAS coverage, § 12:6
Initial finding of noncompliance. CFAO compliance determinations, above
Internal controls, § 12:32

COST ACCOUNTING STANDARDS (CAS)—Cont'd
Mergers and acquisitions, pricing adjustments, § 18:8
Modification
  accounting changes, above
  CAS coverage, modified, § 12:7
Overbilling on cost contracts and invoices, § 12:27
Overhead cost certifications, § 12:23
Progress payment billings, errors in, § 12:26
Proposals, false statements by contractors, § 12:21, 12:24
Qualified employees, § 12:33
Recognition of problem, § 12:29, 12:30
Recommendations, § 12:35
Solicitation representations and certifications, § 12:20
Waiver, § 12:5

COST ALLOWABILITY
Generally, § 11:1-11:20
Accounting department, compliance initiatives, § 11:19
Accounting rules, § 11:7
Allowable costs defined, § 11:4
Apportionment of costs, § 11:6
Certificate of final indirect costs, § 11:9
Compliance initiatives
  generally, § 11:15-11:20
  accounting department, § 11:19
  middle management, § 11:17
  nonsupervisory employees, § 11:18
  recommendations, § 11:20
  supervisors, § 11:17
  upper management, § 11:16
Coverage, § 11:3
Definition, § 11:4
Disallowance of unallowable costs, § 11:8
Fair cost principles
  generally, § 11:2-11:7
  accounting rules, § 11:7
  allowable costs defined, § 11:4
  apportionment of costs, § 11:6

COST ALLOWABILITY—Cont'd
Fair cost principles—Cont'd
  coverage, § 11:3
  restricted costs, § 11:5
  unallowable costs, § 11:5
Final indirect cost certifications, § 11:9
Fraud and deceit, § 11:11
Frequently asked questions, § 11:12
Management
  middle management, § 11:17
  supervisors, § 11:17
  upper management, § 11:16
Middle management, compliance initiatives, § 11:17
Nonsupervisory employees, compliance initiatives, § 11:18
Penalties for unallowable costs clause, § 11:10, Appx M
Progress payments, § 14:10
Recognition of problem, § 11:13, 11:14
Recommendations, § 11:20
Restricted costs, § 11:5
Supervisors, compliance initiatives, § 11:17
Unallowable costs
  generally, § 11:8-11:11
  certificate of final indirect costs, § 11:9
  disallowance, § 11:8
  fair cost principles, § 11:5
  fraud and deceit, § 11:11
  penalties for unallowable costs clause, § 11:10, Appx M
Upper management, compliance initiatives, § 11:16

COSTS
Apportionment and Allocation of Costs (this index)
Certification
  final indirect cost certifications, below
  solicitation representations and certifications, § 12:20
  Truth in Negotiations Act, § 9:6
Compliance costs, recovery of, § 4:8

Index-9

COSTS—Cont'd

Cost Accounting Standards (CAS) (this index)
Cost Allowability (this index)
Final indirect cost certifications allowability, § 11:9
  cost accounting standards (CAS), false statements by contractors, § 12:23
  text of FAR 52.242-4, § **Appx L**
Foreign Military Sales (FMS) (this index)
Instructions for submitting cost/price proposals, § **Appx J**
Mergers and Acquisitions (this index)
Notice of contract costs suspended or disapproved, § **Appx K**
Overhead. Final indirect cost certifications, above
Pricing, Defective (this index)
Progress Payments (this index)
Proposals (this index)
Time Charging (this index)

COUNTRY OF ORIGIN
Domestic and Foreign Products (this index)

CREDIT-FINANCED SALES
Foreign Military Sales (FMS) (this index)

CRIMINAL LAW
Generally, § 1:1-1:59
Administrative proceedings pending, obstruction of, § 1:39
Audits, federal, obstruction of, § 1:34, 1:35
Bidding. **Collusive Bidding** (this index)
Bribery and Illegal Gratuities (this index)
Collusive Bidding (this index)
Conflicts of Interest (this index)
Conspiracy, § 1:12, 1:13
Constitutional law. **Investigations** (this index)
Corruption (this index)
Espionage, § 1:32, 6:13

CRIMINAL LAW—Cont'd
Field interviews, § 2:9
Fines and Penalties (this index)
Foreign Corrupt Practices Act (this index)
Fraud and Deceit (this index)
Global settlements, § 3:12
Grand Jury (this index)
Gratuities. **Bribery and Illegal Gratuities** (this index)
Interviews, § 2:9
Investigations (this index)
Judicial proceedings, obstruction of, § 1:36, 1:37
Kickbacks (this index)
Lobbying Restrictions (this index)
Obstruction of Justice (this index)
Pending administrative proceedings, obstruction of, § 1:39
Perjury, § 1:40, 1:41
Privileges (this index)
Procurement Integrity Act (this index)
Racketeer Influenced and Corrupt Organizations Act (RICO), § 1:44, 1:45
Revolving-door statutes, § 8:13
Scope, § 1:1
Search and Seizure (this index)
Self-incrimination privilege, § 2:32
Sentence and Punishment (this index)
Sentence of Fine statute, § 1:43
Subpoenas (this index)
Theft of government property, § 1:31, 6:12
Wiretaps, § 2:8
Witnesses (this index)

DEBARMENT
Generally, § 1:53-1:55
Global settlements, § 3:14-3:16
Pricing, defective, § 9:23

DEEMED EXPORTS
Export regulations, § 19:3; 19:11
International traffic in arms regulations, § 19:3

INDEX

DEFENSE CONTRACTORS
  Certification
    contract claims, certification of, § 16:7
    Defense Security Cooperation Agency, certification and agreement with, § Appx Y
    foreign military sales (FMS), certification of credit-financed (FMF) sales, § 20:10
  Collusive bidding, defense production pools, § 7:31
  Compliance programs, § 4:4
  Contract claims, certification of, § 16:7
  Criminal investigations, § 2:3
  Defense Security Cooperation Agency
    certification and agreement, § Appx Y
    foreign military financing guidelines, § Appx X
  Domestic and foreign products, DOD end products, § 17:13
  Export Regulations (this index)
  Foreign Military Sales (FMS) (this index)
  Fraud and deceit
    Defense Department fraud investigations, § Appx S
    Department of Army memorandum, procurement fraud information, § Appx I
    indicators of fraud in DOD procurement, § Appx T
    Hotline poster, Department of Defense, § Appx F
  International Sales (this index)
  Mergers and acquisitions, costs, § 18:7
  Procurement fraud information, Department of Army memorandum, § Appx I
  Security assistance management manual form letter of Defense Department, § Appx W

DEFENSES
  Foreign Corrupt Practices Act, bribery, § 19:21

DEFENSES—Cont'd
  Parallel proceedings, inconsistent defenses, § 3:6
  Pricing, defective, § 9:18

DELINQUENT PAYMENTS OF COSTS
  Progress payments, § 14:19

DELIVERABLES
  Compliance audits, § 5:5

DEPARTMENT OF ARMY MEMORANDUM
  Procurement fraud information, § Appx I

DEPARTMENT OF DEFENSE
  Defense Contractors (this index)

DEPRECIATION
  Mergers and acquisitions, depreciation of combined assets, § 18:5

DESIGNATED COUNTRIES
  Domestic and Foreign Products (this index)

DISCIPLINARY ACTION
  Compliance programs, § 4:14

DISCLOSURES
  Cost Accounting Standards (CAS) (this index)
  Lobbying Restrictions (this index)
  Pricing, defective, § 9:27
  Procurement information, disclosure of, § 6:3
  Voluntary disclosures of wrongdoing, § 2:40

DOCUMENTS
  Antiboycott provisions, § 19:38
  Compliance audits, documentation of, § 5:11
  Contract claims, documentation of, § 16:16
  Grand jury, document subpoenas, § 2:41
  Investigations, preparation for, § 2:10

DOMESTIC AND FOREIGN PRODUCTS
  Generally, § 17:1-17:34

DOMESTIC AND FOREIGN PRODUCTS—Cont'd
BAA requirements
  generally, § 17:3
  country of origin
    domestic end products, § 17:12
    qualifying country end products, § 17:13
  exceptions, § 17:8
  penalties, § 17:17
Berry Amendment, § 17:4
Compliance initiatives
  generally, § 17:28-17:34
  history of end products and components, § 17:29
  inventories, separate, § 17:30
  monitoring and oversight procedures, § 17:31
  on-site review, § 17:33
  planning ahead, § 17:32
  policies and procedures, § 17:31
  recommendations, § 17:34
Contract performance, § 17:26
Country of origin
  generally, § 17:11-17:16
  BAA requirements, above
  DOD end products, § 17:13
  FAR v. Customs, § 17:16
  NAFTA marking rules, § 17:16
  qualifying country end products, § 17:13
  TAA designated country end products, § 17:14
  United States-made end products, § 17:15
Designated countries
  end products, § 17:14
  list of designated countries, § Appx V
DOD end products, § 17:13
End products
  country of origin, above
  history of end products and components, § 17:29
  identification of end products, § 17:10
Exceptions, § 17:7-17:9
Export Regulations (this index)

DOMESTIC AND FOREIGN PRODUCTS—Cont'd
FAR v. Customs, § 17:16
Fines and penalties
  BAA penalties, § 17:17
  made in USA labels, § 17:22
  TAA penalties, § 17:18
Free trade agreements, § 17:6
Frequently asked questions
  generally, § 17:19
  made in USA labels, § 17:23
FTC requirements, made in USA labels, § 17:21
Identification of end products, § 17:10
International Sales (this index)
Inventories, separate, § 17:30
Labels. Made in USA labels, below
Made in USA labels
  generally, § 17:20-17:23
  frequently asked questions, § 17:23
  FTC requirements, § 17:21
  penalties, § 17:22
Monitoring and oversight procedures, § 17:31
NAFTA marking rules, § 17:16
Offers to supply products, § 17:25
On-site review, § 17:33
Penalties. Fines and penalties, above
Performance of contracts, § 17:26
Planning ahead, § 17:32
Policies and procedures, § 17:31
Postaward activities, § 17:26
Qualifying countries
  Defense Department qualifying countries, list of, § Appx U
  end products, § 17:13
Recognition of problem, § 17:24-17:27
Recommendations, § 17:34
Records and recording
  history of end products and components, § 17:29
  inventories, separate, § 17:30
Separate inventories, § 17:30
Statutory provisions, § 17:2-17:6

INDEX

DOMESTIC AND FOREIGN PRODUCTS—Cont'd
TAA requirements
generally, § 17:5
designated country end products, § 17:14
exceptions, § 17:9
penalties, § 17:18
Treaties, § 17:2-17:6
United States-made end products
country of origin, § 17:15
made in USA labels, above
WTO GPA requirements, § 17:5

DUE DILIGENCE REVIEW
Mergers and acquisitions, § 18:21, 18:22

EDUCATIONAL INSTITUTIONS
Cost accounting standards (CAS), § 12:10

EDUCATION OF EMPLOYEES
Employment (this index)

EMPLOYMENT
Bribery and Illegal Gratuities (this index)
Compliance Programs (this index)
Cost accounting standards (CAS), CAS-qualified employees, § 12:33
Education and training of employees
antiboycott provisions, § 19:37
compliance programs, § 4:17
cost accounting standards (CAS), § 12:34
Foreign Corrupt Practices Act, § 19:28
investigations, § 2:12
procurement information compliance initiatives, § 6:18, 6:19
time charging, compliance initiatives, § 13:23
Former Employees (this index)
Interviews of employees
compliance audits, § 5:8
Investigations (this index)
Investigations (this index)
Time Charging (this index)

EMPLOYMENT—Cont'd
Training. Education and training of employees, above

EMPLOYMENT CONTRACTS
Procurement Integrity Act, § 6:5

ENVIRONMENTAL VIOLATIONS
Mergers and acquisitions, § 18:15

ESPIONAGE
Generally, § 1:32, 6:13

ESTIMATES
Pricing, Defective (this index)
Progress payments, actual profit less than estimated, § 14:21

ETHICS
Compliance programs, code of corporate ethics, § 4:9
Conflicts of Interest (this index)
Investigations, advice to government investigators as to local ethics rules, § 2:26
Sample code of business ethics and conduct, § Appx E

EXECUTIVE ORDERS
Commercial items, § 10:11

EXEMPTIONS
Commercial Items (this index)
Cost accounting standards (CAS), § 12:4

EXPORT REGULATIONS
Generally, § 19:2-19:18
Antiboycott Provisions (this index)
Brokering, § 19:6
Compliance initiatives, § 19:18
Deemed exports, § 19:3; 19:11
International traffic in arms regulations, § 19:2-19:9
Penalties, § 19:9; 19:15
Re-exports, § 19:4; 19:12
Registration, § 19:7
Significant military equipment, § 19:5
Temporary imports, § 19:8

Index-13

FALSE CLAIMS
Cost Accounting Standards (CAS) (this index)
Fraud and Deceit (this index)

FALSE STATEMENTS
Cost Accounting Standards (CAS) (this index)
Fraud and Deceit (this index)
Perjury, § 1:40, 1:41

FAR V. CUSTOMS
Generally, § 17:16

FEDERAL AUDITS
Investigations by federal auditors, § 2:15
Obstruction of federal audits, § 1:34, 1:35

FEDERAL INSPECTORS GENERAL
List of federal inspectors general, § Appx D

FEDERAL TRADE COMMISSION (FTC)
Collusive bidding, § 7:26
Made in USA labels, § 17:21

FIELD INTERVIEWS
Generally, § 2:9

FINAL INDIRECT COST CERTIFICATIONS
Costs (this index)

FINANCIAL CONDITION
Progress payments, § 14:17

FINANCING
Foreign Military Sales (FMS) (this index)

FINANCING COSTS
Mergers and acquisitions, § 18:4

FINDINGS
Cost Accounting Standards (CAS) (this index)

FINES AND PENALTIES
Administrative penalties
generally, § 1:53-1:50

FINES AND PENALTIES—Cont'd
Administrative penalties—Cont'd
contractual remedies, § 1:59
Debarment (this index)
Procurement Integrity Act, § 6:9
Suspension (this index)
Civil penalties
generally, § 1:49-1:52
contracts, voiding, § 1:52
Foreign Assistance Act, § 1:51
forfeiture of claims, § 1:50
global settlements, § 3:12
Procurement Integrity Act, § 6:8
Conflicts of Interest (this index)
Contractual remedies
administrative penalties, § 1:59
civil penalties, voiding contracts, § 1:52
Costs, penalties for unallowable costs clause, § 11:10, Appx M
Criminal penalties
generally, § 1:42-1:48
global settlements, § 3:12
Procurement Integrity Act, § 6:7
Racketeer Influenced and Corrupt Organizations Act (RICO), § 1:44, 1:45
Sentence and Punishment (this index)
Sentence of Fine statute, § 1:43
Debarment (this index)
Domestic and Foreign Products (this index)
Export Regulations (this index)
Foreign Assistance Act, § 1:51
Foreign Corrupt Practices Act (this index)
Forfeiture of claims, § 1:50
Global Settlements (this index)
International Sales (this index)
Kickbacks, § 7:41
Pricing, Defective (this index)
Procurement Integrity Act (this index)
Product Substitution (this index)
Racketeer Influenced and Corrupt Organizations Act (RICO), § 1:44, 1:45

INDEX

FINES AND PENALTIES—Cont'd
  Sentence and Punishment (this index)
  Suspension (this index)
  Time Charging (this index)

FMF
  Foreign Military Sales (FMS) (this index)

FMS
  Foreign Military Sales (FMS) (this index)

FOLLOW-UP
  Compliance audits, § 5:15

FOREIGN ACQUISITIONS
  Mergers and Acquisitions (this index)

FOREIGN ASSISTANCE ACT
  Fines and penalties, § 1:51
  Fraud and deceit, § 1:22

FOREIGN CORRUPT PRACTICES ACT
  Generally, § 1:28, 19:19 et seq,
  Accounts and accounting
    generally, § 19:24, 19:25
    penalties, § 19:25
    recordkeeping, § 19:24
  Advisory government opinions, § 30
  Awareness of misconduct, § 19:29
  Bribery
    generally, § 19:19-19:23
    defenses, § 19:21
    penalties, § 19:22
    permitted payments, § 19:20
    prohibited payments, § 19:19
  Compliance initiatives
    generally, § 19:28-19:31
    advisory government opinions, § 19:30
    awareness of misconduct, § 19:29
    education of employees, § 19:28
    recordkeeping, § 19:31
  Defenses to bribery, § 19:21
  Education of employees, § 19:28
  Fines and penalties
    accounts and accounting, § 19:25

FOREIGN CORRUPT PRACTICES ACT—Cont'd
  Fines and penalties—Cont'd
    bribery, § 19:22
  Recognition of problem, § 19:26, 19:27
  Recordkeeping
    accounts and accounting, § 19:24
    compliance initiatives, § 19:31

FOREIGN MILITARY SALES (FMS)
  Generally, § 20:1-20:25
  Agents. Commissions and contingent fees of agents, below
  Bona fide agent contingent fees, § 20:6
  Certification of credit-financed (FMF) sales, § 20:10
  Commissions and contingent fees of agents
    generally, § 20:6
    credit-financed (FMF) sales, § 20:11
  Compliance initiatives
    generally, § 20:22-20:25
    credit-financed (FMF) sales, § 20:24
    direct commercial sales, § 20:23
    recommendations, § 20:25
  Contingent fees. Commissions and contingent fees of agents, above
  Costs. Recoupment of nonrecurring costs, below
  Credit-financed (FMF) sales
    generally, § 20:8-20:11
    certification, § 20:10
    commissions and contingent fees, § 20:11
    compliance initiatives, § 20:24
    credit guidelines, § 20:9
    guidelines for financing, § **Appx X**
    offsets, § 20:19
  Direct commercial sales
    generally, § 20:7-20:11
    compliance initiatives, § 20:23
    credit-financed (FMF) sales, above
    financing guidelines, § **Appx X**

FOREIGN MILITARY SALES (FMS)—Cont'd
Financing. Credit-financed (FMF) sales, above
FMF sales. Credit-financed (FMF) sales, above
Mechanics of sale, § 20:3
Offsets
　generally, § 20:16-20:19
　FMF offsets, § 20:19
　FMS offsets, § 20:18
　reporting requirements, § 20:17
Pricing, § 20:5
Pseudo FMS cases, § 20:12
Qualifying countries, Defense Department list of, § Appx U
Recognition of problem, § 20:20, 20:21
Recommendations, § 20:25
Recoupment of nonrecurring costs
　generally, § 20:13-20:15
　background, § 20:13
　policy, § 20:14
　waiver of recoupment charges, § 20:15
Reporting requirements as to offsets, § 20:17
Requirements, § 20:2-20:6
Statutory provisions, § 20:2
Types of government-to-government FMS sales, § 20:4
Waiver of recoupment charges, § 20:15

FOREIGN PRODUCTS
Domestic and Foreign Products (this index)

FORFEITURE OF CLAIMS
Generally, § 1:50

FORMER EMPLOYEES
Conflicts of interest, one-year ban on hiring former agency officials, § 8:3
Investigations (this index)

FRAUD AND DECEIT
Civil fraud
　generally, § 1:14-1:24
　false claims, § 1:15, 1:16

FRAUD AND DECEIT—Cont'd
Civil fraud—Cont'd
　Foreign Assistance Act, § 1:22
　pricing, defective, § 9:21
　Program Fraud Civil Remedies Act, § 1:23, 1:24
　qui tam actions, below
Contract claims, § 16:10
Costs, unallowable, § 11:11
Criminal fraud
　generally, § 1:2-1:11
　false claims, § 1:10, 1:11
　false statements, § 1:3-1:5
　mail fraud, § 1:6, 1:7
　major fraud against United States, § 1:8, 1:9
　pricing, defective, § 9:22
　wire fraud, § 1:6, 1:7
Defense Contractors (this index)
Defense Department fraud investigations, § Appx S
False claims
　civil fraud, § 1:15, 1:16
　criminal fraud, § 1:10, 1:11
Foreign Assistance Act, § 1:22
Mail fraud, § 1:6, 1:7
Major fraud against United States, § 1:8, 1:9
Pricing, Defective (this index)
Procurement fraud information, Department of Army memorandum, § Appx I
Program Fraud Civil Remedies Act, § 1:23, 1:24
Progress payments, substantial evidence of fraud, § 14:22
Qui tam actions
　generally, § 1:17-21
　procedure, § 1:19
　relators, § 1:18
　whistleblower protections, § 1:20
United States, major fraud against, § 1:8, 1:9
Wire fraud, § 1:6, 1:7

FREE TRADE AGREEMENTS
Domestic and foreign products, § 17:6

GLOBAL SETTLEMENTS
Generally, § 3:8-3:17
Benefits, § 3:9
Civil penalties, § 3:13
Criminal liability, § 3:12
Debarment, § 3:14-3:16
Elements, § 3:11
Fines and penalties
  civil penalties, § 3:13
  criminal penalties, § 3:12
Frequently asked questions, § 3:17
Mitigating factors, § 3:18, 3:19
Negotiations, § 3:10
Ombudsman, § 3:15
Reporting requirements, § 3:16
Suspension, § 3:14-3:16

GOVERNMENT AGENCIES
Former agency officials, one-year ban on hiring, § 8:3
Investigators, § 2:3

GRAND JURY
Generally, § 2:5, 2:41-2:44
Averting indictments, § 2:44
Document subpoenas, § 2:41
Indictments, averting, § 2:44
Motions to quash or modify subpoenas, § 2:42
Preparation of witnesses, § 2:43
Subpoenas
  generally, § 2:41
  motions to quash or modify subpoenas, § 2:42
  receipt of subpoenas, § 2:18
Witnesses
  preparation of witnesses, § 2:43
  subpoenas, above

GRATUITIES
Bribery and Illegal Gratuities (this index)

GSA
Commercial Items (this index)

GUIDELINES
Foreign military sales (FMS), credit guidelines, § 20:9

GUIDELINES—Cont'd
Sentence and Punishment (this index)

HOTLINES
Company Hotlines (this index)
Department of Defense hotline poster, § **Appx F**

IDENTIFICATION
Domestic and foreign products, § **17:10**

INCONSISTENT DEFENSES
Parallel proceedings, § 3:6

INDEMNIFICATION
Investigations, preparation for, § 2:25

INDICTMENTS AND INFORMATIONS
Averting indictments, § 2:44

INDUSTRIAL FUNDING FEE
MAS program, § 10:19

INFLUENCING GOVERNMENT ACTIONS
Generally, § 7:1-7:48
Bribery and Illegal Gratuities (this index)
Collusive Bidding (this index)
Kickbacks (this index)
Lobbying Restrictions (this index)

INFORMATION
Access to Government Property and Information (this index)
Antiboycott provisions, refusal to supply boycott-related information, § **19:39**

INSPECTIONS
Product Substitution (this index)

INSTRUCTIONS AND DIRECTIONS
Cost/price proposals, instructions for submitting, § **Appx J**

INSURANCE
Investigations, preparation for, § 2:25

INTENT
  Conflicts of interest, communications and appearances with intent to influence, § 8:8

INTERNAL INVESTIGATIONS
  Investigations (this index)

INTERNAL REVENUE CODE
  Antiboycott provisions, § 19:34

INTERNATIONAL SALES
  Generally, § 19:1-19:46
  Agents and representatives
    generally, § 19:42-19:46
    antiboycott provisions, monitoring agents and partners, § 19:40
    compliance initiatives, § 19:45, 19:46
    examples, § 19:44
    recognition of problem, § 19:43
    recommendations, § 19:46
  Antiboycott Provisions (this index)
  Compliance initiatives
    agents and representatives, § 19:46, 19:46
    Antiboycott Provisions (this index)
    Export Regulations (this index)
    Foreign Corrupt Practices Act (this index)
    Foreign Military Sales (FMS) (this index)
  Defense contractors
    Export Regulations (this index)
    Foreign Military Sales (FMS) (this index)
  Export Regulations (this index)
  Fines and penalties
    Export Regulations (this index)
    Foreign Corrupt Practices Act (this index)
  Foreign Corrupt Practices Act (this index)
  Foreign Military Sales (FMS) (this index)
  Recognition of problem
    agents and representatives, § 19:43
    antiboycott provisions, § 19:35, 19:36

INTERNATIONAL SALES—Cont'd
  Recognition of problem—Cont'd
    Foreign Corrupt Practices Act, § 19:26, 19:27
  Recommendations
    agents and representatives, § 19:46
    foreign military sales (FMS), § 20:25

INTERNATIONAL TRAFFIC IN ARMS REGULATIONS
  Generally, § 19:2-19:9
  Brokering, § 19:6
  Deemed exports, § 19:3
  Penalties, § 19:9
  Re-exports, § 19:4
  Registration, § 19:7
  Significant military equipment, § 19:5
  Temporary imports, § 19:8

INTERVIEWS
  Employment (this index)
  Field interviews, § 2:9

INVENTORY
  Domestic and foreign products, separate inventories, § 17:30
  Progress payments, excessive inventory, § 14:18

INVESTIGATIONS
  Generally, § 2:1-2:44
  Advice to employees, § 2:28
  Arrival of investigators, § 2:21
  Attorneys
    employment, below
    selection of counsel, § 2:22
  Auditors, federal, § 2:15
  Avoidance of obstruction of justice, § 2:23
  Civilian agency investigators, § 2:3
  Communications with prosecutor, § 2:39
  Company hotline calls, § 2:19
  Compliance Programs (this index)
  Constitutional law
    generally, § 2:30-2:33
    counsel, employees' right to, § 2:33

INDEX

INVESTIGATIONS—Cont'd
Constitutional law—Cont'd
  search and seizure, § **2:31**
  self-incrimination privilege, § **2:32**
Contracting officers, allegations by, § **2:16**
Counsel. Attorneys, above
Defense agency investigators, § **2:3**
Defense Department fraud investigations, § **Appx S**
Detection of investigations
  generally, § **2:14-2:20**
  actions by employees or former employees, § **2:20**
  auditors, federal, § **2:15**
  company hotline calls, § **2:19**
  contracting officers, allegations by, § **2:16**
  employee interviews, requests for, § **2:17**
  grand jury subpoenas, § **2:18**
  hotline calls, § **2:19**
Devices, § **2:4-2:9**
Disclosures of wrongdoing, voluntary, § **2:40**
Documents, retention of, § **2:10**
Education of employees, § **2:12**
Employment
  actions by employees or former employees, § **2:20**
  advice to employees, § **2:28**
  attorneys. Counsel for employees, below in this group
  counsel for employees
    generally, § **2:29**
    right of employees to counsel, § **2:33**
  education of employees, § **2:12**
  former employees, below
  internal investigations, employee interviews, § **2:37**
  interviews, below
  notice to employees of investigation, § **2:27**
  requests for employee interviews, § **2:17**
Ethics rules, advice to government investigators, § **2:26**
Field interviews, § **2:9**

INVESTIGATIONS—Cont'd
Former employees
  actions by employees or former employees, § **2:20**
  internal investigations, interviews of former employees, § **2:37**
  preparation for investigations, contact with former employees, § **2:13**
Grand Jury (this index)
Hotline calls, § **2:19**
Indemnification, § **2:25**
Insurance, § **2:25**
Internal investigations
  generally, § **2:34-2:40**
  authorization by company management, § **2:35**
  communications with prosecutor, § **2:39**
  disclosures of wrongdoing, voluntary, § **2:40**
  employee interviews, § **2:37**
  former employees, interviews of, § **2:37**
  investigators, selection of, § **2:36**
  management authorization, § **2:35**
  preliminary internal investigations, § **2:24**
  prosecutor, communications with, § **2:39**
  reports of investigations, § **2:38**
  selection of investigators, § **2:36**
  voluntary disclosures of wrongdoing, § **2:40**
Interviews
  employee interviews
    internal investigations, § **2:37**
    requests for employee interviews, § **2:17**
  field interviews, § **2:9**
Investigators
  generally, § **2:2**
  arrival of investigators, § **2:21**
  civilian agency investigators, § **2:3**
  defense agency investigators, § **2:3**
  ethics rules, advice to government investigators, § **2:26**
  internal investigations, § **2:36**

Index-19

INVESTIGATIONS—Cont'd
Local ethics rules, advice to government investigators, § 2:26
Management authorization of internal investigations, § 2:35
Notice to employees of investigation, § 2:27
Obstruction of justice, avoidance of, § 2:23
Preliminary internal inquiry, § 2:24
Preparation for investigations
   generally, § 2:10-2:13
   advice to employees, § 2:28
   arrival of investigators, § 2:21
   attorneys, above
   avoidance of obstruction of justice, § 2:23
   constitutional law, above
   counsel. Attorneys, above
   detection of investigations, above
   documents, retention of, § 2:10
   employment, above
   ethics rules, advice to government investigators, § 2:26
   former employees, above
   indemnification, § 2:25
   insurance, § 2:25
   internal inquiry, § 2:24
   local ethics rules, advice to government investigators, § 2:26
   notice to employees of investigation, § 2:27
   obstruction of justice, avoidance of, § 2:23
   preliminary internal inquiry, § 2:24
   records custodian, appointment of, § 2:11
Prosecutor, communications with, § 2:39
Records custodian, appointment of, § 2:11
Reports of internal investigations, § 2:38
Requests for employee interviews, § 2:17
Search and Seizure (this index)
Self-incrimination privilege, § 2:32

INVESTIGATIONS—Cont'd
Subpoenas
   generally, § 2:6
   Grand Jury (this index)
Voluntary disclosures of wrongdoing, § 2:40
Wiretaps, § 2:8
Witnesses (this index)

JOINT VENTURES
Collusive bidding, § 7:30

JUDICIAL PROCEEDINGS
Obstruction of judicial proceedings, § 1:36, 1:37

JUSTICE
Obstruction of Justice (this index)

KICKBACKS
Generally, § 1:27, 7:37-7:48
Anti-Kickback Act, § 7:38-7:41
Audits, § 7:47
Compliance initiatives
   generally, § 7:45-7:48
   audits, § 7:47
   policies and procedures, § 7:46, 7:47
   recommendations, § 7:48
Contractor responsibilities, § 7:40
Elements, § 7:39
Fines and penalties, § 7:41
Frequently asked questions, § 7:42
Policies and procedures, § 7:46, 7:47
Recognition of problem, § 7:43, 7:44
Recommendations, § 7:48
Statutory provisions, § 7:37-7:41

LABELS
Domestic and Foreign Products (this index)

LICENSES AND PERMITS
Export Regulations (this index)

LOBBYING RESTRICTIONS
Generally, § 1:29, 7:13-7:22
Byrd Amendment
   generally, § 7:14
   compliance initiatives, § 7:20

INDEX

LOBBYING RESTRICTIONS
—Cont'd
Compliance initiatives
generally, § 7:19-7:22
Byrd Amendment, § 7:20
Lobbying Disclosure Act, § 7:21
recommendations, § 7:22
Disclosures. Lobbying Disclosure Act, below
Frequently asked questions, § 7:16
Lobbying Disclosure Act
generally, § 7:15
compliance initiatives, § 7:21
Recognition of problem, § 7:17, 7:18
Recommendations, § 7:22
Statutory provisions, § 7:13-7:15

LOCAL ETHICS RULES
Investigations, § 2:26

LOSS CONTRACTS
Progress payments, § 14:13

MAIL FRAUD
Generally, § 1:6, 1:7

MANAGEMENT
Cost Allowability (this index)
Internal investigations, authorization by company management, § 2:35
Middle Management (this index)
Product Substitution (this index)
Progress Payments (this index)
Time Charging (this index)
Upper Management (this index)

MAS PROGRAM
Commercial Items (this index)

MATERIAL CONTRACTS
Progress payments, § 14:16

MERGERS AND ACQUISITIONS
Generally, § 18:1-18:22
Access to classified information, foreign acquisitions of United States companies, § 18:19, 18:20
Actions and remedies, prior actions of acquired company, § 18:16

MERGERS AND ACQUISITIONS
—Cont'd
Classified information, foreign acquisitions of United States companies, § 18:19, 18:20
Conflicts of interest, organizational, § 18:12
Contracts, performance of, § 18:14
Costs
generally, § 18:2-18:8
cost accounting standards (CAS), pricing adjustments, § 18:8
defense contractors, § 18:7
depreciation of combined assets, § 18:5
execution costs, § 18:3
financing costs, § 18:4
money, cost of, § 18:6
planning costs, § 18:3
restructuring costs, § 18:7
Defense contractors, costs, § 18:7
Depreciation of combined assets, § 18:5
Due diligence review, § 18:21, 18:22
Environmental violations, § 18:15
Execution costs, § 18:3
Failure to execute novation agreement, § 18:11
Financing costs, § 18:4
Foreign acquisitions of United States companies
generally, § 18:17-18:20
access to classified information, § 18:19, 18:20
classified information, § 18:19, 18:20
ownership restrictions, § 18:18
Money, cost of, § 18:6
Novation agreements
generally, § 18:9-18:11
failure to execute novation agreement, § 18:11
requirements, § 18:10
Ownership restrictions, foreign acquisitions of United States companies, § 18:18
Performance of contracts, § 18:14
Planning costs, § 18:3
Restructuring costs, § 18:7

MERGERS AND ACQUISITIONS
—Cont'd
Resulting company
generally, § 18:12-18:16
conflicts of interest, organizational, § 18:12
contracts, performance of, § 18:14
environmental violations, § 18:15
performance of contracts, § 18:14
prior actions of acquired company, § 18:16
small business, § 18:13
Small business, § 18:13

MIDDLE MANAGEMENT
Cost allowability, compliance initiatives, § 11:17
Product substitution, compliance initiatives, § 15:14
Time Charging (this index)

MILITARY SERVICES
Defense Contractors (this index)

MITIGATION
Debarment, § 1:55
Global settlements, § 3:18, 3:19
Parallel proceedings, § 3:18, 3:19

MODIFICATION
Compliance programs, future modifications of, § 4:6
Cost Accounting Standards (CAS) (this index)
Grand jury subpoenas, motions to quash or modify subpoenas, § 2:42

MONITORING
Antiboycott provisions, monitoring agents and partners, § 19:40
Bribery and illegal gratuities, monitoring employee activities, § 7:10
Domestic and foreign products, § 17:31
Progress payments, monitoring performance of contracts, § 14:32

MONOPOLIES
Antitrust (this index)

MOTIONS
Grand jury, motions to quash or modify subpoenas, § 2:42

NAFTA
Marking rules, § 17:16

NEGOTIATIONS
Contract claims, § 16:17
Global settlements, § 3:10
Pricing, Defective (this index)

NOTICE
Contract costs suspended or disapproved, notice of, § **Appx K**
Investigations, notice to employees, § 2:27

NOVATION AGREEMENTS
Mergers and Acquisitions (this index)

OATHS AND AFFIRMATIONS
Perjury, § 1:40, 1:41

OBSTRUCTION OF JUSTICE
Generally, § 1:33-1:41
Administrative proceedings pending, obstruction of, § 1:39
Audits, federal, obstruction of, § 1:34, 1:35
Avoidance of obstruction of justice, § 2:23
Investigations, avoidance of obstruction of justice, § 2:23
Judicial proceedings, obstruction of, § 1:36, 1:37
Pending administrative proceedings, obstruction of, § 1:39
Perjury, § 1:40, 1:41
Witness tampering, § 1:38

OFFERS
Domestic and foreign products, offers to supply, § 17:25

OFFICERS
Compliance officer, § 4:11

OFFSETS
Foreign Military Sales (FMS) (this index)
Pricing, defective, § 9:19

INDEX

OFFSETS—Cont'd
Progress payments, § 14:23

OMBUDSMAN
Global settlements, § 3:15

OVERBILLING
Cost accounting standards (CAS), false claims by contractors, § 12:27

OVERHEAD
Costs (this index)

PARALLEL PROCEEDINGS
Generally, § 3:1-3:7
Burdensome litigation, § 3:5
Frequently asked questions, § 3:7
Inconsistent defenses, § 3:6
Mitigation, § 3:18, 3:19
Privileges, § 3:4
Transfer of information, § 3:3

PAYMENTS
Bribery and Illegal Gratuities (this index)
Kickbacks (this index)
Progress Payments (this index)

PENALTIES
Export regulations, § 19:9; 19:15
Fines and Penalties (this index)
International traffic in arms regulations, § 19:9

PENDING PROCEEDINGS
Obstruction of pending administrative proceedings, § 1:39

PERFORMANCE OF CONTRACTS
Cost Accounting Standards (CAS) (this index)
Cost Allowability (this index)
Domestic and foreign products, § 17:26
Mergers and acquisitions, § 18:14
Product Substitution (this index)
Progress payments, § 14:32
Time Charging (this index)

PERJURY
Generally, § 1:40, 1:41

POLICIES AND PROCEDURES
Compliance Programs (this index)

POSTAWARD ACTIVITIES
Domestic and foreign products, § 17:26

PRELIMINARY INTERNAL INQUIRY
Preparation for government investigations, § 2:24

PREPARATION
Investigations (this index)

PRICING
Certificate of independent price determination clause, § **Appx H**
Commercial Items (this index)
Contract Claims (this index)
Defective pricing. **Pricing, Defective** (this index)
Foreign military sales (FMS), § **20:5**
Instructions for submitting cost/price proposals, § **Appx J**
Proposals (this index)

PRICING, DEFECTIVE
Generally, § **9:1-9:32**
Adequate price competition, § **9:8**
Adjustments for defective pricing
  generally, § **9:15-9:19**
  amount of government recovery, § **9:17**
  burden of proof, § **9:16**
  contract claims, § **16:9**
  defenses, § **9:18**
  offset, § **9:19**
Certification
  data, certification of, § **9:6**
  independent price determination clause, certificate of, § **Appx H**
Commercial Items (this index)
Compliance initiatives
  generally, § **9:31**
  recommendations, § **9:32**
Contract Claims (this index)
Correction, § **9:28**
Criminal fraud, § **9:22**
Debarment, § **9:23**

Index-23

PRICING, DEFECTIVE—Cont'd
Defenses, adjustments for defective pricing, § 9:18
Disclosures, § 9:27
Estimating systems
  generally, § 9:25-9:28
  applicability, § 9:26
  correction, § 9:28
  disclosures, § 9:27
  government review, § 9:27
Fines and penalties
  generally, § 9:20-9:23
  debarment, § 9:23
  fraud and deceit, below
  suspension, § 9:23
Fraud and deceit
  civil fraud, § 9:21
  criminal fraud, § 9:22
Frequently asked questions, § 9:24
Law or regulation, price set by, § 9:9
Modification, § 9:12
Negotiations. Truth in Negotiations Act, below
Offset, adjustments for defective pricing, § 9:19
Recognition of problem, § 9:29, 9:30
Recommendations, § 9:32
Subcontracts, § 9:14
Suspension, § 9:23
Truth in Negotiations Act
  generally, § 9:2-9:23
  adequate price competition, § 9:8
  adjustments for defective pricing, above
  applicability, § 9:3
  certification of data, § 9:6
  commercial item acquisition, § 9:10, 10:9
  competition, § 9:8
  definition of cost or pricing data, § 9:4
  exceptional case waiver, § 9:11
  exceptions, § 9:7-9:12
  information other than cost or pricing data, § 9:13
  law or regulation, price set by, § 9:9
  modification, § 9:12

PRICING, DEFECTIVE—Cont'd
Truth in Negotiations Act—Cont'd
  subcontractor data, § 9:14
  submission of data, § 9:5
  waiver, § 9:12
Waiver, Truth in Negotiations Act, § 9:12

PRIME CONTRACTS
Commercial items, § 10:6

PRIVILEGES
Parallel proceedings, § 3:4
Self-incrimination privilege, § 2:32

PROCUREMENT INFORMATION
Compliance initiatives
  generally, § 6:16-6:20
  education and training of employees, § 6:18, 6:18
  policies and procedures, establishment of, § 6:17
Department of Army memorandum, § Appx I
Education and training of employees, § 6:18, 6:19
Espionage, § 1:32, 6:13
Improper access to government property and information, § 1:30-1:32, 6:12, 6:13
Policies and procedures, § 6:17
Procurement Integrity Act (this index)
Recognition of problem, § 6:14, 6:15
Recommendations, § 6:20
Summary of criminal and civil statutes, § Appx A
Theft of government property, § 1:31, 6:12

PROCUREMENT INTEGRITY ACT
Generally, § 1:30, 6:1-6:11
Administrative penalties, § 6:9
Compensation, prohibition on official's acceptance of, § 6:6
Conflicts of Interest (this index)
Criminal penalties, § 6:7
Disclosure of procurement information, restrictions on, § 6:3

PROCUREMENT INTEGRITY ACT—Cont'd

Employment contracts, restrictions on, § 6:5
Fines and penalties
  administrative penalties, § 6:9
  civil penalties, § 6:8
  criminal penalties, § 6:7
Frequently asked questions, § 6:11
Obtaining procurement information, restrictions on, § 6:4
Protests, restrictions on, § 6:10
Public officers, compensation of, § 6:6

PRODUCT SUBSTITUTION

Generally, § 15:1-15:16
Commercial items, contractor inspection requirements, § 15:4
Compliance initiatives
  generally, § 15:12-15:16
  middle management, § 15:14
  quality assurance personnel, § 15:15
  recommendations, § 15:16
  upper management, § 15:13
Fines and penalties
  generally, § 15:8-15:10
  companies, penalties for, § 15:10
  individuals, penalties for, § 15:9
Inspections. Quality control, below
Management
  middle management, § 15:14
  upper management, § 15:13
Middle management, compliance initiatives, § 15:14
Quality control
  generally, § 15:2-15:7
  commercial items, contractor inspection requirements, § 15:4
  compliance initiatives, quality assurance personnel, § 15:15
  contractor responsibilities, § 15:2
  higher-level quality requirements, § 15:7
  small contracts, contractor inspection requirements, § 15:5

PRODUCT SUBSTITUTION—Cont'd

Quality control—Cont'd
  standard inspection requirements, § 15:6
  types of contract quality requirements, § 15:3
Recognition of problem, § 15:11
Recommendations, § 15:16
Small contracts, contractor inspection requirements, § 15:5
Upper management, § 15:13

PROFITS

Progress payments, actual profit less than estimated, § 14:21

PROGRAM FRAUD CIVIL REMEDIES ACT

Generally, § 1:23, 1:24

PROGRESS PAYMENTS

Generally, § 14:1-14:36
Accounting department, compliance initiatives, § 14:34
Accounts and accounting
  records, retaining, § 14:33
  submission of accounting data, § 14:4
Actual profit less than estimated, § 14:21
Allowable costs, § 14:10
Auditors, internal, § 14:35
Certification of requests for progress payments, § 14:5
Compliance initiatives
  generally, § 14:27-14:36
  accounting department, § 14:34
  accounting records, retaining, § 14:33
  allowable costs, segregation of, § 14:31
  auditors, internal, § 14:35
  cut-off dates for accumulation of costs, § 14:30
  management. Upper management, below in this group
  performance of contracts, monitoring, § 14:32
  recommendations, § 14:36

PROGRESS PAYMENTS—Cont'd
Compliance initiatives—Cont'd
  segregation
    allowable costs, segregation of, § 14:31
    subcontractor progress payments, segregation of, § 14:29
  subcontractor progress payments, segregation of, § 14:29
  upper management
    generally, § 14:28-14:33
    accounting records, retaining, § 14:33
    allowable costs, segregation of, § 14:31
    cut-off dates for accumulation of costs, § 14:30
    performance of contracts, monitoring, § 14:32
    subcontractor progress payments, segregation of, § 14:29
Computation, § 14:7-14:10
Contracts
  loss contracts, § 14:13
  material contract requirement, noncompliance with, § 14:16
  subcontractor progress payments, below
Costs
  allowable, reasonable, and allocable costs, § 14:10
  cut-off dates for accumulation of costs, § 14:30
  errors in billings, cost accounting standards (CAS), § 12:26
Cumulative total costs, § 14:8
Cut-off dates for accumulation of costs, § 14:30
Delinquent payments of costs, § 14:19
Estimated profit, actual profit less than, § 14:21
Evidence of fraud, § 14:22
Failure to make progress, § 14:17
Fair value of work, unliquidated payments exceeding, § 14:20
False claims by contractors, § 12:26

PROGRESS PAYMENTS—Cont'd
Financial condition, unsatisfactory, § 14:17
Fraud, substantial evidence of, § 14:22
Frequently asked questions, § 14:24
Inventory, excessive, § 14:18
Liquidation of progress payments
  generally, § 14:11
  subcontractors, progress payments to, § 14:12
Loss contracts, § 14:13
Management. Compliance initiatives, above
Material contract requirement, noncompliance with, § 14:16
Performance of contracts, monitoring, § 14:32
Profit less than estimated, § 14:21
Rate of progress payments, § 14:6
Reasonable costs, § 14:10
Recognition of problem, § 14:25, 14:26
Recommendations, § 14:36
Requests for progress payments
  generally, § 14:3-14:5
  certification, § 14:5
  Standard Form 1443, § **Appx R**
  submission of accounting data, § 14:4
Requirements, § 14:2-14:24
Setoff, § 14:23
Subcontractor progress payments
  computation, § 14:9
  liquidation of progress payments, § 14:12
  segregation of subcontractor progress payments, § 14:29
Submission of accounting data, § 14:4
Substantial evidence of fraud, § 14:22
Suspension and reduction of progress payments
  generally, § 14:15-14:23
  actual profit less than estimated, § 14:21
  delinquent payments of costs, § 14:19

INDEX

PROGRESS PAYMENTS—Cont'd
Suspension and reduction of progress payments—Cont'd
estimated profit, actual profit less than, § 14:21
evidence of fraud, § 14:22
failure to make progress, § 14:17
fair value of work, unliquidated payments exceeding, § 14:20
financial condition, unsatisfactory, § 14:17
fraud, substantial evidence of, § 14:22
inventory, excessive, § 14:18
material contract requirement, noncompliance with, § 14:16
profit less than estimated, § 14:21
setoff, § 14:23
substantial evidence of fraud, § 14:22
unliquidated payments exceeding fair value of work, § 14:20
value of work, unliquidated payments exceeding, § 14:20
Title to property, § 14:14
Unliquidated payments exceeding fair value of work, § 14:20
Upper management. Compliance initiatives, above
Value of work, unliquidated payments exceeding, § 14:20

PROJECT NUMBERS
Time charging, compliance initiatives, § 13:31

PROPERTY
Access to Government Property and Information (this index)
Progress payments, title to property, § 14:14

PROPOSALS
False statements by contractors, cost accounting standards (CAS), § 12:21, 12:24
Instructions for submitting cost/price proposals, § Appx J

PROTESTS
Procurement Integrity Act, § 6:10

QUALIFICATIONS
Cost accounting standards (CAS), CAS-qualified employees, § 12:33
Domestic and Foreign Products (this index)

QUALITY CONTROL
Product Substitution (this index)

RACKETEER INFLUENCED AND CORRUPT ORGANIZATIONS ACT (RICO)
Criminal penalties, § 1:44, 1:45

REASONABLE COSTS
Progress payments, § 14:10

RECOMMENDATIONS
Compliance Programs (this index)

RECORDS AND RECORDING
Contract claims, compliance initiatives, § 16:15
Custodian, appointment of, § 2:11
Foreign Corrupt Practices Act (this index)
Time charging, adjustments in recorded time entries, § 13:11

RECOUPMENT
Foreign Military Sales (FMS) (this index)

REEXPORTS
Export Regulations (this index)

RE-EXPORTS
Export regulations, § 19:4; 19:12
International traffic in arms regulations, § 19:4

REGISTRATION
Export regulations, § 19:7
International traffic in arms regulations, § 19:7

RELATORS
Fraud and deceit, qui tam actions, § 1:18

REPORTS
Antiboycott provisions, § 19:41

Index-27

REPORTS—Cont'd
Compliance audits, reporting audit results to government, § 5:16
Compliance programs, reporting violations to government, § 4:15
Foreign military sales (FMS), offsets, § 20:17
Global settlements, § 3:16
Internal investigations, reports of, § 2:38

REPRESENTATIONS
Chart of representations and certifications, § **Appx B**
Commercial items, § 10:12

REVOLVING-DOOR STATUTES
Conflicts of interest, § 8:13

SCREENING
Compliance programs, employee screening, § 4:7

SEARCH AND SEIZURE
Constitutional law, § 2:31
Warrants, § 2:7

SELF-INCRIMINATION PRIVILEGE
Generally, § 2:32

SENTENCE AND PUNISHMENT
Federal sentencing guidelines
  generally, § 1:44
  individuals, sentencing of, § 1:45
  organizations, sentencing of, § 1:45
  text, § **Appx C**
Guidelines. Federal sentencing guidelines, above
Sentence of Fine statute, § 1:43

SENTENCE OF FINE STATUTE
Generally, § 1:43

SETOFFS
Offsets (this index)

SETTLEMENTS
Compromise and Settlement (this index)

SHERMAN ANTITRUST ACT
Collusive bidding, § 7:24

SMALL BUSINESS
Mergers and acquisitions, § 18:13

SMALL CONTRACTS
Commercial Items (this index)

SOLICITATIONS
Cost accounting standards (CAS), false statements by contractors, § 12:20

SPECIAL CONTRACTING METHODS
Commercial Items (this index)

SUBCONTRACTS
Commercial Items (this index)
Pricing, defective, § 9:14
Progress Payments (this index)

SUBPOENAS
Grand Jury (this index)
Investigations (this index)

SUBSTITUTION
Product Substitution (this index)

SUPERVISORS
Cost allowability, compliance initiatives, § 11:17

SUSPENSION
Generally, § 1:56-1:58
Global settlements, § 3:14-3:16
Notice of contract costs suspended or disapproved, § **Appx K**
Pricing, defective, § 9:23

TAA REQUIREMENTS
Domestic and Foreign Products (this index)

TEAMING AGREEMENTS
Collusive bidding, § 7:30

TECHNICAL DATA
Commercial items, § 10:14

TELEPHONE CALLS
Hotlines (this index)

TEMPORARY IMPORTS
International traffic in arms regulations, § **19:8**

TESTING CONTROLS
Compliance audits, § **5:9**

THEFT OF GOVERNMENT PROPERTY
Generally, § **1:31, 6:12**

TIME CARDS
Time Charging (this index)

TIME CHARGING
Generally, § **13:1-13:34**
Accounting department. Compliance initiatives, below
Adjustments
 changes in time charging, below
 labor standards, unexplained adjustments in, § **13:15**
Administrative requirements, § **13:3**
Allocation of costs, § **13:22**
Audits, internal, § **13:24**
Automation of systems, compliance initiatives, § **13:32**
Budgetary controls, overly rigid, § **13:16**
Certifications, § **13:4**
Changes in time charging
 dramatic changes, § **13:9**
 lack of change over extended period, § **13:10**
 recorded time entries, adjustments in, § **13:11**
Compliance initiatives
 generally, § **13:20-13:34**
 accounting department
  generally, § **13:30-13:33**
  automation of systems, § **13:32**
  invalid charges, screening for, § **13:30, 13:33**
  project numbers, designation of, § **13:31**
 allocation of costs, § **13:22**
 audits, internal, § **13:24**
 automation of systems, § **13:32**
 cost allocation policy, § **13:22**
 education of employees, § **13:23**

TIME CHARGING—Cont'd
Compliance initiatives—Cont'd
 invalid charges, screening for, § **13:30, 13:33**
 middle management
  generally, § **13:25-13:28**
  review of charges, § **13:25**
  time cards, review and approval of, § **13:27**
  transfers of labor charges, review of, § **13:28**
  work assignments, § **13:26**
 nonsupervisory employees, § **13:29**
 policies and procedures, § **13:21, 13:22**
 project numbers, designation of, § **13:31**
 recommendations, § **13:34**
 review of charges, § **13:25**
 screening for invalid charges, § **13:30, 13:33**
 system of accumulating and reporting labor costs, § **13:20**
 time cards
  middle management, review and approval of time cards, § **13:27**
  nonsupervisory employees, § **13:29**
  sample time cards, § **Appx P; Appx Q**
  time card analysis attribute test, § **Appx O**
 transfers of labor charges, review of, § **13:28**
 upper management
  generally, § **13:21-13:24**
  audits, internal, § **13:24**
  cost allocation policy, § **13:22**
  education of employees, § **13:23**
  policies and procedures, § **13:21, 13:22**
  work assignments, § **13:26**
Contracts, § **13:17, 13:18**
Cost accounting standards (CAS) disclosure statement, § **13:14**
Cost allocation policy, compliance initiatives, § **13:22**

TIME CHARGING—Cont'd
Disclosure statements, CAS, § 13:14
Education of employees, compliance initiatives, § 13:23
Employee reclassification by labor category, § 13:13
Fines and penalties
  companies, penalties for mischarging for, § 13:5
  individuals, penalties for mischarging for, § 13:6
Frequently asked questions, § 13:7
Invalid charges, screening for, § 13:30, 13:33
Labor category, reclassification of employees by, § 13:13
Labor standards, unexplained adjustments in, § 13:15
Management. Compliance initiatives, above
Middle management. Compliance initiatives, above
Policies and procedures, compliance initiatives, § 13:21, 13:22
Project numbers, designation of, § 13:31
Reclassification of employees by labor category, § 13:13
Recognition of problem, § 13:8-13:19
Recommendations, § 13:34
Recorded time entries, adjustments in, § 13:11
Requirements, § 13:2-13:7
Review of charges, compliance initiatives, § 13:25
Screening for invalid charges, § 13:30, 13:33
System of accumulating and reporting labor costs, § 13:20
Time cards. Compliance initiatives, above
Transfers of labor charges, review of, § 13:28
Undercharging to visible account, § 13:12
Unexplained adjustments in labor standards, § 13:15

TIME CHARGING—Cont'd
Upper management. Compliance initiatives, above
Work assignments, compliance initiatives, § 13:26

TITLE TO PROPERTY
Progress payments, § 14:14

TRAINING
Employment (this index)

TREATIES
Domestic and foreign products, § 17:2-17:6

TRUTH IN NEGOTIATIONS ACT
Commercial items, § 10:9
Pricing, Defective (this index)

UNDERCHARGING
Time charging, undercharging to visible account, § 13:12

UPDATING
Compliance programs, § 4:18

UPPER MANAGEMENT
Cost allowability, compliance initiatives, § 11:16
Product substitution, compliance initiatives, § 15:13
Progress Payments (this index)
Time Charging (this index)

VOIDING CONTRACTS
Civil penalties, § 1:52

WAIVER
Cost accounting standards (CAS), § 12:5
Foreign military sales (FMS), waiver of recoupment charges, § 20:15
Pricing, Truth in Negotiations Act, § 9:12

WARRANTS
Search warrants, § 2:7

WEAPONS AND FIREARMS
Defense Contractors (this index)

INDEX

WHISTLEBLOWER PROTECTIONS
Fraud and deceit, qui tam actions, § 1:20

WIRE FRAUD
Generally, **§ 1:6, 1:7**

WIRETAPS
Investigations, § 2:8

WITNESSES
Grand Jury (this index)

WITNESSES—Cont'd
Perjury, **§ 1:40, 1:41**
Tampering with witnesses, **§ 1:38**

WORK ASSIGNMENTS
Time charging, compliance initiatives, **§ 13:26**

WORK PROGRAMS
Compliance audits, **§ 5:4**

WTO GPA REQUIREMENTS
Domestic and foreign products, **§ 17:5**